Automata, Computability and Complexity

THEORY AND APPLICATIONS

Elaine Rich

Pearson

ISBN 978-81-317-8822-6

First Impression, 2012
Fifth Impression, 2018
Sixth Impression, 2019

Published by Pearson India Education Services Pvt Ltd, CIN: U72200TN2005PTC057128

Head Office: 15th Floor, Tower-B, World Trade Tower, Plot No. 1, Block-C, Sector 16, Noida 201301, Uttar Pradesh, India.
Registered Office: 4th Floor, Software Block, Elnet Software City, TS-140, Block 2 and 9, Rajiv Gandhi Salai, Taramani, Chennai 600 113, Tamil Nadu, India. Fax: 080-30461003, Phone: 080-30461060
Website: in.pearson.com, Email id: companysecretary.india@pearson.com

Printed in India by Gopsons Papers Ltd

CONTENTS

PREFACE

This book has three goals:

1. To introduce students to the elegant theory that underlies modern computing.
2. To motivate students by showing them that the theory is alive. While much of it has been known since the early days of digital computers (and some of it even longer), the theory continues to inform many of the most important applications that are considered today.
3. To show students how to start looking for ways to exploit the theory in their own work.

The core of the book, as a standard textbook, is Parts I through V. They address the first of the stated goals. They contain the theory that is being presented. There is more material in them than can be covered in a one-semester course. Sections that are marked with a ● are optional, in the sense that later material does not, for the most part, depend on them. The Course Plans section on page xv suggests ways of selecting sections that are appropriate for some typical computer science courses.

Then there are seventeen appendices:

- Appendix A reviews the mathematical concepts on which the main text relies. Students should be encouraged to review it during the first week of class.
- Appendix B describes techniques for working with logical formulas (both Boolean and first-order).
- Appendices C, D, E and F treat selected theoretical concepts in greater depth. In particular, they contain the details of some proofs that are only sketched in the main text.
- Appendices G through Q address the second and third goals. They describe applications of the techniques that are described in the main body of the book. They also contain some interesting historical material. Although they are long (at least in comparison to the space that is devoted to applications in most other books in this area), they only skim the surface of the applications that they present. But my hope is that that is enough. The World Wide Web has completely changed our ability to access knowledge. What matters now is to know that something exists and thus to look for it. The short discussions that are presented in these appendices will, I hope, give students that understanding.

There is a Web site that accompanies this book: http://www.theoryandapplications.org/. It is organized into the same sections as the book, so that it is easy to follow the two in parallel. The symbol 💻 following a concept in the text means that additional material is available on the Web site.

Throughout the text, you'll find pointers to the material in the appendices, as well as to material on the book's Web site. There are also some standalone application notes. These pointers and notes are enclosed in boxes, and refer you to the appropriate appendix and page number or to the Web. The appendix references look like this:

> This technique really is useful. (H. 1. 2.)

Notation

It is common practice to write definitions in the following form:

A something is a ***special something*** if it possesses property P.

This form is used even though property P is not only a sufficient but also a necessary condition for being a special something. For clarity we will, in those cases, write "if and only if", abbreviated "iff", instead of "if". So we will write:

A something is a ***special something*** iff it possesses property P.

Throughout the book we will, with a few exceptions, use the following naming conventions:

		Examples
sets	capital letters, early in the alphabet, plus S	A, B, C, D, S
logical formulas	capital letters, middle of the alphabet	P, Q, R
predicates and relations	capital letters, middle of the alphabet	P, Q, R
logical constants	subscripted X's and specific names	X_1, X_2, John, Smoky
functions	lower case letters or words	$f, g, convert$
integers	lower case letters, middle of the alphabet	i, j, k, l, m, n
string-valued variables	lower case letters, late in the alphabet	s, t, u, v, w, x, y
literal strings	written in computer font	`abc`, `aabbb`
language-valued variables	upper case letters starting with L	L, L_1, L_2
specific languages	nonitalicized strings	$\mathrm{A^nB^n}$. WW
regular expressions	lower case Greek letters	α, β, γ
states	lower case letters, middle of the alphabet	p, q, r, s, t
nonterminals in grammar rules	upper case letters	A, B, C, S, T
working strings in grammatical derivations	lower case Greek letter	α, β, γ
strings representing a PDA's stack	lower case Greek letter	α, β, γ
other variables	lower case letters, late in the alphabet	x, y, z

Programs and algorithms will appear throughout the book, stated at varying levels of detail. We will use the following formats for describing them:

- Exact code in some particular programming language will be written the same way other strings are written.

- Algorithms that are described in pseudocode will be written as:

  Until an even-length string is found do:

    Generate the next string in the sequence.

When we want to be able to talk about the steps, they will be numbered, so we will write:

1. Until an even-length string is found do:

  1.1. Generate the next string in the sequence.

2. Reverse the string that was found.

When comments are necessary, as for example in code or in grammars, they will be preceded by the string /*.

Course Plans

Appendix A summarizes the mathematical concepts on which the rest of the book relies. Depending on the background of the students, it may be appropriate to spend one or more lectures on this material. At the University of Texas, our students have had two prior courses in logic and discrete structures before they arrive in my class, so I have found that it is sufficient just to ask the students to read Appendix A and to work a selection of the exercises that are provided at the end of it.

Part I lays the groundwork for the rest of the book. Chapter 2 is essential, since it defines the fundamental structures: strings and languages. I have found that it is very useful to cover Chapter 3, which presents a roadmap for the rest of the material. It helps students see where we are going and how each piece of the theory fits into the overall picture of a theory of computation. Chapter 4 introduces three ideas that become important later in the book. I have found that it may be better to skip Chapter 4 at the beginning of my class and to return to each of its sections once or twice later, as the concepts are required.

If the optional sections are omitted, Chapters 5, 6, 8, 9, 11–14, 17–21, and, optionally, 23 and/or 24 cover the material in a standard course in Automata Theory. Chapter 15 (Context-Free Parsing) contains material that many computer science students need to see and it fits well into an Automata Theory course. I used to include much of it in my class. But that material is often taught in a course on Programming Languages or Compilers. In that case, it makes sense to omit it from the Automata Theory course. In its place, I now cover the optional material in Chapter 5, particularly the section on stochastic finite automata. I also cover Chapter 22. I've found that students are more motivated to tackle the difficult material (particularly the design of reduction proofs) in Chapter 21 if they can see ways in which the theory of undecidability applies to problems that are, to them, more intriguing than questions about the behavior of Turing machines.

This text is also appropriate for a broader course that includes the core of the classic theory of automata plus the modern theory of complexity. Such a course might cover Chapters 2–3, 5, 8, 11, 13, 17–21, and 27–30, omitting sections as time pressures require.

This text is unique in the amount of space it devotes to applications of the core theoretical material. In order to make the application discussions coherent, they are separated from the main text and occur in the appendices at the end of the book. But I have found that I can substantially increase student interest in my course by sprinkling application discussions throughout the term. The application references that occur in the main text suggest places where it makes sense to do that.

Resources for Instructors

There is a website, www.prenhall.com/rich, that contains materials that have been designed to make it easy to teach from this book. In particular, it contains:

- a complete set of Powerpoint slides,
- solutions to many of the Exercises, and
- additional problems, many of them with solutions.

I would like to invite instructors who use this book to send me additional problems that can be shared with other users.

ACKNOWLEDGMENTS

This book would not have been possible without the help of many people. When I first began teaching CS 341, Automata Theory, at the University of Texas, I was given a collection of notes that had been written by Bob Wall and Russell Williams. Much of the material in this book has evolved from those notes. I first learned automata theory from [Hopcroft and Ullman 1969]. Over the years that I have taught CS 341, I have used several textbooks, most frequently [Lewis and Papadimitriou 1988] and [Sipser 2006]. Much of what I have written here has been heavily influenced by the treatment of this material in those books.

Several of my friends, colleagues, and students have provided examples, answered numerous questions, and critiqued what I have written. I am particularly indebted to Don Baker, Volker Bandke, Jim Barnett, Jon Bentley, Gary Bland, Jaime Carbonell, Alan Cline, Martin Cohn, Dan Connolly, Ann Daniel, Chris Edmonson-Yurkanan, Scott Fahlman, Warren Gish, Mohamed Gouda, Jim Hendler, Oscar Hernandez, David Jefferson, Ben Kuipers, Greg Lavender, Tim Maxwell, Andy Mills, Jay Misra, Luay Nakhleh, Gordon Novak, Gabriela Ochoa, Dewayne Perry, Brian Reid, Bob Rich, Mike Scott, Cathy Stacy, Peter Stone, Lynda Trader, and David Zuckerman. Luay Nakhleh, Dan Tamir, and Bob Wall have used drafts of this book in their classes. I thank them for their feedback and that of their students.

I would also like to thank all of the students and teaching assistants who have helped me understand both why this material is hard and why it is exciting and useful. A couple of years ago, Tarang Mittal and Mat Crocker finished my class and decided that they should create an organized automata theory tutoring program the following fall. They got the program going and it continues to make a big difference to many students. I'd like to thank Tarang and Mat and the other tutors: Jason Pennington, Alex Menzies, Tim Maxwell, Chris St. Clair, Luis Guimbarda, Peter Olah, Eamon White, Kevin Kwast, Catherine Chu, Siddharth Natarajan, Daniel Galvan, Elton Pinto, and Jack Djeu.

My students have helped in many other ways as well. Oscar Hernandez helped me with several of the application appendices and made the Powerpoint slides that accompany the book. Caspar Lam designed the Web site for the book. David Reaves took pictures. My quilt, Blue Tweed, appears on the book's cover and on the Web site and slides. David took all the pictures that we used.

I would not have been in a position to write this book without the support of my father, who introduced me to the elegance of mathematics, Andy van Dam for my undergraduate experience at Brown, and Raj Reddy for my graduate experience at CMU. I cannot thank them enough.

Special thanks go to my family and friends, particularly my husband, Alan Cline, and my father, Bob Rich, for countless meals taken over by discussions of this material, proofreading more drafts than I can count, and patience while living with someone who is writing a book.

CREDITS

On the Cover:

A quilt, Blue Tweed (1996, 53" x 80", cotton, machine pieced and quilted), made by the author. Notice that your eye fills in the vertical lines, so they appear to run the length of the quilt, even though the colors in the middle of the quilt are all about the same. Quilt photography by David Reaves.

Photo Credits:

- Photograph of a fragment of the Antikythera Mechanism and two photographs of the reconstructed model of it, Figures P.1 and P2: copyright of the Antikythera Mechanism Research Project.
- Photo of DNA and RNA, Figure K.2, page 965: © Dorling Kindersley.
- Photos of Prague orlog, Figure P.3, page 1056: Ing. Karel Mayr.
- Photo of abacus, Figure P.4, page 1057: David Reaves.
- Photo of Jacquard loom, Figure P.5, page 1058: Stan Sherer.
- Photo of Sony Aibo robot, Figure P.10, page 1062: Alan Cline.

Credits for Exercises:

- Alan Cline: Exercise 27.9.
- [Brachman and Levesque 2004]: Exercise 33.10.
- Jay Misra: Exercise 20.10.
- Luay Nakhleh: Exercises 8.17, 17.5, 17.12, 21.18, 21.21, 21.22.
- Cathy Stacy: Exercise 5.3.
- David Zuckerman: Exercises 22.5, 28.11, 28.16, 28.23(d), 28.26, 29.3, 30.1

Other Credits:

- IBM 7090 example, page 2: Brian Reid.
- IBM 360 JCL, page 3: Volker Bandke, http://www.bsp-gmbh.com/hercules/herc_jcl.html.
- The Java example, page 3: Mike Scott.
- Example 5.10, page 64: from [Misra 2004].
- The poem, "The Pumping Lemma for DFAs", page 198: Martin Cohn.
- The drawings generated by Lindenmayer systems, pages 547–549: Generated by Alan Cline in MATLAB®.
- Graph showing the growth rates of functions, page 598: Generated by Alan Cline in MATLAB®.
- Progression of closures given in Example A.11, pages 777–778: Alan Cline.
- Example A.19, page 784: Alan Cline.
- Analysis of iterative deepening, page 861: Alan Cline.
- The proofs in Section F.1, pages 869–875: Alan Cline.
- The network protocol diagrams and corresponding state machines, pages 919–924: Oscar Hernandez.
- A very long English sentence, page 984: http://www.plainenglish.co.uk/longsentences.htm.

- Drawing of girl with cat, page 995: Lynda Trader.
- Drawing of bear with rifle, page 997: Lynda Trader.
- Sound wave for the word "cacophony", page 1000: Alan Cline.
- Simplified HMM for speech understanding, page 1002: Jim Barnett.
- Drawing of the Towers of Hanoi, page 1058: Alan Cline.
- The schematic diagram and the finite state diagram of a binary multiplier, page 1061: Oscar Hernandez.
- Diagram of the FSM robot controller, page 1063: Peter Stone.

P A R T I

INTRODUCTION

CHAPTER 1

Why Study the Theory of Computation?

In this book, we present a theory of what can be computed and what cannot. We also sketch some theoretical frameworks that can inform the design of programs to solve a wide variety of problems. But why do we bother? We don't we just skip ahead and write the programs that we need? This chapter is a short attempt to answer that question.

1.1 The Shelf Life of Programming Tools

Implementations come and go. In the somewhat early days of computing, programming meant knowing how to write code like:[1]

```
ENTRY     SXA     4,RETURN
          LDQ     X
          FMP     A
          FAD     B
          XCA
          FMP     X
          FAD     C
          STO     RESULT
RETURN    TRA     0

A         BSS     1
B         BSS     1
C         BSS     1
X         BSS     1
TEMP      BSS     1
STORE     BSS     1
          END
```

[1]This program was written for the IBM 7090. It computes the value of a simple quadratic $ax^2 + bx + c$.

In 1957, Fortran appeared and made it possible for people to write programs that looked more straightforwardly like mathematics. By 1970, the IBM 360 series of computers was in widespread use for both business and scientific computing. To submit a job, one keyed onto punch cards a set of commands in OS/360 JCL (Job Control Language). Guruhood attached to people who actually knew what something like this meant:[2]

```
//MYJOB     JOB (COMPRESS),'VOLKER BANDKE', CLASS=P,COND=(0,NE)
//BACKUP   EXEC PGM=IEBCOPY
//SYSPRINT DD   SYSOUT=*
//SYSUT1    DD  DISP=SHR,DSN=MY.IMPORTNT.PDS
//SYSUT2    DD  DISP=(,CATLG),DSN=MY.IMPORTNT.PDS.BACKUP,
//              UNIT=3350,VOL=SER=DISK01,
//              DCB=MY.IMPORTNT.PDS,SPACE=(CYL,(10,10,20))
//COMPRESS EXEC PGM=IEBCOPY
//SYSPRINT DD   SYSOUT=*
//MYPDS     DD  DISP=OLD,DSN=*.BACKUP.SYSUT1
//SYSIN     DD  *
COPY INDD=MYPDS,OUTDD=MYPDS
//DELETE2 EXEC PGM=IEFBR14
//BACKPDS   DD  DISP=(OLD,DELETE,DELETE),DSN=MY.IMPORTNT.PDS.BACKUP
```

By the turn of the millennium, gurus were different. They listened to different music and had never touched a keypunch machine. But many of them did know that the following Java method (when compiled with the appropriate libraries) allows the user to select a file, which is read in and parsed using whitespace delimiters. From the parsed file, the program builds a frequency map, which shows how often each word occurs in the file:

```
public static TreeMap<String, Integer> create() throws IOException
    public static TreeMap<String, Integer> create() throws
                IOException
    {  Integer freq;
       String word;
       TreeMap<String, Integer> result = new TreeMap<String, Integer>();
       JFileChooser c = new JFileChooser();
       int retval = c.showOpenDialog(null);
       if (retval == JFileChooser.APPROVE_OPTION)
            {  Scanner s = new Scanner( c.getSelectedFile());
               while( s.hasNext() )
               {   word = s.next().toLowerCase();
                   freq = result.get(word);
                   result.put(word, (freq == null ? 1 : freq + 1));
               }
            }
       return result;
    }
}
```

[2]It safely reorganizes and compresses a partitioned dataset.

Along the way, other programming languages became popular, at least within some circles. There was a time when some people bragged that they could write code like:[3]

```
(⌈/V)>(+/V)-⌈/V
```

Today's programmers can't read code from 50 years ago. Programmers from the early days could never have imagined what a program of today would look like. In the face of that kind of change, what does it mean to learn the science of computing?

The answer is that there are mathematical properties, both of problems and of algorithms for solving problems, that depend on neither the details of today's technology nor the programming fashion *du jour*. The theory that we will present in this book addresses some of those properties. Most of what we will discuss was known by the early 1970s (barely the middle ages of computing history). But it is still useful in two key ways:

- It provides a set of abstract structures that are useful for solving certain classes of problems. These abstract structures can be implemented on whatever hardware/software platform is available.
- It defines provable limits to what can be computed, regardless of processor speed or memory size. An understanding of these limits helps us to focus our design effort in areas in which it can pay off, rather than on the computing equivalent of the search for a perpetual motion machine.

In this book our focus will be on analyzing problems, rather than on comparing solutions to problems. We will, of course, spend a lot of time solving problems. But our goal will be to discover fundamental properties of the problems themselves:

- Is there any computational solution to the problem? If not, is there a restricted but useful variation of the problem for which a solution does exist?
- If a solution exists, can it be implemented using some fixed amount of memory?
- If a solution exists, how efficient is it? More specifically, how do its time and space requirements grow as the size of the problem grows?
- Are there groups of problems that are equivalent in the sense that if there is an efficient solution to one member of the group there is an efficient solution to all the others?

[3] An expression in the programming language APL 🖳. It returns 1 if the largest value in a three element vector is greater than the sum of the other two elements, and 0 otherwise [Gillman and Rose 1984, p. 326]. Although APL is not one of the major programming languages in use today, its inventor, Kenneth Iverson, received the 1979 Turing Award for its development.

1.2 Applications of the Theory Are Everywhere

Computers have revolutionized our world. They have changed the course of our daily lives, the way we do science, the way we entertain ourselves, the way that business is conducted, and the way we protect our security. The theory that we present in this book has applications in all of those areas. Throughout the main text, you will find notes that point to the more substantive application-focused discussions that appear in Appendices G–Q. Some of the applications that we'll consider are:

- Languages, the focus of this book, enable both machine/machine and person/machine communication. Without them, none of today's applications of computing could exist.

> Network communication protocols are languages. (I. 1) Most web pages are described using the Hypertext Markup Language, HTML. (Q.1.2) The Semantic Web, whose goal is to support intelligent agents working on the Web, exploits additional layers of languages, such as RDF and OWL, that can be used to describe the content of the Web. (I. 3) Music can be viewed as a language, and specialized languages enable composers to create new electronic music. (N.1) Even very unlanguage-like things, such as sets of pictures, can be viewed as languages by, for example, associating each picture with the program that drew it. (Q.1.3)

- Both the design and the implementation of modern programming languages rely heavily on the theory of context-free languages that we will present in Part III. Context-free grammars are used to document the languages' syntax and they form the basis for the parsing techniques that all compilers use.

> The use of context-free grammars to define programming languages and to build their compilers is described in Appendix G.

- People use natural languages, such as English, to communicate with each other. Since the advent of word processing, and then the Internet, we now type or speak our words to computers. So we would like to build programs to manage our words, check our grammar, search the World Wide Web, and translate from one language to another. Programs to do that also rely on the theory of context-free languages that we present in Part III.

> A sketch of some of the main techniques used in natural language processing can be found in Appendix L.

- Systems as diverse as parity checkers, vending machines, communication protocols, and building security devices can be straightforwardly described as finite state machines, which we'll describe in Chapter 5.

> A vending machine is described in Example 5.1. A family of network communication protocols is modeled as finite state machines in I.1. An example of a simple building security system, modeled as a finite state machine, can be found in J.1. An example of a finite state controller for a soccer-playing robot can be found in P.4.

- Many interactive video games are (large, often nondeterministic) finite state machines.

> An example of the use of a finite state machine to describe a role playing game can be found in N.3.1.

- DNA is the language of life. DNA molecules, as well as the proteins that they describe, are strings that are made up of symbols drawn from small alphabets (nucleotides and amino acids, respectively). So computational biologists exploit many of the same tools that computational linguists use. For example, they rely on techniques that are based on both finite state machines and context-free grammars.

> For a very brief introduction to computational biology see Appendix K.

- Security is perhaps the most important property of many computer systems. The undecidability results that we present in Part IV show that there cannot exist a general purpose method for automatically verifying arbitrary security properties of programs. The complexity results that we present in Part V serve as the basis for powerful encryption techniques.

> For a proof of the undecidability of the correctness of a very simple security model, see J.2. For a short introduction to cryptography, see J.3.

- Artificial intelligence programs solve problems in task domains ranging from medical diagnosis to factory scheduling. Various logical frameworks have been proposed for representing and reasoning with the knowledge that such programs exploit. The undecidability results that we present in Part IV show that there cannot exist a general theorem prover that can decide, given an arbitrary statement in first order logic, whether or not that statement follows from the system's axioms. The complexity results that we present in Part V show that, if we back off to the far less expressive system of Boolean (propositional) logic, while it becomes possible to decide the validity of a given statement, it is not possible to do so, in general, in a reasonable amount of time.

> For a discussion of the role of undecidability and complexity results in artificial intelligence, see Appendix M. The same issues plague the development of the Semantic Web. (I.3)

- Clearly documented and widely accepted standards play a pivotal role in modern computing systems. Getting a diverse group of users to agree on a single standard is never easy. But the undecidability and complexity results that we present in Parts IV and V mean that, for some important problems, there is no single right answer for all uses. Expressively weak standard languages may be tractable and decidable, but they may simply be inadequate for some tasks. For those tasks, expressively powerful languages, that give up some degree of tractability and possibly decidability, may be required. The provable lack of a one-size-fits-all language makes the standards process even more difficult and may require standards that allow alternatives.

> We'll see one example of this aspect of the standards process when we consider, in I.3, the design of a description language for the Semantic Web.

- Many natural structures, including ones as different as organic molecules and computer networks, can be modeled as graphs. The theory of complexity that we present in Part V tells us that, while there exist efficient algorithms for answering some important questions about graphs, other questions are "hard", in the sense that no efficient algorithm for them is known nor is one likely to be developed.

> We'll discuss the role of graph algorithms in network analysis in I.2.

- The complexity results that we present in Part V contain a lot of bad news. There are problems that matter yet for which no efficient algorithm is likely ever to be found. But practical solutions to some of these problems exist. They rely on a variety of approximation techniques that work pretty well most of the time.

> An almost optimal solution to an instance of the traveling salesman problem with 1,904,711 cities has been found, as we'll see in Section 27.1. Randomized algorithms can find prime numbers efficiently, as we'll see in Section 30.2.4. Heuristic search algorithms find paths in computer games (N.3.2) and move sequences for champion chess-playing programs. (N.2.5)

CHAPTER 2

Languages and Strings

In the theory that we are about to build, we are going to analyze problems by casting them as instances of the more specific question, "Given some string s and some language L, is s in L?" Before we can formalize what we mean by that, we need to define our terms.

An ***alphabet***, often denoted Σ, is a finite set. We will call the members of Σ ***symbols*** or ***characters***.

2.1 Strings

A ***string*** is a finite sequence, possibly empty, of symbols drawn from some alphabet Σ. Given any alphabet Σ, the shortest string that can be formed from Σ is the empty string, which we will write as ε. The set of all possible strings over an alphabet Σ is written Σ^*. This notation exploits the Kleene star operator, which we will define more generally below.

EXAMPLE 2.1 Alphabets

Alphabet name	Alphabet symbols	Example strings
The English alphabet	{a, b, c, . . . , z}	ε, aabbcg, aaaaa
The binary alphabet	{0, 1}	ε, 0, 001100
A star alphabet	{★, ✪, ✫, ✯, ✭, ✡, ☆}	ε, ✪✪, ✪✭✭☆★☆
A music alphabet	{𝅝, 𝅗𝅥, ♩, ♪, 𝅘𝅥𝅯, 𝅘𝅥𝅰}	ε, 𝅝|𝅗𝅥𝅗𝅥|𝅗𝅥♩♩|

In running text, we will indicate literal symbols and strings by writing them `like this`.

2.1.2 Functions on Strings

The ***length*** of a string s, which we will write as $|s|$, is the number of symbols in s. For example:

$$|\varepsilon| = 0$$
$$|1001101| = 7$$

For any symbol c and string s, we define the function $\#_c(s)$ to be the number of times that the symbol c occurs in s. So, for example, $\#_a(\text{abbaaa}) = 4$.

The ***concatenation*** of two strings s and t, written $s\,||\,t$ or simply st, is the string formed by appending t to s. For example, if x = good and y = bye, then xy = goodbye. So $|xy| = |x| + |y|$.

The empty string, ε, is the identity for concatenation of strings. So $\forall x\ (x\varepsilon = \varepsilon x = x)$.

Concatenation, as a function defined on strings, is associative. So $\forall s, t, w\ ((st)w = s\,(tw))$.

Next we define string ***replication***. For each string w and each natural number i, the string w^i is defined as:

$$w^0 = \varepsilon$$
$$w^{i+1} = w^i w$$

For example:

a^3 = aaa
$(\text{bye})^2$ = byebye
a^0b^3 = bbb

Finally we define string ***reversal***. For each string w, the reverse of w, which we will write w^R, is defined as:

If $|w| = 0$ then $w^R = w = \varepsilon$.
If $|w| \geq 1$ then $\exists a \in \Sigma\ (\exists u \in \Sigma^*\ (w = ua))$, (i.e., the last character of w is a.)
Then define $w^R = au^R$.

THEOREM 2.1 Concatenation and Reverse of Strings

Theorem: If w and x are strings, then $(wx)^R = x^R w^R$.
For example, $(\text{nametag})^R = (\text{tag})^R(\text{name})^R$ = gateman.

Proof: The proof is by induction on $|x|$:

Base case: $|x| = 0$. Then $x = \varepsilon$, and $(wx)^R = (w\varepsilon)^R = (w)^R = \varepsilon w^R = \varepsilon^R w^R = x^R w^R$.

Prove: $\forall n \geq 0\ (((|x| = n) \rightarrow ((wx)^R = x^R w^R)) \rightarrow ((|x| = n + 1) \rightarrow\ ((wx)^R = x^R w^R)))$.

Consider any string x, where $|x| = n + 1$. Then $x = ua$ for some character a and $|u| = n$. So:

$$
\begin{aligned}
(wx)^R &= (w(ua))^R && \text{rewrite } x \text{ as } ua\\
&= ((wu)a)^R && \text{associativity of concatenation}\\
&= a(wu)^R && \text{definition of reversal}\\
&= a(u^R w^R) && \text{induction hypothesis}\\
&= (au^R)w^R && \text{associativity of concatenation}\\
&= (ua)^R w^R && \text{definition of reversal}\\
&= x^R w^R && \text{rewrite } ua \text{ as } x
\end{aligned}
$$

2.1.3 Relations on Strings

A string s is a ***substring*** of a string t iff s occurs contiguously as part of t. For example:

aaa	is a substring of	aaabbbaaa
aaaaaa	is not a substring of	aaabbbaaa

A string s is a ***proper substring*** of a string t iff s is a substring of t and $s \neq t$. Every string is a substring (although not a proper substring) of itself. The empty string, ε, is a substring of every string.

A string s is a ***prefix*** of t iff $\exists x \in \Sigma^* \ (t = sx)$. A string s is a ***proper prefix*** of a string t iff s is a prefix of t and $s \neq t$. Every string is a prefix (although not a proper prefix) of itself. The empty string, ε, is a prefix of every string. For example, the prefixes of abba are: ε, a, ab, abb, abba.

A string s is a ***suffix*** of t iff $\exists x \in \Sigma^* \ (t = xs)$. A string s is a ***proper suffix*** of a string t iff s is a suffix of t and $s \neq t$. Every string is a suffix (although not a proper suffix) of itself. The empty string, ε, is a suffix of every string. For example, the suffixes of abba are: ε, a, ba, bba, abba.

2.2 Languages

A ***language*** is a (finite or infinite) set of strings over a finite alphabet Σ. When we are talking about more than one language, we will use the notation Σ_L to mean the alphabet from which the strings in the language L are formed.

EXAMPLE 2.2 Defining Languages Given an Alphabet

Let Σ = {a, b}. Σ* = {ε, a, b, aa, ab, ba, bb, aaa, aab, ...}.

Some examples of languages over Σ are:

∅, {ε}, {a, b}, {ε, a, aa, aaa, aaaa, aaaaa},
{ε, a, aa, aaa, aaaa, aaaaa, ...}

2.2.2 Techniques for Defining Languages

We will use a variety of techniques for defining the languages that we wish to consider. Since languages are sets, we can define them using any of the set-defining techniques that are described in A.2. For example, we can specify a characteristic function, i.e., a predicate that is *True* of every element in the set and *False* of everything else.

EXAMPLE 2.3 All a's Precede All b's

Let $L = \{w \in \{\texttt{a},\texttt{b}\}^* : \text{all a's precede all b's in } w\}$. The strings ε, a, aa, aabbb, and bb are in L. The strings aba, ba, and abc are not in L. Notice that some strings trivially satisfy the requirement for membership in L. The rule says nothing about there having to be any a's or any b's. All it says is that any a's there are must come before all the b's (if any). If there are no a's or no b's, then there can be none that violate the rule. So the strings ε, a, aa, and bb trivially satisfy the rule and are in L.

EXAMPLE 2.4 Strings That End in a

Let $L = \{x : \exists y \in \{\texttt{a},\texttt{b}\}^* \ (x = y\texttt{a})\}$. The strings a, aa, aaa, bbaa, and ba are in L. The strings ε, bab, and bca are not in L. L consists of all strings that can be formed by taking some string in $\{\texttt{a},\texttt{b}\}^*$ and concatenating a single a onto the end of it.

EXAMPLE 2.5 The Perils of Using English to Describe Languages

Let $L = \{x\#y : x, y \in \{0, 1, 2, 3, 4, 5, 6, 7, 8, 9\}^*$ and, when x and y are viewed as the decimal representations of natural numbers, $square(x) = y\}$. The strings 3#9 and 12#144 are in L. The strings 3#8, 12, and 12#12#12 are not in L. But what about the string #? Is it in L? It depends on what we mean by the phrase, "when x and y are viewed as the decimal representations of natural numbers." Is ε the decimal representation of some natural number? It is possible that an algorithm that converts strings to numbers might convert ε to 0. In that case, since 0 is the square of 0, # is in L. If, on the other hand, the string-to-integer converter fails to accept ε as a valid input, # is not in L. This example illustrates the dangers of using English descriptions of sets. They are sometimes ambiguous. We will strive to use only unambiguous terms. We will also, as we discuss below, develop other definitional techniques that do not present this problem.

EXAMPLE 2.6 The Empty Language

Let $L = \{\} = \varnothing$. L is the language that contains no strings.

EXAMPLE 2.7 The Empty Language is Different From the Empty String

Let $L = \{\varepsilon\}$, the language that contains a single string, ε. Note that L is different from $\varnothing$.

All of the examples we have considered so far fit the definition that we are using for the term *language*: a set of strings. They're quite different, though, from the everyday use of the term. Everyday languages are also languages under our definition.

EXAMPLE 2.8 English Isn't a Well-Defined Language

Let $L = \{w : w \text{ is a sentence in English}\}$.

Examples:	Kerry hit the ball.	/* Clearly in L.
	Colorless green ideas sleep furiously.[4]	/* The syntax is correct but what could it mean?
	The window needs fixed.	/* In some dialects of L.
	Ball the Stacy hit blue.	/* Clearly not in L.

The problem with languages like English is that there is no clear agreement on what strings they contain. We will not be able to apply the theory that we are about to build to any language for which we cannot first produce a formal specification. Natural languages, like English or Spanish or Chinese, while hard to specify, are of great practical importance, though. As a result, substantial effort has been expended in creating formal and computationally effective descriptions of them that are good enough to be used as the basis for applications such as grammar checking and text database retrieval.

To the extent that formal descriptions of natural languages like English can be created, the theory that we are about to develop can be applied, as we will see in Parts II and III and Appendix L.

[4] This classic example of a syntactically correct but semantically anomalous sentence is from [Chomsky 1957].

EXAMPLE 2.9 A Halting Problem Language

Let $L = \{w : w \text{ is a C program that halts on all inputs}\}$. L is substantially more complex than, for example, $\{x \in \{\texttt{a},\texttt{b}\}^*: \text{all a's precede all b's}\}$. But, unlike English, there does exist a clear formal specification of it. The theory that we are about to build will tell us something very useful about L.

We can use the relations that we have defined on strings as a way to define languages.

EXAMPLE 2.10 Using the Prefix Relation

We define the following languages in terms of the prefix relation on strings:

$L_1 = \{w \in \{\texttt{a}, \texttt{b}\}^* : \text{no prefix of } w \text{ contains } \texttt{b}\}$

$= \{\varepsilon, \texttt{a}, \texttt{aa}, \texttt{aaa}, \texttt{aaaa}, \texttt{aaaaa}, \texttt{aaaaaa}, \ldots\}$.

$L_2 = \{w \in \{\texttt{a}, \texttt{b}\}^* : \text{no prefix of } w \text{ starts with } \texttt{b}\}$

$= \{w \in \{\texttt{a}, \texttt{b}\}^* : \text{the first character of } w \text{ is } \texttt{a}\} \cup \{\varepsilon\}$.

$L_3 = \{w \in \{\texttt{a}, \texttt{b}\}^* : \text{every prefix of } w \text{ starts with } \texttt{b}\}$

$= \varnothing$.

L_3 is equal to $\varnothing$ because ε is a prefix of every string. Since ε does not start with b, no strings meet L_3's requirement.

Recall that we defined the replication operator on strings: For any string s and integer n, $s^n = n$ copies of s concatenated together. For example, $(\texttt{bye})^2 = \texttt{byebye}$. We can use replication as a way to define a language, rather than a single string, if we allow n to be a variable, rather than a specific constant.

EXAMPLE 2.11 Using Replication to Define a Language

Let $L = \{\texttt{a}^n : n \geq 0\}$. $L = \{\varepsilon, \texttt{a}, \texttt{aa}, \texttt{aaa}, \texttt{aaaa}, \texttt{aaaaa}, \ldots\}$.

Languages are sets. So, if we want to provide a computational definition of a language, we could specify either:

- a language generator, which enumerates (lists) the elements of the language, or
- a language recognizer, which decides whether or not a candidate string is in the language and returns *True* if it is and *False* if it isn't.

For example, the logical definition, $L = \{x : \exists y \in \{\text{a, b}\}^* \ (x = y\text{a})\}$ can be turned into either a language generator (enumerator) or a language recognizer.

In some cases, when considering an enumerator for a language L, we may care about the order in which the elements of L are generated. If there exists a total order D of the elements of Σ_L (as there does, for example, on the letters of the Roman alphabet or the symbols for the digits 0 – 9), then we can use D to define on L a useful total order called ***lexicographic order*** (written $<_L$):

- Shorter strings precede longer ones: $\forall x \ (\forall y \ ((|x| < |y|) \rightarrow (x <_L y)))$, and
- Of strings that are the same length, sort them in dictionary order using D.

When we use lexicographic order in the rest of this book, we will assume that D is the standard sort order on letters and numerals. If D is not obvious, we will state it.

We will say that a program ***lexicographically enumerates*** the elements of L iff it enumerates them in lexicographic order.

EXAMPLE 2.12 Lexicographic Enumeration

Let $L = \{x \in \{\texttt{a, b}\}^* : \text{all a's precede all b's}\}$. The lexicographic enumeration of L is:

ε, a, b, aa, ab, bb, aaa, aab, abb, bbb, aaaa, aaab, aabb, abbb, bbbb, aaaaa, ...

In Parts II, III, and IV of this book, we will consider a variety of formal techniques for specifying both generators (enumerators) and recognizers for various classes of languages.

2.2.3 What is the Cardinality of a Language?

How large is a language? The smallest language over any alphabet is $\varnothing$, whose cardinality is 0. The largest language over any alphabet Σ is Σ^*. What is $|\Sigma^*|$? Suppose that $\Sigma = \varnothing$. Then $\Sigma^* = \{\varepsilon\}$ and $|\Sigma^*| = 1$. But what about the far more useful case in which Σ is not empty?

THEOREM 2.2 The Cardinality of Σ^*

Theorem: If $\Sigma \neq \varnothing$ then Σ^* is countably infinite.

Proof: The elements of Σ^* can be lexicographically enumerated by a straightforward procedure that:

- Enumerates all strings of length 0, then length 1, then length 2, and so forth.
- Within the strings of a given length, enumerates them in dictionary order.

This enumeration is infinite since there is no longest string in Σ^*. By Theorem A.1, since there exists an infinite enumeration of Σ^*, it is countably infinite. ◼

Since any language over Σ is a subset of Σ^*, the cardinality of every language is at least 0 and at most $\aleph_0$. So all languages are either finite or countably infinite.

2.2.4 How Many Languages Are There?

Let Σ be an alphabet. How many different languages are there that are defined on Σ? The set of languages defined on Σ is $\mathcal{P}(\Sigma^*)$, the power set of Σ^*, or the set of all subsets of Σ^*. If $\Sigma = \varnothing$ then Σ^* is $\{\varepsilon\}$ and $\mathcal{P}(\Sigma^*)$ is $\{\varnothing, \{\varepsilon\}\}$. But, again, what about the useful case in which Σ is not empty?

THEOREM 2.3 An Uncountably Infinite Number of Languages

Theorem: If $\Sigma \neq \varnothing$ then the set of languages over Σ is uncountably infinite.

Proof: The set of languages defined on Σ is $\mathcal{P}(\Sigma^*)$. By Theorem 2.2, Σ^* is countably infinite. By Theorem A.4, if S is a countably infinite set, $\mathcal{P}(S)$ is uncountably infinite. So $\mathcal{P}(\Sigma^*)$ is uncountably infinite. ◼

2.2.5 Functions on Languages

Since languages are sets, all of the standard set operations are well-defined on languages. In particular, we will find union, intersection, difference, and complement to be useful. Complement will be defined with Σ^* as the universe unless we explicitly state otherwise.

EXAMPLE 2.13 Set Functions Applied to Languages

Let: $\Sigma = \{\mathrm{a}, \mathrm{b}\}$.
$L_1 = \{$strings with an even number of a's$\}$.
$L_2 = \{$strings with no b's$\} = \{\varepsilon$, a, aa, aaa, aaaa, aaaaa, aaaaaa, $\ldots\}$.

$L_1 \cup L_2 = \{$all strings of just a's plus strings that contain b's and an even number of a's$\}$.

$L_1 \cap L_2 = \{\varepsilon$, aa, aaaa, aaaaaa, aaaaaaaa, $\ldots\}$.

$L_2 - L_1 = \{$a, aaa, aaaaa, aaaaaaa, $\ldots\}$.

$\neg(L_2 - L_1) = \{$strings with at least one b $\} \cup \{$strings with an even number of a's$\}$.

Because languages are sets of strings, it makes sense to define operations on them in terms of the operations that we have already defined on strings. Three useful ones to consider are concatenation, Kleene star, and reverse.

Let L_1 and L_2 be two languages defined over some alphabet Σ. Then their ***concatenation***, written L_1L_2 is:

$$L_1L_2 = \{w \in \Sigma^* : \exists s \in L_1 (\exists t \in L_2 (w = st))\}.$$

EXAMPLE 2.14 Concatenation of Languages

Let: L_1 = {cat, dog, mouse, bird}.
L_2 = {bone, food}.

L_1L_2 = {catbone, catfood, dogbone, dogfood, mousebone, mousefood, birdbone, birdfood}.

The language $\{\varepsilon\}$ is the identity for concatenation of languages. So, for all languages L, $L\{\varepsilon\} = \{\varepsilon\}L = L$.

The language $\varnothing$ is a zero for concatenation of languages. So, for all languages L, $L\varnothing = \varnothing L = \varnothing$. That $\varnothing$ is a zero follows from the definition of the concatenation of two languages as the set consisting of all strings that can be formed by selecting some string s from the first language and some string t from the second language and then concatenating them together. There are no ways to select a string from the empty set.

Concatenation, as a function defined on languages, is associative. So, for all languages L_1, L_2, and L_3:

$$((L_1L_2)L_3 = L_1(L_2L_3)).$$

It is important to be careful when concatenating languages that are defined using replication. Recall that we used the notation $\{\mathtt{a}^n : n \geq 0\}$ to mean the set of strings composed of zero or more a's. That notation is a shorthand for a longer, perhaps clearer expression, $\{w : \exists n \geq 0\ (w = \mathtt{a}^n)\}$. In this form, it is clear that n is a variable bound by an existential quantifier. We will use the convention that the scope of such quantifiers is the entire expression in which they occur. So multiple occurrences of the same variable letter are the same variable and must take on the same value. Suppose that $L_1 = \{\mathtt{a}^n : n \geq 0\}$ and $L_2 = \{\mathtt{b}^n : n \geq 0\}$. By the definition of language concatenation, $L_1L_2 = \{w : w$ consists of a (possibly empty) a region followed by a (possibly empty) b region$\}$. $L_1L_2 \neq \{\mathtt{a}^n\mathtt{b}^n : n \geq 0\}$, since every string in $\{\mathtt{a}^n\mathtt{b}^n : n \geq 0\}$ must have the same number of b's as a's. The easiest way to avoid confusion is simply to rename conflicting variables before attempting to concatenate the expressions that contain them. So $L_1L_2 = \{\mathtt{a}^n\mathtt{b}^m : n, m \geq 0\}$. In Chapter 6 we will define a convenient notation that will let us write this as a*b*.

Let L be a language defined over some alphabet Σ. Then the ***Kleene star*** of L, written L^* is:

$$L^* = \{\varepsilon\} \cup \{w \in \Sigma^* : \exists k \geq 1\ (\exists w_1, w_2, \ldots w_k \in L\ (w = w_1w_2 \ldots w_k))\}.$$

In other words, L^* is the set of strings that can be formed by concatenating together zero or more strings from L.

EXAMPLE 2.15 Kleene Star

Let L = {dog, cat, fish}. Then:

L^* = {ε, dog, cat, fish, dogdog, dogcat,..., fishdog,..., fishcatfish, fishdogfishcat,...}.

EXAMPLE 2.16 Kleene Star, Again

Let $L = \{w \in \{\mathsf{a}, \mathsf{b}\}^* : \#_{\mathsf{a}}(w)$ is odd and $\#_{\mathsf{b}}(w)$ is even$\}$. Then $L^* = \{w \in \{\mathsf{a}, \mathsf{b}\}^* : \#_{\mathsf{b}}(w)$ is even$\}$. The constraint on the number of a's disappears in the description of L^* because strings in L^* are formed by concatenating together any number of strings from L. If an odd number of strings are concatenated together, the result will contain an odd number of a's. If an even number are used, the result will contain an even number of a's.

L^* always contains an infinite number of strings as long as L is not equal to either $\varnothing$ or $\{\varepsilon\}$ (i.e., as long as there is at least one nonempty string any number of which can be concatenated together). If $L = \varnothing$, then $L^* = \{\varepsilon\}$, since there are no strings that could be concatenated to ε to make it longer. If $L = \{\varepsilon\}$, then L^* is also $\{\varepsilon\}$.

It is sometimes useful to require that at least one element of L be selected. So we define:

$$L^+ = LL^*.$$

Another way to describe L^+ is that it is the closure of L under concatenation. Note that $L^+ = L^* - \{\varepsilon\}$ iff $\varepsilon \notin L$.

EXAMPLE 2.17 L^+

Let $L = \{0, 1\}^+$ be the set of binary strings. L does not include ε.

Let L be a language defined over some alphabet Σ. Then the ***reverse*** of L, written L^R is:

$$L^R = \{w \in \Sigma^* : w = x^R \text{ for some } x \in L\}.$$

In other words, L^R is the set of strings that can be formed by taking some string in L and reversing it.

Since we have defined the reverse of a language in terms of the definition of reverse applied to strings, we expect it to have analogous properties.

THEOREM 2.4 Concatenation and Reverse of Languages

Theorem: If L_1 and L_2 are languages, then $(L_1L_2)^R = L_2{}^R L_1{}^R$.

Proof: If x and y are strings, then $\forall x\, (\forall y\, ((xy)^R = y^R x^R))$ Theorem 2.1

$(L_1L_2)^R = \{(xy)^R : x \in L_1 \text{ and } y \in L_2\}$	Definition of concatenation of languages
$= \{y^R x^R : x \in L_1 \text{ and } y \in L_2\}$	Lines 1 and 2
$= L_2{}^R L_1{}^R$	Definition of concatenation of languages

We have now defined the two important data types, string and language, that we will use throughout this book. In the next chapter, we will see how we can use them to define a framework that will enable us to analyze computational problems of all sorts (not just ones you may naturally think of in terms of strings).

2.2.6 Assigning Meaning to the Strings of a Language

Sometimes we are interested in viewing a language just as a set of strings. For example, we'll consider some important formal properties of the language we'll call $A^nB^n = \{a^nb^n: n \geq 0\}$. In other words, A^nB^n is the language composed of all strings of a's and b's such that all the a's come first and the number of a's equals the number of b's. We won't attempt to assign meanings to any of those strings.

But some languages are useful precisely because their strings do have meanings. We use natural languages like English and Chinese because they allow us to communicate ideas. A program in a language like Java or C^{++} or Perl also has a meaning. In the case of a programming language, one way to define meaning is in terms of some other (typically closer to machine architecture) language. So, for example, the meaning of a Java program can be described as a Java Virtual Machine program. An alternative is to define a program's meaning in a logical language.

Philosophers and linguists (and others) have spent centuries arguing about what sentences in natural languages like English (or Sanskrit or whatever) mean. We won't attempt to solve that problem here. But if we are going to work with formal languages, we need a precise way to map each string to its meaning (also called its ***semantics***). We'll call a function that assigns meanings to strings a ***semantic interpretation function***. Most of the languages we'll be concerned with are infinite because there is no bound on the length of the strings that they contain. So it won't, in general, be possible to define meanings by a table that pairs each string with its meaning.

We must instead define a function that knows the meanings of the language's basic units and can combine those meanings, according to some fixed set of rules, to build meanings for larger expressions. We call such a function, which can be said to "compose" the meanings of simpler constituents into a single meaning for a larger expression, a ***compositional semantic interpretation function***. There arguably exists a mostly compositional semantic interpretation function for English. Linguists fight about the gory details of what such a function must look like. Everyone agrees that words have meanings and that one can build a meaning for a simple sentence by combining the meanings of the subject and the verb. For example, speakers of English would have no trouble assigning a meaning to the sentence, "I gave him the fizding," provided that they are told what the meaning of the word "fizding" is. Everyone also agrees that the meaning of idioms, like "I'm going to give him a piece of my mind," cannot be derived compositionally. Some other issues are more subtle.

Languages whose strings have meaning pervade computing and its applications. Boolean logic and first-order logic are languages. Programming languages are languages. (G.1) Network protocols are languages. (I.1) Database query languages are languages. (Q.1.1) HTML is a language for defining

Web pages. (Q.1.2) XML is a more general language for marking up data. (Q.1.2) OWL is a language for defining the meaning of tags on the Web. (I.3.6) BNF is a language that can be used to specify the syntax of other languages. (G.1.1) DNA is a language for describing proteins. (K.1.2) Music is a language based on sound. (N.1)

When we define a formal language for a specific purpose, we design it so that there exists a compositional semantic interpretation function. So, for example, there exist compositional semantic interpretation functions for programming languages like Java and C^{++}. There exists a compositional semantic interpretation function for the language of Boolean logic. It is specified by the truth tables that define the meanings of whichever operators (e.g., $\wedge$, $\vee$, $\neg$ and $\rightarrow$) are allowed.

One significant property of semantic interpretation functions for useful languages is that they are generally not one-to-one. Consider:

- English: The sentences, "Chocolate, please," "I'd like chocolate," "I'll have chocolate," and "I guess chocolate today," all mean the same thing, at least in the context of ordering an ice cream cone.
- Java: The following chunks of code all do the same thing:

```
int x = 4;     int x = 4;     int x = 4;        int x = 4;
x++;           ++x;           x = x + 1;        x = x --1;
```

The semantic interpretation functions that we will describe later in this book, for example for the various grammar formalisms that we will introduce, will not be one-to-one either.

Exercises

1. Consider the language $L = \{1^n2^n : n > 0\}$. Is the string 122 in L?

2. Let $L_1 = \{\mathtt{a}^n\mathtt{b}^n : n > 0\}$. Let $L_2 = \{\mathtt{c}^n : n > 0\}$. For each of the following strings, state whether or not it is an element of L_1L_2:

a. ε.

b. aabbcc.

c. abbcc.

d. aabbcccc.

3. Let $L_1 = \{\mathtt{peach}, \mathtt{apple}, \mathtt{cherry}\}$ and $L_2 = \{\mathtt{pie}, \mathtt{cobbler}, \varepsilon\}$. List the elements of L_1L_2 in lexicographic order.

4. Let $L = \{w \in \{\mathtt{a}, \mathtt{b}\}^* : |w| \equiv_3 0\}$. List the first six elements in a lexicographic enumeration of L.

5. Consider the language L of all strings drawn from the alphabet $\{\mathtt{a}, \mathtt{b}\}$ with at least two different substrings of length 2.

a. Describe L by writing a sentence of the form $L = \{w \in \Sigma^* : P(w)\}$, where Σ is a set of symbols and P is a first-order logic formula. You may use the function $|s|$ to return the length of s. You may use all the standard relational symbols (e.g., $=$, $\neq$, $<$, etc.), plus the predicate *Substr*(s, t), which is *True* iff s is a substring of t.

b. List the first six elements of a lexicographic enumeration of L.

6. For each of the following languages L, give a simple English description. Show two strings that are in L and two that are not (unless there are fewer than two strings in L or two not in L, in which case show as many as possible).

a. $L = \{w \in \{\text{a}, \text{b}\}^* : \text{exactly one prefix of } w \text{ ends in a}\}$.

b. $L = \{w \in \{\text{a}, \text{b}\}^* : \text{all prefixes of } w \text{ end in a}\}$.

c. $L = \{w \in \{\text{a}, \text{b}\}^* : \exists x \in \{\text{a}, \text{b}\}^+ (w = \text{a}x\text{a}\}$.

7. Are the following sets closed under the following operations? If not, what are their respective closures?

a. The language $\{\text{a}, \text{b}\}$ under concatenation.

b. The odd length strings over the alphabet $\{\text{a}, \text{b}\}$ under Kleene star.

c. $L = \{w \in \{\text{a}, \text{b}\}^*\}$ under reverse.

d. $L = \{w \in \{\text{a}, \text{b}\}^* : w \text{ starts with a}\}$ under reverse.

e. $L = \{w \in \{\text{a}, \text{b}\}^* : w \text{ ends in a}\}$ under concatenation.

8. For each of the following statements, state whether it is *True* or *False*. Prove your answer.

a. $\forall L_1, L_2 (L_1 = L_2 \text{ iff } L_1^* = L_2^*)$.

b. $(\varnothing \cup \varnothing^*) \cap (\neg\varnothing - (\varnothing\varnothing^*)) = \varnothing$ (where $\neg\varnothing$ is the complement of $\varnothing$).

c. Every infinite language is the complement of a finite language.

d. $\forall L\, ((L^R)^R = L)$.

e. $\forall L_1, L_2 ((L_1 L_2)^* = L_1^* L_2^*)$.

f. $\forall L_1, L_2 ((L_1^* L_2^* L_1^*)^* = (L_2 \cup L_1)^*)$.

g. $\forall L_1, L_2 ((L_1 \cup L_2)^* = L_1^* \cup L_2^*)$.

h. $\forall L_1, L_2, L_3 ((L_1 \cup L_2) L_3 = (L_1 L_3) \cup (L_2 L_3))$.

i. $\forall L_1, L_2, L_3 ((L_1 L_2) \cup L_3 = (L_1 \cup L_3)(L_2 \cup L_3))$.

j. $\forall L\, ((L^+)^* = L^*)$.

k. $\forall L\, (\varnothing L^* = \{\varepsilon\})$.

l. $\forall L\, (\varnothing \cup L^+ = L^*)$.

m. $\forall L_1, L_2 ((L_1 \cup L_2)^* = (L_2 \cup L_1)^*)$.

CHAPTER 3

The Big Picture: A Language Hierarchy

Our goal, in the rest of this book, is to build a framework that lets us examine a new problem and be able to say something about how intrinsically difficult it is. In order to do this, we need to be able to compare problems that appear, at first examination, to be wildly different. Apples and oranges come to mind. So the first thing we need to do is to define a single framework into which any computational problem can be cast. Then we will be in a position to compare problems and to distinguish between those that are relatively easy to solve and those that are not.

3.1 Defining the Task: Language Recognition

The unifying framework that we will use is language recognition. Assume that we are given:

- The definition of a language L. (We will consider about half a dozen different techniques for providing this definition.)
- A string w.

Then we must answer the question: "Is w in L?" This question is an instance of a more general class that we will call decision problems. A ***decision problem*** is simply a problem that requires a yes or no answer.

In the rest of this book, we will discuss programs to solve decision problems specifically of the form, "Is w in L?" We will see that, for some languages, a very simple program suffices. For others, a more complex one is required. For still others, we will prove that no program can exist.

3.2 The Power of Encoding

The question that we are going to ask, "Is w in L?" may seem, at first glance, way too limited to be useful. What about problems like multiplying numbers, sorting lists, and retrieving values from a database? And what about real problems like air traffic control or inventory management? Can our theory tell us anything interesting about them?

The answer is yes and the key is encoding. With an appropriate encoding, other kinds of problems can be recast as the problem of deciding whether a string is in a language. We will show some examples to illustrate this idea. We will divide the examples into two categories:

- Problems that are already stated as decision problems. For these, all we need to do is to encode the inputs as strings and then define a language that contains exactly the set of inputs for which the desired answer is yes.
- Problems that are not already stated as decision problems. These problems may require results of any type. For these, we must first reformulate the problem as a decision problem and then encode it as a language recognition task.

3.2.1 Everything is a String

Our stated goal is to build a theory of computation. What we are actually about to build is a theory specifically of languages and strings. Of course, in a computer's memory, everything is a (binary) string. So, at that level, it is obvious that restricting our attention to strings does not limit the scope of our theory. Often, however, we will find it easier to work with languages with larger alphabets.

Each time we consider a new problem, our first task will be to describe it in terms of strings. In the examples that follow, and throughout the book, we will use the notation $<X>$ to mean a string encoding of some object X. We'll use the notation $<X, Y>$ to mean the encoding, into a single string, of the two objects X and Y.

The first three examples we'll consider are of problems that are naturally described in terms of strings. Then we'll look at examples where we must begin by constructing an appropriate string encoding.

EXAMPLE 3.1 Pattern Matching on the Web

- Problem: Given a search string w and a web document d, do they match? In other words, should a search engine, on input w, consider returning d?
- The language to be decided: $\{<w, d> : d \text{ is a candidate match for the query } w\}$.

EXAMPLE 3.2 Question-Answering on the Web

- Problem: Given an English question q and a web document d (which may be in English or Chinese), does d contain the answer to q?
- The language to be decided: $\{<q, d> : d \text{ contains the answer to } q\}$.

The techniques that we will describe in the rest of this book are widely used in the construction of systems that work with natural language (e. g., English or Spanish or Chinese) text and speech inputs. (Appendix L)

EXAMPLE 3.3 Does a Program Always Halt?

- Problem: Given a program p, written in some standard programming language, is p guaranteed to halt on all inputs?
- The language to be decided: $\text{HP}_{\text{ALL}} = \{p : p \text{ halts on all inputs}\}$.

A procedure that could decide whether or not a string is in HP_{ALL} could be an important part of a larger system that proves the correctness of a program. Unfortunately, as we will see in Theorem 21.3, no such procedure can exist.

EXAMPLE 3.4 Primality Testing

- Problem: Given a nonnegative integer n, is it prime? In other words, does it have at least one positive integer factor other than itself and 1?
- An instance of the problem: Is 9 prime?
- Encoding of the problem: We need a way to encode each instance. We will encode each nonnegative integer as a binary string.
- The language to be decided: $\text{PRIMES} = \{w : w \text{ is the binary encoding of a prime number}\}$.

Prime numbers play an important role in modern cryptography systems. (J.3) We'll discuss the complexity of PRIMES in Section 28.1.7 and again in Section 30.2.4.

EXAMPLE 3.5 Verifying Addition

- Problem: Verify the correctness of the addition of two numbers.
- Encoding of the problem: We encode each of the numbers as a string of decimal digits. Each instance of the problem is a string of the form:

$$<\mathit{integer}_1> + <\mathit{integer}_2> = <\mathit{integer}_3>.$$

EXAMPLE 3.5 (*Continued*)

- The language to be decided:

  INTEGERSUM = {*w* of the form: <*integer*$_1$>+ <*integer*$_2$> = <*integer*$_3$> : each of the substrings <*integer*$_1$>, <*integer*$_2$> and <*integer*$_3$> is an element of {0, 1, 2, 3, 4, 5, 6, 8, 9} and *integer*$_3$ is the sum of *integer*$_1$ and *integer*$_2$}.
- Examples of strings in *L*: `2 + 4 = 6` `23 + 47 = 70.`
- Examples of strings not in *L*: `2 + 4 = 10` `2 + 4.`

EXAMPLE 3.6 Graph Connectivity

- Problem: Given an undirected graph *G*, is it connected? In other words, given any two distinct vertices *x* and *y* in *G*, is there a path from *x* to *y*?
- Instance of the problem: Is the following graph connected?

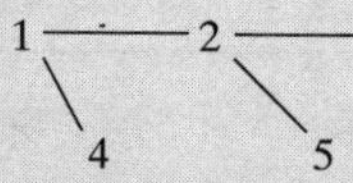

- Encoding of the problem: Let *V* be a set of binary numbers, one for each vertex in *G*. Then we construct <*G*> as follows:
  - Write $|V|$ as a binary number.
  - Write a list of edges, each of which is represented by a pair of binary numbers corresponding to the vertices that the edge connects.
  - Separate all such binary numbers by the symbol /.

For example, the graph shown above would be encoded by the following string, which begins with an encoding of 5 (the number of vertices) and is followed by four pairs corresponding to the four edges:

`101/1/10/10/11/1/100/10/101.`

- The language to be decided:

  CONNECTED = $\{w \in \{0, 1, /\}^* : w = n_1/n_2/\ldots n_i$, where each n_i is a binary string and w encodes a connected graph, as described above$\}$.

EXAMPLE 3.7 Protein Sequence Alignment

- Problem: Given a protein fragment *f* and a complete protein molecule *p*, could *f* be a fragment from *p*?

- Encoding of the problem: Represent each protein molecule or fragment as a sequence of amino acid residues. Assign a letter to each of the 20 possible amino acids. So a protein fragment might be represented as AGHTYWDNR.
- The language to be decided: {<*f*, *p*> *f* could be a fragment from *p*}.

> The techniques that we will describe in the rest of this book are widely used in computational biology. (Appendix K)

In each of these examples, we have chosen an encoding that is expressive enough to make it possible to describe all of the instances of the problem we are interested in. But have we chosen a good encoding? Might there be another one? The answer to this second question is yes. And it will turn out that the encoding we choose may have a significant impact on what we can say about the difficulty of solving the original problem. To see an example of this, we need look no farther than the addition problem that we just considered. Suppose that we want to write a program to examine a string in the addition language that we proposed above. Suppose further that we impose the constraint that our program reads the string one character at a time, left to right. It has only a finite (bounded in advance, independent of the length of the input string) amount of memory. These restrictions correspond to the notion of a finite state machine, as we will see in Chapter 5. It turns out that no machine of this sort can decide the language that we have described. We'll see how to prove results such as this in Chapter 8.

But now consider a different encoding of the addition problem. This time we encode each of the numbers as a binary string, and we write the digits, from lowest order to highest order, left to right (i.e., backwards from the usual way). Furthermore, we imagine the three numbers aligned in the way they often are when we draw an addition problem. So we might encode 10 + 4 = 14 as:

```
 0101   writing 1010 backwards
+0010   writing 0100 backwards
 0111   writing 1110 backwards
```

We now encode each column of that sum as a single character. Since each column is a sequence of three binary digits, it may take on any one of 8 possible values. We can use the symbols a, b, c, d, e, f, g, and h to correspond to 000, 001, 010, 011, 100, 101, 110, and 111, respectively. So we could encode the 10 + 4 = 14 example as afdf.

It is easy to design a program that reads such a string, left to right, and decides, as each character is considered, whether the sum so far is correct. For example, if the first character of a string is c, then the sum is wrong, since 0 + 1 cannot be 0 (although it could be later if there were a carry bit from the previous column).

> This idea is the basis for the design of binary adders, as well as larger circuits, like multipliers, that exploit them. (P.3)

In Part V of this book we will be concerned with the efficiency (stated in terms of either time or space) of the programs that we write. We will describe both time and space requirements as functions of the length of the program's input. When we do that, it may matter what encoding scheme we have picked since some encodings produce longer strings than others do. For example, consider the integer 25. It can be encoded:

- In decimal as: 25,
- In binary as: 11001, or
- In unary as: 1111111111111111111111111.

We'll return to this issue in Section 27.3.1.

3.2.2 Casting Problems as Decision Questions

Problems that are not already stated as decision questions can be transformed into decision questions. More specifically, they can be reformulated so that they become language recognition problems. The idea is to encode, into a single string, both the inputs and the outputs of the original problem P. So, for example, if P takes two inputs and produces one result, we could construct strings of the form $i_1; i_2; r$. Then a string $s = x; y; z$ is in the language L that corresponds to P iff z is the result that P produces given the inputs x and y.

EXAMPLE 3.8 Casting Addition as Decision

- Problem: Given two nonnegative integers, compute their sum.
- Encoding of the problem: We transform the problem of adding two numbers into the problem of checking to see whether a third number is the sum of the first two. We can use the same encoding that we used in Example 3.5.
- The language to be decided:

  INTEGERSUM = $\{w$ of the form: $<\mathit{integer}_1>+<\mathit{integer}_2>=<\mathit{integer}_3>$, where each of the substrings $<\mathit{integer}_1>$, $<\mathit{integer}_2>$, and $<\mathit{integer}_3>$ is an element of $\{0, 1, 2, 3, 4, 5, 6, 7, 8, 9\}^+$ and $\mathit{integer}_3$ is the sum of $\mathit{integer}_1$ and $\mathit{integer}_2\}$.

EXAMPLE 3.9 Casting Sorting as Decision

- Problem: Given a list of integers, sort it.
- Encoding of the problem: We transform the problem of sorting a list into the problem of examining a pair of lists and deciding whether the second corresponds to the sorted version of the first.

- The language to be decided:

$$L = \{w_1 \# w_2 : \exists n \geq 1\ (w_1 \text{ is of the form } int_1, int_2, \ldots int_n,\ w_2 \text{ is of the form } int_1, int_2, \ldots int_n, \text{ and } w_2 \text{ contains the same objects as } w_1 \text{ and } w_2 \text{ is sorted})\}.$$

- Example of a string in L: `1,5,3,9,6#1,3,5,6,9`.
- Example of a string not in L: `1,5,3,9,6#1,2,3,4,5,6,7`.

EXAMPLE 3.10 Casting Database Querying as Decision

- Problem: Given a database and a query, execute the query against the database.
- Encoding of the problem: We transform the task of executing the query into the problem of evaluating a reply to see if it is correct.
- The language to be decided:

$$L = \{d \# q \# a : d \text{ is an encoding of a database, } q \text{ is a string representing a query, and } a \text{ is the correct result of applying } q \text{ to } d\}.$$

- Example of a string in L:

```
(name, age, phone), (John, 23, 567-1234) (Mary, 24, 234-9876 )#
(select name age=23) #
(John).
```

Given each of the problems that we have just considered, there is an important sense in which the encoding of the problem as a decision question is equivalent to the original formulation of the problem: Each can be reduced to the other. We'll have a lot more to say about the idea of reduction in Chapter 21. But, for now, what we mean by ***reduction*** of one problem to another is that, if we have a program to solve the second, we can use it to build a program to solve the first. For example, suppose that we have a program P that adds a pair of integers. Then the following program decides the language INTEGERSUM, which we described in Example 3.8:

Given a string of the form $<integer_1>+<integer_2>=<integer_3>$ do:

1. Let x = *convert-to-integer* ($<integer_1>$).
2. Let y = *convert-to-integer* ($<integer_2>$).
3. Let $z = P(x, y)$.
4. If z = *convert-to-integer* ($<integer_3>$) then accept. Else reject.

Alternatively, if we have a program *T* that decides INTEGERSUM, then the following program computes the sum of two integers *x* and *y*:

1. Lexicographically enumerate the strings that represent decimal encodings of nonnegative integers.
2. Each time a string *s* is generated, create the new string <*x*>+<*y*>=*s*.
3. Feed that string to *T*.
4. If *T* accepts <*x*>+<*y*>=*s*, halt and return *convert-to-integer*(*s*).

3.3 A Machine-Based Hierarchy of Language Classes

In Parts II, III, and IV, we will define a hierarchy of computational models, each more powerful than the last. The first model is simple: Programs written for it are generally easy to understand, they run in linear time, and algorithms exist to answer almost any question we might wish to ask about such programs. The second model is more powerful, but still limited. The last model is powerful enough to describe anything that can be computed by any sort of real computer. All of these models will allow us to write programs whose job is to accept some language *L*. In this section, we sketch this machine hierarchy and provide a short introduction to the language hierarchy that goes along with it.

3.3.1 The Regular Languages

The first model we will consider is the ***finite state machine*** or ***FSM***. Figure 3.1 shows a simple FSM that accepts strings of a's and b's, where all a's come before all b's.

The input to an FSM is a string, which is fed to it one character at a time, left to right. The FSM has a start state, shown in the diagram with an unlabelled arrow leading to it, and some number (zero or more) of accepting states, which will be shown in our diagrams with double circles. The FSM starts in its start state. As each character is read, the FSM changes state based on the transitions shown in the figure. If an FSM *M* is in an accepting state after reading the last character of some input string *s*, then *M* accepts *s*. Otherwise it rejects it. Our example FSM stays in state 1 as long as it is reading a's. When it sees a b, it moves to state 2, where it stays as long as it continues seeing b's. Both state 1 and state 2 are accepting states. But if, in state 2, it sees an a, it goes to state 3, a nonaccepting state, where it stays until it runs out of input. So, for example, this machine will accept aab, aabbb, and bb. It will reject ba.

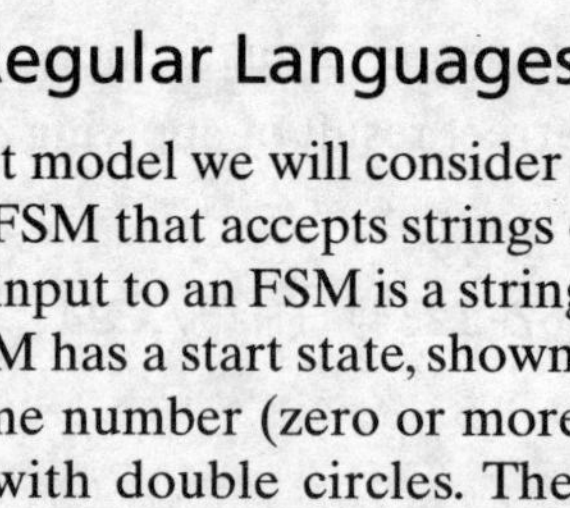

FIGURE 3.1 A simple FSM.

We will call the class of languages that can be accepted by some FSM ***regular***. As we will see in Part II, many useful languages are regular, including binary strings with even parity, syntactically well-formed floating point numbers, and sequences of coins that are sufficient to buy a soda.

3.3.2 The Context-Free Languages

But there are useful simple languages that are not regular. Consider, for example, Bal, the language of balanced parentheses. Bal contains strings like (()) and ()(); it does not contain strings like ()))(. Because it's hard to read strings of parentheses, let's consider instead the related language $A^nB^n = \{a^nb^n : n \geq 0\}$. In any string in A^nB^n, all the a's come first and the number of a's equals the number of b's. We could try to build an FSM to accept A^nB^n. But the problem is, "How shall we count the a's so that we can compare them to the b's?" The only memory in an FSM is in the states and we must choose a fixed number of states when we build our machine. But there is no bound on the number of a's we might need to count. We will prove in Chapter 8 that it is not possible to build an FSM to accept A^nB^n.

But languages like Bal and A^nB^n are important. For example, almost every programming language and query language allows parentheses, so any front end for such a language must be able to check to see that the parentheses are balanced. Can we augment the FSM in a simple way and thus be able to solve this problem? The answer is yes. Suppose that we add one thing, a single stack. We will call any machine that consists of an FSM, plus a single stack, a ***pushdown automaton*** or ***PDA***.

We can easily build a PDA M to accept A^nB^n. The idea is that, each time it sees an a, M will push it onto the stack. Then, each time it sees a b, it will pop an a from the stack. If it runs out of input and stack at the same time and it is in an accepting state, it will accept. Otherwise, it will reject. M will use the same state structure that we used in our FSM example above to guarantee that all the a's come before all the b's. In diagrams of PDAs, read an arc label of the form $x/y/z$ to mean, "if the input is an x, and it is possible to pop y off the stack, then take the transition, do the pop of y, and push z". If the middle argument is ε, then don't bother to check the stack. If the third argument is ε, then don't push anything. Using those conventions, the PDA shown in Figure 3.2 accepts A^nB^n.

Using a very similar sort of PDA, we can build a machine to accept Bal and other languages whose strings are composed of properly nested substrings. For example, a ***palindrome*** is a string that reads the same right-to-left as it does left-to right. We can easily build a PDA to accept the language PalEven $= \{ww^R : w \in \{a, b\}^*\}$, the

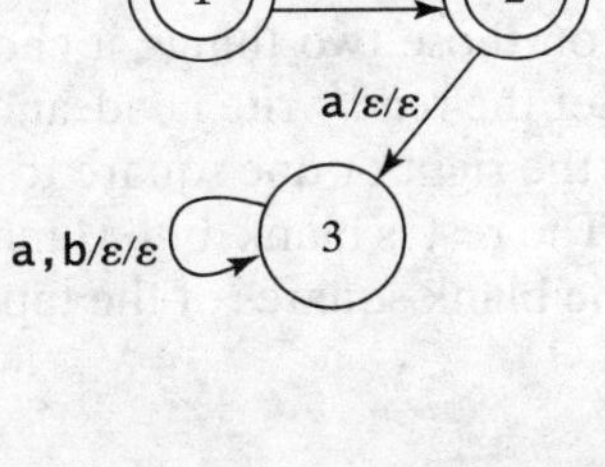

FIGURE 3.2 A simple PDA that accepts A^nB^n.

language of even-length palindromes of a's and b's. The PDA for PalEven simply pushes all the characters in the first half of its input string onto the stack, guesses where the middle is, and then starts popping one character for each remaining input character. If there is a guess that causes the pushed string (which will be popped off in reverse order) to match the remaining input string, then the input string is in PalEven.

But we should note some simple limitations to the power of the PDA. Consider the language WW $= \{ww : w \in \{\text{a}, \text{b}\}^*\}$, which is just like PalEven except that the second half of each of its strings is an exact copy of the first half (rather than the reverse of it). Now, as we'll prove in Chapter 13, it is not possible to build an accepting PDA (although it would be possible to build an accepting machine if we could augment the finite state controller with a first-in, first-out queue rather than a stack).

We will call the class of languages that can be accepted by some PDA ***context-free***. As we will see in Part III, many useful languages are context-free, including most programming languages, query languages, and markup languages.

3.3.3 The Decidable and Semidecidable Languages

But there are useful straightforward languages that are not context-free. Consider, for example, the language of English sentences in which some word occurs more than once. As an even simpler (although probably less useful) example, consider another language to which we will give a name. Let $\text{A}^n\text{B}^n\text{C}^n = \{\text{a}^n\text{b}^n\text{c}^n : n \geq 0\}$, i.e., the language composed of all strings of a's, b's, and c's such that all the a's come first, followed by all the b's, then all the c's, and the number of a's equals the number of b's equals the number of c's. We could try to build a PDA to accept $\text{A}^n\text{B}^n\text{C}^n$. We could use the stack to count the a's, just as we did for A^nB^n. We could pop the stack as the b's come in and compare them to the a's. But then what shall we do about the c's? We have lost all information about the a's and the b's since, if they matched, the stack will be empty. We will prove in Chapter 13 that it is not possible to build a PDA to accept $\text{A}^n\text{B}^n\text{C}^n$.

But it is easy to write a program to accept $\text{A}^n\text{B}^n\text{C}^n$. So, if we want a class of machines that can capture everything we can write programs to compute, we need a model that is stronger than the PDA. To meet this need, we will introduce a third kind of machine. We will get rid of the stack and replace it with an infinite tape. The tape will have a single read/write head. Only the tape square under the read/write head can be accessed (for reading or for writing). The read/write head can be moved one square in either direction on each move. The resulting machine is called a ***Turing machine***. We will also change the way that input is given to the machine. Instead of streaming it, one character at a time, the way we did for FSMs and PDAs, we will simply write the input string onto the tape and then start the machine with the read/write head just to the left of the first input character. We show the structure of a Turing machine in Figure 3.3. The arrow under the tape indicates the location of the read/write head.

At each step, a Turing machine M considers its current state and the character that is on the tape directly under its read/write head. Based on those two things, it chooses its next state, chooses a character to write on the tape under the read/write head, and chooses whether to move the read/write head one square to the right or one square to the left. A finite segment of M's tape contains the input string. The rest is blank, but M may move the read/write head off the input string and write on the blank squares of the tape.

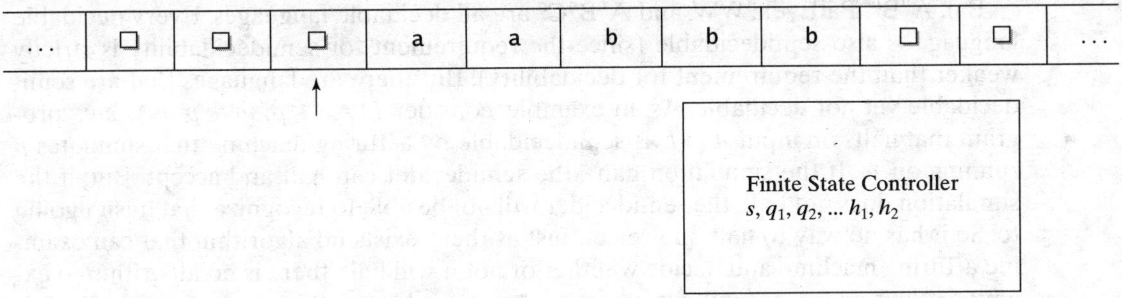

FIGURE 3.3 The structure of a Turing machine.

There exists a simple Turing machine that accepts $A^nB^nC^n$. It marks off the leftmost a, scans to the right to find a b, marks it off, continues scanning to the right, finds a c, and marks it off. Then it goes back to the left, marks off the next a, and so forth. When it runs out of a's, it makes one final pass to the right to make sure that there are no extra b's or c's. If that check succeeds, the machine accepts. If it fails, or if at any point the machine failed to find a required b or c, it rejects. For the details of how this machine operates, see Example 17.8.

Finite state machines and pushdown automata (with one technical exception that we can ignore for now) are guaranteed to halt. They must do so when they run out of input. Turing machines, on the other hand, carry no such guarantee. The input simply sits on the tape. A Turing machine may (and generally does) move back and forth across its input many times. It may move back and forth forever. Or it may simply move in one direction, off the input onto the blank tape, and keep going forever. Because of its flexibility in using its tape to record its computation, the Turing machine is a more powerful model than either the FSM or the PDA. In fact, we will see in Chapter 18 that any computation that can be written in any programming language or run on any modern computer can be described as a Turing machine. However, when we work with Turing machines, we must be aware of the fact that they cannot be guaranteed to halt. And, unfortunately we can prove (as we will do in Chapter 19) that there exists no algorithm that can examine a Turing machine and tell whether or not it will halt (on any one input or on all inputs). This fundamental result about the limits of computation is known as the undecidability of the halting problem.

We will use the Turing machine to define two new classes of languages:

- A language L is ***decidable*** iff there exists a Turing machine M that halts on all inputs, accepts all strings that are in L, and rejects all strings that are not in L. In other words, M can always say yes or no, as appropriate.
- A language L is ***semidecidable*** iff there exists a Turing machine M that accepts all strings that are in L and fails to accept every string that is not in L. Given a string that is not in L, M may reject or it may loop forever. In other words, M can recognize a solution and then say yes, but it may not know when it should give up looking for a solution and say no.

Bal, A^nB^n, PalEven, WW, and $A^nB^nC^n$ are all decidable languages. Every decidable language is also semidecidable (since the requirement for semidecidability is strictly weaker than the requirement for decidability). But there are languages that are semidecidable yet not decidable. As an example, consider $L = \{<p, w>: p$ is a Java program that halts on input $w\}$. L is semidecidable by a Turing machine that simulates p running on w. If the simulation halts, the semidecider can halt and accept. But, if the simulation does not halt, the semidecider will not be able to recognize that it isn't going to. So it has no way to halt and reject. Just as there exists no algorithm that can examine a Turing machine and decide whether or not it will halt, there is no algorithm to examine a Java program (without having to run it) and make that determination. So L is semidecidable but not decidable.

3.3.4 The Computational Hierarchy and Why It Is Important

We have now defined four language classes:

1. Regular languages, which can be accepted by some finite state machine.
2. Context-free languages, which can be accepted by some pushdown automaton.
3. Decidable (or simply D) languages, which can decided by some Turing machine that always halts.
4. Semidecidable (or SD) languages, which can be semidecided by some Turing machine that halts on all strings in the language.

Each of these classes is a proper subset of the next class, as illustrated in the diagram shown in Figure 3.4.

As we move outward in the language hierarchy, we have access to tools with greater and greater expressive power. So, for example, we can define A^nB^n as a context-free language but not as a regular one. We can define $A^nB^nC^n$ as a decidable language but not as a context-free or a regular one. This matters because expressiveness generally comes at a price. The price may be:

- ***Computational efficiency***: Finite state machines run in time that is linear in the length of the input string. A general context-free parser based on the idea of a pushdown automaton requires time that grows as the cube of the length of the input string. A Turing machine may require time that grows exponentially (or faster) with the length of the input string.
- ***Decidability***: There exist procedures to answer many useful questions about finite state machines. For example, does an FSM accept some particular string? Is an FSM minimal (i.e., is it the simplest machine that does the job it does)? Are two FSMs identical? A subset of those questions can be answered for pushdown automata. None of them can be answered for Turing machines.
- ***Clarity***: There exist tools that enable designers to draw and analyze finite state machines. Every regular language can also be described using the (often very convenient) regular expression pattern language that we will define in Chapter 6. Every context-free language, in addition to being recognizable by some pushdown

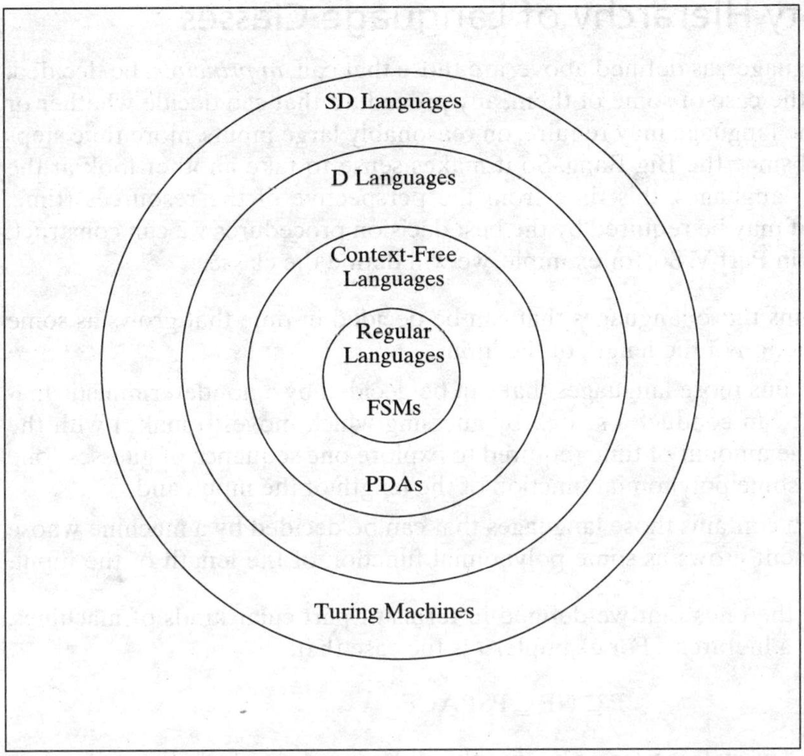

FIGURE 3.4 A hierarchy of language classes.

automaton, can (as we will see in Chapter 11) be described with a context-free grammar. For many important kinds of languages, context-free grammars are sufficiently natural that they are commonly used as documentation tools. No corresponding tools exist for the broader classes of decidable and semidecidable languages.

So, as a practical as well as a theoretical matter, it makes sense, given a particular problem, to describe it using the simplest (i.e., expressively weakest) formalism that is adequate to the job.

> ***The Rule of Least Power***[5]: "Use the least powerful language suitable for expressing information, constraints or programs on the World Wide Web."

Although stated in the context of the World Wide Web, the Rule of Least Power applies far more broadly. We're appealing to a generalization of it here. We'll return to a discussion of it in the specific context of the Semantic Web in I.3.

In Parts II, III, and IV of this book, we explore the language hierarchy that we have just defined. We will start with the smallest class, the regular languages, and move outwards.

[5]Quoted from [Berners-Lee and Mendelsohn 2006].

3.4 A Tractability Hierarchy of Language Classes

The decidable languages, as defined above, are those that can, *in principle*, be decided. Unfortunately, in the case of some of them, any procedure that can decide whether or not a string is in the language may require, on reasonably large inputs, more time steps than have elapsed since the Big Bang. So it makes sense to take another look at the class of decidable languages, this time from the perspective of the resources (time, space, or both) that may be required by the best decision procedures we can construct.

We will do that in Part V. So, for example, we will define the classes:

- ***P***, which contains those languages that can be decided in time that grows as some polynomial function of the length of the input,
- ***NP***, which contains those languages that can be decided by a nondeterministic machine (one that can conduct a search by guessing which move to make) with the property that the amount of time required to explore one sequence of guesses (one path) grows as some polynomial function of the length of the input, and
- ***PSPACE***, which contains those languages that can be decided by a machine whose space requirement grows as some polynomial function of the length of the input.

These classes, like the ones that we defined in terms of particular kinds of machines, can be arranged in a hierarchy. For example, it is the case that:

$$\text{P} \subseteq \text{NP} \subseteq \text{PSPACE}$$

Unfortunately, as we will see, less is known about the structure of this hierarchy than about the structure of the hierarchy we drew in the last section. For example, perhaps the biggest open question of theoretical computer science is whether P = NP. It is possible, although generally thought to be very unlikely, that every language that is in NP is also in P. For this reason, we won't draw a picture here. Any picture we could draw might suggest a situation that will eventually turn out not to be true.

Exercises

1. Consider the following problem: Given a digital circuit *C*, does *C* output 1 on all inputs? Describe this problem as a language to be decided.
2. Using the technique we used in Example 3.8 to describe addition, describe square root as a language recognition problem.
3. Consider the problem of encrypting a password, given an encryption key. Formulate this problem as a language recognition problem.
4. Consider the optical character recognition (OCR) problem: Given an array of black and white pixels and a set of characters, determine which character best matches the pixel array. Formulate this problem as a language recognition problem.
5. Consider the language $\text{A}^n\text{B}^n\text{C}^n = \{\text{a}^n\text{b}^n\text{c}^n : n \geq 0\}$, discussed in Section 3.3.3. We might consider the following design for a PDA to accept $\text{A}^n\text{B}^n\text{C}^n$: As each a

is read, push two a's onto the stack. Then pop one a for each b and one a for each c. If the input and the stack come out even, accept. Otherwise reject. Why doesn't this work?

6. Define a PDA-2 to be a PDA with two stacks (instead of one). Assume that the stacks can be manipulated independently and that the machine accepts iff it is in an accepting state and both stacks are empty when it runs out of input. Describe the operation of a PDA-2 that accepts $A^nB^nC^n = \{a^n b^n c^n : n \geq 0\}$. (*Note*: We will see, in Section 17.5.2, that the PDA-2 is equivalent to the Turing machine in the sense that any language that can be accepted by one can be accepted by the other.)

CHAPTER 4

Computation

Our goal in this book is to be able to make useful claims about problems and the programs that solve them. Of course, both problem specifications and the programs that solve them take many different forms. Specifications can be written in English, or as a set of logical formulas, or as a set of input/output pairs. Programs can be written in any of a wide array of common programming languages. As we said in the last chapter, in this book we are, for the most part, going to depart from those standard methods and, instead

- Define problems a languages to be decided, and
- Define programs as state machines whose input is a string and whose output is *Accept* or *Reject*.

Both because of this change in perspective and because we are going to introduce two ideas that are not common in everyday programming practice, we will pause, in this chapter, and look at what we mean by computation and how we are going to go about it. In particular, we will examine three key ideas:

1. Decision procedures.
2. Nondeterminism.
3. Functions on languages (alternatively, programs that operate on other programs).

Once we have finished this discussion, we will begin our examination of the language classes that we outlined in Chapter 3.

4.1 Decision Procedures

Recall that a ***decision problem*** is one for which we must make a yes/no decision. An ***algorithm*** is a detailed procedure that accomplishes some clearly specified task. A ***decision procedure*** is an algorithm to solve a decision problem. Put another way, it is a program whose result is a Boolean value. Note that, in order to be guaranteed to return a Boolean value, a decision procedure must be guaranteed to halt on all inputs.

This book is about decision procedures. We will spend most of our time discussing decision procedures to answer questions of the form:

- Is string s in language L?

But we will also attempt to answer other questions, in particular ones that ask about the machines that we will build to answer the first group of questions. So we may ask questions such as:

- Given a machine (an FSM, a PDA, or a Turing machine), does it accept any strings?
- Given two machines, do they accept the same strings?
- Given a machine, is it the smallest (simplest) machine that does its job?

If we have in mind a decision problem to which we want an answer, there are three things we may want to know:

1. Does there exist a decision procedure (i.e., an algorithm) to answer the question? A decision problem is ***decidable*** iff the answer to this question is yes. A decision problem is ***undecidable*** iff the answer to this question is no. A decision problem is ***semidecidable*** iff there exists an algorithm that halts and returns *True* iff *True* is the answer. When *False* is the answer, it may either halt and return *False* or it may loop. Some undecidable problems are semidecidable; some are not even that.
2. If any decision procedures exist, find one.
3. Again, if any decision procedures exist, what is the most efficient one and how efficient is it?

In the early part of this book, we will ask questions for which decision procedures exist and we will often skip directly to question 2. But, as we progress, we will begin to ask questions for which, provably, no decision procedure exists. It is because there are such problems that we have articulated question 1.

Decision procedures are programs. They must possess two correctness properties:

1. The program must be guaranteed to halt on all inputs.
2. When the program halts and returns an answer, it must be the correct answer for the given input.

Let's consider some examples.

EXAMPLE 4.1 Checking for Even Numbers

Is the integer x even? This one is easy. Assume that / performs (truncating) integer division. Then the following program answers the question:

even (x : integer)=

If $(x/2)*2 = x$ then return *True* else return *False*.

EXAMPLE 4.2 Checking for Prime Numbers

Is the positive integer x prime? Given an appropriate string encoding, this problem corresponds to the language PRIMES that we defined in Example 3.4. Defining a procedure to answer this question is not hard, although it will require a loop and so it will be necessary to prove that the loop always terminates. Several algorithms that solve this problem exist. Here's an easy one:

```
prime (x: positive integer) =
    For i = 2 to ceiling (sqrt(x)) do:
        If (x/i) * i = x then return False.
    Return True.
```

The function *ceiling*(x), also written $\lceil x \rceil$ returns the smallest integer that is greater than or equal to x. This program is guaranteed to halt. The natural numbers between 0 and *ceiling* (*sqrt*(x))-2 form a well-ordered set under $\leq$. Let *index* correspond to *ceiling* (*sqrt*(x))$-i$. At the beginning of the first pass through the loop, the value of *index* is *ceiling* (*sqrt*(x))-2. The value of *index* decreases by one each time through the loop. The loop ends when that value becomes 0. It's worth pointing out that, while this program is simple and it is easy to prove that it is correct, it is not the most efficient program that we could write. We'll have more to say about this problem in Sections 28.1.7 and 30.2.4.

For our next few examples we need a definition. The sequence:

$$F_n = 2^{2^n} + 1, n \geq 0,$$

defines the ***Fermat numbers*** 💻. The first few Fermat numbers are:

$$F_0 = 3, F_1 = 5, F_2 = 17, F_3 = 257, F_4 = 65{,}537, F_5 = 4{,}294{,}967{,}297.$$

EXAMPLE 4.3 Checking for Small Prime Fermat Numbers

Are there any prime Fermat numbers less than 1,000,000? There exists a simple decision procedure to answer this question:

```
fermatSmall() =
    i = 0.
    Repeat:
        candidate = (2**(2**i)) + 1.
        If candidate is prime then return True.
```

$i = i + 1$.

until *candidate* $\geq$ 1,000,000.

Return *False*.

This algorithm is guaranteed to halt because the value of *candidate* increases each time through the loop and the loop terminates when its value exceeds a fixed bound. We will skip the proof that the correct answer is returned.

EXAMPLE 4.4 Checking for Large Prime Fermat Numbers

Are there any prime Fermat numbers greater than 1,000,000? This question is different in one important way from the previous one. Does there exist a decision procedure to answer this question? What about:

fermatLarge ()=

$i = 0$.

Repeat:

candidate = (2** (2** *i*)) + 1.

If *candidate* > 1,000,000 and is prime then return *True*.

$i = i + 1$.

Return *False*.

What can we say about this program? If there is a prime Fermat number greater than 1,000,000, *fermatLarge* will find it and will halt. But suppose that there is no such number. Then the program will loop forever. *FermatLarge* is not capable of returning *False* even if *False* is the correct answer. So, is *fermatLarge* a decision procedure? No. A decision procedure must halt and return the correct answer, whatever that is.

Can we do better? Is there a decision procedure to answer this question? Yes. Since this question takes no arguments, it has a simple answer, either *True* or *False*. So either

fermatYes ()=

Return *True*,

or

fermatNo ()=

Return *False*.

correctly answers the question. Our problem now is, "Which one?" No one knows. Fermat himself was only able to generate the first five Fermat numbers, and, on

EXAMPLE 4.4 *(Continued)*

that basis, conjectured that all Fermat numbers are prime. If he had been right, then *fermatYes* answers the question. However, it now seems likely that there are no prime Fermat numbers greater than 65,537. A substantial effort continues to be devoted to finding one, but so far the only discoveries have been larger and larger composite Fermat numbers. But there is also no proof that a larger prime one does not exist nor is there an algorithm for finding one. We simply do not know.

EXAMPLE 4.5 Checking for Programs That Halt on a Particular Input

Now consider a problem that is harder and that cannot be solved by a simple constant function such as *fermatYes* or *fermatNo*. Given an arbitrary Java program p that takes a string w as an input parameter, does p halt on some particular value of w? Here's a candidate for a decision procedure:

haltsOnw (p: program, w: string) =

1. Simulate the execution of p on w.

2. If the simulation halts return *True* else return *False*.

Is *haltsOnw* a decision procedure? No, because it can never return the value *False*. Yet *False* is sometimes the correct answer (since there are (p, w) pairs such that p fails to halt on w). When *haltsOnw* should return *False*, it will loop forever in step 1. Can we do better? No. It is possible to prove, as we will do in Chapter 19, that no decision procedure for this question exists.

Define a ***semidecision procedure*** to be a procedure that halts and returns *True* whenever *True* is the correct answer. But, whenever *False* is the correct answer, it may return *False* or it may loop forever. In other words, a semidecision procedure knows when to say yes but it is not guaranteed to know when to say no. A ***semidecidable problem*** is a problem for which a semidecision procedure exists. Example 4.5 is a semidecidable problem. While some semidecidable problems are also decidable, that one isn't.

EXAMPLE 4.6 Checking for Programs That Halt on All Inputs

Now consider an even harder problem: Given an arbitrary Java program that takes a single string as an input parameter, does it halt on all possible input values? Here's a candidate for a decision procedure:

haltsOnAll (*program*) =

1. For $i = 1$ to infinity do:

Simulate the execution of *program* on all possible input strings of length i.

2. If all of the simulations halt return *True* else return *False*.

HaltsOnAll will never halt on any program since, to do so, it must try running the program on an infinite number of strings. And there is not a better procedure to answer this question. We will show, in Chapter 21, that it is not even semidecidable.

The bottom line is that there are three kinds of questions:

- Those for which a decision procedure exists.
- Those for which no decision procedure exists but a semidecision procedure exists.
- Those for which not even a semi-decision procedure exists.

As we move through the language classes that we will consider in this book, we will move from worlds in which there exist decision procedures for just about every question we can think of to worlds in which there exist some decision procedures and perhaps some semidecision procedures, all the way to worlds in which there do not exist even semidecision procedures.

But keep in mind throughout that entire progression what a *decision* procedure is. It is an algorithm that is *guaranteed* to halt on all inputs.

4.2 Determinism and Nondeterminism

Imagine adding to a programming language the function *choose*, which may be written in either of the following forms:

- *choose* (action 1;;
  action 2;;
  ...
  action n)
- *choose* (x from S: $P(x)$)

In the first form, *choose* is presented with a finite list of alternatives, each of which will return either a successful value or the value *False*. *Choose* will:

- Return some successful value, if there is one.
- If there is no successful value, then choose will:

- Halt and return *False* if all the actions halt and return *False*.
- Fail to halt if any of the actions fails to halt. We want to define *choose* this way since any path that has not halted still has the potential to return a successful value.

In the second form, *choose* is presented with a set S of values. S may be finite or it may be infinite if it is specified by a generator. *Choose* will:

- Return some element x of S such that $P(x)$ halts with a value other than *False*, if there is one.
- If there is no such element, then *choose* will:
  - Halt and return *False* if it can be determined that, for all elements x of S, $P(x)$ is not satisfied. This will happen if S is finite and there is a procedure for checking P that always halts. It may also happen, even if S is infinite, if there is some way, short of checking all the elements, to determine that no elements that satisfy P exist.
  - Fail to halt if there is no mechanism for determining that no elements of S that satisfy P exist. This may happen either because S is infinite or because there is no algorithm, guaranteed to halt on all inputs, that checks for P and returns *False* when necessary.

In both forms, the job of *choose* is to find a successful value (which we will define to be any value other than *False*) if there is one. When we don't care which successful value we find (or how we find it), *choose* is a useful abstraction, as we will see in the next few examples.

We will call programs that are written in our new language, which includes *choose*, ***nondeterministic***. We will call programs that are written without using *choose* ***deterministic***.

Real computers are, of course, deterministic. So, if *choose* is going to be useful, there must exist a way to implement it on a deterministic machine. For now, however, we will be noncommittal as to how that is done. It may try the alternatives one at a time, or it may pursue them in parallel. If it tries them one at a time, it may try them in the order listed, in some random order, or in some order that is carefully designed to maximize the chances of finding a successful value without trying all the others. The only requirement is that it must pursue the alternatives in some fashion that is guaranteed to find a successful value if there is one. The point of the *choose* function is that we can separate the design of the choosing mechanism from the design of the program that needs a value and calls *choose* to find it one.

EXAMPLE 4.7 Nondeterministically Choosing a Travel Plan

Suppose that we regularly plan medium length trips. We are willing to drive or to fly and rent a car or to take a train and use public transportation if it is available when we get there, as long as the total cost of the trip and the total time required are reasonable. We don't care about small differences in time or cost enough to make it worth exhaustively exploring all the options every time. We can define the function *trip-plan* to solve our problem:

trip-plan (*start*, *finish*)=

Return ($choose$ ($fly\text{-}major\text{-}airline\text{-}and\text{-}rent\text{-}car$ ($start, finish$);;
$fly\text{-}regional\text{-}airline\text{-}and\text{-}rent\text{-}car$ ($start, finish$);;
$take\text{-}train\text{-}and\text{-}use\text{-}public\text{-}transportation$ ($start, finish$);;
$drive$ ($start,finish$))).

Each of the four functions *trip-plan* calls returns with a successful value iff it succeeds in finding a plan that meets the cost and time requirements. Probably the first three of them are implemented as an Internet agent that visits the appropriate Web sites, specifies the necessary parameters, and waits to see if a solution can be found. But notice that *trip-plan* can return a result as soon as at least one of the four agents finds an acceptable solution. It doesn't care whether the four agents can be run in parallel or are tried sequentially. It just wants to know if there's a solution and, if so, what it is.

A good deal of the power of choose comes from the fact that it can be called recursively. So it can be used to describe a search process, without having to specify the details of how the search is conducted.

EXAMPLE 4.8 Nondeterministically Searching a Space of Puzzle Moves

Suppose that we want to solve the 15-puzzle 💻. We are given two configurations of the puzzle, for example the ones shown here labeled (a) and (b). The goal is to begin in configuration (a) and, through a sequence of moves, reach configuration (b). The only allowable move is to slide a numbered tile into the blank square.

5	2	15	9
7	8	4	12
13	1	6	11
10	14	3	

1	2	3	4
5	6	7	8
9	10	11	12
13	14	15	

EXAMPLE 4.8 (*Continued*)

Using *choose*, we can easily write *solve-15*, a program that finds a solution if there is one. The idea is that *solve*-15 will guess at a first move. From the board configuration that results from that move, it will guess at a second move. From there, it will guess at a third move, and so on. If it reaches the goal configuration, it will report the sequence of moves that got it there.

Using the second form of *choose* (in which values are selected from a set that can be generated each time a new choice must be made), we can define *solve*-15 so that it returns an ordered list of board positions. The first element of the list corresponds to the initial configuration. Following that, in order, are the configurations that result from each of the moves. The final configuration will correspond to the goal. So the result of a call to *solve*-15 will describe a move sequence that corresponds to a solution to the original problem. We'll invoke *solve*-15 with a list that contains just the initial configuration. So we define:

solve-15 (*position-list*)=

/* Explore moves available from the last board configuration to have been generated.

current = *last* (*position-list*).

If *current* = *solution* then return (*position-list*).

/* Assume that *successors* (*current*) returns the set of configurations that can be generated by one legal move from *current*. Then *choose* picks one with the property that, once it has been appended to *position-list*, *solve-15* can continue and find a solution. We assume that *append* destructively modifies its first argument.

choose (*x* from *successors* (*current*): *solve-15* (*append* (*position-list*, *x*))).

Return *position-list*.

If there is a solution to a particular instance of the 15-puzzle, *solve-15* will find it. If we care about how efficiently the solution is found, then we can dig inside the implementation of *choose* and try various strategies, including:

- Checking to make sure we don't generate a board position that has already been explored, or
- Sorting the successors by how close they are to the goal.

But if we don't care about how *choose* works, we don't have to.

> 15-puzzle configurations can be divided into two equivalence classes. Every configuration can be transformed into every other configuration in the same class and into none of the configurations in the other class 💻.

Many decision problems can be solved straightforwardly using *choose*.

EXAMPLE 4.9 Nondeterministically Searching for a Satisfying Assignment

A wff in Boolean logic is ***satisfiable*** iff it is true for at least one assignment of truth values to the literals it contains. Now consider the following problem, which we'll call SAT: Given a Boolean wff w, decide whether or not w is satisfiable.

To see how we might go about designing a program to solve the SAT problem, consider an example wff $w = P \wedge (Q \vee R) \wedge \neg (R \vee S) \rightarrow Q$. We can build a program that considers the predicate symbols (in this case P, Q, R, and S) in some order. For each one, it will pick one of the two available values, *True* or *False*, and assign it to all occurrences of that predicate symbol in w. When no predicate symbols remain, all that is necessary is to use the truth table definitions of the logical operators to simplify w until it has evaluated to either *True* or *False*. If *True*, then we have found an assignment of values to the predicates that makes w true; w is satisfiable. If *False*, then this path fails to find such an assignment and it fails. This procedure must halt because w contains only a finite number of predicate symbols, one is eliminated at each step, and there are only two values to choose from at each step. So either some path will return *True* or all paths will eventually halt and return *False*.

The following algorithm returns *True* if the answer to the question is yes and *False* if the answer to the question is no:

decideSAT (w : Boolean wff)=

  If there are no predicate symbols in w then:

    Simplify w until it is either *True* or *False*.

    Return w.

  Else:

    Find P, the first predicate symbol in w.

    /* Let $w/P/x$ mean the wff w with every instance of P replaced by x.

    Return *choose* (*decideSAT* ($w/P/True$);;
                decideSAT ($w/P/False$)).

One way to envision the execution of a program like *solve*-15 or *decideSAT* is as a search tree. Each node in the tree corresponds to a snapshot of *solve*-15 or *decideSAT* and each path from the root to a leaf node corresponds to one computation that *solve*-15 or *decideSAT* might perform. For example, if we invoke *decideSAT* on the input $P \wedge \neg R$, the set of possible computations can be described by the tree in Figure 4.1. The first level in the tree corresponds to guessing a value for P and the second level corresponds to guessing a value for R.

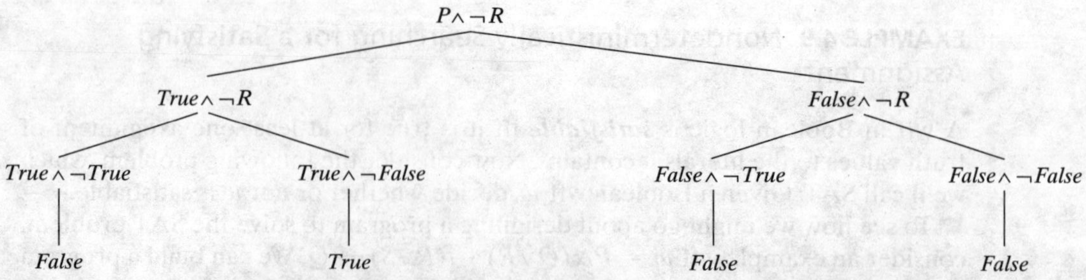

FIGURE 4.1 A search tree created by *decideSAT* on the input $P \wedge \neg R$.

Since there exists at least one computational path that succeeds (i.e., returns a value other than *False*), *decideSAT* will pick the value returned by one such path and return it. So *decideSAT* will return *True*. It may do so after exploring all four of the paths shown above (if it is unlucky choosing an order in which to explore the paths). Or it may guess correctly and find the successful path without considering any of the others.

> Efficient algorithms for solving Boolean satisfiability problems are important in a wide variety of domains. No general and efficient algorithms are known. But, in B.1.3, we'll describe ordered binary decision diagrams (OBDDs), which are used in SAT solvers that work, in practice, substantially more efficiently than *decideSAT* does.

One of the most important properties of programs that exploit *choose* is clear from the simple tree that we just examined: Guesses that do not lead to a solution can be effectively ignored in any analysis that is directed at determining the program's result.

Does adding *choose* to our programming language let us solve any problems that we couldn't solve without it? The answer to that question turns out to depend on what else the programming language already lets us do.

Suppose, for example, that we are describing our programs as finite state machines (FSMs). One way to add *choose* to the FSM model is to allow two or more transitions, labeled with the same input character, to emerge from a single state. We show a simple example in Figure 4.2.

We'll say that a nondeterministic FSM M (i.e., one that may exploit *choose*) accepts iff at least one of its paths accepts. It will reject iff all of its paths reject. So M's job is to

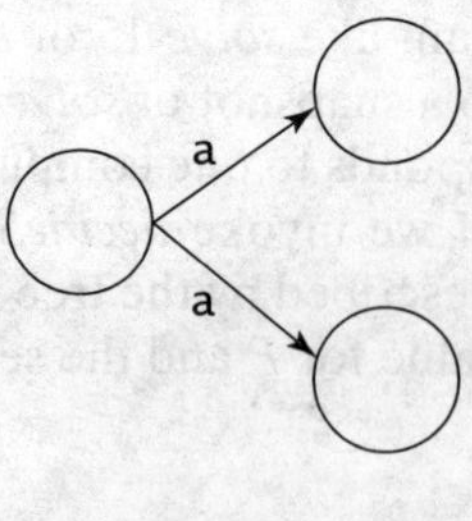

FIGURE 4.2 A nondeterministic FSM with two competing transitions labeled a.

find an accepting path if there is one. If it succeeds, it can ignore all other paths. If *M* exploits *choose* and does contain competing transitions, then one way to view its behavior is that it makes a guess and chooses an accepting path if it can.

While we will find it very convenient to allow nondeterminism like this in finite state machines, we will see in Section 5.4 that, whenever there is a nondeterministic FSM to accept some language *L*, there is also a (possibly much larger and more complicated) deterministic FSM that accepts *L*. So adding *choose* doesn't change the class of languages that can be accepted.

Now suppose that we are describing our programs as pushdown automata (PDAs). Again we will add *choose* to the model by allowing competing transitions coming out of a state. As we will see in Chapter 13, now the answer is that adding *choose* adds power. There are languages that can be accepted by PDAs that exploit *choose* that cannot be accepted by any PDA that does not exploit it.

Lastly, suppose that we are describing our programs as Turing machines or as code in a standard, modern programming language. Then, as we will see in Chapter 17, we are back to the situation we were in with FSMs. Nondeterminism is a very useful design tool that lets us specify complex programs without worrying about the details of how the search is managed. But, if there is a nondeterministic Turing machine that solves a problem, then there is a deterministic one (one that does not exploit *choose*) that also solves the problem.

In the two cases (FSMs and Turing machines) in which adding *choose* does not add computational power to our model, we will see that it does add descriptive power. We'll see examples for which a very simple nondeterministic machine can do the work of a substantially more complex deterministic one. We'll present algorithms, for both FSMs and Turing machines, that construct, given an arbitrary nondeterministic machine, an equivalent deterministic one. Thus we can use nondeterminism as an effective design tool and leave the job of building a deterministic program to a compiler.

In Part V, we will take a different look at analyzing problems and the programs that solve them. There we will be concerned with the complexity of the solution: How much running time does it take or how much memory does it require? In that analysis, nondeterminism will play another important role. It will enable us to separate our solution to a problem into two parts:

1. The complexity of an individual path through the search tree that *choose* creates. Each such path will typically correspond to checking one complete guess to see if it is a solution to the problem we are trying to solve.
2. The total complexity of the entire search process.

So, although nondeterminism may at first seem at odds with our notion of effective computation, we will find throughout this book that it is a very useful tool in helping us to analyze problems and see how they fit into each of the models that we will consider.

For some problems, it is useful to extend *choose* to allow probabilities to be associated with each of the alternatives. For example, we might write:

choose ((.5) action 1;;
          (.3) action 2;;
          (.2) action 3)

For some applications, the semantics we will want for this extended form of *choose* will be that exactly one path should be pursued. Let Pr(n) be the probability associated with alternative n. Then *choose* will select alternative n with probability Pr(n). For other applications, we will want a different semantics: All paths should be pursued and a total probability should be associated with each path as a function of the set of probabilities associated with each step along the path. We will have more to say about how these probabilities actually work when we talk about specific applications.

4.3 Functions on Languages and Programs

In Chapter 2, we described some useful functions on languages. We considered simple functions such as complement, concatenation, union, intersection, and Kleene star. All of those were defined by straightforward extension of the standard operations on sets and strings. Functions on languages are not limited to those, however. In this section, we mention a couple of others, which we'll come back to at various points throughout this book.

EXAMPLE 4.10 The Function *chop*

Define $chop(L) = \{w : \exists x \in L\,(x = x_1cx_2 \wedge x_1 \in \Sigma_L{}^* \wedge x_2 \in \Sigma_L{}^* \wedge c \in \Sigma_L \wedge |x_1| = |x_2| \wedge w = x_1x_2)\}$. In other words, *chop*(L) is all the odd length strings in L with their middle character chopped out.

Recall the language $\mathrm{A^nB^n} = \{\mathrm{a}^n\mathrm{b}^n : n \geq 0\}$. What is *chop* ($\mathrm{A^nB^n}$)? The answer is $\varnothing$, since there are no odd length strings in $\mathrm{A^nB^n}$.

What about $\mathrm{A^nB^nC^n} = \{\mathrm{a}^n\mathrm{b}^n\mathrm{c}^n : n \geq 0\}$? What is *chop* ($\mathrm{A^nB^nC^n}$)? Approximately half of the strings in $\mathrm{A^nB^nC^n}$ have odd length and so can have their middle character chopped out. Strings in $\mathrm{A^nB^nC^n}$ contribute strings to *chop* ($\mathrm{A^nB^nC^n}$) as follows:

n	in $\mathrm{A^nB^nC^n}$	in *chop* $\mathrm{A^nB^nC^n}$
0	ε	
1	abc	ac
2	aabbcc	
3	aaabbbccc	aaabbccc
4	aaaabbbbcccc	
5	aaaaabbbbbccccc	aaaaabbbbccccc

So, *chop* ($\mathrm{A^nB^nC^n}$) $= \{\mathrm{a}^{2n+1}\mathrm{b}^{2n}\mathrm{c}^{2n+1} : n \geq 0\}$.

EXAMPLE 4.11 The Function *firstchars*

Define $firstchars(L) = \{w : \exists y \in L\ (y = cx \wedge c \in \Sigma_L \wedge x \in \Sigma_L{}^* \wedge w \in c^*)\}$. So we could determine *firstchars*(*L*) by looking at all the strings in *L*, finding all the characters that start such strings, and then, for each such character *c*, adding to *firstchars*(*L*) all the strings in *c**. Let's look at *firstchars* applied to some languages:

L	$firstchars(L)$
$\varnothing$	$\varnothing$
$\{\varepsilon\}$	$\varnothing$
{a}	{a}*
A^nB^n	{a}*
{a, b}*	{a}* ∪ {b}*

Given some function *f* on languages, we may want to ask the question, "If *L* is a member of some language class *C*, what can we say about *f*(*L*)? Is it too a member of *C*? Alternatively, is the class *C* closed under *f*?"

EXAMPLE 4.12 Are Language Classes Closed Under Various Functions?

Consider two classes of languages, INF (the set of infinite languages) and FIN (the set of finite languages). And consider four of the functions we have discussed: union, intersection, *chop* and *firstchars*. We will ask the question, "Is class *C* closed under function *f*?" The answers are (with the number in each cell pointing to an explanation below for the corresponding answer):

	FIN	INF
union	yes (1)	yes (5)
intersection	yes (2)	no (6)
chop	yes (3)	no (7)
firstchars	no (4)	yes (8)

1. For any sets A and B, $|A \cup B| \leq |A| + |B|$.
2. For any sets A and B, $|A \cap B| \leq min\,(|A|, |B|)$.
3. Each string in L can generate at most one string in *chop* (L), so $|chop\ (L)| \leq |L|$.

EXAMPLE 4.12 (*Continued*)

4. To show that any class C is not closed under some function f it is sufficient to show a single counter example: a language L where $L \in C$ but $f(L) \notin C$. We showed such a counter example above: *firstchars* ({a}) = {a}*.
5. For any sets A and B, $|A \cup B| \geq |A|$.
6. We show one counterexample: Let L_1 = {a}* and L_2 = {b}*. L_1 and L_2 are infinite. But $L_1 \cap L_2 = \{\varepsilon\}$, which is finite.
7. We have already shown a counterexample: $\mathrm{A^nB^n}$ is infinite. But *Chop* ($\mathrm{A^nB^n}$) = $\varnothing$, which is finite.
8. If L is infinite, then it contains at least one string of length greater than 0. That string has some first character c. Then $\{c\}^* \subseteq$ *firstchars* (L) and $\{c\}^*$ is infinite.

In the rest of this book, we will discuss the four classes of languages: regular, context-free, decidable, and semidecidable, as described in Chapter 3. One of the questions we will ask for each of them is whether they are closed under various operations.

Given some function f on languages, how can we:

1. Implement f?
2. Show that some class of languages is closed under f?

The answer to question 2 is generally by construction. In other words, we will show an algorithm that takes a description of the input language(s) and constructs a description of the result of applying f to that input. We will then use that constructed description to show that the resulting language is in the class we care about. So our ability to answer both questions 1 and 2 hinges on our ability to define an algorithm that computes f, given a description of its input (which is one or more languages).

In order to define an algorithm A to compute some function f, we first need a way to define the input to A. Defining A is going to be very difficult if we allow, for example, English descriptions of the language(s) on which A is supposed to operate. What we need is a formal model that is exactly powerful enough to describe the languages on which we would like A to be able to run. Then A could use the description(s) of its input language(s) to build a new description, using the same model, of the result of applying f.

EXAMPLE 4.13 Representing Languages So That Functions Can Be Applied

Suppose that we wish to compute the function union. It will be very hard to implement union if we allow input language description such as:

- $\{w \in \{\mathrm{a}, \mathrm{b}\}^* : w$ has an odd number of characters$\}$.

- $\{w \in \{\mathsf{a}, \mathsf{b}\}^* : w$ has an even number of a's$\}$.
- $\{w \in \{\mathsf{a}, \mathsf{b}\}^* :$ all a's in w precede all b's$\}$.

Suppose, on the other hand, that we describe each of these languages as a finite state machine that accepts them. So, for example, language 1 would be represented as

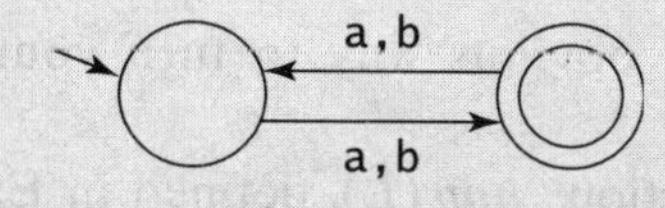

In Chapter 8, we will show an algorithm that, given two FSMs, corresponding to two regular languages, L_1 and L_2, constructs a new FSM that accepts the union of L_1 and L_2.

If we use finite state machines (or pushdown automata or Turing machines) as input I to an algorithm A that computes some function f, then what A will do is to manipulate those FSMs (or PDAs or Turing machines) and produce a new one that accepts the language $f(I)$. If we think of the input FSMs (or PDAs or Turing machines) as programs, then A is a program whose input and output are other programs.

Lisp is a programming language that makes it easy to write programs that manipulate programs. (G.5)

Programs that write other programs are not particularly common, but they are not fundamentally different from programs that work with any other data type. Programs in any conventional programming language can be expressed as strings, so any program that can manipulate strings can manipulate programs. Unfortunately, the syntax of most programming languages makes it relatively difficult to design programs that can effectively manipulate other programs. As we will see later, the FSM, PDA, and Turing machine formalisms that we are going to focus on are reasonably easy to work with. Programs that perform functions on FSMs, PDAs, and Turing machines will be an important part of the theory that we are about to build.

Programs that write other programs play an important role in some application areas, including mathematical modeling of such things as oil wells and financial markets. (G. 8)

Exercises

1. Describe in clear English or pseudocode a decision procedure to answer the question, "Given a list of integers N and an individual integer n, is there any element of N that is a factor of n?"
2. Given a Java program p and the input 0, consider the question, "Does p ever output anything?"
   a. Describe a semidecision procedure that answers this question.
   b. Is there an obvious way to turn your answer to part a into a decision procedure?
3. Recall the function $chop(L)$, defined in Example 4.10. Let $L = \{w \in \{\mathrm{a}, \mathrm{b}\}^* : w = w^R\}$. What is $chop(L)$?
4. Are the following sets closed under the following operations? Prove your answer. If a set is not closed under the operation, what is its closure under the operation?
   a. $L = \{w \in \{\mathrm{a}, \mathrm{b}\}^* : w \text{ ends in a}\}$ under the function *odds*, defined on strings as follows: $odds(s)$ = the string that is formed by concatenating together all of the odd numbered characters of s. (Start numbering the characters at 1.) For example, $odds(\mathrm{ababbbb}) = \mathrm{aabb}$.
   b. FIN (the set of finite languages) under the function *oddsL*, defined on languages as follows:

$$oddsL\ (L) = \{w : \exists x \in L\ (w = odds\ (x))\}.$$

   c. INF (the set of infinite languages) under the function *oddsL*.
   d. FIN under the function *maxstring*, defined in Example 8.22.
   e. INF under the function *maxstring*.
5. Let $\Sigma = \{\mathrm{a}, \mathrm{b}\}$. Let S be the set of all languages over Σ. Let f be a binary function defined as follows:

$$f: S \times S \rightarrow S.$$

$$f(x, y) = x - y.$$

   Answer each of the following questions and justify your answer:
   a. Is f one-to-one?
   b. Is f onto?
   c. Is f commutative?
6. Describe a program, using *choose*, to:
   a. Play Sudoku, described in N. 2.2.
   b. Solve Rubik's Cube®.

P A R T   I I

FINITE STATE MACHINES AND REGULAR LANGUAGES

In this section, we begin our exploration of the language hierarchy. We will start in the inner circle, which corresponds to the class of regular languages.

We will explore three techniques, which we will prove are equivalent, for defining the regular languages:

- Finite state machines.
- Regular languages.
- Regular grammars.

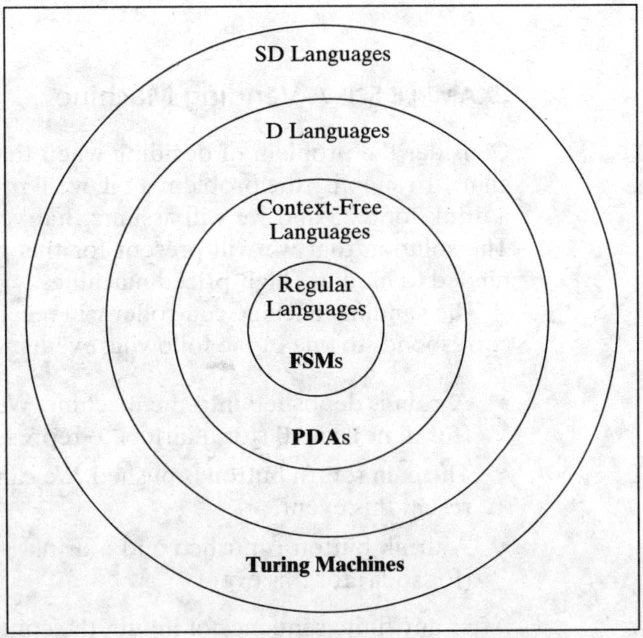

C H A P T E R 5

Finite State Machines

The simplest and most efficient computational device that we will consider is the finite state machine (or FSM).

EXAMPLE 5.1 A Vending Machine

Consider the problem of deciding when to dispense a drink from a vending machine. To simplify the problem a bit, we'll pretend that it were still possible to buy a drink for \$.25 and we will assume that vending machines do not take pennies. The solution that we will present for this problem can straightforwardly be extended to modern, high-priced machines.

The vending machine controller will receive a sequence of inputs, each of which corresponds to one of the following events:

- A coin is deposited into the machine. We can use the symbols N (for nickel), D (for dime), and Q (for quarter) to represent these events.
- The coin return button is pushed. We can use the symbol R (for return) to represent this event.
- A drink button is pushed and a drink is dispensed. We can use the symbol S (for soda) for this event.

After any finite sequence of inputs, the controller will be in either:

- A dispensing state, in which it is willing to dispense a drink if a drink button is pushed.
- A nondispensing state, in which not enough money has been inserted into the machine.

While there is no bound on the length of the input sequence that a drink machine may see in a week, there is only a finite amount of history that its controller must remember in order to do its job. It needs only to be able to answer the question, "Has enough money been inserted, since the last time a drink was dispensed, to purchase the next drink?" It is of course possible for someone to keep inserting money without ever pushing a dispense-drink button. But we can design a controller that will simply reject any money that comes in after the amount required to buy a drink has been recorded and before a drink has actually been dispensed. We will however assume that our goal is to design a customer-friendly drink machine. For example, the thirsty customer may have only dimes. So we'll build a machine that will accept up to \$.45. If more than the necessary \$.25 is inserted before a dispensing button is pushed, our machine will remember the difference and leave a "credit" in the machine. So, for example, if a customer inserts three dimes and then asks for drink, the machine will remember the balance of \$.05.

Notice that the drink controller does not need to remember the actual sequence of coins that it has received. It need only remember the total *value* of the coins that have been inserted since the last drink was dispensed.

The drink controller that we have just described needs 10 states, corresponding to the possible values of the credit that the customer has in the machine: 0, 5, 10, 15, 20, 25, 30, 35, 40, and 45 cents. The main structure of the controller is then:

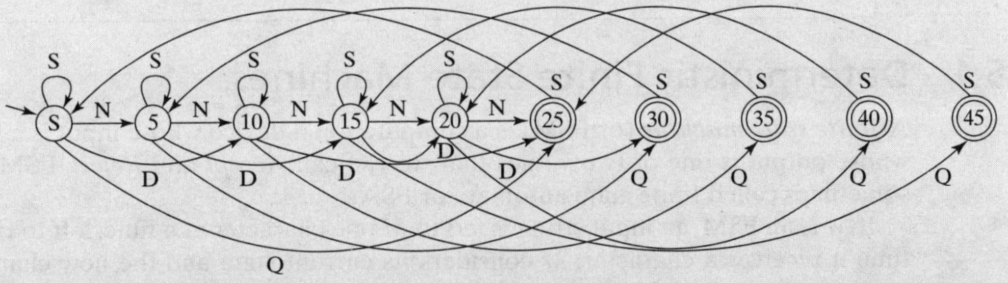

The state that is labeled *S* is the start state. Transitions from one state to the next are shown as arrows and labeled with the event that causes them to take place. As coins are deposited, the controller's state changes to reflect the amount of money that has been deposited. When the drink button is pushed (indicated as *S* in the diagram) and the customer has a credit of less than \$.25, nothing happens. The machine's state does not change. If the drink button is pushed and the customer has a credit of \$.25 or more, the credit is decremented by \$.25 and a drink is dispensed. The drink-dispensing states, namely those that correspond to "enough money", can be thought of as goal or accepting states. We have shown them in the diagram with double circles.

Not all of the required transitions have been shown in the diagram. It would be too difficult to read. We must add to the ones shown all of the following:

- From each of the accepting states, a transition back to itself labeled with each coin value. These transitions correspond to our decision to reject additional coins once the machine has been fed the price of a drink.

EXAMPLE 5.1 *(Continued)*

- From each state, a transition back to the start state labeled R. These transitions will be taken whenever the customer pushes the coin return button. They correspond to the machine returning all of the money that it has accumulated since the last drink was dispensed.

The drink controller that we have just described is an example of a finite state machine. We can think of it as a device to solve a problem (dispense drinks). Or we can think of it as a device to recognize a language (the "enough money" language that consists of the set of strings, such as NDD, that drive the machine to an accepting state in which a drink can be dispensed). In most of the rest of this chapter, we will take the language recognition perspective. But it does also make sense to imagine a finite state machine that actually acts in the world (for example, by outputting a coin or a drink). We will return to that idea in Section 5.9.

> The history of finite state machines substantially predates modern computers. (P. 1)

5.1 Deterministic Finite State Machines

A ***finite state machine*** (or FSM) is a computational device whose input is a string and whose output is one of two values that we can call *Accept* and *Reject*. FSMs are also sometimes called finite state automata or FSAs.

If M is an FSM, an input string is fed to M one character at a time, left to right. Each time it receives a character, M considers its current state and the new character and chooses a next state. One or more of M's states may be marked as accepting states. If M runs out of input and is in an accepting state, it accepts. If, however, M runs out of input and is not in an accepting state, it rejects. The number of steps that M executes on input w is exactly equal to $|w|$, so M always halts and either accepts or rejects.

We begin by defining the class of FSMs whose behavior is deterministic. In such machines, there is always exactly one move that can be made at each step; that move is determined by the current state and the next input character. In Section 5.4, we will relax this restriction and introduce nondeterministic FSMs (also called NDFSMs), in which there may, at various points in the computation, be more than one move from which the machine may choose. We will continue to use the term FSM to include both deterministic and nondeterministic FSMs.

> A telephone switching circuit can easily be modeled as a DFSM.

Formally, a ***deterministic FSM*** (or ***DFSM***) M is a quintuple $(K, \Sigma, \delta, s, A)$, where:

- K is a finite set of states,
- Σ is the input alphabet,

- $s \in K$ is the start state,
- $A \subseteq K$ is the set of accepting states, and
- δ is the transition function. It maps from:

$$\underset{\text{state}}{K} \quad \times \quad \underset{\text{input symbol}}{\Sigma} \quad \text{to} \quad \underset{\text{state}}{K}.$$

A ***configuration*** of a DFSM M is an element of $K \times \Sigma^*$. Think of it as a snapshot of M. It captures the two things that can make a difference to M's future behavior:

- Its current state.
- The input that is still left to read.

The ***initial configuration*** of a DFSM M, on input w, is (s_M, w), where s_M is the start state of M. (We can use the subscript notation to refer to components of a machine M's definition, although, when the context makes it clear what machine we are talking about, we may omit the subscript.)

The transition function δ defines the operation of a DFSM M one step at a time. We can use it to define the sequence of configurations that M will enter. We start by defining the relation *yields-in-one-step*, written $|-_M$. *Yields-in-one-step* relates *configuration*$_1$ to *configuration*$_2$ iff M can move from *configuration*$_1$ to *configuration*$_2$ in one step. Let c be any element of Σ and let w be any element of Σ^*. Then,

$$(q_1, cw) \mid-_M (q_2, w) \text{ iff } ((q_1, c), q_2) \in \delta.$$

We can now define the relation *yields*, written $|-_M{}^*$ to be the reflexive, transitive closure of $|-_M$. So configuration C_1 yields configuration C_2 iff M can go from C_1 to C_2 in zero or more steps. In this case, we will write:

$$C_1 \mid-_M{}^* C_2.$$

A ***computation*** by M is a finite sequence of configurations $C_0, C_1, \ldots, C_n$ for some $n \geq 0$ such that:

- C_0 is an initial configuration,
- C_n is of the form (q, ε), for some state $q \in K_M$ (i.e., the entire input string has been read), and
- $C_0 \mid-_M C_1 \mid-_M C_2 \mid-_M \ldots \mid-_M C_n$.

Let w be an element of Σ^*. Then we will say that:

- ***M accepts*** w iff $(s, w) \mid-_M{}^* (q, \varepsilon)$, for some $q \in A_M$. Any configuration (q, ε), for some $q \in A_M$, is called an ***accepting configuration*** of M.
- ***M rejects*** w iff $(s, w) \mid-_M{}^* (q, \varepsilon)$, for some $q \notin A_M$. Any configuration (q, ε), for some $q \notin A_M$, is called an ***rejecting configuration*** of M.

M halts whenever it enters either an accepting or a rejecting configuration. It will do so immediately after reading the last character of its input.

The ***language accepted by*** M, denoted $L(M)$, is the set of all strings accepted by M.

EXAMPLE 5.2 A Simple Language of a's and b's

Let $L = \{w \in \{\mathsf{a}, \mathsf{b}\}^* :$ every a is immediately followed by a b$\}$. L can be accepted by the DFSM $M = (\{q_0, q_1, q_2\}, \{\mathsf{a}, \mathsf{b}\}, \delta, q_0, \{q_0\})$, where:

$$\begin{aligned}\delta = \{&((q_0, \mathsf{a}), q_1),\\ &((q_0, \mathsf{b}), q_0),\\ &((q_1, \mathsf{a}), q_2),\\ &((q_1, \mathsf{b}), q_0),\\ &((q_2, \mathsf{a}), q_2),\\ &((q_2, \mathsf{b}), q_2))\}.\end{aligned}$$

The tuple notation that we have just used for δ is quite hard to read. We will generally find it useful to draw δ as a transition diagram instead. When we do that, we will use two conventions:

1. The start state will be indicated with an unlabeled arrow pointing into it.
2. The accepting states will be indicated with double circles.

With those conventions, a DFSM can be completely specified by a transition diagram. So M is:

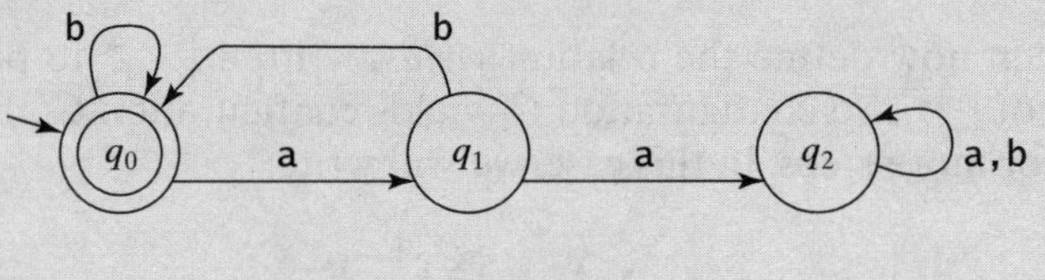

We will use the notation a, b as a shorthand for two transitions, one labeled a and one labeled b.

As an example of M's operation, consider the input string abbabab. M's computation is the sequence of configurations: $(q_0,$ abbabab$)$, $(q_1,$ bbabab$)$, $(q_0,$ babab$)$, $(q_0,$ abab$)$, $(q_1,$ bab$)$, $(q_0,$ ab$)$, $(q_1,$ b$)$, (q_0, ε). Since q_0 is an accepting state, M accepts.

If we look at the three states in M, the machine that we just built, we see that they are of three different sorts:

1. State q_0 is an accepting state. Every string that drives M to state q_0 is in L.
2. State q_1 is not an accepting state. But every string that drives M to state q_1 could turn out to be in L if it is followed by an appropriate continuation string, in this case, one that starts with a b.

3. State q_2 is what we will call a ***dead state***. Once M enters state q_2, it will never leave. State q_2 is not an accepting state, so any string that drives M to state q_2 has already been determined not to be in L, *no matter what comes next*. We will often name our dead states d.

EXAMPLE 5.3 Even Length Regions of a's

Let $L = \{w \in \{a, b\}^* :$ every a region in w is of even length$\}$. L can be accepted by the DFSM M:

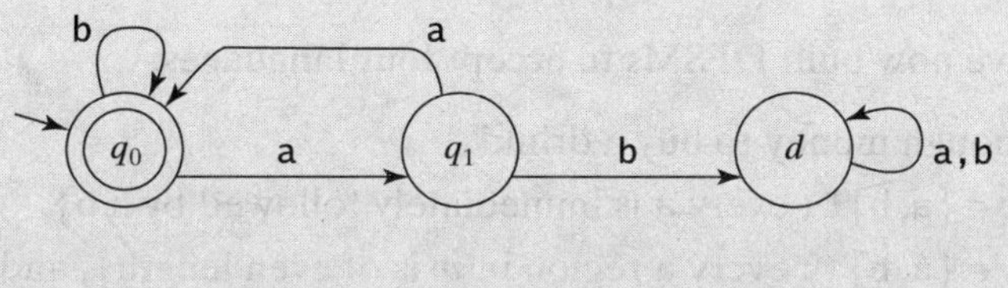

If M sees a b in state q_1, then there has been an a region whose length is odd. So, no matter what happens next, M must reject. So it goes to the dead state d.

A useful way to prototype a complex system is as a finite state machine. See P. 4 for one example: the controller for a soccer-playing robot.

Because objects of other data types are encoded in computer memories as binary strings, it is important to be able to check key properties of such strings.

EXAMPLE 5.4 Checking for Odd Parity

Let $L = \{w \in \{0, 1\}^* : w$ has odd parity$\}$. A binary string has odd parity iff the number of 1's in it is odd. So L can be accepted by the DFSM M:

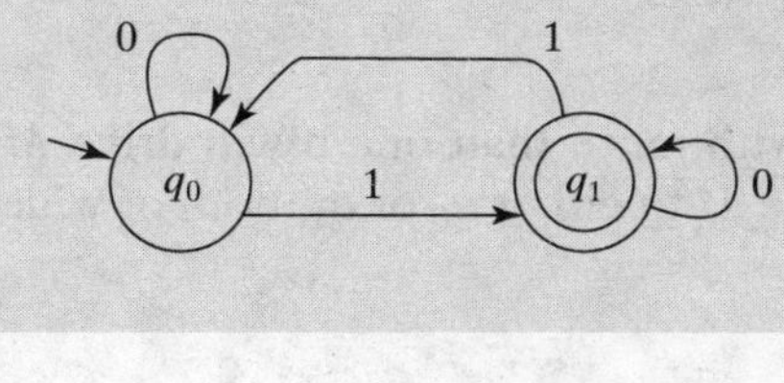

One of the most important properties of finite state machines is that they are guaranteed to halt on any input string of finite length. While this may seem obvious, it is worth noting since, as we'll see later, more powerful computational models may not share this property.

THEOREM 5.1 DFSMs Halt

Theorem: Every DFSM M, on input w, halts after $|w|$ steps.

Proof: On input w, M executes some computation $C_0 \mid\!-_M C_1 \mid\!-_M C_2 \mid\!-_M \ldots \mid\!-_M C_n$, where C_0 is an initial configuration and C_n is of the form (q, ε), for some state $q \in K_M$. C_n is either an accepting or a rejecting configuration, so M will halt when it reaches C_n. Each step in the computation consumes one character of w. So $n = |w|$. Thus M will halt after $|w|$ steps.

5.2 The Regular Languages

We have now built DFSMs to accept four languages:

- "enough money to buy a drink",
- $\{w \in \{\mathsf{a}, \mathsf{b}\}^* :$ every a is immediately followed by a b$\}$,
- $\{w \in \{\mathsf{a}, \mathsf{b}\}^* :$ every a region in w is of even length$\}$, and
- binary strings with odd parity.

These four languages are typical of a large class of languages that can be accepted by finite state machines.

We define the set of ***regular languages*** to be exactly those that can be accepted by some DFSM.

EXAMPLE 5.5 No More Than One b

Let $L = \{w \in \{\mathsf{a}, \mathsf{b}\}^* : w$ contains no more than one b$\}$. L is regular because it can be accepted by the DFSM M:

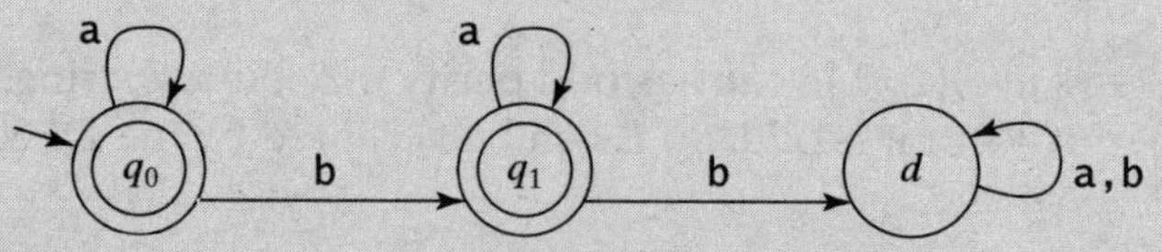

Any string with more than one b will drive M to the dead state d. All other strings will drive M to either q_0 or q_1, both of which are accepting states.

EXAMPLE 5.6 No Two Consecutive Characters Are the Same

Let $L = \{w \in \{\mathsf{a}, \mathsf{b}\}^* :$ no two consecutive characters are the same$\}$. L is regular because it can be accepted by the DFSM M:

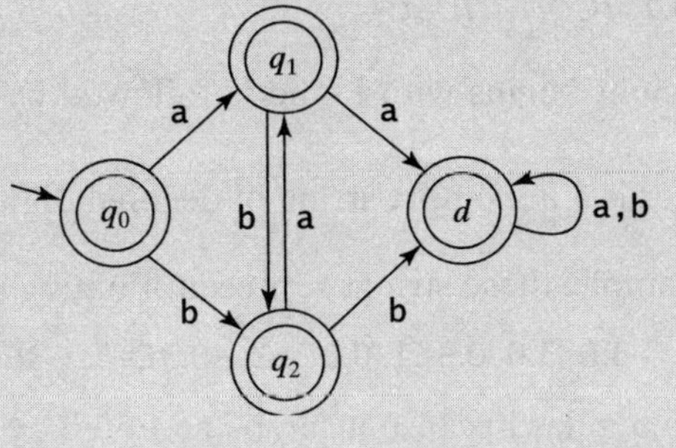

The start state, q_0, is the only state in which both a and b are legal inputs. M will be in state q_1 whenever the consecutive characters rule has not been violated and the last character it has read was a. At that point, the only legal next character is b. M will be in state q_2 whenever the consecutive characters rule has not been violated and the last character it has read was b. At that point, the only legal next character is a. Any other inputs drive M to d.

Simple languages of a's and b's, like the ones in the last two examples, are useful for practice in designing DFSMs. But the real power of the DFSM model comes from the fact that the languages that arise in many real-world applications are regular.

> The language of universal resource identifiers (URIs), used to describe objects on the World Wide Web, is regular. (I.3.1)

To describe less trivial languages will sometimes require DFSMs that are hard to draw if we include the dead state. In those cases, we will omit it from our diagrams. This doesn't mean that it doesn't exist. δ is a function that must be defined for all (state, input) pairs. It just means that we won't bother to draw the dead state. Instead, our convention will be that if there is no transition specified for some (state, input) pair, then that pair drives the machine to a dead state.

EXAMPLE 5.7 Floating Point Numbers

Let FLOAT $= \{w : w$ is the string representation of a floating point number$\}$. Assume the following syntax for floating point numbers:

- A floating point number is an optional sign, followed by a decimal number, followed by an optional exponent.
- A decimal number may be of the form x or $x.y$, where x and y are nonempty strings of decimal digits.

EXAMPLE 5.7 *(Continued)*

- An exponent begins with E and is followed by an optional sign and then an integer.
- An integer is a nonempty string of decimal digits.

So, for example, these strings represent floating point numbers:

+3.0, 3.0, 0.3E1, 0.3E+1, −0.3E+1, −3E8

FLOAT is regular because it can be accepted by the DFSM:

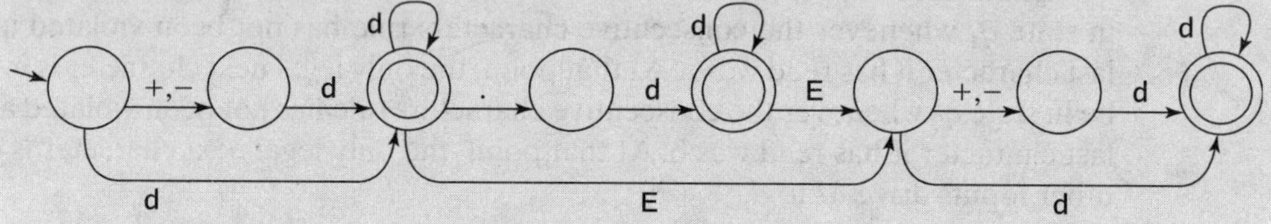

In this diagram, we have used the shorthand d to stand for any one of the decimal digits (0 − 9). And we have omitted the dead state to avoid arrows crossing over each other.

EXAMPLE 5.8 A Simple Communication Protocol

Let L be a language that contains all the legal sequences of messages that can be exchanged between a client and a server using a simple communication protocol. We will actually consider only a very simplified version of such a protocol, but the idea can be extended to a more realistic model.

Let Σ_L = {Open, Request, Reply, Close}. Every string in L begins with Open and ends with Close. In addition, every Request, except possibly the last, must be followed by Reply and no unsolicited Reply's may occur.

L is regular because it can be accepted by the DFSM:

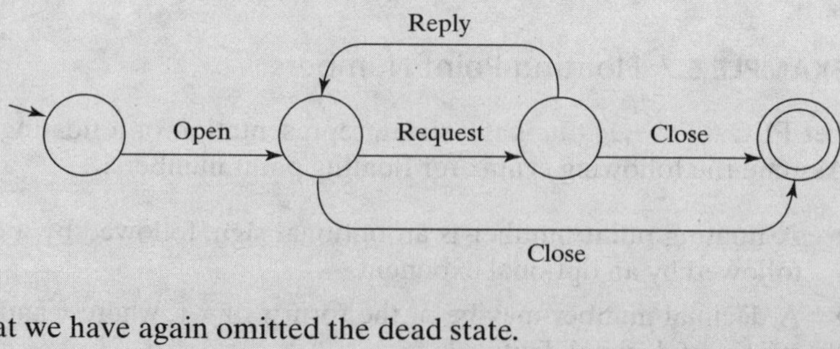

Note that we have again omitted the dead state.

More realistic communication protocols can also be modeled as FSMs. (I.1)

5.3 Designing Deterministic Finite State Machines

Given some language L, how should we go about designing a DFSM to accept L? In general, as in any design task, there is no magic bullet. But there are two related things that it is helpful to think about:

- Imagine any DFSM M that accepts L. As a string w is being read by M, what properties of the part of w that has been seen so far are going to have any bearing on the ultimate answer that M needs to produce? Those are the properties that M needs to record. So, for example, in the "enough money" machine, all that matters is the amount of money since the last drink was dispensed. Which coins came in and the order in which they were deposited make no difference.
- If L is infinite but M has a finite number of states, strings must "cluster". In other words, multiple different strings will all drive M to the same state. Once they have done that, none of their differences matter anymore. If they've driven M to the same state, they share a fate. No matter what comes next, either all of them cause M to accept or all of them cause M to reject. In Section 5.7 we will show that the smallest DFSM for any language L is the one that has exactly one state for every group of initial substrings that share a common fate. For now, however, it helps to think about what those clusters are. We'll do that in our next example.

A building security system can be described as a DFSM that sounds an alarm if given an input sequence that signals an intruder. (J.1)

EXAMPLE 5.9 Even a's, Odd b's

Let $L = \{w \in \{\texttt{a}, \texttt{b}\}^* : w$ contains an even number of a's and an odd number of b's$\}$. To design a DFSM M to accept L, we need to decide what history matters. Since M's goal is to separate strings with even a's and odd b's from strings that fail to meet at least one of those requirements, all it needs to remember is whether the count of a's so far is even or odd and whether the count of b's is even or odd. So, since there are two clusters based on the number of a's so far (even and odd) and two clusters based on the number of b's, there are four distinct clusters.

That suggests that we need a four-state DFSM. Often it helps to name the states with a description of the clusters to which they correspond. The following DFSM M accepts L:

EXAMPLE 5.9 *(Continued)*

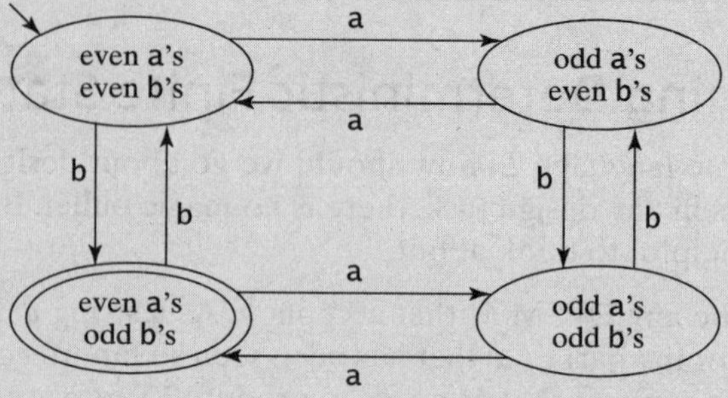

Notice that, once we have designed a machine that analyzes an input string with respect to some set of properties we care about, it is relatively easy to build a different machine that accepts strings based on different values of those properties. For example, to change M so that it accepts exactly the strings with both even a's and even b's, all we need to do is to change the accepting state.

EXAMPLE 5.10 All the Vowels in Alphabetical Order

Let $L = \{w \in \{\texttt{a} - \texttt{z}\}^*$: all five vowels, a, e, i, o, and u, occur in w in alphabetical order$\}$. So L contains words like `abstemious`, `facetious`, and `sacrilegious`. But it does not contain `tenacious`, which does contain all the vowels, but not in the correct order. It is hard to write a clear, elegant program to accept L. But designing a DFSM is simple. The following machine M does the job. In this description of M, let the label "$\Sigma - \{\texttt{a}\}$" mean "all elements of Σ except a" and let the label "Σ" mean "all elements of Σ":

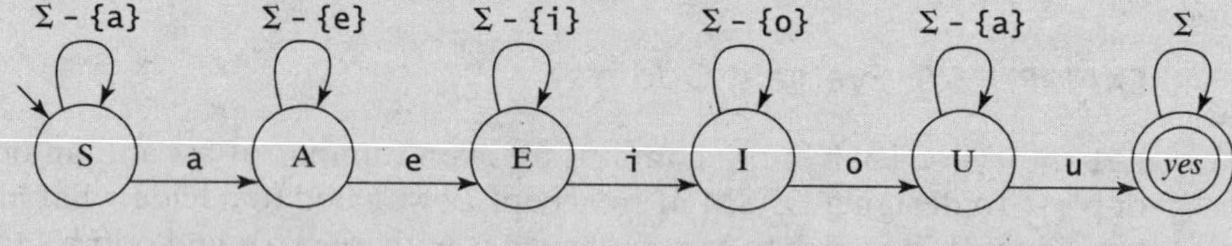

Notice that the state that we have labeled *yes* functions exactly opposite to the way in which the dead state works. If M ever reaches *yes*, it has decided to accept no matter what comes next.

Sometimes an easy way to design an FSM to accept a language L is to begin by designing an FSM to accept the complement of L. Then, as a final step, we swap the accepting and the nonaccepting states.

EXAMPLE 5.11 A Substring that Doesn't Occur

Let $L = \{w \in \{a, b\}^* : w$ does not contain the substring aab$\}$. It is straightforward to design an FSM that looks for the substring aab. So we can begin building a machine to accept L by building the following machine to accept $\neg L$:

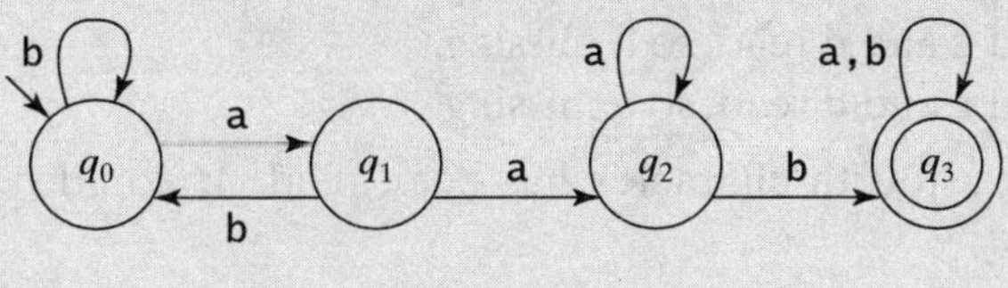

Then we can convert this machine into one that accepts L by making states q_0, q_1, and q_2 accepting and state q_3 nonaccepting.

In Section 8.3 we'll show that the regular languages are closed under complement (i.e., the complement of every regular language is also regular). The proof will be by construction and the last step of the construction will be to swap accepting and nonaccepting states, just as we did in the last example.

Sometimes the usefulness of the DFSM model, as we have so far defined it, breaks down before its formal power does. There are some regular languages that seem quite simple when we state them but that can only be accepted by DFSMs of substantial complexity.

EXAMPLE 5.12 The Missing Letter Language

Let $\Sigma = \{a, b, c, d\}$. Let $L_{Missing} = \{w :$ there is a symbol $a_i \in \Sigma$ not appearing in $w\}$. $L_{Missing}$ is regular. We can begin writing out a DFSM M to accept it. We will need the following states:

- The start state: all letters are still missing.

After one character has been read, M could be in any one of:

- a read, so b, c, and d still missing.
- b read, so a, c, and d still missing.
- c read, so a, b, and d still missing.
- d read, so a, b, and c still missing.

After a second character has been read, M could be in any of the previous states or one of:

- a and b read, so c and d still missing.
- a and c read, so b and d still missing.
- and so forth. There are six of these.

EXAMPLE 5.12 *(Continued)*

After a third character has been read, M could be in any of the previous states or one of:

- a and b and c read, so d missing.
- a and b and d read, so c missing.
- a and c and d read, so b missing.
- b and c and d read, so a missing.

After a fourth character has been read, M could be in any of the previous states or:

- All characters read, so nothing is missing.

Every state except the last is an accepting state. M is complicated but it would be possible to write it out. Now imagine that Σ were the entire English alphabet. It would still be possible to write out a DFSM to accept $L_{Missing}$, but it would be so complicated it would be hard to get it right. The DFSM model is no longer very useful.

5.4 Nondeterministic FSMs

To solve the problem that we just encountered in the missing letter example, we will modify our definition of an FSM to allow nondeterminism. Recall our discussion of nondeterminism in Section 4.2. We will now introduce our first specific use of the ideas we discussed there. We'll see that we can easily build a nondeterministic FSM M to accept $L_{Missing}$. Any string in $L_{Missing}$ must be missing at least one letter. We'll design M so that it simply guesses at which letter that is. If there is a missing letter, then at least one of M's guesses will be right and the corresponding path will accept. So M will accept.

5.4.1 What Is a Nondeterministic FSM?

A nondeterministic FSM (or NDFSM) M is a quintuple $(K, \Sigma, \Delta, s, A)$, where:

- K is a finite set of states,
- Σ is an alphabet,
- $s \in K$ is the start state,
- $A \subseteq$ is the set of final states, and
- Δ is the transition relation. It is a finite subset of: $(K \times (\Sigma \cup \{\varepsilon\})) \times K$.

In other words, each element of Δ contains a (state, input symbol or ε) pair, and a new state.

We define configuration, initial configuration, accepting configuration, *yields-in-one-step*, *yields*, and computation analogously to the way that we defined them for DFSMs.

Let w be an element of Σ^*. Then we will say that:

- M ***accepts*** w iff *at least one* of its computations accepts.
- M ***rejects*** w iff none of its computations accepts.

The ***language accepted by*** M, denoted $L(M)$, is the set of all strings accepted by M.

There are two key differences between DFSMs and NDFSMs. In every configuration, a DFSM can make exactly one move. However, because Δ can be an arbitrary relation (that may not also be a function), that is not necessarily true for an NDFSM. Instead:

- An NDFSM M may enter a configuration in which there are still input symbols left to read but from which *no* moves are available. Since any sequence of moves that leads to such a configuration cannot ever reach an accepting configuration, M will simply halt without accepting. This situation is possible because Δ is not a function. So there can be (state, input) pairs for which no next state is defined.
- An NDFSM M may enter a configuration from which *two or more* competing moves are possible. The competition can come from either or both of the following properties of the transition relation of an NDFSM:
  - An NDFSM M may have one or more transitions that are labeled ε, rather than being labeled with a character from Σ. An ε-transition out of state q may (but need not) be followed, without consuming any input, whenever M is in state q. So an ε-transition from a state q competes with all other transitions out of q. One way to think about the usefulness of ε-transitions is that they enable M to guess at the correct path before it actually sees the input. Wrong guesses will generate paths that will fail but that can be ignored.
  - Out of some state q, there may be more than one transition with a given label. These competing transitions give M another way to guess at a correct path.

Consider the fragment, shown in Figure 5.1, of an NDFSM M. If M is in state q_0 and the next input character is an a, then there are three moves that M could make:

1. It can take the ε-transition to q_1 before it reads the next input character,
2. It can read the next input character and take the transition to q_2, or
3. It can read the next input character and take the transition to q_3.

One way to envision the operation of M is as a tree, as shown in Figure 5.2. Each node in the tree corresponds to a configuration of M. Each path from the root corresponds to a sequence of moves that M might make. Each path that leads to a configuration in which the entire input string has been read corresponds to a computation of M.

An alternative is to imagine following all paths through M in parallel. Think of M as being in a *set* of states at each step of its computation. If, when M runs out of input, the set of states that it is in contains at least one accepting state, then M will accept.

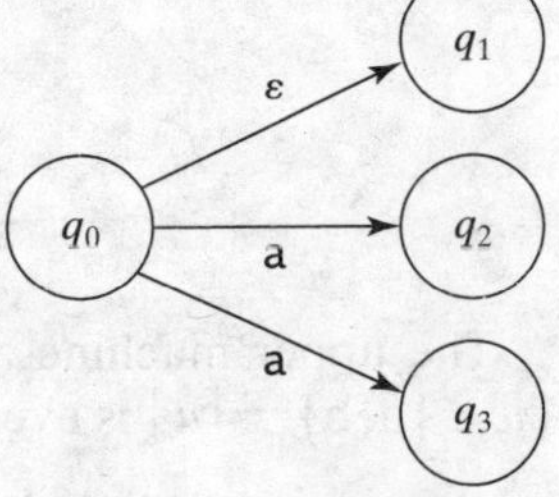

FIGURE 5.1 An NDFSM with two kinds of nondeterminism.

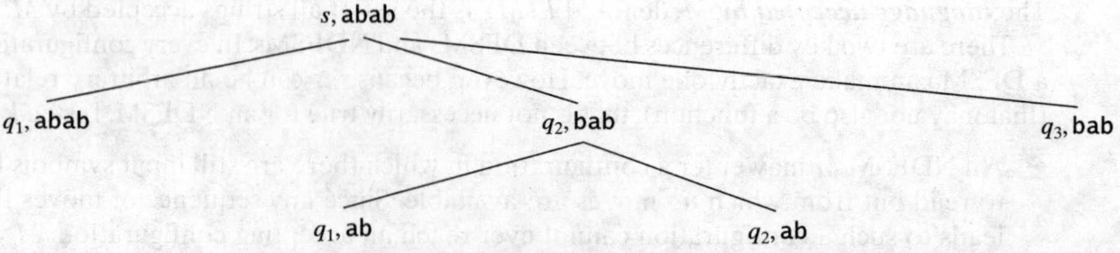

FIGURE 5.2 Viewing nondeterminism as search through a space of computation paths.

EXAMPLE 5.13 An Optional Initial a

Let $L = \{w \in \{\text{a, b}\}^* : w$ is made up of an optional a followed by aa followed by zero or more b's$\}$. The following NDFSM M accepts L:

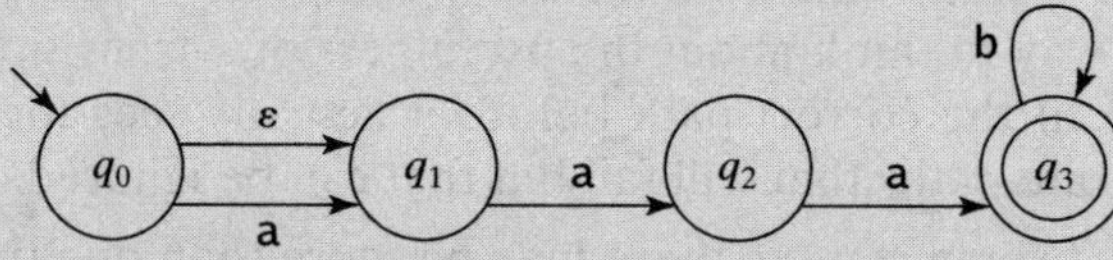

M may (but is not required to) follow the ε-transition from state q_0 to state q_1 before it reads the first input character. In effect, it must guess whether or not the optional a is present.

EXAMPLE 5.14 Two Different Sublanguages

Let $L = \{w \in \{\text{a, b}\}^* : w = \text{aba}$ or $|w|$ is even$\}$. An easy way to build an FSM to accept this language is to build FSMs for each of the individual sublanguages and then "glue" them together with ε-transitions. In essence, the machine guesses, when processing a string, which sublanguage the string might be in. So we have:

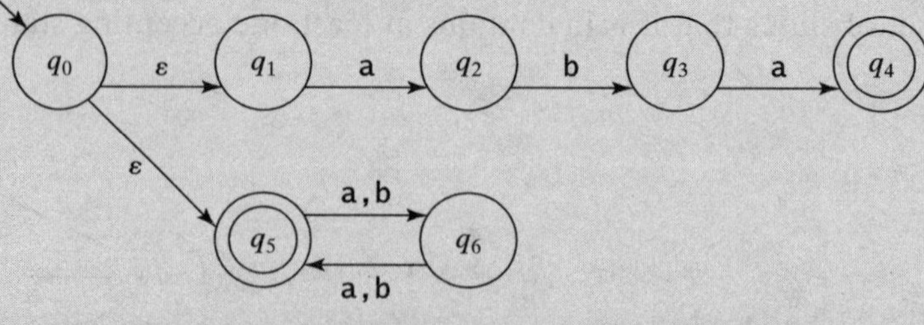

The upper machine accepts $\{w \in \{\text{a, b}\}^* : w = \text{aba}\}$. The lower one accepts $\{w \in \{\text{a, b}\}^* : |w| \text{ is even}\}$.

By exploiting nondeterminism, it may be possible to build a simple FSM to accept a language for which the smallest deterministic FSM is complex. A good example of a language for which this is true is the missing letter language that we considered in Example 5.12.

EXAMPLE 5.15 The Missing Letter Language, Again

Let $\Sigma = \{\texttt{a, b, c, d}\}$. $L_{Missing} = \{w$: there is a symbol $a_i \in \Sigma$ not appearing in $w\}$. The following simple NDFSM M accepts $L_{Missing}$:

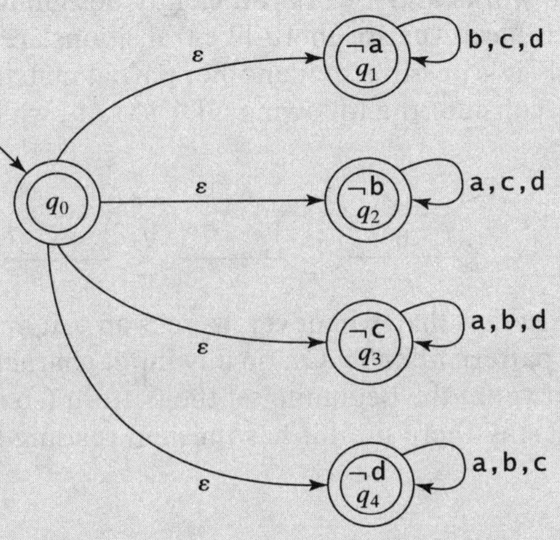

M works by guessing which letter is going to be the missing one. If any of its guesses is right, it will accept. If all of them are wrong, then all paths will fail and M will reject.

5.4.2 NDFSMs for Pattern and Substring Matching

Nondeterministic FSMs are a particularly effective way to define simple machines to search a text string for one or more patterns or substrings.

EXAMPLE 5.16 Exploiting Nondeterminism for Keyword Matching

Let $L = \{w \in \{\texttt{a, b, c}\}^* : \exists x, y \in \{\texttt{a, b, c}\}^* \ (w = x\ \texttt{abcabb}\ y)\}$. In other words, w must contain at least one occurrence of the substring abcabb. The following DFSM M_1 accepts L:

EXAMPLE 5.16 (*Continued*)

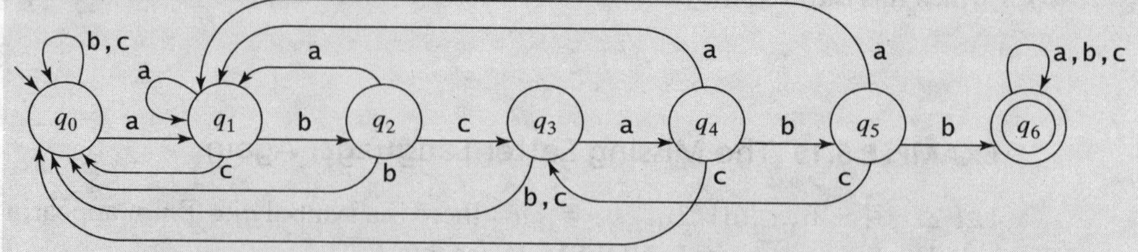

While M_1 works, and it works efficiently, designing machines like M_1 and getting them right is hard. The spaghetti-like transitions are necessary because, whenever a match fails, it is possible that another partial match has already been found.

But now consider the following NDFSM M_2, which also accepts L:

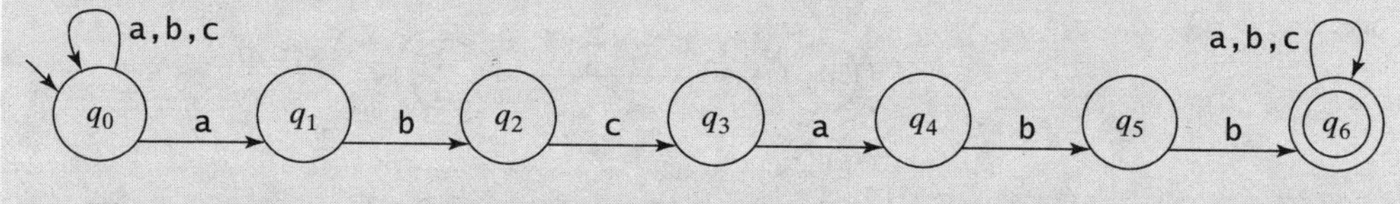

The idea here is that, whenever M_2 sees an a, it may guess that it is at the beginning of the pattern abcabb. Or, on any input character (including a), it may guess that it is not yet at the beginning of the pattern (so it stays in q_0). If it ever reaches q_6, it will stay there until it has finished reading the input. Then it will accept.

Of course, practical string search engines need to be small and deterministic. But NDFSMs like the one we just built can be used as the basis for constructing such efficient search machines. In Section 5.4.4, we will describe an algorithm that converts an arbitrary NDFSM into an equivalent DFSM. It is likely that that machine will have more states than it needs. But, in Section 5.7, we will present an algorithm that takes an arbitrary DFSM and produces an equivalent minimal one (i.e., one with the smallest number of states). So one effective way to build a correct and efficient string-searching machine is to build a simple NDFSM, convert it to an equivalent DFSM, and then minimize the result. One alternative to this three-step process is the Knuth-Morris-Pratt string search algorithm, which we will present in Example 27.5.

String searching is a fundamental operation in every word processing or text editing system.

Now suppose that we have not one pattern but several. Hand crafting a DFSM may be even more difficult. One alternative is to use a specialized, keyword-search FSM-building algorithm that we will present in Section 6.2.4. Another is to build a simple NDFSM, as we show in the next example.

EXAMPLE 5.17 Multiple Keywords

Let $L = \{w \in \{\mathtt{a},\mathtt{b}\}^* : \exists x, y \in \{\mathtt{a},\mathtt{b}\}^* \; ((w = x\,\mathtt{abbaa}\; y) \vee (w = x\,\mathtt{baba}\; y))\}$. In other words, w contains at least one occurrence of the substring abbaa or the substring baba. The following NDFSM M accepts L:

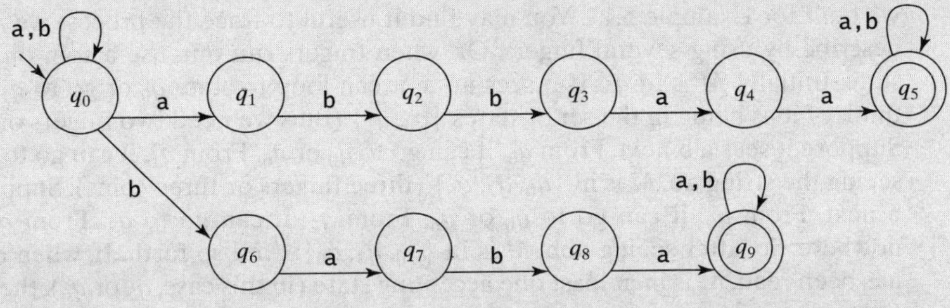

The idea here is that, whenever M sees an a, it may guess that it is at the beginning of the substring abbaa. Whenever it sees a b, it may guess that it is at the beginning of the substring baba. Alternatively, on either a or b, it may guess that it is not yet at the beginning of either substring (so it stays in q_0).

NDFSMs are also a natural way to search for other kinds of patterns, as we can see in the next example.

EXAMPLE 5.18 Other Kinds of Patterns

Let $L = \{w \in \{\mathtt{a}, \mathtt{b}\}^* :$ the fourth from the last character is a$\}$. The following NDFSM M accepts L:

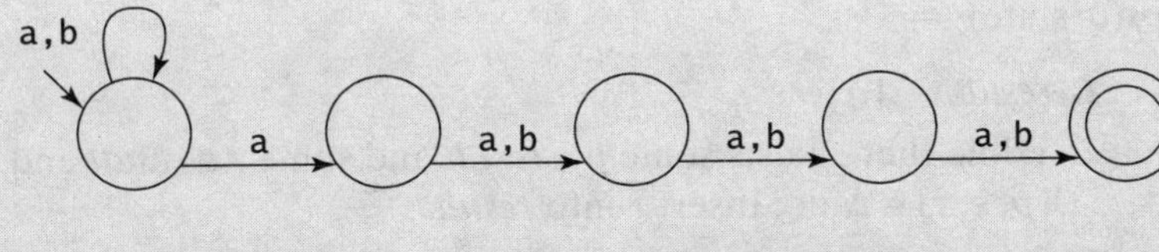

The idea here is that, whenever it sees an a, one of M's paths guesses that it is the fourth from the last character (and so proceeds along the path that will read the last three remaining characters). The other path guesses that it is not (and so stays in the start state).

It is enlightening to try designing DFSMs for the last two examples. We leave that as an exercise. If you try it, you'll appreciate the value of the NDFSM model as a high-level tool for describing complex systems.

5.4.3 Analyzing Nondeterministic FSMs

Given an NDFSM M, such as any of the ones we have just considered, how can we analyze it to determine what strings it accepts? One way is to do a depth-first search of the paths through the machine. Another is to imagine tracing the execution of the original NDFSM M by following all paths in parallel. To do that, think of M as being in a set of states at each step of its computation. For example, consider again the NDFSM that we built for Example 5.17. You may find it useful to trace the process we are about to describe by using several fingers. Or, when fingers run out, use a coin on each active state. Initially, M is in q_0. If it sees an a, it can loop to state q_0 or go to q_1. So we will think of it as being in the set of states $\{q_0, q_1\}$ (thus we need two fingers or two coins). Suppose it sees a b next. From q_0, it can go to q_0 or q_6. From q_1, it can go to q_2. So, after seeing the string ab, M is in $\{q_0, q_2, q_6\}$ (three fingers or three coins). Suppose it sees a b next. From q_0, it can go to q_0 or q_6. From q_2, it can go to q_3. From q_6, it can go nowhere. So, after seeing abb, M is in $\{q_0, q_3, q_6\}$. And so forth. If, when all the input has been read, M is in at least one accepting state (in this case, q_5 or q_9), then it accepts. Otherwise it rejects.

Handling ε-Transitions

But how shall we handle ε-transitions? The construction that we just sketched assumes that all paths have read the same number of input symbols. But if, from some state q, one transition is labeled ε and another is labeled with some element of Σ, M consumes no input as it takes the first transition and one input symbol as it takes the second transition. To solve this problem, we introduce the function eps: $K_M \rightarrow \mathcal{P}(K_M)$. We define $eps(q)$, where q is some state in M, to be the set of states of M that are reachable from q by following zero or more ε-transitions. Formally:

$$eps\,(q) = \{p \in K : (q, w) \mid\!-_M{}^* \, (p, w)\}.$$

Alternatively, $eps(q)$ is the closure of $\{q\}$ under the relation $\{(p, r) :$ there is a transition $(p, \varepsilon, r) \in \Delta\}$. The following algorithm computes eps:

$eps(q$: state$)$ =

1. $result = \{q\}$.
2. While there exists some $p \in result$ and some $r \notin result$ and some transition $(p, \varepsilon, r) \in \Delta$ do: Insert r into $result$.
3. Return $result$.

This algorithm is guaranteed to halt because, each time through the loop, it adds an element to $result$. It must halt when there are no elements left to add. Since there is only a finite number of candidate elements, namely the finite set of states in M, and no element can be added more than once, the algorithm must eventually run out of elements to add, at which point it must halt. It correctly computes $eps(q)$ because, by the condition associated with the while loop:

- It can add no element that is not reachable from q following only ε-transitions.
- It will add all elements that are reachable from q following only ε-transitions.

EXAMPLE 5.19 Computing *eps*

Consider the following NDFSM M:

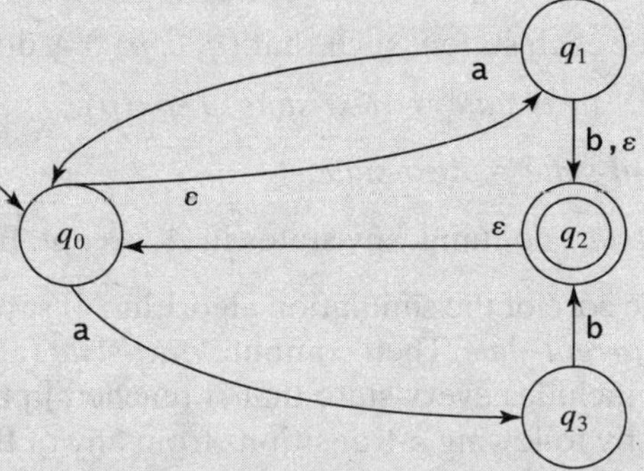

To compute $eps(q_0)$, we initially set *result* to $\{q_0\}$. Then q_1 is added, producing $\{q_0, q_1\}$. Then q_2 is added, producing $\{q_0, q_1, q_2\}$. There is an ε-transition from q_2 to q_0, but q_0 is already in *result*. So the computation of $eps(q_0)$ halts.

The result of running *eps* on each of the states of M is:

$$eps(q_0) = \{q_0, q_1, q_2\}.$$
$$eps(q_1) = \{q_0, q_1, q_2\}.$$
$$eps(q_2) = \{q_0, q_1, q_2\}.$$
$$eps(q_3) = \{q_3\}.$$

Example 5.19 illustrates clearly why we chose to define the *eps* function, rather than treating ε-transitions like other transitions and simply following them whenever we could. The machine we had to consider in that example contains what we might choose to call an ***ε-loop:*** a loop that can be traversed by following only ε-transitions. Since such transitions consume no input, there is no limit to the number of times the loop could be traversed. So, if we were not careful, it would be easy to write a simulation algorithm that did not halt. The algorithm that we presented for *eps* halts whenever it runs out of unvisited states to add, which must eventually happen since the set of states is finite.

A Simulation Algorithm

With the *eps* function in hand, we can now define an algorithm for tracing all paths in parallel through an NDFSM M:

ndfsmsimulate (M: NDFSM, w: string) =

1. *current-state* = *eps*(s). /*Start in the set that contains M's start state and any other states that can be reached from it following only ε-transitions.

2. While any input symbols in w remain to be read do:

   2.1. c = get-next-symbol(w).

   2.2. *next-state* = $\varnothing$.

   2.3. For each state q in *current-state* do:

   For each state p such that $(q, c, p) \in \Delta$ do:

   next-state = *next-state* $\cup$ *eps* (p).

   2.4. *current-state* = *next-state*.

3. If *current-state* contains any states in A, accept. Else reject.

Step 2.3 is the core of the simulation algorithm. It says: Follow every arc labeled c from every state in *current-state*. Then compute *next-state* (and thus the new value of *current-state*) so that it includes every state that is reached in that process, plus every state that can be reached by following ε-transitions from any of those states. For more on how this step can be implemented, see the more detailed description of *ndfsmsimulate* that we present in Section 5.6.2.

5.4.4 The Equivalence of Nondeterministic and Deterministic FSMs

In this section, we explore the relationship between the DFSM and NDFSM models that we have just defined.

THEOREM 5.2 If There is a DFSM for *L*, There is an NDFSM for *L*

Theorem: For every DFSM there is an equivalent NDFSM.

Proof: Let M be a DFSM that accepts some language L. M is also an NDFSM that happens to contain no ε-transitions and whose transition relation happens to be a function. So the NDFSM that we claim must exist is simply M.

But what about the other direction? The nondeterministic model that we have just introduced makes it substantially easier to build FSMs to accept some kinds of languages, particularly those that involve looking for instances of complex patterns. But real computers are deterministic. What does the existence of an NDFSM to accept a language L tell us about the existence of a deterministic program to accept L? The answer is given by the following theorem:

THEOREM 5.3 If There is an NDFSM for *L*, There is a DFSM for *L*

Theorem: Given an NDFSM $M = (K, \Sigma, \Delta, s, A)$ that accepts some language L, there exists an equivalent DFSM that accepts L.

Proof: The proof is by construction of an equivalent DFSM M'. The construction is based on the function *eps* and on the simulation algorithm that we described in the last section. The states of M' will correspond to sets of states in M. So $M' = (K', \Sigma, \delta', s', A')$, where:

- K' contains one state for each element of $\mathcal{P}(K)$.
- $s' = eps(s)$.
- $A' = \{Q \subseteq K : Q \cap A \neq \varnothing\}$.
- $\delta'(Q, c) = \cup\{eps(p) : \exists q \in Q\ ((q, c, p) \in \Delta)\}$.

We should note the following things about this definition:

- In principle, there is one state in K' for each element of $\mathcal{P}(K)$. However, in most cases, many of those states will be unreachable from s' (and thus unnecessary). So we will present a construction algorithm that creates states only as it needs to.
- We'll name each state in K' with the element of $\mathcal{P}(K)$ to which it corresponds. That will make it relatively straightforward to see how the construction works. But keep in mind that those labels are just names. We could have called them anything.
- To decide whether a state in K' is an accepting state, we see whether it corresponds to an element of $\mathcal{P}(K)$ that contains at least one element of A, i.e., one accepting state from K.
- M' accepts whenever it runs out of input and is in a state that contains at least one accepting state of M. Thus it implements the definition of an NDFSM, which accepts iff at least one path through it accepts.
- The definition of δ' corresponds to step 2.3 of the simulation algorithm we presented above.

The following algorithm computes M' given M:

ndfsmtodfsm(M: NDFSM) =

1. For each state q in K do:

Compute $eps(q)$. /* These values will be used below.

2. $s' = eps(s)$.

3. Compute δ':

a. *active-states* $= \{s'\}$. /* We will build a list of all states that are reachable from the start state. Each element of *active-states* is a set of states drawn from K.

b. $\delta' = \varnothing$.

c. While there exists some element Q of *active-states* for which δ' has not yet been computed do:

For each character c in Σ do:

new-state $= \varnothing$.

For each state q in Q do:

For each state p such that $(q, c, p) \in \Delta$ do:

$new\text{-}state = new\text{-}state \cup eps(p)$.

Add the transition $(Q, c, new\text{-}state)$ to δ'.

If $new\text{-}state \notin active\text{-}states$ then insert it into *active-states*.

4. $K' = active\text{-}states$.

5. $A' = \{Q \in K' : Q \cap A \neq \varnothing\}$.

The core of *ndfsmtodfsm* is the loop in step 3.3. At each step through it, we pick a state that we know is reachable from the start state but from which we have not yet computed transitions. Call it Q. Then compute the paths from Q for each element c of the input alphabet as follows: Q is a set of states in the original NDFSM M. So consider each element q of Q. Find all transitions from q labeled c. For each state p that is reached by such a transition, find all additional states that are reachable by following only ε-transitions from p. Let *new-state* be the set that contains all of those states. Now we know that whenever M' is in Q and it reads a c, it should go to *new-state*.

The algorithm *ndfsmtodfsm* halts on all inputs and constructs a DFSM M' that accepts exactly $L(M)$, the language accepted by M.

A rigorous construction proof requires a proof that the construction algorithm is correct. We will generally omit the details of such proofs. But we show them for this case as an example of what these proofs look like. (Appendix C)

The algorithm *ndfsmtodfsm* is important for two reasons:

- It proves the theorem that, for every NDFSM there exists an equivalent DFSM.
- It lets us use nondeterminism as a design tool, even though we may ultimately need a deterministic machine. If we have an implementation of *ndfsmtodfsm*, then, if we can build an NDFSM to solve our problem, *ndfsmtodfsm* can easily construct an equivalent DFSM.

EXAMPLE 5.20 Using *ndfsmtodfsm* to Build a Deterministic FSM

Consider the NDFSM M shown on the next page. To get a feel for M, simulate it on the input string bbbacb, using coins to keep track of the states it enters.

We can apply *ndfsmtodfsm* to M as follows:

1. Compute $eps(q)$ for each state q in K_M:

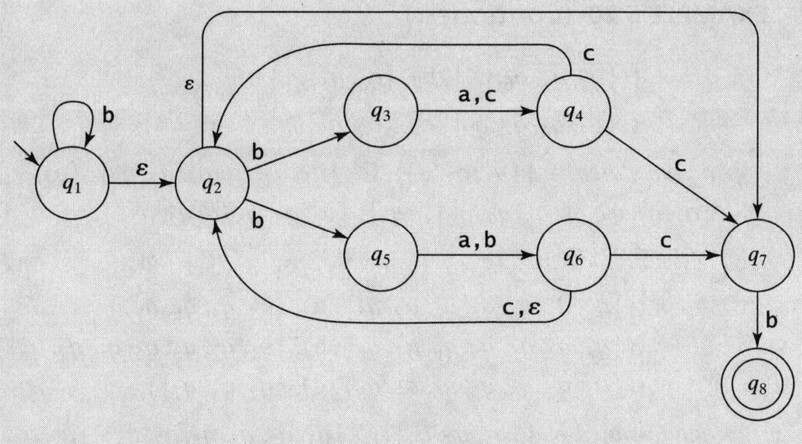

$eps\ (q_1) = \{q_1, q_2, q_7\}$, $eps\ (q_2) = \{q_2, q_7\}$, $eps\ (q_3) = \{q_3\}$, $eps\ (q_4) = \{q_4\}$,
$eps\ (q_5) = \{q_5\}$, $eps\ (q_6) = \{q_2, q_6, q_7\}$, $eps\ (q_7) = \{q_7\}$, $eps\ (q_8) = \{q_8\}$.

2. $s' = eps\ (s) = \{q_1, q_2, q_7\}$.

3. Compute δ':

active-states $= \{\{q_1, q_2, q_7\}\}$. Consider $\{q_1, q_2, q_7\}$:

$((\{q_1, q_2, q_7\}, \mathsf{a}), \varnothing)$.
$((\{q_1, q_2, q_7\}, \mathsf{b}), \{q_1, q_2, q_3, q_5, q_7, q_8\})$.
$((\{q_1, q_2, q_7\}, \mathsf{c}), \varnothing)$.

active-states $= \{\{q_1, q_2, q_7\}, \varnothing, \{q_1, q_2, q_3, q_5, q_7, q_8\}\}$. Consider $\varnothing$:

$((\varnothing, \mathsf{a}), \varnothing)$. /* $\varnothing$ is a dead state and we will generally omit it.
$((\varnothing, \mathsf{b}), \varnothing)$.
$((\varnothing, \mathsf{c}), \varnothing)$.

active-states $= \{\{q_1, q_2, q_7\}, \varnothing, \{q_1, q_2, q_3, q_5, q_7, q_8\}\}$. Consider $\{q_1, q_2, q_3, q_5, q_7, q_8\}$:

$((\{q_1, q_2, q_3, q_5, q_7, q_8\}, \mathsf{a}), \{q_2, q_4, q_6, q_7\})$.
$((\{q_1, q_2, q_3, q_5, q_7, q_8\}, \mathsf{b}), \{q_1, q_2, q_3, q_5, q_6, q_7, q_8\})$.
$((\{q_1, q_2, q_3, q_5, q_7, q_8\}, \mathsf{c}), \{q_4\})$.

active-states $= \{\{q_1, q_2, q_7\}, \varnothing, \{q_1, q_2, q_3, q_5, q_7, q_8\}, \{q_2, q_4, q_6, q_7\}, \{q_1, q_2, q_3, q_5, q_6, q_7, q_8\}, \{q_4\}\}$. Consider $\{q_2, q_4, q_6, q_7\}$:

$((\{q_2, q_4, q_6, q_7\}, \mathsf{a}), \varnothing)$.

EXAMPLE 5.20 *(Continued)*

$((\{q_2, q_4, q_6, q_7\}, \text{b}), \{q_3, q_5, q_8\})$.

$((\{q_2, q_4, q_6, q_7\}, \text{c}), \{q_2, q_7\})$.

active-states $= \{\{q_1, q_2, q_7\}, \varnothing, \{q_1, q_2, q_3, q_5, q_7, q_8\}, \{q_2, q_4, q_6, q_7\}, \{q_1, q_2, q_3, q_5, q_6, q_7, q_8\}, \{q_4\}, \{q_3, q_5, q_8\}, \{q_2, q_7\}\}$.

Consider $\{q_1, q_2, q_3, q_5, q_6, q_7, q_8\}$:

$((\{q_1, q_2, q_3, q_5, q_6, q_7, q_8\}, \text{a}), \{q_2, q_4, q_6, q_7\})$.

$((\{q_1, q_2, q_3, q_5, q_6, q_7, q_8\}, \text{b}), \{q_1, q_2, q_3, q_5, q_6, q_7, q_8\})$.

$((\{q_1, q_2, q_3, q_5, q_6, q_7, q_8\}, \text{c}), \{q_2, q_4, q_7\})$.

active-states $= \{\{q_1, q_2, q_7\}, \varnothing, \{q_1, q_2, q_3, q_5, q_7, q_8\}, \{q_2, q_4, q_6, q_7\}, \{q_1, q_2, q_3, q_5, q_6, q_7, q_8\}, \{q_4\}, \{q_3, q_5, q_8\}, \{q_2, q_7\}, \{q_2, q_4, q_7\}\}$. Consider $\{q_4\}$:

$((\{q_4\}, \text{a}), \varnothing)$.

$((\{q_4\}, \text{b}), \varnothing)$.

$((\{q_4\}, \text{c}), \{q_2, q_7\})$.

active-states did not change. Consider $\{q_3, q_5, q_8\}$:

$((\{q_3, q_5, q_8\}, \text{a}), \{q_2, q_4, q_6, q_7\})$.

$((\{q_3, q_5, q_8\}, \text{b}), \{q_2, q_6, q_7\})$.

$((\{q_3, q_5, q_8\}, \text{c}), \{q_4\})$.

active-states $= \{\{q_1, q_2, q_7\}, \varnothing, \{q_1, q_2, q_3, q_5, q_7, q_8\}, \{q_2, q_4, q_6, q_7\}, \{q_1, q_2, q_3, q_5, q_6, q_7, q_8\}, \{q_4\}, \{q_3, q_5, q_8\}, \{q_2, q_7\}, \{q_2, q_4, q_7\}, \{q_2, q_6, q_7\}\}$.

Consider $\{q_2, q_7\}$:

$((\{q_2, q_7\}, \text{a}), \varnothing)$.

$((\{q_2, q_7\}, \text{b}), \{q_3, q_5, q_8\})$.

$((\{q_2, q_7\}, \text{c}), \varnothing)$.

active-states did not change. Consider $\{q_2, q_4, q_7\}$:

$((\{q_2, q_4, q_7\}, \text{a}), \varnothing)$.

$((\{q_2, q_4, q_7\}, \text{b}), \{q_3, q_5, q_8\})$.

$((\{q_2, q_4, q_7\}, \text{c}), \{q_2, q_7\})$.

active-states did not change. Consider $\{q_2, q_6, q_7\}$:

$((\{q_2, q_6, q_7\}, \text{a}), \varnothing)$.

$((\{q_2, q_6, q_7\}, \text{b}), \{q_3, q_5, q_8\})$.

$((\{q_2, q_6, q_7\}, \text{c}), \{q_2, q_7\})$.

active-states did not change. δ has been computed for each element of *active-states*.

4. $K' = \{\{q_1, q_2, q_7\}, \varnothing, \{q_1, q_2, q_3, q_5, q_7, q_8\}, \{q_2, q_4, q_6, q_7\}, \{q_1, q_2, q_3, q_5, q_6, q_7, q_8\}, \{q_4\}, \{q_3, q_5, q_8\}, \{q_2, q_7\}, \{q_2, q_4, q_7\}, \{q_2, q_6, q_7\}\}$.

5. $A' = \{\{q_1, q_2, q_3, q_5, q_7, q_8\}, \{q_1, q_2, q_3, q_5, q_6, q_7, q_8\}, \{q_3, q_5, q_8\}\}$.

Notice that, in Example 5.20, the original NDFSM had 8 states. So $|\mathcal{P}(K)| = 256$. There could have been that many states in the DFSM that was constructed from the original machine. But only 10 of those are reachable from the start state and so can play any role in the operation of the machine. We designed the algorithm *ndfsmtodfsm* so that only those 10 would have to be built.

Sometimes, however, all or almost all of the possible subsets of states are reachable. Consider again the NDFSM of Example 5.15, the missing letter machine. Let's imagine a slight variant that considers all 26 letters of the alphabet. That machine M has 27 states. So, in principle, the corresponding DFSM could have 2^{27} states. And, this time, all subsets are possible except that M can not be in the start state, q_0, at any time except before the first character is read. So the DFSM that we would build if we applied *ndfsmtodfsm* to M would have $2^{26} + 1$ states. In Section 5.6, we will describe a technique for interpreting NDFSMs without converting them to DFSMs first. Using that technique, highly nondeterministic machines, like the missing letter one, are still practical.

What happens if we apply *ndfsmtodfsm* to a machine that is already deterministic? It must work, since every DFSM is also a legal NDFSM. You may want to try it on one of the machines in Section 5.3. What you will see is that the machine that *ndfsmtodfsm* builds, given an input DFSM M, is identical to M except for the names of the states.

5.5 From FSMs to Operational Systems

An FSM is an abstraction. We can describe an FSM that solves a problem without worrying about many kinds of implementation details. In fact, we don't even need to know whether it will be etched into silicon or implemented in software.

> Statecharts, which are based on the idea of hierarchically structured transition networks, are widely used in software engineering precisely because they enable system designers to work at varying levels of abstraction. (H.2)

FSMs for real problems can be turned into operational systems in any of a number of ways:

- An FSM can be translated into a circuit design and implemented directly in hardware. For example, it makes sense to implement the parity checking FSM of Example 5.4 in hardware.

- An FSM can be simulated by a general purpose interpreter. We will describe designs for such interpreters in the next section. Sometimes all that is required is a simulation. In other cases, a simulation can be used to check a design before it is translated into hardware.
- An FSM can be used as a specification for some critical aspect of the behavior of a complex system. The specification can then be implemented in software just as any specification might be. And the correctness of the implementation can be shown by verifying that the implementation satisfies the specification (i.e., that it matches the FSM).

> Many network communication protocols, including the Alternating Bit protocol and TCP, are described as FSMs. (I.1)

5.6 Simulators for FSMs ●

Once we have created an FSM to solve a problem, we may want to simulate its execution. In this section, we consider techniques for doing that, starting with DFSMs, and then extending our ideas to handle nondeterminism.

5.6.1 Simulating Deterministic FSMs

We begin by considering only deterministic FSMs. One approach is to think of an FSM as the specification for a simple, table-driven program and then proceed to write the code.

EXAMPLE 5.21 Hardcoding a Deterministic FSM

Consider the following deterministic FSM M that accepts the language $L = \{w \in \{\text{a}, \text{b}\}^* : w$ contains no more than one $\text{b}\}$.

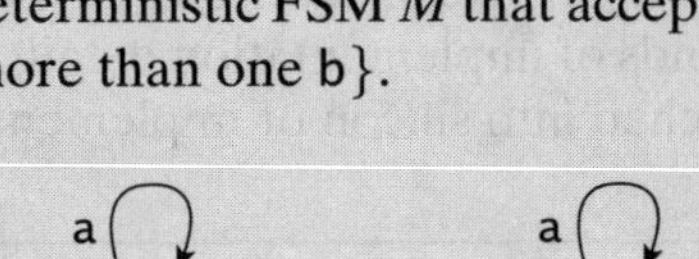

We could view M as a specification for the following program:

Until accept or reject do:
S: s = get-next-symbol.
If s = end-of-file then accept.
Else if s = a then go to *S*.
Else if s = b then go to *T*.

```
T:      s = get-next-symbol.
        If s = end-of-file then accept.
        Else if s = a then go to T.
        Else if s = b then reject.

End.
```

Given an FSM M with states K, this approach will create a program of length $= 2 + (|K| \cdot (|\Sigma| + 2))$. The time required to analyze an input string w is $\mathcal{O}(|w| \cdot |\Sigma|)$. The biggest problem with this approach is that we must generate new code for every FSM that we wish to run. Of course, we could write an FSM compiler that did that for us. But we don't need to. We can, instead, build an interpreter that executes the FSM directly.

Here's a simple interpreter for a deterministic FSM $M = (K, \Sigma, \delta, s, A)$:

dfsmsimulate(M: DFSM, w: string) =

1. $st = s$.

2. Repeat:

  2.1. c = get-next-symbol(w).

  2.2. If $c \neq$ end-of-file then:

    2.2.1. $st = \delta(st, c)$.

  until c = end-of-file.

3. If $st \in A$ then accept else reject.

The algorithm *dfsmsimulate* runs in time approximately $\mathcal{O}(|w|)$, if we assume that the lookup in step 2.2.1 can be implemented in constant time.

5.6.2 Simulating Nondeterministic FSMs

Now suppose that we want to execute an NDFSM M. One solution is:

ndfsmconvertandsimulate(M : NDFSM) =

$$dfsmsimulate(ndfsmtodfsm(M)).$$

But, as we saw in Section 5.4, converting an NDFSM to a DFSM can be very inefficient in terms of both time and space. If M has k states, it could take time and space equal to $\mathcal{O}(2^k)$ just to do the conversion, although the simulation, after the conversion, would take time equal to $\mathcal{O}(|w|)$. So we would like a better way. We would like an algorithm that directly simulates an NDFSM M without converting it to a DFSM first.

We sketched such an algorithm *ndfsmsimulate* in our discussion leading up to the definition of the conversion algorithm *ndfsmtodfsm*. The idea is to simulate being in sets of states at once. But, instead of generating all of the reachable sets of states right away, as *ndfsmtodfsm* does, it generates them on the fly, as they are needed, being careful not to get stuck chasing ε-loops.

We give here a more detailed description of *ndfsmsimulate*, which simulates an NDFSM $M = (K, \Sigma, \Delta, s, A)$ running on an input string w:

ndfsmsimulate(M: NDFSM, w: string) =

1. Declare the set *st*. /* *st* will hold the current state (a set of states from K).

2. Declare the set *st*1. /* *st*1 will be built to contain the next state.

3. $st = eps(s)$. /* Start in all states reachable from s via only ε-transitions.

4. Repeat:

    c = get-next-symbol (w).
    If $c \neq$ end-of-file then do:
        $st1 = \varnothing$.
        For all $q \in st$ do: /* Follow paths from all states M is currently in.
            For all $r : (q, c, r) \in \Delta$ do: /* Find all states reachable from q via a transition labeled c.
                $st1 = st1 \cup eps(r)$. /* Follow all ε-transitions from there.
        $st = st1$. /* Done following all paths. So *st* becomes M's new state.
        If $st = \varnothing$ then exit. /* If all paths have died, quit.
    until c = end-of-file.

5. If $st \cap A \neq \varnothing$ then accept else reject.

Now there is no conversion cost. To analyze a string w requires $|w|$ passes through the main loop in step 4. In the worst case, M is in all states all the time and each of them has a transition to every other one. So one pass could take as many as $\mathcal{O}(|K|^2)$ steps, for a total cost of $\mathcal{O}(w \cdot |K|^2)$.

There is also a third way we could build a simulator for an NDFSM. We could build a depth-first search program that examines the paths through M and stops whenever either it finds a path that accepts or it has tried all the paths there are.

5.7 Minimizing FSMs ◆

If we are going to solve a real problem with an FSM, we may want to find the smallest one that does the job. We will say that a DFSM M is ***minimal*** iff there is no other DFSM M' such that $L(M) = L(M')$ and M' has fewer states than M does.

We might want to be able to ask:

1. Given a language, L, is there a minimal DFSM that accepts L?

2. If there is a minimal machine, is it unique?

3. Given a DFSM M that accepts some language L, can we tell whether M is minimal?

4. Given a DFSM M, can we construct a minimal equivalent DFSM M'?

The answer to all four questions is yes. We'll consider questions 1 and 2 first, and then consider questions 3 and 4.

5.7.1 Building a Minimal DFSM for a Language

Recall that in Section 5.3 we suggested that an effective way to think about the design of a DFSM M to accept some language L over an alphabet Σ is to cluster the strings in Σ^* in such a way that strings that share a future will drive M to the same state. We will now formalize that idea and use it as the basis for constructing a minimal DFSM to accept L.

We will say that x and y are ***indistinguishable*** with respect to L, which we will write as $x \approx_L y$ iff:

$$\forall z \in \Sigma^* \text{ (either both } xz \text{ and } yz \in L \text{ or neither is).}$$

In other words, $\approx_L$ is a relation that is defined so that $x \approx_L y$ precisely in case, if x and y are viewed as prefixes of some longer string, no matter what continuation string z comes next, either both xz and yz are in L or both are not.

EXAMPLE 5.22 How $\approx_L$ Depends on L

If $L = \{\text{a}\}^*$, then a $\approx_L$ aa $\approx_L$ aaa. But if $L = \{w \in \{\text{a}, \text{b}\}^* : |w| \text{ is even}\}$, then a $\approx_L$ aaa, but it is not the case that a $\approx_L$ aa because, if $z =$ a, we have aa $\in L$ but aaa $\notin L$.

We will say that x and y are ***distinguishable*** with respect to L, iff they are not indistinguishable. So, if x and y are distinguishable, then there exists at least one string z such that one but not both of xz and yz is in L.

Note that $\approx_L$ is an equivalence relation because it is:

- Reflexive: $\forall x \in \Sigma^* (x \approx_L x)$, because $\forall x, z \in \Sigma^* (xz \in L \leftrightarrow xz \in L)$.
- Symmetric: $\forall x, y \in \Sigma^* (x \approx_L y \rightarrow y \approx_L x)$, because $\forall x, y, z \in \Sigma^* ((xz \in L \leftrightarrow yz \in L) \leftrightarrow (yz \in L \leftrightarrow xz \in L))$.
- Transitive: $\forall x, y, z \in \Sigma^* (((x \approx_L y) \wedge (y \approx_L w)) \rightarrow (x \approx_L w))$, because: $\forall x, y, z \in \Sigma^* (((xz \in L \leftrightarrow yz \in L) \wedge (yz \in L \leftrightarrow wz \in L)) \rightarrow (xz \in L \leftrightarrow wz \in L))$.

We will use three notations to describe the equivalence classes of $\approx_L$:

- [1], [2], etc. will refer to explicitly numbered classes.
- $[x]$ describes the equivalence class that contains the string x.
- [some logical expression P] describes the equivalence class of strings that satisfy P.

Since $\approx_L$ is an equivalence relation, its equivalence classes constitute a partition of the set Σ^*. So:

- No equivalence class of $\approx_L$ is empty, and
- Every string in Σ^* is in exactly one equivalence class of $\approx_L$.

What we will see soon is that the equivalence classes of $\approx_L$ correspond exactly to the states of the minimum DFSM that accepts L. So every string in Σ^* will drive that DFSM to exactly one state.

Given some language L, how can we determine $\approx_L$? Any pair of strings x and y are related via $\approx_L$ unless there exists some z that could follow them and cause one to be in L and the other not to be. So it helps to begin the analysis by considering simple strings and seeing whether they are distinguishable or not. One way to start this process is to begin lexicographically enumerating the strings in Σ^* and continue until a pattern has emerged.

EXAMPLE 5.23 Determining $\approx L$

Let $\Sigma = \{\text{a}, \text{b}\}$. Let $L = \{w \in \Sigma^* : \text{every a is immediately followed by a b}\}$.

To determine the equivalence classes of $\approx_L$, we begin by creating a first class [1] and arbitrarily assigning ε to it. Now consider a. It is distinguishable from ε since $\varepsilon\text{ab} \in L$ but aab $\notin L$. So we create a new equivalence class [2] and put a in it. Now consider b. b $\approx_L \varepsilon$ since every string is in L unless it has an a that is not followed by a b. Neither of these has an a that could have that problem. So they are both in L as long as their continuation doesn't violate the rule. If their continuation does violate the rule, they are both out. So b goes into [1].

Next we try aa. It is distinguishable from the strings in [1] because the strings in [1] are in L but aa is not. So, consider ε as a continuation string. Take any string in [1] and concatenate ε. The result is still in L. But aaε is not in L. We also notice that aa is distinguishable from a, and so cannot be in [2], because a still has a chance to become in L if it is followed by a string that starts with a b. But aa is out, no matter what comes next. We create a new equivalence class [3] and put aa in it. We continue in this fashion until we discover the property that holds of each equivalence class.

The equivalence classes of $\approx_L$ are:

[1]	[ε, b, abb, ...]	[all strings in L].
[2]	[a, abbba, ...]	[all strings that end in a and have no prior a that is not followed by a b].
[3]	[aa, abaa, ...]	[all strings that contain at least one instance of aa].

Even this simple example illustrates three key points about $\approx_L$:

- No equivalence class can contain both strings that are in L and strings that are not. This is clear if we consider the continuation string ε. If $x \in L$ then $x\varepsilon \in L$. If $y \notin L$ then $y\varepsilon \notin L$. So x and y are distinguishable by ε.
- If there are strings that would take a DFSM for L to the dead state (in other words, strings that are out of L no matter what comes next), then there will be one equivalence class of $\approx_L$ that corresponds to the dead state.
- Some equivalence class contains ε. It will correspond to the start state of the minimal machine that accepts L.

EXAMPLE 5.24 When More Than One Class Contains Strings in *L*

Let $\Sigma = \{$a, b$\}$. Let $L = \{w \in \{$a, b$\}^*$: no two adjacent characters are the same$\}$. The equivalence classes of $\approx_L$ are:

[1]	[ε]	[ε].
[2]	[a, aba, ababa, . . .]	[all nonempty strings that end in a and have no identical adjacent characters].
[3]	[b, ab, bab, abab, . . .]	[all nonempty strings that end in b and have no identical adjacent characters].
[4]	[aa, abaa, ababb . . .]	[all strings that contain at least one pair of identical adjacent characters].

From this example, we make one new observation about $\approx_L$:

- While no equivalence class may contain both strings that are in L and strings that are not, there may be more than one equivalence class that contains strings that are in L. For example, in this last case, all the strings in classes [1], [2], and [3] are in L. Only those that are in [4], which corresponds to the dead state, are not in L. That is because of the structure of L: Any string is in L until it violates the rule, and then it is hopelessly out.

Does $\approx_L$ always have a finite number of equivalence classes? It has in the two examples we have considered so far. But let's consider another one.

EXAMPLE 5.25 $\approx_L$ for A^nB^n

Let $\Sigma = \{a, b\}$. Let $L = A^nB^n = \{a^nb^n : n \geq 0\}$.

We can begin constructing the equivalence classes of $\approx_L$:

[1] [ε].
[2] [a].
[3] [aa].
[4] [aaa].

But we seem to be in trouble. Each new string of a's has to go in an equivalence class distinct from the shorter strings because each string requires a different continuation string in order to become in L. So the set of equivalence classes of $\approx_L$ must include at least all of the following classes:

$$\{[n] : n \text{ is a positive integer and } [n] \text{ contains the single string } a^{n-1}\}$$

Of course, classes that include strings that contain b's are also required.

So, if $L = A^nB^n$, then $\approx_L$ has an infinite number of equivalence classes. This should come as no surprise. A^nB^n is not regular, as we will prove in Chapter 8. If the equivalence classes of $\approx_L$ are going to correspond to the states of a machine to accept L, then there will be a finite number of equivalence classes precisely in case L is regular.

We are now ready to talk about DFSMs and to examine the relationship between $\approx_L$ and any DFSM that accepts L. To help do that we will say that a state q of a DFSM M ***contains*** the set of strings s such that M, when started in its start state, lands in q after reading s.

THEOREM 5.4 $\approx_L$ Imposes a Lower Bound on the Minimum Number of States of a DFSM for L

Theorem: Let L be a regular language and let $M = (K, \Sigma, \delta, s, A)$ be a DFSM that accepts L. The number of states in M is greater than or equal to the number of equivalence classes of $\approx_L$.

Proof: Suppose that the number of states in M were less than the number of equivalence classes of $\approx_L$. Then, by the pigeonhole principle, there must be at least one state q that contains strings from at least two equivalence classes of $\approx_L$. But then M's future behavior on those strings will be identical, which is not consistent with the fact that they are in different equivalence classes of $\approx_L$.

So now we know a lower bound on the number of states that are required to build an FSM to accept a language L. But is it always possible to find a DFSM M such that $|K_M|$ is exactly equal to the number of equivalence classes of $\approx_L$? The answer is yes.

THEOREM 5.5 There Exists a Unique Minimal DFSM for Every Regular Language

Theorem: Let L be a regular language over some alphabet Σ. Then there is a DFSM M that accepts L and that has precisely n states where n is the number of equivalence classes of $\approx_L$. Any other DFSM that accepts L must either have more states than M or it must be equivalent to M except for state names.

Proof: The proof is by construction of $M = (K, \Sigma, \delta, s, A)$, where:

- K contains n states, one for each equivalence class of $\approx_L$.
- $s = [\varepsilon]$, the equivalence class of ε under $\approx_L$.
- $A = \{[x] : x \in L\}$.
- $\delta([x], a) = [xa]$. In other words, if M is in the state that contains some string x, then, after reading the next symbol a, it will be in the state that contains xa.

For this construction to prove the theorem, we must show:

- K is finite. Since L is regular, it is accepted by some DFSM M'. M' has some finite number of states m. By Theorem 5.4, $n \leq m$. So K is finite.
- δ is a function. In other words, it is defined for all (state, input) pairs and it produces, for each of them, a unique value. The construction defines a value of δ for all (state, input) pairs. The fact that the construction guarantees a unique such value follows from the definition of $\approx_L$.
- $L = L(M)$. In other words, M does in fact accept the language L. To prove this, we must first show that $\forall s, t\ (([\varepsilon], st) \mid\!-_M{}^* ([s], t))$. In other words, when M starts in its start state and has a string that we are describing as having two parts, s and t, to read, it correctly reads the first part s and lands in the state $[s]$, with t left to read. We do this by induction on $|s|$. If $|s| = 0$ then we have $([\varepsilon], \varepsilon t) \mid\!-_M{}^* ([\varepsilon], t)$, which is true since M simply makes zero moves. Assume that the claim is true if $|s| = k$. Then we consider what happens when $|s| = k + 1$. $|s| \geq 1$, so we can let $s = yc$ where $y \in \Sigma^*$ and $c \in \Sigma$. We have:

  /* M reads the first k characters:

  $([\varepsilon], yct) \mid\!-_M{}^* ([y], ct)$ (induction hypothesis, since $|y| = k$).

  /* M reads one more character:

  $([y], ct) \mid\!-_M{}^* ([yc], t)$ (definition of δ_M).

  /* Combining those two, after M has read $k + 1$ characters:

  $([\varepsilon], yct) \mid\!-_M{}^* ([yc], t)$ (transitivity of $\mid\!-_M{}^*$).

  $([\varepsilon], st) \mid\!-_M{}^* ([s], t)$ (definition of s as yc).

Now let t be ε. (In other words, we are examining M's behavior after it reads its entire input string.) Let s be any string in Σ^*. By the claim we just proved, $([\varepsilon], s) \mid\!-_M{}^* ([s], \varepsilon)$. M will accept s iff $[s] \in A$, which, by the way in which A was constructed, it will be if the strings in $[s]$ are in L. So M accepts precisely those strings that are in M.

- There exists no smaller machine $M\#$ that also accepts L. This follows directly from Theorem 5.4, which says that the number of equivalence classes of $\approx_L$ imposes a lower bound on the number of states in any DFSM that accepts L.
- There is no different machine $M\#$ that also has n states and that accepts L. Consider any DFSM $M\#$ with n states. We show that either $M\#$ is identical to M (up to state names) or $L(M\#) \neq L(M)$.

Since we do not care about state names, we can standardize them. Call the start state of both M and $M\#$ state 1. Define a lexicographic ordering on the elements of Σ. Number the rest of the states in both M and $M\#$ as follows:

Until all states have been numbered do:

Let q be the lowest numbered state from which there are transitions that lead to an as yet unnumbered state.

List the transitions that lead out from q to any unnumbered state. Sort those transitions lexicographically by the symbol on them.

Go through the sorted transitions (q, a, p), in order, and, for each, assign the next unassigned number to state p.

Note that $M\#$ has n states and there are n equivalence classes of $\approx_L$. Since none of those equivalence classes is empty (by the definition of equivalence classes), $M\#$ either wastes no states (i.e., every state contains at least one string) or, if it does waste any states, it has at least one state that contains strings in different equivalence classes of $\approx_L$. If the latter, then $L(M\#) \neq L$. So we assume the former. Now suppose that $M\#$ is different from M. Then there would have to be at least one state q and one input symbol c such that M has a transition (q, c, r) and $M\#$ has a transition (q, c, t) and $r \neq t$. Call the set of strings that r contains $[r]$. Since $M\#$ has no unused states (i.e., states that contain no strings), by the pigeonhole principle, $M\#$'s transition (q, c, t) must send some string s in $[r]$ to a state, t, that also contains strings that are not in $[r]$. All strings in $[t]$ will then share all futures with s. But s is distinguishable from the strings in $[t]$. If two strings that are distinguishable with respect to L share all futures in $M\#$, then $L(M\#) \neq L$. Contradiction.

The construction that we used to prove Theorem 5.5 is useful in its own right: We can us it, if we know $\approx_L$, to construct a minimal DFSM for L.

EXAMPLE 5.26 Building a Minimal DFSM from $\approx_L$

We consider again the language of Example 5.24: Let $\Sigma = \{a, b\}$. Let $L = \{w \in \{a, b\}^* :$ no two adjacent characters are the same$\}$.

The equivalence classes of $\approx_L$ are:

[1]	[ε]	{ε}.
[2]	[a, aba, ababa, ...]	{all nonempty strings that end in a and have no identical adjacent characters}.
[3]	[b, ab, bab, abab, ...]	{all nonempty strings that end in b and have no identical adjacent characters}.
[4]	[aa, abaa, ababb ...]	{all strings that contain at least one pair of identical adjacent characters; these strings are not in L, no matter what comes next}.

We build a minimal DFSM M to accept L as follows:

- The equivalence classes of $\approx_L$ become the states of M.
- The start state is $[\varepsilon] = [1]$.
- The accepting states are all equivalence classes that contain strings in L, namely [1], [2], and [3].
- $\delta([x], a) = [xa]$. So, for example, equivalence class [1] contains the string ε. If the character a follows ε, the resulting string, a, is in equivalence class [2]. So we create a transition from [1] to [2] labeled a. Equivalence class [2] contains the string a. If the character b follows a, the resulting string, ab, is in equivalence class [3]. So we create a transition from [2] to [3] labeled b. And so forth.

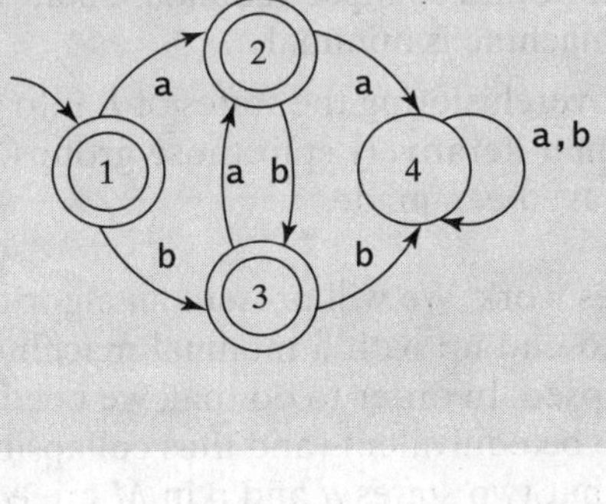

The fact that it is always possible to construct a minimum DFSM M to accept any language L is good news. As we will see later, the fact that that minimal DFSM is unique up to state names is also useful. In particular, we will use it as a basis for an algorithm that checks two DFSMs to see if they accept the same language. The theorem that we have just proven is also useful because it gives us an easy way to prove the following result, which goes by two names, Nerode's theorem and the Myhill-Nerode theorem.

THEOREM 5.6 Myhill-Nerode Theorem

Theorem: A language is regular iff the number of equivalence classes of $\approx_L$ is finite.

Proof: We do two proofs to show the two directions of the implication:

L regular $\rightarrow$ the number of equivalence classes of $\approx_L$ is finite: If L is regular, then there exists some DFSM M that accepts L. M has some finite number of states m. By Theorem 5.4, the number of equivalence classes of $\approx_L \leq m$. So the number of equivalence classes of $\approx_L$ is finite.

The number of equivalence classes of $\approx_L$ is finite $\rightarrow$ L regular: If the number of equivalence classes of $\approx_L$ is finite, then the construction that was described in the proof of Theorem 5.5 will build a DFSM that accepts L. So L must be regular.

The Myhill-Nerode theorem gives us our first technique for proving that a language L, such as A^nB^n, is not regular. It suffices to show that $\approx_L$ has an infinite number of equivalence classes. But using the Myhill-Nerode theorem rigorously is difficult. In Chapter 8, we will introduce other methods that are harder to use incorrectly.

5.7.2 Minimizing an Existing DFSM

Now suppose that we already have a DFSM M that accepts L. In fact, possibly M is the only definition we have of L. In this case, it makes sense to construct a minimal DFSM to accept L by starting with M rather than with $\approx_L$. There are two approaches that we could take to constructing a minimization algorithm:

1. Begin with M and collapse redundant states, getting rid of one at a time until the resulting machine is minimal.
2. Begin by overclustering the states of L into just two groups, accepting and nonaccepting. Then iteratively split those groups apart until all the distinctions that L requires have been made.

Both approaches work. We will present an algorithm that takes the second one.

Our goal is to end up with a minimal machine in which all equivalent states of M have been collapsed. In order to do that, we need a precise definition of what it means for two states to be equivalent (and thus collapsible). We will use the following:

We will say that two states q and p in M are ***equivalent***, which we will write $q \equiv p$, iff for all strings $w \in \Sigma^*$, either w drives M to an accepting state from both q and p or it drives M to a rejecting state from both q and p. In other words, no matter what continuation string comes next, M behaves identically from both states. Note that $\equiv$ is an equivalence relation over states, so it will partition the states of M into a set of equivalence classes.

EXAMPLE 5.27 A Nonminimal DFSM with Two Equivalent States

Let $\Sigma = \{\mathtt{a}, \mathtt{b}\}$. Let $L = \{w \in \Sigma^* : |w| \text{ is even}\}$. Consider the following FSM that accepts L:

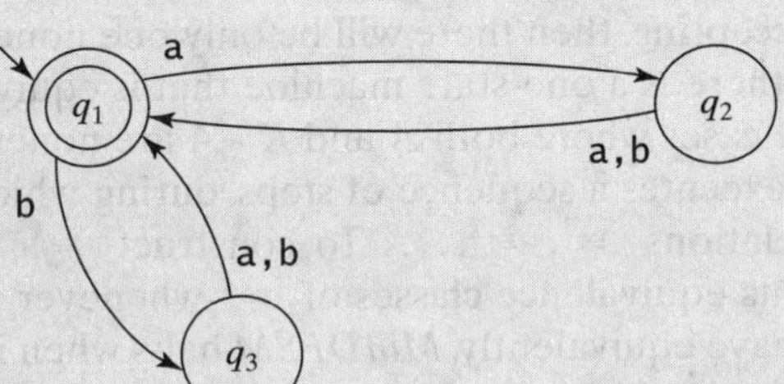

In this machine state $q_2 \equiv$ state q_3.

For two states q and p to be equivalent, they must yield the same outcome for all possible continuation strings. We can't claim an algorithm for finding equivalent states that works by trying all possible continuation strings since there is an infinite number of them (assuming that Σ is not empty). Fortunately, we can show that it is necessary to consider only a finite subset of them. In particular, we will consider them one character at a time, and quit when considering another character has no effect on the machine we are building.

We define a series of equivalence relations $\equiv^n$, for values of $n \geq 0$. For any two states p and q, $p \equiv^n q$ iff p and q yield the same outcome for all strings of length n. So:

- $p \equiv^0 q$ iff they behave equivalently when they read ε. In other words, if they are both accepting or both rejecting states.
- $p \equiv^1 q$ iff they behave equivalently when they read any string of length 1. In other words, if any single character sends both of them to an accepting state or both of them to a rejecting state. Note that this is equivalent to saying that any single character sends them to states that are $\equiv^0$ to each other.
- $p \equiv^2 q$ iff they behave equivalently when they read any string of length 2, which they will do if, when they read the first character they land in states that are $\equiv^1$ to each other. By the definition of $\equiv^1$, they will then yield the same outcome when they read the single remaining character.
- And so forth.

We can state this definition concisely as follows. For all $p, q \in K$:

- $p \equiv^0 q$ iff they are both accepting or both rejecting states.
- For all $n \geq 1$, $q \equiv^n p$ iff:
  - $q \equiv^{n-1} p$, and
  - $\forall a \in \Sigma(\delta(p, a) \equiv^{n-1} \delta(q, a))$.

We will define *minDFSM*, a minimization algorithm that takes as its input a DFSM $M = (K, \Sigma, \delta, s, A)$. *MinDFSM* will construct a minimal DFSM M' that is equivalent to M. It begins by constructing $\equiv^0$, which divides the states of M into at most two equivalence classes, corresponding to A and K - A. If M has no accepting states or if all its states are accepting, then there will be only one nonempty equivalence class and we can quit since there is a one-state machine that is equivalent to M. We consider therefore only those cases where both A and K - A are nonempty.

MinDFSM executes a sequence of steps, during which it constructs the sequence of equivalence relations $\equiv^1$, $\equiv^2$, ... To construct $\equiv^{k+1}$, *minDFSM* begins with $\equiv^k$. But then it splits equivalence classes of $\equiv^k$ whenever it discovers some pair of states that do not behave equivalently. *MinDFSM* halts when it discovers that $\equiv^n$ is the same as $\equiv^{n+1}$. Any further steps would operate on the same set of equivalence classes and so would also fail to find any states that need to be split.

We can now state the algorithm:

minDFSM(*M*: DFSM) =

1. *classes* = $\{A, K{-}A\}$. /* Initially, just two classes of states, accepting and rejecting.
2. Repeat until a pass at which no change to *classes* has been made:

   2.1. *newclasses* = $\varnothing$. /* At each pass, we build a new set of classes, splitting the old ones as necessary. Then this new set becomes the old set, and the process is repeated.

   2.2. For each equivalence class *e* in *classes*, if *e* contains more than one state, see if it needs to be split:

   For each state *q* in *e* do: /* Look at each state and build a table of what it does. Then the tables for all states in the class can be compared to see if there are any differences that force splitting.

   For each character *c* in Σ do:

   Determine which element of *classes* *q* goes to if *c* is read.

   If there are any two states *p* and *q* such that there is any character *c* such that, when *c* is read, *p* goes to one element of *classes* and *q* goes to another, then *p* and *q* must be split. Create as many new equivalence classes as are necessary so that no state remains in the same class with a state whose behavior differs from its. Insert those classes into *newclasses*.

If there are no states whose behavior differs, no splitting is necessary. Insert *e* into *newclasses*.

2.3. *classes* = *newclasses*.

/* The states of the minimal machine will correspond exactly to the elements of *classes* at this point. We use the notation $[q]$ for the element of *classes* that contains the original state q.

3. Return $M' = (classes, \Sigma, \delta, [s_M], \{[q\text{: the elements of } q \text{ are in } A_M]\})$, where $\delta_{M'}$ is constructed as follows:

$$\text{if } \delta_M(q, c) = p, \text{ then } \delta_{M'}([q], c) = [p].$$

Clearly, no class that contains a single state can be split. So, if $|K|$ is k, then the maximum number of times that *minDFSM* can split classes is $k - 1$. Since *minDFSM* halts when no more splitting can occur, the maximum number of times it can go through the loop is $k - 1$. Thus *minDFSM* must halt in a finite number of steps. M' is the minimal DFSM that is equivalent to M since:

- M' is minimal: It splits classes and thus creates new states only when necessary to simulate M, and
- $L(M') = L(M)$: The proof of this is straightforward by induction on the length of the input string.

EXAMPLE 5.28 Using *minDFSM* to Find a Minimal Machine

Let $\Sigma = \{a, b\}$. Let $M =$

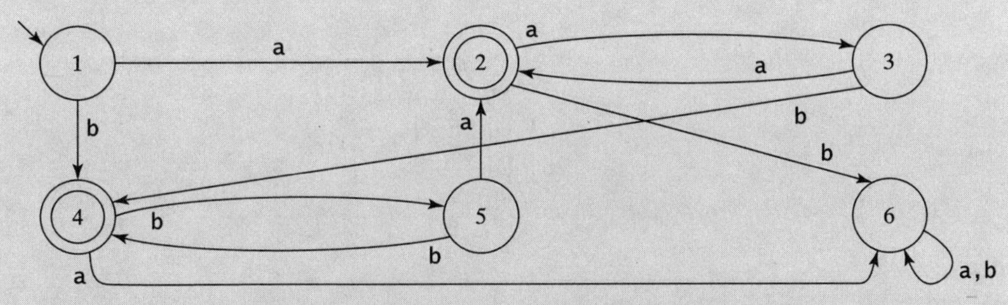

We will show the operation of *minDFSM* at each step:

Initially, *classes* = {[2, 4], [1, 3, 5, 6]}.

At step 1:

((2, a), [1, 3, 5, 6])	((4, a), [1, 3, 5, 6])	No splitting required here.
((2, b), [1, 3, 5, 6])	((4, b), [1, 3, 5, 6])	

EXAMPLE 5.28 *(Continued)*

((1, a), [2, 4]) ((3, a), [2, 4]) ((5, a), [2, 4]) ((6, a), [1, 3, 5, 6])
((1, b), [2, 4]) ((3, b), [2, 4]) ((5, b), [2, 4]) ((6, b), [1, 3, 5, 6])

There are two different patterns, so we must split into two classes, [1, 3, 5] and [6]. Note that, although [6] has the same behavior as [2, 4] after reading a single character, it cannot be combined with [2, 4] because they do not share behavior after reading no characters.

Classes = {[2, 4], [1, 3, 5], [6]}.

At step 2:

((2, a), [1, 3, 5]) ((4, a), [6]) These two must be split.
((2, b), [6]) ((4, b), [1, 3, 5])

((1, a), [2, 4]) ((3, a), [2, 4]) ((5, a), [2, 4]) No splitting required.
((1, b), [2, 4]) ((3, b), [2, 4]) ((5, b), [2, 4])

Classes = {[2], [4], [1, 3, 5], [6]}.

At step 3:

((1, a), [2]) ((3, a), [2]) ((5, a), [2]) No splitting required.
((1, b), [4]) ((3, b), [4]) ((5, b), [4])

So *minDFSM* returns *M'* =

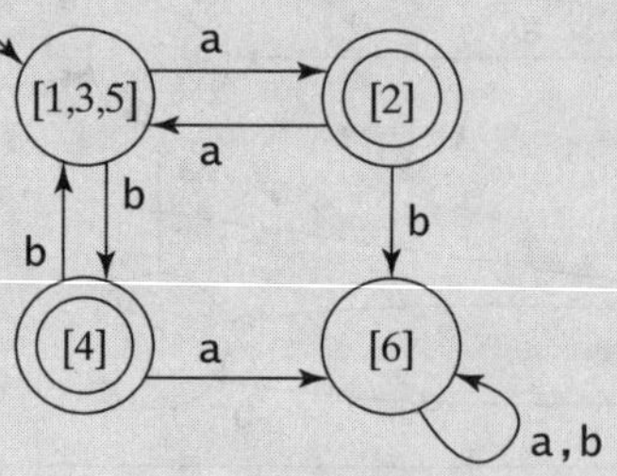

5.8 A Canonical Form for Regular Languages

A ***canonical form*** for some set of objects *C* assigns exactly one representation to each class of "equivalent" objects in *C*. Further, each such representation is distinct, so two objects in *C* share the same representation iff they are "equivalent" in the sense for which we define the form.

> The ordered binary decision diagram (OBDD) is a canonical form for Boolean expressions that makes it possible for model checkers to verify the correctness of very large concurrent systems and hardware circuits. (B.1.3)

Suppose that we had a canonical form for FSMs with the property that two FSMs share a canonical form iff they accept the same language. Further suppose that we had an algorithm that on input M, constructed M's canonical form. Then some questions about FSMs would become easy to answer. For example, we could test whether two FSMs are equivalent (i.e., they accept the same language). It would suffice to construct the canonical form for each of them and test whether the two forms are identical.

The algorithm *minDFSM* constructs, from any DFSM M, a minimal machine that accepts $L(M)$. By Theorem 5.5, all minimal machines for $L(M)$ are identical except possibly for state names. So, if we could define a standard way to name states, we could define a canonical machine to accept $L(M)$ (and thus any regular language). The following algorithm does this by using the state-naming convention that we described in the proof of Theorem 5.5:

buildFSMcanonicalform(M: FSM) =

1. $M' = ndfsmtodfsm(M)$.

2. $M\# = minDFSM(M')$.

3. Create a unique assignment of names to the states of $M\#$ as follows:

  3.1. Call the start state q_0.

  3.2. Define an order on the elements of Σ.

  3.3 Until all states have been named do:

  Select the lowest numbered named state that has not yet been selected. Call it q.

  Create an ordered list of the transitions out of q by the order imposed on their labels.

  Create an ordered list of the as yet unnamed states that those transitions enter by doing the following: If the first transition is (q, c_1, p_1), then put p_1 first. If the second transition is (q, c_2, p_2) and p_2 is not already on the list, put it next. If it is already on the list, skip it. Continue until all transitions have been considered. Remove from the list any states that have already been named.

  Name the states on the list that was just created: Assign to the first one the name q_k, where k is the smallest index that hasn't yet been used. Assign the next name to the next state and so forth until all have been named.

4. Return $M\#$.

Given two FSMs M_1 and M_2, *buildFSMcanonicalform* (M_1) = *buildFSMcanonical form* (M_2) iff $L(M_1) = L(M_2)$. We'll see, in Section 9.1.4, one important use for this canonical form: It provides the basis for a simple way to test whether an FSM accepts any strings or whether two FSMs are equivalent.

5.9 Finite State Transducers ✹

So far, we have used finite state machines as language recognizers. All we have cared about, in analyzing a machine M, is whether or not M ends in an accepting state. But it is a simple matter to augment our finite state model to allow for output at each step of a machine's operation. Often, once we do that, we may cease to care about whether M actually accepts any strings. Many finite state transducers are loops that simply run forever, processing inputs.

One simple kind of finite state transducer associates an output with each state of a machine M. That output is generated whenever M enters the associated state. Deterministic finite state transducers of this sort are called Moore machines, after their inventor Edward Moore. A ***Moore machine*** M is a seven-tuple $(K, \Sigma, O, \delta, D, s, A)$, where:

- K is a finite set of states,
- Σ is an input alphabet,
- O is an output alphabet,
- $s \in K$ is the start state,
- $A \subseteq K$ is the set of accepting states (although for some applications this designation is not important),
- δ is the transition function. It is function from $(K \times \Sigma)$ to (K), and
- D is the display or output function. It is a function from (K) to (O^*).

A Moore machine M computes a function $f(w)$ iff, when it reads the input string w, its output sequence is $f(w)$.

EXAMPLE 5.29 A Typical United States Traffic Light

Consider the following controller for a single direction of a very simple U.S. traffic light (which ignores time of day, traffic, the need to let emergency vehicles through, etc.). We will also ignore the fact that a practical controller has to manage all directions for a particular intersection. In Exercise 5.16, we will explore removing some of these limitations.

The states in this simple controller correspond to the light's colors: green, yellow and red. Note that the definition of the start state is arbitrary. There are three inputs, all of which are elapsed time.

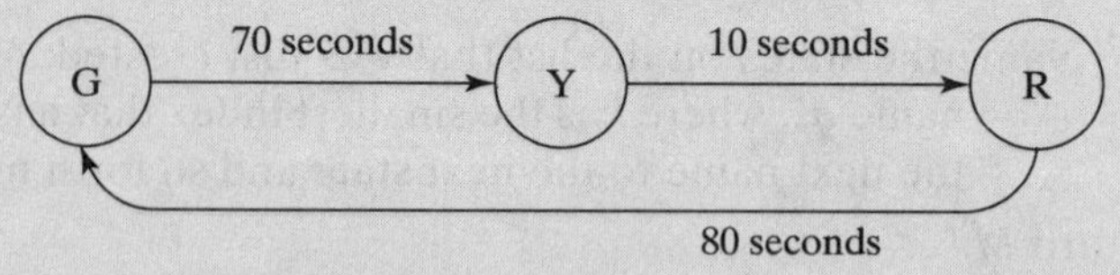

A different definition for a deterministic finite state transducer permits each machine to output any finite sequence of symbols as it makes each transition (in other words, as it reads each symbol of its input). FSMs that associate outputs with transitions are called Mealy machines, after their inventor George Mealy. A ***Mealy machine*** M is a six-tuple $(K, \Sigma, \mathrm{O}, \delta, s, A)$, where:

- K is a finite set of states,
- Σ is an input alphabet,
- O is an output alphabet,
- $s \in K$ is the start state,
- $A \subseteq$ is the set of accepting states, and
- δ is the transition function. It is a function from $(K \times \Sigma)$ to $(K \times O^*)$.

A Mealy machine M computes a function $f(w)$ iff, when it reads the input string w, its output sequence is $f(w)$.

EXAMPLE 5.30 Generating Parity Bits

The following Mealy machine adds an odd parity bit after every four binary digits that it reads. We will use the notation a/b on an arc to mean that the transition may be followed if the input character is a. If it is followed, then the string b will be generated.

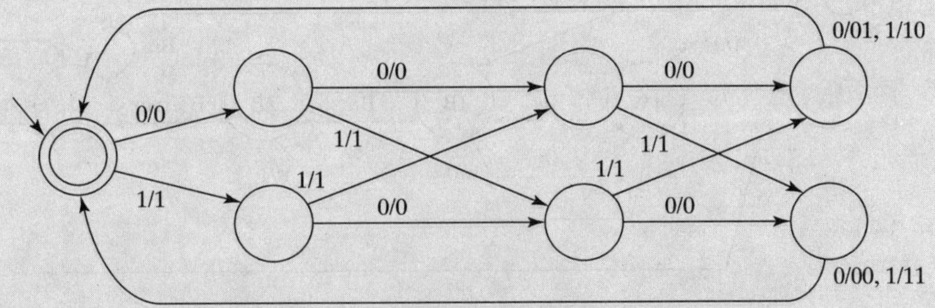

Digital circuits can be modeled as transducers using either Moore or Mealy machines. (P. 3)

EXAMPLE 5.31 A Bar Code Reader

Bar codes are ubiquitous. We consider here a simplification: a bar code system that encodes just binary numbers. Imagine a bar code such as:

EXAMPLE 5.31 *(Continued)*

It is composed of columns, each of the same width. A column can be either white or black. If two black columns occur next to each other, it will look to us like a single, wide, black column, but the reader will see two adjacent black columns of the standard width. The job of the white columns is to delimit the black ones. A single black column encodes 0. A double black column encodes 1.

We can build a finite state transducer to read such a bar code and output a string of binary digits. We'll represent a black bar with the symbol `B` and a white bar with the symbol `W`. The input to the transducer will be a sequence of those symbols, corresponding to reading the bar code left to right. We'll assume that every correct bar code starts with a black column, so white space ahead of the first black column is ignored. We'll also assume that after every complete bar code there are at least two white columns. So the reader should, at that point, reset to be ready to read the next code. If the reader sees three or more black columns in a row, it must indicate an error and stay in its error state until it is reset by seeing two white columns.

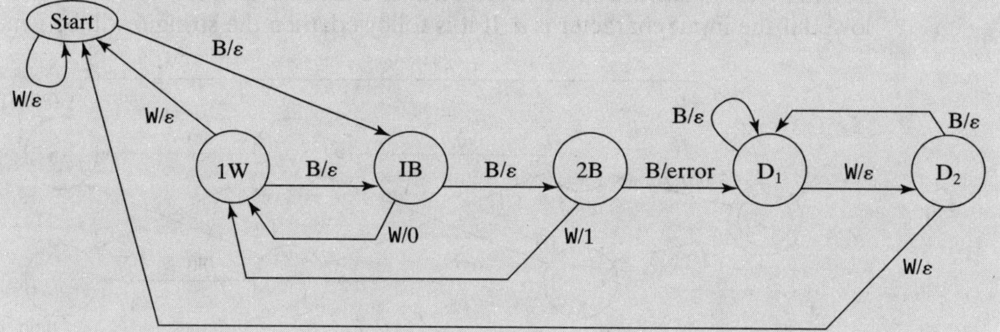

Interpreters for finite state transducers can be built using techniques similar to the ones that we used in Section 5.6 to build interpreters for finite state machines.

5.10 Bidirectional Transducers ◆

A process that reads an input string and constructs a corresponding output string can be described in a variety of different ways. Why should we choose the finite state transducer model? One reason is that it provides a declarative, rather than a procedural, way to describe the relationship between inputs and outputs. Such a declarative model can then be run in two directions. For example:

- To read an English text requires transforming a word like "liberties" into the root word "liberty" and the affix PLURAL. To generate an English text requires transforming a root word like "liberty" and the semantic marker "PLURAL" into the surface word "liberties". If we could specify, in a single declarative model, the relationship between surface words (the ones we see in text) and underlying root words and affixes, we could use it for either application.

> The facts about English spelling rules and morphological analysis can be described with a bidirectional finite state transducer. (L.1)

- The Soundex system, described below in Example 5.33, groups names that sound alike. To create the Soundex representation of a name requires a set of rules for mapping the spelling of the name to a unique four character code. To find other names that sound like the one that generated a particular code requires running those same rules backwards.
- Many things we call translators need to run in both directions. For example, consider translating between Roman numerals 💻 and Arabic ones.

If we expand the definition of a Mealy machine to allow nondeterminism, then any of these bidirectional processes can be represented. A nondeterministic Mealy machine can be thought of as defining a relation between one set of strings (for example, English surface words) and a second set of strings (for example, English underlying root words, along with affixes). It is possible that we will need a machine that is nondeterministic in one or both directions because the relationship between the two sets may not be able to be described as a function.

EXAMPLE 5.32 Letter Substitution

When we define a regular language, it doesn't matter what alphabet we use. Anything that is true of a language L defined over the alphabet {a, b} will also be true of the language L' that contains exactly the strings in L except that every a has been replaced by a 0 and every b has been replaced by a 1. We can build a simple bidirectional transducer that can convert strings in L to strings in L' and vice versa.

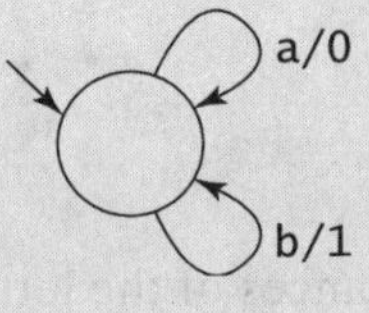

Of course, the real power of bidirectional finite state transducers comes from their ability to model more complex processes.

EXAMPLE 5.33 Soundex: A Way to Find Similar Sounding Names

People change the spelling of their names. Sometimes the spelling was changed for them when they immigrated to a country with a different language, a different set of sounds, and maybe a different writing system. For various reasons, one

EXAMPLE 5.33 *(Continued)*

might want to identify other people to whom one is related. But because of spelling changes, it isn't sufficient simply to look for people with exactly the same last name. The Soundex system was patented by Margaret O'Dell and Robert C. Russell in 1918 as a solution to this problem. The system maps any name to a four character code that is derived from the original name but that throws away details of the sort that often get perturbed as names evolve. So, to find related names, one can run the Soundex transducer in one direction, from a starting name to its Soundex code and then, in the other direction, from the code to the other names that share that code. For example, if we start with the name Kaylor, we will produce the Soundex code K460. If we then use that code and run the transducer backwards, we can generate the names Kahler, Kaler, Kaylor, Keeler, Kellar, Kelleher, Keller, Kelliher, Kilroe, Kilroy, Koehler, Kohler, Koller, and Kyler.

The Soundex system is described by the following set of rules for mapping from a name to a Soundex code:

1. If two or more adjacent letters (including the first in the name) would map to the same number if rule 3.1 were applied to them, remove all but the first in the sequence.
2. The first character of the Soundex code will be the first letter of the name.
3. For all other letters of the name do:

   3.1. Convert the letters B, P, F, V, C, S, G, J, K, Q, X, Z, D, T, L, M, N, and R to numbers using the following correspondences:

   B, P, F, V = 1.

   C, S, G, J, K, Q, X, Z = 2.

   D, T = 3.

   L = 4.

   M, N = 5.

   R = 6.

   3.2. Delete all instances of the letters A, E, I, O, U, Y, H, and W.

4. If the string contains more than three numbers, delete all but the leftmost three.
5. If the string contains fewer than three numbers, pad with 0's on the right to get three.

Here's an initial fragment of a finite-state transducer that implements the relationship between names and Soundex codes. The complete version of this machine can input a name and output a code by interpreting each transition labeled x/y as saying that the transition can be taken on input x and it will output y. Going the other direction, it can input a code and output a name if it interprets each transition the other way: On input y, take the transition and output x. To simplify the diagram, we've used two conventions: The symbol # stands for any one of the letters A,E,I,O,U,Y,H, or W. And a label of the form *x*, *y*, *z*/*a* is a shorthand for three transitions labeled *x*/*a*, *y*/*a*, and *z*/*a*. Also, the states are named to indicate how many code symbols have been generated/read.

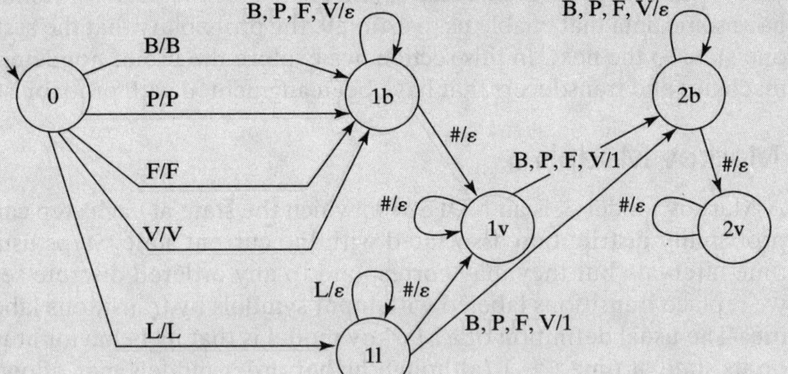

Notice that in one direction (from names to codes), this machine operates deterministically. But, because information is lost in that direction, if we run the machine in the direction that maps from codes to names, it becomes nondeterministic. For example, the ε-transitions can be traversed any number of times to generate vowels that are not represented in the code. Because the goal, in running the machine in the direction from code to names is to generate actual names, the system that does this is augmented with a list of names found in U.S. census reports. It can then follow paths that match those names.

The Soundex system was designed for the specific purpose of matching names in United States census data from the early part of the twentieth century and before. Newer systems, such as Phonix and Metaphone 💻, are attempts to solve the more general problem of identifying words that sound similar to each other. Such systems are used in a variety of applications, including ones that require matching a broader range of proper names (e.g., genealogy and white pages look up) as well as more general word matching tasks (e.g., spell checking).

5.11 Stochastic Finite Automata: Markov Models and HMMs ◆

Most of the finite state transducers that we have considered so far are deterministic. But that is simply a property of the kinds of applications to which they are put. We do not want to live in a world of nondeterministic traffic lights or phone switching circuits. So we typically design controllers (i.e., machines that run things) to be deterministic. For some applications though, nondeterminism can be useful. For example, it can add entertainment value.

> Nondeterministic (possibly stochastic) FSMs can form the basis of video games. (N.3.1)

But now consider problems like the name-evolution one we just discussed. Now we are not attempting to build a controller that drives the world. Instead we are trying to build a model that describes and predicts a world that we are not in control of. Nondeterministic finite state models are often very useful tools in solving such problems. And typically, although we do not know enough to predict with certainty how the behavior of the model will change from one step to the next (thus the need for nondeterminism), we do have some data that enable us to estimate the probability that the system will move from one state to the next. In this section, we explore the use of nondeterministic finite state machines and transducers that have been augmented with probabilistic information.

5.11.1 Markov Models

A Markov model 💻 is an NDFSM in which the state at each step can be predicted by a probability distribution associated with the current state. Steps usually correspond to time intervals, but they may correspond to any ordered discrete sequence. In essence we replace transitions labeled with input symbols by transitions labeled with probabilities. The usual definition of a Markov model is that its behavior at time t depends only on its state at time $t - 1$ (although higher-order models may allow any finite number of past states to play a role). Of course, if we eliminate an input sequence, that is exactly the property that characterizes an FSM.

> Markov models have been used in music composition. (N.1.1) They have also been used to model the generation of many other sorts of content, including Web pages 💻.

Formally a ***Markov model*** is a triple $M = (K, \pi, A)$, where:

- K is a finite set of states,
- π is a vector that contains the initial probabilities of each of the states, and
- A is a matrix that represents the transition probabilities. $A[p, q] = \Pr(\textit{state } q \text{ at time } t \mid \text{state } p \text{ at time } t - 1)$. In other words $A[p, q]$ is the probability that, if M is in state p, it will go to state q next.

Some definitions specify a unique start state, but this definition is more general. If there is a unique start state, then its initial probability is 1 and the initial probabilities of all other states are 0.

Notice that we have not mentioned any output alphabet. We will assume that the output at each step is simply the name of the state of the machine at that step. The sequence of outputs produced by a Markov model is often called a ***Markov chain***.

> The link structure of the World Wide Web can be modeled as a Markov chain, where the states correspond to Web pages and the probabilities describe the likelihood, in a random walk, of going from one page to the next. Google's PageRank is based on the limits of those probabilities 💻.

Given a Markov model that describes some random process, we can answer either of the following questions:

- What is the probability that we will observe a particular sequence $s_1 s_2 \ldots s_n$ of states? We can compute this as follows, using the probability that s_1 is the start state and then multiplying by the probabilities of each of the transitions:

$$\Pr(s_1 s_2 \ldots s_n) = \pi[s_1] \cdot \prod_{i=2}^{n} A[s_{i-1}, s_i].$$

- If the process runs for an arbitrarily long sequence of steps, what is likely to be the result? More specifically, for each state in the system, what is the probability that the system will land in that state?

EXAMPLE 5.34 A Simple Markov Model of the Weather

Suppose that we have the following model for the weather where we live. This model assumes that the weather on day t is influenced only by the weather on day $t - 1$.

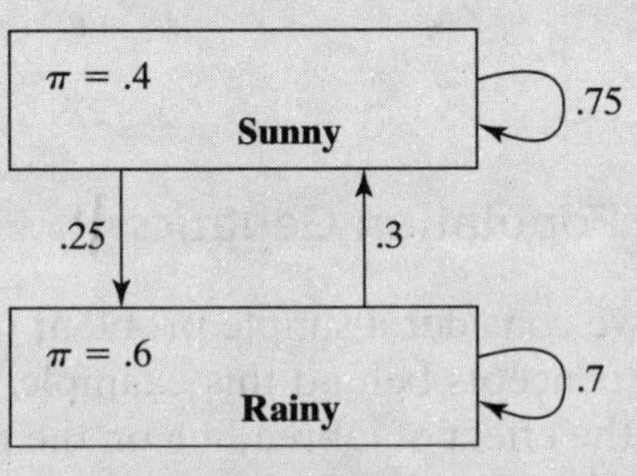

We are considering a five day camping trip and want to know the probability of five sunny days in a row. So we want to know the probability of the sequence Sunny Sunny Sunny Sunny Sunny. The model tells us that it is:

$$.4 \cdot (.75)^4 = .1266$$

Or we could ask, given that it's sunny today, what is the probability that, if we leave now, it will stay sunny for four more days. Now we assume that the model starts in state Sunny, so we compute:

$$(.75)^4 = .316$$

EXAMPLE 5.35 A Simple Markov Model of System Performance

Markov models are used extensively to model the performance of complex systems of all kinds, including computers, electrical grids, and manufacturing plants. While real models are substantially more complex, we can see how these models work by taking Example 5.34 and renaming the states:

EXAMPLE 5.35 (*Continued*)

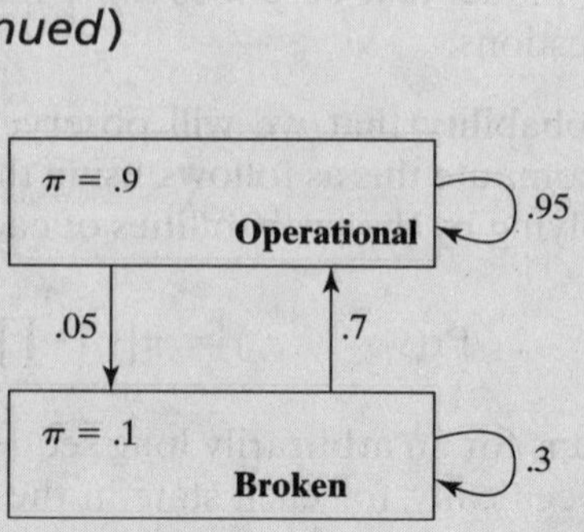

To make it a bit more realistic, we've changed the probabilities so that they describe a system that actually works most of the time. We'll also use smaller time intervals, say seconds. Now we might ask, "Given that the system is now up, what is the probability that the system will stay up for an hour (i.e., for 3600 time steps). The (possibly surprising) answer is:

$$.95^{3600} = 6.3823 \cdot 10^{-81}$$

EXAMPLE 5.36 Population Genetics

In this example we consider a simple problem in population genetics. For a survey of the biological concepts behind this example, see Appendix K. Suppose that we are interested in the effect of inbreeding on the gene pool of a diploid organism (an organism, such as humans, in which each individual has two copies of each gene). Consider the following simple model of the inheritance of a single gene with two alleles (values): A and B. There are potentially three kinds of individuals in the population: the AA organisms, the BB organisms, and the AB organisms. Because we are studying inbreeding, we'll make the assumption that individuals always mate with others who are genetically similar to themselves and so possess the same gene pair.

To simplify our model, we will assume that one couple mates, has two children, and dies. So we can think of each individual as replacing itself and then dying. We can build the following Markov model of a chain of descendents. Each step now corresponds to a generation.

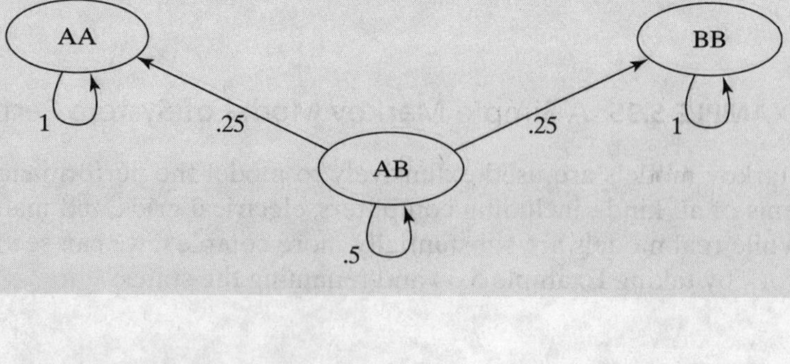

AA pairs can produce only AA offspring. BB pairs can produce only BB offspring. But what about AB pairs? What is their fate? We can answer this question by considering the probability that the model, if it starts in state AB and runs for some number of generations, will land in state AB. That probability is $.5^n$, where n is the number of generations. As n grows, that number approaches 0. We show how quickly it does so in the following table:

n	Pr(AB)
1	.5
5	.03125
10	.0009765625
100	$7.8886 \cdot 10^{-31}$

After only 10 generations, very few heterozygous individuals (i.e., possessing two different alleles) remain. After 100 generations, almost none do. If there is survival advantage in being heterozygous, this could be a disaster for the population. The disaster can be avoided, of course, if individuals mate with genetically different individuals.

Where do the probabilities in a Markov model come from? In some simple cases, they may be computed by hand and added to the system. In most cases, however, they are computed by examining real datasets and discovering the probabilities that best describe those data. So, for example, the probabilities we need for the system performance model of Example 5.35 could be extracted from a log of system behavior over some recent period of time. To see how this can be done, suppose that we have observed the output sequences: T P T Q P Q T and S S P T P Q Q P S T Q P T T P. The correct value for A[P, Q] is the number of times the pair P Q appears in the sequence divided by the total number of times that P appears in any position except the last. Similarly, the correct value for π[P] is the total number of times that P is the first symbol in a sequence divided by the total number of sequences. In realistic problem contexts, the models are huge and they evolve over time. There exist more computationally tractable algorithms for updating the probabilities (and, when necessary the states) of such models.

Substantial work has been done on efficient techniques for updating the huge Markov model of the World Wide Web that is used to compute Google's PageRanks 🖳. Note here that both the state set (corresponding to the set of pages on the Web) as well as the probabilities (which depend on the link structure of the Web) must be regularly revised.

All of the Markov models we have presented so far have the property that their behavior at step t is a function only of their state at step $t - 1$. Such models are called first-order. To build a first-order model with k states requires that we specify k^2 transition probabilities. Now suppose that we wish to describe a situation in which what happens next depends on the previous two states. Or the previous three. Using the same techniques that we used to build a first-order model, we can build models that consider the previous n states for any fixed n. Such models are called n^{th} order Markov models. Notice that an nth order model requires k^{n+1} transition probabilities. But if there are enough data available to train a higher-order model (i.e., to assign appropriate probabilities to all of the required transitions), it may be possible to build a system that quite accurately mimics the behavior of a very complex system.

> A third-order Markov model, trained on about half of this book, used word frequencies to generate the text "The Pumping Theorem is a useful way to define a precedence hierarchy for the operators + and *." (L.3.2) A clever application of a higher order Markov model of English is in producing spam that is hard to detect. (L.3.2)

> Early work on the use of Markov models for musical composition suggested that models of order four or less tended to create works that seemed random, while models of order seven or more tended to create works that felt just like copies of works on which the model was trained. (N.1.1)

Whenever we build a Markov model to describe a naturally occurring process, there is a sense in which we are using probabilities to hide an underlying lack of understanding that would enable us to build a deterministic model of the phenomenon. So, for example, if we know that our computer system is more likely to crash in the morning than in the evening, that may show up as a pair of different probabilities in a Markov model, even if we have no clue why the time of day affects system performance. Some Markov models that do a pretty good job of mimicking nature may seem silly to us for exactly that reason. The one that generates random English text is a good example of that. But now suppose that we had a model that did a very good job of predicting earthquakes. Although we might rather have a good structural model that tells us why earthquakes happen, a purely statistical, predictive model would be a very useful tool. It is because of cases like this that Markov models can be extremely valuable tools for anyone studying complex systems (be they naturally occurring ones like plate tectonics or engineering artifacts like computer systems).

5.11.2 Hidden Markov Models

Now suppose that we are interested in analyzing a system that can be described with a Markov model with one important difference: The states of the system are not directly observable. Instead the model has a separate set of output symbols, which are emitted, with specified probabilities, whenever the system enters one of its now "hidden" states. Now we must base our analysis of the system on an observed sequence of output symbols, from which we can infer, with some probability, the actual sequence of states of the underlying model.

Examples of significant problems that can be described in this way include:

- ***DNA and protein evolution:*** A protein is a sequence of amino acids that is manufactured in living organisms according to a DNA blueprint. Mutations that change the blueprint can occur, with the result that one amino acid may be substituted for another, one or more amino acids may be deleted, or one or more additional amino acids may be inserted. When we examine a DNA fragment or a protein, we'd like to be able to reconstruct the evolutionary process so that we can find other proteins that are functionally related to the current one, even though its details may be different. But the process isn't visible; only its result is.

> HMMs are used for DNA and protein sequence alignment in the face of mutations and other kinds of evolutionary change. (K.3.3)

- ***Speech understanding:*** When we talk, our mouths map from the sentences we want to say into sequences of sounds. The mapping is complex and nondeterministic since multiple words may map to the same sound, words are pronounced differently as a function of the words before and after them, we all form sounds slightly differently, and so forth. All a listener can hear is the sequence of sounds. (S)he would like to reconstruct the mapping (backwards) in order to determine what words we were attempting to say.

> HMMs are used extensively in speech understanding systems. (L.5)

- ***Optical character recognition (OCR)*** 💻: When we write, our hands map from an idealized symbol to some set of marks on a page. The marks are observable, but the process that generates them isn't. Imagine that we could describe a probabilistic process corresponding to each symbol that we can write. Then, to interpret the marks, we must select the process that is most likely to have generated the marks we can see.

What is a Hidden Markov Model?

A powerful technique for solving problems such as this is the ***hidden Markov model*** or ***HMM*** 💻. An HMM is a nondeterministic finite state transducer that has been augmented with three kinds of probabilistic information:

- Each state is labeled with the probability that the machine will be in that state when it starts.
- Each transition from some state p to some (possibly identical) state q is labeled with the probability that, whenever the machine is in state p, it will go next to state q. We

can specify M's transition behavior completely by defining these probabilities. If it is not possible for M to go from some state p to some other state q, then we simply state the probability of going from p to q as 0.

- Each output symbol c at each state q is labeled with the probability that the machine, if it is in state q, will output c.

Formally, an HMM M is a quintuple (K, O, π, A, B), where:

- K is a finite set of states.
- O is the output alphabet.
- π is a vector that contains the initial probabilities of each of the states.
- A is a matrix that represents the transition probabilities. $A[p, q] = \Pr(\text{state } q \text{ at time } t \mid \text{state } p \text{ at time } t - 1)$.
- B, sometimes called the confusion matrix, represents the output probabilities. $B[q, o] = \Pr(\text{output } o \mid \text{state } q)$. Note that outputs are associated with states (as in Moore machines).

The name "hidden Markov model" derives from the two key properties of such devices:

- They are Markov models. Their state at time t is a function solely of their state at time $t - 1$.
- The actual progression of the machine from one state to the next is hidden from all observers. Only the machine's output string can be observed.

To use an HMM as the basis for an application program, we typically have to solve some or all of the following problems:

- ***The decoding problem:*** Given an observation sequence O and an HMM M, discover the path through M that is most likely to have produced O. For example, O might be a string of words that form a sentence. We might have an HMM that describes the structure of naturally occurring English sentences. Each state in M corresponds to a part of speech, such as noun, verb, or adjective. It's not possible to tell, just by looking at O, what sequence of parts of speech generated it, since many words can have more than one part of speech. (Consider, for example, the simple English sentence, "Hit the fly ball.") But we need to infer the parts of speech (a process called part of speech or POS tagging) before we can parse the sentence. We can do that if we can find the path through the HMM that is the most likely to have generated the observed sentence. This problem can be solved efficiently using a dynamic programming algorithm called the Viterbi algorithm, described below.

HMMs are often used for part of speech tagging. (L.2)

Suppose that the sequences that we observe correspond to original sequences that have been altered in some way. The alteration may have been done intentionally (we'll call this "obfuscation") or it may be the result of a natural phenomenon like evolution or a noisy transmission channel. In either case, if we want to know what the original sequence was, we have an instance of the decoding problem. We seek to find the original sequence that is most likely to have been the one that got transformed into the observed sequence.

> In the Internet era, an important application of obfuscation is the generation of spam. If specific words are known to trigger spam filters, they can be altered, by changing vowels, introducing special characters, or whatever, so that they are still recognizable to people but unrecognizable, at least until the next patch, to the spam filters. HMMs can be used to perform "deobfuscation" in an attempt to foil the obfuscators. 💻.

- ***The evaluation problem:*** Given an observation sequence O and a set of HMMs that describe a collection of possible underlying models, choose the HMM that is most likely to have generated O. For example, O might be a sequence of sounds. We might have one HMM for each of the words that we know. We need to choose the word model that is most likely to have generated O. As another example, consider again the protein problem: Now we have one HMM for each family of related proteins. Given a new sample, we want to find the family to which it is most likely to be related. So we look for the HMM that is most likely to have generated it. This problem can be solved efficiently using the forward algorithm, which is very similar to the Viterbi algorithm except that it considers all paths through a candidate HMM, rather than just the most likely one.
- ***The training problem:*** We typically assume, in crafting an HMM M, that the set K of states is built by hand. But where do all the probabilities in π, A, and B come from? Fortunately, there are algorithms that can learn them from a set of training data (i.e., a set of observed output sequences O). One of the most commonly used algorithms is the Baum-Welch algorithm 💻, also called the forward-backward algorithm. Its goal is to tune π, A, and B so that the resulting HMM M has the property that, out of all the HMMs whose state set is equal to K, M is the one most likely to have produced the outputs that constitute the training set. Because the states cannot be directly observed (as they can be in a standard Markov model), the training technique that we described in Section 5.11.1 won't work here. Instead, the Baum-Welch algorithm employs a technique called ***expectation maximization*** or EM. It is an iterative method, so it begins with some initial set of values for π, A, and B. Then it runs the forward algorithm, along with a related backward algorithm, on the training data. The result of this step is a set of probabilities that describe the likelihood that the existing machine, with the current values of π, A, and B, would have output the training set. Using those probabilities, Baum-Welch updates π, A, and B to increase those probabilities. The process continues until no changes to the parameter values can be made.

The Viterbi Algorithm

Given an HMM M and an observed output sequence O, a solution to the decoding problem is the path through M that is most likely to have produced O. One way to find that most likely path is to explore all paths of length $|O|$, keeping track of the accumulated probabilities, and then report the path whose probability is the highest. This approach is straightforward, but may require searching a tree with $|K_M|^{|O|}$ nodes, so the time required may grow exponentially in the length of O.

A more efficient approach uses a dynamic programming technique in which the most likely path of some length, say t, is computed once and then extended by one more step to find the most likely path of length $t + 1$. The Viterbi algorithm uses this approach. It solves the decoding problem by computing, for each step t and for each state q in M:

- The most likely path to q of all the ones that would have generated $O_1 \ldots O_t$.
- The probability of that path.

Once it has done that for each step for which an output was observed, it traces the path backwards. It assumes that the last state is the one at the end of the overall most likely path. The next to the last state is the one that preceded that one on the most likely path, and so forth.

Assume, at each step t, that the algorithm has already considered all paths of length $t - 1$ that could have generated $O_1 \ldots O_{t-1}$. From those paths, it has selected, for each state p, the most likely path to p and it has recorded the probability of the model taking that path, reaching p, and producing $O_1 \ldots O_{t-1}$. We assume further that the algorithm has also recorded, at each state p, the state that preceded p on that most likely path. Before the first output symbol is observed, the probability that the system has reached some state p is simply $\pi(p)$ and there is no preceding state.

Because the model is Markovian, the only thing that affects the probability of the next state is the previous state. In constructing the model, we assumed that prior history doesn't matter (although that may be only an approximation to reality for some problems). So, at step t, we compute, for each state q, the probability that the best path so far that is consistent with $O_1 \ldots O_t$ ends in q and outputs the first t observed symbols. We do this by considering each state p that the model could have been in at step $t - 1$. We already know the probability that the best path up to step $t - 1$ landed in p and produced the observed output sequence. So, to add one more step, we multiply that probability by $A[p, q]$, the probability that the model, if it were in p, would go next to q. But we have one more piece of information: the next output symbol. So, to compute the probability that the model went through p, landed in q, and output the next symbol o, we multiply by $B[p, o]$. Once these numbers have been computed for all possible preceding states p, we choose the most likely one (i.e., the one with the highest score as described above). We record that score at q and we record at q that the most likely predecessor state is the one that produced that highest score.

Although we've described the output function as a function of the state the model is in, we don't actually consider it until we compute the next step, so it may be easier to think of the outputs as associated with the transitions rather than with the states. In particular, the computation that we have just described will end by choosing the state in which the model is most likely to land just after it outputs the final observed symbol. That last state will not generate any output.

Once all steps have been considered, we can choose the overall most likely path as follows: Consider all states. The model is most likely to have ended in the one that, at the final time step, has the highest score as described above. Call that highest scoring state the last state in the path. Find the state that was marked as immediately preceding that one. Continue backwards to the start state.

We can summarize this process, known as the ***Viterbi algorithm***, as follows: Given an observed output sequence O, we will consider each time step between 1 and the length of O. At each such step t, we will set $score(q, t)$ to the highest probability associated with any path of length t that lands M in q, having output the first t symbols in O. We will set $backptr(q, t)$ to the state that immediately preceded q along that best path. Once *score* and *backptr* have been computed for each state at each time step t, we can start at the most likely final state and trace backwards to find the sequence *states* that describes the most likely path through M consistent with O. So the Viterbi algorithm is:

Viterbi(M: Markov model, O: output sequence) =

1. For $t = 0$, for each state q, set $score[q, t]$ to $\pi[q]$.

2. /* Trace forward recording the best path at each step:

For $t = 1$ to $|O|$ do:

2.1. For each state q in K do:

2.1.1. For each state p in K that could have immediately preceded q:

$$candidatescore[p] = score[p, t-1] * A[p, q] * B[p, O_t].$$

2.1.2. /* Record score along most likely path:

$$score[q, t] = \max_{p \in K} candidatescore[p].$$

2.1.3. /* Set q's *backptr*. The function argmax returns the value of the argument p that produced the maximum value of $candidatescore[p]$:

$$backptr[q, t] = \operatorname{argmax}_{p \in K} candidatescore[p].$$

/* Retrieve the best path by going backwards from the most likely last state:

3. $states[|O|]$ = the state q with the highest value of $score[q, |O|]$.

4. For $t = |O| - 1$ to 0 do:

4.1. $states[t] = backptr[states[t + 1], t + 1]$.

5. Return $states[0: |O| - 1]$. /* Ignore the last state since its output was not observed.

The Forward Algorithm

Now suppose that we want to solve the evaluation problem: Given a set of HMMs and an observed output sequence O, decide which HMM had the highest probability of producing O. This problem can be solved with the ***forward algorithm***, which is very similar to the Viterbi algorithm except that, instead of finding the single best path through an HMM M, it computes the probability that M could have output O along *any* path. In step 2.1.2, the Viterbi algorithm selects the highest score associated with any one path to q. The forward algorithm, at that point, sums all the scores. The other big difference between the Viterbi algorithm and the forward algorithm is that the forward algorithm does not need to find a particular path. So it will not have to bother maintaining the *backptr* array. We can state the algorithm as follows:

forward(M: Markov model, O: output sequence) =

1. For $t = 0$, for each state q, set *forward-score*$[q, t]$ to $\pi[q]$.

2. /* Trace forward recording, at each step, the total probability associated with all paths to each state:

For $t = 1$ to $|O|$ do:

2.1. For each state q in K do:

2.1.1. Consider each state p in K that could have immediately preceded q:

$$candidatescore[p] = forwardscore[p, t-1] * A[p, q] * B[p, O_t].$$

2.1.2. /* Sum scores over all paths:

$$forwardscore[q, t] = \sum_p candidatescore[p].$$

3. /* Find the total probability of going through M along any path, landing in any of M's states, and emitting O. This is simply the sum of the probability of landing in state 1 having emitted O, plus the probability of landing in state 2 having emitted O, and so forth. So:

$$totalprob = \sum_{q \in K} forwardscore[q, |O|].$$

4. Return *totalprob*.

To solve the evaluation problem, we run the forward algorithm on all of the contending HMMs and return the one with the highest final score.

The Complexity of the Viterbi and the Forward Algorithms

Analyzing the complexity of the Viterbi and the forward algorithms is straightforward. In both cases, the outer loop of step 2 is executed once for each observed output, so $|O|$ times. Within that loop, the computation of *candidatescore* is done once for each state pair. So if M has k states, it is done k^2 times. The computation of *score*/*forwardscore* takes $\mathcal{O}(k)$ steps, as does the computation of *backptr* in the Viterbi algorithm. The final operation of the Viterbi algorithm (computing the list of states to be returned) takes $\mathcal{O}(|O|)$ steps. The final operation of the forward algorithm (computing the total probability of producing the observed output) takes $\mathcal{O}(k)$ steps. So, in both cases, the total time complexity is $\mathcal{O}(k^2 \cdot |O|)$.

An Example of How These Algorithms Work

The real power of HMMs is in solving complex, real-world problems in which probability estimates can be derived from large datasets. So it is hard to illustrate the effectiveness of HMMs on small problems, but the idea should be clear from the following simple example of the use of the Viterbi algorithm.

EXAMPLE 5.37 Using the Viterbi Algorithm to Guess the Weather

Suppose that you are a state department official in a small country. Each day, you receive a report from each of your consular offices telling you whether or not any of your passports were reported missing that day. You know that the probability of a passport getting lost or stolen is a function of the weather, since people tend to stay inside (and thus manage to keep track of their passports) when the weather is bad. But they tend to go out and thus risk getting their passport lost or stolen if the weather is good. So it amuses you to try to infer the weather in your favorite cities by watching the lost passport reports. We'll use the symbol L to mean that a passport was lost and the symbol # to mean that none was. So, for example, a report for a week might look like LL##L###.

We'll consider just two cities, London and Athens. We can build an HMM for each. Both HMMs have two states, Sunny and Rainy.

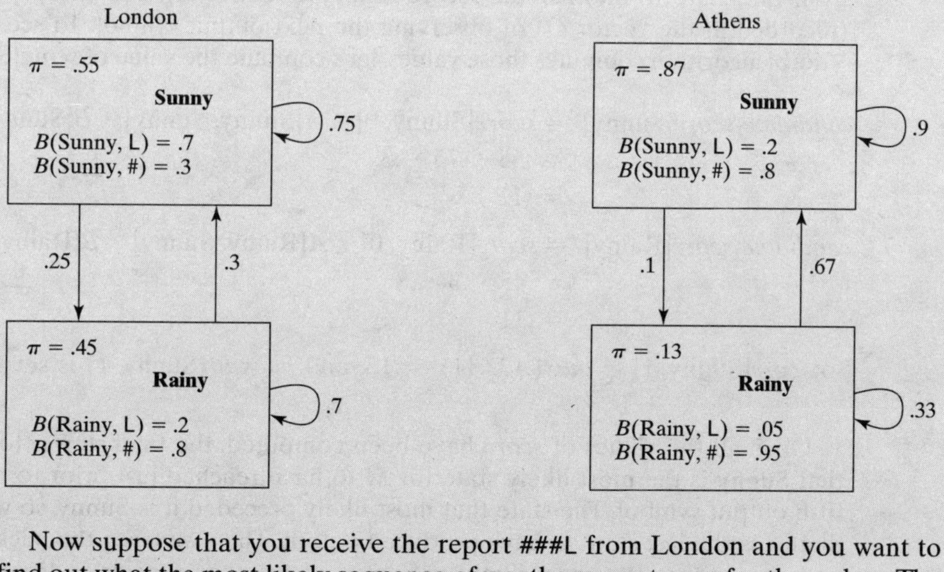

Now suppose that you receive the report ###L from London and you want to find out what the most likely sequence of weather reports was for those days. The Viterbi algorithm will solve the problem.

The easiest way to envision the way that *Viterbi* works is to imagine a lattice, in which each column corresponds to a step and each row corresponds to a state in *M*:

EXAMPLE 5.37 *(Continued)*

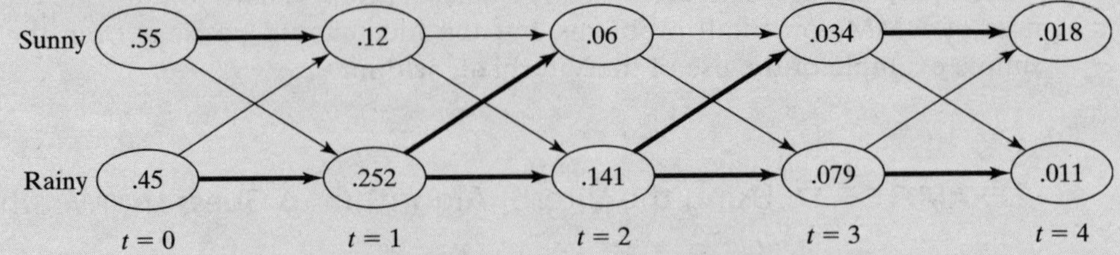

The number shown at each point (q, t) is the value that *Viterbi* computes for *score*$[q, t]$. So we can think of Viterbi as creating this lattice left to right, and filling in scores as it goes along. The arrows represent possible transitions in M. The heavy arrows indicate the path that is recorded in the matrix *backptr*.

At $t = 0$, the probabilities recorded in *score* are just the initial probabilities, as given in π. So the sum of the values in column 1 is 1. At later steps, the sum is less than 1 because we are considering only the probabilities of paths through M that result in the observed output sequence. Other paths could have produced other output sequences.

At all times $t > 0$, the values for *score* can be computed by considering the probabilities at the previous time (as recorded in *score*), the probabilities of moving from one state to another (as recorded in the matrix A), and the probabilities (recorded in the vector O) of observing the next output symbol. To see how the Viterbi algorithm computes those values, let's compute the value of *score*[Sunny, 1]:

$$\begin{aligned} \textit{candidate-score}[\text{Sunny}] &= \textit{score}[\text{Sunny}, 0] \cdot A[\text{Sunny}, \text{Sunny}] \cdot B[\text{Sunny}, \#] \\ &= .55 \cdot .75 \cdot .3 \\ &= .12 \end{aligned}$$

$$\begin{aligned} \textit{candidate-score}[\text{Rainy}] &= \textit{score}[\text{Rainy}, 0] \cdot A[\text{Rainy}, \text{Sunny}] \cdot B[\text{Rainy}, \#] \\ &= .45 \cdot .3 \cdot .8 \\ &= .11 \end{aligned}$$

So *score*[Sunny, 1] = *max*(.12, .11) = .12, and *backptr*(Sunny, 1) is set to Sunny.

Once all the values of *score* have been computed, the final step is to observe that Sunny is the most likely state for M to have reached just prior to reading a fifth output symbol. The state that most likely preceded it is Sunny, so we report Sunny as the last state to have produced output. Then we trace the backpointers and report that the most likely sequence of weather reports is Rainy, Rainy, Rainy, Sunny.

Now suppose that the fax machine was broken and the reports for last week came in with the city names chopped off the top. You have received the report ###L and you want to know whether it is more likely that it came from London or from Athens. To solve this problem, you use the forward algorithm. You run the output sequence ###L through the London model and through the Athens model, this time computing the total probability (as opposed to just the probability along the best path) of reaching each state from any path that is consistent with the output sequence. The most likely source of this report is the model with the highest final probability.

5.12 Finite Automata, Infinite Strings: Büchi Automata ◆

So far, we have considered, as input to our machines, only strings of finite length. Thus we have focused on problems for which we expect to write programs that read an input, compute a result, and halt. Many problems are of that sort, but some are not. For example, consider:

- An operating system.
- An air traffic control system.
- A factory process control system.

Ideally, such systems never halt. They should accept an infinite string of inputs and continue to function. Define Σ^ω to be the set of infinite length strings drawn from the alphabet Σ. For the rest of this discussion, define a language to be a set of such infinite-length strings.

To model the behavior of processes that do not halt, we can extend our notion of an NDFSM to define a machine whose inputs are elements of Σ^ω. Such machines are sometimes called ω-automata (or omega automata).

We'll define one particular kind of ω-automaton: A ***Büchi automaton*** is a quintuple $(K, \Sigma, \Delta, S, A)$, where:

- K is a finite set of states.
- Σ is the input alphabet.
- $S \subseteq K$ is a set of start states.
- $A \subseteq K$ is the set of accepting states.
- Δ is the transition relation. It is a finite subset of:

$$(K \times \Sigma) \times K.$$

Note that, unlike NDFSMs, Büchi automata may have more than one start state. Note also that the definition of a Büchi automaton does not allow ε-transitions.

We define configuration, initial configuration, yields-in-one-step, and yields exactly as we did for NDFSMs. A ***computation*** of a Büchi automaton M is an infinite sequence of configurations $C_0, C_1, \ldots$ such that:

- C_0 is an initial configuration, and
- $C_0 \mid\!-_M C_1 \mid\!-_M C_2 \mid\!-_M \ldots$

But now we must define what it means for a Büchi automaton M to accept a string. We can no longer define acceptance by the state of M when it runs out of input, since it won't. Instead, we'll say that M accepts a string $w \in \Sigma^\omega$ iff, in at least one of its computations, there is some accepting state q such that, when processing w, M enters q an infinite number of times. So note that it is not required that M enter an accepting state and stay there. But it is not sufficient for M to enter an accepting state just once (or any finite number of times). As before, the language accepted by M, denoted $L(M)$, is the set of all strings accepted by M. A language L is ***Büchi-acceptable*** iff it is accepted by some Büchi automaton.

Büchi automata can be used to model concurrent systems, hardware devices, and their specifications. Then programs called model checkers can verify that those systems correctly conform to a set of stated requirements. (H.1.2)

EXAMPLE 5.38 Büchi Automata for Event Sequences

Suppose that there are five kinds of events that can occur in the system that we wish to model. We'll call them a, b, c, d, and e. So let $\Sigma = \{a, b, c, d, e\}$.

We first consider the case in which we require that event e occur at least once. The following (nondeterministic) Büchi automaton accepts all and only the elements of Σ^ω that contain at least one occurrence of e:

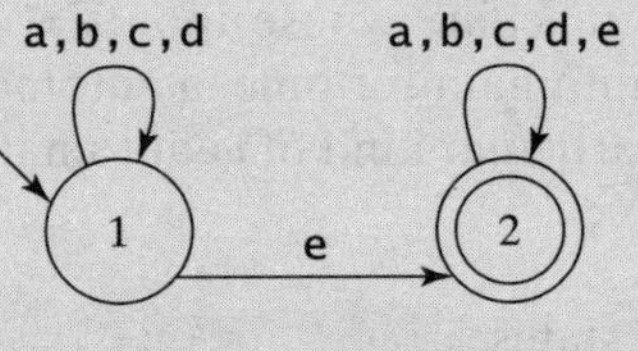

Now suppose that we require that there come a point after which only e's can occur. The following Büchi automaton (described using our convention that the dead state need not be written explicitly) accepts all and only the elements of Σ^ω that eventually reach a point after which no events other than e's occur:

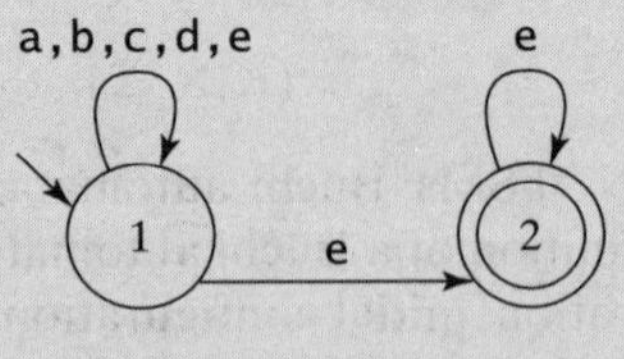

Finally, suppose that we require that every c event be immediately followed by an e event. The following Büchi automaton (this time with the dead state, 3, shown explicitly) accepts all and only the elements of Σ^ω that satisfy that requirement:

EXAMPLE 5.38 *(Continued)*

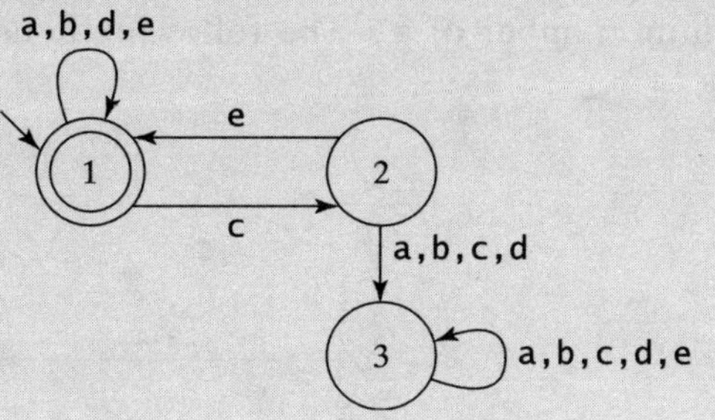

EXAMPLE 5.39 Mutual Exclusion

Suppose that we want to model a concurrent system with two processes and enforce the constraint, often called a mutual exclusion property, that it never happens that both processes are in their critical regions at the same time. We could do this in the usual way, using an alphabet of atomic symbols such as {`Both`, `NotBoth`}, where the system receives the input `Both` at any time interval at which both processes are in their critical region and the input `NotBoth` at any other time interval. But a more direct way to model the behavior of complex concurrent systems is to allow inputs that correspond to Boolean expressions that capture the properties of interest. That way, the same Boolean predicates can be combined into different expressions in different machines that correspond to different desirable properties. To capture the mutual exclusion constraint, we'll use two Boolean predicates, CR_0, which will be *True* iff $process_0$ is in its critical region and CR_1, which will be *True* iff $process_1$ is in its critical region. The inputs to the system will then be drawn from a set of three Boolean expressions: $\{(CR_0 \wedge CR_1), \neg(CR_0 \wedge CR_1), True\}$. The following Büchi automaton accepts all and only the input sequences that satisfy the property that $(CR_0 \wedge CR_1)$ never occurs:

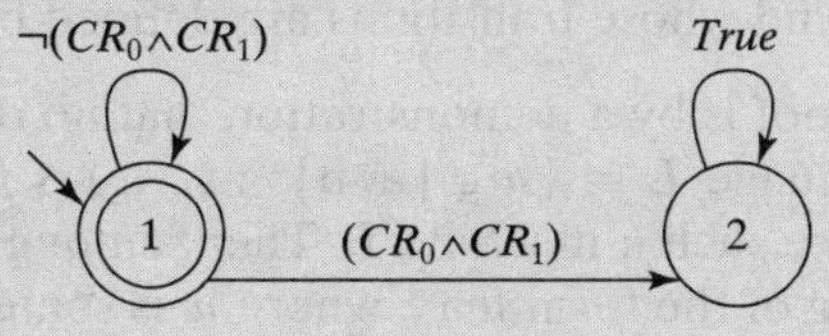

While there is an obvious similarity between Büchi automata and FSMs, and the languages they accept are related, as described below, there is one important difference. For Büchi automata, nondeterminism matters.

EXAMPLE 5.40 For Büchi Automata, Nondeterminism Matters

Let $L = \{w \in \{\text{a, b}\}^\omega : \#_b\ (w) \text{ is finite}\}$. Note that every string in L must contain an infinite number of a's. The following nondeterministic Büchi automaton accepts L:

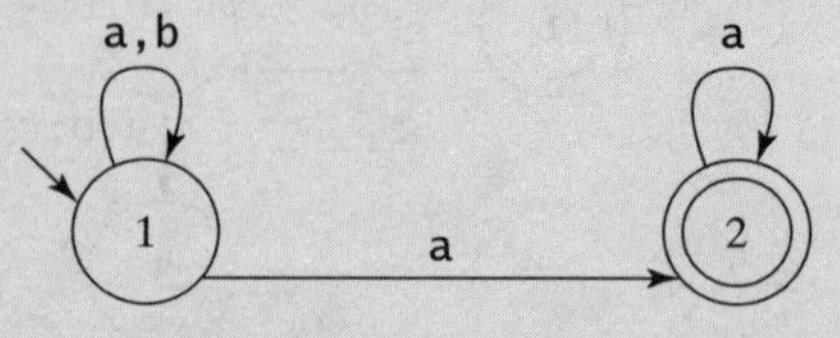

We can try to build a corresponding deterministic machine by using the construction that we used in the proof of Theorem 5.3 (which says that for every NDFSM there does exist an equivalent DFSM). The states of the new machine will then correspond to subsets of states of the original machine and we'll have:

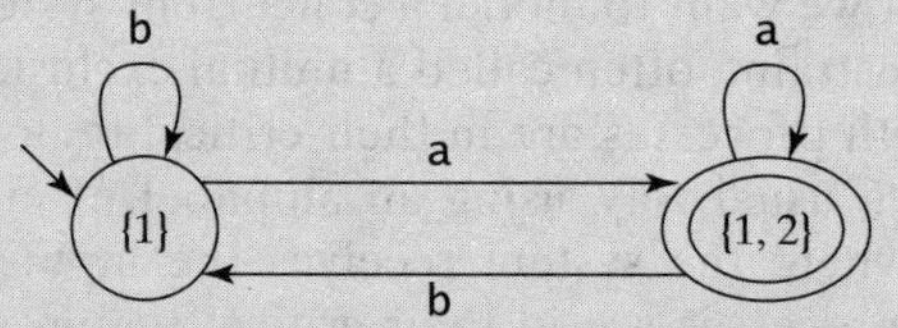

This new machine is indeed nondeterministic and it does accept all strings in L. Unfortunately, it also accepts an infinite number of strings that are not in L, including $(\text{ba})^\omega$. More unfortunately, we cannot do any better.

THEOREM 5.7 Nondeterministic versus Deterministic Büchi Automata

Theorem: There exist languages that can be accepted by a nondeterministic Büchi automaton (i.e., one that meets the definition we have given), but for which there exists no equivalent deterministic Büchi automaton (i.e., one that has a single start state and whose transitions are defined by a function from $(K \times \Sigma)$ to K).

Proof: The proof is by a demonstration that no deterministic Büchi automaton accepts the language $L = \{w \in \{\text{a, b}\}^\omega : \#_b(w)\ \textit{is finite}\}$ of Example 5.40. Suppose that there were such a machine B. Then, among the strings accepted by B, would be every string of the form $w\text{a}^\omega$, where w is some finite string in $\{\text{a, b}\}^*$. This must be true since all such strings contain only a finite number of b's. Remove from B any states that are not reachable from the start state. Now consider any remaining state q in B. Since q is reachable from the start state, there must exist at least one finite string that drives B from the start state to q. Call that string w. Then, as we just observed, wa^ω is in L and so must be accepted by B. In order for B to accept it, there must be at least one accepting state q_a that occurs infinitely often in the computation of B on wa^ω. That accepting state must be reachable from q (the state of B when just w has been read) by some finite number, which we'll call a_q, of a's (since B has only a finite of states). Compute a_q for every state q in B. Let m be the maximum of the a_q values.

We can now show that B accepts the string $(ba^m)^\omega$, which is not in L. Since B is deterministic, its transition function is defined on all (state, input) pairs, so it must run forever on all strings including $(ba^m)^\omega$. From the last paragraph we know that, from any state, there is a string of m or fewer a's that can drive B to an accepting state. So, in particular, after each time it reads a b, followed by a sequence of a's, B must reach some accepting state within m a's. But B has only a finite number of accepting states. So, on input $(ba^m)^\omega$, B reaches some accepting state an infinite number of times and it accepts.

There is a natural relationship between the languages of infinite strings accepted by Büchi automata and the regular languages (i.e., the languages of finite strings accepted by FSMs). To describe this relationship requires an understanding of the closure properties of the regular languages that we will present in Section 8.3, as well as some of the decision procedures for regular languages that we will present in Chapter 9. It would be helpful to read those sections before continuing to read this discussion of Büchi automata.

Any Büchi-acceptable language can be described in terms of regular languages. To see how, observe that any Büchi automaton B can almost be viewed as an FSM, if we simply consider input strings of finite length. The only reason that that can't quite be done is that Büchi automata may have multiple start states. So, from any Büchi automaton B, we can build what we'll call the ***mirror FSM*** M to B as follows: Let $M = B$ except that, if B has more than one start state, then, in M, create a new start state that has an ε-transition to each of the start states of B. Notice that the set of finite length strings that can drive B from a start state to some state q is identical to the set of finite length strings that can drive M from its start state to state q.

Now consider any Büchi automaton B and any string w that B accepts. Since w is accepted, there is some accepting state in B that is visited an infinite number of times while B processes w. Call that state q. (There may be more than one such state. Pick one.) Then we can divide w into two parts, x and y. The first part, x, has finite length and it drives B from a start state to q for the first time. The second part, y, has infinite length and it simply pushes B through one loop after another, each of which starts and ends in q (although there may be more than one path that does this). The set of possible values for x is regular: It is exactly the set that can be accepted by the FSM M that mirrors B, if we let q be M's only accepting state. Call a path from q back to itself ***minimal*** iff it does not pass through q. Then we also notice that the set of strings that can force B through such a minimal path is also regular. It is the set accepted by the FSM M that mirrors B, if we let q be both M's start state and its only accepting state. These observations lead to the following theorem:

THEOREM 5.8 Büchi-Acceptable and Regular Languages

Theorem: L is a Büchi-acceptable language iff it is the finite union of sets each of which is of the form XY^ω, where each X and Y is a regular language.

Proof: Given any Büchi automaton $B = (K, \Sigma, \Delta, S, A)$, let $W_{q_0q_1}$ be the set of all strings that drive B from state q_0 to state q_1. Then, by the definition of what it means for a Büchi automaton to accept a string, we have:

$$L(B) = \bigcup_{s\in S}\bigcup_{q\in A} W_{sq}(W_{qq})^\omega.$$

If L is a Büchi-acceptable language, then there is some Büchi automaton B that accepts it. So the only-if part of the claim is true since:

- S and A are both finite,
- For each s and q, W_{sq} is regular since it is the set of strings accepted by B's mirror FSM M with start state s and single accepting state q,
- $W_{qq} = Y^*$, where Y is the set of strings that can force B along a minimal path from q back to q,
- Y is regular since it is the set of strings accepted by B's mirror FSM M with q as its start state and its only accepting state, and
- The regular languages are closed under Kleene star so $W_{qq} = Y^*$ is also regular.

The if part follows from a set of properties of the Büchi-acceptable and regular languages that are described in Theorem 5.9.

THEOREM 5.9 Closure Properties of Büchi Automata

Theorem and Proof: The Büchi-acceptable languages (like the regular languages) are closed under:

- Concatenation with a regular language: If L_1 is a regular language and L_2 is a Büchi-acceptable language, then L_1L_2 is Büchi-acceptable. The proof is similar to the proof that the regular languages are closed under concatenation except that, since ε transitions are not allowed, the machines for the two languages must be "glued together" differently. If q is a state in the FSM that accepts L_1, and there is a transition from q, labeled c, to some accepting state, then add a transition from q, labeled c, to each start state of the Büchi automaton that accepts L_2.
- Union: If L_1 and L_2 are Büchi-acceptable, then $L_1 \cup L_2$ is also Büchi-acceptable. The proof is analogous to the proof that the regular languages are closed under union. Again, since ε transitions are not allowed, we must use a slightly different glue. The new machine we will build will have transitions directly

from a new start state to the states that the original machines can reach after reading one input character.

- Intersection: If L_1 and L_2 are Büchi-acceptable, then $L_1 \cap L_2$ is also Büchi-acceptable. The proof is by construction of a Büchi automaton that effectively runs a Büchi automaton for L_1 in parallel with one for L_2.
- Complement: If L is Büchi-acceptable, then $\neg L$ is also Büchi-acceptable. The proof of this claim is less obvious. It is given in [Thomas 1990].

Further, if L is a regular language, then L^ω is Büchi-acceptable. The proof is analogous to the proof that the regular languages are closed under Kleene star, but we must again use the modification that was used above in the proof of closure under concatenation.

Büchi automata are useful as models for computer systems whose properties we wish to reason about because a set of important questions can be answered about them. In particular, Büchi automata share with FSMs the existence of decision procedures for all of the properties described in the following theorem:

THEOREM 5.10 Decision Procedures for Büchi Automata

Theorem: There exist decision procedures for all of the following properties:

- Emptiness: Given a Büchi automaton B, is $L(B)$ empty?
- Nonemptiness: Given a Büchi automaton B, is $L(B)$ nonempty?
- Inclusion: Given two Büchi automata B_1 and B_2, is $L(B_1) \subseteq L(B_2)$?
- Equivalence: Given two Büchi automata B_1 and B_2, is $L(B_1) = L(B_2)$?

Proof: The proof of each of these claims can be found in [Thomas 1990].

Exercises

1. Give a clear English description of the language accepted by the following DFSM:

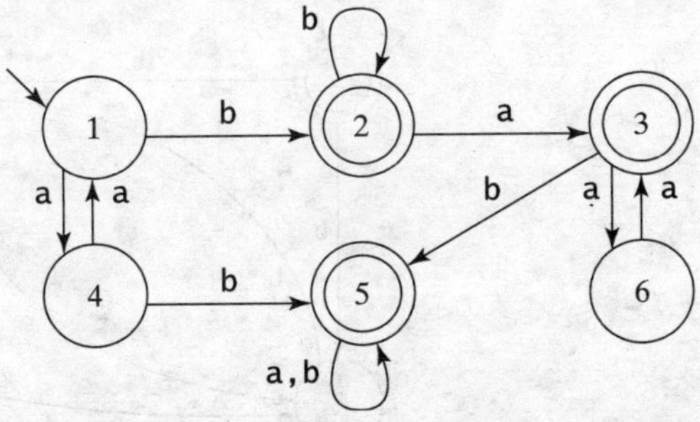

2. Show a DFSM to accept each of the following languages:

a. $\{w \in \{\text{a}, \text{b}\}^* :$ every a in w is immediately preceded and followed by b$\}$.

b. $\{w \in \{\text{a}, \text{b}\}^* : w$ does not end in ba$\}$.

c. $\{w \in \{0, 1\}^* : w$ corresponds to the binary encoding, without leading 0's, of natural numbers that are evenly divisible by 4$\}$.

d. $\{w \in \{0, 1\}^* : w$ corresponds to the binary encoding, without leading 0's, of natural numbers that are powers of 4$\}$.

e. $\{w \in \{0\text{-}9\}^* : w$ corresponds to the decimal encoding, without leading 0's, of an odd natural number$\}$.

f. $\{w \in \{0, 1\}^* : w$ has 001 as a substring$\}$.

g. $\{w \in \{0, 1\}^* : w$ does not have 001 as a substring$\}$.

h. $\{w \in \{\text{a}, \text{b}\}^* : w$ has bbab as a substring$\}$.

i. $\{w \in \{\text{a}, \text{b}\}^* : w$ has neither ab nor bb as a substring$\}$.

j. $\{w \in \{\text{a}, \text{b}\}^* : w$ has both aa and bb as a substrings$\}$.

k. $\{w \in \{\text{a}, \text{b}\}^* : w$ contains at least two b's that are not immediately followed by an a$\}$.

l. $\{w \in \{0, 1\}^* : w$ has no more than one pair of consecutive 0's and no more than one pair of consecutive 1's$\}$.

m. $\{w \in \{0, 1\}^* :$ none of the prefixes of w ends in 0$\}$.

n. $\{w \in \{\text{a}, \text{b}\}^* : (\#_\text{a}(w) + 2 \cdot \#_\text{b}(w)) \equiv_5 0\}$. ($\#_\text{a}(w)$ is the number of a's in w).

3. Consider the children's game Rock, Paper, Scissors 🖳. We'll say that the first player to win two rounds wins the game. Call the two players A and B.

a. Define an alphabet Σ and describe a technique for encoding Rock, Paper, Scissors games as strings over Σ. (*Hint*: Each symbol in Σ should correspond to an ordered pair that describes the simultaneous actions of A and B.)

b. Let L_{RPS} be the language of Rock, Paper, Scissors games, encoded as strings as described in part (a), that correspond to wins for player A. Show a DFSM that accepts L_{RPS}.

4. If M is a DFSM and $\varepsilon \in L(M)$, what simple property must be true of M?

5. Consider the following NDFSM M:

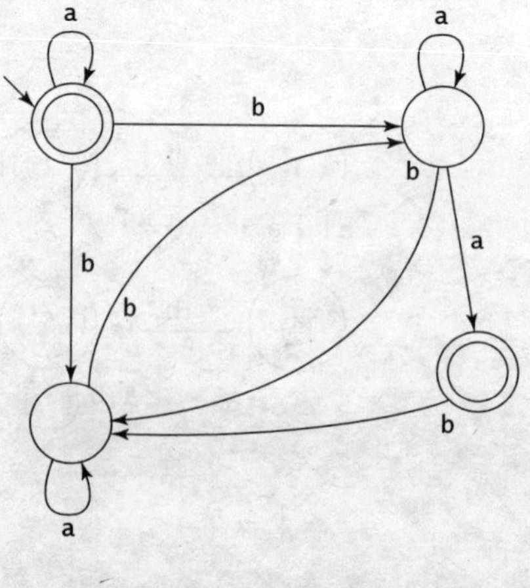

For each of the following strings w, determine whether $w \in L(M)$:

a. aabbba.

b. bab.

c. baba.

6. Show a possibly nondeterministic FSM to accept each of the following languages:

a. $\{\texttt{a}^n\texttt{b}\texttt{a}^m : n, m \geq 0, n \equiv_3 m\}$.

b. $\{w \in \{\texttt{a}, \texttt{b}\}^* : w$ contains at least one instance of aaba, bbb or ababa$\}$.

c. $\{w \in \{\texttt{0-9}\}^* : w$ corresponds to the decimal encoding of a natural number whose encoding contains, as a substring, the encoding of a natural number that is divisible by 3$\}$.

d. $\{w \in \{\texttt{0}, \texttt{1}\}^* : w$ contains both 101 and 010 as substrings$\}$.

e. $\{w \in \{\texttt{0}, \texttt{1}\}^* : w$ corresponds to the binary encoding of a positive integer that is divisible by 16 or is odd$\}$.

f. $\{w \in \{\texttt{a, b, c, d, e}\}^* : |w| \geq 2$ and w begins and ends with the same symbol$\}$.

7. Show an FSM (deterministic or nondeterministic) that accepts $L = \{w \in \{\texttt{a, b, c}\}^* : w$ contains at least one substring that consists of three identical symbols in a row$\}$. For example:

- The following strings are in L: aabbb, baacccbbb.
- The following strings are not in L: ε, aba, abababab, abcbcab.

8. Show a DFSM to accept each of the following languages. The point of this exercise is to see how much harder it is to build a DFSM for tasks like these than it is to build an NDFSM. So do not simply build an NDFSM and then convert it. But do, after you build a DFSM, build an equivalent NDFSM.

a. $\{w \in \{\texttt{a}, \texttt{b}\}^* :$ the fourth from the last character is a$\}$.

b. $\{w \in \{\texttt{a}, \texttt{b}\}^* : \exists x, y \in \{\texttt{a}, \texttt{b}\}^* : ((w = x\ \texttt{abbaa}\ y) \vee (w = x\ \texttt{baba}\ y))\}$.

9. For each of the following NDFSMs, use *ndfsmtodfsm* to construct an equivalent DFSM. Begin by showing the value of *eps*(q) for each state q:

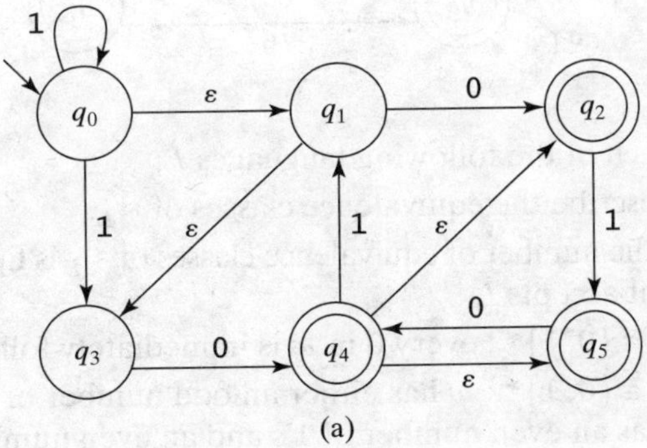

(a)

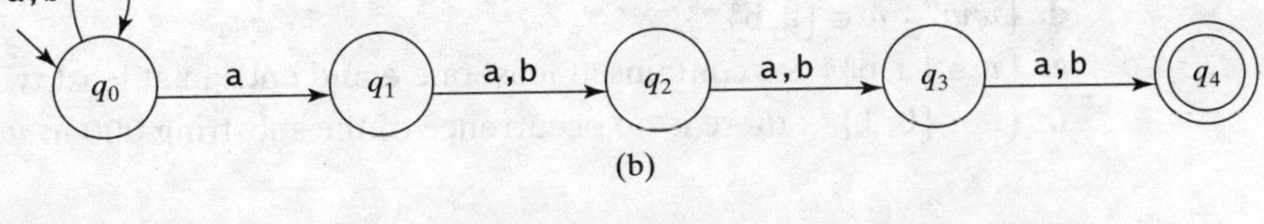

(b)

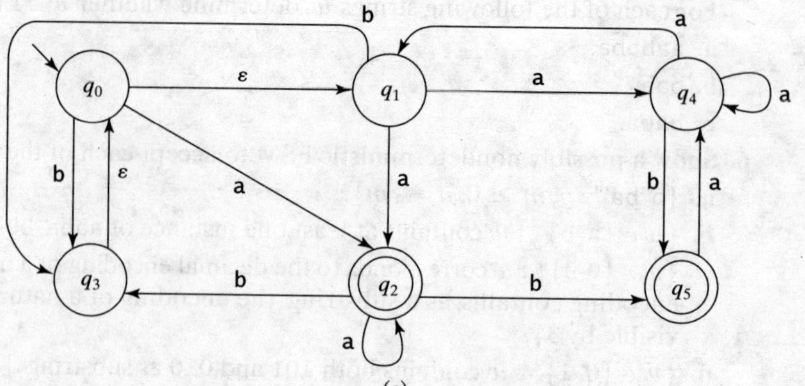

(c)

10. Let M be the following NDFSM. Construct (using *ndfsmtodfsm*), a DFSM that accepts $\neg L(M)$.

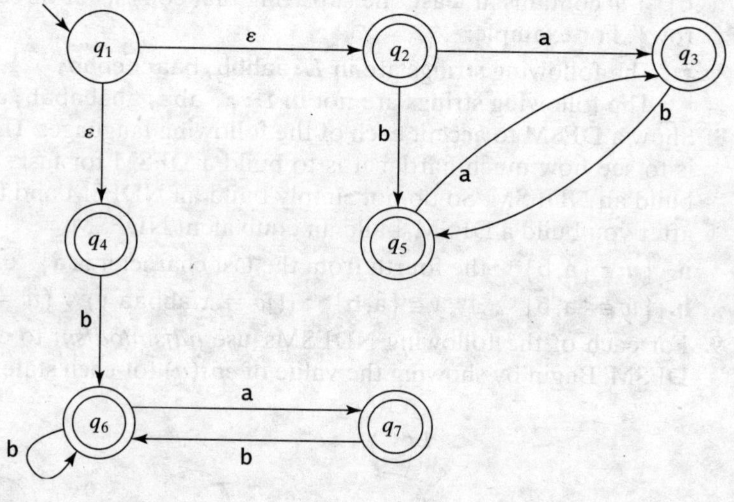

11. For each of the following languages L:

(i) Describe the equivalence classes of $\approx_L$.

(ii) If the number of equivalence classes of $\approx_L$ is finite, construct the minimal DFSM that accepts L.

a. $\{w \in \{0, 1\}^* :$ every 0 in w is immediately followed by the string 11$\}$.

b. $\{w \in \{0, 1\}^* : w$ has either an odd number of 1's and an odd number of 0's or it has an even number of 1's and an even number of 0's$\}$.

c. $\{w \in \{a, b\}^* : w$ contains at least one occurrence of the string aababa$\}$.

d. $\{ww^R : w \in \{a, b\}^*\}$.

e. $\{w \in \{a, b\}^* : w$ contains at least one a and ends in at least two b's$\}$.

f. $\{w \in \{0, 1\}^* :$ there is no occurrence of the substring 000 in $w\}$.

12. Let M be the following DFSM. Use *minDFSM* to minimize M.

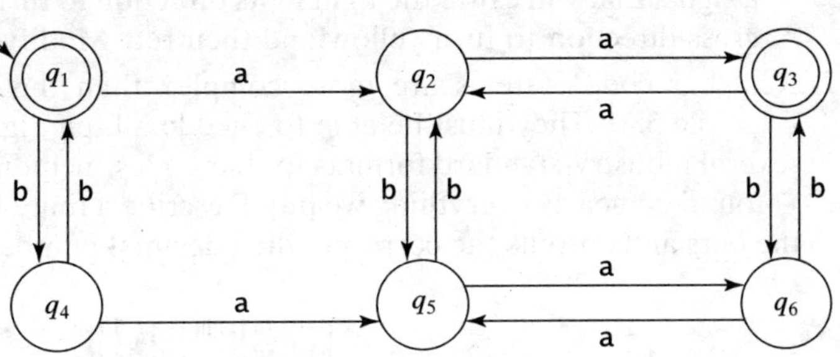

13. Construct a deterministic finite state transducer with input alphabet {a, b} for each of the following tasks:

a. On input w, produce 1^n, where $n = \#_a(w)$.

b. On input w, produce 1^n, where $n = \#_a(w)/2$.

c. On input w, produce 1^n, where n is the number of occurrences of the substring aba in w.

14. Construct a deterministic finite state transducer that could serve as the controller for an elevator. Clearly describe the input and output alphabets, as well as the states and the transitions between them.

15. Consider the problem of counting the number of words in a text file that may contain letters plus any of the following non-letter characters:

<blank><linefeed><end-of-file>, . ; : ?!

Define a word to be a string of letters that is preceded by either the beginning of the file or some non-letter character and that is followed by some non-letter character. For example, there are 11 words in the following text:

The *<blank><blank>* cat *<blank><linefeed>*
saw *<blank>* the *<blank><blank><blank>* rat *<linefeed>*
<blank> with
<linefeed> a*<blank>* hat *<linefeed>*
on *<blank>* the *<blank><blank>* mat *<end-of-file>*

Describe a very simple finite-state transducer that reads the characters in the file one at a time and solves the word-counting problem. Assume that there exists an output symbol with the property that, every time it is generated, an external counter gets incremented.

16. Real traffic light controllers are more complex than the one that we drew in Example 5.29.

a. Consider an intersection of two roads controlled by a set of four lights (one in each direction). Don't worry about allowing for a special left-turn signal. Design a controller for this four-light system.

b. As an emergency vehicle approaches an intersection, it should be able to send a signal that will cause the light in its direction to turn green and the light in the cross direction to turn yellow and then red. Modify your design to allow this.

17. Real bar code systems are more complex than the one that we sketched in Example 5.31. They must be able to encode all ten digits, for example. There are several industry-standard formats for bar codes, including the common UPC code found on nearly everything we buy. Describe a finite state transducer that reads the bars and outputs the corresponding decimal number.

0 12345 67890 5

18. Extend the description of the Soundex FSM that was started in Example 5.33 so that it can assign a code to the name Pfifer. Remember that you must take into account the fact that every Soundex code is made up of exactly four characters.

19. Consider the weather/passport HMM of Example 5.37. Trace the execution of the Viterbi and forward algorithms to answer the following questions:

a. Suppose that the report ###L is received from Athens. What was the most likely weather during the time of the report?

b. Is it more likely that ###L came from London or from Athens?

20. Construct a Büchi automaton to accept each of the following languages of infinite length strings:

a. $\{w \in \{\text{a}, \text{b}, \text{c}\}^\omega$: after any occurrence of an a there is eventually an occurrence of a b$\}$.

b. $\{w \in \{\text{a}, \text{b}, \text{c}\}^\omega$: between any two consecutive a's there is an odd number of b's$\}$.

c. $\{w \in \{\text{a}, \text{b}, \text{c}\}^\omega$: there never comes a time after which no b's occur$\}$.

21. In H.2, we describe the use of statecharts as a tool for building complex systems. A statechart is a hierarchically structured transition network model. Statecharts aren't the only tools that exploit this idea. Another is Simulink®, which is one component of the larger programming environment MATLAB®. Use Simulink to build an FSM simulator.

22. In I.1.2, we describe the Alternating Bit protocol for handling message transmission in a network. Use the FSM that describes the sender to answer the question, "Is there any upper bound on the number of times a message may be retransmitted?"

23. In J.1, we show an FSM model of a simple intrusion detection device that could be part of a building security system. Extend the model to allow the system to have two zones that can be armed and disarmed independently of each other.

CHAPTER 6

Regular Expressions

Let's now take a different approach to categorizing problems. Instead of focusing on the power of a computing device, let's look at the task that we need to perform. In particular, let's consider problems in which our goal is to match finite or repeating patterns. For example, consider:

- The first step of compiling a program: This step is called lexical analysis. Its job is to break the source code into meaningful units such as keywords, variables, and numbers. For example, the string `void` may be a keyword, while the string `23E-12` should be recognized as a floating point number.
- Filtering email for spam.
- Sorting email into appropriate mailboxes based on sender and/or content words and phrases.
- Searching a complex directory structure by specifying patterns that are known to occur in the file we want.

In this chapter, we will define a simple ***pattern language***. It has limitations. But its strength, as we will soon see, is that we can implement pattern matching for this language using finite state machines.

> In his classic book, *A Pattern Language* 💻, Christopher Alexander described common patterns that can be found in successful buildings, towns and cities. Software engineers read Alexander's work and realized that the same is true of successful programs and systems. Patterns are ubiquitous in our world.

6.1 What is a Regular Expression?

The regular expression language that we are about to describe is built on an alphabet that contains two kinds of symbols:

- A set of special symbols to which we will attach particular meanings when they occur in a regular expression. These symbols are $\varnothing$, $\cup$, ε, (,), *, and $^+$.
- An alphabet Σ, which contains the symbols that regular expressions will match against.

A ***regular expression*** is a string that can be formed according to the following rules:

1. $\varnothing$ is a regular expression.
2. ε is a regular expression.
3. Every element in Σ is a regular expression.
4. Given two regular expressions α and β, $\alpha\beta$ is a regular expression.
5. Given two regular expressions α and β, $\alpha \cup \beta$ is a regular expression.
6. Given a regular expression α, α^* is a regular expression.
7. Given a regular expression α, α^+ is a regular expression.
8. Given a regular expression α, (α) is a regular expression.

So, if we let $\Sigma = \{\text{a}, \text{b}\}$, the following strings are regular expressions:

$$\varnothing, \varepsilon, \text{a}, \text{b}, (\text{a} \cup \text{b})^*, \text{abba} \cup \varepsilon.$$

The language of regular expressions, as we have just defined it, is useful because every regular expression has a meaning (just like every English sentence and every Java program). In the case of regular expressions, the meaning of a string is another language. In other words, every string α (such as abba $\cup\, \varepsilon$) in the regular expression language has, as its meaning, some new language that contains exactly the strings that match the pattern specified in α.

To make it possible to determine that meaning, we need to describe a semantic interpretation function for regular expressions. Fortunately, the regular expressions language is simple. So designing a compositional semantic interpretation function (as defined in Section 2.2.6) for it is straightforward. As you read the definition that we are about to present, it will become clear why we chose the particular symbol alphabet we did. In particular, you will notice the similarity between the operations that are allowed in regular expressions and the operations that we defined on languages in Section 2.2.

Define the following semantic interpretation function L for the language of regular expressions:

1. $L(\varnothing) = \varnothing$, the language that contains no strings.
2. $L(\varepsilon) = \{\varepsilon\}$, the language that contains just the empty string.
3. For any $c \in \Sigma$, $L(c) = \{c\}$, the language that contains the single, one-character string c.

4. For any regular expressions α and β, $L(\alpha\beta) = L(\alpha)\,L(\beta)$. In other words, to form the meaning of the concatenation of two regular expressions, first determine the meaning of each of the constituents. Both meanings will be languages. Then concatenate the two languages together. Recall that the concatenation of two languages L_1 and L_2 is $\{w = xy$, where $x \in L_1$ and $y \in L_2\}$. Note that, if either $L(\alpha)$ or $L(\beta)$ is equal to $\varnothing$, then the concatenation will also be equal to $\varnothing$.
5. For any regular expressions α and β, $L(\alpha \cup \beta) = L(\alpha) \cup L(\beta)$. Again we form the meaning of the larger expression by first determining the meaning of each of the constituents. Each of them is a language. The meaning of $\alpha \cup \beta$ then, as suggested by our choice of the character $\cup$ as an operator, is the union of the two constituent languages.
6. For any regular expression α, $L(\alpha^*) = (L(\alpha))^*$, where * is the Kleene star operator defined in Section 2.2.5. So $L(\alpha^*)$ is the language that is formed by concatenating together zero or more strings drawn from $L(\alpha)$.
7. For any regular expression α, $L(\alpha^+) = L(\alpha\alpha^*) = L(\alpha)(L(\alpha))^*$. If $L(\alpha)$ is equal to $\varnothing$, then $L(\alpha^+)$ is also equal to $\varnothing$. Otherwise $L(\alpha^+)$ is the language that is formed by concatenating together one or more strings drawn from $L(\alpha)$.
8. For any regular expression α, $L((\alpha)) = L(\alpha)$. In other words, parentheses have no effect on meaning except to group the constituents in an expression.

If the meaning of a regular expression α is the language L, then we say that α ***defines*** or ***describes*** L.

The definition that we have just given for the regular expression language contains three kinds of rules:

- Rules 1, 3, 4, 5, and 6 give the language its power to define sets, starting with the basic sets defined by rules 1 and 3, and then building larger sets using the operators defined by rules 4, 5, and 6.
- Rule 8 has as its only role grouping other operators.
- Rules 2 and 7 appear to add functionality to the regular expression language. But in fact they don't—they serve only to provide convenient shorthands for languages that can be defined using only rules 1, 3-6, and 8. Let's see why.

First consider rule 2: The language of regular expressions does not need the symbol ε because it has an alternative mechanism for describing $L(\varepsilon)$. Observe that $L(\varnothing^*) = \{w : w$ is formed by concatenating together zero or more strings from $\varnothing\}$. But how many ways are there to concatenate together zero or more strings from $\varnothing$? If we select zero strings to concatenate, we get ε. We cannot select more than zero since there aren't any to choose from. So $L(\varnothing^*) = \{\varepsilon\}$. Thus, whenever we would like to write ε, we could instead write $\varnothing^*$. It is much clearer to write ε, and we shall. But, whenever we wish to make a formal statement about regular expressions or the languages they define, we need not consider rule 2 since we can rewrite any regular expression that contains ε as an equivalent one that contains $\varnothing^*$ instead.

Next consider rule 7: As we showed in the statement of rule 7 itself, the regular expression α^+ is equivalent to the slightly longer regular expression $\alpha\alpha^*$. The form α^+ is a convenient shortcut, and we will use it. But we need not consider rule 7 in any analysis that we may choose to do of regular expressions or the languages that they generate.

The compositional semantic interpretation function that we just defined lets us map between regular expressions and the languages that they define. We begin by analyzing the smallest subexpressions and then work outward to larger and larger expressions.

EXAMPLE 6.1 Analyzing a Simple Regular Expression

$$\begin{aligned} L((\mathtt{a} \cup \mathtt{b})^*\mathtt{b}) &= L((\mathtt{a} \cup \mathtt{b})^*)L(\mathtt{b}) \\ &= (L((\mathtt{a} \cup \mathtt{b})))^*L(\mathtt{b}) \\ &= (L(\mathtt{a}) \cup L(\mathtt{b}))^*L(\mathtt{b}) \\ &= (\{\mathtt{a}\} \cup \{\mathtt{b}\})^*\{\mathtt{b}\} \\ &= \{\mathtt{a}, \mathtt{b}\}^*\{\mathtt{b}\}. \end{aligned}$$

So the meaning of the regular expression $(\mathtt{a} \cup \mathtt{b})^*\mathtt{b}$ is the set of all strings over the alphabet $\{\mathtt{a}, \mathtt{b}\}$ that end in b.

One straightforward way to read a regular expression and determine its meaning is to imagine it as a procedure that generates strings. Read it left to right and imagine it generating a string left to right. As you are doing that, think of any expression that is enclosed in a Kleene star as a loop that can be executed zero or more times. Each time through the loop, choose any one of the alternatives listed in the expression. So we can read the regular expression of the last example, $(\mathtt{a} \cup \mathtt{b})^*\mathtt{b}$, as, "Go through a loop zero or more times, picking a single a or b each time. Then concatenate b." Any string that can be generated by this procedure is in $L((\mathtt{a} \cup \mathtt{b})^*\mathtt{b})$.

Regular expressions can be used to scan text and pick out email addresses. (O.2)

EXAMPLE 6.2 Another Simple Regular Expression

$$\begin{aligned} L(((\mathtt{a} \cup \mathtt{b})(\mathtt{a} \cup \mathtt{b}))\mathtt{a}(\mathtt{a} \cup \mathtt{b})^*) &= L(((\mathtt{a} \cup \mathtt{b})(\mathtt{a} \cup \mathtt{b})))L(\mathtt{a})\ L((\mathtt{a} \cup \mathtt{b})^*) \\ &= L((\mathtt{a} \cup \mathtt{b})(\mathtt{a} \cup \mathtt{b}))\ \{\mathtt{a}\}\ (L((\mathtt{a} \cup \mathtt{b})))^* \\ &= L((\mathtt{a} \cup \mathtt{b}))L((\mathtt{a} \cup \mathtt{b}))\ \{\mathtt{a}\}\ \{\mathtt{a}, \mathtt{b}\}^* \\ &= \{\mathtt{a}, \mathtt{b}\}\ \{\mathtt{a}, \mathtt{b}\}\ \{\mathtt{a}\}\ \{\mathtt{a}, \mathtt{b}\}^* \end{aligned}$$

So the meaning of the regular expression ((a ∪ b)(a ∪ b))a(a ∪ b)* is:

$$\{xay : x \text{ and } y \text{ are strings of a's and b's and } |x| = 2\}.$$

Alternatively, it is the language that contains all strings of a's and b's such that there exists a third character and it is an a.

EXAMPLE 6.3 Given a Language, Find a Regular Expression

Let $L = \{w \in \{a, b\}^* : |w| \text{ is even}\}$. There are two simple regular expressions both of which define L:

((a ∪ b)(a ∪ b))*	This one can be read as, "Go through a loop zero or more times. Each time through, choose an a or b, then choose a second character (a or b)."
(aa ∪ ab ∪ ba ∪ bb)*	This one can be read as, "Go through a loop zero or more times. Each time through, choose one of the two-character sequences."

From this example, it is clear that the semantic interpretation function we have defined for regular expressions is not one-to-one. In fact, given any language L, if there is one regular expression that defines it, there is an infinite number that do. This is trivially true since, for any regular expression α, the regular expression $\alpha \cup \alpha$ defines the same language α does.

Recall from our discussion in Section 2.2.6 that this is not unusual. Semantic interpretation functions for English and for Java are not one-to-one. The practical consequence of this phenomenon for regular expressions is that, if we are trying to design a regular expression that describes some particular language, there will be more than one right answer. We will generally seek the simplest one that works, both for clarity and to make pattern matching fast.

EXAMPLE 6.4 More than One Regular Expression for a Language

Let $L = \{w \in \{a, b\}^* : w \text{ contains an odd number of a's}\}$. Two equally simple regular expressions that define L are:

b* (ab*ab*)* a b*.

b* a b* (ab*ab*)*.

EXAMPLE 6.4 *(Continued)*

Both of these expressions require that there be a single a somewhere. There can also be other a's, but they must occur in pairs, so the result is an odd number of a's. In the first expression, the last a in the string is viewed as the required "odd a". In the second, the first a plays that role.

The regular expression language that we have just defined provides three operators. We will assign the following precedence order to them (from highest to lowest):

1. Kleene star,
2. concatenation, and
3. union.

So the expression (a ∪ bb*a) will be interpreted as (a ∪ (b(b*a))).

All useful languages have idioms: common phrases that correspond to common meanings. Regular expressions are no exception. In writing them, we will often use the following:

$(\alpha \cup \varepsilon)$	Can be read as "optional α", since the expression can be satisfied either by matching α or by matching the empty string.
(a ∪ b)*	Describes the set of all strings composed of the characters a and b. More generally, given any alphabet $\Sigma = \{c_1, c_2, \ldots, c_n\}$, the language Σ^* is described by the regular expression: $$(c_1 \cup c_2 \cup \cdots \cup c_n)^*.$$

When writing regular expressions, the details matter. For example:

a* ∪ b* ≠ (a ∪ b)*	The language on the right contains the string ab, while the language on the left does not. Every string in the language on the left contains only a's or only b's.
(ab)* ≠ a*b*	The language on the left contains the string abab, while the language on the right does not. The language on the right contains the string aaabbbb, while the language on the left does not.

The regular expression a* is simply a string. It is different from the language $L(\text{a}^*) = \{w : w \text{ is composed of zero or more a's}\}$. However, when no confusion will result, we will use regular expressions to stand for the languages that they describe and we will no longer write the semantic interpretation function explicitly. So we will be able to say things like, "The language a* is infinite."

6.2 Kleene's Theorem

The regular expression language that we have just described is significant for two reasons:

- It is a useful way to define patterns.
- The languages that can be defined with regular expressions are, as the name perhaps suggests, exactly the regular languages. In other words, any language that can be defined by a regular expression can be accepted by some finite state machine. And any language that can be accepted by a finite state machine can be defined by some regular expressions.

In this section, we will state and prove as a theorem the claim that we just made: The class of languages that can be defined with regular expressions is exactly the regular languages. This is the first of several claims of this sort that we will make in this book. In each case, we will assert that some set A is identical to some very different looking set B. The proof strategy that we will use in all of these cases is the same. We will first prove that every element of A is also an element of B. We will then prove that every element of B is also an element of A. Thus, since A and B contain the same elements, they are the same set.

6.2.1 Building an FSM from a Regular Expression

THEOREM 6.1 For Every Regular Expression There is an Equivalent FSM

Theorem: Any language that can be defined with a regular expression can be accepted by some FSM and so is regular.

Proof: The proof is by construction. We will show that, given a regular expression α, we can construct an FSM M such that $L(\alpha) = L(M)$.

We first show that there exists an FSM that corresponds to each primitive regular expression:

- If α is any $c \in \Sigma$, we construct for it the simple FSM shown in Figure 6.1 (a).
- If α is $\varnothing$, we construct for it the simple FSM shown in Figure 6.1 (b).
- Although it's not strictly necessary to consider ε since it has the same meaning as $\varnothing^*$ we'll do so since we don't usually think of it that way. So, if α is ε, we construct for it the simple FSM shown in Figure 6.1 (c),

Next we must show how to build FSMs to accept languages that are defined by regular expressions that exploit the operations of concatenation, union, and Kleene star. Let β and γ be regular expressions that define languages over the alphabet Σ. If $L(\beta)$ is regular, then it is accepted by some FSM $M_1 = (K_1, \Sigma, \delta_1, s_1, A_1)$. If $L(\gamma)$ is regular, then it is accepted by some FSM $M_2 = (K_2, \Sigma, \delta_2, s_2, A_2)$.

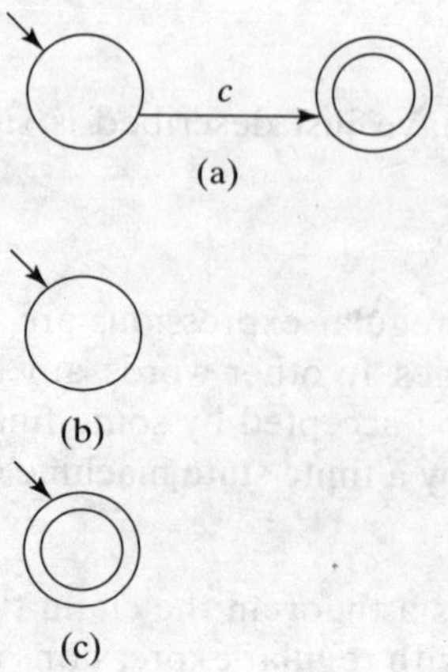

FIGURE 6.1 FSMs for primitive regular expressions.

- If α is the regular expression $\beta \cup \gamma$ and if both $L(\beta)$ and $L(\gamma)$ are regular, then we construct $M_3 = (K_3, \Sigma, \delta_3, s_3, A_3)$ such that $L(M_3) = L(\alpha) = L(\beta) \cup L(\gamma)$. If necessary, rename the states of M_1 and M_2 so that $K_1 \cap K_2 = \varnothing$. Create a new start state, s_3, and connect it to the start states of M_1 and M_2 via ε-transitions. M_3 accepts iff either M_1 or M_2 accepts. So $M_3 = (\{s_3\} \cup K_1 \cup K_2, \Sigma, \delta_3, s_3, A_1 \cup A_2)$, where $\delta_3 = \delta_1 \cup \delta_2 \cup \{((s_3, \varepsilon), s_1), ((s_3, \varepsilon), s_2)\}$.
- If α is the regular expression $\beta\gamma$ and if both $L(\beta)$ and $L(\gamma)$ are regular, then we construct $M_3 = (K_3, \Sigma, \delta_3, s_3, A_3)$ such that $L(M_3) = L(\alpha) = L(\beta)L(\gamma)$. If necessary, rename the states of M_1 and M_2 so that $K_1 \cap K_2 = \varnothing$. We will build M_3 by connecting every accepting state of M_1 to the start state of M_2 via an ε-transition. M_3 will start in the start state of M_1 and will accept iff M_2 does. So $M_3 = (K_1 \cup K_2, \Sigma, \delta_3, s_1, A_2)$, where $\delta_3 = \delta_1 \cup \delta_2 \cup \{((q, \varepsilon), s_2) : q \in A_1\}$.
- If α is the regular expression β^* and if $L(\beta)$ is regular, then we construct $M_2 = (K_2, \Sigma, \delta_2, s_2, A_2)$ such that $L(M_2) = L(\alpha) = L(\beta)^*$. We will create a new start state s_2 and make it accepting, thus assuring that M_2 accepts ε. (We need a new start state because it is possible that s_1, the start state of M_1, is not an accepting state. If it isn't and if it is reachable via any input string other than ε, then simply making it an accepting state would cause M_2 to accept strings that are not in $(L(M_1))^*$.) We link the new s_2 to s_1 via an ε-transitions. Finally, we create ε-transitions from each of M_1's accepting states back to s_1. So $M_2 = (\{s_2\} \cup K_1, \Sigma, \delta_2, s_2, \{s_2\} \cup A_1)$, where $\delta_2 = \delta_1 \cup \{((s_2, \varepsilon), s_1)\} \cup \{((q, \varepsilon), s_1) : q \in A_1\}$.

Notice that the machines that these constructions build are typically highly nondeterministic because of their use of ε-transitions. They also typically have a large number of unnecessary states. But, as a practical matter, that is not a problem since, given an arbitrary NDFSM M, we have an algorithm that can construct an equivalent DFSM M'. We also have an algorithm that can minimize M'.

Based on the constructions that have just been described, we can define the following algorithm to construct, given a regular expression α, a corresponding (usually nondeterministic) FSM:

regextofsm(α: regular expression) =

Beginning with the primitive subexpressions of α and working outwards until an FSM for all of α has been built do:

Construct an FSM as described above.

> The fact that regular expressions can be transformed into executable finite state machines is important. It means that people can specify programs as regular expressions and then have those expressions "compiled" into efficient processes. For example, hierarchically structured regular expressions, with the same formal power as the regular expressions we have been working with, can be used to describe a lightweight parser for analyzing legacy software. (H.4.1)

EXAMPLE 6.5 Building an FSM from a Regular Expression

Consider the regular expression (b ∪ ab)*. We use *regextofsm* to build an FSM that accepts the language defined by this regular expression:

An FSM for b

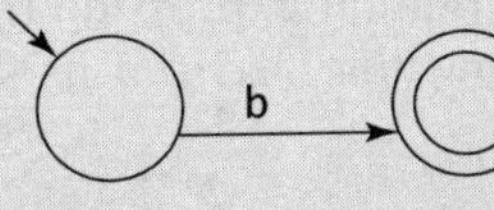

An FSM for a

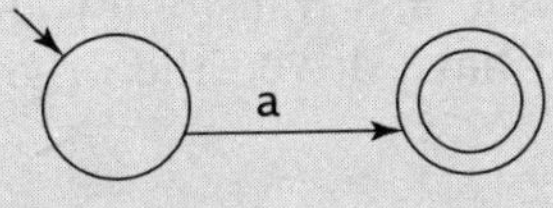

An FSM for b

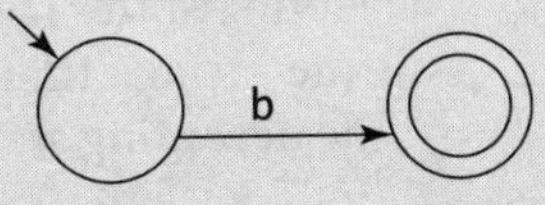

An FSM for ab:

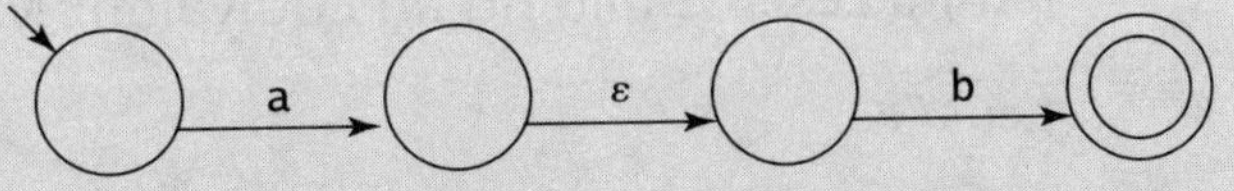

An FSM for (b ∪ ab):

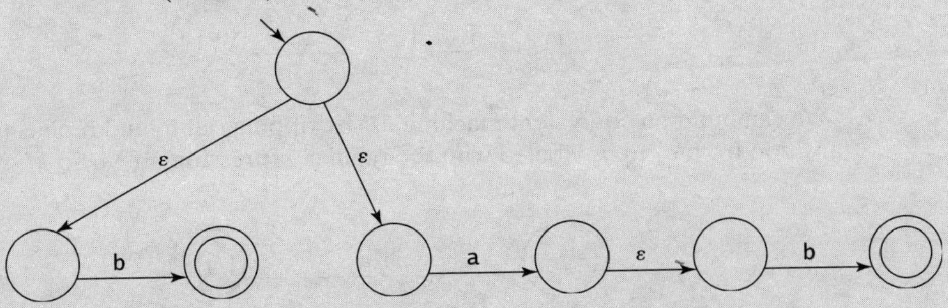

EXAMPLE 6.5 ***(Continued)***

An FSM for (b ∪ ab)*

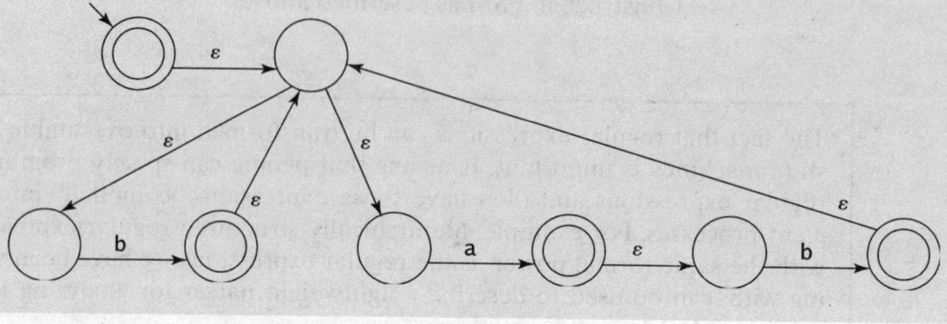

6.2.2 Building a Regular Expression from an FSM

Next we must show that it is possible to go the other direction, namely to build, from an FSM, a corresponding regular expression. The idea behind the algorithm that we are about to present is the following: Instead of limiting the labels on the transitions of an FSM to a single character or ε, we will allow entire regular expressions as labels. The goal of the algorithm is to construct, from an input FSM M, an output machine M' such that M and M' are equivalent and M' has only two states, a start state and a single accepting state. It will also have just one transition, which will go from its start state to its accepting state. The label on that transition will be a regular expression that describes all the strings that could have driven the original machine M from its start state to some accepting state.

EXAMPLE 6.6 Building an Equivalent Machine *M*

Let M be:

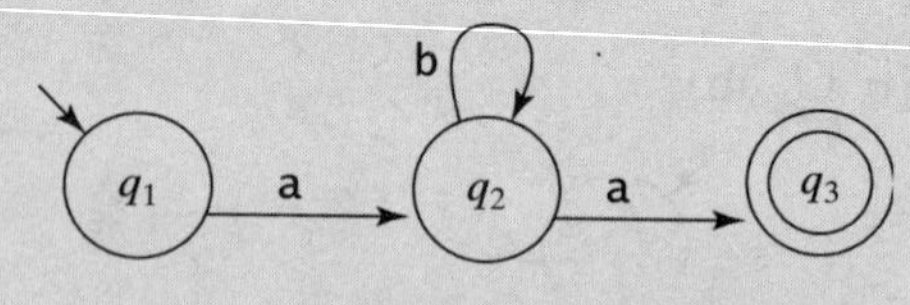

We can build an equivalent machine M' by ripping out q_2 and replacing it by a transition from q_1 to q_3 labeled with the regular expression ab *a. So M' is:

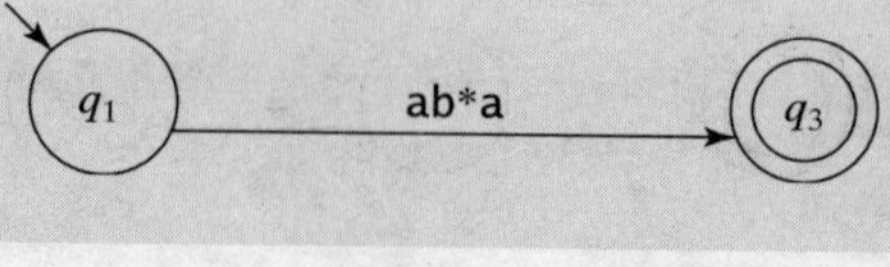

Given an arbitrary FSM M, M' will be built by starting with M and then removing, one at a time, all the states that lie in between the start state and an accepting state. As each such state is removed, the remaining transitions will be modified so that the set of strings that can drive M' from its start state to some accepting state remains unchanged.

The following algorithm creates a regular expression that defines $L(M)$, provided that step 6 can be executed correctly:

fsmtoregexheuristic(M: FSM) =

1. Remove from M any states that are unreachable from the start state.
2. If M has no accepting states then halt and return the simple regular expression $\varnothing$.
3. If the start state of M is part of a loop (i.e., it has any transitions coming into it), create a new start state s and connect s to M's start state via an ε-transition. This new start state s will have no transitions into it.
4. If there is more than one accepting state of M or if there is just one but there are any transitions out of it, create a new accepting state and connect each of M's accepting states to it via an ε-transition. Remove the old accepting states from the set of accepting states. Note that the new accepting state will have no transitions out from it.
5. If, at this point, M has only one state, then that state is both the start state and the accepting state and M has no transitions. So $L(M) = \{\varepsilon\}$. Halt and return the simple regular expression ε.
6. Until only the start state and the accepting state remain do:
   - **6.1.** Select some state *rip* of M. Any state except the start state or the accepting state may be chosen.
   - **6.2.** Remove *rip* from M.
   - **6.3.** Modify the transitions among the remaining states so that M accepts the same strings. The labels on the rewritten transitions may be any regular expression.
7. Return the regular expression that labels the one remaining transition from the start state to the accepting state.

EXAMPLE 6.7 Building a Regular Expression from an FSM

Let M be:

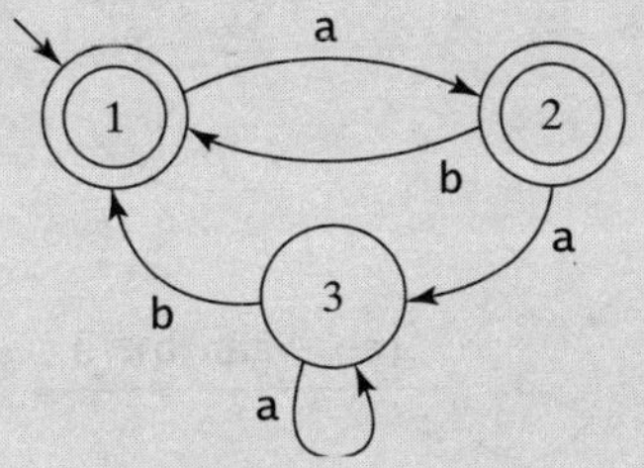

EXAMPLE 6.7 *(Continued)*

Create a new start state and a new accepting state and link them to M:

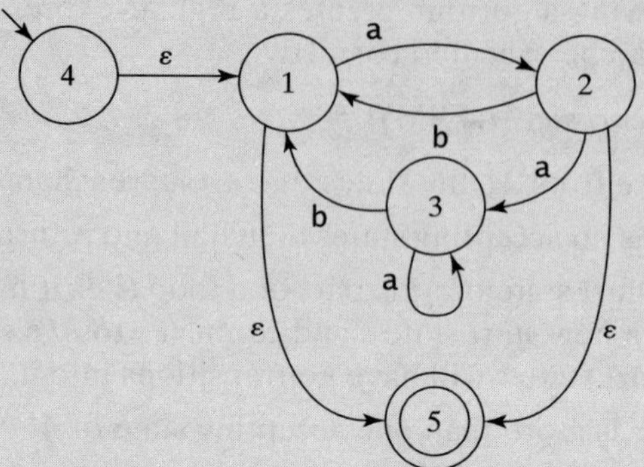

Remove state 3:

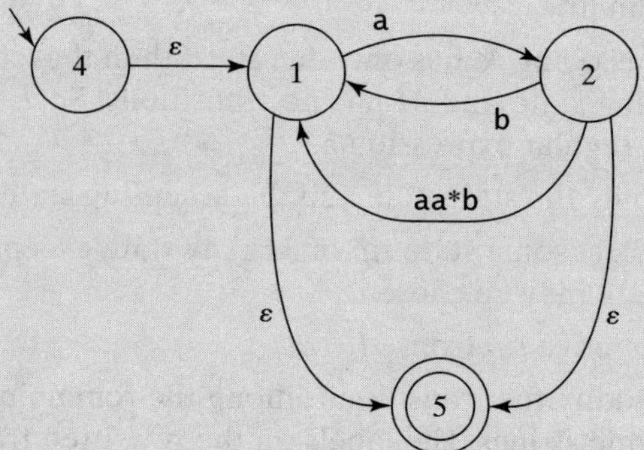

Remove state 2:

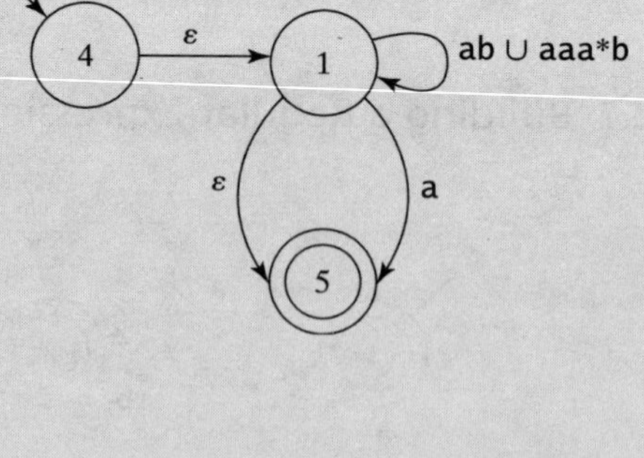

Remove state 1:

EXAMPLE 6.8 A Simple FSM With No Simple Regular Expression

Let M be the FSM that we built in Example 5.9 for the language $L = \{w \in \{\text{a}, \text{b}\}^* : w$ contains an even number of a's and an odd number of b's$\}$. M is:

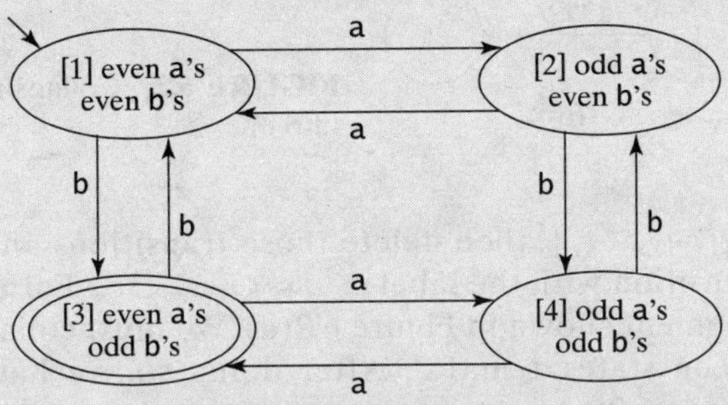

Try to apply *fsmtoregexheuristic* to M. It will not be easy because it is not at all obvious how to implement step 6.3. For example, if we attempt to remove state [2], this changes not just the way that M can move from state [1] to state [4]. It also changes, for example, the way that M can move from state [1] to state [3] because it changes how M can move from state [1] back to itself.

To prove that for every FSM there exists a corresponding regular expression will require a construction in which we make clearer what must be done each time a state is removed and replaced by a regular expression. The algorithm that we are about to describe has that property, although it comes at the expense of simplicity in easy cases such as the one in Example 6.7.

THEOREM 6.2 For Every FSM There is an Equivalent Regular Expression

Theorem: Every regular language (i.e., every language that can be accepted by some FSM) can be defined with a regular expression.

Proof: The proof is by construction. Given an FSM $M = (K, \Sigma, \delta, s, A)$, we can construct a regular expression α such that $L(M) = L(\alpha)$.

As we did in *fsmtoregexheuristic*, we will begin by assuring that M has no unreachable states and that it has a start state that has no transitions into it and a single accepting state that has no transitions out from it. But now we will make a further important modification to M before we start removing states: From every state other than the accepting state there must be exactly one transition to every state (including itself) except the start state. And into every state other than the start state there must be exactly one transition from every state (including itself) except the accepting state. To make this true, we do two things:

- If there is more than one transition between states p and q, collapse them into a single transition. If the set of labels on the original set of such transitions is

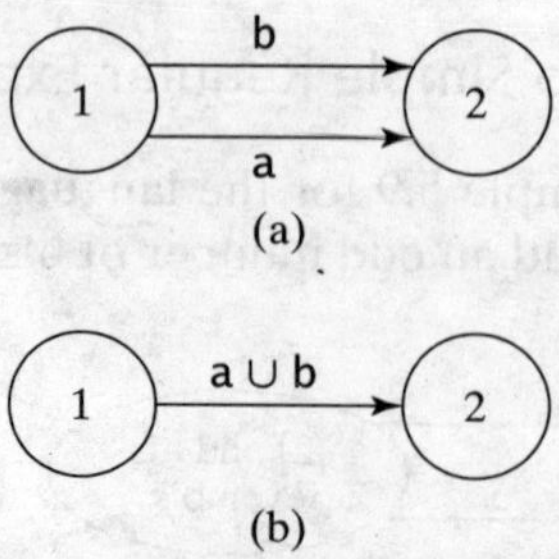

FIGURE 6.2 Collapsing multiple transitions into one.

$\{c_1, c_2, \ldots, c_n\}$, then delete those transitions and replace them by a single transition with the label $c_1 \cup c_2 \cup \ldots \cup c_n$. For example, consider the FSM fragment shown in Figure 6.2(a). We must collapse the two transitions between states 1 and 2. After doing so, we have the fragment shown in Figure 6.2(b).

- If any of the required transitions are missing, add them. We can add all of those transitions without changing $L(M)$ by labeling all of the new transitions with the regular expression $\varnothing$. So there is no string that will allow them to be taken. For example, let M be the FSM shown in Figure 6.3(a). Several new transitions are required. When we add them, we have the new FSM shown in Figure 6.3(b).

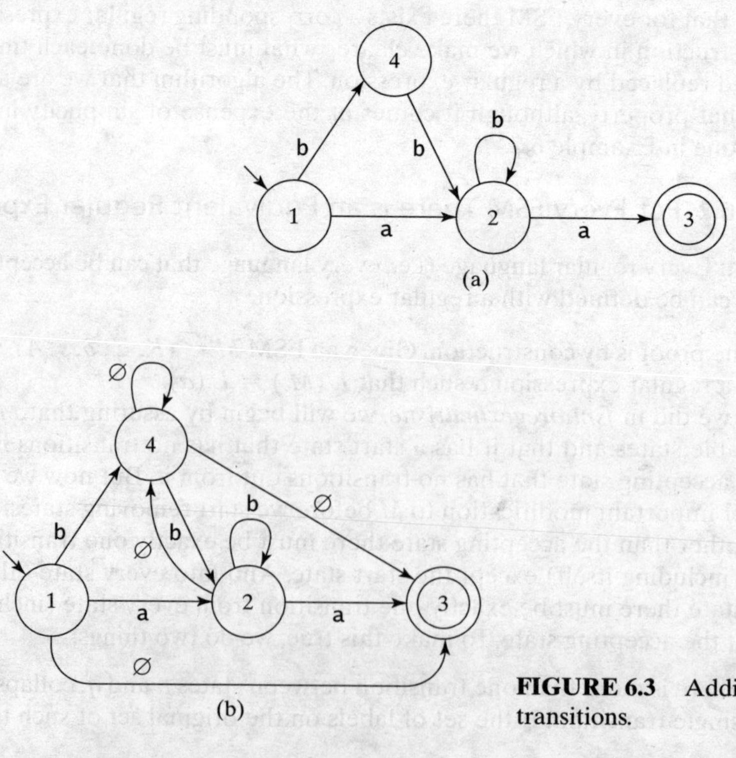

FIGURE 6.3 Adding all the required transitions.

Now suppose that we select a state *rip* and remove it and the transitions into and out of it. Then we must modify every remaining transition so that *M*'s function stays the same. Since *M* already contains a transition between each pair of states (except the ones that are not allowed into and out of the start and accepting states), if all those transitions are modified correctly then *M*'s behavior will be correct.

So, suppose that we remove some state that we will call *rip*. How should the remaining transitions be changed? Consider any pair of states *p* and *q*. Once we remove *rip*, how can *M* get from *p* to *q*?

- It can still take the transition that went directly from *p* to *q*, or
- It can take the transition from *p* to *rip*. Then, it can take the transition from *rip* back to itself zero or more times. Then it can take the transition from *rip* to *q*.

Let $R(p, q)$ be the regular expression that labels the transition in *M* from *p* to *q*. Then, in the new machine M' that will be created by removing *rip*, the new regular expression that should label the transition from *p* to *q* is:

$R(p, q)$	/* Go directly from *p* to *q*,
$\cup$	/* or
$R(p, rip)$	/* go from *p* to *rip*, then
$R(rip, rip)^*$	/*go from *rip* back to itself any number of times, then
$R(rip, q)$	/* go from *rip* to *q*.

We'll denote this new regular expression $R'(p, q)$. Writing it out without the comments, we have:

$$R' = R(p, q) \cup R(p, rip)R(rip, rip)^*R(rip, q).$$

EXAMPLE 6.9 Ripping States Out One at a Time

Again, let *M* be:

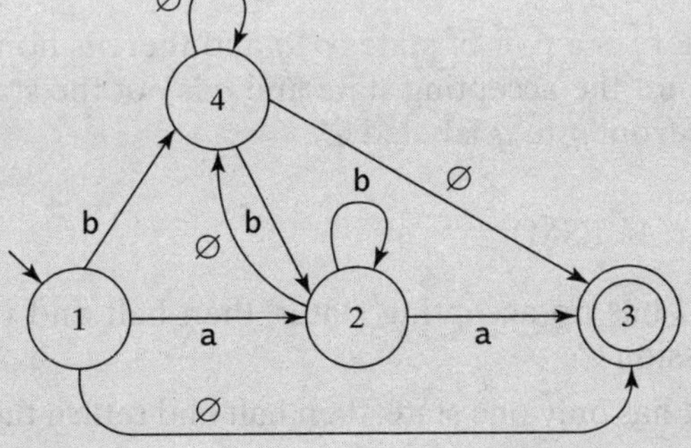

Let *rip* be state 2. Then:

$$R'(1, 3) = R(1, 3) \cup R(1, rip)R(rip, rip)^*R(rip, 3).$$
$$= R(1, 3) \cup R(1, 2)R(2, 2)^*R(2, 3).$$

EXAMPLE 6.9 *(Continued)*

$= \varnothing \cup a \quad b^* \quad a.$

$= ab^*a.$

Notice that ripping state 2 also changes another way the original machine had to get from state 1 to state 3: It could have gone from state 1 to state 4 to state 2 and then to state 3. But we don't have to worry about that in computing $R'(1, 3)$. The required change to that path will occur when we compute $R'(4, 3)$.

When all states except the start state s and the accepting state a have been removed, $R(s, a)$ will describe the set of strings that can drive M from its start state to its accepting state. So $R(s, a)$ will describe $L(M)$.

We can now define an algorithm to build, from any FSM $M = (K, \Sigma, \delta, s, A)$, a regular expression that describes $L(M)$. We'll use two subroutines, *standardize*, which will convert M to the required form, and *buildregex*, which will construct, from the modified machine M, the required regular expression.

standardize(M: FSM) =

1. Remove from M any states that are unreachable from the start state.
2. If the start state of M is part of a loop (i.e., it has any transitions coming into it), create a new start state s and connect s to M's start state via an ε-transition.
3. If there is more than one accepting state of M or if there is just one but there are any transitions out of it, create a new accepting state and connect each of M's accepting states to it via an ε-transition. Remove the old accepting states from the set of accepting states.
4. If there is more than one transition between states p and q, collapse them into a single transition.
5. If there is a pair of states p, q and there is no transition between them and p is not the accepting state and q is not the start state, then create a transition from p to q labeled $\varnothing$.

buildregex(M: FSM) =

1. If M has no accepting states, then halt and return the simple regular expression $\varnothing$.
2. If M has only one state, then halt and return the simple regular expression ε.
3. Until only the start state and the accepting state remain do:

   3.1. Select some state *rip* of M. Any state except the start state or the accepting state may be chosen.

3.2. For every transition from some state p to some state q, if both p and q are not *rip* then, using the current labels given by the expressions R, compute the new label R' for the transition from p to q using the formula:

$$R'(p, q) = R(p, q) \cup R(p, rip)R(rip, rip)^*R(rip, q).$$

3.3. Remove *rip* and all transitions into and out of it.

4. Return the regular expression that labels the one remaining transition from the start state to the accepting state.

We can show that the new FSM that is built by *standardize* is equivalent to the original machine (i.e., that they accept the same language) by showing that the language that is accepted is preserved at each step of the procedure. We can show that *buildregex*(M) builds a regular expression that correctly defines $L(M)$ by induction on the number of states that must be removed before it halts. Using those two procedures, we can now define:

fsmtoregex(M: FSM) =

1. M' = *standardize* (M).
2. Return *buildregex*(M').

6.2.3 The Equivalence of Regular Expressions and FSMs

The last two theorems enable us to prove the next one, due to Stephen Kleene 🖳.

THEOREM 6.3 Kleene's Theorem

Theorem: The class of languages that can be defined with regular expressions is exactly the class of regular languages.

Proof: Theorem 6.1 says that every language that can be defined with a regular expression is regular. Theorem 6.2 says that every regular language can be defined by some regular expression.

6.2.4 Kleene's Theorem, Regular Expressions, and Finite State Machines

Kleene's Theorem tells us that there is no difference between the formal power of regular expressions and finite state machines. But, as some of the examples that we just considered suggest, there is a practical difference in their effectiveness as problem solving tools:

- As we said in the introduction to this chapter, the regular expression language is a pattern language. In particular, regular expressions must specify the order in which a sequence of symbols must occur. This is useful when we want to describe patterns such as phone numbers (it matters that the area code comes first) or email addresses (it matters that the user name comes before the domain).

- But there are some applications where order doesn't matter. The vending machine example that we considered at the beginning of Chapter 5 is an instance of this class of problem. The order in which the coins were entered doesn't matter. Parity checking is another. Only the total number of 1 bits matters, not where they occur in the string. Finite state machines can be very effective in solving problems such as this. But the regular expressions that correspond to those FSMs may be too complex to be useful.

The bottom line is that sometimes it is easy to write a finite state machine to describe a language. For other problems, it may be easier to write a regular expression.

Sometimes Writing Regular Expressions is Easy

Because, for some problems, regular expressions are easy to write, Kleene's theorem is useful. It gives us a second way to show that a language is regular. We need only show a regular expression that defines it.

EXAMPLE 6.10 No More Than One b

Let $L = \{w \in \{\text{a}, \text{b}\}^* : \text{there is no more than one b}\}$. L is regular because it can be described with the following regular expression:

$$\text{a}^* \ (\text{b} \cup \varepsilon) \ \text{a}^*.$$

EXAMPLE 6.11 No Two Consecutive Letters are the Same

Let $L = \{w \in \{\text{a}, \text{b}\}^* : \text{no two consecutive letters are the same}\}$. L is regular because it can be described with either of the following regular expressions:

$$(\text{b} \cup \varepsilon) \ (\text{ab})^* \ (\text{a} \cup \varepsilon).$$

$$(\text{a} \cup \varepsilon) \ (\text{ba})^* \ (\text{b} \cup \varepsilon).$$

EXAMPLE 6.12 Floating Point Numbers

Consider again FLOAT, the language of floating point numbers that we described in Example 5.7. Kleene's Theorem tells us that, since FLOAT is regular, there must be some regular expression that describes it. In fact, regular expressions can be used easily to describe languages like FLOAT. We'll use one shorthand. Let:

D stand for $(0 \cup 1 \cup 2 \cup 3 \cup 4 \cup 5 \cup 6 \cup 7 \cup 8 \cup 9)$.

Then FLOAT is the language described by the following regular expression:

$$(\varepsilon \cup + \cup -)D^+ \ (\varepsilon \cup \ .D^+) \ (\varepsilon \cup \ (\text{E} \ (\varepsilon \cup + \cup -)D^+).$$

It is useful to think of programs, queries, and other strings in practical languages as being composed of a sequence of tokens, where a token is the smallest string that has meaning. So variable and function names, numbers and other constants, operators, and reserved words are all tokens. The regular expression we just wrote for the language FLOAT describes one kind of token. The first thing a compiler does, after reading its input, is to divide it into tokens. That process is called lexical analysis. It is common to use regular expressions to define the behavior of a lexical analyzer. (G.4.1)

Sometimes Building a Deterministic FSM is Easy

Given an arbitrary regular expression, the general algorithms presented in the proof of Theorem 6.1 will typically construct a highly nondeterministic FSM. But there is a useful special case in which it is possible to construct a DFSM directly from a set of patterns. Suppose that we are given a set K of n keywords and a text string s. We want to find occurrences in s of the keywords in K. We can think of K as defining a language that can be described by a regular expression of the form:

$$(\Sigma^*(k_1 \cup k_2 \cup \ldots \cup k_n)\Sigma^*)^+.$$

In other words, we will accept any string in which at least one keyword occurs. For some applications this will be good enough. For others, we may care which keyword was matched. For yet others we'll want to find all substrings that match some keyword in K.

By letting the keywords correspond to sequences of amino acids, this idea can be used to build a fast search engine for protein databases. (K.3)

In any of these special cases, we can build a deterministic FSM M by first building a decision tree out of the set of keywords and then adding arcs as necessary to tell M what to do when it reaches a dead end branch of the tree. The following algorithm builds an FSM that accepts any string that contains at least one of the specified keywords:

buildkeywordFSM(K: set of keywords) =

1. Create a start state q_0.
2. For each element k of K do:

   Create a branch corresponding to k.
3. Create a set of transitions that describe what to do when a branch dies, either because its complete pattern has been found or because the next character is not the correct one to continue the pattern.
4. Make the states at the ends of each branch accepting.

EXAMPLE 6.13 Recognizing a Set of Keywords

Consider the set of keywords {`cat`, `bat`, `cab`}. We can use *buildkeywordFSM* to build a DFSM to accept strings that contain at least one of these keywords. We begin by creating a start state and then a path to accept the first keyword, `cat`:

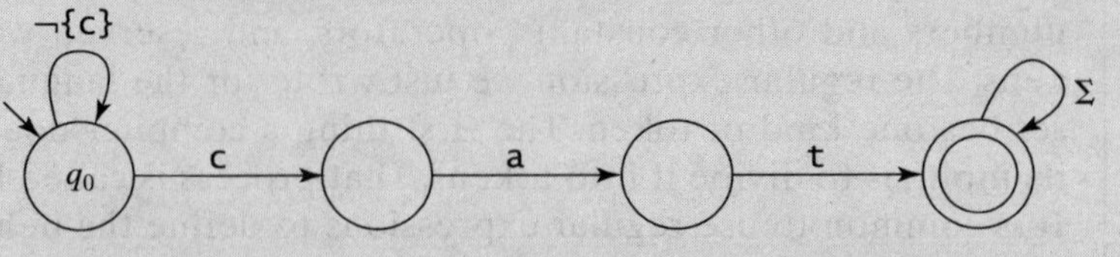

Next we add branches for the remaining keywords, `bat` and `cab`:

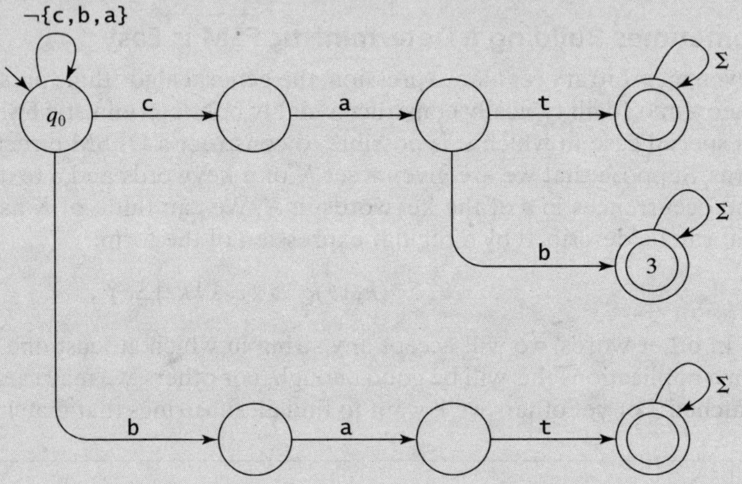

Finally, we add transitions that let the machine recover after a path dies:

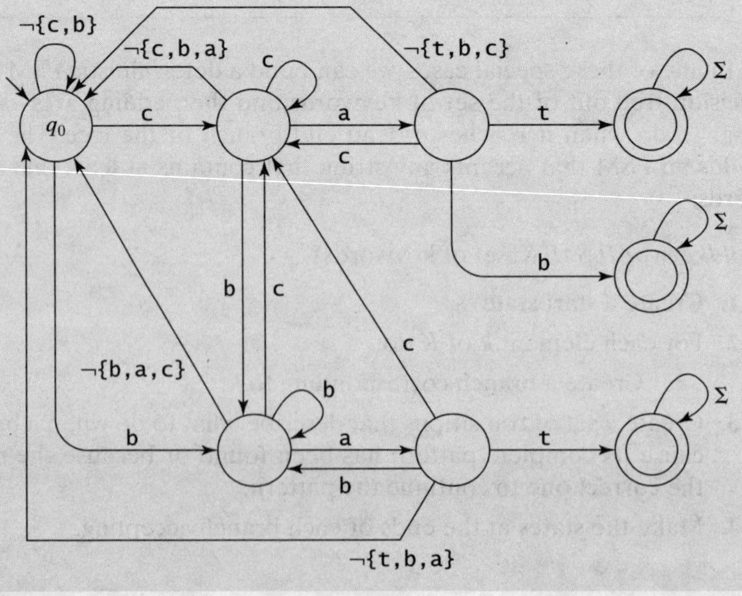

6.3 Applications of Regular Expressions

Patterns are everywhere.

> Regular expressions can be matched against the subject fields of emails to find at least some of the ones that are likely to be spam. (O.1)

Because patterns are everywhere, applications of regular expressions are everywhere. Before we look at some specific examples, one important caveat is required: The term *regular expression* is used in the modern computing world in a much more general way than we have defined it here. Many programming languages and scripting systems provide support for regular expression matching. Each of them has its own syntax. They all have the basic operators union, concatenation, and Kleene star. They typically have others as well. Many, for example, have a substitution operator so that, after a pattern is successfully matched against a string, a new string can be produced. In many cases, these other operators provide enough additional power that languages that are not regular can be described. So, in discussing "regular expressions" or "regexes", it is important to be clear exactly what definition is being used. In the rest of this book, we will use the definition that we presented in Section 6.1, with two additions to be described below, unless we clearly state that, for some particular purpose, we are going to use a different definition.

> The programming language Perl, for example, supports regular expression matching. (Appendix O) In Exercise 6.19, we'll consider the formal power of the Perl regular expression language.

Real applications need more than two or three characters. But we do not want to have to write expressions like:

$$(\mathtt{a} \cup \mathtt{b} \cup \mathtt{c} \cup \mathtt{d} \cup \mathtt{e} \cup \mathtt{f} \cup \mathtt{g} \cup \mathtt{h} \cup \mathtt{i} \cup \mathtt{j} \cup \mathtt{k} \cup \mathtt{l} \cup \mathtt{m} \cup \mathtt{n} \cup \mathtt{o} \cup \mathtt{p} \cup \mathtt{q} \cup \mathtt{r} \cup \mathtt{s} \cup \mathtt{t} \cup \mathtt{u} \cup \mathtt{v} \cup \mathtt{w} \cup \mathtt{x} \cup \mathtt{y} \cup \mathtt{z}).$$

It would be much more convenient to be able to write (a-z). So, in cases where there is an agreed upon collating sequence, we will use the shorthand $(\alpha - \omega)$ to mean $(\alpha \cup \ldots \cup \omega)$, where all the characters in the collating sequence between α and ω are included in the union.

EXAMPLE 6.14 Decimal Numbers

The following regular expression matches decimal encodings of numbers:

$$\texttt{-? ([0-9]}^+\texttt{(\textbackslash.[0-9]*)? | \textbackslash.[0-9]}^+\texttt{)}$$

EXAMPLE 6.14 *(Continued)*

In most standard regular expression dialects, the notation $\alpha?$ is equivalent to $(\alpha \cup \varepsilon)$. In other words, α is optional. So, in this example, the minus sign is optional. So is the decimal point.

Because the symbol . has a special meaning in most regular expression dialects, we must quote it when we want to match it as a literal character. The quote character in most regular expression dialects is \.

> Meaningful "words" in protein sequences are called motifs. They can be described with regular expressions. (K.3.2)

EXAMPLE 6.15 Legal Passwords

Consider the problem of determining whether a string is a legal password. Suppose that we require that all passwords meet the following requirements:

- A password must begin with a letter.
- A password may contain only letters, numbers, and the underscore character.
- A password must contain at least four characters and no more than eight characters.

The following regular expression describes the language of legal passwords. The line breaks have no significance. We have used them just to make the expression easier to read.

((a-z) ∪ (A-Z))
((a-z) ∪ (A-Z) ∪ (0-9) ∪ _)
((a-z) ∪ (A-Z) ∪ (0-9) ∪ _)
((a-z) ∪ (A-Z) ∪ (0-9) ∪ _)
((a-z) ∪ (A-Z) ∪ (0-9) ∪ _ ∪ ε)
((a-z) ∪ (A-Z) ∪ (0-9) ∪ _ ∪ ε)
((a-z) ∪ (A-Z) ∪ (0-9) ∪ _ ∪ ε)
((a-z) ∪ (A-Z) ∪ (0-9) ∪ _ ∪ ε).

While straightforward, the regular expression that we just wrote is a nuisance to write and not very easy to read. The problem is that, so far, we have only three ways to specify how many times a pattern must occur:

- α means that the pattern α must occur exactly once.
- α^* means that the pattern α may occur any number (including zero) of times.
- α^+ means that the pattern α may occur any positive number of times.

What we needed in the previous example was a way to specify how many times a pattern α should occur. We can do this with the following notations:

- $\alpha\{n, m\}$ means that the pattern α must occur at least n times and no more than m times.
- $\alpha\{n\}$ means that the pattern α must occur exactly n times.

Using this notation, we can rewrite the regular expression of Example 6.15 as:

((a-z) ∪ (A-Z)) ((a-z) ∪ (A-Z) ∪ (0-9) ∪ _){3, 7}.

EXAMPLE 6.16 IP Addresses

The following regular expression searches for Internet (IP) addresses:

```
([0-9]{1, 3} (\. [0-9]{1, 3}){3}).
```

In XML, regular expressions are one way to define parts of new document types. (Q.1.2)

6.4 Manipulating and Simplifying Regular Expressions

The regular expressions (a ∪ b)* (a ∪ b)* and (a ∪ b)* define the same language. The second one is simpler than the first and thus easier to work with. In this section we discuss techniques for manipulating and simplifying regular expressions. All of these techniques are based on the equivalence of the languages that the regular expressions define. So we will say that, for two regular expressions α and β, $\alpha = \beta$ if $L(\alpha) = L(\beta)$.

We first consider identities that follow from the fact that the meaning of every regular expression is a language, which means that it is a set:

- Union is commutative: For any regular expressions α and β, $\alpha \cup \beta = \beta \cup \alpha$.
- Union is associative: For any regular expressions α, β, and γ, $(\alpha \cup \beta) \cup \gamma = \alpha \cup (\beta \cup \gamma)$.
- $\varnothing$ is the identity for union: For any regular expression α, $\alpha \cup \varnothing = \varnothing \cup \alpha = \alpha$.
- Union is idempotent: For any regular expression α, $\alpha \cup \alpha = \alpha$.
- Given any two sets A and B, if $B \subseteq A$, then $A \cup B = A$. So, for example, a* ∪ aa = a*, since $L(\text{aa}) \subseteq L(\text{a}^*)$.

Next we consider identities involving concatenation:

- Concatenation is associative: For any regular expressions α, β, and γ, $(\alpha\beta)\gamma = \alpha(\beta\gamma)$.

- ε is the identity for concatenation: For any regular expression α, $\alpha\,\varepsilon = \varepsilon\,\alpha = \alpha$.
- $\varnothing$ is a zero for concatenation: For any regular expression α, $\alpha\,\varnothing = \varnothing\,\alpha = \varnothing$.

Concatenation distributes over union:

- For any regular expressions α, β, and γ, $(\alpha \cup \beta)\gamma = (\alpha\gamma) \cup (\beta\gamma)$. Every string in either of these languages is composed of a first part followed by a second part. The first part must be drawn from $L(\alpha)$ or $L(\beta)$. The second part must be drawn from $L(\gamma)$.
- For any regular expressions α, β, and γ, $\gamma(\alpha \cup \beta) = (\gamma\alpha) \cup (\gamma\beta)$. (By a similar argument.)

Finally, we introduce identities involving Kleene star:

- $\varnothing^* = \varepsilon$.
- $\varepsilon^* = \varepsilon$.
- For any regular expression α, $(\alpha^*)^* = \alpha^*$. $L(\alpha^*)$ contains all and only the strings that are composed of zero or more strings from $L(\alpha)$, concatenated together. All of them are also in $L((\alpha^*)^*)$ since $L((\alpha^*)^*)$ contains, among other things, every individual string in $L(\alpha^*)$. No other strings are in $L((\alpha^*)^*)$ since it can contain only strings that are formed from concatenating together elements of $L(\alpha^*)$, which are in turn concatenations of strings from $L(\alpha)$.
- For any regular expression α, $\alpha^*\alpha^* = \alpha^*$. Every string in either of these languages is composed of zero or more strings from α concatenated together.
- More generally, for any regular expressions α and β, if $L(\alpha^*) \subseteq L(\beta^*)$ then $\alpha^*\beta^* = \beta^*$. For example:

$$a^*(a \cup b)^* = (a \cup b)^*, \text{ since } L(a^*) \subseteq L((a \cup b)^*).$$

  α is redundant because any string it can generate and place at the beginning of a string to be generated by the combined expression $\alpha^*\beta^*$ can also be generated by β^*.
- Similarly, if $L(\beta^*) \subseteq L(\alpha^*)$ then $\alpha^*\beta^* = \alpha^*$.
- For any regular expressions α and β, $(\alpha \cup \beta)^* = (\alpha^*\beta^*)^*$. To form a string in either language, a generator must walk through the Kleene star loop zero or more times. Using the first expression, each time through the loop it chooses either a string from $L(\alpha)$ or a string from $L(\beta)$. That process can be copied using the second expression by picking exactly one string from $L(\alpha)$ and then ε from $L(\beta)$ or one string from $L(\beta)$ and then ε from $L(\alpha)$. Using the second expression, a generator can pick a sequence of strings from $L(\alpha)$ and then a sequence of strings from $L(\beta)$ each time through the loop. But that process can be copied using the first expression by simply selecting each element of the sequence one at a time on successive times through the loop.
- For any regular expressions α and β, if $L(\beta) \subseteq L(\alpha^*)$ then $(\alpha \cup \beta)^* = \alpha^*$. For example, $(a \cup \varepsilon)^* = a^*$, since $\{\varepsilon\} \subseteq L(a^*)$. β is redundant since any string it can generate can also be generated by α^*.

EXAMPLE 6.17 Simplifying a Regular Expression

((a* ∪ ∅)* ∪ aa) (b ∪ bb)* b* ((a ∪ b)* b* ∪ ab) * =	/* L(∅) ⊆ L(a*).
((a*)* ∪ aa) (b ∪ bb)* b* ((a ∪ b)* b* ∪ ab) * =	
(a* ∪ aa) (b ∪ bb)* b* ((a ∪ b)* b* ∪ ab) * =	/* L(aa) ⊆ L(a*).
a* (b ∪ bb)*b* ((a ∪ b)* b* ∪ ab) * =	/* L(bb) ⊆ L(b*).
a* b* b* ((a ∪ b)* b * ∪ ab)* =	
a* b* ((a ∪ b)* b* ∪ ab) * =	/* L(b*) ⊆ L((a ∪ b)*).
a* b* ((a ∪ b)* ∪ ab) * =	/* L(ab) ⊆ L((a ∪ b)*).
a* b* ((a ∪ b)*) * =	
a* b* (a ∪ b)* =	/* L(b*) ⊆ L((a ∪ b)*).
a* (a ∪ b)* =	/* L(a*) ⊆ L((a ∪ b)*).
(a ∪ b)*	

Exercises

1. Describe in English, as briefly as possible, the language defined by each of these regular expressions:
   a. (b ∪ ba) (b ∪ a)* (ab ∪ b).
   b. (((a*b*)*ab) ∪ ((a*b*)*ba))(b ∪ a)*.
2. Write a regular expressions to describe each of the following languages:
   a. $\{w \in \{\mathrm{a}, \mathrm{b}\}^*$: every a in w is immediately preceded and followed by b$\}$.
   b. $\{w \in \{\mathrm{a}, \mathrm{b}\}^*$: w does not end in ba$\}$.
   c. $\{w \in \{0, 1\}^* : \exists y \in \{0, 1\}^* (|xy| \text{ is even})\}$.
   d. $\{w \in \{0, 1\}^*$: w corresponds to the binary encoding, without leading 0s, of natural numbers that are evenly divisible by 4$\}$.
   e. $\{w \in \{0, 1\}^*$: w corresponds to the binary encoding, without leading 0s, of natural numbers that are powers of 4$\}$.
   f. $\{w \in \{0\text{-}9\}^*$: w corresponds to the decimal encoding, without leading 0s, of an odd natural number$\}$.
   g. $\{w \in \{0, 1\}^*$: w has 001 as a substring$\}$.
   h. $\{w \in \{0, 1\}^*$: w does not have 001 as a substring$\}$.
   i. $\{w \in \{\mathrm{a}, \mathrm{b}\}^*$: w has bba as a substring$\}$.
   j. $\{w \in \{\mathrm{a}, \mathrm{b}\}^*$: w has both aa and bb as substrings$\}$.
   k. $\{w \in \{\mathrm{a}, \mathrm{b}\}^*$: w has both aa and aba as substrings$\}$.
   l. $\{w \in \{\mathrm{a}, \mathrm{b}\}^*$: w contains at least two b's that are not followed by an a$\}$.
   m. $\{w \in \{0, 1\}^*$: w has at most one pair of consecutive 0s and at most one pair of consecutive 1s$\}$.

n. $\{w \in \{0, 1\}^* :$ none of the prefixes of w ends in $0\}$.

o. $\{w \in \{a, b\}^* : \#_a(w) \equiv_3 0\}$.

p. $\{w \in \{a, b\}^* : \#_a(w) \leq 3\}$.

q. $\{w \in \{a, b\}^* : w$ contains exactly two occurrences of the substring aa$\}$.

r. $\{w \in \{a, b\}^* : w$ contains no more than two occurrences of the substring aa$\}$.

s. $\{w \in \{a, b\}^* - L\}$, where $L = \{w \in \{a, b\}^* : w$ contains bba as a substring$\}$.

t. $\{w \in \{0, 1\}^* :$ every odd length string in L begins with $11\}$.

u. $\{w \in \{0\text{-}9\}^* : w$ represents the decimal encoding of an odd natural number without leading 0s.

v. $L_1 - L_2$, where $L_1 =$ a*b*c* and $L_2 =$ c*b*a*.

w. The set of legal United States zip codes.

x. The set of strings that correspond to domestic telephone numbers in your country.

3. Simplify each of the following regular expressions:

a. $(a \cup b)^* (a \cup \varepsilon) b^*$.

b. $(\varnothing^* \cup b) b^*$.

c. $(a \cup b)^* a^* \cup b$.

d. $((a \cup b)^*)^*$.

e. $((a \cup b)^+)^*$.

f. $a ((a \cup b)(b \cup a))^* \cup a ((a \cup b) a)^* \cup a ((b \cup a) b)^*$.

4. For each of the following expressions E, answer the following three questions and prove your answer:

i. Is E a regular expression?

ii. If E is a regular expression, give a simpler regular expression.

iii. Does E describe a regular language?

a. $((a \cup b) \cup (ab))^*$.

b. $(a^+ a^n b^n)$.

c. $((ab)^* \varnothing)$.

d. $(((ab) \cup c)^* \cap (b \cup c^*))$.

e. $(\varnothing^* \cup (bb^*))$.

5. Let $L = \{a^n b^n : 0 \leq n \leq 4\}$.

a. Show a regular expression for L.

b. Show an FSM that accepts L.

6. Let $L = \{w \in \{1, 2\}^* :$ for all prefixes p of w, if $|p| > 0$ and $|p|$ is even, then the last character of p is $1\}$.

a. Write a regular expression for L.

b. Show an FSM that accepts L.

7. Use the algorithm presented in the proof of Kleene's Theorem to construct an FSM to accept the language generated by each of the following regular expressions:
   a. (b(b ∪ ε)b)*.
   b. bab ∪ a*.
8. Let L be the language accepted by the following finite state machine:

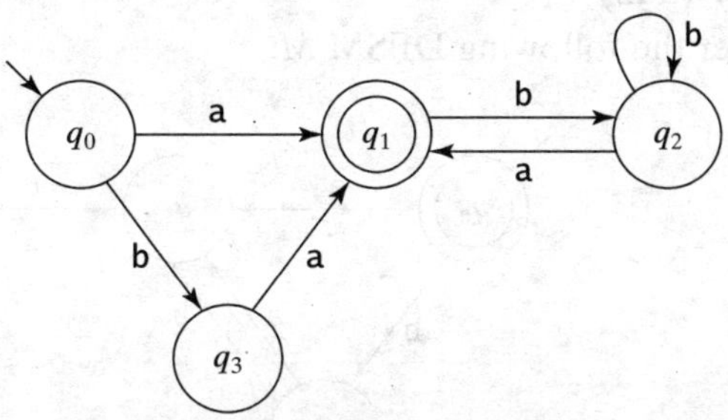

Indicate, for each of the following regular expressions, whether it correctly describes L:
   a. (a ∪ ba)bb*a.
   b. (ε ∪ b)a(bb*a)*.
   c. ba ∪ ab*a.
   d. (a ∪ ba)(bb*a)*.
9. Consider the following FSM M:

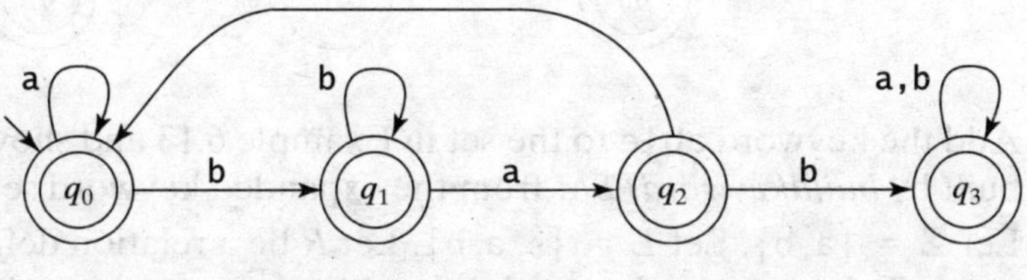

   a. Show a regular expression for $L(M)$.
   b. Describe $L(M)$ in English.
10. Consider the FSM M of Example 5.3. Use *fsmtoregexheuristic* to construct a regular expression that describes $L(M)$.
11. Consider the FSM M of Example 6.9. Apply *fsmtoregex* to M and show the regular expression that results.
12. Consider the FSM M of Example 6.8. Apply *fsmtoregex* to M and show the regular expression that results. (Hint: This one is exceedingly tedious, but it can be done.)
13. Show a possibly nondeterministic FSM to accept the language defined by each of the following regular expressions:
   a. (((a ∪ ba) b ∪ aa)*.
   b. (b ∪ ε)(ab)*(a ∪ ε).
   c. (babb* ∪ a)*.

d. (ba ∪ ((a ∪ bb) a*b)).

e. (a ∪ b)* aa (b ∪ aa) bb (a ∪ b)*.

14. Show a DFSM to accept the language defined by each of the following regular expressions:

a. (aba ∪ aabaa)*.

b. (ab)*(aab)*.

15. Consider the following DFSM M:

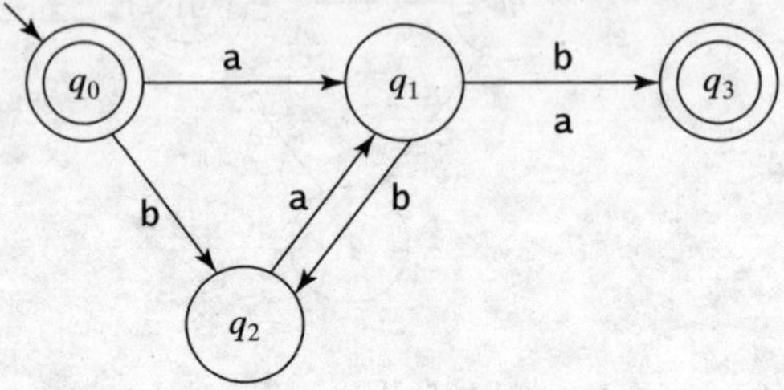

a. Write a regular expression that describes $L(M)$.

b. Show a DFSM that accepts $\neg L(M)$.

16. Given the following DFSM M, write a regular expression that describes $\neg L(M)$:

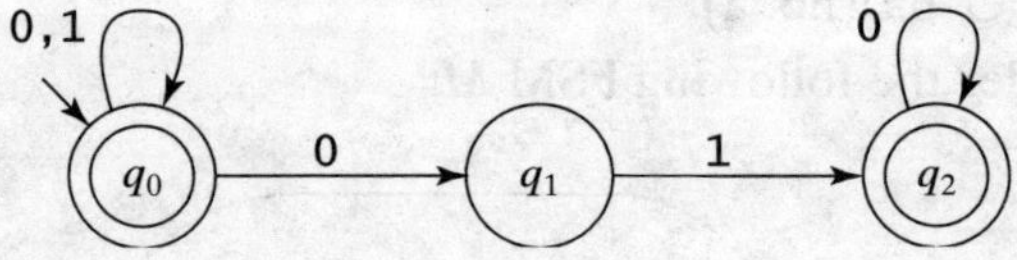

17. Add the keyword able to the set in Example 6.13 and show the FSM that will be built by *buildkeywordFSM* from the expanded keyword set.

18. Let $\Sigma = \{a, b\}$. Let $L = \{\varepsilon, a, b\}$. Let R be a relation defined on Σ^* as follows: $\forall xy\ (xRy \text{ iff } y = xb)$. Let R' be the reflexive, transitive closure of R. Let $L' = \{x : \exists y \in L\ (yR'x)\}$. Write a regular expression for L'.

19. In Appendix O we summarize the main features of the regular expression language in Perl. What feature of that regular expression language makes it possible to write regular expressions that describe languages that aren't regular?

20. For each of the following statements, state whether it is *True* or *False*. Prove your answer.

a. (ab)*a = a(ba)*.

b. (a ∪ b)* b (a ∪ b)* = a* b (a ∪ b)*.

c. (a ∪ b)* b (a ∪ b)* ∪ (a ∪ b)* a (a ∪ b)* = (a ∪ b)*.

d. (a ∪ b)* b (a ∪ b)* ∪ (a ∪ b)* a (a ∪ b)* = (a ∪ b)$^+$.

e. (a ∪ b)* b a (a ∪ b)* ∪ a*b* = (a ∪ b)*.

f. a* b (a ∪ b)* = (a ∪ b)* b (a ∪ b)*.

g. If α and β are any two regular expressions, then $(\alpha \cup \beta)^* = \alpha(\beta\alpha \cup \alpha)$.

h. If α and β are any two regular expressions, then $(\alpha\beta)^*\alpha = \alpha(\beta\alpha)^*$.

CHAPTER 7

Regular Grammars

So far, we have considered two equivalent ways to describe exactly the class of regular languages:

- Finite state machines.
- Regular expressions.

We now introduce a third:

- Regular grammars (sometimes also called right linear grammars).

7.1 Definition of a Regular Grammar

A ***regular grammar*** G is a quadruple (V, Σ, R, S), where:

- V is the rule alphabet, which contains nonterminals (symbols that are used in the grammar but that do not appear in strings in the language) and terminals (symbols that can appear in strings generated by G),
- Σ (the set of terminals) is a subset of V,
- R (the set of rules) is a finite set of rules of the form $X \rightarrow Y$, and
- S (the start symbol) is a nonterminal.

In a regular grammar, all rules in R must:

- have a left-hand side that is a single nonterminal, and
- have a right-hand side that is ε or a single terminal or a single terminal followed by a single nonterminal.

So $S \rightarrow$ a, $S \rightarrow \varepsilon$, and $T \rightarrow$ aS are legal rules in a regular grammar. $S \rightarrow$ aSa and aSa $\rightarrow T$ are not legal rules in a regular grammar.

We will formalize the notion of a grammar generating a language in Chapter 11, when we introduce a more powerful grammatical framework, the context-free grammar. For now, an informal notion will do. The language generated by a grammar $G = (V, \Sigma, R, S)$, denoted $L(G)$, is the set of all strings w in Σ^* such that it is possible to start with S, apply some finite set of rules in R, and derive w.

To make writing grammars easy, we will adopt the convention that, unless otherwise specified, the start symbol of any grammar G will be the symbol on the left-hand side of the first rule in R_G.

EXAMPLE 7.1 Even Length Strings

Let $L = \{w \in \{$a, b$\}^*: |w|$ is even$\}$. The following regular expression defines L:

$$((\text{aa}) \cup (\text{ab}) \cup (\text{ba}) \cup (\text{bb}))^*.$$

The following DFSM M accepts L:

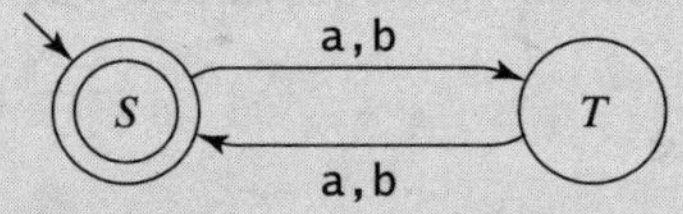

The following regular grammar G also defines L:

$$S \rightarrow \varepsilon$$
$$S \rightarrow \text{a}T$$
$$S \rightarrow \text{b}T$$
$$T \rightarrow \text{a}S$$
$$T \rightarrow \text{b}S$$

In G, the job of the nonterminal S is to generate an even length string. It does this either by generating the empty string or by generating a single character and then creating T. The job of T is to generate an odd length string. It does this by generating a single character and then creating S. S generates ε, the shortest possible even length string. So, if T can be shown to generate all and only the odd length strings, we can show that S generates all and only the remaining even length strings. T generates every string whose length is one greater than the length of some string S generates. So, if S generates all and only the even length strings, then T generates all and only the other odd length strings.

Notice the clear correspondence between M and G, which we have highlighted by naming M's states S and T. Even length strings drive M to state S. Even length strings are generated by G starting with S. Odd length strings drive M to state T. Odd length strings are generated by G starting with T.

7.2 Regular Grammars and Regular Languages

THEOREM 7.1 Regular Grammars Define Exactly the Regular Languages

Theorem: The class of languages that can be defined with regular grammars is exactly the regular languages.

Proof: We first show that any language that can be defined with a regular grammar can be accepted by some FSM and so is regular. Then we must show that every regular language (i.e., every language that can be accepted by some FSM) can be defined with a regular grammar. Both proofs are by construction.

Regular grammar $\rightarrow$ ***FSM:*** The following algorithm constructs an FSM M from a regular grammar $G = (V, \Sigma, R, S)$ and assures that $L(M) = L(G)$:

grammartofsm(G: regular grammar) =

1. Create in M a separate state for each nonterminal in V.
2. Make the state corresponding to S the start state.
3. If there are any rules in R of the form $X \rightarrow w$, for some $w \in \Sigma$, then create an additional state labeled #.
4. For each rule of the form $X \rightarrow wY$, add a transition from X to Y labeled w.
5. For each rule of the form $X \rightarrow w$, add a transition from X to # labeled w.
6. For each rule of the form $X \rightarrow \varepsilon$, mark state X as accepting.
7. Mark state # as accepting.
8. If M is incomplete (i.e., there are some (state, input) pairs for which no transition is defined), M requires a dead state. Add a new state D. For every (q, i) pair for which no transition has already been defined, create a transition from q to D labeled i. For every i in Σ, create a transition from D to D labeled i.

FSM $\rightarrow$ ***Regular grammar*:** The construction is effectively the reverse of the one we just did. We leave this step as an exercise.

EXAMPLE 7.2 Strings that End with aaaa

Let $L = \{w \in \{\mathtt{a}, \mathtt{b}\}^*: w$ ends with the pattern aaaa$\}$. Alternatively, $L = (\mathtt{a} \cup \mathtt{b})^*$ aaaa. The following regular grammar defines L:

$S \rightarrow \mathtt{a}S$ /* An arbitrary number of a's and b's can be generated
$S \rightarrow \mathtt{b}S$ before the pattern starts.

$S \rightarrow \mathtt{a}B$ /* Generate the first a of the pattern.

EXAMPLE 7.2 ***(Continued)***

$B \rightarrow$ aC /* Generate the second a of the pattern.

$C \rightarrow$ aD /* Generate the third a of the pattern.

$D \rightarrow$ a /* Generate the last a of the pattern and quit.

Applying *grammartofsm* to this grammar, we get, omitting the dead state:

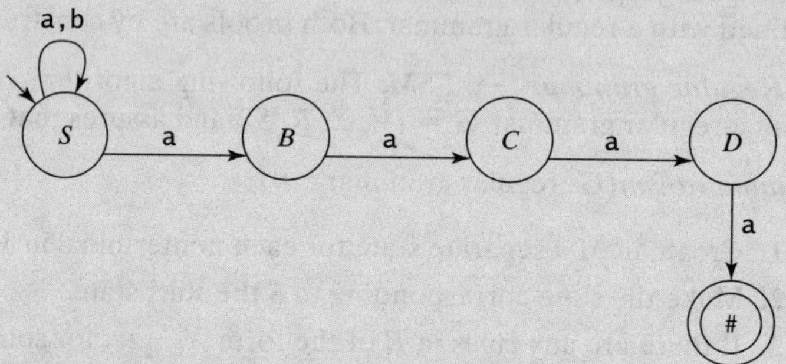

Notice that the machine that *grammartofsm* builds is not necessarily deterministic.

EXAMPLE 7.3 The Missing Letter Language

Let Σ = {a, b, c}. Let L be $L_{Missing}$ = {w : there is a symbol $a_i \in \Sigma$ not appearing in w}, which we defined in Example 5.12. The following grammar G generates $L_{Missing}$:

$S \rightarrow \varepsilon$
$S \rightarrow$ aB
$S \rightarrow$ aC
$S \rightarrow$ bA
$S \rightarrow$ bC
$S \rightarrow$ cA
$S \rightarrow$ cB
$A \rightarrow$ bA
$A \rightarrow$ cA
$A \rightarrow \varepsilon$
$B \rightarrow$ aB
$B \rightarrow$ cB

$B \rightarrow \varepsilon$

$C \rightarrow$ aC

$C \rightarrow$ bC

$C \rightarrow \varepsilon$

The job of S is to generate some string in $L_{Missing}$. It does that by choosing a first character of the string and then choosing which other character will be missing. The job of A is to generate all strings that do not contain any a's. The job of B is to generate all strings that do not contain any b's. And the job of C is to generate all strings that do not contain any c's.

If we apply *grammartofsm* to G, we get M =

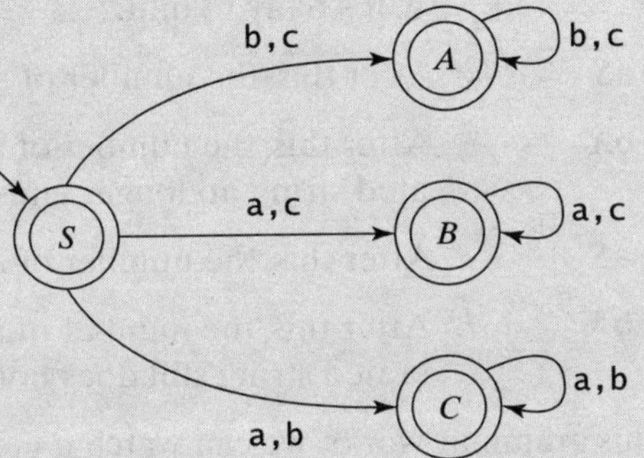

M is identical to the NDFSM we had previously built for $L_{Missing}$ except that it waits to guess whether to go to A, B or C until it has seen its first input character.

Our proof of the first half of Theorem 7.1 clearly describes the correspondence between the nonterminals in a regular grammar and the states in a corresponding FSM. This correspondence suggests a natural way to think about the design of a regular grammar. The nonterminals in such a grammar need to "remember" the relevant state of a left-to-right analysis of a string.

EXAMPLE 7.4 Satisfying Multiple Criteria

Let $L = \{w \in \{$a, b$\}^*$: w contains an odd number of a's and w ends in a$\}$. We can write a regular grammar G that defines L. G will contain four nonterminals, each with a unique function (corresponding to the states of a simple FSM that accepts L). So, in any derived string, if the remaining nonterminal is:

- S, then the number of a's so far is even. We don't have worry about whether the string ends in a since, to derive a string in L, it will be necessary to generate at least one more a anyway.

EXAMPLE 7.4 (*Continued*)

- T, then the number of a's so far is odd and the derived string ends in a.
- X, then the number of a's so far is odd and the derived string does not end in a.

Since only T captures the situation in which the number of a's so far is odd and the derived string ends in a, T is the only nonterminal that can generate ε. G contains the following rules:

$S \rightarrow$ bS /* Initial b's don't matter.

$S \rightarrow$ aT /* After this, the number of a's is odd and the generated string ends in a.

$T \rightarrow \varepsilon$ /* Since the number of a's is odd, and the string ends in a, it's okay to quit.

$T \rightarrow$ aS /* After this, the number of a's will be even again.

$T \rightarrow$ bX /* After this, the number of a's is still odd but the generated string no longer ends in a.

$X \rightarrow$ aS /* After this, the number of a's will be even.

$X \rightarrow$ bX /* After this, the number of a's is still odd and the generated string still does not end in a.

To see how this grammar works, we can watch it generate the string baaba:

$S \Rightarrow$ bS /* Still an even number of a's.

$\Rightarrow$ ba$T$ /* Now an odd number of a's and ends in a. The process could quit now since the derived string, ba, is in L.

$\Rightarrow$ baa$S$ /* Back to having an even number of a's, so it doesn't matter what the last character is.

$\Rightarrow$ baab$S$ /* Still even a's.

$\Rightarrow$ baaba$T$ /* Now an odd number of a's and ends in a. The process can quit, by applying the rule $T \rightarrow \varepsilon$.

$\Rightarrow$ baaba

So now we know that regular grammars define exactly the regular languages. But regular grammars are not often used in practice. The reason, though, is not that they couldn't be. It is simply that there is something better. Given some regular language L, the structure of a reasonable FSM for L very closely mirrors the structure of a reasonable regular grammar for it. And FSMs are easier to work with. In addition, there exist regular expressions. In Parts III and IV, as we move outward to larger classes of languages, there will no longer exist a technique like regular expressions.

At that point, particularly as we are considering the context-free languages, we will see that grammars are a very important and useful way to define languages.

Exercises

1. Show a regular grammar for each of the following languages:
   a. $\{w \in \{\mathsf{a}, \mathsf{b}\}^*$: w contains an even number of a's and an odd number of b's$\}$.
   b. $\{w \in \{\mathsf{a}, \mathsf{b}\}^*$: w does not end in aa$\}$.
   c. $\{w \in \{\mathsf{a}, \mathsf{b}\}^*$: w contains the substring abb$\}$.
   d. $\{w \in \{\mathsf{a}, \mathsf{b}\}^*$: if w contains the substring aa then $|w|$ is odd$\}$.
   e. $\{w \in \{\mathsf{a}, \mathsf{b}\}^*$: w does not contain the substring aabb$\}$.
2. Consider the following regular grammar G:

   $S \rightarrow \mathsf{a}T$
   $T \rightarrow \mathsf{b}T$
   $T \rightarrow \mathsf{a}$
   $T \rightarrow \mathsf{a}W$
   $W \rightarrow \varepsilon$
   $W \rightarrow \mathsf{a}T$

   a. Write a regular expression that generates $L(G)$.
   b. Use *grammartofsm* to generate an FSM M that accepts $L(G)$.
3. Consider again the FSM M shown in Exercise 5.1. Show a regular grammar that generates $L(M)$.
4. Show by construction that, for every FSM M there exists a regular grammar G such that $L(G) = L(M)$.
5. Let $L = \{w \in \{\mathsf{a}, \mathsf{b}\}^*$: every a in w is immediately followed by at least one b$\}$.
   a. Write a regular expression that describes L.
   b. Write a regular grammar that generates L.
   c. Construct an FSM that accepts L.

CHAPTER 8

Regular and Nonregular Languages

The language a*b* is regular. The language $A^nB^n = \{a^nb^n : n \geq 0\}$ is not regular (intuitively because it is not possible, given some finite number of states, to count an arbitrary number of a's and then compare that count to the number of b's). The language $\{w \in \{a, b\}^* :$ every a is immediately followed by a b$\}$ is regular. The similar sounding language $\{w \in \{a, b\}^* :$ every a has a matching b somewhere and no b matches more than one a$\}$ is not regular (again because it is now necessary to count the a's and make sure that the number of b's is at least as great as the number of a's.)

Given a new language L, how can we know whether or not it is regular? In this chapter, we present a collection of techniques that can be used to answer that question.

8.1 How Many Regular Languages Are There?

First, we observe that there are *many* more nonregular languages than there are regular ones:

THEOREM 8.1 The Regular Languages are Countably Infinite

Theorem: There is a countably infinite number of regular languages.

Proof: We can lexicographically enumerate all the syntactically legal DFSMs with input alphabet Σ. Every regular language is accepted by at least one of them. So there cannot be more regular languages than there are DFSMs. Thus there are at most a countably infinite number of regular languages. There is not a one-to-one relationship between regular languages and DFSMs since there is an infinite number of machines that accept any given language. But the number of regular languages is infinite because it includes the following infinite set of languages:

$$\{a\}, \{aa\}, \{aaa\}, \{aaaa\}, \{aaaaa\}, \{aaaaaa\}, \ldots$$

But, by Theorem 2.3, there is an uncountably infinite number of languages over any nonempty alphabet So there are many more nonregular languages than there are regular ones.

8.2 Showing That a Language Is Regular

But many languages *are* regular. How can we know which ones? We start with the simplest cases.

THEOREM 8.2 The Finite Languages

Theorem: Every finite language is regular.

Proof: If L is the empty set, then it is defined by the regular expression $\varnothing$ and so is regular. If it is any finite language composed of the strings $s_1, s_2, \ldots s_n$ for some positive integer n, then it is defined by the regular expression:

$$s_1 \cup s_2 \cup \cdots \cup s_n$$

So it too is regular.

EXAMPLE 8.1 The Intersection of Two Infinite Languages

Let $L = L_1 \cap L_2$, where $L_1 = \{\mathrm{a}^n\mathrm{b}^n : n \geq 0\}$ and $L_2 = \{\mathrm{b}^n\mathrm{a}^n : n \geq 0\}$. As we will soon be able to prove, neither L_1 nor L_2 is regular. But L is. $L = \{\varepsilon\}$, which is finite.

EXAMPLE 8.2 A Finite Language We May Not Be Able to Write Down

Let $L = \{w \in \{0 - 9\}^* : w$ is the social security number of a living US resident$\}$. L is regular because it is finite. It doesn't matter that no individual or organization happens, at any given instant, to know what strings are in L.

Note, however, that although the language in Example 8.2 is formally regular, the techniques that we have described for recognizing regular languages would not be very useful in building a program to check for a valid social security number. Regular expressions are most useful when the elements of L match one or more patterns. FSMs are most useful when the elements of L share some simple structural properties. Other techniques, like hash tables, are better suited to handling finite languages whose elements are chosen by our world, rather than by rule.

EXAMPLE 8.3 Santa Clause, God, and the History of the Americas

Let:

- $L_1 = \{w \in \{0 - 9\}^* : w$ is the social security number of the current US president$\}$.
- $L_2 = \{1$ if Santa Claus exists and 0 otherwise$\}$.
- $L_3 = \{1$ if God exists and 0 otherwise$\}$.
- $L_4 = \{1$ if there were people in North America more than 10,000 years ago and 0 otherwise$\}$.
- $L_5 = \{1$ if there were people in North America more than 15,000 years ago and 0 otherwise$\}$.
- $L_6 = \{w \in \{0 - 9\}^+ : w$ is the decimal representation, without leading 0's, of a prime Fermat number$\}$.

L_1 is clearly finite, and thus regular. There exists a simple FSM to accept it, even though none of us happens to know what that FSM is. L_2 and L_3 are perhaps a little less clear, but that is because the meanings of "Santa Claus" and "God" are less clear. Pick a definition for either of them. Then something that satisfies that definition either does or does not exist. So either the simple FSM that accepts $\{0\}$ and nothing else or the simple FSM that accepts $\{1\}$ and nothing else accepts L_2. And one of them (possibly the same one, possibly the other one) accepts L_3. L_4 is clear. It is the set $\{1\}$. L_5 is also finite, and thus regular. Either there were people in North America by 15,000 years ago or there were not, although the currently available fossil evidence 🖳 is unclear as to which. So we (collectively) just don't know yet which machine to build. L_6 is similar, although this time what is lacking is mathematics, as opposed to fossils. Recall from Section 4.1 that the Fermat numbers are defined by

$$F_n = 2^{2^n} + 1, n \geq 0.$$

The first five elements of F_n are $\{3, 5, 17, 257, 65{,}537\}$. All of them are prime. It appears likely 🖳 that no other Fermat numbers are prime. If that is true, then L_6 is finite and thus regular. If it turns out that the set of Fermat numbers is infinite, then it is almost surely not regular.

Not every regular language is computationally tractable. Consider the Towers of Hanoi language. (P. 2)

But, of course, most interesting regular languages are infinite. So far, we've developed four techniques for showing that a (finite or infinite) language L is regular:

- Exhibit a regular expression for L.
- Exhibit an FSM for L.

- Show that the number of equivalence classes of $\approx_L$ is finite.
- Exhibit a regular grammar for L.

8.3 Some Important Closure Properties of Regular Languages

We now consider one final technique, which allows us, when analyzing complex languages, to exploit the other techniques as subroutines. The regular languages are closed under many common and useful operations. So, if we wish to show that some language L is regular and we can show that L can be constructed from other regular languages using those operations, then L must also be regular.

THEOREM 8.3 Closure under Union, Concatenation and Kleene Star

Theorem: The regular languages are closed under union, concatenation, and Kleene star.

Proof: By the same constructions that were used in the proof of Kleene's theorem.

THEOREM 8.4 Closure under Complement, Intersection, Difference, Reverse and Letter Substitution

Theorem: The regular languages are closed under complement, intersection, difference, reverse, and letter substitution.

Proof:

- The regular languages are closed under complement. If L_1 is regular, then there exists a DFSM $M_1 = (K, \Sigma, \delta, s, A)$ that accepts it. The DFSM $M_2 = (K, \Sigma, \delta, s, K - A)$, namely M_1 with accepting and nonaccepting states swapped, accepts $\neg(L(M_1))$ because it rejects all strings that M_1 accepts and rejects all strings that M_1 accepts.

  Given an arbitrary (possibly nondeterministic) FSM $M_1 = (K_1, \Sigma, \Delta_1, s_1, A_1)$, we can construct a DFSM $M_2 = (K_2, \Sigma, \delta_2, s_2, A_2)$ such that $L(M_2) = \neg(L(M_1))$. We do so as follows: From M_1, construct an equivalent deterministic FSM $M' = (K_{M'}, \Sigma, \delta_{M'}, s_{M'}, A_{M'})$, using the algorithm *ndfsmtodfsm*, presented in the proof of Theorem 5.3. (If M_1 is already deterministic, $M' = M_1$.) M' must be stated completely, so if it is described with an implied dead state, add the dead state and all required transitions to it. Begin building M_2 by setting it equal to M'. Then swap the accepting and the nonaccepting states. So $M_2 = (K_{M'}, \Sigma, \delta_{M'}, s_{M'}, K_{M'} - A_{M'})$.

- The regular languages are closed under intersection. We note that:

$$L(M_1) \cap L(M_2) = \neg(\neg L(M_1) \cup \neg L(M_2)).$$

  We have already shown that the regular languages are closed under both complement and union. Thus they are also closed under intersection.

It is also possible to prove this claim by construction of an FSM that accepts $L(M_1) \cap L(M_2)$. We leave that proof as an exercise.

- The regular languages are closed under set difference (subtraction). We note that:

$$L(M_1) - L(M_2) = L(M_1) \cap \neg L(M_2).$$

We have already shown that the regular languages are closed under both complement and intersection. Thus they are also closed under set difference.

This claim too can also be proved by construction, which we leave as an exercise.

- The regular languages are closed under reverse. Recall that $L^{\mathrm{R}} = \{w \in \Sigma^* : w = x^R \text{ for some } x \in L\}$. We leave the proof of this as an exercise.
- The regular languages are closed under letter substitution, defined as follows: Consider any two alphabets, Σ_1 and Σ_2. Let *sub* be any function from Σ_1 to $\Sigma_2{}^*$. Then *letsub* is a letter substitution function from L_1 to L_2 iff $letsub(L_1) = \{w \in \Sigma_2{}^* : \exists y \in L_1 \; (w = y$ except that every character c of y has been replaced by $sub(c))\}$. For example, suppose that $\Sigma_1 = \{\mathtt{a}, \mathtt{b}\}$, $\Sigma_2 = \{\mathtt{0}, \mathtt{1}\}$, $sub(\mathtt{a}) = \mathtt{0}$, and $sub(\mathtt{b}) = \mathtt{11}$. Then $letsub(\{\mathtt{a}^n\mathtt{b}^n : n \geq 0\}) = \{\mathtt{0}^n\mathtt{1}^{2n} : n \geq 0\}$. We leave the proof that the regular languages are closed under letter substitution as an exercise.

EXAMPLE 8.4 Closure Under Complement

Consider the following NDFSM M =

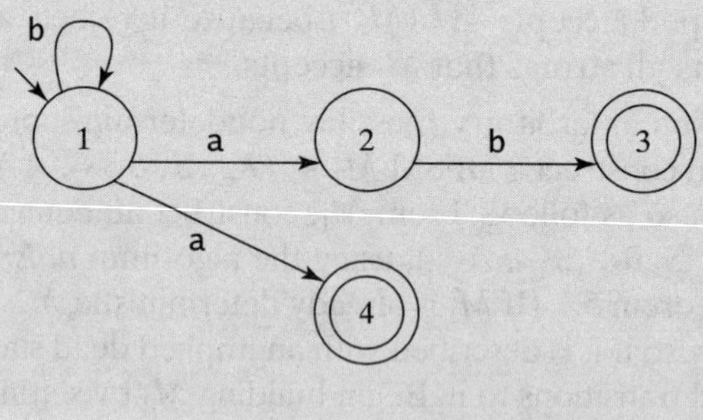

If we use the algorithm that we just described to convert M to a new machine M' that accepts $\neg L(M)$, the last step is to swap the accepting and the nonaccepting states. A quick look at M makes it clear why it is necessary first to make M deterministic and then to complete it by adding the dead state. M accepts the input a in state 4. If we simply swapped accepting and nonaccepting states, without making the other changes, M' would also accept a. It would do so in state 2. The problem is that M is nondeterministic, and has one path along which a is accepted and one along which it is rejected.

To see why it is necessary to add the dead state, consider the input string aba. M rejects it since the path from state 3 dies when M attempts to read the final a and the path from state 4 dies when it attempts to read the b. But, if we don't add the dead state, M' will also reject it since, in it too, both paths will die.

The closure theorems that we have now proved make it easy to take a divide-and-conquer approach to showing that a language is regular. They also let us reuse proofs and constructions that we've already done.

EXAMPLE 8.5 The Divide-and-Conquer Approach

Let $L = \{w \in \{a, b\}^* : w$ contains an even number of a's and an odd number of b's and all a's come in runs of three$\}$. L is regular because it is the intersection of two regular languages. $L = L_1 \cap L_2$, where:

- $L_1 = \{w \in \{a, b\}^* : w$ contains an even number of a's and an odd number of b's $\}$, and
- $L_2 = \{w \in \{a, b\}^* :$ all a's come in runs of three$\}$.

We already know that L_1 is regular, since we showed an FSM that accepts it in Example 5.9:

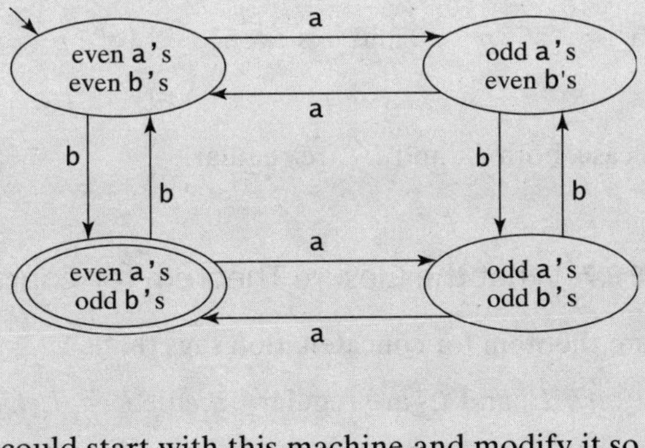

Of course, we could start with this machine and modify it so that it accepts L. But an easier way is exploit a divide-and-conquer approach. We'll just use the machine we have and then build a second simple machine, this one to accept L_2.

EXAMPLE 8.5 *(Continued)*

Then we can prove that L is regular by exploiting the fact that the regular languages are closed under intersection. The following machine accepts L_2:

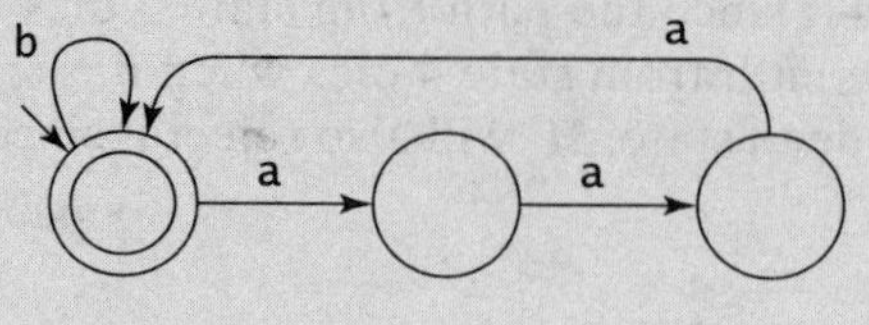

The closure theorems are powerful, but they say only what they say. We have stated each of the closure theorems in as strong a form as possible. Any similar claims that are not implied by the theorems as we have stated them are almost certainly false, which can usually be shown easily by finding a simple counterexample.

EXAMPLE 8.6 What the Closure Theorem for Union Does Not Say

The closure theorem for union says that:

$$\textit{if} \quad L_1 \text{ and } L_2 \text{ are regular} \quad \textit{then} \quad L = L_1 \cup L_2 \text{ is regular.}$$

The theorem says nothing, for example, about what happens if L is regular. Does that mean that L_1 and L_2 are also? The answer is maybe. We know that a^+ is regular. We will consider two cases for L_1 and L_2. First, let them be:

$$\mathrm{a}^+ = \{\mathrm{a}^p : p > 0 \text{ and } p \text{ is prime}\} \cup \{\mathrm{a}^p : p > 0 \text{ and } p \text{ is not prime}\}.$$

$$\mathrm{a}^+ = \quad L_1 \quad \cup \quad L_2.$$

As we will see in the next section, neither L_1 nor L_2 is regular. But now consider:

$$\mathrm{a}^+ = \{\mathrm{a}^p : p > 0 \text{ and } p \text{ is even}\} \cup \{\mathrm{a}^p : p > 0 \text{ and } p \text{ is odd}\}.$$

$$\mathrm{a}^+ = \quad L_1 \quad \cup \quad L_2.$$

In this case, both L_1 and L_2 are regular.

EXAMPLE 8.7 What the Closure Theorem for Concatenation Does Not Say

The closure theorem for concatenation says that:

$$\textit{if} \quad L_1 \text{ and } L_2 \text{ are regular} \quad \textit{then} \quad L = L_1L_2 \text{ is regular.}$$

But the theorem says nothing, for example, about what happens if L_2 is not regular. Does that mean that L isn't regular either? Again, the answer is maybe. We first consider the following example:

$$\{\mathrm{aba}^n\mathrm{b}^n : n \geq 0\} = \{\mathrm{ab}\}\{\mathrm{a}^n\mathrm{b}^n : n \geq 0\}.$$

$$L \quad = \quad L_1 \quad L_2.$$

As we'll see in the next section, L_2 is not regular. And, in this case, neither is L. But now consider:

$$\{\text{aaa*}\} = \{\text{a*}\}\{\text{a}^p : p \text{ is prime}\}.$$
$$L \quad = \quad L_1 \qquad L_2.$$

While again L_2 is not regular, now L is.

8.4 Showing That a Language is Not Regular

We can show that a language is regular by exhibiting a regular expression or an FSM or a finite list of the equivalence classes of $\approx_L$ or a regular grammar, or by using the closure properties that we have proved hold for the regular languages. But how shall we show that a language is not regular? In other words, how can we show that none of those descriptions exists for it? It is not sufficient to argue that we tried to find one of them and failed. Perhaps we didn't look in the right place. We need a technique that does not rely on our cleverness (or lack of it).

What we can do is to make use of the following observation about the regular languages: Every regular language L can be accepted by an FSM M with a finite number of states. If L is infinite, then there must be at least one loop in M. All sufficiently long strings in L must be characterized by one or more repeating patterns, corresponding to the substrings that drive M through its loops. It is also true that, if L is infinite, then any regular expression that describes L must contain at least one Kleene star, but we will focus here on FSMs.

To help us visualize the rest of this discussion, consider the FSM M_{LOOP}, shown in Figure 8.1 (a). M_{LOOP} has 5 states. It can accept an infinite number of strings. But the longest one that it can accept without going through any loops has length 4. Now consider the slightly different FSM M_ε, shown in Figure 8.1 (b). M_ε also has 5 states and one loop. But it accepts only one string, aab. The only string that can drive M_ε through its loop is ε. No matter how many times M_ε goes through the loop, it cannot accept any longer strings.

To simplify the following discussion, we will consider only DFSMs, which have no ε-transitions. Each transition step that a DFSM takes corresponds to exactly one character in its input. Since any language that can be accepted by an NDFSM can also be accepted by a DFSM, this restriction will not affect our conclusions.

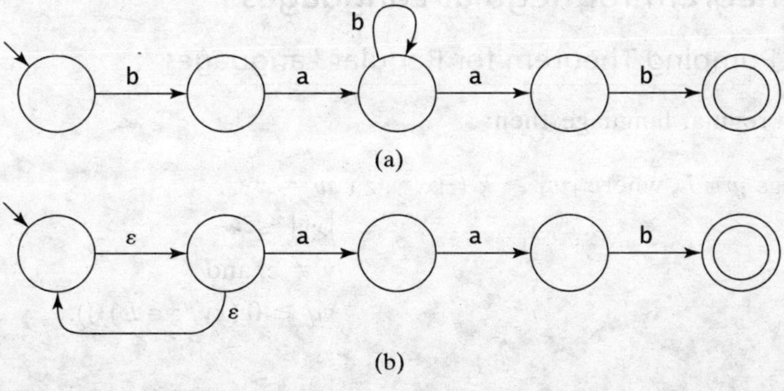

FIGURE 8.1 What is the longest string that a 5-state FSM can accept?

THEOREM 8.5 Long Strings Force Repeated States

Theorem: Let $M = (K, \Sigma, \delta, s, A)$ be any DFSM. If M accepts any string of length $|K|$ or greater, then that string will force M to visit some state more than once (thus traversing at least one loop).

Proof: M must start in one of its states. Each time it reads an input character, it visits some state. So, in processing a string of length n, M creates a total of $n + 1$ state visits (the initial one plus one for each character it reads). If $n + 1 > |K|$, then, by the pigeonhole principle, some state must get more than one visit. So, if $n \geq |K|$, then M must visit at least one state more than once.

Let $M = (K, \Sigma, \delta, s, A)$ be any DFSM. Suppose that there exists some "long" string w (i.e., $|w| \geq |K|$) such that $w \in L(M)$. Then M must go through at least one loop when it reads w. So there is some substring y of w that drove M through at least one loop. Suppose we excise y from w. The resulting string must also be in $L(M)$ since M can accept it just as it accepts w but skipping one pass through one loop. Further, suppose that we splice in one or more extra copies of y, immediately adjacent to the original one. All the resulting strings must also be in $L(M)$ since M can accept them by going through its loop one or more additional times. Using an analogy with a pump, we'll say that we can ***pump*** y out once or in an arbitrary number of times and the resulting string must still be in L.

To make this concrete, let's look again at M_{LOOP}, which accepts, for example, the string babbab. babbab is "long" since its length is 6 and $|K| = 5$. The second b drove M_{LOOP} through its loop. Call the string (in this case b) that drove M_{LOOP} through its loop y. We can pump it out, producing babab, which is also accepted by M_{LOOP}. Or we can pump in as many copies of b as we like, generating such strings as babbbab, babbbbbab, and so forth. M_{LOOP} also accepts all of them. Returning to the original string babbab, the third b also drove M_{LOOP} through its loop. We could also pump it (in or out) and get a similar result.

This property of FSMs, and the languages that they can accept, is the basis for a powerful tool for showing that a language is not regular. If a language contains even one long (to be defined precisely below) string that cannot be pumped in the fashion that we have just described, then it is not accepted by any FSM and so is not regular. We formalize this idea, as the Pumping Theorem, in the next section.

8.4.1 The Pumping Theorem for Regular Languages

THEOREM 8.6 The Pumping Theorem for Regular Languages

Theorem: If L is a regular language, then:

$$\exists k \geq 1 \, (\forall \text{ strings } w \in L, \text{ where } |w| \geq k \, (\exists x, y, z \, (w = xyz, \; |xy| \leq k, \; y \neq \varepsilon, \text{ and } \forall q \geq 0 \, (xy^q z \in L))))$$

Proof: The proof is the argument that we gave above: If L is regular then it is accepted by some DFSM $M = (K, \Sigma, \delta, s, A)$. Let k be $|K|$. Let w be any string in L of length k or greater. By Theorem 8.5, to accept w, M must traverse some loop at least once. We can carve w up and assign the name y to the first substring to drive M through a loop. Then x is the part of w that precedes y and z is the part of w that follows y. We show that each of the last three conditions must then hold:

- $|xy| \leq k$: M must not only traverse a loop eventually when reading w, it must do so for the first time by at least the time it has read k characters. It can read $k - 1$ characters without revisiting any states. But the kth character must, if no earlier character already has, take M to a state it has visited before. Whatever character does that is the last in one pass through some loop.
- $y \neq \varepsilon$: Since M is deterministic, there are no loops that can be traversed by ε.
- $\forall q \geq 0\ (xy^q z \in L)$: y can be pumped out once (which is what happens if $q = 0$) or in any number of times (which happens if q is greater than 1) and the resulting string must be in L since it will be accepted by M. It is possible that we could chop y out more than once and still generate a string in L, but without knowing how much longer w is than k, we don't know any more than that it can be pumped out once.

The Pumping Theorem tells us something that is true of every regular language. Generally, if we already know that a language is regular, we won't particularly care about what the Pumping Theorem tells us about it. But suppose that we are interested in some language L and we want to know whether or not it is regular. If we could show that the claims made in the Pumping Theorem are not true of L, then we would know that L is not regular. It is in arguments such as this that we will find the Pumping Theorem very useful. In particular, we will use it to construct ***proofs by contradiction***. We will say, "If L were regular, then it would possess certain properties. But it does not possess those properties. Therefore, it is not regular."

EXAMPLE 8.8 A^nB^n is not Regular

Let L be $A^nB^n = \{a^nb^n : n \geq 0\}$. We can use the Pumping Theorem to show that L is not regular. If it were, then there would exist some k such that any string w, where $|w| \geq k$, must satisfy the conditions of the theorem. We show one string w that does not. Let $w = a^kb^k$. Since $|w| = 2k$, w is long enough and it is in L, so it must satisfy the conditions of the Pumping Theorem. So there must exist x, y, and z, such that $w = xyz$, $|xy| \leq k$, $y \neq \varepsilon$, and $\forall q \geq 0\ (xy^q z \in L)$. But we show that no such x, y, and z exist. Since we must guarantee that $|xy| \leq k$, y must occur within the first k characters and so $y = a^p$ for some p. Since we must guarantee that $y \neq \varepsilon$, p must be greater than 0. Let $q = 2$. (In other words, we pump in one extra copy of y.) The resulting string is $a^{k+p}b^k$. The last condition of the Pumping Theorem states that this string must be in L, but it is not since it has more a's than b's. Thus there exists at least one long string in L that fails to satisfy the conditions of the Pumping Theorem. So $L = A^nB^n$ is not regular.

The Pumping Theorem is a powerful tool for showing that a language is not regular. But, as with any tool, using it effectively requires some skill. To see how the theorem can be used, let's state it again in its most general terms:

For any language L, if L is regular, then every "long" string in L is pumpable.

So, to show that L is not regular, it suffices to find a single long string w that is in L but is not pumpable. To show that a string is not pumpable, we must show that there is no way to carve it up into x, y, and z in such a way that all three of the conditions of the theorem are met. It is not sufficient to pick a particular y and show that it doesn't work. (We focus on y since, once it has been chosen, everything to the left of it is x and everything to the right of it is z). We must show that there is *no* value for y that works. To do that, we consider all the logically possible classes of values for y (sometimes there is only one such class, but sometimes several must be considered). Then we show that each of them fails to satisfy at least one of the three conditions of the theorem. Generally we do that by assuming that y does satisfy the first two conditions, namely that it occurs within the first k characters and is not ε. Then we consider the third requirement, namely that, for all values of q, xy^qz is in L. To show that it is not possible to satisfy that requirement, it is sufficient to find a single value of q such that the resulting string is not in L. Typically, this can be done by setting q to 0 (thus pumping out once) or to 2 (pumping in once), although sometimes some other value of q must be considered.

In a nutshell then, to use the Pumping Theorem to show that a language L is not regular, we must:

1. Choose a string w, where $w \in L$ and $|w| \geq k$. Note that we do not know what k is; we know only that it exists. So we must state w in terms of k.
2. Divide the possibilities for y into a set of equivalence classes so that all strings in a class can be considered together.
3. For each such class of possible y values, where $|xy| \leq k$ and $y \neq \varepsilon$:
   Choose a value for q such that xy^qz is not in L.

In Example 8.8, y had to fall in the initial a region of w, so that was the only case that needed to be considered. But, had we made a less judicious choice for w, our proof would not have been so simple. Let's look at another proof, with a different w:

EXAMPLE 8.9 A Less Judicious Choice for *w*

Again let L be $A^nB^n = \{a^nb^n : n \geq 0\}$. If A^nB^n were regular, then there would exist some k such that any string w, where $|w| \geq k$, must satisfy the conditions of the theorem. Let $w = a^{\lceil k/2 \rceil}b^{\lceil k/2 \rceil}$. (We must use $\lceil k/2 \rceil$, i.e., the smallest integer greater than $k/2$, rather than truncating the division, since k might be odd.) Since $|w| \geq k$ and w is in L, w must satisfy the conditions of the Pumping Theorem. So, there must exist x, y, and z, such that $w = xyz$, $|xy| \leq k$, $y \neq \varepsilon$, and $\forall q \geq 0\ (xy^qz \in L)$. We show that no such x, y, and z exist. This time, if they did, y

could be almost anywhere in w (since all the Pumping Theorem requires is that it occur in the first k characters and there are only at most $k + 1$ characters). So we must consider three cases and show that, in all three, there is no y that satisfies all conditions of the Pumping Theorem. A useful way to describe the cases is to imagine w divided into two regions:

aaaaa.....aaaaaa | bbbbb.....bbbbbb
1 | 2

Now we see that y can fall:

- Exclusively in region 1: In this case, the proof is identical to the proof we did for Example 8.8.
- Exclusively in region 2: then $y = \text{b}^p$ for some p. Since $y \neq \varepsilon$, p must be greater than 0. Let $q = 2$. The resulting string is a^kb^{k+p}. But this string is not in L, since it has more b's than a's.
- Straddling the boundary between regions 1 and 2: Then $y = \text{a}^p\text{b}^r$ for some non-zero p and r. Let $q = 2$. The resulting string will have interleaved a's and b's, and so is not in L.

There exists at least one long string in L that fails to satisfy the conditions of the Pumping Theorem. So $L = \text{A}^n\text{B}^n$ is not regular.

To make maximum use of the Pumping Theorem's requirement that y fall in the first k characters, it is often a good idea to choose a string w that is substantially longer than the k characters required by the theorem. In particular, if w can be chosen so that there is a uniform first region of length at least k, it may be possible to consider just a single case for where y can fall.

> The Pumping Theorem inspires poets 💻, as we'll see in Chapter 10.

A^nB^n is a simple language that illustrates the kind of property that characterizes languages that aren't regular. It isn't of much practical importance, but it is typical of a family of languages, many of which are of more practical significance. In the next example, we consider Bal, the language of balanced parentheses. The structure of Bal is very similar to that of A^nB^n. Bal is important because most languages for describing arithmetic expressions, Boolean queries, and markup systems require balanced delimiters.

EXAMPLE 8.10 The Balanced Parenthesis Language is Not Regular

Let L be Bal $= \{w \in \{), (\}^* :$ the parentheses are balanced$\}$. If L were regular, then there would exist some k such that any string w, where $|w| \geq k$, must satisfy the conditions of the theorem. Bal contains complex strings like (())(()()). But it is

EXAMPLE 8.10 *(Continued)*

almost always easier to use the Pumping Theorem if we pick as simple a string as possible. So, let $w = (^k)^k$. Since $|w| = 2k$ and w is in L, w must satisfy the conditions of the Pumping Theorem. So there must exist x, y, and z, such that $w = xyz$, $|xy| \leq k$, $y \neq \varepsilon$, and $\forall q \geq 0\ (xy^qz \in L)$. But we show that no x, y, and z exist. Since $|xy| \leq k$, y must occur within the first k characters and so $y = (^p$ for some p). Since $y \neq \varepsilon$, p must be greater than 0. Let $q = 2$. (In other words, we pump in one extra copy of y.) The resulting string is $(^{k+p})^k$. The last condition of the Pumping Theorem states that this string must be in L, but it is not since it has more ('s than)'s. There exists at least one long string in L that fails to satisfy the conditions of the Pumping Theorem. So L = Bal is not regular.

EXAMPLE 8.11 The Even Palindrome Language is Not Regular

Let L be PalEven = $\{ww^R : w \in \{\texttt{a}, \texttt{b}\}^*\}$. PalEven is the language of even-length palindromes of a's and b's. We can use the Pumping Theorem to show that PalEven is not regular. If it were, then there would exist some k such that any string w, where $|w| \geq k$, must satisfy the conditions of the theorem. We show one string w that does not. (Note here that the variable w used in the definition of L is different from the variable w mentioned in the Pumping Theorem.) We will choose w so that we only have to consider one case for where y could fall. Let $w = \texttt{a}^k\texttt{b}^k\texttt{b}^k\texttt{a}^k$. Since $|w| = 4k$ and w is in L, w must satisfy the conditions of the Pumping Theorem. So there must exist x, y, and z, such that $w = xyz$, $|xy| \leq k$, $y \neq \varepsilon$, and $\forall q \geq 0\ (xy^qz \in L)$. Since $|xy| \leq k$, y must occur within the first k characters and so $y = \texttt{a}^p$ for some p. Since $y \neq \varepsilon$, p must be greater than 0. Let $q = 2$. The resulting string is $\texttt{a}^{k+p}\texttt{b}^k\texttt{b}^k\texttt{a}^k$. If p is odd, then this string is not in PalEven because all strings in PalEven have even length. If p is even then it is at least 2, so the first half of the string has more a's than the second half does, so it is not in PalEven. So L = PalEven is not regular.

The Pumping Theorem says that, for any language L, if L is regular, then all long strings in L must be pumpable. Our strategy in using it to show that a language L is not regular is to find *one* string that fails to meet that requirement. Often, there are many long strings that *are* pumpable. If we try to work with them, we will fail to derive the contradiction that we seek. In that case, we will know nothing about whether or not L is regular. To find a w that is not pumpable, think about what property of L is not checkable by an FSM and choose a w that exhibits that property. Consider again our last example. The thing that an FSM cannot do is to remember an arbitrarily long first half and check it against the second half. So we chose a w that would have forced it to do that. Suppose instead that we had let $w = \texttt{a}^k\texttt{a}^k$. It is in L and long enough. But y could be aa and we could pump it out or in and all the resulting strings would be in L.

So far, all of our Pumping Theorem proofs have set q to 2. But that is not always the thing to do. Sometimes it will be necessary to set it to 0. (In other words, we will pump y out).

EXAMPLE 8.12 The Language with More a's Than b's is Not Regular

Let $L = \{\text{a}^n\text{b}^m : n > m\}$. We can use the Pumping Theorem to show that L is not regular. If it were, then there would exist some k such that any string w, where $|w| \geq k$, must satisfy the conditions of the theorem. We show one string w that does not. Let $w = \text{a}^{k+1}\text{b}^k$. Since $|w| = 2k + 1$ and w is in L, w must satisfy the conditions of the Pumping Theorem. So there must exist x, y, and z, such that $w = xyz$, $|xy| \leq k$, $y \neq \varepsilon$, and $\forall q \geq 0\ (xy^qz \in L)$. Since $|xy| \leq k$, y must occur within the first k characters and so $y = \text{a}^p$ for some p. Since $y \neq \varepsilon$, p must be greater than 0. There are already more a's than b's, as required by the definition of L. If we pump in, there will be even more a's and the resulting string will still be in L. But we can set q to 0 (and so pump out). The resulting string is then $\text{a}^{k+1-p}\text{b}^k$. Since $p > 0$, $k + 1 - p \leq k$, so the resulting string no longer has more a's than b's and so is not in L. There exists at least one long string in L that fails to satisfy the conditions of the Pumping Theorem. So L is not regular.

Notice that the proof that we just did depended on our having chosen a w that is just barely in L. It had exactly one more a than b. So y could be any string of up to k a's. If we pumped in extra copies of y, we would have gotten strings that were still in L. But if we pumped out even a single a, we got a string that was not in L, and so we were able to complete the proof.. Suppose, though, that we had chosen $w = \text{a}^{2k}\text{b}^k$. Again, pumping in results in strings in L. And now, if y were simply a, we could pump out and get a string that was still in L. So that proof attempt fails. In general, it is a good idea to choose a w that barely meets the requirements for L. That makes it more likely that pumping will create a string that is not in L.

Sometimes values of q other than 0 or 2 may also be required.

EXAMPLE 8.13 The Prime Number of a's Language is Not Regular

Let L be $\text{Prime}_\text{a} = \{\text{a}^n : n \text{ is prime}\}$. We can use the Pumping Theorem to show that L is not regular. If it were, then there would exist some k such that any string w, where $|w| \geq k$, must satisfy the conditions of the theorem. We show one string w that does not. Let $w = \text{a}^j$, where j is the smallest prime number greater than $k + 1$. Since $|w| > k$, w must satisfy the conditions of the Pumping Theorem. So there must exist x, y, and z, such that $w = xyz$, $|xy| \leq k$ and $y \neq \varepsilon$. $y = \text{a}^p$ for some p. The Pumping Theorem further requires that $\forall q \geq 0\ (xy^qz \in L)$. So, $\forall q \geq 0$ $(\text{a}^{|x|+|z|+q|y|}$ must be in L). That means that $|x| + |z| + q \cdot |y|$ must be prime.

EXAMPLE 8.13 ***(Continued)***

But suppose that $q = |x| + |z|$. Then:

$$|x| + |z| + q \cdot |y| = |x| + |z| + (|x| + |z|) \cdot y$$
$$= (|x| + |z|) \cdot (1 + |y|),$$

which is composite (non-prime) if both factors are greater than 1. $(|x| + |z|) > 1$ because $|w| > k + 1$, and $|y| \leq k$. $(1 + |y|) > 1$ because $|y| > 0$. So, for at least that one value of q, the resulting string is not in L. So L is not regular.

When we do a Pumping Theorem proof that a language L is not regular, we have two choices to make: a value for w and a value for q. As we have just seen, there are some useful heuristics that can guide our choices:

- To choose w:
  - Choose a w that is in the part of L that makes it not regular.
  - Choose a w that is only barely in L.
  - Choose a w with as homogeneous as possible an initial region of length at least k.
- To choose q:
  - Try letting q be either 0 or 2.
  - If that doesn't work, analyze L to see if there is some other specific value that will work.

8.4.2 Using Closure Properties

Sometimes the easiest way to prove that a language L is not regular is to use the closure theorems for regular languages, either alone or in conjunction with the Pumping Theorem. The fact that the regular languages are closed under intersection is particularly useful.

EXAMPLE 8.14 Using Intersection to Force Order Constraints

Let $L = \{w \in \{\mathrm{a}, \mathrm{b}\}^* : \#_\mathrm{a}(w) = \#_\mathrm{b}(w)\}$. If L were regular, then $L' = L \cap \mathrm{a}^*\mathrm{b}^*$ would also be regular. But $L' = \{\mathrm{a}^n\mathrm{b}^n : n \geq 0\}$, which we have already shown is not regular. So L isn't either.

EXAMPLE 8.15 Using Closure Under Complement

Let $L = \{\mathrm{a}^i\mathrm{b}^j : i, j \geq 0 \text{ and } i \neq j\}$. It seems unlikely that L is regular since any machine to accept it would have to count the a's. It is possible to use the Pumping

Theorem to prove that L is not regular but it is not easy to see how. Suppose, for example, that we let $w = \mathrm{a}^{k+1}\mathrm{b}^k$. But then y could be aa and it would pump since $\mathrm{a}^{k-1}\mathrm{b}^k$ is in L, and so is $\mathrm{a}^{k+1+2(q-1)}\mathrm{b}^k$, for all nonnegative values of q.

Instead, let $w = \mathrm{a}^k\mathrm{b}^{k+k!}$. Then $y = \mathrm{a}^p$ for some nonzero p. Let $q = (k!/p) + 1$ (in other words, pump in $(k!/p)$ times). Note that $(k!/p)$ must be an integer because $p < k$. The number of a's in the resulting string is $k + (k!/p)p = k + k!$. So the resulting string is $\mathrm{a}^{k+k!}\mathrm{b}^{k+k!}$, which has equal numbers of a's and b's and so is not in L.

The closure theorems provide an easier way. We observe that if L were regular, then $\neg L$ would also be regular, since the regular languages are closed under complement. $\neg L = \{\mathrm{a}^n\ \mathrm{b}^n : n \geq 0\} \cup \{$ strings of a's and b's that do not have all a's in front of all b's$\}$. If $\neg L$ is regular, then $\neg L \cap \mathrm{a}^*\mathrm{b}^*$ must also be regular. But $\neg L \cap \mathrm{a}^*\mathrm{b}^* = \{\mathrm{a}^n\mathrm{b}^n : n \geq 0\}$, which we have already shown is not regular. So neither is $\neg L$ or L.

Sometimes, using the closure theorems is more than a convenience. There are languages that are not regular but that do meet all the conditions of the Pumping Theorem. The Pumping Theorem alone is insufficient to prove that those languages are not regular, but it may be possible to complete a proof by exploiting the closure properties of the regular languages.

EXAMPLE 8.16 Sometimes We Must Use the Closure Theorems

Let $L = \{\mathrm{a}^i\ \mathrm{b}^j\ \mathrm{c}^k : i, j, k \geq 0 \text{ and } (\text{if } i = 1 \text{ then } j = k)\}$. Every string of length at least 1 that is in L is pumpable. It is easier to see this if we rewrite the final condition as $(i \neq 1)$ or $(j = k)$. Then we observe:

- If $i = 0$ then: If $j \neq 0$, let y be b; otherwise, let y be c. Pump in or out. Then i will still be 0 and thus not equal to 1, so the resulting string is in L.
- If $i = 1$ then: Let y be a. Pump in or out. Then i will no longer equal 1, so the resulting string is in L.
- If $i = 2$ then: Let y be aa. Pump in or out. Then i cannot equal 1, so the resulting string is in L.
- If $i > 2$ then: Let y be a. Pump out once or in any number of times. Then i cannot equal 1, so the resulting string is in L.

But L is not regular. One way to prove this is to use the fact that the regular languages are closed under intersection. So, if L were regular, then $L' = L \cap \mathrm{ab}^*\mathrm{c}^*$ $= \{\ \mathrm{ab}^j\ \mathrm{c}^k : j, k \geq 0 \text{ and } j = k\}$ would also be regular. But it is not, which we can show using the Pumping Theorem. Let $w = \mathrm{ab}^k\mathrm{c}^k$. Then y must occur in the first k characters of w. If y includes the initial a, pump in once. The resulting string is not in L' because it contains more than one a. If y does not include the initial a, then it must be b^p, where $0 < p < k$. Pump in once. The resulting string is not in L' because it contains more b's than c's. Since L' is not regular, neither is L.

EXAMPLE 8.16 *(Continued)*

Another way to show that L is not regular is to use the fact that the regular languages are closed under reverse. $L^R = \{\mathrm{c}^k\ \mathrm{b}^j\ \mathrm{a}^i : i, j, k \geq 0 \text{ and (if } i = 1 \text{ then } j = k)\}$. If L were regular then L^R would also be regular. But it is not, which we can show using the Pumping Theorem. Let $w = \mathrm{c}^k\ \mathrm{b}^k\ \mathrm{a}$. y must occur in the first k characters of w, so $y = \mathrm{c}^p$, where $0 < p \leq k$. Set q to 0. The resulting string contains a single a, so the number of b's and c's must be equal for it to be in L^R. But there are fewer c's than b's. So the resulting string is not in L^R. L^R is not regular. Since L^R is not regular, neither is L.

8.5 Exploiting Problem-Specific Knowledge

Given some new language L, the theory that we have been describing provides the skeleton for an analysis of L. If L is simple, that may be enough. But if L is based on a real problem, any analysis of it will also depend on knowledge of the task domain. We got a hint of this in Example 8.13, where we had to use some knowledge about numbers and algebra. Other problems also require mathematical facts.

EXAMPLE 8.17 The Octal Representation of a Number Divisible by 7

Let $L = \{w \in \{0, 1, 2, 3, 4, 5, 6, 7\}^* : w$ is the octal representation of a nonnegative integer that is divisible by 7$\}$. The first several strings in L are: 0, 7, 16, 25, 34, 43, 52, and 61. Is L regular? Yes, because there is a simple, 7-state DFSM M that accepts L. The structure of M takes advantage of the fact that w is in L iff the sum of its digits, viewed as numbers, is divisible by 7. So the states of M correspond to the modulo 7 sum of the digits so far. We omit the details.

Sometimes L corresponds to a problem from a domain other than mathematics, in which case facts from that domain will be important.

EXAMPLE 8.18 A Music Language

Let Σ = {𝅝, 𝅗𝅥, ♩, ♪, 𝅘𝅥𝅯, 𝅘𝅥𝅰}. Let $L = \{w : w$ represents a song written in 4/4 time$\}$. L is regular. It can be accepted by an FSM that checks for 4 beats between measure bars, where 𝅝 counts as 4, 𝅗𝅥 counts as 2, ♩ counts as 1, ♪ counts as $^1/_2$, 𝅘𝅥𝅯 counts as $^1/_4$, and 𝅘𝅥𝅰 counts as 1/8.

Other techniques described in this book can also be applied to the language of music. (N.1)

EXAMPLE 8.19 English

Is English a regular language? If we assume that there is a longest sentence, then English is regular because it is finite. If we assume that there is not a longest sentence and that the recursive constructs in English can be arbitrarily nested, then it is easy to show that English is not regular. We consider a very small subset of English, sentences such as:

- `The rat ran.`
- `The rat that the cat saw ran.`
- `The rat that the cat that the dog chased saw ran.`

There is a limit on how deeply nested sentences such as this can be if people are going to be able to understand them easily. But the grammar of English imposes no hard upper bound. So we must allow any number of embedded sentences. Let A = {`cat`, `rat`, `dog`, `bird`, `bug`, `pony`} and let V = {`ran`, `saw`, `chased`, `flew`, `sang`, `frolicked`}. If English were regular, then L = English ∩ {`The` A (`that the` A)*V*V } would also be regular. But every English sentence of this form has the same number of nouns as verbs. So we have that:

$$L = \{\texttt{The}\ A(\texttt{that the}\ A)^n\, V^n V, n \geq 0\}.$$

We can show that L is not regular by pumping. The outline of the proof is the same as the one we used in Example 8.9 to show that A^nB^n is not regular. Let w = `The cat (that the rat)`^{k} `saw`^{k} `ran`. y must occur within the first k characters of w. If y is anything other than (`the` A `that`)^p, or (A `that the`)^p, or (`that the` A)^p, for some nonzero p, pump in once and the resulting string will not be of the correct form. If y is equal to one of those strings, pump in once and the number of nouns will no longer equal the number of verbs. In either case the resulting string is not in L. So English is not regular.

Is there a longest English sentence? Are there other ways of showing that English isn't regular? Would it be useful to describe English as a regular language even if we could? (L.3.1)

8.6 Functions on Regular Languages

In Section 8.3, we considered some important functions that can be applied to the regular languages and we showed that the class of regular languages is closed under them. In this section, we will look at some additional functions and ask whether the regular languages are closed under them. In some cases, we will see that the answer is yes. We will prove that the answer is yes by showing a construction that builds one FSM from another. In other cases, we will see that the answer is no, which we now have the tools to prove.

EXAMPLE 8.20 The Function *firstchars*

Consider again the function *firstchars*, which we defined in Example 4.11. Recall that $firstchars(L) = \{w : \exists y \in L\ (y = cx, c \in \Sigma_L, x \in \Sigma_L^*, \text{ and } w \in c^*)\}$. In other words, to compute *firstchars*(L), we find all the characters that can be initial characters of some string in L. For each such character c, $c^* \subseteq firstchars(L)$.

The regular languages are closed under *firstchars*. The proof is by construction. If L is a regular language, then there exists some DFSM $M = (K, \Sigma, \delta, s, A)$ that accepts L. We construct, from M, a new DFSM $M' = (K', \Sigma, \delta', s', A')$ that accepts *firstchars*(L). The algorithm to construct M' is:

1. Mark all the states in M from which there exists some path to some accepting state.

/* Find all the characters that are initial characters in some string in L.

2. $clist = \varnothing$.
3. For each character c in Σ do:

    If there is a transition from s, with label c, to some state q, and q was marked in step 1 then:

    $clist = clist \cup \{c\}$.

/* Build M'.

4. If $clist = \varnothing$ then construct M' with a single state s', which is not accepting.
5. Else do:

    Create a start state s' and make it the first state in A'.

    For each character c in *clist* do:

    Create a new state q_c and add it to A'.
    Add a transition from s' to q_c labeled c.
    Add a transition from q_c to q_c labeled c.

M' accepts exactly the strings in *firstchars*(L), so *firstchars*(L) is regular.

We can also prove that *firstchars*(L) must be regular by showing how to construct a regular expression that describes it. We begin by computing $clist = \{c_1, c_2, \ldots, c_n\}$ as described above. Then a regular expression that describes *firstchars*(L) is:

$$c_1^* \cup c_2^* \cup \cdots \cup c_n^*.$$

The algorithm that we just presented constructs one program (a DFSM), using another program (another DFSM) as a starting point. The algorithm is straightforward. We have omitted a detailed proof of its correctness, but that proof is also straightforward. Suppose that, instead of representing an input language L as a DFSM, we had represented it as an arbitrary program (written in C++ or Java or whatever) that accepted it. It would not have been as straightforward to have designed a corresponding algorithm to convert that program into one that accepted *firstchars*(L). We have just seen another advantage of the FSM formalism.

EXAMPLE 8.21 The Function *chop*

Consider again the function *chop*, defined in Example 4.10. $Chop(L) = \{w : \exists x \in L(x = x_1 c x_2, x_1 \in \Sigma_L^*, x_2 \in \Sigma_L^*, c \in \Sigma_L, |x_1| = |x_2|, \text{ and } w = x_1 x_2)\}$. In other words, *chop*(L) is all the odd length strings in L with their middle character chopped out.

The regular languages are not closed under *chop*. To show this, it suffices to show one counterexample, i.e., one regular language L such that *chop*(L) is not regular. Let L = a*db*. L is regular since it can be described with a regular expression.

What is *chop*(a*db*)? Let w be some string in a*db*. Now we observe:

- If $|w|$ is even, then there is no middle character to chop so w contributes no string to *chop* (a*db*).
- If $|w|$ is odd and w has an equal number of a's and b's, then its middle character is d. Chopping out the d produces, and contributes to *chop*(a*db*), a string in $\{a^n b^n : n \geq 0\}$.
- If $|w|$ is odd and w does not have an equal number of a's and b's, then its middle character is not d. Chopping out the middle character produces a string that still contains one d. Also note that, since $|w|$ is odd and the number of a's differs from the number of b's, it must differ by at least two. So, when w's middle character is chopped out, the resulting string will still have different numbers of a's and b's.

So *chop*(a*db*) contains all strings in $\{a^n b^n : n \geq 0\}$ plus some strings in $\{w \in a^*db^* : |w| \text{ is even and } \#_a(w) \neq \#_b(w)\}$. We can now show that *chop*(a*db*) is not regular. If it were, then the language L' = *chop*(a*db*) ∩ a*b*, would also be regular since the regular languages are closed under intersection. But $L' = \{a^n b^n : n \geq 0\}$, which we have already shown is not regular. So neither is *chop*(a*db*). Since there exists at least one regular language L with the property that *chop*(L) is not regular, the regular languages are not closed under *chop*.

EXAMPLE 8.22 The Function *maxstring*

Define $maxstring(L) = \{w : w \in L \text{ and } \forall z \in \Sigma^*(z \neq \varepsilon \rightarrow wz \notin L)\}$. In other words, *maxstring*(L) contains exactly those strings in L that cannot be extended on the right and still be in L. Let's look at *maxstring* applied to some languages:

L	*maxstring*(*L*)
∅	∅
a*b*	∅
ab*a	ab*a
a*b*a	a*b⁺a

EXAMPLE 8.23 The Function *mix*

Define $mix(L) = \{w : \exists x, y, z\,(x \in L, x = yz, |y| = |z|, w = yz^R)\}$. In other words, $mix(L)$ contains exactly those strings that can be formed by taking some even length string in L and reversing its second half. Let's look at mix applied to some languages:

L	$mix(L)$
$\varnothing$	$\varnothing$
(a ∪ b)*	((a ∪ b)(a ∪ b))*
(ab)*	$\{(\text{ab})^{2n+1} : n \geq 0\} \cup \{(\text{ab})^n(\text{ba})^n : n \geq 0\}$
(ab)*a(ab)*	$\varnothing$

The regular languages are closed under *maxstring*. They are not closed under *mix*. We leave the proof of these claims as an exercise.

Exercises

1. For each of the following languages L, state whether L is regular or not and prove your answer:
   a. $\{\text{a}^i\text{b}^j : i, j \geq 0 \text{ and } i + j = 5\}$.
   b. $\{\text{a}^i\text{b}^j : i, j \geq 0 \text{ and } i - j = 5\}$.
   c. $\{\text{a}^i\text{b}^j : i, j \geq 0 \text{ and } |i - j| \equiv_5 0\}$.
   d. $\{w \in \{0, 1, \#\}^* : w = x\#y, \text{ where } x, y \in \{0, 1\}^* \text{ and } |x| \cdot |y| \equiv_5 0\}$.
   e. $\{\text{a}^i\,\text{b}^j : 0 \leq i < j < 2000\}$.
   f. $\{w \in \{\text{Y}, \text{N}\}^* : w$ contains at least two Y's and at most two N's$\}$.
   g. $\{w = xy : x, y \in \{\text{a}, \text{b}\}^* \text{ and } |x| = |y| \text{ and } \#_\text{a}(x) \geq \#_\text{a}(y)\}$.
   h. $\{w = xyzy^\text{R}x : x, y, z \in \{\text{a}, \text{b}\}^*\}$.
   i. $\{w = xyzy : x, y, z \in \{0, 1\}^+\}$.
   j. $\{w \in \{0, 1\}^* : \#_0(w) \neq \#_1(w)\}$.
   k. $\{w \in \{\text{a}, \text{b}\}^* : w = w^\text{R}\}$.
   l. $\{w \in \{\text{a}, \text{b}\}^* : \exists x \in \{\text{a}, \text{b}\}^+\ (w = x\,x^\text{R}x)\}$.
   m. $\{w \in \{\text{a}, \text{b}\}^*$: the number of occurrences of the substring ab equals the number of occurrences of the substring ba$\}$.
   n. $\{w \in \{\text{a}, \text{b}\}^* : w$ contains exactly two more b's than a's$\}$.
   o. $\{w \in \{\text{a}, \text{b}\}^* : w = xyz, |x| = |y| = |z|$, and $z = x$ with every a replaced by b and every b replaced by a$\}$. Example: abbbabbaa $\in L$, with $x =$ abb, $y =$ bab, and $z =$ baa.
   p. $\{w\text{: } w \in \{\text{a} - \text{z}\}^*$ and the letters of w appear in reverse alphabetical order$\}$. For example, spoonfeed $\in L$.

q. $\{w: w \in \{\text{a} - \text{z}\}^*$ every letter in w appears at least twice$\}$. For example, unprosperousness $\in L$.

r. $\{w : w$ is the decimal encoding of a natural number in which the digits appear in a non-decreasing order without leading zeros$\}$.

s. $\{w$ of the form: <*integer*$_1$> + <*integer*$_2$> = <*integer*$_3$>, where each of the substrings <*integer*$_1$>, <*integer*$_2$>, and <*integer*$_3$> is an element of $\{0 - 9\}^*$ and *integer*$_3$ is the sum of *integer*$_1$ and *integer*$_2\}$. For example, 124+5=129 $\in L$.

t. L_0^*, where $L_0 = \{\text{ba}^i\,\text{b}^j\,\text{a}^k, j \geq 0, 0 \leq i \leq k\}$.

u. $\{w : w$ is the encoding of a date that occurs in a year that is a prime number$\}$. A date will be encoded as a string of the form *mm*/*dd*/*yyyy*, where each m, d, and y is drawn from $\{0\text{–}9\}$.

v. $\{w \in \{1\}^* : w$ is, for some $n \geq 1$, the unary encoding of $10^n\}$. (So $L = \{1111111111, 1^{100}, 1^{1000}, \ldots\}$.)

2. For each of the following languages L, state whether L is regular or not and prove your answer:

a. $\{w \in \{\text{a, b, c}\}^* :$ in each prefix x of w, $\#_\text{a}(x) = \#_\text{b}(x) = \#_\text{c}(x))\}$.

b. $\{w \in \{\text{a, b, c}\}^* : \exists$ some prefix x of w $(\#_\text{a}(x) = \#_\text{b}(x) = \#_\text{c}(x))\}$.

c. $\{w \in \{\text{a, b, c}\}^* : \exists$ some prefix x of w $(x \neq \varepsilon$ and $\#_\text{a}(x) = \#_\text{b}(x) = \#_\text{c}(x))\}$.

3. Define the following two languages:

$$L_\text{a} = \{w \in \{\text{a, b}\}^* : \text{in each prefix } x \text{ of } w, \#_\text{a}(x) \geq \#_\text{b}(x)\}.$$

$$L_\text{b} = \{w \in \{\text{a, b}\}^* : \text{in each prefix } x \text{ of } w, \#_\text{b}(x) \geq \#_\text{a}(x)\}.$$

a. Let $L_1 = L_\text{a} \cap L_\text{b}$. Is L_1 regular? Prove your answer.

b. Let $L_2 = L_\text{a} \cup L_\text{b}$. Is L_2 regular? Prove your answer.

4. For each of the following languages L, state whether L is regular or not and prove your answer:

a. $\{uww^\text{R}v : u, v, w \in \{\text{a, b}\}^+\}$.

b. $\{xyzy^\text{R}x : x, y, z \in \{\text{a, b}\}^+\}$.

5. Use the Pumping Theorem to complete the proof, given in L.3.1, that English isn't regular.

6. Prove *by construction* that the regular languages are closed under:

a. intersection.

b. set difference.

7. Prove that the regular languages are closed under each of the following operations:

a. $\textit{pref}(L) = \{w : \exists x \in \Sigma^*(wx \in L)\}$.

b. $\textit{suff}(L) = \{w : \exists x \in \Sigma^*(xw \in L)\}$.

c. $\textit{reverse}(L) = \{x \in \Sigma^* : x = w^\text{R}$ for some $w \in L\}$.

d. letter substitution (as defined in Section 8.3).

8. Using the defintions of *maxstring* and *mix* given in Section 8.6, give a precise definition of each of the following languages:

a. *maxstring*($A^n B^n$).
b. *maxstring*($a^i b^j c^k, 1 \leq k \leq j \leq i$).
c. *maxstring*(L_1L_2), where $L_1 = \{w \in \{a, b\}^* : w$ contains exactly one a$\}$ and $L_2 = \{a\}$.
d. *mix*((aba)*).
e. *mix*(a*b*).

9. Prove that the regular languages are not closed under *mix*.

10. Recall that $maxstring(L) = \{w : w \in L \text{ and } \forall z \in \Sigma^*(z \neq \varepsilon \rightarrow wz \notin L)\}$.
a. Prove that the regular languages are closed under *maxstring*.
b. If *maxstring*(L) is regular, must L also be regular? Prove your answer.

11. Define the function $midchar(L) = \{c : \exists w \in L(w = ycz, c \in \Sigma_L, y \in \Sigma_L^*, z \in \Sigma_L^*, |y| = |z|)\}$. Answer each of the following questions and prove your answer:
a. Are the regular languages closed under *midchar*?
b. Are the nonregular languages closed under *midchar*?

12. Define the function $twice(L) = \{w : \exists x \in L$ (x can be written as $c_1c_2 \ldots c_n$, for some $n \geq 1$, where each $c_i \in \Sigma_L$, and $w = c_1c_1c_2c_2 \ldots c_nc_n$)$\}$.
a. Let $L = (1 \cup 0)^*1$. Write a regular expression for *twice*(L).
b. Are the regular languages closed under *twice*? Prove your answer.

13. Define the function $shuffle(L) = \{w : \exists x \in L$ (w is some permutation of x)$\}$. For example, if $L = \{$ab, abc$\}$, then $shuffle(L) = \{$ab, abc, ba, acb, bac, bca, cab, cba$\}$. Are the regular languages closed under *shuffle*? Prove your answer.

14. Define the function $copyandreverse(L) = \{w : \exists x \in L(w = xx^R)\}$. Are the regular languages closed under *copyandreverse*? Prove your answer.

15. Let L_1 and L_2 be regular languages. Let L be the language consisting of strings that are contained in exactly one of L_1 and L_2. Prove that L is regular.

16. Define two integers i and j to be ***twin primes*** iff both i and j are prime and $|j - i| = 2$.
a. Let $L = \{w \in \{1\}^* : w$ is the unary notation for a natural number n such that there exists a pair p and q of twin primes, both $> n.\}$ Is L regular?
b. Let $L = \{x, y : x$ is the decimal encoding of a positive integer i, y is the decimal encoding of a positive integer j, and i and j are twin primes$\}$. Is L regular?

17. Consider any function $f(L_1) = L_2$, where L_1 and L_2 are both languages over the alphabet $\Sigma = \{0, 1\}$. A function f is ***nice*** iff whenever L_2 is regular, L_1 is regular. For each of the following functions, f, state whether or not it is nice and prove your answer.
a. $f(L) = L^R$.
b. $f(L) = \{w : w$ is formed by taking a string in L and replacing all 1's with 0's and leaving the 0's unchanged$\}$.
c. $f(L) = L \cup 0^*$.
d. $f(L) = \{w : w$ is formed by taking a string in L and replacing all 1's with 0's and all 0's with 1's (simultaneously)$\}$.

e. $f(L) = \{w : \exists x \in L\ (w = x00)\}$.

f. $f(L) = \{w : w$ is formed by taking a string in L and removing the last character$\}$.

18. We'll say that a language L over an alphabet Σ is ***splitable*** iff the following property holds: Let w be any string in L that can be written as $c_1c_2 \ldots c_{2n}$, for some $n \geq 1$, where each $c_i \in \Sigma$. Then $x = c_1c_3 \ldots c_{2n-1}$ is also in L.

a. Give an example of a splitable regular language.

b. Is every regular language splitable?

c. Does there exist a nonregular language that is splitable?

19. Define the class IR to be the class of languages that are both infinite and regular. Tell whether the class IR closed under:

a. union.

b. intersection.

c. Kleene star.

20. Consider the language $L = \{x0^ny\ 1^nz : n \geq 0, x \in P, y \in Q, z \in R$, where P, Q, and R are nonempty sets over the alphabet $\{0, 1\}\}$. Can you find regular sets P, Q, and R such that L is not regular? Can you find regular sets P, Q, and R such that L is regular?

21. For each of the following claims, state whether it is *True* or *False*. Prove your answer.

a. There are uncountably many non-regular languages over $\Sigma = \{\mathtt{a}, \mathtt{b}\}$.

b. The union of an infinite number of regular languages must be regular.

c. The union of an infinite number of regular languages is never regular.

d. If L_1 and L_2 are not regular languages, then $L_1 \cup L_2$ is not regular.

e. If L_1 and L_2 are regular languages, then $L_1 \otimes L_2 = \{w : w \in (L_1 - L_2)$ or $w \in (L_2 - L_1)\}$ is regular.

f. If L_1 and L_2 are regular languages and $L_1 \subseteq L \subseteq L_2$, then L must be regular.

g. The intersection of a regular language and a nonregular language must be regular.

h. The intersection of a regular language and a nonregular language must not be regular.

i. The intersection of two nonregular languages must not be regular.

j. The intersection of a finite number of nonregular languages must not be regular.

k. The intersection of an infinite number of regular languages must be regular.

l. It is possible that the concatenation of two nonregular languages is regular.

m. It is possible that the union of a regular language and a nonregular language is regular.

n. Every nonregular language can be described as the intersection of an infinite number of regular languages.

o. If L is a language that is not regular, then L^* is not regular.

p. If L^* is regular, then L is regular.

q. The nonregular languages are closed under intersection.

r. Every subset of a regular language is regular.

s. Let $L_4 = L_1L_2L_3$. If L_1 and L_2 are regular and L_3 is not regular, it is possible that L_4 is regular.

t. If L is regular, then so is $\{xy : x \in L \text{ and } y \notin L\}$.

u. Every infinite regular language properly contains another infinite regular language.

CHAPTER 9

Algorithms and Decision Procedures for Regular Languages

So far, we have considered five important properties of regular languages:

1. FSMs and regular expressions are useful design tools.
2. The fact that nondeterminism can be "compiled out" of an FSM makes it even easier, for many kinds of tasks, to design a simple machine that can relatively easily be shown to be correct.
3. DFSMs run in time that is linear in the length of the input.
4. There exists an algorithm to minimize a DFSM.
5. The regular languages are closed under many useful operators, so we can talk about programs that manipulate FSMs to construct new ones.

And now we will consider a sixth:

6. There exist decision procedures for many questions that we would like to ask about FSMs and regular expressions.

9.1 Fundamental Decision Procedures

Recall from Section 4.1 that a decision procedure is an algorithm whose result is a Boolean value. A decision procedure must be guaranteed to halt on all inputs and to return the correct value.

In this section, we describe some of the most useful decision procedures for regular languages:

9.1.1 Membership

Given an FSM M and a string w, does M accept w? This is the most basic question we can ask about an FSM. It can be answered by running M on w, provided that we do so in a fashion that guarantees that the simulation halts. Recall that the simulation of an NDFSM M might not halt if M contains ε-loops that are not handled properly by the simulator.

EXAMPLE 9.1 ε-Loops Can Cause Trouble in NDFSMs

If we are not careful, the simulation of the following NDFSM on input aa might get stuck chasing the ε-loop between q_0 and q_1, never reading any input characters:

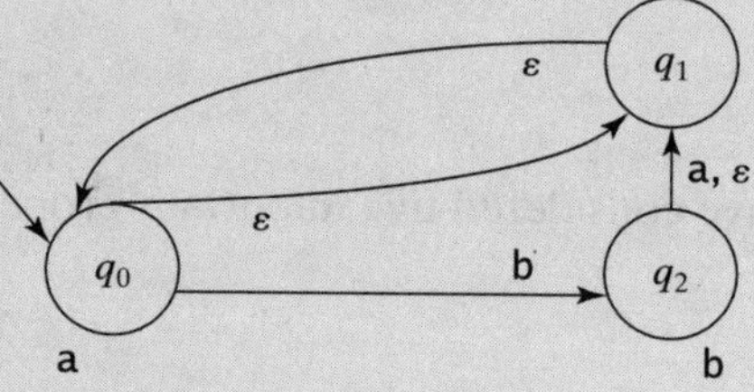

THEOREM 9.1 Decidability of Regular Languages

Theorem: Given a regular language L (represented as an FSM or a regular expression or a regular grammar) and a string w, there exists a decision procedure that answers the question, is $w \in L$?

Proof: If L is represented as an FSM, we can answer the question using either of the simulation techniques described in Section 5.6. We'll choose to use *ndfsmsimulate*:

decideFSM (M: FSM, w: *string*) =

If *ndfsmsimulate*(M, w) accepts then return *True* else return *False*.

Any question that can be answered about an FSM can be answered about a regular expression by first converting the regular expression into an FSM. So if L is represented as a regular expression α, we can answer the question, "Does α generate w?" using the procedure *decideregex* defined as follows:

decideregex (α: regular expression, w: *string*) =

1. From α, use *regextofsm* to construct an FSM M such that $L(\alpha) = L(M)$.
2. Return *decideFSM*(M, w).

The same is true of regular grammars: Any regular grammar G can be converted to an FSM that accepts $L(G)$.

While the solution to this problem was simple, the question itself is very important. We will see later that, in the case of some more powerful computational models (in particular the Turing machine), the basic membership question is not decidable. This fact is yet another powerful argument for the use of an FSM whenever one exists.

In the remainder of this discussion, we will focus on answering questions about FSMs. Each question that is decidable for FSMs is also decidable for regular expressions and for regular grammars because a regular expression or a regular grammar can be converted to an equivalent FSM.

9.1.2 Emptiness and Totality

The next question we will consider is, "Given an FSM M, is $L(M) = \varnothing$?" There are two approaches that we could take to answering a question like this about the overall behavior of M:

1. View M as a directed graph in which the states are the vertices and the transitions are directed edges. Find some property of the graph that corresponds to the situation in which $L(M) = \varnothing$.
2. Run M on some number of strings and observe its behavior.

Both work. Let's consider the first approach in which we do a static analysis of M, without running it on any strings. We observe that $L(M)$ will be empty if K_M contains no accepting states. But then we realize that, for $L(M)$ not to be empty, it is not sufficient for there to be at least one accepting state. That state must be reachable, via some path, from the start state. So we can state the following algorithm for testing whether $L(M) = \varnothing$:

emptyFSMgraph (M: FSM) =

1. Mark all states that are reachable via some path from the start state of M.
2. If at least one marked state is an accepting state, return *False*. Else return *True*.

Another way to use the graph-testing method is to exploit the fact there exists a canonical form for FSMs. Recall that, in Section 5.8, we described the algorithm *buildFSMcanonicalform*, which built, from any FSM M, an equivalent unique minimal DFSM whose states are named in a standard way so that all equivalent FSMs will generate the same minimal deterministic machine. We can use that canonical form as the basis for a simple emptiness checker, since we note that $L(M)$ is empty iff the canonical form of M is the one-state FSM that accepts nothing. So we can define:

emptyFSMcanonicalgraph (M: FSM) =

1. Let $M\# = $ *buildFSMcanonicalform* (M).
2. If $M\#$ is the one-state FSM that accepts nothing, return *True*. Else return *False*.

The second, very different, approach to answering the emptiness question is to run M on some strings and see whether or not it accepts. We might start by running M on all strings in Σ^* to see if it accepts any of them. But there is an infinite number of possible strings (assuming that Σ_M is not empty). A decision procedure must be guaranteed to halt in a finite number of steps, even if the answer is *False*. But we make the same observation here that we used as the basis for the Pumping Theorem: If a DFSM M accepts any "long" strings, then it also accepts the strings that result from pumping out from those long strings the substrings that drove M through a loop. More precisely, if a DFSM M accepts any strings of length greater than or equal to $|K_M|$, then it must also accept at least one string of length less than $|K_M|$. In other words, it must accept at least one string without going through any loops. So we can define *emptyFSMsimulate*:

emptyFSMsimulate (M: FSM) =

1. Let $M' = ndfsmtodfsm\ (M)$.
2. For each string w in Σ^* such that $|w| < |K_{M'}|$ do:
   Run *decideFSM* (M', w).
3. If M' accepts at least one such string, return *False*; else return *True*.

This definition of *emptyFSMsimulate* exploits a powerful technique that we'll use in other decision procedures. We'll call it ***bounded simulation***. It answers a question about $L(M)$ by simulating the execution of M. For bounded simulation to serve as the basis of a decision procedure, two things must be true:

- The simulation of M on a particular input string must be guaranteed to halt. DFSMs always halt, so this requirement is easily met. We'll see later, however, that when we are considering more powerful machines, such as pushdown automata and Turing machines, this condition may not be satisfied.
- It must be possible to determine the answer we seek by simulating M on some *finite* number strings. So we need to be able to do an analysis, of the sort we did above, that shows that once we know how M works on some particular finite set of strings, we can conclude some more general property of its behavior.

The algorithms that we have just presented enable us to prove the following theorem:

THEOREM 9.2 Decidability of Emptiness

Theorem: Given an FSM M, there exists a decision procedure that answers the question, is $L\ (M) = \varnothing$?

Proof: All three algorithms, *emptyFSMgraph*, *emptyFSMcanonicalgraph*, and *emptyFSMsimulate*, can easily be shown to be correct. We can pick any one of them and use it to define the procedure *emptyFSM*. We'll use *emptyFSMsimulate*:

emptyFSM (M: FSM) =

Return *emptyFSMsimulate*(M).

At the other extreme, we might like to ask the question, "Given an FSM M, is $L\ (M) = \Sigma^*$?" In other words, does M accept everything? The answer is yes iff $\neg L\ (M) = \varnothing$. So we have the following theorem:

THEOREM 9.3 Decidability of Totality

Theorem: Given an FSM M, there exists a decision procedure that answers the question, is $L\ (M) = \Sigma^*$?

Proof: The following procedure answers the question:

totalFSM (M: FSM) =

1. Construct M' to accept $\neg L(M)$.
2. Return *emptyFSM* (M').

9.1.3 Finiteness

Suppose that $L(M)$ is not empty. Then we might like to ask, "Is $L(M)$ finite?" Again, we can attempt to answer the question either by analyzing M as a graph or by running it on strings.

Let's consider the graph approach first. $L(M)$ is clearly finite if M contains no loops. But the mere presence of a loop does not guarantee that $L(M)$ is infinite. The loop might be:

- labeled only with ε,
- unreachable from the start state, or
- not on a path to an accepting state.

In any of those cases, the loop will not force M to accept an infinite number of strings. Taking all of those issues into account, we can build the following correct graph-based algorithm to answer the question:

finiteFSMgraph (M: FSM) =

1. M' = *ndfsmtodfsm* (M).
2. M'' = *minDFSM* (M'). /* At this point, there are no ε-transitions and no unreachable states.
3. Mark all states in M'' that are on a path to an accepting state.
4. Considering only marked states, determine whether there are any cycles in M''.
5. If there are cycles, return *False*. Else return *True*.

While it is possible, as we have just seen, to design algorithms to answer questions about FSMs by analyzing them as graphs, it is quite easy to make mistakes, as we would have done had we not considered the three cases in which a loop does not mean that an infinite number of strings can be accepted.

It is often easier to design an algorithm and prove its correctness by appealing to the simulation strategy instead. Pursuing that approach, it may be tempting to try to answer the finiteness question by running M on all possible strings to see if it ever stops accepting. But, again, we can only use simulation in a decision procedure if we can put an upper bound on the amount of simulation that is required. Fortunately, we can do that in this case. Again we appeal to the argument that we used to prove the Pumping Theorem. We begin by making M deterministic so that we do not have to worry about ε-loops. Then observe that $L(M)$ is infinite iff it contains any strings that force M through some loop. Any string of length greater than $|K_M|$ must force M through a loop. So, if M accepts even one string of length greater than $|K_M|$, then $L(M)$ is infinite. Note also that if $L(M)$ is infinite then it contains no longest string.

So it must contain an infinite number of strings of length greater than $|K_M|$. So $L(M)$ is infinite iff M accepts even one string of length greater than $|K_M|$.

Unfortunately, there is an infinite number of such long strings. So we cannot try them all. But suppose that M accepts some "very long" string, i.e., one that forces M through a loop twice. Then we could pump out the substring that corresponds to the first time through the loop. We'd then have a shorter string that is also accepted by M. So if M accepts any strings that force it through a loop twice, it must also accept at least one string that forces it through a loop only once. The longest loop M could contain would be one that drives it through all its states a second time. So, $L(M)$ is infinite iff M accepts at least one string w where:

$$|K_M| \leq |w| \leq 2 \cdot |K_M| - 1.$$

We can now define a simulation-based procedure to determine whether $L(M)$ is finite:

finiteFSMsimulate (M: FSM) =

1. $M' = ndfsmtodfsm\ (M)$.
2. For each string w in Σ^* such that $|K_{M'}| \leq w \leq 2 \cdot |K_{M'}| - 1$ do
   Run *decideFSM* (M', w).
3. If M' accepts at least one such string, return *False* (since L is infinite and thus not finite); else return *True*.

THEOREM 9.4 Decidability of Finiteness

Theorem: Given an FSM M, there exists a decision procedure that answers the questions, "Is $L(M)$ finite?" and "Is $L(M)$ infinite?"

Proof: We can pick either *finiteFSMgraph* or *finiteFSMsimulate* and use it to define the procedure *finiteFSM*:

finiteFSM (M: FSM) =
    Return *finiteFSMsimulate*(M).

Of course, if we can decide whether $L(M)$ is finite, we can decide whether it is infinite:

infiniteFSM (M: FSM) =
    Return $\neg$(*finiteFSMsimulate*(M)).

9.1.4 Equivalence

Given two FSMs M_1 and M_2,, are they equivalent? In other words, is $L(M_1) = L(M_2)$? We can describe two different algorithms for answering this question.

The first algorithm takes advantage of the existence of a canonical form for FSMs. It works as follows:

equalFSMs$_1$ (M_1: FSM, M_2: FSM) =

1. M_1' = *buildFSMcanonicalform* (M_1).
2. M_2' = *buildFSMcanonicalform* (M_2).
3. If M_1' and M_2' are equal, return *True*, else return *False*.

The second algorithm depends on the following observation: Let L_1 and L_2 be the languages accepted by M_1 and M_2. Then M_1 and M_2 are equivalent iff $(L_1 - L_2) \cup (L_2 - L_1) = \varnothing$. Since the regular languages are closed under difference and union, we can build an FSM to accept $(L_1 - L_2) \cup (L_2 - L_1)$. We can then test to see whether that FSM accepts any strings. So we have:

equalFSMs$_2$ (M_1: FSM, M_2: FSM) =

1. Construct M_A to accept $L(M_1) - L(M_2)$.
2. Construct M_B to accept $L(M_2) - L(M_1)$.
3. Construct M_C to accept $L(M_A) \cup L(M_B)$.
4. Return *emptyFSM* (M_C).

THEOREM 9.5 Decidability of Equivalence

Theorem: Given two FSMs M_1 and M_2, there exists a decision procedure that answers the question, "Is $L(M_1) = L(M_2)$?"

Proof: We can pick the approach of either *equalFSMs*$_1$ or *equalFSMs*$_2$ and use it to define the procedure *equalFSMs*. Choosing *equalFSMs*$_2$, we get:

equalFSMs (M_1: FSM, M_2: FSM) =
Return *equalFSMs*$_2$ (M_1, M_2).

9.1.5 Minimality

THEOREM 9.6 Decidability of Minimality

Theorem: Given a DFSM M, there exists a decision procedure that answers the question, "Is M minimal?"

Proof: The proof is by construction. We define:

minimalFSM (M: FSM) =

1. M' = *minDFSM* (M).
2. If $|K_M| = |K_{M'}|$ return *True*; else return *False*.

Note that it is easy to modify *minimalFSM* so that, if M is not minimal, it returns $|K_M| - |K_{M'}|$.

9.1.6 Combining the Basics to Ask Specific Questions

With these fundamental decision algorithms in hand, coupled with the other functions (such as *ndfsmtodfsm* and *minDFSM*) that we have also defined, it is possible to answer a wide range of specific questions that might be of interest in a particular context.

EXAMPLE 9.2 Combining Algorithms and Decision Procedures

Suppose that we would like to know, for two arbitrary patterns, whether there are any nontrivial (which we may define, for example, as not equal to ε) strings that could match both patterns. This might come up if we are attempting to categorize strings in such a way that no string falls into more than one category. We can formalize that question as, "Given two regular expressions α_1 and α_2, is $(L(\alpha_1) \cap L(\alpha_2)) - \{\varepsilon\} \neq \varnothing$?" An algorithm to answer that question is:

1. From α_1, construct an FSM M_1 such that $L(\alpha_1) = L(M_1)$.
2. From α_2, construct an FSM M_2 such that $L(\alpha_2) = L(M_2)$.
3. Construct M' such that $L(M') = L(M_1) \cap L(M_2)$.
4. Construct M_ε such that $L(M_\varepsilon) = \{\varepsilon\}$.
5. Construct M'' such that $L(M'') = L(M') - L(M_\varepsilon)$.
6. If $L(M'')$ is empty return *False*; else return *True*.

9.2 Summary of Algorithms and Decision Procedures for Regular Languages

Sprinkled throughout our discussion of regular languages has been a collection of algorithms that can be applied to FSMs, regular expressions, and regular grammars. Together, those algorithms make it possible to:

- optimize FSMs,
- construct new FSMs and regular expressions from existing ones, thus enabling us to decompose complex problems into simpler ones and to reuse code that has already been written, and
- answer a wide variety of questions about any regular language or about the class of regular languages.

Because there are so many of these algorithms and they have been spread out over several chapters, we present a concise list of them here:

- Algorithms that operate on FSMs without altering the language that is accepted:
  - *Ndfsmtodfsm*: Given an NDFSM M, construct a DFSM M' such that $L(M) = L(M')$.
  - *MinDFSM*: Given a DFSM M, construct a minimal DFSM M', such that $L(M) = L(M')$.

- Algorithms that compute functions of languages defined as FSMs:
  - Given two FSMs M_1 and M_2, construct a new FSM M_3 such that $L(M_3) = L(M_2) \cup L(M_1)$.
  - Given two FSMs M_1 and M_2, construct a new FSM M_3 such that $L(M_3) = L(M_2)L(M_1)$ (i.e., the concatenation of $L(M_2)$ and $L(M_1)$).
  - Given an FSM M, construct a new FSM M' such that $L(M') = (L(M))^*$.
  - Given an FSM M, construct a new FSM M' such that $L(M') = \neg L(M)$.
  - Given two FSMs M_1 and M_2, construct a new FSM M_3 such that $L(M_3) = L(M_2) \cap L(M_1)$.
  - Given two FSMs M_1 and M_2, construct a new FSM M_3 such that $L(M_3) = L(M_2) - L(M_1)$.
  - Given an FSM M, construct a new FSM M' such that $L(M') = (L(M))^R$ (i.e., the reverse of $L(M)$).
  - Given an FSM M, construct an FSM M' that accepts *letsub*($L(M)$), where *letsub* is a letter substitution function.

- Algorithms that convert between FSMs and regular expressions:
  - Given a regular expression α, construct an FSM M such that $L(\alpha) = L(M)$.
  - Given an FSM M, construct a regular expression α such that $L(\alpha) = L(M)$.

- Algorithms that convert between FSMs and regular grammars:
  - Given a regular grammar G, construct an FSM M such that $L(G) = L(M)$.
  - Given an FSM M, construct a regular grammar G such that $L(G) = L(M)$.

- Algorithms that implement operations on languages defined by regular expressions or regular grammars: Any operation that can be performed on languages defined by FSMs can be implemented by converting all regular expressions or regular grammars to equivalent FSMs and then executing the appropriate FSM algorithm.

- Decision procedures that answer questions about languages defined by FSMs:
  - Given an FSM M and a string w, is w is accepted by M?
  - Given an FSM M, is $L(M) = \varnothing$?

- Given an FSM M, is $L(M) = \Sigma^*$?
- Given an FSM M, is $L(M)$ finite (or infinite)?
- Given two FSMs, M_1 and M_2, is $L(M_1) = L(M_2)$?
- Given a DFSM M, is M minimal?

- Decision procedures that answer questions about languages defined by regular expressions or regular grammars: Again, convert the regular expressions or regular grammars to FSMs and apply the FSM algorithms.

This list is important and it represents a strong argument for describing problems as regular languages and solutions as FSMs or regular expressions. As we will soon see, a few of these algorithms (but not most) exist for context-free languages and their associated representations (as pushdown automata or as context-free grammars). None of them exists for general purpose programming languages or Turing machines.

> At this point, we are concerned primarily with the existence of the algorithms that we need. In Part V, we'll expand our inquiry to include the complexity of the algorithms that we have found. But we can note here that not all of the algorithms that we have presented so far are efficient in the common sense of running in time that is polynomial in the length of the input. For example, *ndfsmtodfsm* may construct a DFSM whose size grows exponentially in the size of the input NDFSM. Thus its time requirement (in the worst case) is also exponential.

Exercises

1. Define a decision procedure for each of the following questions. Argue that each of your decision procedures gives the correct answer and terminates.

a. Given two DFSMs M_1 and M_2, is $L(M_1) = L(M_2)^R$?

b. Given two DFSMs M_1 and M_2 is $|L(M_1)| < |L(M_2)|$?

c. Given a regular grammar G and a regular expression α, is $L(G) = L(\alpha)$?

d. Given two regular expressions, α and β, do there exist any even length strings that are in $L(\alpha)$ but not $L(\beta)$?

e. Let $\Sigma = \{\texttt{a}, \texttt{b}\}$ and let α be a regular expression. Does the language generated by α contain all the even length strings in Σ^*.

f. Given an FSM M and a regular expression α, is it true that both $L(M)$ and $L(\alpha)$ are finite and M accepts exactly two more strings than α generates?

g. Let $\Sigma = \{\mathtt{a}, \mathtt{b}\}$ and let α and β be regular expressions. Is the following sentence true:

$$(L(\beta) = \mathtt{a}^*) \vee (\forall w\ (w \in \{\mathtt{a}, \mathtt{b}\}^* \wedge |w| \text{ even}) \rightarrow w \in L\ (\alpha)).$$

h. Given a regular grammar G, is $L(G)$ regular?

i. Given a regular grammar G, does G generate any odd length strings?

CHAPTER 10

Summary and References

Theoretically, every machine we build is a finite state machine. There is only a finite number (probably about 10^{79}) of atoms in the observable universe (that part of the universe that is within a distance of the speed of light times the age of the universe). So we have access to only a finite number of molecules with which to build computer memories, hard drives, and external storage devices. That doesn't mean that every real problem should be described as a regular language or solved with an FSM. FSMs and regular expressions are powerful tools for describing problems that possess the kind of repetitive patterns that FSMs and regular expressions can capture. To handle other problems and languages, we will need the more powerful models that we will introduce in Parts III and IV. The abstract machines that are built using those models will be equipped with infinite storage devices. Describing problems using those devices may be useful even if there exists some practical upper bound on the size of the actual inputs that need to be considered (and so some bound on the amount of memory required to solve the problem).

A lighthearted view of the theory of automata and computability has inspired a collection of poems by Martin Cohn and Harry Mairson. We include one of the poems here. Unfortunately, the names of the important concepts aren't standard and the poem uses some that are different from ours. So:

- DFA (Deterministic Finite Automaton) is equivalent to DFSM.
- The symbol p is used as we used k in the pumping theorem.
- The term r.e. (recursively enumerable), in the last line, refers to the class of languages we are calling semidecidable.

The Pumping Lemma for DFAs By Martin Cohn

Any regular language L has a magic number p
And any long-enough 'word' in L has the following property:
Amongst its first p symbols is a segment you can find
Whose repetition or omission leaves 'word' amongst its kind.

So if you find a language L which fails this acid test,
And some long word you pump becomes distinct from all the rest,

By contradiction you have shown that language L is not
A regular L, resilient to the damage you have wrought.

But if, upon the other hand, 'word' stays within its L,
Then either L is regular, or else you chose not well.
For 'word' is parsed as xyz, and y cannot be null,
And y must come before p symbols have been read in full.

You cannot choose the length of y, nor can you specify
Just where within the word you chose it happens just to lie.
The DFA locates string y to your discomfiture.
Recall this moral to the grave: You can't fool Mother Nature.

As postscript mathematical, addendum to the wise:
The basic proof we outlined here does surely generalize.
So there's a pumping lemma for languages context-free,
But sadly we do not have the same for those that are r.e.

References

The idea of a finite state computer grew out of an early (i.e., predating modern computers) attempt [McCulloch and Pitts 1943] to describe the human brain as a logical computing device. The artificial neuron model 💻 described in that paper inspired the development of the modern neural networks that play an important role in artificial intelligence systems today. It also laid the groundwork for the development of the general model of finite state computing that we have discussed. About a decade after the McCulloch and Pitts paper, several independent formulations of finite state computers appeared. Mealy and Moore machines were defined in [Mealy 1955] and [Moore 1956], respectively. [Kleene 1956] described the McCulloch and Pitts neurons as FSMs. It also defined regular expressions and then proved the result that we state as Theorem 6.3 and call Kleene's Theorem, namely that the class of languages that can be defined by regular expressions is identical to the class that can be accepted by finite state machines.

Many of the early results in finite automata, including Theorem 5.3 (that, for every nondeterministic FSM there exists an equivalent deterministic one) were given in [Rabin and Scott 1959]. For this work, Rabin and Scott received the 1976 Turing Award. The citation read, "For their joint paper "Finite Automata and Their Decision Problem," which introduced the idea of nondeterministic machines, which has proved to be an enormously valuable concept. Their classic paper has been a continuous source of inspiration for subsequent work in this field."

The definition of the missing letter language that we discussed in Example 5.12 and Example 5.15 and the proof given in Appendix C for the correctness of *ndfsmtodfsm* were taken from [Lewis and Papadimitriou 1998].

[Aho and Corasick 1975] presents a set of algorithms for building a finite state transducer that finds and reports all instances of a set of keywords in a target string. The algorithm *buildkeywordFSM* is derived from those algorithms, so the details of how it words can be found in the original paper.

The Myhill-Nerode Theorem was proved in [Myhill 1957] and [Nerode 1958].

Markov chains were first described (in Russian) by A. A. Markov in 1906. The mathematical theory of Hidden Markov models was described in [Baum, Petrie, Soules, and Weiss 1970]. The Viterbi algorithm was presented in [Viterbi 1967].

Büchi automata were described in [Büchi 1960a] and [Büchi 1960b]. For a comprehensive discussion of them, as well as other automata on infinite strings, see [Thomas 1990] or [Khoussainov and Nerode 2001]. The Büchi automaton that describes the mutual exclusion property and that we presented in Example 5.39 is taken from [Clarke, Grumberg, and Peled 2000], which is a good introduction to model checking. The proof we presented for Theorem 5.7 is taken from [Roggenbach 2002], which presents a comprehensive discussion of nondeterminism in ω-automata, including a discussion of alternative models, including Muller and Rabin automata. Theorem 5.8 was stated in [Büchi 1960a]. Our presentation of it and of Theorem 5.9 and Theorem 5.10 is taken from [Thomas 1990], which supplies more details.

Regular grammars were defined as part of what we now call the Chomsky hierarchy (see Section 24.2) in [Chomsky 1959]. The equivalence of FSMs and regular grammars was shown in [Chomsky and Miller 1958].

The Pumping Theorem for regular languages (along with one for context-free languages that we will discuss in Section 13.3) was stated and proved in [Bar-Hillel, Perles, and Shamir 1961]. The Pumping Theorem proof in Example 8.15 was taken from [Sipser 2006].

P A R T I I I

CONTEXT-FREE LANGUAGES AND PUSHDOWN AUTOMATA

In this section, we move out one level and explore the class of context-free languages.

This class is important. For most programming languages, the set of syntactically legal statements is (except possibly for type checking) a context-free language. The set of well-formed Boolean queries is a context-free language. A great deal of the syntax of English can be described in the context-free framework that we are about to discuss. To describe these languages, we need more power than the regular language definition allows. For example, to describe both programming language statements and Boolean queries requires the ability to specify that parentheses be balanced. Yet we showed in Section 8.4 that it is not possible to define a regular language that contains exactly the set of strings of balanced parentheses.

We will begin our discussion of the context-free languages by defining a grammatical formalism that can be used to describe every language in the class (which, by the way, does include the language of balanced parentheses). Then, in Chapter 12, we will return to the question of defining machines that can accept strings in the language. At that point, we'll see that the pushdown automaton, an NDFSM augmented with a single stack, can accept

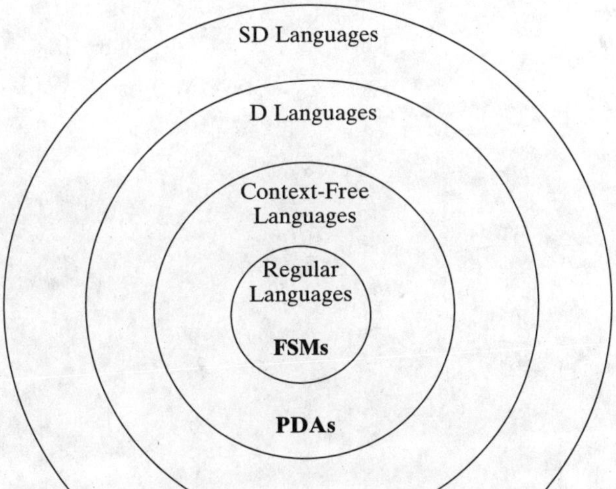

exactly the class of context-free languages that we are about to describe. In Chapter 13, we will see that the formalisms that we have presented stop short of the full power that is provided by a more general computational model. So we'll see that there are straightforward languages that are not context-free. But, because of the restrictions that the context-free formalism imposes, it will turn out to be possible to define algorithms that perform at least the most basic operations on context-free languages, including deciding whether a string is in a language. We'll summarize those algorithms in Chapters 14 and 15.

The theory that we are about to present for the context-free languages is not as straightforward and elegant as the one that we have just described for the regular languages. We'll see, for example, that there doesn't exist an algorithm that compares two pushdown automata to see if they are equivalent. Given an arbitrary context-free grammar *G*, there doesn't exist a linear-time algorithm that decides whether a string *w* is an element of *L*(*G*). But there does exist such an algorithm if we restrict our attention to a useful subset of the context-free languages. The context-free languages are not closed under many common operations like intersection and complement.

On the other hand, because the class of context-free languages includes most programming languages, query languages, and a host of other languages that we use daily to communicate with computers, it is worth taking the time to work through the theory that is presented here, even though it is less clear than the one we were able to build in Part II.

CHAPTER 11

Context-Free Grammars

We saw, in our discussion of the regular languages in Part II, that there are substantial advantages to using descriptive frameworks (in that case, FSMs, regular expressions, and regular grammars) that offer less power and flexibility than a general purpose programming language provides. Because the frameworks were restrictive, we were able to describe a large class of useful operations that could be performed on the languages that we defined.

We will begin our discussion of the context-free languages with another restricted formalism, the context-free grammar. But before we define it, we will pause and answer the more general question, "What is a grammar?"

11.1 Introduction to Rewrite Systems and Grammars

We'll begin with a very general computational model: Define a ***rewrite system*** (also called a ***production system*** or a ***rule-based system***) to be a list of rules and an algorithm for applying them. Each rule has a left-hand side and a right-hand side. For example, the following could be rewrite-system rules:

$$S \rightarrow aSb$$
$$aS \rightarrow \varepsilon$$
$$aSb \rightarrow bSabSa$$

In the discussion that follows, we will focus on rewrite system that operate on strings. But the core ideas that we will present can be used to define rewrite systems that operate on richer data structures. Of course, such data structures can be represented as strings, but the power of many practical rule-based systems comes from their ability to manipulate other structures directly.

Expert systems, (M.3.3) are programs that perform tasks in domains like engineering, medicine, and business, that require expertise when done by people. Many kinds of expertise can naturally be modeled as sets of condition/action rules. So many expert systems are built using tools that support rule-based programming.

Rule based systems are also used to model business practices (M.3.4) and as the basis for reasoning about the behavior of nonplayer characters in computer games. (N.3.3)

When a rewrite system R is invoked on some initial string w, it operates as follows:

simple-rewrite(R: rewrite system, w: initial string) =

1. Set *working-string* to w.

2. Until told by R to halt do:

- **2.1.** Match the left-hand side of some rule against some part of *working-string*.
- **2.2.** Replace the matched part of *working-string* with the right-hand side of the rule that was matched.

3. Return *working-string*.

If *simple-rewrite*(R, w) can return some string s then we'll say that R can ***derive*** s from w or that there exists a ***derivation*** in R of s from w.

Rewrite systems can model natural growth processes, as occur, for example, in plants. In addition, evolutionary algorithms can be applied to rule sets. Thus rewrite systems can model evolutionary processes. (Q.2.2)

We can define a particular ***rewrite-system formalism*** by specifying the form of the rules that are allowed and the algorithm by which they will be applied. In most of the rewrite-system formalisms that we will consider, a rule is simply a pair of strings. If the string on the left-hand side matches, it is replaced by the string on the right-hand side. But more flexible forms are also possible. For example, variables may be allowed. Let x be a variable. Then consider the rule:

$$\text{a}x\text{a} \rightarrow \text{aa}$$

This rule will squeeze out whatever comes between a pair of a's.

Another useful form allows regular expressions as left-hand sides. If we do that, we can write rules like the following, which squeezes out b's between a's:

$$\text{ab*ab*a} \rightarrow \text{aaa}$$

The extended form of regular expressions that is supported in programming languages like Perl is often used to write substitution rules. (Appendix O)

In addition to describing the form of its rules, a rewrite-system formalism must describe how its rules will be applied. In particular, a rewrite-system formalism will define the conditions under which *simple-rewrite* will halt and the method by which it will choose a match in step 2.1. For example, one rewrite-system formalism might specify that any rule that matches may be chosen. A different formalism might specify that the rules have to be tried in the order in which they are written, with the first one that matches being the one that is chosen next.

Rewrite systems can be used to define functions. In this case, we write rules that operate on an input string to produce the required output string. Rewrite systems can also be used to define languages. In this case, we define a unique start symbol. The rules then apply and we will say that the language L that is generated by the system is exactly the set of strings, over L's alphabet, that can be derived by *simple-rewrite* from the start symbol.

> A rewrite-system formalism can be viewed as a programming language and some such languages turn out to be useful. For example, Prolog (M.2.3) supports a style of programming called logic programming. A logic program is a set of rules that correspond to logical statements of the form A if B. The interpreter for a logic program reasons backwards from a goal (such as A), chaining rules together until each right-hand side has been reduced to a set of facts (axioms) that are already known to be true.

The study of rewrite systems has played an important role in the development of the theory of computability. We'll see in Part V that there exist rewrite-system formalisms that have the same computational power as the Turing machine, both with respect to computing functions and with respect to defining languages. In the rest of our discussion in this chapter, however, we will focus just on their use to define languages.

A rewrite system that is used to define a language is called a ***grammar***. If G is a grammar, let $L(G)$ be the language that G generates. Like every rewrite system, every grammar contains a list (almost always treated as a set, i.e., as an unordered list) of rules. Also, like every rewrite system, every grammar works with an alphabet, which we can call V. In the case of grammars, we will divide V into two subsets:

- a ***terminal alphabet***, generally called Σ, which contains the symbols that make up the strings in $L(G)$, and
- a ***nonterminal alphabet***, the elements of which will function as working symbols that will be used while the grammar is operating. These symbols will disappear by the time the grammar finishes its job and generates a string.

One final thing is required to specify a grammar. Each grammar has a unique start symbol, often called S.

> Grammars can be used to describe phenomena as different as English (L.3), programming languages like Java (G.1), music (N.1), dance (Q.2.1), the growth of living organisms (Q.2.2), and the structure of RNA. (K.4)

A ***grammar formalism*** (like any rewrite-system formalism) specifies the form of the rules that are allowed and the algorithm by which they will be applied. The grammar formalisms that we will consider vary in the form of the rules that they allow. With one exception (Lindenmayer systems, which we'll describe in Section 24.4), all of the grammar formalisms that we will consider include a control algorithm that ignores rule order. Any rule that matches may be applied next.

To generate strings in $L(G)$, we invoke *simple-rewrite* (G, S). *Simple-rewrite* will begin with S and will apply the rules of G, which can be thought of (given the control algorithm we just described) as licenses to replace one string by another. At each step of one of its derivations, some rule whose left-hand side matches somewhere in *working-string* is selected. The substring that matched is replaced by the rule's right-hand side, generating a new value for *working string*.

> Grammars can be used to define languages that, in turn, define sets of things that don't look at all like strings. For example, SVG (Q.1.3) is a language that is used to describe two-dimensional graphics. SVG can be described with a context-free grammar.

We will use the symbol $\Rightarrow$ to indicate steps in a derivation. So, for example, suppose that G has the start symbol S and the rules $S \rightarrow \mathrm{a}S\mathrm{b}$, $S \rightarrow \mathrm{b}S\mathrm{a}$, and $S \rightarrow \varepsilon$. Then a derivation could begin with:

$$S \Rightarrow \mathrm{a}S\mathrm{b} \Rightarrow \mathrm{aa}S\mathrm{bb} \Rightarrow \ldots$$

At each step, it is possible that more than one rule's left-hand side matches the working string. It is also possible that a rule's left-hand side matches the working string in more than one way. In either case, there is a derivation corresponding to each alternative. It is precisely the existence of these choices that enables a grammar to generate more than one string.

Continuing with our example, there are three choices at the next step:

$$S \Rightarrow \mathrm{a}S\mathrm{b} \Rightarrow \mathrm{aa}S\mathrm{bb} \Rightarrow \mathrm{aaa}S\mathrm{bbb} \quad \text{(using the first rule),}$$
$$S \Rightarrow \mathrm{a}S\mathrm{b} \Rightarrow \mathrm{aa}S\mathrm{bb} \Rightarrow \mathrm{aab}S\mathrm{abb} \quad \text{(using the second rule), and}$$
$$S \Rightarrow \mathrm{a}S\mathrm{b} \Rightarrow \mathrm{aa}S\mathrm{bb} \Rightarrow \mathrm{aabb} \quad \text{(using the third rule).}$$

The derivation process may end whenever one of the following things happens:

1. The working string no longer contains any nonterminal symbols (including, as a special case, when the working string is ε), or
2. There are nonterminal symbols in the working string but there is no match with the left-hand side of any rule in the grammar. For example, if the working string were $A\mathrm{a}B\mathrm{b}$, this would happen if the only left-hand side were C.

In the first case, but not the second, we say that the working string is ***generated*** by the grammar. Thus, the ***language*** that a grammar generates includes only strings over the terminal alphabet (i.e., strings in Σ^*). In the second case, we have a blocked or nonterminated derivation but no generated string.

It is also possible that, in a particular case, neither 1 nor 2 is achieved. Suppose, for example, that a grammar contained only the rules $S \rightarrow B\text{a}$ and $B \rightarrow \text{b}B$, with S the start symbol. Then all derivations proceed in the following way:

$$S \Rightarrow B\text{a} \Rightarrow \text{b}B\text{a} \Rightarrow \text{bb}B\text{a} \Rightarrow \text{bbb}B\text{a} \Rightarrow \text{bbbb}B\text{a} \Rightarrow \cdots$$

The working string is always rewriteable (in only one way, as it happens), and so this grammar can produce no terminated derivations consisting entirely of terminal symbols (i.e., generated strings). Thus this grammar generates the language $\varnothing$.

11.2 Context-Free Grammars and Languages

We've already seen our first specific grammar formalism. In Chapter 7, we defined a regular grammar to be one in which every rule must:

- have a left-hand side that is a single nonterminal, and
- have a right-hand side that is ε or a single terminal or a single terminal followed by a single nonterminal.

We now define a ***context-free grammar*** (or CFG) to be a grammar in which each rule must:

- have a left-hand side that is a single nonterminal, and
- have a right-hand side.

To simplify the discussion that follows, define an A rule, for any nonterminal symbol A, to be a rule whose left-hand side is A.

Next we must define a control algorithm of the sort we described at the end of the last section. A derivation will halt whenever no rule's left-hand side matches against *working-string*. At every step, any rule that matches may be chosen.

Context-free grammar rules may have any (possibly empty) sequence of symbols on the right-hand side. Because the rule format is more flexible than it is for regular grammars, the rules are more powerful. We will soon show some examples of languages that can be generated with context-free grammars but that can not be generated with regular ones.

All of the following are allowable context-free grammar rules (assuming appropriate alphabets):

$$S \rightarrow \text{a}S\text{b}$$
$$S \rightarrow \varepsilon$$
$$T \rightarrow T$$
$$S \rightarrow \text{a}S\text{bb}TT$$

The following are not allowable context-free grammar rules:

$$ST \rightarrow \text{a}S\text{b}$$
$$\text{a} \rightarrow \text{a}S\text{b}$$
$$\varepsilon \rightarrow \text{a}$$

The name for these grammars, "context-free," makes sense because, using these rules, the decision to replace a nonterminal by some other sequence is made without looking at the context in which the nonterminal occurs. In Chapters 23 and 24 we will consider less restrictive grammar formalisms in which the left-hand sides of the rules may contain several symbols. For example, the rule aSa → aTa would be allowed. This rule says that S can be replaced by T when it is surrounded by a's. One of those formalisms is called "context-sensitive" because its rules allow context to be considered.

> Programming language syntax is typically described using context-free grammars, as we'll see below and in Appendix G.

Formally, a context-free grammar G is a quadruple (V, Σ, R, S), where:

- V is the rule alphabet, which contains nonterminals (symbols that are used in the grammar but that do not appear in strings in the language) and terminals,
- Σ (the set of terminals) is a subset of V,
- R (the set of rules) is a finite subset of $(V - \Sigma) \times V^*$, and
- S (the start symbol) can be any element of $V - \Sigma$.

Given a grammar G, define $x \Rightarrow_G y$ (abbreviated $\Rightarrow$ when G is clear from context) to be the binary relation *derives-in-one-step*, defined so that:

$$\forall x, y \in V^* (x \Rightarrow_G y \text{ iff } x = \alpha A \beta,\ y = \alpha\gamma\beta, \text{ and there exists a rule } A \rightarrow \gamma \text{ in } R_G).$$

Any sequence of the form $w_0 \Rightarrow_G w_1 \Rightarrow_G w_2 \Rightarrow_G \ldots \Rightarrow_G w_n$ is called a ***derivation*** in G. Let $\Rightarrow_G{}^*$ be the reflexive, transitive closure of $\Rightarrow_G$. We'll call $\Rightarrow_G{}^*$ the ***derives*** relation.

The ***language generated by G***, denoted $L(G)$, is $\{w \in \Sigma^* : S \Rightarrow_G{}^* w\}$. In other words, the language generated by G is the set of all strings of terminals that can be derived from S using zero or more applications of rules in G.

A language L is ***context-free*** iff it is generated by some context-free grammar G. The context-free languages (or CFLs) are a proper superset of the regular languages. In the next several examples, we will see languages that are context-free but not regular. Then, in Chapter 13, we will prove the other part of this claim, namely that every regular language is also context-free.

EXAMPLE 11.1 The Balanced Parentheses Language

Consider Bal $= \{w \in \{), (\}^* :$ the parentheses are balanced$\}$. We showed in Example 8.10 that Bal is not regular. But it is context-free because it can be generated by the grammar $G = (\{S,), (\}, \{), (\}, R, S)$, where:

$$R = \{S \rightarrow (S)$$
$$S \rightarrow SS$$
$$S \rightarrow \varepsilon\}.$$

Some example derivations in G:

$S \Rightarrow (S) \Rightarrow ()$.

$S \Rightarrow (S) \Rightarrow (SS) \Rightarrow ((S)S) \Rightarrow (()S) \Rightarrow (()(S)) \Rightarrow (()())$.

So, $S \Rightarrow^* ()$ and $S \Rightarrow^* (()())$.

The syntax of Boolean query languages is describable with a context-free grammar. (Q.11)

EXAMPLE 11.2 A^nB^n

Consider $A^nB^n = \{a^nb^n : n \geq 0\}$. We showed in Example 8.8 that A^nB^n is not regular. But it is context-free because it can be generated by the grammar $G = \{\{S, a, b\}, \{a, b\}, R, S\}$, where:

$$R = \{S \rightarrow aSb \\ S \rightarrow \varepsilon\}.$$

What is it about context-free grammars that gives them the power to define languages like Bal and A^nB^n?

We can begin answering that question by defining a rule in a grammar G to be ***recursive*** iff it is of the form $X \rightarrow w_1Yw_2$, where $Y \Rightarrow_G{}^* w_3Xw_4$ and all of w_1, w_2, w_3, and w_4 may be any element of V^*. A grammar is recursive iff it contains at least one recursive rule. For example, the grammar we just presented for *Bal* is recursive because it contains the rule $S \rightarrow (S)$. The grammar we presented for A^nB^n is recursive because it contains the rule $S \rightarrow aSb$. A grammar that contained the rule $S \rightarrow aS$ would also be recursive. So the regular grammar whose rules are $\{S \rightarrow aT, T \rightarrow aW, W \rightarrow aS, W \rightarrow a\}$ is recursive. Recursive rules make it possible for a finite grammar to generate an infinite set of strings.

Let's now look at an important property that gives context-free grammars the power to define languages that aren't regular. A rule in a grammar G is ***self-embedding*** iff it is of the form $X \rightarrow w_1Yw_2$, where $Y \Rightarrow_G{}^* w_3Xw_4$ and both w_1w_3 and w_4w_2 are in Σ^+. A grammar is self-embedding iff it contains at least one self-embedding rule. So now we require that a nonempty string be generated on each side of the nested X. The grammar we presented for *Bal* is self-embedding because it contains the rule $S \rightarrow (S)$. The grammar we presented for A^nB^n is self-embedding because it contains the rule $S \rightarrow aSb$. The presence of a rule like $S \rightarrow aS$ does not by itself make a grammar self-embedding. But the rule $S \rightarrow aT$ is self-embedding in any grammar G that also contains the rule $T \rightarrow Sb$, since $S \rightarrow aT$ and $T \Rightarrow_G{}^* Sb$. Self-embedding grammars are able to define languages like Bal, A^nB^n, and others whose strings must contain pairs of matching regions, often of the form uv^ixy^iz. No regular language can impose such a requirement on its strings.

The fact that a grammar G is self-embedding does not guarantee that $L(G)$ isn't regular. There might be a different grammar G' that also defines $L(G)$ and that is not self-embedding. For example, $G_1 = (\{S, a\}, \{a\}, \{S \rightarrow \varepsilon, S \rightarrow a, S \rightarrow aSa\}, S)$ is self-embedding, yet it defines the regular language a^*. However, we note the following two important facts:

- If a grammar G is not self-embedding then $L(G)$ is regular. Recall that our definition of regular grammars did not allow self-embedding.

- If a language L has the property that every grammar that defines it is self-embedding, then L is not regular.

The rest of the grammars that we will present in this chapter are self-embedding.

EXAMPLE 11.3 Even Length Palindromes

Consider PalEven $= \{ww^R : w \in \{\text{a}, \text{b}\}^*\}$, the language of even-length palindromes of a's and b's. We showed in Example 8.11 that PalEven is not regular. But it is context-free because it can be generated by the grammar $G = \{\{S, \text{a}, \text{b}\}, \{\text{a}, \text{b}\}, R, S\}$, where:

$$
\begin{aligned}
R = \{&S \rightarrow \text{a}S\text{a} \\
&S \rightarrow \text{b}S\text{b} \\
&S \rightarrow \varepsilon\}.
\end{aligned}
$$

EXAMPLE 11.4 Equal Numbers of a's and b's

Let $L = \{w \in \{\text{a}, \text{b}\}^* : \#_{\text{a}}(w) = \#_{\text{b}}(w)\}$. We showed in Example 8.14 that L is not regular. But it is context-free because it can be generated by the grammar $G = \{\{S, \text{a}, \text{b}\}, \{\text{a}, \text{b}\}, R, S\}$, where:

$$
\begin{aligned}
R = \{&S \rightarrow \text{a}S\text{b} \\
&S \rightarrow \text{b}S\text{a} \\
&S \rightarrow SS \\
&S \rightarrow \varepsilon\}.
\end{aligned}
$$

These simple examples are interesting because they capture, in a couple of lines, the power of the context-free grammar formalism. But our real interest in context-free grammars comes from the fact that they can describe useful and powerful languages that are substantially more complex.

It quickly becomes apparent, when we start to build larger grammars, that we need a more flexible grammar-writing notation. We'll use the following two extensions when they are helpful:

- The symbol | should be read as "or". It allows two or more rules to be collapsed into one. So the following single rule is equivalent to the four rules we wrote in Example 11.4:

$$S \rightarrow \text{a}S\text{b} \mid \text{b}S\text{a} \mid SS \mid \varepsilon$$

- We often require nonterminal alphabets that contain more symbols than there are letters. To solve that problem, we will allow a nonterminal symbol to be any sequence of characters surrounded by angle brackets. So <program> and <variable> could be nonterminal symbols using this convention.

BNF (or Backus Naur form) is a widely used grammatical formalism that exploits both of these extensions. It was created in the late 1950s as a way to describe the programming language ALGOL 60. It has since been extended and several dialects developed. (G.1.1)

EXAMPLE 11.5 BNF for a Small Java Fragment

Because BNF was originally designed when only a small character set was available, it uses the three symbol sequence ::= in place of →. The following BNF-style grammar describes a highly simplified and very small subset of Java:

```
<block> ::= {<stmt-list>} | {}
<stmt-list> ::= <stmt> | <stmt-list> <stmt>
<stmt> ::= <block> | while (<cond>) <stmt> |
           if (<cond>) <stmt> |
           do <stmt> while (<cond>); | <assignment-stmt>; |
           return | return <expression> |
           <method-invocation>;
```

The rules of this grammar make it clear that the following block may be legal in Java (assuming that the appropriate declarations have occurred):

```
{       while (x < 12) {
                hippo.pretend(x);
                x = x + 2;
        }}
```

On the other hand, the following block is not legal:

```
{       while x < 12}) (
                hippo.pretend(x);
                x = x + 2;
        }}
```

Many other kinds of practical languages are also context-free. For example, HTML can be described with a context-free grammar using a BNF-style grammar. (Q.1.2)

EXAMPLE 11.6 A Fragment of an English Grammar

Much of the structure of an English sentence can be described by a (large) context-free grammar. For historical reasons, linguistic grammars typically use a

EXAMPLE 11.6 (*Continued*)

slightly different notational convention. Nonterminals will be written as strings whose first symbol is an upper case letter. So the following grammar describes a tiny fragment of English. The symbol *NP* will derive noun phrases; the symbol *VP* will derive verb phrases:

$S \rightarrow NP\ VP$
$NP \rightarrow$ `the` $Nominal$ | `a` $Nominal$ | $Nominal$ | $ProperNoun$ | $NP\ PP$
$Nominal \rightarrow N \mid Adjs\ N$
$N \rightarrow$ `cat` | `dogs` | `bear` | `girl` | `chocolate` | `rifle`
$ProperNoun \rightarrow$ `Chris` | `Fluffy`
$Adjs \rightarrow Adj\ Adjs \mid Adj$
$Adj \rightarrow$ `young` | `older` | `smart`
$VP \rightarrow V \mid V\ NP \mid VP\ PP$
$V \rightarrow$ `like` | `likes` | `thinks` | `shot` | `smells`
$PP \rightarrow Prep\ NP$
$Prep \rightarrow$ `with`

> Is English (or German or Chinese) really context-free? (L.3.3)

11.3 Designing Context-Free Grammars

In this section, we offer a few simple strategies for designing straightforward context-free grammars. Later we'll see that some grammars are better than others (for various reasons) and we'll look at techniques for finding "good" grammars. For now, we will focus on finding some grammar.

The most important rule to remember in designing a context-free grammar to generate a language L is the following:

- If L has the property that every string in it has two regions and those regions must bear some relationship to each other (such as being of the same length), then the two regions must be generated in tandem. Otherwise, there is no way to enforce the necessary constraint.

  Keeping that rule in mind, there are two simple ways to generate strings:

- To generate a string with multiple regions that must occur in some fixed order but do not have to correspond to each other, use a rule of the form:

$$A \rightarrow BC\ldots$$

  This rule generates two regions, and the grammar that contains it will then rely on additional rules to describe how to form a B region and how to form a C region. Longer rules, like $A \rightarrow BCDE$, can be used if additional regions are necessary.

- To generate a string with two regions that must occur in some fixed order and that must correspond to each other, start at the outside edges of the string and generate toward the middle. If there is an unrelated region in between the related ones, it must be generated after the related regions have been produced.

> The outside-in structure of context-free grammars makes them well suited to describing physical things, like RNA molecules, that fold. (K.4)

EXAMPLE 11.7 Concatenating Independent Sublanguages

Let $L = \{a^n b^n c^m : n, m \geq 0\}$. Here, the c^m portion of any string in L is completely independent of the $a^n b^n$ portion, so we should generate the two portions separately and concatenate them together. So let $G = (\{S, N, C, a, b, c\}, \{a, b, c\}, R, S\}$ where:

$R = \{S \rightarrow NC$ /* Generate the two independent portions.
$N \rightarrow aNb$ /* Generate the $a^n b^n$ portion, from the outside in.
$N \rightarrow \varepsilon$
$C \rightarrow cC$ /* Generate the c^m portion.
$C \rightarrow \varepsilon\}$.

EXAMPLE 11.8 The Kleene Star of a Language

Let $L = \{a^{n_1} b^{n_1} a^{n_2} b^{n_2} \ldots a^{n_k} b^{n_k} : k \geq 0 \text{ and } \forall i\ (n_i \geq 0)\}$. For example, the following strings are in L: ε, abab, aabbaaabbbabab. Note that $L = \{a^n b^n : n \geq 0\}^*$, which gives a clue how to write the grammar we need. We know how to produce individual elements of $\{a^n b^n : n \geq 0\}$, and we know how to concatenate regions together. So a solution is $G = (\{S, M, a, b\}, \{a, b\}, R, S\}$ where:

$R = \{S \rightarrow MS$ /* Each M will generate one $\{a^n b^n : n \geq 0\}$ region.
$S \rightarrow \varepsilon$
$M \rightarrow aMb$ /* Generate one region.
$M \rightarrow \varepsilon\}$.

11.4 Simplifying Context-Free Grammars ◆

In this section, we present two algorithms that may be useful for simplifying context-free grammars.

Consider the grammar $G = (\{S, A, B, C, D, a, b\}, \{a, b\}, R, S)$, where:

$R = \{S \rightarrow AB \mid AC$
$A \rightarrow aAb \mid \varepsilon$

$$B \rightarrow \mathrm{b}A$$
$$C \rightarrow \mathrm{b}C\mathrm{a}$$
$$D \rightarrow AB\}.$$

G contains two useless variables: C is useless because it is not able to generate any strings in Σ^*. (Every time a rule is applied to a C, a new C is added.) D is useless because it is unreachable, via any derivation, from S. So any rules that mention either C or D can be removed from G without changing the language that is generated. We present two algorithms, one to find and remove variables like C that are unproductive, and one to find and remove variables like D that are unreachable.

Given a grammar $G = (V, \Sigma, R, S)$, we define *removeunproductive*(G) to create a new grammar G', where $L(G') = L(G)$ and G' does not contain any unproductive symbols. Rather than trying to find the unproductive symbols directly, *removeunproductive* will find and mark all the productive ones. Any that are left unmarked at the end are unproductive. Initially, all terminal symbols will be marked as productive since each of them generates a terminal string (itself). A nonterminal symbol will be marked as productive when it is discovered that there is at least one way to rewrite it as a sequence of productive symbols. So *removeunproductive* effectively moves backwards from terminals, marking nonterminals along the way.

removeunproductive(G: CFG) =

1. $G' = G$.
2. Mark every nonterminal symbol in G' as unproductive.
3. Mark every terminal symbol in G' as productive.
4. Until one entire pass has been made without any new symbol being marked do:

    For each rule $X \rightarrow \alpha$ in R do:

        If every symbol in α has been marked as productive and X has not yet been marked as productive, then mark X as productive.

5. Remove from $V_{G'}$ every unproductive symbol.
6. Remove from $R_{G'}$ every rule with an unproductive symbol on either the left-hand side or the right-hand side.
7. Return G'

Removeunproductive must halt because there is only some finite number of nonterminals that can be marked as productive. So the maximum number of times it can execute step 4 is $|V - \Sigma|$. Clearly $L(G') \subseteq L(G)$ since G' can produce no derivations that G could not have produced. And $L(G') = L(G)$ because the only derivations that G can perform but G' cannot are those that do not end with a terminal string.

Notice that it is possible that S is unproductive. This will happen precisely in case $L(G) = \varnothing$. We will use this fact in Section 14.1.2 to show the existence of a procedure that decides whether or not a context-free language is empty.

Next we'll define an algorithm for getting rid of unreachable symbols like D in the grammar we presented above. Given a grammar $G = (V, \Sigma, R, S)$, we define *removeunreachable*(G) to create a new grammar G', where $L(G') = L(G)$ and G'

does not contain any unreachable nonterminal symbols. What *removeunreachable* does is to move forward from S, marking reachable symbols along the way.

removeunreachable(G: CFG) =

1. $G' = G$.
2. Mark S as reachable.
3. Mark every other nonterminal symbol as unreachable.
4. Until one entire pass has been made without any new symbol being marked do:
   For each rule $X \rightarrow \alpha A \beta$ (where $A \in V - \Sigma$ and $\alpha, \beta \in V^*$) in R do:
   If X has been marked as reachable and A has not, then mark A as reachable.
5. Remove from $V_{G'}$ every unreachable symbol.
6. Remove from $R_{G'}$ every rule with an unreachable symbol on the left-hand side.
7. Return G'.

Removeunreachable must halt because there is only some finite number of nonterminals that can be marked as reachable. So the maximum number of times it can execute step 4 is $|V - \Sigma|$. Clearly $L(G') \subseteq L(G)$ since G' can produce no derivations that G could not have produced. And $L(G') = L(G)$ because every derivation that can be produced by G can also be produced by G'.

11.5 Proving That a Grammar is Correct ✹

In the last couple of sections, we described some techniques that are useful in designing context-free languages and we argued that the grammars that we built were correct (i.e., that they correctly describe languages with certain properties). But, given some language L and a grammar G, can we actually prove that G is correct (i.e., that it generates exactly the strings in L)? To do so, we need to prove two things:

1. G generates only strings in L, and
2. G generates all the strings in L.

The most straightforward way to do step 1 is to imagine the process by which G generates a string as the following loop (a version of *simple-rewrite*, using *st* in place of *working-string*):

1. *st* = S.
2. Until no nonterminals are left in *st* do:
   Apply some rule in R to *st*.
3. Output *st*.

Then we construct a loop invariant I and show that:

- I is true when the loop begins,
- I is maintained at each step through the loop (i.e., by each rule application), and
- $I \wedge$ (*st* contains only terminal symbols) $\rightarrow$ *st* $\in L$.

Step 2 is generally done by induction on the length of the generated strings.

EXAMPLE 11.9 The Correctness of the A^nB^n Grammar

In Example 11.2, we considered the language A^nB^n. We built for it the grammar $G = \{\{S, a, b\}, \{a, b\}, R, S\}$, where:

$$R = \{S \rightarrow aSb \quad (1)$$
$$S \rightarrow \varepsilon\}. \quad (2)$$

We now show that G is correct. We first show that every string w in $L(G)$ is in A^nB^n: Let *st* be the working string at any point in a derivation in G. We need to define I so that it captures the two features of every string in A^nB^n: The number of a's equals the number of b's and the letters are in the correct order. So we let I be:

$$(\#_a(st) = \#_b(st)) \wedge (st \in a^*(S \cup \varepsilon)b^*).$$

Now we prove:

- I is true when $st = S$: In this case, $\#_a(st) = \#_b(st)) = 0$ and *st* is of the correct form.
- If I is true before a rule fires, then it is true after the rule fires: To prove this, we consider the rules one at a time and show that each of them preserves I. Rule (1) adds one a and one b to *st*, so it does not change the difference between the number of a's and the number of b's. Further, it adds the a to the left of S and the b to the right of S, so if the form constraint was satisfied before applying the rule it still is afterwards. Rule (2) adds nothing so it does not change either the number of a's or b's or their locations.
- If I is true and *st* contains only terminal symbols, then $st \in A^nB^n$: In this case, *st* possesses the three properties required of all strings in A^nB^n: They are composed only of a's and b's, $(\#_a(st) = \#_b(st))$, and all a's come before all b's.

Next we show that every string w in A^nB^n can be generated by G: Every string in A^nB^n is of even length, so we will prove the claim only for strings of even length. The proof is by induction on $|w|$:

- Base case: If $|w| = 0$, then $w = \varepsilon$, which can be generated by applying rule (2) to S.
- Prove: If every string in A^nB^n of length k, where k is even, can be generated by G, then every string in A^nB^n of length $k + 2$ can also be generated. Notice that, for any even k, there is exactly one string in A^nB^n of length k : $a^{k/2}b^{k/2}$. There is also only one string of length $k + 2$, namely $aa^{k/2}b^{k/2}b$, that can be generated by first applying rule (1) to produce aSb, and then applying to S whatever rule sequence generated $a^{k/2}b^{k/2}$. By the induction hypothesis, such a sequence must exist.

EXAMPLE 11.10 The Correctness of the Equal a's and b's Grammar

In Example 11.4 we considered the language $L = \{w \in \{\mathrm{a}, \mathrm{b}\}^* : \#_{\mathrm{a}}(w) = \#_{\mathrm{b}}(w)\}$. We built for it the grammar $G = \{\{S, \mathrm{a}, \mathrm{b}\}, \{\mathrm{a}, \mathrm{b}\}, R, S\}$, where:

$$
\begin{aligned}
R = \{ & S \rightarrow \mathrm{a}S\mathrm{b} && (1)\\
& S \rightarrow \mathrm{b}S\mathrm{a} && (2)\\
& S \rightarrow SS && (3)\\
& S \rightarrow \varepsilon\}. && (4)
\end{aligned}
$$

This time it is perhaps less obvious that G is correct. In particular, does it generate every sequence where the number of a's equals the number of b's? The answer is yes, which we now prove.

To make it easy to describe this proof, we define the following function:

$$\Delta(w) = \#_{\mathrm{a}}(w) - \#_{\mathrm{b}}(w).$$

Note that a string w is in L iff $w \in \{\mathrm{a}, \mathrm{b}\}^*$ and $\Delta(w) = 0$.

We begin by showing that every string w in $L(G)$ is in L: Again, let st be the working string at any point in a derivation in G. Let I be:

$$st \in \{\mathrm{a}, \mathrm{b}, S\}^* \wedge \Delta(st) = 0.$$

Now we prove:

- I is true when $st = S$: In this case, $\#_{\mathrm{a}}(st) = \#_{\mathrm{b}}(st)) = 0$. So $\Delta(st) = 0$.
- If I is true before a rule fires, then it is true after the rule fires: The only symbols that can be added by any rule are a, b, and S. Rules (1) and (2) each add one a and one b to st, so neither of them changes $\Delta(st)$. Rules (3) and (4) add neither a's nor b's to the working string, so $\Delta(st)$ does not change.
- If I is true and st contains only terminal symbols, then $st \in L$: In this case, st possesses the two properties required of all strings in L: They are composed only of a's and b's and $\Delta(st) = 0$.

It is perhaps less obviously true that G generates every string in L. Can we be sure that there are no permutations that it misses? Yes, we can. We next we show that every string w in L can be generated by G. Every string in L is of even length, so we will prove the claim only for strings of even length. The proof is by induction on $|w|$.

- Base case: If $|w| = 0$, $w = \varepsilon$, which can be generated by applying rule (4) to S.
- Prove that if every string in L of length $\leq k$, where k is even, can be generated by G, then every string w in L of length $k + 2$ can also be generated: Since w has length $k + 2$, it can be rewritten as one of the following: axb, bxa, axa, or bxb, for some $x \in \{\mathrm{a}, \mathrm{b}\}^*$. $|x| = k$. We consider two cases:
    - $w =$ axb or bxa. If $w \in L$, then $\Delta(w) = 0$ and so $\Delta(x)$ must also be 0. $|x| = k$. So, by the induction hypothesis, G generates x. Thus G can also generate w: It first applies either rule (1) (if $w =$ axb) or rule (2) (if $w =$ bxa). It then applies to S whatever rule sequence generated x. By the induction hypothesis, such a sequence must exist.

EXAMPLE 11.10 (*Continued*)

- w = axa, or bxb. We consider the former case. The argument is parallel for the latter. Note that any string in L, of either of these forms, must have length at least 4. We will show that $w = vy$, where both v and y are in L, $2 \leq |v| \leq k$, and $2 \leq |y| \leq k$. If that is so, then G can generate w by first applying rule (3) to produce SS, and then generating v from the first S and y from the second S. By the induction hypothesis, it must be possible for it to do that since both v and y have length $\leq k$.

  To find v and y, we can imagine building w (which we've rewritten as axa) up by concatenating one character at a time on the right. After adding only one character, we have just a. Δ(a) $= 1$. Since $w \in L$, $\Delta(w) = 0$. So Δ (ax) $= -1$ (since it is missing the final a of w). The value of Δ changes by exactly 1 each time a symbol is added to a string. Since Δ is positive when only a single character has been added and becomes negative by the time the string ax has been built, it must at some point before then have been 0. Let v be the shortest nonempty prefix of w to have a value of 0 for Δ. Since v is nonempty and only even length strings can have Δ equal to $0, 2 \leq |v|$. Since Δ became 0 sometime before w became ax, v must be at least two characters shorter than w (it must be missing at least the last character of x plus the final a), so $|v| \leq k$. Since $\Delta(v) = 0, v \in L$. Since $w = vy$, we know bounds on the length of y: $2 \leq |y| \leq k$. Since $\Delta(w) = 0$ and $\Delta(v) = 0$, $\Delta(y)$ must also be 0 and so $y \in L$.

11.6 Derivations and Parse Trees

Context-free grammars do more than just describe the set of strings in a language. They provide a way of assigning an internal structure to the strings that they derive. This structure is important because it, in turn, provides the starting point for assigning meanings to the strings that the grammar can produce.

The grammatical structure of a string is captured by a ***parse tree***, which records which rules were applied to which nonterminals during the string's derivation. In Chapter 15, we will explore the design of programs, called ***parsers***, that, given a grammar G and a string w, decide whether $w \in L(G)$ and, if it is, create a parse tree that captures the process by which G could have derived w.

A parse tree, derived by a grammar $G = (V, \Sigma, R, S)$, is a rooted, ordered tree in which:

- Every leaf node is labeled with an element of $\Sigma \cup \{\varepsilon\}$,
- The root node is labeled S,
- Every other node is labeled with some element of $V - \Sigma$, and
- If m is a nonleaf node labeled X and the children of m are labeled $x_1, x_2, \ldots, x_n$, then R contains the rule $X \rightarrow x_1, x_2, \ldots, x_n$.

Define the ***branching factor*** of a grammar G to be length (the number of symbols) of the longest right-hand side of any rule in G. Then the branching factor of any parse tree generated by G is less than or equal to the branching factor of G.

EXAMPLE 11.11 The Parse Tree of a Simple English Sentence

Consider again the fragment of an English grammar that we wrote in Example 11.6. That grammar can be used to produce the following parse tree for the sentence `the smart cat smells chocolate`:

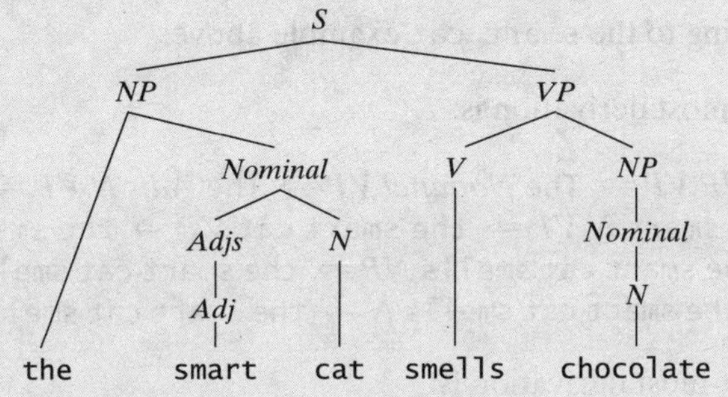

Notice that, in Example 11.11, the constituents (the subtrees) correspond to objects (like some particular cat) that have meaning in the world that is being described. It is clear from the tree that this sentence is not about cat smells or smart cat smells.

Because parse trees matter, it makes sense, given a grammar G, to distinguish between:

- G's ***weak generative capacity***, defined to be the set of strings, $L(G)$, that G generates, and
- G's ***strong generative capacity***, defined to be the set of parse trees that G generates.

When we design grammars it will be important that we consider both their weak and their strong generative capacities.

In our last example, the process of deriving the sentence `the smart cat smells chocolate` began with:

$$S \Rightarrow NP\ VP \Rightarrow \ldots$$

Looking at the parse tree, it isn't possible to tell which of the following happened next:

$$S \Rightarrow NP\ VP \Rightarrow \texttt{The}\ Nominal\ VP \Rightarrow$$
$$S \Rightarrow NP\ VP \Rightarrow NP\ V\ NP \Rightarrow$$

Parse trees are useful precisely because they capture the important structural facts about a derivation but throw away the details of the order in which the nonterminals were expanded.

While it's true that the order in which nonterminals are expanded has no bearing on the structure that we wish to assign to a string, order will become important when we attempt to define algorithms that work with context-free grammars. For example, in Chapter 15 we will consider various parsing algorithms for context-free languages. Given an input string w, such algorithms must work systematically through the space of possible derivations in search of one that could have generated w. To make it easier to describe such algorithms, we will define two useful families of derivations:

- A ***left-most derivation*** is one in which, at each step, the leftmost nonterminal in the working string is chosen for expansion.
- A ***right-most derivation*** is one in which, at each step, the rightmost nonterminal in the working string is chosen for expansion.

Returning to the `smart cat` example above:

- A left-most derivation is:

$$\begin{gathered} S \Rightarrow NP\ VP \Rightarrow \texttt{The}\ Nominal\ VP \Rightarrow \texttt{The}\ Adjs\ N\ VP \Rightarrow \texttt{The}\ Adj\ N\ VP \Rightarrow \\ \texttt{The smart}\ N\ VP \Rightarrow \texttt{the smart cat}\ VP \Rightarrow \texttt{the smart cat}\ V\ NP \Rightarrow \\ \texttt{the smart cat smells}\ NP \Rightarrow \texttt{the smart cat smells}\ Nominal \Rightarrow \\ \texttt{the smart cat smells}\ N \Rightarrow \texttt{the smart cat smells chocolate} \end{gathered}$$

- A right-most derivation is:

$$\begin{gathered} S \Rightarrow NP\ VP \Rightarrow NP\ V\ NP \Rightarrow NP\ V\ Nominal \Rightarrow NP\ V\ N \Rightarrow NP\ V\ \texttt{chocolate} \Rightarrow \\ NP\ \texttt{smells chocolate} \Rightarrow \texttt{the}\ Nominal\ \texttt{smells chocolate} \Rightarrow \\ \texttt{the}\ Adjs\ N\ \texttt{smells chocolate} \Rightarrow \texttt{The}\ Adjs\ \texttt{cat smells chocolate} \Rightarrow \\ \texttt{the}\ Adj\ \texttt{cat smells chocolate} \Rightarrow \texttt{the smart cat smells chocolate} \end{gathered}$$

11.7 Ambiguity

Sometimes a grammar may produce more than one parse tree for some (or all) of the strings it generates. When this happens, we say that the grammar is ambiguous. More precisely, a grammar G is ***ambiguous*** iff there is at least one string in $L(G)$ for which G produces more than one parse tree. It is easy to write ambiguous grammars if we are not careful. In fact, we already have.

EXAMPLE 11.12 The Balanced Parentheses Grammar is Ambiguous

Recall the language Bal $= \{w \in \{), (\}^* :$ the parentheses are balanced$\}$, for which we wrote the grammar $G = \{\{S,), (\}, \{), (\}, R, S)$, where:

$$\begin{aligned} R = \{ & S \rightarrow (S) \\ & S \rightarrow SS \\ & S \rightarrow \varepsilon\}. \end{aligned}$$

G can produce both of the following parse trees for the string (())():

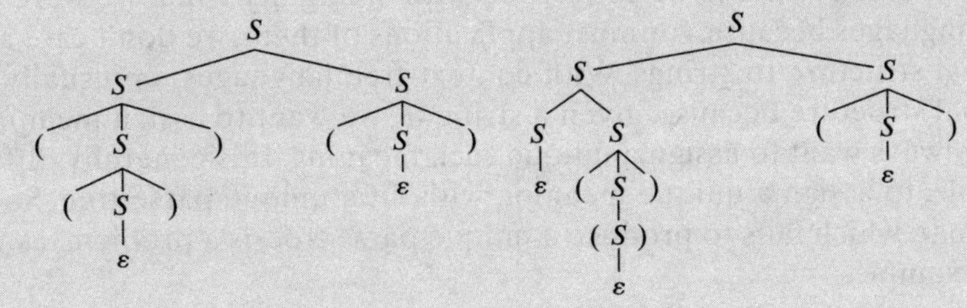

In fact, G can produce an infinite number of parse trees for the string (())().

A grammar G is unambiguous iff, for all strings w, at every point in a leftmost or rightmost derivation of w, only one rule in G can be applied. The grammar that we just presented in Example 11.12 clearly fails to meet this requirement. For example, here are two leftmost derivations of the string (())():

- $S \Rightarrow SS \Rightarrow (S)S \Rightarrow ((S))S \Rightarrow (())S \Rightarrow (())(S) \Rightarrow (())()$.
- $S \Rightarrow SS \Rightarrow SSS \Rightarrow SS \Rightarrow (S)S \Rightarrow ((S))S \Rightarrow (())S \Rightarrow (())(S) \Rightarrow (())()$.

11.7.1 Why Is Ambiguity a Problem?

Why are we suddenly concerned with ambiguity? Regular grammars can also be ambiguous. And regular expressions can often derive a single string in several distinct ways.

EXAMPLE 11.13 Regular Expressions and Grammars Can Be Ambiguous

Let $L = \{w \in \{a, b\}^* : w$ contains at least one a$\}$. L is regular. It can be defined with both a regular expression and a regular grammar. We show two ways in which the string aaa can be generated from the regular expression we have written and two ways in which it can be generated by the regular grammar:

Regular Expression	**Regular Grammar**
(a ∪ b)*a (a ∪ b)*.	$S \rightarrow$ a
	$S \rightarrow$ bS
choose a from (a ∪ b), then	$S \rightarrow$ aS
choose a from (a ∪ b), then	$S \rightarrow$ aT
choose a, then	$T \rightarrow$ a
choose ε from (a ∪ b)*.	$T \rightarrow$ b
or	$T \rightarrow$ aT
	$T \rightarrow$ bT
choose ε from (a ∪ b)*, then	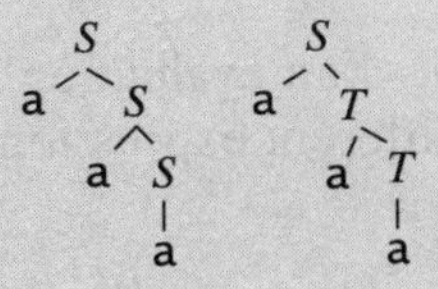
choose a, then	
choose a from (a ∪ b), then	
choose a from (a ∪ b).	

We had no reason to be concerned with ambiguity when we were discussing regular languages because, for most applications of them, we don't care about assigning internal structure to strings. With context-free languages, we usually do care about internal structure because, given a string w, we want to assign meaning to w. We almost always want to assign a unique such meaning. It is generally difficult, if not impossible, to assign a unique meaning without a unique parse tree. So an ambiguous grammar, which fails to produce a unique parse tree, is a problem, as we'll see in our next example.

EXAMPLE 11.14 An Ambiguous Expression Grammar

Consider E_{xpr}, which we'll define to be the language of simple arithmetic expressions of the kind that could be part of anything from a small calculator to a programming language. We can define E_{xpr} with the following context-free grammar $G = \{\{E, \texttt{id}, +, *, (,)\}, \{\texttt{id}, +, *, (,)\}, R, E\}$, where:

$$
\begin{aligned}
R = \{&E \rightarrow E + E\\
&E \rightarrow E * E\\
&E \rightarrow (E)\\
&E \rightarrow \texttt{id}\ \}.
\end{aligned}
$$

So that we can focus on the issues we care about, we've used the terminal symbol `id` as a shorthand for any of the numbers or variables that can actually occur as the operands in the expressions that G generates. Most compilers and interpreters for expression languages handle the parsing of individual operands in a first pass, called lexical analysis, which can be done with an FSM. We'll return to this topic in Chapter 15.

Consider the string 2 + 3 * 5, which we will write as `id + id * id`. Using G, we can get two parses for this string:

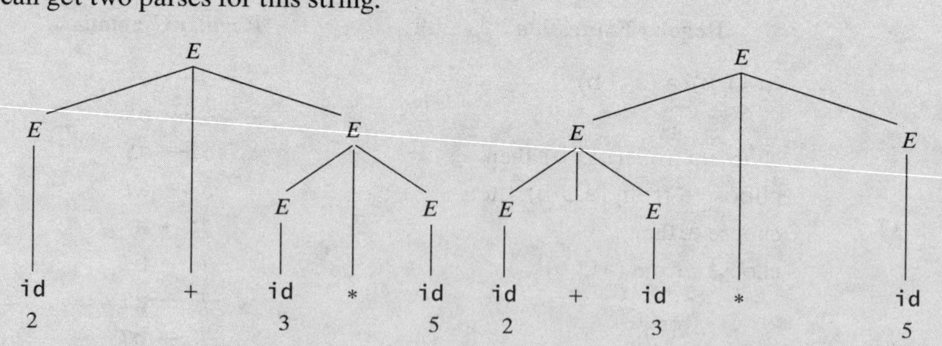

Should an evaluation of this expression return 17 or 25? (See Example 11.19 for a different expression grammar that fixes this problem.)

Natural languages, like English and Chinese, are not explicitly designed. So it isn't possible to go in and remove ambiguity from them. See Example 11.22 and L.3.4.

Designers of practical languages must be careful that they create languages for which they can write unambiguous grammars.

11.7.2 Inherent Ambiguity

In many cases, when confronted with an ambiguous grammar G, it is possible to construct a new grammar G' that generates $L(G)$ and that has less (or no) ambiguity. Unfortunately, it is not always possible to do this. There exist context-free languages for which no unambiguous grammar exists. We call such languages ***inherently ambiguous***.

EXAMPLE 11.15 An Inherently Ambiguous Language

Let $L = \{\text{a}^i\text{b}^j\text{c}^k : i, j, k \geq 0, i = j \text{ or } j = k\}$. An alternative way to describe it is $\{\text{a}^n\text{b}^n\text{c}^m : n, m \geq 0\} \cup \{\text{a}^n\text{b}^m\text{c}^m : n, m \geq 0\}$. Every string in L has either (or both) the same number of a's and b's or the same number of b's and c's. L is inherently ambiguous. One grammar that describes it is $G = (\{S, S_1, S_2, A, B, \text{a}, \text{b}, \text{c}\}, \{\text{a}, \text{b}, \text{c}\}, R, S\}$, where:

$$
\begin{aligned}
R = \{ & S \rightarrow S_1 \mid S_2 \\
& S_1 \rightarrow S_1\text{c} \mid A && \text{/* Generate all strings in } \{\text{a}^n\text{b}^n\text{c}^m : n, m \geq 0\}. \\
& A \rightarrow \text{a}A\text{b} \mid \varepsilon \\
& S_2 \rightarrow \text{a}S_2 \mid B && \text{/* Generate all strings in } \{\text{a}^n\text{b}^m\text{c}^m : n, m \geq 0\}. \\
& B \rightarrow \text{b}B\text{c} \mid \varepsilon\}.
\end{aligned}
$$

Now consider the strings in $\text{A}^\text{n}\text{B}^\text{n}\text{C}^\text{n} = \{\text{a}^n\text{b}^n\text{c}^n : n \geq 0\}$. They have two distinct derivations, one through S_1 and the other through S_2. It is possible to prove that L is inherently ambiguous: Given any grammar G that generates L there is at least one string with two derivations in G.

EXAMPLE 11.16 Another Inherently Ambiguous Language

Let $L = \{\text{a}^i\text{b}^j\text{a}^k\text{b}^l : i, j, k, l \geq 0, i = k \text{ or } j = l\}$. L is also inherently ambiguous.

Unfortunately, there are no clean fixes for the ambiguity problem for context-free languages. In Section 22.5 we'll see that both of the following problems are undecidable:

- Given a context-free grammar G, is G ambiguous?
- Given a context-free language L, is L inherently ambiguous?

11.7.3 Techniques for Reducing Ambiguity ✹

Despite the negative theoretical results that we have just mentioned, it is usually very important, when we are designing practical languages and their grammars, that we come up with a language that is not inherently ambiguous and a grammar for it that is unambiguous. Although there exists no general purpose algorithm to test for ambiguity in a grammar or to remove it when it is found (since removal is not always possible), there do exist heuristics that we can use to find some of the more common sources of ambiguity and remove them. We'll consider here three grammar structures that often lead to ambiguity:

1. ε rules like $S \rightarrow \varepsilon$.
2. Rules like $S \rightarrow SS$ or $E \rightarrow E + E$. In other words recursive rules whose right-hand sides are symmetric and contain at least two copies of the nonterminal on the left-hand side.
3. Rule sets that lead to ambiguous attachment of optional postfixes.

Eliminating ε-Rules

In Example 11.12, we showed a grammar for the balanced parentheses language. That grammar is highly ambiguous. Its major problem is that it is possible to apply the rule $S \rightarrow SS$ arbitrarily often, generating unnecessary instances of S, which can then be wiped out without a trace using the rule $S \rightarrow \varepsilon$. If we could eliminate the rule $S \rightarrow \varepsilon$, we could eliminate that source of ambiguity. We'll call any rule whose right-hand side is ε an ε-rule.

We'd like to define an algorithm that could remove ε-rules from a grammar G without changing the language that G generates. Clearly if $\varepsilon \in L(G)$, that won't be possible. Only an ε-rule can generate ε. However, it is possible to define an algorithm that eliminates ε-rules from G and leaves $L(G)$ unchanged except that, if $\varepsilon \in L(G)$, it will be absent from the language generated by the new grammar. We will show such an algorithm. Then we'll show a simple way to add ε back in, when necessary, without adding back the kind of ε-rules that cause ambiguity.

Let $G = (V, \Sigma, R, S)$ be any context-free grammar. The following algorithm constructs a new grammar G' such that $L(G') = L(G) - \{\varepsilon\}$ and G' contains no ε-rules:

removeEps (G: CFG) =

1. Let $G' = G$.
2. Find the set N of nullable variables in G'. A variable X is ***nullable*** iff either:
   (1) there is a rule $X \rightarrow \varepsilon$, or
   (2) there is a rule $X \rightarrow PQR\ldots$ such that $P, Q, R, \ldots$ are all nullable.

   So compute N as follows:

   2.1. Set N to the set of variables that satisfy (1).

   2.2. Until an entire pass is made without adding anything to N do:

   Evaluate all other variables with respect to (2). If any variable satisfies (2) and is not in N, insert it.

3. Define a rule to be ***modifiable*** iff it is of the form $P \rightarrow \alpha Q \beta$ for some Q in N and any α, β in V^*. Since Q is nullable, it could be wiped out by the application of ε-rules. But those rules are about to be deleted. So one possibility should be that Q just doesn't get generated in the first place. To make that happen requires adding new rules. So, repeat until G' contains no modifiable rules that haven't been processed:
   - **3.1.** Given the rule $P \rightarrow \alpha Q \beta$, where $Q \in N$, add the rule $P \rightarrow \alpha\beta$ if it is not already present and if $\alpha\beta \neq \varepsilon$ and if $P \neq \alpha\beta$. This last check prevents adding the useless rule $P \rightarrow P$, which would otherwise be generated if the original grammar contained, for example, the rule $P \rightarrow PQ$ and Q were nullable.
4. Delete from G' all rules of the form $X \rightarrow \varepsilon$.
5. Return G'.

If *removeEps* halts, $L(G') = L(G) - \{\varepsilon\}$ and G' contains no ε-rules. And *removeEps* must halt. Since step 2 must add a nonterminal to N at each pass and it cannot add any symbol more than once, it must halt within $|V - \Sigma|$ passes. Step 3 may have to be done once for every rule in G and once for every new rule that it adds. But note that, whenever it adds a new rule, that rule has a shorter right-hand side than the rule from which it came. So the number of new rules that can be generated by some original rule in G is finite. So step 3 can execute only a finite number of times.

EXAMPLE 11.17 Eliminating ε-Rules

Let $G = \{\{S, T, A, B, C, \text{a}, \text{b}, \text{c}\}, \{\text{a}, \text{b}, \text{c}\}, R, S)$, where:

$$
\begin{aligned}
R = \{S &\rightarrow \text{a}T\text{a} \\
T &\rightarrow ABC \\
A &\rightarrow \text{a}A \mid C \\
B &\rightarrow B\text{b} \mid C \\
C &\rightarrow \text{c} \mid \varepsilon\}.
\end{aligned}
$$

On input G, *removeEps* behaves as follows: Step 2 finds the set N of nullable variables by initially setting N to $\{C\}$. On its first pass through step 2.2 it adds A and B to N. On the next pass, it adds T (since now A, B, and C are all in N). On the next pass, no new elements are found, so step 2 halts with $N = \{C, A, B, T\}$. Step 3 adds the following new rules to G':

$S \rightarrow \text{aa}$	/* Since T is nullable.
$T \rightarrow BC$	/* Since A is nullable.
$T \rightarrow AC$	/* Since B is nullable.
$T \rightarrow AB$	/* Since C is nullable.
$T \rightarrow C$	/* From $T \rightarrow BC$, since B is nullable. Or from $T \rightarrow AC$.
$T \rightarrow B$	/* From $T \rightarrow BC$, since C is nullable. Or from $T \rightarrow AB$.

EXAMPLE 11.17 (*Continued*)

$T \rightarrow A$ /* From $T \rightarrow AC$, since C is nullable. Or from $T \rightarrow AB$.

$A \rightarrow$ a /* Since A is nullable.

$B \rightarrow$ b /* Since B is nullable.

Finally, step 4 deletes the rule $C \rightarrow \varepsilon$.

Sometimes $L(G)$ contains ε and it is important to retain it. To handle this case, we present the following algorithm, which constructs a new grammar G'', such that $L(G'') = L(G)$. If $L(G)$ contains ε, then G'' will contain a single ε-rule that can be thought of as being "quarantined". Its sole job is to generate the string ε. It can have no interaction with the other rules of the grammar.

atmostoneEps (G: CFG) =

1. $G'' =$ *removeEps* (G).
2. If S_G is nullable then: /* This means that $\varepsilon \in L(G)$.
   2.1. Create in G'' a new start symbol $S*$.
   2.2. Add to $R_{G''}$ the two rules: $S* \rightarrow \varepsilon$ and $S* \rightarrow S_G$.
3. Return G''.

EXAMPLE 11.18 Eliminating ε-Rules from the Balanced Parens Grammar

We again consider Bal $= \{w \in \{), (\}^* :$ the parentheses are balanced$\}$ and the grammar $G = (\{S,), (\}, \{), (\}, R, S)$, where:

$$R = \{S \rightarrow (S) \quad (1)$$
$$S \rightarrow SS \quad (2)$$
$$S \rightarrow \varepsilon\}. \quad (3)$$

We would like to eliminate the ambiguity in G. Since $\varepsilon \in L(G)$, we call *atmostoneEps*(G), which begins by applying *removeEps* to G:

- In step 2, $N = \{S\}$.
- In step 3, rule (1) causes us to add the rule $S \rightarrow ()$. Rule (2) causes us to consider adding the rule $S \rightarrow S$, but we omit adding rules whose right-hand sides and left-hand sides are the same.
- In step 4, we delete the rule $S \rightarrow \varepsilon$.

So *removeEps*(G) returns the grammar $G' = (\{S,), (\}, \{), (\}, R, S)$, where $R =$

$$\{S \rightarrow (S)$$
$$S \rightarrow ()$$
$$S \rightarrow SS\}.$$

In its step 2, *atmostoneEps* creates the new start symbol $S*$. In step 3, it adds the two rules $S* \rightarrow \varepsilon$, $S* \rightarrow S$. So *atmostoneEps* returns the grammar $G'' = \{\{S*, S,), (\}, \{), (\}, R, S*)$, where:

$$R = \{S* \rightarrow \varepsilon \\ S* \rightarrow S \\ S \rightarrow (S) \\ S \rightarrow () \\ S \rightarrow SS\}.$$

The string (())() has only one parse in G''.

Eliminating Symmetric Recursive Rules

The new grammar that we just built for Bal is better than our original one. But it is still ambiguous. The string ()()() has two parses, shown in Figure 11.1. The problem now is the rule $S \rightarrow SS$, which must be applied $n - 1$ times to generate a sequence of n balanced parentheses substrings. But, at each time after the first, there is a choice of which existing S to split.

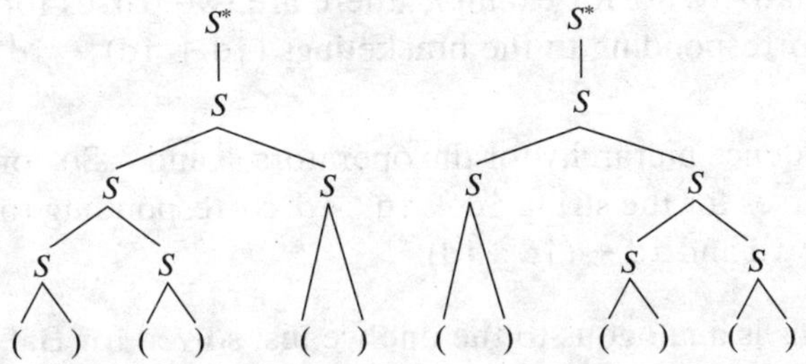

FIGURE 11.1 Two parse trees for the string ()()().

The solution to this problem is to rewrite the grammar so that there is no longer a choice. We replace the rule $S \rightarrow SS$ with one of the following rules:

$S \rightarrow SS_1$ /* force branching to the left.

$S \rightarrow S_1S$ /* force branching to the right.

Then we add the rule $S \rightarrow S_1$ and replace the rules $S \rightarrow (S)$ and $S \rightarrow ()$ with the rules $S_1 \rightarrow (S)$ and $S_1 \rightarrow ()$. What we have done is to change the grammar so that branching can occur only in one direction. Every S that is generated can branch, but no S_1 can. When all the branching has happened, S rewrites to S_1 and the rest of the derivation can occur.

So one unambiguous grammar for Bal is $G = \{\{S,), (\}, \{), (\}, R, S)$, where:

$R = \{S* \rightarrow \varepsilon$ (1)
$S* \rightarrow S$ (2)
$S \rightarrow SS_1$ (3) /* Force branching to the left.
$S \rightarrow S_1$ (4)
$S_1 \rightarrow (S)$ (5)
$S_1 \rightarrow ()\}$. (6)

The technique that we just used for Bal is useful in any situation in which ambiguity arises from a recursive rule whose right-hand side contains two or more copies of the left-hand side. An important application of this idea is to expression languages, like the language of arithmetic expressions that we introduced in Example 11.14.

EXAMPLE 11.19 An Unambiguous Expression Grammar

Consider again the language E_{xpr}, which we defined with the following context-free grammar $G = \{\{E, \texttt{id}, +, *, (,)\}, \{\texttt{id}, +, *, (,)\}, R, E\}$, where:

$$
\begin{aligned}
R = \{&E \rightarrow E + E\\
&E \rightarrow E * E\\
&E \rightarrow (E)\\
&E \rightarrow \texttt{id}\ \}.
\end{aligned}
$$

G is ambiguous in two ways:

1. It fails to specify associativity. So, for example, there are two parses for the string id + id + id, corresponding to the bracketings (id + id) + id and id + (id + id).
2. It fails to define a precedence hierarchy for the operators + and *. So, for example, there are two parses for the string id + id * id, corresponding to the bracketings (id + id) * id and id + (id * id).

The first of these problems is analogous to the one we just solved for Bal. We could apply that solution here, but then we'd still have the second problem. We can solve both of them with the following grammar $G' = \{\{E, T, F, \texttt{id}, +, *, (,)\}, \{\texttt{id}, +, *, (,)\}, R, E\}$, where:

$$
\begin{aligned}
R = \{&E \rightarrow E + T\\
&E \rightarrow T\\
&T \rightarrow T * F\\
&T \rightarrow F\\
&F \rightarrow (E)\\
&F \rightarrow \texttt{id}\}.
\end{aligned}
$$

Just as we did for Bal, we have forced branching to go in a single direction (to the left) when identical operators are involved. And, by adding the levels T (for term) and F (for factor) we have defined a precedence hierarchy: Times has higher precedence than plus does. Using G', there is now a single parse for the string `id` + `id` * `id`:

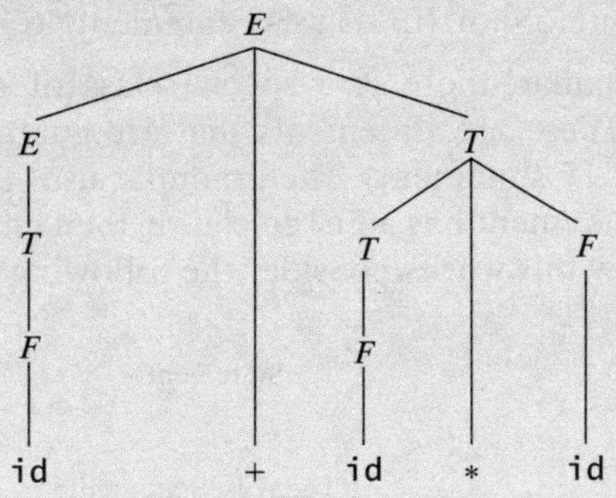

Ambiguous Attachment

The third source of ambiguity that we will consider arises when constructs with optional fragments are nested. The problem in such cases is then, "Given an instance of the optional fragment, at what level of the parse tree should it be attached?"

Probably the most often described instance of this kind of ambiguity is known as the ***dangling else problem***. Suppose that we define a programming language with an `if` statement that can have either of the following forms:

<stmt> ::= `if` <cond> `then` <stmt>
<stmt> ::= `if` <cond> `then` <stmt> `else` <stmt>

In other words, the `else` clause is optional. Then the following statement, with just a single `else` clause, has two parses:

`if` $cond_1$ `then` `if` $cond_2$ `then` st_1 `else` st_2

In the first parse, the single `else` clause goes with the first `if`. (So it attaches high in the parse tree.) In the second parse, the single `else` clause goes with the second `if`. (In this case, it attaches lower in the parse tree.)

EXAMPLE 11.20 The Dangling Else Problem in Java

Most programming languages that have the dangling else problem (including C, C++, and Java) specify that each `else` goes with the innermost `if` to which it can be attached. The Java grammar forces this to happen by changing the rules to something like these (presented here in a simplified form that omits many of the statement types that are allowed):

<Statement> ::= <IfThenStatement> | <IfThenElseStatement> |
<IfThenElseStatementNoShortIf> | ...
<StatementNoShortIf> ::= <block> | <IfThenElseStatementNoShortIf> | ...
<IfThenStatement> ::= `if` (<Expression>) <Statement>
<IfThenElseStatement> ::= `if` (<Expression>) <StatementNoShortIf> `else`
<Statement>

EXAMPLE 11.20 (*Continued*)

<IfThenElseStatementNoShortIf> ::= `if` (<Expression>)
<StatementNoShortIf> `else` <StatementNoShortIf>

In this grammar, there is a special class of statements called <Statement NoShortIf>. These are statements that are guaranteed not to end with a short (i.e., `else`-less `if` statement). The grammar uses this class to guarantee that, if a top-level `if` statement has an `else` clause, then any embedded `if` must also have one. To see how this works, consider the following parse tree:

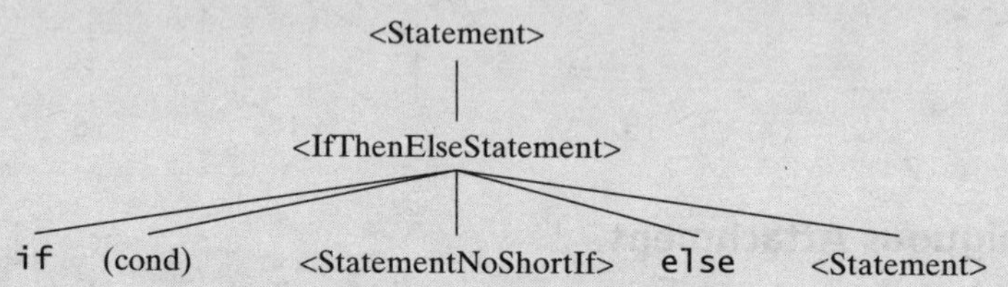

The top-level `if` statement claims the `else` clause for itself by guaranteeing that there will not be an embedded `if` that is missing an `else`. If there were, then that embedded `if` would grab the one `else` clause there is.

> For a discussion of other ways in which programming languages can solve this problem, see G.3.

Attachment ambiguity is also a problem for parsers for natural languages such as English, as we'll see in Example 11.22

Proving that a Grammar is Unambiguous

While it is undecidable, *in general*, whether a grammar is ambiguous or unambiguous, it may be possible to prove that a *particular* grammar is either ambiguous or unambiguous. A grammar G can be shown to be ambiguous by exhibiting a single string for which G produces two parse trees. To see how it might be possible to prove that G is unambiguous, recall that G is unambiguous iff every string derivable in G has a single leftmost derivation. So, if we can show that, during any leftmost derivation of any string $w \in L(G)$, exactly one rule can be applied, then G is unambiguous.

EXAMPLE 11.21 The Final Balanced Parens Grammar is Unambiguous

We return to the final grammar G that we produced for Bal. G = {{S,), (}, {), (}, R, S), where:

$$
\begin{aligned}
R = \{S^* &\rightarrow \varepsilon && (1)\\
S^* &\rightarrow S && (2)\\
S &\rightarrow SS_1 && (3)\\
S &\rightarrow S_1 && (4)\\
S_1 &\rightarrow (S) && (5)\\
S_1 &\rightarrow ()\}. && (6)
\end{aligned}
$$

We prove that G is unambiguous. Given the leftmost derivation of any string w in $L(G)$, there is, at each step of the derivation, a unique symbol, which we'll call X, that is the leftmost nonterminal in the working string. Whatever X is, it must be expanded by the next rule application, so the only rules that may be applied next are those with X on the left-hand side. There are three nonterminals in G. We show, for each of them, that the rules that expand them never compete in the leftmost derivation of a particular string w. We do the two easy cases first:

- S^*: The only place that S^* may occur in a derivation is at the beginning. If $w = \varepsilon$, then rule (1) is the only one that can be applied. If $w \neq \varepsilon$, then rule (2) is the only one that can be applied.
- S_1: If the next two characters to be derived are (), S_1 must expand by rule (6). Otherwise, it must expand by rule (5).

In order discuss S, we first define, for any matched set of parentheses m, the ***siblings*** of m to be the smallest set that includes any matched set p adjacent, on the right, to m and all of p's siblings. So, for example, consider the string:

$$\underbrace{\left(\underbrace{()}_{1}\,\underbrace{()}_{2}\right)}_{5}\;\underbrace{()}_{3}\,\underbrace{()}_{4}$$

The set () labeled 1 has a single sibling, 2. The set (()()) labeled 5 has two siblings, 3 and 4. Now we can consider S. We observe that:

- S must generate a string in Bal and so it must generate a matched set, possibly with siblings.
- So the first terminal character in any string that S generates is (. Call the string that starts with that (and ends with the) that matches it, s.
- The only thing that S_1 can generate is a single matched set of parentheses that has no siblings.
- Let n be the number of siblings of s. In order to generate those siblings, S must expand by rule (3) exactly n times (producing n copies of S_1) before it expands by rule (4) to produce a single S_1, which will produce s. So, at every step in a derivation, let p be the number of occurrences of S_1 to the right of S. If $p < n$, S must expand by rule (3). If $p = n$, S must expand by rule (4).

Going Too Far

We must be careful, in getting rid of ambiguity, that we don't do so at the expense of being able to generate the parse trees that we want. In both the arithmetic expression example and the dangling else case, we were willing to force one interpretation. Sometimes, however, that is not an acceptable solution.

EXAMPLE 11.22 Throwing Away The Parses That We Want

Let's return to the small English grammar that we showed in Example 11.6. That grammar is ambiguous. It has an ambiguous attachment problem, similar to the dangling else problem. Consider the following two sentences:

```
Chris likes the girl with a cat.

Chris shot the bear with a rifle.
```

Each of these sentences has two parse trees because, in each case, the prepositional phrase `with a` *N*, can be attached either to the immediately preceding *NP* (`the girl` or `the bear`) or to the *VP*. The correct interpretation for the first sentence is that there is a girl with a cat and Chris likes her. In other words, the prepositional phrase attaches to the *NP*. Almost certainly, the correct interpretation for the second sentence is that there is a bear (with no rifle) and Chris used a rifle to shoot it. In other words, the prepositional phrase attaches to the *VP*. See L.3.4 for additional discussion of this example.

For now, the key point is that we could solve the ambiguity problem by eliminating one of the choices for *PP* attachment. But then, for one of our two sentences, we'd get a parse tree that corresponds to nonsense. In other words, we might still have a grammar with the required weak generative capacity, but we would no longer have one with the required strong generative capacity. The solution to this problem is to add some additional mechanism to the context-free framework. That mechanism must be able to choose the parse that corresponds to the most likely meaning.

> English parsers must have ways to handle various kinds of attachment ambiguities, including those caused by prepositional phrases and relative clauses. (L.3.4)

11.8 Normal Forms ✱

So far, we've imposed no restrictions on the form of the right-hand sides of our grammar rules, although we have seen that some kinds of rules, like those whose right-hand side is ε, can make grammars harder to use. In this section, we consider what happens if we carry the idea of getting rid of ε-productions a few steps farther.

Normal forms for queries and data can simplify database processing. (H.5) Normal forms for logical formulas can simplify automated reasoning in artificial intelligence systems (M.2) and in program verification systems. (H.1.1)

Let C be any set of data objects. For example, C might be the set of context-free grammars. Or it could be the set of syntactically valid logical expressions or a set of database queries. We'll say that a set F is a ***normal form*** for C iff it possesses the following two properties:

- For every element c of C, except possibly a finite set of special cases, there exists some element f of F such that f is equivalent to c with respect to some set of tasks.
- F is simpler than the original form in which the elements of C are written. By "simpler" we mean that at least some tasks are easier to perform on elements of F than they would be on elements of C.

We define normal forms in order to make other tasks easier. For example, it might be easier to build a parser if we could make some assumptions about the form of the grammar rules that the parser will use. Recall that, in Section 5.8, we introduced the notion of a canonical form for a set of objects. A normal form is a weaker notion, since it does not require that there be a unique representation for each object in C, nor does it require that "equivalent" objects map to the same representation. So it is sometimes possible to define useful normal forms when no useful canonical form exists. We'll now do that for context-free grammars.

11.8.1 Normal Forms for Grammars

We'll define the following two useful normal forms for context-free grammars:

- ***Chomsky Normal Form***: In a Chomsky normal form grammar $G = (V, \Sigma, R, S)$, all rules have one of the following two forms:
  - $X \rightarrow a$, where $a \in \Sigma$, or
  - $X \rightarrow BC$, where B and C are elements of $V - \Sigma$.

  Every parse tree that is generated by a grammar in Chomsky normal form has a branching factor of exactly 2, except at the branches that lead to the terminal nodes, where the branching factor is 1. This property makes Chomsky normal form grammars useful in several ways, including:

  - Parsers can exploit efficient data structures for storing and manipulating binary trees.
  - Every derivation of a string w contains $|w| - 1$ applications of some rule of the form $X \rightarrow BC$, and $|w|$ applications of some rule of the form $X \rightarrow a$. So it is straightforward to define a decision procedure to determine whether w can be generated by a Chomsky normal form grammar G.

In addition, because the form of all the rules is so restricted, it is easier than it would otherwise be to define other algorithms that manipulate grammars.

- ***Greibach Normal Form***: In a Greibach normal form grammar $G = (V, \Sigma, R, S)$, all rules have the following form:
  - $X \rightarrow a\beta$, where $a \in \Sigma$ and $\beta \in (V - \Sigma)^*$.

  In every derivation that is produced by a grammar in Greibach normal form, precisely one terminal is generated for each rule application. This property is useful in several ways, including:
  - Every derivation of a string w contains $|w|$ rule applications. So again it is straightforward to define a decision procedure to determine whether w can be generated by a Greibach normal form grammar G.
  - As we'll see in Theorem 14.2, Greibach normal form grammars can easily be converted to pushdown automata with no ε-transitions. This is useful because such PDAs are guaranteed to halt.

THEOREM 11.1 Chomsky Normal Form

Theorem: Given a context-free grammar G, there exists a Chomsky normal form grammar G_C such that $L(G_C) = L(G_C) - \{\varepsilon\}$.

Proof: The proof is by construction, using the algorithm *converttoChomsky* presented below.

THEOREM 11.2 Greibach Normal Form

Theorem: Given a context-free grammar G, there exists a Greibach normal form grammar G_G such that $L(G_G) = L(G) - \{\varepsilon\}$.

Proof: The proof is also by construction. We present it in D.1.

11.8.2 Converting to a Normal Form

Normal forms are useful if there exists a procedure for converting an arbitrary object into a corresponding object that meets the requirements of the normal form. Algorithms to convert grammars into normal forms generally begin with a grammar G and then operate in a series of steps as follows:

1. Apply some transformation to G to get rid of undesirable property 1. Show that the language generated by G is unchanged.
2. Apply another transformation to G to get rid of undesirable property 2. Show that the language generated by G is unchanged *and* that undesirable property 1 has not been reintroduced.
3. Continue until the grammar is in the desired form.

Because it is possible for one transformation to undo the work of an earlier one, the order in which the transformation steps are performed is often critical to the correctness of the transformation algorithm.

One transformation that we will exploit in converting grammars both to Chomsky normal form and to Greibach normal form is based on the following observation. Consider a grammar that contains the three rules:

$X \rightarrow \mathrm{a}Y\mathrm{c}$
$Y \rightarrow \mathrm{b}$
$Y \rightarrow ZZ$

We can construct an equivalent grammar by replacing the X rule with the rules:

$X \rightarrow \mathrm{abc}$
$X \rightarrow \mathrm{a}ZZ\mathrm{c}$

Instead of letting X generate an instance of Y, X immediately generates whatever Y could have generated. The following theorem generalizes this claim.

THEOREM 11.3 Rule Substitution

Theorem: Let $G = (V, \Sigma, R, S)$ be a context-free grammar that contains a rule r of the form $X \rightarrow \alpha Y \beta$, where α and β are elements of V^* and $Y \in (V - \Sigma)$. Let $Y \rightarrow \gamma_1 | \gamma_2 | \ldots | \gamma_n$ be all of G's rules whose left-hand side is Y. And let G' be the result of removing from R the rule r and replacing it by the rules $X \rightarrow \alpha\gamma_1\beta, X \rightarrow \alpha\gamma_2\beta, \ldots, X \rightarrow \alpha\gamma_n\beta$. Then $L(G') = L(G)$.

Proof: We first show that every string in $L(G)$ is also in $L(G')$: Suppose that w is in $L(G)$. If G can derive w without using rule r, then G' can do so in exactly the same way. If G can derive w using rule r, then one of its derivations has the following form, for some value of k between 1 and n:

$$S \Rightarrow \ldots \Rightarrow \delta X \phi \Rightarrow \delta\alpha Y \beta\phi \Rightarrow \delta\alpha\gamma_k\beta\phi \Rightarrow \ldots \Rightarrow w.$$

Then G' can derive w with the derivation:

$$S \Rightarrow \ldots \Rightarrow \delta X \phi \Rightarrow \qquad \delta\alpha\gamma_k\beta\phi \Rightarrow \ldots \Rightarrow w.$$

Next we show that only strings in $L(G)$ can be in $L(G')$. This must be so because the action of every new rule $X \rightarrow \alpha\gamma_k\beta$ could have been performed in G by applying the rule $X \rightarrow \alpha Y \beta$ and then the rule $Y \rightarrow \gamma_k$.

11.8.3 Converting to Chomsky Normal Form

There exists a straightforward four-step algorithm that converts a grammar $G = (V, \Sigma, R, S)$ into a new grammar G_C such that G_C is in Chomsky normal form and $L(G_C) = L(G) - \{\varepsilon\}$. Define:

converttoChomsky(G: CFG) =

1. Let G_C be the result of removing from G all ε-rules, using the algorithm *removeEps*, defined in Section 11.7.4.
2. Let G_C be the result of removing from G_C all unit productions (rules of the form $A \rightarrow B$), using the algorithm *removeUnits* defined below. It is important that *removeUnits* run after *removeEps* since *removeEps* may introduce unit

productions. Once this step has been completed, all rules whose right-hand sides have length 1 are in Chomsky normal form (i.e., they are composed of a single terminal symbol).

3. Let G_C be the result of removing from G_C all rules whose right-hand sides have length greater than 1 and include a terminal (e.g., $A \rightarrow$ aB or $A \rightarrow B$aC). This step is simple and can be performed by the algorithm *removeMixed* given below. Once this step has been completed, all rules whose right-hand sides have length 1 or 2 are in Chomsky normal form.
4. Let G_C be the result of removing from G_C all rules whose right-hand sides have length greater than 2 (e.g., $A \rightarrow BCDE$). This step too is simple. It can be performed by the algorithm *removeLong* given below.
5. Return G_C.

A ***unit production*** is a rule whose right-hand side consists of a single nonterminal symbol. The job of *removeUnits* is to remove all unit productions and to replace them by a set of other rules that accomplish the job previously done by the unit productions. So, for example, suppose that we start with a grammar G that contains the following rules:

$S \rightarrow XY$
$X \rightarrow A$
$A \rightarrow B \mid$ a
$B \rightarrow$ b

Once we get rid of unit productions, it will no longer be possible for X to become A (and then B) and thus to go on to generate a or b. So X will need the ability to go directly to a and b, without any intermediate steps. We can define *removeUnits* as follows:

removeUnits(G: CFG) =

1. Let $G' = G$.
2. Until no unit productions remain in G' do:
   2.1. Choose some unit production $X \rightarrow Y$.
   2.2. Remove it from G'.
   2.3. Consider only rules that still remain in G'. For every rule $Y \rightarrow \beta$, where $\beta \in V^*$, do:
   Add to G' the rule $X \rightarrow \beta$ unless that is a rule that has already been removed once.
3. Return G'.

Notice that we have not bothered to check to make sure that we don't insert a rule that is already present. Since R, the set of rules, is a set, inserting an element that is already in the set has no effect.

At each step of its operation, *removeUnits* is performing the kind of rule substitution described in Theorem 11.3. (It happens that both α and β are empty.) So that theorem tells us that, at each step, the language generated by G' is unchanged from the previous step. If *removeUnits* halts, it is clear that all unit productions have been removed. It is less obvious that *removeUnits* can be guaranteed to halt. At each step, one unit production is removed, but several new rules may be added, including new unit productions. To see that *removeUnit* must halt, we observe that there is a bound $= |V - \Sigma|^2$ on the number of unit productions that can be formed from a fixed set $V - \Sigma$ of nonterminals. At each step, *removeUnits* removes one element from that set and that element can never be reinserted. So *removeUnits* must halt in at most $|V - \Sigma|^2$ steps.

EXAMPLE 11.23 Removing Unit Productions

Let $G = (V, \Sigma, R, S)$, where:

$$R = \{S \rightarrow XY$$
$$X \rightarrow A$$
$$A \rightarrow B \mid \text{a}$$
$$B \rightarrow \text{b}$$
$$Y \rightarrow T$$
$$T \rightarrow Y \mid \text{c}\}.$$

The order in which *removeUnits* chooses unit productions to remove doesn't matter. We'll consider one order it could choose:

Remove $X \rightarrow A$. Since $A \rightarrow B \mid \text{a}$, add $X \rightarrow B \mid \text{a}$.
Remove $X \rightarrow B$. Add $X \rightarrow \text{b}$.
Remove $Y \rightarrow T$. Add $Y \rightarrow Y \mid \text{c}$. Notice that we've added $Y \rightarrow Y$, which is useless, but it will be removed later.
Remove $Y \rightarrow Y$. Consider adding $Y \rightarrow T$, but don't since it has previously been removed.
Remove $A \rightarrow B$. Add $A \rightarrow \text{b}$.
Remove $T \rightarrow Y$. Add $T \rightarrow \text{c}$, but with no effect since it was already present.

At this point, the rules of G are:

$$S \rightarrow XY$$
$$A \rightarrow \text{a} \mid \text{b}$$
$$B \rightarrow \text{b}$$
$$T \rightarrow \text{c}$$
$$X \rightarrow \text{a} \mid \text{b}$$
$$Y \rightarrow \text{c}$$

No unit productions remain, so *removeUnits* halts.

We must now define the two straightforward algorithms that are required by steps 3 and 4 of the conversion algorithm that we sketched above. We begin by defining:

removeMixed (G: CFG) =

1. Let $G' = G$.
2. Create a new nonterminal T_a for each terminal a in Σ.
3. Modify each rule in G' whose right-hand side has length greater than 1 and that contains a terminal symbol by substituting T_a for each occurrence of the terminal a.
4. Add to G', for each T_a, the rule $T_a \rightarrow a$.
5. Return G'.

EXAMPLE 11.24 Removing Mixed Productions

The result of applying *removeMixed* to the grammar:

$A \rightarrow \text{a}$
$A \rightarrow \text{a}B$
$A \rightarrow B\text{a}C$
$A \rightarrow B\text{b}C$

is the grammar:

$A \rightarrow \text{a}$
$A \rightarrow T_aB$
$A \rightarrow BT_aC$
$A \rightarrow BT_bC$
$T_a \rightarrow \text{a}$
$T_b \rightarrow \text{b}$

Finally we define *removeLong*. The idea for *removeLong* is simple. If there is a rule with n symbols on its right-hand side, replace it with a set of rules. The first rule generates the first symbol followed by a new symbol that will correspond to "the rest". The next rule rewrites that symbol as the second of the original symbols, followed by yet another new one, again corresponding to "the rest", and so forth, until there are only two symbols left to generate. So we define:

removeLong (G: CFG) =

1. Let $G' = G$.
2. For each G' rule r^k of the form $A \rightarrow N_1N_2N_3N_4 \ldots N_n$, $n > 2$, create new nonterminals $M^k{}_2, M^k{}_3, \ldots M^k{}_{n-1}$.
3. In G', replace r^k with the rule $A \rightarrow N_1M^k{}_2$.
4. To G', add the rules $M^k{}_2 \rightarrow N_2M^k{}_3$, $M^k{}_3 \rightarrow N_3M^k{}_4, \ldots M^k{}_{n-1} \rightarrow N_{n-1}N_n$.
5. Return G'.

When we illustrate this algorithm, we typically omit the superscripts on the M's, and, instead, guarantee that we use distinct nonterminals by using distinct subscripts.

EXAMPLE 11.25 Removing Rules with Long Right-hand Sides

The result of applying *removeLong* to the single rule grammar:

$$A \rightarrow BCDEF$$

is the grammar with rules:

$$A \rightarrow BM_2$$
$$M_2 \rightarrow CM_3$$
$$M_3 \rightarrow DM_4$$
$$M_4 \rightarrow EF$$

We can now illustrate the four steps of *converttoChomsky*.

EXAMPLE 11.26 Converting a Grammar to Chomsky Normal Form

Let $G = (\{S, A, B, C, \text{a}, \text{c}\}, \{A, B, C\}, R, S)$, where:

$$R = \{S \rightarrow \text{a}AC\text{a}$$
$$A \rightarrow B \mid \text{a}$$
$$B \rightarrow C \mid \text{c}$$
$$C \rightarrow \text{c}C \mid \varepsilon\}.$$

We convert G to Chomsky normal form. Step 1 applies *removeEps* to eliminate ε-productions. We compute N, the set of nullable variables. Initially $N = \{C\}$. Because of the rule $B \rightarrow C$, we add B. Then, because of the rule $A \rightarrow B$, we add A. So $N = \{A, B, C\}$. Since both A and C are nullable, we derive three new rules from the first original rule, giving us:

$$S \rightarrow \text{a}AC\text{a} \mid \text{a}A\text{a} \mid \text{a}C\text{a} \mid \text{aa}$$

We add $A \rightarrow \varepsilon$ and $B \rightarrow \varepsilon$, but both of them will disappear at the end of this step. We also add $C \rightarrow$ c. So *removeEps* returns the rule set:

$$S \rightarrow \text{a}AC\text{a} \mid \text{a}A\text{a} \mid \text{a}C\text{a} \mid \text{aa}$$
$$A \rightarrow B \mid \text{a}$$
$$B \rightarrow C \mid \text{c}.$$
$$C \rightarrow \text{c}C \mid \text{c}$$

Next we apply *removeUnits*:

Remove $A \rightarrow B$. Add $A \rightarrow C \mid \text{c}$.
Remove $B \rightarrow C$. Add $B \rightarrow \text{c}C$ (and $B \rightarrow \text{c}$, but it was already there).
Remove $A \rightarrow C$. Add $A \rightarrow \text{c}C$ (and $A \rightarrow \text{c}$, but it was already there).

So *removeUnits* returns the rule set:

$$S \rightarrow \text{a}AC\text{a} \mid \text{a}A\text{a} \mid \text{a}C\text{a} \mid \text{aa}$$
$$A \rightarrow \text{a} \mid \text{c} \mid \text{c}C$$
$$B \rightarrow \text{c} \mid \text{c}C$$
$$C \rightarrow \text{c}C \mid \text{c}$$

Next we apply *removeMixed*, which returns the rule set:

$$S \rightarrow T_aACT_a \mid T_aAT_a \mid T_aCT_a \mid T_aT_a$$
$$A \rightarrow \text{a} \mid \text{c} \mid T_cC$$
$$B \rightarrow \text{c} \mid T_cC$$
$$C \rightarrow T_cC \mid \text{c}$$

EXAMPLE 11.26 (*Continued*)

$T_a \rightarrow$ a
$T_c \rightarrow$ c

Finally, we apply *removeLong*, which returns the rule set:

$S \rightarrow T_a S_1$ $\quad S \rightarrow T_a S_3$ $\quad S \rightarrow T_a S_4$ $\quad S \rightarrow T_a T_a$
$S_1 \rightarrow A S_2$ $\quad S_3 \rightarrow A T_a$ $\quad S_4 \rightarrow C T_a$
$S_2 \rightarrow C T_a$
$A \rightarrow$ a | c | $T_c C$
$B \rightarrow$ c | $T_c C$
$C \rightarrow T_c C$ | c
$T_a \rightarrow$ a
$T_c \rightarrow$ c

From Example 11.26 we see that the Chomsky normal form version of a grammar may be longer than the original grammar was. How much longer? And how much time may be required to execute the conversion algorithm? We can answer both of these questions by answering them for each of the steps that the conversion algorithm executes. Let n be the length of an original grammar G. Then we have:

1. Use *removeEps* to remove ε-rules: Suppose that G contains a rule of the form $X \rightarrow A_1 A_2 A_3 \ldots A_k$. If all of the variables A_1 through A_k are nullable, this single rule will be rewritten as $2^k - 1$ rules (since each of the k nonterminals can either be present or not, except that they cannot all be absent). Since k can grow as n, we have that the length of the grammar that *removeEps* produces (and thus the amount of time that *removeEps* requires) is $\mathcal{O}(2^n)$ In this worst case, the conversion algorithm becomes impractical for all but toy grammars. We can prevent this worst case from occurring though. Suppose that all right-hand sides can be guaranteed to be short. For example, suppose they all have length at most 2. Then no rule will be rewritten as more than 3 rules. We can make this guarantee if we modify *converttoChomsky* slightly. We will run *removeLong* as step 1 rather than as step 4. Note that none of the other steps can create a rule whose right-hand side is longer than the right-hand side of some rule that already exists. So it is not necessary to rerun *removeLong* later. With this change, *removeEps* runs in linear time.
2. Use *removeUnits* to remove unit productions: We've already shown that this step must halt in at most $|V - \Sigma|^2$ steps. Each of those steps takes constant time and may create one new rule. So the length of the grammar that *removeUnits* produces, as well as the time required for it to run, is $\mathcal{O}(n^2)$.
3. Use *removeMixed* to remove rules with right-hand sides of length greater than 1 and that contain a terminal symbol: This step runs in linear time and constructs a grammar whose size grows linearly.

4. Use *removeLong* to remove rules with long right-hand sides: This step runs in linear time and constructs a grammar whose size grows linearly.

So, if we change *converttoChomsky* so that it does step 4 first, its time complexity is $\mathcal{O}(n^2)$ and the size of the grammar that it produces is also $\mathcal{O}(n^2)$.

11.8.4 The Price of Normal Forms

While normal forms are useful for many things, as we will see over the next few chapters, it is important to keep in mind that they exact a price and it's one that we may or may not be willing to pay, depending on the application. If G is an arbitrary context-free grammar and G' is an equivalent grammar in Chomsky (or Greibach) normal form, then G and G' generate the same set of strings, but only in rare cases (for example if G happened already to be in normal form) do they assign to those strings the same parse trees. Thus, while converting a grammar to a normal form has no effect on its weak generative capacity, it may have a significant effect on its strong generative capacity.

11.9 Island Grammars ✹

Suppose that we want to parse strings that possess one or more of the following properties:

- Some (perhaps many) of them are ill-formed. In other words, while there may be a grammar that describes what strings are "supposed to look like", there is no guarantee that the actual strings we'll see conform to those rules. Consider, for example, any grammar you can imagine for English. Now imagine picking up the phone and hearing something like, "Um, I uh need a copy of uh my bill for er Ap, no May, I think, or June, maybe all of them uh, I guess that would work." Or consider a grammar for HTML. It will require that tags be properly nested. But strings like `<b><i>bold italic</b></i>` show up not infrequently in HTML documents. Most browsers will do the right thing with them, so they never get debugged.
- We simply don't know enough about them to build an exact model, although we do know something about some patterns that we think the strings will contain.
- They may contain substrings in more than one language. For example, bi(multi)lingual people often mix their speech. We even give names to some of the resulting hybrids: Spanglish, Japlish, Hinglish, etc. Or consider a typical Web page. It may contain fragments of HTML, Java script, or other languages, interleaved with each other. Even when parsing strings that are all in the same "language", dialectical issues may arise. For example, in response to the question, "Are you going to fix dinner tonight?" an American speaker of English might say, "I could," while a British speaker of English might say, "I could do." Similarly, in analyzing legacy software, there are countless dialects of languages like Fortran and Cobol.
- They may contain some substrings we care about, interleaved with other substrings we don't care about and don't want to waste time parsing. For example, when parsing an XML document to determine its top level structure, we may have no interest in the text or even in many of the tags.

Island grammars can play a useful role in reverse engineering software systems. (H.4.2)

In all of these cases, the role of any grammar we might build is different than the role a grammar plays, say, in a compiler. In the latter case, the grammar is prescriptive. A compiler can simply reject inputs that do not conform to the grammar it is given. Contrast that with a tool whose job is to analyze legacy software or handle customer phone calls. Such a tool must do the best it can with the input that it sees. When building tools of that sort, it may make sense to exploit what is called an island grammar. An ***island grammar*** is a grammar that has two parts:

- A set of detailed rules that describe the fragments that we care about. We'll call these fragments ***islands***.
- A set of flexible rules that can match everything else. We'll call everything else the ***water***.

A very simple form of island grammar is a regular expression that just describes the patterns that we seek. A regular expression matcher ignores those parts of the input string that do not match the patterns. But suppose that the patterns we are looking for cannot be described with regular expressions. For example, they may require balanced parentheses. Or suppose that we want to assign structure to the islands. In that case, we need something more powerful than a regular expression (or a regular grammar). One way to view a context-free island grammar is that it is a hybrid between a context-free grammar and a set of regular expressions.

To see how island grammars work, consider the problem of examining legacy software to determine patterns of static subroutine invocation. To solve this problem, we could use the following island grammar, which is a simplification and modification of one presented in [Moonen 2001]:

[1]	<input> → <chunk>*	
[2]	<chunk> → CALL <id> (<expr>)	{cons(CALL)}
[3]	<chunk> → CALL ERROR (<expr>)	{reject}
[4]	<chunk> → <water>	
[5]	<water> → Σ*	{avoid}

Rule 1 says that a complete input file is a set of chunks. The next three rules describe three kinds of chunks:

- Rule 2 describes the chunks we are trying to find. Assume that another set of rules (such as the ones we considered in Example 11.19) defines the valid syntax for expressions. Those rules may exploit the full power of a context-free grammar, for example to guarantee that parenthesized expressions are properly nested. Then rule 2 will find well-formed function calls. The action associated with it, {cons (CALL)}, tells the parser what kind of node to build whenever this rule is used.

- Rule 3 describes chunks that, although they could be formed by rule 2, are structures that we know we are not interested in. In this case, there is a special kind of error call that we want to ignore. The action {reject} says that whenever this rule matches, its result should be ignored.
- Rule 4 describes water, i.e., the chunks that correspond to the parts of the program that aren't CALL statements. Rule 5 is used to generate the water. But notice that it has the {avoid} action associated with it. That means that it will not be used to match any text that can be matched by some other, non-avoiding rule.

Island grammars can be exploited by appropriately crafted parsers. But we should note here, to avoid confusion, that there is also a somewhat different notion, called ***island parsing***, in which the goal is to use a standard grammar to produce a complete parse given an input string. But, while conventional parsers read and analyze their inputs left-to-right, an island parser first scans its input looking for one or more regions where it seems likely that a correct parse tree can be built. Then it grows the parse tree outward from those "islands" of (relative) certainty. If the input is ill-formed (as is likely to happen, for example, in the case of spoken language understanding), then the final output of the parser will be a sequence of islands, rather than a complete parse. So island grammars and island parsing are both techniques for coping with ill-formed and unpredictable inputs. Island grammars approach the task by specifying, at grammar-writing time, which parts of the input should be analyzed and which should be ignored. Island parsers, in this other sense, approach the task by using a full grammar and deciding, at parse time, which input fragments appear to be parsable and which don't.

11.10 Stochastic Context-Free Grammars ✸

Recall that, at the end of our discussion of finite state machines in Chapter 5, we introduced the idea of a stochastic FSM: an NDFSM whose transitions have been augmented with probabilities that describe some phenomenon that we want to model. We can apply that same idea to context-free grammars: We can add probabilities to grammar rules and so create a ***stochastic context-free grammar*** (also called a ***probabilistic context-free grammar***) that generates strings whose distribution matches some naturally occurring distribution with which we are concerned.

> A stochastic context-free grammar can be used to generate random English text that may seem real enough to fool some people 💻.

A stochastic context-free grammar G is a quintuple (V, Σ, R, S, D), where:

- V is the rule alphabet, which contains nonterminals (symbols that are used in the grammar but that do not appear in strings in the language) and terminals,
- Σ (the set of terminals) is a subset of V,
- R (the set of rules) is a finite subset of $(V - \Sigma) \times V^*$,
- S (the start symbol) can be any element of $V - \Sigma$, and

- D is a function from R to $[0 - 1]$. So D assigns a probability to each rule in R. D must satisfy the requirement that, for every nonterminal symbol X, the sum of the probabilities associated with all rules whose left-hand side is X must be 1.

EXAMPLE 11.27 A Simple Stochastic Grammar

Recall PalEven $= \{ww^R : w \in \{\texttt{a}, \texttt{b}\}^*\}$, the language of even-length palindromes of a's and b's. Suppose that we want to describe the specific case in which a's occur three times as often as b's do. Then we might write the grammar $G = (\{S, \texttt{a}, \texttt{b}\}, \{\texttt{a}, \texttt{b}\}, R, S, D)$, where R and D are defined as follows:

$$S \rightarrow \texttt{a}S\texttt{a} \quad [.72]$$
$$S \rightarrow \texttt{b}S\texttt{b} \quad [.24]$$
$$S \rightarrow \varepsilon \quad [.04]$$

Given a grammar G and a string s, the probability of a particular parse tree t is the product of the probabilities associated with the rules that were used to generate it. In other words, if we let C be the collection (in which duplicates count) of rules that were used to generate t and we let $\Pr(r)$ be the probability associated with rule r, then:

$$\Pr(t) = \prod_{r \in C} \Pr(r).$$

Stochastic context-free grammars play an important role in natural language processing. (L.3.6)

Stochastic grammars can be used to answer two important kinds of questions:

- In an error-free environment, we know that we need to analyze a particular string s. So we want to solve the following problem: Given s, find the most likely parse tree for it.
- In a noisy environment, we may not be sure exactly what string we need to analyze. For example, suppose that it is possible that there have been spelling errors, so the true string is similar but not identical to the one we have observed. Or suppose that there may have been transmission errors. Or suppose that we have transcribed a spoken string and it is possible that we didn't hear it correctly. In all of these cases we want to solve the following problem: Given a set of possible true strings X and an observed string o, find the particular string s (and possibly also the most likely parse for it) that is most likely to have been the one that was actually generated. Note that the probability of generating any particular string w is the sum of the probabilities of generating each possible parse tree for w. In other words, if T is the set of possible parse trees for w, then the total probability of generating w is:

$$\Pr(w) = \sum_{t \in T} Pr(t).$$

Then the sentence s that is most likely to have been generated, given the observation o, is the one with the highest conditional probability given o. Recall that argmax of w returns the value of the argument w that maximizes the value of the function it is given. So the highest probability sentence s is:

$$s = \underset{w \in X}{\text{argmax}}\ Pr\ (w|o)$$

$$= \underset{w \in X}{\text{argmax}} \frac{\Pr\ (o|w) \Pr\ (w)}{\Pr\ (o)}.$$

> Stochastic context-free grammars can be used model the three-dimensional structure of RNA. (K.4)

In Chapter 15, we will discuss techniques for parsing context-free languages that are defined by standard (i.e., without probabilistic information) context-free grammars. Those techniques can be extended to create techniques for parsing using stochastic grammars. So they can be used to answer both of the questions that we just presented.

Exercises

1. Let Σ = {a, b}. For the languages that are defined by each of the following grammars, do each of the following:

   i. List five strings that are in L.

   ii. List five strings that are not in L (or as many as there are, whichever is greater).

   iii. Describe L concisely. You can use regular expressions, expressions using variables (e.g., $a^n b^n$, or set theoretic expressions (e.g., $\{x: \ldots\}$).

   iv. Indicate whether or not L is regular. Prove your answer.

   a. $S \rightarrow$ aS | Sb | ε

   b. $S \rightarrow$ aSa | bSb | a | b

   c. $S \rightarrow$ aS | bS | ε

   d. $S \rightarrow$ aS | aSbS | ε

2. Let G be the grammar of Example 11.12. Show a third parse tree that G can produce for the string (())().

3. Consider the following grammar G:

$$S \rightarrow 0S1|SS|10$$

Show a parse tree produced by G for each of the following strings:

   a. 010110.

   b. 00101101.

4. Consider the following context free grammar G:

$$S \rightarrow aSa$$

$$S \rightarrow T$$
$$S \rightarrow \varepsilon$$
$$T \rightarrow \mathtt{b}T$$
$$T \rightarrow \mathtt{c}T$$
$$T \rightarrow \varepsilon$$

One of these rules is redundant and could be removed without altering $L(G)$. Which one?

5. Using the simple English grammar that we showed in Example 11.6, show two parse trees for each of the following sentences. In each case, indicate which parse tree almost certainly corresponds to the intended meaning of the sentence:

a. `The bear shot Fluffy with the rifle.`

b. `Fluffy likes the girl with the chocolate.`

6. Show a context-free grammar for each of the following languages L:

a. BalDelim $= \{w : \text{where } w \text{ is a string of delimiters: (,), [,], \{, \}, that are properly balanced}\}$.

b. $\{\mathtt{a}^i\mathtt{b}^j : 2i = 3j + 1\}$.

c. $\{\mathtt{a}^i\mathtt{b}^j : 2i \neq 3j + 1\}$.

d. $\{w \in \{\mathtt{a}, \mathtt{b}\}^* : \#_{\mathtt{a}}(w) = 2 \cdot \#_{\mathtt{b}}(w)\}.\}$.

e. $L = \{w \in \{\mathtt{a}, \mathtt{b}\}^* : w = w^{\mathrm{R}}\}$.

f. $\{\mathtt{a}^i\mathtt{b}^j\mathtt{c}^k : i, j, k \geq 0 \text{ and } (i \neq j \text{ or } j \neq k)\}$.

g. $\{\mathtt{a}^i\mathtt{b}^j\mathtt{c}^k : i, j, k \geq 0 \text{ and } (k \leq i \text{ or } k \leq j)\}$.

h. $\{w \in \{\mathtt{a}, \mathtt{b}\}^* : \text{every prefix of } w \text{ has at least as many a's as b's}\}$.

i. $\{\mathtt{a}^n\mathtt{b}^m : m \geq n, m\text{-}n \text{ is even}\}$.

j. $\{\mathtt{a}^m\mathtt{b}^n\mathtt{c}^p\mathtt{d}^q : m, n, p, q \geq 0 \text{ and } m + n = p + q\}$.

k. $\{x\mathtt{c}^n : x \in \{\mathtt{a}, \mathtt{b}\}^* \text{ and } (\#_{\mathtt{a}}(x) = n \text{ or } \#_{\mathtt{b}}(x) = n)\}$.

l. $\{b_i\#b_{i+1}^{\mathrm{R}} : b_i$ is the binary representation of some integer i, $i \geq 0$, without leading zeros$\}$. (For example `101#011` $\in L$.)

m. $\{x^{\mathrm{R}}\#y : x, y \in \{\mathtt{0}, \mathtt{1}\}^* \text{ and } x \text{ is a substring of } y\}$.

7. Let G be the ambiguous expression grammar of Example 11.14. Show at least three different parse trees that can be generated from G for the string `id+id*id*id`.

8. Consider the unambiguous expression grammar G' of Example 11.19.

a. Trace a derivation of the string `id+id*id*id` in G'.

b. Add exponentiation (**) and unary minus ($-$) to G', assigning the highest precedence to unary minus, followed by exponentiation, multiplication, and addition, in that order.

9. Let $L = \{w \in \{\mathtt{a}, \mathtt{b}, \cup, \varepsilon, (,), *, ^+\}^* : w$ is a syntactically legal regular expression$\}$.

a. Write an unambiguous context-free grammar that generates L. Your grammar should have a structure similar to the arithmetic expression grammar G' that we presented in Example 11.19. It should create parse trees that:

- Associate left given operators of equal precedence, and
- Correspond to assigning the following precedence levels to the operators (from highest to lowest):
  - $*$ and $^+$
  - concatenation
  - $\cup$

b. Show the parse tree that your grammar will produce for the string (a ∪ b) ba*.

10. Let $L = \{w \in \{\mathsf{A} - \mathsf{Z}, \neg, \wedge, \vee, \rightarrow, (,)\}^* : w$ is a syntactically legal Boolean expression$\}$.

a. Write an unambiguous context-free grammar that generates L and that creates parse trees that:

- Associate left given operators of equal precedence, and
- Correspond to assigning the following precedence levels to the operators (from highest to lowest): $\neg$, $\wedge$, $\vee$, and $\rightarrow$.

b. Show the parse tree that your grammar will produce for the string:

$$\neg \mathsf{P} \vee \mathsf{R} \rightarrow \mathsf{Q} \rightarrow \mathsf{S}$$

11. In I.3.1, we present a simplified grammar for URIs (Uniform Resource Identifiers), the names that we use to refer to objects on the Web.

a. Using that grammar, show a parse tree for:

`https://www.mystuff.wow/widgets/fradgit#sword`

b. Write a regular expression that is equivalent to the grammar that we present.

12. Prove that each of the following grammars is correct:

a. The grammar, shown in Example 11.3, for the language PalEven.

b. The grammar, shown in Example 11.1, for the language Bal.

13. For each of the following grammars G, show that G is ambiguous. Then find an equivalent grammar that is not ambiguous.

a. $(\{S, A, B, T, \mathsf{a}, \mathsf{c}\}, \{\mathsf{a}, \mathsf{c}\}, R, S)$, where $R = \{S \rightarrow AB, S \rightarrow BA, A \rightarrow \mathsf{a}A, A \rightarrow \mathsf{ac}, B \rightarrow T\mathsf{c}, T \rightarrow \mathsf{a}T, T \rightarrow \mathsf{a}\}$.

b. $(\{S, \mathsf{a}, \mathsf{b}\}, \{\mathsf{a}, \mathsf{b}\}, R, S)$, where $R = \{S \rightarrow \varepsilon, S \rightarrow \mathsf{a}S\mathsf{a}, S \rightarrow \mathsf{b}S\mathsf{b}, S \rightarrow \mathsf{a}S\mathsf{b}, S \rightarrow \mathsf{b}S\mathsf{a}, S \rightarrow SS\}$.

c. $\{\{S, A, B, T, \mathsf{a}, \mathsf{c}\}, \{\mathsf{a}, \mathsf{c}\}, R, S)$, where $R = \{S \rightarrow AB, A \rightarrow AA, A \rightarrow \mathsf{a}, B \rightarrow T\mathsf{c}, T \rightarrow \mathsf{a}T, T \rightarrow \mathsf{a}\}$.

d. $(\{S, \mathsf{a}, \mathsf{b}\}, \{\mathsf{a}, \mathsf{b}\}, R, S)$, where $R = \{S \rightarrow \mathsf{a}S\mathsf{b}, S \rightarrow \mathsf{b}S\mathsf{a}, S \rightarrow SS, S \rightarrow \varepsilon\}$. ($G$ is the grammar that we presented in Example 11.10 for the language $L = \{w \in \{\mathsf{a,b}\}^* : \#_{\mathsf{a}}(w) = \#_{\mathsf{b}}(w)\}$.)

e. $(\{S, \mathsf{a}, \mathsf{b}\}, \{\mathsf{a}, \mathsf{b}\}, R, S)$, where $R = \{S \rightarrow \mathsf{a}S\mathsf{b}, S \rightarrow \mathsf{aa}S\mathsf{b}, S \rightarrow \varepsilon\}$.

14. Let G be any context-free grammar. Show that the number of strings that have a derivation in G of length n or less, for any $n > 0$, is finite.

15. Consider the fragment of a Java grammar that is presented in Example 11.20. How could it be changed to force each `else` clause to be attached to the outermost possible `if` statement?

16. How does the COND form in Lisp, as described in G.5, avoid the dangling else problem?

17. Consider the grammar G' of Example 11.19.

a. Convert G' to Chomsky normal form.

b. Consider the string `id*id+id`.

i. Show the parse tree that G' produces for it.

ii. Show the parse tree that your Chomsky normal form grammar produces for it.

18. Convert each of the following grammars to Chomsky normal form:

a. $S \rightarrow \mathrm{a}S\mathrm{a}$
$S \rightarrow B$
$B \rightarrow \mathrm{bb}C$
$B \rightarrow \mathrm{bb}$
$C \rightarrow \varepsilon$
$C \rightarrow \mathrm{c}C$

b. $S \rightarrow ABC$
$A \rightarrow \mathrm{a}C \mid D$
$B \rightarrow \mathrm{b}B \mid \varepsilon \mid A$
$C \rightarrow A\mathrm{c} \mid \varepsilon \mid C\mathrm{c}$
$D \rightarrow \mathrm{aa}$

c. $S \rightarrow \mathrm{a}TV\mathrm{a}$
$T \rightarrow \mathrm{a}T\mathrm{a} \mid \mathrm{b}T\mathrm{b} \mid \varepsilon \mid V$
$V \rightarrow \mathrm{c}V\mathrm{c} \mid \varepsilon$

CHAPTER 12

Pushdown Automata

Grammars define context-free languages. We'd also like a computational formalism that is powerful enough to enable us to build an acceptor for every context-free language. In this chapter, we describe such a formalism.

12.1 Definition of a (Nondeterministic) PDA

A pushdown automaton, or PDA, is a finite state machine that has been augmented by a single stack. In a minute, we will present the formal definition of the PDA model that we will use. But, before we do that, one caveat to readers of other books is in order. There are several competing PDA definitions, from which we have chosen one to present here. All are provably equivalent, in the sense that, for all i and j, if there exists a version_i PDA that accepts some language L then there also exists a version_j PDA that accepts L. We'll return to this issue in Section 12.5, where we will mention a few of the other models and sketch an equivalence proof. For now, simply beware of the fact that other definitions are also in widespread use.

We will use the following definition: A ***pushdown automaton*** (or ***PDA***) M is a sextuple $(K, \Sigma, \Gamma, \Delta, s, A)$, where:

- K is a finite set of states,
- Σ is the input alphabet,
- Γ is the stack alphabet,
- $s \in K$ is the start state,
- $A \subseteq K$ is the set of accepting states, and
- Δ is the transition relation. It is a finite subset of:

$$(K \times (\Sigma \cup \{\varepsilon\}) \times \Gamma^*) \times (K \times \Gamma^*).$$

$(K$	$(\Sigma \cup \{\varepsilon\})$	$\Gamma^*)$	$(K$	$\Gamma^*)$
state	input or ε	string of symbols to pop from top of stack	state	string of symbols to push on top of stack

A ***configuration*** of a PDA M is an element of $K \times \Sigma^* \times \Gamma^*$. It captures the three things that can make a difference to M's future behavior:

- its current state,
- the input that is still left to read, and
- the contents of its stack.

The ***initial configuration*** of a PDA M, on input w, is (s, w, ε).

We will use the following notational convention for describing M's stack as a string: The top of the stack is to the left of the string. So:

c		
a	will be written as	cab
b		

If a sequence $c_1 c_2 \ldots c_n$ of characters is pushed onto the stack, they will be pushed rightmost first, so if the value of the stack before the push was s, the value after the push will be $c_1 c_2 \ldots c_n s$.

Analogously to what we did for FSMs, we define the relation *yields-in-one-step*, written $|\text{-}_M$. *Yields-in-one-step* relates *configuration*$_1$ to *configuration*$_2$ iff M can move from *configuration*$_1$ to *configuration*$_2$ in one step. Let c be any element of $\Sigma \cup \{\varepsilon\}$, let γ_1, γ_2 and γ be any elements of Γ^*, and let w be any element of Σ^*. Then:

$$(q_1, cw, \gamma_1\gamma)|\text{-}_M (q_2, w, \gamma_2\gamma) \text{ iff } ((q_1, c, \gamma_1), (q_2, \gamma_2)) \in \Delta.$$

Note two things about what a transition $((q_1, c, \gamma_1), (q_2, \gamma_2))$ says about how M manipulates its stack:

- M may only take the transition if the string γ_1 matches the current top of the stack. If it does, and the transition is taken, then M pops γ_1 and then pushes γ_2. M cannot "peek" at the top of its stack without popping off the values that it examines.
- If $\gamma_1 = \varepsilon$, then M must match ε against the top of the stack. But ε matches everywhere. So letting γ_1 be ε is equivalent to saying "without bothering to check the current value of the stack." It is not equivalent to saying, "if the stack is empty." In our definition, there is no way to say that directly, although we will see that we can create a way by letting M, before it does anything else, push a special marker onto the stack. Then, whenever that marker is on the top of the stack, the stack is otherwise empty.

The relation *yields*, written $|\text{-}_M{}^*$, is the reflexive, transitive closure of $|\text{-}_M$. So configuration C_1 yields configuration C_2 iff:

$$C_1 |\text{-}_M{}^* C_2.$$

A ***computation*** by M is a finite sequence of configurations $C_0, C_1, \ldots, C_n$ for some $n \geq 0$ such that:

- C_0 is an initial configuration,
- C_n is of the form (q, ε, γ), for some state $q \in K$ and some string γ in Γ^*, and
- $C_0 |\text{-}_M C_1 |\text{-}_M C_2 |\text{-}_M \ldots |\text{-}_M C_n$.

Note that we have defined the behavior of a PDA M by a transition relation Δ, not a transition function. Thus we allow nondeterminism. If M is in some configuration (q_1, s, γ), it is possible that:

- Δ contains exactly one transition that matches. In that case, M makes the specified move.
- Δ contains more than one transition that matches. In that case, M chooses one of them. Each choice defines one computation that M may perform.
- Δ contains no transition that matches. In that case, the computation that led to that configuration halts.

Let C be a computation of M on input $w \in \Sigma^*$. Then we will say that:

- C is an ***accepting computation*** iff $C = (s, w, \varepsilon) |\text{-}_M{}^* (q, \varepsilon, \varepsilon)$, for some $q \in A$. Note the strength of this requirement: A computation accepts only if it runs out of input when it is in an accepting state *and* the stack is empty.
- C is a ***rejecting computation*** iff $C = (s, w, \varepsilon) |\text{-}_M{}^* (q, w', \alpha)$, where C is not an accepting computation and where M has no moves that it can make from (q, w', α). A computation can reject only if the criteria for accepting have not been met *and* there are no further moves (including following ε-transitions) that can be taken.

Let w be a string that is an element of Σ^*. Then we will say that:

- ***M accepts*** w iff *at least one* of its computations accepts.
- ***M rejects*** w iff all of its computations reject.

The ***language accepted by*** M, denoted $L(M)$, is the set of all strings accepted by M. Note that it is possible that, on input w, M neither accepts nor rejects.

In all the examples that follow, we will draw a transition $((q_1, c, \gamma_1), (q_2, \gamma_2))$ as an arc from q_1 to q_2, labeled $c/\gamma_1/\gamma_2$. So such a transition should be read to say, "If c matches the input and γ_1 matches the top of the stack, the transition from q_1 to q_2 can be taken, in which case c should be removed from the input, γ_1 should be popped from the stack, and γ_2 should be pushed onto it." If $c = \varepsilon$, then the transition can be taken without consuming any input. If $\gamma_1 = \varepsilon$, the transition can be taken without checking the stack or popping anything. If $\gamma_2 = \varepsilon$, nothing is pushed onto the stack when the transition is taken. As we did with FSMs, we will use a double circle to indicate accepting states.

Even very simple PDAs may be able to accept languages that cannot be accepted by any FSM. The power of such machines comes from the ability of the stack to count.

EXAMPLE 12.1 The Balanced Parentheses Language

Consider again Bal = $\{w \in \{), (\}^* :$ the parentheses are balanced$\}$. The following one-state PDA M accepts Bal. M uses its stack to count the number of left parentheses that have not yet been matched. We show M graphically and then as a sextuple:

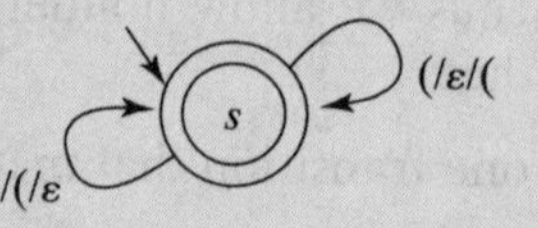

$M = (K, \Sigma, \Gamma, \Delta, s, A)$, where:

$K = \{s\}$,	(the states)
$\Sigma = \{(,)\}$,	(the input alphabet)
$\Gamma = \{(\}$,	(the stack alphabet)
$A = \{s\}$, and	(the accepting state)
$\Delta = \{((s, (, \varepsilon), (s, ( )),$	
$((s,), ( ), (s, \varepsilon))\}$.	

If M sees a (, it pushes it onto the stack (regardless of what was already there). If it sees a) and there is a (that can be popped off the stack, M does so. If it sees a) and there is no (to pop, M halts without accepting. If, after consuming its entire input string, M's stack is empty, M accepts. If the stack is not empty, M rejects.

PDAs, like FSMs, can use their states to remember facts about the structure of the string that has been read so far. We see this in the next example.

EXAMPLE 12.2 A^nB^n

Consider again $A^nB^n = \{a^nb^n : n \geq 0\}$. The following PDA M accepts A^nB^n. M uses its states to guarantee that it only accepts strings that belong to a*b*. It uses its stack to count a's so that it can compare them to the b's. We show M graphically:

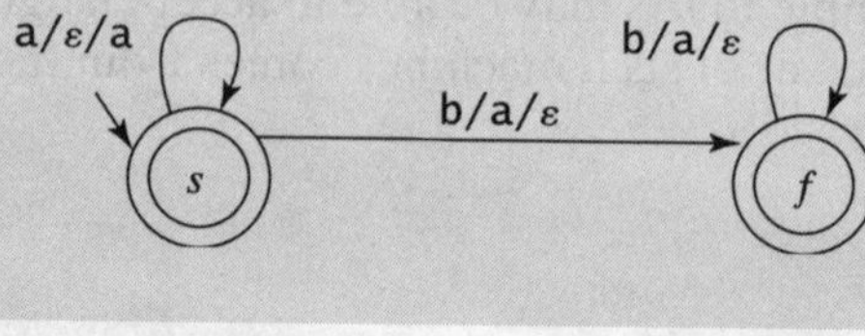

Writing it out, we have $M = (K, \Sigma, \Gamma, \Delta, s, A)$, where:

$K = \{s, f\}$,	(the states)
$\Sigma = \{\mathsf{a}, \mathsf{b})\}$,	(the input alphabet)
$\Gamma = \{\mathsf{a}\}$,	(the stack alphabet)
$A = \{s, f\}$, and	(the accepting states)

$$\Delta = \{((s, \mathsf{a}, \varepsilon), (s, \mathsf{a})),$$
$$((s, \mathsf{b}, \mathsf{a}), (f, \varepsilon)),$$
$$((f, \mathsf{b}, \mathsf{a}), (f, \varepsilon))\}.$$

Remember that M only accepts if, when it has consumed its entire input string, it is in an accepting state *and* its stack is empty. So, for example, M will reject aaa, even though it will be in state s, an accepting state, when it runs out of input. The stack at that point will contain aaa.

EXAMPLE 12.3 WcW^{R}

Let WcW^{R} $= \{wcw^R : w \in \{\mathsf{a}, \mathsf{b}\}^*\}$. The following PDA M accepts WcW^{R}:

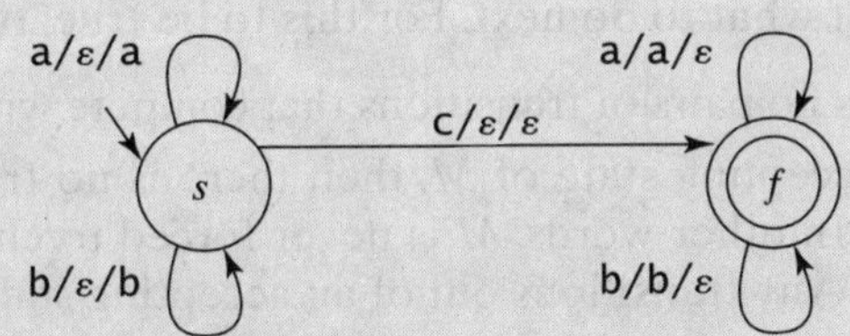

M moves from state s, in which it is recording w, to state f, in which it is checking for w^R, when it sees the character c. Since every string in WcW^{R} must contain the middle c, state s is not an accepting state.

The definition that we have chosen to use for a PDA is flexible; it allows several symbols to be pushed or popped from the stack in one move. This will turn out to be particularly useful when we attempt to build PDAs that correspond to practical grammars that contain rules like $T \rightarrow T * F$ (the multiplication rule that was part of the arithmetic expression grammar that we defined in Example 11.19). But we illustrate the use of this flexibility here on a simple case.

EXAMPLE 12.4 A^{n}B$^{\mathsf{2n}}$

Let A^{n}B$^{\mathsf{2n}}$ $= \{\mathsf{a}^n\mathsf{b}^{2n} : n \geq 0\}$. The following PDA M accepts A^{n}B$^{\mathsf{2n}}$ by pushing two a's onto the stack for every a in the input string. Then each b pops a single a:

EXAMPLE 12.4 (*Continued*)

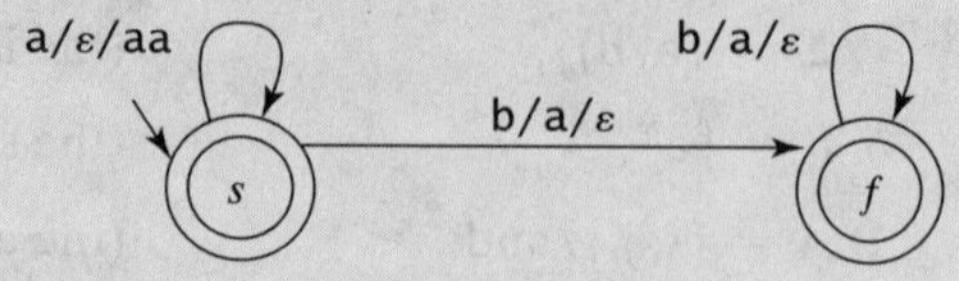

12.2 Deterministic and Nondeterministic PDAs

The definition of a PDA that we have presented allows nondeterminism. It sometimes makes sense, however, to restrict our attention to deterministic PDAs. In this section we will define what we mean by a deterministic PDA. We also show some examples of the power of nondeterminism in PDAs. Unfortunately, in contrast to the situation with FSMs, and as we will prove in Theorem 13.13, there exist nondeterministic PDAs for which no equivalent deterministic PDA exists.

12.2.1 Definition of a Deterministic PDA

Define a PDA M to be ***deterministic*** iff there exists no configuration of M in which M has a choice of what to do next. For this to be true, two conditions must hold:

1. Δ_M contains no pairs of transitions that compete with each other.
2. If q is an accepting state of M, then there is no transition $((q, \varepsilon, \varepsilon), (p, a))$ for any p or a. In other words, M is never forced to choose between accepting and continuing. Any transitions out of an accepting state must either consume input (since, if there is remaining input, M does not have the option of accepting) or pop something from the stack (since, if the stack is not empty, M does not have the option of accepting).

So far, all of the PDAs that we have built have been deterministic. So each machine followed only a single computational path.

12.2.2 Exploiting Nondeterminism

But a PDA may be designed to have multiple competing moves from a single configuration. As with FSMs, the easiest way to envision the operation of a nondeterministic PDA M is as a tree, as shown in Figure 12.1. Each node in the tree corresponds to a configuration of M and each path from the root to a leaf node may correspond to one computation that M might perform.

Notice that the state, the stack, and the remaining input can be different along different paths. As a result, it will not be possible to simulate all paths in parallel, the way we did for NDFSMs.

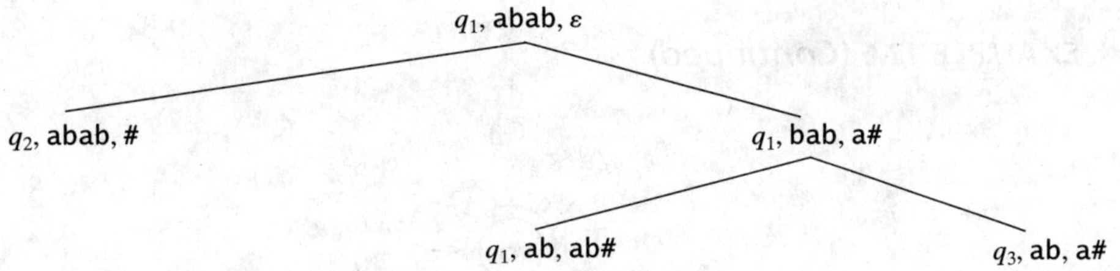

FIGURE 12.1 Viewing nondeterminism as search through a space of computation paths.

EXAMPLE 12.5 Even Length Palindromes

Consider again PalEven $= \{ww^R : w \in \{\text{a, b}\}^*\}$, the language of even-length palindromes of a's and b's. The following nondeterministic PDA M accepts PalEven:

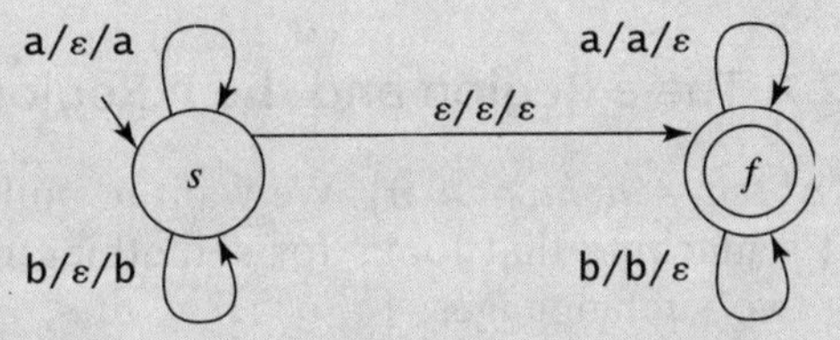

M is nondeterministic because it cannot know when it has reached the middle of its input. Before each character is read, it has two choices: It can guess that it has not yet gotten to the middle. In that case, it stays in state s, where it pushes each symbol it reads. Or it can guess that it has reached the middle. In that case, it takes the ε-transition to state f, where it pops one symbol for each symbol that it reads.

EXAMPLE 12.6 Equal Numbers of a's and b's

Let $L = \{w \in \{\text{a, b}\}^* : \#_a(w) = \#_b(w)\}$. Now we don't know the order in which the a's and b's will occur. They can be interleaved. So for example, any PDA to accept L must accept aabbba. The only way to count the number of characters that have not yet found their mates is to use the stack. So the stack will sometimes count a's and sometimes count b's. It will count whatever it has seen more of. The following simple PDA accepts L:

EXAMPLE 12.6 ***(Continued)***

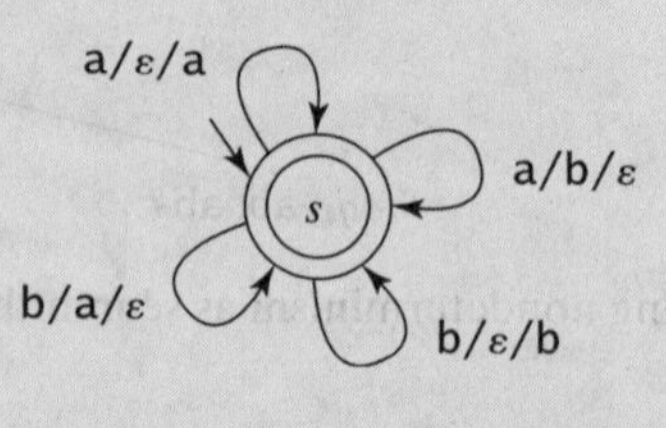

This machine is highly nondeterministic. Whenever it sees an a in the input, it can either push it (which is the right thing to do if it should be counting a's) or attempt to pop a b (which is the right thing to do if it should be counting b's). All the computations that make the wrong guess will fail to accept since they will not succeed in clearing the stack. But if $\#_a(w) = \#_b(w)$, there will be one computation that will accept.

EXAMPLE 12.7 The a Region and the b Region are Different

Let $L = \{a^m b^n : m \neq n; m, n > 0\}$. We want to build a PDA M to accept L. It is hard to build a machine that looks for something negative, like $\neq$. But we can break L into two sublanguages: $\{a^m b^n : 0 < m < n\}$ and $\{a^m b^n : 0 < n < m\}$. Either there are more a's or more b's. M must accept any string that is in either of those sublanguages. So M is:

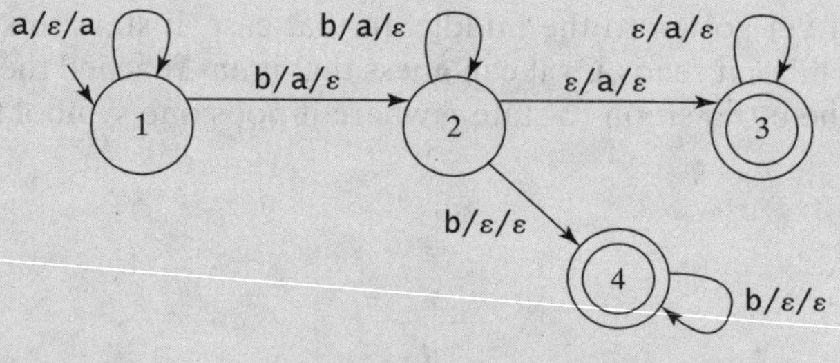

As long as M sees a's, it stays in state 1 and pushes each a onto the stack. When it sees the first b, it goes to state 2. It will accept nothing but b's from that point on. So far, its behavior has been deterministic. But, from state 2, it must make choices. Each time it sees another b and there is an a on the stack, it should consume the b and pop the a and stay in state 2. But, in order to accept, it must eventually either read at least one b that does not have a matching a or pop an a that does not have a matching b. It should do the former (and go to state 4) if there is a b in the input stream when the stack is empty. But we have no way to specify that a move can be taken only if the stack is empty. It should do the latter (and go to state 3) if there is an a on the stack but the input stream is empty. But we have no way to specify that the input stream is empty.

As a result, in most of its moves in state 2, *M* will have a choice of three paths to take. All but the correct one will die out without accepting. But a good deal of computational effort will be wasted first.

In the next section, we present techniques for reducing nondeterminism caused by the two problems we've just presented:

- A transition that should be taken only if the stack is empty, and
- A transition that should be taken only if the input stream is empty.

But first we present one additional example of the power of nondeterminism.

EXAMPLE 12.8 $\neg A^nB^nC^n$

Let's first consider $A^nB^nC^n = \{a^nb^nc^n : n \geq 0\}$. If we try to think about building a PDA to accept $A^nB^nC^n$, we immediately run into trouble. We can use the stack to count a's and then compare them to the b's. But then the stack will be empty and it won't be possible to compare the c's. We can try to think of something clever to get around this problem, but we will fail. We'll prove in Chapter 13 that no PDA exists to accept this language.

But now let $L = \neg A^nB^nC^n$. There is a PDA that accepts L. $L = L_1 \cup L_2$, where:

- $L_1 = \{w \in \{a, b, c\}^* :$ the letters are out of order$\}$.
- $L_2 = \{a^ib^jc^k : i, j, k \geq 0$ and $(i \neq j$ or $j \neq k)\}$ (in other words, not equal numbers of a's, b's, and c's).

A simple FSM can accept L_1. So we focus on L_2. It turns out to be easier to check for a mismatch in the number of a's, b's, and c's than to check for a match because, to detect a mismatch, it is sufficient to find one thing wrong. It is not necessary to compare everything. So a string w is in L_2 iff *either* (or both) the a's and b's don't match or the b's and c's don't match. We can build PDAs, such as the one we built in Example 12.7, to check each of those conditions. So we can build a straightforward PDA for L. It first guesses which condition to check for. Then submachines do the checking. We sketch a PDA for L here and leave the details as an exercise:

EXAMPLE 12.8 (*Continued*)

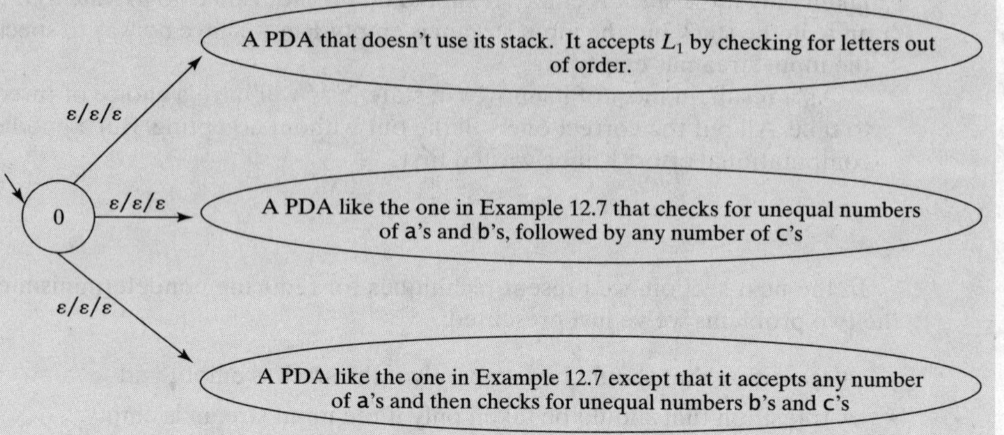

This last example is significant for two reasons:

- It illustrates the power of nondeterminism.
- It proves that the class of languages acceptable by PDAs is not closed under complement. We'll have more to say about that in Section 13.4.

An important fact about the context-free languages, in contrast to the regular ones, is that nondeterminism is more than a convenient design tool. In Section 13.5 we will define the ***deterministic context-free languages*** to be those that can be accepted by some deterministic PDA that may exploit an end-of-string marker. Then we will prove that there are context-free languages that are not deterministic in this sense. Thus there exists, for the context-free languages, no equivalent of the regular language algorithm *ndfsmtodfsm*. There are, however, some techniques that can be used to reduce nondeterminism in many of the kinds of cases that often occur. We'll sketch two of them in the next section.

12.2.3 Techniques for Reducing Nondeterminism ✸

In Example 12.7, we saw nondeterminism arising from two very specific circumstances:

- A transition that should be taken only if the stack is empty competes against one or more moves that require a match of some string on the stack, and
- A transition that should be taken only if the input stream is empty competes against one or more moves that require a match against a specific input character.

Both of these circumstances are common, so we would like to find a way to reduce or eliminate the nondeterminism that they cause.

We first consider the case in which the nondeterminism could be eliminated if it were possible to check for an empty stack. Although our PDA model does not provide a way to do that directly, it is easy to simulate. Any PDA M that would like to be able to check for empty stack can simply, before it does anything else, push a special character onto the stack. The stack is then logically empty iff that special character is at the top of the stack. The only thing we must be careful about is that, before M can accept a string, its stack must be completely empty. So the special character must be popped whenever M reaches an accepting state.

EXAMPLE 12.9 Using a Bottom of Stack Marker

We can use the special, bottom-of-stack marker technique to reduce the nondeterminism in the PDA that we showed in Example 12.7. We'll use # as the marker. When we do that, we get the following PDA M':

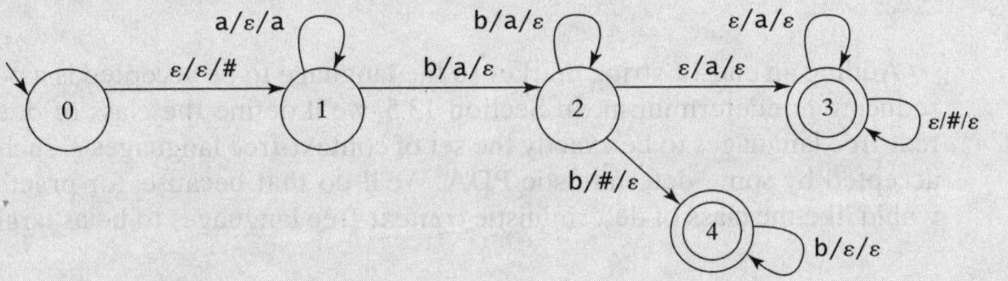

Now the transition back to state 2 no longer competes with the transition to state 4, which can only be taken when the # is the only symbol left on the stack. M' is still nondeterministic though, because the transition back to state 2 competes with the transition to state 3. We still don't have a way to specify that M' should go to state 3 only if it has run out of input.

Next we consider the "out of input" problem. To solve that one, we will make a change to the input language. Instead of building a machine to accept a language L, we'll build one to accept $L\$$, where \$ is a special end-of-string marker. In any practical system, we would probably choose *<newline>* or *<cr>* or *<enter>*, rather than \$, but we'll use \$ here because it is easy to see.

EXAMPLE 12.10 Using an End-of-String Marker

We can use the end-of-string marker technique to eliminate the remaining nondeterminism in the PDAs that we showed in Example 12.7 and Example 12.9. When we do that, we get the following PDA M'':

EXAMPLE 12.10 (*Continued*)

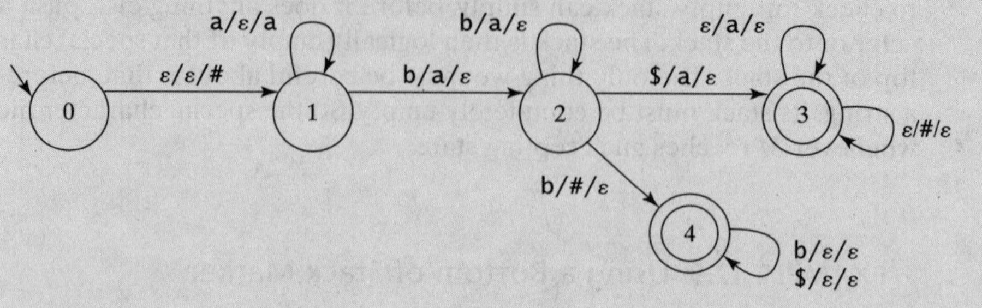

Now the transition back to state 2 no longer competes with the transition to state 3, since the latter can only be taken when the $ is read. Notice that we must be careful to read the $ on all paths, not just the one where we needed it.

Adding an end-of-string marker to the language to be accepted is a powerful tool for reducing nondeterminism. In Section 13.5, we'll define the class of deterministic context-free languages to be exactly the set of context-free languages L such that $L\$$ can be accepted by some deterministic PDA. We'll do that because, for practical reasons, we would like the class of deterministic context-free languages to be as large as possible.

12.3 Equivalence of Context-Free Grammars and PDAs

So far, we have shown PDAs to accept several of the context-free languages for which we wrote grammars in Chapter 11. This is no accident. In this section we'll prove, as usual by construction, that context-free grammars and pushdown automata describe exactly the same class of languages.

12.3.1 Building a PDA from a Grammar

THEOREM 12.1 For Every CFG There Exists an Equivalent PDA

Theorem: Given a context-free grammar $G = (V, \Sigma, R, S)$, there exists a PDA M such that $L(M) = L(G)$.

Proof: The proof is by construction. There are two equally straightforward ways to do this construction, so we will describe both of them. Either of them can be converted to a practical parser (a recognizer that returns a parse tree if it accepts) by adding simple tree-building operations associated with each stack operation. We'll see how in Chapter 15.

Top-down parsing: A top-down parser answers the question, "Could G generate w?" by starting with S, applying the rules of R, and seeing whether w can be derived. We can build a PDA that does exactly that. We will define the algorithm *cfgtoPDAtopdown*(G), which, from a grammar G, builds a corresponding PDA M that, on input w, simulates G attempting to produce a leftmost derivation of w. M will have two states. The only purpose of the first state is to push S onto the stack and then go to the second state. M's stack will actually do all the work by keeping track of what G is trying derive. Initially, of course, that is S, which is why M begins by pushing S onto the stack. But suppose that R contains a rule of the form $S \rightarrow \gamma_1\gamma_2 \ldots \gamma_n$. Then M can replace its goal of generating an S by the goal of generating a γ_1, followed by a γ_2, and so forth. So M can pop S off the stack and replace it by the sequence of symbols $\gamma_1\gamma_2 \ldots \gamma_n$ (with γ_1 on top). As long as the symbol on the top of the stack is a nonterminal in G, this process continues, effectively applying the rules of G to the top of the stack (thus producing a left-most derivation).

The appearance of a terminal symbol c on the top of the stack means that G is attempting to generate c. M only wants to pursue paths that generate its input string w. So, at that point, it pops the top symbol off the stack, reads its next input character, and compares the two. If they match, the derivation that M is pursuing is consistent with generating w and the process continues. If they don't match, the path that M is currently following ends without accepting. So, at each step, M either applies a grammar rule, without consuming any input, or it reads an input character and pops one terminal symbol off the stack.

When M has finished generating each of the constituents of the S it pushed initially, its stack will become empty. If that happens at the same time that M has read all the characters of w, G can generate w, so M accepts. It will do so since its second state will be an accepting state. Parsers with a structure like M's are called top-down parsers. We'll have more to say about them in Section 15.2.

As an example, suppose that R contains the rules $A \rightarrow$ a, $B \rightarrow$ b and $S \rightarrow AAB$. Assume that the input to M is aab. Then M first shifts S onto the stack. Next it applies its third rule, pops S off, and replaces it by AAB. Then it applies its first rule, pops off A, and replaces it by a. The stack is then aAB. At that point, it reads the first character of its input, pops a, compares the two characters, sees that they match, and continues. The stack is then AB. Again M applies its first rule, pops off A, and replaces it by a. The stack then is aB. Then it reads the next character of its input, pops a, compares the two characters, sees that they match, and continues. The stack is then B. M applies its second rule, pops off B, and replaces it by b. It reads the last input character, pops off b, compares the two characters, and sees that they match. At that point, M is in an accepting state and both the stack and the input stream are empty, so M accepts. The outline of M is shown in Figure 12.2.

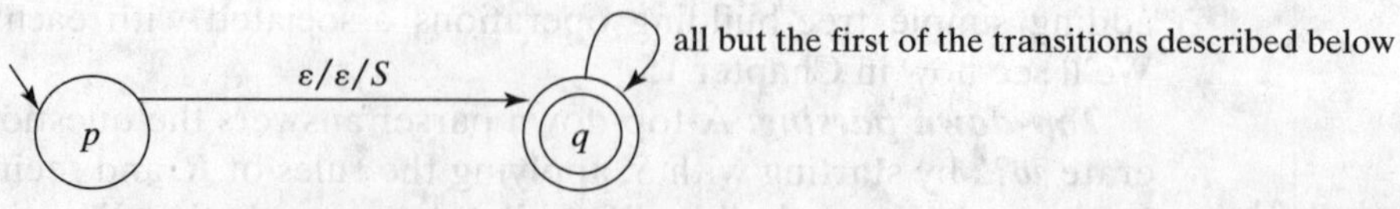

FIGURE 12.2 A PDA that parses top-down.

Formally, $M = (\{p, q\}, \Sigma, V, \Delta, p, \{q\})$, where Δ contains:

- The start-up transition $((p, \varepsilon, \varepsilon), (q, S))$, which pushes the start symbol onto the stack and goes to state q.
- For each rule $X \rightarrow \gamma_1\gamma_2 \ldots \gamma_n$ in R, the transition $((q, \varepsilon, X), (q, \gamma_1\gamma_2 \ldots \gamma_n))$, which replaces X by $\gamma_1\gamma_2 \ldots \gamma_n$. If $n = 0$ (i.e., the right-hand side of the rule is ε), then the transition is $((q, \varepsilon, X), (q, \varepsilon))$.
- For each character $c \in \Sigma$, the transition $((q, c, c), (q, \varepsilon))$, which compares an expected character from the stack against the next input character and continues if they match.

So we can define:

cfgtoPDAtopdown (G: CFG) =
    From G, construct M as defined above.

Bottom-up parsing: A bottom-up parser answers the question, "Could G generate w?" by starting with w, applying the rules of R backwards, and seeing whether S can be reached. We can build a PDA that does exactly that. We will define the algorithm *cfgtoPDAbottomup*(G), which, from a grammar G, builds a corresponding PDA M that, on input w, simulates the construction, backwards, of a rightmost derivation of w in G. Again, M will have two states, but this time all the work will happen in the first one. In the top-down approach that we described above, the entries in the stack corresponded to expectations: to constituents that G was trying to derive. In the bottom-up approach that we are describing now, the objects in the stack will correspond to constituents that have actually been found in the input. If M ever finds a complete S that covers its entire input, then it should accept. So if, when M runs out of input, the stack contains a single S, it will accept. M will be able to perform two kinds of actions:

- M can read an input symbol and ***shift*** it onto the stack.
- Whenever a sequence of elements at the top of the stack matches, in reverse, the right-hand side of some rule r in R, M can pop that sequence off and replace it by the left-hand side of r. When this happens, we say that M has ***reduced*** by rule r.

Because of the two actions that it can perform, a parser based on a PDA like M is called a ***shift-reduce parser***. We'll have more to say about how such parsers work in Section 15.3. For now, we just observe that they simulate, backwards, a right-most derivation.

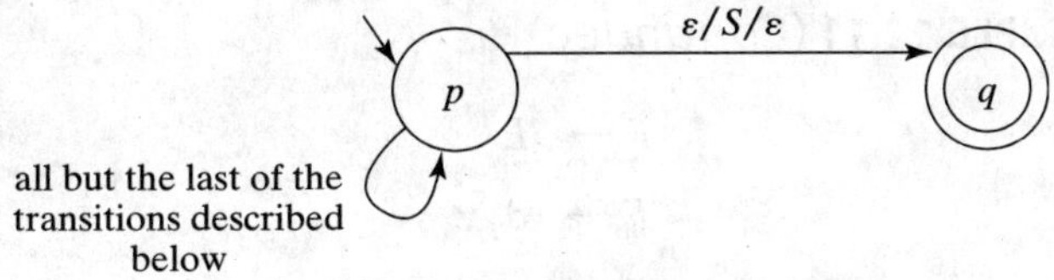

FIGURE 12.3 A PDA that parses bottom-up.

To see how M might work, suppose that R contains the rules $A \rightarrow$ a, $B \rightarrow$ b and $S \rightarrow AAB$. Assume that the input to M is aab. Then M first shifts a onto the stack. The top of the stack matches the right-hand side of the first rule. So M can apply the rule, pop off a, and replace it with A. Then it shifts the next a, so the stack is aA. It reduces by the first rule again, so the stack is AA. It shifts the b, applies the second rule, and leaves the stack as BAA. At that point, the top of the stack matches, in reverse, the right-hand side of the third rule. The string is reversed because the leftmost symbol was read first and so is at the bottom of the stack. M will pop off BAA and replace it by S.

To accept, M must pop S off the stack, leave the stack empty, and go to its second state, which will accept. The outline of M is shown in Figure 12.3.

Formally, $M = (\{p, q\}, \Sigma, V, \Delta, p, \{q\})$, where Δ contains:

- The shift transitions: $((p, c, \varepsilon), (p, c))$, for each $c \in \Sigma$.
- The reduce transitions: $((p, \varepsilon, (\gamma_1\gamma_2 \ldots \gamma_n)^R), (p, X))$, for each rule: $X \rightarrow \gamma_1\gamma_2 \ldots \gamma_n$ in R.
- The finish up transition: $((p, \varepsilon, S), (q, \varepsilon))$.

So we can define:

cfgtoPDAbottomup (G: CFG) =

From G, construct M as defined above.

EXAMPLE 12.11 Using *cfgtoPDAtopdown* and *cfgtoPDAbottomup*

Consider E_{xpr}, our simple expression language, defined by $G = \{\{E, T, F, \texttt{id}, +, *, (,)\}, \{\texttt{id}, +, *, (,)\}, R, E\}$, where:

$$R = \quad E \rightarrow E + T$$
$$E \rightarrow T$$
$$T \rightarrow T * F$$
$$T \rightarrow F$$

EXAMPLE 12.11 (*Continued*)

$$F \rightarrow E$$

$$F \rightarrow \texttt{id}\}.$$

We show two PDAs, M_a and M_b, that accept E_{xpr}. We can use the function *cfgtoPDAtopdown*(G) to build M_a =

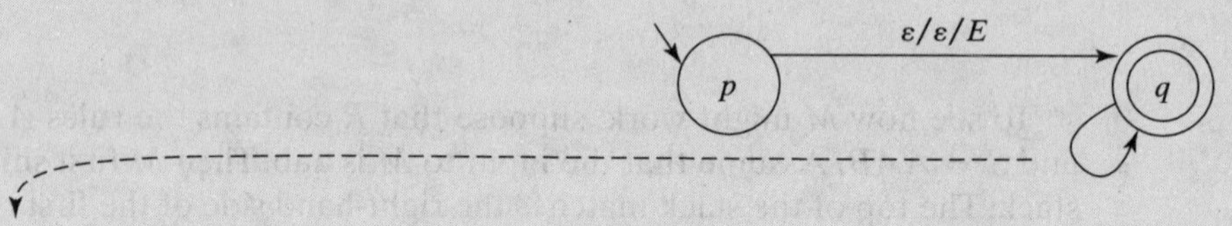

(1) $(q, \varepsilon, E), (q, E + T)$

(2) $(q, \varepsilon, E), (q, T)$

(3) $(q, \varepsilon, T), (q, T * F)$

(4) $(q, \varepsilon, T), (q, F)$

(5) $(q, \varepsilon, F), (q, (E))$

(6) $(q, \varepsilon, F), (q, \texttt{id})$

(7) $(q, \texttt{id}, \texttt{id}), (q, \varepsilon)$

(8) $(q, (, (), (q, \varepsilon)$

(9) $(q,),)), (q, \varepsilon)$

(10) $(q, +, +), (q, \varepsilon)$

(11) $(q, *, *), (q, \varepsilon)$

We can use *cfgtoPDAbottomup*(G) to build M_b =

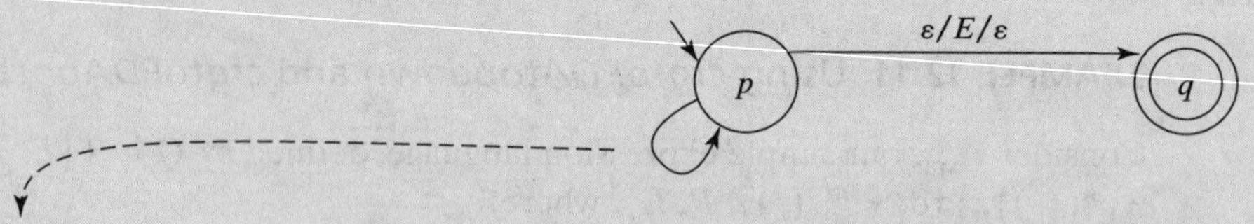

(1) $(p, \texttt{id}, \varepsilon), (p, \texttt{id})$

(2) $(p, (, \varepsilon), (p, ()$

(3) $(p,), \varepsilon), (p,))$

(4) $(p, +, \varepsilon), (p, +)$

(5) $(p, *, \varepsilon), (p, *)$

(6) $(p, \varepsilon, T + E), (p, E)$

(7) $(p, \varepsilon, T), (p, E)$

(8) $(p, \varepsilon, F * T), (p, T)$

(9) $(p, \varepsilon, F), (p, T)$

(10) $(p, \varepsilon,)E(\,), (p, F)$

(11) $(p, \varepsilon, \texttt{id}), (p, F)$

The theorem that we just proved is important for two very different kinds of reasons:

- It is theoretically important because we will use it to prove one direction of the claim that context-free grammars and PDAs describe the same class of languages. For this purpose, all we care about is the truth of the theorem.
- It is of great practical significance. The languages we use to communicate with programs are, in the main, context-free. Before an application can assign meaning to our programs, our queries, and our marked up documents, it must parse the statements that we have written. Consider either of the PDAs that we built in our proof of this theorem. Each stack operation of either of them corresponds to the building of a piece of the parse tree that corresponds to the derivation that the PDA found. So we can go a long way toward building a parser by simply augmenting one of the PDAs that we just built with a mechanism that associates a tree-building operation with each stack action. Because the PDAs follow the structure of the grammar, we can guarantee that we get the parses we want by writing appropriate grammars. In truth, building efficient parsers is more complicated than this. We'll have more to say about the issues in Chapter 15.

12.3.2 Building a Grammar from a PDA ◆

We next show that it is possible to go the other way, from a PDA to a grammar. Unfortunately, the process is not as straightforward as the grammar-to-PDA process. Fortunately, for applications, it is rarely (if ever) necessary to go in this direction.

Restricted Normal Form

The grammar-creation algorithm that we are about to define must make some assumptions about the structure of the PDA to which it is applied. So, before we present that algorithm, we will define what we'll call ***restricted normal form*** for PDAs. A PDA M is in restricted normal form iff:

1. M has a start state s' that does nothing except push a special symbol onto the stack and then transfer to a state s from which the rest of the computation begins. There must be no transitions back to s'. The special symbol must not be used in any other way in M. We will use # to stand for such a symbol.
2. M has a single accepting state a. All transitions into a pop # and read no input.
3. Every transition in M, except the one from s', pops exactly one symbol from the stack.

As with other normal forms, in order for restricted normal form to be useful, we must define an algorithm that converts an arbitrary PDA $M = (K, \Sigma, \Gamma, \Delta, s, A)$ into it. Given M, *convertPDAtorestricted* builds a new PDA M' such that $L(M') = L(M)$ and M' is in restricted normal form.

convertPDAtorestricted (M: PDA) =

1. Initially, let $M' = M$.

/* Establish property 1:

2. Create a new start state s'.
3. Add the transition $((s', \varepsilon, \varepsilon), (s, \#))$.

/* Establish property 2:

4. Create a new accepting state a.
5. For each accepting state q in M do:
   - **5.1.** Create the transition $((q, \varepsilon, \#), (a, \varepsilon))$.
   - **5.2.** Remove q from the set of accepting states (making a the only accepting state in M').

/* Establish property 3:

/* Assure that no more than one symbol is popped at each transition:

6. For every transition t that pops k symbols, where $k > 1$ do:
   - **6.1.** Replace t with k transitions, each of which pops a single symbol. Create additional states as necessary to do this. Only if the last of the k symbols can be popped should any input be read or any new symbols pushed. Specifically, let $qq_1, qq_2, \ldots, qq_{k-1}$ bc new state names. Then:

     Replace $((q_1, c, \gamma_1\gamma_2 \ldots \gamma_n), (q_2, \gamma_P))$ with:

     $$((q_1, \varepsilon, \gamma_1), (qq_1, \varepsilon)), ((qq_1, \varepsilon, \gamma_2), (qq_2, \varepsilon)), \ldots,$$
     $$((qq_{k-1}, c, \gamma_n), (q_2, \gamma_P)).$$

/* Assure that exactly one symbol is popped at each transition. We already know that no more than one will be. But perhaps none were. In that case, what

M' needs to do instead is to pop whatever was on the top of the stack and then just push it right back. So we'll need one new transition for every symbol that might be on the top of the stack. Note that, because of existence of the bottom of stack marker #, we are guaranteed that the stack will not be empty so there will always be a symbol that can be popped.

7. For every transition $t = ((q_1, c, \varepsilon), (q_2, \gamma))$ do:

7.1. Replace t with $|\Gamma_{M'}|$ transitions, each of which pops a single symbol and then pushes it back on. Specifically, for each symbol α in $\Gamma_M \cup \{\#\}$, add the transition $((q_1, c, \alpha), (q_2, \gamma\alpha))$.

8. Return M'.

EXAMPLE 12.12 Converting to Restricted Normal Form

Let $\mathrm{WcW^R} = \{wcw^R : w \in \{\mathtt{a}, \mathtt{b}\}^*\}$. A straightforward PDA M that accepts $\mathrm{WcW^R}$ is the one we showed in Example 12.3:

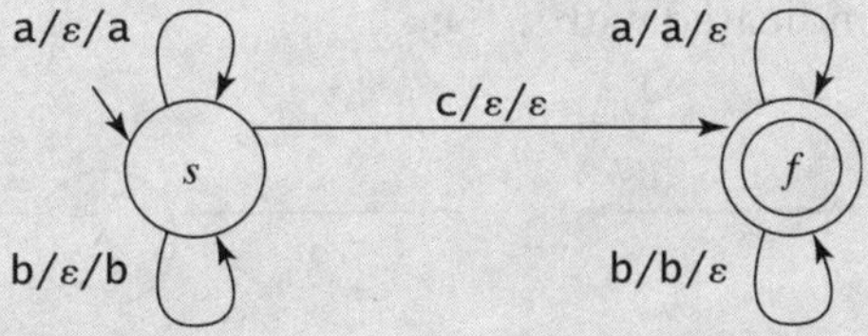

M is not in restricted normal form. To create an equivalent PDA M', we first create new start and accepting states and connect them to M:

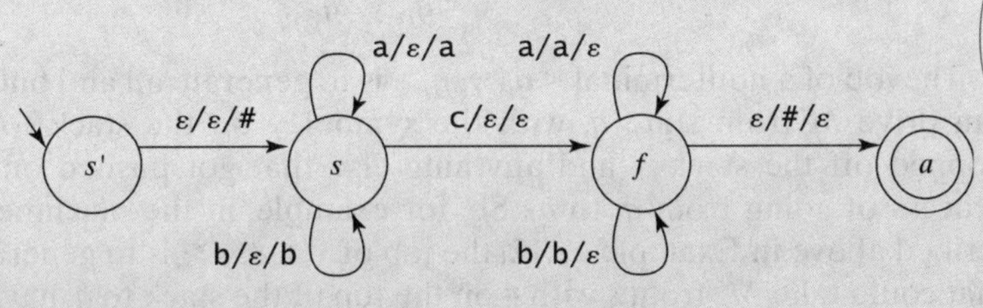

M' contains no transitions that pop more than one symbol. And it contains no transitions that push more than one symbol. But it does contain transitions that pop nothing. Since $\Gamma_{M'} = \{\mathtt{a}, \mathtt{b}, \#\}$, the three transitions from state s must be replaced by the following nine transitions:

((*s*, a, #),(*s*, a#)), #((*s*, a, a),(*s*, aa)), #((*s*, a, b),(*s*, ab)),

((*s*, b, #),(*s*, b#)), #((*s*, b, a),(*s*, ba)), #((*s*, b, b),(*s*, bb)),

((*s*, c, #),(*f*, #)), #((*s*, c, a),(*f*, a)), #((*s*, c, b),(*f*, b)).

Building the Grammar

Since we have now shown that any PDA can be converted into an equivalent one in restricted normal form, we can show that, for any PDA M, there exists a context-free grammar that generates $L(M)$ by first converting M to restricted normal form and then constructing a grammar.

THEOREM 12.2 For Every PDA There Exists an Equivalent CFG

Theorem: Given a PDA $M = (K, \Sigma, \Gamma, \Delta, s, A)$, there exists a CFG $G = (V, \Sigma, R, S)$ such that $L(G) = L(M)$.

Proof: The proof is by construction. In the proof of Theorem 12.1, we showed how to use a PDA to simulate a grammar. Now we show how to use a grammar to simulate a PDA. The basic idea is simple: The productions of the grammar will simulate the moves of the PDA. Unfortunately, the details get messy.

The first step of the construction of G will be to build from M, using the algorithm *convertPDAtorestricted* that we just defined, an equivalent PDA M', where M' is in restricted normal form. So every machine that the grammar-construction algorithm must deal with will look like this (with the part in the middle that actually does the work indicated with . . .):

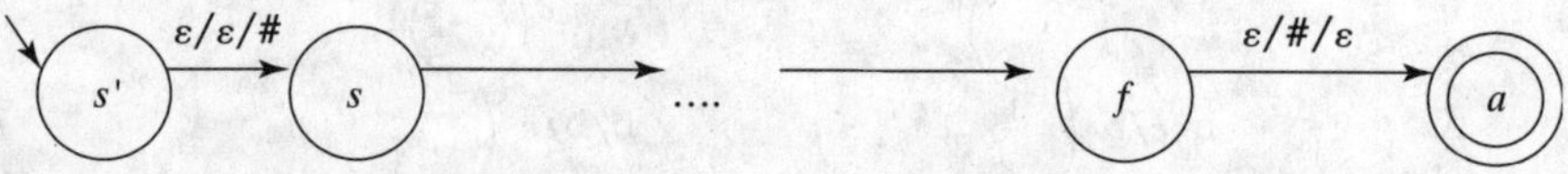

G, the grammar that we will build, will exploit a collection of nonterminal symbols to which we will give names of the following form:

$$<q_i, \gamma, q_j>.$$

The job of a nonterminal $<q_i, \gamma, q_j>$ is to generate all and only the strings that can drive M from state q_i with the symbol γ on the stack to state q_j, having popped off the stack γ and anything else that got pushed on top of it in the process of going from q_i to q_j. So, for example, in the machine M' that we described above in Example 12.12, the job of $<s, \#, a>$ is to generate all the strings that could take M' from s with # on the top of the stack to a, having popped the # (and anything else that got pushed along the way) off the stack. But notice that that is exactly the set of strings that M' will accept. So G will contain the rule:

$$S \rightarrow <s, \#, a>.$$

Now we need to describe the rules that will have $<s, \#, a>$ on their left-hand sides. They will make use of additional nonterminals. For example, M' from Example 12.12 must go through state f on its way to a. So there will be the nonterminal $<f, \#, a>$, which describes the set of strings that can drive M' from f to a, popping #. That set is, of course, $\{\varepsilon\}$.

How can an arbitrary machine M get from one state to another? Because M is in restricted normal form, we must consider only the following three kinds of transitions, all of which pop exactly one symbol:

- Transitions that push no symbols: Suppose that there is a such a transition $((q, c, \gamma), (r, \varepsilon))$, where $c \in \Sigma \cup \{\varepsilon\}$. We consider how such a transition can participate in a computation of M:

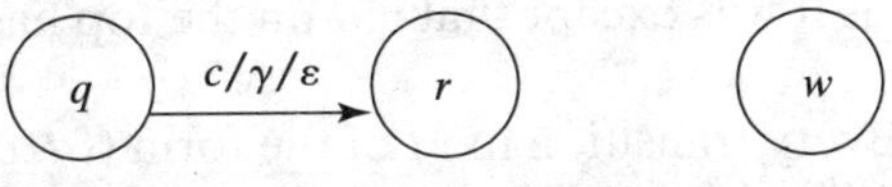

  If this transition is taken, then M reads c, pops γ, and then moves to r. After doing that, it may follow any available paths from r to any next state w, where w may be q or r or any other state. So consider the nonterminal $<q, \gamma, w>$, for any state w. Its job is to generate all strings that drive M from q to w while popping off γ. We now know how to describe at least some of those strings: They are the ones that start with c and are followed by any string that could drive M from r to w without popping anything (since the only thing we need to pop, γ, has already been popped). So we can write the rule:

$$<q, \gamma, w> \rightarrow c<r, \varepsilon, w>.$$

  Read this rule to say that M can go from q to w, leaving the stack just as it was except that a γ on the top has been popped, by reading c, popping γ, going to r, and then somehow getting from r to w, leaving the stack just as it was. Since M reads c, G must generate it.

  Every transition in M of the form $((q, c, \gamma), (r, \varepsilon))$ generates one grammar rule, like the one above, for every state w in M, except s'.

- Transitions that push one symbol: This situation is similar to the case where M pushes no symbols except that whatever computation follows must pop the symbol that this transition pushes. So, suppose that M contains:

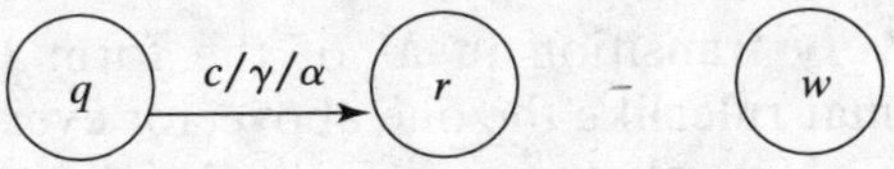

  If this transition is taken, then M reads the character c, pops γ, pushes α, and then moves to r. After doing that, it may follow any available paths from r to any next state w, where w may be q or r or any other state. So consider the nonterminal $<q, \gamma, w>$, for any state w. Its job is to generate all strings that drive M from q to w while popping off γ. We now know how to describe at least some of those strings: They are the ones that start with c and are followed by any string that could drive M from r to w while popping the α that just got pushed. So we can write the rule:

$$<q, \gamma, w> \rightarrow c<r, \alpha, w>.$$

Read this rule to say that M can go from q to w, leaving the stack just as it was except that a γ on the top has been popped, by reading c, popping γ, pushing α, going to r, and then somehow getting from r to w, leaving the stack just as it was except that a α on the top has been popped.

Every transition in M of the form $((q, c, \gamma), (r, \alpha))$ generates one grammar rule, like the one above, for every state w in M, except s'.

- Transitions that push two symbols: This situation is a bit more complicated since two symbols are pushed and must then be popped.

If this transition is taken, then M reads c, pops γ, pushes two characters $\alpha\beta$, and then moves to r. Now suppose that we again want to consider strings that drive M from q to w, where the only change to the stack is to pop the γ that gets popped on the way from q to r. This time, two symbols have been pushed, so both must subsequently be popped. Since M is in restricted normal form, it can pop only a single symbol on each transition. So the only way to go from r to w and pop both symbols is to visit another state in between the two. Call it v, as shown in the figure. We now know how to describe at least some of the strings that drive M from q to w, popping γ: They are the ones that start with c and are followed first by any string that could drive M from r to v while popping α and then by any string that could drive M from v to w while popping β. So we can write the rule:

$$<q, \gamma, w> \rightarrow c<r, \alpha, v><v, \beta, w>$$

Every transition in M of the form $((q, c, X), (r, \alpha\beta))$ generates one grammar rule, like the one above, for every pair of states v and w in M, except s'. Note that v and w may be the same and either or both of them could be q or r.

- Transitions that push more than two symbols: These transitions can be treated by extending the technique for two symbols, adding one additional state for each additional symbol.

The last situation that we need to consider is how to stop. So far, every rule we have created has some nonterminal on its right-hand side. If G is going to generate strings composed solely of terminal symbols, it must have a way to eliminate the final nonterminals once all the terminal symbols have been generated. It can do this with one rule for every state q in M:

$$<q, \varepsilon, q> \rightarrow \varepsilon.$$

Read these rules to say that M can start in q, remain in q, having popped nothing, without consuming any input.

We can now define *buildgrammar*(M), which assumes that M is in restricted normal form:

buildgrammar(M: PDA in restricted normal form) =

1. Set Σ_G to Σ_M.
2. Set the start symbol of G to S.
3. Build R as follows:
   3.1. Insert the rule $S \rightarrow <s, \#, a>$.
   3.2. For every transition $((q, c, \gamma), (r, \varepsilon))$ (i.e., every transition that pushes no symbols), and every state w, except s', in M do:
   Insert the rule $<q, \gamma, w> \rightarrow c<r, \varepsilon, w>$.
   3.3. For every transition $((q, c, \gamma), (r, \alpha))$ (i.e., every transition that pushes one symbol), except the one from s', and every state w, except s', in M do:
   Insert the rule $<q, \gamma, w> \rightarrow c<r, \alpha, w>$.
   3.4. For every transition $((q, c, \gamma), (r, \alpha\beta))$ (i.e., every transition that pushes two symbols), except the one from s', and every pair of states v and w, except s', in M do:
   Insert the rule $<q, \gamma, w> \rightarrow c<r, \alpha, v><v, \beta, w>$.
   3.5. In a similar way, create rules for transitions that push more than two symbols.
   3.6. For every state q, except s', in M do:
   Insert the rule $<q, \varepsilon, q> \rightarrow \varepsilon$.
4. Set V_G to $\Sigma_M \cup \{$nonterminal symbols mentioned in the rules inserted into $R\}$.

The algorithm *buildgrammar* creates all the nonterminals and all the rules required for G to generate exactly the strings in $L(M)$. We should note, however, that it generally also creates many nonterminals that are useless because they are either unreachable or unproductive (or both). For example, suppose that, in M, there is a transition $((q_6, c, \gamma), (q_7, \alpha))$ from state q_6 to state q_7, but no path from state q_7 to state q_8. Nevertheless, in step 3.3, *buildgrammar* will insert the rule $<q_6, \gamma, q_8> \rightarrow c<q_7, \alpha, q_8>$. But $<q_7, \alpha, q_8>$ is unproductive since there are no strings that drive M from q_7 to q_8.

Finally, for an arbitrary PDA M, we define *PDAtoCFG*:

PDAtoCFG (M: PDA) =

1. Return *buildgrammar*(*convertPDAtorestricted*(M)).

EXAMPLE 12.13 Building a Grammar from a PDA

In Example 12.12, we showed a simple PDA for WcW^R = {wcw^R : $w \in$ {a, b}*}. Then we converted that PDA to restricted normal form and got M':

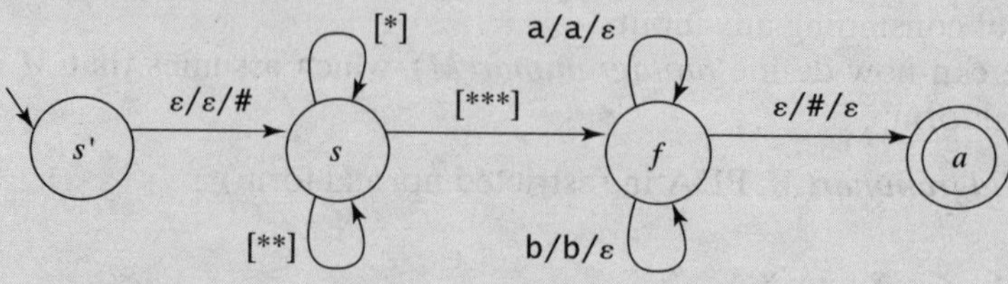

Each of the bracket-labeled arcs corresponds to:

[*] ((s, a, #), (s, a#)), ((s, a, a), (s, aa)), ((s, a, b), (s, ab)),

[**] ((s, b, #), (s, b#)), ((s, b, a), (s, ba)), ((s, b, b), (s, bb)), and

[***] ((s, c, #), (f, #)), ((s, c, a), (f, a)), ((s, c, b), (f, b)).

Buildgrammar constructs a grammar G from M'. To see how G works, consider the parse tree that it builds for the input string abcba. The numbers in brackets at each node indicate the rule that is applied to the nonterminal at the node.

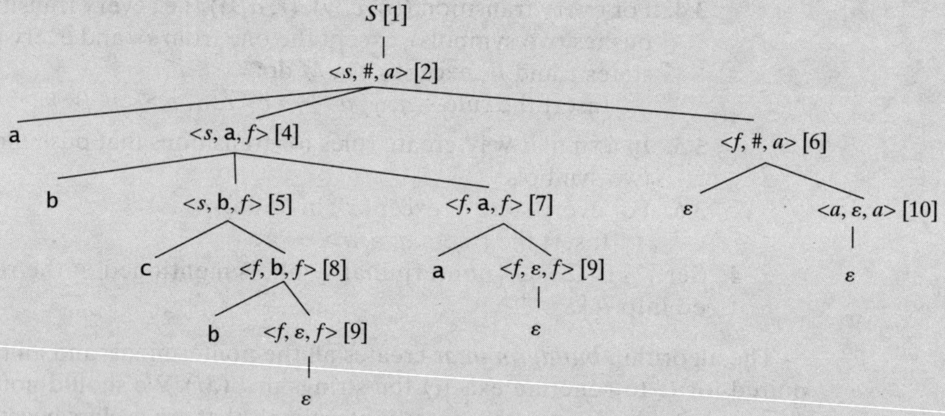

Here are some of the rules in G. On the left are the transitions of M'. The middle column contains the rules derived from each transition. The ones marked [x] in the right column contain useless nonterminals and so cannot be part of any derivation of a string in $L(G)$. Because there are so many useless rules, we have omitted the ones generated from all transitions after the first.

		$S \rightarrow <s, \#, a>$	[1]
	$((s', \varepsilon, \varepsilon), (s, \#))$	no rules based on the transition from s''	
[*]	$((s, \mathrm{a}, \#), (s, \mathrm{a}\#))$	$<s, \#, s> \rightarrow \mathrm{a} <s, \mathrm{a}, s> <s, \#, s>$	[x]
		$<s, \#, s> \rightarrow \mathrm{a} <s, \mathrm{a}, f> <f, \#, s>$	[x]
		$<s, \#, s> \rightarrow \mathrm{a} <s, \mathrm{a}, a> <a, \#, s>$	[x]
		$<s, \#, f> \rightarrow \mathrm{a} <s, \mathrm{a}, s> <s, \#, f>$	[x]
		$<s, \#, f> \rightarrow \mathrm{a} <s, \mathrm{a}, f> <f, \#, f>$	[x]
		$<s, \#, f> \rightarrow \mathrm{a} <s, \mathrm{a}, a> <a, \#, f>$	[x]
		$<s, \#, a> \rightarrow \mathrm{a} <s, \mathrm{a}, s> <s, \#, a>$	[x]
		$<s, \#, a> \rightarrow \mathrm{a} <s, \mathrm{a}, f> <f, \#, a>$	[2]
		$<s, \#, a> \rightarrow \mathrm{a} <s, \mathrm{a}, a> <a, \#, a>$	[x]
	$((s, \mathrm{a}, \mathrm{a}), (s, \mathrm{aa}))$	$<s, \mathrm{a}, f> \rightarrow \mathrm{a} <s, \mathrm{a}, f> <f, \mathrm{a}, f>$	[3]
	$((s, \mathrm{a}, \mathrm{b}), (s, \mathrm{ab}))$	$<s, \mathrm{b}, f> \rightarrow \mathrm{a} <s, \mathrm{a}, f> <f, \mathrm{b}, f>$	[14]
[**]	$((s, \mathrm{b}, \#), (s, \mathrm{b}\#))$	$<s, \#, f> \rightarrow \mathrm{b} <s, \mathrm{b}, f> <f, \#, f>$	[15]
	$((s, \mathrm{b}, \mathrm{a}), (s, \mathrm{ba}))$	$<s, \mathrm{a}, f> \rightarrow \mathrm{b} <s, \mathrm{b}, f> <f, \mathrm{a}, f>$	[4]
	$((s, \mathrm{b}, \mathrm{b}), (s, \mathrm{bb}))$	$<s, \mathrm{b}, f> \rightarrow \mathrm{b} <s, \mathrm{b}, f> <f, \mathrm{b}, f>$	[16]
[***]	$((s, \mathrm{c}, \#), (f, \#))$	$<s, \#, f> \rightarrow \mathrm{c} <f, \#, f>$	[17]
	$((s, \mathrm{c}, \mathrm{a}), (f, \mathrm{a}))$	$<s, \mathrm{a}, f> \rightarrow \mathrm{c} <f, \mathrm{a}, f>$	[18]
	$((s, \mathrm{c}, \mathrm{b}), (f, \mathrm{b}))$	$<s, \mathrm{b}, f> \rightarrow \mathrm{c} <f, \mathrm{b}, f>$	[5]
	$((f, \varepsilon, \#), (a, \varepsilon))$	$<f, \#, a> \rightarrow \varepsilon <\mathrm{a}, \varepsilon, a>$	[6]
	$((f, \mathrm{a}, \mathrm{a}), (f, \varepsilon))$	$<f, \mathrm{a}, f> \rightarrow \mathrm{a} <f, \varepsilon, f>$	[7]
	$((f, \mathrm{b}, \mathrm{b}), (f, \varepsilon))$	$<f, \mathrm{b}, f> \rightarrow \mathrm{b} <f, \varepsilon, f>$	[8]
		$<s, \varepsilon, s> \rightarrow \varepsilon$	[19]
		$<f, \varepsilon, f> \rightarrow \varepsilon$	[9]
		$<a, \varepsilon, a> \rightarrow \varepsilon$	[10]

12.3.3 The Equivalence of Context-free Grammars and PDAs

THEOREM 12.3 PDAs and CFGs Describe the Same Class of Languages

Theorem: A language is context-free iff it is accepted by some PDA.

Proof: Theorem 12.1 proves the only if part. Theorem 12.2 proves the if part.

12.4 Nondeterminism and Halting

Recall that a computation C of a PDA $M = (K, \Sigma, \Gamma, \Delta, s, A)$ on a string w is an accepting computation iff:

$$C = (s, w, \varepsilon)|\text{-}_M{}^* (q, \varepsilon, \varepsilon), \text{ for some } q \in A.$$

We'll say that a computation C of M ***halts*** iff at least one of the following conditions holds:

- C is an accepting computation, or
- C ends in a configuration from which there is no transition in Δ that can be taken.

We'll say that M ***halts*** on w iff every computation of M on w halts. If M halts on w and does not accept, then we say that M rejects w.

For every context-free language L, we've proven that there exists a PDA M such that $L(M) = L$. Suppose that we would like to be able to:

- Examine a string and decide whether or not it is in L.
- Examine a string that is in L and create a parse tree for it.
- Examine a string that is in L and create a parse tree for it in time that is linear in the length of the string.
- Examine a string and decide whether or not it is in the complement of L.

Do PDAs provide the tools we need to do those things? When we were at a similar point in our discussion of regular languages, the answer to that question was yes. For every regular language L, there exists a minimal deterministic FSM that accepts it. That minimal DFSM halts on all inputs, accepts all strings that are in L, and rejects all strings that are not in L.

Unfortunately, the facts about context-free languages and PDAs are different from the facts about regular languages and FSMs. Now we must face the following:

1. There are context-free languages for which no deterministic PDA exists. We'll prove this as Theorem 13.13.
2. It is possible that a PDA may
   - not halt, or
   - not ever finish reading its input.

So, let M be a PDA that accepts some language L. Then, on input w, if $w \in L$ then M will halt and accept. But if $w \notin L$, while M will not accept w, it is possible that it will not reject it either. To see how this could happen, let $\Sigma = \{\text{a}\}$ and consider the PDA M, shown in Figure 12.4. $L(M) = \{\text{a}\}$. The computation (1, a, ε) |- (2, a, a) |- (3, ε, ε) will cause M to accept a. But consider any other input except a. Observe that:

- M will never halt. There is no accepting configuration, but there is always at least one computational path that has not yet halted. For example, on input aa, one such path is:

  (1, aa, ε) |- (2, aa, a) |- (1, aa, aa) |- (2, aa, aaa) |- (1, aa, aaaa) |- (2, aa, aaaaa) |-...

- M will never finish reading its input unless its input is ε. On input aa, for example, there is no computation that will read the second a.

3. There exists no algorithm to minimize a PDA. In fact, it is undecidable whether a PDA is already minimal.

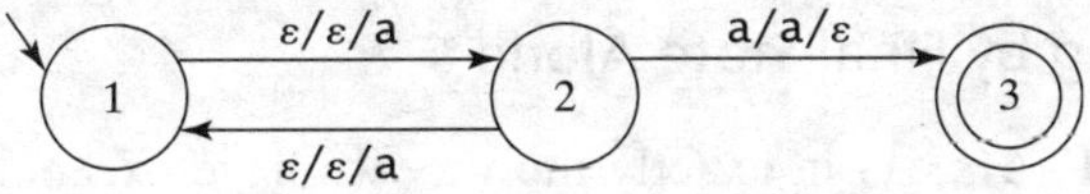

FIGURE 12.4 A PDA that may neither accept nor reject.

Problem 2 is especially critical. This same problem also arose with NDFSMs. But there we had a choice of two solutions:

- Use *ndfsmtodfsm* to convert the NDFSM to an equivalent deterministic one. A DFSM halts on input w in $|w|$ steps.
- Simulate the NDFSM using *ndfsmsimulate*, which ran all computational paths in parallel and handled ε-transitions in a way that guaranteed that the simulation of an NDFSM M on input w halted in $|w|$ steps.

Neither of those approaches works for PDAs. There may not be an equivalent deterministic PDA. And it is not possible to simulate all paths in parallel on a single PDA because each path would need its own stack. So what can we do? Solutions to these problems fall into two classes:

- Formal ones that do not restrict the class of languages that are being considered. Unfortunately, these approaches generally do restrict the *form* of the grammars and PDAs that can be used. For example, they may require that grammars be in Chomsky or Greibach normal form. As a result, parse trees may not make much sense. We'll see some of these techniques in Chapter 14.
- Practical ones that work only on a subclass of the context-free languages. But the subset is large enough to be useful and the techniques can use grammars in their natural forms. We'll see some of these techniques in Chapters 13 and 15.

12.5 Alternative Equivalent Definitions of a PDA ✸

We could have defined a PDA somewhat differently. We list here a few reasonable alternative definitions. In all of them a PDA M is a sextuple $(K, \Sigma, \Gamma, \Delta, s, A)$:

- We allow M to pop and to push any string in Γ^*. In some definitions, M may pop only a single symbol but it may push any number of them. In some definitions, M may pop and push only a single symbol.
- In our definition, M accepts its input w only if, when it finishes reading w, it is in an accepting state and its stack is empty. There are two alternatives to this:
  - Accept if, when the input has been consumed, M lands in an accepting state, regardless of the contents of the stack.
  - Accept if, when the input has been consumed, the stack is empty, regardless of the state M is in.

All of these definitions are equivalent in the sense that, if some language L is accepted by a PDA using one definition, it can be accepted by some PDA using each of the other definitions.

We can prove this claim for any pair of definitions by construction. To do so, we show an algorithm that transforms a PDA of one sort into an equivalent PDA of the other sort.

EXAMPLE 12.14 Accepting by Final State Alone

Define a PDA $M = (K, \Sigma, \Gamma, \Delta, s, A)$ in exactly the way we have except that it will accept iff it lands in an accepting state, regardless of the contents of the stack. In other words, if $(s, w, \varepsilon) \vdash_M{}^* (q, \varepsilon, \gamma)$ and $q \in A$, then M accepts.

To show that this model is equivalent to ours, we must show two things: For each of our machines, there exists an equivalent one of these, and, for each of these, there exists an equivalent one of ours. We'll do the first part to show how such a construction can be done. We leave the second as an exercise.

Given a PDA M that accepts by accepting state and empty stack, construct a new PDA M' that accepts by accepting state alone, where $L(M') = L(M)$. M' will have a single accepting state q_a. The only way for M' to get to q_a will be to land in an accepting state of M when the stack is logically empty. But there is no way to check that the stack is empty. So M' will begin by pushing a bottom-of-stack marker #, onto the stack. Whenever # is the top symbol on the stack, the stack is logically empty.

So the construction proceeds as follows:

1. Initially, let $M' = M$.
2. Create a new start state s'. Add the transition $((s', \varepsilon, \varepsilon), (s, \#))$.
3. Create a new accepting state q_a.
4. For each accepting state a in M do:
   Add the transition $((a, \varepsilon, \#), (q_a, \varepsilon))$.
5. Make q_a the only accepting state in M'.

It is easy to see that M' lands in its only accepting state (q_a) iff M lands in some accepting state with an empty stack. Thus M' and M accept the same strings.

As an example, we apply this algorithm to the PDA we built for the balanced parentheses language Bal:

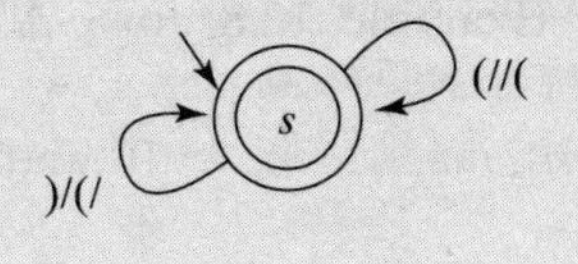

becomes

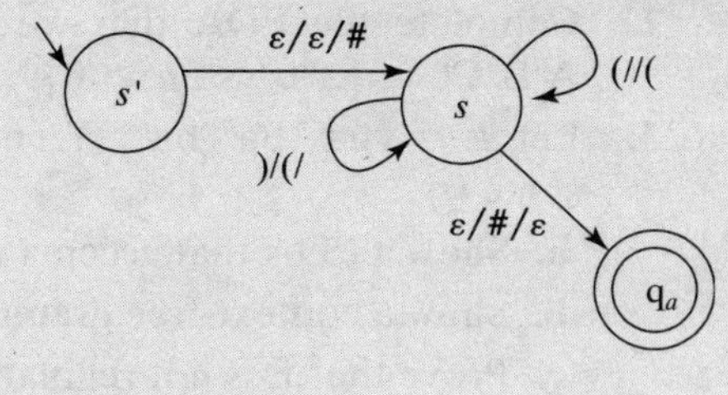

Notice, by the way, that while M is deterministic, M' is not.

12.6 Alternatives that are Not Equivalent to the PDA ✱

We defined a PDA to be a finite state machine to which we add a single stack. We mention here two variants of that definition, each of which turns out to define a more powerful class of machine. In both cases, we'll still start with an FSM.

For the first variation, we add a first-in, first-out (FIFO) queue in place of the stack. Such machines are called tag systems or Post machines. As we'll see in Section 18.2.3, tag systems are equivalent to Turing machines in computational power.

For the second variation, we add two stacks instead of one. Again, the resulting machines are equivalent in computational power to Turing machines, as we'll see in Section 17.5.2.

Exercises

1. Build a PDA to accept each of the following languages L:
   - **a.** BalDelim = $\{w$: where w is a string of delimiters: (,), [,], {, }, that are properly balanced$\}$.
   - **b.** $\{\mathrm{a}^i\mathrm{b}^j : 2i = 3j + 1\}$.
   - **c.** $\{w \in \{\mathrm{a}, \mathrm{b}\}^* : \#_\mathrm{a}(w) = 2 \cdot \#_\mathrm{b}(w)\}$.
   - **d.** $\{\mathrm{a}^n\mathrm{b}^m : m \leq n \leq 2m\}$.
   - **e.** $\{w \in \{\mathrm{a}, \mathrm{b}\}^* : w = w^R\}$.
   - **f.** $\{\mathrm{a}^i\mathrm{b}^j\mathrm{c}^k : i, j, k \geq 0 \text{ and } (i \neq j \text{ or } j \neq k)\}$.
   - **g.** $\{w \in \{\mathrm{a}, \mathrm{b}\}^*$: every prefix of w has at least as many a's as b's$\}$.
   - **h.** $\{\mathrm{a}^n\mathrm{b}^m\mathrm{a}^n : n, m \geq 0 \text{ and } m \text{ is even}\}$.
   - **i.** $\{x\mathrm{c}^n : x \in \{\mathrm{a}, \mathrm{b}\}^*, \#_\mathrm{a}(x) = n \text{ or } \#_\mathrm{b}(x) = n\}$.
   - **j.** $\{\mathrm{a}^n\mathrm{b}^m : m \geq n, m\text{-}n \text{ is even}\}$.
   - **k.** $\{\mathrm{a}^m\mathrm{b}^n\mathrm{c}^p\mathrm{d}^q : m, n, p, q \geq 0 \text{ and } m + n = p + q\}$.

l. $\{b_i\#b_{i+1}{}^{\mathrm{R}} : b_i$ is the binary representation of some integer i, $i \geq 0$, without leading zeros$\}$. (For example 101#011 $\in L$.)

m. $\{x^{\mathrm{R}}\#y : x, y \in \{0,1\}^*$ and x is a substring of $y\}$.

n. $L_1{}^*$, where $L_1 = \{xx^{\mathrm{R}} : x \in \{\mathrm{a,b}\}^*\}$.

2. Complete the PDA that we sketched, in Example 12.8, for $\neg\mathrm{A^nB^nC^n}$, where $\mathrm{A^nB^nC^n} = \{\mathrm{a}^n\mathrm{b}^n\mathrm{c}^n : n \geq 0\}$.

3. Let $L = \{\mathrm{ba}^{m_1}\mathrm{ba}^{m_2}\mathrm{ba}^{m_3}\ldots\ \mathrm{ba}^{m_n} : n \geq 2, m_1, m_2, \ldots, m_n \geq 0$, and $m_i \neq m_j$ for some $i, j\}$.

a. Show a PDA that accepts L.

b. Show a context-free grammar that generates L.

c. Prove that L is not regular.

4. Consider the language $L = L_1 \cap L_2$, where $L_1 = \{ww^{\mathrm{R}} : w \in \{\mathrm{a, b}\}^*\}$ and $L_2 = \{\mathrm{a}^n\mathrm{b}^*\mathrm{a}^n : n \geq 0\}$.

a. List the first four strings in the lexicographic enumeration of L.

b. Write a context-free grammar to generate L.

c. Show a natural PDA for L. (In other words, don't just build it from the grammar using one of the two-state constructions presented in this chapter.)

d. Prove that L is not regular.

5. Build a deterministic PDA to accept each of the following languages:

a. $L\$$, where $L = \{w \in \{\mathrm{a, b}\}^* : \#_{\mathrm{a}}(w) = \#_{\mathrm{b}}(w)\}$.

b. $L\$$ where $L = \{\mathrm{a}^n\mathrm{b}^+\mathrm{a}^m : n \geq 0$ and $\exists k \geq 0\ (m = 2k + n)\}$.

6. Complete the proof that we started in Example 12.14. Specifically, show that if M is a PDA that accepts by accepting state alone, then there exists a PDA M' that accepts by accepting state and empty stack (our definition) where $L(M') = L(M)$.

CHAPTER 13

Context-Free and Noncontext-Free Languages

The language $A^nB^n = \{a^nb^n : n \geq 0\}$ is context-free. The language $A^nB^nC^n = \{a^nb^nc^n : n \geq 0\}$ is not context free (intuitively because a PDA's stack cannot count all three of the letter regions and compare them). PalEven $= \{ww^R : w \in \{a, b\}^*\}$ is context-free. The similar language WW $= \{ww : w \in \{a, b\}^*\}$ is not context-free (again, intuitively, because a stack cannot pop the characters of w off in the same order in which they were pushed).

Given a new language L, how can we know whether or not it is context-free? In this chapter, we present a collection of techniques that can be used to answer that question.

13.1 Where Do the Context-Free Languages Fit in the Big Picture?

First, we consider the relationship between the regular languages and the context-free languages.

THEOREM 13.1 The Context-Free Languages Properly Contain the Regular Languages

Theorem: The regular languages are a proper subset of the context-free languages.

Proof: We first show that every regular language is context-free. We then show that there exists at least one context-free language that is not regular.

We show that every regular language is context-free by construction. If L is regular, then it is accepted by some DFSM $M = (K, \Sigma, \delta, s, A)$. From M we construct a PDA $M' = (K', \Sigma', \Gamma', \Delta', s', A')$ to accept L. In essence, M' will simply be M and will ignore the stack. Let M' be $(K, \Sigma, \varnothing, \Delta', s, A)$, where Δ' is constructed as follows: For every transition (q_i, c, q_j) in δ, add to Δ' the transition

$((q_i, c, \varepsilon), (q_j, \varepsilon))$. M' behaves identically to M, so $L(M) = L(M')$. So the regular languages are a subset of the context-free languages.

The regular languages are a *proper* subset of the context-free languages because there exists at least one language, A^nB^n, that is context-free but not regular.

Next, we observe that there are *many* more noncontext-free languages than there are context-free ones:

THEOREM 13.2 How Many Context-Free Languages are There?

Theorem: There is a countably infinite number of context-free languages.

Proof: Every context-free language is generated by some context-free grammar $G = (V, \Sigma, R, S)$. We can encode the elements of V as binary strings, so we can lexicographically enumerate all the syntactically legal context-free grammars. There cannot be more context-free languages than there are context-free grammars, so there is at most a countably infinite number of context-free languages. There is not a one-to-one relationship between context-free languages and context-free grammars since there is an infinite number of grammars that generate any given language. But, by Theorem 13.1, every regular language is context-free. And, by Theorem 8.1, there is a countably infinite number of regular languages. So there is at least and at most a countably infinite number of context-free languages.

But, by Theorem 2.3, there is an uncountably infinite number of languages over any nonempty alphabet Σ. So there are many more noncontext-free languages than there are regular ones.

13.2 Showing That a Language is Context-Free

We have so far seen two techniques that can be used to show that a language L is context-free:

- Exhibit a context-free grammar for it.
- Exhibit a (possibly nondeterministic) PDA for it.

There are also closure theorems for context-free languages and they can be used to show that a language is context-free if it can be described in terms of other languages whose status is already known. Unfortunately, there are fewer closure theorems for the context-free languages than there are for the regular languages. In order to be able to discuss both the closure theorems that exist, as well as the ones we'd like but don't have, we will wait and consider the issue of closure theorems in Section 13.4, after we have developed a technique for showing that a language is not context-free.

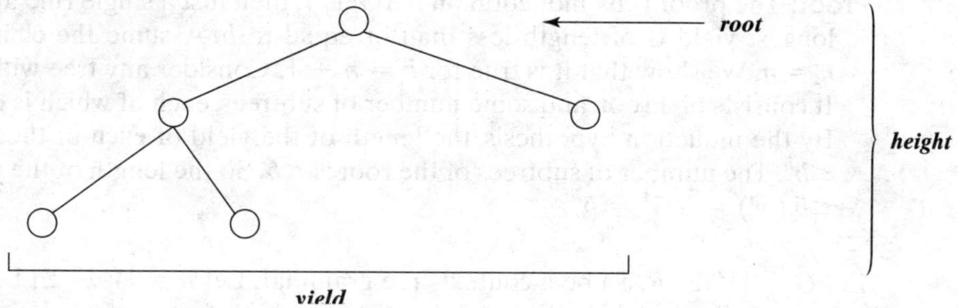

FIGURE 13.1 The structure of a parse tree.

13.3 The Pumping Theorem for Context-Free Languages

Suppose we are given a language and we want to prove that it is not context-free. Just as with regular languages, it is not sufficient simply to claim that we tried to build a grammar or a PDA and we failed. That doesn't show that there isn't some other way to approach the problem.

Instead, we will again approach this problem from the other direction. We will articulate a property that is provably true of all context-free languages. Then, if we can show that a language L does not possess this property, then we know that L is not context-free. So, just as we did when we used the Pumping Theorem for regular languages, we will construct ***proofs by contradiction***. We will say, "If L were context-free, then it would possess certain properties. But it does not possess those properties. Therefore, it is not context-free."

This time we exploit the fact that every context-free language is generated by some context-free grammar. The argument we are about to make is based on the structure of parse trees. Recall that a parse tree, derived by a grammar $G = (V, \Sigma, R, S)$, is a rooted, ordered tree in which:

- Every leaf node is labeled with an element of $\Sigma \cup \{\varepsilon\}$,
- The root node is labeled S,
- Every other node is labeled with some element of $V - \Sigma$, and
- If m is a nonleaf node labeled X and the children of m are labeled $x_1, x_2, \ldots, x_n$, then the rule $X \rightarrow x_1x_2 \ldots, x_n$ is in R.

Consider an arbitrary parse tree, as shown in Figure 13.1 The ***height*** of a tree is the length of the longest path from the root to any leaf. The ***branching factor*** of a tree is the largest number of daughters of any node in the tree. The ***yield*** of a tree is the ordered sequence of its leaf nodes.

THEOREM 13.3 The Height of A Tree and its Branching Factor Put A Bound On its Yield

Theorem: The length of the yield of any tree T with height h and branching factor b is $\leq b^h$.

Proof: The proof is by induction on h. If h is 1, then just a single rule applies. So the longest yield is of length less than or equal to b. Assume the claim is true for $h = n$. We show that it is true for $h = n + 1$. Consider any tree with $h = n + 1$. It consists of a root, and some number of subtrees, each of which is of height $\leq n$. By the induction hypothesis, the length of the yield of each of those subtrees is $\leq b^n$. The number of subtrees of the root is $\leq b$. So the length of the yield must be $\leq b\,(b^n) = b^{n+1} = b^h$.

Let $G = (V, \Sigma, R, S)$ be a context-free grammar. Let $n = |V - \Sigma|$ be the number of nonterminal symbols in G. Let b be the branching factor of G, defined to be the length of the longest right-hand side of any rule in R.

Now consider any parse tree T generated by G. Suppose that no nonterminal appears more than once on any one path from the root of T to a nonterminal. Then the height of T is $\leq n$. So the longest string that could correspond to the yield of T has length $\leq b^n$.

Now suppose that w is a string in $L(G)$ and $|w| > b^n$. Then any parse tree that G generates for w must contain at least one path that contains at least one repeated nonterminal. Another way to think of this is that, to derive w , G must have used at least one recursive rule. So any parse tree for w must look like the one shown in Figure 13.2, where X is some repeated nonterminal. We use dotted lines to make it clear that the derivation may not be direct but may, instead, require several steps. So, for example, it is possible that the tree shown here was derived using a grammar that contained the rules $X \rightarrow$ aYb, $Y \rightarrow$ bXa, and $X \rightarrow$ ab.

Of course, it is possible that w has more than one parse tree. For the rest of this discussion we will pick some tree such that G generates no other parse tree for w that has fewer nodes. Within that tree it is possible that there are many repeated nonterminals and that some of them are repeated more than once. We will assume only that we have chosen point [1] in the tree such that X is the first repeated nonterminal on any path, coming up from the bottom, in the subtree rooted at [1]. We'll call the rule that was applied at [1] $rule_1$ and the rule that was applied at [2] $rule_2$.

We can sketch the derivation that produced this tree as:

$$S \Rightarrow^* uXz \Rightarrow^* uvXyz \Rightarrow^* uvxyz.$$

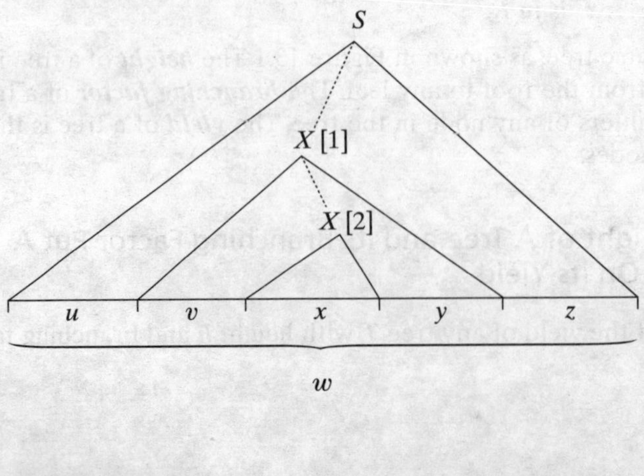

FIGURE 13.2 A parse tree whose height is greater than n.

So we have carved w up into five pieces: u, v, x, y, and z. We observe that:

- There is another derivation in G, $S \Rightarrow^* uXz \Rightarrow^* uxz$, in which, at the point labeled [1], the nonrecursive $rule_2$ is used. So uxz is also in $L(G)$.
- There are infinitely many derivations in G, such as $S \Rightarrow^* uXz \Rightarrow^* uvXyz \Rightarrow^* uvvXyyz \Rightarrow^* uvvxyyz$, in which the recursive $rule_1$ is applied one or more additional times before the nonrecursive $rule_2$ is used. Those derivations produce the strings, uv^2xy^2z, uv^3xy^3z, etc. So all of those strings are also in $L(G)$.
- It is possible that $v = \varepsilon$, as it would be, for example if $rule_1$ were $X \rightarrow X\text{a}$. It is also possible that $y = \varepsilon$, as it would be, for example if $rule_1$ were $X \rightarrow \text{a}X$. But it is not possible that both v and y are ε. If they were, then the derivation $S \Rightarrow^* uXz \Rightarrow^* uxz$ would also yield w and it would create a parse tree with fewer nodes. But that contradicts the assumption that we started with a tree with the smallest possible number of nodes.
- The height of the subtree rooted at [1] is at most $n + 1$ (since there is one repeated nonterminal and every other nonterminal can occur no more than once). So $|vxy| \leq b^{n+1}$.

These observations are the basis for the context-free Pumping Theorem, which we state next.

THEOREM 13.4 The Pumping Theorem for Context-Free Languages

Theorem: If L is a context-free language, then:

$$\exists k \geq 1\ (\forall \text{ strings } w \in L, \text{ where } |w| \geq k\ (\exists u, v, x, y, z\ (w = uvxyz,\ vy \neq \varepsilon,\ |vxy| \leq k, \text{ and } \forall q \geq 0\ (uv^qxy^qz \text{ is in } L)))).$$

Proof: The proof is the argument that we gave above: If L is context-free, then it is generated by some context-free grammar $G = (V, \Sigma, R, S)$ with n nonterminal symbols and branching factor b. Let k be b^{n+1}. Any string that can be generated by G and whose parse tree contains no paths with repeated nonterminals must have length less than or equal to b^n. Assuming that $b \geq 2$, it must be the case that $b^{n+1} > b^n$. So let w be any string in $L(G)$ where $|w| \geq k$. Let T be any smallest parse tree for w (i.e., a parse tree such that no other parse tree for w has fewer nodes). T must have height at least $n + 1$. Choose some path in T of length at least $n + 1$. Let X be the bottommost repeated nonterminal along that path. Then w can be rewritten as $uvxyz$ as shown in the tree diagram of Figure 13.2. The tree rooted at [1] has height at most $n + 1$. Thus its yield, vxy, has length less than or equal to b^{n+1}, which is k. Further, $vy \neq \varepsilon$ since if vy were ε then there would be a smaller parse tree for w and we chose T so that that wasn't so. Finally, v and y can be pumped: uxz must be in L because $rule_2$ could have been used immediately at [1]. And, for any $q \geq 1$, uv^qxy^qz must be in L because $rule_1$ could have been used q times before finally using $rule_2$.

So, if L is a context-free language, every "long" string in L must be pumpable. Just as with the Pumping Theorem for regular languages, the pumped region can be pumped out once or pumped in any number of times, in all cases resulting in another string that is also in L. So, if there is even one "long" string in L that is not pumpable, then L is not context-free.

Note that the value k plays two roles in the Pumping Theorem. It defines what we mean by a "long" string and it imposes an upper bound on $|vxy|$. When we set k to b^{n+1}, we guaranteed that it was large enough so that we could prove that it served both of those purposes. But we should point out that a smaller value would have sufficed as the definition for a "long" string, since any string of length greater than b^n must be pumpable.

There are a few important ways in which the context-free Pumping Theorem differs from the regular one:

- The most obvious is that two regions, v and y, must be pumped in tandem.
- We don't know anything about where the strings v and y will fall. All we know is that they are reasonably "close together", i.e., $|vxy| \leq k$.
- Either v or y could be empty, although not both.

EXAMPLE 13.1 $A^nB^nC^n$ is Not Context-Free

Let $L = A^nB^nC^n = \{a^nb^nc^n : n \geq 0\}$. We can use the Pumping Theorem to show that L is not context-free. If it were, then there would exist some k such that any string w, where $|w| \geq k$, must satisfy the conditions of the theorem. We show one string w that does not. Let $w = a^kb^kc^k$, where k is the constant from the Pumping Theorem. For w to satisfy the conditions of the Pumping Theorem, there must be some u, v, x, y, and z such that $w = uvxyz$, $vy \neq \varepsilon$, $|vxy| \leq k$, and $\forall q \geq 0$ (uv^qxy^qz is in L). We show that no such u, v, x, y, and z exist. If either v or y contains two or more different characters, then set q to 2 (i.e., pump in once) and the resulting string will have letters out of order and thus not be in $A^nB^nC^n$. (For example, if v is aabb and y is cc, then the string that results from pumping will look like aaa... aaabbaabbccc...ccc.) If both v and y each contain at most one distinct character then set q to 2. Additional copies of at most two different characters are added, leaving the third unchanged. There are no longer equal numbers of the three letters, so the resulting string is not in $A^nB^nC^n$. There is no way to divide w into $uvxyz$ such that all the conditions of the Pumping Theorem are met. So $A^nB^nC^n$ is not context-free.

As with the Pumping Theorem for regular languages, it requires some skill to design simple and effective proofs using the context-free Pumping Theorem. As before, the choices that we can make, when trying to show that a language L is not context-free are:

- We choose w, the string to be pumped. It is important to choose w so that it is in the part of L that captures the essence of why L is not context-free.
- We choose a value for q that shows that w isn't pumpable.

- We may apply closure theorems before we start, so that we show that L is not context-free by showing that some other language L' isn't. We'll have more to say about this technique later.

EXAMPLE 13.2 The Language of Strings with n² a's is Not Context-Free

Let $L = \{a^{n^2} : n \geq 0\}$. We can use the Pumping Theorem to show that L is not context-free. If it were, then there would exist some k such that any string w, where $|w| \geq k$, must satisfy the conditions of the theorem. We show one string w that does not. Let n (in the definition of L) be k^2. So $n^2 = k^4$ and $w = a^{k^4}$. For w to satisfy the conditions of the Pumping Theorem, there must be some u, v, x, y, and z, such that $w = uvxyz$, $vy \neq \varepsilon$, $|vxy| \leq k$, and $\forall q \geq 0$ (uv^qxy^qz is in L). We show that no such u, v, x, y, and z exist. Since w contains only a's, $vy = \text{a}^p$, for some nonzero p. Set q to 2. The resulting string, which we'll call s, is a^{k^4+p}, which must be in L. But it isn't because it is too short. If a^{k^4}, which contains $(k^2)^2$ a's, is in L, then the next longer element of L contains $(k^2 + 1)^2$ a's. That's $k^4 + 2k^2 + 1$ a's. So there are no strings in L with length between k^4 and $k^4 + 2k^2 + 1$. But $|s| = k^4 + p$. So, for s to be in L, $p = |vy|$ would have to be at least $2k^2 + 1$. But $|vxy| \leq k$, so p can't be that large. Thus s is not in L. There is no way to divide w into $uvxyz$ such that all the conditions of the Pumping Theorem are met. So L is not context-free.

When using the Pumping Theorem, we focus on v and y. Once they are specified, so are u, x, and z.

To show that there exists no v, y pair that satisfies all of the conditions of the Pumping Theorem, it is sometimes necessary to enumerate a set of cases and rule them out one at a time. Sometimes the easiest way to do this is to imagine the string to be pumped as divided into a set of regions. Then we can consider all the ways in which v and y can fall across those regions.

EXAMPLE 13.3 Dividing the String w Into Regions

Let $L = \{\text{a}^n\text{b}^m\text{a}^n : n, m \geq 0 \text{ and } n \geq m\}$. We can use the Pumping Theorem to show that L is not context-free. If it were, then there would exist some k such that any string w, where $|w| \geq k$, must satisfy the conditions of the theorem. We show one string w that does not. Let $w = \text{a}^k\text{b}^k\text{a}^k$, where k is the constant from the Pumping Theorem. For w to satisfy the conditions of the Pumping Theorem, there must be some u, v, x, y, and z, such that $w = uvxyz$, $vy \neq \varepsilon$, $|vxy| \leq k$, and $\forall q \geq 0$ (uv^qxy^qz is in L). We show that no such u, v, x, y, and z exist. Imagine w divided into three regions as follows:

```
aaa ... aaabbb ... bbbaaa ...aaa
|    1      |     2     |    3    |
```

EXAMPLE 13.3 ***(Continued)***

We consider all the cases for where v and y could fall and show that in none of them are all the conditions of the theorem met:

- If either v or y crosses regions, then set q to 2 (thus pumping in once). The resulting string will have letters out of order and so not be in L. So in all the remaining cases we assume that v and y each falls within a single region.
- (1, 1): Both v and y fall in region 1. Set q to 2. In the resulting string, the first group of a's is longer than the second group of a's. So the string is not in L.
- (2, 2): Both v and y fall in region 2. Set q to 2. In the resulting string, the b region is longer than either of the a regions. So the string is not in L
- (3, 3): Both v and y fall in region 3. Set q to 0. The same argument as for (1, 1).
- (1, 2): Nonempty v falls in region 1 and nonempty y falls in region 2. (If either v or y is empty, it does not matter where it falls. So we can treat it as though it falls in the same region as the nonempty one. We have already considered all of those cases.) Set q to 2. In the resulting string, the first group of a's is longer than the second group of a's. So the string is not in L.
- (2, 3): Nonempty v falls in region 2 and nonempty y falls in region 3. Set q to 2. In the resulting string the second group of a's is longer than the first group of a's. So the string is not in L.
- (1, 3): Nonempty v falls in region 1 and nonempty y falls in region 3. If this were allowed by the other conditions of the Pumping Theorem, we could pump in a's and still produce strings in L. But if we pumped out, we would violate the requirement that the a regions be at least as long as the b region. More importantly, this case violates the requirement that $|vxy| \leq k$. So it need not be considered.

There is no way to divide w into $uvxyz$ such that all the conditions of the Pumping Theorem are met. So L is not context-free.

Consider the language PalEven $= \{ww^R : w \in \{\text{a}, \text{b}\}^*\}$, the language of even-length palindromes of a's and b's, which we introduced in Example 11.3. Let w be any string in PalEven. Then substrings of w are related to each other in a perfectly nested way, as shown in Figure 13.3 (a). Nested relationships of this sort can naturally be described with a context-free grammar, so languages whose strings are structured in this way are typically context-free.

But now consider the case in which the relationships are not properly nested but instead cross. For example, consider the language WcW $= \{w\text{c}w : w \in \{\text{a}, \text{b}\}^*\}$. Now let w be any string in WcW. Then substrings of w are related to each other as shown in Figure 13.3 (b). We call such dependencies, where lines cross each other, ***cross-serial dependencies***. Languages whose strings are characterized by cross serial dependencies are typically not context-free.

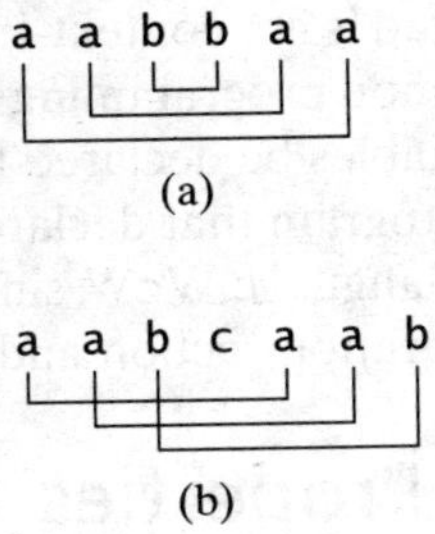

FIGURE 13.3 Nested versus cross-serial dependencies.

EXAMPLE 13.4 WcW is Not Context-Free

Let WcW $= \{wcw : w \in \{\text{a, b}\}^*\}$. WcW is not context-free. All its nonempty strings contain cross-serial dependencies.

We can use the Pumping Theorem to show that WcW is not context-free. If it were, then there would exist some k such that any string w, where $|w| \geq k$, must satisfy the conditions of the theorem. We show one string w that does not. Let $w = \text{a}^k\text{b}^k\text{ca}^k\text{b}^k$, where k is the constant from the Pumping Theorem. For w to satisfy the conditions of the Pumping Theorem, there must be some u, v, x, y, and z, such that $w = uvxyz$, $vy \neq \varepsilon$, $|vxy| \leq k$, and $\forall q \geq 0$ (uv^qxy^qz is in WcW). We show that no such u, v, x, y, and z exist. Imagine w divided into five regions as follows:

```
aaa ... aaabbb ... bbbcaaa ... aaabbb ... bbb
|    1    |    2    |3|    4    |    5    |
```

Call the part before the c the left side and the part after the c the right side. We consider all the cases for where v and y could fall and show that in none of them are all the conditions of the theorem met:

- If either v or y overlaps region 3, set q to 0. The resulting string will no longer contain a c and so is not in WcW.
- If both v and y occur before region 3 or they both occur after region 3, then set q to 2. One side will be longer than the other and so the resulting string is not in WcW.
- If either v or y overlaps region 1, then set q to 2. In order to make the right side match, something would have to be pumped into region 4. But any v, y pair that did that would violate the requirement that $|vxy| \leq k$.
- If either v or y overlaps region 2, then set q to 2. In order to make the right side match, something would have to be pumped into region 5. But any v, y pair that did that would violate the requirement that $|vxy| \leq k$.

There is no way to divide w into $uvxyz$ such that all the conditions of the Pumping Theorem are met. So WcW is not context-free.

Are programming languages like C++ and Java context-free? (G.2)

The language WcW, which we just showed is not context-free, is important because of its similarity to the structure of many common programming languages. Consider a programming language that requires that variables be declared before they are used. If we consider just a single variable w , then a program that declares w and then uses it has a structure very similar to the strings in the language WcW, since the string w must occur in exactly the same form in both the declaration section and the body of the program.

13.4 Some Important Closure Properties of Context-Free Languages

It helps to be able to analyze a complex language by decomposing it into simpler pieces. Closure theorems, when they exist, enable us to do that. We'll see in this section that, while the context-free languages are closed under some common operations, we cannot prove as strong a set of closure theorems as we were able to prove for the regular languages.

13.4.1 The Closure Theorems

THEOREM 13.5 Closure Under Union, Concatenation, Kleene Star, Reverse, and Letter Substitution

Theorem: The context-free languages are closed under union, concatenation, Kleene star, reverse, and letter substitution.

Proof: We prove each of the claims separately by construction:

- The context-free languages are closed under union: If L_1 and L_2 are context-free languages, then there exist context-free grammars $G_1 = (V_1, \Sigma_1, R_1, S_1)$ and $G_2 = (V_2, \Sigma_2, R_2, S_2)$ such that $L_1 = L(G_1)$ and $L_2 = L(G_2)$. If necessary, rename the nonterminals of G_1 and G_2 so that the two sets are disjoint and so that neither includes the symbol S. We will build a new grammar G such that $L(G) = L(G_1) \cup L(G_2)$. G will contain all the rules of both G_1 and G_2. We add to G a new start symbol, S, and two new rules, $S \rightarrow S_1$ and $S \rightarrow S_2$. The two new rules allow G to generate a string iff at least one of G_1 or G_2 generates it. So $G = (V_1 \cup V_2 \cup \{S\}, \Sigma_1 \cup \Sigma_2, R_1 \cup R_2 \cup \{S \rightarrow S_1, S \rightarrow S_2\}, S)$.
- The context-free languages are closed under concatenation: If L_1 and L_2 are context-free languages, then there exist context-free grammars $G_1 = (V_1, \Sigma_1, R_1, S_1)$ and $G_2 = (V_2, \Sigma_2, R_2, S_2)$ such that $L_1 = L(G_1)$ and $L_2 = L(G_2)$. If necessary, rename the nonterminals of G_1 and G_2 so that the two sets are disjoint and so that neither includes the symbol S. We will build a new grammar G such that $L(G) = L(G_1)\, L(G_2)$. G will contain all the rules of both G_1 and G_2. We add to G a new start symbol, S, and one new rule, $S \rightarrow S_1S_2$. So $G = (V_1 \cup V_2 \cup \{S\}, \Sigma_1 \cup \Sigma_2, R_1 \cup R_2 \cup \{S \rightarrow S_1 S_2\}, S)$.
- The context-free languages are closed under Kleene star: If L_1 is a context-free language, then there exists a context-free grammar $G_1 = (V_1, \Sigma_1, R_1, S_1)$

such that $L_1 = L(G_1)$. If necessary, rename the nonterminals of G_1 so that V_1 does not include the symbol S. We will build a new grammar G such that $L(G) = L(G_1)^*$. G will contain all the rules of G_1. We add to G a new start symbol, S, and two new rules, $S \rightarrow \varepsilon$ and $S \rightarrow S\,S_1$. So $G = (V_1 \cup \{S\}, \Sigma_1, R_1 \cup \{S \rightarrow \varepsilon, S \rightarrow S\,S_1\}, S)$.

- The context-free languages are closed under reverse: Recall that $L^R = \{w \in \Sigma^* : w = x^R \text{ for some } x \in L\}$. If L is a context-free language, then it is generated by some Chomsky normal form grammar $G = (V, \Sigma, R, S)$. Every rule in G is of the form $X \rightarrow BC$ or $X \rightarrow a$, where X, B, and C are elements of $V - \Sigma$ and $a \in \Sigma$. In the latter case $L(X) = \{a\}$. $\{a\}^R = \{a\}$. In the former case, $L(X) = L(B)L(C)$. By Theorem 2.4, $(L(B)L(C))^R = L(C)^R L(B)^R$. So we construct, from G, a new grammar G', such that $L(G') = L^R$. $G' = (V_G, \Sigma_G, R', S_G)$, where R' is constructed as follows:
  - For every rule in G of the form $X \rightarrow BC$, add to R' the rule $X \rightarrow CB$.
  - For every rule in G of the form $X \rightarrow a$, add to R' the rule $X \rightarrow a$.
- The context-free languages are closed under letter substitution, defined as follows: Consider any two alphabets, Σ_1 and Σ_2. Let *sub* be any function from Σ_1 to Σ_2^*. Then *letsub* is a letter substitution function from L_1 to L_2 iff $letsub(L_1) = \{w \in \Sigma_2^* : \exists y \in L_1 (w = y$ except that every character c of y has been replaced by $sub(c))\}$. We leave the proof of this as an exercise.

As with regular languages, we can use these closure theorems as a way to prove that a more complex language is context-free if it can be shown to be built from simpler ones using operations under which the context-free languages are closed.

THEOREM 13.6 Nonclosure Under Intersection, Complement, and Difference

Theorem: The context-free languages are not closed under intersection, complement, or difference.

Proof:

- The context-free languages are not closed under intersection: The proof is by counterexample. Let:

$L_1 = \{a^n b^n c^m : n, m \geq 0\}$. /* equal a's and b's.

$L_2 = \{a^m b^n c^n : n, m \geq 0\}$. /* equal b's and c's.

Both L_1 and L_2 are context-free since there exist straightforward context-free grammars for them.

But now consider:

$$L = L_1 \cap L_2 = \{a^n b^n c^n \;:\; n \geq 0\}.$$

If the context-free languages were closed under intersection, L would have to be context-free. But we proved, in Example 13.1, that it isn't.

- The context-free languages are not closed under complement: Given any sets L_1 and L_2,

$$L_1 \cap L_2 = \neg(\neg L_1 \cup \neg L_2).$$

The context-free languages are closed under union. So, if they were also closed under complement, they would necessarily be closed under intersection. But we just showed that they are not. Thus they are not closed under complement either. We've also seen an example that proves this claim directly. $\neg A^nB^nC^n$ is context-free. We showed a PDA that accepts it in Example 12.8. But $\neg(\neg A^nB^nC^n) = A^nB^nC^n$ is not context-free.

- The context-free languages are not closed under difference (subtraction): Given any language L,

$$\neg L = \Sigma^* - L.$$

Σ^* is context-free. So, if the context-free languages were closed under difference, the complement of any context-free language would necessarily be context-free. But we just showed that that is not so.

Recall that, in using the regular Pumping Theorem to show that some language L was not regular, we sometimes found it useful to begin by intersecting L with another regular language to create a new language L'. Since the regular languages are closed under intersection, L' would necessarily be regular if L were. We then showed that L', designed to be simpler to work with, was not regular. And so neither was L.

It would be very useful to be able to exploit this technique when using the context-free Pumping Theorem. Unfortunately, as we have just shown, the context-free languages are not closed under intersection. Fortunately, however, they are closed under intersection with the regular languages. We'll prove this result next and then, in Section 13.4.2, we'll show how it can be exploited in a proof that a language is not context-free.

THEOREM 13.7 Closure Under Intersection With the Regular Languages

Theorem: The context-free languages are closed under intersection with the regular languages.

Proof: The proof is by construction. If L_1 is context-free, then there exists some PDA $M_1 = (K_1, \Sigma, \Gamma_1, \Delta_1, s_1, A_1)$ that accepts it. If L_2 is regular then there exists a DFSM $M_2 = (K_2, \Sigma, \delta, s_2, A_2)$ that accepts it. We construct a new PDA, M_3 that accepts $L_1 \cap L_2$. M_3 will work by simulating the parallel execution of M_1 and M_2. The states of M_3 will be ordered pairs of states of M_1 and M_2. As each input character is read, M_3 will simulate both M_1 and M_2 moving appropriately to a new state. M_3 will have a single stack, which will be controlled by M_1. The only slightly tricky thing is that M_1 may contain ε-transitions. So M_3 will have to allow M_1 to follow them while M_2 just stays in the same state and waits until the next input symbol is read.

$M_3 = (K_1 \times K_2, \Sigma, \Gamma_1, \Delta_3, (s_1, s_2), A_1 \times A_2)$, where Δ_3 is built as follows:

- For each transition $((q_1, \quad a, \beta), \ (p_1, \quad \gamma))$ in Δ_1, and each transition $((q_2, \quad a \quad), \ p_2 \quad)$ in δ, add to Δ_3 the transition: $(((q_1, q_2), a, \beta), ((p_1, p_2), \gamma))$.
- For each transition $((q_1, \quad \varepsilon, \beta), \ (p_1, \quad \gamma)$ in Δ_1, and each state q_2 in K_2, add to Δ_3 the transition: $(((q_1, q_2), \varepsilon, \beta), \ ((p_1, q_2), \gamma))$.

We define *intersectPDAandFSM* as follows:

intersectPDAandFSM (M_1: PDA, M_2: FSM) =
Build M_3 as defined in the proof of Theorem 13.7.

THEOREM 13.8 Closure Under Difference with the Regular Languages

Theorem: The difference $(L_1 - L_2)$ between a context-free language L_1 and a regular language L_2 is context-free.

Proof: $L_1 - L_2 = L_1 \cap \neg L_2$. If L_2 is regular, then, since the regular languages are closed under complement, $\neg L_2$ is also regular. Since L_1 is context-free, by Theorem 13.7, $L_1 \cap \neg L_2$ is context-free.

The last two theorems are important tools, both for showing that a language is context-free and for showing that a language is not context-free.

EXAMPLE 13.5 Using Closure Theorems to Prove A Language Context-Free

Consider the perhaps contrived language $L = \{a^n b^n : n \geq 0 \text{ and } n \neq 1776\}$. Another way to describe L is that it is $\{a^n b^n : n \geq 0\} - \{a^{1776} b^{1776}\}$. $A^n B^n = \{a^n b^n : n \geq 0\}$ is context-free. We have shown both a simple grammar that generates it and a simple PDA that accepts it. $\{a^{1776} b^{1776}\}$ is finite and thus regular. So, by Theorem 13.8, L is context free.

Generalizing that example a bit, from Theorem 13.8 it follows that any language that can be described as the result of subtracting a finite number of elements from some language known to be context-free must also be context-free.

13.4.2 Using the Pumping Theorem in Conjunction with the Closure Properties

Languages that impose no specific order constraints on the symbols contained in their strings are not always context-free. But it may be hard to prove that one isn't just by using the Pumping Theorem. In such a case, it is often useful to exploit Theorem 13.7, which tells us that the context-free languages are closed under intersection with the regular languages.

Recall our notational convention from Section 13.3: (n, n) means that all nonempty substrings of vy occur in region n. This may happen either because v and y are both nonempty and they both occur in region n. Or it may happen because one or the other is empty and the nonempty one occurs in region n.

Are natural languages like English or Chinese or German context-free? (L.3.3)

EXAMPLE 13.6 WW is Not Context-Free

Let WW $= \{ww : w \in \{\mathsf{a}, \mathsf{b}\}^*\}$. WW is similar to WcW $= \{w\mathsf{c}w : w \in \{\mathsf{a}, \mathsf{b}\}^*\}$, except that there is no longer a middle marker. Because, like WcW, it contains cross-serial dependencies, it is not context-free. We could try proving that by using the Pumping Theorem alone. Here are some attempts, using various choices for w:

- Let $w = (\mathsf{ab})^{2k}$. If $v = \varepsilon$ and $y = \mathsf{ab}$, pumping works fine.
- Let $w = \mathsf{a}^k\mathsf{ba}^k\mathsf{b}$. If $v =$ a and is in the first group of a's and $y =$ a and is in the second group of a's, pumping works fine.
- Let $w = \mathsf{a}^k\mathsf{b}^k\mathsf{a}^k\mathsf{b}^k$. Now the constraint that $|vxy| \leq k$ prevents v and y from both being in the two a regions or the two b regions. This choice of w will lead to a successful Pumping Theorem proof. But there are four regions in w and we must consider all the ways in which v and y could overlap those regions, including all those in which either or both of v and y occur on a region boundary. While it is possible to write out all those possibilities and show, one at a time, that every one of them violates at least one condition of the Pumping Theorem, there is an easier way.

If WW were context-free, then $L' =$ WW $\cap\ \mathsf{a}^*\mathsf{b}^*\mathsf{a}^*\mathsf{b}^*$ would also be context-free. But it isn't, which we can show using the Pumping Theorem. If it were, then there would exist some k such that any string w, where $|w| \geq k$, must satisfy the conditions of the theorem. We show one string w that does not. Let $w = \mathsf{a}^k\mathsf{b}^k\mathsf{a}^k\mathsf{b}^k$, where k is the constant from the Pumping Theorem. For w to satisfy the conditions of the Pumping Theorem, there must be some u, v, x, y, and z, such that $w = uvxyz$, $vy \neq \varepsilon$, $|vxy| \leq k$, and $\forall q \geq 0$ (uv^qxy^qz is in L'). We show that no such u, v, x, y, and z exist. Imagine w divided into four regions as follows:

aaa . . . aaabbb . . . bbbaaa . . . aaabbb . . . bbb

| 1 | 2 | 3 | 4 |

We consider all the cases for where v and y could fall and show that in none of them are all the conditions of the theorem met:

- If either v or y overlaps more than one region, set q to 2. The resulting string will not be in a*b*a*b* and so is not in L'.
- If $|vy|$ is not even then set q to 2. The resulting string will have odd length and so not be in L'. We assume in all the other cases that $|vy|$ is even.
- $(1, 1), (2, 2), (1, 2)$: Set q to 2. The boundary between the first half and the second half will shift into the first b region. So the second half will start with a b, while the first half still starts with an a. So the resulting string is not in L'.
- $(3, 3), (4, 4), (3, 4)$: Set q to 2. This time the boundary shifts into the second a region. The first half will end with an a while the second half still ends with a b. So the resulting string is not in L'.
- $(2, 3)$: Set q to 2. If $|v| \neq |y|$ then the boundary moves and, as argued above, the resulting string is not in L'. If $|v| = |y|$ then the first half contains more b's and the second half contains more a's. Since they are no longer the same, the resulting string is not in L'.
- $(1, 3), (1, 4)$, and $(2, 4)$ violate the requirement that $|vxy| \leq k$.

There is no way to divide w into $uvxyz$ such that all the conditions of the Pumping Theorem are met. So L' is not context-free. So neither is WW.

> One reason that context-free grammars are typically too weak to describe musical structures is that they cannot describe constraints such as the one that defines WW. (N.1.2)

EXAMPLE 13.7 A Simple Arithmetic Language is Not Context-Free

Let $L = \{x \# y = z : x, y, z \in \{0, 1\}^*$ and, if x, y and z are viewed as positive binary numbers without leading zeros, then $xy = z^R\}$. For example, 100#111 = 00111 $\in L$. (We do this example instead of the more natural one in which we require that $xy = z$ because it seems as though it might be more likely to be context-free. As we'll see, however, even this simpler variant is not.)

If L were context-free, then $L' = L \cap$ 10*#1* = 0*1* would also be context-free. But it isn't, which we can show using the Pumping Theorem. If it were, then there would exist some k such that any string w, where $|w| \geq k$, must satisfy the conditions of the theorem. We show one string w that does not. Let $w = 10^k \# 1^k = 0^k 1^k$, where k is the constant from the Pumping Theorem. Note that $w \in L$ because $10^k \cdot 1^k = 1^k 0^k$.

EXAMPLE 13.7 *(Continued)*

For w to satisfy the conditions of the Pumping Theorem, there must be some u, v, x, y, and z, such that $w = uvxyz$, $vy \neq \varepsilon$, $|vxy| \leq M$, and $\forall q \geq 0$ (uv^qxy^qz is in L). We show that no such u, v, x, y, and z exist. Imagine w divided into seven regions as follows:

```
1 000 ... 000 # 111 ... 111 = 000 ... 000111 ... 111
|1|    2     |3|    4     |5|     6      |   7     |
```

We consider all the cases for where v and y could fall and show that in none of them are all the conditions of the theorem met:

- If either v or y overlaps region 1, 3, or 5 then set q to 0. The resulting string will not be in 10*#1* = 0*1* and so is not in L'.
- If either v or y contains the boundary between 6 and 7, set q to 2. The resulting string will not be in 10*#1* = 0*1* and so is not in L'. So the only cases left to consider are those where v and y each occur within a single region.
- (2, 2), (4, 4), (2, 4): Set q to 2. Because there are no leading zeros, changing the left side of the string changes its value. But the right side doesn't change to match. So the resulting string is not in L'.
- (6, 6), (7, 7), (6, 7): Set q to 2. The right side of the equality statement changes value but the left side doesn't. So the resulting string is not in L'.
- (4, 6): Note that, because of the first argument to the multiplication, the number of 1's in the second argument must equal the number of 1's after the =. Set q to 2. The number of 1's in the second argument changed but the number of 1's in the result did not. So the resulting string is not in L'.
- (2, 6), (2, 7), and (4, 7) violate the requirement that $|vxy| \leq k$.

There is no way to divide w into $uvxyz$ such that all the conditions of the Pumping Theorem are met. So L is not context-free.

Sometimes the closure theorems can be used to reduce the proof that a new language L is not context-free to the proof that some other language L' is not context-free, where we have already proven the case for L'.

EXAMPLE 13.8 Using Intersection to Force Order Constraints

Let $L = \{w \in \{\mathrm{a, b, c}\}^* : \#_{\mathrm{a}}(w) = \#_{\mathrm{b}}(w) = \#_{\mathrm{c}}(w)\}$. If L were context-free, then $L' = L \cap \mathrm{a^*b^*c^*}$ would also be context-free. But $L' = \mathrm{A^nB^nC^n}$, which is not context-free, so neither is L.

13.5 Deterministic Context-Free Languages ◆

The regular languages are closed under complement, intersection, and difference. Why are the context-free languages different? In a nutshell, because the machines that accept them may necessarily be nondeterministic. Recall the technique that we used, in the proof of Theorem 8.4, to show that the regular languages are closed under complement: Given a (possibly nondeterministic) FSM M_1, we used the following procedure to construct a new FSM M_2 such that $L(M_2) = \neg L(M_1)$:

1. From M_1, construct an equivalent DFSM M', using the algorithm *ndfsmtodfsm*, presented in the proof of Theorem 5.3. (If M_1 is already deterministic, $M' = M_1$.)
2. M' must be stated completely, so if it is described with an implied dead state, add the dead state and all required transitions to it.
3. Begin building M_2 by setting it equal to M'. Then swap the accepting and the nonaccepting states. So $M_2 = (K_{M'}, \Sigma, \delta_{M'}, s_{M'}, K_{M'} - A_{M'})$.

We have no PDA equivalent of *ndfsmtodfsm*, so we cannot simply adapt this construction for PDAs. Our proofs that the regular languages are closed under intersection and difference relied on the fact that they were closed under complement, so we cannot adapt those proofs here either.

We have no PDA equivalent of *ndfsmtodfsm* because there provably isn't one, as we will show shortly. Recall that, in Section 12.2, we defined a PDA M to be ***deterministic*** iff:

- Δ_M contains no pairs of transitions that compete with each other, and
- if q is an accepting state of M, then there is no transition $((q, \varepsilon, \varepsilon), (p, a))$ for any p or a.

In other words, M never has a choice between two or more moves, nor does it have a choice between moving and accepting. There exist context-free languages that cannot be accepted by any deterministic PDA. But suppose that we restrict our attention to the ones that can.

What is a Deterministic Context-Free Language?

We are about to define the class of deterministic context-free languages. Because this class is useful, we would like it to be as large as possible. So let \$ be an end-of-string marker. We could use any symbol that is not in Σ_L (for example *<line feed>* or *<cr>*), but \$ is easier to read. A language L is ***deterministic context-free*** iff $L\$$ can be accepted by some deterministic PDA.

To see why we have defined the deterministic context-free languages to exploit an end-of-string marker, consider the following example of a straightforward language for which no deterministic PDA exists unless an end-of-string marker is used.

EXAMPLE 13.9 Why an End-of-String Marker is Useful

Let $L = \texttt{a}^* \cup \{\texttt{a}^n\texttt{b}^n : n > 0\}$. Consider any PDA M that accepts L. When it begins reading a's, M must push them onto the stack in case there are going to be b's. But, if it runs out of input without seeing b's, it needs a way to pop those a's from the stack before it can accept. Without an end-of-string marker, there is no way to allow that popping to happen *only* when all the input has been read. So, for example, the following PDA accepts L, but it is nondeterministic because the transition to state 3 (where the a's will be popped) can compete with both of the other transitions from state 1.

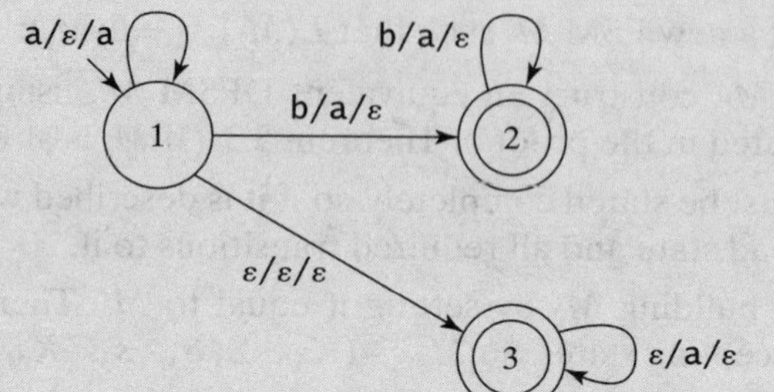

With an end-of-string marker, we can build the following deterministic PDA, which can only take the transition to state 3, the a-popping state, when it sees the $:

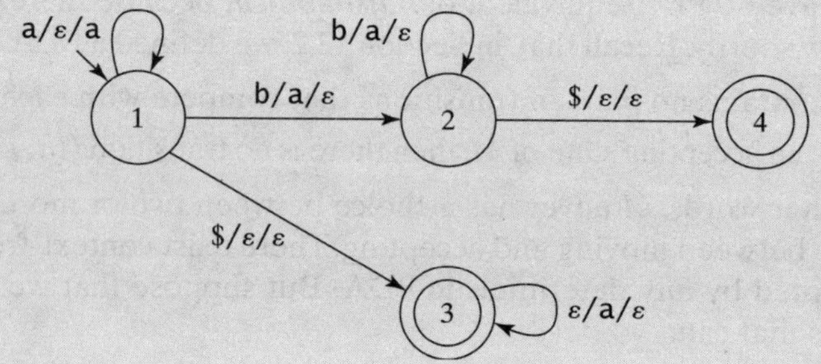

Before we go any farther, we have to be sure of one thing. We introduced the end-of-string marker to make it easier to build PDAs that are deterministic. We need to make sure that it doesn't make it possible to build a PDA for a language L that was not already context-free. In other words, adding the end-of-string marker cannot convert a language that was not context-free into one that is. We do that next.

THEOREM 13.9 CFLs and Deterministic CFLs

Theorem: Every deterministic context-free language (as just defined) is context-free.

Proof: If L is deterministic context-free, then $L\$$ is accepted by some deterministic PDA $M = (K, \Sigma, \Gamma, \Delta, s, A)$. From M, we construct M' such that $L(M') = L$. The idea is that, whatever M can do on reading \$, M' can do on reading ε (i.e., by simply guessing that it is at the end of the input). But, as soon as M' makes that guess, it cannot read any more input. It may perform the rest of its computation (such as popping its stack), but any path that pretends it has seen the \$ before it has read all of its input will fail to accept. To enable M' to perform whatever stack operations M could have performed, but not to read any input, M' will be composed of two copies of M: The first copy will be identical to M, and M' will operate in that part of itself until it guesses that it is at the end of the input; the second copy will be identical to M except that it contains only the transitions that do not consume any input. The states in the first copy will be labeled as in M. Those in the second copy will have the prime symbol appended to their names. So, if M contains the transition $((q, \varepsilon, \gamma_1), (p, \gamma_2))$, M' will contain the transition $((q', \varepsilon, \gamma_1), (p', \gamma_2))$. The two copies will be connected by finding, in the first copy of M, every \$-transition from some state q to some state p. We replace each such transition with an ε-transition into the second copy. So the new transition goes from q to p'.

We can define the following procedure to construct M':

without\$(M: PDA) =

1. Initially, set M' to M.

/* Make the copy that does not read any input.

2. For every state q in M, add to M' a new state q'.
3. For every transition $((q, \varepsilon, \gamma_1), (p, \gamma_2))$ in Δ_M do:
   3.1. Add to $\Delta_{M'}$ the transition $((q', \varepsilon, \gamma_1), (p', \gamma_2))$.

/* Link up the two copies.

4. For every transition $((q, \$, \gamma_1), (p, \gamma_2))$ in Δ_M do:
   4.1. Add to $\Delta_{M'}$ the transition $((q, \varepsilon, \gamma_1), (p', \gamma_2))$.
   4.2. Remove $((q, \$, \gamma_1), (p, \gamma_2))$ from $\Delta_{M'}$.

/* Set the accepting states of M'.

5. $A_{M'} = \{q' : q \in A\}$.

Closure Properties of the Deterministic Context-Free Languages

The deterministic context-free languages are practically very significant because it is possible to build deterministic, linear time parsers for them. They also possess additional formal properties that are important, among other reasons, because they enable us to prove that not all context-free languages are deterministic context-free. The most important of these is that the deterministic context-free languages, unlike the larger class of context-free languages, are closed under complement.

THEOREM 13.10 Closure Under Complement

Theorem: The deterministic context-free languages are closed under complement.

Proof: The proof is by construction. If L is a deterministic context-free language over the alphabet Σ, then $L\$$ is accepted by some deterministic PDA $M = (K, \Sigma \cup \{\$\}, \Gamma, \Delta, s, A)$. We need to describe an algorithm that constructs a new deterministic PDA that accepts $(\neg L)\$$. To prove Theorem 8.4 (that the regular languages are closed under complement), we defined a construction that proceeded in two steps: Given an arbitrary FSM, convert it to an equivalent DFSM, and then swap accepting and nonaccepting states. We can skip the first step here, but we must solve a new problem. A deterministic PDA may fail to accept an input string w for any one of several reasons:

1. Its computation ends before it finishes reading w.
2. Its computation ends in an accepting state but the stack is not empty.
3. Its computation loops forever, following ε-transitions, without ever halting in either an accepting or a nonaccepting state.
4. Its computation ends in a nonaccepting state.

If we simply swap accepting and nonaccepting states we will correctly fail to accept every string that M would have accepted (i.e., every string in $L\$$). But we will not necessarily accept every string in $(\neg L)\$$. To do that, we must also address issues 1 through 3 above.

An additional problem is that we don't want to accept $\neg L(M)$. That includes strings that do not end in \$. We must accept only strings that do end in \$ and that are in $(\neg L)\$$.

A construction that solves these problems is given in D.2.

What else can we say about the deterministic context-free languages? We know that they are closed under complement. What about union and intersection? We observe that $L_1 \cap L_2 = \neg(\neg L_1 \cup \neg L_2)$. So, if the deterministic context-free languages were closed under union, they would necessarily be closed under intersection also. But they are not closed under union. The context-free languages are closed under union, so the union of two deterministic context-free languages must be context-free. It may, however not be deterministic. The deterministic context-free languages are also not closed under intersection. In fact, when two deterministic context-free languages are intersected, the result may not even be context-free.

THEOREM 13.11 Nonclosure Under Union

Theorem: The deterministic context-free languages are not closed under union.

Proof: We show a counterexample:

$$\text{Let } L_1 = \{\mathrm{a}^i\mathrm{b}^j\mathrm{c}^k : i, j, k \geq 0 \text{ and } i \neq j\}.$$

$$\text{Let } L_2 = \{\mathrm{a}^i\mathrm{b}^j\mathrm{c}^k : i, j, k \geq 0 \text{ and } j \neq k\}.$$

$$\text{Let } L' = L_1 \cup L_2.$$
$$= \{\mathrm{a}^i\mathrm{b}^j\mathrm{c}^k : i, j, k \geq 0 \text{ and } ((i \neq j) \text{ or } (j \neq k))\}.$$

$$\text{Let } L'' = \neg L'.$$
$$= \{\mathrm{a}^i\mathrm{b}^j\mathrm{c}^k : i, j, k \geq 0 \text{ and } i = j = k\} \cup$$
$$\{w \in \{\mathrm{a}, \mathrm{b}, \mathrm{c}\}^* : \text{the letters are out of order}\}.$$

Let $L''' = L'' \cap \text{a}^*\text{b}^*\text{c}^*$.
$= \{\text{a}^n\text{b}^n\text{c}^n : n \geq 0\}$.

L_1 and L_2 are deterministic context-free. Deterministic PDAs that accept $L_1\$$ and $L_2\$$ can be constructed using the same approach we used to build a deterministic PDA for $L = \{\text{a}^m\text{b}^n : m \neq n; m, n > 0\}$ in Example 12.7. Their union L' is context-free but it cannot be deterministic context-free. If it were, then its complement L'' would also be deterministic context-free and thus context-free. But it isn't. If it were context-free, then L''', the intersection of L'' with a*b*c*, would also be context-free since the context-free languages are closed under intersection with the regular languages. But L''' is $\text{A}^n\text{B}^n\text{C}^n = \{\text{a}^n\text{b}^n\text{c}^n : n \geq 0\}$, which we have shown is not context-free.

THEOREM 13.12 Nonclosure Under Intersection

Theorem: The deterministic context-free languages are not closed under intersection.

Proof: We show a counterexample:

Let $L_1 = \{\text{a}^i\text{b}^j\text{c}^k : i, j, k \geq 0 \text{ and } i = j\}$.
Let $L_2 = \{\text{a}^i\text{b}^j\text{c}^k : i, j, k \geq 0 \text{ and } j = k\}$.

Let $L' = L_1 \cap L_2$.
$= \{\text{a}^n\text{b}^n\text{c}^n : n \geq 0\}$.

L_1 and L_2 are deterministic context-free. The deterministic PDA shown in Figure 13.4 accepts $L_1\$$. A similar one accepts L_2. But we have shown that their intersection L' is not context-free, much less deterministic context-free.

A Hierarchy within the Class of Context-Free Languages

The most important result of this section is the following theorem: There are context-free languages that are not deterministic context-free. Since there are context-free languages for which no deterministic PDA exists, there can exist no equivalent of *ndfsmtodfsm* for PDAs. Nondeterminism is a fact of life when working with PDAs unless we are willing to work only with languages that have been designed to be deterministic.

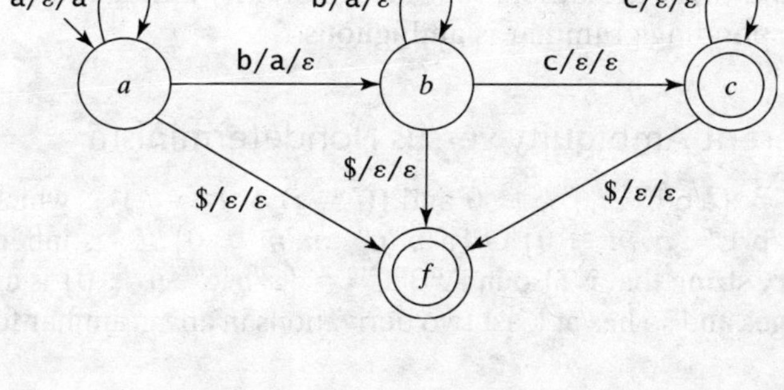

FIGURE 13.4 A deterministic PDA that accepts $\{\text{a}^i\text{b}^j\text{c}^k : i, j, k \geq 0$ and $i = j$.

The fact that there are context-free languages that are not deterministic poses a problem for the design of efficient parsing algorithms. The best parsing algorithms we have sacrifice either generality (i.e., they cannot correctly parse all context-free languages) or efficiency (i.e., they do not run in time that is linear in the length of the input). In Chapter 15, we will describe some of these algorithms.

THEOREM 13.13 Some CFLs are not Deterministic

Theorem: The class of deterministic context-free languages is a *proper* subset of the class of context-free languages. Thus there exist nondeterministic PDAs for which no equivalent deterministic PDA exists.

Proof: By Theorem 13.9, every deterministic context-free language is context-free. So all that remains is to show that there exists at least one context-free language that is not deterministic context-free.

Consider $L = \{a^i b^j c^k : i, j, k \geq 0 \text{ and } ((i \neq j) \text{ or } (j \neq k))\}$. L is context-free. The construction of a grammar for it was an exercise in Chapter 11. But we can show that L is not deterministic context-free by the same argument that we used in the proof of Theorem 13.11. If L were deterministic context-free, then, by Theorem 13.10, its complement $L' = \{a^i b^j c^k : i, j, k \geq 0 \text{ and } i = j = k\} \cup \{w \in \{a, b, c\}^* : \text{the letters are out of order}\}$ would also be deterministic context-free and thus context-free. If L' were context-free, then $L'' = L' \cap a^*b^*c^*$ would also be context-free (since the context-free languages are closed under intersection with the regular languages). But $L'' = A^nB^nC^n = \{a^n b^n c^n : n \geq 0\}$, which is not context-free. So L is context-free but not deterministic context-free.

Since L is context-free, it is accepted by some (nondeterministic) PDA M. M is an example of a nondeterministic PDA for which no equivalent deterministic PDA exists. If such a deterministic PDA did exist and accept L, it could be converted into a deterministic PDA that accepted $L\$$. But, if that machine existed, L would be deterministic context-free and we just showed that it is not.

We get the class of deterministic context-free languages when we think about the context-free languages from the perspective of PDAs that accept them. Recall from Section 11.7.3 that, when we think about the context-free languages from the perspective of the grammars that generate them, we also get a subclass of languages that are, in some sense, "easier" than others: There are context-free languages for which unambiguous grammars exist and there are others that are inherently ambiguous, by which we mean that every corresponding grammar is ambiguous.

EXAMPLE 13.10 Inherent Ambiguity versus Nondeterminism

Recall the language $L_1 = \{a^i b^j c^k : i, j, k \geq 0 \text{ and } ((i = j) \text{ or } (j = k))\}$, which can also be described as $\{a^n b^n c^m : n, m \geq 0\} \cup \{a^n b^m c^m : n, m \geq 0\}$. L_1 is inherently ambiguous because every string that is also in $A^nB^nC^n = \{a^n b^n c^n : n \geq 0\}$ is an element of both sublanguages and so has at least two derivations in any grammar for L_1.

Now consider the slightly different language $L_2 = \{a^n b^n c^m d : n, m \geq 0\} \cup \{a^n b^m c^m e : n, m \geq 0\}$. L_2 is not inherently ambiguous. It is straightforward to write an unambiguous grammar for each of the two sublanguages and any string in L_2 is an element of only one of them (since each such string must end in d or e but not both). L_2 is not, however, deterministic. There exists no PDA that can decide which of the two sublanguages a particular string is in until it has consumed the entire string.

What is the relationship between the deterministic context-free languages and the languages that are not inherently ambiguous? The answer is shown in Figure 13.5. The subset relations shown in the figure are proper:

- There exist deterministic context-free languages that are not regular. These languages are in the innermost donut in the figure. One example is $A^nB^n = \{a^n b^n : n \geq 0\}$.
- There exist languages that are not in the inner donut (i.e., they are not deterministic). But they are context-free and not inherently ambiguous. Two examples of languages in this second donut are:
  - PalEven = $\{ww^R : w \in \{a, b\}^*\}$. The grammar we showed for it in Example 11.3 is unambiguous.
  - $\{a^n b^n c^m d : n, m \geq 0\} \cup \{a^n b^m c^m e : n, m \geq 0\}$.
- There exist languages that are in the outer donut because they are inherently ambiguous. Two examples are:
  - $\{a^i b^j c^k : i, j, k \geq 0 \text{ and } ((i = j) \text{ or } (j = k))\}$.
  - $\{a^i b^j c^k : i, j, k \geq 0 \text{ and } ((i \neq j) \text{ or } (j \neq k))\}$.

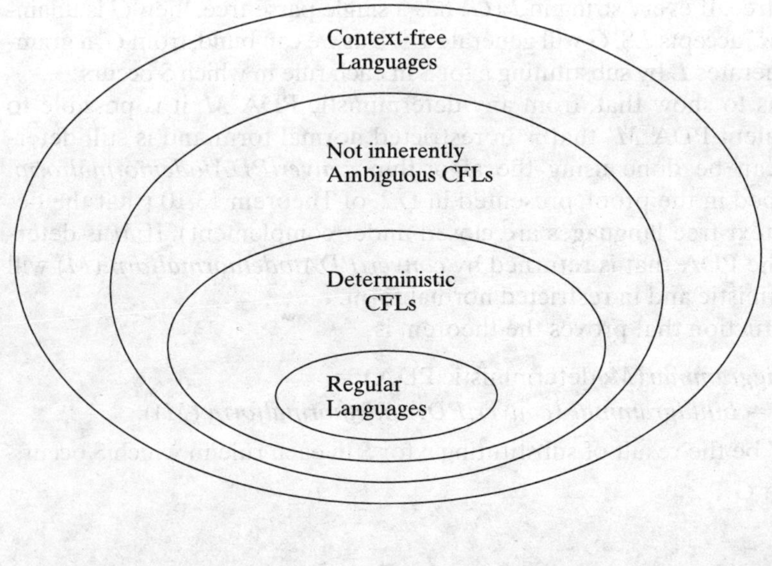

FIGURE 13.5 A hierarchy within the class of context-free languages.

To prove that the figure is properly drawn requires two additional results:

THEOREM 13.14 Every Regular Language is Deterministic Context-Free

Theorem: Every regular language is deterministic context-free.

Proof: The proof is by construction. $\{\$\}$ is regular. So, if L is regular, then so is $L\$$ (since the regular languages are closed under concatenation). So there is a DFSM M that accepts it. Using the construction that we used in the proof of Theorem 13.1 to show that every regular language is context-free, construct, from M a PDA P that accepts $L\$$. P will be deterministic.

THEOREM 13.15 Every Deterministic CFL has an Unambiguous Grammar

Theorem: For every deterministic context-free language there exists an unambiguous grammar.

Proof: If a language L is deterministic context-free, then there exists a deterministic PDA M that accepts $L\$$. We prove the theorem by construction of an unambiguous grammar G such that $L(M) = L(G)$. We construct G using approximately the same technique that we used to build a grammar from a PDA in the proof of Theorem 12.2. The algorithm *PDAtoCFG* that we presented there proceeded in two steps:

1. Invoke *convertPDAtorestricted*(M) to build M', an equivalent PDA in restricted normal form.
2. Invoke *buildgrammar* (M'), to build an equivalent grammar G.

It is straightforward to show that, if M' is deterministic, then the grammar G that *buildgrammar* constructs will be unambiguous: G produces derivations that mimic the operation of M'. Since M' is deterministic, on any input w it can follow only one path. So G will be able to produce only one leftmost derivation for w. Thus w has only one parse tree. If every string in $L(G)$ has a single parse tree, then G is unambiguous. Since M' accepts $L\$$, G will generate $L\$$. But we can build, from G, a grammar G' that generates L by substituting ε for \$ in each rule in which \$ occurs.

So it remains to show that, from any deterministic PDA M, it is possible to build an equivalent PDA M' that is in restricted normal form and is still deterministic. This can be done using the algorithm *convertPDAtodetnormalform*, which is described in the proof, presented in D.2, of Theorem 13.10 (that the deterministic context-free languages are closed under complement). If M is deterministic, then the PDA that is returned by *convertPDAtodetnormalform*(M) will be both deterministic and in restricted normal form.

So the construction that proves the theorem is:

buildunambiggrammar$(M$: deterministic PDA$)$ =

1. Let G = *buildgrammar* (*convertPDAtodetnormalform* (M)).
2. Let G' be the result of substituting ε for \$ in each rule in which \$ occurs.
3. Return G'.

13.6 Ogden's Lemma

The context-free Pumping Theorem is a useful tool for showing that a language is not context-free. However, there are many languages that are not context-free but that cannot be proven so just with the Pumping Theorem. In this section we consider a more powerful technique that may be useful in those cases.

Recall that the Pumping Theorem for regular languages imposed the constraint that the pumpable region y had to fall within the first k characters of any "long" string w. We exploited that fact in many of our proofs. But notice that the Pumping Theorem for context-free languages imposes no similar constraint. The two pumpable regions, v and y must be reasonably close together, but, as a group, they can fall anywhere in w. Sometimes there is a region that is pumpable, even though other regions aren't, and this can happen even in the case of long strings drawn from languages that are not context-free.

EXAMPLE 13.11 Sometimes Pumping Isn't Strong Enough

Let $L = \{a^i b^i c^j : i, j \geq 0, i \neq j\}$. We could attempt to use the context-free Pumping Theorem to show that L is not context-free. Let $w = a^k b^k c^{k+k!}$. (The reason for this choice will be clear soon.) Divide w into three regions, the a's, the b's, and the c's, which we'll call regions 1, 2, and 3, respectively. If either v or y contains two or more distinct symbols, then set q to 2. The resulting string will have letters out of order and thus not be in L. We consider the remaining possibilities:

- (1, 1), (2, 2), (1, 3), (2, 3): Set q to 2. The number of a's will no longer equal the number of b's, so the resulting string is not in L.
- (1, 2): If $|v| \neq |y|$ then set q to 2. The number of a's will no longer equal the number of b's, so the resulting string is not in L. If $|v| = |y|$ then set q to $(k!/|v|) + 1$. Note that $(k!/|v|)$ must be an integer since $|v| \leq k$. The string that results from pumping is $a^X b^X c^{k+k!}$, where $X = k + (q - 1) \cdot |v| = k + (k!/|v|) \cdot |v| = k + k!$. So the number of a's and of b's equals the number of c's. This string is not in L. So far, the proof is going well. But now we must consider:
- (3, 3): Pumping in will result in even more c's than a's and b's, so it will produce a string that is still in L. And, while pumping out can reduce the number of c's, it can't reduce it all the way down to k because $|vxy| \leq k$. So the maximum number of c's that can be pumped out is k, which would result in a string with $k!$ c's. But, as long as $k \geq 3$, $k! > k$. So the resulting string is in L and we have failed to show that L is not context-free.

What we need is a way to prevent v and y from falling in the c region of w.

Ogden's Lemma is a generalization of the Pumping Theorem. It lets us mark some number of symbols in our chosen string w as ***distinguished***. Then at least one of v and y must contain at least one distinguished symbol. So, for example, we could complete the proof that we started in Example 13.11 if we could force at least one of v or y to contain at least one a.

THEOREM 13.16 Ogden's Lemma

Theorem: If L is a context-free language, then:

$\exists k \geq 1$ ($\forall$ strings $w \in L$, where $|w| \geq k$, if we mark at least k symbols of w as distinguished then:

$$(\exists u, v, x, y, z\ (w = uvxyz,$$
$$vy \text{ contains at least one distinguished symbol,}$$
$$vxy \text{ contains at most } k \text{ distinguished symbols, and}$$
$$\forall q \geq 0\ \ (uv^q xy^q z \text{ is in } L))).$$

Proof: The proof is analogous to the one we did for the context-free Pumping Theorem except that we consider only paths that generate the distinguished symbols. If L is context-free, then it is generated by some context-free grammar $G = (V, \Sigma, R, S)$ with n nonterminal symbols and branching factor b. Let k be b^{n+1}. Let w be any string in $L(G)$ such that $|w| \geq k$. A parse tree T for w might look like the one shown in Figure 13.6.

Suppose that we mark at least b^{n+1} symbols as distinguished. The distinguished symbols are marked with a ✓ (Ignore the fact that there aren't enough of them in the picture. Its only role is to make it easier to visualize the process.) Call the sequence of distinguished nodes the ***distinguished subsequence*** of w. In this example, that is bje. Note that the distinguished subsequence is not necessarily a substring. The characters in it need not be contiguous. The length of the distinguished subsequence is at least b^{n+1}. We can now mark the nonleaf nodes that branched in a way that enabled the distinguished subsequence to grow to at least length b^{n+1}. Mark every nonleaf node that has at least two daughters that contain a distinguished leaf. In this example, we mark X_2, and X_1, as indicated by the symbol ♦. It is straightforward to prove by induction that T must contain at least one path that contains at least $n + 1$ marked

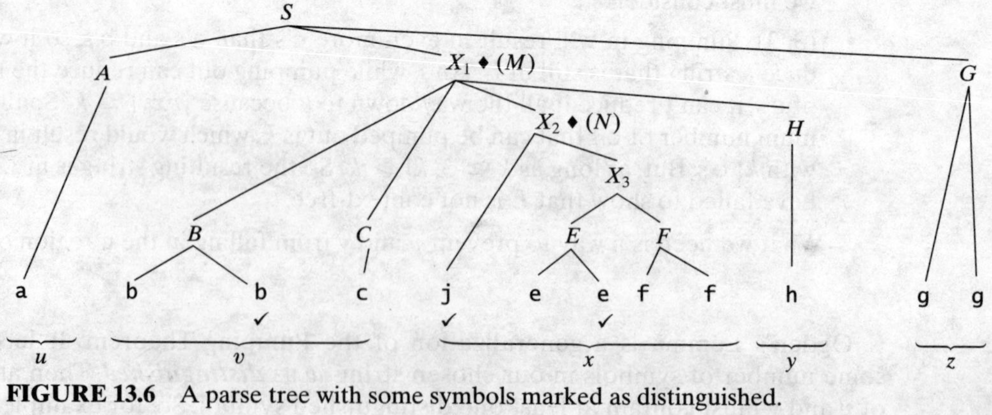

FIGURE 13.6 A parse tree with some symbols marked as distinguished.

nonleaf nodes since its yield contains b^{n+1} distinguished symbols. Choose one such path such that there is no longer one. That path must contain at least two nodes labeled with the same nonterminal symbol. Choose the two nodes that are labeled with the bottom-most pair of repeated marked nonterminals. Call the lower one N and the higher one M. In the example, M is X_1 and N is X_2. As shown in the diagram, divide w into $uvxyz$, such that x is the yield of N and vxy is the yield of M. Now observe that:

- vy contains at least one distinguished symbol because the root of the subtree with yield vxy has at least two daughters that contain distinguished symbols. One of them may be in the subtree whose yield is x, but that leaves at least one that must be in either v or y. There may be distinguished symbols in both, although, as in our example T, that is not necessary.
- vxy contains at most k (b^{n+1}) distinguished symbols because there are at most $n + 1$ marked internal nodes on a longest path in the subtree that dominates it. Only marked internal nodes create branches that lead to more than one distinguished symbol, and no internal node can create more than b branches.
- $\forall q \geq 0$ ($uv^q xy^q z$ is in L), by the same argument that we used in the proof of the context-free Pumping Theorem.

Notice that the context-free Pumping Theorem describes the special case in which all symbols of the string w are marked.

Ogden's Lemma is the tool that we need to complete the proof that we started in Example 13.11.

EXAMPLE 13.12 Ogden's Lemma May Work When Pumping Doesn't

Now we can use Ogden's Lemma to complete the proof that $L = \{\mathrm{a}^i\mathrm{b}^i\mathrm{c}^j : i, j \geq 0, i \neq j\}$ is not context-free. Let $w = \mathrm{a}^k\mathrm{b}^k\mathrm{c}^{k+k!}$. Mark all the a's in w as distinguished. If either v or y contains two or more distinct symbols, then set q to 2. The resulting string will have letters out of order and thus not be in L. We consider the remaining possibilities:

- (1, 1), (1, 3): Set q to 2. The number of a's will no longer equal the number of b's, so the resulting string is not in L.
- (1, 2): If $|v| \neq |y|$ then set q to 2. The number of a's will no longer equal the number of b's, so the resulting string is not in L. If $|v| = |y|$ then set q to $(k!/|v|) + 1$. Note that $(k!/|v|)$ must be an integer since $|v| \leq k$. The string that results from pumping is $\mathrm{a}^{k+(q-1)\cdot|v|}\,\mathrm{b}^{k+(q-1)\cdot|v|}\,\mathrm{c}^{k+k!} = \mathrm{a}^{k+(k!/|v|)\cdot|v|}\,\mathrm{b}^{k+(k!/|v|)\cdot|v|}\,\mathrm{c}^{k+k!} = \mathrm{a}^{k+k!}\,\mathrm{b}^{k+k!}\,\mathrm{c}^{k+k!}$. So the number of a's and of b's equals the number of c's. This string is not in L.
- (2, 2), (2, 3), (3, 3) fail to satisfy the requirement that at least one symbol in vy be marked as distinguished.

There is no way to divide w into vxy such that all the conditions of Ogden's Lemma are met. So L is not context-free.

13.7 Parikh's Theorem ◆

Suppose that we consider a language L not from the point of view of the exact strings it contains but instead by simply counting, for each string w in L, how many instances of each character in Σ w contains. So, from this perspective, the strings aaabbba and abababa are the same. If Σ is {a, b}, then both strings can be described with the pair (4, 3) since they contain 4 a's and 3 b's. We can build such descriptions by defining a family of functions ψ_Σ, with domain Σ^* and range $\{(i_1, i_2, \ldots i_k)\}$, where $k = |\Sigma|$:

$\psi_\Sigma(w) = (i_1, i_2, \ldots i_k)$ where, for all j, i_j = the number of occurrences in w of the jth element of Σ.

So, if Σ = {a, b, c, d}, then ψ_Σ(aabbbbddd) = (2, 4, 0, 3).

Now consider some language L, which is a set of strings over some alphabet Σ. Instead of considering L as a set of strings, we can consider it as the set of vectors that are produced by applying ψ_Σ to the strings it contains. To do this, we define another family of functions Ψ_Σ, with domain $\mathcal{P}(\Sigma^*)$ and range $\mathcal{P}\{(i_1, i_2, \ldots i_k)\}$:

$$\Psi_\Sigma(L) = \{(i_1, i_2, \ldots i_k) : \exists w \in L\ (\psi_\Sigma(w) = (i_1, i_2, \ldots i_k))\}.$$

If Σ is fixed, then there is a single function ψ and a single function Ψ. In that case, we will omit Σ and refer to the functions just as ψ and Ψ.

We will say that two languages L_1 and L_2, over the alphabet Σ^*, are ***letter-equivalent*** iff $\Psi_\Sigma(L_1) = \Psi_\Sigma(L_2)$. In other words, L_1 and L_2 contain the same strings if we disregard the order in which the symbols occur in the strings.

EXAMPLE 13.13 Letter Equivalence

Let Σ = {a, b}. Then, for example, ψ(a) = (1, 0). ψ(b) = (0, 1). ψ(ab) = (1, 1). ψ(aaabbbb) = (3, 4).

Now consider Ψ:

- Let $L_1 = \text{A}^\text{n}\text{B}^\text{n} = \{\text{a}^n\text{b}^n : n \geq 0\}$. Then $\Psi(L_1) = \{(i, i) : 0 \leq i\}$.
- Let L_2 = (ab)*. Then $\Psi(L_2) = \{(i, i) : 0 \leq i\}$.
- Let $L_3 = \{\text{a}^n\text{b}^n\text{a}^n : n \geq 0\}$. Then $\Psi(L_3) = \{(2i, i) : 0 \leq i\}$.
- Let $L_4 = \{\text{a}^{2n}\text{b}^n : n \geq 0\}$. Then $\Psi(L_4) = \{(2i, i) : 0 \leq i\}$.
- Let L_5 = (aba)*. Then $\Psi(L_5) = \{(2i, i) : 0 \leq i\}$.

L_1 and L_2 are letter-equivalent. So are L_3, L_4 and L_5.

Just looking at the five languages we considered in Example 13.13, we can observe that it is possible for two languages with different formal properties (for example a regular language and a context-free but not regular one) to be letter equivalent to each other. L_3 is not context-free. L_4 is context-free but not regular. is regular. But the three of them are letter equivalent to each other.

Parikh's Theorem, which we are about to state formally and then prove, tells us that that example is far from unique. In fact, given any context-free language L, there exists some regular language L' such that L and L' are letter-equivalent to each other. So A^nB^n is letter equivalent to (ab)*. The language $\{a^{2n}b^n : n \geq 0\}$ is letter equivalent to (aba)* and to (aab)*. And PalEven = $\{ww^R : w \in \{a, b\}^*\}$ is letter equivalent to (aa ∪ bb)* since Ψ(PalEven) = Ψ((aa ∪ bb)*) = $\{(2i, 2j) : 0 \leq i \wedge 0 \leq j\}$. The proof of Parikh's Theorem is similar to the proofs we have already given for the Context-free Pumping Theorem and for Ogden's Lemma. It is based on the fact that, if L is context-free, then all the strings in L can be formed by starting with one of a finite set of "short" strings in L and then pumping in some finite number of strings (v, y pairs), all of which are chosen from a finite library of possible values for v and y.

An interesting application of Parikh's theorem is in the proof of a corollary that tells us that every context-free language over a single character alphabet must also be regular. We will add that corollary to our kit of tools for proving that a language is not context-free (by showing that, if it were, then it would also be regular but we know that it isn't).

Notice, by the way, that while we are about to prove that if L is context-free then it is letter-equivalent to some regular language, the converse of that claim is false. A language can be letter-equivalent to some regular language and not be context-free. We prove this by considering two of the languages from Example 13.13: $L_3 = \{a^nb^na^n : n \geq 0\}$ is not context-free, but it is letter-equivalent to $L_5 =$ (aba)*, which is regular.

THEOREM 13.17 Parikh's Theorem

Theorem: Every context-free language is letter-equivalent to some regular language.

Proof: The proof follows an argument similar to the one we used to prove the context-free Pumping Theorem. It is given in D.3.

An algebraic approach to thinking about what ψ and Ψ are doing is the following: We can describe the standard way of looking at strings as starting with a set S of primitive strings (ε and all the one-character strings drawn from Σ) and the single operation of concatenation, which is associative and has ε as an identity. Σ^* is then the closure of S under concatenation. ψ_Σ maps elements of Σ^* to elements of $\{(i_1, i_2, \ldots i_k)\}$, on which is defined the operation of pair wise addition, which is associative and has $(0, 0, \ldots 0)$ as an identity. But addition is also commutative, while concatenation is not. So, while, if we concatenate strings, it matters what order we do it in, if we consider the images of strings under ψ, the order in which we combine them doesn't matter. Parikh's theorem can be described as a special case of more general properties of commutative systems.

When Σ contains just a single character, the order of the characters in a string is irrelevant. So we have the following result:

THEOREM 13.18 Every CFL Over A Single-Character Alphabet is Regular

Theorem: Any context-free language over a single-character alphabet is regular.

Proof: By Parikh's Theorem, if L is context-free then L is letter-equivalent to some regular language L'. Since the order of characters has no effect on strings when all characters are the same, $L = L'$. Since L' is regular, so is L.

EXAMPLE 13.14 A^nA^n is Regular

Let $\Sigma = \{a, b\}$ and consider $L = A^nB^n = \{a^nb^n : n \geq 0\}$. A^nB^n is context-free but not regular.

$$\text{Now let: } \Sigma = \{a\} \text{ and } L' = \{a^na^n, n \geq 0\}.$$
$$= \{a^{2n} : n \geq 0\}.$$
$$= \{w \in \{a\}^* : |w| \text{ is even}\}. \ L' \text{ is regular.}$$

EXAMPLE 13.15 PalEven is Regular if $\Sigma = \{a\}$

Let $\Sigma = \{a, b\}$ and consider $L = \text{PalEven} = \{ww^R : w \in \{a, b\}^*\}$. PalEven is context-free but not regular.

$$\text{Now let: } \Sigma = \{a\} \text{ and } L' = \{ww^R : w \in \{a\}^*\}$$
$$= \{w \in \{a\}^* : |w| \text{ is even}\}. \ L' \text{ is regular.}$$

When we are considering only a single letter alphabet, we can use Theorem 13.18 to show that a language that we already know not to be regular cannot be context-free either.

EXAMPLE 13.16 The Prime Number of a's Language is Not Context-Free

Consider again $\text{Prime}_a = \{a^n : n \text{ is prime}\}$. Prime_a is not context-free. If it were, then, by Theorem 13.18, it would also be regular. But we showed in Example 8.13 that it is not regular. So it is not context-free either.

13.8 Functions on Context-Free Languages ◆

In Section 13.4, we saw that the context-free languages are closed under some important functions, including concatenation, union, and Kleene star. But their closure properties are substantially weaker than are the closure properties of the regular languages. In this section, we consider some other functions that can be applied to languages and we ask whether the context-free languages are closed under them. The proof strategies we will use are the same as the ones we used for the regular languages and for the results we have already obtained for the context-free languages:

- To show that the context-free languages are closed under some function f, we will show an algorithm that constructs, given any context-free language L, either a grammar or a PDA that describes $f(L)$.
- To show that the context-free languages are not closed under some function f, we will exhibit a counterexample, i.e., a language L where L is context-free but $f(L)$ is not.

EXAMPLE 13.17 *Firstchars*

Consider again the function *firstchars* $(L) = \{w : \exists y \in L\ (y = cx \wedge c \in \Sigma_L \wedge x \in \Sigma_L^* \wedge w \in c^*)\}$. The context-free languages are closed under *firstchars*(L). In fact, if L is context-free then *firstchars*(L) is regular. We know that this must be true by an argument similar to the one we used in Example 8.20 to show that the regular languages are closed under *firstchars*. There must be some finite set of characters $\{c_1, c_2, \ldots, c_n\}$ that can begin strings in L (since Σ_L is finite). So there exists some regular expression of the following form that describes *firstchars*(L):

$$c_1^* \cup c_2^* \cup \cdots \cup c_n^*.$$

We can also show a constructive proof that *firstchars*(L) is context-free if L is. If L is a context-free language, then there is some context-free grammar $G = (V, \Sigma, R, S)$ that generates it. We construct a context-free grammar $G' = (V', \Sigma', R', S')$ that generates *firstchars*(L):

1. Convert G to Greibach normal form using the procedure *converttoGreibach*, defined in D.1.
2. Remove from G all unreachable nonterminals and all rules that mention them.
3. Remove from G all unproductive nonterminals and all rules that mention them.
4. Initialize V' to $\{S'\}$, Σ' to $\{\}$, and R' to $\{\}$.
5. For each remaining rule in G of the form $S \rightarrow c\,\gamma$ do:
   - **5.1.** Add to R' the rules $S' \rightarrow C_c$, $C_c \rightarrow c\, C_c$ and $C_c \rightarrow \varepsilon$.
   - **5.2.** Add to Σ' the symbol c.
   - **5.3.** Add to V' the symbol C_c.
6. Return G'.

The idea behind this construction is that, if G is in Greibach normal form, then, each time a rule is applied, the next terminal symbol is generated. So, if we look at G's start symbol S and ask what terminals any of its rules can generate, we'll know exactly what terminals strings in $L(G)$ can start with.

EXAMPLE 13.18 *Maxstring*

Consider again the function $maxstring(L) = \{w : w \in L \text{ and } \forall z \in \Sigma^*(z \neq \varepsilon \rightarrow wz \notin L)\}$. The context-free languages are not closed under $maxstring(L)$. The proof is by counterexample. Consider the language $L = \{a^i b^j c^k : k \leq i \text{ or } k \leq j\}$. L is context-free but $maxstring(L)$ is not. We leave the proof of this as an exercise.

Exercises

1. For each of the following languages L, state whether L is regular, context-free but not regular, or not context-free and prove your answer.
   a. $\{xy : x, y \in \{a, b\}^* \text{ and } |x| = |y|\}$.
   b. $\{(ab)^n a^n b^n : n > 0\}$.
   c. $\{x\#y : x, y \in \{0, 1\}^* \text{ and } x \neq y\}$.
   d. $\{a^i b^n : i, n > 0 \text{ and } i = n \text{ or } i = 2n\}$.
   e. $\{wx : |w| = 2 \cdot |x| \text{ and } w \in a^+b^+ \text{ and } x \in a^+b^+\}$.
   f. $\{a^n b^m c^k : n, m, k \geq 0 \text{ and } m \leq min(n, k)\}$.
   g. $\{xyx^R : x \in \{0, 1\}^+ \text{ and } y \in \{0, 1\}^*\}$.
   h. $\{xwx^R : x, w \in \{a, b\}^+ \text{ and } |x| = |w|\}$.
   i. $\{ww^R w : w \in \{a, b\}^*\}$.
   j. $\{wxw : |w| = 2 \cdot |x| \text{ and } w \in \{a, b\}^* \text{ and } x \in \{c\}^*\}$.
   k. $\{a^i : i \geq 0\}\{b^i : i \geq 0\}\{a^i : i \geq 0\}$.
   l. $\{x \in \{a, b\}^* : |x|$ is even and the first half of x has one more a than does the second half$\}$.
   m. $\{w \in \{a, b\}^* : \#_a(w) = \#_b(w)$ and w does not contain either the substring aaa or abab$\}$.
   n. $\{a^n b^{2n} c^m : n, m \geq 0\} \cap \{a^n b^m c^{2m} : n, m \geq 0\}$.
   o. $\{x \text{ c } y : x, y \in \{0, 1\}^* \text{ and } y \text{ is a prefix of } x\}$.
   p. $\{w : w = uu^R \text{ or } w = ua^n : n = |u|, u \in \{a, b\}^*\}$.
   q. $L(G)$, where $G = S \rightarrow aSa$
   $S \rightarrow SS$
   $S \rightarrow \varepsilon$
   r. $\{w \in$ (A-Z, a-z, ., blank)$^+$: there exists at least one duplicated, capitalized word in w). For example, the string, `The history of China can be viewed from the perspective of an outsider or of someone living in China`, $\in L$.
   s. $\neg L_0$, where $L_0 = \{ww : w \in \{a, b\}^*\}$.
   t. L^*, where $L = \{0^*1^i0^*1^i0^* : i \geq 0\}$.
   u. $\neg A^nB^n$.
   v. $\{ba^jb : j = n^2 \text{ for some } n \geq 0\}$. For example, baaaab $\in L$.
   w. $\{w \in \{a, b, c, d\}^* : \#_b(w) \geq \#_c(w) \geq \#_d(w) \geq 0\}$.

2. Let $L = \{w \in \{\mathtt{a}, \mathtt{b}\}^* :$ the first, middle, and last characters of w are identical$\}$.
   a. Show a context-free grammar for L.
   b. Show a natural PDA that accepts L.
   c. Prove that L is not regular.
3. Let $L = \{\mathtt{a}^n\mathtt{b}^m\mathtt{c}^n\mathtt{d}^m : n, m \geq 1\}$. L is interesting because of its similarity to a useful fragment of a typical programming language in which one must declare procedures before they can be invoked. The procedure declarations include a list of the formal parameters. So now imagine that the characters in $\mathtt{a}^n$ correspond to the formal parameter list in the declaration of procedure 1. The characters in $\mathtt{b}^m$ correspond to the formal parameter list in the declaration of procedure 2. Then the characters in $\mathtt{c}^n$ and $\mathtt{d}^m$ correspond to the parameter lists in an invocation of procedure 1 and procedure 2 respectively, with the requirement that the number of parameters in the invocations match the number of parameters in the declarations. Show that L is not context-free.
4. Without using the Pumping Theorem, prove that $L = \{w \in \{\mathtt{a}, \mathtt{b}, \mathtt{c}\}^* : \#_{\mathtt{a}}(w) = \#_{\mathtt{b}}(w) = \#_{\mathtt{c}}(w)$ and $\#_{\mathtt{a}}(w) > 50\}$ is not context-free.
5. Give an example of a context-free language L ($\neq \Sigma^*$) that contains a subset L_1 that is not context-free. Prove that L is context free. Describe L_1 and prove that it is not context-free.
6. Let $L_1 = L_2 \cap L_3$.
   a. Show values for L_1, L_2, and L_3, such that L_1 is context-free but neither L_2 nor L_3 is.
   b. Show values for L_1, L_2, and L_3, such that L_2 is context-free but neither L_1 nor L_3 is.
7. Give an example of a context-free language L, other than one of the ones in the book, where $\neg L$ is not context-free.
8. Theorem 13.7 tells us that the context-free languages are closed under intersection with the regular languages. Prove that the context-free languages are also closed under union with the regular languages.
9. Complete the proof that the context-free languages are not closed under *maxstring* by showing that $L = \{\mathtt{a}^i\mathtt{b}^j\mathtt{c}^k : k \leq i$ or $k \leq j\}$ is context-free but *maxstring*(L) is not context-free.
10. Use the Pumping Theorem to complete the proof, started in L.3.3, that English is not context-free if we make the assumption that subjects and verbs must match in a "respectively" construction.
11. In N.1.2, we give an example of a simple musical structure that cannot be described with a context-free grammar. Describe another one, based on some musical genre with which you are familiar. Define a sublanguage that captures exactly that phenomenon. In other words, ignore everything else about the music you are considering and describe a set of strings that meets the one requirement you are studying. Prove that your language is not context-free.
12. Define the leftmost maximal P subsequence m of a string w as follows:
    - P must be a nonempty set of characters.
    - A string S is a P subsequence of w iff S is a substring of w and S is composed entirely of characters in P. For example 1, 0, 10, 01, 11, 011, 101, 111, 1111, and 1011 are $\{0, 1\}$ subsequences of 2312101121111.

- Let S be the set of all P subsequences of w such that, for each element t of S, there is no P subsequence of w longer than t. In the example above, $S = \{1111, 1011\}$.
- Then m is the leftmost (within w) element of S. In the example above, $m = 1011$.

a. Let $L = \{w \in \{0\text{-}9\}^* : \text{if } y \text{ is the leftmost maximal } \{0, 1\} \text{ subsequence of } w \text{ then } |y| \text{ is even}\}$. Is L regular (but not context free), context free or neither? Prove your answer.

b. Let $L = \{w \in \{\text{a, b, c}\}^* : \text{the leftmost maximal } \{\text{a, b}\} \text{ subsequence of } w \text{ starts with a}\}$. Is L regular (but not context free), context free or neither? Prove your answer.

13. Are the context-free languages closed under each of the following functions? Prove your answer.

a. $chop(L) = \{w : \exists x \in L\ (x = x_1cx_2 \wedge x_1 \in \Sigma_L^* \wedge x_2 \in \Sigma_L^* \wedge c \in \Sigma_L \wedge |x_1| = |x_2| \wedge w = x_1x_2)\}$

b. $mix(L) = \{w : \exists x, y, z \colon (x \in L, x = yz, |y| = |z|, w = yz^R)\}$

c. $pref(L) = \{w : \exists x \in \Sigma^*(wx \in L)\}$

d. $middle(L) = \{x : \exists y, z \in \Sigma^*(yxz \in L)\}$

e. Letter substitution

f. $shuffle(L) = \{w : \exists x \in L\ (w \text{ is some permutation of } x)\}$

g. $copyreverse\ (L) = \{w : \exists x \in L\ (w = xx^R)\}$

14. Let $alt\ (L) = \{x : \exists y, n\ (y \in L, |y| = n, n > 0, y = a_1 \cdots a_n, \forall i \leq n\ (a_i \in \Sigma)$, and $x = a_1a_3a_5 \cdots a_k$, where $k = (\text{if } n \text{ is even then } n - 1 \text{ else } n))\}$.

a. Consider $L = \text{a}^n\text{b}^n$. Clearly describe $L_1 = alt(L)$.

b. Are the context free languages closed under the function *alt*? Prove your answer.

15. Let $L_1 = \{\text{a}^n\text{b}^m : n \geq m\}$. Let $R_1 = \{(\text{a} \cup \text{b})^* : \text{there is an odd number of a's and an even number of b's}\}$. Use the construction that is described in the proof of Theorem 13.7 to build a PDA that accepts $L_1 \cap R_1$.

16. Let T be a set of languages defined as follows:

$$T = \{L : L \text{ is a context-free language over the alphabet} \{\text{a, b, c}\} \text{ and, if } x \in L, \text{ then } |x| \equiv_3 0\}.$$

Let P be the following function on languages:

$$P(L) = \{w : \exists x \in \{\text{a, b, c}\} \text{ and } \exists y \in L \text{ and } y = xw\}.$$

Is the set T closed under P? Prove your answer.

17. Show that the following languages are deterministic context-free:

a. $\{w : w \in \{\text{a, b}\}^*$ and each prefix of w has at least as many a's as b's$\}$

b. $\{\text{a}^n\text{b}^n : n \geq 0\} \cup \{\text{a}^n\text{c}^n : n \geq 0\}$

18. Show that $L = \{\text{a}^n\text{b}^n : n \geq 0\} \cup \{\text{a}^n\text{b}^{2n} : n \geq 0\}$ is not deterministic context-free.

19. Are the deterministic context-free languages closed under reverse? Prove your answer.

20. Prove that each of the following languages is not context-free. (Hint: Use Ogden's Lemma.)

a. $\{\mathtt{a}^i\mathtt{b}^j\mathtt{c}^k : i \geq 0, j \geq 0, k \geq 0, \text{and } i \neq j \neq k\}$

b. $\{\mathtt{a}^i\mathtt{b}^j\mathtt{c}^k\mathtt{d}^n : i \geq 0, j \geq 0, k \geq 0, n \geq 0, \text{and } (i = 0 \text{ or } j = k = n)\}$

21. Let $\Psi(L)$ be as defined in Section 13.7, in our discussion of Parikh's Theorem. For each of the following languages L, first state what $\Psi(L)$ is. Then give a regular language that is letter-equivalent to L.

a. Bal $= \{w \in \{\mathtt{)}, \mathtt{(}\}^* : \text{the parentheses are balanced}\}$

b. Pal $= \{w \in \{\mathtt{a}, \mathtt{b}\}^* : w \text{ is a palindrome}\}$

c. $\{x^{\mathrm{R}}\#y : x, y \in \{\mathtt{0}, \mathtt{1}\}^* \text{ and } x \text{ is a substring of } y\}$

22. For each of the following claims, state whether it is *True* or *False*. Prove your answer.

a. If L_1 and L_2 are two context-free languages, $L_1 - L_2$ must also be context-free.

b. If L_1 and L_2 are two context-free languages and $L_1 = L_2L_3$, then L_3 must also be context-free.

c. If L is context free and R is regular, $R - L$ must be context-free.

d. If L_1 and L_2 are context-free languages and $L_1 \subseteq L \subseteq L_2$, then L must be context-free.

e. If L_1 is a context-free language and $L_2 \subseteq L_1$, then L_2 must be context-free.

f. If L_1 is a context-free language and $L_2 \subseteq L_1$, it is possible that L_2 is regular.

g. A context-free grammar in Chomsky normal form is always unambiguous.

CHAPTER 14

Algorithms and Decision Procedures for Context-Free Languages

Many questions that we could answer when asked about regular languages are unanswerable for context-free ones. But a few important questions can be answered and we have already presented a useful collection of algorithms that can operate on context-free grammars and PDAs. We'll present a few more here.

14.1 The Decidable Questions

Fortunately, the most important questions (i.e., the ones that must be answerable if context-free grammars are to be of any practical use) are decidable.

14.1.1 Membership

We begin with the most fundamental question, "Given a language L and a string w, is w in L?" Fortunately this question can be answered for every context-free language. By Theorem 12.1, for every context-free language L, there exists a PDA M such that M accepts L. But we must be careful. As we showed in Section 12.4, PDAs are not guaranteed to halt. So the mere existence of a PDA that accepts L does not guarantee the existence of a procedure that decides it (i.e., always halts and says yes or no appropriately).

It turns out that there are two alternative approaches to solving this problem, both of which work:

- Use a grammar: Using facts about every derivation that is produced by a grammar in Chomsky normal form, we can construct an algorithm that explores a finite number of derivation paths and finds one that derives a particular string w iff such a path exists.

- Use a PDA: While not all PDAs halt, it is possible, for any context-free language L, to craft a PDA M that is guaranteed to halt on all inputs and that accepts all strings in L and rejects all strings that are not in L.

Using a Grammar to Decide

We begin by considering the first alternative. We show a straightforward algorithm for deciding whether a string w is in a language L:

decideCFLusingGrammar(L: CFL, w: string) =

1. If L is specified as a PDA, use *PDAtoCFG*, presented in the proof of Theorem 12.2, to construct a grammar G such that $L(G) = L(M)$.

2. If L is specified as a grammar G, simply use G.

3. If $w = \varepsilon$ then if S_G is nullable (as defined in the description of *removeEps* in Section 11.7.4) then accept, otherwise reject.

4. If $w \neq \varepsilon$ then:

4.1. From G, construct G' such that $L(G') = L(G) - \{\varepsilon\}$ and G' is in Chomsky normal form.

4.2. If G derives w, it does so in $2 \cdot |w| - 1$ steps. Try all derivations in G of that number of steps. If one of them derives w, accept. Otherwise reject.

The running time of *decideCFLusingGrammar* can be analyzed as follows: We assume that the time required to build G' is constant, since it does not depend on w. Let $n = |w|$. Let g be the search-branching factor of G', defined to be the maximum number of rules that share a left-hand side. Then the number of derivations of length $2n - 1$ is bounded by g^{2n-1}, and it takes at most $2n - 1$ steps to check each one. So the worst-case running time of *decideCFLusingGrammar* is $\mathcal{O}(n2^n)$. In Section 15.3.1, we will present techniques that are substantially more efficient. We will describe the CKY algorithm, which, given a grammar G in Chomsky normal form, decides the membership question for G in time that is $\mathcal{O}(n^3)$. We will then describe an algorithm that can decide the question in time that is linear in n if the grammar that is provided meets certain requirements.

THEOREM 14.1 Decidability of Context-Free Languages

Theorem: Given a context-free language L (represented as either a context-free grammar or a PDA) and a string w, there exists a decision procedure that answers the question, "Is $w \in L$?"

Proof: The following algorithm, *decideCFL*, uses *decideCFLusingGrammar* to answer the question:

decideCFL(L: CFL, w: string) =

1. If *decideCFLusingGrammar(L, w)* accepts, return *True* else return *False*.

Using a PDA to Decide ✱

It is also possible to solve the membership problem using PDAs. We take a two-step approach. We first show that, for every context-free language L, it is possible to build a PDA that accepts $L - \{\varepsilon\}$ and that has no ε-transitions. Then we show that every PDA with no ε-transitions is guaranteed to halt.

THEOREM 14.2 Elimination of ε-Transitions

Theorem: Given any context-free grammar $G = (V, \Sigma, R, S)$, there exists a PDA M such that $L(M) = L(G) - \{\varepsilon\}$ and M contains no transitions of the form $((q_1, \varepsilon, \alpha), (q_2, \beta))$. In other words, every transition reads exactly one input character.

Proof: The proof is by a construction that begins by converting G to Greibach normal form. Recall that, in any grammar in Greibach normal form, all rules are of the form $X \rightarrow a\,A$, where $a \in \Sigma$ and $A \in (V - \Sigma)^*$. Now consider again the algorithm *cfgtoPDAtopdown*, which builds, from any context-free grammar G, a PDA M that, on input w, simulates G deriving w, starting from S. $M = (\{p, q\}, \Sigma, V, \Delta, p, \{q\})$, where Δ contains:

1. The start-up transition $((p, \varepsilon, \varepsilon), (q, S))$, which pushes the start symbol onto the stack and goes to state q.
2. For each rule $X \rightarrow s_1 s_2 \ldots s_n$ in R, the transition $((q, \varepsilon, X), (q, s_1 s_2 \ldots s_n))$, which replaces X by $s_1 s_2 \ldots s_n$. If $n = 0$ (i.e., the right-hand side of the rule is ε), then the transition $((q, \varepsilon, X), (q, \varepsilon))$.
3. For each character $c \in \Sigma$, the transition $((q, c, c), (q, \varepsilon))$, which compares an expected character from the stack against the next input character and continues if they match.

The start-up transition, plus all the transitions generated in step 2, are ε-transitions. But now suppose that G is in Greibach normal form. If G contains the rule $X \rightarrow c s_2 \ldots s_n$ (where $c \in \Sigma$ and s_2 through s_n are elements of V-Σ), it is not necessary to push c onto the stack, only to pop it with a rule from step 3. Instead, we collapse the push and the pop into a single transition. So we create a transition that can be taken only if the next input character is c. In that case, the string $s_2 \ldots s_n$ is pushed onto the stack.

Now we need only find a way to get rid of the start-up transition, whose job is to push S onto the stack so that the derivation process can begin. Since G is in Greibach normal form, any rules with S on the left-hand side must have the form $S \rightarrow c s_2 \ldots s_n$. So instead of reading no input and just pushing S, M will skip pushing S and instead, if the first input character is c, read it and push the string $s_2 \ldots s_n$.

Since terminal symbols are no longer pushed onto the stack, we no longer need the transitions created in step 3 of the original algorithm.

So $M = (\{p, q\}, \Sigma, V, \Delta, p, \{q\})$, where Δ contains:

1. The start-up transitions: For each rule $S \rightarrow cs_2 \ldots s_n$, the transition $((p, c, \varepsilon), (q, s_2 \ldots s_n))$.
2. For each rule $X \rightarrow cs_2 \ldots s_n$ (where $c \in \Sigma$ and s_2 through s_n are elements of $V - \Sigma$), the transition $((q, c, X), (q, s_2 \ldots s_n))$.

The following algorithm builds the required PDA:

cfgtoPDAnoeps(G: context-free grammar) =

1. Convert G to Greibach normal form, producing G'.
2. From G' build the PDA M described above.

THEOREM 14.3 Halting Behavior of PDAs Without ε-Transitions

Theorem: Let M be a PDA that contains no transitions of the form $((q_1, \varepsilon, s_1), (q_2, s_2))$, i.e., no ε-transitions. Consider the operation of M on input $w \in \Sigma^*$. M must halt and either accept or reject w. Let $n = |w|$. We make three additional claims:

a. Each individual computation of M must halt within n steps.

b. The total number of computations pursued by M must be less than or equal to b^n, where b is the maximum number of competing transitions from any state in M.

c. The total number of steps that will be executed by all computations of M is bounded by nb^n.

Proof:

a. Since each computation of M must consume one character of w at each step and M will halt when it runs out of input, each computation must halt within n steps.

b. M may split into at most b branches at each step in a computation. The number of steps in a computation is less than or equal to n. So the total number of computations must be less than or equal to b^n.

c. Since the maximum number of computations is b^n and the maximum length of each is n, the maximum number of steps that can be executed before all computations of M halt is nb^n.

So a second way to answer the question, "Given a context-free language L and a string w, is w in L?" is to execute the following algorithm:

decideCFLusingPDA(L: CFL, w: string) =

1. If L is specified as a PDA, use *PDAtoCFG*, as presented in the proof of Theorem 12.2, to construct a grammar G such that $L(G) = L(M)$.
2. If L is specified as a grammar G, simply use G.

3. If $w = \varepsilon$ then if S_G is nullable (as defined in the description of *removeEps* in Section 11.7.4) then accept, otherwise reject.

4. If $w \neq \varepsilon$ then:

4.1. From G, construct G' such that $L(G') = L(G) - \{\varepsilon\}$ and G' is in Greibach normal form.

4.2. From G' construct, using *cfgtoPDAnoeps*, the algorithm described in the proof of Theorem 14.2, a PDA M' such that $L(M') = L(G')$ and M' has no ε-transitions.

4.3. By Theorem 14.3, all paths of M' are guaranteed to halt within a finite number of steps. So run M' on w. Accept if M' accepts and reject otherwise.

The running time of *decideCFLusingPDA* can be analyzed as follows: We will take as a constant the time required to build M', since that can be done once. It need not be repeated for each string that is to be analyzed. Given M', the time required to analyze a string w is then the time required to simulate all paths of M' on w. Let $n = |w|$. From Theorem 14.3, we know that the total number of steps that will be executed by all paths of M is bounded by nb^n, where b is the maximum number of competing transitions from any state in M'. But is that number of steps required? If one state has a large number of competing transitions but the others do not, then the average branching factor will be less than b, so fewer steps will be necessary. But if b is greater than 1, the number of steps still grows exponentially with n. The exact number of steps also depends on how the simulation is done. A straightforward depth-first search of the tree of possibilities will explore b^n steps, which is less than nb^n because it does not start each path over at the beginning. But it still requires time that is $\mathcal{O}(b^n)$. In Section 15.2.3, we present an alternative approach to top-down parsing that runs in time that is linear in n if the grammar that is provided meets certain requirements.

14.1.2 Emptiness and Finiteness

While many interesting questions are not decidable for context-free languages, two others, in addition to membership are: emptiness and finiteness.

THEOREM 14.4 Decidability of Emptiness and Finiteness

Theorem: Given a context-free language L, there exists a decision procedure that answers each of the following questions:

1. Given a context-free language L, is $L = \varnothing$?
2. Given a context-free language L, is L infinite?

Since we have proven that there exists a grammar that generates L iff there exists a PDA that accepts it, these questions will have the same answers whether we ask them about grammars or about PDAs.

Proof:

1. Let $G = (V, \Sigma, R, S)$ be a context-free grammar that generates L. $L(G) = \varnothing$ iff S is unproductive (i.e., not able to generate any terminal strings). The following algorithm exploits the procedure *removeunproductive*, defined in Section 11.4, to remove all unproductive nonterminals from G. It answers the question, "Given a context-free language L, is $L = \varnothing$?"

   decideCFLempty(G: context-free grammar) =

   1. Let $G' = removeunproductive\,(G)$.
   2. If S is not present in G' then return *True* else return *False*.

2. Let $G = (V, \Sigma, R, S)$ be a context-free grammar that generates L. We use an argument similar to the one that we used to prove the context-free Pumping Theorem. Let n be the number of nonterminals in G. Let b be the branching factor of G. The longest string that G can generate without creating a parse tree with repeated nonterminals along some path is of length b^n. If G generates no strings of length greater than b^n, then $L(G)$ is finite. If G generates even one string w of length greater than b^n, then, by the same argument we used to prove the Pumping Theorem, it generates an infinite number of strings since $w = uvxyz$, $|vy| > 0$, and $\forall q \geq 0\ (uv^qxy^qz$ is in $L)$. So we could try to test to see whether L is infinite by invoking *decideCFL*(L, w) on all strings in Σ^* of length greater than b^n. If it returns *True* for any such string, then L is infinite. If it returns *False* on all such strings, then L is finite.

   But, assuming Σ is not empty, there is an infinite number of such strings. Fortunately, it is necessary to try only a finite number of them. Suppose that G generates even one string of length greater than $b^{n+1} + b^n$. Let t be the shortest such string. By the Pumping Theorem, $t = uvxyz$, $|vy| > 0$, and uxz (the result of pumping vy out once) $\in L$. Note that $|uxz| < |t|$ since some nonempty vy was pumped out of t to create it. Since, by assumption, t is the shortest string in L of length greater than $b^{n+1} + b^n$, $|uxz|$ must be less than or equal to $b^{n+1} + b^n$. But the Pumping Theorem also tells us that $|vxy| \leq k$ (i.e., b^{n+1}), so no more than b^{n+1} strings could have been pumped out of t. Thus we have that $b^n < |uxz| \leq b^{n+1} + b^n$. So, if L contains any strings of length greater than b^n, it must contain at least one string of length less than or equal to $b^{n+1} + b^n$. We can now define *decideCFLinfinite* to answer the question, "Given a context-free language L, is L infinite?":

   decideCFLinfinite(G: context-free grammar) =

   1. Lexicographically enumerate all strings in Σ^* of length greater than b^n and less than or equal to $b^{n+1} + b^n$.
   2. If, for any such string w, *decideCFL*(L, w) returns *True* then return *True*. L is infinite.
   3. If, for all such strings w, *decideCFL*(L, w) returns *False* then return *False*. L is not infinite.

14.1.3 Equality of Deterministic Context-Free languages

THEOREM 14.5 Decidability of Equivalence for Deterministic Context-Free Languages

Theorem: Given two *deterministic* context-free languages L_1 and L_2, there exists a decision procedure to determine whether $L_1 = L_2$.

Proof: This claim was not proved until 1997 and the proof [Sénizergues 2001] is beyond the scope of this book, but see 🖳.

14.2 The Undecidable Questions

Unfortunately, we will prove in Chapter 22 that there exists no decision procedure for many other questions that we might like to be able to ask about context-free languages, including:

- Given a context-free language L, is $L = \Sigma^*$?
- Given a context-free language L, is the complement of L context-free?
- Given a context-free language L, is L regular?
- Given two context-free languages L_1 and L_2, is $L_1 = L_2$? (Theorem 14.5 tells us that this question is decidable for the restricted case of two deterministic context-free languages. But it is undecidable in the more general case.)
- Given two context-free languages L_1 and L_2, is $L_1 \subseteq L_2$?
- Given two context-free languages L_1 and L_2, is $L_1 \cap L_2 = \varnothing$?
- Given a context-free language L, is L inherently ambiguous?
- Given a context-free grammar G, is G ambiguous?

14.3 Summary of Algorithms and Decision Procedures for Context-Free Languages

Although we have presented fewer algorithms and decision procedures for context-free languages than we did for regular languages, there are many important ones, which we summarize here:

- Algorithms that transform grammars:
  - *removeunproductive*(G: context-free grammar): Construct a grammar G' that contains no unproductive nonterminals and such that $L(G') = L(G)$.
  - *removeunreachable*(G: context-free grammar): Construct a grammar G' that contains no unreachable nonterminals and such that $L(G') = L(G)$.

- *removeEps*(G: context-free grammar): Construct a grammar G' that contains no rules of the form $X \rightarrow \varepsilon$ and such that $L(G') = L(G) - \{\varepsilon\}$.
- *atmostoneEps*(G: context-free grammar): Construct a grammar G' that contains no rules of the form $X \rightarrow \varepsilon$ except possibly $S^* \rightarrow \varepsilon$, in which case there are no rules whose right-hand side contains S^*, and such that $L(G') = L(G)$.
- *converttoChomsky*(G: context-free grammar): Construct a grammar G' in Chomsky normal form, where $L(G') = L(G) - \{\varepsilon\}$.
- *converttoGreibach*(G: context-free grammar): Construct a grammar G' in Greibach normal form, where $L(G') = L(G) - \{\varepsilon\}$.
- *removeUnits*(G: context-free grammar): Construct a grammar G' that contains no unit productions, where $L(G') = L(G)$.

- Algorithms that convert between context-free grammars and PDAs:
  - *cfgtoPDAtopdown*(G: context-free grammar): Construct a PDA M such that $L(M) = L(G)$ and M operates top-down to simulate a left-most derivation in G.
  - *cfgtoPDAbottomup*(G: context-free grammar): Construct a PDA M such that $L(M) = L(G)$ and M operates bottom up to simulate, backwards, a right-most derivation in G.
  - *cfgtoPDAnoeps*(G: context-free grammar): Construct a PDA M such that M contains no transitions of the form $((q_1, \varepsilon, s_1), (q_2, s_2))$ and $L(M) = L(G) - \{\varepsilon\}$.

- Algorithms that transform PDAs:
  - *convertPDAtorestricted*(M: PDA): Construct a PDA M' in restricted normal form where $L(M') = L(M)$.

- Algorithms that compute functions of languages defined as context-free grammars:
  - Given two grammars G_1 and G_2, construct a new grammar G_3 such that $L(G_3) = L(G_1) \cup L(G_2)$.
  - Given two grammars G_1 and G_2, construct a new grammar G_3 such that $L(G_3) = L(G_1)L(G_2)$.
  - Given a grammar G, construct a new grammar G' such that $L(G') = (L(G))^*$.
  - Given a grammar G, construct a new grammar G' such that $L(G') = (L(G))^R$.
  - Given a grammar G, construct a new grammar G' that accepts *letsub*($L(G)$), where *letsub* is a letter substitution function.

- Miscellaneous algorithms for PDAs:
  - *intersectPDAandFSM* (M_1: PDA, M_2: FSM): Construct a PDA M_3 such that $L(M_3) = L(M_1) \cap L(M_2)$.
  - *without$*($M$: PDA): If M accepts $L\$$, construct a PDA M' such that $L(M') = L$.
  - *complementdetPDA*(M: DPDA): If M accepts $L\$$, construct a PDA M' such that $L(M') = (\neg L)\$$.

- Decision procedures that answer questions about context-free languages:
  - *decideCFLusingPDA*(L: CFL, w : string): Decide whether w is in L.
  - *decideCFLusingGrammar*(L: CFL, w: string): Decide whether w is in L.
  - *decideCFL*(L: CFL, w: string): Decide whether w is in L.
  - *decideCFLempty*(G: context-free grammar): Decide whether $L(G) = \varnothing$.
  - *decideCFLinfinite*(G: context-free grammar): Decide whether $L(G)$ is infinite.j

Exercises

1. Give a decision procedure to answer each of the following questions:
   a. Given a regular expression α and a PDA M, is the language accepted by M a subset of the language generated by α?
   b. Given a context-free grammar G and two strings s_1 and s_2, does G generate s_1s_2?
   c. Given a context-free grammar G, does G generate at least three strings?
   d. Given a context-free grammar G, does G generate any even length strings?
   e. Given a regular grammar G, is $L(G)$ context-free?

CHAPTER 15

Context-Free Parsing◆

Programming languages are (mostly) context-free. Query languages are usually context-free. English can, in large part, be considered context-free. Strings in these languages need to be analyzed and interpreted by compilers, query engines, and various other kinds of application programs. So we need an algorithm that can, given a context-free grammar G:

1. Examine a string and decide whether or not it is a syntactically well-formed member of $L(G)$, and
2. If it is, assign to it a parse tree that describes its structure and thus can be used as the basis for further interpretation.

Are programming languages really context-free? (G.2)

In Section 14.1.1, we described two techniques that can be used to construct, from a grammar G, a decision procedure that answers the question, "Given a string w, is w in $L(G)$?" But we aren't done. We must still deal with the following issues:

- The first procedure, *decideCFLusingGrammar*, requires a grammar that is in Chomsky normal form. The second procedure, *decideCFLusingPDA*, requires a grammar that is in Greibach normal form. We would like to use a natural grammar so that the parsing process can produce a natural parse tree.
- Both procedures require search and take time that grows exponentially in the length of the input string. But we need efficient parsers, preferably ones that run in time that is linear in the length of the input string.
- All either procedure does is to determine membership in $L(G)$. It does not produce parse trees.

Query languages are context-free. (Q.1.1)

In this chapter we will sketch solutions to all of these problems. The discussion will be organized as follows:

- Easy issues:
  - Actually building parse trees: All of the parsers we will discuss work by applying grammar rules. So, to build a parse tree, it suffices to augment the parser with a function that builds a chunk of tree every time a rule is applied.
  - Using lookahead to reduce nondeterminism: It is often possible to reduce (or even eliminate) nondeterminism by allowing the parser to look ahead at the next one or more input symbols before it makes a decision about what to do.
- Lexical analysis: a preprocessing step in which strings of individual input characters are divided into strings of larger units, called tokens, that can be input to a parser.
- Top-down parsers:
  - A simple but inefficient recursive descent parser.
  - Modifying a grammar for top-down parsing.
  - LL parsing.
- Bottom-up parsers:
  - The simple but not efficient enough Cocke-Kasami-Younger (CKY) algorithm.
  - LR parsing.
- Parsers for English and other natural languages.

As we'll see, the bottom line on the efficiency of context-free parsing is the following. Let n be the length of the string to be parsed. Then:

- There exists a straightforward algorithm (CKY) that can parse any context-free language in $\mathcal{O}(n^3)$ time. While this is substantially better than the exponential time required to simulate the kind of nondeterministic PDAs that we built in Section 12.3, it isn't good enough for many practical applications. In addition, CKY requires its grammar to be in Chomsky normal form. There exists a much less straightforward version of CKY that can parse any context-free language in close to $\mathcal{O}(n^2)$ time.
- There exist algorithms that can parse large subclasses of context-free languages (including many of the ones we care about, like most programming languages and query languages) in $\mathcal{O}(n)$ time. There are reasonably straightforward top-down algorithms that can be built by hand. There are more efficient, more complicated bottom-up ones. But there exist tools that make building practical bottom-up parsers very easy.
- Parsing English, or any other natural language, is harder than parsing most artificial languages, which can be designed with parsing efficiency in mind.

```
level = observation - 17.5;
```

(a)

id	=	id	-	id	;

(b)

FIGURE 15.1 Lexical analysis.

15.1 Lexical Analysis

Consider the input string shown in Figure 15.1 (a). It contains 27 characters, including blanks. The job of lexical analysis is to convert it into a sequence of symbols like the one shown in Figure 15.1 (b).

We call each of the symbols that the lexical analyzer produces a ***token***. So, in this simple example, there are 6 tokens. In addition to creating a token stream, the lexical analyzer must be able to associate, with each token, some information about how it was formed. That information will matter when it comes time to assign meaning to the input string (for example by generating code).

In principle, we could skip lexical analysis. We could instead extend every grammar to include the rules by which simple constituents like identifiers and numbers are formed.

EXAMPLE 15.1 Specifying *id* with a Grammar

We could change our arithmetic expression grammar (from Example 11.19) so that *id* is a nonterminal rather than a terminal. We'd then have to add rules such as:

id → *identifier* | *integer* | *float*

identifier → *letter alphanum* /* a letter followed by zero or more alphanumerics.

alphanum → *letter alphnum* | *digit alphnum* | ε

integer → *-unsignedint* | *unsignedint* /* an optional minus sign followed by an unsigned integer.

unsignedint → *digit* | *digit unsignedint*

digit → 0 | 1 | 2 | 3 | 4 | 5 | 6 | 7 | 8 | 9

....

But there is an easier way to handle this early part of the parsing problem. We can write regular expressions that define legal identifiers and numbers. Those regular expressions can then be compiled into deterministic finite state machines, which can run in time that is linear in the length of the input.

Useful tools for building lexical analyzers, also called ***lexers***, are widely available. Lex is a good example of such a tool. The input to Lex is a set of rules. The left-hand side of each rule is a regular expression that describes the input strings to which the rule should apply. The right-hand side of each rule (enclosed in curly brackets) describes the output that should be created whenever the rule matches. The output of Lex is a lexical analyzer. When the analyzer runs, it matches its rules against an input stream. Any text that is not matched by any rule is simply echoed back into the output stream. Any text that is matched is replaced in the output stream by the right-hand side of the matching rule. The analyzer assumes a specific pattern of run-time communication between itself and a context-free parser to which it will be streaming tokens. In particular, it assumes the existence of a few shared variables, including one called *yylval*, into which the value that corresponds to the current token can be placed.

EXAMPLE 15.2 Some Simple Lex Rules

Here are some simple Lex rules:

```
1. [ \t]+;                                                  /* Get rid of blanks
                                                               and tabs.
2. [A-Za-z][A-Za-z0-9]*   { return(ID);   }                 /* Find identifiers.
3. [0-9]+                 { sscanf(yytext, "%d", &yylval);
                            return (INTEGER);  }            /* Return INTEGER
                                                               and put the value
                                                               in yylval.
```

- Rule 1 has just a left-hand side, which matches any string composed of just blanks and tabs. Since it has an empty right-hand side, the string it matches will be replaced by the empty string. So it could be used to get rid of blanks and tabs in the input if their only role is as delimiters. In this case, they will not correspond to any symbols in the grammar that the parser will use.
- Rule 2 has a left-hand side that can match any alphanumeric string that starts with a letter. Any substring it matches will be replaced by the value of its right-hand side, namely the token *id*. So this rule could be used to find identifiers. But since no information about what identifier was found is recorded, this rule is too simple for most applications.
- Rule 3 could be used to find integers. It returns the token INTEGER. But it also places the specific value that it matched into the shared variable *yylval*.

If two Lex rules match against a single piece of input text, the analyzer chooses between them as follows:

- A longer match is preferred over a shorter one.
- Among rules that match the same number of input characters, the one that was written first in the input to Lex is preferred.

EXAMPLE 15.3 How Lex Chooses Which Rule to Apply

Suppose that Lex has been give the following two rules:

1. `integer` {action 1}
2. `[a-z]+` {action 2}

Now consider what the analyzer it builds will do on the following input sequences:

`integers`	take action 2 because rule (2) matches the entire string `integers`, while rule (1) matches only the first 7 characters.
`integer`	take action 1 because both patterns match all 7 characters and rule (1) comes first.

Lex was specifically designed as a tool for building lexical analyzers to work with parsers generated with the parser-building tool Yacc, which we will describe in Section 15.3.

15.2 Top-Down Parsing

A top-down parser for a language defined by a grammar G works by creating a parse tree with a root labeled S_G. It then builds the rest of the tree, working downward from the root, using the rules in R_G. Whenever it creates a node that is labeled with a terminal symbol, it checks to see that it matches the next input symbol. If it does, the parser continues until it has built a tree that spans the entire input string. If the match fails, the parser terminates that path and tries an alternative way of applying the rules. If it runs out of alternatives, it reports failure. For some languages, described with certain kinds of grammars, it is possible to do all of this without ever having to consider more than one path, generally by looking one character ahead in the input stream before a decision about what to do next is made. We'll begin by describing a very general parser that conducts a depth-first search and typically requires backtracking. Then we'll consider grammar restrictions that may make deterministic top-down parsing possible.

15.2.1 Depth-First Search

We begin by describing a simple top-down parser that works in essentially the same way that the top-down PDAs that we built in Section 12.3.1 did. It attempts to reconstruct a left-most derivation of its input string. The only real difference is that it is now necessary to describe how nondeterminism will be handled. We'll use depth-first search with backtracking. The algorithm that we are about to present is similar to *decideCFLusingPDA*. They are both nondeterministic, top-down algorithms. But the one we present here, in contrast to *decideCFLusingPDA*, does not require a grammar in any particular form.

EXAMPLE 15.4 Top-Down, Depth-First Parsing

To see how a how a depth-first, top-down parser works, let's consider an English grammar that is even simpler than the one we used in Example 11.6. This time, we will require that every sentence end with the end-of-string marker $:

$S \rightarrow NP\,VP\,\$$

$NP \rightarrow$ `the` $N \mid N \mid ProperNoun$

$N \rightarrow$ `cat` | `dogs` | `bear` | `girl` | `chocolate` | `rifle`

$ProperNoun \rightarrow$ `Chris` | `Fluffy`

$VP \rightarrow V \mid V\ NP$

$V \rightarrow$ `like` | `likes` | `thinks` | `shot` | `smells`

On input `the cat likes chocolate` $, the parser, given these rules, will behave as follows:

- Build an *S* using the only rule available:

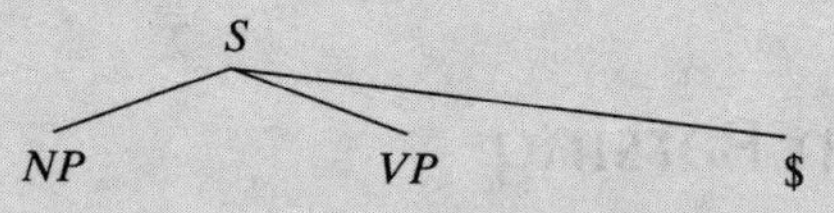

- Build an *NP*. Start with the first alternative, which successfully matches the first input symbol:

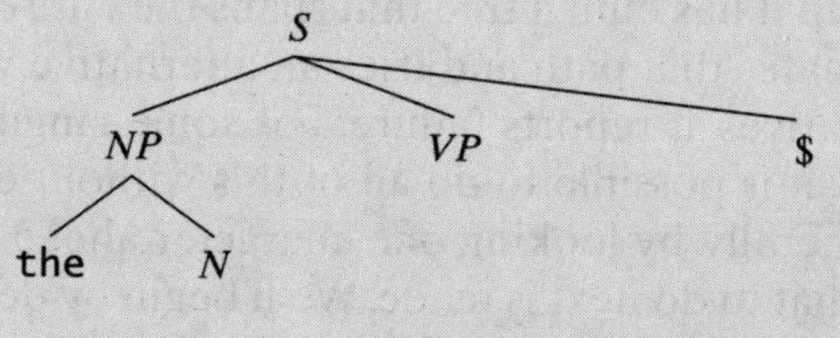

- Build an *N*. Start with the first alternative, which successfully matches the next input symbol:

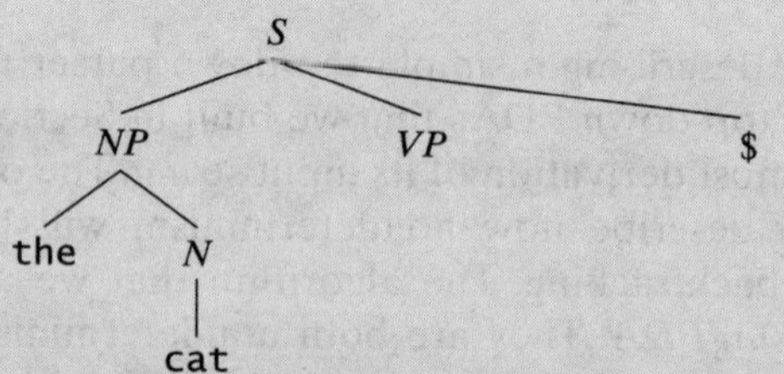

- Build a *VP*. Start with the first alternative:

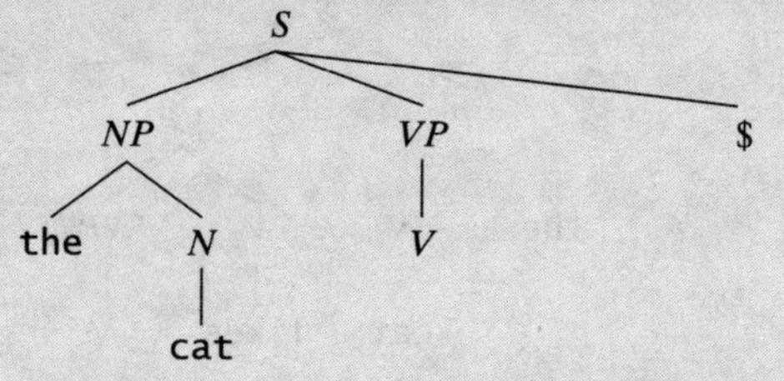

- Build a *V*. The first alternative, `like`, fails to match the input. The second, `likes`, matches:

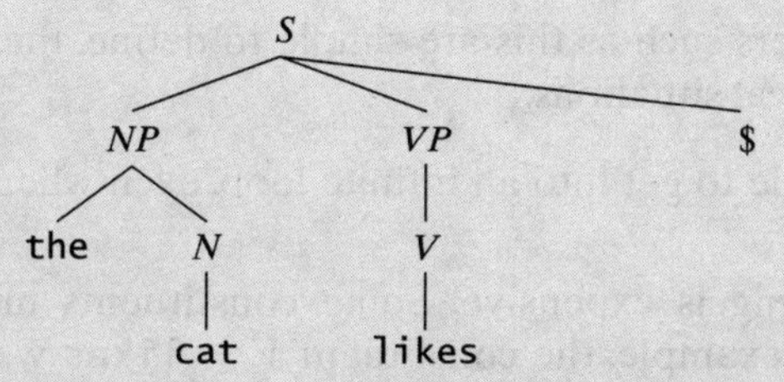

- Match $. This fails, since the word `chocolate` remains in the input. So the process undoes decisions, in order, until it has backtracked to:

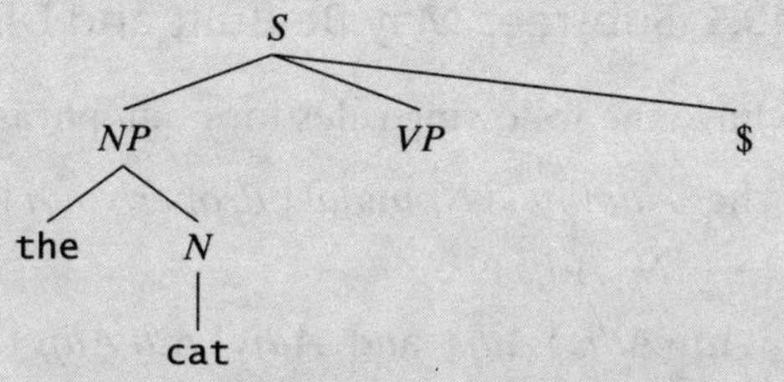

- Build a *VP*. This time, try the second alternative:

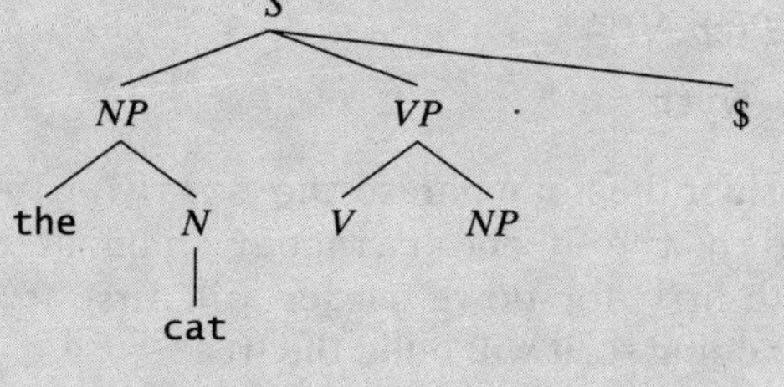

- Continue until a tree that spans the entire input has been built:

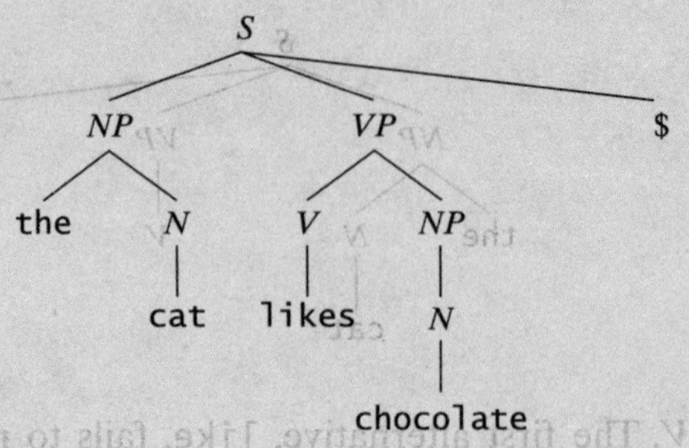

While parsers such as this are simple to define, there are two problems with using them in practical situations:

- It is possible to get into an infinite loop, even when there is a correct parse for the input.
- Backtracking is expensive. Some constituents may be built and unbuilt many times. For example, the constituent *V* → `likes` was built twice in the simple sentence shown in Example 15.4. We'll illustrate this problem on a larger scale in the next example.

EXAMPLE 15.5 Subtrees May Be Built and Discarded Many Times

Suppose we have the following rules for noun phrases:

NP → `the` *Nominal* | *Nominal* | *ProperNoun* | *NP PP*

Nominal → *N* | *Adjs N*

Adjs → *Adv Adjs* | *Adjs* `and` *Adjs* | *Adj Adjs* | *Adj*

N → `student` | `raincoat`

Adj → `tall` | `self-possessed` | `green`

Adv → `strikingly`

PP → *Prep NP*

Prep → `with`

Now consider the noun phrase `the strikingly tall and self-possessed student with the green raincoat`. In an attempt to parse this phrase as an *NP*, a depth-first, top-down parser will first try to use the rule *NP* → `the` *Nominal*. In doing so, it will build the tree:

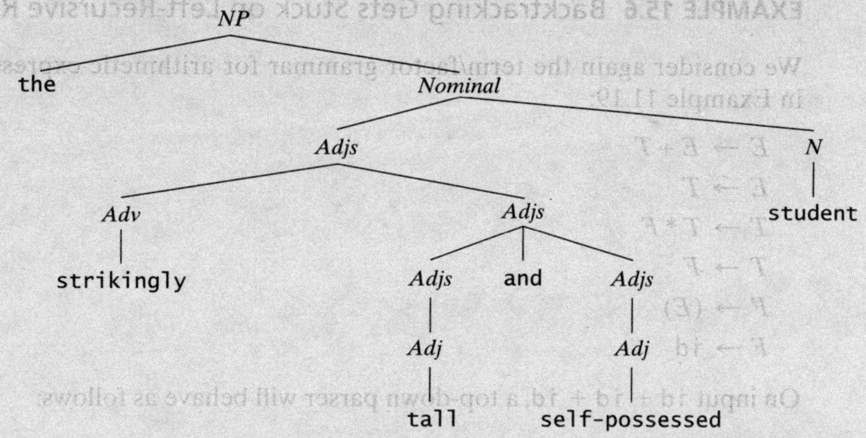

Then it will notice that four symbols, `with the green raincoat`, remain. At that point, it will have to back all the way up to the top *NP* and start over, this time using the rule *NP* → *NP PP*. It will eventually build an *NP* that spans the entire phrase[6]. But that *NP* will have, as a constituent, the one we just built and threw away. So the entire tree we showed above will have to be rebuilt from scratch.

Because constituents may be built and rebuilt many times, the depth-first algorithm that we just sketched may take time that is $\mathcal{O}(g^n)$, where g is the maximum number of alternatives for rewriting any nonterminal in the grammar and n is the number of input symbols.

Both the problem of infinite loops and the problem of inefficient rebuilding of constituents during backtracking can sometimes be fixed by rearranging the grammar and/or by looking ahead one or more characters before making a decision. In the next two sections we'll see how this may be done.

15.2.2 Modifying a Grammar for Top-Down Parsing

Some grammars are better than others for top-down parsing. In this section we consider two issues: preventing the parser from getting into an infinite loop and using lookahead to reduce nondeterminism.

Left-Recursive Rules and Infinite Loops

A top-down parser can get into an infinite loop and fail to find a complete parse tree, even when there is one.

[6]A separate issue is that this phrase is ambiguous. We've shown the parse that corresponds to the bracketing `strikingly (tall and self-possessed)`. An alternative parse corresponds to the bracketing `(strikingly tall) and self-possessed`.

EXAMPLE 15.6 Backtracking Gets Stuck on Left-Recursive Rules

We consider again the term/factor grammar for arithmetic expressions shown in Example 11.19:

$E \rightarrow E + T$

$E \rightarrow T$

$T \rightarrow T * F$

$T \rightarrow F$

$F \rightarrow (E)$

$F \rightarrow$ id

On input id + id + id, a top-down parser will behave as follows:

- Build an E, using the first alternative:

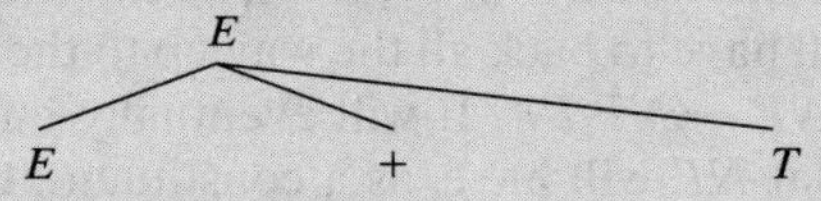

- Build an E, using the first alternative:

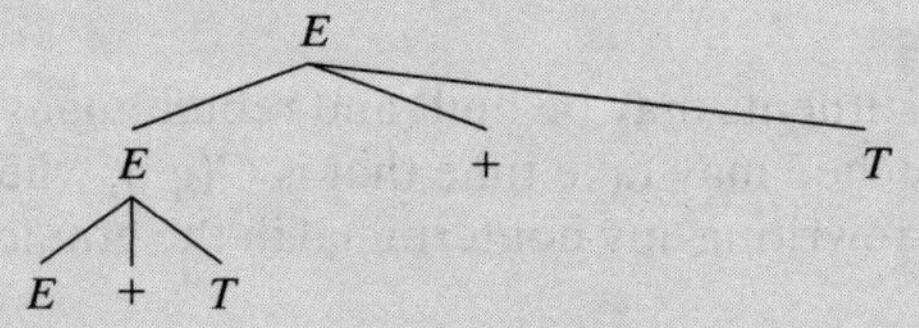

- Build an E, using the first alternative, and so forth, forever, expanding the left-most E as $E + T$.

The problem is the existence in the grammar of left-recursive rules like $E \rightarrow E + T$ and $T \rightarrow T * F$. Paralleling the definition we gave in Section 11.2 for a recursive rule, we say that a grammar rule is ***left-recursive*** iff it is of the form $X \rightarrow Yw_2$ and $Y \Rightarrow_G^* Xw_4$, where w_2 and w_4 may be any element of V^*. If the rules were rewritten so that the recursive symbols were on the right of the right-hand side rather than on the left of it, the parser would be able to make progress and consume the input symbols.

We first consider direct recursion, i.e., rules of the form $X \rightarrow Xw_2$. This case includes the rules $E \rightarrow E + T$ and $T \rightarrow T * F$. Suppose that such a rule is used to derive a string in $L(G)$. For example, let's use the rule $E \rightarrow E + T$. Then there is a derivation that looks like:

$$E \Rightarrow E + T \Rightarrow E + T + T \Rightarrow \ldots \Rightarrow T + T \ldots + T \Rightarrow \ldots.$$

In other words, the left-recursive rule is applied some number of times but then the recursion stops and some nonrecursive rule with the same left-hand side is applied. In this example, it was the rule $E \rightarrow T$. The left-most symbol in the string we just derived came from the nonrecursive rule. So an alternative way to generate that string would be to generate that leftmost T first, by applying once a new rule $E \rightarrow T\,E'$. Then we can generate the rest by applying, as many times as necessary, a new recursive (but not left-recursive) rule $E' \rightarrow +T\,E'$, followed by a clean-up rule $E' \rightarrow \varepsilon$, which will stop the recursion.

Applying this idea to our arithmetic expression grammar, we get the new grammar:

$E \rightarrow T E'$
$E' \rightarrow +T E'$
$E' \rightarrow \varepsilon$
$T \rightarrow F T'$
$T' \rightarrow *F T'$
$T' \rightarrow \varepsilon$
$F \rightarrow (E)$
$F \rightarrow$ id

We can describe what we just did more generally as follows: Given any context-free grammar G, if G contains any left-recursive rule with left-hand side A, then consider all rules in G with left-hand side A. Divide them into two groups, the left-recursive ones and the others. Replace all of them with new rules, as shown in Table 15.1.

If, in addition to removing left-recursion, we want to avoid introducing ε-rules, we can use a variant of this algorithm. Instead of always generating A' and then erasing it at the end of the recursive part of a derivation, we create rules that allow it not to be generated. So we replace each original left-recursive rule, $A \rightarrow A\alpha_k$, with *two* new rules: $A' \rightarrow \alpha_k A'$ and $A' \rightarrow \alpha_k$. Instead of replacing each original nonleft-recursive rule, $A \rightarrow \beta_k$, we keep it and add the new rule: $A \rightarrow \beta_k A'$. We do not add the rule $A' \rightarrow \varepsilon$. Because we will have another use for this variant of the algorithm (in converting grammars to Greibach normal form), we will give it the name *removeleftrecursion*(N: nonterminal symbol).

Table 15.1 Eliminating left-recursive rules.

Original left-recursive rules:	***Replace with:***
$A \rightarrow A\alpha_1$ $A \rightarrow A\alpha_2$ … $A \rightarrow A\alpha_n$	$A' \rightarrow \alpha_1 A'$ $A' \rightarrow \alpha_2 A'$ … $A' \rightarrow \alpha_n A'$ $A' \rightarrow \varepsilon$
Original nonleft-recursive rules:	***Replace with:***
$A \rightarrow \beta_1$ $A \rightarrow \beta_2$ … $A \rightarrow \beta_m$	$A \rightarrow \beta_1 A'$ $A \rightarrow \beta_2 A'$ … $A \rightarrow \beta_m A'$

Unfortunately, the technique that we have just presented, while it does eliminate direct left recursion, does not solve the entire problem. Consider the following grammar G:

$$S \rightarrow Y\mathrm{a}$$
$$Y \rightarrow S\mathrm{a}$$
$$Y \rightarrow \varepsilon$$

G contains no directly left-recursive rules. But G does contain left-recursive rules, and a top-down parser that used G would get stuck building the infinite left-most derivation $S \Rightarrow Y\mathrm{a} \Rightarrow S\mathrm{aa} \Rightarrow Y\mathrm{aaa} \Rightarrow S\mathrm{aaaa} \Rightarrow \ldots.$ It is possible to eliminate this kind of left-recursion as well by using an algorithm that loops through all the nonterminal symbols in G and applies the algorithm that we just presented to eliminate direct left-recursion.

So left-recursion can be eliminated and the problem of infinite looping in top-down parsers can be solved. Unfortunately, the elimination of left-recursion comes at a price. Consider the input string `id` + `id` + `id`. Figure 15.2(a) shows the parse trees that will be produced for it using our original expression grammar. Figure 15.2(b) shows the new one, with no left-recursive rules.

Notice that, in the original parse tree, the + operator associates left, while in the new parse tree it associates right. Since the goal of producing a parse tree is to serve as the first step toward assigning meaning to the input string (for example, by writing code to correspond to it), this change is significant. In order to solve our parsing problem, we've changed the meaning of at least some strings in the language we are trying to parse.

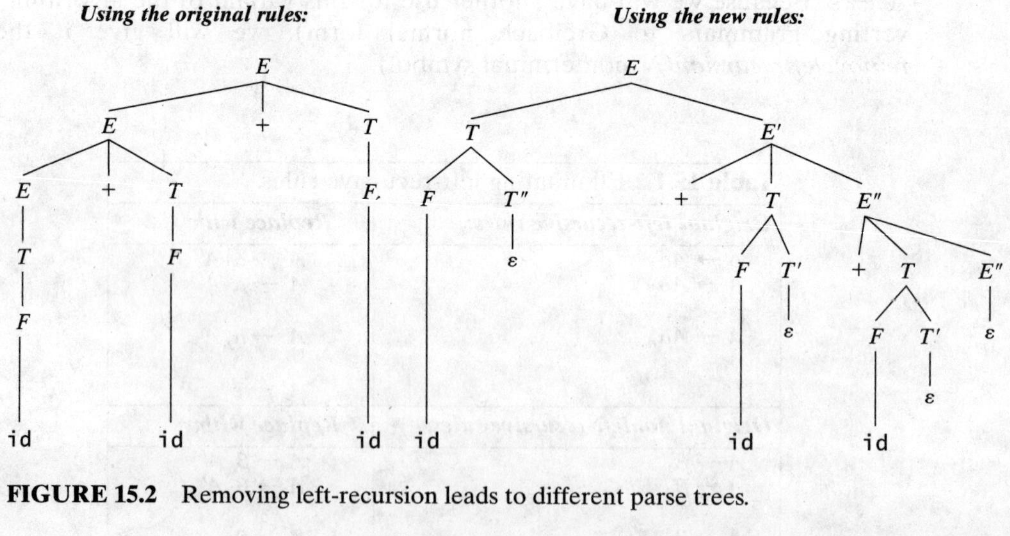

FIGURE 15.2 Removing left-recursion leads to different parse trees.

Using Lookahead and Left Factoring to Reduce Nondeterminism

As we saw in Example 15.4 (the simple English example), a depth-first, top-down parser may have to explore multiple derivations before it finds the one that corresponds to the current input string. The process we just described for getting rid of left-recursive rules does nothing to affect that. So we would still like to find a technique for reducing or eliminating the need for search. Sometimes it is possible to analyze a grammar in advance and determine that some paths will never lead to a complete derivation of a string of terminal symbols. But the more important case arises, as it did even with our very simple grammar of English, when the correct derivation depends on the current input string. When that happens, the best source of guidance for the parser is the input string itself and its best strategy is to procrastinate branching as long as possible in order to be able to use the input to inform its decisions. To implement this strategy, we'll consider doing two things:

- Changing the parsing algorithm so that it exploits the ability to look one symbol ahead in the input before it makes a decision about what to do next, and
- Changing the grammar to help the parser procrastinate decisions.

We can explore both of these issues by considering just a fragment of our arithmetic-expression grammar, which we'll augment with one new rule that describes simple function calls. So consider just the following set of three rules:

1. $F \rightarrow (E)$

2. $F \rightarrow$ `id`

3. $F \rightarrow$ `id`(E) /* This is a new rule that describes a call to a unary function.

If a top-down parser needs to expand a node labeled F, which rule should it use? If it can look one symbol ahead in the input before deciding, it can choose between rule 1, which it should apply if the next character is (, and rules 2 and 3, one of which should be applied if the next symbol is `id`.

But how can a parser choose between rules 2 and 3 if it can look only one symbol ahead? The answer is to change the grammar so that the decision can be procrastinated. In particular, we will rewrite the grammar as:

1. $F \rightarrow (E)$

1.1. $F \rightarrow$ `id` X

2. $X \rightarrow \varepsilon$

3. $X \rightarrow (E)$

Now, if the lookahead symbol is `id`, the parser will apply rule 1.1. Then it will match the `id` and set the lookahead symbol to the following symbol. Next it must decide whether to expand X by rule 2 or rule 3. But it is one symbol farther along in the input as it faces this decision. If the next input symbol is (, it is possible that either rule should be chosen (although see below for an additional technique that may resolve this conflict as well). But if the next input symbol is anything else, only rule 2 can possibly lead to a complete parse.

The operation that we just did is called ***left factoring***. It can be described as follows: Let G be a context-free grammar that contains two or more rules with the same left-hand side and the same initial sequence of symbols on the right-hand side. Suppose those rules are:

$$A \rightarrow \alpha\beta_1$$
$$A \rightarrow \alpha\beta_2$$
$$\ldots$$
$$A \rightarrow \alpha\beta_n$$

where $\alpha \neq \varepsilon$ and $n \geq 2$. We remove those rules from G and replace them with the rules:

$$A \rightarrow \alpha A'$$
$$A' \rightarrow \beta_1$$
$$A' \rightarrow \beta_2$$
$$\ldots$$
$$A' \rightarrow \beta_n$$

A parser that uses this new grammar will still have to make a decision about what to do after it has read the input sequence α. But it will probably be farther along in the input string by the time it has to do that.

15.2.3 Deterministic Top-Down Parsing with LL(1) Grammars

Can we do better? We know, from Theorem 13.13, that there exist context-free languages for which no deterministic PDA exists. So there will be context-free languages for which the techniques that we have just described will not be able to remove all sources of nondeterminism. But do we care about them? Could we build a deterministic, linear-time parser for:

1. A typical programming language like Java or C++ or Haskell?
2. A typical database query language?
3. A typical Web search query language?
4. English or Chinese?

The answer to questions 1 through 3 is yes. The answer to question 4 is mostly no, although there have been some partially successful attempts to do so. Using techniques such as the ones we just described, it is sometimes possible to craft a grammar for which a deterministic top-down parser exists. Such parsers are often also called ***predictive parsers***. To simplify the rest of this discussion, assume that every input string ends with the end-of-string marker \$. This means that, until after the \$ is reached, there is always a next symbol, which we will call the lookahead character.

It will be possible to build a predictive top-down parser for a grammar G precisely in case every string that is generated by G has a unique left-most derivation and it is possible to determine each step in that derivation by looking ahead some fixed number k of characters in the input stream. In this case, we say that G is **LL(*k*)**, so named because an LL(k) grammar allows a predictive parser that scans its input left to right (the origin of the first L in the name) to build a left-most derivation (the origin of the second L) if it is allowed k lookahead symbols. Note that every LL(k) grammar is unambiguous (because every string it generates has a unique left-most derivation). It is not the case, however, that every unambiguous grammar is LL(k).

Most predictive parsers use a single lookahead symbol. So we are interested in determining whether or not a grammar G is LL(1). To do so, it is useful to define two functions:

- Given a grammar G and a sequence of symbols α, define $first(\alpha)$ to be the set of all terminal symbols that can occur as the first symbol in any string derived from α using R_G. If α derives ε, then $\varepsilon \in first(\alpha)$.
- Given a grammar G and a nonterminal symbol A, define $follow(A)$ to be the set of all terminal symbols that can immediately follow whatever A produces in some string in $L(G)$.

EXAMPLE 15.7 Computing *First* and *Follow*

Consider the following simple grammar G:

$$S \rightarrow AXB\$$$
$$A \rightarrow \text{a}A \mid \varepsilon$$
$$X \rightarrow \text{c} \mid \varepsilon$$
$$B \rightarrow \text{b}B \mid \varepsilon$$

- $first(S) = \{\text{a}, \text{c}, \text{b}, \$\}$.
- $first(A) = \{\text{a}, \varepsilon\}$.
- $first(AX) = \{\text{a}, \text{c}, \varepsilon\}$.
- $first(AXB) = \{\text{a}, \text{c}, \text{b}, \varepsilon\}$.
- $follow(S) = \varnothing$.
- $follow(A) = \{\text{c}, \text{b}, \$\}$.
- $follow(X) = \{\text{b}, \$\}$.
- $follow(B) = \{\$\}$.

We can now state the conditions under which a grammar G is LL(1). It is iff, whenever G contains two competing rules $A \rightarrow \alpha$ and $A \rightarrow \beta$, all of the following are true:

- There is no terminal symbol that is an element of both *first*(α) and *first*(β).
- ε cannot be derived from both α and β.
- If ε can be derived from one of α or β, assume it is α. Then there may be two competing derivations:

$$\begin{aligned} S &\Rightarrow \gamma_1 A \gamma_2 \\ &\Rightarrow \gamma_1 \alpha \gamma_2 \\ &\Rightarrow \gamma_1 \quad \gamma_2 \end{aligned} \qquad \text{and} \qquad \begin{aligned} S &\Rightarrow \gamma_1 A \gamma_2 \\ &\Rightarrow \gamma_1 \beta \gamma_2 \end{aligned}$$

Consider the information available to a predictive parser when it has to choose how to expand A. It has consumed the input up through γ_1. So, when it looks one character ahead, it will find the first character of γ_2 (in case $A \Rightarrow \alpha \Rightarrow \varepsilon$) or it will find the first character of β (in case $A \Rightarrow \beta$). So we require that there be no terminal symbol that is an element of both *follow*(A) (which describes the possible first terminal symbols in γ_2) and *first*(β).

We define a language to be LL(k) iff there exists an LL(k) grammar for it. Not all context-free languages are LL(k) for any fixed k. In particular, no inherently ambiguous one is, since every LL(k) grammar is unambiguous. There are also languages for which there exists an unambiguous grammar but no LL(k) one. For example, consider $\{a^n b^n c^m d : n, m \geq 0\} \cup \{a^n b^m c^m e : n, m \geq 0\}$, which is unambiguous, but not LL(k), for any k, since there is no fixed bound on the number of lookahead symbols that must be examined in order to determine whether a given input string belongs to the first or the second sublanguage. There are even deterministic context-free languages that are not LL(k), for any k. One such example is $\{a^n b^n, n \geq 0\} \cup \{a^n c^n, n \geq 0\}$. (Intuitively, the problem there is that, given a string w, it is not possible to determine the first step in the derivation of w until either a b or a c is read.) But many practical languages are LL(k). In fact, many are LL(1), so it is worth looking at ways to exploit this property in the design of a top-down parser.

There are two reasonably straightforward ways to go about building a predictive parser for a language L that is described by an LL(1) grammar G. We consider each of them briefly here.

Recursive Descent Parsing

A ***recursive-descent parser*** contains one function for each nonterminal symbol A in G. The argument of each such function is a parse tree node labeled A, and the function's job is to create the appropriate parse tree beneath the node that it is given. The function corresponding to the nonterminal A can be thought of as a case statement, with one alternative for each of the ways that A can be expanded. Each such alternative checks whether the next chunk of input could have been derived from A using the rule in question. It checks each terminal symbol directly. To check each nonterminal symbol, it invokes the function that is defined for it. The name "recursive descent" comes from the fact that most context-free grammars contain recursive rules, so the parser will typically exploit recursive function calls.

EXAMPLE 15.8 Recursive Descent Parsing

Let G include the rules:

$A \rightarrow BA \mid \mathsf{a}$

$B \rightarrow \mathsf{b}B \mid \mathsf{b}$

The function associated with A will then be (ignoring many details, including how the next lookahead symbol is computed, how the parse tree is actually built, and what happens on input strings that are not in $L(G)$):

A(n: parse tree node labeled A) =

case (lookahead = b : /* Use the rule $A \rightarrow BA$.
Invoke B on a new daughter node labeled B.
Invoke A on a second new daughter node labeled A.

lookahead = a : /* Use the rule $A \rightarrow$ a.
Create a new daughter node labeled a.

Table-Driven LL(1) Parsing

Instead of letting a set of recursive function calls implicitly maintain a stack, we could build a parser that works in much the same way that the top-down PDAs of Section 12.3.1 do. Such a parser would maintain its stack explicitly.

Consider all of the transitions that such a parser can take. We can index them in a table called a ***parse table***, which contains one row for each nonterminal that could be on the top of the stack and one column for each terminal symbol that could correspond to the lookahead symbol. Then we can build a straightforward table-driven parser that chooses its next move by using the current top-of-stack and lookahead symbols as indices into the table.

EXAMPLE 15.9 Building a Parse Table

Let G be:

$S \rightarrow AB\$ \mid AC\$$

$A \rightarrow \mathsf{a}A \mid \mathsf{a}$

$B \rightarrow \mathsf{b}B \mid \mathsf{b}$

$C \rightarrow \mathsf{c}$

The parse table for G would be:

Lookahead symbol / *Top of stack*	a	b	c	\$
S	$S \rightarrow AB\$$ $S \rightarrow AC\$$			
A	$A \rightarrow$ aA $A \rightarrow$ a			
B		$B \rightarrow$ bB $B \rightarrow$ b		
C			$C \rightarrow$ c	

Notice two things about the parse table that we just built:

- Many of the cells are empty. If the parser looks in the table and finds an empty cell, it knows that it has hit a dead-end: The path it is currently following will never succeed in parsing the input string.
- Some of the cells contain more than one rule. A parser that used that table as the basis for choosing its next move would thus be nondeterministic. Suppose, on the other hand, we could guarantee that the table contained at most one rule in each cell. Then a parser that was driven by it would be deterministic.

Given any LL(1) grammar G, it is possible to build a parse table with at most one rule in each cell. Thus it is possible to build a deterministic (predictive) table-driven parser for G. The parser simply consults the table at each step and applies the rule that is specified.

Note that the grammar of Example 15.9 is not LL(1) because a is an element of both *first*(AB\$) and *first*(AC\$). Thus there are two ways to expand S if the lookahead symbol is a. There are also two ways to expand A if the lookahead symbol is a and two ways to expand B if the lookahead symbol is b. But the language described by that grammar is LL(1). We leave the construction of an LL(1) grammar for it as an exercise.

LL(1) parsers can be built by hand, but there exist tools 🖳 that greatly simplify the process.

15.3 Bottom-Up Parsing

Rather than parsing top-down, as we have just described, an alternative is to parse bottom-up, and thus drive the process directly by the current string of input symbols.

A bottom-up parser for a language defined by a grammar G works by creating the bottom nodes of a parse tree and labeling them with the terminal symbols in the input. Then it attempts to build a complete parse tree above those nodes. It does this by applying the rules in R_G backwards. In other words, suppose that a sequence of nodes labeled $x_1, x_2, \ldots x_n$ has already been built and R_G contains the rule:

$$X \rightarrow x_1, x_2, \ldots x_n$$

Then the parser can build a node, label it X, and insert the nodes labeled $x_1, x_2, \ldots x_n$ as its children. If the parser succeeds in building a tree that spans the entire input and whose root is labeled S_G, then it has succeeded. If there is no path by which it can do that, it fails and reports that the input string is not in $L(G)$.

Since there may be choices for which rule to apply at any point in this process, a bottom-up parser patterned after the PDAs that we built in Section 12.3.1 may be nondeterministic and its running time may grow exponentially in the length of the input string. That is clearly unacceptable for a practical parser. In the next section we describe a straightforward bottom-up parsing algorithm with running time that is $\mathcal{O}(n^3)$. But even that may not be good enough. Fortunately, just as we did for top-down parsing, we can construct a deterministic parser that runs in time that is $\mathcal{O}(n)$ if we impose some restrictions on the grammars that we use.

15.3.1 The Cocke-Kasami-Younger Algorithm

A straightforward, bottom-up parser that handles nondeterminism by backtracking typically wastes a lot of time building and rebuilding nodes as it backtracks. An alternative is a dynamic programming approach in which each possible constituent is built (bottom-up) exactly once and then made available to any later rules that want to use it.

The Cocke-Kasami-Younger algorithm (also called CKY or CYK) works by storing such constituents in a two dimensional table T that contains one column for each input symbol and one row for each possible substring length. Call the input string w and let its length be n. Then T contains one row and one column for each integer between 1 and n. We will number the rows of T starting at the bottom and the columns starting from the left. For all i and j between 1 and n, each cell $T[i, j]$ corresponds to the substring of w that extends for i symbols and starts in position j. The value that will eventually fill each such cell will be the set of nonterminal symbols that could derive the string to which the cell corresponds. For example, to parse the string id + id ∗ id, we would need to fill in the cells in Table 15.2. Note that each cell is labeled with the substring to which it corresponds, not with the value it will eventually take on.

Let G be the grammar that is to be used. Initially, each cell in T will be blank. The parser will begin filling in T, starting from the bottom, and then moving upward to row n. When it is complete, each cell in the lower triangle of T will contain the set of nonterminal symbols that could have generated the corresponding substring. If the start symbol of G occurs in $T[n, 1]$, then G can generate the substring that starts in position 1 and has length n. But that is exactly w. So G can generate w.

Table 15.2 The table that a CKY parser builds. Each cell will eventually contain the set of nonterminals that can derive the constituent, shown here, to which the cell corresponds.

Row 5	id + id ∗ id				
Row 4	id + id ∗	+ id ∗ id			
Row 3	id + id	+ id ∗	id ∗ id		
Row 2	id+	+ id	id ∗	∗ id	
Row 1	id	+	id	∗	id
Input string:	**id**	+	**id**	∗	**id**

The CKY algorithm requires that the grammar that it uses be in Chomsky normal form. Recall that, in a Chomsky normal form grammar, all rules have one of the following two forms:

- $X \rightarrow a$, where $a \in \Sigma$, or
- $X \rightarrow BC$, where B and C are elements of $V - \Sigma$.

So we need two separate techniques for filling in T:

- To fill in row 1, use rules of the form $X \rightarrow a$. In particular, if $X \rightarrow a$ and a is the symbol associated with column j, then add X to $T[1, j]$.
- To fill in rows 2 through n, use rules of the form $X \rightarrow BC$, since they are the ones that can combine constituents to form larger ones. Suppose the parser is working on some cell in row k. It wants to determine whether the rule $X \rightarrow BC$ can be used to generate the corresponding substring s of length k. If it can, then there must be some way to divide s into exactly two constituents, one corresponding to B and the other corresponding to C. Since both of those constituents must be shorter than s, any ways there are of building them must already be represented in cells in rows below k.

We can now state the CKY algorithm as follows:

$CKY(G$: Chomsky normal form grammar, $w = a_1a_2 \ldots a_n$: string) =

/* Fill in the first (bottom-most) row of T, checking each symbol in w and finding all the nonterminals that could have generated it.

1. For $j = 1$ to n do:
    If G contains the rule $X \rightarrow a_j$, then add X to $T[1, j]$.

/* Fill in the remaining rows, starting with row 2 and going upward.

2. For $i = 2$ to n do: /* For each row after the first
    For $j = 1$ to $n - i + 1$ do: /* For each column in the lower triangle of T
        For $k = 1$ to $i - 1$ do: /* For each character after which there could be a split into two constituents
            For each rule $X \rightarrow YZ$ do:
If $Y \in T[k, j]$ and $Z \in T[i - k, j + k]$, then: /* Y and Z found.
                Insert X into $T[i, j]$.

3. If $S_G \in T[n, 1]$ then accept else reject.

The core matching operation occurs in the step flagged with ####. The parser must determine whether X could have generated the substring that starts in position j and has length i. It is currently considering splitting that substring after the kth symbol. So it checks whether Y could have generated the first piece, namely the one that starts in position j and has length k. And it checks whether Z could have generated the second piece, namely the one that starts in position $j + k$ and whose length is equal to the length of the original substring minus the part that Y matched. That is $i - k$.

EXAMPLE 15.10 The CKY Algorithm

Consider parsing the string aab with the grammar:

$S \rightarrow A\ B$
$A \rightarrow A\ A$
$A \rightarrow$ a
$B \rightarrow$ a
$B \rightarrow$ b

CKY begins by filling in the bottom row of T as follows:

Row 3			
Row 2			
Row 1	A, B	A, B	B
Input string:	a	a	b

Notice that, at this point, the algorithm has no way of knowing whether the a's were generated by A or by B.

Next, the algorithm moves on to step 2. Setting i to 2, it fills in the second row, corresponding to substrings of length 2, as follows: When i is 2 and j is 1, it is considering ways of generating the initial substring aa. Setting k to 1, it considers splitting it into a and a. Then, considering the rule $S \rightarrow AB$, it finds the A and the B that it needs in row 1, so it adds S to $T[2, 1]$. Similarly for the rule $A \rightarrow AA$, so it adds A to $T[2, 1]$. It then sets j to 2 and looks at ways of generating substrings that start in position 2. Setting k to 1, it considers splitting ab into a and b. Considering the rule $S \rightarrow AB$, it finds the A and the B that it needs, so it adds S to $T[2, 2]$. At this point, T is:

Row 3			
Row 2	S, A	S	
Row 1	A, B	A, B	B
Input string:	a	a	b

Next CKY sets i to 3. So it is considering strings of length 3. There is only one, namely the one that starts at position 1. So the only value of j that will be considered is 1. There are now two values of k to consider, since there are two ways that the string aba can be split in two. Setting k to 1, it is considering the constituents a and ab. Considering the rule $S \rightarrow AB$, it looks for an A of length 1 starting in position 1 (which it finds) and a B of length 2 starting in position 2 (which it fails to find). It then considers the other rule, $A \rightarrow AA$. For this rule to succeed there would have to be an A of length 1 in position 1 (which it finds) and a second A of length 2 starting in position 2 (which it fails to find). Notice that, since it needs an A of length 2, it must look in row 2. The A in row 1 doesn't help. So it has found

EXAMPLE 15.10 (*Continued*)

nothing by breaking the string after position 1. It sets k to 2 and considers breaking it, after position 2, into aa and b. Now it again tries the first rule, $S \rightarrow AB$. It looks in row 2 for an A that generated aa and in row 1 for a B that generated b. It finds both and inserts S into $T[3, 1]$. So it accepts.

The algorithm that we just presented does not actually build a parse tree. It simply decides whether the string w is in $L(G)$. It can easily be modified to build parse trees as it applies rules. Then the final parse tree for w is the one associated with the start symbol in $T[n, 1]$. If G is ambiguous, there may be more than one such tree.

We can analyze the complexity of CKY as follows: We will assume that the size of the grammar G is a constant, so any operation whose complexity is dependent only on the size of G takes constant time. This means that the code inside the loop of step 1 and the testing of all grammar rules that is done inside the loop of step 2 each take constant time. Step 1 takes time that is $\mathcal{O}(n)$. Step 2 can be analyzed as follows:

- The outer loop (i) is executed $n - 1$ times.
- The next loop (j) is executed, on average $n/2$ times and at most $n - 1$ times.
- The next loop (k) is also executed, on average $n/2$ times and at most $n - 1$ times.
- The inner loop takes constant time.

So step 2 takes time that is $\mathcal{O}((n - 1)(n/2)(n/2)) = \mathcal{O}(n^3)$. Step 3 takes constant time. So the total time is $\mathcal{O}(n^3)$.

If we also want to consider the size of G, then let $|G|$ be the number of rules in G. If G is in Chomsky Normal form, CKY takes time that is $\mathcal{O}(n^3 \cdot |G|)$. But if G is not already in Chomsky Normal form, it must first be converted, and that process can take time that is $\mathcal{O}(\cdot |G|^2)$. So we have that the total time required by CKY is $\mathcal{O}(n^3 \cdot |G|^2)$.

15.3.2 Context-Free Parsing and Matrix Multiplication

The CKY algorithm can be described in terms of Boolean matrix multiplication. Stated that way, its time efficiency depends on the efficiency of Boolean matrix multiplication. In particular, again assuming that the size of the grammar is constant, the running time becomes $\mathcal{O}(M(n))$, where $M(n)$ is the time required to multiply two $n \times n$ Boolean matrices. Straightforward matrix multiplication algorithms (such as Gaussian elimination) take time that is $\mathcal{O}(n^3)$, so this recasting of the algorithm has no effect on its complexity. But faster matrix multiplication algorithms exist. For example, Strassen's algorithm (described in Exercise 27.9) reduces the time to $\mathcal{O}(n^{2.807})$, but at a price of increased complexity and a structure that makes it less efficient for small to medium values of n. The fastest known technique, the Coppersmith-Winograd algorithm 💻, has worst case running time that is $\mathcal{O}(n^{2.376})$, but it is too complex to be practical.

More recently, a further result 💻 that links matrix multiplication and context-free parsing has been shown: Let P be any context-free parser with time complexity $\mathcal{O}(gn^{3-\varepsilon})$, where g is the size of the grammar and n is the length of the input string. Then

P can be efficiently converted into an algorithm to multiply two $n \times n$ Boolean matrices in time $\mathcal{O}(n^{3-\varepsilon/3})$. So, if there were a fast algorithm for parsing arbitrary context-free languages, there would also be a fast matrix multiplication algorithm. Substantial effort over the years has been expended looking for a fast matrix multiplication algorithm, and none has been found. So it appears relatively unlikely that there is a fast general algorithm for context-free parsing.

15.3.3 Shift-Reduce Parsing

The CKY algorithm works for any context-free language, but it has two important limitations:

- It is not efficient enough for many applications. We'd like a deterministic parser that runs in time that is linear in the length of the input.
- It requires that the grammar it uses be stated in Chomsky normal form. We'd like to be able to use more natural grammars and thus to extract more natural parse trees.

We'll next consider a bottom-up technique that can be made deterministic for a large, practically significant set of languages.

The parser that we are about to describe is called a ***shift-reduce parser***. It will read its input string from left to right and can perform two basic operations:

1. Shift an input symbol onto the parser's stack and build, in the parse tree, a terminal node labeled with that input symbol.
2. Reduce a string of symbols from the top of the stack to a nonterminal symbol, using one of the rules of the grammar. Each time it does this, it also builds the corresponding piece of the parse tree.

We'll begin by considering a shift-reduce parser that may have to explore more than one path. Then we'll look at ways to make it deterministic in cases where that is possible.

To see how a shift-reduce parser might work, let's trace its operation on the string `id + id * id`, using our original term/factor grammar for arithmetic expressions:

1. $E \rightarrow E + T$
2. $E \rightarrow T$
3. $T \rightarrow T * F$
4. $T \rightarrow F$
5. $F \rightarrow (E)$
6. $F \rightarrow$ `id`

We'll number the main steps in this process so that we can refer to them later.

Step 1: When we start, the parser's stack is empty, so our only choice is to shift the first input symbol, `id`, onto the stack. Next, we have a choice. We can either use rule 6 to reduce `id` to F, or we can get the next input symbol and shift it onto the stack. It's clear that we need to apply rule 6 now. Why? Because there are no other rules that can consume an `id` directly. So we have to do this reduction before we can do anything else with `id`. But could we wait and do it later? No, because reduction always applies to the symbols at the top of the stack. If we push anything on before we reduce id, we'll never again get id at the top of the stack. It will just sit there, unable to participate in any rules. So we reduce id to *F*, giving us a stack containing just *F*, and the parse tree (remember we're building it up from the bottom):

The reasoning we just did is going to be the basis for the design of a "smart" deterministic bottom up parser. Without that reasoning, a dumb, brute force parser would have had to consider both paths at this first choice point: the one we took, as well as the one that fails to reduce and instead pushes + onto the stack. That second path will eventually reach a dead end, so even a brute force parser will eventually get the right answer. But our goal is to eliminate search.

Step 2: At this point, the parser's stack contains *F* and the remaining input is + id $*$ id. Again we must choose between reducing the top of the stack or shifting on the next input symbol. Again, by looking ahead and analyzing the grammar, we can see that eventually we will need to apply rule 1. To do so, the first id will have to have been reduced to a *T* and then to an *E*. So let's next reduce by rule 4 and then again by rule 2, giving the parse tree and stack:

Step 3: At this point, there are no further reductions to consider, since there are no rules whose right-hand side is just *E*. So we must consume the next input symbol + and shift it onto the stack. Having done that, there are again no available reductions. So we shift the next input symbol. The stack then contains id + *E* (writing the stack with its top to the left). Again, we need to reduce id before we can do anything else, so we reduce it to *F* and then to *T*. Now we've got:

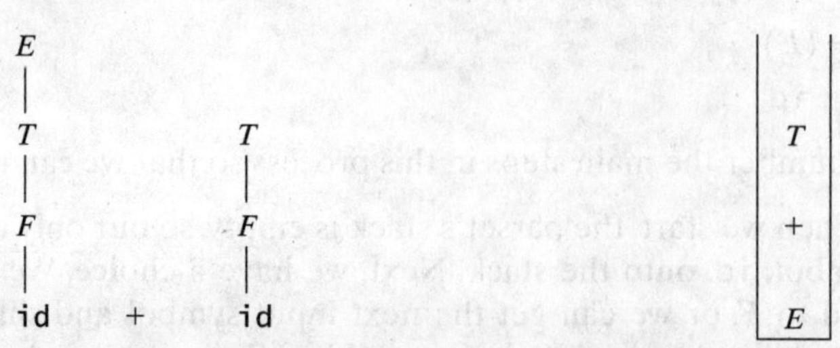

Notice that we have three parse tree fragments. Since we're working up from the bottom, we don't know yet how they'll get put together. We now have three choices: Reduce T to E using rule 2, reduce $T + E$ to E using rule 1 or shift on the next input symbol. Note, by the way, that we will always be matching the right-hand sides of the rules in reverse because the last symbol we read (and thus the right-most one we'll match) is at the top of the stack.

Step 4: In considering whether to reduce or shift at this point, we realize that, for the first time, there isn't one correct answer for all input strings. When there was just one universally correct answer, we could compute it simply by examining the grammar. Now we can't do that. In the example we're working with, we don't want to do either of the reductions, since the next input symbol is $*$. We know that the only complete parse tree for this input string will correspond to the interpretation in which $*$ is applied before $+$. That means that $+$ must be at the top of the tree. If we reduce now, it will be at the bottom. So we need to shift $*$ onto the stack and do a reduction that will build the multiplication piece of the parse tree before we do a reduction involving $+$. But if the input string had been `id` + `id` + `id`, we'd want to reduce now in order to cause the first $+$ to be done first, thus producing left associativity. So we appear to have reached a point where we'll have to branch. If we choose the wrong path, we'll eventually hit a dead end and have to back up. We'd like not to waste time exploring dead end paths, however. We'll come back later to the question of how we can make a parser know how to avoid dead ends. For now, let's just forge ahead and do the right thing and see what happens.

As we said, what we want to do here is not to reduce but instead to shift $*$ onto the stack. Once we do that, the stack will contain $* \; T + E$. At this point, there are no available reductions (since there are no rules whose right-hand side contains $*$ as the last symbol), so we shift the next symbol, resulting in the stack `id` $* \; T + E$. Clearly we next have to reduce `id` to F (following the same argument that we used above), so we've got:

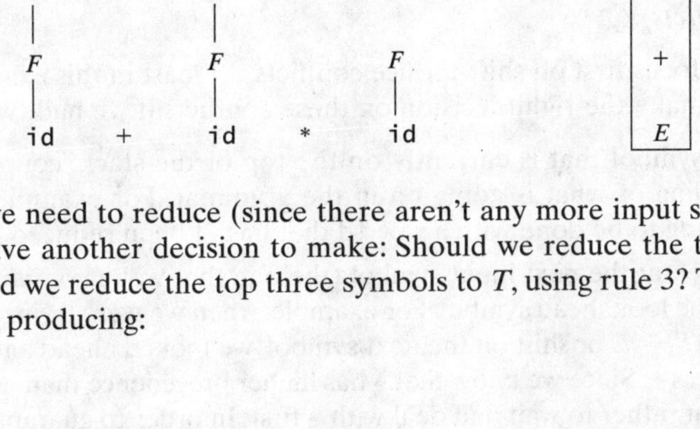

Step 5: Next, we need to reduce (since there aren't any more input symbols to shift), but now we have another decision to make: Should we reduce the top F to T, using rule 4, or should we reduce the top three symbols to T, using rule 3? The right answer is to use rule 3, producing:

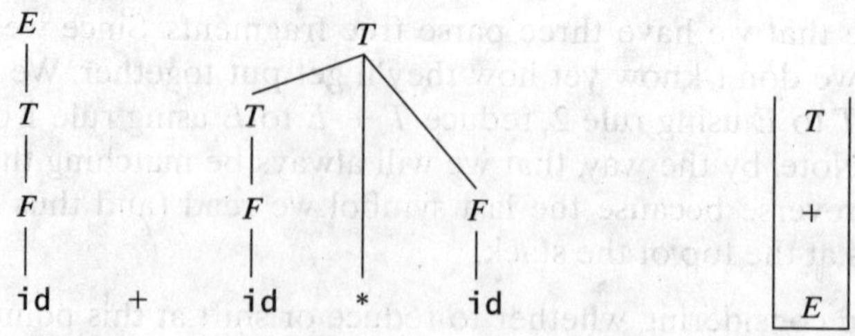

Step 6: Finally, we need to apply rule 1, to produce the single symbol E on the top of the stack, and the parse tree:

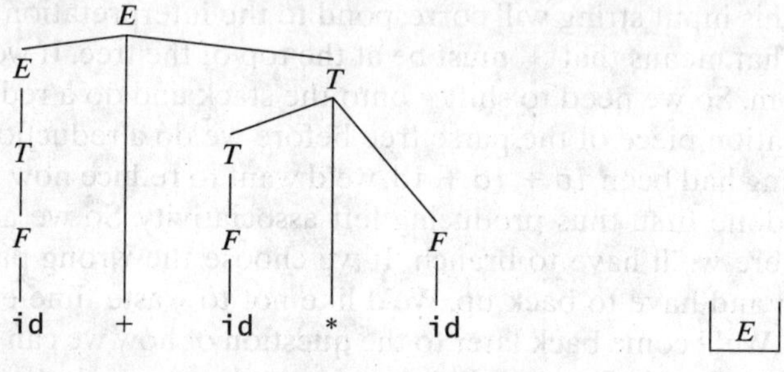

The job of a shift-reduce parser is complete once it has:

- built a parse tree that spans the entire input string, and
- produced a stack that contains just the start symbol.

So we are done, although we'll discuss below extending the input to include an end-of-input symbol $. In that case, we will usually have a final rule that consumes the $ and pops the start symbol from the stack.

Now let's return to the question of how we can build a parser that makes the right choices at each step of the parsing process. As we walked through the example parse above, there were two kinds of decisions that we had to make:

- Whether to shift or reduce (we'll call these ***shift-reduce conflicts***).
- Which of several available reductions to perform (we'll call these ***reduce-reduce conflicts***).

Let's focus first on shift-reduce conflicts. At least in this example, it was always possible to make the right decision on these conflicts if we had two kinds of information:

- The symbol that is currently on the top of the stack, coupled with a good understanding of what is going on in the grammar. For example, we noted that there's nothing to be done with a raw `id` that hasn't been reduced to an F.
- A peek at the next input symbol (the one that we're considering shifting), which we call the lookahead symbol. For example, when we were trying to decide whether to reduce $T + E$ or shift on the next symbol, we looked ahead and saw that the next symbol was $*$. Since we know that $*$ has higher precedence than $+$, we knew not to reduce $+$, but rather to wait and deal with $*$ first. In order to guarantee that there always is a

lookahead symbol, even after the last real input symbol has been read, we'll assume from now on that every string ends with \$, a special end-of-input symbol.

If the decision about whether to shift or to reduce is dependent only on the current top of stack symbol and the current lookahead symbol, then we can define a procedure for resolving shift-reduce conflicts by specifying a precedence relation $P \subseteq V \times \{\Sigma \cup \$\}$. P will contain the pair (s, c) iff, whenever the top of stack symbol is s and the lookahead symbol is c, the parser should reduce. If the current situation is described by a pair that is not in P, then the parser will shift the lookahead symbol onto the stack.

An easy way to encode a precedence relation is as a table, which we'll call a ***precedence table***. As an example, consider the following precedence table for our arithmetic expression grammar, augmented with \$:

	(	)	id	+	*	\$
(						
)		**R**		**R**	**R**	**R**
id		**R**		**R**	**R**	**R**
+						
*						
E						
T		**R**		**R**		**R**
F		**R**		**R**	**R**	**R**

This table should be read as follows: Compare the left-most column to the top of the stack and find the row that matches. Now compare the symbols along the top of the chart to the lookahead symbol and find the column that matches. If there's an **R** in the corresponding square of the table, then reduce. Otherwise, shift.

Let's now go back to the problem of parsing our example input string, `id` + `id` ∗ `id`. Remember that we had a shift/reduce conflict at step 4, when the stack's contents were $T + E$ and the next input symbol was ∗. We can now resolve that conflict by checking the precedence table. We look at the next to the last row of the table, the one that has T as the top of stack symbol. Then we look at the column headed ∗. There's no **R**, so we don't reduce. But notice that if the lookahead symbol had been +, we'd have found an **R**, telling us to reduce, which is exactly what we'd want to do. Thus this table captures the precedence relationships between the operators ∗ and +, plus the fact that we want to associate left when faced with operators of equal precedence.

Now consider the problem of resolving reduce-reduce conflicts. Here's a simple strategy called the ***longest-prefix heuristic***: Given a choice of right-hand sides that match the current stack, choose the longest one.

Returning to our example parse, we encountered a reduce-reduce conflict at step 5. The longest-prefix heuristic tells us to reduce $F * T$ rather than just F, which is the right thing to do.

15.3.4 Deterministic, Bottom-UP LR Parsing

There is a large and very useful class of languages for which it is possible to build a deterministic, bottom-up parser by extending the notion of a precedence table so that it includes even more information about paths that will eventually succeed versus those that will eventually fail. We'll call the resulting table a ***parse table***.

We define a grammar G to be **LR(k)**, for any positive integer k, iff it is possible to build a deterministic parser for G that scans its input left to right (thus the L in the name) and, for any input string in $L(G)$, builds a rightmost derivation (thus the R in the name), looking ahead at most k symbols. We define a language to be LR(k) iff there exists an LR(k) grammar for it. We'll state here, without proof, two important facts about the LR(k) languages:

- The class of LR(k) languages is exactly the class of deterministic context-free languages, as defined in Section 13.5.
- If a language is LR(k), for some k, then it is also LR(1).

Given an LR(1) grammar, it is possible to build a parse table that can serve as the basis for a deterministic shift-reduce parser. The parse table, like the precedence table we built in the last section, tells the parser when to shift and when to reduce. It also tells it how to resolve reduce-reduce conflicts. Unfortunately, for many LR(1) languages, the parse table is too large to be practical.

But there is a technique, called LALR (lookahead LR) parsing, that works on a restricted class of LR(1) grammars. LALR parsers are deterministic, shift-reduce parsers. They are widely used for a combination of three important reasons:

- Most practical languages can be described by an LALR grammar.
- The parse tables that are required by an LALR parser are reasonably small.
- There exist powerful tools to build those tables. So efficient parsers are very easy to build.

This last point is key. While it is possible to build parse tables for top-down LL parsers by hand, it isn't possible, for any but the simplest grammars, to build LALR parse tables by hand. As a result, bottom-up parsing was not widely used until the development of parser-generation tools. The most influential such tool has been Yacc, which is designed to work together with Lex (described briefly in Section 15.1) to build a combined lexical analyzer/parser. There have been many implementations of Yacc and it has many descendants.

15.4 Parsing Natural Languages

Programming languages are artificial. They are designed by human designers, who are free to change them so that they possess various desirable properties, including parsability. But now consider English or Spanish or Chinese or Swahili. These languages are natural. They have evolved to serve a purpose, but that purpose is communication among people. The need to build programs to analyze them, index them, retrieve them, translate them, and so forth, has been added very late in the game. It should therefore come as little surprise that the efficient parsing techniques that we have described in the last two sections do not work as well for natural languages as they do for artificial ones.

15.4.1 The Problems

Parsers for natural languages must face at least five problems that are substantially more severe in the case of natural languages than they are for artificial ones:

- Ambiguity: There do not exist unambiguous grammars with the power to generate all the parse trees that correspond to the meanings of sentences in the language. Many sentences are syntactically ambiguous. (Recall Example 11.22.) Choosing the correct parse tree for a sentence generally requires appeal to facts about the larger context in which the sentence occurs and facts about what makes sense. Those facts can be encoded in separate functions that choose from among a set of parse trees or partial parse trees. Or they may be encoded probabilistically in a stochastic grammar, as described in Section 11.10. Even when the information required to make a choice is available in the input string, it may be many words away, so the single symbol lookahead that we used in LL and LR parsing is rarely adequate.
- Gaps: In the sentence, `What did Jen eat?`, the word `What` is the object of the verb `eat` but it is not near it in the sentence. See L.3.3 for a discussion of this issue.
- Dialect: English is not one language. It is hundreds at least. Chinese is worse. There is no ISO standard for English or Chinese. So what language should we build a grammar for?
- Evolution: Natural languages change as they are used. The sentences, `You wanted to do that why?` and `They're open 24/7`, are fine American English sentences today. But they wouldn't have been twenty years ago.
- Errors: Even among speakers who agree completely on how they ought to talk, what they actually say is a different story. While it is acceptable (and even desirable) for a compiler to throw out syntactically ill-formed programs, imagine the usefulness of a translating telephone that objected to every sentence that stopped in the middle, started over, and got a pronoun wrong. Parsers for natural languages must be robust in a way that parsers for artificial languages are not required to be.

In addition, natural languages share with many artificial languages the problem of checking for agreement between various constituents:

- For programming languages, it is necessary to check variable declarations against uses.
- For natural languages, it is necessary to check for agreement between subject and verb, for agreement between nouns and modifiers (in languages like Spanish), and so forth.

In G.2, we prove that one typical programming language, Java, is not context-free because of the requirement that variables be declared before they are used. So parsers for programming languages exploit additional mechanisms, such as symbol tables, to check such features. In L.3.3, we address the question of whether natural languages such as English are formally context-free. There are no proofs, consistent with the empirical facts about how people actually talk, that English is not context-free. There is, on the other hand, a proof that one grammatical feature of one natural language, Swiss German, is not context-free. But, even for English, it is more straightforward to describe agreement features, just as we do for Java, with additional mechanisms that check agreement features.

15.4.2 The Earley Algorithm

Despite the problems we just described, context-free parsers, augmented as necessary, are widely used in natural language processing systems. Although efficient parsing is important, deterministic parsing is generally not possible. So LL and LR techniques won't work. And it is usually not acceptable to require grammars to be in Chomsky normal form (because parsers based on such grammars will not generate natural parse trees). So the CKY algorithm can't be used. The Earley algorithm, which we present next, is a reasonably efficient ($\mathcal{O}(n^3)$) algorithm that works with an arbitrary context-free grammar. Because of its importance in natural language processing, we'll describe this algorithm as it operates on English sentences. But it can be applied to any context-free language. So, for example, to imagine it being used in a compiler, substitute the term "token" each time we mention a "word" here.

The Earley algorithm, like the CKY algorithm, is a dynamic programming technique. It works top-down but, unlike the simple depth-first search algorithm that we discussed in Section 15.2.1, it builds each potential constituent only once (and then may reuse smaller constituents as it explores alternative ways to build larger ones). The structure that is used to record the constituents as they are found can be thought of as a simple chart. So parsers that are based on the Earley algorithm, and on others that are related to it, are often called ***chart parsers***.

To describe the way that the Earley algorithm works, we introduce the dot notation, which we will use to indicate the progress that the parser has made so far in matching the right-hand side of a grammar rule against the input. Let:

$A \rightarrow \alpha \bullet \beta\gamma$ describe an attempt to apply the rule $A \rightarrow \alpha\beta\gamma$, where everything before the • has already matched against the input and the parser is still trying match everything after the •.

$A \rightarrow \bullet\, \alpha\beta\gamma$ describe a similar attempt except that nothing has yet matched against the input.

$A \rightarrow \alpha\beta\gamma \bullet$ describe a similar attempt except that the entire right-hand side (and thus also A) has matched against the input.

The overall progress of the parsing process can be described by listing each rule that is currently being attempted and indicating, for each:

- Where in the sentence the parser is trying to match the right hand side, and
- How much progress (as indicated by the position of the dot) has been made in doing that matching.

All of this information can be summarized in a chart with $n + 1$ rows, where n is the number of words in the input string. In creating the chart, we won't assign indices to the words of the input string. Instead we'll assign the indices to the points in between the words. So, for example, we might have:

```
0   Jen   1   saw   2   Bill   3
```

We'll let row i of the chart contain every instance of an attempt to match a rule whose • is in position i. The easiest way to envision the chart is to imagine that it also has $n + 1$ columns, which will correspond to the location in the input at which the partial match began. We'll reverse our usual convention and list the column index first so that the pair describes the start and then the end of a partial match. So associating the indices $[i, j]$ with a rule $A \rightarrow \alpha \bullet \beta\gamma$ means that the parser began matching α in position i and the • is currently in position j.

The Earley algorithm works top-down. So it starts by inserting into the chart every rule whose left-hand side is the start symbol of the grammar. The indices associated with each such rule are [0, 0], since the parser must try to match the right-hand side starting before the first word (i.e., in position 0) and it has so far matched nothing. The job of the parser is to find a match, for the right-hand side of at least one of those rules, that spans the entire sentence. In other words, for at least one of those initial rules, the • must move all the way to the right and the index pair $[0, n]$, indicating a match starting before the first word and ending after the last one, must be assigned to the rule.

To see how the algorithm works, we'll trace its operation on the simple sentence we showed above, given the following grammar:

$S \rightarrow NP\ VP$

$NP \rightarrow ProperNoun$

$VP \rightarrow V\ NP$

After initialization, the chart will be:

3	
2	
1	
0	$S \rightarrow \bullet\ NP\ VP$ [0, 0]

0 `Jen` 1 `saw` 2 `Bill` 3

Next, the algorithm predicts that an *NP* must occur, starting at position 0. So it looks for rules that tell it how to construct such an *NP*. It finds one, and adds it to the chart, giving:

3	
2	
1	
0	$NP \rightarrow \bullet\ ProperNoun$ [0, 0] $S \rightarrow \bullet\ NP\ VP$ [0, 0]

0 `Jen` 1 `saw` 2 `Bill` 3

Now it predicts the existence of a *ProperNoun* that starts in position 0. It isn't generally practical to handle part of speech tags like *ProperNoun* by writing a rule like *ProperNoun* → `Jen` | `Bill` | `Chris` |... Instead, we'll assume that the input has already been tagged with part of speech markers like *Noun*, *ProperNoun*, *Verb*, and so forth. (See L.2 for a discussion of how this is process, called part of speech or POS tagging is done.) So, whenever the next symbol the parser is looking for is a part of speech tag, it will simply check the next input symbol and see whether it has the required tag. If it does, a match has occurred and the parser will behave as though it just matched the implied rule. If it does not, then no match has been found and the rule can make no progress. In this case, `Jen` is a *ProperNoun*, so there is a match. The parser can apply the implied rule *ProperNoun* → `Jen`. Notice that whenever the parser actually matches against the input, the • moves. So the parser adds this new rule to the next row of the chart, which now becomes:

4	
3	
2	
1	*ProperNoun* → `Jen` • [0, 1]
0	*NP* → • *ProperNoun* [0, 0] *S* → • *NP VP* [0, 0]

ProperNoun *V, N* *ProperNoun*
0 `Jen` 1 `saw` 2 `Bill` 3

The parser has now finished considering both of the rules in row 0, so it moves on to row 1. It notices that it has found a complete *ProperNoun*. Whenever it finds a complete constituent, it must look back to see what rules predicted the occurrence of that constituent (and thus are waiting for it). The new, complete constituent starts at position 0, so the parser looks for rules whose • is in position 0, indicating that they are waiting for a constituent that starts there. So it looks back in row 0. It finds that the *NP* rule is waiting for a *ProperNoun*. Since a *ProperNoun* has just been found, the parser can create the rule *NP* → *ProperNoun* • [0, 1] and add it to row 1. Then it looks at that rule and realizes that it has found a complete *NP* starting in position 0. So it looks back in row 0 again, this time to see what rule is waiting for an *NP*. It finds that *S* is, so it creates the rule *S* → *NP* • *VP* [0, 1]. At this point, the chart looks like this (using ✓ to mark rules that have already been processed):

3	
2	
1	*S* → *NP* • *VP* [0, 1] ✓ *NP* → *ProperNoun* • [0, 1] ✓ *ProperNoun* → `Jen` • [0, 1]
0	✓ *NP* → • *ProperNoun* [0, 0] ✓ *S* → • *NP VP* [0, 0]

ProperNoun *V, N* *ProperNoun*
0 `Jen` 1 `saw` 2 `Bill` 3

The remaining unprocessed rule tells the parser that it needs to predict again. It needs to find a *VP* starting in position 1. Because no progress has been made in finding a *VP*, any rule that could describe one will have its • still in position 1. So the parser adds the rule *VP* → • *V NP* [1, 1] to row 1 of the chart. At this point, the chart will be:

3	
2	
1	*VP* → • *V NP* [1, 1] ✓ *S* → *NP* • *VP* [0, 1] ✓ *NP* → *ProperNoun* • [0, 1] ✓ *ProperNoun* → `Jen` • [0, 1]
0	✓ *NP* → • *ProperNoun* [0, 0] ✓ *S* → • *NP VP* [0, 0]

	ProperNoun		*V, N*		*ProperNoun*	
0	`Jen`	1	`saw`	2	`Bill`	3

In processing the next rule, the parser notices that the predicted symbol is a part of speech, so it checks the next input word to see if it can be a *V*erb. Saw has been tagged as a possible *V*erb or a possible *N*oun. So a new rule is added, this time to row 2 since the • moves to the right to indicate that the match has moved one word farther in the input. Notice that because the Earley algorithm works top-down, it will ignore part of speech tags (such as `saw` as a *N*oun) that don't fit in the larger sentence context. The chart is now:

3	
2	*V* → `saw` • [1, 2]
1	✓ *VP* → • *V NP* [1, 1] ✓ *S* → *NP* • *VP* [0, 1] ✓ *NP* → *ProperNoun* • [0, 1] ✓ *ProperNoun* → `Jen` • [0, 1]
0	✓ *NP* → • *ProperNoun* [0, 0] ✓ *S* → • *NP VP* [0, 0]

	ProperNoun				*ProperNoun*	
0	`Jen`	1	`saw`	2	`Bill`	3

Having found a complete constituent (the *V*), starting in position 1, the parser looks back to row 1 to find rules that are waiting for it. It finds one: *VP* → • *V NP* [1, 1]. So it can advance this rule's • and create the rule *VP* → *V* • *NP* [1, 2], which can be added to row 2. That rule will be processed next. It will predict the existence of an *NP* starting in position 2, so the parser will create rules that describe the possible structures for such an *NP*. Our simple grammar has only one *NP* rule, so the parser will create the rule *NP* → • *ProperNoun* [2, 2] and add it to the chart in row 2. Next the parser looks for, and finds, a *ProperNoun*, `Bill`, starting in position 2 and ending at position 3. So it enters it in row 3. At this point, the chart will be:

3		*ProperNoun* → `Bill` • [2,3]
2	✓	*NP* → • *ProperNoun* [2,2]
	✓	*VP* → *V* • *NP* [1,2]
	✓	*V* → `saw` • [1,2]
1	✓	*VP* → • *VNP* [1,1]
	✓	*S* → *NP* • *VP* [0,1]
	✓	*NP* → *ProperNoun* • [0,1]
	✓	*ProperNoun* → `Jen` • [0,1]
0	✓	*NP* → • *ProperNoun* [0,0]
	✓	*S* → • *NP VP* [0,0]

	ProperNoun		*V,N*		*ProperNoun*	
0	`Jen`	1	`saw`	2	`Bill`	3

Having found a complete constituent (the *ProperNoun*), starting in position 2, the parser looks in row 2 to find rules that are waiting for a *ProperNoun* starting in position 2. It finds one: *NP* → • *ProperNoun* [2, 2]. It can advance that rule's • and add the rule *NP* → *ProperNoun* • [2, 3] to row 3. This rule tells the parser that another complete constituent, an *NP*, has been found, starting in position 2. So it again looks back to row 2 and finds that the rule *VP* → *V* • *NP* [1, 2] is looking for that *NP*. So its • can be advanced, and the rule *VP* → *V NP* • [1, 3] can be added to row 3. That rule describes yet another complete constituent, a *VP*, starting back in position 1. So the parser looks back at row 1 to find a rule that is waiting for that *VP*. It finds *S* → *NP* • *VP* [0, 1]. So its • can be advanced, and the rule *S* → *NP VP* • [0, 3] can be added to row 3. Now the chart is:

3		*S* → *NP VP* • [0,3]
	✓	*VP* → *V NP* • [1,3]
	✓	*NP* → *ProperNoun* • [2,3]
	✓	*ProperNoun* → `Bill` • [2,3]
2	✓	*NP* → • *ProperNoun* [2,2]
	✓	*VP* → *V* • *NP* [1,2]
	✓	*V* → `saw` • [1,2]
1	✓	*VP* → • *VNP* [1,1]
	✓	*S* → *NP* • *VP* [0,1]
	✓	*NP* → *ProperNoun* • [0,1]
	✓	*ProperNoun* → `Jen` • [0,1]
0	✓	*NP* → • *ProperNoun* [0,0]
	✓	*S* → • *NP VP* [0,0]

	ProperNoun		*V,N*		*ProperNoun*	
0	`Jen`	1	`saw`	2	`Bill`	3

At this point, the parsing process halts. A complete *S* that spans the entire input has been found. In this simple example, there is only one parse. Given a more complex sentence and a more realistic grammar, there could be several parses. If we want to find them all, the parser can be allowed to continue until no new edges can be added.

We can now state the algorithm that we have just described:

Earleyparse(w: input string containing n words, G: context-free grammar) =

1. For every rule in G of the form $S \rightarrow \alpha$, where S is the start symbol of G, do: /* Initialize *chart*.
   insert(*chart*, $S \rightarrow \bullet \alpha$ [0, 0]). /* Insert the rule $S \rightarrow \bullet \alpha$ [0, 0] into row 0 of *chart*.
2. For $i = 0$ to n do: /* Go through the rows one at a time.
   For each rule r in row_i of *chart* do:
      If r corresponds to finding a complete constituent, then
         extendothers(*chart*, r).
      Else if the symbol after the • of r is a part of speech tag, then
         scaninput(w, *chart*, r).
      Else *predict*(*chart*, r).

insert(*chart*, r [j, k]: rule that spans from j to k in chart) =
   If r is not already on chart, spanning from j to k, then add it in row k.

extendothers(*chart*: chart, r [j, k]: rule of the form $A \rightarrow \alpha \bullet$ that spans from j to k in chart) =
   For each rule p of the form $X \rightarrow \beta \bullet A\gamma[i, j]$ on *chart* do: /* Find rules waiting for A starting at j.
      insert(*chart*, $X \rightarrow \beta A \bullet \gamma[i, k]$). /* Move the • one symbol to the right and add rule to row_k.

scaninput(w: input string, *chart*: chart, r [j, k]: rule of the form $A \rightarrow \beta \bullet A\gamma$, where A is a part of speech tag, and the rule spans from j to k in chart) =
   If w_k (the kth word of the input) has been labeled with the tag A then:
      insert(*chart*, $A \rightarrow w_k \bullet [k, k + 1]$). /* Add this one to the next row.

predict(*chart*: chart, r [j, k]: rule of the form $A \rightarrow \alpha \bullet B\beta$ that spans from j to k in chart) =
   For each rule in G of the form $B \rightarrow \gamma$ do:
      insert(*chart*, $B \rightarrow \bullet \gamma[k, k]$). /* Try to find a B starting at k.

As we have presented it, *Earleyparse* doesn't actually build a parse tree. It simply decides whether a parse exists. But it is straightforward to modify it so that the parse tree(s) that correspond to successful S rules can be extracted.

Notice that *Earleyparse* avoids the two major pitfalls of the more straightforward top-down parsing algorithm that exploits simple depth-first search. First, we observe that it will always halt, even if provided with a grammar that contains left-recursive rules. This must be true because a rule cannot be added to the chart at a given location more than once. Since there is a finite number of rules and a finite number of locations in the chart, only a finite number of rules can be placed on the chart and *Earleyparse* terminates after it has processed each of them.

Second, we observe that *Earleyparse* avoids the wasted effort of backtracking search. Instead it reuses constituents. How it does so may not have been obvious in the very simple example that we just considered. But suppose that we added to our grammar a few more *NP* rules, the necessary prepositional phrase (*PP*) rules and the rule:

$VP \rightarrow V\dot{P}\ PP$

Now suppose that we try to parse the sentence `Jen saw Bill through the window`. A backtracking, top-down parser would try the $VP \rightarrow V\ NP$ rule first (assuming it was listed first). It would build an *S* using that *VP* and then realize that the *S* didn't span the entire sentence. So it would back up and throw away all the work it did to build the *VP*, including building the *NP* that dominates `Bill`. In this simple example, that *NP* doesn't represent a lot of work, but in a less trivial sentence, it might. Then the parser would start over to build a *VP* using the new rule that allows for a prepositional phrase. *Earleyparse*, on the other hand, will build each of those constituents once. Since rules are never removed from the chart, they can be reused as necessary by other, higher-level rules. We leave working out the details of this example as an exercise.

We can analyze the complexity of *Earleyparse* as follows: The loop of step 2 is executed *n* times. The inner loop is executed once for each rule that is already in the row. There are $\mathcal{O}(n)$ of them. Whenever *extendothers* is called, it must compare its edge to all the other edges in the row. And there are $\mathcal{O}(n)$ of them. Multiplying these together, we get that the total number of steps is $\mathcal{O}(n^3)$. If we want to consider the size of *G*, then let $|G|$ be the number of rules in *G*. The total number of steps executed by *Earleyparse* becomes $\mathcal{O}(n^3 \cdot |G|^2)$.

Exercises

1. Consider the following grammar that we presented in Example 15.9:

$S \rightarrow AB\$ \mid AC\$$
$A \rightarrow \mathtt{a}A \mid \mathtt{a}$
$B \rightarrow \mathtt{b}B \mid \mathtt{b}$
$C \rightarrow \mathtt{c}$

Show an equivalent grammar that is LL(1) and prove that it is.

2. Assume the grammar:

$S \rightarrow NP\ VP$
$NP \rightarrow ProperNoun$
$NP \rightarrow Det\ N$
$VP \rightarrow V\ NP$
$VP \rightarrow VP\ PP$
$PP \rightarrow Prep\ NP$

Assume that `Jen` and `Bill` have been tagged *ProperNoun*, `saw` has been tagged *V*, `through` has been tagged *Prep*, `the` has been tagged *Det*, and `window` has been tagged *N*. Trace the execution of *Earleyparse* on the input sentence `Jen saw Bill through the window.`

3. Trace the execution of *Earleyparse* given the string and grammar of Example 15.5.
4. Trace the execution of a CKY parser on the input string `id + id * id`, given the unambiguous arithmetic expression grammar shown in Example 11.19, by:
   a. Converting the grammar to Chomsky normal form.
   b. Showing the steps of the parser.

CHAPTER 16

Summary and References

The theory of context-free languages is not as tidy as the theory of regular languages. Interesting subsets, including the deterministic context-free languages and the context-free languages that are not inherently ambiguous, can be shown to be only proper subsets of the larger class of context-free languages. The context-free languages are not closed under many common operations. There is no algorithm for minimizing PDAs. There is no fast recognition algorithm that works for arbitrary context-free languages. There are no decision procedures for many important questions. Yet substantial effort has been invested in studying the context-free languages because they are useful. The results that we have presented here have been developed by many people, including theoreticians (who were particularly interested in the formal properties of the set), linguists (who were interested in modeling natural languages and who found context-free grammars to be a useful tool), and compiler writers (who were interested in building efficient parsers for programming languages). The theory that was developed out of the confluence of those efforts continues to provide the basis for practical parsing systems today.

Table 16.1 summarizes the properties of the context-free languages and compares them to the regular languages:

References

The context-free grammar formalism grew out of the efforts of linguists to describe the structure of sentences in natural languages such as English. By the mid 1940's, it was widely understood that sentences could be described hierarchically, with a relatively small number of immediate constituents (or ICs) at each level. For example, many English sentences can be described as a noun phrase followed by a verb phrase. Each such IC, until the smallest ones, could in turn be further described as a set of smaller constituents, and so forth. [Chomsky 1956] introduced phrase structure (production-rule) grammars as a way to describe such a structural analysis of a sentence. In [Chomsky 1959], Chomsky defined a four-level hierarchy of language classes based on the form of the grammar rules that are allowed. Context-free grammars, in the sense in which we have defined them, with their particular restrictions on the form of the rules, were described there. We'll say more about the Chomsky hierarchy in Section 24.2.

Table 16.1 Comparing the regular and the context-free languages.

	Regular	***Context-Free***
Automaton	FSM	PDA
Grammar(s)	Regular grammar Regular expressions	Context-free grammar
ND = D?	Yes	No
Closed under:		
Concatenation	Yes	Yes
Union	Yes	Yes
Kleene star	Yes	Yes
Complement	Yes	No
Intersection	Yes	No
∩ with Regular	Yes	Yes
Decidable:		
Membership	Yes	Yes
Emptiness	Yes	Yes
Finiteness	Yes	Yes
$= \Sigma^*$	Yes	No
Equivalence	Yes	No

Chomsky normal form was also introduced in [Chomsky 1959]. Greibach normal form was introduced in [Greibach 1965].Island grammars are described in [Moonen 2001]. There are many other applications of them as well □. Two early uses of the related idea, island parsing, are described in [Carroll 1983] and [Stock, Falcone and Insinnamo 1988]. For a discussion of stochastic (probabilistic) context-free grammars and parsing techniques, see [Jurafsky and Martin 2000].

The idea of using a pushdown stack to process naturally recursive structures, like formulas in logic or in programming languages, was developed independently by many people in the 1950s. (For a brief discussion of this history, as well as many other aspects of the theory of context-free languages, see [Greibach 1981].) The pushdown automaton was described both in [Oettinger 1961] (where it was used for the syntactic analysis of natural language sentences as part of a machine translation system) and in [Schutzenberger 1963]. The proof of the equivalence of context-free grammars and PDAs appeared independently in [Evey 1963], [Chomsky 1962] and [Schutzenberger 1963].

Many key properties of context-free languages, including the Pumping Theorem and the fact that the context-free languages are closed under intersection with the regular languages, were described in [Bar-Hillel, Perles and Shamir 1961]. Our claim that, if a grammar G is not self-embedding then $L(G)$ is regular, is proved in [Hopcroft and Ullman 1969]. The fact that the context-free languages are closed under union but not under intersection and complement was shown in [Scheinberg 1960]. Ogden's Lemma appeared in [Ogden 1968]. Parikh's Theorem was presented in [Parikh 1966]. The fact that every context-free language over a single character alphabet is regular is from [Ginsburg and Rice 1962]. For a comprehensive treatment of the mathematical theory of context-free languages, see [Ginsburg 1966].

[Parikh 1966] proved that there exist inherently ambiguous context-free languages. It showed that $\{a^i b^j a^k b^l : i, j, k, l \geq 0, i = k \text{ or } j = l\}$ is inherently ambiguous. The claim that $\{a^i b^j c^k : i, j, k \geq 0, i = j \text{ or } j = k\}$ is inherently ambiguous is proved in [Harrison 1978] and in [Du and Ko 2001], using Ogden's Lemma.

The proof in Example 11.10 is taken from [Martin 2003].

See [Aho, Sethi and Ullman 1986] for a more detailed treatment of the issues that arise in parsing artificial context-free languages, as well as a good survey of the history of the development of parsing techniques, including the definition of LL(k) and LR(k) languages. In particular, algorithms for computing *first* and *follow* and for eliminating all left recursion are presented there. Lex is described in [Lesk and Schmidt 1979]. Yacc is described in [Johnson 1979]. The CKY algorithm was independently discovered by John Cocke, Daniel Younger, and Tadao Kasami, and described in [Younger 1967] and [Kasami 1965]. [Valiant 1975] showed that context-free parsing could be recast as matrix multiplication. Strassen's algorithm for fast matrix multiplication was described in [Strassen 1969]. The $\mathcal{O}(n^{2.376})$ matrix multiplication algorithm was presented in [Coppersmith and Winograd 1990]. The claim that if there were a fast context-free parsing algorithm there would be a fast algorithm for Boolean matrix multiplication is proved in [Lee 2002]. The claims we made about the LR(k) languages are proved in [Hopcroft and Ullman 1969].

Earley's algorithm for general top-down parsing was first presented in [Earley 1970]. The version given here is patterned after the one in [Jurafsky and Martin 2000].

PART IV

TURING MACHINES AND UNDECIDABILITY

We are about to begin our exploration of the two outer circles of the language hierarchy, as well as the background, the area outside all of the circles.

Up until now, we have been placing limitations on what we could do in order that we could discover simple solutions when they exist.

Now we are going to tear down all the barriers and explore the full power of formal computation. We will discover a whole range of problems that become solvable once we do that. We will also discover that there are fundamental limitations on what we can compute, regardless of the specific model with which we choose to work.

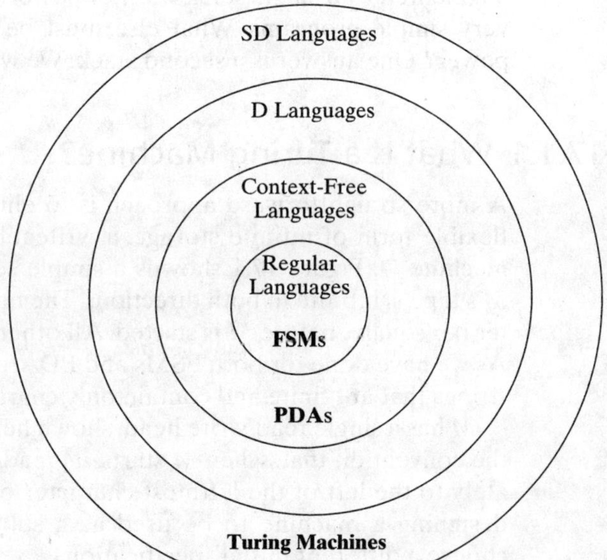

CHAPTER 17

Turing Machines

We need a new kind of automaton that has two properties:

- It must be powerful enough to describe all computable things. In this respect, it should be like real computers and unlike FSMs and PDAs.
- It must be simple enough that we can reason formally about it. In this respect, it should be like FSMs and PDAs and unlike real computers.

17.1 Definition, Notation and Examples

In our discussion of pushdown automata, it became clear that a finite state controller augmented by a single stack was not powerful enough to be able to execute even some very simple programs. What else must be added in order to acquire the necessary power? One answer is a second stack. We will explore that idea in Section 17.5.2.

17.1.1 What Is a Turing Machine?

A more straightforward approach is to eliminate the stack and replace it by a more flexible form of infinite storage, a writeable tape. When we do that, we get a Turing machine 💻. Figure 17.1 showns a simple schematic diagram of a Turing machine *M*. *M*'s tape is infinite in both directions. The input to *M* is written on the tape, one character per square, before *M* is started. All other squares of the tape are initially blank (❑). As we have done for both FSMs and PDAs, *M*'s behavior will be defined only on input strings that are finite and contain only characters in *M*'s input alphabet.

M has a single read/write head, shown here with an arrow. We will almost always use the convention that, when *M* starts, its read/write head will be over the blank immediately to the left of the leftmost character of the input. But occasionally, when we are designing a machine to be used as a subroutine by some other machine, we may choose a different initial specification.

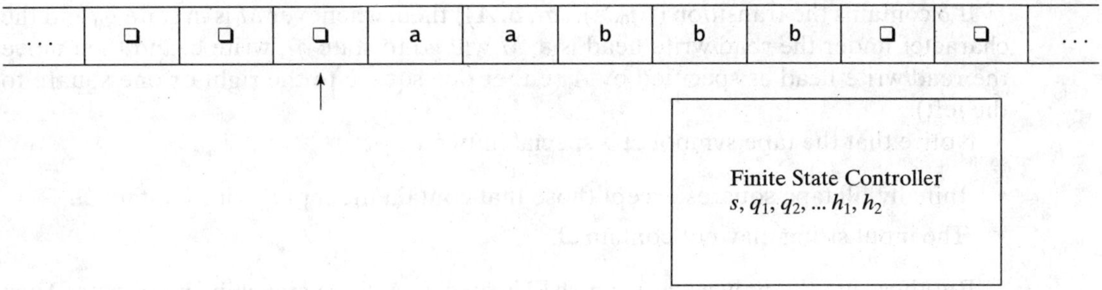

FIGURE 17.1 The structure of a Turing machine.

M begins in its start state. At each step of its operation, *M* must:

- choose its next state,
- write on the current square, and
- move the read/write head left or right one square.

M can move back and forth on its tape, so there is no longer the idea that it consumes all of its input characters one at a time and then halts. *M* will continue to execute until it reaches a special state called a halting state. It is possible that *M* may never reach a halting state, in which case it will execute forever.

Notice that there will always be a finite number of nonblank squares on *M*'s tape. This follows from the fact that, before *M* starts, only a finite number of squares are nonblank. Then, at each step of its operation, *M* can write on at most one additional square. So, after any finite number of steps, only a finite number of squares can be nonblank. And, even if *M* never halts, at any point in its computation it will have executed only a finite number of steps.

In Chapter 18 we are going to argue that the Turing machine, as we have just described it, is as powerful as any other reasonable model of computation, including modern computers. So, in the rest of this discussion, although our examples will be simple, remember that we are now talking about computation, broadly conceived.

We are now ready to provide a formal definition. A ***Turing machine*** (or ***TM***) *M* is a sixtuple $(K, \Sigma, \Gamma, \delta, s, H)$, where:

- K is a finite set of states,
- Σ is the input alphabet, which does not contain ❑,
- Γ is the tape alphabet, which must, at a minimum, contain ❑ and have Σ as a subset,
- $s \in K$ is the start state,
- $H \subseteq K$ is the set of halting states, and
- δ is the transition function. It maps from:

$$\begin{array}{ccccccccc} (K - H) & \times & \Gamma & \text{to} & K & \times & \Gamma & \times & \{\rightarrow, \leftarrow\}. \\ \textit{non-halting state} & \times & \textit{tape character} & & \textit{state} & \times & \textit{tape character} & \times & \textit{action}(R \textit{ or } L) \end{array}$$

If δ contains the transition $((q_0, \text{a}), (q_1, \text{b}, A))$ then, whenever M is in state q_0 and the character under the read/write head is a, M will go to state q_1, write b, and then move the read/write head as specified by A (either one square to the right or one square to the left).

Notice that the tape symbol ❑ is special in two ways:

- Initially, all tape squares except those that contain the input string contain ❑.
- The input string may not contain ❑.

But those are the only ways in which ❑ is special. A Turing machine may write ❑ just as it writes any other symbol in its tape alphabet Γ. Be careful, though, if you design a Turing machine M that does write ❑. Make sure that M can tell the difference between running off the end of the input and hitting a patch of ❑'s within the part of the tape it is working on. Some books use a definition of a Turing machine that does not allow writing ❑. But we allow it because it can be quite useful if you are careful. In addition, this definition allows a Turing machine to output a string that is shorter than its input by writing ❑'s as necessary.

Define the ***active tape*** of a Turing machine M to be the shortest fragment of M's tape that includes the square under the read/write head and all the nonblank squares.

We require that δ be defined for all (state, input) pairs unless the state is a halting state. Notice that δ is a function, not a relation. So this is a definition for deterministic Turing machines.

One other important observation: A Turing machine can produce output, namely the contents of its tape when it halts.

EXAMPLE 17.1 Add b's to Make Them Match the a's

Design a Turing machine M that takes as input a string in the language $\{\text{a}^i\text{b}^j : 0 \leq j \leq i\}$ and adds b's as required to make the number of b's equal the number of a's. The input to M will look like this:

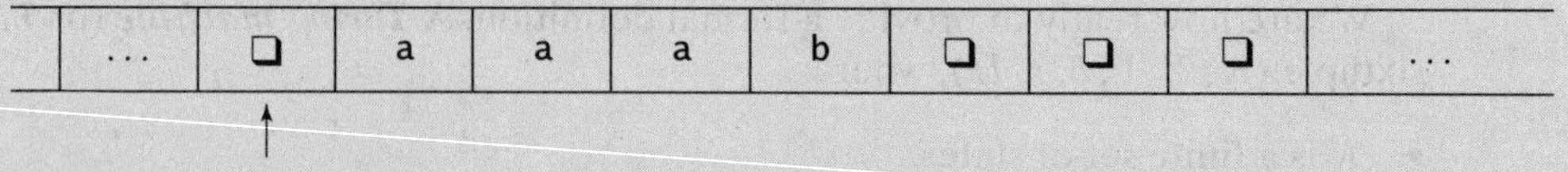

On that input, the output (the contents of the tape when M halts) should be:

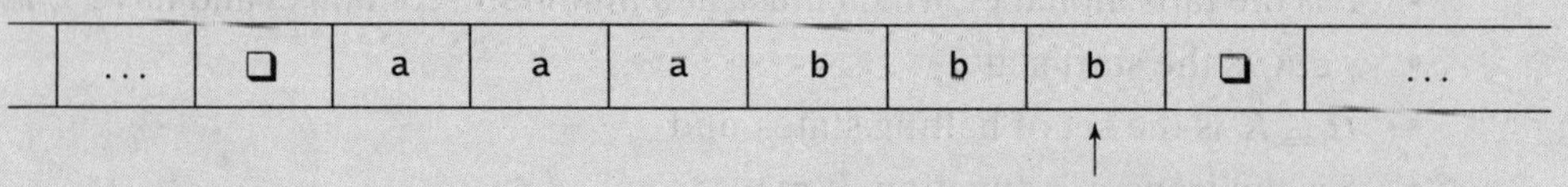

M will operate as follows:

1. Move one square to the right. If the character under the read/write head is ❑, halt. Otherwise, continue.

2. Loop:

2.1. Mark off an a with a $.

2.2. Scan rightward to the first b or ❑.

- If b, mark it off with a # and get ready to go back and find the next matching a, b pair.
- If ❑, then there are no more b's but there are still a's that need matches. So it is necessary to write another b on the tape. But that b must be marked so that it cannot match another a. So write a #. Then get ready to go back and look for remaining unmarked a's.

2.3. Scan back leftward looking for a or ❑. If a, then go back to the top of the loop and repeat. If ❑, then all a's have been handled. Exit the loop. (Notice that the specification for M guarantees that there will not be more b's than a's.)

3. Make one last pass all the way through the nonblank area of the tape, from left to right, changing each $ to an a and each # to a b.

4. Halt.

M = ({1, 2, 3, 4, 5, 6}, {a, b}, {a, b, ❑, $, #}, δ, 1, {6}), where δ =

(((1, ❑), (2, ❑, →)),
((1, a), (2, q, →))
((1, b), (2, q, →)),
((1, $), (2, ❑, →)),
((1, #), (2, ❑, →)),

{These four transitions are required because M must be defined for every state/ input pair, but since it isn't possible to see anything except ❑ in state 1, it doesn't matter what they do.}

((2, ❑), (6, $, →)),
((2, a), (3, $, →)),
((2, b), (3, $, →)),
((2, $), (3, $, →)),
((2, #), (3, $, →)),

{Three more unusable elements of δ. We'll omit the rest here for clarity.}

((3, ❑), (4, #, ←)),
((3, a), (3, a, →)),
((3, b), (4, #, ←)),
((3, $), (3, $, →)),
((3, #), (3, #, →)),
((4, ❑), (5, ❑, →)),
((4, a), (3, $, →)),
((4, $), (4, $, ←)),
((4, #), (4, #, ←)),
((5, ❑), (6, ❑, ←)), }

{State 6 is a halting state and so has no transitions out of it}

((5, $), (5, a, →)),
((5, #), (5, b, →)))

People find it nearly impossible to read transition tables like this one, even for very simple machines. So we will adopt a graphical notation similar to the one we used for both FSMs and PDAs. Since each element of δ has five components, we need a notation for labeling arcs that includes all the required information. Let $x/t/a$ on an arc of M mean that the transition can be taken if the character currently under the read/write head is x. If it is taken, write t and then move the read/write head as specified by a. We will also adopt the convention that we will omit unusable transitions, such as $((1, a), (2, \square, \rightarrow))$ in the example above, from our diagrams so that they are easier to read.

EXAMPLE 17.2 Using the Graphical Language

Here is a graphical description, using the notation we just described, of the machine from Example 17.1:

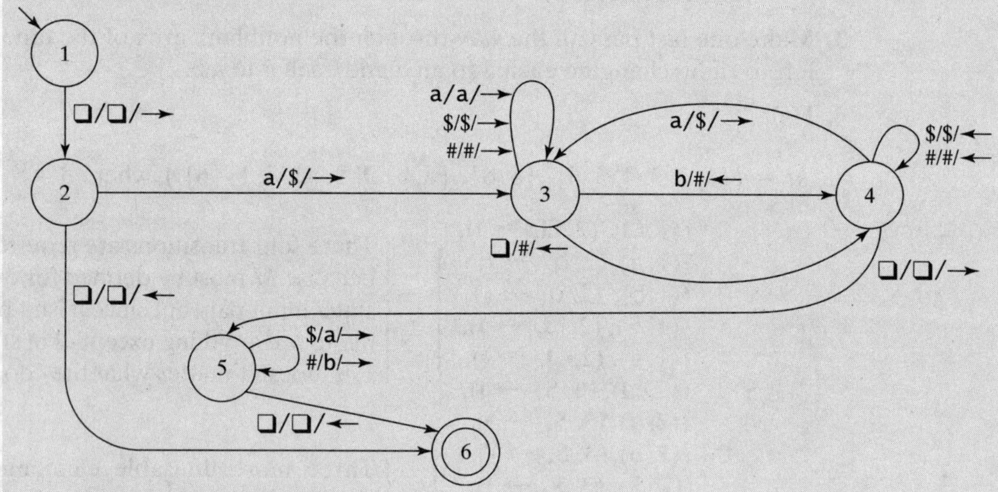

17.1.2 Programming Turing Machines

Although there is a lot less practical motivation for learning to program a Turing machine than there is for learning to build FSMs, regular expressions, context-free grammars, and parsers, it is interesting to see how a device that is so simple can actually be made to compute whatever we can compute using the fastest machines in our labs today. It seems to highlight the essence of what it takes to compute.

In Chapter 18, we will argue that anything computable can be computed by a Turing machine. So we should not expect to find simple nuggets that capture everything a Turing machine programmer needs to know. But, at least for the fairly straightforward language recognition problems that we will focus on, there are a few common programming idioms. The example we have just shown illustrates them:

- A computation will typically occur in phases: When phase 1 finishes, phase 2 begins, and so forth.

- One phase checks for corresponding substrings by moving back and forth, marking off corresponding characters.
- There are two common ways to go back and forth. Suppose the input string is aaaabbbb and we want to mark off the a's and make sure they have corresponding b's. Almost any sensible procedure marks the first a, scans right, and marks the first b. There are then two ways to approach doing the rest. We could:
  - Scan left to the first a we find and process the rest of the a's right to left. That is the approach we took in Example 17.1 discussed previously.
  - Scan all the way left until we find the first marked a. Bounce back one square to the right and mark the next a. In this approach, we process all the a's left to right.

  Both ways work. Sometimes it seems easier to use one, sometimes the other.
- If we care about the machine's output (as opposed to caring just about whether it accepts or rejects), then there is a final phase that makes one last pass over the tape and converts the marked characters back to their proper form.

17.1.3 Halting

We make the following important observations about the three kinds of automata that we have so far considered:

- A DFSM M, on input w, is guaranteed to halt in $|w|$ steps. We proved this result as Theorem 5.1. An arbitrary NDFSM can be simulated by *ndfsmsimulate* and that simulation will also halt in $|w|$ steps.
- An arbitrary PDA, on input w, is not guaranteed to halt. But, as we saw in Chapter 14, for any context-free language L there exists a PDA M that accepts L and that is guaranteed to halt.
- A Turing machine M, on input w, is not guaranteed to halt. It could, instead, bounce back and forth forever on its tape. Or it could just blast its way, in a single direction, through the input and off forever into the infinite sequence of blanks on the tape. And now, unlike with PDAs, there exists no algorithm to find an equivalent Turing machine that is guaranteed to halt.

This fundamental property of Turing machines, that they cannot be guaranteed to halt, will drive a good deal of our discussion about them.

17.1.4 Formalizing the Operation of a Turing Machine

In this section we will describe formally the computation process that we outlined in the last section.

A ***configuration*** of a Turing machine $M = (K, \Sigma, \Gamma, \delta, s, H)$ is a 4-tuple that is an element of:

K	$\times$	$((\Gamma - \{\square\})\Gamma^*) \cup \{\varepsilon\}$	$\times$	Γ	$\times$	$(\Gamma^*(\Gamma - \{\square\})) \cup \{\varepsilon\}$.
state		includes all of M's active tape to the left of the read/write head		square under the read/write head		includes all of M's active tape to the right of the read/write head

Notice that, although M's tape is infinite, the description of any configuration is finite because we include in that description the smallest contiguous tape fragment that includes all the nonblank squares and the square under the read/write head.

We will use the following shorthand for configurations: (q, s_1, a, s_2) will be written as $(q, s_1\underline{a}s_2)$.

The initial configuration of any Turing machine M with start state s and input w is $(s, \underline{\square}\, w)$. Any configuration whose state is an element of H is a halting configuration.

EXAMPLE 17.3 Using the 4-Tuple Notation and the Shorthand

Tape (head position underlined)	As a 4-tuple	Shorthand
… ❑ a b <u>b</u> b ❑ ❑ …	$(q, \text{ab}, \text{b}, \text{b})$	$(q, \text{ab}\underline{\text{b}}\text{b})$
… <u>❑</u> a a b b ❑ …	$(q, \varepsilon, \square, \text{aabb})$	$(q, \underline{\square}\text{abbb})$

The transition function δ defines the operation of a Turing machine M one step at a time. We can use it to define the sequence of configurations that M will enter. We start by defining the relation *yields-in-one-step*, written $|-_M$, which relates configuration c_1 to configuration c_2 iff M can move from configuration c_1 to configuration c_2 in one step. So, just as we did with FSMs and PDAs, we define:

$$(q_1, w_1)|-_M (q_2, w_2) \text{ iff } (q_2, w_2) \text{ is derivable, via } \delta, \text{ in one step.}$$

We can now define the relation ***yields***, written $|-_M{}^*$, to be the reflexive, transitive closure of $|-_M$. So configuration C_1 yields configuration C_2 if:

$$C_1 |-_M{}^* C_2.$$

A ***path*** through M is a sequence of configurations $C_0, C_1, C_2, \ldots$ such that C_0 is an initial configuration of M and:

$$C_0 |-_M C_1 |-_M C_2 |-_M \ldots$$

A ***computation*** by M is a path that halts. So it is a sequence of configurations $C_0, C_1, \ldots, C_n$ for some $n \geq 0$, such that C_0 is an initial configuration of M, C_n is a halting configuration of M, and:

$$C_0 |-_M C_1 |-_M C_2 |-_M \ldots |-_M C_n.$$

If a computation halts in n steps, we will say that it has length n and we will write:

$$C_0 |-_M{}^n C_n$$

17.1.5 A Macro Notation for Turing Machines

Writing even very simple Turing machines is time consuming and reading a description of one and making sense of it is even harder. Sometimes we will simply describe, at a high level, how a Turing machine should operate. But there are times when we would like to be able to specify a machine precisely. So, in this section, we present a macro language that will make the task somewhat easier. If you don't care about the details of how Turing machines work, you can skip this section. In most of the rest of our examples, we will give the high level description first, followed (when it's feasible) by a description in this macro language.

The key idea behind this language is the observation that we can combine smaller Turing machines to build more complex ones. We begin by defining simple machines that perform the basic operations of writing on the tape, moving the read/write head, and halting:

- Symbol writing machines: For each $x \in \Gamma$, define M_x, written just x, to be a Turing machine that writes x on the current square of the tape and then halts. So, if $\Gamma = \{a, b, \square\}$, there will be three simple machines: a, b, and ❑. (A technical note: Given our definition of a Turing machine, each of these machines must actually make two moves. In the first move, it writes the new symbol on the tape and moves right. In the next move, it rewrites whatever character was there and then moves left. These two moves are necessary because our machines must move at each step. But this is a detail with which we do not want to be concerned when we are writing Turing machine programs. This notation hides it from us.)
- Head moving machines: There are two of these: R rewrites whatever character was on the tape and moves one square to the right. L rewrites whatever character was on the tape and moves one square to the left.
- Machines that simply halt: Each of our machines halts when it has nothing further to do (i.e., it has entered a state on which δ is undefined), but there are times when we'll need to indicate halting explicitly. We will use three simple halting machines:
  - h, which simply halts. We will use h when we want to make it clear that some path of a machine halts, but we do not care about accepting or rejecting.
  - n, which halts and rejects.
  - y, which halts and accepts.

Next we need to describe how to:

- Check the tape and branch based on what character we see, and
- Combine the basic machines to form larger ones.

We can do both of these things with a notation that is very similar to the one we have used for all of our state machines so far. We will use two basic forms:

- M_1M_2: Begin in the start state of M_1. Run M_1 until it halts. If it does, begin M_2 in its start state (without moving the read/write head) and run M_2 until it halts. If it does, then halt. If either M_1 or M_2 fails to halt, M_1M_2 will fail to halt.

- $M_1 \xrightarrow{\textit{condition}} M_2$: Begin in the start state of M_1. Run M_1 until it halts. If it does, check *condition*. If it is true, then begin M_2 in its start state (without moving the read/write head) and run M_2 until it halts. The simplest condition will be the presence of a specific character under the read/write head, although we will introduce some others as well. A machine with this structure will fail to halt if either:
  - M_1 fails to halt, or
  - *condition* is true and M_2 fails to halt.

We will use the symbol $>$ to indicate where the combination machine begins.

EXAMPLE 17.4 The Macro Language Lets Machines be Composed

Let M =

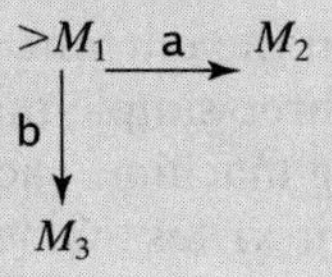

So M:

- Starts in the start state of M_1.
- Computes until M_1 reaches a halting state.
- Examines the tape. If the current symbol is a, then it transfers control to M_2. If the current symbol is b, it transfers control to M_3.

To make writing our machines a bit easier, we introduce some shorthands:

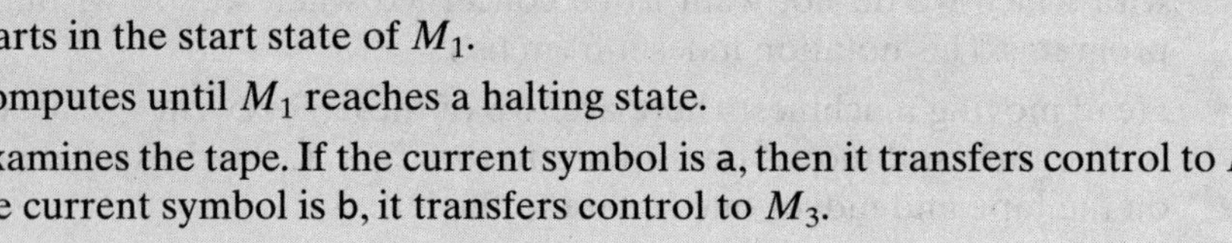

Next we provide a simple mechanism for storing values in variables. Each variable will hold just a single character. A standard Turing machine can remember values for any finite number of such variables either by writing them someplace on its tape or by branching to a different state for each possible value. This second solution avoids having to scan back and forth on the tape, but it can lead to an explosion in the number of states since there must be effectively a new copy of the machine for each combination of values that a set of variables can have. We will hide the mechanism by which variables are implemented by allowing them to be named and explicitly referenced in the conditions on the arcs of our machines. So we have:

$M_1 \xrightarrow[\text{except a}]{\text{all elements of } \Gamma} M_2$ becomes $M_1 \xrightarrow{x \leftarrow \neg \text{a}} M_2$

and x takes on the value of the current square.

$M_1 \xrightarrow{\text{a, b}} M_2$ becomes $M_1 \xrightarrow{x \leftarrow \text{a, b}} M_2$

and x takes on the value of the current square.

We can use the value of a variable in two ways. The first is as a condition on a transition. So we can write:

$$M_1 \xrightarrow{x = y} M_2$$

if $x = y$ then take the transition.

Note that we use $\leftarrow$ for assignment and $=$ and $\neq$ for Boolean comparison. We can also write the value of a variable. We'll indicate that with the variable's name.

EXAMPLE 17.5 Using Variables to Remember Single Characters

Let $M=$

$$> \xrightarrow{x \leftarrow \neg \square} \text{R}x$$

If the current square is not blank, M remembers its value in the variable x, goes right one square, and copies it by writing the value of x. (If the current square is blank, M has nothing to do. So it halts.)

Next we define some very useful machines that we can build from the primitives we have so far:

$>\text{R} \circlearrowleft \neg\square$ Move right. If the character under the read/write head is not $\square$, repeat. If it is $\square$, no further action is specified, so halt. In other words, find the first blank square to the right of the current square. We will abbreviate this $\text{R}_{\square}$

$>\text{L} \circlearrowleft \neg\square$ Move left. If the character under the read/write head is not $\square$, repeat. If it is $\square$, no further action is specified, so halt. In other words, find the first blank square to the left of the current square. We will abbreviate this $\text{L}_{\square}$.

$>\text{R} \circlearrowleft \square$ Similarly, but find the first nonblank square to the right of the current square. We will abbreviate this $\text{R}_{\neg\square}$.

$>\text{L} \circlearrowleft \square$ Similarly, but find the first nonblank square to the left of the current square. We will abbreviate this $\text{L}_{\neg\square}$.

We can do the same thing we have just done for ❑ with any other character in Γ. So we can write:

L_a	Find the first occurrence of a to the left of the current square.
$R_{a,b}$	Find the first occurrence of a or b to the right of the current square.
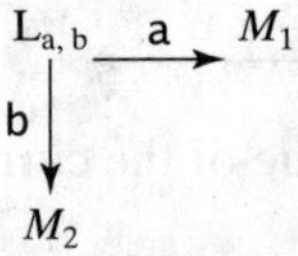	Find the first occurrence of a or b to the left of the current square, then go to M_1 if the detected character is a; go to M_2 if the detected character is b.
$L_{x \leftarrow a,b}$	Find the first occurrence of a or b to the left of the current square and set x to the value found.
$L_{x \leftarrow a,b}Rx$	Find the first occurrence of a or b to the left of the current square, set x to the value found, move one square to the right, and write x (a or b).

EXAMPLE 17.6 Triplicating a String

We wish to build M with the following specification: Input: ❑w $w \in \{1\}^*$

Output: ❑w^3

Example: Input: ❑111 Output: ❑111111111

M will operate as follows on input w:

1. Loop
   - **1.1.** Move right to the first 1 or ❑.
   - **1.2.** If the current character is ❑, all the 1s have been copied. Exit the loop. Otherwise the current character must be a 1. Mark it off with # (so it won't get copied again), move right to the first blank, and write two more #'s.
   - **1.3.** Go left back to the blank in front of the string.
2. Make one final pass through the string converting the #'s back to 1's

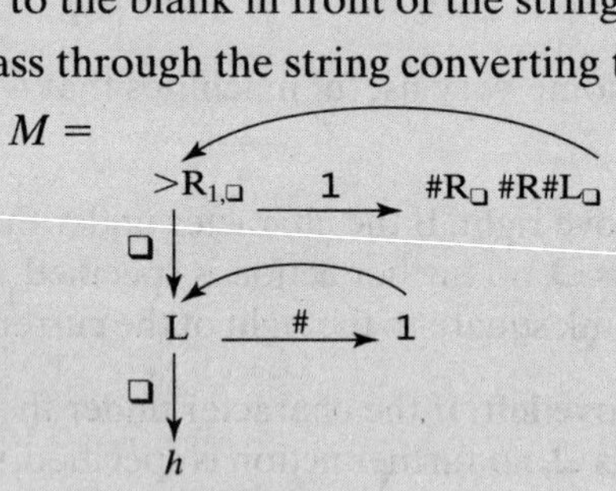

EXAMPLE 17.7 Shifting Left One Square

We wish to build a shifting machine $S_{\leftarrow}$ with the following specification, where u and w are strings that do not contain any ❑'s:

Input:	❑*u*❑*w*❑
Output:	❑*uw*❑

Example: Input: 11❑00

Output: 1100❑

$S_{\leftarrow}$ moves left to right through w, copying each character onto the square immediately to its left:

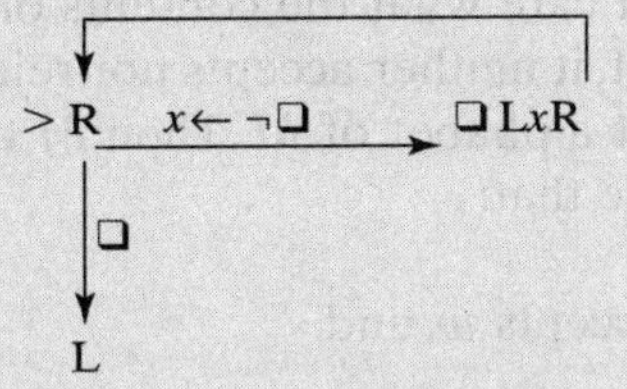

17.2 Computing With Turing Machines

Now that we know how Turing machines work, we can describe how to use a Turing machine to:

- recognize a language, or
- compute a function.

17.2.1 Turing Machines as Language Recognizers

Given a language L, we would like to be able to design a Turing machine M that takes as input (on its tape) some string w and tells us whether or not $w \in L$. There are many languages for which it is going to be possible to do this. Among these are all of the noncontext-free languages that we discussed in Part III (as well as all the regular and context-free languages for which we have built FSMs and PDAs).

However, as we will see in Chapter 19 and others that follow it, there are many languages for which even the power of the Turing machine is not enough. In some of those cases, there is absolutely nothing better that we can do. There exists no Turing machine that can distinguish between strings that are in L and strings that are not. But there are other languages for which we can solve part of the problem. For each of these languages we can build a Turing machine M that looks for the property P (whatever it is) of being in L. If M discovers that its input possesses P, it halts and accepts. But if P does not hold for some input string w, then M may keep looking forever. It may not be able to tell that it is not going to find P and thus it should halt and reject.

In this section we will define what it means for a Turing machine to decide a language (i.e., for every string, accept or reject as appropriate) and for a Turing machine to semidecide a language (i.e., to accept when it should).

Deciding a Language

Let M be a Turing machine with start state s and two halting states that we will call y and n. Let w be an element of Σ^*. Then we will say that:

- ***M accepts*** w iff $(s, \square w) \vdash_M^* (y, w')$ for some string w'. We call any configuration (y, w') an ***accepting configuration***.
- ***M rejects*** w iff $(s, \square w) \vdash_M^* (n, w')$ for some string w'. We call any configuration (n, w') a ***rejecting configuration***.

Notice that we do not care what the contents of M's tape are when it halts. Also note that if M does not halt, it neither accepts nor rejects.

Let Σ be the input alphabet of M. Then M ***decides*** a language $L \subseteq \Sigma^*$ iff, for any string $w \in \Sigma^*$, it is true that:

- If $w \in L$ then M accepts w, and
- If $w \notin L$ then M rejects w.

Since every string in Σ^* is either in L or not in L, any deciding machine M must halt on all inputs. A language L is ***decidable*** iff there is a Turing machine M that decides it.

We define the set D to be the set of all decidable languages. So a language L is in D iff there is a Turing machine that decides it. In some books, the set D is called R, or the set of ***recursive languages***.

EXAMPLE 17.8 $A^nB^nC^n$

Recall the language $A^nB^nC^n = \{a^nb^nc^n : n \geq 0\}$, which we showed was not context-free and so could not be recognized with a PDA. $A^nB^nC^n$ is decidable. We can build a straightforward Turing machine M to decide it. M will work as follows on input w:

1. Move right onto w. If the first character is $\square$, halt and accept.

2. Loop:

2.1. Mark off an a with a 1.

2.2. Move right to the first b and mark it off with a 2. If there isn't one, or if there is a c first, halt and reject.

2.3. Move right to the first c and mark it off with a 3. If there isn't one, or if there is an a first, halt and reject.

2.4. Move all the way back to the left, then right again past all the 1s (the marked off a's). If there is another a, go back to the top of the loop. If there isn't, exit the loop.

3. All a's have found matching b's and c's and the read/write head is just to the right of the region of marked off a's. Continue moving left to right to verify that all b's and c's have been marked. If they have, halt and accept. Otherwise halt and reject.

In our macro language, *M* is:

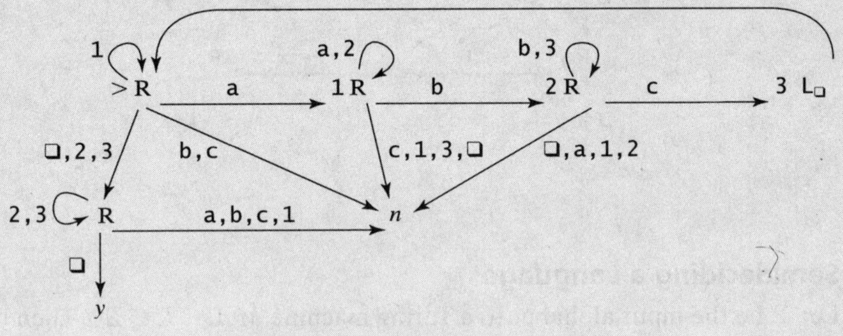

EXAMPLE 17.9 WcW

Consider again WcW = $\{wcw : w \in \{a, b\}^*\}$. We can build *M* to decide WcW as follows:

1. Loop:

   1.1. Move right to the first character. If it is c, exit the loop. Otherwise, overwrite it with ❑ and remember what it is.

   1.2. Move right to the c. Then continue right to the first unmarked character. If it is ❑, halt and reject. (This will happen if the string to the right of c is shorter than the string to the left.) If it is anything else, check to see whether it matches the remembered character from the previous step. If it does not, halt and reject. If it does, mark it off with #.

   1.3. Move back leftward to the first ❑.

2. There are no characters remaining before the c. Make one last sweep left to right checking that there are no unmarked characters after the c and before the first blank. If there are, halt and reject. Otherwise, halt and accept.

EXAMPLE 17.9 (*Continued*)

In our macro language, *M* is:

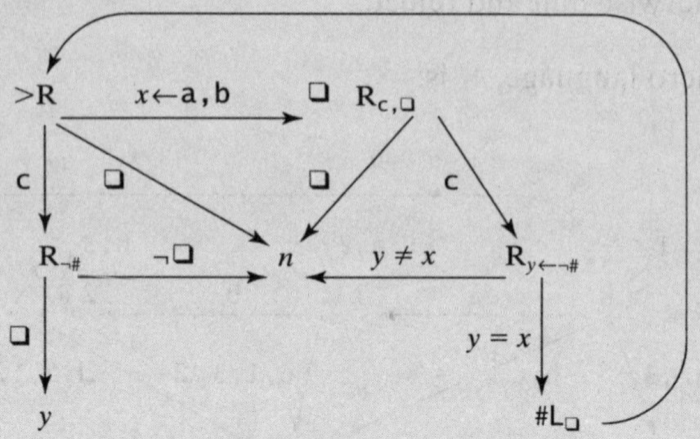

Semideciding a Language

Let Σ be the input alphabet to a Turing machine *M*. Let $L \subseteq \Sigma^*$. Then we will say that *M* ***semidecides*** *L* iff, for any string $w \in \Sigma^*$:

- If $w \in L$ then *M* accepts *w*, and
- If $w \notin L$ then *M* does not accept *w*. In this case, *M* may explicitly reject or it may loop.

A language *L* is ***semidecidable*** iff there is a Turing machine that semidecides it. We define the set SD to be the set of all semidecidable languages. So a language *L* is in SD iff there is a Turing machine that semidecides it. In some books, the set SD is called RE, or the set of ***recursively enumerable languages*** or the set of ***Turing-recognizable languages***.

EXAMPLE 17.10 Semideciding by Running Off the Tape

Let $L = \mathtt{b^*a(a \cup b)^*}$. So, any machine that accepts *L* must look for at least one a. We can build *M* to semidecide *L*:

1. Loop:
   Move one square to the right. If the character under the read/write head is an a, halt and accept.

In our macro language, *M* is:

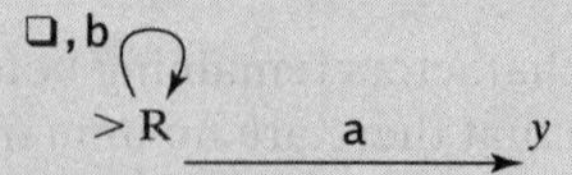

Of course, for *L*, we can do better than *M*. *M#* decides *L*:

1. Loop:
   Move one square to the right. If the character under the read/write head is an a, halt and accept. If it is ❑, halt and reject.

In our macro language, *M#* is:

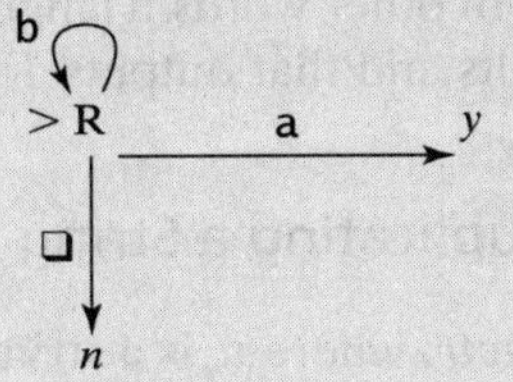

As we will prove later, there are languages that are in SD but not D and so a semideciding Turing machine is the best we will be able to build for those languages.

17.2.2 Turing Machines Compute Functions

When a Turing machine halts, there is a value on its tape. When we build deciding and semideciding Turing machines, we ignore that value. But we don't have to. Instead, we can define what it means for a Turing machine to compute a function. We'll begin by defining what it means for a Turing machine to compute a function whose domain and range are sets of strings. Then we'll see that, by using appropriate encodings of other data types and of multiple input values, we can define Turing machines to compute a wide variety of functions.

In this section, we consider only Turing machines that always halt. In Chapter 25 we will expand this discussion to include Turing machines that sometimes fail to halt.

Let M be a Turing machine with start state s, halting state h, and input alphabet Σ. The initial configuration of M will be $(s, \underline{\square} w)$, where $w \in \Sigma^*$.

Define $M(w) = z$ iff $(s, \underline{\square} w) \mid\!-_M{}^* (h, \underline{\square} z)$. In other words $M(w) = z$ iff M, when started on a string w in Σ^*, halts with z on its tape and its read/write head is just to the left of z.

Let $\Sigma' \subseteq \Gamma$ be M's output alphabet (i.e., the set of symbols that M may leave on its tape when it halts).

Now, let f be any function that maps from Σ^* to Σ'^*. We say that a Turing machine ***M computes*** a function f iff, for all $w \in \Sigma^*$:

- If w is an input on which f is defined, $M(w) = f(w)$. In other words, M halts with $f(w)$ on its tape.
- Otherwise $M(w)$ does not halt.

A function f is ***recursive*** or ***computable*** iff there is a Turing machine M that computes it and that always halts. The term *computable* more clearly describes the essence of these functions. The traditional name for them, however, is *recursive*. We will see why that is in Chapter 25. In the meantime, we will use the term *computable*.[7]

[7]In some other treatments of this subject, a function f is ***computable*** iff there is some Turing machine M (which may not always halt) that computes it. Specifically, if there are values for which f is undefined, M will fail to halt on those values. We will say that such a function is ***partially computable*** and we will reserve the term *computable* for that subset of the partially computable functions that can be computed by a Turing machine that always halts.

There is a natural correspondence between the use of Turing machines to compute functions and their use as language deciders. A language is decidable iff its characteristic function is computable. In other words, a language L is decidable iff there exists a Turing machine that always halts and that outputs *True* if its input is in L and *False* otherwise.

EXAMPLE 17.11 Duplicating a String

Let $duplicate(w) = ww$, where w is a string that does not contain ❑.

A Turing machine to compute *duplicate* can be built easily if we have two subroutines:

- The copy machine C, which will perform the following operation:

$$\underline{\square}w\square\square\square\square\square\square \quad \rightarrow \quad \square w\underline{\square}w\square$$

C will work by moving back and forth on the tape, copying characters one at a time:

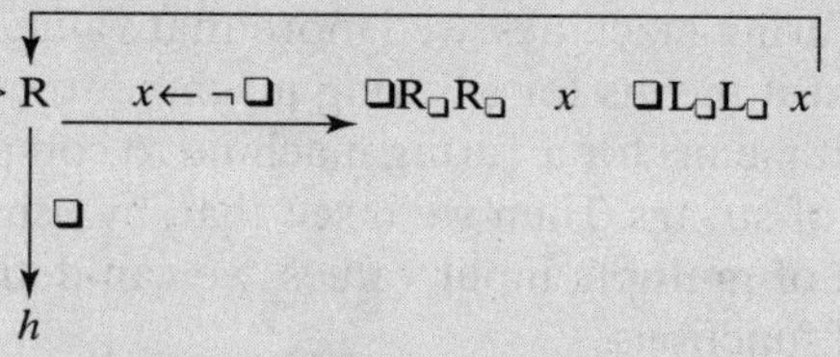

We define C this way because the copy process is straightforward if there is a character (we use ❑) to delimit the two copies.

- The $S_{\leftarrow}$ machine, which we described in Section 17.1.5. We will use $S_{\leftarrow}$ to shift the second copy of w one square to the left.

M, defined as follows, computes *duplicate*:

$$> CS_{\leftarrow} L_{\square}$$

Now suppose that we want to compute functions on values other than strings. All we need to do is to encode those values as strings. To make it easy to describe functions on such values, define a family of functions, $value_k(n)$. For any positive integer k, $value_k(n)$ returns the nonnegative integer that is encoded, base k, by the string n. For example, $value_2(101) = 5$ and $value_8(101) = 65$. We will say that a Turing machine M computes a function f from $\mathbb{N}^m$ to $\mathbb{N}$ provided that, for some k, $value_k(M(n_1; n_2; \ldots n_m)) = f(value_k(n_1), \ldots value_k(n_m))$.

Not all functions with straightforward definitions are computable. For example, the busy beaver functions described in Section 25.1.4 measure the "productivity" of Turing machines by returning the maximum amount of work (measured in steps or in number of symbols on the tape) that can be done by a Turing machine with n states. The busy beaver functions are not computable.

EXAMPLE 17.12 The Successor Function

Consider the successor function $succ(n) = n + 1$. On input ❑n❑, M should output ❑$n + 1$❑.

We will represent n in binary without leading zeros. So $n \in 0 \cup 1\{0,1\}^*$ and $f(n) = m$, where $value_2(m) = value_2(n) + 1$.

We can now define the Turing machine M to compute *succ*:

1. Scan right until the first ❑. Then move one square back left so that the read/write head is on the last digit of n.
2. Loop:
   - **2.1.** If the digit under the read/write head is a 0, write a 1, move the read/write head left to the first blank, and halt.
   - **2.2.** If the digit under the read/write head is a 1, we need to carry. So write a 0, move one square to the left, and go back to the top of the loop.
   - **2.3.** If the digit under the read/write head is a ❑, we have carried all the way to the left. Write a 1, move one square to the left, and halt.

In our macro language, M is:

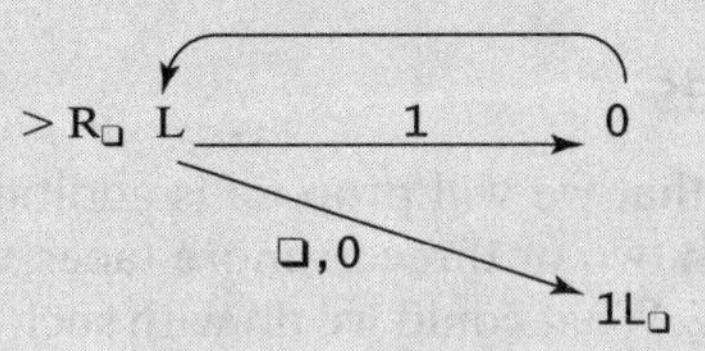

We can build Turing machines to compute functions of two or more arguments by encoding each of the arguments as a string and then concatenating them together, separated by a delimiter.

EXAMPLE 17.13 Binary Addition

Consider the *plus* function defined on the integers. On input ❑x;y❑, M should output the sum of x and y.

We will represent x and y in binary without leading zeros. So, for example, we'll encode the problem $5 + 8$ as the input string 101;1000. On this input, M should halt with 1101 on its tape. More generally, M should compute $f(n_1, n_2) = m$, where $value_2(m) = value_2(n_1) + value_2(n_2)$.

We leave the design of M as an exercise.

17.3 Adding Multiple Tapes and Nondeterminism

We have started with a very simple definition of a Turing machine. In this section we will consider two important extensions to that basic model. Our goal in describing the extensions is to make Turing machines easier to program. But we don't want to do that if it forces us to give up the simple model that we carefully chose because it would be easy to prove things about. So we are not going to add any fundamental power to the model. For each of the extensions we consider, we will prove that, given a Turing machine M that exploits the extension, there exists a Turing machine M' that is equivalent to M and that does not exploit the new feature. Each of these proofs will be by construction, from M to M'. This will enable us to place a bound on any change in time complexity that occurs when we transform M to M'.

There will be a bottom line at the end of this chapter. The details of the definition of a Turing machine don't matter in the sense that they don't affect what can be computed. In fact, there is a large family of other computational models that look even more unlike the basic definition than our extended machines do but that are still equivalent in power. We will articulate that principle in the following chapter. We will see, however, that the details may matter if we are concerned about the efficiency of the computations that we do. Even here, though, the details matter less than one might initially think. With one exception (the addition of nondeterminism), we'll see that adding features changes the time complexity of the resulting programs by at most a polynomial factor.

17.3.1 Multiple Tapes

The first extension that we will propose is additional tapes. Suppose we could build a Turing machine with two or three or more tapes, each with its own read/write head, as shown in Figure 17.2. What could we do with such a machine? One answer is, "a lot less going back and forth on the tape."

A k-tape Turing machine, just like a 1-tape Turing machine, is a sixtuple $M = (K, \Sigma, \Gamma, \delta, s, H)$. A configuration of a k-tape machine M is a $k + 1$ tuple: (*state*, *tape*$_1, \ldots,$ *tape*$_k$), where each tape description is identical to the description

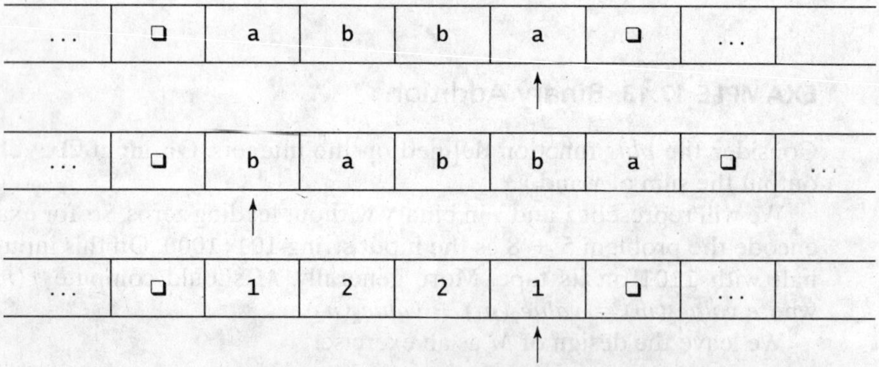

FIGURE 17.2 A multiple tape Turing machine.

we gave in Section 17.1.4 for a 1-tape machine. *M*'s initial configuration will be (s, ❑w, ❑, ..., ❑). In other words, its input will be on tape 1; all other tapes will initially be blank, with their read/write heads positioned on some blank square. If *M* halts, we will define its output to be the contents of tape 1; the contents of the other tapes will be ignored.

At each step, *M* will examine the square under each of its read/write heads. The set of values so obtained, along with the current state, determines *M*'s next action. It will write and then move on each of the tapes simultaneously. Sometimes *M* will want to move along one or more of its tapes without moving on others. So we will now allow the move action, stay put, which we will write as ↑. So δ is a function from:

$$
\begin{array}{lcl}
((K - H) \times \Gamma_1 & \text{to} & (K \times \Gamma_1 \times \{\leftarrow, \rightarrow, \uparrow\} \\
\quad \times \Gamma_2 & & \times \Gamma_2 \times \{\leftarrow, \rightarrow, \uparrow\} \\
\quad \times \ldots & & \times \ldots \\
\quad \times \ldots & & \times \ldots \\
\quad \times \Gamma_k) & & \times \Gamma_k \times \{\leftarrow, \rightarrow, \uparrow\}).
\end{array}
$$

EXAMPLE 17.14 Exploiting Two Tapes to Duplicate a String

Suppose that we want to build a Turing machine that, on input ❑$\underline{w}$❑, outputs ❑ww❑. In Example 17.11 we saw how we could do this with a conventional, one-tape machine that went back and forth copying each character of w one at a time. To copy a string of length n took n passes, each of which took n steps, for a total of n^2 steps. But to make that process straightforward, we left a blank between the two copies. So then we had to do a second pass in which we shifted the copy one square to the left. That took an additional n steps. So the entire process took $\mathcal{O}(n^2)$ steps. We now show how to do the same thing with a two tape machine M_C in $\mathcal{O}(n)$ steps.

Let w be the string to be copied. Initially, w is on tape 1 with the read/write head just to its left. The second tape is empty. The operation of M_C is shown in the following series of snapshots:

...	❑	a	b	b	a	❑	❑	❑	❑	...
	↑									

...	❑	❑	❑	❑	❑	❑	❑	❑	❑	...
	↑									

The first thing M_C will do is to move to the right on both tapes, one square at a time, copying the character from tape 1 onto the corresponding square of tape 2. This phase of the processing takes $|w|$ steps. At the end of this phase, the tapes will look like this, with both read/write heads on the blank just to the right of w:

EXAMPLE 17.14 (*Continued*)

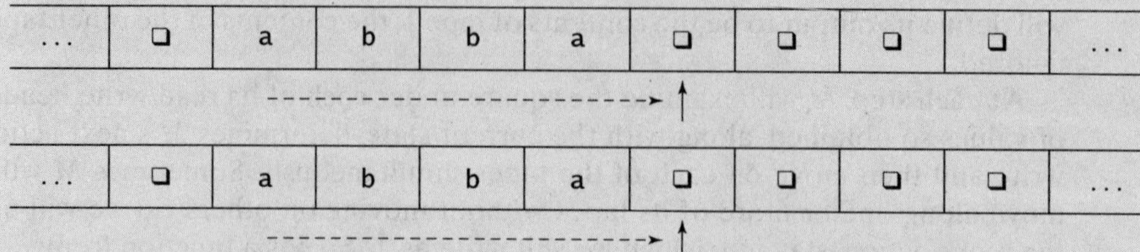

Next M_C moves tape 2's read/write head all the way back to the left. This phase also takes $|w|$ steps. At the end of it, the tapes will look like this:

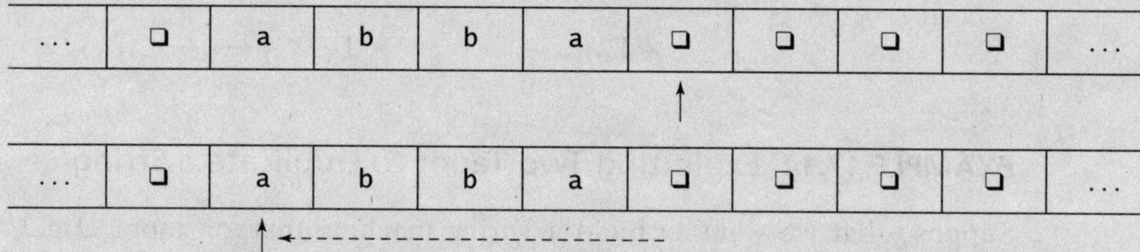

In its final phase, M_C will sweep to the right, copying w from tape 2 to tape 1. This phase also takes $|w|$ steps. At the end of it, the tapes will look like this:

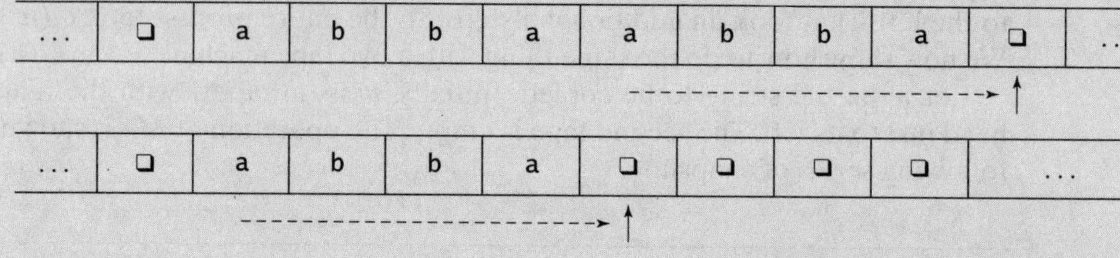

M_C takes $3 \cdot |w| = \mathcal{O}(|w|)$ steps.

EXAMPLE 17.15 Exploiting Two Tapes for Addition

Exercise 17.3(a) asks you to construct a standard one-tape Turing machine to add two binary numbers. Let's now build a 2-tape Turing machine M_A to do that. Let x and y be arbitrary binary strings. On input $\underline{❑}x; y$, M_A should output $\underline{❑}z$, where z is the binary encoding of the sum of the numbers represented by x and y.

For example, let $x = 5$ and $y = 6$. The initial configuration of tape 1 will be $\underline{❑}$ 101;110. The second tape is empty:

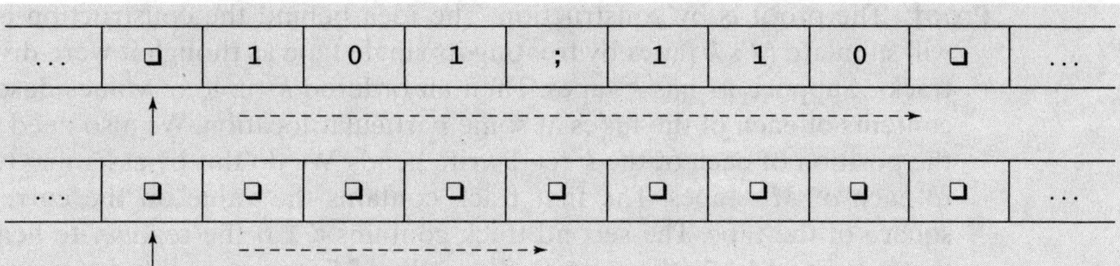

In its first phase, M_A moves the read/write head of tape 1 all the way to the right, copying x onto tape 2 and replacing it, on tape 1, with ❑s. It also replaces the ; with a ❑. It then moves both read/write heads rightward to the last nonblank square. At the end of this phase, y is on tape 1; x is on tape 2, and each read/write head is pointing to the low-order digit of its number:

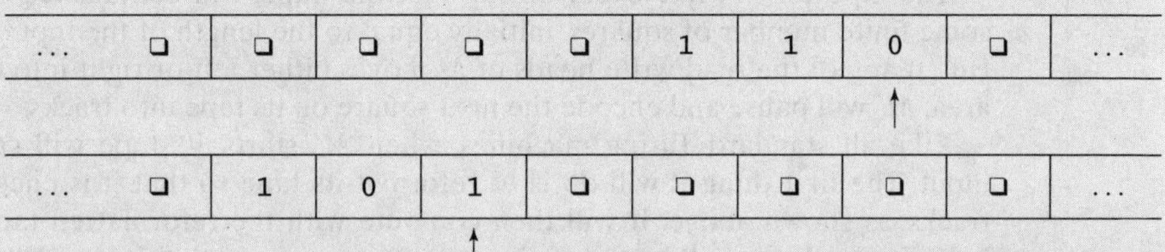

In its second phase, M_A moves back to the left, considering one pair of digits at a time. It sums them, treating a ❑ on either tape as a 0, records the result on tape 1, and remembers the carry digit for the next sum. Once it has encountered a blank on both tapes, it writes the carry digit if necessary and then it halts. At that point, its tapes are:

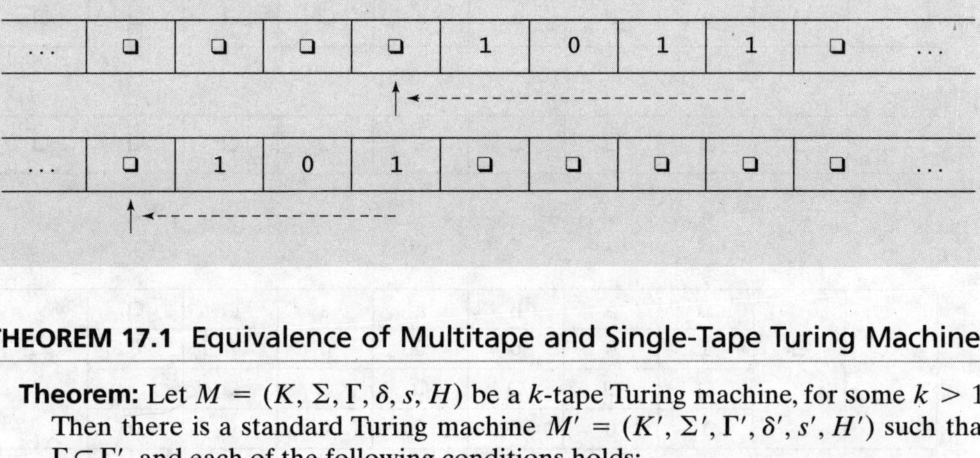

THEOREM 17.1 Equivalence of Multitape and Single-Tape Turing Machines

Theorem: Let $M = (K, \Sigma, \Gamma, \delta, s, H)$ be a k-tape Turing machine, for some $k > 1$. Then there is a standard Turing machine $M' = (K', \Sigma', \Gamma', \delta', s', H')$ such that $\Gamma \subseteq \Gamma'$, and each of the following conditions holds:

- For any input string x, M on input x halts with output z on the first tape iff M' on input x halts at the same halting state (y, n, or h) and with z on its tape.
- If, on input x, M halts after n steps, then M' halts in $\mathcal{O}(n^2)$ steps.

Proof: The proof is by construction. The idea behind the construction is that M' will simulate M's k tapes by treating its single tape as though it were divided into tracks. Suppose M has k tapes. Then an ordered k-tuple of values describes the contents of each of the tapes at some particular location. We also need to record the position of each of the k read/write heads. We do this by assigning two tracks to each of M's tapes. The first track contains the value on the corresponding square of the tape. The second track contains a 1 if the read/write head is over that square and a 0 otherwise. Because all of M's tapes are infinite, we need a way to line them up in order to be able to represent a slice through them. We will do this by starting with M's initial configuration and then lining up the tapes so that all the read/write heads form a single column.

To see how this works, let $k = 2$. Then M's initial configuration is shown in Figure 17.3(a). M' will encode that pair of tapes on its single tape as shown in Figure 17.3(b).

The tape for M', like every Turing machine tape, will contain □s on all but some finite number of squares, initially equal to the length of the input string w. But, if any of the read/write heads of M moves either left or right into the blank area, M' will pause and encode the next square on its tape into tracks.

Like all standard Turing machines, when M' starts, its tape will contain its input. The first thing it will do is to reformat its tape so that it is encoded as k tracks, as shown above. It will then compute with the reformatted tape until it halts. Its final step will be to reformat the tape again so that its result (the string that is written on its simulated tape 1) is written, without the track encoding, on the tape. So M' will need a tape alphabet that can encode both the initial and final situations (a single character per tape square) and the encoding of k tapes (with k values plus k read/write head bits per tape square). So M' needs a tape alphabet that has a unique symbol for each element of $\Gamma \cup (\Gamma \times \{0, 1\})^k$. Thus

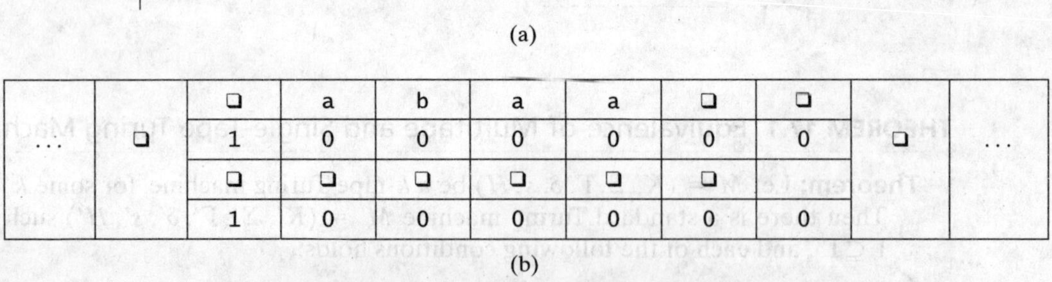

FIGURE 17.3 Encoding multiple tapes as multiple tracks.

$|\Gamma'| = |\Gamma| + (2 \cdot |\Gamma|)^k$. For example, to do the encoding shown above requires that Γ′ contain symbols for ❑, a, b, (❑, 1, ❑, 1), (a, 0, ❑, 0), (b, 0, ❑, 0), and so forth. $|\Gamma'| = 3 + 6^2 = 39$.

M′ operates as follows:

1. Set up the multitrack tape:

1.1. Move one square to the right to the first nonblank character on the tape.

1.2. While the read/write head is positioned over some non-❑ character *c* do:

Write onto the square the symbol that corresponds to a *c* on tape 1 and ❑s on every other track. On the first square, use the encoding that places a 1 on each even-numbered track (corresponding to the simulated read/write heads). On every other square, use the encoding that places a 0 on each even-numbered track.

2. Simulate the computation of *M* until (if) *M* would halt: (Each step will start with the read/write head for *M′* on the ❑ immediately to the right of the divided tape.)

2.1. Scan left and store in the state the *k*-tuple of characters under the simulated read/write heads. Move back to the ❑ immediately to the right of the divided tape.

2.2. Scan left and update each track as required by the appropriate transition of *M*. If necessary, subdivide a new square into tracks.

2.3. Move back right.

3. When *M* would halt, reformat the tape to throw away all but track 1, position the read/write head correctly, and then go to *M*'s halting state.

The construction that we just presented proves that any computation that can be performed by a *k*-tape Turing machine can be performed by a 1-tape machine. So adding any finite number of tapes adds no power to the Turing machine model. But there is a difference: The 1-tape machine must execute multiple steps for each single step taken by the *k*-tape machine. How many more? This question is only well defined if *M* (and so *M′*) halts. So, if *M* halts, let:

- *w* be the input string to *M*, and
- *n* be the number of steps *M* executes before it halts.

Each time *M′* executes step 2, it must make two passes over the nonblank segment of its tape. How long is that segment? It starts out with length $|w|$ but if *M* ever moves off its input then *M′* will extend the encoded area and have to sweep over the new section on each succeeding pass. So we do not know exactly the length of the nonblank (encoded) part of the *M′* tape, but we can put an upper bound on it by observing that *M* (and thus *M′*) can write on at most one additional square at each step. So an upper bound on the length of encoded tape is $|w| + n$.

We can now compute an upper bound on the number of steps it will take *M′* to simulate the execution of *M* on *w*:

Step 1 (initialization):	=	$\mathcal{O}(\lvert w\rvert)$.
Step 2 (computation):		
Number of passes	=	n.
Steps at each pass:		
For step 2.1	=	$2\cdot$(length of tape).
	=	$2\cdot(\lvert w\rvert + n)$.
For step 2.2	=	$2\cdot(\lvert w\rvert + n)$.
Total	=	$\mathcal{O}(n\cdot(\lvert w\rvert + n))$.
Step 3 (clean up):	=	$\mathcal{O}$(length of tape).
Total:	=	$\mathcal{O}(n\cdot(\lvert w\rvert + n))$.

If $n \geq |w|$ (which it will be most of the time, including in all cases in which M looks at each square of its input at least once), then the total number of steps executed by M' is $\mathcal{O}(n^2)$.

17.3.2 Nondeterministic Turing Machines

So far, all of our Turing machines have been deterministic. What happens if we relax that restriction? Before we answer that question, let's review what we know so far about nondeterminism:

- With FSMs, we saw that nondeterminism is a very useful programming tool. It makes the task of designing certain classes of machines, including pattern matchers, easy. So it reduces the likelihood of programmer error. But nondeterminism adds no real power. For any NDFSM M, there exists an equivalent deterministic one M'. Furthermore, although the number of states in M' may be as many as 2^K, where K is the number of states in M, the time it takes to execute M' on some input string w is $\mathcal{O}(|w|)$, just as it is for M.
- With PDAs, on the other hand, we saw that nondeterminism adds power. There are context-free languages that can be recognized by a nondeterministic PDA for which no equivalent deterministic PDA exists.

So, now, what about Turing machines? The answer here is mixed:

- Nondeterminism adds no power in the sense that any computation that can be performed by a nondeterministic Turing machine can be performed by a corresponding deterministic one.
- But complexity is an issue. It may take exponentially more steps to solve a problem using a deterministic Turing machine than it does to solve the same problem with a nondeterministic Turing machine.

A ***nondeterministic Turing machine*** is a sixtuple $(K, \Sigma, \Gamma, \Delta, s, H)$, where K, Σ, Γ, s, and H are as for standard Turing machines, and Δ is a subset of

$((K - H) \times \Gamma) \times (K \times \Gamma \times \{\leftarrow, \rightarrow\})$. In other words, we have replaced the transition *function* δ by the transition *relation* Δ, in much the same way we did when we defined nondeterministic FSMs and PDAs. The primary difference between our definition of nondeterminism for FSMs and PDAs and our definition of nondeterminism for Turing machines is that, since the operation of a Turing machine is not tied to the read-only, one-at-a-time consumption of its input characters, the notion of an ε-transition no longer makes sense.

But, just as before, we now allow multiple competing moves from a single configuration. And, as before, the easiest way to envision the operation of a nondeterministic Turing machine M is as a tree, as shown in Figure 17.4. Each node in the tree corresponds to a configuration of M and each path from the root corresponds to one sequence of configurations that M might enter.

Just as with PDAs, both the state and the data (in this case the tape) can be different along different paths.

Next we must define what it means for a nondeterministic Turing machine to:

- Decide a language.
- Semidecide a language.
- Compute a function.

We will consider each of these in turn.

Nondeterministic Deciding

What does it mean for a nondeterministic Turing machine to decide a language? What happens if the various paths disagree? The definition we will use is analogous to the one we used for both FSMs and PDAs. Recall that a computation of M is a sequence of configurations, starting in an initial configuration and ending in a halting configuration.

Let $M = (K, \Sigma, \Gamma, \Delta, s, H)$ be a nondeterministic Turing machine. Let w be an element of Σ^*. Then we will say that:

- M ***accepts*** w iff *at least one* of its computations accepts.
- M ***rejects*** w iff all of its computations reject.

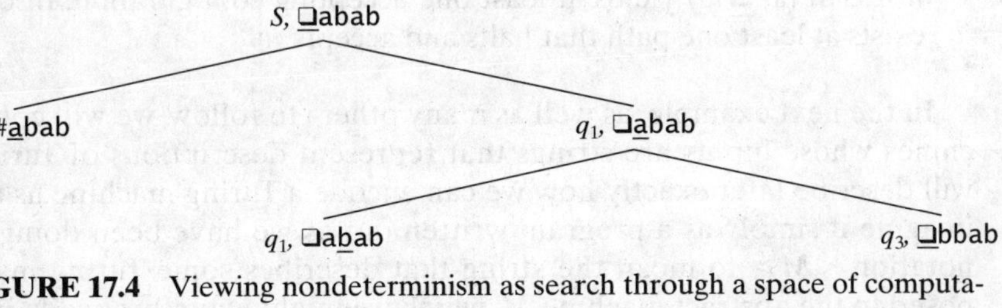

FIGURE 17.4 Viewing nondeterminism as search through a space of computation paths.

M ***decides*** a language $L \subseteq \Sigma^*$ iff, $\forall w \in \Sigma^*$:

- There is a finite number of paths that *M* can follow on input *w*,
- All of those paths are computations (i.e., they halt), and
- $w \in L$ iff *M* accepts *w*.

EXAMPLE 17.16 Exploiting Nondeterminism For Finding Factors

Let COMPOSITES = $\{w \in \{0, 1\}^* : w$ is the binary encoding of a composite number$\}$. We can build a nondeterministic Turing machine *M* to decide COMPOSITES. *M* operates as follows on input *w*:

1. Nondeterministically choose two binary numbers *p* and *q*, both greater than 1, such that $|p|$ and $|q| \leq |w|$. Write them on the tape, after *w*, separated by ;. For example, consider the input string 110011. After this step, *M*'s tape, along one of its paths, will look like:
   ❑110011;111;1111❑❑
2. Multiply *p* and *q* and put the answer, *A*, on the tape, in place of *p* and *q*. At this point, *M*'s tape will look like:
   ❑110011;1101001❑❑
3. Compare *A* and *w*. If they are equal, accept (i.e., go to *y*); else reject (i.e., go to *n*).

Nondeterministic Semideciding

Next we must decide what it means for a nondeterministic Turing machine to semidecide a language. What happens if the various paths disagree? In particular, what happens if some paths halt and others don't. Again, the definition that we will use requires only that there exist at least one accepting path. We don't care how many nonaccepting (looping or rejecting) paths there are. So we will say:

A nondeterministic Turing machine $M = (K, \Sigma, \Gamma, \Delta, s, H)$ ***semidecides*** a language $L \subseteq \Sigma^*$ iff, $\forall w \in \Sigma^*$:

- $w \in L$ iff $(s, \underline{❑}w)$ yields at least one accepting configuration. In other words, there exists at least one path that halts and accepts *w*.

In the next example, as well as many others to follow, we will consider Turing machines whose inputs are strings that represent descriptions of Turing machines. We will describe later exactly how we can encode a Turing machine as a string. For now, imagine it simply as a program written out as we have been doing. We will use the notation <*M*> to mean the string that describes some Turing machine *M* (as opposed to the abstract machine *M*, which we might actually encode in a variety of different ways).

EXAMPLE 17.17 Semideciding by Simulation

Let $L = \{<M> : M$ is a Turing machine that halts on at least one string$\}$. We will describe later how one Turing machine can simulate another. Assuming that we can in fact do that, a Turing machine S to semidecide L will work as follows on input $<M>$:

1. Nondeterministically choose a string w in Σ^* and write it on the tape.
2. Run M on w.
3. Accept.

Any individual branch of S will halt iff M halts on that branch's string. If a branch halts, it accepts. So at least one branch of S will halt and accept iff there is at least one string on which M halts.

As we will see in Chapter 21, semideciding is the best we are going to be able to do for L. We will also see that the approach that we have taken to designing S, namely to simulate some other machine and see whether it halts, will be one that we will use a lot when semideciding is the best that we can do.

Nondeterministic Function Computation

What about Turing machines that compute functions? Suppose, for example, that there are two paths through some Turing machine M on input w and they each return a different value. What value should M return? The first one it finds? Some sort of average of the two? Neither of these definitions seems to capture what we mean by a computation. And what if one path halts and the other doesn't? Should we say that M halts and returns a value? We choose a strict definition:

A nondeterministic Turing machine $M = (K, \Sigma, \Gamma, \Delta, s, H)$ ***computes*** a function f iff, $\forall w \in \Sigma^*$:

- All paths that M can follow on input w halt (i.e., all paths are computations), and
- All of M's computations result in $f(w)$.

Does Nondeterminism Add Power?

One of the most important results that we will prove about Turing machines is that nondeterminism adds no power to the original model. Nondeterministic machines may be easier to design and they may run substantially faster, but there is nothing that they can do that cannot be done with some equivalent deterministic machine.

THEOREM 17.2 Nondeterminism in Deciding and Semideciding Turing Machines

Theorem: If a nondeterministic Turing machine $M = (K, \Sigma, \Gamma, \Delta, s, H)$ decides a language L, then there exists a deterministic Turing machine M' that decides L. If a nondeterministic Turing machine M semidecides a language L, then there exists a deterministic Turing machine M' that semidecides L.

Proof Strategy: The proof will be by construction. The first idea we consider is the one we used to show that nondeterminism does not add power to FSMs. There we showed how to construct a new FSM M' that simulated the parallel execution of all of the paths of the original FSM M. Since M had a finite number of states, the number of sets of states that M' could be in was finite. So we simply constructed M' so that its states corresponded to sets of states from M. But that simple technique will not work for Turing machines because we must now consider the tape. Each path will need its own copy of the tape. Perhaps we could solve that problem by exploiting the technique from Section 17.3.1, where we used a single tape to encode multiple tapes. But that technique depended on advance knowledge of k, the number of tapes to be encoded. Since each path of M' will need a new copy of the tape, it isn't possible to put an *a priori* bound on k. So we must reject this idea.

A second idea we might consider is simple depth-first search. If any path rejects, M' will back up and try an alternative. If any path accepts, M' will halt and accept. If M' explores the entire tree and all paths have rejected, then it rejects. But there is a big problem with this approach. What if one of the early paths is one that doesn't halt? Then M' will get stuck and never find some accepting path later in the tree. If we are concerned only with finding deterministic equivalents for nondeterministic *deciding* Turing machines, this is not an issue since all paths of any deciding machine must halt. But we must also show that every nondeterministic *semideciding* Turing machine has an equivalent deterministic machine. So we must abandon the idea of a depth-first search.

But we can build an M' that conducts a breadth-first search of the tree of computational paths that M generates. Suppose that there are never more than b competing moves available from any configuration of M. And suppose that h is the length of the longest path that M might have to follow before it can accept. Then M' may require $\mathcal{O}(b^{h+1})$ moves to find a solution since it may have to explore an entire tree of height h. Is an exponential increase in the time it takes a deterministic machine to simulate the computation of a nondeterministic one the best we can do? No one knows. Most people will bet yes. Yet no one has been able to prove that no better approach exists. A proof of the correctness of either a yes or a no answer to this question is worth \$1,000,000 💻. We will return to this question in Part V. There we will see that the standard way in which this question is asked is, "Does P = NP?"

For now though we will continue with the search-based approach. To complete this proof with such a construction requires that we show how to implement the search process on a Turing machine. Because breadth-first search requires substantial bookkeeping that is difficult to describe, we'll use an alternative but computationally similar technique, iterative deepening. We describe the construction in detail in E.1.

THEOREM 17.3 Nondeterminism in Turing Machines That Compute Functions

Theorem: If a nondeterministic Turing machine $M = (K, \Sigma, \Gamma, \Delta, s, H)$ computes a function *f* then there exists a deterministic Turing machine M' that computes *f*.

Proof: The proof is by construction. It is very similar to the proof of Theorem 17.2 and is left as an exercise.

17.4 Simulating a "Real" Computer ✸

We've now seen that adding multiple tapes does not increase the power of Turing Machines. Neither does adding nondeterminism. What about adding features that would make a Turing Machine look more like a standard computer? Consider, for example, a simple computer that is composed of:

- An unbounded number of memory cells addressed by the integers starting at 0. These memory cells may be used to contain both program instructions and data. We'll encode both in binary. Assume no limit on the number of bits that are stored in each cell.
- An instruction set composed of basic operations including read (R), move input pointer right or left (MIR, MIL), load (L), store (ST), add (A), subtract (S), jump (JUMP), conditional jump (CJUMP), and halt (H). Here's a simple example program:

```
R      10       /* Read 2 bits from the input tape and put them
                   into the accumulator.
MIR    10       /* Move the input pointer two bits to the right.
CJUMP  1001     /* If the value in the accumulator is 0, jump to
                   location 1001.
A      10111    /* Add to the value in the accumulator the value
                   at location 10111.
ST     10111    /* Store the result back in location 10111.
```

- A program counter.
- An address register.
- An accumulator in which operations are performed.
- A small fixed number of special purpose registers.
- An input file.
- An output file.

Can a Turing machine simulate the operation of such a computer? The answer is yes.

THEOREM 17.4 A Real Computer Can be Simulated by a Turing Machine

Theorem: A random-access, stored program computer can be simulated by a Turing Machine. If the computer requires n steps to perform some operation, the Turing Machine simulation will require $\mathcal{O}(n^6)$ steps.

Proof: The proof is by construction of a simulator we'll call *simcomputer*. The simulator *simcomputer* will use 7 tapes:

- Tape 1 will hold the computer's memory. It will be organized as a series of (address, value) pairs, separated by the delimiter #. The addresses will be represented in binary. The values will also be represented in binary. This means that we need a binary encoding of programs such as the addition one we saw above. We'll use the first 4 bits of any instruction word for the operation code. The remainder of the word will store the address. So tape 1 will look like this:

  #0,$value_0$#1,$value_1$#10,$value_2$#11,$value_3$#100,$value_4$#...#

  With an appropriate assignment of operations to binary encodings, our example program, if stored starting at location 0, would look like:

  #0,000110010#1,11111001#10,001110011#11,001010111#....

  Notice that we must explicitly delimit the words because there is no bound on their length. Addresses may get longer as the simulated program uses more words of its memory. Numeric values may increase as old values are added to produce new ones.

- Tape 2 will hold the program counter, which is just an index into the memory stored on tape 1.
- Tape 3 will hold the address register.
- Tape 4 will hold the accumulator.
- Tape 5 will hold the operation code of the current instruction.
- Tape 6 will hold the input file.
- Tape 7 will hold the output file, which will initially be blank.

Like all other multitape Turing machines, *simcomputer* will begin with its input on tape 1 and all other tapes blank. *Simcomputer* requires two inputs, the program to be simulated and the input on which the simulation is to be run. So we will encode them both on tape 1, separated by a special character that we will write as %.

We will assume that the program is stored starting in memory location 0, so the program counter will initially need to be initialized to 0. The simulator *simcomputer* operates as follows:

simcomputer(*program*) =

/* Initialize.

1. Move the input string to tape 6.

2. Initialize the program counter (tape 2) to 0.

/* Execute one pass through this loop for every instruction executed by *program*.

3. Loop:

3.1. Starting at the left of the nonblank portion of tape 1, scan to the right looking for an index that matches the contents of tape 2 (the program counter).

/* Decode the current instruction and increment the program counter.

3.2. Copy the operation code to tape 5.
3.3. Copy the address to tape 3.
3.4. Add 1 to the value on tape 2.

/* Retrieve the operand.

3.5. Starting at the left again, scan to the right looking for the address that is stored on tape 3.

/* Execute the instruction.

3.6. If the operation is Load, copy the operand to tape 4 (the accumulator).
3.7. If the operation is Add, add the operand to the value on tape 4.
3.8. If the operation is Jump, copy the value on tape 3 to tape 2 (the program counter).
3.9. And so forth for the other operations.

How many steps must *simcomputer* execute to simulate a program that runs in n steps? It executes the outer loop of step 3 n times. How many steps are required at each pass through the loop? Step 3.1 may take t steps, if t is the length of tape 1. Step 3.2 takes a constant number of steps. Step 3.3 may take a steps if a is the number of bits required to store the longest address that is used on tape 1. Step 3.4 may also take a steps. Step 3.5 again may have to scan all of tape 1, so it may take t steps. The number of steps required to execute the instruction varies:

- Addition takes v steps if v is the length of the longer operand.
- Load takes v steps if v is the length of the value to be loaded.
- Store generally takes v steps if v is the length of the value to be stored. However, suppose that the value to be stored is longer than the value that is already stored at that location. Then *simcomputer* must shift the remainder of Tape 1 one square to the right in order to have room for the new value. So executing a Store instruction could take t steps (where t is the length of tape 1).

The remainder of the operations can be analyzed similarly. Notice that we have included no complex operations like multiply. (But this is not a limitation. Multiply can be implemented as a sequence of additions.) So it is straightforward to see that the number of steps required to perform any of the operations that we have defined is, in the worst case, a linear function of t, the length of tape 1.

So how long is tape 1? It starts out at some length k. Each instruction has the ability to increase the number of memory locations by 1 since a store instruction can store to an address that was not already represented on the tape. And each instruction has the ability to increase by 1 the length of a machine "word", since the add instruction can create a value that is one bit longer than either of its operands.

So, after n simulated steps, t, the length of the tape, could be $k + n^2$ (if new words are created and each word gets longer). If we assume that $n \geq k$, we can say that the length of the tape, after n steps, is $\mathcal{O}(n^2)$. So the number of steps that *simcomputer* must execute to simulate each step of the original program is $\mathcal{O}(n^2)$. Since *simcomputer* must simulate n steps of the original program, the total number of steps executed by *simcomputer* is $\mathcal{O}(n^3)$.

The simulator *simcomputer* uses 7 tapes. We know, from Theorem 17.1, that a k-tape Turing machine that executes n steps can be simulated in $\mathcal{O}(n^2)$ steps by a one-tape, standard Turing Machine. So the total number of steps it would take a one-tape standard Turing Machine to simulate one of our programs executing n steps is $\mathcal{O}(n^6)$. While this represents a nontrivial increase in the number of steps, it is important to note that the increase is a polynomial function of n. It does not grow exponentially, the way the simulation of a nondeterministic Turing Machine did.

Any program that can be written in any modern programming language can be compiled into code for a machine such as the simple random access machine that we have just described. Since we have shown that any such machine can be simulated by a Turing machine, we will begin to use clear pseudocode to define Turing machines.

17.5 Alternative Turing Machine Definitions ✸

We have provided one definition for what a Turing machine is and how it operates. There are many equivalent alternatives. In this section we will explore two of them.

17.5.1 One-Way vs. Two-Way Infinite Tape

Many books define a Turing machine to have a tape that is infinite in only one direction. We use a two-way infinite tape. Does this difference matter? In other words, are there any problems that one kind of machine can solve that the other one cannot? The answer is no.

THEOREM 17.5 A One-Way Infinite Tape is Equivalent to a Two-Way Infinite Tape

Theorem: Any computation by a Turing machine with a two-way infinite tape can be simulated by a Turing machine with a one-way infinite tape.

Proof: Let M be a Turing machine with a two-way infinite tape. We describe M', an equivalent machine whose tapes are infinite in only one direction. M' will use three tapes. The first will hold that part of M's tape that starts with the square under the read/write head and goes to the right. The second M' tape will hold that part of M's tape to the left of the read/write head. The third tape will count, in unary, the number of moves that M has made so far. An example of this encoding is shown in Figure 17.5.

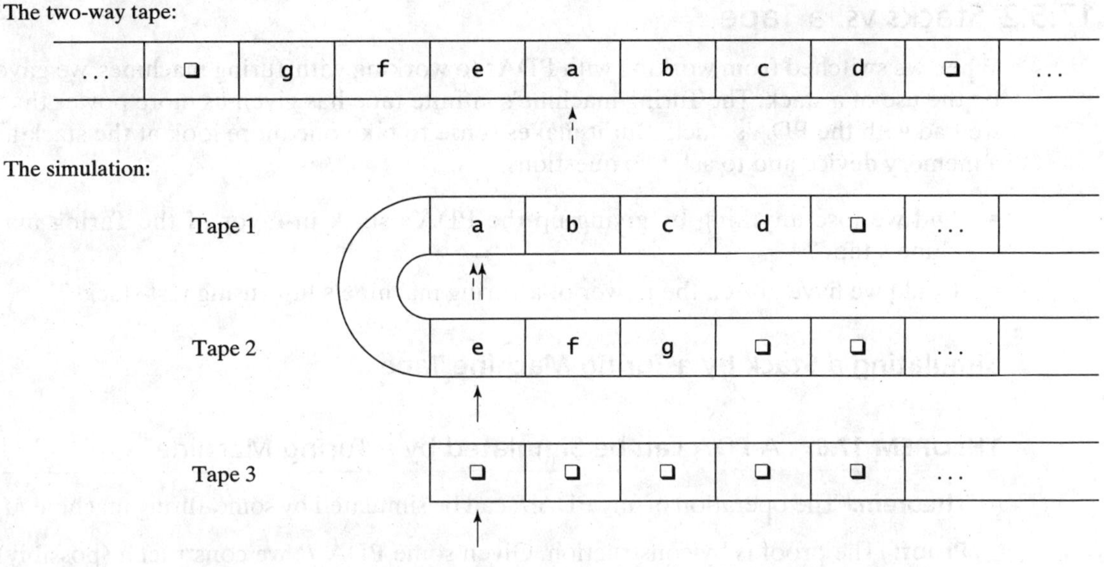

FIGURE 17.5 Simulating a two-way infinite tape on a one-way infinite tape.

M's read/write head is shown above as a dashed arrow. M' has three read/write heads (shown as dark arrows above), one for each tape. It will use its finite state controller to keep track of whether the simulated read/write head is on tape 1 or tape 2. If the simulated read/write head is on tape 1, square t, then the M' tape 1 read/write head will be on square t and its tape 2 read/write head will be on the leftmost square. Similarly if the simulated read/write head is on tape 2.

Initially, M' tape 1 will be identical to M's tape, M' tape 2 will be blank, and the M' tape 3 will also be blank (since no moves have yet been made).

The simulation: M' simulates each step of M. If M attempts to move to the left, off the end of its tape, M' will begin writing at the left end of tape 2. If M continues to move left, M' will move right on tape 2. If M moves right and goes back onto its original tape, M' will begin moving right on tape 1. If M would halt, then M' halts the simulation.

But, if M' is computing a function, then M' must also make sure, when it halts, that its tape 1 contains exactly what M's tape would have contained. Some of that may be on tape 2. If it is, then the contents of tape 1 must be shifted to the right far enough to allow the contents of tape 2 to be moved up. The maximum number of symbols that M' may have written on tape 2 is n, where n is the number of steps executed by M. Tape 3 contains n. So M' moves n squares to the right on tape 2. Then it moves leftward, one square at a time as long as it reads only blanks. Each time it moves to the left, it erases a 1 from tape 3. When it hits the first nonblank character, tape 3 will contain the unary representation of the number of times M' must shift tape 1 one square to the right and then copy one symbol from tape 2 to tape 1. M' executes this shifting process the required number of times and then halts.

17.5.2 Stacks vs. a Tape

When we switched from working with PDAs to working with Turing machines, we gave up the use of a stack. The Turing machine's infinite tape has given us more power than we had with the PDA's stack. But it makes sense to take one more look at the stack as a memory device and to ask two questions:

- Did we lose anything by giving up the PDA's stack in favor of the Turing machine's tape?
- Could we have gotten the power of a Turing machine's tape using just stacks?

Simulating a Stack by a Turing Machine Tape

THEOREM 17.6 A PDA can be Simulated by a Turing Machine

Theorem: The operation of any PDA P can be simulated by some Turing machine M.

Proof: The proof is by construction. Given some PDA P, we construct a (possibly) nondeterministic Turing machine M to simulate the operation of P. Since there is a finite number of states in P, M can keep track of the current state of P in its own finite state controller.

Each branch of M will use two tapes, one for the input and one for the stack, as shown in Figure 17.6. Tape 1 will function just like the read-only stream of input that is fed to the PDA. M will never write on tape 1 and will only move to the right, one square at a time. Tape 2 will mimic the behavior of M's stack, with its read/write head moving back and forth as symbols are pushed onto and popped from the stack.

M will operate as follows:

1. Initialization: Write #, indicating the bottom of the stack, under the read/write head of Tape 2. Tape 2's read/write head will always remain positioned on the top of the stack. Set the simulated state S_{sim} to s.

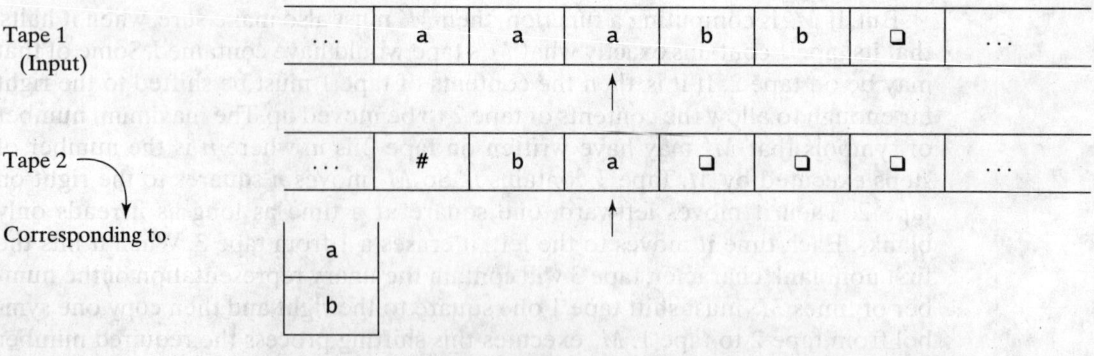

FIGURE 17.6 Simulating a PDA by a Turing machine.

2. Simulation: Let the character under the read/write head of Tape 1 be c. At each step of the operation of P do:

2.1. If $c = \square$, halt and accept if S_{sim} is an accepting state of P and reject otherwise.

2.2. Nondeterministically choose from Δ a transition of the form $((S_{sim}, c, pop), (q_2, push))$ or $((S_{sim}, \varepsilon, pop), (q_2, push))$. In other words, chose some transition from the current state that either reads the current input character or reads ε.

2.3. Scan left on Tape 2 $|pop|$ squares, blanking out each square and checking to see whether Tape 2 matches *pop*. If it does not, terminate this path. If it does, then move right on Tape 2 $|push|$ squares copying *push* onto Tape 2.

2.4. If we are not following an ε-transition, move the read/write head of Tape 1 one square to the right and set c to the character on that square.

2.5. Set S_{sim} to q_2 and repeat.

So we gave up no power when we abandoned the PDA's stack in favor of the Turing machine's tape.

Simulating a Turing Machine Tape by Using Two Stacks

What about the other way around? Is there any way to use stacks to get the power of an infinite, writeable tape? The answer is yes. Any Turing machine M can be simulated by a PDA P with two stacks. Suppose that M's tape is as shown in Figure 17.7 (a). Then P's two stacks will be as shown in Figure 17.7 (b).

Stack 1 contains M's active tape up to and including the square that is currently under the read/write head. Stack 2 contains the remainder of M's active tape. If M moves to the left, the top character from stack 1 is popped and then pushed onto stack 2. If M moves

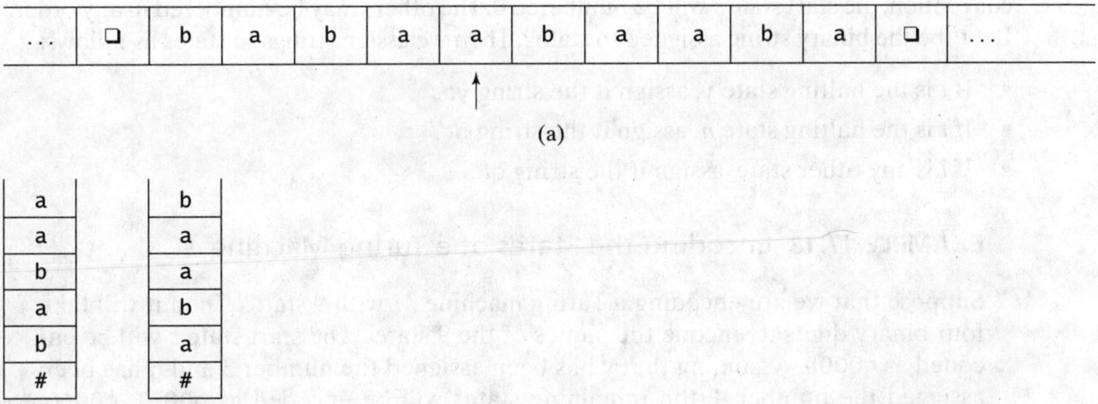

FIGURE 17.7 Simulating a Turing machine tape with two stacks.

onto the blank region to the left of its tape, then the character that it writes is simply pushed onto the top of stack 1. If M moves to the right, the top character from stack 2 is popped and then pushed onto stack 1. If M moves onto the blank region to the right of its tape, then the character that it writes is simply pushed onto the top of stack 1.

17.6 Encoding Turing Machines as Strings

So far, all of our Turing machines have been hardwired (just like early computers). Does it make sense, just as it did with real computers, to develop a programmable Turing machine: a single Turing machine that accepts as input a (M: Turing machine, s: input string) pair and outputs whatever M would output when started up on s? The answer is yes. We will call such a device the ***universal Turing machine*** or simply U.

To define U we need to do two things:

1. Define an encoding scheme that can be used to describe to U a (Turing machine, input string) pair.
2. Describe the operation of U given such an encoded pair.

17.6.1 An Encoding Scheme for Turing Machines

We need to be able to describe an arbitrary Turing machine $M = (K, \Sigma, \Gamma, \delta, s, H)$ as a string that we will write as $<M>$. When we define the universal Turing machine, we will have to assign it a fixed input alphabet. But the machines we wish to input to it may have an arbitrary number of states and they may exploit alphabets of arbitrary size. So we need to find a way to encode an arbitrary number of states and a tape alphabet of arbitrary size using some new alphabet of fixed size. The obvious solution is to encode both state sets and alphabets as binary strings.

We begin with K. We will determine i, the number of binary digits required to encode the numbers from 0 to $|K| - 1$. Then we will number the states from 0 to $|K| - 1$ and assign to each state the binary string of length i that corresponds to its assigned number. By convention, the start state s will be numbered 0. The others may be numbered in any order. Let t' be the binary string assigned to state t. Then we assign strings to states as follows:

- If t is the halting state y, assign it the string yt'.
- If t is the halting state n, assign it the string nt'.
- If t is any other state, assign it the string qt'.

EXAMPLE 17.18 Encoding the States of a Turing Machine

Suppose that we are encoding a Turing machine M with 9 states. Then it will take four binary digits to encode the names of the 9 states. The start state s will be encoded as q0000. Assuming that y has been assigned the number 3 and n has been assigned the number 4, the remaining states will be encoded as q0001, q0010, y0011, n0100, q0101, q0110, q0111, and q1000.

Next we will encode the tape alphabet in a similar fashion. We will begin by determining j, the number of binary digits required to encode the numbers from 0 to $|\Gamma| - 1$. Then we will number the characters (in any order) from 0 to $|\Gamma| - 1$ and assign to each character the binary string of length j that corresponds to its assigned number. Finally, we will assign to each symbol y the string ay', where y' is the binary string already assigned to y.

EXAMPLE 17.19 Encoding the Tape Alphabet of a Turing Machine

Suppose that we are encoding a Turing machine M with $\Gamma = \{\square, \text{a}, \text{b}, \text{c}\}$. Then it will take two binary digits to encode the names of the four characters. The assignment of numbers to the characters is arbitrary. It just must be done consistently throughout the encoding. So, for example, we could let:

❑ = a00

a = a01

b = a10

c = a11

Next we need a way to encode the transitions of δ, each of which is a 5-tuple: (state, input character, state, output character, move). We have just described how we will encode states and tape characters. There are only two allowable moves, $\rightarrow$ and $\leftarrow$, so we can just use those two symbols to stand for their respective moves. We will encode each transition in δ as a string of exactly the form (state, character, state, character, move), using the state, character, and move encodings that we have just described. Then we can specify δ as a list of transitions separated by commas.

With these conventions, we can completely specify almost all Turing machines simply as a list of transitions. But we must also consider the special case of the simple Turing machine M_{none}, shown in Figure 17.8. M_{none} has no transitions but it is a legal Turing machine (that semidecides Σ^*). To enable us to represent machines like M_{none}, we add one more convention: When encoding a Turing machine M, for any state q in M that has no incoming transitions, add to M's encoding the substring (q). So M_{none} would be encoded as simply (q0).

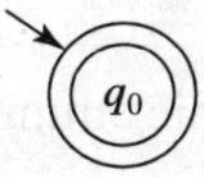

FIGURE 17.8 Encoding a Turing machine with no transitions.

EXAMPLE 17.20 Encoding a Complete Turing Machine Description

Consider $M = (\{s, q, h\}, \{a, b, c\}, \{\square, a, b, c\}, \delta, s, \{h\})$, where δ =

state	symbol	δ
s	$\square$	$(q, \square, \rightarrow)$
s	a	$(s, \text{b}, \rightarrow)$
s	b	$(q, \text{a}, \leftarrow)$
s	c	$(q, \text{b}, \leftarrow)$
q	$\square$	$(s, \text{a}, \rightarrow)$
q	a	$(q, \text{b}, \rightarrow)$
q	b	$(q, \text{b}, \leftarrow)$
q	c	$(h, \text{a}, \leftarrow)$

We start encoding M by determining encodings for each of its states and tape symbols:

state/symbol	representation
s	q00
q	q01
h	q10
$\square$	a00
a	a01
b	a10
c	a11

The complete encoding of M, which we will denote by $<M>$, is then:

(q00,a00,q01,a00, $\rightarrow$), (q00,a01,q00,a10, $\rightarrow$), (q00,a10,q01,a01, $\leftarrow$), (q00,a11,q01,a10, $\leftarrow$), (q01,a00,q00,a01, $\rightarrow$), (q01,a01,q01,a10, $\rightarrow$), (q01,a10,q01,a10, $\leftarrow$), (q01,a11,q10,a01, $\leftarrow$).

17.6.2 Enumerating Turing Machines

Now that we have an encoding scheme for Turing machines, it is possible to create an enumeration of them.

THEOREM 17.7 We can Lexicographically Enumerate the Valid Turing Machines

Theorem: There exists an infinite lexicographic enumeration of:

a. All syntactically valid Turing machines.

b. All syntactically valid Turing machines whose input alphabet is some particular set Σ.

c. All syntactically valid Turing machines whose input alphabet is some particular set Σ and whose tape alphabet is some particular set Γ.

Proof: Fix an alphabet $\Sigma = \{$(,), a, q, y, n, 0, 1, comma, $\rightarrow$, $\leftarrow\}$, i.e., the set of characters that are used in the Turing machine encoding scheme that we just described. Let the symbols in Σ be ordered as shown in the list we just gave. The following procedure lexicographically enumerates all syntactically valid Turing machines:

1. Lexicographically enumerate the strings in Σ^*.
2. As each string s is generated, check to see whether it is a syntactically valid Turing machine description. If it is, output it.

To enumerate just those Turing machines whose input and/or tape alphabets are limited to the symbols in some particular sets Σ and Γ, add, to step 2, a check to see that only alphabets of the appropriate sizes are allowed.

With this procedure in hand, we can now talk about the ith Turing machine. It is the ith element generated by the enumeration procedure.

17.6.3 Another Win of Encoding

Our motivation for defining what we mean by $<M>$ was that we would like to be able to input a definition of M to the universal Turing machine U, which will then execute M. But it turns out that, now that we have a well-defined string encoding $<M>$ for any Turing machine M, we can pass $<M>$ as input to programs other than U and ask those programs to operate on M. So we can talk about some Turing machine T that takes the description of another Turing machine (say M_1) as input and transforms it into a description of a different machine (say M_2) that performs some different, but possibly related task. We show this schematically in Figure 17.9.

We will make extensive use of this idea of transforming one Turing machine into another when we discuss the use of reduction to show that various problems are undecidable.

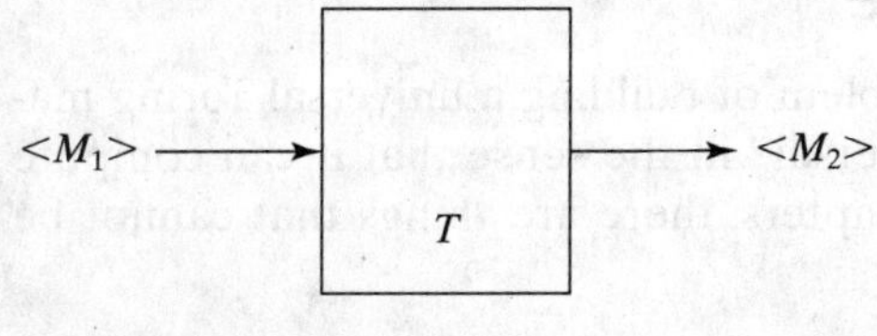

FIGURE 17.9 Turing machine T takes one Turing machine as input and creates another as its output.

EXAMPLE 17.21 One Turing Machine Operates on the Description of Another

Define a Turing machine T whose specifications are:

Input: $<M_1>$, where M_1 is a Turing machine that reads its input tape and performs some operation P on it.

Output: $<M_2>$, where M_2 is a Turing machine that performs P on an empty input tape.

The job of T is shown in the following diagram. We have, for convenience here, described $<M_2>$ using our macro language, but we could have written out the detailed string encoding of it.

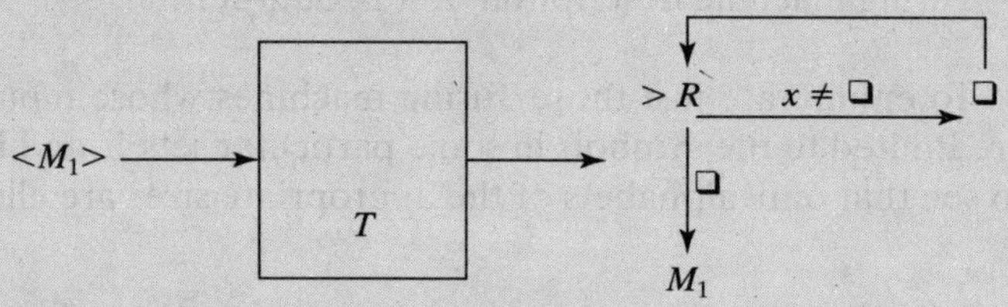

T constructs the machine M_2 that starts by erasing its input tape. Then it passes control to M_1. So we can define T as follows:

$T(<M_1>) =$

Output the machine shown on the right above.

17.6.4 Encoding Multiple Inputs to a Turing Machine

Every Turing machine takes a single string as its input. Sometimes, however, we wish to define a Turing machine that operates on more than one object. For example, we are going to define the universal Turing machine U to accept a machine M and a string w and to simulate the execution of M on w. To do this, we need to encode both arguments as a single string. We can easily do that by encoding each argument separately and then concatenating them together, separated by some character that is not in any of the alphabets used in forming the individual strings. For example, we could encode the pair $(<M>, <\mathtt{aabb}>)$ as $<M>; <\mathtt{aabb}>$. We will use the notation $<x_1, x_2, \ldots x_n>$ to mean a single string that encodes the sequence of individual values $x_1, x_2, \ldots x_n$.

17.7 The Universal Turing Machine

We are now in a position to return to the problem of building a universal Turing machine, which we'll call U. U is not truly "universal" in the sense that it can compute "everything." As we'll see in the next few chapters, there are things that cannot be computed by any Turing machine. U is, however, universal in the sense that, given an arbitrary Turing machine M and an input w, U will simulate the operation of M on w.

We can state U's specification as follows: On input <M, w>, U must:

- Halt iff M halts on w.
- If M is a deciding or a semideciding machine, then:
  - If M accepts, accept.
  - If M rejects, reject.
- If M computes a function, then U(<M, w>) must equal $M(w)$.

U will use three tapes to simulate the execution of M on w:

- Tape 1 will correspond to M's tape.
- Tape 2 will contain <M>, the "program" that U is running.
- Tape 3 will contain the encoding of the state that M is in at any point during the simulation. Think of tape 3 as holding the program counter.

When U begins, it will have <M, w> on tape 1. (Like all multitape machines, it starts with its input on tape 1 and all other tapes blank.) Figure 17.10 (a) illustrates U's three tapes when it begins. It uses the multitrack encoding of three tapes that we described in Section 17.3.1.

U's first job is to initialize its tapes. To do so, it must do the following:

1. Transfer <M> from tape 1 to tape 2 (erasing it from tape 1).
2. Examine <M> to determine the number of states in M and thus i, the number of binary digits required to encode M's states. Write $\mathsf{q}0^i$ (corresponding to the start state of M) on tape 3.

Assume that it takes three bits to encode the states of M. Then, after initialization, U's tapes will be as shown in Figure 17.10 (b).

U begins simulating M with the read/write heads of its three tapes as described above. More generally, it will start each step of its simulation with the read/write heads placed as follows:

- Tape 1's read/write head will be over the a that is the first character of the encoding of the current character on M's tape.
- Tape 2's read/write head will be at the beginning of <M>.
- Tape 3's read/write head will be over the q of the program counter.

Following initialization as described above, U operates as follows:

1. Until M would halt do:

1.1. Scan tape 2 for a quintuple that matches the current state, input pair.

	<M---	------	------	---M,	w---	------	---w>		
	1	0	0	0	0	0	0		
❑	❑	❑	❑	❑	❑	❑	❑	❑	❑
	1	0	0	0	0	0	0		
	❑	❑	❑	❑	❑	❑	❑		
	1	0	0	0	0	0	0		

(a)

	❑	❑	❑	❑	<w---	------	---w>		
	0	0	0	0	1	0	0		
❑	<M---	------	---M>		❑	❑	❑	❑	❑
	1	0	0	0	0	0	0		
	q	0	0	0	❑	❑	❑		
	1	❑	❑	❑	❑	❑	❑		

(b)

FIGURE 17.10 The tapes of the universal Turing machine U.

1.2. Perform the associated action, by changing tapes 1 and 3. If necessary, extend the simulated tape that is encoded on tape 1.

1.3. If no matching quintuple found, halt.

2. Report the same result M would report:

- If M is viewed as a deciding or semideciding machine for some language L: If the simulated state of M is y, then accept. If the simulated state is n, then reject.
- If M is viewed as a machine that computes a function: Reformat the tape so that the value of tape 1 is all that is left.

How long does it take U to simulate the computation of M? If M would halt in k steps, then U must go through its loop k times. Each time through the loop, it must scan <M> to find out what to do. So U takes $\mathcal{O}(|M| \cdot k)$ steps.

Now we know that if we wanted to build real Turing machines we could build one physical machine and feed it descriptions of any other Turing machines that we wanted to run. So this is yet another way in which the Turing machine is a good general model of computation.

The existence of U enables us to prove the following theorem:

THEOREM 17.8 One Turing Machine Can Simulate Another

Theorem: Given any Turing machine M and input string w, there exists a Turing machine M' that simulates the execution of M on w and:

- halts iff M halts on w, and
- if it halts, returns whatever result M returns.

Proof: Given a particular M and w, we construct a specific M' to operate as follows:

$M'(x) =$

Invoke the universal Turing machine U on the string $<M, w>$.

Notice that M' ignores its own input (which we've called x). It is a constant function. M' halts iff U halts and, if it halts, will return the result of executing M on w.

Theorem 17.8 enables us to write, in a Turing machine definition, the pseudocode, "Run M on w," and then branch based on whether or not M halts (and, if it halts, what it returns).

If the universal Turing machine is a good idea, what about universal other things? Could we, for example, define a universal FSM? Such an FSM would accept the language $L = \{<F, w> : F$ is a finite state machine and $w \in L(F).\}$ The answer is no. Since any FSM has only a finite amount of memory, it has no way to remember and then execute a program of arbitrary length. We have waited until now to introduce the idea of a universal machine because we had to.

Exercises

1. Give a short English description of what each of these Turing machines does:

a. $\Sigma_M = \{a, b\}$. $M =$

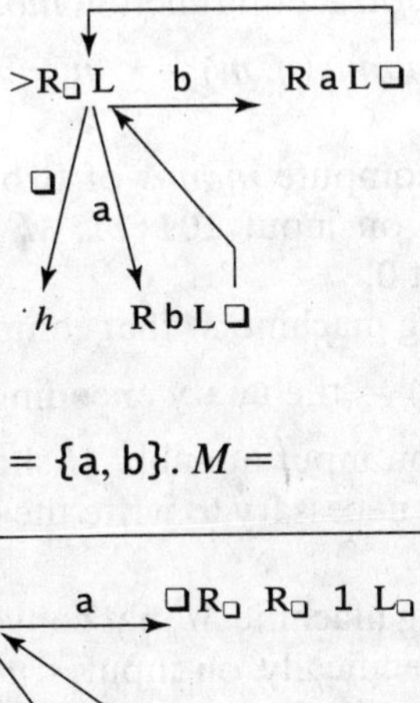

b. $\Sigma_M = \{a, b\}$. $M =$

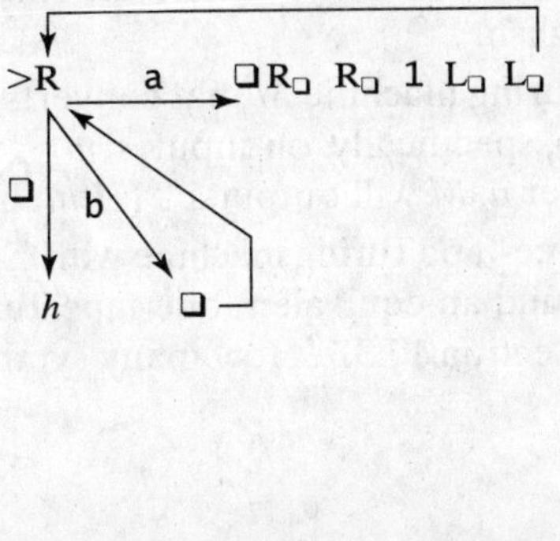

2. Construct a standard, deterministic, one-tape Turing machine M to decide each of the following languages L. You may find it useful to define subroutines. Describe M in the macro language defined in Section 17.1.5.

a. $\{x * y = z : x, y, z \in 1^+$ and, when x, y, and z are viewed as unary numbers, $xy = z\}$. For example, the string $1111 * 11 = 11111111 \in L$.

b. $\{a^i b^j c^i d^j, i, j \geq 0\}$.

c. $\{w \in \{a, b, c, d\}^*: \#_b(w) \geq \#_c(w) \geq \#_d(w) \geq 0\}$.

3. Construct a standard, deterministic, one-tape Turing machine M to compute each of the following functions:

a. The function sub_3, which is defined as follows:

$$sub_3(n) = n - 3 \text{ if } n > 2$$
$$0 \text{ if } n \leq 2.$$

Specifically, compute sub_3 of a natural number represented in binary. For example, on input 10111, M should output 10100. On input 11101, M should output 11010. (*Hint*: You may want to define a subroutine.)

b. Addition of two binary natural numbers (as described in Example 17.13). Specifically, given the input string <x>;<y>, where <x> is the binary encoding of a natural number x and <y> is the binary encoding of a natural number y, M should output <z>, where z is the binary encoding of $x + y$. For example, on input 101;11, M should output 1000.

c. Multiplication of two unary numbers. Specifically, given the input string <x>;<y>, where <x> is the unary encoding of a natural number x and <y> is the unary encoding of a natural number y, M should output <z>, where z is the unary encoding of xy. For example, on input 111;1111, M should output 111111111111.

d. The proper subtraction function *monus*, which is defined as follows:

$$monus(n, m) = \begin{cases} n - m & \text{if } n > m \\ 0 & \text{if } n \leq m. \end{cases}$$

Specifically, compute *monus* of two natural numbers represented in binary. For example, on input 101;11, M should output 10. On input 11;101, M should output 0.

4. Construct a Turing machine M that computes the function $f: \{a, b\}^* \rightarrow N$, where:

$$f(x) = \text{the unary encoding of } max(\#_a(x), \#_b(x)).$$

For example, on input aaaabb, M should output 1111. M may use more than one tape. It is not necessary to write the exact transition function for M. Describe it in clear English.

5. Construct a Turing machine M that converts binary numbers to their unary representations. So, specifically, on input <w>, where w is the binary encoding of a natural number n, M will output 1^n. (*Hint*: Use more than one tape.)

6. Let M be a three-tape Turing machine with $\Sigma = \{a, b, c\}$ and $\Gamma = \{a, b, c, \square, 1, 2\}$. We want to build an equivalent one-tape Turing machine M' using the technique described in Section 17.3.1. How many symbols must there be in Γ'?

7. In Example 13.2, we showed that the language $L = \{a^{n^2}, n \geq 0\}$ is not context-free. Show that it is in D by describing, in clear English, a Turing machine that decides it. (*Hint*: Use more than one tape.)

8. In Example 17.9, we showed a Turing machine that decides the language WcW. If we remove the middle marker c, we get the language WW. Construct a Turing machine M that decides WW. You may want to exploit nondeterminism. It is not necessary to write the exact transition function for M. Describe it in clear English.

9. In Example 4.9, we described the Boolean satisfiability problem and we sketched a nondeterministic program that solves it using the function *choose*. Now define the language SAT = {<*w*>: *w* is a wff in Boolean logic and *w* is satisfiable}. Describe in clear English the operation of a nondeterministic (and possibly n-tape) Turing machine that decides SAT.

10. Prove Theorem 17.3.

11. Prove rigorously that the set of regular languages is a *proper* subset of D.

12. In this question, we explore the equivalence between function computation and language recognition as performed by Turing machines. For simplicity, we will consider only functions from the nonnegative integers to the nonnegative integers (both encoded in binary). But the ideas of these questions apply to any computable function. We'll start with the following definition:

- Define the *graph* of a function f to be the set of all strings of the form $[x, f(x)]$, where x is the binary encoding of a nonnegative integer, and $f(x)$ is the binary encoding of the result of applying f to x.

For example, the graph of the function *succ* is the set $\{[0,1],[1,10],[10,11],\ldots\}$.

a. Describe in clear English an algorithm that, given a Turing machine M that computes f, constructs a Turing machine M' that decides the language L that contains exactly the graph of f.

b. Describe in clear English an algorithm that, given a Turing machine M that decides the language L that contains the graph of some function f, constructs a Turing machine M' that computes f.

c. A function is said to be partial if it may be undefined for some arguments. If we extend the ideas of this exercise to partial functions, then we do not require that the Turing machine that computes f halt if it is given some input x for which $f(x)$ is undefined. Then L (the graph language for f), will contain entries of the form $[x, f(x)]$ for only those values of x for which f is defined. In that case, it may not be possible to decide L, but it will be possible to semidecide it. Do your constructions for parts (a) and (b) work if the function f is partial? If not, explain how you could modify them so they will work correctly. By "work", we mean:

- For part (a): Given a Turing machine that computes $f(x)$ for all values on which f is defined, build a Turing machine that semidecides the language L that contains exactly the graph of f;
- For part (b): Given a Turing machine that semidecides the graph language of f (and thus accepts all strings of the form$[x, f(x)]$ when $f(x)$ is defined), build a Turing machine that computes f.

13. What is the minimum number of tapes required to implement a universal Turing machine?

14. Encode the following Turing Machine as an input to the universal Turing machine that is described in Section 17.7:

$M = (K, \Sigma, \Gamma, \delta, q_0, \{h\})$, where:

$K = \{q_0, q_1, h\}$,

$\Sigma = \{\text{a}, \text{b}\}$,

$\Gamma = \{\text{a}, \text{b}, \text{c}, \square\}$, and

δ is given by the following table:

q	σ	$\delta(q, \sigma)$
q_0	a	$(q_1, \text{b}, \rightarrow)$
q_0	b	$(q_1, \text{a}, \rightarrow)$
q_0	$\square$	$(h, \square, \rightarrow)$
q_0	c	$(q_0, \text{c}, \rightarrow)$
q_1	a	$(q_0, \text{c}, \rightarrow)$
q_1	b	$(q_0, \text{b}, \leftarrow)$
q_1	$\square$	$(q_0, \text{c}, \rightarrow)$
q_1	c	$(q_1, \text{c}, \rightarrow)$

C H A P T E R 18

The Church-Turing Thesis

The Turing machine is the most powerful of the models of computation that we have so far considered. There are problems that can be solved by a Turing machine that cannot be solved by a PDA, just as there are problems that could be solved by a PDA but not by an FSM. Is this the end of the line, or should we expect a sequence of even more powerful models?

One way of looking at things suggests that we should expect to keep going. A simple counting argument shows that there are more languages than there are Turing machines:

- There is at most a countably infinite number of Turing machines since we can lexicographically enumerate all the strings that correspond to syntactically legal Turing machines.
- There is an uncountably infinite number of languages over any nonempty alphabet.
- Thus there are more languages than there are Turing machines.

So there are languages that cannot be recognized by any Turing machine. But can we do better by creating some new formalism? If any such new formalism shares with Turing machines the property that each instance of it has a finite description (for example a finite length Java program or a finite length grammar) then the same argument will apply to it and there will still be languages that it cannot describe.

But there might be some alternative model in which we could write finite length programs and for which no equivalent Turing machine exists. Is there? We showed in the last chapter that there are several features (e.g., multiple tapes, nondeterminism) that we could add to our definition of a Turing machine without increasing its power. But does that mean that there is nothing we could add that would make a difference? Or might there be some completely different model that has more power than the Turing machine?

18.1 The Thesis

Another way to ask the question about the existence of a more powerful model is this: Recall that we have defined an ***algorithm*** to be a detailed procedure that accomplishes some clearly specified task. Note that this definition is general enough to include decision procedures (functions that return Boolean values), as well as functions that return values of other types. In fact, it is general enough to include recipes for beef Wellington. We will, however, focus just on tasks that involve computation. Now we can restate our question: "Is there any computational algorithm that cannot be implemented by some Turing machine? Then, if there is, can we find some more powerful model in which we could implement that algorithm?" Note that we are assuming here that both real-world inputs and real-world outputs can be appropriately encoded into symbols that can be written onto a device such as the Turing machine's tape. We are not talking about whether an abstract Turing machine can actually chop mushrooms, take pictures, produce sound waves, or turn a steering wheel.

During the first third of the 20th century, a group of influential mathematicians was focused on developing a completely formal basis for mathematics. Out of this effort emerged, among other things, *Principia Mathematica* [Whitehead and Russell 1910, 1912, 1913], which is often described as the most influential work on logic ever written. Among its achievements was the introduction of a theory of types that offers a way out of Russell's paradox.[8] The continuation and the ultimate success of this line of work depended on positive answers to two key questions:

1. Is it possible to axiomatize all of the mathematical structures of interest in such a way that every true statement becomes a theorem? We will allow the set of axioms to be infinite, but it must be decidable. In other words, there must exist an algorithm that can examine a string and determine whether or not it is an axiom.
2. Does there exist an algorithm to decide, given a set of axioms, whether a given statement is a theorem? In other words, does there exist an algorithm that always halts and that returns *True* when given a theorem and *False* otherwise?

> *Principia Mathematica* played a landmark role in the development of mathematical logic in the early part of the 20th century. Forty-five years later it played another landmark role, this time in a discipline that Whitehead and Russell could never have imagined. In 1956, the Logic Theorist, often regarded as the first artificial intelligence program, proved most of the theorems in Chapter 2 of *Principia Mathematica*. (M.2.2)

It was widely believed that the answer to both of these questions was yes. Had it been, perhaps the goal of formalizing all of mathematics could have been attained. But the answer to both questions is no. Three papers that appeared within a few years of each other shattered that dream.

Kurt Gödel showed, in the proof of his Incompleteness Theorem [Gödel 1931], that the answer to question 1 is no. In particular, he showed that there exists no decidable axiomatization of Peano arithmetic (the natural numbers plus the operations *plus* and *times*) that is both consistent and complete. By complete we mean that all true statements in the language of the theory are theorems. Note that an infinite set of axioms is

[8] Let M be "the set of all sets that are not members of themselves." Is M a member of M? The fact that either answer to this question leads to a contradiction was noticed by Bertrand Russell in about 1901. The question is called "Russell's paradox."

allowed, but it must be decidable. So an infinite number of true statements can be made theorems simply by adding new axioms. But Gödel showed that, no matter how often that is done, there must remain other true statements that are unprovable.

Question 2 had been clearly articulated a few years earlier in a paper by David Hilbert and Wilhelm Ackermann [Hilbert and Ackermann 1928]. They called it the ***Entscheidungsproblem***. (*Entscheidungsproblem* is German for "decision problem.") There are three equivalent ways to state the problem:

- "Does there exist an algorithm to decide, given an arbitrary sentence w in first order logic, whether w is valid (i.e., true in all interpretations)?"
- "Given a set of axioms A and a sentence w, does there exist an algorithm to decide whether w is entailed by A?" Note that this formulation is equivalent to the first one since the sentence $A \rightarrow w$ is valid iff w is entailed by A.
- "Given a set of axioms A and a sentence w , does there exist an algorithm to decide whether w can be proved from A?" Note that this formulation is equivalent to the second one since Gödel's Completeness Theorem tells us that there exists, for first-order logic, an inference procedure that is powerful enough to derive, from A, every sentence that is entailed by A.

Note that questions 1 and 2 (i.e., "Can the facts be axiomatized?" and "Can theoremhood be decided?"), while related, are different in an important way. The fact that the answer to question 1 is no does not obviously imply that the answer to the Entscheidungsproblem is no. While some true statements are not theorems, it might still have turned out to be possible to define an algorithm that distinguishes theorems from nontheorems.

The Entscheidungsproblem had captured the attention of several logicians of the time, including Alan Turing and Alonzo Church. Turing and Church, working independently, realized that, in order to solve the Entscheidungsproblem, it was necessary first to formalize what was meant by an algorithm. Turing's formalization was what we now call a Turing machine. Church's formalization was the ***lambda calculus***, which we will discuss briefly below. The two formalizations look very different. But Turing showed that they are equivalent in power. Any problem that can be solved in one can be solved in the other. As it turns out ([Turing 1936] and [Church 1936]), the Entscheidungsproblem can be solved in neither. We'll see why this is so in Chapter 19.

But out of the negative results that formed the core of the Church and Turing papers emerged an important new idea: Turing machines and the lambda calculus are equivalent. Perhaps that observation can be extended.

The ***Church-Turing thesis***, or sometimes just ***Church's thesis***, states that all formalisms powerful enough to describe everything we think of as a computational algorithm are equivalent.

We should point out that this statement is stronger than anything that either Church or Turing actually said. This version is based on a substantial body of work that has occurred since Turing and Church's seminal papers. Also note that we have carefully used the word *thesis* here, rather than *theorem*. There exists no proof of the Church-Turing thesis because its statement depends on our informal definition of a computational algorithm. It is in principle possible that someone may come up with a more powerful model.

Many very different models have been proposed over the years. We will examine a few of them below. All have been shown to be no more powerful than the Turing machine.

The Church-Turing thesis is significant. In the next several chapters, we are going to prove that there are important problems whose solutions cannot be computed by any Turing machine. The Church-Turing thesis tells us that we should not expect to find some other reasonable computational model in which those same problems can be solved. Moreover, the equivalence proofs that support the thesis tell us that it is certain that those problems cannot be solved in any of the specific computational models that have so far been considered and compared to the Turing machine.

18.2 Examples of Equivalent Formalisms ◆

All of the following models have been shown to be equivalent to our basic definition of a Turing machine:

- Modern computers, if we assume that there is an unbounded amount of memory available.
- Lambda calculus.
- Partial recursive functions (in which the class of computable functions is built from a small number of primitive functions and a small set of combining operations).
- Tag systems (in which we augment an FSM with a FIFO queue rather than a stack).
- Unrestricted grammars (in which we remove the constraint that the left-hand side of each production must consist of just a single nonterminal).
- Post production systems (in which we allow grammar-like rules with variables).
- Markov algorithms.
- Conway's Game of Life.
- One dimensional cellular automata.
- Various theoretical models of DNA-based computing.
- Lindenmayer systems.

We will describe recursive functions in Chapter 25, unrestricted grammars in Chapter 23, and Lindenmayer systems (also called L-systems) in Section 24.4. In the remainder of this chapter and we will briefly discuss the others.

18.2.1 Modern Computers

We showed in Section 17.4 that the functionality of modern "real" computers can be implemented with Turing machines. This observation suggests a slightly different way to define the decidable languages (i.e., those that are in D). A language L is decidable if there exists a decision procedure for it.

18.2.2 Lambda Calculus

Alonzo Church developed the lambda calculus 💻 as a way to formalize the notion of an algorithm. While Turing's solution to that same problem has the feel of a procedure, Church's solution feels more like a mathematical specification.

> The lambda calculus is the basis for modern functional programming languages like Lisp, Scheme, ML, and Haskell. (G.5)

The lambda calculus is an expression language. Each expression defines a function of a single argument, which is written as a variable bound by the operator λ. For example, the following simple lambda calculus expression describes the successor function:

$$(\lambda\, x.\, x + 1).$$

Functions can be applied to arguments by binding each argument to a formal parameter. So:

$$(\lambda\, x.\, x + 1)\; 3.$$

is evaluated by binding 3 to x and computing the result, 4.

Functions may be arguments to other functions and the value that is computed by a function may be another function. One of the most common uses of this feature is to define functions that we may think of as taking more than one argument. For example, we can define a function to add two numbers by writing:

$$(\lambda\, x.\, \lambda y.\, x + y)$$

Function application is left associative. So we can apply the addition function that we just described by writing, for example:

$$(\lambda\, x.\, \lambda y.\, x + y)\; 3\; 4$$

This expression is evaluated by binding 3 to x to create the new function $(\lambda\, y.\, 3 + y)$, which is then applied to 4 to return 7.

In the pure lambda calculus, there is no built-in data type number. All expressions are functions. But the natural numbers can be defined as lambda calculus functions. So the lambda calculus can effectively describe numeric functions just as we have done.

The lambda calculus can be shown to be equivalent in power to the Turing machine. In other words, the set of functions that can be defined in the lambda calculus is equal to the set of functions that can be computed by a Turing machine. Because of this equivalence, any problem that is undecidable for Turing machines is also undecidable for the lambda calculus. For example, we'll see in Chapter 21 that it is undecidable whether two Turing machines are equivalent. It is also undecidable whether two expressions in the lambda calculus are equivalent. In fact, Church's proof of that result was the first formal undecidability proof. (It appeared months before Turing's proof of the undecidability of questions involving Turing machines.)

18.2.3 Tag Systems

In the 1920s, a decade or so before the pioneering work of Gödel, Turing, and Church was published, the Polish logician Emil Post began working on the decidability of logical theories. Out of his work emerged two formalisms that are now known to be equivalent to the Turing machine. We'll mention the first, tag systems, here and the second, Post production systems, in the next section.

Post, and others, defined various versions (with differing restrictions on the alphabet and on the form of the operations that are allowed) of the basic tag system architecture. We describe the simplest here: A ***tag system***, sometimes now called a ***Post machine***, is a finite state machine that is augmented with a first-in, first out (FIFO) queue. In other words, it's a PDA with a FIFO queue rather than a stack.

It is easy to see that there are languages that are not context-free (and so cannot be accepted by any PDA) but that can be accepted by a tag system. Recall that while PalEven $= \{ww^R : w \in \{a, b\}^*\}$ is context-free, its cousin, WW $= \{ww : w \in \{a, b\}^*\}$, in which the second half of the string is not reversed, is not context-free. We could not build a PDA for WW because, using a stack, there was no way to compare the characters in the second half of a string to the characters in the first half except by reversing them. If we can use a FIFO queue instead of a stack, we no longer have this problem. So a simple tag system to accept WW writes the first half of its input string into its queue and then removes characters from the head of the queue, one at a time, and checks each of them against the characters in the second half of the input string.

But have we simply traded one set of languages for another? Or can we build a tag system to accept PalEven as well as WW? The answer is that, while there is not a simple tag system to accept PalEven, there is a tag system. In fact, any language that can be accepted by a Turing machine can also be accepted by a tag system. To see why, we'll sketch a technique for simulating a Turing machine with a tag system. Let the tag system's queue correspond to the Turing machine's active tape plus a blank on either side and let the head of the tag system's queue contain the square that is under the Turing machine's read/write head.

Now we just need a way to move both left and right in the queue, which would be easy if the tag system's queue were a loop (i.e., if its front and back were glued together). It isn't a loop, but we can treat it as though it were. To simulate a Turing machine that moves its head one square to the right, remove the symbol at the head of the queue and add it to the tail. To simulate a Turing machine that moves its head one square to the left, consider a queue that contains n symbols. One at a time, remove the first $n - 1$ symbols from the head of the queue and add them to the tail. To simulate a Turing machine that moves onto the blank region of its tape, exploit the fact that a tag system is allowed to push more than one symbol onto the end of its queue. So push two, one of which corresponds to the newly nonblank square.

18.2.4 Post Production Systems

We next consider a second formalism that is derived from Post's early work. This one is based on the idea of a rewrite or production or rule-based system. A Post production system (or simply Post system), as such systems have come to be known (although Post never called them that), shares with the grammar formalisms that we have considered the property that computation is accomplished by applying a set of production rules whose left-hand sides are matched against a current working string and whose right-hand sides are used to rewrite the working string.

Post's early work inspired the development of many modern rule-based systems, including context-free grammars described in BNF (G.1.1), rule-based expert systems (M.3), production rule-based cognitive architectures (M.3.2), and rule-based specifications for the behavior of NPCs in interactive games. (N.3.3)

Based on the ideas described in Post's work, we define a ***Post system*** P to be a quintuple (V, Σ, X, R, S), where:

- V is the rule alphabet, which contains nonterminal and terminal symbols,
- Σ (the set of terminals) is a subset of V,
- X is a set of variables whose values are drawn from V^*,
- R (the set of rules) is a finite subset of $(V \cup X)^* \times (V \cup X)^*$, with the additional constraint that every variable that occurs on the right-hand side of a rule must also have occurred on the left-hand side, and
- S (the start symbol) can be any element of $V - \Sigma$.

There are three important differences between Post systems, as just defined, and both the regular and context-free grammar formalisms that we have already considered:

1. In a Post system, the left-hand side of a rule may contain two or more symbols.
2. In a Post system, rules may contain variables. When a variable occurs on the left-hand side of a rule, it may match any element of V^*. When a variable occurs on the right-hand side, it will generate whatever value it matched.
3. In a Post system, a rule may be applied only if its left-hand side matches the entire working string. When a rule is applied, the entire working string is replaced by the string that is specified by the rule's right-hand side. Note that this contrasts with the definition of rule application that we use in our other rule-based formalisms. In them, a rule may match any substring of the working string and just that substring is replaced as directed by the rule's right-hand side. So, suppose that we wanted to write a rule $A \rightarrow B$ that replaced an A anywhere in the string with a B. We would have to write instead the rule $XAY \rightarrow XBY$. The variables X and Y can match everything before the A and after it, respectively.

As with regular and context-free grammars, let $x \Rightarrow_P y$ mean that the string y can be derived from the string x by applying a single rule in R_P. Let $x \Rightarrow_P{}^* y$ mean that y can be derived from x by applying zero or more rules in R_P. The language generated by P, denoted $L(P)$ is $\{w \in \Sigma^* : S \Rightarrow_P{}^* w\}$.

EXAMPLE 18.1 A Post System for WW

Recall the language WW = $\{ww : w \in \{\text{a}, \text{b}\}^*\}$, which is in D (i.e., it is decidable) but is not context-free. We can build a Post system P that generates WW. $P = (\{S, \text{a}, \text{b}\}, \{\text{a}, \text{b}\}, \{X\}, R, S)$, where R =

(1) $XS \rightarrow X\text{a}S$ /* Generate $(\text{a} \cup \text{b})^*$ S.

(2) $XS \rightarrow X\text{b}S$ "

(3) $XS \rightarrow XX$ /* Create a second copy of X.

This Post system can generate, for example, the string abbabb. It does so as follows:

$S \Rightarrow$ (using rule (1) and letting X match ε)

a$S \Rightarrow$ (using rule (2) and letting X match a)

ab$S \Rightarrow$ (using rule (2) and letting X match ab)

abb$S \Rightarrow$ (using rule (3) and letting X match abb)

abbabb

Post systems, as we have just defined them, are equivalent in power to Turing machines. The set of languages that can be generated by a Post system is exactly SD, the set of semidecidable languages. The proof of this claim is by construction. For any Post system P, it is possible to build a Turing machine M that simulates P. And, for any Turing machine M, it is possible to build a Post system P that simulates M.

18.2.5 Unrestricted Grammars

While the availability of variables in Post systems is convenient, variables are not actually required to give Post systems their power. In Chapter 23, we will describe another formalism that we will call an unrestricted grammar. The rules in an unrestricted grammar may not contain variables, but their left-hand sides may contain any number of terminal and nonterminal symbols, subject to the sole constraint that there be at least one symbol. Unrestricted grammars have exactly the same power as do Post systems and Turing machines. They can generate exactly the semidecidable (SD) languages. In Example 23.3 we'll show an unrestricted grammar that generates WW (the language we considered above in Example 18.1).

18.2.6 Markov Algorithms

Next we consider yet another formalism based on rewrite rules. A Markov algorithm 💻 (named for its inventor, Andrey A. Markov, Jr., the son of the inventor of the stochastic Markov model that we described in Section 5.11.1), is simply an ordered list of rules, each of which has a left-hand side that is a single string and a right-hand side that is also a single string. Formally a Markov algorithm M is a triple (V, Σ, R), where:

- V is the rule alphabet, which contains both working symbols and input symbols. Whenever the job of M is to semidecide or decide a language (as opposed to compute a function), V will contain two special working symbols, *Accept* and *Reject*.
- Σ (the set of input symbols) is a subset of V, and
- R (the rules) is an ordered list of rules, each of which is an element of $V^* \times V^*$. There are two kinds of rules, continuing and terminating. Whenever a terminating rule is applied, the algorithm halts. We will write continuing rules, as usual, as $X \rightarrow Y$. We will write terminating rules by adding a dot after the arrow. So we will have $X \rightarrow \bullet\, Y$.

Notice that there is no start symbol. Markov algorithms, like Turing machines, are given an input string. The job of the algorithm is to examine its input and return the appropriate result.

The rules are interpreted by the following algorithm:

Markovalgorithm(M: Markov algorithm, w : input string) =

1. Until no rules apply or the process has been terminated by executing a terminal rule do:
   - **1.1.** Find the first rule in the list R that matches against w. If that rule matches w in more than one place, choose the leftmost match.
   - **1.2.** If no rule matches then exit.
   - **1.3.** Apply the matched rule to w by replacing the substring that matched the rule's left-hand side with the rule's right-hand side.
   - **1.4.** If the matched rule is a terminating rule, exit.
2. If w contains the symbol *Accept* then accept.
3. If w contains the symbol *Reject* then reject.
4. Otherwise, return w.

Notice that a Markov algorithm (unlike a program in any of the other rule-based formalisms that we have considered so far) is completely deterministic. At any step, either no match exists, in which case the algorithm halts, or exactly one match can be selected.

> The logic programming language Prolog executes programs (sets of rules) in very much the same way that the Markov algorithm interpreter does. Programs are deterministic and programmers control the order in which rules are applied by choosing the order in which to write them. (M.2.3)

The Markov algorithm formalism is equivalent in power to the Turing machine. This means that Markov algorithms can semidecide exactly the set of SD languages (in which case they may accept or reject) and they can compute exactly the set of computable functions (in which case they may return a value). The proof of this claim is by construction: It is possible to show that a Markov algorithm can simulate the universal Turing machine *U*, and vice versa.

EXAMPLE 18.2 A Markov Algorithm for $A^nB^nC^n$

We show a Markov algorithm *M* to decide the language $A^nB^nC^n = \{a^nb^nc^n : n \geq 0\}$. Let $M = (\{a, b, c, \#, \%, ?, Accept, Reject\}, \{a, b, c\}, R)$, where $R =$

1. #a → %	/*If the first character is an a, erase it and look for a b next.
2. #b →• *Reject*	/* If the first character is a b, reject.
3. #c →• *Reject*	/* If the first character is a c, reject.
4. %a → a%	/* Move the % past the a's until it finds a b.
5. %b → ?	/* If it finds a b, erase it and look for a c next.
6. % →• *Reject*	/* No b found. Just c's or end of string. Reject.
7. ?b → b?	/* Move the ? past the b's until it finds a c.
8. ?c → ε	/* If it finds a c, erase it. Then only rule (11) can fire next.
9. ? →• *Reject*	/* No c found. Just a's or b's or end of string. Reject.
10. # →• *Accept*	/* A # was created but there are no input characters left. Accept.
11. ε → #	/* This one goes first since none of the others can.

When *M* begins, the only rule that can fire is 11, since all the others must match some working symbol. So rule 11 matches at the far left of the input string and adds a # to the left of the string. If the first input character is an a, it will be picked up by rule 1, then erased and replaced by a new working symbol . The job of the % is to sweep past any other a's and find the first b. If there is no b or if a c comes first, *M* will reject. If there is a b, it will be picked up by rule 5, then erased and replaced by a third working symbol ?, whose job is to sweep past any remaining b's and find the first c. If there is no c, *M* will reject. If there is, it will be erased by rule 8. At that point, there are no remaining working symbols, so the only thing that can happen is that rule 11 fires and the process repeats until all matched sets of a's, b's, and c's have been erased. If that happens, the final # that rule 11 adds will be the only symbol left. Rule 10 will fire and accept.

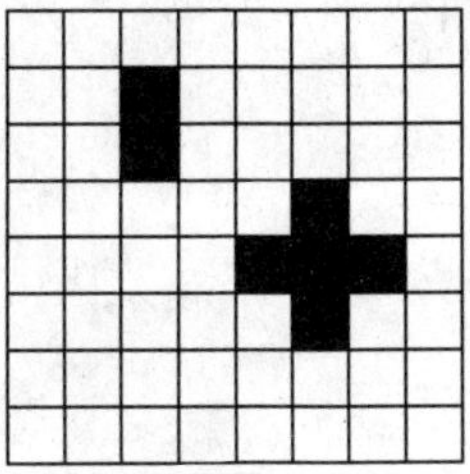

FIGURE 18.1 An example of the Game of Life.

18.2.7 Conway's Game of Life

The Game of Life was first proposed by John Conway. In the game, the board (the world) starts out in some initial configuration in which each square is either alive (shown in black) or dead (shown in white). A simple example is shown in Figure 18.1.

Life is not a game in the usual sense of having players. It is more like a movie that we can watch. It proceeds in discrete steps. At each step, the value for each cell is determined by computing the number of immediate neighbors (including the four on the diagonals, so up to a maximum of eight) it currently has, according to the following rules:

- A dead cell with exactly three live neighbors becomes a live cell (birth).
- A live cell with two or three live neighbors stays alive (survival).
- In all other cases, a cell dies or remains dead (overcrowding or loneliness).

Once values for all the cells at the next step have been determined, all of them change values simultaneously. Then the next step begins.

> Life is fascinating to watch.

Life can be played on a board of any size and it can be given any desired starting configuration. Depending on the starting configuration, Life may end (all the cells die), it may reach some other stable configuration (it looks the same from one step to the next), or it may enter a cycle of configurations. We'll say that the game of Life halts iff it reaches some stable configuration.

We can imagine the Life simulator as a computing device that takes the initial board configuration as input, knows one operation (namely how to move from one configuration to the next), may or may not halt, and if it halts, produces some stable configuration as its result. Conway and others have shown that, with an appropriate encoding of Turing machines and input strings as board configurations, the operation of any Turing machine can be simulated by the game of Life. And a Life simulator can be written as a Turing machine. So Life is equivalent in power to a Turing machine.

18.2.8 One Dimensional Elementary Cellular Automata

The game of Life can be thought of as a two-dimensional cellular automaton. Each square looks at its neighboring cells in two dimensions to decide what should happen to it at the next step. But we don't need two dimensions to simulate a Turing machine. Wolfram [2002] describes one-dimensional cellular automata that look like the one shown in Figure 18.2.

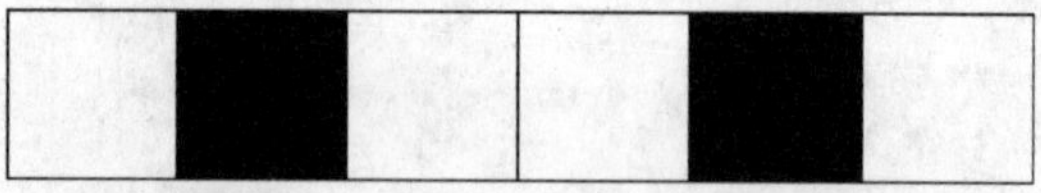

FIGURE 18.2 A one-dimensional cellular automaton.

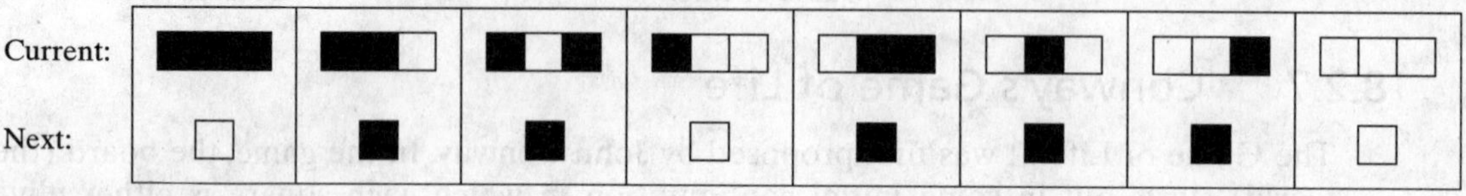

FIGURE 18.3 Rule 110.

As in the game of Life, each cell is either on or off (black or white), an initial configuration is specified, and the configuration of the automaton at each later step t is determined by independently computing the value for each cell, which in turn is a function solely of the values of itself and its neighbors (in this case two) at step $t - 1$.

In the game of Life, Conway specified the rule that is to be used to compute the value of each cell at the next step. What rule shall we use for these one-dimensional automata? Since each cell can have one of the two values (black or white) and each cell's next configuration depends on the current configuration of three cells (itself and its two neighbors), there are 256 (2^8) rules that we could use. Each rule contains 8 (2^3) parts, specifying what should happen next for each of the 8 possible current situations. Figure 18.2 shows the rule that Wolfram numbers 110. Wolfram describes a proof that Rule 110, with an appropriate (and complex) encoding of Turing machines and strings as cellular automata, is equivalent in power to the Turing machine.

18.2.9 DNA Computing

See K.1 for a very short introduction to molecular biology and genetics.

In 1993, Len Adleman observed that DNA molecules and Turing machine tapes both do the same thing: They encode information as strings. Further, he observed that both nature and the Turing machine offer simple operations for manipulating those strings. So he wondered, can DNA compute? To begin to answer that question, he performed a fascinating experiment 🖳. In a laboratory, he solved an instance of the Hamiltonian path problem[9] using DNA molecules. More precisely, what he did was the following:

[9] The definition that Adleman uses for the Hamiltonian path problem is the following: Let G be a directed graph, with one node s designated as the start node and another node d designated as the end node. A Hamiltonian path through G is a path that begins at s, ends at d, and visits each other node in G exactly once. A Hamiltonian path problem is then the following decision problem: Given a directed graph G, with designated s and d, does there exist a Hamiltonian path through it? We will return to this problem in Part V. There we will use a slightly different definition that asks for any Hamiltonian path through G. It will not specify a particular start and end vertex.

1. He chose a particular graph G (with 7 vertices and 14 edges).
2. He encoded each vertex of G as a sequence of 8 nucleotides. For example, a vertex might be represented as ACCTGCAG.
3. He encoded each directed edge of G as a sequence of 8 nucleotides, namely the last four from the encoding of the start vertex and the first four from the encoding of the end vertex. So, for example, if there was an edge from ACTTGCAG to TCGGACTG, then it would be encoded as GCAGTCGG.
4. He synthesized many copies of each of the edge sequences, as well as many copies of the DNA complements[10] of all the vertex encodings. So for example, since one of the vertices was encoded as ACTTGCAG, its complement, the sequence TGAACGTC, was synthesized.
5. He combined the vertex-complement molecules and the edge molecules in a test tube, along with water, salt, some important enzymes, and a few other chemicals required to support the natural biological processes.
6. He allowed to happen the natural process by which complementary strands of DNA in solution will meet and stick together (anneal). So for example, consider again the edge GCAGTCGG. It begins at the vertex whose encoding is ACTTGCAG and it ends at a vertex whose encoding is TCGGACTG. The complements of those vertices are TGAACGTC and AGCCTGAC. So, in solution, the edge strands will anneal with the vertex-complement strands to produce the double strand:

   path of length one (i.e., one edge): GCAGTCGG
   complement of sequence of two vertices: TGAACGTC AGCCTGAC

   But then, suppose that there is an edge from the second vertex to some third one. Then that edge will anneal to the lower string that was produced above, generating:

   path of length two: GCAGTCGG ACTGGGCT
   complement of sequence of two vertices: TGAACGTC AGCCTGAC

   Then a third vertex may anneal to the right end of the path sequence. And so forth. Eventually, if there is a path from the start vertex to the end one, there will be a sequence of fragments, like our top one, that corresponds to that path.
7. He allowed a second biological reaction to occur. The enzyme ligase that had been added to the mixture joins adjacent sequences of DNA. So instead of strands of fragments, as above, the following strands will be produced:

   path of length two: GCAGTCGGACTGGGCT
   complement of sequence of three vertices: TGAACGTCAGCCTGACCCGATACA

[10] Each DNA molecule is a double strand of nucleotide sequences. Each nucleotide contains one of the four bases: adenine (A), thymine (T), guanine (G) and cytosine (C). Each of these has a complement: C and G are complements and A and T are complements. When a double strand of DNA is examined as a sequence of base pairs (one from each strand), every base occurs across from its complement. So, whenever one strand has a C, the other has a G. And whenever one strand has an A, the other has a T.

8. He used the polymerase chain reaction (PCR) technique to make massive numbers of copies of exactly those sequences that started at the start vertex and ended at the end one. Other sequences were still present in the mix after this step, but in much lower numbers.
9. He used gel electrophoresis to select only those molecules whose length corresponded to a Hamiltonian path through the graph.
10. He checked that each of the vertices other than the source and the destination did in fact occur in the selected molecules. To do this required one pass through the following procedure for each intermediate vertex:
    - **10.1.** Use a DNA "probe" that attracts molecules that contain a particular DNA sequence (i.e., the one for the vertex that is being checked).
    - **10.2.** Use a magnet to attract the probes.
    - **10.3.** Throw away the rest of the solution, thus losing those molecules that were not attached to the probe.
11. He checked that some DNA molecules remained at the end. Only molecules that corresponded to paths that started at the start vertex, ended at the end vertex, had the correct length for a path that visited each vertex exactly once, and contained each of the vertices could still be present. So if any DNA was left, a Hamiltonian path existed.

Since that early experiment, other scientists have tried other ways of encoding information in DNA molecules and using biological operations to compute with it 🖳. The question then arises: Is DNA computing Turing-equivalent? The answer depends on exactly what we mean by DNA computing. In particular, what operations are allowed? For example, must the model be limited only to operations that can be performed only by naturally occurring enzymes? It has been shown that, given some reasonable assumptions about allowed operations, DNA computing is Turing-equivalent.

Exercises

1. Church's Thesis makes the claim that all reasonable formal models of computation are equivalent. And we showed in, Section 17.4, a construction that proved that a simple accumulator/register machine can be implemented as a Turing machine. By extending that construction, we can show that any computer can be implemented as a Turing machine. So the existence of a decision procedure (stated in any notation that makes the algorithm clear) to answer a question means that the question is decidable by a Turing machine.

   Now suppose that we take an arbitrary question for which a decision procedure exists. If the question can be reformulated as a language, then the language will be in D iff there exists a decision procedure to answer the question. For each of the following problems, your answers should be a precise description of an algorithm. It need not be the description of a Turing Machine:

   a. Let $L = \{<M> : M$ is a DFSM that doesn't accept any string containing an odd number of 1's$\}$. Show that L is in D.

b. Let $L = \{<E> : E$ is a regular expression that describes a language that contains at least one string w that contains 111 as a substring$\}$. Show that L is in D.

c. Consider the problem of testing whether a DFSM and a regular expression are equivalent. Express this problem as a language and show that it is in D.

2. Consider the language $L = \{w = xy : x, y \in \{\mathtt{a}, \mathtt{b}\}^*$ and y is identical to x except that each character is duplicated$\}$. For example, ababaabbaabb $\in L$.

a. Show that L is not context-free.

b. Show a Post system (as defined in Section 18.2.4) that generates L.

3. Show a Post system that generates $A^nB^nC^n$.

4. Show a Markov algorithm (as defined in Section 18.2.6) to subtract two unary numbers. For example, on input 111-1, it should halt with the string 11. On input 1-111, it should halt with the string -11.

5. Show a Markov algorithm to decide WW.

6. Consider Conway's Game of Life, as described in Section 18.2.7. Draw an example of a simple Life initial configuration that is an oscillator, meaning that it changes from step to step but it eventually repeats a previous configuration.

CHAPTER 19

The Unsolvability of the Halting Problem

So far, we have focused on solvable problems and we have described an increasingly powerful sequence of formal models for computing devices that can implement solutions to those problems. Our last attempt is the Turing machine and we've shown how to use Turing machines to solve several of the problems that were not solvable with a PDA or an FSM. The Church-Turing thesis suggests that, although there are alternatives to Turing machines, none of them is any more powerful. So, are we done? Can we build a Turing machine to solve any problem we can formally describe?

Until a bit before the middle of the 20th century, western mathematicians believed that it would eventually be possible to prove any true mathematical statement and to define an algorithm to solve any clearly stated mathematical problem. Had they been right, our work would be done. But they were wrong. And, as a consequence, the answer to the question in the last paragraph is no. There are well-defined problems for which no Turing machine exists.

In this chapter we will prove our first result that shows the limits of what we can compute. In later chapters, we will discuss other unsolvable problems and we will see how to analyze new problems and then prove either that they are solvable or that they are not. We will do this by showing that there are languages that are not decidable (i.e., they are not in D). So, recall the definitions of the sets D and SD that we presented in Chapter 17:

- A Turing machine M with input alphabet Σ ***decides*** a language $L \subseteq \Sigma^*$ (or, alternatively, implements a decision procedure for L) iff, for any string $w \in \Sigma^*$:
    - if $w \in L$ then M accepts w, and
    - if $w \notin L$ then M rejects w.

  A language L is ***decidable*** (and thus an element of D) iff there is a Turing machine M that decides it.

- A Turing machine M with input alphabet Σ ***semidecides*** a language $L \subseteq \Sigma^*$ (or, alternatively, implements a semidecision procedure for L) iff for any string $w \in \Sigma^*$:
  - if $w \in L$ then M accepts w, and
  - if $w \notin L$ then M does not accept w. (Note that M may fail to accept either by rejecting or by failing to halt.)

  A language L is ***semidecidable*** (and thus an element of SD) iff there is a Turing machine that semidecides it.

Many of the languages that we are about to consider are composed of strings that correspond, at least in part, to encodings of Turing machines. Some of them may also contain other fragments. So we will be considering languages such as:

- $L_1 = \{<M, w> :$ Turing machine M halts on input string $w\}$.
- $L_2 = \{<M> :$ there exists no string on which Turing machine M halts$\}$.
- $L_3 = \{<M_a, M_b> : M_a$ and M_b are Turing machines that halt on the same strings$\}$.

Recall that $<M>$ is the notation that we use for the encoding of a Turing machine M using the scheme described in Section 17.6. $<M, w>$ means the encoding of a pair of inputs: a Turing machine M and an input string w. $<M_a, M_b>$ means the encoding of a pair of inputs, both of which are Turing machines.

Consider L_1 above. It consists of the set of strings that encode a (Turing machine, string) pair with the property that the Turing machine M, when started with w on its tape, halts. So, in order for some string s to be in language L_1, it must possess two properties:

- It must be syntactically well-formed.
- It must encode a machine M and a string w such that M would halt if started on w.

We will be attempting to find Turing machines that can decide (or semidecide) languages like L_1, L_2, and L_3. Building a Turing machine to check for syntactic validity is easy. We would like to focus on the other part. So, in our discussion of languages such as these, we will define the universe from which we are drawing strings to be the set that contains only those strings that meet the syntactic requirements of the language definition. For example, that could be the set that contains descriptions of Turing machines (strings of the form $<M>$), or the set that contains descriptions of a Turing machine and a string (strings of the form $<M, w>$). This contrasts with the convention we have been using up until now, in which the universe was Σ^*, where Σ is the alphabet over which L is defined.

This change in convention will be important whenever we talk about the complement of a language such as L_1, L_2, or L_3. So, for example, we have:

$$\neg L_1 = \{<M, w> : \text{Turing machine } M \textit{ does not halt} \text{ on input string } w\}.$$

Note that this convention has no impact on the decidability of any of these languages since the set of syntactically valid strings is in D. So it is straightforward to build a precondition checker that accepts exactly the syntactically well-formed strings and rejects all others.

19.1 The Language H is Semidecidable but Not Decidable

We begin by considering the language we called L_1 in the last section. We're now going to call it H, the halting problem language. So, define:

- H = {<M, w> : Turing machine M halts on input string w}.

H is:

- Easy to state and to understand.
- Of great practical importance since a program to decide H could be a very useful part of a program-correctness checker. You don't want to go online to pay a bill and have the system go into an infinite loop after it has debited your bank account and before it credits the payment to your electric bill.
- Semidecidable.
- Not decidable.

We need to prove these last two claims. Before we attempt to do that, let's consider them. H would be decidable if there existed an algorithm that could take as input a program M and an input w and decide whether M will halt on w. It is easy to define such an algorithm that works some of the time. For example, it would be easy to design an algorithm that could discover that the following program (and many others like it that contain no loops) halts on all inputs:

1. Concatenate 0 to the end of the input string.
2. Halt.

It would also be easy to design an algorithm that could discover that the following program (and many others like it) halts on no inputs:

1. Concatenate 0 to the end of the input string.
2. Move right one square.
3. Go to step 1.

But, for H to be decidable, we would need an algorithm that decides the question in all cases. Consider the following program:

times3(x: positive integer) =
  While $x \neq 1$ do:
    If x is even then $x = x/2$.
    Else $x = 3x + 1$.

It is easy to prove that *times3* halts on any positive integer that is a power of 2. In that case, x decreases each time through the loop and must eventually hit 1. But what about other inputs? Will it halt, for example on 23,478? It is conjectured that, for any positive integer input, the answer to this question is yes. But, so far, no one has been able either to prove that conjecture or to find a counterexample. The problem of determining whether *times3* must always halt is called the ***3x + 1 problem***.

So there appear to be programs whose halting behavior is difficult to determine. We now prove that the problem of deciding halting behavior for an arbitrary (machine, input) pair is semidecidable but not decidable.

THEOREM 19.1 Semidecidability of the Halting Problem

Theorem: The language H = {<M, w> : Turing machine M halts on input string w} is semidecidable.

Proof: The proof is by construction of a semideciding Turing machine M_{SH}. The design of M_{SH} is simple. All it has to do is to run M on w and accept if M halts. So:

M_{SH}(<M, w>) =

1. Run M on w.
2. Accept.

M_{SH} accepts iff M halts on w. Thus M_{SH} semidecides H.

But H is not decidable. This single fact is going to turn out to be the cornerstone of the entire theory of undecidability that we will discuss in the next several chapters.

> Compilers check for various kinds of errors in programs. But, because H is undecidable, no compiler can offer a guarantee that a program is free of infinite loops. (G.4.4)

THEOREM 19.2 Undecidability of the Halting Problem

Theorem: The language H = {<M, w> : Turing machine M halts on input string w} is not decidable.

Proof: If H were decidable, then there would be some Turing machine M_H that decided it. M_H would implement the following specification:

halts(<M: string, w : string>) =
If <M> is the description of a Turing machine that halts on input w, then accept; else reject.

Note that we have said nothing about how M_H would work. It might use simulation. It might examine M for loops. It might use a crystal ball. The only claim we are making about M_H is that it can implement *halts*. In other words, it can decide somehow whether M halts on w and report *True* if it does and *False* if it does not.

Now suppose that we write the specification for a second Turing machine, which we'll call *Trouble*:

Trouble(*x*: string) =
 If *halts* accepts <*x*, *x*>, then loop forever; else halt.

If there exists some M_H that computes the function *halts*, then the Turing machine *Trouble* also exists. We can easily write the code for it as follows: Assume that $C_\#$ is a Turing machine (similar to the copy machine that we showed in Example 17.11) that writes onto its tape a second copy of its input, separated from the first by a comma. Also assume that M_H exploits the variable *r*, into which it puts 1 if it is about to halt and accept and 0 if it is about to halt and reject. Then, using the notation defined in Section 17.1.5, *Trouble* is shown in Figure 19.1.

Trouble takes a single string *x* as its input. It makes a copy of that string, moves its read/write head all the way back to the left, and then invokes M_H on *x*, *x*. M_H will treat the first copy as a Turing machine and the second one as the input to that Turing machine. When M_H halts (which it must, since we've assumed that it is a deciding machine), *Trouble* will either halt immediately or loop forever, depending on whether M_H stored a 0 or a 1 in *r*.

What happens if we now invoke *Trouble*(<*Trouble*>)? In other words, we invoke *Trouble* on the string that corresponds to its own description, as shown in the figure. Then *Trouble* will invoke M_H(<*Trouble*, *Trouble*>). Since the second argument of M_H can be any string, this is a valid invocation of the function. What should M_H say?

- If M_H reports that *Trouble*(<*Trouble*>) halts (by putting a 1 in the variable *r*), then what *Trouble* actually does is to loop.
- But if M_H reports that *Trouble*(<*Trouble*>) does not halt (by putting a 0 in the variable *r*), then what *Trouble* actually does is to halt.

Thus there is no response that M_H can make that accurately predicts the behavior of *Trouble*(<*Trouble*>). So we have found at least one input on which any implementation of *halts* must fail to report the correct answer. Thus there exists no correct implementation of *halts*. This means that M_H does not exist. So H is not decidable.

FIGURE 19.1 A Turing machine that implements the function *Trouble*.

Table 19.1 Using diagonalization to construct *Trouble*.

	i_1	i_2	i_3	...	*<Trouble>*	...
machine$_1$	1					
machine$_2$		1				
machine$_3$					1	
...				1		
Trouble			1			1
...	1	1	1			
...				1		

There is another way to state this proof that makes it clearer that what we have just done is to use diagonalization. Consider Table 19.1. To form column 0, we lexicographically enumerate all Turing machines, using the procedure that was defined in Section 17.6.2. To form row 0, we lexicographically enumerate all possible input strings over the alphabet Σ that we used to encode inputs to the universal Turing machine. The cell $[i, j]$ of the table contains the value 1 if TM_i halts on the jth input string and is blank otherwise.

This table is infinite in both directions, so it will never be explicitly constructed. But, if we claim that the Turing machine M_H exists, we are claiming that it can compute the correct value for any cell in this table on demand. *Trouble* must correspond to some row in the table and so, in particular, M_H must be able to compute the values for that row. The string <*Trouble*> must correspond to some column in the table. What value should occur in the black cell of the picture? There is no value that correctly describes the behavior of *Trouble*, since we explicitly constructed it to look at the black cell and then do exactly the opposite of what that cell says.

So we have just proven (twice) a very important result that can be stated in any one of three ways:

- The language H is not decidable.
- The halting problem is unsolvable (i.e., there can exist no implementation of the specification we have given for the *halts* function).
- The membership problem for the SD languages (i.e., those that can be accepted by some Turing machine) is not solvable.

Recall that we have seen many times that any decision problem that we can state formally can be restated as a language recognition task. So it comes as no surprise that this one can. In the rest of this book, we will use whichever version of this result is clearer at each point.

19.2 Some Implications of the Undecidability of H

We now have our first example, H, of a language that is semidecidable (i.e., it is in SD) but that is not decidable (i.e., it is not in D). What we will see in the rest of this section is that H is far more than an anomaly. It is the key to the fundamental distinction between the classes D and SD.

THEOREM 19.3 H is the Key to the Difference Between D and SD

Theorem: If H were in D then every SD language would be in D.

Proof: Let L be any SD language. Since L is in SD, there exists a Turing machine M_L that semidecides it. Suppose H were also in D. Then it would be decided by some Turing machine that we can call O (for oracle). To decide whether some string w is in L, we can appeal to O and ask it whether M_L will halt on the input w. If the answer is yes, we can (without risk of getting into an infinite loop) run M_L on w and see whether or not it accepts. So, given M_L (the machine that semidecides L), we can build a new Turing machine M' that decides L by appeal to O:

M'(w: string) =

1. Run O on $<M_L, w>$.
2. If O accepts (which it will iff M_L halts on w), then:
   - 2.1. Run M_L on w.
   - 2.2. If it accepts, accept. Else reject.
3. Else reject.

Since O is a deciding machine for H, it always halts. If it reports that M would halt on w, then M' can run M on w to see whether it accepts or rejects. If, on the other hand, O reports that M would not halt then it certainly cannot accept, so M' rejects. So M' always halts and returns the correct answer. Thus, if H were in D, all SD languages would be.

But H is not in D. And as we are about to see, it is not alone.

19.3 Back to Turing, Church, and the Entscheidungsproblem

At the beginning of Chapter 18, we mentioned that Turing invented the Turing machine because he was attempting to answer the question, "Given a set of axioms A and a sentence s, does there exist an algorithm to decide whether s is entailed by A?" To do that, he needed a formal definition of an algorithm, which the Turing machine provided. As an historical aside, we point out here that in Turing's model, machines (with the exception of a universal machine that could simulate other machines) were always started on a blank tape. So, while in H we ask whether a Turing machine M halts on some particular input w, Turing would ask simply whether it halts. But note that this is not a significant change. In our model, all inputs are of finite length. So it is possible to encode any particular input in the states of a machine that is to operate on it. That machine can start out with a blank tape, write the desired input on its tape, and then continue as though the tape had contained the input.

Having defined the Turing machine (which he called simply a "computing machine"), Turing went on to show the unsolvability of the halting problem. He then used that result to show that no solution to the Entscheidungsproblem (the problem of deciding whether s is entailed by A) can exist. An outline of Turing's proof is the following:

1. If we could solve the problem of determining whether a given Turing machine ever prints the symbol 0, then we could solve the problem of determining whether a given Turing machine halts. Turing presented the technique by which this could be done.
2. But we can't solve the problem of determining whether a given Turing machine halts, so neither can we solve the problem of determining whether it ever prints 0.
3. Given a Turing machine M, we can construct a logical formula F that is a theorem, given the axioms of Peano arithmetic, iff M ever prints the symbol 0. Turing also presented the technique by which this could be done.
4. If there were a solution to the Entscheidungsproblem, then we would be able to determine the theoremhood of any logical sentence and so, in particular, we could use it to determine whether F is a theorem. We would thus be able to decide whether M ever prints the symbol 0.
5. But we know that there is no procedure for determining whether M ever prints 0.
6. So there is no solution to the Entscheidungsproblem.

This proof is an example of the technique that we will use extensively in Chapter 21 to show that problems are not decidable. We reduce a problem that is already known not to be decidable to a new problem whose decidability is in question. In other words, we show that if the new problem were decidable by some Turing machine M, then we could use M as the basis for a procedure to decide the old problem. But, since we already know that no solution to the old problem can exist, no solution for the new one can exist either. The proof we just sketched uses this technique twice: once in steps 1 and 2 to show that we cannot solve the problem of determining whether a Turing machine ever prints the symbol 0, and a second time, in steps 3 through 6, to show that we cannot solve the Entscheidungsproblem.

Exercises

1. Consider the language L = {<M> : Turing machine M accepts at least two strings}.

   a. Describe in clear English a Turing machine M that semidecides L.

   b. Now change the definition of L just a bit. Consider:

   L' = {<M> : Turing machine M accepts *exactly* 2 strings>.

   Can you tweak the Turing machine you described in part a to semidecide L'?

2. Consider the language $L = \{<M>:$ Turing machine M accepts the binary encodings of the first three prime numbers$\}$.

a. Describe in clear English a Turing machine M that semidecides L.

b. Suppose (contrary to fact, as established by Theorem 19.2) that there were a Turing machine *Oracle* that decided H. Using it, describe in clear English a Turing machine M that decides L.

CHAPTER 20

Decidable and Semidecidable Languages

Now that we have shown that the halting problem is undecidable, it should be clear why we introduced the notion of a semidecision procedure. For some problems, it is the best we will be able to come up with. In this chapter we explore the relationship between the classes D and SD, given what we now know about the limits of computation.

20.1 D: The Big Picture

First, we observe that the class D includes the regular and the context-free languages. More precisely:

THEOREM 20.1 All Context-Free Languages, Plus Others, are in D

Theorem: The set of context-free languages is a proper subset of D.

Proof: By Theorem 14.1, the membership problem for the context-free languages is decidable. So the context-free languages are a subset of D. And there is at least one language, $A^nB^nC^n$, that is decidable but not context-free. So the context-free languages are a *proper* subset of D.

20.2 SD: The Big Picture

Now what can we say about the relationship between D and the larger class SD? Almost every language you can think of that is in SD is also in D. Examples include:

- $A^nB^nC^n = \{a^nb^nc^n : n \geq 0\}$,
- $WcW = \{wcw : w \in \{a, b\}^*\}$,

- WW = $\{ww : w \in \{a, b\}^*\}$, and
- $\{w$ of the form: $x{*}y = z$, where: $x, y, z \in \{0, 1\}^*$ and, when x, y, and z are viewed as binary numbers, $x \cdot y = z\}$.

But there are languages that are in SD but not in D. We already know one:

- H = $\{<M, w> :$ Turing machine M halts on input string $w\}$.

What about others? It isn't possible to come up with any physical examples since there are only finitely many molecules in the observable universe. So every physical set is finite and thus regular. But unless we want to model all our real world problems using only the power of a finite state machine, we generally ignore the fact that the true language is finite and model it as a more complex set that is unbounded and thus, for all practical purposes, infinite. If we do that, then here's a language that is effectively in SD and has the look and feel of many SD languages:

- $L = \{w : w$ is the email address of someone who will respond to a message you just posted to your newsgroup$\}$.

If someone responds, you know that their email address is in L. But if your best friend hasn't responded yet, you don't know that she isn't going to. All you can do is wait.

In Chapter 21 we will see that any question that asks about the result of running a Turing machine is undecidable (and so its corresponding language formulation is not in D). In a nutshell, if you can't think of a way to answer the question by simulating the Turing machine, it is very likely that there is no other way to do it and the question is undecidable. But keep in mind that we said that the question must ask about the *result of running* the Turing machine. Questions that ask simply about the Turing machine itself (e.g., how many states does it have) or about its behavior partway through its computation (e.g., what does it do after exactly 100 steps) are generally decidable.

In Chapter 22 we will see some examples of undecidable problems that do not ask questions about Turing machines. If you'd like to be convinced that this theory applies to more than the analysis of Turing machines (or of programs in general), skip ahead briefly to Chapter 22.

In this chapter we will look at properties of four classes of languages and see how they relate to each other. The classes we will consider are shown in Figure 20.1. They are:

- D, corresponding to the inner circle of the figure, the set of decidable languages.
- SD, corresponding to the outer circle of the figure, the set of semidecidable languages.
- SD/D, corresponding to the donut in the figure, the set of languages that are in SD but not D.
- ¬SD, corresponding to the grey area in the figure, the set of languages that are not even semidecidable.

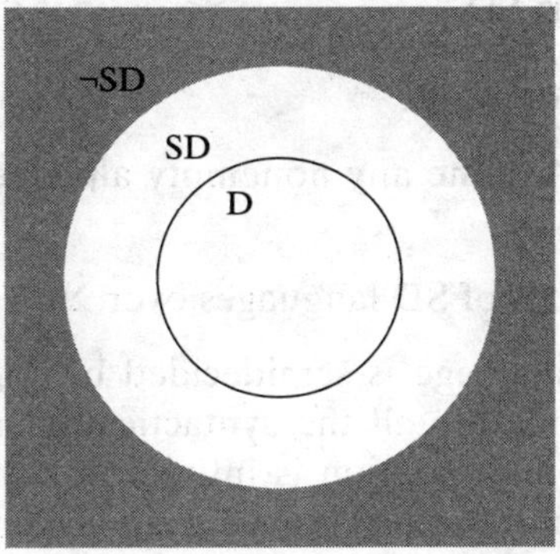

FIGURE 20.1 The relationships between D and SD.

20.3 Subset Relationships between D and SD

The picture that we just considered implicitly makes three claims about the relationship between the classes *D* and SD. From the inside out they are:

1. D is a subset of SD. In other words, every decidable language is also semidecidable.
2. There exists at least one language that is in SD but not D and so the donut in the picture is not empty.
3. There exist languages that are not in SD. In other words, the gray area of the figure is not empty.

We have already proven the second of these claims: In Chapter 19 we described H = {<*M*, *w*> : Turing machine *M* halts on input string *w*} and showed that H is not in D but is in SD. We now consider each of the other two claims.

THEOREM 20.2 D is a Subset of SD

Theorem: Every decidable language is also semidecidable.

Proof: The proof follows directly from the definitions of deciding and semideciding Turing machines. If *L* is in D, then it is decided by some Turing machine *M*. *M* therefore accepts all and only the strings in *L*. So *M* is also a semideciding machine for *L*. Since there is a Turing machine that semidecides *L*, it is in SD.

Next we consider whether the class SD includes all languages or whether there are languages that are not even semidecidable. As Figure 20.1 suggests (by the existence of the gray region), the answer is that there are languages that are not in SD.

THEOREM 20.3 Not All Languages are in SD

Theorem: There exist languages that are not in SD.

Proof: We will use a counting argument. Assume any nonempty alphabet Σ. First we prove the following lemma:

Lemma: There is a countably infinite number of SD languages over Σ.

Proof of Lemma: Every semidecidable language is semidecided by some Turing machine. We can lexicographically enumerate all the syntactically legal Turing machines with input alphabet Σ. That enumeration is infinite, so, by Theorem A.1, there is a countably infinite number of semideciding Turing machines. There cannot be more SD languages than there are semideciding Turing machines, so there is at most a countably infinite number of SD languages. There is not a one-to-one correspondence between SD languages and semideciding Turing machines since there is an infinite number of machines that semidecide any given language. But the number of SD languages must be infinite because it includes (by Theorem 20.1 and Theorem 20.2) all the context-free languages and, by Theorem 13.2, there are an infinite number of them. So there is a countably infinite number of SD languages.

Proof of Theorem: There is an uncountably infinite number of languages over Σ (by Theorem 2.2). So there are more languages over Σ than there are in SD. Thus there must exist at least one language that is in $\neg$SD.

We will see our first example of a language that is in $\neg$SD in the next section.

20.4 The Classes D and SD Under Complement

The regular languages are closed under complement. The context free languages are not. What about the decidable (D) languages and the semidecidable (SD) languages?

THEOREM 20.4 The Decidable Languages are Closed Under Complement

Theorem: The class D is closed under complement.

Proof: The proof is by a construction that is analogous to the one we used to show that the regular languages are closed under complement. Let L be any decidable language. Since L is in D, there is some deterministic Turing machine M that decides it. Recall that a deterministic Turing machine must be completely specified (i.e., there must be a transition from every nonhalting state on every character in the tape alphabet), so there is no need to worry about a dead state. From M we construct M' to decide $\neg L$. Initially, let $M' = M$. Now swap the y and n states. M' halts and accepts whenever M would halt and reject; M' halts and rejects whenever M would halt and accept. Since M always halts, so does M'. And M' accepts exactly those strings that M would reject, i.e., $\neg L$. Since there is a deciding machine for $\neg L$, it is in D.

THEOREM 20.5 The Semidecidable Languages are not Closed Under Complement

Theorem: The class SD is not closed under complement.

Proof: The proof is by contradiction. Suppose the class SD were closed under complement. Then, given any language L in SD, $\neg L$ would also be in SD. So there would be a Turing machine M that semidecides L and another Turing machine M' that semidecides $\neg L$. From those two we could construct a new a Turing machine $M\#$ that decides L. On input w, $M\#$ will simulate M and M', in parallel, running on w. Since w must be an element of either L or $\neg L$, one of M or M' must eventually accept. If M accepts, then $M\#$ halts and accepts. If M' accepts, then $M\#$ halts and rejects. So, if the SD languages were closed under complement, then all SD languages would also be in D. But we know from Chapter 19 that H = {<M, w> : Turing machine M halts on input string w} is in SD but not D.

These last two theorems give us a new way to prove that a language L is in D (or, in fact, a way to prove that a language is not in SD):

THEOREM 20.6 L and ¬L Both in SD is Equivalent to L is in D

Theorem: A language L is in D iff both it and its complement $\neg L$ are in SD.

Proof: We prove each direction of the implication:

Proof that L in D implies L and ¬L are in SD: Because L is in D, it must also be in SD by Theorem 20.2. But what about $\neg L$? By Theorem 20.4, the class D is closed under complement, so $\neg L$ is also in D. And so, using Theorem 20.2 again, it is also in SD.

Proof that L and ¬L are in SD implies L is in D: The proof is by construction and uses the same construction that we used to prove Theorem 20.5: Since L and $\neg L$ are in SD, they each have a semideciding Turing machine. Suppose L is semidecided by M and $\neg L$ is semidecided by M'. From those two we construct a new Turing machine $M\#$ that decides L. On input w, $M\#$ will simulate M and M', in parallel, running on w. Since w must be an element of either L or $\neg L$, one of M_1 or M_2 must eventually accept. If M_1 accepts, then $M\#$ halts and accepts. If M_2 accepts, then $M\#$ halts and rejects. Since $M\#$ decides L, L is in D.

We can use Theorem 20.6 to prove our first example of a language that is not in SD:

THEOREM 20.7 ¬H is not in SD

Theorem: The language ¬H, (the complement of H) = {<M, w> : Turing machine M does not halt on input string w} is not in SD.

Proof: Recall that we are defining the complement of languages involving Turing machine descriptions with respect to the universe of syntactically well-formed strings. From Theorem 19.1, we know that H is in SD (since we showed a semideciding Turing machine for it). By Theorem 20.6 we know that if ¬H were also in SD then H would be in D. But, by Theorem 19.2, we know that H is not in D. So ¬H is not in SD.

20.5 Enumerating a Language

In most of our discussion so far, we have defined a language by specifying either a grammar that can generate it or a machine that can accept it. But it is also possible to specify a machine that is a generator. Its job is to enumerate (in some order) the strings of the language. We will now explore how to use a Turing machine to do that.

20.5.1 Enumerating in Some Undefined Order

To generate a language L, we need a Turing machine M whose job is to start with a blank tape, compute for a while, place some string in L on the tape, signal that we should snapshot the tape to record its contents, and then go back and do it all that again. If L is finite, we can construct M so that it will eventually halt. If L is infinite, M must continue generating forever. If a Turing machine M behaves in this way and outputs all and only the strings in L, then we say that M ***enumerates*** L. Any enumerating Turing machine M must have a special state that we will call p (for print). Whenever M enters p, the shortest string that contains all the nonblank characters on M's tape will be considered to have been enumerated by M. Note that p is not a halting state. It merely signals that the current contents of the tape should be viewed as a member of L. M may also have a halting state if L is finite. Formally, we say that a Turing machine M enumerates L iff, for some fixed state p of M,

$$L = \{w : (s, \square) |-_{M}{}^{*} (p, w)\}$$

A language L is ***Turing-enumerable*** iff there is a Turing machine that enumerates it. Note that we are making no claim here about the order in which the strings in L are generated.

To make it easy to describe enumerating Turing machines in our macro language, we'll define the simple subroutine P, shown in Figure 20.2. It simply enters the state p and halts.

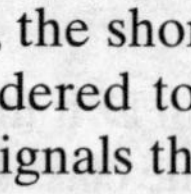

FIGURE 20.2 A subroutine that takes a snapshot of the tape.

EXAMPLE 20.1 Enumerating in Lexicographic and in Random Order

Consider the language a*. Here are two different Turing machines that enumerate it:

M_1:

$>P$aR

M_2:

$>P$aP□RaRaRaP□P

M_1 enumerates a* in lexicographic order. M_2 enumerates it in a less straightforward order. It will produce the sequence ε, a, aaa, aa, aaaaa, aaaa, ...

So now we have one mechanism for using a Turing machine to generate a language and a separate mechanism for using a Turing machine to accept one. Is there any relationship between the class of Turing-enumerable languages and either the class of decidable languages (D) or the class of semidecidable languages (SD)? The answer is yes. The class of languages that can be enumerated by a Turing machine is identical to SD.

THEOREM 20.8 Turing Enumerable is Equivalent to Semidecidable

Theorem: A language is in SD (i.e., it can be semidecided by some Turing machine) iff it is Turing-enumerable.

Proof: We must do two proofs, one that shows that if a language is Turing enumerable then it is in SD and another that shows that if a language is in SD then it is Turing enumerable.

Proof that if a language is Turing enumerable then it is in SD: If a language L is Turing enumerable then there is some Turing machine M that enumerates it. We convert M to a machine M' that semidecides L:

$M'(w : \text{string}) =$

1. Save input w on a second tape.
2. Invoke M, which will enumerate L. Each time an element of L is enumerated, compare it to w. If they match, halt and accept. Otherwise, continue with the enumeration.

Because there is a Turing machine that semidecides L, it is in SD. Figure 20.3 illustrates how M' works.

Proof that if a language is in SD then it is Turing enumerable: If $L \subseteq \Sigma^*$ (for some Σ) is in SD, then there is a Turing machine M that semidecides it. We will use M to construct a new machine M' that enumerates L. The idea behind M' is

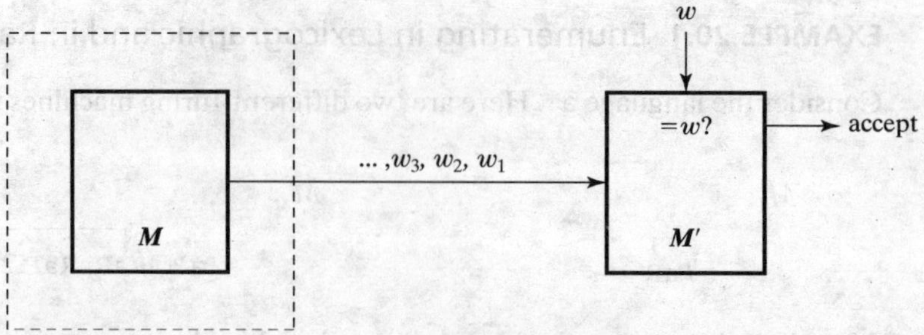

FIGURE 20.3 Using an enumerating machine in a semidecider.

that it will lexicographically enumerate Σ^*. It will consider each of the strings it enumerates as a candidate for membership in L. So it will pass each such string to M. Whenever M accepts some string w, M' will output it. The problem is that M is not guaranteed to halt. So what happens if M' invokes M on a string that is not in L and M loops? If we are not careful, M' will wait forever and never give other strings a chance.

To solve this problem, M' will not just invoke M and sit back and wait to see what happens. It will carefully control the execution of M. In particular, it will invoke M on $string_1$ and let it compute one step. Then it will consider $string_2$. It will allow M to compute one step on $string_2$ and also one more step on $string_1$. Then it will consider $string_3$, this time trying the new $string_3$ for one step and applying one more step to the computations on $string_2$ and on $string_1$. Anytime M accepts some string in this sequence, M' will output that string. If there is some string s that is not in L, then the computation corresponding to s will either halt and reject or fail to halt. In either case, M' will never output s.

This pattern is shown in Figure 20.4. Each column corresponds to a candidate string and each row corresponds to one stage of the process. At each stage, a new string is added and one more step is executed for each string that is already being considered but on which M has not yet halted. The number of steps that have been executed on each string so far is shown in brackets. If M does halt on some string (as, for example, b, in the chart below), that column will simply be skipped at future stages.

We will call the technique that we just described ***dovetailing***. It will turn out to be useful for other similar kinds of proofs later.

ε [1]					
ε [2]	a [1]				
ε [3]	a [2]	b [1]			
ε [4]	a [3]	b [2]	aa [1]		
ε [5]	a [4]	b [3]	aa [2]	ab [1]	
ε [6]	a [5]		aa [3]	ab [2]	ba [1]

FIGURE 20.4 Using dovetailing to control simulation.

So a description of M' is:

$M'() =$

1. Enumerate all $w \in \Sigma^*$ lexicographically. As each string w_j is enumerated:
   1.1. Start up a copy of M with w_j as its input.
   1.2. Execute one step of each M_i initiated so far, excluding only those that have previously halted.
2. Whenever an M_i accepts, output w_i.

20.5.2 Enumerating in Lexicographic Order

So far, we have said nothing about the order in which the strings in L are enumerated by M. But now suppose we do. We say that M ***lexicographically enumerates*** L iff M enumerates the elements of L in lexicographic order. A language L is ***lexicographically Turing-enumerable*** iff there is a Turing machine that lexicographically enumerates it.

Now we can ask whether there is any relationship between the class of lexicographically Turing-enumerable languages and any of the other classes we have already defined. Just as we found in the last section, in the case of unordered enumeration, we discover that the answer is yes. The class of languages that can be lexicographically enumerated by a Turing machine is identical to D.

THEOREM 20.9 Lexicographically Turing Enumerable is Equivalent to Being Decidable

Theorem: A language is in D iff it is lexicographically Turing-enumerable.

Proof: Again we must do two proofs, one for each direction of the implication.

Proof that if a language is in D then it is lexicographically Turing enumerable: If a language $L \subseteq \Sigma^*$ (for some Σ) is in D, then there is some Turing machine M that decides it. Using M, we can build M', which lexicographically generates the strings in Σ^* and tests them, one at a time by passing them to M. Since M is a deciding machine, it halts on all inputs, so dovetailing is not required here. If, on string w, M halts and accepts, then M' outputs w. If M halts and rejects, then M' just skips w and goes on to the next string in the lexicographic enumeration. Thus M' lexicographically enumerates L. The relationship between M and M' can be seen in Figure 20.5.

Proof that if a language is lexicographically Turing enumerable then it is in D: If a language L is lexicographically Turing enumerable, then there is some Turing machine M that lexicographically enumerates it. Using M, we can build M', which, on input w, starts up M and waits until either M generates w (in which case M' accepts w), M generates a string that comes after w in the enumeration (in which

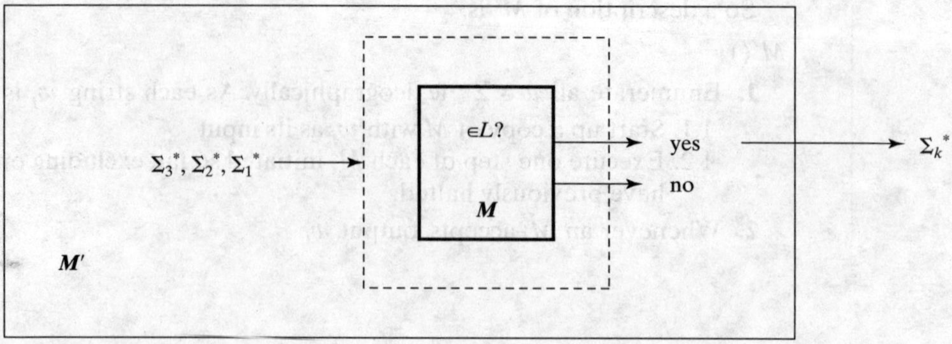

FIGURE 20.5 Using a decider in a lexicographic enumerator.

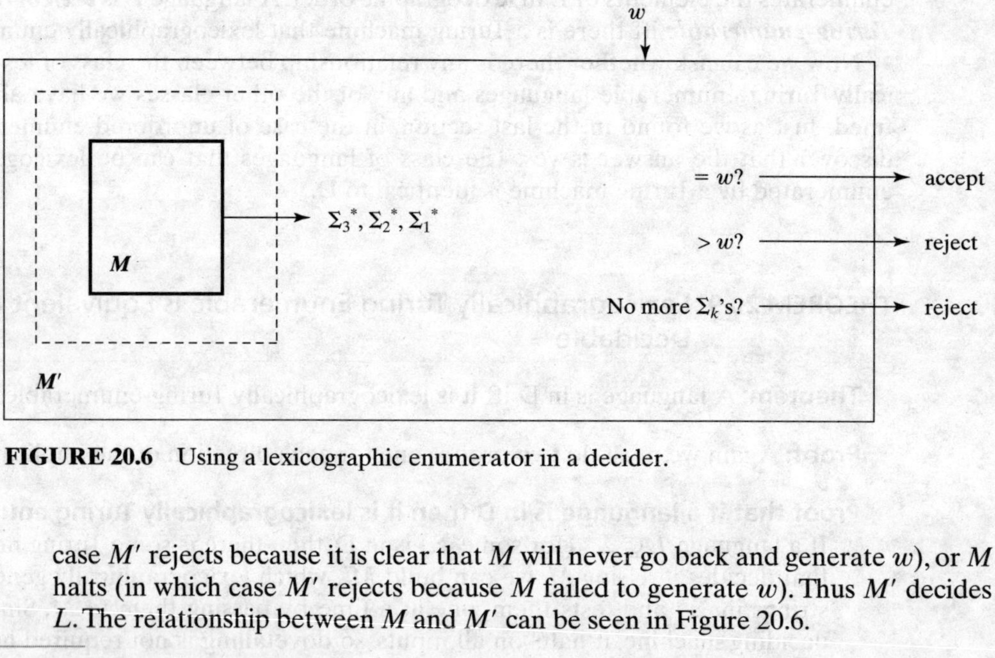

FIGURE 20.6 Using a lexicographic enumerator in a decider.

case M' rejects because it is clear that M will never go back and generate w), or M halts (in which case M' rejects because M failed to generate w). Thus M' decides L. The relationship between M and M' can be seen in Figure 20.6.

20.6 Summary

In this chapter we have considered several ways in which the classes D and SD are related and we have developed theorems that give us ways to prove that a specific language L is in D and/or SD. Figure 20.7 attempts to summarize these results. The column labeled IN lists our techniques for proving that a language is in the corresponding language class. The column labeled OUT lists our techniques for proving that a language is not in the corresponding language class. We have listed reduction here for completeness. We will present reduction as a proof technique in Chapter 21. And we

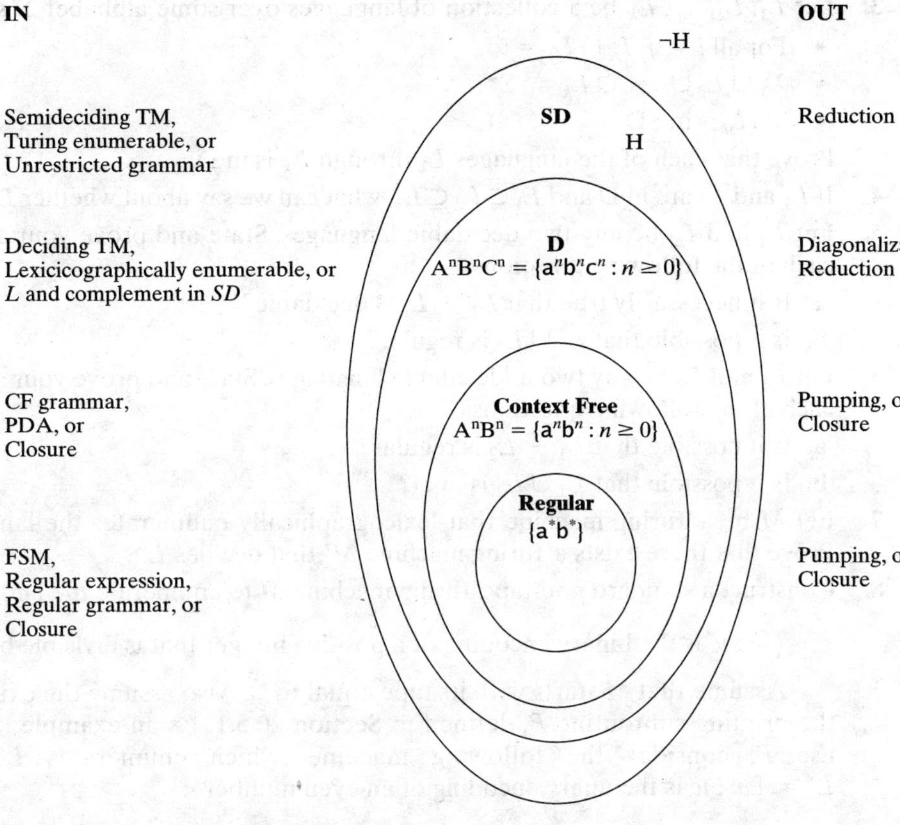

FIGURE 20.7 Relating four language classes.

have mentioned unrestricted grammars, which we will discuss in Chapter 23. You'll also note, in the figure, one example language in each class.

Exercises

1. Show that the set D (the decidable languages) is closed under:
   a. Union
   b. Concatenation
   c. Kleene star
   d. Reverse
   e. Intersection
2. Show that the set SD (the semidecidable languages) is closed under:
   a. Union
   b. Concatenation
   c. Kleene star
   d. Reverse
   e. Intersection

3. Let $L_1, L_2, \ldots, L_k$ be a collection of languages over some alphabet Σ such that:
    - For all $i \neq j$, $L_i \cap L_j = \varnothing$.
    - $L_1 \cup L_2 \cup \ldots \cup L_k = \Sigma^*$.
    - $\forall i$ (L_i is in SD).

   Prove that each of the languages L_1 through L_k is in D.
4. If L_1 and L_3 are in D and $L_1 \subseteq L_2 \subseteq L_3$, what can we say about whether L_2 is in D?
5. Let L_1 and L_2 be any two decidable languages. State and prove your answer to each of the following questions:
    a. Is it necessarily true that $L_1 - L_2$ is decidable?
    b. Is it possible that $L_1 \cup L_2$ is regular?
6. Let L_1 and L_2 be any two undecidable languages. State and prove your answer to each of the following questions:
    a. Is it possible that $L_1 - L_2$ is regular?
    b. Is it possible that $L_1 \cup L_2$ is in D?
7. Let M be a Turing machine that lexicographically enumerates the language L. Prove that there exists a Turing machine M' that decides L^R.
8. Construct a standard one-tape Turing machine M to enumerate the language:

   $$\{w : w \text{ is the binary encoding of a positive integer that is divisible by } 3\}.$$

   Assume that M starts with its tape equal to ❑. Also assume the existence of the printing subroutine P, defined in Section 20.5.1. As an example of how to use P, consider the following machine, which enumerates L', where $L' = \{w : w \text{ is the unary encoding of an even number}\}$:

   $$> P\, R\, 1\, R\, 1$$

   You may find it useful to define other subroutines as well.
9. Construct a standard one-tape Turing machine M to enumerate the language A^nB^n. Assume that M starts with its tape equal to ❑. Also assume the existence of the printing subroutine P, defined in Section 20.5.1.
10. If w is an element of $\{0, 1\}^*$, let $\neg w$ be the string that is derived from w by replacing every 0 by 1 and every 1 by 0. So, for example, $\neg 011 = 100$. Consider an infinite sequence S defined as follows:

    $$S_0 = 0.$$
    $$S_{n+1} = S_n \neg S_n.$$

    The first several elements of S are 0, 01, 0110, 01101001, 0110100110010110. Describe a Turing machine M to output S. Assume that M starts with its tape equal to ❑. Also assume the existence of the printing subroutine P, defined in Section 20.5.1, but now with one small change: If M is a multitape machine, P will output the value of tape 1. (*Hint*: Use two tapes.)

11. Recall the function *mix*, defined in Example 8.23. Neither the regular languages nor the context-free languages are closed under *mix*. Are the decidable languages closed under *mix*? Prove your answer.
12. Let $\Sigma = \{\mathtt{a}, \mathtt{b}\}$. Consider the set of all languages over Σ that contain only even length strings.
    a. How many such languages are there?
    b. How many of them are semidecidable?
13. Show that every infinite semidecidable language has a subset that is not decidable.

CHAPTER 21

Decidability and Undecidability Proofs

We now know two languages that are not in D:

- $H = \{<M, w> : \text{Turing machine } M \text{ halts on input } w\}$
- $\neg H = \{<M, w> : \text{Turing machine } M \text{ does not halt on input } w\}$ (which also isn't in SD)

In this chapter we will see that they are not alone. Recall that we have two equivalent ways to describe a question: as a language (in which case we ask whether it is in D), and as a problem (in which case we ask whether it is decidable or whether it can be solved). Although all of our proofs will be based on the language formulation, it is sometimes easier, particularly for programmers, to imagine the question in its problem formulation. Table 21.1 presents a list, stated both ways, of some of the undecidable questions that we will consider in this and succeeding chapters.

Table 21.1 The problem and the language view.

The Problem View	***The Language View***
Given a Turing machine *M* and a string *w*, does *M* halt on *w*?	$H = \{<M, w> : \text{TM } M \text{ halts on input } w\}$
Given a Turing machine *M* and a string *w*, does *M* not halt on *w*?	$\neg H = \{<M, w> : \text{TM } M \text{ does not halt on input } w\}$
Given a Turing machine *M*, does *M* halt on the empty tape?	$H_\varepsilon = \{<M> : \text{TM } M \text{ halts on } \varepsilon\}$
Given a Turing machine *M*, is there any string on which *M* halts?	$H_{ANY} = \{<M> : \text{there exists at least one string on which TM } M \text{ halts}\}$
Given a Turing machine *M*, does *M* accept all strings?	$A_{ALL} = \{<M> : L(M) = \Sigma^*\}$
Given two Turing machines M_a and M_b, do they accept the same languages?	$EqTMs = \{<M_a, M_b> : L(M_a) = L(M_b)\}$
Given a Turing machine *M*, is the language that *M* accepts regular?	$TM_{REG} = \{<M> : L(M) \text{ is regular}\}$

Some of these languages are also not in SD. We will return to them in Section 21.6, where we will see how to prove that languages are not in SD.

The primary technique that we will use here to show that a language L is not in D is reduction. We will show that if L were in D, we could use its deciding machine to decide some other language that we already know is not decidable. Thus we can conclude that L is not decidable either.

21.1 Reduction

We ***reduce*** a problem to one or more other problems when we describe a solution to the first problem in terms of solutions to the others. We generally choose to reduce to simpler problems, although sometimes it makes sense to pick problems just because we already have solutions for them. Reduction is ubiquitous in everyday life, puzzle solving, mathematics, and computing.

EXAMPLE 21.1 Calling Jen

We want to call our friend Jen but don't have her number. But we know that Jim has it. So we reduce the problem of finding Jen's number to the problem of getting hold of Jim.

The most important property of a reduction is clear even in the very simple example of finding Jen's number:

> The reduction exists AND there is a procedure that works for getting hold of Jim IMPLIES we will have Jen's number.

But what happens if there is no way to get hold of Jim? Does that mean that we cannot find Jen's number? No. There may be some other way to get it.

If, on the other hand, we knew (via some sort of oracle) that there is no way we could ever end up with Jen's number, and if we still believed in the reduction (i.e., we believed that Jim knows Jen's number and would be willing to give it to us), we would be forced to conclude that there exists no effective procedure for getting hold of Jim.

EXAMPLE 21.2 Crisis Detection

Suppose that we want to know whether there is some sort of crisis brewing in the world, our city, or the company we work for. We'd like to ask the Pentagon, the city council, or top management, but they probably won't tell us. But perhaps we can reduce this question to one we can answer: Has there been a spike this week in orders for middle-of-the-night pizza delivery to: the Pentagon, the town hall, corporate headquarters? This reduction will work provided all of the following are true:

EXAMPLE 21.2 (*Continued*)

- There will be all-nighters at the specified locations if and only if there is a crisis.
- There will be a spike in middle-of-the-night pizza orders if and only if there are all-nighters there.
- It is possible to find out about pizza orders.

The crisis-detection example illustrates a common use of reduction: We wish to solve a problem but have no direct way of doing so. So we look for a way to transform the problem we care about into some other problem that we can solve. The transformation must have the property that the answer to this new problem provides the answer to the original one.

EXAMPLE 21.3 Fixing Dinner

We can reduce the problem of fixing dinner to a set of simpler problems: Fix the entrée, fix the salad, and fix the dessert.

EXAMPLE 21.4 Theorem Proving

Suppose that we want to establish $Q(A)$ and that we have, as a theorem:

$$\forall x(R(x) \wedge S(x) \wedge T(x) \rightarrow Q(x)).$$

Then we can reduce the problem of proving $Q(A)$ to three new ones: proving $R(A)$, $S(A)$, and $T(A)$.

> Backward chaining solves problems by reducing complex goals to simpler ones until direct solutions can be found. It is used in theorem provers and in a variety of kinds of automatic reasoning and intelligent systems. (M.2.3)

These last two examples illustrate an important kind of reduction, often called ***divide and conquer***. One problem is reduced to two or more problems, all of which must be solved in order to produce a solution to the original problem. But each of the new problems is assumed to be easier to solve than the original one was.

EXAMPLE 21.5 Nim

Nim[11] starts with one or more piles of sticks. Two players take turns removing sticks from the piles. At each turn, a player chooses a pile and may remove some or all of the sticks from that pile. The player who is left with no sticks to remove loses. For example, an initial configuration of a Nim game could be the following, in which the sticks are arranged in three piles:

Consider the problem of determining whether there is any move that we can make that will guarantee that we can win. The obvious way to solve this problem is to search the space of legal moves until we find a move that makes it impossible for the other player to win. If we find such a move, we know that we can force a win. If we don't, then we know that we cannot. But the search tree can be very large and keeping track of it is nearly impossible for people. So how can we answer the question?

We can reduce the problem of searching a Nim game tree to a simple problem in Boolean arithmetic. We represent the number of sticks in each pile as a binary number, arrange the numbers in a column, lining up their low-order digits, and then apply the exclusive-or (XOR) operator to each column. So, in the example above, we'd have:

100 (4)
010 (2)
101 (5)
———
011

If the resulting string is in 0^+, then the current board position is a guaranteed loss for the current player. If the resulting string is not in 0^+, then there is a move by which the current player can assure that the next position will be a guaranteed loss for the opponent. So, given a Nim configuration, we can decide whether we can guarantee a win by transforming it into the XOR problem we just described and then checking to see that the result of the XOR is not in 0^+.

In addition, we can easily extend this approach so that it tells us what move we should make. All that is required is to choose one number (i.e., one pile of sticks) and subtract from it some number such that the result of XORing together the new counts will yield some string in 0^+. There may be more than one such move,

[11] This description is taken from [Misra 2004].

EXAMPLE 21.5 *(Continued)*

but it suffices just to find the first one. So we try the rows one at a time. In our example, we quickly discover that if we remove one stick from the second pile (the one currently containing two sticks), then we get:

100	(4)
001	(1)
101	(5)
000	

So we remove one stick from the second pile. No search of follow-on moves is required.

> Some combinatorial problems can be solved easily by reducing them to graph problems. (E.3)

EXAMPLE 21.6 Computing a Function

Suppose that we have access only to a very simple calculator that can perform integer addition but not multiplication. We can reduce the problem of computing xy to the problem of computing $a + b$ as follows:

multiply(x: integer, y: integer) =
 answer = 0.
 For $i = 1$ to y do:
  answer = *answer* + x.
 Return *answer*.

21.2 Using Reduction to Show that a Language is Not Decidable

So far, we have used reduction to show that problem$_1$ *is* solvable if problem$_2$ is. Now we will turn the idea around and use it to show that problem$_2$ is not solvable given that we already know that problem$_1$ isn't. Reduction, as we are about to use it, is a ***proof by contradiction*** technique. We will say, "Suppose that problem$_2$ were decidable. Then we could use its decider as a subroutine that would enable us to solve problem$_1$. But we already know that there is no way to solve problem$_1$. So there isn't any way to solve problem$_2$ either."

In the rest of this chapter, we are going to construct arguments of exactly this form to show that various languages are not in D because $H = \{<M, w> :$ Turing machine M halts on input string $w\}$ isn't. We'll then extend the technique to show that some languages are not in SD either (because ¬H isn't). But, before we do that, we should note one very

EXAMPLE 21.7 Dividing an Angle

Given an arbitrary angle, divide it into sixths, using only a straightedge and a compass. We show that there exists no general procedure to solve this problem. Suppose that there were such a procedure, which we'll call *sixth*. Then we could define the following procedure to trisect an arbitrary angle:

trisect(a: angle) =

1. Divide a into six equal parts by invoking *sixth*(a).
2. Ignore every other line, thus dividing a into thirds.

So we have reduced the problem of trisecting an angle to the problem of dividing it into sixths. But we know that there exists no procedure for trisecting an arbitrary angle using only a straightedge and compass. The proof of that claim relies on a branch of mathematics known as Galois theory 💻, after the French mathematician Evariste Galois, who was working on the problem of discovering solutions for polynomials of arbitrary degree. An interesting tidbit from the history of mathematics: Galois's work in this area was done while he was still a teenager, but was not published during his lifetime, which ended when he was killed in a duel in 1832 at age 20.

If *sixth* existed, then *trisect* would exist. But we know that *trisect* cannot exist. So neither can *sixth*.

important thing about arguments of this sort: Solvability (and decidability) results can hinge on the details of the specifications of the problems involved. For example, let's reconsider the angle trisection problem. This time, instead of the requirement, "using only a straight edge and a compass," we'll change the rules to "in origami." Now, it turns out that it is possible to trisect an angle using the paper folding and marking operations that origami provides 💻. We will have to be very careful to state exactly what we mean in specifying the languages that we are about to consider.

In the rest of this chapter, we are going to use reduction in a very specific way. The goal of a reduction is to enable us to describe a decision procedure for a language L_1 by using a decision procedure (which we will call *Oracle*) that we hypothesize exists for some other language L_2. Furthermore, since our goal is to develop a decision procedure (i.e., design a Turing machine), we are interested only in reductions that are themselves computable (i.e., can be implemented as a Turing machine that is guaranteed to halt). So the precise meaning of reduction that we will use in the rest of this book is the following:

A ***reduction*** R from L_1 to L_2 consists of one or more Turing machines with the following property: If there exists a Turing machine *Oracle* that decides (or semidecides) L_2, then the Turing machines in R can be composed with *Oracle* to build a deciding (or a semideciding) Turing machine for L_1. The idea is that the machines in R perform the straightforward parts of the task, while we assume that *Oracle* can do a good deal of the work.[12]

[12]It is common to define a reduction as a function, rather than as a Turing machine. But, when that is done, we require that the function be computable. Since the computable functions are exactly the functions that can be computed by some Turing machine, these two definitions are equivalent.

We will focus on the existence of deciding Turing machines now. Then, in Section 21.2, we will use this same idea when we explore the existence of semideciding machines. We will use the notation $P \leq P'$ to mean that P is reducible to P'. While we require that a reduction be one or more Turing machines, we will allow the use of clear pseudocode as a way to specify the machines. Because the key property of a reduction, as we have just defined it, is that it be computable by Turing machines, reducibility in this sense is sometimes called ***Turing reducibility***.

Since our focus in the rest of Part IV is on answering the question, "Does there exist a Turing machine to decide (or semidecide) some language L?" we will accept as a reduction any collection of Turing machines that meets the definition that we just gave. If, in addition, we cared about the efficiency of our (semi)deciding procedure, we would also have to care about the efficiency of the reduction. We will discuss that issue in Part V.

Having defined reduction precisely in terms of Turing machines, we can now return to the main topic of the rest of this chapter: How can we use reduction to show that some language L_2 is not decidable? When we reduce L_1 to L_2 via a reduction R, we show that if L_2 is in D then so is L_1 (because we can decide it with a composition of the machines in R with the *Oracle* that decides L_2). So what if we already know that L_1 is not in D? Then we have just shown that L_2 isn't either.

To see why this is so, recall that the definition of reduction tells us that:

$$(R \text{ is a reduction from } L_1 \text{ to } L_2) \wedge (L_2 \text{ is in D}) \rightarrow (L_1 \text{ is in D}).$$

If (L_1 is in D) is false, then at least one of the two antecedents of that implication must be false. So if we know that (R is a reduction from L_1 to L_2) is true, then (L_2 is in D) must be false.

We now have a way to show that some new language L_2 is not in D: We find a language that is reducible to L_2 and that is known not to be in D. We already have one language, H, that is not in D. So we can use it to prove that other languages aren't either.

Figure 21.1 shows the form of this argument graphically. The solid arrow indicates the reduction R from L_1 to L_2. The other two arrows correspond to implication. So the diagram says that if L_1 is reducible to L_2 then we know (as shown in the upward implication) that if L_2 is in D, so is L_1. But L_1 is known not to be in D. So (as shown in the downward implication) we know that L_2 is not in D either.

The important thing about this diagram is the direction of the arrows. We reduce L_1 to L_2 to show that the undecidability of L_1 guarantees that L_2 is also undecidable. As we do our reduction proofs, we must be careful always to reduce a known undecidable language to the unknown one. The most common mistake in doing reduction proofs is to do them backwards.

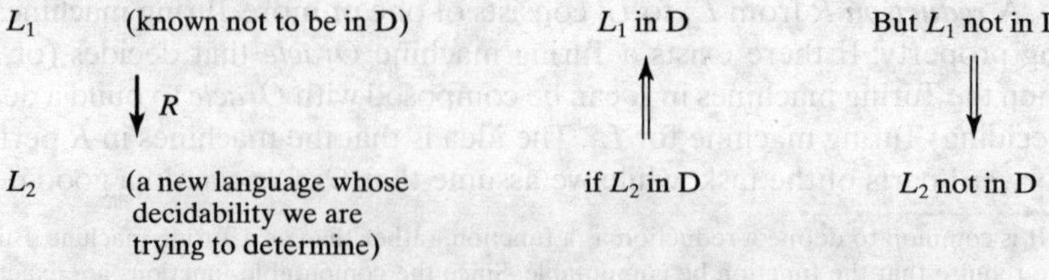

FIGURE 21.1 Using reduction for undecidability.

Summarizing what we have said: To use reduction to show that a language L_2 is not in D, we need to do three things:

1. Choose a language L_1 to reduce from. We must choose an L_1
   - that is already known not to be in D, and
   - that can be reduced to L_2 (i.e., there would be a deciding machine for it if there existed a deciding machine for L_2).
2. Define the reduction R and describe the composition C of R with *Oracle*, the machine that we hypothesize decides L_2.
3. Show that C does correctly decide L_1 if *Oracle* exists. We do this by showing
   - that R can be implemented as one or more Turing machines, and
   - that C is correct, meaning that it correctly decides whether its input x is an element of L_1. To do this, we must show that:
     - If $x \in L_1$, then $C(x)$ accepts, and
     - If $x \notin L_1$, then $C(x)$ rejects.

21.2.2 Mapping Reducibility

The most straightforward way to reduce one problem, which we'll call A, to another, which we'll call B, is to find a way to transform instances of A into instances of B. Then we simply hand the transformed input to the program that solves B and return the result. In Example 21.5, we illustrated this idea in our solution to the problem of determining whether or not we could force a win in the game of Nim. We transformed a problem involving a pile of sticks into a Boolean XOR problem. And we did it in such a way that a procedure that determined whether the result of the XOR was nonzero would also tell us whether we could force a win. So our reduction consisted of a single procedure *transform*. Then we argued that, if *XORsolve* solved the Boolean XOR problem, then *XOR-solve*(*transform*(x)) correctly decided whether x was a position from which we could guarantee a win.

In the specific context of attempting to solve decision procedures, we can formalize this idea as follows: Given an alphabet Σ, we will say that L_1 is ***mapping reducible*** to L_2, which we will write as $L_1 \leq_M L_2$, iff there exists some computable function f such that:

$$\forall x \in \Sigma^* (x \in L_1 \text{ iff } f(x) \in L_2).$$

In general, the function f gives us a way to transform any value x into a new value x' so that we can answer the question, "Is x in L_1?" by asking instead the question, "Is x' in L_2?" If f can be computed by some Turing machine R, then R is a ***mapping reduction*** from L_1 to L_2. So, if $L_1 \leq_M L_2$ and there exists a Turing machine *Oracle* that decides L_2, then the following Turing machine C, which is simply the composition of *Oracle* with R, will decide L_1:

$$C(x) = Oracle(R(x)).$$

The first several reduction proofs that we will do use mapping reducibility. In the first few, we show that a new language L_2 is not in D because H can be reduced to it. Once we have done several of those proofs, we'll have a collection of languages, all of which have been shown not to be in D. Then, for a new proof that some language L_2 is not in D, it will suffice to show that any one of the others can be reduced to it.

THEOREM 21.1 "Does *M* Halt on ε?" is Undecidable

Theorem: The language $H_\varepsilon = \{<M> : \text{Turing machine } M \text{ halts on } \varepsilon\}$ is in SD/D.

Proof: We will first show that H_ε is in SD. Then we will show that it is not in D.

We show that H_ε is in SD by exhibiting a Turing machine *T* that semidecides it. *T* operates as follows:

$T(<M>) =$

1. Run M on ε.
2. Accept.

T accepts <*M*> iff *M* halts on ε, so *T* semidecides H_ε.

Next we show that $H \leq_M H_\varepsilon$ and so H_ε is not in D. We will define a mapping reduction *R* whose job will be to map instances of H to instances of H_ε in such a way that, if there exists a Turing machine (which we will call *Oracle*) that decides H_ε, then *Oracle*(*R*(<*M*, *w*>)) will decide H.

R will transform any input of the form <*M*, *w*> into a new string, of the form <*M*>, suitable as input to *Oracle*. Specifically, what *R* does is to build a new Turing machine, which we will call *M*#, that halts on ε iff *M* halts on *w*. One way to do that is to build *M*# so that it completely ignores its own input. That means that it will halt on everything (including ε) or nothing. And we need for it to halt on everything precisely in case *M* would halt on *w*. That's easy. Let *M*# simply run *M* on *w*. It will halt on everything iff *M* halts on *w*. Note that *M*#, like every Turing machine has an input, namely whatever is on its tape when it begins to execute. So we'll define a machine *M*#(*x*), where *x* is the name we'll give to *M*#'s input tape. We must do that even though, in this and some other cases we'll consider, it happens that the behavior of *M*# doesn't depend on what its input tape contains.

So let *R* be a mapping reduction from H to H_ε defined as follows:

$R(<M, w>) =$

1. Construct the description <*M*#> of a new Turing machine *M*#(*x*) that, on input *x*, operates as follows:
   - **1.1.** Erase the tape.
   - **1.2.** Write *w* on the tape.
   - **1.3.** Run *M* on *w*.
2. Return <*M*#>.

We claim that if *Oracle* exists and decides H_ε, then $C = Oracle(R(<M, w>))$ decides H. To complete the proof, we need to show that *R* corresponds to a computable function (i.e., that it can be implemented by a Turing machine) and that *C* does in fact decide H:

- *R* can be implemented as a Turing machine: *R* must construct <*M#*> from <*M*, *w*>. To see what *M#* looks like, suppose that *w* = aba. Then *M#* will sweep along its input tape, blanking it out. Then it will write the string aba, move its read/write head back to the left, and, finally, pass control to *M*. So, in our macro language, *M#* will be:

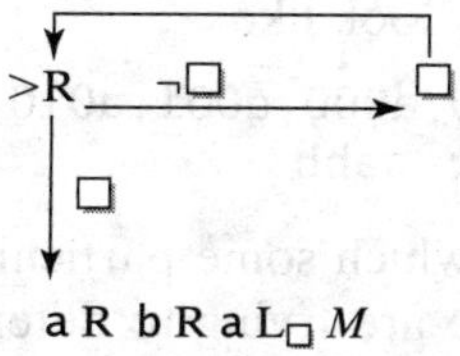

  The procedure for constructing *M#*, given an arbitrary *M* and *w*, is:

  1. Write the following code, which erases the tape:

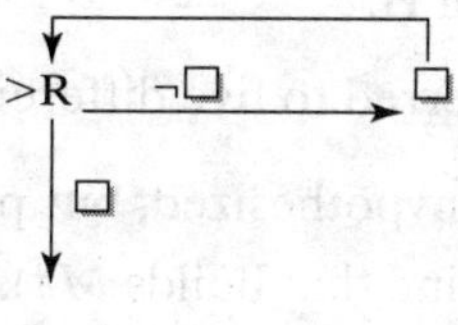

  2. For each character *c* in *w* do:
    2.2. Write *c*.
    2.3. If *c* is not the last character in *w*, write R.
  3. Write $L_{\square}$ *M*.

- *C* is correct: *M#* ignores its own input. It halts on everything or nothing. Think of its step 1.3 as a gate. The computation only makes it through the gate if *M* halts on *w*. If that happens then *M#* halts, no matter what its own input was. Otherwise, it loops in step 1.3. So:
  - If <*M*, *w*> ∈ H: *M* halts on *w*, so *M#* halts on everything. In particular, it halts on ε. *Oracle*(<*M#*>) accepts.
  - If <*M*, *w*> ∉ H: *M* does not halt on *w*, so *M#* halts on nothing and thus not on ε. *Oracle*(<*M#*>) rejects.

But no machine to decide H can exist, so neither does *Oracle*.

This result may seem surprising. It says that if we could decide whether some Turing machine *M* halts on the specific string ε, then we could solve the more general problem of deciding whether a machine *M* halts on an arbitrary input. Clearly, the other way around is true: If we could decide H (which we cannot), then we could decide whether *M* halts on any one particular string. But doing a reduction in that direction would tell us nothing about whether H_{ε} is decidable. The significant thing that we just saw in this proof is that there also exists a reduction in the direction that does tell us that H_ε is not decidable.

To understand the reduction proof that we just did (and all the others that we are about to do), keep in mind that it involves two different kinds of languages:

- H and H_ε: The strings in H_ε are encodings of Turing machines, so they look like

  `(q000,a000,q001,a010, ←), (q000,a000,q001,a010, →), ...`

  The strings in H are similar, except that they also include a particular w, so they look like

  `q000,a000,q001,a010, ←), (q000,a000,q001,a010, →),`
  `...; aabb`

- The language on which some particular Turing machine M, whose membership in either H or H_ε we are trying to determine, halts: Since M can be any Turing machine, the set of strings on which M halts can be anything. It might, for example, be A^nB^n, in which case it would contain strings like aaabbb. It could also, of course, be a language of Turing machine descriptions, but it will help to keep from getting confused if you think of M's whose job is to recognize languages like A^nB^n that are very different from H.

  The proof also referred to five different Turing machines:

  1. *Oracle* (the hypothesized, but provably nonexistent, machine to decide H_ε).
  2. *R* (the machine that builds *M#*). This one actually exists.
  3. *C* (the composition of *R* with *Oracle*).
  4. *M#* (the machine whose description we will pass as input to *Oracle*). Note that *M#* will never actually be executed.
  5. *M* (the machine whose behavior on the input string w we are interested in determining). Its description is input to *R*.

Figure 21.2 shows a block diagram of *C*. It illustrates the relationship among the five machines.

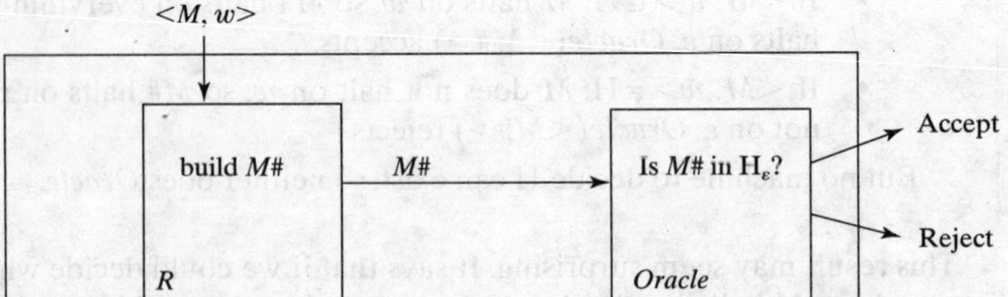

FIGURE 21.2 The relationships among *C*, *R*, and *Oracle*.

THEOREM 21.2 "Does *M* Halt on Anything?" is Undecidable

Theorem: The language $\text{H}_{\text{ANY}} = \{<M> :$ there exists at least one string on which Turing machine M halts$\}$ is in SD/D.

Proof: Again, we will first show that H_{ANY} is in SD. Then we will show that it is not in D.

We show that H_{ANY} is in SD by exhibiting a Turing machine T that semidecides it. We could try building T so that it simply runs M on all strings in Σ^* in lexicographic order. If it finds one that halts, it halts. But, of course, the problem with this approach is that if M fails to halt on the first string T tries, T will get stuck and never try any others. So we need to try the strings in Σ^* in a way that prevents T from getting stuck. We build T so that it operates as follows:

$T(<M>) =$

1. Use the dovetailing technique described in the proof of Theorem 20.8 to try M on all of the elements of Σ^* until there is one string on which M halts. Recall that, in dovetailing, we run M on one step of the first string, then another step on that string plus one step on the next, and so forth, as shown here (assuming $\Sigma = \{\text{a}, \text{b}\}$):

```
ε [1]
ε [2]  a [1]
ε [3]  a [2]  b [1]
ε [4]  a [3]  b [2]  aa [1]
ε [5]  a [4]  b [3]  aa [2]  ab [1]
ε [6]  a [5]                 aa [3]  ab [2]  ba [1]
```

2. If any instance of M halts, halt and accept.

T will accept iff M halts on at least one string. So T semidecides H_{ANY}.

Next we show that $\text{H} \leq_{\text{M}} \text{H}_{\text{ANY}}$ and so H_{ANY} is not in D. Let R be a mapping reduction from H to H_{ANY} defined as follows:

$R(<M, w>) =$

1. Construct the description $<M\#>$ of a new Turing machine $M\#(x)$ that, on input x, operates as follows:

   1.1. Examine x.

   1.2. If $x = w$, run M on x, else loop.

2. Return $<M\#>$.

If *Oracle* exists and decides H_{ANY}, then $C = Oracle(R(<M, w>))$ decides H:

- R can be implemented as a Turing machine: The proof is similar to that for Theorem 21.1. We will omit it in this and future proofs unless it is substantially different from the one we have already done.
- C is correct: $M\#$'s behavior depends on its input. The only string on which $M\#$ has a chance of halting is w. So:
  - If $<M, w> \in \text{H}$: M halts on w, so $M\#$ halts on w. So there exists at least one string on which $M\#$ halts. $Oracle(<M\#>)$ accepts.

- If $<M, w> \in$ H: M does not halt on w, so neither does $M\#$. So there exists no string on which $M\#$ halts. *Oracle*($<M\#>$) rejects.

But no machine to decide H can exist, so neither does *Oracle*.

Sometimes there is more than one straightforward reduction that works. For example, here is an alternative proof that H_{ANY} is not in D:

Proof: We show that H_{ANY} is not in D by reduction from H. Let R be a mapping reduction from H to H_{ANY} defined as follows:

$R(<M, w>) =$

1. Construct the description $<M\#>$ of a new Turing machine $M\#(x)$ that, on input x, operates as follows:

1.1. Erase the tape.

1.2. Write w on the tape.

1.3. Run M on w.

2. Return $<M\#>$.

If *Oracle* exists and decides H_{ANY}, then $C = Oracle(R(<M, w>))$ decides H. R can be implemented as a Turing machine. And C is correct. $M\#$ ignores its own input. It halts on everything or nothing. So:

- If $<M, w> \in$ H: M halts on w, so $M\#$ halts on everything. So it halts on at least one string. *Oracle*($<M\#>$) accepts.
- If $<M, w> \notin$ H: M does not halt on w, so $M\#$ halts on nothing. So it does not halt on at least one string. *Oracle*($<M\#>$) rejects.

But no machine to decide H can exist, so neither does *Oracle*.

Notice that we used the same reduction in this last proof that we used for Theorem 21.1. This is not uncommon. The fact that a single construction may be the basis for several reduction proofs is important. It derives from the fact that several quite different looking problems may in fact be distinguishing between the same two cases.

Recall the steps in doing a reduction proof of undecidability:

1. Choose an undecidable language L_1 to reduce from.

2. Define the reduction R.

3. Show that the composition of R with *Oracle* correctly decides L_1.

We make choices at steps 1 and 2. Our last example showed that there may be more than one reasonable choice for step 2. There may also be more than one reasonable choice for step 1. So far, we have chosen to reduce from H. But now that we know other languages that are not in D, we could choose to use one of them. We want to pick one that makes step 2, constructing R, as straightforward as possible.

THEOREM 21.3 "Does *M* Halt on Everything?" is Undecidable

Theorem: The language $H_{ALL} = \{<M> : \text{Turing machine } M \text{ halts on } \Sigma^*\}$ is not in D. (Note: H_{ALL} is also not in SD, which we will show in Section 21.6.)

Proof: We show that $H_\varepsilon \leq_M H_{ALL}$ and so H_{ALL} is not in D. We have chosen to use H_ε rather than H because H_ε looks more like H_{ALL} than H does. Both of them contain strings composed of a single Turing machine description, without reference to a particular string *w*. It is possible to do this proof by reduction from H instead. We leave that as an exercise.

Let *R* be a mapping reduction from H_ε to H_{ALL} defined as follows:

$R(<M>) =$

1. Construct the description $<M\#>$ of a new Turing machine $M\#(x)$ that, on input *x*, operates as follows:
   - **1.1.** Erase the tape.
   - **1.2.** Run *M*.
2. Return $<M\#>$.

If *Oracle* exists and decides H_{ALL}, then $C = Oracle(R(<M>))$ decides H_ε. *R* can be implemented as a Turing machine. And *C* is correct. *M#* runs *M* on ε. It halts on everything or nothing, depending on whether *M* halts on ε. So:

- If $<M> \in H_\varepsilon$: *M* halts on ε, so *M#* halts on all inputs. $Oracle(<M\#>)$ accepts.
- If $<M> \notin H_\varepsilon$: *M* does not halt on ε, so *M#* halts on nothing. $Oracle(<M\#>)$ rejects.

But no machine to decide H_ε can exist, so neither does *Oracle*.

Are safety and security properties of complex systems decidable? (J.2)

We next define a new language that corresponds to the membership question for Turing machines:

- $A = \{<M, w> : \text{Turing machine } M \text{ accepts } w\}$

Note that A is different from H, since it is possible that *M* halts but does not accept. Accepting is a stronger condition than halting. An alternative definition of *A* is then:

- $A = \{<M, w> : M \text{ is a Turing machine and } w \in L(M)\}$.

Recall that, for finite state machines and pushdown automata, the membership question was decidable. In other words, there exists an algorithm that, given *M* (an FSM or a PDA) and a string *w*, answers the question, "Does *M* accept *w*?" We're about to show that the membership question for Turing machines is undecidable.

THEOREM 21.4 "Does *M* accept *w*?" is Undecidable

Theorem: The language A = {<*M*, *w*> : *M* is a Turing machine and $w \in L(M)$} is not in D.

Proof: We show that $H \leq_M A$ and so A is not in D. Since H and A are so similar, it may be tempting to define a mapping reduction *R* simply as the identity function:

R(<*M*, *w*>) =

1. Return <*M*, *w*>.

But this won't work, as we see immediately when we try to prove that *C* = *Oracle*(*R*(<*M*, *w*>)) decides *A*:

- If <*M*, *w*> ∈ H: *M* halts on *w* . It may either accept or reject. If *M* accepts *w*, then *Oracle*(<*M*, *w*>) accepts. But if *M* rejects *w*, *Oracle*(<*M*, *w*>) will reject.

So we cannot guarantee that *Oracle* will accept whenever *M* halts on *w*. We need to construct *R* so that it passes to *Oracle* a machine *M#* that is guaranteed both to halt and to accept whenever *M* would halt on *w*.

We can make that happen by defining *R*, a mapping reduction from H to A, as follows:

R(<*M*, *w*>) =

1. Construct the description <*M#*> of a new Turing machine *M#*(*x*) that, on input *x*, operates as follows:

  1.1. Erase the tape.

  1.2. Write *w* on the tape.

  1.3. Run *M* on *w*.

  1.4. Accept. /* This step is new. It is important since the hypothesized *Oracle* will decide whether *M#* accepts *w*, not just whether it halts on *w*.

2. Return <*M#*, *w*>. /* Note that *R* returns not just a description of *M#*. It returns a string that encodes both *M#* and an input string. This is important since any decider for A will accept only strings of that form. We chose *w* somewhat arbitrarily. We could have chosen any other string, for example ε.

If *Oracle* exists and decides A, then *C* = *Oracle*(*R*(<*M*, *w*>)) decides H. *R* can be implemented as a Turing machine. And *C* is correct. *M#* ignores its own input. It accepts everything or nothing, depending on whether it makes it through the gate at step 1.3, and thus to step 1.4. So:

- If <*M*, *w*> ∈ H: *M* halts on *w*, so *M#* accepts everything. In particular, it accepts *w*. *Oracle*(<*M#*, *w*>) accepts.
- If <*M*, *w*> ∉ H: *M* does not halt on *w*. *M#* gets stuck in step 1.3 and so accepts nothing. In particular, it does not accept *w*. *Oracle*(<*M#*, *w*>) rejects.

But no machine to decide H can exist, so neither does *Oracle*.

We can also define A_ε, A_{ANY}, and A_{ALL}, in a similar fashion and show that they too are not in D:

THEOREM 21.5 "Does *M* Accept ε?" is Undecidable

Theorem: The language $A_\varepsilon = \{<M> : \text{Turing machine } M \text{ accepts } \varepsilon\}$ is not in D.

Proof: Analogous to that for H_ε. It is left as an exercise.

THEOREM 21.6 "Does *M* Accept Anything?" is Undecidable

Theorem: The language $A_{ANY} = \{<M> : \text{there exists at least one string that Turing machine } M \text{ accepts}\}$ is not in D.

Proof: Analogous to that for H_{ANY}. It is left as an exercise.

The fact that A_{ANY} is not in D means that there exists no decision procedure for the emptiness question for the SD languages. Note that, in this respect, they are different from both the regular and the context-free languages, for which such a procedure does exist.

THEOREM 21.7 "Does *M* Accept Everything?" is Undecidable

Theorem: The language $A_{ALL} = \{<M> : M \text{ is a Turing machine and } L(M) = \Sigma^*\}$ is not in D.

Proof: Analogous to that for H_{ALL}. It is left as an exercise.

So far, we have discovered that many straightforward questions that we might like to ask about the behavior of Turing machines are undecidable. It should come as no surprise then to discover that the equivalence question for Turing machines is also undecidable. Consider the language:

- EqTMs $= \{<M_a, M_b> : M_a \text{ and } M_b \text{ are Turing machines and } L(M_a) = L(M_b)\}$.

We will show that EqTMs is not in D. How can we use reduction to do that? So far, all the languages that we know are not in D involve the description of a single Turing machine. So suppose that EqTMs were decidable by some Turing machine *Oracle*. How could we use *Oracle*, which compares two Turing machines, to answer questions about a single machine, as we must do to solve H or A or any of the other languages we have been considering? The answer is that our reduction *R* must create a second machine *M#* whose behavior it knows completely. Then it can answer questions about some other machine by comparing it to *M#*. We illustrate this idea in our proof of the next theorem.

Consider the problem of virus detection. Suppose that a new virus *V* is discovered and its code is determined to be <*V*>. Is it sufficient for antivirus software to check solely for occurrences of <*V*>? (J.4)

THEOREM 21.8 "Are Two Turing Machines Equivalent?" is Undecidable

Theorem: The language EqTMs = $\{<M_a, M_b> : M_a$ and M_b are Turing machines and $L(M_a) = L(M_b)\}$ is not in D.

Proof: We show that $A_{ALL} \leq_M$ EqTMs and so EqTMs is not in D. Let R be a mapping reduction from A_{ALL} to EqTMs defined as shown below. Since R must invoke *Oracle* on a pair of Turing machines, it will create one new one, $M\#$, which can be compared to M. The idea is that $M\#$ will be designed so that it simply halts and accepts, whatever its input is. By comparing M to $M\#$, we can determine M's behavior:

$R(<M>) =$

1. Construct the description $<M\#>$ of a new Turing machine $M\#(x)$ that, on input x, operates as follows:
   1.1. Accept.
2. Return $<M, M\#>$.

If *Oracle* exists and decides EqTMs, then $C = Oracle(R(<M>))$ decides A_{ALL}. R can be implemented as a Turing machine. And C is correct. $M\#$ accepts everything. So if $L(M) = L(M\#)$, M must also accept everything. So:

- If $<M> \in A_{ALL}$: $L(M) = L(M\#)$. $Oracle(<M, M\#>)$ accepts.
- If $<M> \notin A_{ALL}$: $L(M) \neq L(M\#)$. $Oracle(<M, M\#>)$ rejects.

But no machine to decide A_{ALL} can exist, so neither does *Oracle*.

Consider the problem of grading programs that are written as exercises in programming classes. We would like to compare each student program to a "correct" program written by the instructor and accept those programs that behave identically to the one written by the instructor. Theorem 21.8 says that a perfect grading program cannot exist.

We should point out here that EqTMs is not only not in D, it is also not in SD. We leave the proof of that as an exercise.

21.2.3 Reductions That are Not Mapping Reductions

The general definition of reducibility that we provided at the beginning of Section 21.2 is strictly more powerful than the more restricted notion of mapping reducibility that we have used in the examples that we have considered so far. We'll next consider a case where no mapping reduction exists, but a more general one does. Recall that the more general definition of a reduction from L_1 to L_2 may consist of two or more functions that can be composed to decide L_1 if *Oracle* exists and decides L_2. We'll see that one particularly useful thing to do is to exploit a second function that applies to the output of *Oracle* and flips it (i.e., it turns an *Accept* into a *Reject* and vice versa).

THEOREM 21.9 "Does *M* Accept No Even Length Strings?" is Undecidable

Theorem: The language $L_2 = \{<M> :$ Turing machine M accepts no even length strings$\}$ is not in D.

Proof: We show that $\text{H} \leq L_2$ and so L_2 is not in D. As in the other examples we have considered so far, we need to define a reduction from H to L_2. But this time we are going to run into a glitch. We can try to implement a straightforward mapping reduction *R* between H and L_2, just has we have done for our other examples. But, when we do that and then pass its result to *Oracle*, we'll see that *Oracle* will return the opposite of the answer we need to decide H. But that is an easy problem to solve. Since *Oracle* is (claimed to be) a deciding machine, it always halts. So we can add to the reduction a second Turing machine that runs after *Oracle* and just inverts *Oracle*'s response. We'll call that second machine simply ¬. Define:

$R(<M, w>) =$

1. Construct the description <*M*#> of a new Turing machine *M*#(x) that, on input x, operates as follows:

  1.1. Erase the tape.
  1.2. Write w on the tape.
  1.3. Run *M* on w.
  1.4. Accept.

2. Return <*M*#>.

$\{R, \neg\}$ is a reduction from H to L_2. If *Oracle* exists and decides L_2, then $C = \neg Oracle(R(<M, w>))$ decides H. *R* and ¬ can be implemented as a Turing machines. And *C* is correct. *M*# ignores its own input. It accepts everything or nothing, depending on whether it makes it to step 1.4. So:

- If $<M, w> \in$ H: *M* halts on w, so *M*# accepts everything, including some even length strings. *Oracle*(<*M*#>) rejects so *C* accepts.
- If $<M, w> \notin$ H: does not halt on w. *M*# gets stuck in step 1.3 and accepts nothing, and so, in particular, no even length strings. *Oracle*(<*M*#>) accepts. So *C* rejects.

But no machine to decide H can exist, so neither does *Oracle*. So L_2 is not in D. It is also not in SD. We leave the proof of that as an exercise.

We have just shown that there exists a reduction from H to $L_2 = \{<M> :$ Turing machine M accepts no even length strings$\}$. It is possible to prove that this is a case where it was necessary to exploit the greater power offered by the more general definition of reducibility. We leave as an exercise the proof that no mapping reduction from H to L_2 exists. To see why this might be so, it is important to keep in mind the definition of mapping reducibility: $L_1 \leq_M L_2$ iff there exists some computable function f such that:

$$\forall x (x \in L_1 \text{ iff } f(x) \in L_2).$$

Note that, if such an f exists, it is also a mapping reduction from $\neg L_1$ to $\neg L_2$.

21.3 Are All Questions About Turing Machines Undecidable?

By now it should be clear that many interesting properties of the behavior of Turing machines are undecidable. Is it true that any question that asks about a Turing machine or its behavior is undecidable? No.

First, we observe that questions that ask just about a Turing machine's physical structure, rather than about its behavior, are likely to be decidable.

EXAMPLE 21.8 The Number of States of M is Decidable

Let $L_A = \{<M> : \text{Turing machine } M \text{ contains an even number of states}\}$. L_A is decidable by the following procedure:

1. Make a pass through $<M>$, counting the number of states in M.
2. If even, accept; else reject.

Next we'll consider two questions that do ask about a Turing machine's behavior but are, nevertheless, decidable.

EXAMPLE 21.9 Whether M Halts in Some Fixed Time is Decidable

Let $L_B = \{<M, w> : \text{Turing machine } M \text{ halts on } w \text{ within 3 steps}\}$. L_B is decidable by the following procedure:

1. Simulate M for 3 steps.
2. If it halted, accept; else reject.

EXAMPLE 21.10 Exactly How M Works May be Decidable

Let $L_C = \{<M, w> : \text{Turing machine } M \text{ moves right exactly twice while running on } w\}$.

Notice that M must move either to the right or the left on each move. We make the usual assumption that M's read/write head is positioned immediately to the left of the leftmost input character when M starts. If M cannot move right more than twice, it can read no more than two characters of its input. But it may loop forever moving left. As it moves left, it can write on the tape, but it cannot go back more than two squares to read what it has written. So the only part of the tape that can affect M's future behavior is the current square, two squares to the right and two squares to the left (since all other squares to the left still contain ❑). Let K be the set of states of M and let Γ be M's tape alphabet. Then the number of effectively distinct configurations of M is $maxconfigs = |K_M| \cdot |\Gamma_M|^5$. If we simulate M running for *maxconfigs* moves, it will have entered, at least once, each configuration that it is ever going to reach. If it has not halted, then it is in an infinite loop. Each time through the loop it will do the same thing it did the last time.

If, in simulating *maxconfigs* moves, M moved right more than twice, we can reject. If it did not move right at all, or if it moved right once, we can reject. If it moved right twice, we need to find out whether either of those moves occurred during some loop. We can do that by running M for up to *maxconfigs* more moves. In the extreme case of a maximally long loop, it will move right once more. If there is a shorter loop, M may move right several times more. So the following procedure decides L_C:

1. Run M on w for $|K_M| \cdot |\Gamma_M|^5$ moves or until M halts or moves right three times:

1.2. If M moved right exactly twice, then:
Run M on w for another $|K_M| \cdot |\Gamma_M|^5$ moves or until it moves right.
If M moved right any additional times, reject; otherwise accept.

1.3. If M moved right some other number of times, reject.

What is different about languages such as L_A, L_B, and L_C (in contrast to H, H_ε, H_{ANY}, H_{ALL}, and the other languages we have proven are not in D)? The key is that, in the case of L_A, the question is not about M's behavior at all. It involves just its structure. In the case of L_B and L_C, the question we must answer is not about the language that the Turing machine M halts on or accepts. It is about a detail of M's behavior as it is computing. In the case of L_B, it has to do with the exact number of steps in which M might halt. In the case of L_C, it is about the way that M goes about solving the problem (specifically how often it moves right). It turns out that questions like those can be decided. We'll see, though, in Section 21.5, that we must be careful about this. Some questions that appear to be about the details of how M operates can be recast as questions about M's output and so are not decidable.

Rice's Theorem, which we present next, articulates the difference between languages like H and languages like L_A, L_B, and L_C.

21.4 Rice's Theorem ◆

Consider the set SD of semidecidable languages. Suppose that we want to ask any of the following questions about some language L in that set:

- Does L contain some particular string w?
- Does L contain ε?
- Does L contain any strings at all?
- Does L contain all strings over some alphabet Σ?

In order to consider building a program to answer any of those questions, we first need a way to specify formally what L is. Since the SD languages are, by definition, exactly the languages that can be semidecided by some Turing machine, one way to specify a language L is to give a semideciding Turing machine for it. If we do that, then we can restate each of those questions as:

- Given a semideciding Turing machine M, does M accept some particular string w?
- Given a semideciding Turing machine M, does M accept ε?
- Given a semideciding Turing machine M, does M accept anything?
- Given a semideciding Turing machine M, does M accept all strings in Σ^*?

We can encode each of those decision problems as a language to be decided, yielding:

- $A = \{<M, w> : \text{Turing machine } M \text{ accepts } w\}$.
- $A_\varepsilon = \{<M> : \text{Turing machine } M \text{ accepts } \varepsilon\}$.
- $A_{ANY} = \{<M> : \text{there exists at least one string that Turing machine } M \text{ accepts}\}$.
- $A_{ALL} = \{<M> : \text{Turing machine } M \text{ accepts all inputs}\}$.

We have already seen that none of these languages is in D, so none of the corresponding questions is decidable. Rice's Theorem, which we are about to state and prove, tells us that not only these languages, but any language that can be described as $\{<M>: P(L(M)) = True\}$, for any nontrivial property P, is not in D. By a *nontrivial property* we mean a property that is not simply *True* for all languages or *False* for all languages.

But we can state Rice's Theorem even more generally than that. The questions we have just considered are questions we can ask of any semidecidable language, independently of how we describe it. We have used semideciding Turing machhnes as our descriptions. But we could use some other descriptive form. (For example, in Chapter 23, we will consider a grammar formalism that describes exactly the SD languages.) The key is that the property we are evaluating is a property of the language itself and not a property of some particular Turing machine that happens to semidecide it.

So an alternative way to state Riae's Theorem is:

No nontrivial property of the SD languages is decidable.

> Just as languages that are defined in terms of the behavior of Turing machines are generally not decidable, functions that describe the way that Turing machines behave are likely not to be computable. See, for example, the ***busy beaver functions*** described in Section 25.1.4.

To use Rice's Theorem to show that a language L of the form $\{<M>: P(L(M)) = True\}$ is not in D we must:

- Specify property P.
- Show that the domain of P is the set of SD languages.
- Show that P is nontrivial:
  - P is true of at least one language.
  - P is false of at least one language.

Let M, M_a, and M_b be Turing machines. We'll consider each of the following languages and see whether Rice's Theorem applies to it:

1. $\{<M>$: M is a Turing machine and $L(M)$ contains only even length strings$\}$.
2. $\{<M>$: M is a Turing machine and $L(M)$ contains an odd number of strings$\}$.
3. $\{<M>$: M is a Turing machine and $L(M)$ contains all strings that start with a$\}$.
4. $\{<M>$: M is a Turing machine and $L(M)$ is infinite$\}$.
5. $\{<M>$: M is a Turing machine and $L(M)$ is regular$\}$.
6. $\{<M>$: Turing machine M contains an even number of states$\}$.
7. $\{<M>$: Turing machine M has an odd number of symbols in its tape alphabet$\}$.
8. $\{<M>$: Turing machine M accepts ε within 100 steps$\}$.
9. $\{<M>$: Turing machine M accepts $\varepsilon\}$.
10. $\{<M_a, M_b>$: M_a and M_b are Turing machines and $L(M_a) = L(M_b)\}$.

In cases 1 through 5, we can easily state P. For example, in case 1, P is, "*True* if L contains only even length strings and *False* otherwise". In all five cases, the domain of P is the set of SD languages and P is nontrivial. For example, in case 1, P is *True* of $\{$aa, bb$\}$ and *False* of $\{$a, aa$\}$.

But now consider cases 6 through 8. In case 6, P is, "*True* if M has an even number of states and *False* otherwise". P is no longer a property of a language. It is a property of some specific machine, independent of the language that the machine accepts. The same is true in cases 7 and 8. So Rice's Theorem tells us nothing about whether those languages are in D. They may or may not be. As it turns out, all three of these examples are in D and languages that look like them usually are. But Rice's Theorem does not tell us that. It simply tells us nothing.

Next consider case 9. In form, it looks something like case 8. But it is in fact like 1–5. An alternative way to state P is, "$\varepsilon \in L(M)$". It is not the wording of the description that matters. It is the property P itself that counts.

Finally consider case 10. We have already shown that this language, which we have named EqTMs, is not in D. But Rice's Theorem does not tell us that. Again, it says nothing since now we are asking about a property whose domain is SD $\times$ SD, rather than simply SD. So when Rice's Theorem doesn't apply, it is possible that we are dealing with a language in D. It is also possible we are dealing with one not in D. Without additional investigation, we just don't know.

Rice's Theorem is not going to give us a way to prove anything we couldn't have proven with reduction. Although it is an alternative proof strategy, its main value is its insight. We know immediately, when confronted with a question about the SD languages, that it will not be decidable.

The proof of Rice's Theorem is by reduction from H. It is a bit more complex than any of the reductions we have done so far, but the principle is exactly the same. What we are going to do is to show that if it were possible to decide *any* property P (without regard to what P is except that it is nontrivial), then it would be possible to decide H. It may seem surprising that we can show this without appeal to any information about what P tells us. But we can.

THEOREM 21.10 Rice's Theorem

Theorem: For any nontrivial P, the language $L = \{<M>: P(L(M)) = True\}$ is not in D.

Proof: We prove Rice's Theorem by showing that $H \leq_M L$. Let P be any nontrivial property of the SD languages. We do not know what P is. But, whatever it is, either $P(\varnothing) = True$ or $P(\varnothing) = False$. Assume it is *False*. We leave the proof that the theorem holds if $P(\varnothing) = True$ as an exercise. Since P is nontrivial, there is some SD language L_T such that $P(L_T)$ is *True*. Since L_T is in SD, there exists some Turing machine K that semidecides it.

We need to define a mapping reduction R from H to L. The main idea in this reduction is that R will build a machine $M\#$ that first runs M on w as a sort of filter. If it makes it by that step, then it considers its own input and either accepts it or not. If we can design $M\#$'s action at that second step so that we can tell whether it makes it there, we will know whether M halted on w.

Let R be a reduction from H to L defined as follows:

$R(<M, w>) =$

1. Construct the description $<M\#>$ of a new Turing machine $M\#(x)$ that, on input x, operates as follows:
   1.1. Copy its input x to a second tape.
   1.2. Erase the tape.
   1.3. Write w on the tape.
   1.4. Run M on w.
   1.5. Put x back on the first tape and run K (the Turing machine that semidecides L_T, a language of which P is *True*) on x.
2. Return $<M\#>$.

If *Oracle* exists and decides L, then $C = Oracle(R(<M, w>))$ decides H. R can be implemented as a Turing machine. And C is correct:

- If $<M, w> \in H$: M halts on w, so $M\#$ makes it to step 1.5. So $M\#$ does whatever K would do. So $L(M\#) = L(K)$ and $P(L(M\#)) = P(L(K))$. We chose K precisely to assure that $P(L(K))$ is *True*, so $P(L(M\#))$ must also be *True*. *Oracle* decides P. $Oracle(<M\#>)$ accepts.

- If <M, w> $\notin$ H: M does not halt on w. $M\#$ gets stuck in step 1.4 and so accepts nothing. $L(M\#) = \varnothing$. By assumption, $P(\varnothing) =$ *False*. *Oracle* decides P. *Oracle*(<$M\#$>) rejects.

But no machine to decide H can exist, so neither does *Oracle*.

Now that we have proven the theorem, we can use it as an alternative to reduction in proving that a language L is not in D.

THEOREM 21.11 "Is $L(M)$ Regular?" is Undecidable

Theorem: Given a Turing machine M, the question, "Is $L(M)$ regular?" is not decidable. Alternatively, the language TM_{REG} = {<M> : M is a Turing machine and $L(M)$ is regular} is not in D.

Proof: By Rice's Theorem. We define P as follows:

- Let P be defined on the set of languages accepted by some Turing machine M. Let it be *True* if $L(M)$ is regular and *False* otherwise.
- The domain of P is the set of SD languages since it is the set of languages accepted by some Turing machine.
- P is nontrivial:
  - $P(a^*) =$ *True*.
  - $P(A^nB^n) =$ *False*.

Thus we can conclude that {<M>: M is a Turing machine and $L(M)$ is regular} is not in D.

We can also prove this by reduction from H. The reduction we will use exploits two functions, R and $\neg$. R will map instances of H to instances of TM_{REG}. It will use a strategy that is very similar to the one we used in proving Rice's Theorem. As in the proof of Theorem 21.9, $\neg$ will simply invert *Oracle*'s response (turning an *Accept* into a *Reject* and vice versa). So define:

R(<M, w>) =

1. Construct the description <$M\#$> of a new Turing machine $M\#(x)$ that, on input x, operates as follows:

1.1. Copy its input x to a second tape.
1.2. Erase the tape.
1.3. Write w on the tape.
1.4. Run M on w.
1.5. Put x back on the first tape.
1.6. If $x \in A^nB^n$ then accept, else reject.

2. Return <$M\#$>.

{R, $\neg$} is a reduction from H to TM_{REG}. If *Oracle* exists and decides TM_{REG}, then $C = \neg$*Oracle*(R(<M, w>)) decides H. R and $\neg$ can be implemented as

Turing machines. In particular, it is straightforward to build a Turing machine that decides whether a string x is in A^nB^n. And C is correct:

- If $<M, w> \in H$: M halts on w, so $M\#$ makes it to step 1.5. Then it accepts x iff $x \in A^nB^n$. So $M\#$ accepts A^nB^n, which is not regular. *Oracle*($<M\#>$) rejects. C accepts.
- If $<M, w> \notin H$: M does not halt on w. $M\#$ gets stuck in step 1.4 and so accepts nothing. $L(M\#) = \varnothing$, which is regular. *Oracle*($<M\#>$) accepts. C rejects.

But no machine to decide H can exist, so neither does *Oracle*.

It turns out that we can also make a stronger statement about TM_{REG}. It is not only not in D, it is not in SD. We leave the proof of that as an exercise.

21.5 Undecidable Questions About Real Programs

The real practical impact of the undecidability results that we have just presented is the following: The programming environments that we actually use every day are equal in computational power to the Turing machine. So questions that are undecidable when asked about Turing machines are equally undecidable when asked about Java programs or C++ programs, or whatever. The undecidability of a question about real programs can be proved by reduction from the corresponding question about Turing machines. We'll show one example of doing this.

THEOREM 21.12 "Are Two Programs Equivalent?" is Undecidable

Theorem: The language EqPrograms $= \{<P_a, P_b> : P_a$ and P_b are programs in any standard programming language *PL* and $L(P_a) = L(P_b)\}$ is not in D.

Proof: Recall that EqTMs $= \{<M_a, M_b> : M_a$ and M_b are Turing machines and $L(M_a) = L(M_b)\}$. We show that EqTMs $\leq_M$ EqPrograms and so EqPrograms is not in D (since EqTMs isn't). It is straightforward to build, in any standard programming language, an implementation of the universal Turing machine U. Call that program *SimUM*. Now let R be a mapping reduction from EqTMs to EqPrograms defined as follows:

$R(<M_a, M_b>) =$

1. Build P_1, a *PL* program that, on input w, invokes *SimUM*(M_a, w) and returns its result.
2. Build P_2, a *PL* program that, on input w, invokes *SimUM*(M_b, w) and returns its result.
3. Return $<P_1, P_2>$.

If *Oracle* exists and decides EqPrograms, then $C =$ *Oracle*($R(<M_a, M_b>)$) decides EqTMs. R can be implemented as a Turing machine. And C is correct. $L(P_1) = L(M_a)$ and $L(P_2) = L(M_b)$. So:

- If $<M_a, M_b> \in$ EqTMs: $L(M_a) = L(M_b)$. So $L(P_1) = L(P_2)$. *Oracle*($<P_1, P_2>$) accepts.
- If $<M_a, M_b> \notin$ EqTMs: $L(M_a) \neq L(M_b)$. So $L(P_1) \neq L(P_2)$. *Oracle*($<P_1, P_2>$) rejects.

But no machine to decide EqTMs can exist, so neither does *Oracle*.

The United States Patent Office issues patents on software. But, before the Patent Office can issue any patent, it must check for prior art. The theorem we have just proved suggests that there can exist no general purpose program that can do that checking automatically.

Because the undecidability of questions about real programs follows from the undecidability of those questions for Turing machines, we can show, for example, that all of the following questions are undecidable:

1. Given a program P and input x, does P, when running on x, halt?
2. Given a program P, might P get into an infinite loop on some input?
3. Given a program P and input x, does P, when running on x, ever output a 0? Or anything at all?
4. Given two programs, P_1 and P_2, are they equivalent?
5. Given a program P, input x, and a variable n, does P, when running on x, ever assign a value to n? We need to be able to answer this question if we want to be able to guarantee that every variable is initialized before it is used.
6. Given a program P and code segment S in P, does P ever reach S on any input (in other words, can we chop S out)?
7. Given a program P and code segment S in P, does P reach S on every input (in other words, can we guarantee that S happens)?

We've already proved that questions 1, 2, and 4 are undecidable for Turing machines. Question 3 (about printing 0) is one that Turing himself asked and showed to be undecidable. We leave that proof as an exercise.

Is it possible to build a program verification system that can determine, given an arbitrary specification S and program P whether or not P correctly implements S? (H.1)

But what about questions 5, 6, and 7? They appear to be about details of how a program operates, rather than about the result of running the program (i.e., the language it accepts or the function it computes). We know that many questions of that sort are decidable, either by inspecting the program or by running it for some bounded number of steps. So why are these questions undecidable? Because they cannot be answered either by inspection or by bounded simulation. We can prove that each of them is undecidable by showing that some language that we already know is not in D can be reduced to it. To do this, we'll return to the Turing machine representation for programs. We'll show that question 6 is undecidable and leave the others as exercises.

Can a compiler check for dead code and eliminate it? (G.4.3)

THEOREM 21.13 "Does *M* Ever Reach Some Particular State?" is Undecidable

Theorem: The language $L = \{<M, q> :$ Turing machine M reaches state q on some input$\}$ is not in D.

Proof: We show that $\text{H}_{\text{ANY}} \leq_{\text{M}} L$ and so L is not in D. Let R be a mapping reduction from H_{ANY} to L defined as follows:

$R(<M>) =$

1. From $<M>$, construct the description $<M\#>$ of a new Turing machine $M\#$ that will be identical to M except that, if M has a transition $((q_1, c_1), (q_2, c_2, a))$ and q_2 is a halting state other than h, replace that transition with $((q_1, c_1), (h, c_2, a))$.
2. Return $<M\#, h>$.

If *Oracle* exists and decides L, then $C = Oracle(R(<M>))$ decides H_{ANY}. R can be implemented as a Turing machine. And C is correct: $M\#$ will reach the halting state h iff M would reach some halting state. So:

- If $<M> \in \text{H}_{\text{ANY}}$: There is some string on which M halts. So there is some string on which $M\#$ reaches state h. $Oracle(<M\#, h>)$ accepts.
- If $<M> \notin \text{H}_{\text{ANY}}$: There is no string on which M halts. So there is no string on which $M\#$ reaches state h. $Oracle(<M\#, h>)$ rejects.

But no machine to decide H_{ANY} can exist, so neither does *Oracle*.

21.6 Showing That a Language is Not Semidecidable

We know, from Theorem 20.3, that there exist languages that are not in SD. In fact, we know that there are uncountably many of them. And we have seen one specific example, ¬H. In this section we will see how to show that other languages are also not in SD. Although we will first discuss a couple of other methods of proving that a language is not in SD (which we will also write as in ¬SD), we will again make extensive use of reduction. This time, the basis for our reduction proofs will be ¬H. We will show that if some new language L were in SD, ¬H would also be. But it is not.

Before we try to prove that a language L is not in SD (or that it is), we need an intuition that tells us what to prove. A good way to develop such an intuition is to think about trying to write a program to solve the problem. Languages that are not in SD generally involve either infinite search, or knowing that a Turing machine will infinite loop, or both. For example, the following languages are not in SD:

- $\neg$H = {<M, w> : Turing machine M does *not* halt on w}. To solve this one by simulation, we would have to run M forever.
- {<M> : $L(M) = \Sigma^*$}. To solve this one by simulation, we would have to try all strings in Σ^*. But there are infinitely many of them.
- {<M> : there does *not* exist a string on which Turing machine M halts}. To solve this one by simulation, we would have to try an infinite number of strings and show that all of them fail to halt. Even to show that one fails to halt would require an infinite number of steps.

In the rest of this section, we present a collection of techniques that can be used to prove that a language is not in SD.

21.6.1 Techniques Other Than Reduction ✸

Sometimes we can show that a language L is not in SD by giving a proof by contradiction that does not exploit reduction. We will show one such example here. For this example, we need to make use of a theorem that we will prove in Section 25.3: The recursion theorem tells us that there exists a subroutine, *obtainSelf*, available to any Turing machine M, that constructs <M>, the description of M.

We have not so far said anything about minimizing Turing machines. The reason is that no algorithm to do so exists. In fact, given a Turing machine M, it is undecidable whether M is minimal. Alternatively, the language of descriptions of minimal Turing machines is not in SD. More precisely, define a Turing machine M to be ***minimal*** iff there exists no other Turing machine M' such that $|$<M'>$| < |$<M>$|$ and M' is equivalent to M.

THEOREM 21.14 "Is M Minimal?" is Not Semidecidable

Theorem: The language TM_{MIN} = {<M>: Turing machine M is minimal} is not in SD.

Proof: If TM_{MIN} were in SD, then (by Theorem 20.8) there would exist some Turing machine *ENUM* that enumerates its elements. Define the following Turing machine:

$M\#(x) =$

1. Invoke *obtainSelf* to produce <$M\#$>.
2. Run *ENUM* until it generates the description of some Turing machine M' whose description is longer than $|$<$M\#$>$|$.
3. Invoke the universal Turing machine U on the string <M', x>.

Since TM_{MIN} is infinite, *ENUM* must eventually generate a string that is longer than $|<M\#>|$. So $M\#$ makes it to step 3 and so is equivalent to M' since it simulates M'. But, since $|<M\#>| < |<M'>|$, M' cannot be minimal. Yet it was generated by *ENUM*. Contradiction.

Another way to prove that a language is not in SD is to exploit Theorem 20.6, which tells us that a language L is in D iff both it and its complement, $\neg L$, are in SD. This is true because, if we could semidecide both L and $\neg L$, we could run the two semideciders in parallel, wait until one of them halts, and then either accept (if the semidecider for L accepted) or reject (if the semidecider for $\neg L$ accepted).

So suppose that we are considering some language L. We want to know whether L is in SD and we already know:

- $\neg L$ is in SD, and
- at least one of L or $\neg L$ is not in D.

Then we can conclude that L is not in SD, because, if it were, it would force both itself and its complement into D, and we know that cannot be true. This is the technique that we used to prove that $\neg$H is not in SD. We can use it for some other languages as well, which we will do in our proof of the next theorem.

THEOREM 21.15 "Does There Exist No String On Which *M* Halts?" is Not Semidecidable

Theorem: $\text{H}_{\neg\text{ANY}} = \{<M> :$ there does ***not*** exist any string on which Turing machine M halts$\}$ is not in SD.

Proof: Recall that we said, at the beginning of Chapter 19, that we would define the complement of a language of Turing machine descriptions with respect to the universe of syntactically valid Turing machine descriptions. So the complement of $\text{H}_{\neg\text{ANY}}$ is $\text{H}_{\text{ANY}} = \{<M> :$ there exists at least one string on which Turing machine M halts$\}$. From Theorem 21.2, we know:

- $\neg\text{H}_{\neg\text{ANY}}$ (namely, H_{ANY}) is in SD.
- $\neg\text{H}_{\neg\text{ANY}}$ (namely, H_{ANY}) is not in D.

So $\text{H}_{\neg\text{ANY}}$ is not in SD because, if it were, then H_{ANY} would be in D but it isn't.

21.6.2 Reduction

The most general technique that we can use for showing that a language is not in SD is reduction. Our argument will be analogous to the one we used to show that a language is not in D. It is:

- To prove that a language L_2 is not in SD, find a reduction R from some language L_1 that is already known not to be in SD to L_2.

If L_2 were in SD, then there would exist some Turing machine *Oracle* that semidecides it. Then the composition of R and *Oracle* would semidecide L_1. But there can exist no Turing machine that semidecides L_1. So *Oracle* cannot exist. So L_2 is not in SD.

There are two differences between reductions that show that a language is not in SD and those that show that a language not in D:

1. We must choose to reduce from a language that is already known not to be in SD (as opposed to choosing one where all we can prove is that it is not in D). We already have one example of such a language: ¬H. So we have a place to start.
2. We hypothesize the existence of a *semi*deciding machine *Oracle*, rather than a deciding one.

The second of these will sometimes turn out to be critical. In particular, the function ¬ (which inverts the output of *Oracle*), can no longer be implemented as a Turing machine. Since *Oracle* is claimed only to be a semideciding machine, there is no guarantee that it halts. Since *Oracle* may loop, there is no way to write a procedure that accepts iff *Oracle* doesn't. So we won't be able to include ¬ in any of our reductions.

We will need to find a way around this problem when it arises. But let's first do a very simple example where there is no need to do the inversion. We begin with a reduction proof of Theorem 21.15. We show that $\neg H \leq_M H_{\neg ANY}$. Let R be a mapping reduction from ¬H to $H_{\neg ANY}$ defined as follows.

$R(<M, w>) =$

1. Construct the description $<M\#>$ of a new Turing machine $M\#(x)$ that, on input x, operates as follows:
   1.1. Erase the tape.
   1.2. Write w on the tape.
   1.3. Run M on w.
2. Return $<M\#>$.

If *Oracle* exists and semidecides $H_{\neg ANY}$, then $C = Oracle(R(<M, w>))$ semidecides ¬H. R can be implemented as a Turing machine. And C is correct: $M\#$ ignores its input. It halts on everything or nothing, depending on whether M halts on w. So:

- If $<M, w> \in \neg H$: M does not halt on w, so $M\#$ halts on nothing. *Oracle*($<M\#>$) accepts.
- If $<M, w> \notin \neg H$: M halts on w, so $M\#$ halts on everything. *Oracle*($<M\#>$) does not accept.

But no machine to semidecide ¬H can exist, so neither does *Oracle*.

Straightforward reductions of this sort can be used to show that many other languages, particularly those that are defined by the failure of a Turing machine to halt, are also not in SD.

THEOREM 21.16 "Does M Fail to Halt On ε?" is Not Semidecidable

Theorem: $\neg H_\varepsilon = \{<M> : \text{Turing machine } M \text{ does not halt on } \varepsilon\}$ is not in SD.

Proof: The proof is by reduction from ¬H. We leave it as an exercise.

Sometimes, however, finding a reduction that works is a bit more difficult. We next consider the language:

- $A_{anbn} = \{<M> : M \text{ is a Turing machine and } L(M) = A^nB^n = \{a^nb^n : n \geq 0\}\}$.

Note that A_{anbn} contains strings that look like:

```
(q00,a00,q01,a00,→),(q00,a01,q00,a10,→),(q00,a10,q01,a01,←),
(q00,a11,q01,a10,←),(q01,a00,q00,a01,→),
(q01,a01,q01,a10,→),(q01,a10,q01,a11,←),(q01,a11,q11,a01,←)
```

It does not contain strings like aaabbb. But A^nB^n does.

We are going to have to try a couple of times to find a correct reduction that can be used to prove that A_{anbn} is not in SD.

THEOREM 21.17 "Is $L(M) = A^nB^n$?" is Not Semidecidable

Theorem: The language $A_{anbn} = \{<M> : M \text{ is a Turing machine and } L(M) = A^nB^n\}$ is not in SD.

Proof: We show that $\neg H \leq_M A_{anbn}$ and so A_{anbn} is not in SD. We will build a mapping reduction R from $\neg H$ to A_{anbn}. R needs to construct the description of a new Turing machine $M\#$ so that $M\#$ is an acceptor for A^nB^n if M does not halt on w and it is something else if M does halt on w. We can try the simple $M\#$ that first runs M on w as a gate that controls access to the rest of the program:

Reduction Attempt 1: Define:

$R(<M, w>) =$

1. Construct the description $<M\#>$ of a new Turing machine $M\#(x)$ that, on input x, operates as follows:
   - **1.1.** Copy the input x to a second tape.
   - **1.2.** Erase the tape.
   - **1.3.** Write w on the tape.
   - **1.4.** Run M on w.
   - **1.5.** Put x back on the first tape.
   - **1.6.** If $x \in A^nB^n$ then accept; else loop.
2. Return $<M\#>$.

Now we must show that, if some Turing machine *Oracle* semidecides A_{anbn}, then $C = Oracle(R(<M, w>))$ semidecides $\neg H$. But we encounter a problem when we try to show that C is correct. If M halts on w, then $M\#$ makes it to step 1.5 and becomes an A^nB^n acceptor, so $Oracle(<M\#>)$ accepts. If M does not halt on w, then $M\#$ accepts nothing. It is therefore not an A^nB^n acceptor, so $Oracle(<M\#>)$ does not accept. The reduction R has succeeded in capturing the correct distinction: *Oracle* returns one answer when $<M, w> \in \neg H$ and another answer when $<M, w> \notin \neg H$. But the answer is backwards. And this time we can't simply add the function $\neg$ to the reduction and define C to return $\neg Oracle(R(<M, w>))$. *Oracle* is only hypothesized to be a semideciding machine so there is no way for $\neg$ to accept if *Oracle* fails to accept (since it may loop).

There is an easy way to fix this. We build *M#* so that it either accepts just A^nB^n (if *M* does not halt on *w*) or everything (if *M* does halt on *w*). We make that happen by putting the gate *after* the code that accepts A^nB^n instead of before.

Reduction Attempt 2: Define:

R(<*M*, *w*>) =

1. Construct the description <*M#*> of a new Turing machine *M#*(*x*) that, on input *x*, operates as follows:
   - **1.2.** If $x \in A^nB^n$ then accept. Else:
   - **1.2.** Erase the tape.
   - **1.3.** Write *w* on the tape.
   - **1.4.** Run *M* on *w*.
   - **1.5.** Accept.
2. Return <*M#*>.

If *Oracle* exists and semidecides A_{anbn}, then *C* = *Oracle*(*R*(<*M*, *w*>)) semidecides ¬H. *R* can be implemented as a Turing machine. And *C* is correct: *M#* immediately accepts all strings in A^nB^n. If *M* does not halt on *w*, those are the only strings that *M#* accepts. If *M* does halt on *w*, *M#* accepts everything. So:

- If <*M*, *w*> ∈ ¬H: *M* does not halt on *w*, so *M#* accepts A^nB^n in step 1.1. Then it gets stuck in step 1.4, so it accepts nothing else. It is an A^nB^n acceptor. *Oracle*(<*M#*>) accepts.
- If <*M*, *w*> ∉ ¬H: *M* halts on *w*, so *M#* accepts everything. $L(M\#) \neq A^nB^n$. *Oracle*(<*M#*>) does not accept.

But no machine to semidecide ¬H can exist, so neither does *Oracle*.

Sometimes, however, the simple gate technique doesn't work, as we will see in the next example.

THEOREM 21.18 "Does *M* Halt On Everything?" is Not Semidecidable

Theorem: H_{ALL} = {<*M*> : Turing machine *M* halts on Σ^*} is not in SD.

Proof: We show that H_{ALL} is not in SD by reduction from ¬H.

Reduction Attempt 1: Define:

R(<*M*, *w*>) =

1. Construct the description <*M#*> of a new Turing machine *M#(x)* that, on input *x*, operates as follows:
   - **1.1.** Erase the tape.
   - **1.2.** Write *w* on the tape.
   - **1.3.** Run *M* on *w*.
2. Return <*M#*>.

We can attempt to show that, if *Oracle* exists and semidecides H_{ALL}, then C = *Oracle*(*R*(<*M*, *w*>)) correctly semidecides ¬H. The problem is that it doesn't:

- If <*M*, *w*> ∈ ¬H: *M* does not halt on *w*, so *M#* gets stuck in step 1.3 and halts on nothing. *Oracle*(<*M#*>) does not accept.
- If <*M*, *w*> ∉ ¬H: *M* halts on *w*, so *M#* halts on everything. *Oracle*(<*M#*>) accepts.

This is backwards. We could try halting on something before running *M* on *w*, the way we did on the previous example. But the only way to make *M#* into a machine that halts on everything would be to have it halt immediately, before running *M*. But then its behavior would not depend on whether *M* halts on *w*. We need a new technique.

Reduction Attempt 2: Define:

R(<*M*, *w*>) =

1. Construct the description <*M#*> of a new Turing machine *M#*(*x*) that, on input *x*, operates as follows:
   - **1.1.** Copy the input *x* to a second tape.
   - **1.2.** Erase the tape.
   - **1.3.** Write *w* on the tape.
   - **1.4.** Run *M* on *w* for $|x|$ steps or until it naturally halts.
   - **1.5.** If *M* naturally halted, then loop.
   - **1.6.** Else halt.
2. Return <*M#*>.

We build *M#* so that it runs the simulation of *M* on *w* for some finite number of steps and observes whether *M* would have halted in that time. If *M* would have halted, *M#* loops. If *M* would *not* have halted, *M#* promptly halts. This is where we flip from halting to looping and vice versa. It works because the simulation always halts, so *M#* never gets stuck running it. But for how many steps should we run the simulation? If *M* is going to halt, we don't know how long it will take for it to do so. We need to guarantee that we don't quit too soon and think that *M* isn't going to halt when it actually will. Here's the insight: The language Σ^* is infinite. So if *M#* is going to halt on every string in Σ^*, it will have to halt on an infinite number of strings. It's okay if *M#* gets fooled into thinking that *M* will halt some of the time as long as it does not do so for all possible inputs. So *M#* will run the simulation of *M* on *w* for a number of steps equal to the length of its (*M#*'s) own input. It may be fooled into thinking *M* is going to halt on *w* when it is invoked on short strings. But, if *M* does eventually halt, it does so in some number of steps *n*. When started on any strings of length *n* or more, *M#* will try long enough and will discover that *M* on *w* would have halted. Then it will loop. So it will not halt on all strings in Σ^*.

If *Oracle* exists and semidecides H_{ALL}, then C = *Oracle*(*R*(<*M*, *w*>)) semidecides ¬H. *R* can be implemented as a Turing machine. And *C* is correct:

- If <*M*, *w*> ∈ ¬H: *M* does not halt on *w*. So, no matter how long *x* is, *M* will not halt in $|x|$ steps. So, for all inputs *x*, *M#* makes it to step 1.6. So it halts on everything. *Oracle*(<*M#*>) accepts.

- If $<M, w> \notin \neg$H: M halts on w. It does so in some number of steps n. On inputs of length less than n, $M\#$ will make it to step 1.6 and halt. But on all inputs of length n or greater, $M\#$ will loop in step 1.5. So it fails to halt on everything. *Oracle*($<M\#>$) does not accept.

But no machine to semidecide ¬H can exist, so neither does *Oracle*.

21.6.3 Is L in D, SD/D, or ¬SD?

Throughout this chapter, we have seen examples of languages that are decidable (i.e., they are in D), are semidecidable but not decidable (i.e., they are in SD/D), and, most recently, are not even semidecidable (i.e., they are in ¬SD). We have seen some heuristics that are useful for analyzing a language and determining what class it is in. In applying those heuristics, it is critical that we look closely at the language definition. Small changes can make a big difference to the decidability of the language. For example, consider the following four languages (where, in each case, M is a Turing machine):

1. $\{<M> : M$ has an even number of states$\}$.
2. $\{<M> : |<M>|$ is even$\}$.
3. $\{<M> : |L(M)|$ is even$\}$ (i.e., $L(M)$ contains an even number of strings).
4. $\{<M> : M$ accepts all even length strings$\}$.

Language 1 is in D. A simple examination of $<M>$ will tell us how many states M has. Language 2 is also in D. To decide it, all we need to do is to examine $<M>$, the string description of M, and determine whether that string is of even length. Rice's Theorem does not apply in either of those cases since the property we care about involves the physical Turing machine M, not the language it accepts. But languages 3 and 4 are different. To decide either of them requires evaluating a property of the language that a Turing machine M accepts. Rice's Theorem tells us, therefore, that neither of them is in D. In fact, neither of them is in SD either. The intuition here is that to semidecide them by simulation would require trying an infinite number of strings. We leave the proof of this claim as an exercise.

Now consider another set:

1. $\{<M, w> :$ Turing machine M does not halt on input string $w\}$. (This is just ¬H.)
2. $\{<M, w> :$ Turing machine M rejects $w\}$.
3. $\{<M, w> :$ Turing machine M is a deciding Turing machine and M rejects $w\}$.

We know that ¬H is in ¬SD. What about language 2? It seems similar. But it is different in a crucial way and is therefore in SD/D. The following Turing machine semidecides it: Run M on w; if it halts and rejects, accept. The key difference is that now, instead of needing to detect that M loops, we need to detect that M halts and rejects. We can detect halting (but not looping) by simulation. Now consider language 3. If it were somehow possible to know that M were a deciding machine, then there would be a decision procedure to determine whether or not it rejects w: Run M on w. It must halt (since it's a deciding machine). If it rejects, accept, else reject. That would mean language 3 would be in D. But language 3 is, in fact, in ¬SD. It is harder than language 2. The problem is that there is not even a semideciding procedure for the question, "Is M a deciding machine?" That question is equivalent to asking whether M halts on all inputs, which we have shown is not semidecidable.

21.7 Summary of D, SD/D and ¬SD Languages that Include Turing Machine Descriptions

At the beginning of this chapter, we presented a table with a set of questions that we might like to ask about Turing machines and we showed the language formulation of each question. We have now proven where most of those languages fall in the D, SD/D, ¬SD hierarchy that we have defined. (The rest are given as exercises.) So we know whether there exists a decision procedure, a semidecision procedure, or neither, to answer the corresponding question. Because many of these questions are very important as we try to understand the power of the Turing machine formalism, we summarize in Table 21.2 the status of those initial questions, along with some of the others that we have considered in this chapter.

Table 21.2 The problem and the language view.

The Problem View	*The Language View*	*Status*
Does TM M have an even number of states?	$\{<M> : \text{TM } M \text{ has an even number of states}\}$	D
Does TM M halt on w?	$H = \{<M, w> : \text{TM } M \text{ halts on } w\}$	SD/D
Does TM M halt on the empty tape?	$H_\varepsilon = \{<M> : \text{TM } M \text{ halts on } \varepsilon\}$	SD/D
Is there any string on which TM M halts?	$H_{ANY} = \{<M> : \text{there exists at least one string on which TM } M \text{ halts}\}$	SD/D
Does TM M halt on all strings?	$H_{ALL} = \{<M> : \text{TM } M \text{ halts on } \Sigma^*\}$	¬SD
Does TM M accept w?	$A = \{<M, w> : \text{TM } M \text{ accepts } w\}$	SD/D
Does TM M accept ε?	$A_\varepsilon = \{<M> : \text{TM } M \text{ accepts } \varepsilon\}$	SD/D
Is there any string that TM M accepts?	$A_{ANY}\ \{<M> : \text{there exists at least one string that TM } M \text{ accepts}\}$	SD/D
Does TM M fail to halt on w?	$\neg H = \{<M, w> : \text{TM } M \text{ does not halt on } w\}$	¬SD
Does TM M accept all strings?	$A_{ALL} = \{<M> : L(M) = \Sigma^*\}$	¬SD
Do TMs M_a and M_b, accept the same languages?	$\text{EqTMs} = \{<M_a, M_b> : L(M_a) = L(M_b)\}$	¬SD
Is it the case that TM M does not halt on any string?	$H_{\neg ANY} = \{<M> : \text{there does not exist any string on which TM } M \text{ halts}\}$	¬SD
Does TM M fail to halt on its own description?	$\{<M> : \text{TM } M \text{ does not halt on input } <M>\}$	¬SD
Is TM M minimal?	$TM_{MIN} = \{<M> : \text{TM } M \text{ is minimal}\}$	¬SD
Is the language that TM M accepts regular?	$TM_{REG} = \{<M> : L(M) \text{ is regular}\}$	¬SD
Is $L(M) = A^nB^n$?	$A_{anbn} = \{<M> : L(M) = A^nB^n\}$	¬SD

Exercises

1. For each of the following languages L, state whether L is in D, SD/D, or $\neg$SD. Prove your claim. Assume that any input of the form $<M>$ is a description of a Turing machine.

   a. $\{\mathtt{a}\}$

   b. $\{<M> : \mathtt{a} \in L(M)\}$

   c. $\{<M> : L(M) = \{\mathtt{a}\}\}$

   d. $\{<M_a, M_b> : M_a \text{ and } M_b \text{ are Turing machines and } \varepsilon \in L(M_a) - L(M_b)\}$

   e. $\{<M_a, M_b> : M_a \text{ and } M_b \text{ are Turing machines and } L(M_a) = L(M_b) - \{\varepsilon\}\}$

   f. $\{<M_a, M_b> : M_a \text{ and } M_b \text{ are Turing machines and } L(M_a) \neq L(M_b)\}$

   g. $\{<M, w> : M$, when operating on input w, never moves to the right on two consecutive moves$\}$

   h. $\{<M> : M \text{ is the only Turing machine that accepts } L(M)\}$

   i. $\{<M> : L(M) \text{ contains at least two strings}\}$

   j. $\{<M> : M \text{ rejects at least two even length strings}\}$

   k. $\{<M> : M \text{ halts on all palindromes}\}$

   l. $\{<M> : L(M) \text{ is context-free}\}$

   m. $\{<M> : L(M) \text{ is not context-free}\}$

   n. $\{<M> : A_{\#}(L(M)) > 0\}$, where $A_{\#}(L) = |L \cap \{\mathtt{a}^*\}|$

   o. $\{<M> : |L(M)| \text{ is a prime integer} > 0\}$

   p. $\{<M> : \text{there exists a string } w \text{ such that } |w| < |<M>| \text{ and that } M \text{ accepts } w\}$

   q. $\{<M> : M \text{ does not accept any string that ends with } 0\}$

   r. $\{<M> :$ there are at least two strings w and x such that M halts on both w and x within some number of steps s, and $s < 1000$ and s is prime$\}$

   s. $\{<M> : \text{there exists an input on which } M \text{ halts in fewer than } |<M>| \text{ steps}\}$

   t. $\{<M> : L(M) \text{ is infinite}\}$

   u. $\{<M> : L(M) \text{ is uncountably infinite}\}$

   v. $\{<M> : M \text{ accepts the string } <M, M> \text{ and does not accept the string } <M>\}$

   w. $\{<M> : M \text{ accepts at least two strings of different lengths}\}$

   x. $\{<M> : M \text{ accepts exactly two strings and they are of different lengths}\}$

   y. $\{<M, w> : M \text{ accepts } w \text{ and rejects } w^R\}$

   z. $\{<M, x, y> : M \text{ accepts } xy\}$

   aa. $\{<D> : <D> \text{ is the string encoding of a deterministic FSM } D \text{ and } L(D) = \varnothing\}$

2. In E.3, we describe a straightforward use of reduction that solves a grid coloring problem by reducing it to a graph problem. Given the grid G shown here:

   a. Show the graph that corresponds to G.

   b. Use the graph algorithm we describe to find a coloring of G.

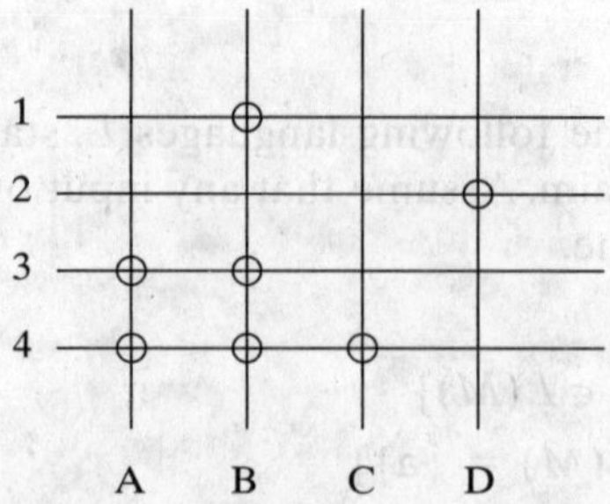

3. In this problem, we consider the relationship between H and a very simple language {a}.

a. Show that {a} is *mapping* reducible to H.

b. Is it possible to reduce H to {a}? Prove your answer.

4. Show that H_{ALL} = {<*M*>: Turing machine *M* halts on Σ^*} is not in D by reduction from H.

5. Show that each of the following languages is not in D.

a. A_ε

b. A_{ANY}

c. A_{ALL}

d. {<*M*, *w*> : Turing machine *M* rejects *w*}

e. {<*M*, *w*> : Turing machine *M* is a deciding Turing machine and *M* rejects *w*}

6. Show that *L* = {<*M*> : Turing machine *M*, on input ε, ever writes 0 on its tape} is in D iff H is in D. In other words, show that $L \leq$ H and H $\leq L$.

7. Show that each of the following questions is undecidable by recasting it as a language recognition problem and showing that the corresponding language is not in D.

a. Given a program *P*, input *x*, and a variable *n*, does *P*, when running on *x*, ever assign a value to *n*?

> Can a compiler check to make sure every variable is initialized before it is used? (G.4.4)

b. Given a program *P* and code segment *S* in *P*, does *P* reach *S* on every input (in other words, can we guarantee that *S* happens)?

c. Given a program *P* and a variable *x*, is *x* always initialized before it is used?

d. Given a program *P* and a file *f*, does *P* always close *f* before it exits?

e. Given a program *P* with an array reference of the form *a*[*i*], will *i*, at the time of the reference, always be within the bounds declared for the array?

f. Given a program *P* and a database of objects *d*, does *P* perform the function *f* on all elements of *d*?

8. Theorem J.1 tells us that the safety of even a very simple security model is undecidable. Its proof is by reduction from H_ε. Show an alternative proof that reduces $A = \{<M, w> : M \text{ is a Turing machine and } w \in L(M)\}$ to the language Safety.
9. Show that each of the following languages is not in SD.
   a. $\neg H_\varepsilon$
   b. EqTMs
   c. TM_{REG}
   d. $\{<M> : |L(M)| \text{ is even}\}$
   e. $\{<M> : \text{Turing machine } M \text{ accepts all even length strings}\}$
   f. $\{<M> : \text{Turing machine } M \text{ accepts no even length strings}\}$
   g. $\{<M> : \text{Turing machine } M \text{ does not halt on input } <M>\}$
   h. $\{<M, w> : M \text{ is a deciding Turing machine and } M \text{ rejects } w\}$
10. Do the other half of the proof of Rice's Theorem. In other words, show that the theorem holds if $P(\varnothing) = True$.
11. For each of the following languages L, do two things:
    i. State whether or not Rice's Theorem has anything to tell us about the decidability of L.
    ii. State whether L is in D, SD/D, or not in SD.
    a. $\{<M> : \text{Turing machine } M \text{ accepts all strings that start with } \mathtt{a}\}$.
    b. $\{<M> : \text{Turing machine } M \text{ halts on } \varepsilon \text{ in no more than 1000 steps}\}$.
    c. $\neg L_1$, where $L_1 = \{<M> : \text{Turing machine } M \text{ halts on all strings in no more than 1000 steps}\}$.
    d. $\{<M, w> : \text{Turing machine } M \text{ rejects } w\}$.
12. Use Rice's Theorem to prove that each of the following languages L is not in D:
    a. $\{<M> : \text{Turing machine } M \text{ accepts at least two odd length strings}\}$.
    b. $\{<M> : M \text{ is a Turing machine and } |L(M)| = 12\}$.
13. Prove that there exists no mapping reduction from H to the language L_2 that we defined in Theorem 21.9.
14. Let $\Sigma = \{\mathtt{1}\}$. Show that there exists at least one undecidable language with alphabet Σ.
15. Give an example of a language L such that neither L nor $\neg L$ is decidable.
16. Let *repl* be a function that maps from one language to another. It is defined as follows:

$$repl(L) = \{w : \exists x \in L \text{ and } w = xx\}.$$

    a. Are the context free languages closed under *repl*? Prove your answer.
    b. Are the decidable languages closed under *repl*? Prove your answer.
17. For any nonempty alphabet Σ, let L be any decidable language other than $\varnothing$ or Σ^*. Prove that $L \leq_M \neg L$.
18. We will say that L_1 is doubly reducible to L_2, which we will write as $L_1 \leq_D L_2$, iff there exist two computable functions f_1 and f_2 such that:

$$\forall x \in \Sigma^*((x \in L_1) \text{ iff } (f_1(x) \in L_2 \text{ and } f_2(x) \notin L_2)).$$

Prove or disprove each of the following claims:

a. If $L_1 \leq L_2$ and $L_2 \neq \Sigma^*$, then $L_1 \leq_D L_2$.

b. If $L_1 \leq_D L_2$ and $L_2 \in D$, then $L_1 \in D$.

c. For every language L_2, there exists a language L_1 such that $\neg(L_1 \leq_D L_2)$.

19. Let L_1 and L_2 be any two SD/D languages such that $L_1 \subset L_2$. Is it possible that L_1 is reducible to L_2? Prove your answer.

20. If L_1 and L_2 are decidable languages and $L_1 \subseteq L \subseteq L_2$, must L be decidable? Prove your answer.

21. Goldbach's conjecture states that every even integer greater than 2 can be written as the sum of two primes. (Consider 1 to be prime.) Suppose that A = $\{<M, w> : M$ is a Turing machine and $w \in L(M)\}$ were decidable by some Turing machine *Oracle*. Define the following function:

$G()$ = *True* if Goldbach's conjecture is true,

False otherwise.

Use *Oracle* to describe a Turing machine that computes G. You may assume the existence of a Turing machine P that decides whether a number is prime.

22. A language L is ***D-complete*** iff (1) L is in D, and (2) for every language L' in D, $L' \leq_M L$. Consider the following claim: If $L \in D$ and $L \neq \Sigma^*$ and $L \neq \varnothing$, then L is D-complete. Prove or disprove this claim.

C H A P T E R 22

Decidability of Languages That Do Not (Obviously) Ask Questions about Turing Machines◆

If the only problems that were undecidable were questions involving the behavior of Turing Machines (and thus programs written in any reasonable formalism), we would still care. After all, being able to prove properties of the programs that we write is of critical importance when bugs could mean the loss of millions of dollars or hundreds of lives. But Turing Machines do not own the market in undecidable problems. In this chapter, we will look at some examples of undecidable problems that do not (at least directly) ask questions about Turing Machines.

Although the problems we will consider here do not appear to involve Turing Machines, each of the undecidability proofs that we will describe is based, either directly or indirectly, on a reduction from a language (such as H, A, or $\neg H_\varepsilon$) whose definition does refer to the behavior of Turing machines. Many of these proofs are based on variants of a single idea, namely the fact that it is possible to encode a Turing machine configuration as a string. For example, the string abq100cd can encode the configuration of a Turing machine that is in state 4, with abcd on the tape and the read/write head positioned on the c. Then we can encode a computation of a Turing machine as a sequence of configurations, separated by delimiters. For example, we might have:

#q0❑abcd#q1abcd#aq1bcd#

Or we can encode a computation as a table, where each row corresponds to a configuration. So, for example, we might have:

#q0❑abcd#

#❑q1abcd#

#❑aq1bcd#

To show that a new language is not decidable, we will then define a reduction that maps from one of these representations of a Turing machine's computations to some essential structure of the new problem. We will design the reduction so that the new problem's structure possesses some key property iff the Turing machine's computation enters a halting state (or an accepting state) or fails to enter a halting state, or whatever it is we need to check. So, if there is a procedure to decide whether an instance of the new problem possesses the key property, then there is also a way to check whether a Turing machine halts (or accepts or whatever). So, for example, suppose that we are using the table representation and that M, the Turing machine whose computation we have described, does not halt. Then the table will have an infinite number of rows. In the proof we'll sketch in Section 22.3, the cells of the table will correspond to tiles that must be arranged according to a small set of rules. So, if we could tell whether an infinite arrangement of tiles exists, we could tell whether the table is infinite (and thus whether M fails to halt).

22.1 Diophantine Equations and Hilbert's 10th Problem

In 1900, the German mathematician David Hilbert presented a list of 23 problems that he argued should be the focus of mathematical research as the new century began. The 10th of his problems 💻 concerned systems of Diophantine equations (polynomials in any number of variables, all with integer coefficients), such as:

$$4x^3 + 7xy + 2z^2 - 23x^4z = 0.$$

A Diophantine problem is, "Given a system of Diophantine equations, does it have an integer solution?" Hilbert asked whether there exists a decision procedure for Diophantine problems. Diophantine problems are important in applications in which the variables correspond to quantities of indivisible objects in the world. For example, suppose x is the number of shares of stock A to be bought, y is the number of shares of stock B, and z is the number of shares of stock C. Since it is not generally possible to buy fractions of shares of stock, any useful solution to an equation involving x, y, and z would necessarily assign integer values to each variable.

We can recast the Diophantine problem as the language TENTH = $\{<w> : w$ is a system of Diophantine equations that has an integer solution$\}$. In 1970, Yuri Matiyasevich proved a general result from which it follows that the answer to Hilbert's question is no: TENTH is not in D. Using the Fibonacci sequence (defined in Example 24.4), Matiyasevich proved that every semidecidable set S is Diophantine, by which we mean that there is a reduction from S to the problem of deciding whether some system of Diophantine equations has an integer solution. So, if the Diophantine problem were decidable, every semidecidable set would be decidable. But we know that there are semidecidable sets (e.g., the language H) that are not decidable. So the Diophantine problem is not decidable either.

As an aside, however, we should point out that when all of the terms are of degree 1, Diophantine problems are decidable, which is good news for the writers of puzzle problems of the sort:

> A farmer buys 100 animals for \$100.00. The animals include at least one cow, one pig, and one chicken, but no other kind. If a cow costs \$10.00, a pig costs \$3.00, and a chicken costs \$0.50, how many of each did he buy? 💻

It is also true that Diophantine problems that involve just a single variable are decidable. And quadratic Diophantine problems of two variables are decidable. These are problems of the form $ax^2 + by = c$, where a, b, and c are positive integers and we ask whether there exist integer values of x and y that satisfy the equation.

We will return to the question of the solvability of Diophantine problems in Part V. There we will see that:

- Diophantine problems of degree 1 (like the cows, pigs, and chickens problem) and Diophantine problems of a single variable of the form $ax^k = c$ are not only solvable, they are efficiently solvable (i.e., there exists a polynomial-time algorithm to solve them).
- Quadratic Diophantine problems are solvable, but there appears to exist no polynomial-time algorithm for doing so. The quadratic Diophantine problem belongs to the complexity class NP-complete.
- The general Diophantine problem is undecidable, so not even an inefficient algorithm for it exists.

22.2 Post Correspondence Problem

Consider two lists of strings over some alphabet Σ. The lists must be finite and of equal length. We can call the two lists X and Y. So we have:

$$X = x_1, x_2, x_3, \ldots, x_n.$$
$$Y = y_1, y_2, y_3, \ldots, y_n.$$

Now we ask a question about the lists: Does there exist some finite sequence of integers that can be viewed as indices of X and Y such that, when elements of X are selected as specified and concatenated together, we get the same string that we get when elements of Y are also concatenated together as specified? For example, if we assert that 1, 3, 4 is such a sequence, we're asserting that $x_1x_3x_4 = y_1y_3y_4$. Any problem of this form is an instance of the ***Post Correspondence Problem*** 🖳, first formulated in the 1940's by Emil Post.

EXAMPLE 22.1 A PCP Instance with a Simple Solution

Let PCP_1 be:

	X	Y
1	b	aab
2	abb	b
3	aba	a
4	baaa	baba

EXAMPLE 22.1 ***(Continued)***

PCP_1 has a very simple solution: 3, 4, 1, which is a solution because (ignoring spaces, which are shown here just to make it clear what is happening):

aba baaa b = a baba aab

It also has an infinite number of other solutions, including 3, 4, 1, 3, 4, 1 and 3, 4, 1, 3, 4, 1, 3, 4, 1.

EXAMPLE 22.2 A PCP Instance with No Solution

Let PCP_2 be:

	X	Y
1	11	011
2	01	0
3	001	110

PCP_2 has no solution. It is straightforward to show this by trying candidate solutions. Mismatched symbols that cause the current path to die are marked with an ×.

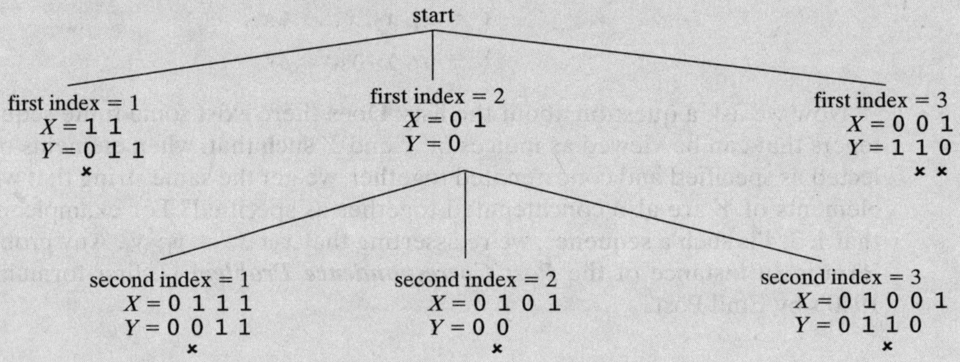

All paths have failed to find a solution.

EXAMPLE 22.3 A PCP Instance with No Simple Solutions

Let PCP_3 be:

	X	Y
1	1101	1
2	0110	11
3	1	110

PCP_3 has solutions (in fact, an infinite number of them), but the shortest one has length 252.

We can formulate the Post Correspondence Problem as a language decision problem. To do that, we need to define a way to encode each instance of the Post Correspondence Problem as a string. Let Σ be any nonempty alphabet. Then an instance of the Post Correspondence Problem is a string $<P>$ of the form:

$$<P> = (x_1, x_2, x_3, \ldots, x_n)(y_1, y_2, y_3, \ldots, y_n), \text{ where } \forall j\,(x_j \in \Sigma^+ \text{ and } y_j \in \Sigma^+).$$

For example, $<PCP_1>$ = (b, abb, aba, baaa)(aab, b, a, baba).

We'll say that a PCP instance has ***size n*** whenever the number of strings in its X list is n. (In this case, the number of strings in its Y list is also n.) A solution to a PCP instance of size n is a finite sequence $i_1, i_2, \ldots i_k$ of integers such that:

$$\forall 1 \leq j \leq k\ (1 \leq i_j \leq n \text{ and } x_{i_1}x_{i_2}\ldots x_{i_k} = y_{i_1}y_{i_2}\ldots y_{i_k}).$$

To define a concrete PCP language, we need to fix an alphabet. We'll let Σ be $\{0, 1\}$ and simply encode any other alphabet in binary. Now the problem of determining whether a particular instance P of the Post Correspondence Problem has a solution can be recast as the problem of deciding the language:

- PCP = $\{<P> : P$ is an instance of the Post correspondence problem and P has a solution$\}$.

THEOREM 22.1 The Undecidability of PCP

Theorem: The language PCP = $\{<P> : P$ is an instance of the Post correspondence problem and P has a solution$\}$ is in SD/D.

Proof: We will first show that PCP is in SD by building a Turing machine $M_{PCP}(<P>)$ that semidecides it. The idea is that M_{PCP} will simply try all possible solutions of length 1, then all possible solutions of length 2, and so forth. If there is any finite sequence of indices that is a solution, M_{PCP} will find it. To describe more clearly how M_{PCP} works, we first observe that any solution to a PCP problem $P = (x_1, x_2, x_3, \ldots, x_n)(y_1, y_2, y_3, \ldots, y_n)$ is a finite sequence of integers between 1 and n. We can build a Turing machine $M\#$ that lexicographically enumerates all such sequences. Now we define:

$M_{PCP}(<P>) =$

1. Invoke $M\#$.

2. As each string is enumerated, see if it is a solution to P. If so, halt.

Next we must prove that PCP is not in D. There are two approaches we could take to doing this proof. One is to use reduction from H. The idea is that, to decide whether $<M, w>$ is in H, we create a PCP instance that simulates the computation history of M running on w. We do the construction in such a way that there exists a finite sequence that solves the PCP problem iff the computation halts. So, if we could decide PCP, we could decide H. An alternative is to make use of the grammar formalism that we will define in the next chapter. We'll show there that unrestricted grammars generate all and only the SD languages. So the problem of deciding whether a grammar G generates a string w is equivalent to deciding whether a Turing machine M accepts w and is thus undecidable. Given that result, we can prove that PCP is not in D by a construction that maps a grammar to a PCP instance in such a way that there exists a finite sequence that solves the PCP problem iff there is a finite derivation of w using the rules of G. This second approach is somewhat easier to explain, so it is the one we'll use. We give the proof in E.4.

It turns out that some special cases of PCP are decidable. For example, if we restrict our attention to problems of size 2, then PCP is decidable. A bounded version of PCP is also decidable. Define the language:

- BOUNDED-PCP = $\{<P, k> : P$ is an instance of the Post Correspondence problem that has a solution of length less than or equal to $k\}$.

While BOUNDED-PCP is decidable (by a straightforward algorithm that simply tries all candidate solutions of length up to k), it appears not to be efficiently decidable. It is a member of the complexity class NP-complete, which we will define in Section 28.2.

The fact that PCP is not decidable in general is significant. As we will see in Section 22.5.3, reduction from PCP is a convenient way to show the undecidability of other kinds of problems, including some that involve context-free languages.

22.3 Tiling Problems

Consider a class of tiles called Wang tiles or Wang dominos 🖳. A Wang tile is a square that has been divided into four regions by drawing two diagonal lines, as shown in Figure 22.1. Each region is colored with one of a fixed set of colors.

Now suppose that you are given a finite set of such tile designs, all of the same size, for example the set of three designs shown here. Further suppose that you have an infinite supply of each type of tile. Then we may ask whether or not it is possible to tile an arbitrary surface in the plane with the available designs while adhering to the following rules:

1. Each tile must be placed so that it is touching its neighbors on all four sides (if such neighbors exist). In other words, no gaps or overlaps are allowed.
2. When two tiles are placed so that they adjoin each other, the adjoining regions of the two tiles must be the same color.
3. No rotations or flips are allowed.

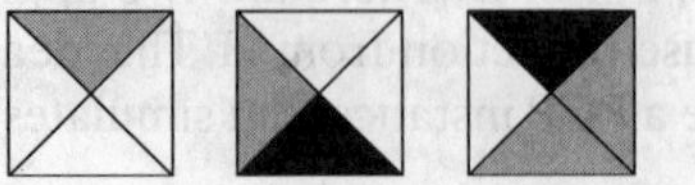

FIGURE 22.1 A tiling problem.

EXAMPLE 22.4 A Set of Tiles that Can Tile the Plane

The set of tiles shown in Figure 22.1 can be used to tile any surface in the plane. Here is a small piece of the pattern that can be built and then repeated as necessary since its right and left sides match, as do its top and bottom:

EXAMPLE 22.5 A Set of Tiles that Cannot Tile the Plane

Now consider a new set of tiles:

Only a small number of small regions can be tiled with this set. To see this, start with tile 1, add a tile below it and then try to extend the pattern sideways. Then start with tile 2 and show the same thing. Then observe that tile 3, the only one remaining, cannot be placed next to itself.

We can formulate the tiling problem, as we have just described it, as a language to be decided. To do that, we need to define a way to encode each instance of the tiling problem (i.e., a set of tile designs) as a string. We will represent each design as an ordered 4-tuple of values drawn from the set {`G`, `W`, `B`}. To describe a design, start in the top region and then go around the tile clockwise. So, for example, the tile set of Figure 22.1 could be represented as:

`(G W W W) (W W B G) (B G G W)`.

Now we can define:

- TILES = {<*T*> : every finite surface on the plane can be tiled, according to the rules, with the tile set *T*}.

The string `(G W W W) (W W B G) (B G G W)`, which corresponds to the tile set of Example 22.4, is in TILES.

The string `(G W W W) (W W G G) (B G B W)`, which corresponds to the tile set of Example 22.5, is not in TILES.

Is TILES in D? In other words, does there exist a decision procedure that determines, for a given set of tiles, whether or not it can be used to tile an arbitrary surface in the plane? Consider the following conjecture, called Wang's conjecture: If a given set of tiles can be used to tile an arbitrary surface, then it can always do so periodically. In other words, there must exist a finite area that can be tiled and then repeated infinitely often to cover any desired surface. For example, the tile set of Example 22.4 covers the plane periodically using the 3×3 grid shown above. If Wang's conjecture were true, then the tiling question would be decidable by considering successively larger square grids in search of one that can serve as the basis for a periodic tiling. If such a grid exists, it will be found. If no such grid exists, then it is possible to prove (using a result known as the König infinity lemma) that there must exist a finite square grid that cannot be tiled at all. So this procedure must eventually halt, either by finding a grid that can be used for a periodic tiling or by finding a grid that cannot be tiled at all (and thus discovering that no periodic tiling exists).

> It is possible to make many kinds of changes to the kinds of tiles that are allowed without altering the undecidability properties of the tiling problem as we have presented it for Wang tiles. Tiling problems, in this broader sense, have widespread applications in the physical world. For example, the growth of crystals can often be described as a tiling.

As it turns out, Wang's conjecture is false. There exist tile sets that can tile an arbitrary area aperiodically (i.e., without any repeating pattern) but for which no periodic tiling exists. Of course, that does not mean that TILES must not be in D. There might exist some other way to decide it. But there does not. TILES is not in D. In fact, it is not even in SD, although ¬TILES is.

THEOREM 22.2 The Undecidability of TILES

Theorem: The language TILES = $\{<T>$: every finite surface on the plane can be tiled, according to the rules, with the tile set $T\}$ is not in D. It is also not in SD. But ¬TILES is in SD.

Proof: We first prove that ¬TILES is in SD. Consider a search space defined as follows: The start state contains no tiles. From any state s, construct the set of successor states, each of which is built by adding one tile, according to the rules, to the configuration in s. We can build a Turing machine M that semidecides ¬TILES by systematically exploring this space. If and only if it ever happens that all the branches reach a dead end in which there is no legal move, then there is no tiling and M accepts.

If TILES were also in SD, then, by Theorem 20.6, it would be in D. But it is not. The proof that it is not is by reduction from $\neg H_{\varepsilon}$. The idea behind the reduction is to describe a way to map an arbitrary Turing machine M into a set of tiles T in such a way that T is in TILES iff M does not halt on ε. The reduction uses a row of tiles to correspond to a configuration of M. It begins by creating a row that corresponds to M's initial configuration when started on a blank tape. Then the next row will correspond to M's next configuration, and so forth. There is always a next configuration of M and thus a next row in the tiling iff M does not halt. T is in TILES iff there is always a next row (i.e., T can tile an arbitrarily large area). So if it were possible to semidecide whether T is in TILES it would be possible to semidecide whether M fails to halt on ε. But we know (from Theorem 21.16) that $\neg H_\varepsilon$ is not in SD. So neither is TILES.

The language TILES corresponds to an unbounded tiling problem. We can also formulate a bounded version: "Given a particular stack of n^2 tiles (for some value of n), is it possible to tile an $n \times n$ surface in the plane?" This problem is clearly decidable by the straightforward algorithm that simply tries all ways of placing the n^2 tiles on the n^2 cells of an $n \times n$ grid. But there is still bad news. The theory of time complexity that we will describe in Chapter 28 provides the basis for formalizing the following claim: The bounded tiling problem is apparently intractable. The time required to solve it by the best known algorithm grows exponentially with n. We will return to this discussion in Exercise 28.20).

22.4 Logical Theories

Even before anyone had seen a computer, mathematicians were interested in the question: "Does there exist an algorithm to determine, given a statement in a logical language, whether or not it is a theorem?" In other words, can it be proved from the available axioms plus the rules of inference. In the case of formulas in first order logic, this problem even had a specific name, the Entscheidungsproblem. With the advent of the computer, the Entscheidungsproblem acquired more than mathematical interest. If such an algorithm existed, it could play a key role in programs that, among other things:

- decide whether other programs are correct.
- determine that a plan for controlling a manufacturing robot is correct.
- accept or reject interpretations for English sentences, based on whether or not they make sense.

22.4.1 Boolean Theories

If we consider only Boolean logic formulas, such as $(P \wedge (Q \vee \neg R) \rightarrow S)$, then there exist procedures to decide all of the following questions:

- Given a well-formed formula (wff) w, is w valid (i.e., is it true for all assignments of truth values to its variables)?
- Given a wff w, is w satisfiable (i.e., is there some assignment of truth values to its variables such that w is true)?
- Given a wff w and a set of axioms A, is w a theorem (i.e., can it be proved from A)?

Alternatively, all of the following languages are in D.

- VALID = {<w> : w is a wff in Boolean logic and w is valid}
- SAT = {<w> : w is a wff in Boolean logic and w is satisfiable}
- PROVABLE = {<A, w> : w is a wff in Boolean logic, A is a set of axioms in Boolean logic and w is provable from A}

> Suppose that the specification for a hardware device or a software system can be described in terms of a finite number of states. Then it can be written as a Boolean formula. Then one way to verify the correctness of a particular implementation is to see whether it satisfies the specification. The fact that SAT is decidable makes this approach, called model checking, possible. (H.1.2)

There is a straightforward procedure for answering all of these questions since each wff contains only a finite number of variables and each variable can take on one of two possible values (*True* or *False*). So it suffices to try all the possibilities. A wff is valid iff it is true in all assignments of truth values to its variables. It is satisfiable iff it is true in at least one such assignment. A wff w is provable from A iff ($A \rightarrow w$) is valid.

Unfortunately, if w contains n variables, then there are 2^n ways of trying all ways of assigning values to those variables. So any algorithm that does that takes time that grows exponentially in the size of w. The best known algorithms for answering any of these questions about an arbitrary wff do take exponential time in the worst case. We'll return to this issue when we consider complexity in Part V. However, we should note that there are techniques that can perform better than exponentially in many cases. One approach (described in B.1.3) represents formulas as ordered binary decision diagrams (OBDDs).

22.4.2 First-Order Logical Theories

If we consider first-order logic (FOL) sentences, such as $\forall x\,(\exists y\,(P(x, y) \wedge Q(y, x) \rightarrow T(x)))$, then none of the questions we asked about Boolean logic (validity, satisfiability, and theoremhood) is decidable.

We'll focus here on the question of deciding, given a sentence w and a decidable set of axioms A, whether w can be proved from A. To do this, we'll define the language:

- $\text{FOL}_{\text{theorem}}$ = {<A, w> : A is a decidable set of axioms in first-order logic, w is a sentence in first-order logic, and w is entailed by A}.

Note that we do not require that the set of axioms be finite, but we do require that it be decidable. For example ***Peano arithmetic*** is a first-order logical theory that describes the natural numbers, along with the functions *plus* and *times* applied to them. Peano arithmetic exploits an infinite but decidable set of axioms.

THEOREM 22.3 First-Order Logic is Semidecidable

Theorem: $FOL_{theorem}$ = {<*A*, *w*> : *A* is a decidable set of axioms in first-order logic, *w* is a sentence in first-order logic, and *w* is entailed by *A*} is in SD.

Proof: The algorithm *proveFOL* semidecides $FOL_{theorem}$:

proveFOL(*A*: decidable set of axioms, *w*: sentence) =

1. Using some complete set of inference rules for first-order logic, begin with the sentences in *A* and lexicographically enumerate the sound proofs. If *A* is infinite, then it will be necessary to embed in that process a subroutine that lexicographically enumerates the sentences in the language of the theory of *A* and checks each to determine whether or not it is an axiom.
2. Check each proof as it is created. If it succeeds in proving *w*, halt and accept.

By Gödel's Completeness Theorem, we know that there does exist a set of inference rules for first order logic that is complete in the sense that they are able to derive, from a set of axioms *A*, all sentences that are entailed by *A*. So step 1 of *proveFOL* can be correctly implemented.

There exist techniques for implementing *proveFOL* in a way that is computationally efficient enough for many practical applications. We describe one of them, resolution, in B.2.2.

Unfortunately, *proveFOL* is not a decision procedure since it may not halt. Also, unfortunately, it is not possible to do better, as we now show.

Logical reasoning provides a basis for many artificial intelligence systems. Does the fact that first-order logic is undecidable mean that artificial intelligence is impossible? (M.2.4)

THEOREM 22.4 First-Order Logic is Not Decidable

Theorem: $FOL_{theorem}$ = {<*A*, *w*> : *A* is a decidable set of axioms in first-order logic, *w* is a sentence in first-order logic, and *w* is entailed by *A*} is not in D.

Proof: Let *T* be any first-order theory with *A* (a decidable set of axioms) and *M* (an interpretation, i.e., a domain and an assignment of meanings to the constant, predicate, and function symbols of *A*). If *T* is not consistent, then all sentences are theorems in *T*. So the simple procedure that always returns *True* decides whether any sentence is a theorem in *T*. We now consider the case in which *T* is consistent.

If *T* is complete then, for any sentence *w*, either *w* or $\neg w$ is a theorem. So the set of theorems is decidable because it can be decided by the following algorithm:

decidecompletetheory(*A*: set of axioms, *w*: sentence) =

1. In parallel, use *proveFOL*, as defined above, to attempt to prove w and $\neg w$.
2. One of the proof attempts will eventually succeed. If the attempt to prove w succeeded, then return *True*. If the attempt to prove $\neg w$ succeeded, then return *False*.

A slightly different way to say this is that if the set of theorems is in SD and the set of nontheorems is also in SD, then by Theorem 20.6, both sets are also in D. But we must also consider the case in which T is not complete. Now it is possible that neither w nor $\neg w$ is a theorem. Does there exist a decision procedure to determine whether w is a theorem? The answer is no, which we will show by exhibiting one particular theory for which no decision procedure exists. We use the theory of Peano arithmetic. Gödel proved (in a result that has come to be known as Gödel's Incompleteness Theorem) that the theory of Peano arithmetic cannot be both consistent and complete.

Following Turing's argument, we show that $H_\varepsilon \leq_M \mathrm{FOL}_{\mathrm{theorem}}$ and so $\mathrm{FOL}_{\mathrm{theorem}}$ is not in D. Let R be a mapping reduction from $H_\varepsilon = \{<M> : \text{Turing machine } M \text{ halts on } \varepsilon\}$ to $\mathrm{FOL}_{\mathrm{theorem}}$ defined as follows:

R(<*M*>) =

1. From (<*M*>), construct a sentence F in the language of Peano arithmetic, such that F is a theorem, provable given the axioms of Peano arithmetic, iff M halts on ε.
2. Let P be the axioms of Peano arithmetic. Return <*P*, *F*>.

If *Oracle* exists and decides $\mathrm{FOL}_{\mathrm{theorem}}$, then C = *Oracle*(*R*(<*M*, *w*>)) decides H_ε:

- There exists an algorithm to implement R. It is based on the techniques described by Turing (although he actually proved first that, because H_ε is undecidable, it is also undecidable whether a Turing machine ever prints 0. He then showed how to create a logical expression that is a theorem of Peano arithmetic iff a Turing machine ever prints 0). We omit the details.
- C is correct:
  - If $<M> \in H_\varepsilon$: M halts on ε. F is a theorem of Peano arithmetic. *Oracle*(<*P*, *F*>) accepts.
  - If $<M> \notin H_\varepsilon$: M does not halt on ε. F is not a theorem of Peano arithmetic. *Oracle*(<*P*, *F*>) rejects.

But no machine to decide H_ε can exist, so neither does *Oracle*.

Is it decidable, given a system of laws, whether some consequence follows from those laws? (M.2.5)

Keep in mind that the fact that $\mathrm{FOL}_{\mathrm{theorem}}$ is undecidable means only that there is no algorithm to *decide* whether an arbitrary sentence is a theorem in an arbitrary theory. $FOL_{theorem}$ is semidecidable and the algorithm, *proveFOL*, that we described in the proof of Theorem 22.3, provides a way to *discover* a proof if one exists. Although efficiency issues arise, we shouldn't write off first-order systems as practical tools, despite the negative results that we have just shown.

Also note that, just as the unsolvability of the halting problem doesn't say that there are not some cases in which we can show that a program halts or other cases in which we can show that it doesn't, the fact that $FOL_{theorem}$ is undecidable doesn't prove that there are not some theories for which it is possible to decide theoremhood.

For example, consider ***Presburger arithmetic***, a theory of the natural numbers and the single function *plus* 🖳. The following is a theorem of Presburger arithmetic (where "number" means natural number):

- The sum of two odd numbers is even:
  $\forall x (\forall y ((\exists u (x = u + u + 1) \land \exists v (y = v + v + 1)) \rightarrow \exists z (x + y = z + z)))$.

Presburger arithmetic is decidable (although unfortunately, as we will see in Section 28.9.3, no *efficient* procedure for deciding it exists).

> Because Presburger arithmetic is decidable, it has been used as a basis for verification systems that prove the correctness of programs. We'll say more about program verification in H.1.

22.5 Undecidable Problems about Context-Free Languages

Recall from Chapter 9 that we were able to find a decision procedure for all of the questions that we asked about regular languages. We have just seen, at the other extreme, that almost all the questions we ask about Turing machines and the languages they define are undecidable. What about context-free languages? In Chapter 14, we described two decision procedures for them:

1. Given a CFL L and a string s, is $s \in L$?
2. Given a CFL L, is $L = \varnothing$?

What about other questions we might like to ask, including:

3. Given a CFL L, is $L = \Sigma^*$?
4. Given two CFLs L_1 and L_2, is $L_1 = L_2$?
5. Given two CFLs L_1 and L_2, is $L_1 \subseteq L_2$?
6. Given a CFL L, is $\neg L$ context-free?
7. Given a CFL L, is L regular?
8. Given two CFLs L_1 and L_2, is $L_1 \cap L_2 = \varnothing$?
9. Given a CFL L, is L inherently ambiguous?

Since we have proven that there exists a grammar that generates L iff there exists a PDA that accepts it, these questions will have the same answers whether we ask them about grammars or about PDAs. In addition, there are questions that we might like to ask specifically about PDAs, including:

10. Given two PDAs M_1 and M_2, is M_2 a minimization of M_1? Define M_2 to be a ***minimization*** of M_1 iff $L(M_1) = L(M_2)$ and there exists no other PDA M' such that $L(M_2) = L(M')$ and M' has fewer states than M_2 has.

And there are other questions specifically about grammars, including:

11. Given a CFG G, is G ambiguous?

Questions 3-11 are all undecidable. Alternatively, if these problems are stated as languages, the languages are not in D. Keep in mind however that just as there are programs that can be shown to halt (or not to halt), there are context-free languages about which various properties can be proven. For example, although question 11 is undecidable (for an arbitrary CFG), some grammars can easily be shown to be ambiguous by finding a single string for which two parses exist. And other grammars can be shown to be unambiguous, for example by showing that they are LL(1), as described in Section 15.2.3.

There are two strategies that we can use to show that these problems are in general undecidable. The first is to exploit the idea of a computation history to enable us to reduce H to one of these problems. The second is to show that a problem is not in D by reduction from the Post Correspondence Problem. We will use both, starting with the computation history approach.

22.5.1 Reduction via Computation History

We will first show that question 3 is undecidable by reducing H to the language $\text{CFG}_{\text{ALL}} = \{<G> : G \text{ is a CFG and } L(G) = \Sigma^*\}$. To do this reduction, we will have to introduce a new technique in which we create strings that correspond to the computation history of some Turing machine M. But, once we have shown that CFG_{ALL} is not in D, the proofs of claims 4, 5, and 10 are quite straightforward. They use reduction from CFG_{ALL}.

Recall from Section 17.1 that a ***configuration*** of a Turing machine M is a 4 tuple (M's current state, the nonblank portion of the tape before the read/write head, the character under the read/write head, the nonblank portion of the tape after the read/write head).

A ***computation*** of M is a sequence of configurations $C_0, C_1, \ldots, C_n$ for some $n \geq 0$ such that C_0 is the initial configuration of M, C_n is a halting configuration of M, and

$$C_0 |-_M C_1 |-_M C_2 |-_M \ldots |-_M C_n.$$

Notice that, under this definition, a computation is a finite sequence of configurations, the last of which must be a halting configuration. So, if M does not halt when started in configuration C_0, there exists no computation that starts in C_0. That doesn't mean that M can't compute from C_0. It just means that there is no finite sequence that records what it does and it is that sequence that we are calling a computation.

A ***computation history*** of M is a string that encodes a computation. We will write each configuration in the history as a 4-tuple, as described above. Then we will encode the entire history by concatenating the configurations together. So, assuming that s is M's start state and h is a halting state, here's an example of a string that could represent a computation history of M:

(s, ε,❑, abba)(q_1, ε, a, bba)(q_2, a, b, ba)(q_2, ab, b, a)(q_2, abb, a, ❑)(h, abba, ❑,❑).

THEOREM 22.5 CFG_{ALL} is Undecidable

Theorem: The language CFG_{ALL} = {<G> : G is a CFG and $L(G)$ = Σ*} is not in D.

Proof: We show that CFG_{ALL} is not in D by reduction from H = {<M, w> : Turing machine M halts on input string w}. The reduction we will use exploits two functions, R and ¬. R will map instances of H to instances of CFG_{ALL}. As in the proof of Theorem 21.9, ¬ will simply invert *Oracle*'s response (turning an accept into a reject and vice versa).

The idea behind R is that it will build a grammar G that generates the language L# composed of all strings in Σ* *except* any that represent a computation history of M on w. If M does not halt on w, there are no computation histories of M on w (since a computation history must be of finite length and end in a halting state) so G generates Σ* and *Oracle* will accept. If, on the other hand, there exists a computation history of M on w, then there will be a string that G will not generate and *Oracle* will reject. So *Oracle* makes the correct distinction but accepts when we need it to reject and vice versa. But since *Oracle* is a deciding machine, ¬ can invert its response.

It turns out to be easier for R to build a PDA to accept L# than it is to build a grammar to generate it. But we have an algorithm to build, from any PDA, the corresponding grammar. So R will first build a PDA P, then convert P to a grammar.

In order for a string s to be a computation history of M on w, it must possess four properties:

1. It must be a syntactically valid computation history.
2. C_0 must correspond to M being in its start state, with w on the tape, and with the read/write head positioned just to the left of w.
3. The last configuration must be a halting configuration.
4. Each configuration after C_0 must be derivable from the previous one according to the rules in M's transition relation δ_M.

We want P to accept any string that is *not* a computation history of M on w. So if P finds even one of these conditions violated it will accept. P will nondeterministically choose which of the four conditions to check. It can then check the one it picked as follows:

1. We can write a regular expression to define the syntax of the language of computation histories. So P can easily check for property 1 and accept if the string is ill-formed.

2. R builds P from a particular pair, so it can hardwire into P what the initial configuration would have to be if s is to be a computation history of M on w.
3. Again, R can hardwire into P what a halting configuration of M is, namely one in which M is in some state in H_M.
4. This is the only hard one. To show that a string s is not composed of configurations that are derivable from each other, it suffices to find even one adjacent pair where the second configuration cannot be derived from the first. So P can nondeterministically pick one configuration and then check to see whether the one that comes after it is not correct, according to the rules of δ_M.

But how exactly, can we implement the test for property 4? Suppose that we have an adjacent pair of configurations. If they are part of a computation history of M, then they must be identical except:

- The state of the second must have changed as specified in δ_M.
- Right around the read/write head, the change specified by δ_M must have occurred on the tape.

So, for example, it is possible, given an appropriate δ_M, that the following string could be part of a computation history:

(q1, aaaa, b, aaaa)(q2, aaa, a, baaaa).

Here M moved the read/write head one square to the left. But it is not possible for the following string to be part of any computation history:

(q1, aaaa, b, aaaa)(q2, bbbb, a, bbbb).

M cannot change any squares other than the one directly under its read/write head.

So P must read the first configuration, remember it, and then compare it to the second. Since a configuration can be of arbitrary length and P is a PDA, the only way P can remember a configuration is on the stack. But then it has a problem. When it tries to pop off the symbols from the first configuration to compare it to the second, they will be backwards.

To solve this problem, we will change slightly our statement of the language that P will accept. Now it will be B#, the ***boustrophedon*** version of L#. In B#, every odd numbered configuration will be written backwards. The word "boustrophedon" aptly describes B#. It is derived from a Greek word that means turning as oxen do in plowing. It is used to describe a writing scheme in which alternate lines are written left to right and then right to left (so that the scribe wastes no effort moving his hand across the page without writing). With this change, P can compare two adjacent configurations and determine whether one could have been derived from the other via δ.

Boustrophedon writing 💻 has been used in ancient Greek texts and for inscriptions on statues on Easter Island. Much more recently, dot matrix printers used back and forth writing, but they adjusted their fonts so that it was not the case that every other line appeared backwards.

We are now ready to state:

$R(<M, w>) =$

1. Construct the description of a PDA P that accepts all strings in $B\#$.
2. From P, construct a grammar G that generates $L(P)$.
3. Return $<G>$.

$\{R, \neg\}$ is a reduction from H to CFG_{ALL}. If *Oracle* exists and decides CFG_{ALL}, then $C = \neg Oracle(R(<M, w>))$ decides H. R can be implemented as a Turing machine. And C is correct:

- If $<M, w> \in H$: M halts on w. So there exists a computation history of M on w. So there is a string that G does not generate. *Oracle*($<G>$) rejects. C accepts.
- If $<M, w> \notin H$: M does not halt on w, so there exists no computation history of M on w. G generates Σ^*. *Oracle*($<G>$) accepts. C rejects.

But no machine to decide H can exist, so neither does *Oracle*.

22.5.2 Using the Undecidability of CFG_{ALL}

Now that we have proven our first result about the undecidability of a question about context-free grammars, others can be proven by reduction from it. For example:

THEOREM 22.6 "Are Two CFGs Equivalent?" is Undecidable

Theorem: The language $GG_= = \{<G_1, G_2> : G_1 \text{ and } G_2 \text{ are CFGs and } L(G_1) = L(G_2)\}$ is not in D.

Proof: We show that $CFG_{ALL} \leq_M GG_=$ and so $GG_=$ is not in D. Let R be a mapping reduction from CFG_{ALL} to $GG_=$ defined as follows:

$R(<G>) =$

1. Construct the description $<G\#>$ of a new grammar $G\#$ that generates Σ^*.
2. Return $<G\#, G>$.

If *Oracle* exists and decides $GG_=$, then $C = Oracle(R(<G>))$ decides CFG_{ALL}:

- R can be implemented as a Turing machine.
- C is correct:
  - If $<G> \in CFG_{ALL}$: G is equivalent to $G\#$, which generates everything. $Oracle(<G\#, G>)$ accepts.
  - If $<G> \notin CFG_{ALL}$: G is not equivalent to $G\#$, which generates everything. $Oracle(<G\#, G>)$ rejects.

But no machine to decide CFG_{ALL} can exist, so neither does *Oracle*.

THEOREM 22.7 "Is One CFL a Subset of Another?" is Undecidable

Theorem: The language $\{<G_1, G_2> : G_1$ and G_2 are context-free grammars and $L(G_1) \subseteq L(G_2)\}$ is not in D.

Proof: The proof is by reduction from $GG_=$ and is left as an exercise.

The undecidability of so many questions about context-free languages makes optimizing programs to work with them more difficult than optimizing FSMs. For example, in Chapter 5 we described an algorithm for minimizing DFSMs. But now, in discussing context-free languages and PDAs, we must accept that the problem of determining whether one PDA is a minimization of another, is undecidable. This result can be proved quite easily by reduction from CFG_{ALL}.

THEOREM 22.8 "Is One PDA a Minimization of Another?" is Undecidable

Theorem: The language $PDA_{MIN} = \{<M_1, M_2>$: PDA M_2 is a minimization of PDA $M_1\}$ is undecidable.

Proof: We show that $CFG_{ALL} \leq_M PDA_{MIN}$ and so PDA_{MIN} is not in D. Before we start the reduction, recall that M_2 is a minimization of M_1 iff:

$$(L(M_1) = L(M_2)) \wedge M_2 \text{ is minimal.}$$

Let R be a mapping reduction from CFG_{ALL} to PDA_{MIN} defined as follows:

$R(<G>) =$

1. Invoke *cfgtoPDAtopdown*(G) to construct the description $<P>$ of a PDA that accepts the language that G generates.
2. Write $<P\#>$ such that $P\#$ is a PDA with a single state s that is both the start state and an accepting state. Make a transition from s back to itself on each input symbol. Never push anything onto the stack. Note that $L(P\#) = \Sigma^*$ and $P\#$ is minimal.
3. Return $<P, P\#>$.

If *Oracle* exists and decides PDA_{MIN}, then $C = Oracle(R(\langle G \rangle))$ decides CFG_{ALL}. *R* can be implemented as a Turing machine. And *C* is correct:

- If $\langle G \rangle \in CFG_{ALL}: L(G) = \Sigma^*$. So $L(P) = \Sigma^*$. Since $L(P\#) = \Sigma^*$, $L(P) = L(P\#)$. And $P\#$ is minimal. Thus $P\#$ is a minimization of *P*. $Oracle(\langle P, P\# \rangle)$ accepts.
- If $\langle G \rangle \notin CFG_{ALL}$: $L(G) \neq \Sigma^*$. So $L(P) \neq \Sigma^*$. But $L(P\#) = \Sigma^*$. So $L(P) \neq L(P\#)$. So $Oracle(\langle P, P\# \rangle)$ rejects.

But no machine to decide CFG_{ALL} can exist, so neither does *Oracle*.

22.5.3 Reductions from PCP

Several of the context-free language problems that we listed at the beginning of this section can be shown not to be decidable by showing that the Post Correspondence Problem is reducible to them. The key observation that forms the basis for those reductions is the following: Consider *P*, a particular instance of PCP. If *P* has a solution, then there is a sequence of indexes that makes it possible to generate the same string from the *X* list and from the *Y* list. If there isn't a solution, then there is no such sequence.

We start by defining a mapping between instances of PCP and context-free grammars. Recall that, given some nonempty alphabet Σ, an instance of PCP is a string of the form:

$$\langle P \rangle = (x_1, x_2, x_3, \ldots, x_n)(y_1, y_2, y_3, \ldots, y_n), \text{ where } \forall j\, (x_j \in \Sigma^+ \text{ and } y_j \in \Sigma^+).$$

To encode solutions to *P*, we'll need a way to represent the integers that correspond to the indexes. Since all the integers must be in the range $1{:}n$, we can do this with *n* symbols. So let Σ_n be a set of *n* symbols such that $\Sigma \cap \Sigma_n = \varnothing$. We'll use the jth element of Σ_n to encode the integer *j*.

Given any PCP instance *P*, we'll define a grammar G_x that generates one string for every candidate solution to *P*. The string will have a second half that is the sequence of indices that is the solution, except that that sequence will be reversed. The first half of the string will be the concatenation of the elements from the *X* list that were selected by the indices. So suppose that $x_1 =$ aaa, $x_2 =$ bbc, and $x_3 =$ dd. Then the index sequence 1, 2, 3 would produce the string aaabbcdd. So G_x will generate the string aaabbcdd321. (Note that the index sequence appears reversed.) We'll also build the grammar G_y, which does the same thing for the sequences that can be formed from the *Y* list. Note that there is no commitment at this point that any of the strings generated by either G_x or G_y corresponds to a solution of *P*. What we'll see in a moment is that a string *s* corresponds to such a solution iff it is generated by both G_x and G_y.

More formally, for any PCP instance *P*, define the following two grammars G_x and G_y:

- $G_x = (\{S_x\} \cup \Sigma \cup \Sigma_n, \Sigma \cup \Sigma_n, R_x, S_x)$, where R_x contains the following two rules for each value of *i* between 1 and *n*:

$$S_x \rightarrow x_i S_x i$$

$$S_x \rightarrow x_i i$$

In both rules, *i* is represented by the ith element of Σ_n.

- $G_y = (\{S_y\} \cup \Sigma \cup \Sigma_n\}, \Sigma \cup \Sigma_n, R_y, S_y)$, where R_y contains the following two rules for each value of i between 1 and n:

$$S_y \rightarrow y_i S_y i$$
$$S_y \rightarrow y_i i$$

In both rules, i is represented by the ith element of Σ_n.

Every string that G_x generates will be of the form $x_{i_1} x_{i_2} \ldots x_{i_k} (i_1, i_2, \ldots i_k)^{\text{R}}$. Every string that G_y generates will be of the form $y_{i_1} y_{i_2} \ldots y_{i_k} (i_1, i_2, \ldots i_k)^{\text{R}}$.

Any solution to P is a finite sequence $i_1, i_2, \ldots i_k$ of integers such that:

$$\forall j (1 \leq i_j \leq n \text{ and } x_{i_1} x_{i_2} \ldots x_{i_k} = y_{i_1} y_{i_2} \ldots y_{i_k}).$$

If any such solution $i_1, i_2, \ldots i_k$ exists, let $w = x_{i_1} x_{i_2} \ldots x_{i_k} = y_{i_1} y_{i_2} \ldots y_{i_k}$. Then both G_x and G_y will generate the string:

$$w(i_1, i_2, \ldots i_k)^R.$$

EXAMPLE 22.6 Defining Grammars for a PCP Instance

Consider PCP_4, defined as follows:

i	X	Y
1	b	bab
2	abb	b
3	aba	a
4	bbaaa	babaaa

PCP_4 is represented as the string (b, abb, aba, bbaaa)(bab, b, a, babaaa).

The rules in G_x	The rules in G_y
$S_x \rightarrow$ bS_x1, $S_x \rightarrow$ b1,	$S_y \rightarrow$ babS_y1, $S_y \rightarrow$ bab1,
$S_x \rightarrow$ abbS_x2, $S_x \rightarrow$ abb2,	$S_y \rightarrow$ bS_y2, $S_y \rightarrow$ b2,
$S_x \rightarrow$ aba S_x3, $S_x \rightarrow$ aba3	$S_y \rightarrow$ aS_y3, $S_y \rightarrow$ a3
$S_x \rightarrow$ bbaaa S_x4, $S_x \rightarrow$ bbaaa4	$S_y \rightarrow$ babaaaS_y4, $S_y \rightarrow$ babaaa4

G_x generates strings of the form $w\ v^R$, where w is a sequence of strings from column X and v is the sequence of indices that were used to form w. G_y does the same for strings from column Y. So, for example, since 1, 2, 3, 1 is a solution to PCP_4, G_x can generate the following string (with blanks inserted to show the structure and with the index sequence reversed):

b abb aba b 1321

G_y can also generate that string, although it derives it differently:

bab b a bab 1321

Using the ideas that we have just described, we are ready to show that some significant questions about the context-free languages are undecidable. We'll do so by converting each question to a language and then exhibiting a reduction from PCP = {<P> : *P* has a solution} to that language.

THEOREM 22.9 "Is the Intersection of Two CFLs Empty?" is Undecidable

Theorem: The language IntEmpty = {<G_1, G_2> : G_1 and G_2 are context-free grammars and $L(G_1) \cap L(G_2) = \varnothing$} is not in D.

Proof: We show that IntEmpty is not in D by reduction from PCP = {<P> : *P* has a solution}. The reduction we will use exploits two functions, R and $\neg$. R will map instances of PCP to instances of IntEmpty. As before, $\neg$ will simply invert *Oracle*'s response (turning an *Accept* into a *Reject* and vice versa).

Define R as follows:

R(<P>) =

1. From P construct G_x and G_y as described above.
2. Return <G_x, G_y>.

{R, $\neg$} is a reduction from PCP to IntEmpty. If *Oracle* exists and decides IntEmpty, then $C = \neg$*Oracle*(R(<P>)) decides PCP. R and $\neg$ can be implemented as Turing machines. And C is correct:

- If <P> $\in$ PCP: P has at least one solution. So both G_x and G_y will generate some string:

$$w(i_1, i_2, \ldots i_k)^R, \text{ where } w = x_{i_1}x_{i_2}\ldots x_{i_k} = y_{i_1}y_{i_2}\ldots y_{i_k}$$

  So $L(G_1) \cap L(G_2) \neq \varnothing$. *Oracle*(<$G_x$, G_y>) rejects, so C accepts.

- If <P> $\notin$ PCP: P has no solution. So there is no string that can be generated by both G_x and G_y. So $L(G_1) \cap L(G_2) = \varnothing$. *Oracle*(<$G_x$, G_y>) accepts, so C rejects.

But no machine to decide PCP can exist, so neither does *Oracle*.

In Chapter 11 we spent a good deal of time worrying about whether the context-free grammars that we built were unambiguous. Yet we never gave an algorithm to determine whether or not a context-free grammar was ambiguous. Now we can understand why. No such algorithm exists.

THEOREM 22.10 "Is a CFG Ambiguous?" is Undecidable

Theorem: The language $\text{CFG}_{\text{UNAMBIG}} = \{<G> : G$ is a context-free grammar and G is ambiguous$\}$ is not in D.

Proof: We show that $\text{PCP} \leq_M \text{CFG}_{\text{UNAMBIG}}$ and so $\text{CFG}_{\text{UNAMBIG}}$ is not in D. Let R be a mapping reduction from PCP to $\text{CFG}_{\text{UNAMBIG}}$ defined as follows:

$R(<P>) =$

1. From P construct G_x and G_y as described above.
2. Construct G as follows:
   - 2.1. Add to G all the symbols and rules of both G_x and G_y.
   - 2.2. Add a new start symbol S and the two rules $S \rightarrow S_x$ and $S \rightarrow S_y$.
3. Return $<G>$.

G generates $L(G_1) \cup L(G_2)$. Further, it does so by generating all the derivations that G_1 can produce as well as all the ones that G_2 can produce, except that each has a prepended $S \Rightarrow S_x$ or $S \Rightarrow S_y$.

If *Oracle* exists and decides $\text{CFG}_{\text{UNAMBIG}}$, then $C = Oracle(R(<P>))$ decides PCP. R can be implemented as a Turing machine. And C is correct:

- If $<P> \in$ PCP: P has at least one solution. So both G_x and G_y will generate some string:

  $$w(i_1, i_2, \ldots i_k)^R, \text{ where } w = x_{i_1}x_{i_2}\ldots x_{i_k} = y_{i_1}y_{i_2}\ldots y_{i_k}$$

  So G can generate that string in two different ways. G is ambiguous. *Oracle*($<G>$) accepts.

- If $<P> \notin$ PCP: P has no solution. So there is no string that can be generated by both G_x and G_y. Since both G_x and G_y are unambiguous, so is G. *Oracle*($<G>$) rejects.

But no machine to decide PCP can exist, so neither does *Oracle*.

Exercises

1. Solve the linear Diophantine farmer problem presented in Section 22.1.
2. Consider the following instance of the Post Correspondence Problem. Does it have a solution? If so, show one.

i	X	Y
1	a	bab
2	bbb	bb
3	aab	ab
4	b	a

3. Prove that, if we consider only PCP instances with a single character alphabet, PCP is decidable.
4. Prove that, if an instance of the Post Correspondence Problem has a solution, it has an infinite number of solutions.
5. Recall that the size of an instance P of the Post Correspondence Problem is the number of strings in its X list. Consider the following claim about the Post Correspondence problem: For any n, if P is a PCP instance of size n and if no string in either its X or its Y list is longer than n, then, if P has any solutions, it has one of length less than or equal to 2^n. Is this claim true or false? Prove your answer.
6. Let TILES = $\{<T>$: any finite surface on the plane can be tiled, according to the rules described in the book, with the tile set $T\}$. Let s be the string that encodes the following tile set:

Is $s \in$ TILES? Prove your answer.
7. For each of the following languages L, state whether or not it is in D and prove your answer.
   a. $\{<G> : G$ is a context-free grammar and $\varepsilon \in L(G)\}$.
   b. $\{<G> : G$ is a context-free grammar and $\{\varepsilon\} = L(G)\}$.
   c. $\{<G_1, G_2> : G_1$ and G_2 are context-free grammars and $L(G_1) \subseteq L(G_2)\}$.
   d. $\{<G> : G$ is a context-free grammar and $\neg L(G)$ is context free$\}$.
   e. $\{<G> : G$ is a context-free grammar and $L(G)$ is regular$\}$.

CHAPTER 23

Unrestricted Grammars ◆

Consider a language like $A^nB^nC^n = \{a^nb^nc^n : n \geq 0\}$. We know that we cannot write a context-free grammar for it. But could we create a new grammar formalism that is powerful enough to describe it and other languages like it? The answer to this question is yes. Recall that we moved from the power to define the regular languages to the power to define the context-free languages by removing constraints on the form of the rules that are allowed. We will do that again now. This time we will remove all constraints. We will prove that the class of languages that can be generated by one of these new, unrestricted grammars is exactly SD.

23.1 Definition and Examples

An ***unrestricted grammar*** G is a quadruple (V, Σ, R, S), where:

- V is an alphabet that may contain terminal and nonterminal symbols,
- Σ (the set of terminals) is a subset of V,
- R (the set of rules) is a finite subset of $V^+ \times V^*$,
- S (the start symbol) is an element of $V - \Sigma$.

Note that now the right-hand side of a rule may contain multiple symbols. So we might, have, for example:

$$a X a \rightarrow a\ a\ a$$
$$b X b \rightarrow a\ b\ a$$

In this case, the derivation of X depends on its context. It is thus common to call rules like this "context-sensitive." We will avoid using this terminology, however, because in the next chapter we will describe another formalism that we will call a context-sensitive grammar. While it, too, allows rules such as these, it does impose one important constraint that is lacking in the definition of an unrestricted grammar. It is thus less powerful, in a formal sense, than the system that we are describing here.

An unrestricted grammar G (just like a context-free grammar) derives strings by applying rules, beginning with its start symbol. So, to describe its behavior, we define the *derives-in-one-step* relation ($\Rightarrow$) analogously to the way we defined it for context-free grammars. Given a grammar $G = (V, \Sigma, R, S)$, define $x \Rightarrow_G y$ to be a binary relation such that:

$$\begin{aligned}\forall x, y \in V^*(x \Rightarrow_G y \text{ iff } x &= \alpha\beta\phi,\\ y &= \alpha\gamma\phi,\\ &\alpha, \phi, \text{and } \gamma \in V^*,\\ &\beta \in V^+, \text{and}\\ &\text{there is a rule } \beta \rightarrow \gamma \text{ in } R).\end{aligned}$$

Any sequence of the form $w_0 \Rightarrow_G w_1 \Rightarrow_G w_2 \Rightarrow_G \ldots \Rightarrow_G w_n$ is called a derivation in G. As before, $\Rightarrow_G{}^*$ is the reflexive, transitive closure of $\Rightarrow_G$.

The language generated by G is $\{w \in \Sigma^* : S \Rightarrow_G {}^*w\}$. So, just as before, $L(G)$ is the set of all strings of terminal symbols derivable from S via the rules of G.

Unrestricted grammars are sometimes called ***phrase structure grammars*** or ***type 0 grammars***, the latter because of their place in the Chomsky hierarchy (which we will describe in Section 24.2). Some books also use the term ***semi-Thue system*** synonymously with unrestricted grammar. While the two formalisms are very similar, they model different computational processes and so must be considered separately. We will describe semi-Thue systems in Section 23.5.

EXAMPLE 23.1 $A^nB^nC^n$

Consider $A^nB^nC^n = \{a^nb^nc^n : n \geq 0\}$. We build a grammar $G = (V, \{a, b, c\}, R, S)$, where V and R are as described below and $L(G) = A^nB^nC^n$. We first observe that any grammar for $A^nB^nC^n$ must generate all and only those strings with two properties:

- equal numbers of a's, b's, and c's, and
- letters in the correct order.

Just as with context-free grammars, the only way to guarantee that there are equal numbers of a's, b's, and c's is to generate them in parallel. The problem, though, is that there is no way to generate them in the correct order. For example, we could try a rule like:

$$S \rightarrow abSc$$

But if we apply that rule twice, we will generate the string ababScc. So what we will have to do is to generate each string in two phases:

1. Generate the correct number of each symbol.
2. Move the symbols around until they are in the correct order. This is the step that is possible in an unrestricted grammar but was not possible in a context-free one.

But we must be careful. As soon as G has generated a string that contains only terminal symbols, it is done, and that string is in $L(G)$. So we must make sure that, until the string is ready, it still contains at least one nonterminal. We can do that by creating one or more nonterminals that will stand in for their corresponding terminals and will be replaced once they have been moved into position. We'll use one such symbol, B.

We begin building the rules of G by inserting into R two rules that will generate strings with equal numbers of a's, b's, and c's:

1. $S \rightarrow$ aBSc
2. $S \rightarrow \varepsilon$

To generate the string $\mathrm{a}^i\mathrm{b}^i\mathrm{c}^i$, we will apply rule 1 i times. Then we will apply rule 2 once. Suppose we want to generate $\mathrm{a}^3\mathrm{b}^3\mathrm{c}^3$. Then we will apply rule 1 three times, then rule 2 once, and we will generate aBaBaBccc. Because of the nonterminal symbol B, this string is not an element of $L(G)$. We still have the opportunity to rearrange the symbols, which we can do by adding one swapping rule:

3. Ba $\rightarrow$ aB

Rule 3 can be applied as many times as necessary to push all the a's to the front of the string. But what *forces* it to be applied? The answer is the B's. Until all the B's are gone, the string that has been generated is not in $L(G)$. So we need rules to transform each B into b. We must design those rules so that they cannot be applied to any B until it is where it belongs. We can assure that with the following two rules:

4. Bc $\rightarrow$ bc
5. Bb $\rightarrow$ bb

Rule 4 transforms the rightmost B into b. Rule 5 transforms a B if it has an already transformed b directly to its right.

Having written a grammar such as the one we just built for $\mathrm{A}^n\mathrm{B}^n\mathrm{C}^n$, can we prove that it is correct (i.e., that it generates exactly the strings in the target language?) Yes. Just as with a context-free grammar, we can prove that a grammar G is correct by:

1. showing that G generates *only* strings in L, and
2. showing that G generates *all* the strings in L.

We show 1 by defining an invariant I that is true of S and is maintained each time a rule in G is fired. Call the string that is being derived *st*. Then to prove the correctness of the grammar we just showed for $\mathrm{A}^n\mathrm{B}^n\mathrm{C}^n$, we let I be:

$\#_{\mathrm{a}}(st) = \#_{\mathrm{b}}(st) + \#_{B}(st) = \#_{\mathrm{c}}(st) \wedge$ all c's occur to the right of all a's, b's, and B's $\wedge$ all b's occur together and immediately to the left of the c region.

We show 2 by induction on n. Both of these steps are straightforward in this simple case. The same general strategy works for other unrestricted grammars, but it may be substantially more difficult to implement.

Next we consider another two examples of unrestricted grammars so that we can get a better idea of how they work.

EXAMPLE 23.2 Equal Numbers of a's, b's and c's

Let $L = \{w \in \{a, b, c\}^* : \#_a(w) = \#_b(w) = \#_c(w)\}$. We build a grammar $G = (V, \{a, b, c\}, R, S)$, where V and R are as described below and $L(G) = L$. L is similar to $A^nB^nC^n$ except that the letters may occur in any order. So, again, we will begin by generating matched sets of a's, b's, and c's. But, this time, we need to allow the second phase of the grammar to perform arbitrary permutations of the characters. So we will start with the rules:

1. $S \rightarrow ABSC$
2. $S \rightarrow \varepsilon$

Next we need to allow arbitrary permutations, so we add the rules:

3. $AB \rightarrow BA$
4. $BA \rightarrow AB$
5. $AC \rightarrow CA$
6. $CA \rightarrow AC$
7. $BC \rightarrow CB$
8. $CB \rightarrow BC$

Finally, we need to generate terminal symbols. Remember that every rule in G must have at least one nonterminal on its left-hand side. In contrast to $A^nB^nC^n$, here the job of the nonterminals is not to *force* reordering but to *enable* it. This means that a nonterminal symbol can be replaced by its corresponding terminal symbol at any time. So we add the rules:

9. $A \rightarrow$ a
10. $B \rightarrow$ b
11. $C \rightarrow$ c

EXAMPLE 23.3 WW

Consider WW $= \{ww : w \in \{a, b\}^*\}$. We build a grammar $G = (V, \{a, b\}, R, S)$, where V and R are as described below and $L(G) =$ WW. The strategy we will use is the following:

1. Generate $w\,C\,w^R\#$, where C will serve as a temporary middle marker and # will serve as a temporary right boundary. This is easy to do with a context-free grammar.
2. Reverse w^R. We will do that by viewing # as a wall and jumping the characters in w^R, *leftmost first*, over the wall.
3. Finally, clean up by removing C and #.

Suppose that, after step 1, we have aab$C$baa#. We let C spawn a pusher P, yielding:

aabCPbaa#.

The job of P is to push the character just to its right rightward to the wall so that it can hop over. To do this, we will write rules that swap Pb with each character between it and the wall. Those rules will generate the following sequence of strings:

aab$C$aPba#

aab$C$aa$P$b#

The last step in getting the pushed character (in this case, b) where it belongs is to jump it over the wall and then erase P, yielding:

aab$C$aa#b

Next, C will spawn another pusher P and use it to push the first a up to the wall. At that point, we will have:

aab$C$aPa#b

Then a jumps the wall, landing immediately after it, yielding:

aab$C$a#ab

Notice that the substring ba has now become ab, as required. Now the remaining a can be pushed and jumped, yielding:

aab$C$#aab

The final step is to erase C# as soon as they become adjacent to each other.

The following set of rules R implements this plan:

$S \rightarrow T\#$	/* Generate the wall exactly once.
$T \rightarrow$ aTa	/* Generate wCw^R.
$T \rightarrow$ bTb	"
$T \rightarrow C$	"
$C \rightarrow CP$	/* Generate a pusher P.

$Paa \rightarrow aPa$	/* Push one character to the right to get ready to jump.
$Pab \rightarrow bPa$	"
$Pba \rightarrow aPb$	"
$Pbb \rightarrow bPb$	"
$Pa\# \rightarrow \#a$	/* Hop a character over the wall.
$Pb\# \rightarrow \#b$	"
$C\# \rightarrow \varepsilon$	

We have described the way that we want G to work. It clearly can do exactly what we have said it will do. But can we be sure that it does nothing else? Remember that, at any point, any rule whose left-hand side matches can be applied. So, for example, what prevents C from spawning a new pusher P before the first character has jumped the wall? Nothing. But the correctness of G is not affected by this. Pushers (and the characters they are pushing) cannot jump over each other. If C spawns more pushers than are necessary, the resulting string cannot be transformed into a string containing just terminal symbols. So any path that does that dies without generating any strings in $L(G)$.

If we want to decrease the number of dead-end paths that a grammar G can generate, we can write rules that have more restrictive left-hand sides. So, for example, we could replace the rule:

$C \rightarrow CP$	/* Generate a pusher P.

with the rules:

$Ca \rightarrow CPa$	/* Generate a pusher P.
$Cb \rightarrow CPb$	"

Now C can only generate one pusher for each character in w^R.

Unrestricted grammars often have a strong procedural feel that is typically absent from restricted grammars. Derivations usually proceed in phases. When we design a grammar G, we make sure that the phases work properly by using nonterminals as flags that tell G what phase it is in. It is very common to have three phases:

- Generate the right number of the various symbols.
- Move them around to get them in the right order.
- Clean up.

In implementing these phases, there are some quite common idioms:

- Begin by creating a left wall, a right wall, or both.
- Reverse a substring by pushing the characters, one at a time, across the wall at the opposite end from where the first character originated.

- Use nonterminals to represent terminals that need additional processing (such as shifting from one place to another) before the final string should be generated.

Now that we have seen the extent to which unrestricted grammars can feel like programs, it may come as no surprise that they are general purpose computing devices. In Section 23.3 we will show how they can be used not just to define languages but also to compute functions. But first we will show that the class of languages that can be generated by an unrestricted grammar is exactly SD. So, sadly, although these grammars can be used to define decidable languages like $A^nB^nC^n$, unfortunately there is no parsing algorithm for them. Given an unrestricted grammar G and a string w, it is undecidable whether G generates w. We will prove that in Section 23.2.

23.2 Equivalence of Unrestricted Grammars and Turing Machines

Recall that, in our discussion of the Church-Turing thesis, we mentioned several formalisms that can be shown to be equivalent to Turing machines. We can now add unrestricted grammars to our list.

> Since rewrite systems can have the same computational power as the Turing machine, they have been used to define programming languages such as Prolog. (M.2.3)

THEOREM 23.1 Turing Machines and Unrestricted Grammars Describe the Same Class of Languages

Theorem: A language L is generated by an unrestricted grammar iff it is semidecided by some Turing machine M.

Proof: We will prove each direction of this claim separately:

a. We show that the existence of an unrestricted grammar G for L implies the existence of a semideciding Turing machine for L. We do this by construction of a nondeterministic Turing machine that, on input x, simulates applying the rules of G, checking at each step to see whether G has generated x.

b. We show that the existence of a semideciding Turing machine M for L implies the existence of an unrestricted grammar for L. We do this by construction of a grammar that mimics the execution of M.

Proof of Claim a: Given an unrestricted grammar $G = (V, \Sigma, R, S)$, we construct a nondeterministic Turing machine M that semidecides $L(G)$. The idea is that M, on input x, will start with S, apply rules in R, and see whether it can generate x. If it ever does, it will halt and accept. M will be nondeterministic so that it can try all possible derivations in G. Each nondeterministic branch will use two tapes:

- Tape 1 holds M's input string x.
- Tape 2 holds the string that has so far been derived using G.

At each step, M nondeterministically chooses a rule to try to apply and a position on tape 2 to start looking for the left-hand side of the rule. If the rule's left-hand side matches, M applies the rule. Then it checks whether tape 2 equals tape 1. If any such branch succeeds in generating x, M accepts. Otherwise, it keeps looking. If a branch generates a string to which no rules in R can apply, it rejects. So some branch of M accepts iff there is a derivation of x in G. Thus M semidecides $L(G)$.

Proof of Claim b: Given a semideciding Turing machine $M = (K, \Sigma, \Gamma, \delta, s, H)$, we construct an unrestricted grammar $G = (\{\#, \text{q}, 0, 1, \text{A}\} \cup \Gamma, \Sigma, R, S)$ such that $L(G) = L(M)$. The idea is that G will exploit a generate-and-test strategy in which it first creates candidate strings in Σ^* and then simulates running M on them. If there is some string s that M would accept, then G will cleanup its working symbols and generate s. G operates in three phases:

- Phase 1 can generate all strings of the following form, where qs is the binary encoding in <M> of M's start state, n is any positive integer, and each of the characters a_1 through a_n is in Σ^*:

  $$\# \square \square \text{ q}s\ a_1 a_1 a_2 a_2 a_3 a_3 \ldots a_n a_n \square \square \#$$

  The #'s will enable G to exploit rules that need to locate the beginning and the end of the string that it has derived so that they can scan the string. The rest of the string directly encodes M's state and the contents of its tape (with each tape symbol duplicated). It also encodes the position of M's read/write head by placing the encoding of the state immediately to the left of the character under the read/write head. So the strings that are generated in Phase 1 can be used in Phase 2 to begin simulating M, starting in state qs, with the string $a_1 a_2 a_3 \ldots a_n$ on its tape and the read/write head positioned immediately to the left of a_1. Each character on the tape is duplicated so that G can use the second instance as though it were on the tape, writing on top of it as necessary. Then, if M accepts, G will use the first instance to reconstruct the input string that was accepted.

- Phase 2 simulates the execution of M on a particular string w. So, for example, suppose that Phase 1 generated the following string:

  # □ □ q000 a a b b c c b b a a □ □ #

  Then Phase 2 begins simulating M on the string abcba. The rules of G are constructed from δ_M. At some point, G might generate

  # □ □ a 1 b 2 c c b 4 q011 a 3 □ □ #

  if M, when invoked on abcba could be in state 3, with its tape equal to 12c43, and its read/write head positioned on top of the final 3.

To implement Phase 2, G contains one or more rules for each element of δ_M. The rules look like these:

`q100 b b → b 2 q101` /* If M, in state 4 looking at b, would rewrite it as 2, go to state 5, and move right.

`a a q011 b 4 → q011 a a b 4` /* If M, in state 3 looking at 4, would rewrite it as 4, go to state 3, and move left. Notice that to encode moving left we must create a separate rule for each pair of characters that could be to the left of the read/write head.

In Phase 2, all of M's states are encoded in their standard binary form except its accepting state(s), all of which will be encoded as A.

- Phase 3 cleans up by erasing all the working symbols if M ever reaches an accepting state. It will leave in its derived string only those symbols corresponding to the original string that M accepted. Once the derived string contains only terminal symbols, G halts and outputs the string.

To implement Phase 3, G contains one rule of the following form for each character other than A and # in its alphabet:

x A → A x /* If M ever reaches an accepting state, sweep A all the way to the left of the string until it is next to #.

It also has one rule of the following form for each pair x, y of characters other than A and #:

#A x y → x #A /* Sweep #A rightward, deleting the working copy of each symbol and keeping the original version.

And then it has the final rule:

#A# → ε /* At the end of the sweep, wipe out the last working symbols.

23.3 Grammars Compute Functions

We have now shown that grammars and Turing machines are equivalent in their power to define languages. But we also know that Turing machines can do something else: They can compute functions by leaving a meaningful result on their tape when they halt. Can unrestricted grammars do that as well? The answer is yes. Suppose that, instead of starting with just the start symbol S, we allow a grammar G to be invoked with some input string w. G would apply its rules as usual. If it then halted, having derived some new string w' that is the result of applying function f to w, we could say that G

computed f. The only details we need to work out are how to format the input so G will be able to work effectively and how to tell when G should halt.

We say that a grammar G ***computes*** f iff, $\forall w, v \in \Sigma^*(SwS \Rightarrow^* v \leftrightarrow v = f(w))$. We use G's start symbol S to solve both of the problems we just mentioned: S serves as a delimiter for the input string so that G will be able to perform actions like, "Start at the left-hand end of the string and move rightward doing something". And, as usual, G continues to apply rules until either there are no more rules that can be applied or the derived string is composed entirely of terminal symbols. So, to halt and report a result, G must continue until both delimiting S's are removed. A function f is called ***grammatically computable*** iff there is a grammar G that computes it.

Recall the family of functions, $value_k(n)$. For any positive integer k, $value_k(n)$ returns the natural number that is encoded, base k, by the string n. For example $value_2(101) = 5$.

EXAMPLE 23.4 Computing the Successor Function in Unary

Let f be the successor function $succ(n)$ on the unary representations of natural numbers. Specifically, define $f(n) = m$, where $value_1(m) = value_1(n) + 1$. If G is to compute f, it will need to produce derivations such as:

$$S1S \Rightarrow^* 11$$

$$S1111S \Rightarrow^* 11111$$

We need to design G so that it adds exactly one more 1 to the input string and gets rid of both S's. The following two-rule grammar $G = (\{S, 1\}, \{1\}, R, S)$ does that with $R =$

$S11 \rightarrow 1S1$	/* Move the first S rightward past all but the last 1.
$S1S \rightarrow 11$	/* When it reaches the last 1, add a 1 and remove the S's.

EXAMPLE 23.5 Multiplying by 2 in Unary

Let $f(n) = m$, where $value_1(m) = 2 \cdot value_1(n)$. G should produce derivations such as:

$$S11S \Rightarrow^* 1111$$

$$S1111S \Rightarrow^* 11111111$$

G needs to go through its input string, turning every 1 into 11. Again, a simple two-rule grammar $G = (\{S, 1\}, \{1\}, R, S)$ is sufficient, with $R =$

$S1 \rightarrow 11S$	/* Starting from the left, duplicate a 1. Shift the initial S so that only the 1's that still need to be duplicated are on its right.
$SS \rightarrow \varepsilon$	/* When all 1's have been duplicated, stop.

EXAMPLE 23.6 Squeezing Out Extra Blanks

Let $f(x\colon x \in \{\mathrm{a}, \mathrm{b}, \square\}^*) = x$ except that extra blanks will be squeezed out. More specifically, blanks will be removed so that there is never more than one ❑ between "words", i.e., sequences of a's and b's, and there are no leading or trailing ❑'s}. G should produce derivations such as:

$$S\mathrm{aa}\square\mathrm{b}\square\square\mathrm{aa}\square\square\square\square\mathrm{b}\square S \Rightarrow^* \mathrm{aa}\square\mathrm{b}\square\mathrm{aa}\square\mathrm{b}$$

$$S\square\mathrm{aa}\square\mathrm{b}\square\square\mathrm{aa}\square\mathrm{b}\square\square S \Rightarrow^* \mathrm{aa}\square\mathrm{b}\square\mathrm{aa}\square\mathrm{b}$$

This time, G is more complex. It must reduce every ❑❑ string to ❑. And it must get rid of *all* ❑'s that occur adjacent to either S.

$G = (\{S, T, \mathrm{a}, \mathrm{b}, \square\}, \{\mathrm{a}, \mathrm{b}, \square\}, R, S)$, where $R =$

$S\square \rightarrow S$	/* Get rid of leading ❑'s. *All* blanks get squeezed, not just repeated ones.
$SS \rightarrow \varepsilon$	/* In case there are no nonblank characters.
$S\mathrm{a} \rightarrow \mathrm{a}T$	/* T replaces S to indicate that we are no longer in a leading ❑'s region. For the rest of G's operation, all characters to the left of T will be correct. Those to the right still need to be processed.
$S\mathrm{b} \rightarrow \mathrm{b}T$	"
$T\mathrm{a} \rightarrow \mathrm{a}T$	/* Sweep T across a's and b's.
$T\mathrm{b} \rightarrow \mathrm{b}T$	"
$T\square\square \rightarrow T\square$	/* Squeeze repeated ❑'s.
$T\square\mathrm{a} \rightarrow \square\mathrm{a}T$	/* Once there is a single ❑, sweep T past it and the first letter after it.
$T\square\mathrm{b} \rightarrow \square\mathrm{b}T$	"
$T\square S \rightarrow \varepsilon$	/* The $T\square\square$ rule will get rid of all but possibly one ❑ at the end of the string.
$TS \rightarrow \varepsilon$	/* If there were no trailing ❑'s, this rule finishes up.

From this last example, it is easy to see how we can construct a grammar G to compute some function f. G can work in very much the way a Turing machine would, sweeping back and forth through its string. In fact, it is often easier to build a grammar to compute a function than it is to build a Turing machine because, with grammars, we do not have to worry about shifting the string if we want to add or delete characters from somewhere in the middle.

Recall that in Section 17.2.2, we defined a ***computable function*** to be a function that can be computed by a Turing machine that always halts and, on input x, leaves $f(x)$ on its tape. We now have an alternative definition:

THEOREM 23.2 Turing Machines and Unrestricted Grammars Compute the Same Class of Functions

Theorem: A function f is computable iff it is grammatically computable. In other words a function f can be computed by a Turing machine iff there is an unrestricted grammar that computes it.

Proof: The proof requires two constructions. The first shows that, for any grammar G, there is a Turing machine M that simulates G, halts whenever G produces a terminal string s, and leaves s on its tape when it halts. The second shows the other direction: For any Turing machine M, there is a grammar G that simulates M and produces a terminal string s whenever M halts with s on its tape. These constructions are similar to the ones we used to prove Theorem 23.1. We omit the details.

23.4 Undecidable Problems About Unrestricted Grammars

Consider the following questions that we might want to ask about unrestricted grammars:

- Given an unrestricted grammar G and a string w, is $w \in L(G)$?
- Given an unrestricted grammar G, is $\varepsilon \in L(G)$?
- Given two unrestricted grammars G_1 and G_2, is $L(G_1) = L(G_2)$?
- Given an unrestricted grammar G, is $L(G) = \varnothing$?

Does there exist a decision procedure to answer any of these questions? Or, formulating these problems as language recognition tasks, are any of these languages decidable?

- $L_a = \{<G, w> : G$ is an unrestricted grammar and $w \in L(G)\}$
- $L_b = \{<G> : G$ is an unrestricted grammar and $\varepsilon \in L(G)\}$
- $L_c = \{<G_1, G_2> : G_1$ and G_2 are unrestricted grammars and $L(G_1) = L(G_2)\}$
- $L_d = \{<G> : G$ is an unrestricted grammar and $L(G) = \varnothing\}$

The answer to all these questions is, "no". If any of these problems involving grammars were solvable, then the corresponding problem involving Turing machines would also be solvable. But it isn't. We can prove each of these cases by reduction. We will do one here and leave the others as exercises. They are very similar.

THEOREM 23.3 Undecidability of Unrestricted Grammars

Theorem: The language $L_a = \{<G, w> : G$ is an unrestricted grammar and $w \in L(G)\}$ is not in D.

Proof: We show that $A \leq_M L_a$ and so L_a is not decidable. Let R be a mapping reduction from $A = \{<M, w> : \text{Turing machine } M \text{ accepts } w\}$ to L_a, defined as follows:

$R(<M, w>) =$

1. From M, construct the description $<G\#>$ of a grammar $G\#$ such that $L(G\#) = L(M)$.
2. Return $<G\#, w>$.

If *Oracle* exists and decides L_a, then $C = Oracle(R(<M, w>))$ decides A. R can be implemented as a Turing machine using the algorithm presented in Section 23.2. And C is correct:

- If $<M, w> \in A$: $M(w)$ halts and accepts. $w \in L(M)$. So $w \in L(G\#)$. $Oracle(<G\#, w>)$ accepts.
- If $<M, w> \notin A$: $M(w)$ does not accept. $w \notin L(M)$. So $w \notin L(G\#)$. $Oracle(<G\#, w>)$ rejects.

But no machine to decide A can exist, so neither does *Oracle*.

So, unrestricted grammars, although powerful, are very much less useful than context-free ones, since even the most basic question, "Given a string w, does G generate w?" is undecidable.

23.5 The Word Problem for Semi-Thue Systems

Unrestricted grammars can generate languages and they can compute functions. A third way of characterizing their computational power has played an important historical role in the development of formal language theory. Define a ***word problem*** to be the following:

> Given two strings, w and v, and a rewrite system T, determine whether v can be derived from w using T.

An important application of the word problem is in logical reasoning. If we can encode logical statements as strings (in the obvious way) and if we can also define a rewrite system T that corresponds to a set of inference rules, then determining whether v can be rewritten as w using T is equivalent to deciding whether the sentence that corresponds to v is entailed by the sentence that corresponds to w.

Any rewrite system whose job is to transform one string into another must to be able to start with an arbitrary string (not just some unique start symbol). Further, since both the starting string and the ending one may contain any symbols in the alphabet of the system, the distinction between terminal symbols and working symbols goes away. Making those two changes to the unrestricted grammar model we get:

A ***semi-Thue system*** T is a pair (Σ, R), where:

- Σ is an alphabet, and
- R (the set of rules) is a subset of $\Sigma^+ \times \Sigma^*$.

Semi-Thue systems were named after their inventor, the Norwegian mathematician Axel Thue. Just as an aside: A ***Thue system*** is a semi-Thue system with the additional property that, if R contains the rule $x \rightarrow y$, then it also contains the rule $y \rightarrow x$.

We define for semi-Thue systems the *derives-in-one-step* relation ($\Rightarrow_T$) and its transitive closure *derives* ($\Rightarrow_T{}^*$) exactly as we did for unrestricted grammars. Since there is no distinguished start symbol, it doesn't make sense to talk about the language that can be derived from a semi-Thue system. It does, however, make sense to talk about the word problem: Given a semi-Thue system T and two strings w and v, determine whether $w \Rightarrow_T{}^* v$. We have already seen that it is undecidable, for an unrestricted grammar with a distinguished start symbol S, whether S derives some arbitrary string w. So too it is undecidable, for a semi-Thue system, whether one arbitrary string can derive another.

THEOREM 23.4 Undecidability of the Word Problem for Semi-Thue Systems

Theorem: The word problem for semi-Thue systems is undecidable. In other words, given a semi-Thue system T and two strings w and v, it is undecidable whether $w \Rightarrow_T{}^* v$.

Proof: The proof is by reduction from the halting problem language H = $\{<M, w>$: Turing machine M halts on input string $w\}$. Given a Turing machine M and an input string w, we will build a semi-Thue system T with the property that M halts on w iff $w \Rightarrow_T{}^*$ S. The construction that is used in the reduction mirrors the construction that we used to prove (Theorem 23.1) that Turing machines and unrestricted grammars define the same class of languages. Given a Turing machine M, we first build a semi-Thue system T whose rules simulate the operation of M. Assume that the symbol S has not been used in the construction so far. We now add rules to T as follows:

- For every halting state q in M, add the rule $q \rightarrow$ S. These rules guarantee that, if M eventually enters some halting state, the symbol S will appear in a string derived by T. Since S is an otherwise unused symbol, that is the only case in which it will appear in a string that T derives.
- For every other symbol c in T's alphabet, add the rules cS $\rightarrow$ S and Sc $\rightarrow$ S. These rules enable T to transform any string containing the symbol S into a string that is just S.

So if, on input w, M would ever enter a halting state, the rules of T will enable w to derive some string that contains the symbol S. That string will then derive the string consisting of only S. And M entering a halting state is the only way to generate an S. So M halts on input w iff $w \Rightarrow_T^* \text{S}$. Thus, if the word problem were decidable, H would also be. But it isn't.

Exercises

1. Show an unrestricted grammar that generates each of the following languages.
   a. $\{a^{2^n}b^{2^n} : n \geq 0\}$
   b. $\{\text{a}^n\text{b}^m\text{c}^{n+m} : n, m > 0\}$
   c. $\{\text{a}^n\text{b}^m\text{c}^{nm} : n, m > 0\}$
   d. $\{\text{a}^n\text{b}^{2n}\text{c}^{3n} : n \geq 1\}$
   e. $\{ww^{\text{R}}w : w \in \{\text{a}, \text{b}\}^*\}$
   f. $\{\text{a}^n\text{b}^n\text{a}^n\text{b}^n : n \geq 0\}$
   g. $\{xy\#x^{\text{R}} : x, y \in \{\text{a}, \text{b}\}^* \text{ and } |x| = |y|\}$
   h. $\{w\text{c}^m\text{d}^n : w \in \{\text{a}, \text{b}\}^* \text{ and } m = \#_\text{a}(w) \text{ and } n = \#_\text{b}(w)\}$

2. Show a grammar that computes each of the following functions (given the input convention described in Section 23.3):
   a. f: $\{\text{a}, \text{b}\}^+ \rightarrow \{\text{a}, \text{b}\}^+$, where $f(s = \text{a}_1\text{a}_2\text{a}_3 \ldots \text{a}_{|s|}) = \text{a}_2\text{a}_3 \ldots \text{a}_{|s|}\text{a}_1$. For example $f(\text{aabbaa}) = \text{abbaaa}$.
   b. f: $\{\text{a}, \text{b}\}^+ \rightarrow \{\text{a}, \text{b}, 1\}^+$, where $f(s) = s1^n$, where $n = \#_\text{a}(s)$. For example $f(\text{aabbaa}) = \text{aabbaa1111}$.
   c. f: $\{\text{a}, \text{b}\}^*\#\{\text{a}, \text{b}\}^* \rightarrow \{\text{a}, \text{b}\}^*$, where $f(x\#y) = xy^{\text{R}}$.
   d. f: $\{\text{a}, \text{b}\}^+ \rightarrow \{\text{a}, \text{b}\}^+$, where $f(s) =$ if $\#_\text{a}(s)$ is even then s, else s^{R}.
   e. f: $\{\text{a}, \text{b}\}^* \rightarrow \{\text{a}, \text{b}\}^*$, where $f(w) = ww$.
   f. f: $\{\text{a}, \text{b}\}^+ \rightarrow \{\text{a}, \text{b}\}^*$, where $f(s) =$ if $|s|$ is even then s, else s with the middle character chopped out. (*Hint:* The answer to this one is fairly long, but it is not very complex. Think about how you would use a Turing machine to solve this problem.)
   g. $f(n) = m$, where $value_1(n)$ is a natural number and $value_1(m) = value_1(\lfloor n/2 \rfloor)$. Recall that $\lfloor x \rfloor$ (read as "floor of x") is the largest integer that is less than or equal to x.
   h. $f(n) = m$, where $value_2(n)$ is a natural number and $value_2(m) = value_2(n) + 5$.

3. Show that, if G, G_1 and G_2 are unrestricted grammars, then each of the following languages, defined in Section 23.4, is not in D:
   a. $L_\text{b} = \{<G> : \varepsilon \in L(G)\}$
   b. $L_\text{c} = \{<G_1, G_2> : L(G_1) = L(G_2)\}$
   c. $L_\text{d} = \{<G> : L(G) = \varnothing\}$

4. Show that, if G is an unrestricted grammar, then each of the following languages is not in D.

a. $\{\langle G\rangle : \text{a}^* \subseteq L(G)\}$

b. $\{\langle G\rangle : G \text{ is ambiguous}\}$ (*Hint*: Prove this by reduction from PCP.)

5. Let G be the unrestricted grammar for the language $\text{A}^n\text{B}^n\text{C}^n = \{\text{a}^n\text{b}^n\text{c}^n : n \geq 0\}$, shown in Example 23.1. Consider the proof, given in E.4, of the undecidability of the Post Correspondence Problem. The proof is by reduction from the membership problem for unrestricted grammars.

a. Define the MPCP instance *MP* that will be produced, given the input $\langle G, \text{abc}\rangle$, by the reduction that is defined in the proof of Theorem E.1.

b. Find a solution for *MP*.

c. Define the PCP instance *P* that will be built from *MP* by the reduction that is defined in the proof of Theorem E.2.

d. Find a solution for *P*.

CHAPTER 24

The Chomsky Hierarchy and Beyond ✸

So far, we have described a hierarchy of language classes, including the regular languages, the context-free languages, the decidable languages (D), and the semidecidable languages (SD). The smaller classes have useful properties, including efficiency and decidability, that the larger classes lack. But they are more limited in what they can do. In particular, PDAs are not powerful enough for most applications. But, to do better, we have jumped to Turing machines and, in so doing, have given up the ability to decide even the most straightforward questions.

The question naturally arises, "Are there other formalisms that can effectively describe useful languages?" The answer is yes and we will consider a few of them in this chapter.

24.1 The Context-Sensitive Languages

We would like a computational formalism that accepts exactly the set D. We have one: The set of Turing machines that always halt. But that set is itself undecidable. What we would like is a computational model that comes close to describing exactly the class D but that is itself decidable in the sense that we can look at a program and tell whether or not it is an instance of our model.

In this section we'll describe the ***context-sensitive languages***, which fit into our existing language hierarchy as shown in Figure 24.1. The context-sensitive languages can be decided by a class of automata called linear bounded automata. They can also be described by grammars we will call context-sensitive (because they allow multiple symbols on the left-hand sides of rules). The good news about the context-sensitive languages is that many interesting languages that are not context-free are context-sensitive. But the bad news is that, while a parsing algorithm for them does exist, no efficient one is known nor is one likely to be discovered.

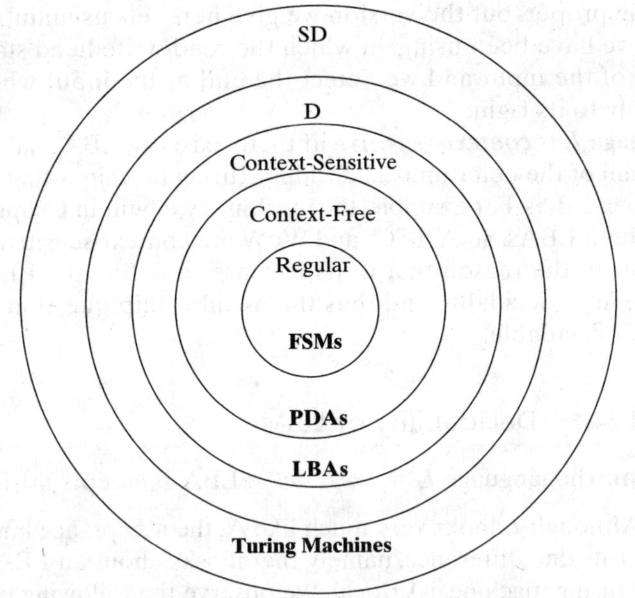

FIGURE 24.1 A hierarchy of language classes.

24.1.1 Linear Bounded Automata

There are two common definitions of a linear bounded automaton (or LBA). The crucial aspect of both is that an LBA is a Turing machine whose tape is limited by the length of its input. The two definitions can be stated informally as:

1. An LBA is a Turing machine that cannot move past the blank square on either side of its input.
2. An LBA is a Turing machine that cannot use more than $k \cdot |w|$ tape squares, where w is its input and k is some fixed positive integer.

The second definition seems, at first glance, to be less restrictive, since it allows for additional working space on the tape. But, in fact, the two definitions are equivalent, since we can implement a definition$_2$ LBA as a definition$_1$ LBA whose tape is divided into tracks to simulate k tapes. So it is just a tradeoff between more tape squares and a larger tape alphabet. Because the first definition is slightly simpler, we will use it.

A ***linear bounded automaton*** (or LBA) $B = (K, \Sigma, \Gamma, \Delta, s, H)$ is a nondeterministic Turing machine that cannot move off the tape region that starts at the blank to the left of the input and ends at the blank immediately after the input. If an LBA attempts to move off that region, the read/write head simply stays where it is. This definition is slightly nonstandard. The usual one restricts the head to the input string proper, but the version we give here lets us maintain the programming style that we have been using, in which the read/write head starts on the blank just to the left of the input and we detect the end of the input when we find the blank immediately to its right.

A language L is ***context-sensitive*** iff there exists an LBA that accepts it.

Almost all of the deterministic deciding Turing machines that we have described so far have been LBAs. For example, the machines we built in Chapter 17 for $A^nB^nC^n$ and WcW are both LBAs. So $A^nB^nC^n$ and WcW are context-sensitive languages.

And now to the reason that it made sense to define the LBA: The halting problem for LBAs is decidable and thus the membership question for context-sensitive languages is decidable.

THEOREM 24.1 Decidability of LBAs

Theorem: The language $L = \{<B, w> : \text{LBA } B \text{ accepts } w\}$ is in D.

Proof: Although L looks very much like A, the acceptance language for Turing machines, its one difference, namely that it asks about an LBA rather than an arbitrary Turing machine, is critical. We observe the following property of an LBA B operating on some input w: B can be in any one of its $|K|$ states. The tape that B can look at has exactly $|w| + 2$ squares. Each of those squares can contain any value in Γ and the read/write head can be on any one of them. So the number of distinct configurations of B is:

$$MaxConfigs = |K| \cdot |\Gamma|^{(|w|+2)} \cdot (|w| + 2).$$

If B ever reaches a configuration that it has been in before, it will do the same thing the second time that it did the first time. So, if it runs for more than *MaxConfigs* steps, it is in a loop and it is not going to halt.

We are now ready to define a nondeterministic Turing machine that decides L:

$M(<B, w>) =$

1. Simulate all paths of B on w, running each for *MaxConfigs* steps or until B halts, whichever comes first.
2. If any path accepted, accept; else reject.

Since, from each configuration of B, there is a finite number of branches and each branch is of finite length, M will be able to try all branches of B in a finite number of steps. M will accept the string $<B, w>$ if any path of B, running on w, accepts (i.e., B itself would accept) and it will reject the string $<B, w>$ if every path of B on w either rejects or loops.

We defined an LBA to be a *nondeterministic* Turing machine with bounded tape. Does nondeterminism matter for LBAs? Put another way, for any nondeterministic LBA B does there exist an equivalent deterministic LBA? No one knows.

24.1.2 Context-Sensitive Grammars

Why have we chosen to call the class of languages that can be accepted by an LBA "context-sensitive"? Because there exists a grammar formalism that exactly describes these languages and this formalism, like the unrestricted grammar formalism on which it is based, allows rules whose left-hand sides describe the context in which the rules may be applied.

A ***context-sensitive grammar*** $G = (V, \Sigma, R, S)$ is an unrestricted grammar in which R satisfies the following constraints:

- The left-hand side of every rule contains at least one nonterminal symbol.
- If R contains the rule $S \rightarrow \varepsilon$ then S does not occur on the right-hand side of any rule.
- With the exception of the rule $S \rightarrow \varepsilon$, if it exists, every rule $\alpha \rightarrow \beta$ in R has the property that $|\alpha| \leq |\beta|$. In other words, with the exception of the rule $S \rightarrow \varepsilon$, there are no length-reducing rules in R.

We should point out here that this definition is a bit nonstandard. The more common definition allows no length-reducing rules at all. But without the exception for $S \rightarrow \varepsilon$, it is not possible to generate any language that contains ε. So the class of languages that could be generated would not include any of the classes that we have so far considered.

We define $\Rightarrow$ (*derives-in-one-step*), $\Rightarrow^*$ (*derives*), and $L(G)$ analogously to the way they were defined for context-free and unrestricted grammars.

Some of the grammars (both context-free and unrestricted) that we have written so far are context-sensitive. But many are not.

EXAMPLE 24.1 A^nB^n

For the language A^nB^n, we wrote the grammar:

$S \rightarrow \text{a}S\text{b}$

$S \rightarrow \varepsilon$

That grammar is not context-sensitive. But the following equivalent grammar is:

$S \rightarrow \varepsilon$

$S \rightarrow S_1$

$S_1 \rightarrow \text{a}S_1\text{b}$

$S_1 \rightarrow \text{ab}$

Because of the prohibition against length-reducing rules, the problem of determining whether a context-sensitive grammar G generates some string w is decidable. Recall that it was not decidable for unrestricted grammars, so this is a significant change.

THEOREM 24.2 Decidability of Context-Sensitive Grammars

Theorem: The language $L = \{<G, w> : \text{context sensitive grammar } G \text{ generates string } w\}$ is in D.

Proof: We construct a nondeterministic Turing machine M to decide L. M will explore all derivations that G can produce starting from its start symbol. Eventually one of the following things must happen on every derivation path:

- G will generate w.
- G will generate a string to which no rules can be applied. The path will end.
- G will keep generating strings of the same length. Since there is a finite number of strings of a given length, G must eventually generate the same one twice. Whenever that happens, the path can be terminated since it is not getting any closer to generating w.
- G will generate a string s that is longer than w. The path can be terminated. Since there are no length-reducing rules, there is no way that w could ever be derived from s. It is this case that distinguishes context-sensitive grammars from unrestricted ones.

Since G has only a finite number of choices at each derivation step and since each path that is generated must eventually end, the Turing machine M that explores all derivation paths will eventually halt. If at least one path generates w, M will accept. If no path generates w, M will reject.

24.1.3 Equivalence of Linear Bounded Automata and Context-Sensitive Grammars

We now have a new computational model, the LBA, and we have shown that it is decidable whether some LBA B accepts a string w. We also have a new grammatical framework, context-sensitive grammars, and we have shown that it is decidable whether or not a context-sensitive grammar G generates some string w. That similarity, along with the terminology that we have been using, should cause the following theorem to come as no surprise:

THEOREM 24.3 Equivalence of LBAs and Context-Sensitive Grammars

Theorem: The class of languages that can be described with a context-sensitive grammar is exactly the same as the class of languages that can be accepted by some LBA. Alternatively, a language is context-sensitive iff it can be generated by some context-sensitive grammar.

Proof: The proof is very similar to the one that we did of Theorem 23.1, which asserted the equivalence of unrestricted grammars and Turing machines. We must do two proofs:

- We show that, given a context-sensitive grammar G, there exists an LBA B such that $L(G) = L(B)$. We do this by construction of B from G. B uses a two-track tape (simulated on one tape). On input w, B keeps w on the first track. On the second track, it nondeterministically constructs a derivation using G, but with one exception. Any path that is about to generate a string that is longer than w will halt immediately. So B never needs a tape longer than $|w|$ and is thus an LBA.

- We show that, given an LBA B, there exists a context-sensitive grammar G such that $L(B) = L(G)$. As in the proof of Theorem 23.1, G will simulate the operation of B. The design of G is a bit more complex now because it cannot use working symbols that get erased at the end. However, that problem can be solved with an appropriate encoding of the nonterminal symbols.

24.1.4 Where Do Context-Sensitive Languages Fit in the Language Hierarchy?

Our motivation in designing the LBA was to get the best of both worlds—something closer to the power of a Turing machine, but with the decidability properties of a PDA. Have we succeeded? Both of the languages $\{<B, w> : \text{LBA } B \text{ accepts } w\}$ and $\{<G, w> : \text{context sensitive grammar } G \text{ generates string } w\}$ are decidable. And we have seen at least one example, $A^nB^nC^n$, of a language that is not context-free but is context-sensitive. In this section, we state and prove two theorems that show that the picture at the beginning of this chapter is correctly drawn.

THEOREM 24.4 The Context-Sensitive Languages are a Proper Subset of D

Theorem: The context-sensitive languages are a proper subset of D.

Proof: We divide the proof into two parts. We first show that every context-sensitive language is in D. Then we show that there exists at least one language that is in D but that is not context-sensitive.

The first part is easy. Every context-sensitive language L is accepted by some LBA B. So the Turing machine that simulates B as described in the proof of Theorem 24.1 decides L.

Second, we must prove that there exists at least one language that is in D but that is not context-sensitive. It is not easy to do this by actually exhibiting such a language. But we can use diagonalization to show that one exists.

We consider only languages with $\Sigma = \{\texttt{a}, \texttt{b}\}$. First we must define an enumeration of all the context-sensitive grammars with $\Sigma = \{\texttt{a}, \texttt{b}\}$. To do that, we need an encoding of them. We can use a technique very much like the one we used to encode Turing machines. Specifically, we will encode a grammar $G = (V, \Sigma, R, S)$ as follows:

- Encode the nonterminal alphabet: Let $k = |V - \Sigma|$ be the number of nonterminal symbols in G. Let n be the number of binary digits required to represent the integers 0 to $k - 1$. Encode the set of nonterminal symbols $(V - \Sigma)$ as $\texttt{x}d_1d_2 \ldots d_n$, where each $d_i \in \{0, 1\}$. Let $\texttt{x}00\ldots0_n$ correspond to S.

- Encode the terminal alphabet, {a, b}, as a and b.
- Encode each rule $\alpha \rightarrow \beta$ in R as: $A \rightarrow B$, where A is the concatenation of the encodings of all of the symbols of α and B is the concatenation of the encodings of all of the symbols of β. So the encoding of a rule might look like:

  ax01b → bx01a

- Finally, encode G by concatenating together its rules, separated by ;'s. So a complete grammar G might be encoded as:

  x00 → ax00a; x00 → x01; x01 → bx01b; x01 → b

Let $Enum_G$ be the lexicographic enumeration of all encodings, as just described, of context-sensitive grammars with $\Sigma = \{\mathrm{a}, \mathrm{b}\}$. Let $Enum_{\mathrm{a,b}}$ be the lexicographic enumeration of $\{\mathrm{a}, \mathrm{b}\}^*$. We can now imagine the infinite table shown in Table 24.1. Column 0 contains the elements of $Enum_G$. Row 0 contains the elements of $Enum_{\mathrm{a,b}}$. Each other cell, with index (i, j) is 1 if $grammar_i$ generates $string_j$ and 0 otherwise. Because {<G, w> : context sensitive grammar G generates string w} is in D, there exists a Turing machine that can compute the values in this table as they are needed.

Now define the language $L_D = \{string_i : string_i \notin L(G_i)\}$. L_D is:

- In D because it is decided by the following Turing machine M:

  $M(x) =$

  1. Find x in the list $Enum_{\mathrm{a,b}}$. Let its index be i. (In other words, column i corresponds to x.)
  2. Lookup cell (i, i) in the table.
  3. If the value is 0, then x is not in $L(G_i)$ so x is in L_D, so accept.
  4. If the value is 1, then x is in $L(G_i)$ so x is not in L_D, so reject.

- Not context-sensitive because it differs, in the case of at least one string, from every language in the table and so is not generated by any context-sensitive grammar.

Table 24.1 Using diagonalization to show that there exist decidable languages that are not context-sensitive.

	$String_1$	$String_2$	$String_3$	$String_4$	$String_5$	$String_6$	...
$Grammar_1$	1	0	0	0	0	0	...
$Grammar_2$	0	1	0	0	0	0	...
$Grammar_3$	1	1	0	0	0	0	...
$Grammar_4$	0	0	1	0	0	0	...
$Grammar_5$	1	0	1	0	0	0	...
...	...	...	...	...	...	...	...

THEOREM 24.5 The Context-Free Languages are a Proper Subset of the Context-Sensitive Languages

Theorem: The context-free languages are a proper subset of the context-sensitive languages.

Proof: We know one language, $A^nB^nC^n$, that is context-sensitive but not context-free. So it remains only to show that every context-free language is context-sensitive.

If L is a context-free language then there exists some context-free grammar $G = (V, \Sigma, R, S)$ that generates it. Convert G to Chomsky normal form, producing G'. G' generates $L - \{\varepsilon\}$. G' is a context-sensitive grammar because it has no length-reducing rules. If $\varepsilon \in L$, then create in G' a new start symbol S' (distinct from any other symbols already in G'), and add the rules $S' \rightarrow \varepsilon$ and $S' \rightarrow S$. G' is still a context-sensitive grammar and it generates L. So L is a context-sensitive language.

24.1.5 Closure Properties of the Context-Sensitive Languages

The context-sensitive languages exhibit strong closure properties. In order to prove that, it is useful first to prove a normal form theorem for context-sensitive grammars. We will do that here, and then go on to prove a set of closure theorems.

A context-sensitive grammar $G = (V, \Sigma, R, S)$ is in ***nonterminal normal form*** iff all rules in R are of one of the following two forms:

- $\alpha \rightarrow c$, where α is an element of $(V - \Sigma)$ and $c \in \Sigma$, or
- $\alpha \rightarrow \beta$, where both α and β are elements of $(V - \Sigma)^+$.

In other words, the set of nonterminals includes one for each terminal symbol and it is the job of that nonterminal simply to generate its associated terminal symbol. G does almost of its work manipulating only nonterminals. At the end, the terminal symbols are generated. Once terminal symbols have been generated, no further rules can apply to them since no rules have any terminals in their left-hand sides.

THEOREM 24.6 Nonterminal Normal Form for Context-Sensitive Grammars

Theorem: Given a context-sensitive grammar G, there exists an equivalent nonterminal normal form grammar G' such that $L(G') = L(G)$.

Proof: The proof is by construction. From G we create G' using the algorithm *converttononterminal* defined as follows:

converttononterminal(G: context-sensitive grammar) =

1. Initially, let $G' = G$.
2. For each terminal symbol c in Σ, create a new nonterminal symbol T_c and add to $R_{G'}$ the rule $T_c \rightarrow c$.

3. Modify each of the original rules (not including the ones that were just created) so that every occurrence of a terminal symbol c is replaced by the nonterminal symbol T_c.
4. Return G'.

Note that no length-reducing rules have been introduced, so if G is a context-sensitive grammar, so is G'.

We can now state a set of closure theorems. The proofs of two of these theorems will exploit nonterminal normal form as just defined.

THEOREM 24.7 Closure Under Union

Theorem: The context-sensitive languages are closed under union.

Proof: The proof is by construction of a context-sensitive grammar. The construction is identical to the one we gave in the proof of Theorem 13.5 that the context-free languages are closed under union: If L_1 and L_2 are context-sensitive languages, then there exist context-sensitive grammars $G_1 = (V_1, \Sigma_1, R_1, S_1)$ and $G_2 = (V_2, \Sigma_2, R_2, S_2)$ such that $L_1 = L(G_1)$ and $L_2 = L(G_2)$. If necessary, rename the nonterminals of G_1 and G_2 so that the two sets are disjoint and so that neither includes the symbol S. We will build a new grammar G such that $L(G) = L(G_1) \cup L(G_2)$. G will contain all the rules of both G_1 and G_2. We add to G a new start symbol, S, and two new rules, $S \rightarrow S_1$ and $S \rightarrow S_2$. The two new rules allow G to generate a string iff at least one of G_1 or G_2 generates it. So $G = (V_1 \cup V_2 \cup \{S\}, \Sigma_1 \cup \Sigma_2, R_1 \cup R_2 \cup \{S \rightarrow S_1, S \rightarrow S_2\}, S)$. Note that no length-reducing rules are introduced, so the grammar that results is a context-sensitive grammar.

THEOREM 24.8 Closure Under Concatenation

Theorem: The context-sensitive languages are closed under concatenation.

Proof: The proof is by construction of a context-sensitive grammar. Again we use the construction of Theorem 13.5: If L_1 and L_2 are context-sensitive languages, then there exist context-sensitive grammars $G_1 = (V_1, \Sigma_1, R_1, S_1)$ and $G_2 = (V_2, \Sigma_2, R_2, S_2)$ such that $L_1 = L(G_1)$ and $L_2 = L(G_2)$. If necessary, rename the nonterminals of G_1 and G_2 so that the two sets are disjoint and so that neither includes the symbol S. We will build a new grammar G such that $L(G) = L(G_1)L(G_2)$. G will contain all the rules of both G_1 and G_2. We add to G a new start symbol, S, and one new rule, $S \rightarrow S_1S_2$. So $G = (V_1 \cup V_2 \cup \{S\}, \Sigma_1 \cup \Sigma_2, R_1 \cup R_2 \cup \{S \rightarrow S_1S_2\}, S)$.

However, now there is one problem that we need to solve: Suppose that one of the original grammars contained a rule with Aa as its left hand side. Figure 24.2 shows a partial parse tree that might be generated by the new grammar. The problem is that Aa can match at the boundary between the substring that was

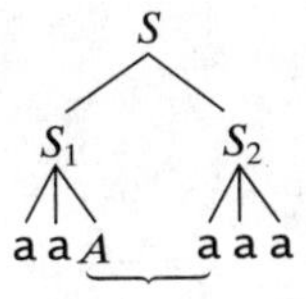

FIGURE 24.2 Two subtrees may interact.

generated from S_1 and the one that was generated from S_2. That could result in a string that is not the concatenation of a string in L_1 with a string in L_2. If only nonterminal symbols could occur on the left-hand side of a rule, this problem would be solved by the renaming step that guarantees that the two sets of nonterminals (in the two original grammars) are disjoint. If G were in nonterminal normal form, then that condition would be met.

So, to build a grammar G such that $L(G) = L(G_1)L(G_2)$, we do the following:

1. Convert both G_1 and G_2 to nonterminal normal form.
2. If necessary, rename the nonterminals of G_1 and G_2 so that the two sets are disjoint and so that neither includes the symbol S.
3. $G = (V_1 \cup V_2 \cup \{S\}, \Sigma_1 \cup \Sigma_2, R_1 \cup R_2 \cup \{S \rightarrow S_1 S_2\}, S)$.

THEOREM 24.9 Closure Under Kleene Star

Theorem: The context-sensitive languages are closed under Kleene star.

Proof: The proof is by construction of a context-sensitive grammar. If L_1 is a context-sensitive language, then there exists a context-sensitive grammar $G_1 = (V_1, \Sigma_1, R_1, S_1)$ such that $L_1 = L(G_1)$. To build a grammar G such that $L(G) = L(G_1)^*$, we can use a construction similar to that of Theorem 13.5, in which we create a new start symbol and let it generate zero or more copies of the original start symbol. But now we have two problems. The first is dealing with ε. To solve it, we'll introduce two new symbols, S and T, instead of one. We'll add to the original grammar G_1 a new start symbol S, which will be able to be rewritten as either ε or T. T will then be recursive and will be able to generate $L(G_1)^+$. If necessary, rename the nonterminals of G_1 so that V_1 does not include the symbol S or T. G will contain all the rules of G_1. Then we add to G a new start symbol, S, another new nonterminal T, and four new rules, $S \rightarrow \varepsilon$, $S \rightarrow T$, $T \rightarrow T S_1$, and $T \rightarrow S_1$.

But we also run into a problem like the one we just solved above for concatenation. Suppose that the partial tree shown in Figure 24.3(a) can be created and that there is a rule whose left-hand side is AA. Then that rule could be applied not just to a string that was generated by S_1 but to a string at the boundary between two instances of S_1. To solve this problem we can again convert the original grammar to nonterminal normal form before we start. But now the two symbols, AA, that are spuriously adjacent to each other were both derived from instances of the same nonterminal (S_1), so creating disjoint sets of nonterminals

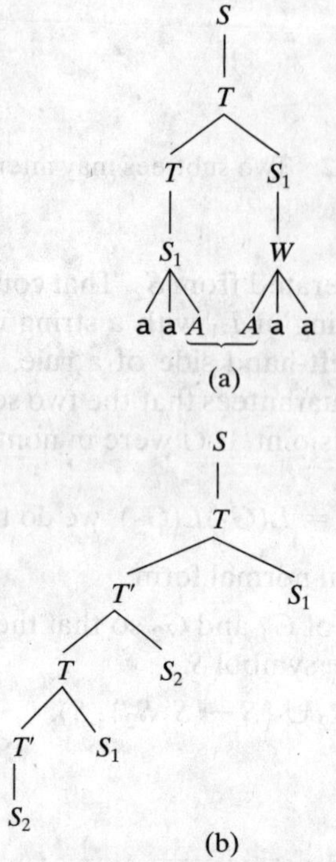

FIGURE 24.3 Preventing two subtrees from interacting.

won't solve the problem. What we have to do this time is to create a copy of the rules that can be used to derive an S_1. Let those rules derive some new nonterminal S_2. The two sets of rules will do exactly the same thing but they will exploit disjoint sets of nonterminals as they do so. Then we'll alternate them. So, for example, to generate a string that is the concatenation of four strings from L_1, we'll create the parse tree shown in Figure 24.3(b). Now, since neither S_1 nor S_2 can generate ε, it can never happen that nonterminals from two separate subtrees rooted by S_1 can be adjacent to each other, nor can it happen from two separate subtrees rooted by S_2.

We can now state the complete construction of a grammar G such that $L(G) = L(G_1)^*$:

1. Convert G_1 to nonterminal normal form.
2. If necessary, rename the nonterminals so they do not include S, T, T', or S_2.
3. Create a new nonterminal S_2 and create copies (with different names) of all the nonterminals and the rules in G_1 so that $L(S_2) = L(S_1)$.
4. $G = (V_1 \cup \{S, T, T'\} \cup \{S_2$ and other nonterminals generated in step 3$\}$,
   Σ_1,
   $R_1 \cup \{S \rightarrow \varepsilon, S \rightarrow T, T \rightarrow T'S_1, T \rightarrow S_1, T' \rightarrow TS_2, T' \rightarrow S_2\}$
   $\cup\ \{$the rules that derive S_2, as generated in step 3$\}$,
   S).

THEOREM 24.10 Closure Under Intersection

Theorem: The context-sensitive languages are closed under intersection.

Proof: This time we cannot pattern a proof after one we did for the context-free languages since the context-free languages are not closed under intersection. But we can do a proof by construction of an LBA. If L_1 and L_2 are context-sensitive languages, then there exist LBAs $B_1 = (K_1, \Sigma_1, \Gamma_1, \Delta_1, s_1, H_1)$ and $B_2 = (K_2, \Sigma_2, \Gamma_2, \Delta_2, s_1, H_1)$ such that $L_1 = L(B_1)$ and $L_2 = L(B_2)$. We construct a new LBA B such that $L(B) = L(B_1) \cap L(B_2)$. B will treat its tape as though it were divided into two tracks. It will first copy its input from track 1 to track 2. Then it will simulate B_1 on track 1. If that simulation accepts, then B will simulate B_2 on track 2. If that simulation also accepts, then B will accept. So B will accept iff both B_1 and B_2 do.

THEOREM 24.11 Closure Under Complement

Theorem: The context-sensitive languages are closed under complement.

Proof: The proof of this claim is based on a complexity argument, so we will delay it until Chapter 29, but see 💻.

24.1.6 Decision Procedures for the Context-Sensitive Languages

We have already shown that the membership question for context-sensitive languages is decidable. Unfortunately, it does not appear to be efficiently decidable. Comparing the situation of context-free languages and context-sensitive languages, we have, where w is a string and G a grammar:

- If G is a context-free grammar, then there exists a $\mathcal{O}(n^3)$ algorithm (as we saw in Chapter 15) to decide whether $w \in L(G)$.
- If G is a context-sensitive grammar, then the problem of deciding whether $w \in L(G)$ can be solved by the algorithm that we presented in the proof of Theorem 24.2. It is not certain that no more efficient algorithm exists, but it is known that the decision problem for context-sensitive languages is PSPACE-complete. (We'll define PSPACE-completeness in Chapter 29.) The fact that the problem is PSPACE-complete means that no polynomial-algorithm exists for it unless there also exist polynomial-time algorithms for large classes of other problems for which no efficient algorithm has yet been found. More precisely, no polynomial-time algorithm for deciding membership in a context-sensitive language exists unless P = NP = PSPACE, which is generally thought to be very unlikely.

Because no efficient parsing techniques for the context-sensitive languages are known, practical parsers for programming languages (G.4.2) and natural languages (L.3.3) typically use a context-free grammar core augmented with specific other mechanisms. They do not rely on context-sensitive grammars.

What about other questions we might wish to ask about context-sensitive languages? We list some questions in Table 24.2, and we show their decidability for the context-sensitive languages and also, for comparison, for the context-free languages.

We prove two of these claims about the context-sensitive languages here and leave the others as exercises. Since we have shown that context-sensitive grammars and LBAs describe the same class of languages, any question that is undecidable for one will also be undecidable for the other. So we can prove the decidability of a question by using either grammars or machines, whichever is more straightforward. We'll do one example of each.

THEOREM 24.12 "Is a Context-Sensitive Language Empty?" is Undecidable

Theorem: The language $L_2 = \{<B> : B \text{ is a LBA and } L(B) = \varnothing\}$ is not in D.

Proof: The proof is by reduction from $H_{\neg ANY} = \{<M> : \text{there does not exist any string on which Turing machine } M \text{ halts}\}$, which we showed, in Theorem 21.15, is not even in SD. We will define *R*, a mapping reduction from $H_{\neg ANY}$ to L_2. The idea is that *R* will use the reduction via computation history technique described in Section 22.5.1. Given a particular Turing machine *M*, it is straightforward to build a new Turing machine *M#* that can determine whether a string *x* is a valid computation history of *M*. *M#* just needs to check four things:

- The string *x* must be a syntactically legal computation history.
- The first configuration of *x* must correspond to *M* being in its start state, with its read/write head positioned just to the left of the input.
- The last configuration of *x* must be a halting configuration.
- Each configuration after the first must be derivable from the previous one according to the rules in *M*'s transition relation δ.

In order to check these things, *M#* need never move off the part of its tape that contains its input, so *M#* is in fact an LBA. Since a computation history must

Table 24.2 Decidability of questions about context-free and context-sensitive languages.

	Decidable for context-free languages?	***Decidable for context-sensitive languages?***
Is $L = \Sigma^*$?	No	No
Is $L_1 = L_2$?	No (but Yes for deterministic CFLs)	No
Is $L_1 \subseteq L_2$?	No	No
Is *L* regular?	No	No
Is $\neg L$ also context-free?	No	
Is $\neg L$ also context-sensitive?		Yes, trivially since the context-sensitive languages are closed under complement.
Is $L = \varnothing$?	Yes	No
Is $L_1 \cap L_2 = \varnothing$?	No	No

end in a halting state, there will be no valid computation histories for M iff M halts on nothing. So R is defined as follows:

$R(<M>) =$

1. Construct the description $<M\#>$ of an LBA $M\#(x)$ that operates as follows:
   1.1. If x is a valid computation history of M, accept, else reject.
2. Return $<M\#>$.

If *Oracle* exists and decides L_2, then $C = Oracle(R(<M>))$ decides $H_{\neg ANY}$:

- R can be implemented as a Turing machine.
- C is correct:
  - If $<M> \in H_{\neg ANY}$: There are no valid computation histories of the Turing machine M, so the LBA $M\#$ accepts nothing. $Oracle(<M\#>)$ accepts.
  - If $<M> \notin H_{ANY}$: There is at least one valid computation history of M, so $M\#$ accepts at least one string. $Oracle<M\#>$ rejects.

But no machine to decide $H_{\neg ANY}$ can exist, so neither does Oracle.

THEOREM 24.13 "Is the Intersection of Two Context-Sensitive Languages Empty?" is Undecidable

Theorem: The language $L_2 = \{<G_1, G_2> : G_1$ and G_2 are context-sensitive grammars and $L(G_1) \cap L(G_2) = \varnothing\}$ is not in D.

Proof: The proof is by reduction from $L_1 = \{<G_1, G_2> : G_1$ and G_2 are context-free grammars and $L(G_1) \cap L(G_2) = \varnothing\}$, which we showed, in Theorem 22.9, is not in D. Let R be a mapping reduction from L_1 to L_2 defined as follows:

$R(<G_1, G_2>) =$

1. Using the procedure that was described in the proof of Theorem 24.5, construct from the two context-free grammars G_1 and G_2, two context-sensitive grammars G_3 and G_4 such that $L(G_3) = L(G_1)$ and $L(G_4) = L(G_2)$.
2. Return $<G_3, G_4>$.

If *Oracle* exists and decides L_2, then $C = Oracle(R(<G_1, G_2>))$ decides L_1. But no machine to decide L_1 can exist, so neither does *Oracle*.

24.2 The Chomsky Hierarchy

In 1956, Noam Chomsky described a slightly different version of the onion diagram that we have been using. Chomsky's version, commonly called the Chomsky hierarchy, is shown In Figure 24.4. This version is appealing because, for each level, there exists both a grammar formalism and a computational structure. Chomsky used the terms

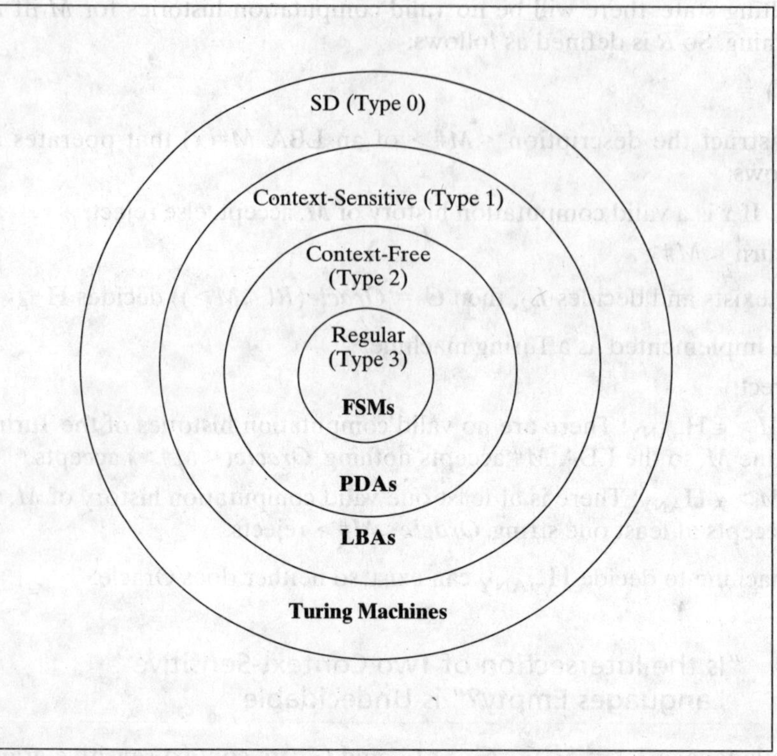

FIGURE 24.4 The Chomsky hierarchy.

type 0, type 1, type 2, and type 3 to describe the four levels in his model and those terms are still used in some treatments of this topic.

The basis for the Chomsky hierarchy is the amount and organization of the memory required to process the languages at each level.

- ***type 0*** (semidecidable): no memory constraint
- ***type 1*** (context-sensitive): memory limited by the length of the input string
- ***type 2*** (context-free): unlimited memory but accessible only in a stack (so only a finite amount is accessible at any point)
- ***type 3*** (regular): finite memory

The Chomsky hierarchy makes an obvious suggestion: Different grammar formalisms offer different descriptive power and may be appropriate for different tasks. In the years since Chomsky published the hierarchy, that idea, coupled with the need to solve real problems, has led to the development of many other formalisms. We will sketch two of them in the rest of this chapter.

24.3 Attribute, Feature, and Unification Grammars

For many applications, context-free grammars are almost, but not quite, good enough. While they may do a good job of describing the primary structure of the strings in a language, they make it difficult, and in some cases impossible, to describe constraints on the way in which sibling constituents may be derived. For example, we saw that no context-free grammar exists for the simple artificial language $A^nB^nC^n = \{a^nb^nc^n : n \geq 0\}$. The context-free grammar formalism provides no way to express the constraint that the numbers of a's, b's, and c's must be equal. We've seen (in Example 23.1) an unrestricted grammar for $A^nB^nC^n$. But we've also seen that unrestricted grammars are impractical.

What we need is a new technique for describing constraints on sets of constituents. The approach that we describe next treats both terminals and nonterminals not as atomic symbols but rather as clusters of ***features*** (or ***attributes***) and associated values. Then it allows rules to:

- Define ways in which features are passed up and down in parse trees.
- Describe constraints on feature values that must be satisfied before the rules can be applied.

EXAMPLE 24.2 An Attribute Grammar for $A^nB^nC^n$

We'll show an attribute grammar G for the language $A^nB^nC^n$. G will be a context-free grammar that has been augmented with one feature, *size*. The rules in G will define how *size* is used. Some rules will compute *size* and pass it up, from the terminal nodes, to the root. The single S rule will contain the description of a *size* constraint that must be satisfied before the rule can be applied.

$$G = (\{S, A, B, C, \text{a}, \text{b}, \text{c}\}, \{\text{a}, \text{b}, \text{c}\}, R, S), \text{ where:}$$

$$\begin{aligned}
R = \{S &\rightarrow ABC & &(size(A) = size(B) = size(C)) \\
A &\rightarrow \text{a} & &(size(A) \leftarrow 1) \\
A &\rightarrow A_2\ \text{a} & &(size(A) \leftarrow size(A_2) + 1) \\
B &\rightarrow \text{b} & &(size(B) \leftarrow 1) \\
B &\rightarrow B_2\ \text{b} & &(size(B) \leftarrow size(B_2) + 1) \\
C &\rightarrow \text{c} & &(size(C) \leftarrow 1) \\
C &\rightarrow C_2\ \text{c} & &(size(C) \leftarrow size(C_2) + 1)\}.
\end{aligned}$$

In this example, each rule has been annotated with an attribute expression. Read the notation A_2 as the name for the daughter constituent, rooted at A, created by the rule that refers to it. This grammar could easily be used by a bottom-up parser that builds the maximal A, B, and C constituents, assigns a size to each, and then attempts to combine the three of them into a single S. The combination will succeed only if all the sizes match.

The fact that it could be useful to augment context-free grammars with various kinds of features and constraints has been observed both by the writers of grammars for programming languages and the writers of grammars of natural languages, such as English. In the programming languages and compilers world, these grammars tend to be called

attribute grammars. In the linguistics world, they tend to be called ***feature grammars*** or ***unification grammars*** (the latter because of their reliance on a matching process, called unification, that decides when there is a match between features and constraints).

EXAMPLE 24.3 A Unification Grammar Gets Subject/Verb Agreement Right

In Example 11.6, we presented a simple fragment of an English grammar. That fragment is clearly incomplete; it fails to generate most of the sentences of English. But it also overgenerates. For example, it can generate the following sentence (marked with an * to show that it is ungrammatical):

```
* The bear like chocolate.
```

The problem is that this sentence was generated using the rule $S \rightarrow NP\ VP$. Because the grammar is context-free, the *NP* and *VP* constituents must be realized independently. So there is no way to implement the English constraint that present tense verbs must agree with their subjects in number and gender.

We can solve this problem by replacing the simple nonterminals *NP* (Noun Phrase) and *VP* (Verb Phrase) by compound ones that include features corresponding to person and number. One common way to do that is to represent everything, including the primary category, as a feature. So, instead of *NP* and *VP*, we might have:

```
CATEGORY NP             [CATEGORY VP
PERSON   THIRD           PERSON    THIRD
NUMBER   SINGULAR]       NUMBER    SINGULAR]
```

Instead of atomic terminal symbols like `bear`, we might have:

```
[CATEGORY  N
 LEX  bear
 PERSON   THIRD
 NUMBER   SINGULAR]
```

Instead of grammar rules like $S \rightarrow NP\ VP$, we will now have rules that are stated in terms of feature sets. The idea is that we will write rules that describe constraints on how features must match in order for constituents to be combined. So, for example the $S \rightarrow NP\ VP$ rule might become:

```
[CATEGORY S] → [CATEGORY NP         [CATEGORY VP
                 NUMBER  x1           NUMBER x1
                 PERSON  x2]          PERSON x2]
```

This rule exploits two variables, x_1 and x_2, to describe the values of the NUMBER and PERSON features. Whenever a particular NP is constructed, it will (by a mechanism that we won't go into) acquire values for its NUMBER and PERSON features from its constituents (usually the head noun, such as bear). The same thing will happen for each individual VP. The scope of the variables x_1 and x_2 should be taken to be the entire rule, which will thus be interpreted to say that an NP and a VP can be combined to form an S iff they have matching values for their NUMBER and PERSON features. We've oversimplified here by suggesting that the only way for values to match is for them to be identical. Practical systems typically exploit a more powerful notion of matching. For example, past tense verbs in English aren't marked for number. So a VP that dominated the verb shot, for instance, would have a NUMBER value that would enable it to combine with an NP whose NUMBER was either SINGULAR or PLURAL.

Several important natural language grammar formalisms are feature (unification)-based. Grammars written in those formalisms exploit features that describe agreement constraints between subjects and verbs, between nouns and their modifiers, and between verbs and their arguments, to name just a few. (L.3.3) They may also use semantic features, both as additional constraints on the way in which sentences can be generated and as the basis for assigning meanings to sentences once they have been parsed.

Both the formal power and the computational efficiency of attribute/feature/unification grammars depend on the details of how features are defined and used. Not all attribute/feature/unification grammar formalisms are stronger than context-free grammars. In particular, consider a formalism that requires that both the number of features and the number of values for each feature must be finite. Then, given any grammar G in that formalism, there exists an equivalent context-free grammar G'. The proof of this claim is straightforward and is left as an exercise. With this restriction then, attribute/feature/unification grammars are simply notational conveniences. In English, there are only two values (singular and plural) for syntactic number and only three values (first, second and third) for person. So the grammar that we showed in Example 24.3 can be rewritten as a (longer and more complex) context-free grammar.

Now consider the grammar that we showed in Example 24.2. The single attribute *size* can take an arbitrary integer value. We know that no context-free equivalent of that grammar exists. When the number of attribute-value pairs is not finite, the power of a grammar formalism depends on the way in which attributes can be computed and evaluated. Some formalisms have the power of Turing machines.

Grammars, augmented with attributes and constraints, can be used in a wide variety of applications. For example, they can describe component libraries and product families.

Particularly in the attribute grammar tradition, it is common to divide attributes into two classes:

- ***synthesized attributes***, which are passed up the parse tree, and
- ***inherited attributes***, which are passed down the tree.

Both of the examples that we have presented use synthesized attributes, which are particularly well-suited to use by bottom-up parsers. Inherited attributes, on the other hand, are well-suited to use by top-down parsers.

One appeal of attribute/feature/unification grammars is that features can be used not just as a way to describe constraints on the strings that can be generated. They may also be used as a way to construct the meanings of strings. Assume that we are working with a language for which a compositional semantic interpretation function (as defined in Section 2.2.6) exists. Then the meaning of anything other than a primitive structure is a function of the meanings of its constituent structures. So, to use attributes as a way to compute meanings for the strings in a language L, we must:

- Create a set of attributes whose values will describe the meanings of the primitives of L. For English, the primitives will typically be words (or possibly smaller units, like morphemes). For programming languages, the primitives will be variables, constants, and the other primitive language constructs.
- Associate with each grammar rule a rule that describes how the meaning attributes of each element of the rule's right hand side should be combined to form the meaning of the left-hand side. For example, the English rule $S \rightarrow NP\ VP$ can specify that the meaning of an S is structure whose subject is the meaning of the constituent NP and whose predicate is the meaning of the constituent VP.

> Attribute grammars for programming languages were introduced as a way to define the semantics of programs that were written in those languages. They can be a useful tool for parser generators.

24.4 Lindenmayer Systems

Lindenmayer systems, or simply L-systems, were first described by Aristid Lindenmayer, a biologist whose goal was to model plant development and growth. L-systems are grammars. They use rules to derive strings. But there are three differences between L-systems and the other grammar formalisms we have discussed so far. These differences arise from the fact that L-systems were designed not to define languages but rather to model ongoing, dynamic processes.

The first difference is in the way in which rules are applied. In all of our other grammar formalisms, rules are applied sequentially. In L-systems, as in the Game of Life and the other cellular automata that we mentioned in Chapter 18, rules are applied, in parallel, to all the symbols in the working string. For example, think of each working string as representing an organism at some time t. At time $t + 1$, each of its cells will have changed according to the rules of cell development. Or think of each working string as representing a population at some time t. At time $t + 1$, each of the individuals will have matured, died, or reproduced according to the rules of population change.

The second difference is in what it means to generate a string. In all our other grammar formalisms, derivation continues at least until no nonterminal symbols remain in the working string. Only strings that contain no nonterminal symbols are considered to have been generated by the grammar. In L-systems, because we are modeling a process, each of the working strings will be considered to have been generated by the grammar. The distinction between terminals and nonterminals disappears, although there may be some symbols that will be treated as constants (i.e., no rules apply to them).

The third difference is that we will start with an initial string (of one or more symbols), rather than just an initial symbol.

An L-system G is a triple (Σ, R, ω), where:

- Σ is an alphabet, which may contain a subset C of constants, to which no rules will apply,
- R is a set of rules, and
- ω (the start sequence) is an element of Σ^+.

Each rule in R is of the form: $\alpha A \beta \rightarrow \gamma$, where:

- $A \in \Sigma$. A is the symbol that is to be rewritten by the rule.
- $\alpha, \beta \in \Sigma^*$. α and β describe context that must be present in order for the rule to fire. If they are equal to ε, no context is checked.
- $\gamma \in \Sigma^*$. γ is the string that will replace A when the rule fires.

The most straightforward way to describe $L(G)$, the set of strings generated by an L-system G is to specify an interpreter for G. We do that as follows:

L-system-interpret(G: L-system) =

1. Set *working-string* to ω.

2. Do forever:

2.1. Output *working-string*.

2.2. *new-working-string* = ε.

2.3. For each symbol c in *working-string* (moving left to right) do:

If possible, choose a rule r whose left-hand side matches c and where c's neighbors (in *working-string*) satisfy any context constraints included in r.

If a rule r was found, concatenate its right-hand side to the right end of *new-working-string*.

If none was found, concatenate c to the right end of *new-working-string*.

2.4. *working-string* = *new-working-string*.

In addition to their original purpose, L-systems have been used for applications ranging from composing music (N.1.2) to predicting protein folding 💻 to designing buildings 💻.

Because each successive string is built by recursively applying the rules to the symbols in the previous string, the strings that L-systems generate typically exhibit a property called ***self-similarity***. We say that an object is self-similar whenever the structure exhibited by its constituent parts is very similar to the structure of the object taken as a whole.

EXAMPLE 24.4 Fibonacci's Rabbits

Let G be the L-system defined as follows:

$\Sigma = \{\texttt{I}, \texttt{M}\}$.

$\omega = \texttt{I}$.

$R = \{\texttt{I} \rightarrow \texttt{M},$

$\quad\quad \texttt{M} \rightarrow \texttt{M I}\}$.

The sequence of strings generated by G begins:

0. `I`
1. `M`
2. `M I`
3. `M I M`
4. `M I M M I`
5. `M I M M I M I M`
6. `M I M M I M I M M I M M I`

If we describe each string by its length, then the sequence that G generates is known as the Fibonacci sequence, defined as:

$Fibonacci_0 = 1$.

$Fibonacci_1 = 1$.

For $n > 1$, $Fibonacci_n = Fibonnaci_{n-1} + Fibonnaci_{n-2}$.

Fibonacci's goal, in defining the sequence that bears his name, was to model the growth of an idealized rabbit population in which no one dies and each mature pair produces a new male-female pair at each time step. Assume that it takes one time step for each rabbit to reach maturity and mate. Also assume that the gestation period of rabbits is one time step and that we begin with one pair of (immature) rabbits. So at time step 0, there is 1 pair. At time step 1 there is still 1 pair, but they have matured and mated. So, at time step 2, the original pair is alive and has produced one new one. At time step 3, all pairs from time step 2 (of which there are 2) are still alive and all pairs (of which there is just 1) that have been around at least two time steps have produced a new pair. So there are $2 + 1 = 3$ pairs. At time step 4, the 3 pairs from the previous step are still alive and the 2 pairs from two steps ago have reproduced, so there are $3 + 2 = 5$ pairs. And so forth.

Notice that the strings that G produces mirror this structure. Each I corresponds to one immature pair of rabbits and each M corresponds to one mature pair. Each string is the concatenation of its immediately preceding string (the survivors) with the string that preceded it two steps back (the breeders).

Leonardo Pisano Fibonacci lived from 1170 to 1250. Much more recently, the L-system that describes the sequence that bears his name has been used to model things as various as plant structure (Q.2.2), limericks and ragtime music .

L-systems can be used to model two and three-dimensional structures by assigning appropriate meanings to the symbols that get generated. For example, the turtle geometry system provides a set of basic drawing primitives. A turtle program is simply a string of those symbols. So we can use L-systems to generate turtle programs and thus to generate two-dimensional images. Three-dimension structures can be built in a similar way.

Fractals are self-similar, recursive structures, so they are easy to generate using L-systems.

EXAMPLE 24.5 Sierpinski Triangle

Let G be the L-system defined as follows:

$$\Sigma = \{\text{A}, \text{B}, +, -\}.$$

$$\omega = \text{A}.$$

$$R = \{\text{A} \rightarrow \text{B} - \text{A} - \text{B},$$

$$\text{B} \rightarrow \text{A} + \text{B} + \text{A}\}.$$

Notice that + and − are constants. No rules transform them so they are simply copied to each successive output string. The sequence of strings generated by G begins:

1. A
2. B − A − B
3. A + B + A − B − A − B − A + B + A
4. B − A − B + A + B + A + B − A − B − A + B + A − B − A − B − A + B + A − B − A − B + A + B + A + B − A − B

We can interpret these strings as turtle programs by choosing a line length k and then attaching meanings to the symbols in Σ as follows:

- A and B mean move forward, drawing a line of length k.
- + means turn to the left 60°.
- − means turn to the right 60°.

Strings 3, 4, 8, and 10 then correspond to turtle programs that can draw the following sequence of figures (scaling k appropriately):

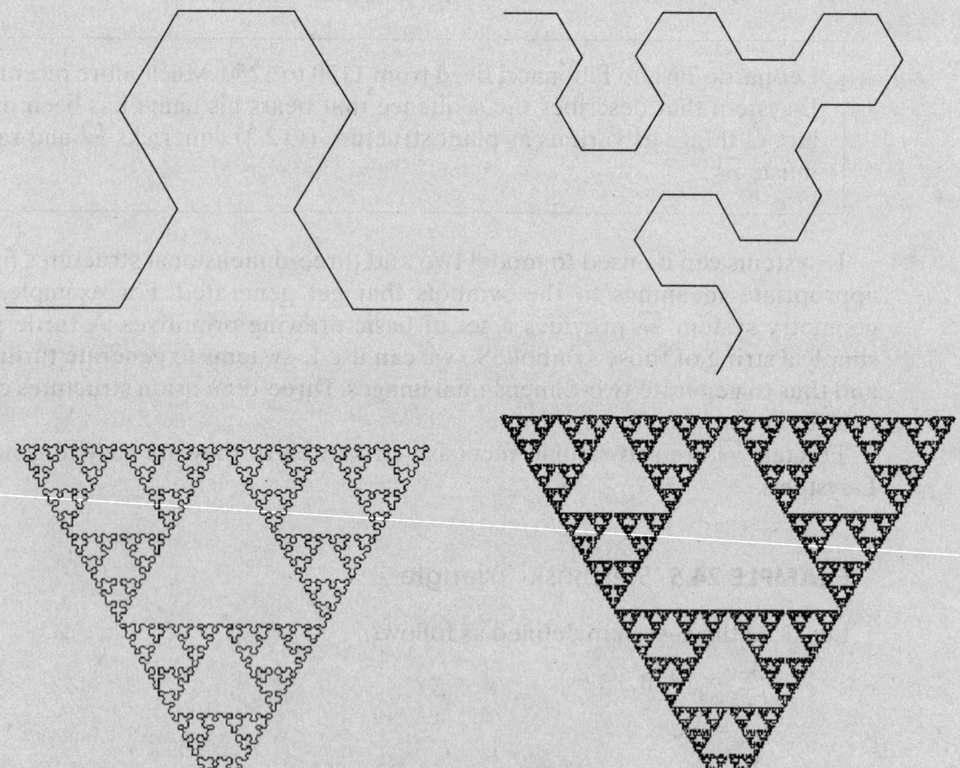

The limit of this sequence (assuming that an appropriate scaling factor is applied at each step) is the fractal known as the ***Sierpinski triangle*** 💻.

The growth of many natural structures can most easily be described as the development of branches, which split into new branches, which split into new branches, and so forth. We can model this process with an L-system by introducing into v two new symbols: [will correspond to a push operation and] will correspond to a pop. If we are interpreting the strings the L-system generates as turtle programs, push will push the current pen position onto a stack. Pop will pop off the top pen position, pick up the pen, return it to the position that is on the top of the stack, and then put it down again.

EXAMPLE 24.6 Trees

Let G be the L-system defined as follows:

$\Sigma = \{\mathsf{F}, +, -, [,]\}$.

$\omega = \mathsf{F}$.

$R = \{ \mathsf{F} \rightarrow \mathsf{F}[-\mathsf{F}]\mathsf{F}[+\mathsf{F}][\mathsf{F}] \}$.

The sequence of strings generated by G begins:

1. F
2. F[− F] F [+ F] [F]
3. F[− F] F [+ F] [F] [− F [− F] F [+ F] [F]] F [− F] F [+ F] [F] [+ F [− F] F [+ F] [F]] [F [− F] F [+ F] [F]]

We can interpret these strings as turtle programs by choosing a line length k and then attaching meanings to the symbols in Σ as follows:

- F means move forward, drawing a line of length k.
- + means turn to the left 36°.
- − means turn to the right 36°.
- [means push the current pen position and direction onto the stack.
-] means pop the top pen position/direction off the stack, lift up the pen, move it to the position that is now on the top of the stack, put it back down, and set its direction to the one on the top of the stack.

Strings 2, 3, 4, and 8 then correspond to turtle programs that can draw the following sequence of figures (scaling k appropriately):

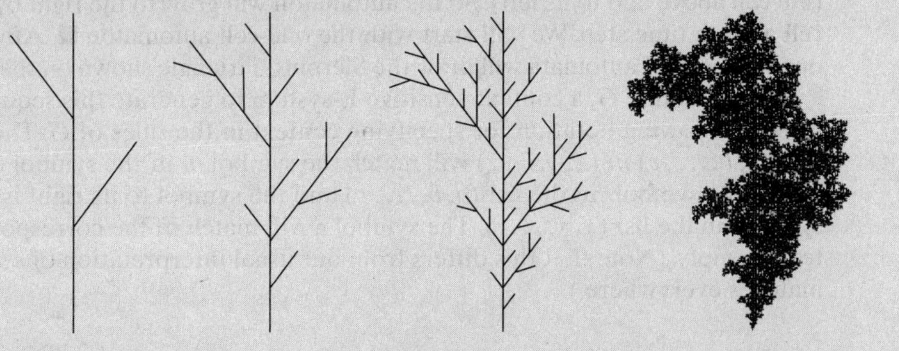

One note about these pictures: The reason that the number of line segments is not consistently a power of 5 is that some lines are drawn on top of others.

Much more realistic trees, as well as other biological structures, can also be described with L-systems. (Q.2.2)

So far, all of the L-systems that we have considered are context-free (because we have put no context requirements on the left-hand sides of any of the rules) and deterministic (because there is no more than one rule that matches any symbol). Deterministic, context-free L-systems are called ***D0L-systems*** and are widely used. But we could, for example, give up determinism and allow competing rules with the same left-hand side. In that case, one common way to resolve the competition is to attach probabilities to the rules and thus to build a stochastic L-system.

We can also build L-systems that are not context-free. In such systems, the left-hand side of a rule may include contextual constraints. These constraints will be checked before a rule can be applied. But the constraints do not participate in the substitution that the rule performs. Each rule still describes how a single symbol is to be rewritten.

EXAMPLE 24.7 Sierpinski Triangle, Again

Imagine a one-dimensional cellular automaton. Each cell may contain the value black or white. At any point in time, the automaton consists of a finite number of cells, although it may grow to the right from one step to the next. We will display successive time steps on successive lines, with each cell immediately below its position at the previous time step. With this arrangement, define the ***parents*** of a cell at time t to be the cell immediately above it (i.e., itself at time $t - 1$) and (if it exists) the one that is one row above it but shifted one cell to the left (i.e., its left neighbor at time $t - 1$). Now we can state the rule for moving from one time step to the next: At each time step after the first, a cell will exist if it would have at least one parent. And its value will be

- black if it has exactly one black parent,
- white otherwise.

Note that, at each time step, one additional cell to the right will have a parent (the cell above and to its left). So the automaton will grow to the right by one black cell at each time step. We will start with the one-cell automaton ■. After 32 steps, our sequence of automata will draw the Sierpinski triangle shown on the next page.

We can define G, a context-sensitive L-system to generate this sequence. We'll use the following notation for specifying context in the rules of G: The left-hand side $(a, b, \ldots, c)\ m\ (x, y, \ldots z)$ will match the symbol m iff the symbol to its left is any of the symbols in the list $(a, b, \ldots, c)$ and the symbol to its right is any of the symbols in the list $(x, y, \ldots z)$. The symbol ε will match iff the corresponding context is empty. (Note that this differs from our usual interpretation of ε, in which it matches everywhere.)

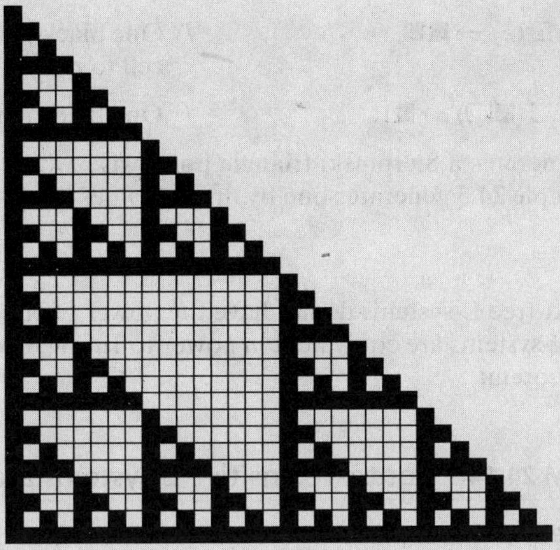

With those conventions, G is:

$\Sigma = \{\blacksquare, \square\}$.

$\omega = \blacksquare$.

$R = \{(\varepsilon \mid \square)\, \blacksquare\, (\varepsilon) \rightarrow \blacksquare\blacksquare,$ /* This square is black with no black one to the left, so at $t + 1$ there's exactly one black parent. The new cell is black. And there's no cell to the right, so add one, which also has one black parent so it too is black.

$(\varepsilon \mid \square)\, \blacksquare\, (\blacksquare \mid \square) \rightarrow \blacksquare,$ /* This square is black and no black one to the left, so at $t + 1$ there's exactly one black parent. The new cell is black.

$(\blacksquare)\, \blacksquare\, (\varepsilon) \rightarrow \square\blacksquare,$ /* Black, plus black to the left. Two black parents. New cell is white. No cell to the right, so add one. It has one black parent so it is black.

$(\blacksquare)\, \blacksquare\, (\blacksquare \mid \square) \rightarrow \square,$ /* Two black parents. New one is white.

$(\varepsilon \mid \square)\, \square\, (\varepsilon) \rightarrow \square\blacksquare,$ /* Two white parents. New one is white. Add cell to right.

$(\varepsilon \mid \square)\, \square\, (\blacksquare \mid \square) \rightarrow \square,$ /* Two white parents. New one is white.

(■) □ (ε) → ■ ■, /* One black parent. New one is white. Add cell to right.

(■) □ (■|□) → ■}. /* One black parent. New one is black.

G generates a Sierpinski triangle point wise, while the L-system we described in Example 24.5 generates one by drawing lines.

Context-free L-systems do not have the power of Turing machines. But, if context is allowed, L-systems are equivalent in power to Turing machines. So we can state the following theorem:

THEOREM 24.14 Context-Sensitive L-Systems are Turing Equivalent

Theorem: The computation of any context-sensitive L-system can be simulated by some Turing machine. And the computation of any Turing machine can be simulated by some deterministic, context-sensitive L-system.

Proof: The computation of any L-system can be simulated by a Turing machine that implements the algorithm *L-system-interpret*. So it remains to show the other direction.

The proof that the execution of any Turing machine can be simulated by some deterministic, context-sensitive L-system is by construction. More precisely, we'll show that Turing machine M, on input w, halts in some halting state q and with tape contents v iff L-system L converges to the static string qv.

If M is not deterministic, create an equivalent deterministic machine and proceed with it. Then, given M and w, define L as follows:

- Let Σ_L be Σ_M, augmented as follows:
  - Add the symbol 0 to encode M's start state.
  - If M has the halting state y, add the symbol y to encode it.
  - If M has the halting state n, add the symbol n to encode it.
  - If M has any other halting states, add the symbol h to encode all of them.
  - Add one distinct symbol for each nonhalting state of M.
- Let ω (L's start string) encode M's initial configuration. Configurations will be encoded by a string that represents M's active tape, plus two blank squares on each end. The symbol that represents M's current state will be inserted into the string immediately to the left of the tape symbol that is under the read/write head. We will follow our usual convention that, just before it starts, M's read/write is on the blank square just to the left of the first input character. So ω = □□0□w□□.
- Let the rules R of L encode M's transitions. To do this, we exploit the fact that the action of a Turing machine is very local. Things only change near the

read/write head. So, letting integers correspond to states, suppose that the working string of L is ga4bcde. This encodes a configuration in which M's read/write head is on the b and M is in state 4. The read/write head can move one square to the left or one square to the right. Whichever way it moves, the character under it can change. So, if it moves left, the a changes to some state symbol, the 4 changes to an a, and the b changes to whatever it gets rewritten as. If, on the other hand, the read/write head moves to the right, the 4 changes to whatever the b gets rewritten as and the b gets rewritten as the new state symbol. To decide how to rewrite some character in the working string, it is sufficient to look at one character to its left and two to its right. If there is no state symbol in that area, the symbol gets rewritten as itself. No rule need be specified to make this happen. For all the combinations that do involve a state symbol, we add to R rules that cause the system to behave as M behaves. Finally, add rules so that, if h, y, or n is ever generated, it will be pushed all the way to the left, leaving the rest of the string unchanged. Add no other rules to R (and in particular no other rules involving any of the halting state symbols).

L will converge to qv iff M halts, in state q, with v on its tape.

Exercises

1. Write context-sensitive grammars for each of the following languages L. The challenge is that, unlike with an unrestricted grammar, it is not possible to erase working symbols.
   a. $A^nB^nC^n = \{ a^nb^nc^n : n \geq 0\}$.
   b. $WW = \{ww : w \in \{a, b\}^*\}$.
   c. $\{w \in \{a, b, c\}^* : \#_a(w) = \#_b(w) = \#_c(w)\}$.
2. Prove that each of the following languages is context-sensitive.
   a. $\{a^n : n \text{ is prime}\}$
   b. $\{a^{n^2} : n \geq 0\}$
   c. $\{xwx^R : x, w \in \{a, b\}^+ \text{ and } |x| = |w|\}$
3. Prove that every context-free language is accepted by some deterministic LBA.
4. Recall the diagonalization proof that we used in the proof of Theorem 24.4, which tells us that the context-sensitive languages are a proper subset of D. Why cannot that same proof technique be used to show that there exists a decidable language that is not decidable or an SD language that is not decidable?
5. Prove that the context-sensitive languages are closed under *reverse*.
6. Prove that each of the following questions is undecidable.
   a. Given a context-sensitive language L, is $L = \Sigma^*$?
   b. Given a context-sensitive language L, is L finite?
   c. Given two context-sensitive languages L_1 and L_2, is $L_1 = L_2$?
   d. Given two context-sensitive languages L_1 and L_2, is $L_1 \subseteq L_2$?
   e. Given a context-sensitive language L, is L regular?

7. Prove the following claim, made in Section 24.3: Given an attribute/feature/unification grammar formalism that requires that both the number of features and the number of values for each feature must be finite and a grammar G in that formalism, there exists an equivalent context-free grammar G'.

8. The following sequence of figures corresponds to a fractal called a ***Koch island***:

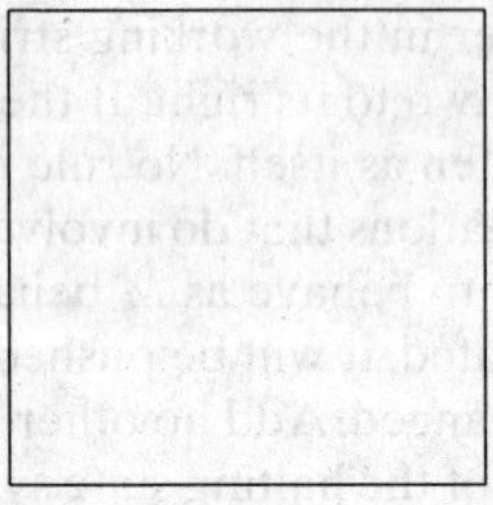

(a)

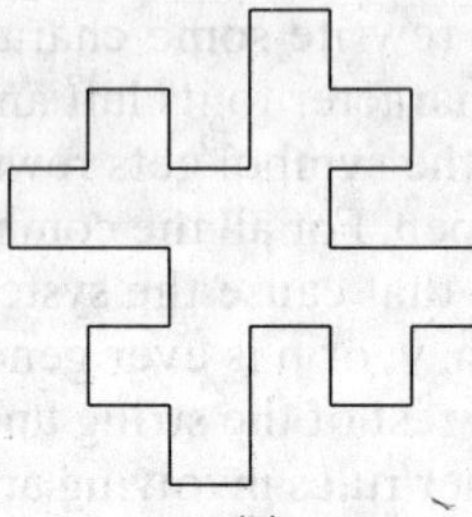

(b)

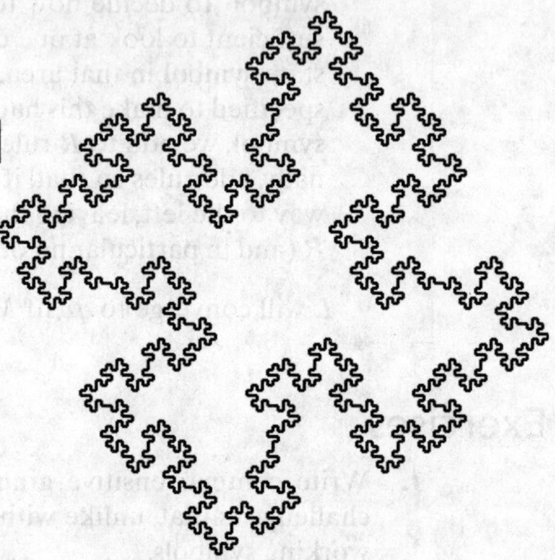

(d)

(c)

These figures were drawn by interpreting strings as turtle programs, just as we did in Example 24.5 and Example 24.6. The strings were generated by an L-system G, defined with:

$$\Sigma = \{\mathsf{F}, +, -\}.$$

$$\omega = \mathsf{F} - \mathsf{F} - \mathsf{F} - \mathsf{F}.$$

To interpret the strings as turtle programs, attach meanings to the symbols in Σ as follows (assuming that some value for k has been chosen):

- F means move forward, drawing a line of length k.
- \+ means turn left 90°.
- − means turn right 90°.

Figure (a) was drawn by the first generation string ω. Figure (b) was drawn by the second generation string, and so forth. R_G contains a single rule. What is it?

CHAPTER 25

Computable Functions ✸

In almost all of our discussion so far, we have focused on exactly one kind of problem: deciding a language. We saw in Chapter 2 that other kinds of problems can be recast as language-decision problems and so can be analyzed within the framework that we have described. But, having introduced the Turing machine, we now also have a way to analyze programs that compute functions whose range is something other than $\{Accept, Reject\}$.

25.1 What is a Computable Function?

Informally, a function is computable if there exists a Turing machine that can compute it. In this section we will formalize that notion.

25.1.1 Total and Partial Functions

We begin by considering two classes of functions. Let f be an arbitrary function. Then:

- f is a ***total function*** on the domain *Dom* iff f is defined on all elements of *Dom*. This is the standard mathematical definition of a function on a domain.
- f is a ***partial function*** on the domain *Dom* iff f is defined on zero or more elements of *Dom*. This definition allows for the existence of elements of the domain on which the function is not defined.

EXAMPLE 25.1 Total and Partial Functions

- Consider the successor function *succ* and the domain $\mathbb{N}$ (the natural numbers). *Succ* is a total function on $\mathbb{N}$. It is also a partial function on $\mathbb{N}$.
- Consider the simple string function *midchar*, which returns the middle character of its argument string if there is one. The *midchar* function is a partial function on the domain of strings. But it is not a total function on the domain of

EXAMPLE 25.1 *(Continued)*

strings, since it is undefined for strings of even length. It is, however, a total function on the smaller domain of odd length strings.

- Consider the function *steps*, defined on inputs of the form $<M, w>$. It returns the number of steps that Turing machine M executes, on input w, before it halts. The *steps* function is a partial function on the domain $\{<M, w>\}$. But it is not a total function on that domain, since it is undefined for values of $<M, w>$ where M does not halt on w. It is, however, a total function on the smaller domain $\{<M, w>$: Turing machine M halts on input $w\}$.

Why do we want to expand the notion of a function to allow for partial functions? A cleaner approach is simply to narrow the domain so that it includes only values on which the function is defined. So, for example, in the case of the *midchar* function, we simply assert that its domain is the set of odd length strings. Then we have a total function and thus a function in the standard mathematical sense. Of course we can do the same thing with the function *steps*: We can refine its domain to include only values on which it is defined. But now we face an important problem given that our task is to write programs (more specifically, to design Turing machines) that can compute functions. The set of values on which *steps* is defined is the language H. And H is not in D (i.e., it is not a decidable set). So, no matter what Turing machine we might build to compute *steps*, there exists no other Turing machine that can examine a value and decide whether the *steps* machine should be able to run.

Another way to think of this problem is that it is impossible for any implementation of *steps* to check its precondition. The only way it is going to be possible to build an implementation of *steps* is going to be to define its domain as some decidable set and then allow that there are elements of that domain for which *steps* will not return a value. Thus *steps* will be a partial and not a total function of the domain on which the program that implements it runs. So any such program will fail to halt on some inputs.

25.1.2 Partially Computable and Computable Functions

Recall that, in Section 17.2.2, we introduced the notion of a Turing machine that computes an arbitrary function. In the rest of this section we will expand on the ideas that we sketched there. In particular, we will now consider functions, like *midchar* and *steps*, that are not defined on all elements of Σ^*.

We begin by restating the basic definitions that we gave in Section 17.2.2:

- Let M be a Turing machine with start state s, halting state h, input alphabet Σ, and tape alphabet Γ. The initial configuration of M will be $(s, \square w)$, where $w \in \Sigma^*$.
- Define $M(w) = z$ iff $(s, \square w) \mid\!-_M{}^* (h, \square z)$. In other words $M(w) = z$ iff M, when started on a string w in Σ^*, halts with z on its tape and its read/write head is just to the left of z.

- We say that a Turing machine M ***computes*** a function f iff, for all $w \in \Sigma^*$:
  - If w is an input on which f is defined, $M(w) = f(w)$. In other words, M halts with $f(w)$ on its tape.
  - Otherwise $M(w)$ does not halt.
- A function f is ***recursive*** or ***computable*** iff there is a Turing machine M that computes it and that always halts.

But what about functions that are not defined on all elements of Σ^*? They are not computable under this definition. Let f be any function defined on some subset of Σ^*. Then f is ***partially computable*** iff there exists a Turing machine M that computes it. In other words, M halts and returns the correct value for all inputs on which f is defined. On all other inputs, M fails to halt.

Let f be any partially computable function whose domain is only a proper subset of Σ^*. Then any Turing machine that computes f will fail to halt on some inputs. But now consider only those functions f such that the set of values *Dom* on which f is defined is decidable. In other words, f is a total function on the decidable set *Dom*. For example, *midchar* is such a function, defined on the decidable set of odd length strings. For any such function f, we define a new function f' that is identical to f except that its range includes one new value, which we will call *Error*. On any input z on which f is undefined, $f'(z) = Error$. Given a Turing machine M that computes f, we can construct a new Turing machine M' that computes f' and that always halts. Let *Dom* be the set of values on which f is defined. Since *Dom* is in D, there is some Turing machine *TF* that decides it. Then the following Turing machine M' computes f':

$M'(x) =$

1. Run *TF* on x.
2. If it rejects, output *Error*.
3. If it accepts, run M on x.

We have simply put a wrapper around M. The job of the wrapper is to check M's precondition and only run M when its precondition is satisfied. This is the technique we use all the time with real programs.

Using the wrapper idea we can now offer a broader and more useful definition of computability: Let f be a function whose domain is some subset of Σ^*. Then f is ***computable*** iff there exists a Turing machine M that computes f' (as described above) and that halts on all inputs. Equivalently, f is computable iff it is partially computable and its domain is a decidable set.

Now suppose that f is a function whose domain and/or range is not a set of strings. For example, both the domain and the range of the successor function *succ* are the integers. Then f is computable iff all of the following conditions hold:

- There exist alphabets Σ and Σ'.
- There exists an encoding of the elements of the domain of f as strings in Σ^*.
- There exists an encoding of the elements of the range of f as strings in Σ'^*.

- There exists some computable function f' with the property that, for every $w \in \Sigma^*$:
  - If $w = <x>$ and x is an element of f's domain, then $f'(w) = <f(x)>$, and
  - If w is not the encoding of any element of f's domain (either because it is not syntactically well formed or because it encodes some value on which f is undefined), then $f'(w) = Error$.

EXAMPLE 25.2 The Successor Function *succ*

Consider again the successor function:

$$succ: \mathbb{N} \rightarrow \mathbb{N},$$
$$succ(x) = x + 1.$$

We can encode both the domain and the range of *succ* in unary (i.e., as strings drawn from {1}*). Then we can define the following Turing machine M to compute it:

$M(x) =$

1. Write 1.
2. Move left once.
3. Halt.

The function *succ* is a total function on $\mathbb{N}$. Every element of $\Sigma^* = \{1\}^*$ is the encoding of some element of $\mathbb{N}$. For each such element x, M computes $f(x)$ and halts. So *succ* is computable.

EXAMPLE 25.3 The Function *midchar*

Consider again the function *midchar* that we introduced in Example 25.1. Recall that *midchar* is a total function on the set of odd length strings and a partial function on the set of strings. Now we want to build a Turing machine M to compute *midchar*.

The most straightforward way to encode a string x as input to M is as itself. If we do that, then we can build a straightforward Turing machine M that behaves as follows on input x:

- If the length of x is odd, compute *midchar*(x).
- If the length of x is even, then what? By the definition of a machine that computes a function f, M should loop on all values for which f is not defined. So it must loop on all even length inputs.

The existence of M proves that *midchar* is partially computable. But *midchar* is also computable because the following Turing machine M', which halts on all inputs, computes *midchar'*:

$M'(x) =$

1. If the length of x is even, output *Error*.
2. Otherwise, find the middle character of x and output it.

EXAMPLE 25.4 The Function *steps*

Consider again the function *steps* that we introduced in Example 25.1. Recall that *steps* is a total function on the set $\{<M, w>$: Turing machine M halts on input $w\}$. It is a partial function on the set $\{<M, w>\}$. And it is also a partial function on the larger set of strings that includes syntactically ill-formed inputs. *Steps* is a partially computable function because the following three-tape Turing machine S computes it:

$S(x) =$

1. If x is not a syntactically well formed $<M, w>$ string then loop.
2. If x is a syntactically well formed $<M, w>$ string then:
   - **2.1.** Copy M to tape 3.
   - **2.2.** Copy w to tape 2.
   - **2.3.** Write 0 on tape 1.
   - **2.4.** Simulate M on w on tape 2, keeping a count on tape 1 of each step that M makes.

S halts whenever its input is well-formed and M halts on w. If it halts, it has the value of *steps*($<M, w>$) on tape 1. By Theorem 17.1, there exists a one-tape Turing machine S' whose output is identical to the value that S placed on tape 1. So S' is a standard Turing machine that computes *steps*. The existence of S' proves that *steps* is partially computable.

But *steps* is not computable. We show that it is not by showing that there exists no Turing machine that computes the function *steps'*, defined as:

steps'(x) = If x is not a syntactically well-formed $<M, w>$ string, then *Error*.
If x is well-formed but *steps*($<M, w>$) is undefined (i.e., M does not halt on w), then *Error*.
If *steps*($<M, w>$) is defined (i.e., M halts on w), then *steps*($<M, w>$).

We prove that no such Turing machine exists by reduction from H. Suppose that there did exist such a machine. Call it ST. Then the following Turing machine

EXAMPLE 25.4 (*Continued*)

DH would decide the language H = {<*M*, *w*> : Turing machine *M* halts on input string *w*}:

DH(<*M*, *w*>) =

1. Run *ST*(<*M*, *w*>).
2. If the result is *Error* then reject. Else accept.

But we know that there can exist no Turing machine to decide H. So *ST* must not exist. So *steps* is not computable.

25.1.3 Functions That Are Not Partially Computable

There exist functions like *succ* and *midchar* that are computable. There exist functions like *steps* that are partially computable but not computable. But there also exist functions that are not even partially computable.

THEOREM 25.1 There Exist Functions That are Not Even Partially Computable

Theorem: There exist (a very large number of) functions that are not partially computable.

Proof: We will use a counting argument similar to the one we used to prove a similar result, Theorem 20.3, which says that there exist languages that are not semidecidable. We will consider only unary functions from some subset of $\mathbb{N}$ (the nonnegative integers) to $\mathbb{N}$. Call the set of all such functions *U*. We will encode both the input to functions in *U* and their outputs as binary strings.

Lemma: There is a countably infinite number of partially computable functions in *U*.

Proof of Lemma: Every partially computable function in *U* is computed by some Turing machine *M* with Σ and Γ equal to $\{0, 1\}$. By Theorem 17.7, there exists an infinite lexicographic enumeration of all such syntactically legal Turing machines. So, by Theorem A.1, there is a countably infinite number of Turing machines that compute functions in *U*. There cannot be more partially computable functions than there are Turing machines, so there is at most a countably infinite number of partially computable functions in *U*. There is not a one-to-one correspondence between partially computable functions and the Turing machines that compute them since there is an infinite number of Turing machines that compute any given function. But the number of partially computable functions in *U* must be infinite because it includes all the constant functions (which are also computable):

$$cf_1(x) = 1, cf_2(x) = 2, cf_3(x) = 3, \ldots$$

So there is a countably infinite number of partially computable functions in *U*.

Lemma: There is an uncountably infinite number of functions in U.

Proof of Lemma: For any element s in $\mathcal{P}(\mathbb{N})$ (the power set of $\mathbb{N}$), let f_s be the characteristic function of s. So $f_s(x) = 1$ if $x \in s$ and 0 otherwise. No two elements of $\mathcal{P}(\mathbb{N})$ have the same characteristic function. By Theorem A.4, there is an uncountably infinite number of elements in $\mathcal{P}(\mathbb{N})$, so there is an uncountably infinite number of such characteristic functions, each of which is in U.

Proof of Theorem: Since there is only a countably infinite number of partially computable functions in U and an uncountably infinite number of functions in U, there is an uncountably infinite number of functions in U that are not partially computable.

Now we know that there exist many functions that are not partially computable. But can we describe one? The answer is yes. One way to do so is by diagonalization. Let E be a lexicographic enumeration of the Turing machines that compute the partially computable functions in U. Let M_i be the ith machine in that enumeration. Define a new function $notcomp(x)$ as follows:

$$notcomp: \mathbb{N} \rightarrow \{0, 1\},$$
$$notcomp(x) = 1 \text{ if } M_x(x) = 0, 0 \text{ otherwise.}$$

So $notcomp(x) = 0$ if either $M_i(x)$ is defined and the value is something other than 0 or if $M_i(x)$ is not defined. This new function $notcomp$ is in U, but it differs, in at least one place, from every function that is computed by a Turing machine whose encoding is listed in E. So there is no Turing machine that computes it. Thus it is not partially computable.

25.1.4 The Busy Beaver Functions

There exist even more straightforward total functions that are not partially computable. One well known example is a family of functions called ***busy beaver functions*** 🖳. To define two of these functions, consider the set T of all standard Turing machines M (i.e., deterministic, one-tape machines of the sort defined in Section 17.1), where M has tape alphabet $\Gamma = \{\square, 1\}$ and M halts on a blank tape. Then:

- $S(n)$ is defined by considering all machines that are in T and that have n nonhalting states. The value of $S(n)$ is the maximum number of steps that are executed by any such n-state machine, when started on a blank tape, before it halts.
- $\Sigma(n)$ is defined by again considering all machines that are in T and that have n nonhalting states. The value of $\Sigma(n)$ is the maximum number of 1's that are left on the tape by any such n-state machine, when started on a blank tape, when it halts.

A variety of other busy beaver functions have also been defined. Some of them allow three or more tape symbols (instead of the two we allow). Some use variants of our Turing machine definition. For example, our versions are called quintuple versions, since our Turing machines both write and move the read/write head at each step (so

Table 25.1 Some values for the busy beaver functions.

n	$S(n)$	$\Sigma(n)$
1	1	1
2	6	4
3	21	6
4	107	13
5	$\geq$47,176,870	4098
6	$\geq 3 \cdot 10^{1730}$	$\geq 1.29 \cdot 10^{865}$

each element of the transition function is a quintuple). One common variant allows machines to write or to move, but not both, at each step (so each element of the transition function is a quadruple). Quadruple machines typically require more steps than quintuple machines require to perform the same task.

All of the busy beaver functions provide a measure of how much work a Turing machine with n states can do before it halts. And none of them is computable. In a nutshell, the reason is that their values grow too fast, as can be seen from Table 25.1, which summarizes some of what is known about the values of S and Σ, as we defined them above. For values of n greater than 4 (in the case of S) or 5 in the case of Σ, the actual values are not known but lower bounds on them are, as shown in the table. For the latest results in determining these bounds, see 💻.

THEOREM 25.2 S and Σ are Total Functions

Theorem: Both S and Σ are total functions on the positive integers.

Proof: For any value n, both $S(n)$ and $\Sigma(n)$ are defined iff there exists some standard Turing machine M, with tape alphabet $\Gamma = \{\square, 1\}$, where:

- M has n nonhalting states, and
- M halts on a blank tape.

We show by construction that such a Turing machine M exists for every integer value of $n \geq 1$. We will name the nonhalting states of M with the integers $1, \ldots, n$. We can build M as follows:

1. Let state 1 be the start state of M.
2. For all i such that $1 < i \leq n$, add to δ_M the transition $((i-1, \square), (i, \square, \rightarrow))$.
3. Let M have a single halting state called h.
4. Add to δ_M the transition $((n, \square), (h, \square, \rightarrow))$.

M is a standard Turing machine with tape alphabet $\Gamma = \{\square, 1\}$, it has n nonhalting states, and it halts on a blank tape. It is shown in Figure 25.1.

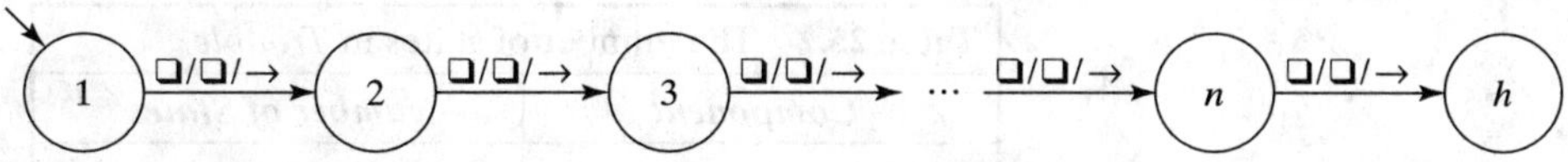

FIGURE 25.1 A halting Turing machine with n nonhalting states.

So both S and Σ are defined on all positive integers. If they are not computable, it is not because their domains are not in D. But they are not computable. We first prove a lemma and then use it to show that both busy beaver functions, S and Σ, are not computable.

THEOREM 25.3 The Busy Beaver Functions are Strictly Monotonically Increasing

Theorem: Both S and Σ are strictly monotonically increasing functions. In other words:

$$S(n) < S(m) \quad \text{iff} \quad n < m, \text{ and}$$
$$\Sigma(n) < \Sigma(m) \quad \text{iff} \quad n < m.$$

Proof: We must prove four claims:

- $n < m \rightarrow S(n) < S(m)$: Let $S(n) = k$. Then there exists an n-state Turing machine TN that runs for k steps and then halts. From TN we can build an m-state Turing machine TM that runs for $k + (m - n)$ steps and then halts. We add $m - n$ states to TN. Let any state that was a halting state of TN cease to be a halting state. Instead, make it go, on any input character, to the first new state, write a 1, and move right. From that first new state, go, on any input character, to the second new state, write a 1, and move right. Continue through all the new states. Make the last one a halting state. This new machine executes k steps, just as TN did, and then an additional $m - n$ steps. Then it halts. So $S(m) \geq S(n) + (m - n)$. Since $m > n$, $(m - n)$ is positive. So $S(m) > S(n)$.
- $S(n) < S(m) \rightarrow n < m$: We can rewrite this as $\neg(n < m) \rightarrow \neg(S(n) < S(m))$ and then as $n \geq m \rightarrow S(n) \geq S(m)$. If $n = m$, then $S(m) = S(n)$. If $n > m$, then by the first claim, proved above, $S(n) > S(m)$.
- $n < m \rightarrow \Sigma(n) < \Sigma(m)$: Analogously to the proof that $n < m \rightarrow S(n) < S(m)$ but substitute Σ for S.
- $\Sigma(n) < \Sigma(m) \rightarrow n < m$: Analogously to the proof that $S(n) < S(m) \rightarrow n < m$, but substitute Σ for S.

THEOREM 25.4 The Busy Beaver Functions are Not Computable

Theorem: Neither S nor Σ is computable.

Proof: We will prove that S is not computable. We leave the proof of Σ as an exercise.

Table 25.2 The number of states in $Trouble_n$

Component	***Number of States***
$Write_n$	$n+1$
;R	1
$Write_n$	$n+1$
$L_{\square}$	2
Multiply	m
$L_{\square}$	2
BB	b
Total	$2n+m+b+7$

Suppose that S were computable. Then there would be some Turing machine *BB*, with some number of states that we can call b, that computes it. For any positive integer n, we can define a Turing machine $Write_n$ that writes n 1's on its tape, one at a time, moving rightwards, and then halts with its read/write head on the blank square immediately to the right of the rightmost 1. $Write_n$ has n non-halting states plus one halting state. We can also define a Turing machine *Multiply* that multiplies two unary numbers, written on its tape and separated by the ; symbol. The design of *Multiply* was an exercise in Chapter 17. Let m be the number of states in *Multiply*.

Using the macro notation we described in Section 17.1.5, we can define, for any positive integer n, the following Turing machine, which we can call $Trouble_n$:

$$>Write_n \; ; \mathrm{R} \; Write_n \; \mathrm{L_q} \; Multiply \; \mathrm{L_q} \; BB$$

$Trouble_n$ first writes a string of the form $1^n;1^n$. It then moves its read/write head back to the left so that it is on the blank square immediately to the left of that string. It invokes *Multiply*, which results in the tape containing a string of exactly n^2 1's. It moves its read/write head back to the left and then invokes *BB*, which outputs $S(n^2)$. The number of states in $Trouble_n$ is shown in Table 25.2.

Since *BB*, the final step of $Trouble_n$, writes a string of length $S(n^2)$ and it can write only one character per step, $Trouble_n$ must run for at least $S(n^2)$ steps. Since, for any $n > 0$, $Trouble_n$ is a Turing machine with $2n + m + b + 7$ states that runs for at least $S(n^2)$ steps, we know that:

$$S(2n + m + b + 7) \geq S(n^2).$$

By Theorem 25.3, we know that S is monotonically increasing, so it must also be true that, for any $n > 0$:

$$2n + m + b + 7 \geq n^2.$$

But, since n^2 grows faster than n does, that cannot be true. In assuming that *BB* exists, we have derived a contradiction. So *BB* does not exist. So S is not computable.

25.1.5 Languages and Functions

It should be clear by now that there is a natural correspondence between languages, which may be in D, SD/D, or ¬ SD, and functions, which may be computable, partially computable, or neither. We can construct Table 25.3. It gives us now three ways to present a computational problem.

25.2 Recursive Function Theory

We have been using the terms:

- *decidable*, to describe languages that can be decided by some Turing machine,
- *semidecidable*, to describe languages that can be semidecided by some Turing machine,
- *partially computable*, to describe functions that can be computed by some Turing machine, and
- *computable*, to describe functions that can be computed by some Turing machine that halts on all inputs.

Table 25.3 The problem, language, and functional views.

The Problem View	***The Language View***	***The Functional View***
Given thrce natural numbers, x, y, and z, is $z = x \cdot y$?	$\{<x> * <y> = <z> :$ $x, y, z \in \{0, 1\}^*$ and $num(x) \cdot num(y) = num(z)\}$.	$f: \mathbb{N} \times \mathbb{N} \rightarrow \mathbb{N}$, $f(x, y) = x \cdot y$.
	D	***Computable***
Given a Turing machine M, does M have an even number of states?	$\{<M> :$ TM M has an even number of states$\}$.	$f: \{<M>\} \rightarrow$ Boolean, $f(<M>) =$ *True* if TM M has an even number of states, *False* otherwise.
	D	***Computable***
Given a Turing machine M and a string w, does M halt on w in n steps?	$\{<M, w, n> :$ TM TM M halts on w in n steps$\}$.	$f: \{<M, w>\} \rightarrow \mathbb{N}$, $f(<M, w>) =$ if TM M halts on w then the number of steps it executes before halting, else undefined.
	SD/D	***Partially computable***
Given a Turing machine M, does M halt on all strings in no more than n steps?	$\{<M, n> :$ TM M halts on each element of Σ^* in no more than n steps$\}$.	$f: \{<M>\} \rightarrow \mathbb{N}$, $f(<M>) =$ if TM M halts on all strings then the maximum number of steps it executes before halting, else undefined.
	¬SD	***Not partially computable***

The more traditional terminology is:

- *recursive* for *decidable*.
- *recursively enumerable* for *semidecidable*. The recursively enumerable languages are often called just the *RE* or *r.e.* languages.
- *partial recursive* for *partially computable*.
- *recursive* for *computable*.

Before we continue, we need to issue one warning about the fact that there is no standard definition for some of these terms. The terms *computable* and *recursive* are used in some discussions, including this one, to refer just to functions that can be computed by a Turing machine that always halts. In some other discussions, they are used to refer to the class we have called the *partial recursive* or the *partially computable* functions.

Why are the computable functions traditionally called *recursive*? The word makes sense if you think of *recursive* as a synonym for *computable*. In this section, we will see why *recursive* is a reasonable synonym for *computable*. In the rest of this section, to be compatible with conventional treatments of this subject, we will use the term *recursive function* to mean *computable function*.

A ***recursive function*** is one that can be computed by a Turing machine that halts on all inputs. A ***partial recursive function*** is one that can be computed by some Turing machine (but one that may loop if there are any inputs on which the function is undefined). So we have definitions, stated in terms of a computational framework, for two important classes of functions. Let's now ask a different question: Are there definitions of the same classes of functions that do not appeal to any model of computation but that can instead be derived from standard mathematical tools, including the definition of a small set of primitive functions and the ability to construct new functions using operators such as composition and recursion? The answer is yes.

In the rest of this section we will develop such a definition for a class of functions that turns out to be exactly, given an appropriate encoding, the recursive functions. And we will develop a similar definition for the class of recursively enumerable functions. We will build a theory of functions, each of which has a domain that is an ordered n-tuple of natural numbers and a range that is the natural numbers. We have already shown that numbers can be represented as strings and strings can be represented as numbers, so there is no fundamental incompatibility between the theory we are about to describe and the one, based on Turing machines operating on strings, that we have already considered.

25.2.1 Primitive Recursive Functions

We begin by defining the ***primitive recursive functions*** to be the smallest class of functions from $\mathbb{N} \times \mathbb{N} \times \cdots \times \mathbb{N}$ to $\mathbb{N}$ that includes:

- the constant function 0,
- the successor function: $succ(n) = n + 1$, and
- a family of projection functions: for any $0 < j \leq k$, $p_{kj}(n_1, n_2, \ldots n_k) = n_j$,

and that is closed under the operations:

- composition of g with $h_1, h_2, \ldots h_k$:

$$g(h_1(\,), h_2(\,), \ldots h_k(\,)).$$

- primitive recursion of f in terms of g and h:
  - $f(n_1, n_2, \ldots n_k, \quad 0) = g(n_1, n_2, \ldots n_k)$. This is the base case.
  - $f(n_1, n_2, \ldots n_k, m + 1) = h(n_1, n_2, \ldots n_k, m, f(n_1, n_2, \ldots n_k, m))$. Note that in this, the recursive case, the function h takes a large number of arguments. It need not, however, use all of them, since the projection functions make it possible to select only those arguments that are needed.

EXAMPLE 25.5 Primitive Recursive Functions Perform Arithmetic

To make these examples easier to read, we will define the constant $1 = succ(0)$. All of the following functions are primitive recursive:

- The function *plus*, which adds two numbers:

$$plus(n, 0) = p_{1,1}(n) = n.$$
$$plus(n, m + 1) = succ(p_{3,3}(n, m, plus(n, m))).$$

For clarity, we will simplify our future definitions by omitting the explicit calls to the projection functions. Doing that here, we get:

$$plus(n, 0) = n.$$
$$plus(n, m + 1) = succ(plus(n, m)).$$

- The function *times*:

$$times(n, 0) = 0.$$
$$times(n, m + 1) = plus(n, times(n, m)).$$

- The function *factorial*, more usually written $n!$:

$$factorial(0) = 1.$$
$$factorial(n + 1) = times(succ(n), factorial(n)).$$

- The function *exp*, more usually written n^m:

$$exp(n, 0) = 1.$$
$$exp(n, m + 1) = times(n, exp(n, m)).$$

- The predecessor function *pred*, which is defined as follows:

$$pred(0) = 0.$$
$$pred(n + 1) = n.$$

Many other straightforward functions are also primitive recursive. We may now wish to ask, "What is the relationship between the primitive recursive functions and the computable functions?" All of the primitive recursive functions that we have considered so far are computable. Are all primitive recursive functions computable? Are all computable functions primitive recursive? We will answer these questions one at a time.

THEOREM 25.5 Every Primitive Recursive Function is Computable

Theorem: Every primitive recursive function is computable.

Proof: Each of the basic functions, as well as the two combining operations can be implemented in a straightforward fashion on a Turing machine or using a standard programming language. We omit the details.

THEOREM 25.6 Not Every Computable Function is Primitive Recursive

Theorem: There exist computable functions that are not primitive recursive.

Proof: The proof is by diagonalization. We will consider only unary functions; we will show that there exists at least one unary computable function that is not primitive recursive.

We first observe that it is possible to create a lexicographic enumeration of the definitions of the unary primitive recursive functions. To do so, we first define an alphabet Σ that contains the symbols 0, 1, the letters of the alphabet (for use as function names), and the special characters (,), = and comma (,). Using the definition of the primitive recursive functions given above, we can build a Turing machine M that decides the language of syntactically legal unary primitive recursive functions. So, to produce the desired lexicographic enumeration of the primitive recursive function definitions, it suffices to enumerate lexicographically all strings over Σ^* and output only those that are accepted by M. We will choose to number the elements of this enumeration (the function definitions) starting with 0.

Using the lexicographic enumeration of the primitive recursive function definitions that we just described and a straightforward lexicographic enumeration of the natural numbers (the possible arguments to those functions), we can imagine Table 25.4 which we will call T. $T[i, j]$ contains the value of f_i applied to j. Since every primitive recursive function is computable, there exists a Turing machine that can compute the value for any cell in T when it is required.

We now define the function $diagonal(n) = succ(T(n, n))$, which can be computed by the following Turing machine M:

$M(n) =$

1. Run the Turing machine that computes f_n on n. Let the value it produces be x.
2. Return $x + 1$.

The function *diagonal* is computable (by M) but it is not in the enumeration of primitive recursive functions since it differs from each of those in at least one place. So there exist computable functions that are not primitive recursive.

Table 25.4 Using diagonalization to prove that there are computable functions that are not primitive recursive.

	0	1	2	3	4	5	...
f_0							
f_1							
f_2							
f_3							
f_4							
f_5							
...							

25.2.2 Ackermann's Function

Now we know that there exists at least one computable function that is not primitive recursive. But are there others? The answer is yes.

Consider Ackermann's function, defined as follows on the domain $\mathbb{N} \times \mathbb{N}$:

$$A(0, y) = y + 1.$$

$$A(x + 1, 0) = A(x, 1).$$

$$A(x + 1, y + 1) = A(x, A(x + 1, y)).$$

Table 25.5 shows a few values for A. Table 25.6 comments on some of the values in the last row of Table 25.5.

So imagine that, at every second since the Big Bang, we had written one digit on every atom in the universe. By now we would have written approximately $3 \cdot 10^{96}$ digits, which is not enough to have written (much less computed) $A(4,3)$.

Ackermann's function, unlike the busy beaver functions of Section 25.1.4, is recursive (computable). Ignoring memory and stack overflow, it is easy to write a program to compute it. But Ackermann's function is not primitive recursive. While it does not grow as fast as the busy beaver functions, it does grow faster than many other fast-growing functions like *fermat*. It is possible to prove that A is not primitive recursive precisely because it grows so quickly and there is an upper bound on the rate at which primitive recursive functions can grow.

Table 25.5 The first few values of Ackermann's function.

x \ y	0	1	2	3	4
0	1	2	3	4	5
1	2	3	4	5	6
2	3	5	7	9	11
3	5	13	29	61	125
4	13	65533	$2^{65536} - 3$	$2^{2^{65536}} - 3$	$2^{2^{2^{65536}}} - 3$

Table 25.6 Ackermann's function grows very fast.

	Decimal digits required to express this value	***To put that number in perspective***
(4, 2)	19,729	There have been about $12 \cdot 10^9$ years or $3 \cdot 10^{17}$ seconds since the Big Bang.
(4, 3)	10^{5940}	There are about 10^{79} atoms in the observable universe.
(4, 4)	$10^{10^{5939}}$	

So A is another example of a computable function that is not primitive recursive.

25.2.3 Recursive (Computable) Functions

Since there are computable functions that are not primitive recursive, we are still looking for a way to define exactly the functions that Turing machines can compute.

We next define the class of μ-recursive functions using the same basic functions that we used to define the primitive recursive functions. We will again allow function composition and primitive recursion. But we will add one way of defining a new function.

We must first define a new notion: The ***minimalization*** f of a function g (of $k + 1$ arguments) is a function of k arguments defined as follows:

$$f(n_1, n_2, \ldots n_k) = \begin{cases} \text{the smallest } m \text{ such that } g(n_1, n_2, \ldots n_k, m) = 1, & \text{if there is such an } m, \\ 0, & \text{otherwise.} \end{cases}$$

Clearly, given any function g and any set of k arguments to it, there either is at least one value m such that $g(n_1, n_2, \ldots n_k, m) = 1$ or there isn't. If there is at least one such value, then there is a smallest one (since we are considering only the natural numbers). So there always exists a function f that is the minimalization of g. If g is computable, then we can build a Turing machine $T_{\min}$ that almost computes f as follows:

$T_{\min}(n_1, n_2, \ldots n_k) =$

1. $m = 0$.
2. While $g(n_1, n_2, \ldots n_k, m) \neq 1$ do:
   $m = m + 1$.
3. Return m.

The problem is that $T_{\min}$ will not halt if no value of m exists. There is no way for $T_{\min}$ to discover that no such value exists and thus return 0.

Since we are trying to build a theory of computable functions (those for which there exists a Turing machine that always halts), we next define the class of minimalizable functions as follows: A function g is ***minimalizable*** iff, for every $n_1, n_2, \ldots n_k$, there is an m such that $g(n_1, n_2, \ldots n_k, m) = 1$. In other words, g is minimalizable if $T_{\min}$, as defined above, always halts.

We define the ***μ*-recursive functions** to be the smallest class of functions from $\mathbb{N} \times \mathbb{N} \times \ldots \times \mathbb{N}$ to $\mathbb{N}$ that includes:

- the constant function 0,
- the successor function: $succ(n) = n + 1$, and
- the family of projection functions: For any $k \geq j > 0$, $p_{k,j}(n_1, n_2, \ldots n_k) = n_j$,

and that is closed under the operations:

- composition of g with $h_1, h_2, \ldots h_k$:

$$g(h_1(\,), h_2(\,), \ldots h_k(\,)),$$

- primitive recursion of f in terms of g and h, and
- minimalization of minimalizable functions.

A good way to get an intuitive understanding of the difference between the primitive recursive functions and the μ-recursive functions is the following:

- In the computation of any primitive recursive function, iteration is always bounded; it can be implemented with a *for* loop that runs for n_k steps, where n_k is the value of the last argument to f. So, for example, computing *times*(2, 3) requires invoking *plus* three times.
- In the computation of a μ-recursive function, on the other hand, iteration may require the execution of a *while* loop like the one in T_{min}. So it is not always possible to impose a bound, in advance, on the number of steps required by the computation.

THEOREM 25.7 Equivalence of μ-Recursion and Computability

Theorem: A function is μ-recursive iff it is computable.

Proof: We must show both directions:

- Every μ-recursive function is computable. We show this by showing how to build a Turing machine for each of the basic functions and for each of the combining operations.
- Every computable function is μ-recursive. We show this by showing how to construct μ-recursive functions to perform each of the operations that a Turing machine can perform.

We will omit the details of both of these steps. They are straightforward but tedious.

We have now accomplished our first goal. We have a functional definition for the class of computable functions.

It is worth pointing out here why the same diagonalization argument that we used in the case of primitive recursive functions cannot be used again to show that there must exist some computable function that is not μ-recursive. The key to the argument in the case of the primitive recursive functions was that it was possible to create a lexicographic enumeration of exactly the primitive recursive function definitions. The reason it was possible is that a simple examination of the syntax of a proposed function tells us whether or not it is primitive recursive. But now consider trying to do the same thing to decide whether a function *f* is μ-recursive. If *f* is defined in terms of the minimalization of some other function *g*, we would first have to check to see whether *g* is minimalizable. To do that, we would need to know whether T_{min} halts on all inputs. That problem is undecidable. So there exists no lexicographic enumeration of the μ-recursive functions.

Next we will attempt to find a functional definition for the class of partially computable functions. We define the ***partial μ-recursive functions*** to be the smallest class of functions from $\mathbb{N} \times \mathbb{N} \times \ldots \times \mathbb{N}$ to $\mathbb{N}$ that includes:

- the constant function 0,
- the successor function: $succ(n) = n + 1$, and
- the family of projection functions: For any $k \geq j > 0$, $p_{k,j}(n_1, n_2, \ldots n_k) = n_j$,

and that is closed under the operations:

- composition of *g* with $h_1, h_2, \ldots h_k$,
- primitive recursion of *f* in terms of *g* and *h*, and
- minimalization.

The only difference between this definition and the one that we gave for the μ-recursive functions is that we now allow minimalization of any function, not just the minimalizable ones. A function that is defined in this way may, therefore, not be a total function. So it is possible that there exists no Turing machine that computes it and that always halts.

THEOREM 25.8 Equivalence of Partial μ-Recursion and Partial Computability

Theorem: A function is a partial μ-recursive function iff it is partially computable.

Proof: We must show both directions:

- Every partial μ-recursive function is partially computable. We show this by showing how to build a Turing machine for each of the basic functions and for each of the combining operations. Note that the Turing machine that implements the minimalization of a function that is not minimalizable will not be guaranteed to halt on all inputs.
- Every partially computable function is partial μ-recursive. We show this by showing how to construct μ-recursive functions to perform each of the operations that a Turing machine can perform.

We will omit the details of both of these steps. They are straightforward but tedious.

25.3 The Recursion Theorem and Its Use

In this section, we prove the existence of a very useful computable (recursive) function: *obtainSelf*. When called as a subroutine by any Turing machine M, *obtainSelf* writes onto M's tape the string encoding of M.

We begin by asking whether there exists a Turing machine that implements the following specification:

virus() =

1. For each address in address book do:

1.1. Write a copy of myself.

1.2. Mail it to the address.

2. Do something fun and malicious like change one bit in every file on the machine.

3. Halt.

In particular, can we implement step 1.1 and build a program that writes a copy of itself? That seems simple until we try. A program that writes any literal string s = "$a_1a_2a_3 \ldots a_n$" is simply:

- Write "$a_1a_2a_3 \ldots a_n$".

But, using that simple string encoding of a program, this program is 8 characters longer than the string it writes. So if we imagined that our original code had length k then the program to write it would have length $k + 8$. But if that code contained the write statement, we would need to write:

- Write "Write" $\|$ "$a_1a_2a_3 \ldots a_n$".

But now we need to write that, and so forth. Perhaps this seems hopeless. But it is not.

First, let's rearrange virus a little bit:

virus() =

1. *copyme* = copy of myself.

2. For each address in address book do:

2.1. Mail *copyme* to the address.

3. Do something fun and malicious like change one bit in every file on the machine.

4. Halt.

If *virus* can somehow get a single copy of itself onto its tape, a simple loop (of fixed length, independent of the length of the copy) can make additional copies, which can then be treated like any other string. The problem is for *virus* to get access to that first copy of itself. Here's how we can solve that problem.

First, we will define a family of printing functions, P_s. For any literal string s, P_s is the description of a Turing machine that writes the string s onto the tape. Think of s as being hardwired into P_s. For example, P_{abbb} = <aRbRbRbR>. Notice that the length of the Turing machine P_s depends on the length of *s*.

Next we define a Turing machine, *createP*, that takes a string *s* as input on one tape and outputs the printing function P_s on a second tape:

createP(*s*) =

1. For each character *c* in *s* (on tape 1) do on tape 2:

1.1. Write *c*.

1.2. Write R.

Notice that the length of *createP* is fixed. It does not need separate code for each character of *s*. It has just one simple loop that reads the characters of *s* one at a time and outputs two characters for each.

Now let's break *virus* down into two parts:

- Step 1: We'll call this step *copy*. It writes on the tape a string that is the description of *virus*.
- Steps 2, 3, and 4, or whatever else *virus* wants to do: We'll call this part *work*. This part begins with *virus*'s description on the tape and does whatever it wants with it.

We will further break step 1, *copy*, down into two pieces that we will call *A* and *B*. *A* will execute first. Its job will be to write <*B*, *work*>, the description of *B* and *work* onto the tape. The string <*B*, *work*> will be hardwired into *A*, so the length of *A* itself depends on |<*B*, *work*>|. When *A* is done, the tape will be as shown in Figure 25.2(a).

The job of *B* will be to write <*A*>, the description of *A*, onto the tape immediately to the left of what *A* wrote. So, after *B* has finished, the job of copying *virus* will be complete and the tape will be as shown in Figure 25.2(b).

Suppose that we knew exactly what *B* was. Then *A* would be $P_{<B><work>}$. Assuming that we describe *A* in our macro language, |<*A*>| would then be $2 \cdot |<B><work>|$, since for each character it must write and then move one square to the right. But what is *B*? It must be a machine that writes <*A*>. And its length must be fixed. It cannot depend on the length of <*A*>, since then the length of <*A*> would depend on the length of <*B*>, which would depend on the length of <*A*> and so forth. So it cannot just be $P_{<A>}$.

Fortunately, we know how to build *B* so that it writes <*A*> and does so with a fixed chunk of code, independent of the length of *A*. Given any string *s* on tape 1, *createP*

<*B*> <*work*>

(a)

<*A*> <*B*> <*work*>

(b)

FIGURE 25.2 The result of running *A* and then *B*.

writes, onto a second tape, the description of a Turing machine that writes *s*. And it does so with a fixed length program. *A* is a program that writes a string. So perhaps *B* could use *createP* to write a description of *A*. That will work if *B* has access to the string *s* that *A* wrote. But it does. *A* wrote <*B*><*work*>, which is exactly what is on the tape when *B* gets control. So we have (expanding out the code for *createP*):

B =

1. /* Invoke *createP* to write onto tape 2 the code that writes the string that is currently on tape 1.

For each character *c* in *s* (on tape 1) do on tape 2:

1.1. Write *c*.

1.2. Write R.

2. /* Copy tape 2 to tape 1, moving right to left. Place this copy to the left of what is already on tape 1.

Starting at the rightmost character *c* on tape 2 and the blank immediately to the left of the leftmost character on tape 1, loop until all characters have been processed:

2.1. Copy *c* to tape 1.

2.2. Move both read/write heads one square to the left.

So the code for *B* (unlike the code for *A*) is independent of the particular Turing machine of which we need to make a copy.

When *B* starts, the two tapes will be as shown in Figure 25.3(a). After step 1, they will be as shown in Figure 25.3(b). Remember that <*A*> is the description of a

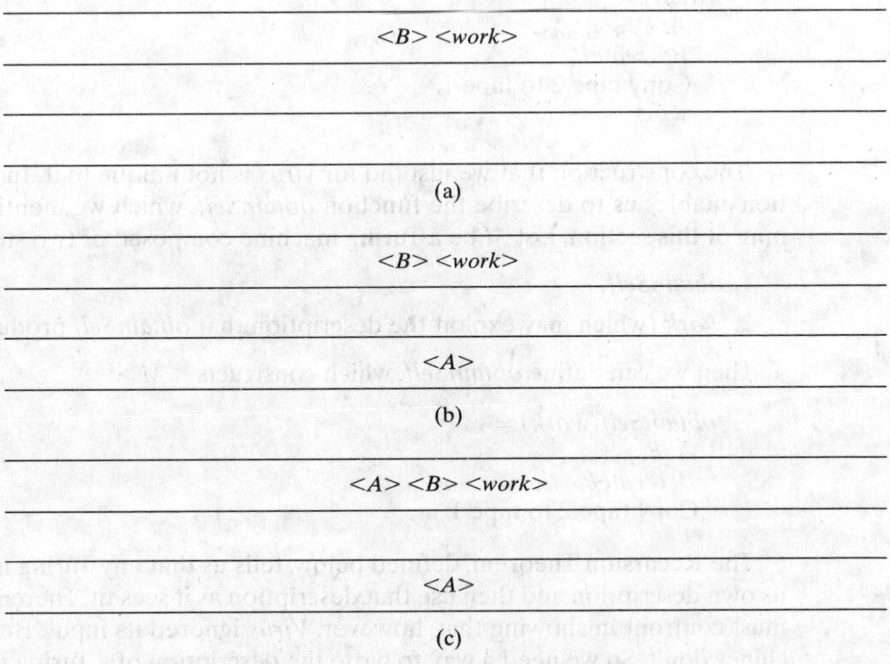

FIGURE 25.3
The tape before, during, and after the execution of *B*.

Turing machine that writes <*B*><*work*>. Then, after step 2, they will be as shown in Figure 25.3(c).

Notice that the code for *B* is fixed. It first writes <*A*> onto tape 2 using a simple loop. Then, starting from the right, it copies <*A*> onto tape 2 just to the left of the string <*B*><*work*> that was already there. Again, it does this with a simple loop.

Now we can describe *virus* exactly as follows. Recall that <*M*> means the string description, written in the macro language described in Section 17.6, of the Turing machine *M*. So <*B*> is the description of the Turing machine labeled *B* here:

virus() =
    A: Write on tape 1 <*B*> <*work*>.
    B: /* *createP*, which will write onto tape 2 the code that writes the string that is currently on tape 1.
        For each character c in *s* (on tape 1) do on tape 2:
            Write *c*.
            Write R.
        /* Copy tape 2 to tape 1, moving right to left. Place this copy to the left of what is already on tape 1.
        Starting at the rightmost character *c* on tape 2 and the blank immediately to the left of the leftmost character on tape 1, loop until all characters have been processed:
            Copy *c* to tape 1.
            Move both read/write heads one square to the left.
    work.

Or, more succinctly, using P_s and *createP*:

virus() =
    A: $P_{<B><work>}$.
    B: *createP*.
    Copy tape 2 to tape 1.
    work.

The construction that we just did for *virus* is not unique to it. In fact, that construction enables us to describe the function *obtainSelf*, which we mentioned at the beginning of this section. Let *M* be a Turing machine composed of two steps:

1. *obtainSelf*.
2. *work* (which may exploit the description that *obtainSelf* produced).

Then we can define *obtainSelf*, which constructs <*M*>:

obtainSelf(work) =
    A: $P_{<B><work>}$.
    B: *createP*.
    Copy tape 2 to tape 1

The Recursion Theorem, defined below, tells us that any Turing machine can obtain its own description and then use that description as it sees fit. There is one issue that we must confront in showing that, however. *Virus* ignored its input. But many Turing machines don't. So we need a way to write the description of a Turing machine *M* onto its tape without destroying its input. This is easy. If *M* is a *k*-tape Turing machine, we build a $k + 2$ tape machine, where the extra two tapes are used, as we have just described, to create a description of *M*.

THEOREM 25.9 The Recursion Theorem

Theorem: For every Turing machine *T* that computes a partially computable function *t* of two string arguments, there exists a Turing machine *R* that computes a partially computable function *r* of one string argument and:

$$\forall x\,(r(x) = t(<R>, x)).$$

To understand the recursion theorem, it helps to see an example. Recall the Turing machine that we specified in our proof of Theorem 21.14 (that the language of descriptions of minimal Turing machines is not in SD):

M#(*x*) =

1. Invoke *obtainSelf* to produce <*M#*>.
2. Run *ENUM* until it generates the description of some Turing machine *M'* whose description is longer than |<*M#*>|.
3. Invoke the universal Turing machine *U* on the string <*M'*, *x*>.

Steps 2 and 3 are the guts of *M#* and correspond to a Turing machine *T* that takes two arguments, <*M#*> and *x*, and computes a function we can call *t*. *M#*, on the other hand, takes a single argument, *x*. But *M#*(*x*) is exactly *T*(<*M#*>, *x*) because in step 1, *M#* constructs <*M#*>, which it then hands to *T* (i.e., steps 2 and 3). So, given that we wish to compute *T*(<*M#*>, *x*), *M#* is the Turing machine *R* that the recursion theorem says must exist. The only difference between *R* and *T* is that *R* constructs its own description and then passes that description, along with its own argument, on to *T*. Since, for any *T*, *R* must exist, it must always be possible for *R* to construct its own description and pass it to *T*.

Proof: The proof is by construction. The construction is identical to the one we showed above in our description of *virus* except that we substitute *T* for *work*.

The Recursion Theorem is sometimes stated in a different form, as a fixed-point theorem. We will state that version as a separate theorem whose proof follows from the recursion theorem as just stated and proved.

THEOREM 25.10 The Fixed-Point Definition of the Recursion Theorem

Theorem: Let *f*: {<*M*> : *M* is a Turing machine description} → {<*M*> : *M* is a Turing machine description} be any computable function on the set of Turing machine descriptions. There exists some Turing machine *F* such that *f*(<*F*>) is the description of some Turing machine *G* and it is the case that *F* and *G* are equivalent (i.e., they behave identically on all inputs). We call *F* a ***fixed point*** of the function *f*, since it does not change when *f* is applied to it.

Proof: The Turing machine F that we claim must exist is:

$F(x) =$

1. Invoke *obtainSelf* to produce <F>.
2. Since f is a computable function, there must be some Turing machine M_f that computes it. Invoke $M_f(<F>)$, which produces the description of some Turing machine we can call G.
3. Run G on x.

Whatever f is, $f(<F>) = <G>$. F and G are equivalent since, on any input x, F halts exactly when G would halt and it leaves on its tape exactly what G leaves.

This theorem says something interesting and, at first glance perhaps, counterintuitive. Let's consider again the *virus* program that we described above. In its *work* section, it changes one bit in every file on its host machine. Consider the files that correspond to programs. Theorem 25.10 says that there exists at least one program whose behavior will not change when it is altered in that way. Of course, most programs will change. That is why *virus* can be so destructive. But there is not only one fixed point for *virus*, there are many, including:

- Every program that infinite loops on all inputs and where the bit that f changes comes after the section of code that went into the loop.
- Every program that has a chunk of redundant code, such as:

  $$a = 5$$
  $$a = 7$$

  where the bit that gets changed is in the first value that is assigned and then overwritten.
- Every program that has a branch that can never be reached and where the bit that f changes is in the unreachable chunk of code.

We have stated and proved the Recursion Theorem in terms of the operation of Turing machines. It can also be stated and proved in the language of recursive functions. When done this way, its proof relies on another theorem that is interesting in its own right. We state and prove it next. To do so, we need to introduce a new technique for describing functions since, so far, we have described them as strings (i.e., the string encodings of the Turing machines that compute them). Yet the theory of recursive functions is a theory of functions on the natural numbers.

We define the following one-to-one function *Gödel* that maps from the set of Turing machines to the positive integers: Let M be a Turing machine that computes some partially computable function. Let <M> be the string description of M, using the encoding mechanism that we defined in Section 17.6.1. That encoding scheme used eleven symbols, which can be encoded in binary using four bits. Rewrite <M> as a binary string. Now view that string as the number it encodes. We note that *Gödel* is a function (since each Turing machine is assigned a unique number); it is one-to-one (since no two

Turing machines are assigned the same number); but it is not onto (since there are numbers that do not encode any Turing machine). A one-to-one function that assigns natural numbers to objects is called a ***Gödel numbering***, since the technique was introduced by Kurt Gödel. It played a key role in the proof of his Incompleteness Theorem.

We'll now create a second Gödel numbering, this time of the partial recursive functions. For each such function, assign to it the smallest number that has been assigned to some Turing machine that computes it. Now define:

φ_k to be the partially computable function with Gödel number k.

Notice that since functions are now represented as numbers, it is straightforward to talk about functions whose inputs and/or outputs are other functions. We'll take advantage of this and describe our next result. Suppose that $f(x_1, x_2, \ldots, x_m, y_1, y_2, \ldots, y_n)$ is an arbitrary function of $m + n$ arguments. Then we'll see that it is always possible, whenever we fix values for $x_1, x_2, \ldots, x_m$, to create a new function f' of only n arguments. The new function f' will behave as though it were f with the fixed values supplied for the first m arguments. One way to think of f' is that it encapsulates f and a set of values $v_1, v_2, \ldots, v_m$. We'll show that there exists a family of functions, one for each pair of values m and n, that, given f and $v_1, v_2, \ldots, v_m$, creates f' as required.

THEOREM 25.11 The *s-m-n* Theorem

Theorem: For all $m, n \geq 1$, there exists a computable function $s_{m,n}$ with the following property: Let k be the Gödel number of some partially computable function of $m + n$ arguments. Then, for all $k, v_1, v_2, \ldots, v_m, y_1, y_2, \ldots, y_n$:

- $s_{m,n}(k, v_1, v_2, \ldots, v_m)$ returns a number j that is the Gödel number of some partially computable function of n arguments, and
- $\varphi_j(y_1, y_2, \ldots, y_n) = \varphi_k(v_1, v_2, \ldots, v_m, y_1, y_2, \ldots, y_n)$.

Proof: We will prove the theorem by defining a family of Turing machines $M_{m,n}$ that compute the $s_{m,n}$ family of functions. On input $(k, v_1, v_2, \ldots, v_m)$, $M_{m,n}$ will construct a new Turing machine M_j that operates as follows on input w: Write $v_1, v_2, \ldots, v_m$ on the tape immediately to the left of w; move the read/write head all the way to the left in front of v_1; and pass control to the Turing machine encoded by k. $M_{m,n}$ will then return j, the Gödel number of the function computed by M_j.

The *s-m-n* Theorem has important applications in the design of functional programming languages. (G.5) In particular, it is the basis for ***currying***, which implements the process we have just described. When a function of $k > 0$ arguments is curried, one or more of its arguments are fixed and a new function, of fewer arguments, is constructed.

Exercises

1. Define the function $pred(x)$ as follows:

$$pred: \mathbb{N} \rightarrow \mathbb{N},$$
$$pred(x) = x - 1.$$

   a. Is *pred* a total function on $\mathbb{N}$?
   b. If not, is it a total function on some smaller, decidable domain?
   c. Show that *pred* is computable by defining an encoding of the elements of $\mathbb{N}$ as strings over some alphabet Σ and then showing a Turing machine that halts on all inputs and that computes either *pred* or *pred'* (using the notion of a primed function as described in Section 25.1.2).

2. Prove that every computable function is also partially computable.
3. Consider $f: A \rightarrow \mathbb{N}$, where $A \subseteq \mathbb{N}$. Prove that, if f is partially computable, then A is semidecidable (i.e., Turing enumerable).
4. Give an example, other than *steps*, of a function that is partially computable but not computable.
5. Define the function $countL(<M>)$ as follows:

$$countL: \{<M> : M \text{ is a Turing machine}\} \rightarrow \mathbb{N} \cup \{\aleph_0\},$$
$$countL(<M>) = \text{the number of input strings that are accepted by } M.$$

   a. Is *countL* a total function on $\{<M> : M \text{ is a Turing machine}\}$?
   b. If not, is it a total function on some smaller, decidable domain?
   c. Is *countL* computable, partially computable, or neither? Prove your answer.

6. Give an example, other than any mentioned in the book, of a function that is not partially computable.
7. Let g be some partially computable function that is not computable. Let h be some computable function and let $f(x) = g(h(x))$. Is it possible that f is a computable function?
8. Prove that the busy beaver function Σ is not computable.
9. Prove that each of the following functions is primitive recursive:
   a. The function $double(x) = 2x$.
   b. The proper subtraction function *monus*, which is defined as follows:

$$monus(n, m) = \begin{cases} n - m & \text{if } n > m \\ 0 & \text{if } n \leq m \end{cases}$$

   c. The function *half*, which is defined as follows:

$$half(n) = \begin{cases} n/2 & \text{if } n \text{ is even} \\ (n-1)/2 & \text{if } n \text{ is odd} \end{cases}$$

10. Let A be Ackermann's function. Verify that $A(4, 1) = 65533$.

CHAPTER 26

Summary and References

One way to think about what we have done in Part IV is to explore the limits of computation. We have considered many different models of "the computable." All of them were described and studied by people who were trying to answer the question, "What can we compute?" Some of the models look similar. For example, Post production systems and unrestricted grammars both define languages by providing a start symbol and a set of production rules that rewrite one string into another. While there are differences (Post systems exploit variables and must match entire strings while unrestricted grammars use only constants and can match substrings), it turns out that the two formalisms are identical: They both define exactly the class of languages that we are calling SD. Similarly, Turing machines and tag systems look similar. One uses a tape with a moveable read/write head, the other uses a first-in, first-out queue. But that difference also turns out not to matter. A machine of either kind can be simulated by a machine of the other kind.

Some of the models look very different. Turing machines seem like sequential computers. Expressions in the lambda calculus read like mathematical function definitions. Unrestricted grammars are rewrite systems. One of the most important structural differences is between the models (such as Turing machines, tag systems, the lambda calculus, semi-Thue systems, and Markov algorithms) that accept inputs, and so compute functions, and those (such as unrestricted grammars, Post systems, and Lindenmayer systems) that include a start symbol and so generate languages. But all of these systems can be viewed as mechanisms for defining languages. The generating systems generate languages; the function-computation systems compute a language's characteristic function. So even that difference doesn't effect the bottom line of what is computable.

Another thing that we did in Part IV was to introduce three new classes of languages: D, SD, and the context-sensitive languages. The table shown in Table 26.1 summarizes the properties of those languages and compares them to the regular and the context-free languages.

Table 26.1 Comparing the classes of languages.

	Regular	***Context-Free***	***Context-Sensitive***	**D**	**SD**
Automaton	FSM	PDA	LBA		TM
Grammar(s)	Regular expressions	Context-free	Context-sensitive		Unrestricted
ND = D?	Yes	No	unknown		Yes
Closed under:					
Concatenation	Yes	Yes	Yes	Yes	Yes
Union	Yes	Yes	Yes	Yes	Yes
Kleene star	Yes	Yes	Yes	Yes	Yes
Complement	Yes	No	Yes	Yes	No
Intersection	Yes	No	Yes	Yes	Yes
∩ with Regular	Yes	Yes	Yes	Yes	Yes
Decidable:					
Membership	Yes	Yes	Yes		No
Emptiness	Yes	Yes	No		No
Finiteness	Yes	Yes	No		No
$= \Sigma^*$	Yes	No	No		No
Equivalence	Yes	No	No		No

References

Gödel's Completeness Theorem was presented in [Gödel 1929]. His Incompleteness Theorem was presented in [Gödel 1931].

The Entscheidungsproblem was articulated in [Hilbert and Ackermann 1928]. In [Church 1936], Alonzo Church defined the lambda calculus and proved that no solution to the Entscheidungsproblem exists. In [Turing 1936], Alan Turing defined the Turing Machine and also proved the unsolvability of the Entscheidungsproblem. Many of the early papers on computability have been reprinted in [Davis 1965]. The Turing machine description language defined in Chapter 17 is patterned closely after one described in [Lewis and Papadimitriou 1998].

Post published his work on tag systems in [Post 1943]. [Minsky 1961] showed that tag systems have the same computational power as Turing machines. As a result, that claim is sometimes called Minsky's Theorem. Post also described his production rule system in [Post 1943]. A good modern treatment can be found in [Taylor 1998].

Markov algorithms were first described (in Russian) in [Markov 1951]. A good treatment in English is [Markov and Nagorny 1988].

A description of Conway's Game of Life was first published in [Gardner 1970]. [Berlekamp, Conway, and Guy 1982] describe a proof of the equivalence of Turing machines and the Game of Life. [Rendell 2000] describes an implementation of a Turing machine in Life.

One dimensional cellular automata are described in detail in [Wolfram 2002].

The first experiment in DNA computing was described in [Adleman 1994] and [Adleman 1998]. A detailed mathematical treatment of the subject can be found in [Păun, Rozenberg and Salomaa 1998].

See [Lagarias 1985] for a comprehensive discussion of the $3x + 1$ problem.

Rice's Theorem was described in [Rice 1953].

Hilbert's 10th problem was shown to be undecidable as a result of Matiyasevich's theorem, published in [Matiyasevich 1970].

The undecidability of the Post Correspondence Problem was shown in [Post 1946]. The proof that we present in E.4 was modeled after the one in [Linz 2001]. The fact that the Post Correspondence Problem is decidable if limited to instances of size two was shown in [Ehrenfeucht, Karhumaki and Rozenberg 1982].

Wang tiles were first described in [Wang 1961]. Also in that paper, Wang articulated the hypothesis we called Wang's conjecture; he proved that, if the conjecture is true, then the tiling problem is decidable. [Berger 1966] showed that Wang's conjecture is false by demonstrating a set of 20,426 tiles that tile the plane only aperiodically. [Culik 1996] showed an aperiodic set of just 13 tiles.

Presburger arithmetic was defined in [Presburger 1929]. [Fischer and Rabin 1974] showed that any decision procedure for Presburger arithmetic requires time that is $\mathcal{O}(2^{2^{cn}})$.

See [Bar-Hillel, Perles and Shamir 1961], [Ginsburg and Rose 1963], and [Hartmanis and Hopcroft 1968] for fundamental results on the undecidability of questions involving context-free languages. The fact that it is undecidable whether a context-free grammar is ambiguous was published independently by [Cantor 1962], [Floyd 1962] and [Chomsky and Schutzenberger 1963].

Theorem 23.4, which tells us that the word problem for semi-Thue systems is undecidable, was proved in [Post 1947].

The Chomsky hierarchy was defined in [Chomsky 1959], with unrestricted grammars as the most powerful of the formalisms to occur in the hierarchy. Also in that paper Chomsky proved Theorem 23.1, which says that the set of languages that can be generated by an unrestricted grammar is equivalent to the set SD.

[Chomsky 1959] also defined the context-sensitive languages to be those that could be described with a context-sensitive grammar. It also proved Theorem 24.4, which says that the context-sensitive languages are a proper subset of D. The equivalence of the context-sensitive languages in that sense and the languages that can be accepted by a (nondeterministic) linear bounded automaton was shown in [Kuroda 1964]. The fact that the context-sensitive languages (unlike the context-free ones) are closed under intersection was proved in [Landweber 1963]. The proofs we give for the closure of the context-sensitive languages under union, concatenation, Kleene star, and intersection are from [Hopcroft and Ullman 1979]. The fact that the membership problem for context-sensitive languages is NP-hard was proved in [Karp 1972].

Attribute grammars as a way to define the semantics of context-free languages were introduced in [Knuth 1968]. For an introduction to the use of feature/unification grammars in natural language processing, see [Jurafsky and Martin 2000].

Lindenmayer systems (L-systems) were first described in [Lindenmayer 1968]. See [Prusinkiewicz and Lindenmayer 1990] for an excellent description of them and of their use as the basis for simulations of plant development. The L-system that generates the trees in Example 24.6 was taken from [Ochoa 1998].

The busy beaver functions were first described in [Rado 1962].

Primitive recursive functions were described in [Dedekind 1888]. See [Martin 2003] for a comprehensive discussion of primitive recursive functions with many examples.

[Ackermann 1928] showed the existence of a function that was computable but not primitive recursive. His original function was one of three variables. Rózsa Péter and Raphael Robinson created the simpler version, of two variables, that now bears Ackermann's name. It was described in [Péter 1967].

The μ-recursive functions are described in [Kleene 1936a]. The *s-m-n* Theorem and the Recursion Theorem are also due to Kleene. See [Kleene 1964]. The constructive proof that we present for Theorem 25.9 follows the one given in [Sipser 2006].

P A R T V

COMPLEXITY

In Part IV we described the distinction between problems that are theoretically solvable and ones that are not. In this section, we will take another look at the class of solvable problems and further distinguish among them. In particular, we will contrast problems that are "practically solvable", in the sense that programs that solve them have resource requirements (in terms of time and or space) that can generally be met, and problems that are "practically unsolvable", at least for large inputs, since their resource requirements grow so quickly that they cannot typically be met. Throughout our discussion, we will generally assume that if resource requirements grow as some polynomial function of problem size, then the problem is practically solvable. If they grow faster than that, then, for all but very small problem instances, the problem will generally be practically unsolvable.

C H A P T E R 27

Introduction to the Analysis of Complexity

Once we know that a problem is solvable (or a language is decidable or a function is computable), we're not done. The next step is to find an efficient algorithm to solve it.

27.1 The Traveling Salesman Problem

The ***traveling salesman problem*** (or TSP for short) is easy to state: Given n cities and the distances between each pair of them, find the shortest tour that returns to its starting point and visits each other city exactly once along the way. We can solve this problem using the straightforward algorithm that first generates all possible paths that meet the requirements and then returns the shortest one. Since we must make a loop through the cities, it doesn't matter what city we start in. So we can pick any one. If there are n cities, there are $n - 1$ cities that could be chosen next. And $n - 2$ that can be chosen after that. And so forth. So, given n cities, the number of different tours is $(n - 1)!$. We can cut the number of tours we examine in half by recognizing that the cost of a tour is the same whether we traverse it forward or backward. That still leaves $(n - 1)!/2$ tours to consider. So this approach quickly becomes intractable as the number of cities grows. To see why, consider the following set of observations: The speed of light is $3 \cdot 10^8$ m/sec. The width of a proton is 10^{-15} m. So, if we perform one operation in the time it takes light to cross a proton, we can perform $3 \cdot 10^{23}$ operations/sec. There have been about $3 \cdot 10^{17}$ seconds since the Big Bang. So, at that rate, we could have performed about $9 \cdot 10^{40}$ operations since the Big Bang. But 36! is $3.6 \cdot 10^{41}$. So there hasn't been enough time since the Big Bang to have solved even a single traveling salesman problem with 37 cities. That's fewer than one city per state in the United States.

One early application of work on the TSP was of concern to farmers rather than salesmen. The task was to conduct a survey of farmlands in Bengal in 1938. One goal of the survey planners was to minimize the cost of transporting the surveyors and their equipment from one place to the next. Another early application was the scheduling of school bus routes so that all the stops were visited and the travel distance among them was minimized.

Of course, one way to make more computations possible is to exploit parallelism. For example, there are about 10^{11} neurons in the human brain. If we think of them as operating independently, then they can perform 10^{11} computations in parallel. Each of them is very slow. But if we imagined the fast operation we described above being performed by 10^{11} computers in parallel, then there would have been time for $9 \cdot 10^{51}$ operations since the Big Bang. $43! = 6 \cdot 10^{52}$. So we still could not have solved an instance of the TSP with one city per state.

In this century, manufacturing applications of the TSP are important. Consider the problem of drilling a set of holes on a board. To minimize manufacturing time, it may be important to minimize the distance that must be traveled by the drill as it moves from one hole to the next. ◻

Over 50 years of research on the traveling salesman problem have led to techniques for reducing the number of tours that must be examined. For example, a dynamic programming approach that reuses partial solutions leads to an algorithm that solves any TSP instance with n cities in time that grows only as $n^2 2^n$. For large n, that is substantially better than $(n - 1)!$. But it still grows exponentially with n and is not efficient enough for large problems. Despite substantial work since the discovery of that approach, there still exists no algorithm that can be guaranteed to solve an arbitrary instance of the TSP exactly and efficiently. We use the term *efficiently* here to mean that the time required to execute the algorithm grows as no more than some polynomial function of the number of cities. Whether or not such an efficient algorithm exists is perhaps the most important open question in theoretical computer science. We'll have a lot more to say about this question, which is usually phrased somewhat differently: "Does P = NP?"

So we do not have a technique for solving the TSP that is efficient and that is guaranteed to find the optimal solution for all problem instances. But suppose that we can compromise. Then it turns out that:

1. there are techniques that are guaranteed to find an optimal solution and that run efficiently on many (although not all) problem instances, and
2. there are techniques that are guaranteed to find a good (although not necessarily optimal) solution and to do so efficiently.

TSP solvers that make the first compromise exploit the idea of linear programming 💻. Given a problem P, a solver of this sort begins by setting up a relaxed version of P (i.e., one in which it is not necessary to satisfy all of the constraints imposed by the original problem P). Then it uses the optimization techniques of linear programming to solve this relaxed problem efficiently. The solution that it finds at this step is optimal, both for the original problem P and for the relaxed problem, but it may not be a legal solution to P. If it is, the process halts with the best tour. If the solution to the relaxed problem is not also a solution to P, it can be used to make a "cut" in the space of possible solutions. The cut is a new linear constraint with the property that the solution that was just found and rejected is on one side of the constraint while all possible solutions to the original problem P are on the other. Ideally, of course, many other candidate solutions that would also have to be rejected will also be on the wrong side of the cut. The cut is then added and a new linear programming problem, again a relaxed (but this time less relaxed) version of P, is solved. This process continues until it finds a solution that meets the constraints of the original problem P. In the worst case, only a single solution will be eliminated every time and an exponential number of tours will have to be considered. When the data come from real problems, however, it usually turns out that the algorithm performs substantially better than that. In 1954, when this idea was first described, it was used to solve an instance of the TSP with 49 cities. Since then, computers have gotten faster and the technique has been improved. In 2004, the Concorde TSP solver, a modern implementation of this idea, was used to find the optimal route that visits 24,978 cities in Sweden 💻.

But what about the second compromise? It often doesn't make sense to spend months finding the perfect tour when a very good one could be found in minutes. Further, if we're solving a problem based on real distances, then we've already approximated the problem by measuring the distances to some finite precision. The notion of an exact optimal solution is theoretically well defined, but it may not be very important for real problems.

If we are willing to accept a "good" solution, then there are reasonably efficient algorithms for solving the TSP. For example, suppose that the distances between the cities satisfy the triangle inequality (i.e., given any three cities a, b, and c, the length of the path that goes directly from a to b is less than or equal to the length of the path that goes from a to c and then to b). If the cities are laid out on a plane and if the distances between them correspond to Euclidean distance (i.e., the standard measure of distance in the plane), then this constraint is met. Then there is a polynomial-time algorithm that finds a minimum spanning tree (as described in Section 28.1.6) for the city graph and uses it to construct a tour whose length is no more than twice the length of an optimal tour. And there is a more sophisticated algorithm that constructs a tour whose distance is guaranteed to be no more than 1.5 times that of the optimal one. So, for all such real-world problems, we have a "pretty good" efficient algorithm. But we'd like to do better and we usually can. For example, a solution that is known to be no more than 0.1% longer than an optimal tour has been found for a problem with 1,904,711 cities 💻.

In several important ways, the TSP is representative of a much larger collection of problems that are of substantial practical interest. As we consider these problems and look for efficient algorithms to solve them, we'll typically consider the following two important questions:

1. What do we mean by efficiency? In particular, are we concerned with:
   - the time required to solve a problem, or
   - the space required to solve it?
2. How intrinsically hard is the problem? In other words, is there some reason to believe that an algorithm that is relatively inefficient, for example one whose time complexity grows exponentially with the size of the input, is the best we are likely to be able to come up with to solve the problem at hand?

In the next three chapters, we will develop a theory that helps us to answer question 2, with respect to both time and space requirements.

27.2 The Complexity Zoo

We are going to discover that, just as we were able to build a hierarchy of language classes based on the power of the automaton required to solve the membership problem, we can build a hierarchy of problem classes based on the complexity of the best algorithm that could exist to solve the problem. We'll consider problems that are intrinsically "easy" or ***tractable***, by which we will mean that they can be solved in time that grows only by some polynomial function of the size of the input. And we'll consider problems (like the traveling salesman problem) that appear to be intrinsically "hard" or ***intractable***, by which we mean that the time required to execute the best known algorithm grows exponentially (or worse) in the size of the input.

Some of the complexity classes that we will describe are large and play important roles in characterizing the practical solvability of the problems that they contain. For example, the first class that we will define is P, the class of problems that can be solved by a deterministic algorithm in polynomial time. All of the context-free languages (including the regular ones) are in P. So is deciding whether a number is prime or whether a graph is connected.

We will also describe a large and important class called NP-complete. No efficient algorithm for solving any NP-complete problem is known. The algorithms that we do have all require some kind of nontrivial search. For example, the traveling salesman problem is NP-complete. So is deciding whether a Boolean formula is satisfiable. (A straightforward search-based approach to solving this problem simply tries all possible assignments of truth values to the variables of an input formula.)

For a variety of reasons, people have found it useful to define many other classes of problems as well. Some of these classes are large and include languages of substantial practical interest. Many others are small and contain problems of more limited interest. There are classes that are known to be subclasses of other classes. There are classes that are known to be mutually disjoint. And there are pairs of classes whose relationship to each other is unknown. The ***Complexity Zoo*** 💻 is a catalogue of known complexity classes. At the time that this sentence is being written, it contains 460 classes, with new ones still being added. We will mention only a small fraction of them in the next few chapters. But the others are defined using the same kinds of techniques that we will use. In each case, the goal is to group together a set of problems that share some significant characteristic(s).

27.3 Characterizing Problems

In order to be able to compare very different kinds of problems, we will need a single framework in which to describe them. Just as we did in Parts II, III, and IV of this book, we will describe problems as languages to be decided. So we will prove complexity results for some of the languages we have already discussed, including:

- $\{w \in \{a, b\}^* :$ no two consecutive characters are the same$\}$ (a typical regular language),
- $\{a^i b^j c^k : i, j, k \geq 0$ and $(i \neq j)$ or $(j \neq k)\}$ (an example of a context-free language),
- $A^nB^nC^n = \{a^n b^n c^n : n \geq 0\}$ (an "easy" language that is not context-free), and
- SAT $= \{<w> : w$ is a wff in Boolean logic and w is satisfiable$\}$ (a "hard" language that is not context-free).

We will describe both time and space complexity in terms of functions that are defined only for deciding Turing machines (i.e., Turing machines that always halt). So our discussion of the complexity of languages will be restricted to the decidable languages. Thus we will not be able to make any claims about the complexity of languages such as:

- H $= \{<M, w> :$ Turing machine M halts on input string $w\}$, or
- PCP $= \{<P> :$ the Post Correspondence Problem instance P has a solution$\}$.

If we were not restricting our attention to decision problems (whose output is a single bit), we might discover problems that appear hard simply because they require very long answers. For example, consider the Towers of Hanoi problem, which we describe in P.2. Suppose that we wanted to describe the complexity of the most efficient algorithm that, on input n, outputs a sequence of moves that would result in n disks being moved from one pole to another. It is possible to prove that the shortest such sequence contains $2^n - 1$ moves. So any algorithm that solves this problem must run for at least $2^n - 1$ steps (assuming that it takes at least one step to write each move). And it needs at least $2^n - 1$ memory cells to store the output sequence as it is being built. Regardless of how efficiently each move can be chosen, both the time complexity and the space complexity of any algorithm that solves this problem must be exponential simply because the length of the required answer is.

Contrast this with the traveling salesman problem. Given n cities, a solution is an ordered list of the n cities. So the length of a solution is approximately the same as the length of the input. The complexity of solving the problem arises not from the need to compose a large answer but from the apparent need to search a large space of possible short answers. By choosing to cast all of our problems as decision problems, we standardize (to one bit) the length of the solutions that will be produced. Then we can compare problems by asking about the complexity, with respect to time or space or both, of computing that one bit. (We will see, at the end of the next section, how the traveling salesman problem can be converted to a decision problem.)

27.3.1 Choosing an Encoding

Recall that we argued, in Section 3.2, that restricting our attention to the broad task of language recognition did not tie our hands behind our backs since other kinds of problems can be encoded as languages to be decided. So, for example, we will prove complexity results for some languages that are derived from questions we might ask about graphs. For example, we can analyze the complexity of:

- CONNECTED = {<*G*> : *G* is an undirected graph and *G* is connected}. An undirected graph is ***connected*** iff there exists a path from each vertex to every other vertex.
- HAMILTONIAN-CIRCUIT = {<*G*> : *G* is an undirected graph and *G* contains a Hamiltonian circuit}. A ***Hamiltonian circuit*** is a path that starts at some vertex *s*, ends back in *s*, and visits each other vertex in *G* exactly once.

When our focus was on decidability, we did not concern ourselves very much with the nature of the encodings that we used. One exception to this arose in Section 3.2, when we showed one encoding for an integer sum problem that makes the resulting language regular, while a different encoding results in a nonregular language.

But now we want to make claims not just about decidability but about the efficiency of decidability. In particular, we are going to want to describe both the time and the space requirements of a deciding program as a function of the length of the program's input. So it may matter what encoding we choose (and thus how long each input string is). Most of the time, it will be obvious what constitutes a reasonable encoding.

One important place where it may not be obvious is the question of what constitutes a reasonable encoding of the natural numbers. We will take as reasonable an encoding in any base greater than or equal to 2. So we'll allow, for example, both binary and decimal encodings. We will not consider unary encodings. The reason for this distinction is straightforward: it takes n characters to encode n in unary (letting the empty string stand for 0, 1 for 1, and so forth). But for any base $b \geq 2$, the string encoding of n base b has length $\lfloor \log_b n \rfloor + 1$ (where $\lfloor x \rfloor$, read as "floor of x", is the largest natural number less than x). So the length of the encoding grows only as the logarithm of n, rather than as n. Looked at from the other direction, the length of the string required to encode n in unary grows as 2^k, where k is the length of the string required to encode n in any base $b \geq 2$.

As long as we consider only bases greater than 1, the choice of base changes the length of any number's encoding only by some constant factor. This is true since, for any two positive integers a and b:

$$\log_a x = \log_a b \cdot \log_b x.$$

As we'll see shortly, we are going to ignore constant factors in almost all of our analyses. So, in particular, the constant $\log_a b$ will not affect the analyses that we will do. We'll get the same analysis with any base $b \geq 2$. With this encoding decision in hand, we'll be able to analyze the complexity of languages such as:

- PRIMES = $\{w : w$ is the binary encoding of a prime number$\}$.

But keep in mind one consequence of this encoding commitment: Consider any program P that implements a function on the natural numbers. Suppose that, given the number k as input, P executes $c_1 \cdot k$ steps (for some constant c_1). It might seem natural to say P executes in time that is linear in the size of its input. But the length of the actual input to P will be $\log_b k$, where b is greater than 1. So, if we describe the number of steps P executes as a function of the length of its input, we will get $c_2 \cdot 2^{\log k}$. Thus P executes in time that grows exponentially in the length of its input.

What about encodings for graph problems such as the ones we mentioned above? We consider two reasonable encodings for a graph $G = (V, E)$, where V is a set of vertices and E is a set of edges. Let $n = |V|$ (the number of vertices in V). For both encodings, we begin by naming the vertices with the integers from 1 to n. Then we may:

- Represent G as a list of edges. This is the technique that we used in Example 3.6. We will represent each vertex with the binary string that encodes its name. We will represent an edge by the pair of binary strings corresponding to the start and the end vertices of the edge. Then we can represent G by a sequence of edges. The binary strings will be separated by the character /, and we'll begin each encoding with the binary encoding of n. Thus the string 101/1/10/10/11/1/100/10/101 would encode a graph with five vertices and four edges. The maximum number of edges in G is n^2 (or $n^2/2$ if G is undirected). The number of characters required to encode a single vertex is $\lfloor \log_2 n \rfloor + 1$. The number of characters required to encode a single edge plus the delimiter ahead of it is then $2 \cdot \lfloor \log_2 n \rfloor + 4$. So the maximum length of the string that encodes G is bounded by:

$$n^2(2 \cdot \log_2 n + 4) + \log_2 n.$$

- Represent G as an adjacency matrix, as described in A.3.2. The matrix will have n rows and n columns. The value stored in cell (i, j) will be 1 if G contains an edge from vertex i to vertex j; it will be 0 otherwise. So the value of each cell can be encoded as a single binary digit and the entire matrix can be encoded as a binary string of length:

$$n^2.$$

In either case, the size of the representation of G is a polynomial function of the number of vertices in G. The main question that we are going to be asking about the problems we consider is whether or not there exists an algorithm that solves the problem in some amount of time that grows as no more than some polynomial function of the size of the input. In that case, the answer will be the same whether we describe the size of G as simply the number of vertices it contains or we describe it as the length of one of the two string encodings (an edge list or an adjacency matrix) that we just described.

27.3.2 Converting Optimization Problems into Languages

But now let's return to the traveling salesman problem. One way to think of the TSP is that it is the Hamiltonian circuit problem with a twist: We've added distances (or, more generally) costs to the edges. And we're no longer interested simply in knowing whether a circuit exists. We insist on finding the shortest (or cheapest) one. We call problems like TSP, in which we must find the "best" solution (for some appropriate definition of "best"), ***optimization problems***.

We can convert an optimization problem into a decision problem by placing a bound on the cost of any solution that we will accept. So, for example, we will be able to analyze the complexity of the language:

- TSP-DECIDE = {<*G*, *cost*> : <*G*> encodes an undirected graph with a positive distance attached to each of its edges and *G* contains a Hamiltonian circuit whose total cost is less than *cost*}.

It may feel that we have lost something in this transformation. Suppose that what we really want to know is how hard it will be to find the best Hamiltonian circuit in a graph. The modified form of the problem that we have described as TSP-DECIDE seems in some sense easier, since we need only answer a yes/no question and we're given a bound above which we need check no paths. If we found an efficient algorithm that decided TSP-DECIDE, we might still not have an efficient way of solving the original problem. If, on the other hand, there is no efficient procedure for deciding TSP-DECIDE, then there can be no efficient procedure for solving the original problem (since any such procedure could be turned into an efficient procedure for deciding TSP-DECIDE). The time required to decide TSP-DECIDE is a lower bound on the time required to solve the original problem. And what we're going to see is that no efficient procedure for deciding TSP-DECIDE is known and it appears unlikely that one exists.

27.4 Measuring Time and Space Complexity

Before we can begin to analyze problems to determine how fundamentally hard they are, we need a way to analyze the time and space requirements of specific programs.

27.4.1 Choosing a Model of Computation

If we are going to say that a program, running on some particular input, executes p steps or uses m memory locations, we need to know what counts as a step or a memory location. Consider, for example, the following simple function *tally*, which returns the product of the integers in an input array:

```
tally (A: vector of n integers, n: integer) =
    result = 1.
    For i = 1 to n do:
        result = result * A[i].
        end.
    Return result.
```

Suppose that *tally* is invoked on an input vector A with 10 elements. How many steps does it run before it halts? One way to answer the question would be to count each line of code once for each time it is executed. So the initialization of *result* is done once. The multiplication is done 10 times. The return statement is executed once. But how shall we count the statement "for $i = 1$ to n do:" and the end statement? We could count the for statement 10 times and thus capture the fact that the index variable is incremented and compared to n 10 times. Then we could skip counting the end statement entirely. Or we could count the end statement 10 times and assume that that's where the index variable is compared to 10. So we might end up with the answer 22 (i.e., 1 + 1 + 10 + 10, which we get if we don't count executions of the end statement). Or we might end up with the answer 32 (i.e., 1 + 1 + 10 + 10 + 10, which we get if we count both the end and the for statement 10 times).

As we'll soon see, this is a difference that won't matter in the kinds of analyses that we will want to do, since, using either metric, we can say that the number of steps grows linearly with the number of elements in *A*. But there is another problem here. Should we say that the amount of time required to increment the index variable is the same as the amount of time required to multiply two (possibly large) numbers? That doesn't seem to make sense. In particular, as the number of elements of *A* increases, the size of *result* increases. So, depending on how integers are represented, a real computer may require more time per multiplication as the number of elements of *A* increases. In that case, it would no longer be true that the number of steps grows only linearly with the length of *A*.

Now consider an analysis of the space requirements of *tally*. One simple way to do such an analysis is to say that, in addition to the memory that holds its inputs, *tally* requires two memory locations, one to hold the index variable *i* and another to hold the accumulated product in *result*. Looked at this way, the amount of additional space required by *A* is a constant (i.e., 2), independent of the size of its input. But what happens if we again consider that the size of *result* may grow as each new element of *A* is multiplied into it. In that case, the number of bits required to encode *result* may also grow as the number of elements of *A* grows. Again the question arises, "Exactly what should we count?"

We will solve both of these problems by choosing one specific model of computation: the Turing machine. We will count execution steps in measuring time and visited tape squares in measuring space. More precisely:

- We will allow Turing machines with any fixed size tape alphabet. Note that if we made a more restrictive assumption and allowed only two tape symbols, the number of steps and tape squares might increase but only by some constant factor.
- We will allow only one-tape Turing machines. Would it matter if we relaxed this restriction and allowed multiple tapes? Recall that we showed, in Section 17.3.1, that the number of steps required to execute a program on a one-tape machine grows as at most the square of the number of steps required to execute the same program on a multiple tape machine. So, if such a factor doesn't matter, we can allow multiple-tape machines for convenience.
- We will consider both deterministic and nondeterministic Turing machines. We will describe different complexity functions for the two of them and explore how they relate to each other. It seems likely, but no one has yet succeeding in proving, that there are problems that require exponentially more steps to solve on a deterministic machine than they do on a nondeterministic one.

Of course, we rarely care about the efficiency of actual Turing machines. (And we know that, even for some simple problems, straightforward Turing machines may seem very inefficient.) We care about the efficiency of real computers. But we showed, in Section 17.4, that the number of steps required to simulate a simple but realistic computer architecture on a one-tape deterministic Turing machine may grow as at most the sixth power of the number of steps required by the realistic machine. Almost all of the complexity analyses that we will do will ignore polynomial factors. When we are doing that, we may therefore describe programs in a more conventional programming style and count steps in the obvious way.

27.4.2 Defining Functions that Measure Time and Space Requirements

If we are given some particular Turing machine M and some particular input w, then we can determine the exact number of steps that M executes when started with w on its tape. We can also determine exactly the number of tape squares that M visits in the process. But we'd like to be able to describe M more generally and ask how it behaves on an arbitrary input.

To do that, we define two functions, *timereq* and *spacereq*. The domain of both functions is the set of Turing machines that halt on all inputs. The range of both is the set of functions that map from the natural numbers to the natural numbers. The function *timereq*(M) measures the time complexity of M; it will return a function that describes how the number of steps that M executes is related to the length of its input. Similarly, the function *spacereq*(M) will define the space complexity of M; it will return a function that describes the number of tape squares that M visits as a function of the length of its input.

Specifically, we define *timereq* as follows:

- If M is a deterministic Turing machine that halts on all inputs, then the value of *timereq*(M) is the function $f(n)$ defined so that, for any natural number n, $f(n)$ is the maximum number of steps that M executes on any input of length n.
- If M is a nondeterministic Turing machine all of whose computational paths halt on all inputs, then think of the set of computations that M might perform as a tree, just as we did in Section 17.3.2. We will not measure the number of steps in the entire tree of computations. Instead we will consider just individual paths and we will measure the length of the longest one. So the value of *timereq*(M) is the function $f(n)$ defined so that, for any natural number n, $f(n)$ is the number of steps on the longest path that M executes on any input of length n.

Analogously, we define *spacereq* as follows:

- If M is a deterministic Turing machine that halts on all inputs, then the value of *spacereq*(M) is the function $f(n)$ defined so that, for any natural number n, $f(n)$ is the maximum number of tape squares that M reads on any input of length n.
- If M is a nondeterministic Turing machine all of whose computational paths halt on all inputs, then the value of *spacereq*(M) is the function $f(n)$ defined so that, for any natural number n, $f(n)$ is the maximum number of tape squares that M reads on any path that it executes on any input of length n.

Notice that both *timereq*(M) and *spacereq*(M), as we have just defined them, measure the worst-case performance of M. In other words they measure the resource requirements of M on the inputs that require the most resources. An alternative approach would be to define both functions to return the average over all inputs. So, for example, we might define *timereqaverage*(M) to be the function $f(n)$ that returns the average number of steps that M executes on inputs of length n.

We have chosen to focus on worst-case performance, both because we would like to know an upper bound on the resources required to solve a problem and because it is, in most cases, easier to determine. We should keep in mind, however, that it is possible for worst-case performance and average-case performance to be very different. For example, an algorithm that exploits a hash table may take, on average, constant time to look up a value. But, if all the entries happen to hash to the same location, it may take time that is proportional to the number of entries in the table.

> The fact that average-case and worst-case may be very different can be exploited by hackers. (J.4.2)

The good news about the difference between average-case and worst-case is that, for many real problems, the worst case is very rare. For example, in Chapter 30, we will describe the design of randomized algorithms that solve some hard problems quickly with probability equal almost to one.

EXAMPLE 27.1 Analyzing the Turing Machine that Decides $A^nB^nC^n$

Consider the deterministic Turing machine M that we built in Example 17.8. It decides the language $A^nB^nC^n = \{a^nb^nc^n : n \geq 0\}$ and it operates as follows:

1. Move right onto w. If the first character is ❑, halt and accept.
2. Loop:
   2.1. Mark off an a with a 1.
   2.2. Move right to the first b and mark it off with a 2. If there isn't one or if there is a c first, halt and reject.
   2.3. Move right to the first c and mark it off with a 3. If there isn't one or if there is an a first, halt and reject.
   2.4. Move all the way back to the left, then right again past all the 1's (the marked off a's). If there is another a, go back to the top of the loop. If there isn't, exit the loop.
3. All a's have found matching b's and c's and the read/write head is just to the right of the region of marked off a's. Continue moving left to right to verify that all b's and c's have been marked. If they have, halt and accept. Otherwise halt and reject.

We can analyze M and determine *timereq*(M) as follows: Let n be the length of the input string w. First, since we must determine the number of steps that M

executes in the worst case, we will not consider the cases in which it exits the loop in statement 2 prematurely. So we consider only cases where there are at least as many b's and c's (in the right order) as there are a's. In all such cases, *M* executes the statement-2 loop once for every a in the input.

Let's continue by restricting our attention to the case where $w \in \mathrm{A^nB^nC^n}$. Then, each time through the loop, *M* must, on its way to the right, visit every square that contains an a, every square that contains a b, and, on average, half the squares that contain a c. And it must revisit them all as it scans back to the left. Since each letter occurs $n/3$ times, the average number of steps executed each time through the loop is $2(n/3 + n/3 + n/6)$. The loop will be executed $n/3$ times, so the total number of steps executed by the loop is $2(n/3)(n/3 + n/3 + n/6)$. Then, in the last execution of statement 2.4, combined with the execution of statement 3, *M* must make one final sweep all the way through w. That takes an additional n steps. So the total number of steps *M* executes is:

$$2(n/3)(n/3 + n/3 + n/6) + n.$$

Now suppose instead that $w \notin \mathrm{A^nB^nC^n}$ because it contains either extra characters after the matched regions or extra a's or b's embedded in the matching regions. So, for example, w might be `aaabbbbbccc` or `aabbcca`. In these cases, the number of steps executed by the loop of statement 2 is less than the number we computed above (because the loop is executed fewer than $n/3$ times). Since *timereq* must measure the number of steps in the worst case, for any input of length n, we can therefore ignore inputs such as these in our analysis. So we can say that:

$$timereq(M) = 2(n/3)(n/3 + n/3 + n/6) + n.$$

Using ideas that we will formalize shortly, we can thus say that the time required to run *M* on an input of length n grows as n^2.

Analyzing *spacereq*(*M*) is simpler. *M* uses only those tape squares that contain its input string, plus the blank on either side of it. So we have:

$$spacereq(M) = n + 2.$$

27.5 Growth Rates of Functions

Let *A* be a program and suppose that $timereq(A) = 2n$. By almost any standard, *A* is efficient. We can probably afford to run *A* on any inputs that anyone can afford to construct. But now consider a program *B*, where $timereq(B) = 2^n$. This second program is a lot less efficient than *A* is. And there are inputs of quite reasonable size on which *B* would not yet have finished if it had started at the instant of the Big Bang. Some functions grow very much faster than others, as shown in Figure 27.1 (in which both the x-axis, corresponding to n, and the y-axis, corresponding $f(n)$, are logarithmic).

As we develop a theory of complexity, we will find that problems that can be solved by algorithms whose time requirement is some polynomial function (e.g., $2n$) will generally

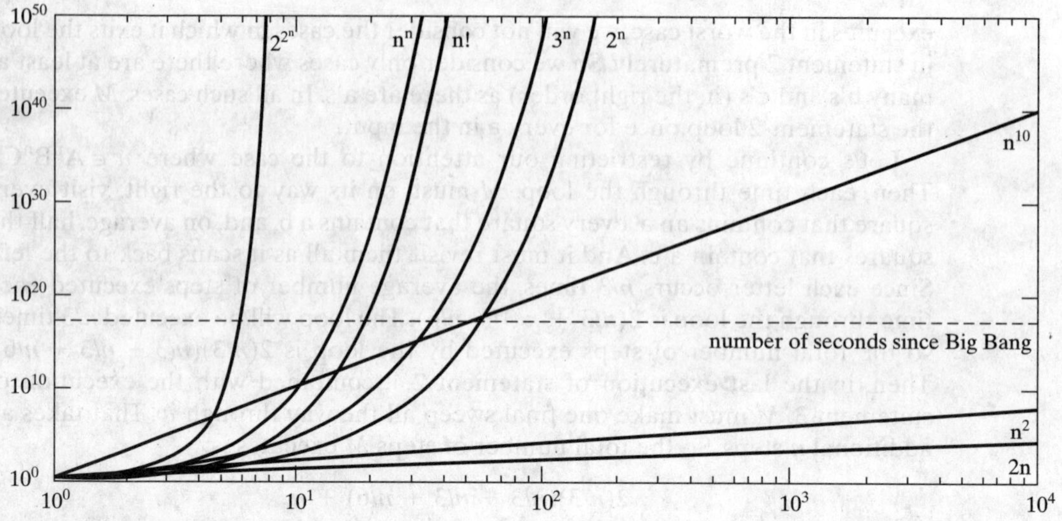

FIGURE 27.1 Growth rates of functions.

be regarded as tractable. Problems for which the best known algorithm has greater than polynomial time complexity (e. g., 2^n) will generally be regarded as intractable.

Problems that are intractable in this sense are likely to remain intractable, even as computers get faster. For example, if computer speed increases by a factor of 10, we can think of *timereq* as decreasing by a factor of 10. The only effect that has on the growth rate chart that we just presented is to shift all the lines down a barely perceptible amount.

It is possible that the one thing that might change the intractability picture for some problems is ***quantum computing*** ▭. So far, the only quantum computers that have been built are so small that quantum computing has not had a practical impact on the solvability of hard problems. Someday, however, they might. But it is important to keep in mind that while quantum computing may break through intractability barriers, it cannot break through computability ones. The proof that we did of the unsolvability of the halting problem made no appeal to the physical structure of the device that was hypothesized to implement the halts function. So it applies to quantum computers as well as to current silicon-based ones.

27.6 Asymptotic Dominance

As we analyze problems and the algorithms that can solve them, we may be interested in one or both of:

- The exact amount of time or space required to run an algorithm on a problem of a given size. In this case, we may care that one algorithm runs twice as fast as another one, or that it uses half as much memory. When this happens, the functions *timereq*(*M*) and *spacereq*(*M*) are exactly what we need.

- The rate at which the required time or space grows as the size of the problem grows. In this case, we may be relatively unconcerned with such things as constant factors, particularly if we are facing that the total required time or space grows exponentially (or worse) with the size of the problem. In this case, *timereq*(M) and *spacereq*(M) provide detail that may obscure the important factors.

In the analyses that we will do in the next two chapters, we will focus on the second of these issues. Thus we will, by and large, ignore constant factors and slowly growing terms. So for example, if $timereq(M_1) = 3n^2 + 23n + 100$ and $timereq(M_2) = 25n^2 + 4n + 3$, we would like to say that the time complexity of both machines grows as n^2. But before we embark on that analysis, we should point out that, when we are considering practical algorithms, constant factors and more slowly growing terms may matter. For instance, in Exercise 27.8, we will compare two algorithms for matrix multiplication. To multiply two $n \times n$ matrices using the obvious algorithm requires time that grows as n^3. An alternative is Strassen's algorithm. We'll see that it requires time that grows as $n^{2.807}$. But we'll also see that Strassen's algorithm can be slower than the straightforward approach until n crosses a threshold that typically occurs between 500 and 1000.

To be able to do the kind of analysis that we wish to focus on, we'll need to be able to compare two functions and ask how they behave as their inputs grow. For example, does one of them grow faster than the other? In other words, after some finite set of small cases, is one of them consistently larger than the other? In that case, we can view the larger function as describing an upper bound on the smaller one. Or perhaps they grow at the same rate. In that case, we can view either as describing a bound on the growth of the other. Or perhaps, after some finite number of small cases, one of them is consistently smaller than the other. In that case, we can view the smaller one as describing a lower bound on the other. Or maybe we can make no consistent claim about the relationship between the two functions. The theory that we are about to present is a general one that relates functions to each other. It is not tied specifically to our use, namely to measure the performance of programs. But it is exactly what we need.

> One reason that we generally choose to ignore constant factors, in particular, is that the Linear Speedup Theorem tells us that, up to a point, any Turing machine can be sped up by any desired constant factor. (F.2)

Consider any two functions f and g from the natural numbers to the positive reals. We define five useful relations that may hold between such functions. The first, $\mathcal{O}$, is introduced in A.7.2. We have been using it informally in the analyses of the algorithms that we have presented in Parts II, III, and IV. The other four are new:

- ***Asymptotic upper bound:*** $f(n) \in \mathcal{O}(g(n))$ iff there exists a positive integer k and a positive constant c such that:

$$\forall n \geq k\,(f(n) \leq c\,g(n)).$$

In other words, ignoring some number of small cases (all those of size less than k), and ignoring some constant factor c, $f(n)$ is bounded from above by $g(n)$. Another way to describe this relationship, if the required limit exists, is:

$$\lim_{n\to\infty} \frac{f(n)}{g(n)} < \infty.$$

In this case, we'll say that f is "big-Oh" of g or that g asymptotically dominates or grows at least as fast as f. We can think of g as describing an upper bound on the growth of f.

- ***Asymptotic strong upper bound:*** $f(n) \in o(g(n))$ iff, for every positive c, there exists a positive integer k such that:

$$\forall n \geq k\,(f(n) < c\,g(n)).$$

In other words, whenever the required limit exists:

$$\lim_{n\to\infty} \frac{f(n)}{g(n)} = 0.$$

In this case, we'll say that f is "little-oh" of g or that g grows strictly faster than f does.

- ***Asymptotic lower bound:*** $f(n) \in \Omega(g(n))$ iff there exists a positive integer k and a positive constant c such that:

$$\forall n \geq k\,(f(n) \geq c\,g(n)).$$

In other words, ignoring some number of small cases (all those of size less than k), and ignoring some constant factor c, $f(n)$ is bounded from below by $g(n)$. Another way to describe this relationship, if the required limit exists, is:

$$\lim_{n\to\infty} \frac{f(n)}{g(n)} > 0.$$

In this case, we'll say that f is "big-Omega" of g or that g grows no faster than f.

- ***Asymptotic strong lower bound:*** $f(n) \in \omega(g(n))$ iff, for every positive c, there exists a positive integer k such that:

$$\forall n \geq k\,(f(n) > c\,g(n)).$$

In other words, whenever the required limit exists:

$$\lim_{n\to\infty} \frac{f(n)}{g(n)} = \infty.$$

In this case, we'll say that f is "little-omega" of g or that g grows strictly slower than f does.

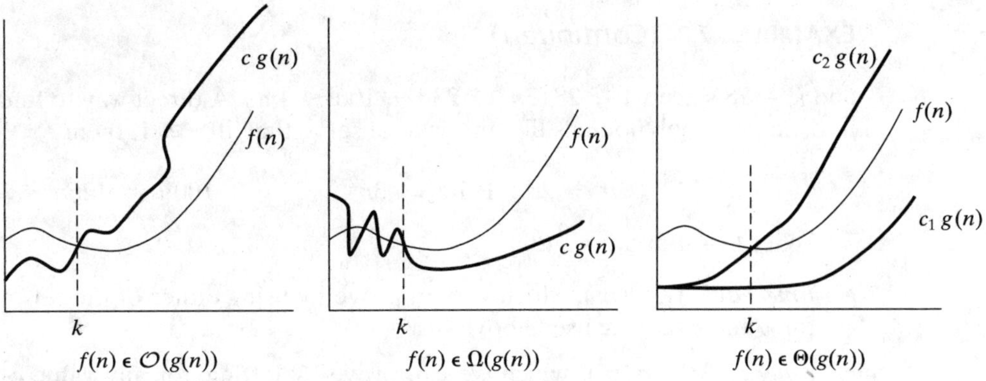

FIGURE 27.2 $\mathcal{O}$, Ω, and Θ.

- ***Asymptotic tight bound:*** $f(n) \in \Theta(g(n))$ iff there exists a positive integer k and positive constants c_1, and c_2 such that:

$$\forall n \geq k\,(c_1\,g(n) \leq f(n) \leq c_2\,g(n)).$$

In other words, again assuming the limit exists:

$$0 < \lim_{n\to\infty} \frac{f(n)}{g(n)} < \infty.$$

In this case, we'll say that f is "Theta" of g or that g is an asymptotically tight bound on f. Equivalently, we can define Θ in terms of $\mathcal{O}$ and Ω in either of the following ways:

- $f(n) \in \Theta(g(n))$ iff $f(n) \in \mathcal{O}(g(n))$ and $f(n) \in \Omega(g(n))$. In other words, $f(n) \in \Theta(g(n))$ iff $g(n)$ is both an upper and a lower bound of $f(n)$.
- $f(n) \in \Theta(g(n))$ iff $f(n) \in \mathcal{O}(g(n))$ and $g(n) \in \mathcal{O}(f(n))$. In other words, $f(n) \in \Theta(g(n))$ iff $f(n)$ and $g(n)$ are upper bounds of each other.

The graphs shown in Figure 27.2 may help in visualizing the bounds that are defined by $\mathcal{O}$, Ω, and Θ.

EXAMPLE 27.2 Determining $\mathcal{O}$, σ, Ω, and Θ from the Definitions

Suppose that we have analyzed the time complexity of some Turing machine M and determined that:

$$timereq(M) = 3n^2 + 23n + 100.$$

Then:

- $timereq(M) \in \mathcal{O}(n^2)$, which we can prove by finding appropriate values for c and k. A bit of experimenting will show that we could, for example, let $c = 4$

EXAMPLE 27.2 ***(Continued)***

and $k = 28$ since $\forall n \geq 28\,(3n^2 + 23n + 100 \leq 4n^2)$. A direct way to find c and k in the case of polynomials like this is to observe that, if $n \geq 1$, then:

$$3n^2 + 23n + 100 \leq 3n^2 + 23n^2 + 100n^2 = 126n^2.$$

So let $k = 1$ and $c = 126$.

- $timereq(M) \in \mathcal{O}(n^3)$, which we can prove by using either of the sets of values for k and c that we used above.
- $timereq(M) \in \sigma(n^3)$, which we can prove by letting, for any value of c, k be $\lceil 126/c \rceil + 1$ (where $\lceil x \rceil$, read as "ceiling of x", is the smallest integer greater than or equal to x). To see why such a k works, again observe that, if $n \geq 1$ then:

$$3n^2 + 23n + 100 \leq 3n^2 + 23n^2 + 100n^2 = 126n^2.$$

So we can assure that $3n^2 + 23n + 100 < c\,n^3$ by assuring that $126n^2 < c\,n^3$. Solving for n, we get $n > 126/c$.

We can guarantee that k is an integer and that it is greater than $126/c$ by setting it to $\lceil 126/c \rceil + 1$. Note that this means that $k \geq 1$, so the condition we required for the first step we did is satisfied.

- $timereq(M) \in \Omega(n)$, which we can prove by letting $c = 1$ and $k = 1$, since $\forall n \geq 1\,(3n^2 + 23n + 100 \geq n)$.
- $timereq(M) \in \Omega(n^2)$, which we can prove by letting $c = 1$ and $k = 1$, since $\forall n \geq 1\,(3n^2 + 23n + 100 \geq n^2)$.
- $timereq(M) \in \Theta(n^2)$, which we can prove by noting that $3n^2 + 23n + 100 \in \mathcal{O}(n^2)$ and $3n^2 + 23n + 100 \in \Omega(n^2)$. Note that $timereq(M) \notin \Theta(n)$ and $timereq(M) \notin \Theta(n^3)$.

Given two functions $f(n)$ and $g(n)$, it is possible to show that $f(n) \in \mathcal{O}(g(n))$ (and similarly for σ, Ω, and Θ) by showing the required constants, as we have just done. But it is much easier to prove such claims by exploiting a set of facts about arithmetic with respect to these relations. We'll state some of these facts in the next two theorems.

THEOREM 27.1 Facts About $\mathcal{O}$

Theorem: Let f, f_1, f_2, g, g_1, and g_2 be functions from the natural numbers to the positive reals, let a and b be arbitrary real constants, and let $c, c_0, c_1, \ldots c_k, s, t$ be any positive real constants. Then:

1. $f(n) \in \mathcal{O}(f(n))$.

2. **Addition:**
   2.1. $\mathcal{O}(f(n)) = \mathcal{O}(f(n) + c_0)$ (if we make the assumption, which will always be true for the functions we will be considering, that $1 \in \mathcal{O}(f(n))$).
   2.2. If $f_1(n) \in \mathcal{O}(g_1(n))$ and $f_2(n) \in \mathcal{O}(g_2(n))$ then $f_1(n) + f_2(n) \in \mathcal{O}(g_1(n) + g_2(n))$.
   2.3. $\mathcal{O}(f_1(n) + f_2(n)) = \mathcal{O}(max(f_1(n), f_2(n)))$.
3. **Multiplication:**
   3.1. $\mathcal{O}(f(n)) = \mathcal{O}(c_0 f(n))$.
   3.2. If $f_1(n) \in \mathcal{O}(g_1(n))$ and $f_2(n) \in \mathcal{O}(g_2(n))$ then $f_1(n)f_2(n) \in \mathcal{O}(g_1(n)\, g_2(n))$.
4. **Polynomials:**
   4.1. If $a \leq b$ then $\mathcal{O}(n^a) \subseteq \mathcal{O}(n^b)$.
   4.2. If $f(n) = c_j n^j + c_{j-1} n^{j-1} + \ldots c_1 n + c_0$ then $f(n) \in \mathcal{O}(n^j)$.
5. **Logarithms:**
   5.1. For a and $b > 1$, $\mathcal{O}(\log_a n) = \mathcal{O}(\log_b n)$.
   5.2. If $0 < a < b$ and $c > 1$ then $\mathcal{O}(n^a) \subseteq \mathcal{O}(n^a \log_c n) \subseteq \mathcal{O}(n^b)$.
6. **Exponentials (including the fact that exponentials dominate polynomials):**
   6.1. If $1 < a \leq b$ then $\mathcal{O}(a^n) \subseteq \mathcal{O}(b^n)$.
   6.2. If $a \geq 0$ and $b > 1$ then $\mathcal{O}(n^a) \subseteq \mathcal{O}(b^n)$.
   6.3. If $f(n) = c_{j+1} 2^n + c_j n^j + c_{j-1} n^{j-1} + \ldots c_1 n + c_0$, then $f(n) \in \mathcal{O}(2^n)$.
   6.4. If $s > 1$ then $\mathcal{O}(n^t 2^n) \subseteq \mathcal{O}(2^{(n^s)})$.
7. **Factorial dominates exponentials:** If $a \geq 1$ then $\mathcal{O}(a^n) \subseteq \mathcal{O}(n!)$.
8. **Transitivity:** If $f(n) \in \mathcal{O}(f_1(n))$ and $f_1(n) \in \mathcal{O}(f_2(n))$ then $f(n) \in \mathcal{O}(f_2(n))$.

Proof: Proofs of these claims, based on the definition of $\mathcal{O}$, are given in F.1 or left as exercises.

We can summarize some of the key facts from Theorem 27.1 as follows, with the caveat that the constants a, b, c, and d must satisfy the constraints given in the theorem:

$$\mathcal{O}(c) \subseteq \mathcal{O}(\log_a n) \subseteq \mathcal{O}(n^b) \subseteq \mathcal{O}(d^n) \subseteq \mathcal{O}(n!).$$

In other words, factorial dominates exponentials, which dominate polynomials, which dominate logarithms, which dominate constants.

THEOREM 27.2 Facts About σ

Theorem: Given any functions f and g from the natural numbers to the positive reals:

- $f(n) \notin \sigma(f(n))$
- $\sigma(f(n)) \subset \mathcal{O}(f(n))$

Proof: Proofs of these claims, based on the definitions of $\mathcal{O}$ and σ, are given in F.1.

EXAMPLE 27.3 Determining $\mathcal{O}$ and σ from the Properties Theorems

In Example 27.1, we analyzed the time complexity of the Turing machine M and determined that:

$$
\begin{aligned}
timereq(M) &= 2(n/3)(n/3 + n/3 + n/6) + n. \\
&= (5/9)n^2 + n.
\end{aligned}
$$

So:

- $timereq(M) \in \mathcal{O}(n^2)$. It is also true that $timereq(M) \in \mathcal{O}(n^3)$.
- $timereq(M) \in \sigma(n^3)$.

We've defined the relations $\mathcal{O}$, σ, Ω, and Θ because each of them is useful in characterizing the way in which $timereq(M)$ and $spacereq(M)$ grow as the length of the input to M increases. $\Theta(f(n))$ provides the most information since it describes the tightest bound on the growth of $f(n)$. But most discussions of complexity rely more extensively on $\mathcal{O}$ for two reasons:

- Even when analyzing a particular machine M, it may be easier to prove a claim about $\mathcal{O}(timereq(M))$ than about $\Theta(timereq(M))$ (and similarly about $spacereq(M)$). In this case, it is conventional to make the strongest claim that can be proved. So, for example, if $timereq(M) \in \mathcal{O}(n^3)$ then it must also be true that $timereq(M) \in \mathcal{O}(n^4)$. But if we can prove the former claim, then that is the one we will make. This is the convention that we have used in analyzing algorithms in Parts II, III, and IV of this book.
- In Chapters 28, 29, and 30, we will move from discussing individual algorithms for deciding a language to making claims about the inherent complexity of a language itself. We'll base those claims on the best known algorithm for deciding the language. Since we often cannot prove that no better algorithm can exist, we will be unable to make any claim about a lower bound on the complexity of the language. Thus $\mathcal{O}$ will be the best that we can do.

It is common to say, informally, "M is $\mathcal{O}(f(n))$," when we mean that $timereq(M) \in \mathcal{O}(f(n))$. We will do this when it causes no confusion. Similarly, we'll say that M is ***polynomial*** or that M implements a ***polynomial-time algorithm*** whenever $timereq(M) \in \mathcal{O}(f(n))$ for some polynomial function f.

27.7 Algorithmic Gaps

Our goal, in the next three chapters, is to characterize problems by their inherent difficulty. We can close the book on the complexity of a problem L if we can show all of the following:

1. There exists an algorithm that decides L and that has complexity C_1.
2. Any algorithm that decides L must have complexity at least C_2.
3. $C_1 = C_2$.

The existence of an algorithm as described in point 1 imposes an upper bound on the inherent complexity of L since it tells us that we can achieve C_1. The existence of a proof of a claim as described in point 2 imposes a lower bound on the inherent complexity of L since it tells us that we can't do better than C_2. If $C_1 = C_2$, we are done.

What we are about to see is that, for many interesting problems, we are not done. For all of the problems we will consider, some algorithm is known. So we have an upper bound on inherent complexity. But, for many of these problems, only very weak lower bounds are known. Proving lower bounds turns out to be a lot harder than proving upper bounds. So, for many problems, there is a gap, and sometimes a very significant one, between the best known lower bound and the best known upper bound. For example, the best known deterministic algorithm for solving the traveling salesman problem exactly has $timereq \in \mathcal{O}(2^{(n^k)})$. But it is unknown whether this is the best we can do. In particular, no one has been able to prove that there could not exist a deterministic, polynomial time algorithm for TSP-DECIDE.

The complexity classes that we are about to define will necessarily be based on the facts that we have. Thus they will primarily be defined in terms of upper bounds. We will group together problems for which algorithms of similar complexity are known. We must remain agnostic, for now, on several questions of the form, "Is class CL_1 equal to class CL_2?" Such questions will only be able to be answered by the discovery of new algorithms that prove stronger upper bounds or by the discovery of new proofs of stronger lower bounds.

27.8 Examples ✹

Suppose that we have a problem that we wish to solve and an algorithm that solves it. But we'd like a more efficient one. We might be happy with one that runs, say, twice as fast as the original one does. But we would be even happier if we could find one for which the required time grew more slowly as the size of the problem increased. For example, the original algorithm might be $\mathcal{O}(2^n)$, while another one might be $\mathcal{O}(n^3)$. Sometimes we will succeed in finding such an algorithm. As we'll see in the next couple of chapters, sometimes we won't.

27.8.1 Polynomial Speedup

We begin with two examples for which we start with a polynomial algorithm but are nevertheless able to improve its running time.

EXAMPLE 27.4 Finding the Minimum and Maximum in a List

We first consider an easy problem: Given a list of n numbers, find the minimum and the maximum elements in the list. We can convert this problem into a language recognition problem by defining the language L = {<*list of numbers*, *number*$_1$, *number*$_2$> : *number*$_1$ is the minimum element of the list and *number*$_2$ is the maximum element}.

EXAMPLE 27.4 *(Continued)*

We'll focus on the core of the decision procedure. Its job is to examine a list and find its minimum and maximum elements. We begin with a simple approach:

```
simplecompare(list: list of numbers) =
    max = list[1].
    min = list[1].
    For i = 2 to length(list) do:
        If list[i] < min then min = list[i].
        If list[i] > max then max = list[i].
```

Rather than trying to count every operation, we'll assume that the time required by all the other operations is dominated by the time required to do the comparisons. The straightforward algorithm that we just presented requires $2(n - 1)$ comparisons. So we can say that *simplecompare* is $\mathcal{O}(2n)$. Or, eliminating the constant, it is $\mathcal{O}(n)$. Can we do better? We notice that if $list[i] < min$ then it cannot also be true that $list[i] > max$. So that comparison can be skipped. We can do even better, though, if we consider the elements of the list two at a time. We first compare $list[i]$ to $list[i + 1]$. Then we compare the smaller of the two to min and the larger of the two to max. This new algorithm requires only $(3/2)(n - 1)$ comparisons. So, while the time complexity of all three algorithms is $\mathcal{O}(n)$, the last one requires 25% fewer comparisons than the first one did.

In the next example we return to a problem we considered in Chapter 5: Given a pattern string and an input text string, does the pattern match anywhere in the text? We know that this question is decidable and that one way to answer it is to use a finite state machine. We now consider another way and examine its efficiency.

EXAMPLE 27.5 String Search and the Knuth-Morris-Pratt Algorithm

Define the language:

- STRING-SEARCH = {<*t*, *p*> : the string *p* (the pattern) exists as a substring somewhere in *t* (the text string)}.

The following straightforward algorithm decides STRING-SEARCH by looking for at least one occurrence of the pattern *p* somewhere in *t*. It starts at the left and shifts *p* one character to the right each time it fails to find a match. (Note that the characters in the strings are numbered starting with 0.)

```
simple-string-search(t, p: strings) =
    i = 0.
    j = 0.
    While i ≤ |t| − |p| do:
```

While $j < |p|$ do:
  If $t[i + j] = p[j]$ then $j = j + 1$. /* Continue the match
    Else exit this loop. /* Match failed. Need to slide the pattern to the right.
If $j = |p|$ then halt and accept. /* The entire pattern matched.
  Else:
    $i = i + 1$. /* Slide the pattern one character to the right.
    $j = 0$. /* Start over again matching pattern characters.
Halt and reject. /* Checked all the way to the end and didn't find a match.

Let n be $|t|$ and let m be $|p|$. In the worst case (in which it doesn't find an early match), *simple-string-search* will go through its outer loop almost n times and, for each of those iterations, it will go through its inner loop m times. So *timereq(simple-string-search)* $\in \mathcal{O}(nm)$.

Can we do better? The answer is yes. We know, from Section 5.4.2, that, given a particular pattern p, we can build a deterministic finite state machine that looks for p in t and executes only n steps. But constructing that machine by hand for each new p isn't feasible if the pattern itself must also be an input to the program. We could use the following algorithm to decide STRING-SEARCH (where both t and p are input to the program):

string-search-using-FSMs(t, p: strings) =

1. Build the simple nondeterministic FSM M that accepts any string that contains p as a substring.
2. Let $M' = ndfsmtodfsm(M)$. /* Make an equivalent deterministic FSM.
3. Let $M'' = minDFSM(M')$. /* Minimize it.
4. Run M'' on t.
5. If it accepts, accept. Else reject.

Step 4 of *string-search-using-FSMs* runs in n steps. And it is true that steps 1 through 3 need only be done once for each pattern p. The resulting machine M'' can then be used to scan as many input strings as we want. But steps 1 through 3 are expensive since the number of states of M' may grow exponentially with the number of states of M (i.e., with the number of characters in p).

So can we beat *string-search-using-FSMs*? In particular, can we design a search algorithm whose matching time is linear in n (the length of t) but that can be efficient in performing any necessary preprocessing of p? The answer to this second question is also yes. One way to do it is to use the *buildkeywordFSM* algorithm,

EXAMPLE 27.5 (*Continued*)

which we presented in Section 6.2.4, to build a deterministic FSM directly from the pattern. An alternative is to search directly without first constructing an FSM.

The Knuth-Morris-Pratt algorithm 🖳 does the latter. It is a variant of *simple-string-search* that is efficient both in preprocessing and in searching. To see how it works, we'll begin with an example. Let t and p be as shown here. *Simple-string-search* begins by trying to match p starting in position 0:

```
        0 1 2 3 4 5 6 7 8
t:      a b c a b a b c a b d

p:      a b c a b d
                  ×
```

We've marked with an × the point at which *simple-string-search* notices that its first attempt to find a match has failed. *Simple-string-search* will increment i by 1, thus shifting the pattern one character to the right, and then it will try again, this time checking:

```
        0 1 2 3 4 5 6 7 8
t:      a b c a b a b c a b d

p:        a b c a b d
          ×
```

But it shouldn't have had to bother doing that. It already knows what the first five characters of t are. The first one doesn't matter since the pattern is going to be shifted past it to the right. But the next four characters, bcab, tell it something. They are not the beginning of the pattern it is trying to match. It makes no sense to try again to match starting with the b or with the c.

Assume that a match fails. When it does, the current value of j is exactly the number of characters that were successfully matched before the failure was detected. We ignore the first of those characters since we will slide the pattern at least one character to the right and so the first matched character will never be considered again. Call the remaining $j - 1$ characters the kernel. In our example, when the first mismatch was detected, j was 5, so the kernel is bcab. Now notice that, given a value for j, we can compute the only possible kernel just from the pattern p. It is independent of t. Specifically, the kernel that corresponds to j is composed of characters 1 through $j - 1$ of p (numbering from 0 again).

Given a kernel from the last match, how do we know how far to the right we can slide the pattern before we have to try again to match it against t? The answer is that we can slide the beginning of the pattern to the right until it is just past the kernel. But then we have to slide it back to the left to account for any overlap between the end of the kernel and the beginning of the pattern. So how far is that? To answer that question, we do the following. Start by placing the kernel on one line and the pattern, immediately to the right of it, on the line below it. So we have, in our example:

```
b c a b
        a b c a b d
```

Now slide the pattern as far to the left as it can go subject to the constraint that, when we stop, any characters that are lined up in a single column must be identical. So, in this example, we can slide the pattern leftward by two characters, producing:

```
b c a b
    a b c a b d
```

Thus, given this particular pattern p, if j is five when a mismatch is detected, then the next match we should try is the one that we get if we shift the pattern five characters to the right minus the two overlap characters. So we slide it three character to the right and we try:

```
       0 1 2 3 4 5 6 7 8
t:     a b c a b a b c a b d

p:           a b c a b d
                 ×
```

Again remember that this analysis of sliding distance is independent of the text string t. So we can preprocess a pattern p to determine what the overlap numbers are for each value of j. We will store those numbers in a table we will call T. Note that if $j = 0$ or 1, the corresponding kernel will be empty. For reasons that will become clear when we see exactly how the table T is going to be used, set $T[0]$ to -1 and $T[1]$ to 0. For the pattern abcabd that we have been considering, T will be:

j	0	1	2	3	4	5
$T[j]$	-1	0	0	0	1	2
the kernel	ε	ε	b	bc	bca	bcab

Now, continuing with our example, notice something else about what should happen on the next match attempt. There were two characters of overlap between the pattern and the kernel. That means that we already know that the first two pattern characters match against the last two kernel characters and that those last two kernel characters are identical to the two text characters we would look at first. We don't need to check them again. So, each time we reposition the pattern on the text string (thus changing the index i in the search algorithm we presented above), we can also compute j, the first character pair we need to check. Rather than resetting it to 0 every time, we can jump it past the known characters and start it at the first character we actually need to check. So how far can we jump? The answer is that the new value of j can be computed by using its previous value as an index into T. The new value of j is exactly $T[j]$, since the size of the overlap is exactly the length of the substring we have already examined and thus can skip.

We can now state our new search algorithm based on these two optimizations (i.e., sliding the pattern to the right as far as possible and starting to check the next match as far to the right as possible):

Knuth-Morris-Pratt(t, p: strings) =

$i = 0$.

$j = 0$.

EXAMPLE 27.5 (*Continued*)

While $i \le |t| - |p|$ do:
  While $j < |p|$ do:
    If $t[i + j] = p[j]$ then $j = j + 1$. /* Continue the match
      Else exit this loop. /* Match failed. Need to slide the pattern to the right.
    If $j = |p|$ then halt and accept. /* The entire pattern matched.
    Else:
* $i = i + j - T[j]$. /* Slide the pattern as far as possible to the right.
* $j = max(0, T[j])$. /* Start j at the first character we actually need to check.
Halt and reject. /* Checked all the way to the end and didn't find a match.

Knuth-Morris-Pratt is identical to *simple-string-search* except in the two lines marked on the left with asterisks. The only difference is in how i and j are updated each time a new match starts.

Looking at the algorithm, it should be clear why we assigned $T[0]$ the value -1. If a match fails immediately, we have to guarantee that the pattern gets shifted one character to the right for the next match. Assigning $T[0]$ the value -1 does that. Unfortunately though, that assignment does mean that we must treat $j = 0$ as a special case in computing the next value for j. That value must be 0, not -1. Thus the use of the *max* function in the expression that defines the next value for j.

Assuming that T can be computed and that it has the values shown above, we can now illustrate the operation of *Knuth-Morris-Pratt* on our example. At each iteration, we show the value of j (i.e., the position at which we start comparing the pattern to the text), with an underline:

```
     0 1 2 3 4 5 6 7 8
t:   a b c a b a b c a b d    Start with i = 0, j = 0.
p:   a b c a b d
               ×              Mismatch found: i = 0, j = 5.
```
Compute new values for next match: $i = i + j - T[j] = 0 + 5 - 2 = 3$.
$j = max(0, T[j]) = 2$.

```
t:   a b c a b a b c a b d
p:         a b c a b d
               ×              Mismatch found immediately: i = 3, j = 2.
```
Compute new values for next match: $i = i + j - T[j] = 3 + 2 - 0 = 5$.
$j = max(0, T[j]) = 0$.

```
t:   a b c a b a b c a b d
p:             a b c a b d
               ×              Complete match will now be found.
```

How much we can slide the pattern each time we try a match depends on the structure of the pattern. The worst case is a pattern like aaaaaab. Notice that every kernel for this pattern will be a string of zero or more a's. That means that the pattern overlaps all the way to the left on every kernel. This is going to mean that it is never possible to slide the pattern more than one character to the right on each new match attempt. Using the technique we described above, we can build T (which describes the number of characters of overlap) for this pattern:

j	0	1	2	3	4	5	6
$T[j]$	−1	0	1	2	3	4	5
the kernel	ε	ε	a	aa	aaa	aaaa	aaaaa

Now consider what happens when we run *Knuth-Morris-Pratt* on the following example using this new pattern:

0 1 2 3 4 5 6 7 8 9 10 ...

t: a a a a a a a a a a a a a a a a a a b   Start with $i = 0, j = 0$.

p: a a a a a a b

×   Mismatch found: $i = 0, j = 6$.

Compute new values for next match: $i = i + j - T[j] = 0 + 6 - 5 = 1$.

$j = max\ (0, T[j]) = 5$.

t: a a a a a a a a a a a a a a a a a a b

p: a a a a a a b

×   Mismatch found almost immediately: $i = 1, j = 6$.

Compute new values for next match: $i = i + j - T[j] = 1 + 6 - 5 = 2$.

$j = max\ (0, T[j]) = 5$.

t: a a a a a a a a a a a a a a a a a a b

p: a a a a a a b

×   Mismatch found almost immediately: $i = 2, j = 6$.

This process continues, shifting the pattern one character to the right each time, until it finds a match at the very end of the string. But notice that, even though we weren't able to advance the pattern more than one character at each iteration, we were able to start j out at 5 each time. So we did skip most of the comparisons that *simple-string-search* would have done.

Analyzing the complexity of *Knuth-Morris-Pratt* is straightforward. Ignore for the moment the complexity of computing the table T. We will discuss that below. Assuming that T has been computed, we can count the maximum number of comparisons that will be done given a text t of length n and a pattern p of length m. Consider each character c of t. If the first comparison of p to c succeeds, then one of the following things must happen next:

- The rest of the pattern also matches. No further match attempts will be made so c will never be examined again.
- Somewhere later the pattern fails. But, in that case, c becomes part of the kernel that will be produced by that failed match. No kernel characters are ever reexamined. So c will never be examined again.

EXAMPLE 27.5 ***(Continued)***

So the number of successful comparisons is no more than n. The number of unsuccessful comparisons is also no more than n since every unsuccessful comparison forces the process to stop and start over, sliding the pattern at least one character to the right. That can happen no more than n times. So the total number of comparisons is no more than $2n$ and so is $\mathcal{O}(n)$.

It remains to describe the algorithm that constructs the table T. The obvious approach is to try matching p against each possible kernel, starting in each possible position. But we would like a technique that is $\mathcal{O}(m)$, i.e., linear in the length of the pattern. Such an algorithm exists. It builds up the entries in T one at a time starting with $T[2]$ (since T[0] is always -1 and $T[1]$ is always 0). The idea is the following: Assume that we have already considered a kernel of length $k - 1$ and we are now considering one of length k. This new kernel is identical to the previous one except that one more character from p has been added to the right. So, returning to our first example, assume we have already processed the kernel of length 3 and observed a one character overlap (shown in the box) with the pattern:

```
kernel:    b c [a]
pattern:       [a] b c a b d
```

To form the next longer kernel we add a b to the right of the previous kernel:

```
kernel:    b c [a] b
pattern:       [a] b c a b d
```

Notice that there is no chance that there is now an overlap that starts to the left of the one we found at the last step. If the pattern didn't match those earlier characters of the kernel before, it still won't. There are only three possibilities:

- The match we found at the previous step can be extended by one character. That is what happens in this case. When this happens, the value of T for the current kernel is one more than it was for the last one.
- The match we found on the previous step cannot be extended. In that case, we check to see whether a new, shorter match can be started.
- Neither can the old match be extended nor a new one started. In this case, the value of T corresponding to the current kernel is 0.

Based on this observation, we can define the following algorithm for computing the table T:

buildoverlap(p: pattern string) =
  $T[0] = -1$.
  $T[1] = 0$.
  $j = 2$ /* j is the index of the element of T we are currently computing. It is the entry for a kernel of length $j - 1$.

```
k = 0.                              /* k is the length of the overlap from the
                                    /*   previous element of T.
While j < |p| do:                   /* When j equals |p|, all elements of T
                                    /*   have been filled in.
    Compare p[j − 1] to p[k].       /* Compare the character that just got
                                    /*   appended to the kernel to the next
                                    /*   character of p to see if the current
                                    /*   match can be extended.
    If they are equal then:         /* Extend the previous overlap by one
                                    /*   character.
        T[j] = k + 1.
        j = j + 1.                  /* We know the answer for this cell and
                                    /*   can go on to the next.
        k = k + 1.                  /* The overlap length just increased by one.
    If they are not equal but       /* See if a shorter match is possible,
    k > 0 then:                     /*   starting somewhere in the box that
                                    /*   enclosed the match we had before.
        k = T[k].                   /* Don't increment j since we haven't
                                    /*   finished this entry yet.
    If they are not equal and k = 0 then:  /* No overlap exists.
        T[j] = 0.
        j = j + 1.                  /* We know the answer for this cell and
                                    /*   can go on to the next.
        k = 0.                      /* The overlap length is back to 0.
```

Buildoverlap executes at most $2m$ comparisons (where m is the length of the pattern p). So the total number of comparisons executed by *Knuth-Morris-Pratt* on a text of length n and a pattern of length m is $\mathcal{O}(n + m)$. Particularly if either n or m is very large, this is a substantial improvement over *simple-string-search*, which required $\mathcal{O}(nm)$ comparisons.

27.8.2 Replacing an Exponential Algorithm with a Polynomial One

Sometimes we can get substantially greater speedup than we did in the last two examples. We may be able to replace one algorithm with another whose asymptotic complexity is much better. We've already seen two important examples of this:

- Given a string w, and a context-free language L, described by a grammar G, an obvious way to decide whether w is an element L is to try all the possible ways in which w might be derived using the rules of G. Alternatively, we could try all paths through the nondeterministic PDA that can be constructed from G. But both of these approaches are $\mathcal{O}(2^n)$. Practical parsers must be substantially more efficient than that. In Chapter 15 we saw that, for many useful context-free languages, we can build linear-time parsers. We also saw that it is possible to retain generality and to parse an arbitrary context-free language in $\mathcal{O}(n^3)$ time using techniques, such as the Cocke-Kasami-Younger algorithm and the Earley algorithm, that exploit dynamic programming.

- Given a hidden Markov model (HMM) M and an observed output sequence O, an obvious way to determine the path through M that was most likely to have produced O is to try all paths through M of length $|O|$, compute their probabilities, and then choose the one with the highest such probability. But, letting n be $|O|$, this approach is $\mathcal{O}(2^n)$. If HMMs are to be useful, particularly in real-time applications like speech understanding, they have to be substantially faster than that. But, again, we can exploit dynamic programming. The Viterbi and the forward algorithms, which we described in Section 5.11.2, run in $\mathcal{O}(k^2 n)$ time, where k is the number of states in M.

Whenever our first attempt to solve a problem yields an exponential-time algorithm, it will be natural to try to do better. The next example is a classic case in which that effort succeeds.

EXAMPLE 27.6 Greatest Common Divisor and Euclid's Algorithm

One of the earliest problems for which an efficient algorithm replaced a very inefficient, but obvious one, is greatest common divisor (or gcd). Let n and m be integers. Then $gcd(n, m)$ is the largest integer k such that k is a factor of both n and m. The obvious way to compute *gcd* is:

gcd-obvious(n, m: integers) =

1. Compute the prime factors of both n and m.
2. Let k be the product of all factors common to n and m (including duplicates).
3. Return k.

So, for example, the prime factors of 40 are $\{2, 2, 2, 5\}$. The prime factors of 60 are $\{2, 2, 3, 5\}$. So $gcd(40, 60) = 2 \cdot 2 \cdot 5 = 20$.

Unfortunately, no efficient (i.e., polynomial-time) algorithm for prime factorization is known. So the obvious solution to the gcd problem is also inefficient.

But there is a better way. The following technique 🖳 was known to the ancient Greeks. Although probably discovered before Euclid, one version of it appeared in Euclid's *Elements* in about 300 B.C. and so the technique is commonly called Euclid's algorithm:

gcd-Euclid(n, m: integers) =

If $m = 0$ return n.

Else return *gcd-Euclid*(m, n (mod m)), where n (mod m) is the remainder after integer division of n by m.

To see that *gcd-Euclid* must eventually halt, observe that $n(mod\ m) < m$. So the second argument to *gcd-Euclid* is strictly decreasing. Since it can never become negative, it must eventually become 0. The proof that *gcd-Euclid* halts with the correct result rests on the observation that, for any integers n and m, if some integer k divides both n and m it must also divide n (mod m). To see why this is so, notice that there exists some natural number j such that $n = jm + (n(mod\ m))$. So, if both n and jm are divisible by k, $n\ (mod\ m)$ must also be.

Next we analyze the time complexity of *gcd-Euclid*. Again, the key is that its second argument is strictly decreasing. The issue is, "How fast?" The answer is based on the observation that $n(mod\ m) \leq n/2$. To see why this is so, consider two cases:

- $m \leq n/2$: We have $n(mod\ m) < m \leq n/2$ and thus $n(mod\ m) \leq n/2$.
- $m > n/2$: Then $n(mod\ m) = n - m$. So $n(mod\ m) \leq n/2$.

We note that *gcd-Euclid* swaps its arguments on each recursive call. So, after each pair of calls, the second argument is cut at least in half. Thus, after at most $2 \cdot \log_2 m$ calls, the second argument will be equal to 0 and *gcd-Euclid* will halt. If we assume that each division has constant cost, then $timereq(gcd\text{-}Euclid) \in \mathcal{O}(\log_2 (max(n, m)))$.

We can turn the gcd problem into a language to be recognized by defining:

- RELATIVELY-PRIME $= \{<n, m> : n$ and m are integers and they are relatively prime$\}$. Two integers are ***relatively prime*** iff their gcd is 1.

The following procedure decides RELATIVELY-PRIME:

REL-PRIMEdecide(<*n*, *m*: integers>) =

If *gcd-Euclid*$(n, m) = 1$ then accept; else reject.

We already know that $timereq(gcd\text{-}Euclid) \in \mathcal{O}(\log_2(max(n, m)))$. But recall that the length of the string encoding of an integer k is $\mathcal{O}(\log k)$. So, if the input to *REL-PRIMEdecide* has length $|<n, m>|$, then $max(n, m)$ may be $2^{|<n, m>|}$. Thus $timereq(REL\text{-}PRIMEdecide) \in \mathcal{O}(\log_2(2^{|<n, m>|}) = \mathcal{O}(|<n, m>|)$. So *REL-PRIMEdecide* runs in linear time.

In Section 28.1, we will see other examples of problems that can be solved in an obvious way using an exponential-time algorithm but for which more efficient, polynomial-time algorithms also exist. But then, in Section 28.2, we'll consider a large family of problems for which no efficient solutions are known, despite the fact that substantial effort has gone into searching for them.

27.8.3 Time-Space Tradeoffs

Space efficiency and time efficiency affect the utility of an algorithm in different ways. In the early days of computing, when memory was expensive, programmers worried about small factors (and even constants) in the amount of memory required by their programs. But, in modern computers, memory is cheap, fast, and plentiful. So while it may matter to us whether one program takes twice as long as another one to run, we rarely care whether it takes twice as much memory. That is we don't care *until* our program runs out of memory and stops dead in its tracks. Time inefficiency may lead to a graceful degradation in system performance. Memory inefficiency may make a program's performance "fall off a cliff". So there are cases where we have no choice but to choose a less time-efficient algorithm in place of a more time-efficient one because the former uses less space. This is particularly likely to happen when we are solving intrinsically hard problems, in other words those where, no matter what we do, the amount of time and/or memory grows very quickly as the size of the problem increases.

EXAMPLE 27.7 Search: Depth-First, Breadth-First, and Iterative Deepening

Consider the problem of searching a tree. We have discussed this problem at various points throughout this book. For example, Theorem 17.2 tells us that, for any nondeterministic deciding or semideciding Turing machine M, there exists an equivalent deterministic one. The proof given in E.1 is by construction of a deterministic machine that conducts a search through the computational paths of M. If it finds an accepting path, then it accepts.

What search algorithm shall we use to solve problems such as this?

- ***Depth-first search*** chooses one branch and follows it until it reaches either a solution or a dead-end. In the latter case, it backs up to the most recent decision point from which there still exists an unexplored branch. Then it picks one such branch and follows it. This process continues until either a solution is found or no unexplored alternatives remain. Depth-first search is easy to implement and it requires very little space (just a stack whose depth equals the length of the path that is currently being considered). But depth-first search can get stuck exploring a bad path and miss exploring a better one. For example, in the proof of Theorem 17.2, we must consider the case in which some of M's paths do not halt. A depth-first search could get stuck in one of them and never get around to finding some other path that halts and accepts. So depth-first search cannot be used to solve this problem.

- ***Breadth-first search*** explores all paths to depth one, storing each of the nodes it generates. Next it expands each of those nodes one more level, generating a new fringe of leaf nodes. Then it returns to those leaf nodes and expands all of them one more level. This process continues until either a solution is found or no leaf nodes have any successors. Breadth-first search cannot get stuck since it explores all paths of length k before considering any paths of length $k + 1$. But breadth-first search must store every partial path in memory. So the amount of space it requires grows exponentially with the depth of the search tree that it is exploring. A Turing machine has an infinite tape, so it will never run out of room. However, managing it and shifting its contents around are difficult. Real computers, though, have finite memory. So, for practical problems, breadth-first search can work very well as long as the available memory is adequate for storing all the partial paths. As soon as it is not, the search process unceremoniously stops.

- ***Iterative deepening*** is a compromise between breadth-first search and depth-first search. It first explores all paths of length 1 using depth-first search. Then it starts over and explores all paths of length 2 using depth-first search. And then all paths of length 3, and so forth. Whenever it finds a solution, at some depth, it halts. The space complexity of iterative deepening is the same as for depth-first search. And its time complexity is only slightly worse than that of breadth-first search. This may seem counterintuitive, since, for each k, the search to depth k starts over; it doesn't use any of the results from the search to depth $k - 1$. We present the algorithm in detail in E.1, and we analyze its complexity in E.2. In a nutshell, the reason that starting the search over every time isn't such a bad idea is that the top part of the search tree is the part that must be generated many times. But the top part is very small compared to the bottom part. Iterative deepening is the technique that we use to prove Theorem 17.2.

Exercises

1. Let M be an arbitrary Turing machine.

a. Suppose that $timereq(M) = 3n^3(n + 5)(n - 4)$. Circle all of the following statements that are true:

i. $timereq(M) \in \mathcal{O}(n)$.
ii. $timereq(M) \in \mathcal{O}(n^6)$.
iii. $timereq(M) \in \mathcal{O}(n^5/50)$.
iv. $timereq(M) \in \Theta(n^6)$.

b. Suppose that $timereq(M) = 5^n \cdot 3n^3$. Circle all of the following statements that are true:

i. $timereq(M) \in \mathcal{O}(n^5)$.
ii. $timereq(M) \in \mathcal{O}(2^n)$.
iii. $timereq(M) \in \mathcal{O}(n!)$.

2. Show a function f, from the natural numbers to the reals, that is $\mathcal{O}(1)$ but that is not constant.

3. Assume the definitions of the variables given in the statement of Theorem 27.1. Prove that if $s > 1$ then:

$$\mathcal{O}(n^t 2^n) \subseteq \mathcal{O}(2^{(n^s)}).$$

4. Prove that, if $0 < a < b$, then $n^b \notin \mathcal{O}(n^a)$.

5. Let M be the Turing machine shown in Example 17.9. M accepts the language WcW $= \{wcw : w \in \{\mathtt{a}, \mathtt{b}\}^*\}$. Analyze $timereq(M)$.

6. Assume a computer that executes 10^{10} operations/second. Make the simplifying assumption that each operation of a program requires exactly one machine instruction. For each of the following programs P, defined by its time requirement, what is the largest size input on which P would be guaranteed to halt within a week?

a. $timereq(P) = 5243n + 649$.
b. $timereq(P) = 5n^2$.
c. $timereq(P) = 5^n$.

7. Let each line of the following table correspond to a problem for which two algorithms, A and B, exist. The table entries correspond to *timereq* for each of those algorithms. Determine, for each problem, the smallest value of n (the length of the input) such that algorithm B runs faster than algorithm A.

A	B
n^2	$572n + 4171$
n^2	$1000n \log_2 n$
$n!$	$450n^2$
$n!$	$3^n + 2$

8. Show that $L = \{<M>: M$ is a Turing machine and $timereq(M) \in \mathcal{O}(n^2)\}$ is not in SD.

9. Consider the problem of multiplying two $n \times n$ matrices. The straightforward algorithm *multiply* computes $C = A \cdot B$ by computing the value for each element of C using the formula:

$$C_{i,j} = \sum_{k=1}^{n} A_{i,k} B_{k,j} \quad \text{for } i, j = 1, \ldots, n.$$

Multiply uses n multiplications and $n - 1$ additions to compute each of the n^2 elements of C. So it uses a total of n^3 multiplications and $n^3 - n^2$ additions. Thus $timereq(multiply) \in \Theta(n^3)$.

We observe that any algorithm that performs at least one operation for each element of C must take at least n^2 steps. So we have an n^2 lower bound and an n^3 upper bound on the complexity of matrix multiplication. Because matrix multiplication plays an important role in many kinds of applications (including, as we saw in Section 15.3.2, some approaches to context-free parsing), the question naturally arose, "Can we narrow that gap?" In particular, does there exist a better than $\Theta(n^3)$ matrix multiplication algorithm? In [Strassen 1969], Volker Strassen showed that the answer to that question is yes.

Strassen's algorithm exploits a divide-and-conquer strategy in which it computes products and sums of smaller submatrices. Assume that $n = 2^k$, for some $k \geq 1$. (If it is not, then we can make it so by expanding the original matrix with rows and columns of zeros, or we can modify the algorithm presented here and divide the original matrix up differently.) We begin by dividing A, B, and C into 2×2 blocks. So we have:

$$A = \begin{bmatrix} A_{1,1} & A_{1,2} \\ A_{2,1} & A_{2,2} \end{bmatrix}, B = \begin{bmatrix} B_{1,1} & B_{1,2} \\ B_{2,1} & B_{2,2} \end{bmatrix}, \text{and } C = \begin{bmatrix} C_{1,1} & C_{1,2} \\ C_{2,1} & C_{2,2} \end{bmatrix},$$

where each $A_{i,j}$, $B_{i,j}$, and $C_{i,j}$ is a $2^{k-1} \times 2^{k-1}$ matrix.

With this decomposition, we can state the following equations that define the values for each element of C:

$$C_{1,1} = A_{1,1}B_{1,1} + A_{1,2}B_{2,1}.$$
$$C_{1,2} = A_{1,1}B_{1,2} + A_{1,2}B_{2,2}.$$
$$C_{2,1} = A_{2,1}B_{1,1} + A_{2,2}B_{2,1}.$$
$$C_{2,2} = A_{2,1}B_{1,2} + A_{2,2}B_{2,2}.$$

So far, decomposition hasn't bought us anything. We must still do eight multiplications and four additions, each of which must be done on matrices of size 2^{k-1}. Strassen's insight was to define the following seven equations:

$$Q_1 = (A_{1,1} + A_{2,2})(B_{1,1} + B_{2,2}).$$
$$Q_2 = (A_{2,1} + A_{2,2})B_{1,1}.$$
$$Q_3 = A_{1,1}(B_{1,2} - B_{2,2}).$$
$$Q_4 = A_{2,2}(B_{2,1} - B_{1,1}).$$
$$Q_5 = (A_{1,1} + A_{1,2})B_{2,2}.$$
$$Q_6 = (A_{2,1} - A_{1,1})(B_{1,1} + B_{1,2}).$$
$$Q_7 = (A_{1,2} - A_{2,2})(B_{2,1} + B_{2,2}).$$

These equations can then be used to define the values for each element of C as follows:

$$C_{1,1} = Q_1 + Q_4 - Q_5 + Q_7.$$
$$C_{1,2} = Q_3 + Q_5.$$
$$C_{2,1} = Q_2 + Q_4.$$
$$C_{2,2} = Q_1 - Q_2 + Q_3 + Q_6.$$

Now, instead of eight matrix multiplications and four matrix additions, we do only seven matrix multiplications, but we must also do eighteen matrix additions (where a subtraction counts as an addition). We've replaced twelve matrix operations with 25. But matrix addition can be done in $\mathcal{O}(n^2)$ time, while matrix multiplication remains more expensive.

Strassen's algorithm applies these formulas recursively, each time dividing each matrix of size 2^k into four matrices of size 2^{k-1}. The process halts when $k = 1$. (Efficient implementations ▭ of the algorithm actually stop the recursion sooner and use the simpler *multiply* procedure on small submatrices. We'll see why in part (e) of this problem.) We can summarize the algorithm as follows:

Strassen(A, B, k: where A and B are matrices of size 2^k) =

If $k = 1$ then compute the Q's using scalar arithmetic. Else, compute them as follows:

$Q_1 = \mathit{Strassen}((A_{1,1} + A_{2,2}), (B_{1,1} + B_{2,2}), k - 1).$

$Q_2 = \mathit{Strassen}((A_{2,1} + A_{2,2}), B_{1,1}, k - 1).$

… /* Compute all the Q matrices as described above.

$Q_7 =$

$C_{1,1} =$

… /* Compute all the C matrices as described above.

$C_{2,2} =$

Return C.

In the years following Strassen's publication of his algorithm, newer ones that use even fewer operations have been discovered 🖳. The fastest known technique is the Coppersmith-Winograd algorithm, whose time complexity is $\mathcal{O}(n^{2.376})$. But it is too complex to be practically useful. There do exist algorithms with better performance than *Strassen*, but, since it opened up this entire line of inquiry, we should understand its complexity. In this problem, we will analyze *timereq* of *Strassen* and compare it to *timereq* of the standard algorithm *multiply*. We should issue two caveats before we start, however: The analysis that we are about to do just counts scalar multiplies and adds. It does not worry about such things as the behavior of caches and the use of pipelining. In practice, it turns out that the crossover point for *Strassen* relative to *multiply* 🖳 is lower than our results suggest. In addition, *Strassen* may not be as numerically stable as *multiply* is, so it may not be suitable for all applications.

a. We begin by defining $mult'(k)$ to be the number of scalar multiplications that will be performed by *Strassen* when it multiplies two $2^k \times 2^k$ matrices. Similarly, let $add'(k)$ be the number of scalar additions. Describe both $mult'(k)$ and $add'(k)$ inductively by stating their value for the base case (when $k = 1$) and then describing their value for $k > 1$ as a function of their value for $k - 1$.

b. To find closed form expressions for $mult'(k)$ and add' requires solving the recurrence relations that were given as answers in part (a). Solving the one for $mult'(k)$ is easy. Solving the one for $add'(k)$ is harder. Prove that the following are correct:

$$mult'(k) = 7^k.$$

$$add'(k) = 6 \cdot (7^k - 4^k).$$

c. We'd like to define the time requirement of *Strassen*, when multiplying two $n \times n$ matrices, as a function of n, rather than as a function of $\log_2 n$, as we have been doing. So define $mult(n)$ to be the number of multiplications that will be performed by *Strassen* when it multiplies two $n \times n$ matrices. Similarly, let $add(n)$ be the number of additions. Using the fact that $k = \log_2 n$, state $mult(n)$ and $add(n)$ as functions of n.

d. Determine values of α and β, each less than 3, such that $mult(k) \in \Theta(n^{\alpha})$ and $add(k) \in \Theta(n^{\beta})$.

e. Let $ops(n) = mult(n) + add(n)$ be the total number of scalar multiplications and additions that *Strassen* performs to multiply two $n \times n$ matrices. Recall that, for the standard algorithm *multiply*, this total operation count is $2n^3 - n^2$. We'd like to find the crossover point, i.e., the point at which *Strassen* performs fewer scalar operations than *multiply* does. So find the smallest value of k such that $n = 2^k$ and $ops(n) < 2n^3 - n^2$. (Hint: Once you have an equation that describes the relationship between the operation counts of the two algorithms, just start trying candidates for k, starting at 1.)

10. In this problem, we will explore the operation of the Knuth-Morris-Pratt string search algorithm that we described in Example 27.5. Let p be the pattern cbacbcc.

a. Trace the execution of *buildoverlap* and show the table T that it builds.

b. Using T, trace the execution of *Knuth-Morris-Pratt*(cbaccbacbcc, cbacbcc).

C H A P T E R 28

Time Complexity Classes

Some problems are easy. For example, every regular language can be decided in linear time (by running the corresponding DFSM). Some problems are harder. For example, the best known algorithm for deciding the Traveling Salesman language TSP-DECIDE takes, in the worst case, time that grows exponentially in the size of the input. In this chapter, we will define a hierarchy of language classes based on the time required by the best known decision algorithm.

28.1 The Language Class P

The first important complexity class that we will consider is the class P, which includes all and only those languages that are decidable by a deterministic Turing machine in polynomial time. So we have:

The Class P: $L \in \mathrm{P}$ iff there exists some deterministic Turing machine M that decides L and $timereq(M) \in \mathcal{O}(n^k)$ for some constant k.

It is common to think of the class P as containing exactly the ***tractable*** problems. In other words, it contains those problems that are not only solvable in principle (i.e., they are decidable) but also solvable in an amount of time that makes it reasonable to depend on solving them in real application contexts.

Of course, suppose that the best algorithm we have for deciding some language L is $\Theta(n^{1000})$ (i.e., its running time grows at the same rate, to within a constant factor, as n^{1000}). It is hard to imagine using that algorithm on anything except a toy problem. But the empirical fact is that we don't tend to find algorithms of this sort. Most problems of practical interest that are known to be in P can be solved by programs that are no worse than $\mathcal{O}(n^3)$ if we are analyzing running times on conventional (random access) computers. And so they're no worse than $\mathcal{O}(n^{18})$ when run on a one-tape, deterministic Turing machine. Furthermore, it often happens that, once some polynomial time algorithm is known, a faster one will be discovered. For example, consider the problem of matrix multiplication. If we count steps on a random access computer, the obvious algorithm for matrix multiplication (based on Gaussian elimination) is $\mathcal{O}(n^3)$. Strassen's algorithm 🖳 is more efficient; it is $\mathcal{O}(n^{2.81})$. Other algorithms whose asymptotic complexity is even lower (approaching $\mathcal{O}(n^2)$) are now known, although they are substantially more complex.

So, as we consider languages that are in P, we will generally discover algorithms whose time requirement is some low-order polynomial function of the length of the input. But we should be clear that not all languages in P have this property. In Section 28.9.1, we'll describe the time hierarchy theorems. One consequence of the Deterministic Time Hierarchy Theorem is that, for any integer $k>1$, there are languages that can be decided by a deterministic Turing machine in $\mathcal{O}(n^k)$ time but not in $\mathcal{O}(n^{k-1})$ time. It just happens that if $k = 5000$, we are unlikely to care.

Going the other direction, if we have a problem that we cannot show to be in P, is it necessarily intractable in practice? Often it is. But there may be algorithms that solve it quickly most of the time or that solve it quickly and return the right answer most of the time. For example, prior to the recent proof (which we will mention in Section 28.1.7) that primality testing can be done in polynomial time, randomized algorithms that performed primality testing efficiently were known and commonly used 🖳. We'll return to this approach in Chapter 30.

28.1.1 Closure of P under Complement

One important property of the class P is that, if a language L is in P, so is its complement:

THEOREM 28.1 P is Closed Under Complement

Theorem: The class P is closed under complement.

Proof: For any language L, if $L \in \text{P}$ then there exists some deterministic Turing machine M that decides L in polynomial time. From M, we can build a new deterministic Turing machine M' that decides $\neg L$ in polynomial time. We use the same construction that we used to prove Theorem 20.4 (which tells us that the decidable languages are closed under complement). M' is simply M with accepting and nonaccepting states swapped. M' will always halt in exactly the same number of steps M would take and it will accept $\neg L$.

For many problems that we are likely to care about, this closure theorem doesn't give us exactly the result we need. For example, we'll show below that the language CONNECTED = {<*G*> : *G* is an undirected graph and *G* is connected} is in P. We'd like then to be able to conclude that the related language NOTCONNECTED = {<*G*> : *G* is an undirected graph and *G* is not connected} is also in P. But we have the same problem that we had in analyzing languages that are defined in terms of a Turing machine's behavior:

- ¬CONNECTED = NOTCONNECTED ∪ {strings that are not syntactically legal descriptions of undirected graphs}.

If, however, we can check for legal syntax in polynomial time, then we can consider the universe with respect to which the complement of CONNECTED is computed to be just those strings whose syntax is legal. Then we can conclude that NOTCONNECTED is in P if CONNECTED is. In all the examples we will consider in this book, such a syntax check can be done in polynomial time. So we will consider the complement of some language L to be the language consisting of strings of the correct syntax but without the property that defines L.

28.1.2 Languages That Are in P

We have already discussed many examples of languages that are in P:

- Every regular language is in P since every regular language can be decided in linear time. We'll prove this claim as Theorem 28.2 below.
- Every context-free language is in P since there exist context-free parsing (and deciding) algorithms that run in $\mathcal{O}(n^3)$ time on a conventional computer (and thus run in $\mathcal{O}(n^{18})$ time on a single-tape Turing machine). We'll prove this claim as Theorem 28.3 below.
- Some languages that are not context-free are also in P. One example of such a language is $A^nB^nC^n = \{a^nb^nc^n : n \geq 0\}$. In Example 27.1, we analyzed M, the Turing machine that we had built to decide $A^nB^nC^n$. We showed that $timereq(M) = 2(n/3)(n/3 + n/3 + n/6) + n$, which, as we showed in Example 27.3, is in $\mathcal{O}(n^2)$.

> The game of Nim (appropriately encoded as a decision problem in which we ask whether there is a guaranteed win for the current player) is in P. But it appears that very few "interesting" games are in P. (N.2)

Many other languages are also in P. In the rest of this section, we show examples of proofs that languages are in P. If we can construct a one-tape, deterministic Turing machine M that decides some language L in polynomial time, then we have a proof that L is in P. But we will generally find it substantially easier just to describe a decision procedure as it would be implemented on a conventional, random access computer. Then we can appeal to Theorem 17.4, which tells us that a deterministic random access program that executes t steps can can be simulated by a seven-tape Turing machine in $\mathcal{O}(t^3)$ steps. We also showed, in Theorem 17.1, that t steps of a k-tape Turing machine can be simulated in $\mathcal{O}(t^2)$ steps of a standard Turing machine. Composing these results, we have that if a random access program runs in t steps, it can be simulated by a standard Turing machine in $\mathcal{O}(t^6)$ steps. Since the composition of two polynomials is a polynomial, if we have a random access algorithm that runs in polynomial time, then it can be simulated in a polynomial number of steps on a deterministic one-tape Turing machine and so the language that it decides is in P.

We'll make one other simplifying assumption as well. It takes $\mathcal{O}(n^2)$ steps to compare two strings of length n on a one-tape Turing machine. It takes $\mathcal{O}(\log^2 n)$ to compare two integers of size n (since their string descriptions have length $\log n$). We can do similar analyses of the time required to perform arithmetic operations on numbers of size n. The key is that all of these operations can be performed in polynomial time. So, if our goal is to show that an algorithm runs in polynomial time, we can assume that all such operations are performed in constant time (which many of them are on real computers). While not strictly true, this assumption will have no effect on any claim we may make that an algorithm runs in polynomial time.

28.1.3 Regular and Context-Free Languages

THEOREM 28.2 Every Regular Language can be Decided in Linear Time

Theorem: Every regular language can be decided in linear time. So every regular language is in P.

Proof: Given any regular language L, there exists some deterministic finite state machine $M = (K, \Sigma, \delta, s, A)$ that decides L. From M, we can construct a deterministic Turing machine $M' = (K \cup \{s', y, n\}, \Sigma, \Sigma \cup \{\square\}, \delta', s', \{y\})$ that decides L in linear time. Roughly, M' simply simulates the steps of M, moving its read/write head one square to the right at each step and making no change to the tape. When M' reads a $\square$, it halts. If it is in an accepting state, it accepts; otherwise it rejects. So, if (q, a, p) is a transition in M, M' will contain the transition $((q, a), (p, a, \rightarrow))$. Because of our convention that the read/write head of M' will be just to the left of the first input character when it begins, M' will need a new start state, s', in which it will read a $\square$ and move right to the first input character. Also, since FSMs halt when they run out of input, while Turing machines halt only when they enter an explicit halting state, M' will need two new states: y, which will halt and accept, and n, which will halt and reject. Finally, M' will need transitions into y and n labeled $\square$. So, if q is a state in M (and thus also in M') and q is an accepting state in M, M' will contain the transition $((q, \square), (y, \square, \rightarrow))$. If, on the other hand, q is not an accepting state in M, M' will contain the transition $((q, \square), (n, \square, \rightarrow))$.

On any input of length n, M' will execute $n + 2$ steps. So $timereq(M') \in \mathcal{O}(n)$.

It is significant that every regular language can be decided in linear time. But the fact that every regular language is in P is also a consequence of the more general fact that we prove next: Every context-free language is in P.

THEOREM 28.3 Every Context-Free Language is in P

Theorem: Every context-free language can be decided in $\mathcal{O}(n^{18})$ time. So every context-free language is in P.

Proof: In Chapter 14, we showed that every context-free language is decidable. Unfortunately, neither of the algorithms that we presented there (*decideCFLusingGrammar* and *decideCFLusingPDA*) runs in polynomial time. But, in Section 15.3, we presented the Cocke-Kasami-Younger (CKY) algorithm, which can parse any context-free language in time that is $\mathcal{O}(n^3)$ if we count operations on a conventional computer. That algorithm can be simulated on a standard, one-tape Turing machine in $\mathcal{O}(n^{18})$ steps.

28.1.4 Connected Graphs

We next consider languages that describe significant properties of graphs. One of the simplest questions we can ask about a graph is whether it is connected. A graph is ***connected*** iff there exists a path from each vertex to each other vertex. We consider here the problem for undirected graphs. (We can also define the related language for directed graphs.) Define the language:

- CONNECTED = {<G> : G is an undirected graph and G is connected}.

THEOREM 28.4 The Problem of Identifying Connected Graphs is in P

Theorem: CONNECTED is in P.

Proof: We prove that CONNECTED is in P by exhibiting a deterministic, polynomial-time algorithm that decides it:

connected(<G : graph with vertices V and edges E>) =

1. Set all vertices to be unmarked.
2. Mark vertex 1.
3. Initialize L (a list that will contain vertices that have been marked but whose successors have not yet been examined) to contain just vertex 1.
4. Initialize *marked-vertices-counter* to 1.
5. Until L is empty do:
   - **5.1.** Remove the first element from L. Call it *current-vertex*.
   - **5.2.** For each edge e that has *current-vertex* as an endpoint do:
     Call the other endpoint of e *next-vertex*. If *next-vertex* is not already marked then do:
       - Mark *next-vertex*.
       - Add *next-vertex* to L.
       - Increment *marked-vertices-counter* by 1.
6. If *marked-vertices-counter* $= |V|$ accept; else reject.

Connected will mark and count the vertices that are reachable from vertex 1. Since G is undirected, if there is a path from vertex 1 to some vertex n, then there is also a path from vertex n back to vertex 1. So, if there is a path from vertex 1 to every other vertex, then there is a path from every other vertex back to vertex 1 and from there to each other vertex. Thus G is connected. If, on the other hand, there is some vertex that is not reachable from vertex 1, G is unconnected.

So it remains to show that the runtime of *connected* is some polynomial function of $|<G>|$:

- Step 1 takes time that is $\mathcal{O}(|V|)$.
- Steps 2, 3, and 4 each take constant time.
- The outer loop of step 5 can be executed at most $|V|$ times since no vertex can be put on L more than once.
    - Step 5.1 takes constant time.
    - The loop in step 5.2 can be executed at most $|E|$ times. Each time through, it requires at most $\mathcal{O}(|V|)$ time (depending on how the vertices are represented and marked).
- Step 6 takes constant time.

So the total time required to execute *connected* is $|V| \cdot \mathcal{O}(|E|) \cdot \mathcal{O}(|V|) = \mathcal{O}(|V|^2|E|)$. But note that $|E| \leq |V|^2$. So the time required to execute *connected* is $\mathcal{O}(|V|^4)$.

28.1.5 Eulerian Paths and Circuits

The Seven Bridges of Königsberg problem 💻 is inspired by the geography of a town once called Königsberg, in Germany, now called Kaliningrad, in Russia. The town straddled the banks of the river Pregel and there were two islands in the river. There were seven bridges connecting the river banks and the islands as shown in Figure 28.1. The problem is this: Can a citizen of Königsberg take a walk through the town (starting anywhere she likes) and cross each bridge exactly once?

In 1736, Leonhard Euler showed that the answer to this question is no. To prove this, he abstracted the map to a graph whose vertices correspond to the land masses and whose edges correspond to the bridges between them. So, in Euler's representation, the town becames the graph shown in Figure 28.2. Vertices 1 and 2 represent the river banks and vertices 3 and 4 represent the two islands.

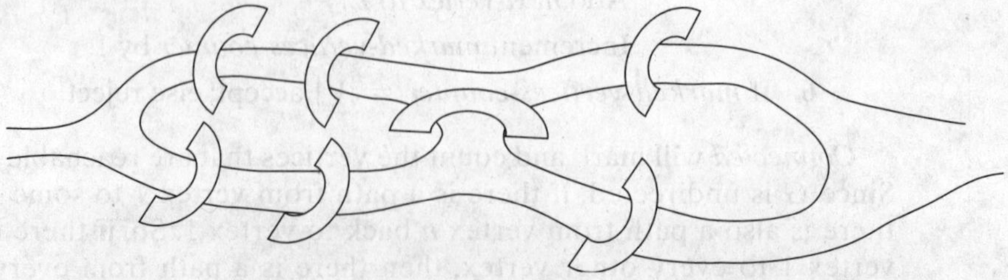

FIGURE 28.1 The Seven Bridges of Königsberg.

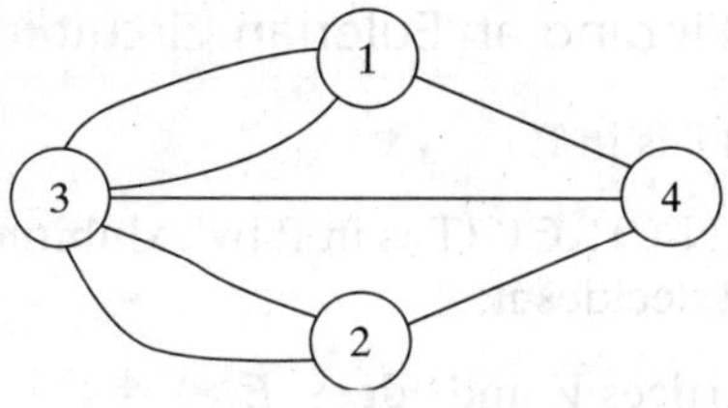

FIGURE 28.2 The Seven Bridges of Königsberg as a graph.

We can now restate the Seven Bridges of Königsberg problem as, "Does there exist a path through the graph such that each edge is traversed exactly once?"

Generalizing to an arbitrary graph, we give the following definitions:

- An ***Eulerian path*** through a graph G is a path that traverses each edge in G exactly once.
- An ***Eulerian circuit*** through a graph G is a path that starts at some vertex s, ends back in s, and traverses each edge in G exactly once. (Note the difference between an Eulerian circuit and a Hamiltonian one: An Eulerian circuit visits each *edge* exactly once. A Hamiltonian circuit visits each *vertex* exactly once.)

> Bridge inspectors, road cleaners, and network analysts can minimize their effort if they traverse their systems by following an Eulerian circuit. (I.2)

We'd now like to determine the computational complexity of deciding, given an arbitrary graph G, whether or not it possesses an Eulerian path (or circuit). Both questions can be answered with a similar technique, so we'll pick the circuit problem and define the following language:

- EULERIAN-CIRCUIT = $\{<G> : G$ is an undirected graph and G contains an Eulerian circuit$\}$.

We'll show next that EULERIAN-CIRCUIT is in P. The algorithm that we will use to prove this claim is based on an observation that Euler made in studying the Königsberg bridge problem. Define the ***degree*** of a vertex to be the number of edges with it as an endpoint. For example, in the Königsberg graph, vertices 1, 2, and 4 have degree 3. Vertex 3 has degree 5. Euler observed that:

- A connected graph possesses an Eulerian path that is not a circuit iff it contains exactly two vertices of odd degree. Those two vertices will serve as the first and last vertices of the path.
- A connected graph possess an Eulerian circuit iff all its vertices have even degree. Because each vertex has even degree, any path that enters it can also leave it without reusing an edge.

It should now by obvious why Euler knew (without explicitly exploring all possible paths) that there existed no path that crossed each of the Königsberg bridges exactly once.

THEOREM 28.5 The Problem of Finding an Eulerian Circuit in a Graph is in P

Theorem: EULERIAN-CIRCUIT is in P.

Proof: We prove that EULERIAN-CIRCUIT is in P by exhibiting a deterministic, polynomial-time algorithm that decides it:

Eulerian(<G: graph with vertices V and edges E>) =

1. If *connected*(G) rejects, reject (since an unconnected graph cannot have an Eulerian circuit). Else:
2. For each vertex v in G do:
   - **2.1.** Count the number of edges that have v as one endpoint but not both.
   - **2.2.** If the count is odd, exit the loop and reject.
3. If all counts are even, accept.

The correctness of *Eulerian* follows from Euler's observations as stated above. We show that *Eulerian* runs in polynomial time as follows:

- We showed in the proof of Theorem 28.4 that *connected* runs in time that is polynomial in $|<V>|$.
- The loop in step 2 is executed at most $|V|$ times. Each time through, it requires time that is $\mathcal{O}(|E|)$.
- Step 3 takes constant time.

So the total time required to execute steps 2 through 3 of *Eulerian* is $|V| \cdot \mathcal{O}(|E|)$. But $|E| \leq |V|^2$. So the time required to execute steps 2-3 of *Eulerian* is $\mathcal{O}(|V|^3)$.

28.1.6 Minimum Spanning Trees ✸

Consider an arbitrary undirected graph G. A ***spanning tree*** T of G is a subset of the edges of G such that:

- T contains no cycles and
- Every vertex in G is connected to every other vertex using just the edges in T.

An unconnected graph (i.e., a graph in which there exist at least two vertices with no path between them) has no spanning trees. A connected graph G will have at least one spanning tree; it may have many.

Define a ***weighted graph*** to be a graph that has a weight (a number) associated with each edge. Typically the weight represents some sort of cost or benefit associated with traversing the edge. Define an ***unweighted graph*** to be a graph that does not associate weights with its edges.

If G is a weighted graph, we can compare the spanning trees of G by defining the cost of a tree to be the sum of the costs (weights) of its edges. Then a tree T is a ***minimum spanning tree*** of G iff it is a spanning tree and there is no other spanning tree whose cost is lower than that of T. Note that, if all edge costs are positive, a minimum spanning tree is also a minimum cost subgraph that connects all the vertices of G since any connected subgraph that contains cycles (i.e., any connected subgraph that is not a tree) must have higher cost than T does.

> The cheapest way to lay cable that connects a set of points is along a minimum spanning tree that connects those points. (I.2)

EXAMPLE 28.1 A Minimum Spanning Tree

Let G be the following graph, in which the edge costs are shown in parentheses next to each edge:

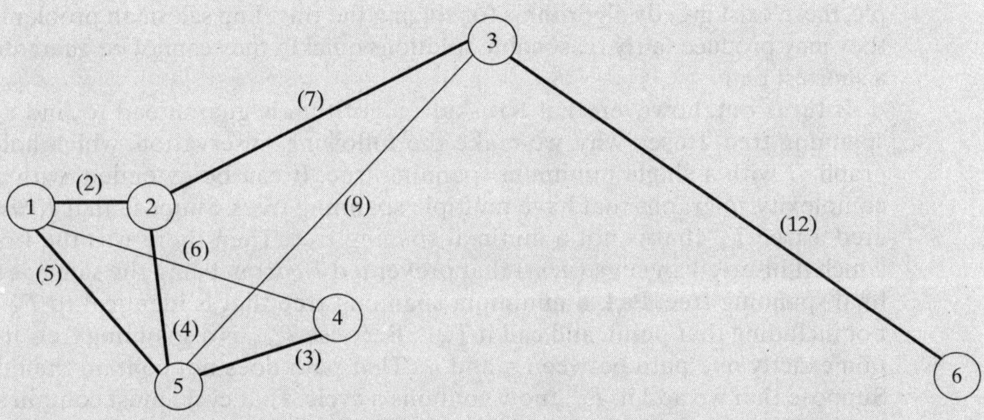

The subgraph shown with heavy lines is a minimum spanning tree of G.

Given a connected graph G, how shall we go about trying to find a minimum spanning tree for it? The most obvious thing to do is to try all subgraphs of G. We can reject any that do not connect all of G's vertices. Of the remaining ones, we can choose the one with the lowest total cost. This procedure works but does not run in time that is polynomial in the size of G. Can we do better? The answer is yes.

One of the simplest reasonable algorithms for finding a minimum spanning tree is Kruskal's algorithm, defined as follows:

Kruskal(G: connected graph with vertices V and edges E) =

1. Sort the edges in E in ascending order by their cost. Break ties arbitrarily.
2. Initialize T to a forest with an empty set of edges.
3. Until all the edges in E have been considered do:
   - **3.1.** Select e, the next edge in E. If the endpoints of e are not connected in T then add e to T
4. Return T.

To show that Kruskal's algorithm finds a minimum spanning tree, we must show that the graph T that it returns is a tree (i.e., it is connected and it contains no cycles), that it is a spanning tree (i.e., that it includes all the vertices of the original graph G), and that there is no lower cost spanning tree of G. T cannot contain cycles because step 3.1 can add an edge only if its two endpoints are not already connected. T must be connected and it must be a spanning tree because we assumed that the input graph G is connected. This means that if we used all of G's edges, every one of G's vertices would be in T and T would be connected. But we do use all of G's edges except ones whose endpoints are already connected in T.

So all that remains is to prove that we have found a minimum spanning tree. Kruskal's algorithm is an example of a ***greedy algorithm***: It attempts to find an optimal global solution by grabbing the best (local) pieces, in this case short edges, and putting them together. Greedy algorithms tend to run quickly because they may do little or no search. But they cannot always be guaranteed to find the best global solution. For example, there exist greedy algorithms for solving the traveling salesman problem. Although they may produce fairly reasonable solutions quickly, they cannot be guaranteed to find a shortest path.

It turns out, however, that Kruskal's algorithm is guaranteed to find a minimum spanning tree. To see why, we make the following observation, which holds for any graph G with a single minimum spanning tree. It can be extended, with a bit more complexity, to graphs that have multiple spanning trees. Suppose that *Kruskal* generated a tree T_K that is not a minimal spaning tree. Then there was the first point at which it inserted an edge (n, m) that prevented T_K from being the same as some minimal spanning tree. Pick a minimum spanning tree that is identical to T_K up to, but not including that point, and call it T_{min}. Because T_{min} is a spanning tree, it must contain exactly one path between n and m. That path does not contain the edge (n, m). Suppose that we add it. T_{min} now contains a cycle. That cycle must contain some edge e that *Kruskal* would have considered after considering (n, m) (since otherwise it would have been chosen instead of (n, m) as a way to connect n and m). Thus the weight of that edge must be at least the weight of (n, m). Remove e from T_{min}. Call the result T_{min}'. T_{min}' is a spanning tree. It contains the edge (n, m) instead of the edge e. Since the weight of (n, m) is less than or equal to the weight of e, the weight of T_{min}' must be less than or equal to the weight of T_{min}. But we assumed that T_{min} was minimal, so it can't be less. It must, therefore be equal. But then adding (n, m) did not prevent T_K, the tree that *Kruskal* built, from being minimal. This contradicts the assumption that it did.

We are now ready to ask the question, "How computationally hard is finding a minimum spanning tree?" Since this is an optimization problem, we'll use the same technique we used to convert the traveling salesman problem into the decision problem TSP-DECIDE: We'll give a cost bound and ask whether there exists a minimum spanning tree whose cost is less than the bound we provide.

Define the language:

MST = $\{<G, cost> : G$ is an undirected graph with a positive cost attached to each of its edges and there exists a minimum spanning tree of G with total cost less than $cost\}$.

THEOREM 28.6 The Problem of Finding a Minimum Spanning Tree with an Acceptable Cost is in P

Theorem: MST is in P.

Proof: We prove that MST is in P by exhibiting a polynomial time algorithm that decides it:

MSTdecide(<*G*: graph with vertices *V* and edges *E*, *cost*: number>) =

1. Invoke *Kruskal*(*G*). Let *T* be the minimum spanning tree that is returned.
2. If the total cost of $T < cost$ then accept, else reject.

MSTdecide runs in polynomial time if each of its two steps does. Step 2 can be done in constant time.

So it remains to analyze Kruskal's algorithm, which we do as follows:

- Step 1, the sorting step, can be done with $|E| \cdot \log |E|$ comparisons and each comparison takes constant time.
- Step 2 takes constant time.
- The loop in step 3 is executed $|E|$ times. The time required at each step to test whether two vertices are disconnected depends on the data structure that is used to represent *T*. A straightforward way to do it is to maintain, for each tree in the forest *T*, a set that contains exactly the vertices that are present in that tree. Each vertex in *V* will be in at most one such set. So, in considering an edge (n, m), we examine each of the sets. If we find one that contains *n*, we look just in that set to see whether *m* is also there. If it is, then *n* and *m* are already connected; otherwise they are not. To find *n*, we may have to look through all the sets, so we may have to examine $|V|$ vertices and, if all the vertices are in the same set, we might have to do that again to look for *m*. So we might examine $\mathcal{O}(|V|)$ vertices to do the check for disconnectedness. Further, if we take this approach, then we must maintain these sets. But, even doing that, the cost of adding *e* to *T* is constant. So step 3 takes a total number of steps that is $\mathcal{O}(|E| \cdot |V|)$.

So the total time required to execute Kruskal's algorithm is $\mathcal{O}(|E| \cdot |V|)$ and so $\mathcal{O}(|<G>|^2)$. With a more efficient implementation of step 3, it is possible to show[13] that it is also $\mathcal{O}(|E| \cdot \log|V|)$.

Kruskal's algorithm proves that MST is in P. And it is very easy to implement. There also exist other algorithms for finding minimum spanning trees that run even faster than Kruskal's algorithm does.

28.1.7 Primality Testing

Prime numbers have fascinated mathematicians since the time of the ancient Greeks. It turns out that some key problems involving prime numbers are known to be solvable in polynomial time, while some others are not now known to be.

[13] For a proof of this claim, see [Corman et al. 2001].

> Prime numbers are of more than theoretical interest. They play a critical role in modern encryption systems. (J. 3)

In Example 27.6, we introduced the language:

- RELATIVELY-PRIME = {<n, m> : n and m are integers and they are relatively prime}. Recall that two integers are relatively prime iff their greatest common divisor is 1.

THEOREM 28.7 RELATIVELY-PRIME is in P

Theorem: RELATIVELY-PRIME is in P.

Proof: RELATIVELY-PRIME can be decided in linear time by the algorithm *REL-PRIMEdecide*, described in Example 27.6.

But now consider the problem of determining whether or not a number is prime. We have encoded that problem as the language:

- PRIMES = $\{w : w$ is the binary encoding of a prime number$\}$.

The obvious way to decide PRIMES is, when given the number k, to consider all the natural numbers between 2 and $\sqrt{k}$. Check each to see whether it divides evenly into k. If any such number does, then k isn't prime. If none does, then k is prime. The time required to implement this approach is $\mathcal{O}(\sqrt{k})$. But n, the length of the string that encodes k, is log k. So this simple algorithm is $\mathcal{O}(2^{n/2})$. Because of the practical significance of primality testing, particularly in cryptography, substantial effort has been devoted to finding a more efficient technique for deciding PRIMES. It turns out that there exist randomized algorithms that can decide PRIMES in polynomial time if we allow an exceedingly small, but nonzero, probability of making an error. We'll describe such an approach in Chapter 30. Such techniques are widely used in practice.

Until very recently, however, the question of whether PRIMES is in P (i.e., whether a provably correct, polynomial-time algorithm for it exists) remained unanswered and it continued to be of theoretical interest. We now know the answer to the question. We can state it as the following theorem:

THEOREM 28.8 PRIMES is in P

Theorem: PRIMES is in P.

Proof: Various proofs of this claim have been proposed. Most have relied on hypotheses that, although widely believed to be true, remained unproven. But [Agrawal, Kayal and Saxena 2004] contains a proof that relies on no unproven assumptions. It describes an algorithm for deciding PRIMES that runs in deterministic $\mathcal{O}((\log n)^{12} \cdot f(\log(\log n)))$ time, where f is a polynomial. The details of the proof are beyond the scope of this book. Since the original algorithm was described, modifications of it that further improve its performance have been discovered.

The class P is closed under complement. So we also have that the following language is in P:

COMPOSITES = $\{w : w$ is the binary encoding of a composite number$\}$. A composite number is a natural number greater than 1 that is not prime.

Unfortunately, the results we have just presented do not close the book on the problem of working with prime and composite numbers. We now know that there exists a polynomial-time algorithm to check whether a number is prime and we continue to exploit randomized algorithms to answer the question in practice. The fact that we can, in polynomial time, tell whether or not a number is prime does not tell us that there exists a polynomial-time algorithm to *discover* the factors of a number that is not prime. No efficient algorithm for factoring using a conventional computer is currently known. Were a practical and efficient algorithm to be discovered, modern encryption techniques that rely on factorization would no longer be effective. One approach to constructing such an algorithm is to exploit quantum computing. Shor's algorithm, for example, factors a number k in $\mathcal{O}((\log k)^3)$ time on a quantum computer. But the largest number that has so far been able to be factored on a quantum computer is 15.

28.2 The Language Class NP

Now suppose that, in our quest for polynomial-time deciding Turing machines, we allow nondeterminism. Will this increase the number of languages for which it is possible to build polynomial-time deciders? No one knows. But it appears likely that it does. For example, consider again the traveling salesman language TSP-DECIDE = $\{w$ of the form: <*G*, *cost*>, where <*G*> encodes an undirected graph with a positive distance attached to each of its edges and *G* contains a Hamiltonian circuit whose total cost is less than *cost*$\}$. Recall that a Hamiltonian circuit is a path that starts at some vertex *s*, ends back in *s*, and visits each other vertex in *G* exactly once. We know of no *deterministic* Turing machine that can decide TSP-DECIDE in polynomial time. But there is a *nondeterministic* Turing machine that does. It works by using nondeterminism to guess the best path. (We'll describe it in detail below.)

28.2.1 Defining the Class NP

TSP-DECIDE is typical of a large class of problems that are of considerable practical interest. All of them share the following three properties:

1. The problem can be solved by searching through a space of partial solutions (such as routes), looking for a complete solution that satisfies all of the given constraints. The size of the space that must be explored in this way grows exponentially with the size of the problem that is being considered.

2. No better (i.e., not based on search) technique for finding an exact solution is known.
3. But, if a proposed solution were suddenly to appear, it could be checked for correctness very efficiently.

The next language class that we will define is called NP. It will include TSP-DECIDE and its cousins, as well as the "easier" languages that are also in P. In Section 28.5.1, we'll define a subset of NP called NP-complete. It will include only those languages, like TSP-DECIDE, that are the "hardest" of the NP languages.

Properties 1 and 3 suggest two superficially quite different ways to define NP. It turns out that the two definitions are equivalent. Because each of them is useful in some contexts, we provide them both.

Nondeterministic Deciding

The first definition we present is based on the idea of search. Nondeterministic Turing machines perform search. So we will define the class NP to include all and only those languages that are decidable by a nondeterministic Turing machine in polynomial time. (The name NP stands for **N**ondeterministic **P**olynomial.) Remember that in defining the time requirement of a nondeterministic Turing machine M, we don't consider the total number of steps that M executes on all of its computational paths; instead we measure just the length of its longest path. Thus we'll say that a language L is in NP iff there is some nondeterministic Turing machine M that decides L and the length of the longest computational path that M must follow on any input of length n grows as some polynomial function of n. So we have:

The Class NP: $L \in$ NP iff there exists some nondeterministic Turing machine M that decides L and $timereq(M) \in \mathcal{O}(n^k)$ for some constant k.

Again consider the language TSP-DECIDE. Given a string $w = <G, cost>$, we can build a nondeterministic Turing machine M that decides whether w is in TSP-DECIDE. M's job is to decide whether there is a Hamiltonian circuit through G whose cost is less than *cost*. M will nondeterministically guess a path through G with length equal to the number of vertices in G. There is a finite number of such paths and each of them has finite length, so all paths of M will eventually halt. M will accept w if it finds at least one path that corresponds to a Hamiltonian circuit whose cost is less than *cost*. Otherwise it will reject. We will show below that $timereq(M) \in \mathcal{O}(n)$. So TSP-DECIDE $\in$ NP.

Deterministic Verifying

But now suppose that (somehow) we find ourselves in possession of a particular path c, along with the claim that c proves that $w = <G, cost>$ is in TSP-DECIDE. In other words, there is a claim that c is a Hamiltonian circuit through G with cost less than *cost*. Our only job now is to check c and verify that it does in fact prove that w is in TSP-DECIDE. We can build a deterministic Turing machine M' that does this in time that is polynomial in the length of w. The input to M' will be the string $(<G, cost, c>)$. Assume that c is represented as a sequence of vertices. Then M' will simply walk through c, one vertex at a time, checking that G does in fact contain the required edge from each vertex to its successor. As it does this, it will keep track of the length of *c* so far. If that length ever exceeds the number of vertices in *G*, *M′* will halt and reject. Also, as it goes along, it will use a list of the vertices in *G* and mark each one as it is visited, checking to make sure that every vertex is visited exactly once. And, finally, it will keep a running total of the costs of the edges that it follows. If every step of *c* follows an edge in *G*, every vertex in *G* is visited once except that *c* starts and ends at the same vertex, and the cost of *c* is less than *cost*, *M′* will accept its input and thus report that *c* does in fact prove that *w* is in TSP-DECIDE. Otherwise *M′* will reject its input and thus report that *c* fails to do that. (But note that this doesn't mean that *w* is not in TSP-DECIDE; we know only that *c* fails to show that it is.) We'll call *M′* a verifier for TSP-DECIDE. We can analyze the complexity of *M* as follows: Let *n* be the number of vertices in *G*. Then *M′* executes its outer loop at most *n* times (since it will quit if the length of *c* exceeds *n*). As it checks each step in *c*, it may take $\mathcal{O}(|<G>|^2)$ steps to check the edges of *G*, to mark the visited vertices, and to update the cost total. So the total time for the main loop is $\mathcal{O}(|<G>|^3)$. The final check takes time that is $\mathcal{O}(|<G>|^2)$. So the total is $\mathcal{O}(|<G>|^3)$.

So we have *M*, a *nondeterministic* polynomial time *decider* for TSP-DECIDE. And we have *M′*, a *deterministic* polynomial time *verifier* for it. The relationship between *M* and *M′* is typical for problems like TSP-DECIDE. The decider works by nondeterministically searching a space of candidate structures (in the case of TSP-DECIDE, candidate paths) and accepting iff it finds at least one that meets the requirements imposed by the language that is being decided. The verifier works by simply checking a single candidate structure (e.g., a path) and verifying that it meets the language's requirements.

The existence of verifiers like *M′* suggests an alternative way to define the class NP. We first define exactly what we mean by a verifier: A Turing machine *V* is a ***verifier*** for a language *L* iff:

$$w \in L \text{ iff } \exists c\, (<w, c> \in L(V)).$$

We'll call *c*, the candidate structure that we provide to the verifier *V*, a ***certificate***. Think of it as a certificate of proof that *w* is in *L*. So *V* verifies *L* precisely in case it accepts at least one certificate for every string in *L* and accepts no certificate for any string that is not in *L*. Since the string we are actually interested in is *w*, we will define *timereq*(*V*), when *V* is a verifier, as a function just of $|w|$, not of $|<w, c>|$.

Now, using the idea of a verifier, we can state the following alternative definition for the class NP:

> ***The Class NP:*** $L \in$ NP iff there exists a deterministic Turing machine *V* such that *V* is a verifier for *L* and $timereq(V) \in \mathcal{O}(n^k)$ for some constant *k* (i.e., *V* is a deterministic polynomial-time verifier for *L*).

Note that, since the number of steps that a polynomial-time *V* executes is bounded by some polynomial function of the length of the input string *w*, the number of certificate characters it can look at is also bounded by the same function. So, when we are considering polynomial time verifiers, we will consider only certificates whose length is bounded by some polynomial function of the length of the input string *w*.

The Two Definitions are Equivalent

Now that we have two definitions for the class NP, we would like to be able use whichever one is more convenient. However, it is not obvious that the two definitions are equivalent. So we must prove that they are.

THEOREM 28.9 The Two Definitions of the Class NP are Equivalent

Theorem: The following two definitions are equivalent:

1. $L \in$ NP iff there exists a nondeterministic, polynomial-time Turing machine that decides it.
2. $L \in$ NP iff there exists a deterministic, polynomial-time verifier for it.

Proof: We must prove that if there exists a nondeterministic decider for L then there exists a deterministic verifier for it, and vice versa:

1. Let L be a language that is in NP by definition 1. Then there exists a nondeterministic, polynomial-time Turing machine M that decides it. Using M, we construct V, a deterministic polynomial time verifier for L. On the input $<w, c>$, V will simulate M running on w except that, every time M would have to make a choice, V will simply follow the path that corresponds to the next symbol of c. V will accept iff M would have accepted on that path. Thus V will accept iff c is a certificate for w. V runs in polynomial time because the length of the longest path M can follow is bounded by some polynomial function of the length of w. So V is a deterministic polynomial-time verifier for L.
2. Let L be a language that is in NP by definition 2. Then there exists a deterministic Turing machine V such that V is a verifier for L and $timereq(V) \in \mathcal{O}(n^k)$ for some k. Using V, we construct a nondeterministic polynomial-time Turing machine M that will decide L. On input w, M will nondeterministically select a certificate c whose length is bounded by the greatest number of steps V could execute on any input of length at most $timereq(V)(|w|)$. (It need not consider any longer certificates since v would not be able to evaluate them.) It will then run V on $<w, c>$. M follows a finite number of computational paths, each of which halts in time that is $\mathcal{O}(n^k)$. So M is a nondeterministic polynomial-time Turing machine that decides L.

In the next section we will see several examples of languages that are in NP. Theorem 28.9 tells us that we can prove a claim of the form, "L is in NP" by exhibiting for L either a nondeterministic polynomial-time decider or a deterministic polynomial-time verifier.

28.2.2 Languages That Are in NP

The class NP is important because it contains many languages that arise naturally in a variety of applications. We'll mention several here. None of these languages is known to be in P. In fact, all of them are in the complexity class NP-complete, which contains the hardest NP languages. We'll define NP-completeness in Section 28.5.

TSP-DECIDE is typical of a large class of graph-based languages that are in NP. This class includes:

- HAMILTONIAN-PATH = {<G> : G is an undirected graph and G contains a Hamiltonian path}. A ***Hamiltonian path*** through G is a path that visits each vertex in G exactly once.
- HAMILTONIAN-CIRCUIT = {<G> : G is an undirected graph and G contains a Hamiltonian circuit}. A ***Hamiltonian circuit*** is a path that starts at some vertex s, ends back in s, and visits each other vertex in G exactly once.
- CLIQUE = {<G, k> : G is an undirected graph with vertices V and edges E, k is an integer, $1 \leq k \leq |V|$, and G contains a k-clique}. A ***clique*** in G is a subset of V with the property that every pair of vertices in the clique is connected by some edge in E. A k-clique is a clique that contains exactly k vertices.

NP includes other kinds of languages as well. Typically a language is in NP if you can imagine deciding it by exploring a well-defined search space looking for at least one value that meets some clear requirement. So, for example, the following language based on an important property of Boolean logic formulas is in NP:

- SAT = {<w> : w is a wff in Boolean logic and w is satisfiable}. We can show that a string w is in SAT by finding a satisfying assignment of values to the variables in the wff that it encodes.

Sets of almost any type can lead to problems that are in NP. We've just mentioned examples based on graphs (sets of vertices and edges) and on logical wffs (sets of variables connected by operators). The following NP language is based on sets of integers:

- SUBSET-SUM = {<S, k> : S is a multiset (i.e., duplicates are allowed) of integers, k is an integer, and there exists some subset of S whose elements sum to k}. For example:
  - <{1256, 45, 1256, 59, 34687, 8946, 17664}, 35988> is in SUBSET-SUM.
  - <{101, 789, 5783, 6666, 45789, 996}, 29876> is not in SUBSET-SUM.

> The SUBSET-SUM problem can be used as the basis for a simple encryption system that could be used, for example, to store password files. We start with a set of say 1000 integers. Call them the base integers. Then suppose that each password can be converted (for example by looking at pairs of symbols) to a multiset of base integers. Then a password checker need not store actual passwords. It can simply store the sum of the base integers that the password generates. When a user enters a password, it is converted to base integers and the sum is computed and checked against the stored sum. But if hackers break in and get access to the stored password sums, they won't be able to reconstruct any of the passwords, even if they know how passwords are mapped to base integers, unless they can (reasonably efficiently) take a sum and find a subset of the base integers that add to form it.

The next example of an NP language is based on sets of anything as long as the objects have associated costs:

- SET-PARTITION = {<S> : *S* is a multiset (i.e., duplicates are allowed) of objects, each of which has an associated cost, and there exists a way to divide *S* into two subsets, *A* and *S-A*, such that the sum of the costs of the elements in *A* equals the sum of the costs of the elements in *S-A*}.

> SET-PARTITION arises in many sorts of resource allocation contexts. For example, suppose that there are two production lines and a set of objects that need to be manufactured as quickly as possible. Let the objects' costs be the time required to make them. Then the optimum schedule divides the work evenly across the two machines. Load balancing in a dual processor computer system can also be described as a set-partition problem.

Our final example is based on sets of anything as long as the objects have associated costs and values:

- KNAPSACK = {<S, v, c> : *S* is a set of objects each of which has an associated cost and an associated value, v and c are integers, and there exists some way of choosing elements of *S* (duplicates allowed) such that the total cost of the chosen objects is at most c and their total value is at least v}. Notice that, if the cost of each item equals its value, then the KNAPSACK problem becomes very similar to the SUBSET-SUM problem.

> The KNAPSACK problem derives its name from the problem of choosing the best way to pack a knapsack with limited capacity in such as way as to maximize the utility of the contents. For example, imagine a thief trying to decide what to steal or a backpacker trying to decide what food to take. The KNAPSACK problem arises in a wide variety of applications in which resources are limited and utility must be maximized. For example, what ads should a company buy? What products should a factory make? How should a company expand its workforce?

In the next three sections we'll prove that TSP-DECIDE, CLIQUE and SAT are in NP. We'll consider HAMILTONIAN-CIRCUIT in Theorem 28.22. We leave the rest as exercises.

28.2.3 TSP

We argued above that there exists a nondeterministic, polynomial-time Turing machine that decides TSP-DECIDE. Now we prove that claim. Just to make it clear how such a machine might work, we will describe in detail the Turing machine *TSPdecide*. Let *V* be the vertices in G and E be its edges. *TSPdecide* will nondeterministically consider all paths through G with length equal to $|V|$. There is a finite number of such paths and each of them has finite length, so all paths of *TSPdecide* will eventually halt. *TSPdecide* will accept w if it finds at least one path that corresponds to a Hamiltonian circuit and that has cost less than *cost*. Otherwise it will reject. *TSPdecide* will use three tapes. The first will store the input G. The second will keep track of the path that is being built. And the third will contain the total cost of the path so far. We define *TSPdecide* as follows:

TSPdecide(<*G*: graph with vertices V and edges E, *cost*: integer>) =

1. Initialize by nondeterministically choosing a vertex in G. Put that vertex on the path that is stored on tape 2. Write 0 on tape 3.
2. Until the number of vertices on the path on tape 2 is equal to $|V| + 1$ or this path fails do:
   2.1. Nondeterministically choose an edge e in E.
   2.2. Check that one endpoint of e is the last vertex on the current path.
   2.3. Check that either:
   - the number of vertices on the path equals $|V|$ and the other endpoint of e is the same as the first vertex in the path, or
   - the number of vertices on the path is less than $|V|$ and the other endpoint of e is not on already on the path.

   2.4. Add the cost of e to the path cost that is stored on tape 3 and check that the result is less than *cost*.
   2.5. If conditions 2.2, 2.3, and 2.4, are satisfied then add the second endpoint of e to the current path.
   2.6. Else this path fails. Exit the loop.
3. If the loop ended normally, accept. If it ended by the path failing, reject.

We analyze *timereq*(*TSPdecide*) as follows: The initialization in step 1 takes $\mathcal{O}(|<G, cost>|)$ time. The longest path that *TSPdecide* will consider contains $|V| + 1$ vertices. (It may also consider some shorter paths if they fail before completing a circuit). So *TSPdecide* goes through the step 2 loop at most $\mathcal{O}(|<G, cost>|)$ times. Each step of that loop takes $\mathcal{O}(|<G, cost>|)$ time. So $timereq(TSPdecide) \in \mathcal{O}(|<G, cost>|^2)$.

We've now described both a nondeterministic decider and a deterministic verifier for TSP-DECIDE. So proving the next theorem is straightforward.

THEOREM 28.10 TSP-DECIDE is in NP

Theorem: TSP-DECIDE = {<*G*, *cost*> : <*G*> encodes an undirected graph with a positive distance attached to each of its edges and *G* contains a Hamiltonian circuit whose total cost is less than *cost*>} is in NP.

Proof: The nondeterministic Turing machine *TSPdecide* decides TSP-DECIDE in polynomial time.

While it is sometimes instructive to describe a decider or a verifier in detail, as a Turing machine, as we have just done, we will generally describe them simply as well-specified algorithms. We will do that in the following examples.

28.2.4 Clique Detection

Recall that, given a graph G with vertices V and edges E, a ***clique*** in G is a subset of V with the property that every pair of vertices in the clique is connected by some edge in E. A ***k-clique*** is a clique that contains exactly k vertices.

> Clique detection, particularly the detection of maximally large cliques, plays an important role in many applications in computational biology.

THEOREM 28.11 CLIQUE is in NP

Theorem: CLIQUE = $\{<G, k> : G$ is an undirected graph with vertices V and edges E, k is an integer, $1 \leq k \leq |V|$, and G contains a k-clique$\}$ is in NP.

Proof: We can prove this claim by describing a deterministic polynomial time verifier, *clique-verify*($<G, k, c>$), that takes three inputs, a graph G, an integer k, and a set of vertices c, where c is a proposed certificate for $<G, k>$. The job of *clique-verify* is to check that c is a clique in G and that it contains k vertices. The first step of *clique-verify* is to count the number of vertices in c. If the number is greater than $|V|$ or not equal to k, it will immediately reject. Otherwise, it will go on to step 2, where it will consider all pairs of vertices in c. For each, it will go through the edges in E and check that there is an edge between the two vertices of the pair. If there is any pair that is not connected by an edge, *clique-verify* will reject. If all pairs are connected, it will accept. Step 1 takes time that is linear in $|c|$, which is bounded by some polynomial function of $|<G, k>|$. Step 2 must consider $|c|^2$ vertex pairs. For each it must examine at most $|E|$ edges. Since both $|c|$ and $|E|$ are bounded by $|<G, k>|$, $timereq(clique\text{-}verify) \in \mathcal{O}(|<G, k>|^3)$. So *clique-verify* is a deterministic polynomial-time verifier for CLIQUE.

28.2.5 Boolean Satisfiability

In Section 22.4.1, we showed that several key questions concerning Boolean formulas are decidable. In particular, we showed that SAT is in D. We can now consider the complexity of SAT. We'll prove here that it and one of its cousins, 3-SAT, are in NP. You may recall that, in Section 22.4.1, we also showed that the problem of deciding whether a Boolean formula is valid (i.e., whether it is true for all assignments of values to its variables) is decidable. It turns out that that problem appears to be harder than the problem of deciding satisfiability. We'll consider the language VALID = $\{<w> : w$ is a wff in Boolean logic and w is valid$\}$ in Section 28.8.

SAT has applications in such domains as computer-aided design, computer-aided manufacturing, robotics, machine vision, scheduling, and hardware and software verification. It is particularly useful in verifying the correctness of digital circuits using a technique called model checking. (H.1.2)

THEOREM 28.12 SAT is in NP

Theorem: SAT = $\{<w> : w$ is a wff in Boolean logic and w is satisfiable$\}$ is in NP.

Proof: SAT is in NP because there exists a deterministic polynomial time verifier for it. $SAT\text{-}verify(<w, c>)$ takes two inputs, a wff w and a certificate c, which is a list of assignments of truth values to the variables of w. The job of *SAT-verify* is to determine whether w evaluates to *True* given the assignments provided by c. For example:

- The wff $w = P \wedge Q \wedge \neg R$ is satisfiable. The string $c = (P = True, Q = True, R = False)$ is a certificate for it, since the expression $True \wedge True \wedge \neg False$ simplifies to *True*. $SAT\text{-}verify(<w, c>)$ will accept.
- The wff $w = P \wedge Q \wedge R$ is satisfiable. But the string $c = (P = True, Q = True, R = False)$ is not a certificate for it, since the expression $True \wedge True \wedge False$ simplifies to *False*. So $SAT\text{-}verify(<w, c>)$ will reject.
- The wff $w = P \wedge \neg P$ is not satisfiable. So for any c, $SAT\text{-}verify(<w, c>)$ will reject.

Let *vars* be the number of distinct variables in w. Let *ops* be the number of operators in w. Then *SAT-verify* behaves as follows: For each assignment in c, it makes one pass through w, replacing all occurrences of the current variable with the value that c assigns to it. Then it makes at most *ops* passes through w, on each pass replacing every operator whose arguments have already been evaluated by the result of applying the operator to its arguments. Then it checks to see whether $w = True$. The first step must consider *vars* variables and each can be processed in $\mathcal{O}(|w|)$ time. Since $vars \leq |w|$, this first step takes $\mathcal{O}(|w|^2)$ time. The second step executes at most *ops* passes and each pass can be done in $\mathcal{O}(|w|)$ time. Since $ops \leq |w|$, the second step takes $\mathcal{O}(|w|^2)$ time. Thus *SAT-verify* takes time $\mathcal{O}(|w|^2)$ and is a deterministic polynomial-time verifier for SAT.

Alternatively, we can build a nondeterministic polynomial-time decider for SAT. It decides whether a string $<w>$ is in SAT by nondeterministically choosing a set of assignments to the variables in w. Then it uses *SAT-verify* to check whether that assignment proves that w is satisfiable.

As far as we know, SAT is not also in P. No polynomial time algorithm to decide it in the general case is known. But very efficient SAT solvers work well in practice. They take advantage of the fact that it is typically not necessary to enumerate all possible assignments of values to the variables. One technique that exploits this observation

Table 28.1 3-CNF and CNF formulas.

	3-CNF	CNF
$(P \vee \neg Q \vee R)$	•	•
$(P \vee \neg Q \vee R) \wedge (\neg P \vee Q \vee \neg R)$	•	•
P		•
$(P \vee \neg Q \vee R \vee S) \wedge (\neg P \vee \neg R)$		•
$P \rightarrow Q$		
$(P \wedge \neg Q \wedge R \wedge S) \vee (\neg P \wedge \neg R)$		
$\neg(P \vee Q \vee R)$		

relies on a clever data structure, the ordered binary decision diagram (or OBDD), which we describe in B.1.3.

We next describe 3-SAT, a variant of SAT that we will find useful in our upcoming discussion of the complexity of several other languages. Before we can define 3-SAT we must define conjunctive normal form for Boolean formulas:

- A ***literal*** is either a variable or a variable preceded by a single negation symbol.
- A ***clause*** is either a single literal or the disjunction of two or more literals.
- A well-formed formula (or wff) of Boolean logic is in ***conjunctive normal form*** (or CNF) iff it is either a single clause or the conjunction of two or more clauses.
- A wff is in ***3-conjunctive normal form*** (or 3-CNF) iff it is in conjunctive normal form and each clause contains exactly three literals.

Table 28.1 illustrates these definitions. The symbol • indicates that the corresponding formula is in the matching form.

Every wff can be converted to an equivalent wff in conjunctive normal form. See B.1.1 for a proof of this claim, as well as more examples of all of the terms that we have just defined.

THEOREM 28.13 3-SAT is in NP

Theorem: 3-SAT = $\{<w> : w$ is a wff in Boolean logic, w is in 3-conjunctive normal form and w is satisfiable$\}$ is in NP.

Proof: 3-SAT is in NP because there exists a deterministic polynomial time verifier for it. $3\text{-}SAT\text{-}verify(<w, c>)$ first checks to make sure that w is in 3-CNF. It can do that in linear time. Then it calls $SAT\text{-}verify(<w, c>)$ to check that c is a certificate for w.

28.3 Does P = NP?

While we know some things about the relationship between P and NP, a complete answer to the question, "Are they equal?" has, so far, remained elusive.

We begin by describing what we do know:

THEOREM 28.14 Every Language in P is also in NP

Theorem: $P \subseteq NP$.

Proof: Let L be an arbitrary language in P. Then there exists a deterministic polynomial time decider M for L. But M is also a nondeterministic polynomial time decider for L. (It just doesn't have to make any guesses.) So L is in NP.

So all of the following languages are in NP:

- every context-free language,
- EULERIAN-CIRCUIT,
- MST, and
- PRIMES.

But what about the other direction? Are there languages that are in NP but that are not in P? Alternatively (since we just showed that $P \subseteq NP$), does P = NP? No one knows. There are languages, like TSP-DECIDE, CLIQUE, and SAT that are known to be in NP but for which no deterministic polynomial time decision procedure exists. But no one has succeeded in proving that those languages, or many others that are in NP, are not also in P.

The question, "Does P = NP?" is one of seven Millennium Problems 🖳; a \$1,000,000 prize awaits anyone who can solve it. By the way, most informed bets are on the answer to the question being, "No." Further, it is widely believed that even if it should turn out to be possible to prove that every language that is in NP is also in P, it is exceedingly unlikely that that proof will lead to the development of practical polynomial time algorithms to decide languages like TSP-DECIDE and SAT. There is widespread consensus that if such algorithms existed they would have been discovered by now given the huge amount of effort that has been spent looking for them.

While we do not know with certainty whether P = NP, we do know something about how the two classes relate to other complexity classes. In particular, define:

- PSPACE: For any language L, $L \in$ PSPACE iff there exists some deterministic Turing machine M that decides L and $spacereq(M) \in \mathcal{O}(n^k)$ for some k.
- NPSPACE: For any language L, $L \in$ NPSPACE iff there exists some nondeterministic Turing machine M that decides L and $spacereq(M) \in \mathcal{O}(n^k)$ for some k.
- EXPTIME: For any language L, $L \in$ EXPTIME iff there exists some deterministic Turing machine M that decides L and $timereq(M) \in \mathcal{O}(2^{(n^k)})$ for some k. We'll consider the class EXPTIME in Section 28.9.

Chapter 29 is devoted to a discussion of space complexity classes, including PSPACE and NPSPACE. We'll mention here just one important result: Savitch's Theorem (which we state as Theorem 29.2) tells us that any nondeterministic Turing machine can be converted to a deterministic one that uses at most quadratically more space. So, in particular, PSPACE = NPSPACE and we can simplify our discussion by considering just PSPACE.

We can summarize what is known about P, NP, and the new classes PSPACE and EXPTIME as follows:

- $\mathrm{P} \subseteq \mathrm{NP} \subseteq \mathrm{PSPACE} \subseteq \mathrm{EXPTIME}$.

In addition, in Section 28.9.1, we will prove the Deterministic Time Hierarchy Theorem, which tell us that $\mathrm{P} \neq \mathrm{EXPTIME}$. So at least one of the inclusions shown above must be proper. It is generally assumed that all of them are, but no proofs of those claims exist.

Because we know that $\mathrm{P} \neq \mathrm{EXPTIME}$, we also know that there exist decidable but intractable problems.

28.4 Using Reduction in Complexity Proofs

In Chapter 21, we used reduction to prove decidability properties of new languages by reducing other languages to them. Since all we cared about then was decidability, we accepted as reductions any Turing machines that implemented computable functions. We were not concerned with the efficiency of those Turing machines. We can also use reduction to prove complexity properties of new languages based on the known complexity properties of other languages. When we do that, though, we will need to place bounds on the complexity of the reductions that we use. In particular, it is important that the complexity of any reduction we use be dominated by the complexity of the language we are reducing to. To guarantee that, we will exploit only deterministic, polynomial-time reductions.

All of the reductions that we will use to prove complexity results will be mapping reductions. Recall, from Section 21.2.2, that a ***mapping reduction*** R from L_1 to L_2 is a Turing machine that implements some computable function f with the property that:

$$\forall x(x \in L_1 \leftrightarrow f(x) \in L_2).$$

Now suppose that R is a mapping reduction from L_1 to L_2 and that there exists a Turing machine M that decides L_2. Then to decide whether some string x is in L_1 we first apply R to x and then invoke M to decide membership in L_2. So $C(x) = M(R(x))$ will decide L_1.

Suppose that there exists a deterministic, polynomial-time mapping reduction R from L_1 to L_2. Then we'll say that L_1 is deterministic, polynomial-time ***reducible*** to L_2, which we'll write as $L_1 \leq_P L_2$. And, whenever such an R exists, we note that:

- L_1 must be in P if L_2 is: If L_2 is in P then there exists some deterministic, polynomial-time Turing machine M that decides it. So $M(R(x))$ is also a deterministic, polynomial-time Turing machine and it decides L_1.
- L_1 must be in NP if L_2 is: If L_2 is in NP then there exists some nondeterministic, polynomial-time Turing machine M that decides it. So $M(R(x))$ is also a nondeterministic, polynomial-time Turing machine and it decides L_1.

Given two languages L_1 and L_2, we can use reduction to:

- Prove that L_1 is in P or in NP because we already know that L_2 is.
- Prove that L_1 would be in P or in NP if we could somehow show that L_2 is. When we do this we cluster languages of similar complexity (even if we're not yet sure what that complexity is).

In many of the reductions that we will do, we will map objects of one sort to objects that appear to be of a very different sort. For example, the first reduction that we show will be from 3-SAT (a language of Boolean wffs) to the graph language INDEPENDENT-SET. On the surface, Boolean formulas and graphs seem quite different. So how should the reduction proceed? The strategy we'll typically use is to exploit gadgets. A ***gadget*** is a structure in the target language that mimics the role of a corresponding structure in the source language. In the 3-SAT to INDEPENDENT-SET reduction, strings in the source language describe formulas that contain literals and clauses. Strings in the target language describe graphs that contain vertices and edges. So we need one gadget that looks like a graph but that mimics a literal and another gadget that looks like a graph but that mimics a clause. Very simple gadgets will work in this case. In some others that we'll see later, more clever constructions will be required.

Consider the language:

- INDEPENDENT-SET = $\{<G, k> : G$ is an undirected graph and G contains an independent set of at least k vertices$\}$.

An ***independent set*** is a set of vertices no two of which are adjacent (i.e., connected by a single edge). So, in the graph shown in Figure 28.3, the circled vertices form an independent set.

> Consider a graph in which the edges represent conflicts between the objects that correspond to the vertices. For example, in a scheduling program the vertices might represent tasks. Then two vertices will be connected by an edge if their corresponding tasks cannot be scheduled at the same time because their resource requirements conflict. We can find the largest number of tasks that can be scheduled at the same time by finding the largest independent set in the task graph.

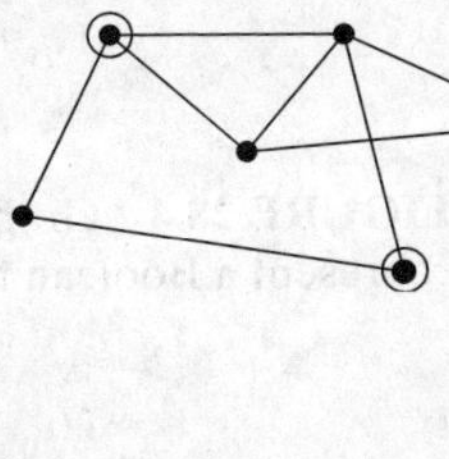

FIGURE 28.3 An independent set.

Notice, by the way, that there is an obvious relationship between INDEPENDENT-SET and CLIQUE. If S is an independent set in some graph G with vertices V and edges E, then S is also a clique in the graph G' with vertices V and edges E', where E' contains an edge between each pair of nodes n and m iff V does not contain such an edge. There is also a relationship between INDEPENDENT-SET and the language CHROMATIC-NUMBER, which we'll define in Section 28.7.6. While INDEPENDENT-SET asks for the maximum number of vertices in any one independent set in G, CHROMATIC-NUMBER asks how many nonintersecting independent sets are required if every vertex in G is to be in one.

THEOREM 28.15 3-SAT is Reducible to INDEPENDENT-SET

Theorem: 3-SAT $\leq_P$ INDEPENDENT-SET

Proof: We show a deterministic, polynomial-time reduction R from 3-SAT to INDEPENDENT-SET. R must map from a Boolean formula to a graph. Let f be a Boolean formula in 3-conjunctive normal form. Let k be the number of clauses in f. R is defined as follows:

$R(<f>) =$

1. Build a graph G by doing the following:
   - **1.1.** Create one vertex for each instance of each literal in f.
   - **1.2.** Create an edge between each pair of vertices that correspond to literals in the same clause.
   - **1.3.** Create an edge between each pair of vertices that correspond to complementary literals (i.e., two literals that are the negation of each other).
2. Return $<G, k>$.

For example, consider the formula $(P \vee \neg Q \vee W) \wedge (\neg P \vee S \vee T)$. From this formula, R will build the graph shown in Figure 28.4.

So each literal gadget is a single vertex and each clause gadget is a set of three vertices plus the edges that connect them.

R runs in polynomial time. To show that it is correct, we must show that $f \in$ 3-SAT iff $R(<f>) \in$ INDEPENDENT-SET.

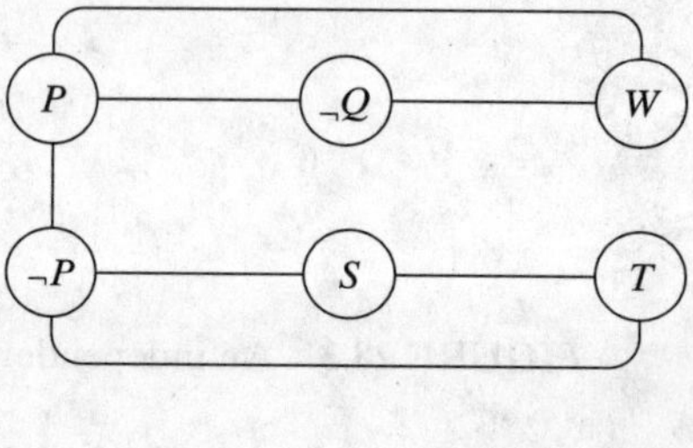

FIGURE 28.4 Graph gadgets represent a Boolean formula.

We first show that $<f> \in$ 3-SAT $\rightarrow R(<f>) \in$ INDEPENDENT-SET. If $<f> \in$ 3-SAT then there exists a satisfying assignment A of values to the variables in f. We can use that assignment to show that G, the graph that R builds, contains an independent set S of size at least (in fact, exactly) k. Build S as follows: From each clause gadget choose one literal that is made positive by A. (There must be one since A is a satisfying assignment.) Add the vertex corresponding to that literal to S. S will contain exactly k vertices. And it is an independent set because:

- No two vertices come from the same clause. So step 1.2 could not have created an edge between them.
- No two vertices correspond to complementary literals. So step 1.3 could not have created an edge between them.

Next we show that $R(<f>) \in$ INDEPENDENT-SET $\rightarrow <f> \in$ 3-SAT. If $R(<f>) \in$ INDEPENDENT-SET then the graph G that R builds contains an independent set S of size at least (again, in fact, exactly) k. We can use that set to show that there exists some satisfying assignment A for f. Notice that no two vertices in S come from the same clause gadget (because, if they did, they would be connected in G). Since S contains at least k vertices, no two are from the same clause, and f contains k clauses, S must contain one vertex from each clause. So build A as follows: Assign the value *True* to each literal that corresponds to a vertex in S. This is possible because no two vertices in S correspond to complementary literals (again because, if they did, they would be connected in G). Assign arbitrary values to all other literals. Since each clause will contain at least one literal whose value is *True*, the value of f will be *True*.

If we want to decide 3-SAT, it is unlikely that we would choose to do so by reducing it to INDEPENDENT-SET and then deciding INDEPENDENT-SET. That wouldn't make sense since none of our techniques for deciding INDEPENDENT-SET run any faster than some obvious methods for deciding 3-SAT. But, having done this reduction, we're in a new position if somehow a fast technique for deciding INDEPENDENT-SET were to be discovered. Then we would instantly also have a fast way to decide 3-SAT.

28.5 NP-Completeness and the Cook-Levin Theorem

We don't know whether P = NP. Substantial effort has been expended both in looking for a proof that the two classes are the same and in trying to find a counterexample (i.e., a language that is in NP but not in P) that proves that they are not. Neither of those efforts has succeeded. But what has emerged from that work is a class of NP languages that are maximally "hard" in the sense that if any one of them should turn out to be in P then every NP language would also be in P (and thus P would equal NP). This class of maximally hard NP languages is called NP-complete.

28.5.1 NP-Complete and NP-Hard Languages

Consider two properties that a language L might possess:

1. L is in NP.
2. Every language in NP is deterministic, polynomial-time reducible to L.

Using those properties, we will define:

The Class NP-hard: L is NP-hard iff it possesses property 2. Any NP-hard language L is at least as hard as every language in NP in the sense that if L should turn out to be in P, every NP language must also be in P. Languages that are NP-hard are generally viewed as being ***intractable***, meaning that it is unlikely that any efficient (i.e., deterministic, polynomial-time) decision procedure for any of them is likely to exit.

The Class NP-complete: L is NP-complete iff it possesses *both* property 1 and property 2. All NP-complete languages can be viewed as being equivalently hard in the sense that all of them can be decided in nondeterministic, polynomial time and, if any one of them can also be decided in deterministic polynomial time, then all of them can.

Note that the difference between the classes NP-hard and NP-complete is that NP-hard contains some languages that appear to be harder than the languages in NP (in the sense that no nondeterministic, polynomial-time decider for them is known to exist). To see the difference, consider two families of languages whose definitions are based on popular games:

The languages that correspond to generalizations of many one-person games (or puzzles) are NP-complete. For example, consider the generalization of Sudoku (described in N.2.2) to an $n \times n$ grid (where n is a perfect square). Then define the following language:

- SUDOKU = {<*b*>: *b* is a configuration of an $n \times n$ grid and *b* has a solution under the rules of Sudoku}.

SUDOKU is in NP because there exists a straightforward verifier that checks a proposed solution. It has also been shown to be NP-complete.

> The complexity of Sudoku is similar to that of other interesting puzzles. (N.2.2)

On the other hand, the languages that correspond to generalizations of many two-person games are NP-hard but thought not to be in NP. For example, consider the generalization of chess to an $n \times n$ board. Then define the language:

- CHESS = {<*b*>: *b* is a configuration of an $n \times n$ chess board and there is a guaranteed win for the current player}.

The complexity of the language CHESS explains the fact that it took almost 50 years between the first attempts at programming computers to play chess and the first time that a program beat a reigning chess champion. Some other games, like Go, are still dominated by human players. (N.2)

In Section 28.9, we'll return to the issue of problems that appear not to be in NP. For now we can just notice that the reason that CHESS appears not to be in NP is that it is not possible to verify that a winning move sequence exists just by checking a single sequence. It appears necessary to check all sequences that result from the choices that could be made by the opposing player. This can be done in exponential time using depth-first search, so CHESS is an element of the complexity class EXPTIME (which we'll define precisely later).

The class NP-complete is important. Many of its members correspond to problems, like the traveling salesman problem, that have substantial practical significance. It is also one of the reasons that it appears unlikely that P = NP. A deterministic, polynomial-time decider for any member of NP-complete would prove that P and NP are the same. Yet, despite substantial effort on many of the known NP-complete problems, no such decider has been found.

But how can we prove that a language L is NP-complete? To do so requires that we show that every other language that is in NP is deterministic, polynomial-time reducible to it We can't show that just by taking some list of known NP languages and cranking out the reductions. There is an infinite number of NP languages.

If we had even one NP-complete language L', then we could show that a new NP language L is NP-complete by showing that L' is deterministic, polynomial-time reducible to it. Then every other NP language could be reduced first to L' and then to L. But how can we get that process started? We need a "first" NP-complete language.

28.5.2 The Cook-Levin Theorem and the NP-Completeness of SAT

Steven Cook and Leonid Levin independently solved the problem of finding a first NP-complete language by showing that SAT is NP-complete. Their proof does not depend on reducing individual NP languages to SAT. Instead it exploits the fact that a language is in NP precisely in case there exists some nondeterministic, polynomial-time Turing machine M that decides it. Cook and Levin showed that there exists a polynomial-time algorithm that, given $<M>$, maps any string w to a Boolean formula that describes the sequence of steps that M executes on input w. They showed further that this reduction guarantees that the formula it constructs is satisfiable iff M ends its computation by accepting w. So, if there exists a deterministic, polynomial-time algorithm that decides SAT, then any NP language (decided by some Turing machine M), can be decided in deterministic, polynomial time by running the reduction (based on $<M>$) on w and then running the SAT decider on the resulting formula.

Because SAT is NP-complete, it is unlikely that a polynomial-time decider for it exists. But Boolean satisfiability is a sufficiently important practical problem that there exists an entire annual conference 💻 devoted to the study of both theoretical and applied research in this area. We'll say more about the development of efficient SAT solvers in B.1.3.

It is interesting to note that the NP-completeness proof that we are about to do is not the first time that we have exploited a reduction that works because an arbitrary Turing machine computation can be simulated using some other (superficially quite different) structure:

- We sketched, in the proof of Theorem 22.4, Turing's argument that the Entscheidungsproblem is not decidable. That proof makes use of a reduction that maps <*M*> to a first-order logic sentence that is provable (given a particular set of axioms) iff *M* ever prints 0. The reduction exploits a construction that builds a formula that describes the sequence of configurations that *M* enters as it computes.
- We showed, in the proof of Theorem 22.1, that PCP, the Post Correspondence Problem language, is not decidable. We did that by defining a reduction that maps an <*M*, *w*> pair to a PCP instance in such a way that the computation of *M* on *w* can be simulated by the process of forming longer and longer partial solutions to the PCP instance. Then we showed that that process ends with a complete solution to the PCP instance iff *M* halts and accepts *w*.
- We argued, in the proof of Theorem 22.2, that TILES, which corresponds to a set of tiling problems, is not even semidecidable. We did that by defining a reduction from a Turing machine to a set of tiles in such a way that each new row of any tiling would correspond to the next configuration of the Turing machine as it performed its computation. So there exists an infinite tiling iff the Turing machine fails to halt.
- We show, in the proof of Theorem J.1, that a simple security model is undecidable. We do that by defining a reduction from an arbitrary Turing machine to an access control matrix. Then we show how the computation of the Turing machine could be simulated by a sequence of operations on the access control matrix in such a way that the property q_f leaks iff the Turing machine halts.

The key difference between those proofs and the one we are about to show for the Cook-Levin Theorem is that the reduction we'll describe here works with a description of a Turing machine *M* that is known to halt (along all computational paths) and to do so in polynomial time.

THEOREM 28.16 Cook-Levin Theorem

Theorem: SAT = {<*w*> : *w* is a wff in Boolean logic and *w* is satisfiable} is NP-complete.

Proof: By Theorem 28.12, SAT is in NP. So it remains to show that it is NP-hard (i.e., that all NP languages are deterministic, polynomial-time reducible to it).

We'll show a generic reduction R from any NP language to SAT. To use R as a reduction from a particular language $L \in \text{NP}$, we will provide it with M, one of the nondeterministic, polynomial-time deciding machines that must exist for L. Then, when R is applied to a particular string w, it will construct a (large but finite) Boolean formula that is satisfiable iff at least one of M's computational paths accepts w.

To see how R works, imagine a two-layer table that describes one computational path that M can follow on some particular input w. An example of such a table is shown in Figure 28.5. Imagine that the second tier, shown in bold, is overlaid on top of the first tier.

Each row of the table corresponds to one configuration of M. The first row corresponds to M's starting configuration (in which the read/write head is positioned on top of the blank immediately to the left of the first symbol of w) and each succeeding row corresponds to the configuration that results from the one before it. Some row will correspond to M's halting configuration and we won't care what any of the rows after that one look like. We don't know how many steps M executes before it halts so we don't know exactly how many rows we will need. But we do know that *timereq*(M) is some polynomial function $f(|w|)$ that is an upper bound on the number of steps. So we'll just let the table have $f(|w|) + 1$ rows.

The lower tier of the table will encode the contents of M's tape. The upper tier will indicate M's current state and the position of M's read/write head. So all the cells of the upper tier will be empty except the one in each row that corresponds to the square that is under the read/write head. Each of those nonempty cells will contain a symbol that corresponds to M's current state. So, in the table shown above, the upper tier is empty except for the cells that contain an expression of the form $q_n/$.

In each configuration, M's tape is infinite in both directions. But only a finite number of squares can be visited by M before it halts. We need only represent the squares that contain the original input plus the others that might be visited. It is possible that M spends all of its steps moving in a single direction. So, after $f(|w|)$ steps, the read/write head might be $f(|w|)$ squares to the left of where it began. Or it might be $f(|w|)$ squares, including the original input string, to the right of where it began. In order to allow room for either of these worst cases, we will include, in each tape description, the $f(|w|)$ tape squares to the left of the initial read/write head position and $max(f(|w|), |w|)$ tape squares to the right of it.

	$f(\lvert w\rvert)$							$max(f(\lvert w\rvert), \lvert w\rvert)$					
$f(\lvert w\rvert) + 1$	☐	☐	☐	☐	☐	☐	q_0/☐	a	a	b	☐	☐	☐
	☐	☐	☐	☐	☐	☐	☐	q_1/a	a	b	☐	☐	☐
	☐	☐	☐	☐	☐	☐	☐	a	q_1/a	b	☐	☐	☐
	☐	☐	☐	☐	☐	☐	☐	a	b	q_1/b	☐	☐	☐
	☐	☐	☐	☐	☐	☐	☐	a	b	b	q_2/☐	☐	☐
	☐	☐	☐	☐	☐	☐	☐	a	b	b	☐	y/☐	☐
	☐	☐	☐	☐	☐	☐	☐	a	b	b	☐	y/☐	☐

FIGURE 28.5 A two-layer table that describes one computational path of M on w.

For example, suppose that, on input aab, one of M's paths runs for 5 steps and halts in the accepting state y. If $f(3) = 6$, then that path might be described in the table shown above (where q_n/c means that the lower tier contains the symbol c and the upper tier contains q_n).

To make it easier to talk about this table, let $rows = f(|w|) + 1$ be the number of rows it contains and let $cols = f(|w|) + max(f(|w|), |w|) + 1$ be the number of columns it contains. Let $padleft = f(|w|)$.

The job of the reduction R, with respect to some particular Turing machine M, is to map a string w to a Boolean formula that describes a table such as the one above. R will guarantee that the formula it builds is satisfiable iff all of the following conditions are met:

1. The formula describes a legal table in the sense that:
   1.1. The upper tier contains exactly one state marker per row.
   1.2. The lower tier contains exactly one symbol per tape square.
2. The formula describes a table whose first row represents the initial configuration of M on input w.
3. The formula describes a table some row of which represents an accepting configuration of M on input w (i.e., the upper tier contains the state y).
4. The formula describes a table that simulates a computation that M could actually perform. So every row, except the first and any that come after the accepting configuration, represents a configuration that, given the transition relation that defines M, can immediately follow the configuration that is described by the preceding row.

Given these constraints, checking whether the formula that R builds is satisfiable is equivalent to checking that there exists some computation of M that accepts w.

It would be easy to write a first-order logic formula that satisfies conditions 1–4. We could write quantified formulas that said things like, "In every row there exists a square that contains a state symbol and every other square in that row does not contain a state symbol." But the key to defining R is to realize that we can also write a Boolean formula that says those same things. The reason we can is that we know that M halts and we have a bound on the number of steps it will execute before it halts. So we know the size of the table that describes its computation. That means that, instead of creating variables that can range over rows or tape squares, we can simply create individual variables for each property of each cell in the table. (Notice, by the way, that if we tried to take the approach we're using here and use it to reduce an arbitrary, i.e., not necessarily NP, language to SAT, it wouldn't work because we would then have no such bound on the size of the table. So, for example, we couldn't try this with the halting language H.)

Imagine the cells in the computation table that we described above as being labeled with a row number i and a column number j. We'll label the cell in the upper left corner (1, 1). Let Γ be M's tape alphabet and let K be the set of its states. We can now define the variables that R will use in mapping a particular input w:

- For each i and j such that $1 \leq i \leq rows$ and $1 \leq j \leq cols$ and for each symbol c in Γ, create the variable $tape_{i,j,c}$. When the variable $tape_{i,j,c}$ is used in a formula that describes a computational table, it will be assigned the value *True* if cell(i, j) contains the tape symbol c. Otherwise it will be *False*. These variables then describe the lower tier of the computational table.

- For each i and j such that $1 \le i \le rows$ and $1 \le j \le cols$ and for each state q in K, create the variable $state_{i,j,q}$. When the variable $state_{i,j,q}$ is used in a formula that describes a computational table, it will be assigned the value *True* if cell(i, j) contains the state symbol q. Otherwise it will be *False*. These variables then describe the upper tier of the computational table.

We're now ready to describe the process by which R maps a string w to a Boolean formula *DescribeMonw*, which will be composed of four conjuncts, each corresponding to one of the four conditions we listed above. In order to be able to state these formulas concisely, we'll define the notations:

$$\bigwedge_{1 \le i \le rows} tape_{i,j,k} \quad \text{and} \quad \bigvee_{1 \le i \le rows} tape_{i,j,k}$$

The first represents the Boolean AND of a set of propositions and the second represents their Boolean OR.

CONJUNCT 1: The first conjunct will represent the constraint that the table must describe a single computational path. Without this constraint it would be possible, if M is nondeterministic, to satisfy all the other constraints and yet describe a table that jumbles multiple computational paths together (thus telling us nothing about any of them).

For each cell (i, j), we need to say that the variable corresponding to some tape symbol c is *True* and all of the ones corresponding to other tape symbols are *False*. So, for a given (i, j), let $T_{i,j}$ say that cell(i, j) contains symbol c_1 and not any others or it contains symbol c_2 and not any others and so forth up to symbol $c_{|\Gamma|}$:

$$T_{i,j} \equiv \bigvee_{c \in \Gamma} (tape_{i,j,c} \wedge (\bigwedge_{\substack{s \in \Gamma \\ s \ne c}} \neg tape_{i,j,s})).$$

Then let *Tapes* say that this is true for all squares in the table. So:

$$Tapes \equiv \bigwedge_{1 \le i \le rows} (\bigwedge_{1 \le j \le cols} T_{i,j}).$$

We also need to say that each row contains exactly one state symbol. So let $Q_{i,j}$ say that cell(i, j) contains exactly one state symbol:

$$Q_{i,j} \equiv \bigvee_{q \in K} (state_{i,j,q} \wedge (\bigwedge_{\substack{p \in K \\ p \ne q}} \neg state_{i,j,p})).$$

Then let *States* say that, for each row, there is exactly one column for which that is true:

$$States \equiv \bigwedge_{1 \le i \le rows} (\bigvee_{1 \le j \le cols} (Q_{i,j} \wedge (\bigwedge_{\substack{1 < k \le cols \\ k \ne j}} \bigwedge_{q \in K} \neg state_{i,k,q}))).$$

So we have:

$$Conjunct_1 \equiv Tapes \wedge States.$$

CONJUNCT 2: The second conjunct will represent the constraint that the first row of the table must correspond to *M*'s initial configuration when started on input w. Assume that *M*'s start state is q_0. We'll first describe the lower tier of the table (the symbols on *M*'s tape). The first $padleft + 1$ squares will be blank. Then the input string w will appear and then all remaining squares will be blank. Let $w[j]$ be the jth symbol in w. Let:

$$Blanks \equiv \Big(\bigwedge_{1 \le j \le padleft+1} tape_{1,j,\text{blank}}\Big) \wedge \Big(\bigwedge_{padleft+|w|+2 \le j \le cols} tape_{1,j,blank}\Big).$$

$$Initialw \equiv \bigwedge_{padleft+2 \le j \le padleft+|w|+1} tape_{1,j,w[j]}.$$

Now we describe the upper tier of the table. We need to say that *M* is in state q_0 with its read/write head immediately to the left of the first square of w. Let:

$$Initialq \equiv state_{1,padleft+1,q0}.$$

Then we have:

$$Conjunct_2 \equiv Blanks \wedge Initialw \wedge Initialq.$$

CONJUNCT 3: The third conjunct will represent the constraint that *M*'s computation must halt in the accepting state y. This means that some cell in the upper tier of the table must contain the state symbol y.

$$Conjunct_3 \equiv \bigvee_{1 \le j \le row} \bigvee_{1 \le j \le cols} state_{i,j,y}.$$

CONJUNCT 4: The fourth and last conjunct will represent the constraint that successive rows of the table must correspond to successive configurations in a possible computation of *M*. To construct this conjunct, our reduction *R* must have access to *M*'s transition relation Δ.

The key to the construction of $conjunct_4$ can be seen by looking through a small window at the large computation table that we are working with. An example of such a window is shown in Figure 28.6. Notice that each successive configuration of *M* is nearly identical to the previous one. The only tape square that can change its value is the one under the read/write head. And the read/write head can move only one square to the left or one square to the right.

•
•

q_1/a	a	a	b	❑	❑
b	q_1/a	a	b	❑	❑
b	a	q_1/a	b	❑	❑
b	a	b	q_1/b	❑	❑
b	a	b	b	q_2/❑	❑

• • • (left and right of the table)

•
•

FIGURE 28.6 A window into a computation table.

Call the first row in which the accepting state y occurs *done*. Now consider all rows from 2 until *done*. (We don't care what happens in any rows after the one in which y appears. They are just in the table because we had to make sure there was enough room for all the rows that matter.) What we want to say is that, comparing row i to row $i - 1$:

- All the tape squares that aren't under the read/write head stayed the same. Let:

  $Sames \equiv \forall 2 \leq i \leq done\ (\forall j\ (\forall c$ (read/write head not in column j in row $i - 1 \rightarrow (tape_{i,j,c} \leftrightarrow tape_{i-1,j,c}))))$.

- The tape square under the read/write head changed in some way that is allowed by Δ:

  $ChangedTape \equiv \forall 2 \leq i \leq done\ (\forall j\ (\forall c$ (read/write head in column j in row $i - 1$ and $tape_{i,j,c} \rightarrow$
  $\exists p$ (state stored in row $i - 1 = p$, and
  $\exists s$ (character in column j in row $i - 1 = s$, and
  $\exists q\ (((p, s),(q, c, (\rightarrow | \leftarrow))) \in \Delta)))))$.

- The state and the read/write head changed in some way that is allowed by Δ. There are two possibilities: Either the read/write head moved one square to the right or it moved one square to the left:

  $ChangedStateAndHead \equiv \forall 2 \leq i \leq done\ (\forall j(\forall q(state_{i,j,q} \rightarrow$
  $moved\text{-}right \vee moved\text{-}left)))$, where:
  $moved\text{-}right \equiv (\exists p$ (state stored in row $i - 1 = p$, and
  $\exists s$ (character in column $j - 1$ in row $i - 1 = s$, and
  $\exists c(((p, s), (q, c, \rightarrow)) \in \Delta))))$.
  $moved\text{-}left \equiv (\exists p$ (state stored in row $i - 1 = p$, and
  $\exists s$ (character in column $j + 1$ in row $i - 1 = s$, and
  $\exists c(((p, s), (q, c, \leftarrow)) \in \Delta))))$.

This last conjunct is the most complex of the four. So we will skip the step in which we convert the quantified formulas we've just presented to equivalent Boolean ones. By now it should be clear that since we are quantifying over a finite set of objects, doing that is straightforward, although tedious. So we have:

$Conjunct_4 \equiv$ the Boolean equivalent of:
$Sames \wedge ChangedTape \wedge ChangedStateAndHead$.

The final formula that* R *produces: We can now state R. On input w, it uses $<M>$ and constructs a description of the Boolean formula:

$$DescribeMonw = Conjunct_1 \wedge Conjunct_2 \wedge Conjunct_3 \wedge Conjunct_4.$$

DescribeMonw will have a satisfying assignment to its variables iff there exists some computational path along which M accepts w. So, for any NP language L, $L \leq$ SAT.

It remains to show that $R(w)$ operates in polynomial time. The number of variables in *DescribeMonw* can be computed as follows: We know that the number of steps that M will execute on input w is bounded by some polynomial function $f(|w|)$. So the number of cells in the computational table is $\mathcal{O}(f(|w|)^2)$. Call that number *cellcount*. To represent the bottom tier of the table requires $cellcount \cdot |\Gamma|$ variables. To represent the top tier of the table requires $cellcount \cdot |K|$ variables. Since both $|\Gamma|$ and $|K|$ are independent of $|w|$, the number of variables is then $\mathcal{O}(f(|w|)^2)$. So the number of characters required to encode each instance of a variable when it occurs in a literal in *DescribeMonw* is $(\mathcal{O}(\log f(|w|)^2))$, which is polynomial in $|w|$.

Constructing each of the conjuncts that form *DescribeMonw* is straightforward. But we must show that the length of each of them is bounded by some polynomial function of w:

- Conjunct 1: Each formula $T_{i,j}$ contains $|\Gamma|^2$ literals. So *Tapes* contains $cellcount \cdot |\Gamma|^2$ literals. Each formula $Q_{i,j}$ contains $|K|^2$ literals. So *States* contains $cellcount \cdot cols \cdot |K|^2 \in \mathcal{O}(f(|w|)^3)$ literals and $Conjunct_1$ contains $\mathcal{O}(f(|w|)^3)$ literals.
- Conjunct 2: We require *cols* literals to describe the tape contents and 1 to describe the state and read/write head. So $Conjunct_2$ contains $\mathcal{O}(f(|w|))$ literals.
- Conjunct 3: $Conjunct_3$ contains $\mathcal{O}(f(|w|)^2)$ literals.
- Conjunct 4: The straightforward way to convert the quantified expressions we have provided into the required Boolean formulas nests ANDs and ORs to correspond to the nested universal and existential quantifiers. If we do that, then we will get formulas with at most $cellcount \cdot |K|^2 \cdot |\Gamma|^2$ literals. Again, since $|K| \cdot$ are $|\Gamma|$ are independent of w, we have that $Conjunct_4$ contains $\mathcal{O}(f(|w|)^2)$ literals.

So $|DescribeMonw|$ is polynomial in $|w|$ and it can be constructed in polynomial time.

28.6 Other NP-Complete Problems

The Cook-Levin theorem gives us our first NP-complete language. In this section we'll see that it is not alone ▭.

28.6.1 A Sampling of NP-Complete Languages

We've already described many languages that can be shown to be NP-complete. In fact every NP language that we have mentioned, except for CHESS and those that we have said are in P, is provably NP-complete. So all of the following languages are NP-complete:

- SAT = {<w> : w is a wff in Boolean logic and w is satisfiable}.
- 3-SAT = {<w> : w is a wff in Boolean logic, w is in 3-conjunctive normal form and w is satisfiable}.

- TSP-DECIDE = {<*G*, *cost*>, where <*G*> encodes an undirected graph with a positive distance attached to each of its edges and *G* contains a Hamiltonian circuit whose total cost is less than *cost*}.
- HAMILTONIAN-PATH = {<*G*> : *G* is an undirected graph and *G* contains a Hamiltonian path}.
- HAMILTONIAN-CIRCUIT = {<*G*> : *G* is an undirected graph and *G* contains a Hamiltonian circuit}.
- CLIQUE = {<*G*, *k*> : *G* is an undirected graph with vertices *V* and edges *E*, *k* is an integer, $1 \leq k \leq |V|$, and *G* contains a *k*-clique}.
- INDEPENDENT-SET = {<*G*, *k*> : *G* is an undirected graph and *G* contains an independent set of at least *k* vertices}.
- SUBSET-SUM = {<*S*, *k*> : *S* is a multiset (i.e., duplicates are allowed) of integers, *k* is an integer, and there exists some subset of *S* whose elements sum to *k*}.
- SET-PARTITION = {<*S*> : *S* is a multiset (i.e., duplicates are allowed) of objects each of which has an associated cost and there exists a way to divide *S* into two subsets, *A* and $S - A$, such that the sum of the costs of the elements in *A* equals the sum of the costs of the elements in $S - A$}.
- KNAPSACK = {<*S*, *v*, *c*> : *S* is a set of objects each of which has an associated cost and an associated value, *v* and *c* are integers, and there exists some way of choosing elements of *S* (duplicates allowed) such that the total cost of the chosen objects is at most *c* and their total value is at least *v*}.
- SUDOKU = {<*b*> : *b* is a configuration of an $n \times n$ Sudoku grid and *b* has a solution}.

Examples of other languages that are also NP-complete include:

- SUBGRAPH-ISOMORPHISM = {<G_1, G_2> : G_1 is isomorphic to some subgraph of G_2}. Two graphs *G* and *H* are ***isomorphic*** to each other iff there exists a way to rename the vertices of *G* so that the result is equal to *H*. Another way to think about isomorphism is that two graphs are isomorphic iff their drawings are identical except for the labels on the vertices.

> The subgraph isomorphism problem arises naturally in many domains. For example, consider the problem of matching two chemical structures to see if one occurs within another.

- BIN-PACKING = {<*S*, *c*, *k*> : *S* is a set of objects each of which has an associated size and it is possible to divide the objects so that they fit into *k* bins, each of which has size *c*}.

> The bin packing problem can be extended to two and three dimensions and it remains NP-complete. The two-dimensional problem arises, for example, in laying out a newsletter with k pages and a set of stories and pictures that need to be placed on the pages. The three-dimensional problem arises, for example, in assigning cargo to a set of trucks or train cars.

- SHORTEST-SUPERSTRING = $\{<S, k> : S$ is a set of strings and there exists some superstring T such that every element of S is a substring of T and T has length less than or equal to $k\}$.

> The shortest superstring problem arises naturally during DNA sequencing. The problem there is to find the most likely larger molecule from which a set of fragments were derived. (K.5)

- BOUNDED-PCP = $\{<P, k> : P$ is an instance of the Post Correspondence problem (as described in Section 22.2) that has a solution of length less than or equal to $k\}$.

28.6.2 Proving That a Language is NP-Complete

To prove that a new language is NP-complete, we will exploit the following theorem. Recall that when we write $L_1 \leq_P L_2$, we mean that L_1 is polynomial-time mapping reducible to L_2.

THEOREM 28.17

Theorem: If L_1 is NP-complete, $L_1 \leq_P L_2$, and L_2 is in NP, then L_2 is also NP-complete.

Proof: If L_1 is NP-complete then every other NP language is deterministic, polynomial-time reducible to it. So let L be any NP language and let R_L be the Turing machine that reduces L to L_1. If $L_1 \leq_P L_2$, let R_2 be the Turing machine that implements that reduction. Then L can be deterministic, polynomial-time reduced to L_2 by first applying R_L and then applying R_2. Since L_2 is in NP and every other language in NP is deterministic, polynomial-time reducible to it, it is NP-complete.

Theorem 28.17 tells us that we can use reduction from any known NP-complete language to show that a new language is also NP-complete. At this point, we have only one such language: SAT. So we will begin by using it. Once we have others, we can use whichever one makes the required reduction easy. In fact, the first thing we will do is to show that 3-SAT, a close relative of SAT, is NP-complete. Then we'll have 3-SAT as a tool to use in our other reductions.

28.6.3 3-SAT

In Section 28.2.5 we defined:

- 3-SAT = {<w> : w is a wff in Boolean logic, w is in 3-conjunctive normal form, and w is satisfiable}.

3-SAT is a somewhat contrived language. It is significant primarily because doing reductions from 3-SAT is often substantially easier than doing them from SAT. 3-SAT's restricted form limits the number of conditions that must be considered, as we saw in the reduction we did, in Theorem 28.15, from 3-SAT to INDEPENDENT-SET.

THEOREM 28.18 3-SAT is NP-Complete

Theorem: 3-SAT is NP-complete.

Proof: We showed, in Theorem 28.13, that 3-SAT is in NP. So all that remains is to show that it is NP-hard (i.e., that every other language in NP is deterministic, polynomial-time reducible to it).

We could show that 3-SAT is NP-hard if we could show a polynomial-time reduction from SAT to it. Define:

R(w: wff of Boolean logic) =

1. Use *conjunctiveBoolean* (as defined in the proof of Theorem B.1) to construct w', where w' is in conjunctive normal form and w' is equivalent to w.
2. Use *3-conjunctiveBoolean* (as defined in the proof of Theorem B.2) to construct w'', where w'' is in 3-conjunctive normal form and w'' is satisfiable iff w' is.
3. Return w''.

If R ran in polynomial time, it would be the reduction that we need. In Exercise 28.4, we show that step two does run in polynomial time. Unfortunately, step one does not. The length of w' (and thus the time required to construct it) can grow exponentially with the length of w. There are two approaches that we could take to solving this problem:

- We can retain the idea of reducing SAT to 3-SAT. We observe that, for R to be a reduction from SAT to 3-SAT, it is not necessary that w' be equivalent to w. It is sufficient to assure that w' is satisfiable iff w is. There exists a polynomial-time algorithm (described in [Hopcroft, Motwani and Ullman 2001]) that constructs, from any wff w, a w' that meets that requirement. If we replace step one of R with that algorithm, R is a polynomial-time reduction from SAT to 3-SAT, so 3-SAT is NP-hard.
- We can prove that 3-SAT is NP-hard directly, using a variant of the proof we offered for the Cook-Levin Theorem. It is possible to modify the reduction R that proves the Cook-Levin Theorem so that it constructs a formula in conjunctive normal form. R will still run in polynomial time. We leave the proof of this claim as Exercise 28.13. Once R has constructed a conjunctive normal

form formula w, we can use *3-conjunctiveBoolean* to construct w' where w' is in 3-conjunctive normal form and w' is satisfiable iff w is. This composition of *3-conjunctiveBoolean* with R shows that any NP language can be reduced to 3-SAT. So 3-SAT is NP-hard.

28.6.4 Independent-Set

Recall that, given a graph G, an independent set is a set of vertices of G, no two of which are adjacent (i.e., connected by a single edge). Using that definition, we defined the following language, which we can now show is NP-complete:

- INDEPENDENT-SET = {<G, k> : G is an undirected graph and G contains an independent set of at least k vertices}.

THEOREM 28.19 INDEPENDENT-SET is NP-Complete

Theorem: INDEPENDENT-SET is NP-complete.

Proof: We must prove that INDEPENDENT-SET is in NP and that it is NP-hard (i.e., that every other language in NP is deterministic, polynomial-time reducible to it).

INDEPENDENT-SET is in NP: We describe *Ver*, a deterministic, polynomial-time verifier for it: Let G be a graph with vertices V and edges E. Let c be a certificate for <G, k>; c will be a list of vertices. On input <G, k, c>, *Ver* checks that the number of vertices in c is at least k and no more than $|V|$. If it is not, it rejects. Next it considers each vertex in c one at a time. For each such vertex v, it finds all edges in E that have v as one endpoint. It then checks that the other endpoint of each of those edges is not in c. $Timereq(Ver) \in \mathcal{O}(|c| \cdot |E| \cdot |c|)$. Both $|c|$ and $|E|$ are polynomial in $|<G, k>|$. So *Ver* runs in polynomial time.

INDEPENDENT-SET is NP-hard because Theorem 28.15 tells us that 3-SAT $\leq_P$ INDEPENDENT-SET.

28.6.5 Vertex-Cover

A vertex cover C of a graph G with vertices V and edges E is a subset of V with the property that every edge in E touches at least one of the vertices in C. Obviously V is a vertex cover of G. But we are typically interested in finding a smaller one. So we define the following language, which we will show is NP-complete:

- VERTEX-COVER = {<G, k>: G is an undirected graph and there exists a vertex cover of G that contains at most k vertices}.

> To be able to test every link in a network, it suffices to place monitors at a set of vertices that form a vertex cover of the network. (I.2)

We will show that VERTEX-COVER (also called NODE-COVER) is NP-complete by reducing 3-SAT to it. The proof will provide another example of the use of carefully constructed gadgets that map the literals and clauses that occur in strings in 3-SAT to the vertices and edges described by strings in VERTEX-COVER. Alternatively, we could prove that VERTEX-COVER is NP-complete with a very simple reduction from INDEPENDENT-SET (since, if S is an independent set in some graph G with vertices V and edges E, then $V - S$ is a vertex cover of G). We leave that alternative proof as an exercise.

THEOREM 28.20 VERTEX-COVER is NP-Complete

Theorem: VERTEX-COVER is NP-complete.

Proof: We must prove that VERTEX-COVER is in NP and that it is NP-hard.

VERTEX-COVER is in NP: We describe *Ver*, a deterministic, polynomial-time verifier for it: Let G be a graph with vertices V and edges E. Let c be a certificate for $<G, k>$; c will be a list of vertices. On input $<G, k, c>$, *Ver* checks that the number of vertices in c is at most $min(k, |V|)$. If it is not, it rejects. Next it considers each vertex in c one at a time. For each such vertex v, it finds all edges in E that have v as one endpoint and it marks each such edge. Finally, it makes one pass through E and checks whether every edge is marked. If all of them are, it accepts; otherwise it rejects. $Timereq(Ver) \in \mathcal{O}(|c| \cdot |E|)$. Both $|c|$ and $|E|$ are polynomial in $|<G, k>|$. So *Ver* runs in polynomial time.

VERTEX-COVER is NP-hard: We prove this by demonstrating a reduction R that shows that:

$$\text{3-SAT} \leq_P \text{VERTEX-COVER}.$$

R's job is to map a Boolean formula f (in 3-conjunctive normal form) to a graph. It will exploit two kinds of gadgets:

- A variable gadget: For each variable x in f, R will build a simple graph with two vertices and one edge between them. Label one of the vertices x and the other one $\neg x$.
- A clause gadget: For each clause c in f, R will build a graph with three vertices, one for each literal in c. There will be an edge between each pair of vertices in this graph.

The variable and clause gadgets must then be connected to correspond to the structure of f. R will build an edge from every vertex in a clause gadget to the vertex of the variable gadget with the same label.

So, for example, given the Boolean formula $(P \vee \neg Q \vee T) \wedge (\neg P \vee Q \vee S)$, R will build the graph shown in Figure 28.7.

Let f be a Boolean formula with c clauses and v variables. Then we can define R as follows:

$R(<f>) =$

1. Build a graph G as described above.

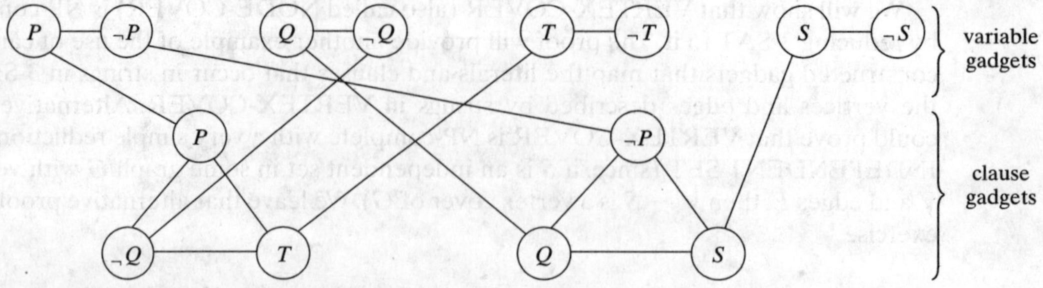

FIGURE 28.7 Reducing 3-SAT to VERTEX-COVER.

2. Let $k = v + 2c$.
3. Return <G, k>.

R runs in polynomial time. To show that it is correct, we must show that <f> ∈ 3-SAT iff R(<f>) ∈ VERTEX-COVER.

We first show that <f> ∈ 3-SAT → R(<f>) ∈ VERTEX-COVER. If <f> ∈ 3-SAT, then there exists a satisfying assignment A of values to the variables in f. We can use that assignment to show that G, the graph that R builds, contains a vertex cover C of size at most (in fact, exactly) k. We can construct C by doing the following:

1. From each variable gadget, select the vertex that corresponds to the literal that is true in A. Add each of those vertices to C.
2. Since A is a satisfying assignment, there must exist at least one true literal in each clause. Pick one and put the vertices corresponding to the other two into C.

C contains exactly k vertices. And it is a cover of G because:

- One vertex from every variable gadget is in C, so all the edges that are internal to the variable gadgets are covered.
- Two vertices from every clause gadget are in C, so all the edges that are internal to the clause gadgets are covered.
- All the edges that connect variable gadgets to clause gadgets are covered because, for each clause gadget:
  - Two of the three emerging edges are covered by the two clause gadget-vertices in C.
  - The other one must be connected to a variable gadget vertex that corresponds to a true literal, so that vertex is in C.

Next we show that R(<f>) ∈ VERTEX-COVER → <f> ∈ 3-SAT. If R(<f>) ∈ VERTEX-COVER, then the graph G that R builds contains a vertex cover C of size at most (again, in fact, exactly) k. Notice that C must:

- Contain at least one vertex from each variable gadget in order to cover the internal edge in the variable gadget.
- Contain at least two vertices from each clause gadget in order to cover all three internal edges in the clause gadget.

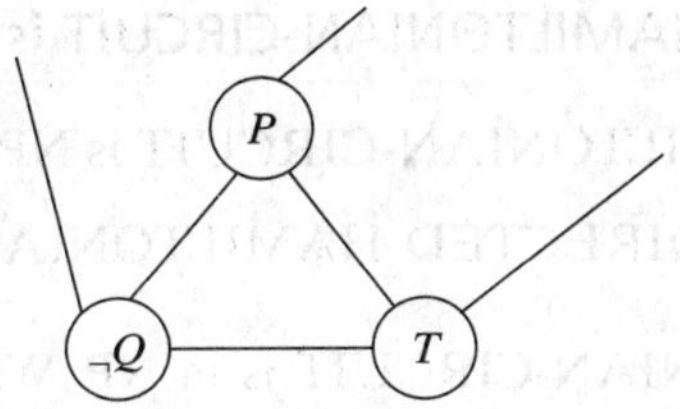

FIGURE 28.8 A clause gadget.

Satisfying those two requirements uses up all k vertices, so the vertices we have just described are the only vertices in C. We can use C to show that there exists some satisfying assignment A for f. Building A is simple: Assign the value *True* to each literal that is the label for one of the vertices in C that comes from a variable gadget. We note that A is a satisfying assignment for f iff it assigns the value *True* to at least one literal in each of f's clauses.

To see why it is certain that A does this, consider an arbitrary clause gadget in G, as shown in Figure 28.8. Since C is a cover for G, all six of the edges that connect to vertices in this gadget must be covered. But we know that only two of the vertices in the gadget are in C. They can cover the three internal edges. But the three edges that connect to the variable gadgets must also be covered. Only two can be covered by a vertex in the clause gadget. The other one must be covered by its other endpoint, which is in some variable gadget. So each clause is connected to some literal whose corresponding vertex is in C. We made each such literal *True* in A. So A assigns the value *True* to at least one literal in each clause. Thus it is a satisfying assignment for f.

28.6.6 HAMILTONIAN-CIRCUIT and the Traveling Salesman Problem

We started our discussion of complexity, at the beginning of Chapter 27, by considering the traveling salesman problem. We observed then that, while there exists an obvious exponential algorithm for solving the problem, there does not exist an *obvious* polynomial algorithm for solving it exactly. While it remains an open question whether *any* polynomial algorithm for the traveling salesman problem does in fact exist, we can now prove a result that suggests that it is relatively unlikely that one does. TSP-DECIDE is NP-complete.

We have already shown that TSP-DECIDE is in NP. But we must also show that it is NP-hard, which we will do by reducing 3-SAT to it. It turns out to be easier to map 3-SAT to appropriate graph structures if the graph edges are directed. So we will introduce a new language:

DIRECTED-HAMILTONIAN-CIRCUIT = {<G> : G is a *directed* graph and G contains a Hamiltonian circuit}.

Then we will prove that:

3-SAT $\geq_P$ DIRECTED-HAMILTONIAN-CIRCUIT $\geq_P$
HAMILTONIAN-CIRCUIT $\geq_P$ TSP-DECIDE.

THEOREM 28.21 DIRECTED-HAMILTONIAN-CIRCUIT is NP-Complete

Theorem: DIRECTED-HAMILTONIAN-CIRCUIT is NP-complete.

Proof: We must prove that DIRECTED-HAMILTONIAN-CIRCUIT is in NP and that it is NP-hard.

DIRECTED-HAMILTONIAN-CIRCUIT is in NP: We describe *Ver*, a deterministic, polynomial-time verifier for it: Let G be a graph with vertices V and edges E. Let c be a certificate for $<G, k>$; c will be a list of vertices. On input $<G, k, c>$, *Ver* checks that the number of vertices in c is $|V| + 1$. If it is not, it rejects. It also rejects if the first and last vertices are not identical. Next it considers each vertex v in c, except the last, one at a time. It marks v in V and rejects if it had previously been marked. It also checks that the required edge to v exists and rejects if it does not. If it finishes without rejecting, it accepts. $Timereq(Ver) \in \mathcal{O}(|c| \cdot (|V| + |E|))$. All of $|c|$, $|V|$, and $|E|$ are polynomial in $|<G, k>|$. So *Ver* runs in polynomial time.

DIRECTED-HAMILTONIAN-CIRCUIT is NP-hard: We prove this by demonstrating a reduction R that shows that:

$$\text{3-SAT} \leq_P \text{DIRECTED-HAMILTONIAN-CIRCUIT}.$$

R's job is to map a Boolean formula Bf (in 3-conjunctive normal form) to a graph. R will exploit two kinds of gadgets, one to correspond to the variables of Bf and the other to correspond to the clauses.

We'll describe the variable gadgets first. Let n be the number of variables in the Boolean formula Bf. If v is the ith such variable, let m be the larger of the number of occurrences of v or of $\neg v$ in Bf. The gadget that corresponds to v will have the structure shown in Figure 28.9. We'll call this gadget V_i.

Now imagine a Hamiltonian path (not a circuit) through V_i. It must enter V_i from the left at a_i and leave it on the right at b_i. There are only two ways to do that. If the path begins by going down to a t vertex, then it must next go straight up to the matching f vertex, then crosswise to the next t vertex, up to the matching f vertex, and so forth. Similarly, if the path begins by going up to an f vertex, it must next go straight down to the matching t vertex, then crosswise to the next f vertex, and so forth. A path that did anything else would not be Hamiltonian since it would not visit all the vertices. So there are two paths through V_i:

- The one that begins by going down to a t vertex. We will use this one to correspond to assigning to the variable v the value *True*
- The one that begins by going up to an f vertex. We will use this one to correspond to assigning to the variable v the value *False*.

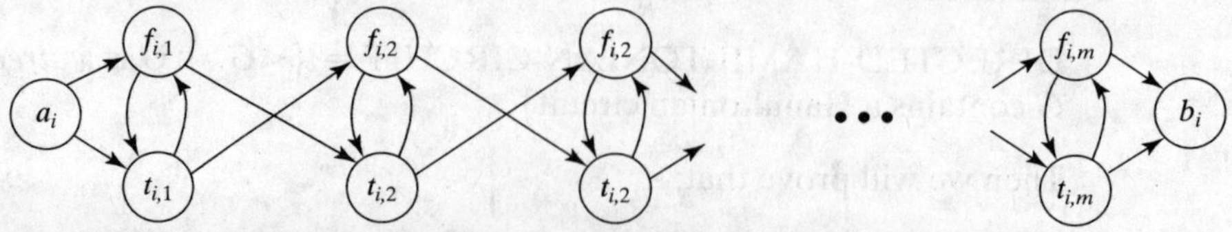

FIGURE 28.9 A variable gadget in the reduction from 3-SAT to DIRECTED-HAMILTONIAN-CIRCUIT.

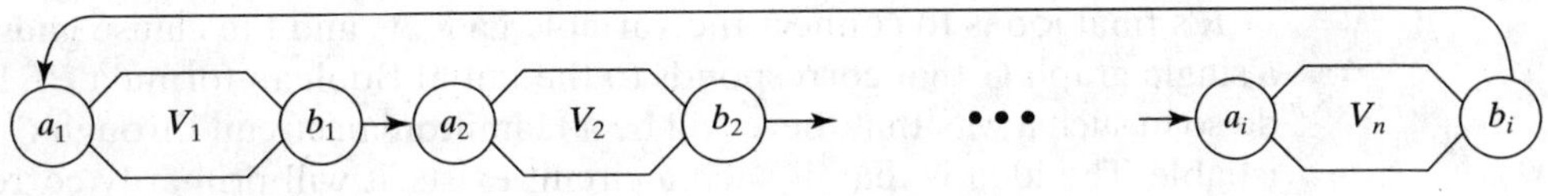

FIGURE 28.10 Stringing the variable gadgets together.

R will build the variable gadgets V_1 through V_n and then combine them into a single structure *V*, as shown in Figure 28.10. Suppose that *H* is a Hamiltonian circuit through *V*. Then *H* must enter each of the variable gadgets exactly once (through its *a* vertex), choose one of the two paths through that gadget (thus effectively choosing to make the corresponding variable either *True* or *False*), leave that variable gadget (through its *b* vertex), and then enter the next one.

Next we must describe the clause gadgets. The gadget that corresponds to the ith clause in the formula *Bf* will have the structure shown in Figure 28.11. We'll call this gadget C_i.

Suppose that C_i is part of a graph *G* that contains some Hamiltonian cycle *H*. *H* must enter through one of C_i's *in* vertices. Further, note that if it enters in column *j* it must also leave through column *j*. To see why this is so, we consider all the paths it could take. From $in_{i,j}$, *H* can:

- Go straight down to $out_{i,j}$ and exit.
- Proceed across to the next *in* vertex and then down to the matching *out* one. From there it can go to the next *out* vertex (which will be $out_{i,j}$) and exit. It cannot simply exit right away because, if it does, there is no way for *H* to reach $out_{i,j}$. The two vertices that could precede it are already in *H* and neither of them went to it. Without $out_{i,j}$, *H* can't be Hamiltonian.
- Proceed across to the next *in* vertex and then the next one. From there it can go down to the matching *out* vertex, then across to the next and then to the next (which will be $out_{i,j}$) and then exit. It cannot exit at either of the other *out* vertices since, if it did, there would again be no way for *H* to reach $out_{i,j}$.

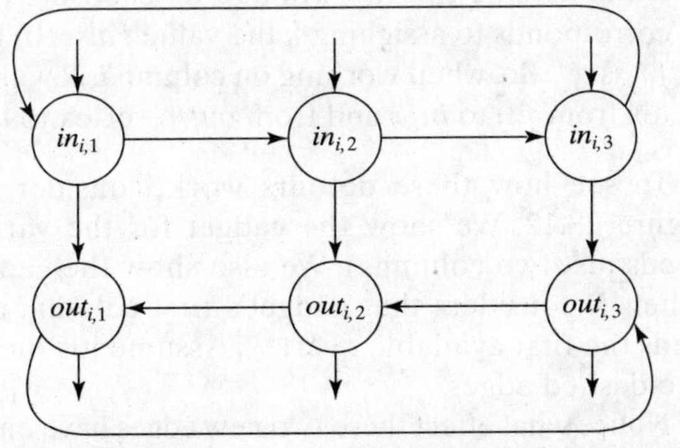

FIGURE 28.11 A clause gadget in the reduction from 3-SAT to DIRECTED-HAMILTONIAN-CIRCUIT.

R's final job is to connect the variable gadgets and the clause gadgets to form a single graph G that corresponds to the initial Boolean formula Bf. Its goal is to do so in such a way that there will be a Hamiltonian circuit through G iff Bf is satisfiable. The idea is that, if such a circuit exists, it will primarily correspond to a circuit through V, the variable gadget graph. As V has been defined, such a circuit exists. In fact, several exist since there are two paths through each of the individual variable gadgets. So what R must do now is to connect V to the clause gadgets so that there will still be a Hamiltonian circuit if Bf is satisfiable. If, on the other hand, Bf is not satisfiable, the introduction of the clause gadgets will produce a graph through which no Hamiltonian circuit exists. What R is going to do is to use the clause gadgets to introduce detours through V so that this is true.

In each clause gadget C, think of the first column as corresponding to its corresponding clause's first literal, the second column as corresponding to the second literal, and the third column as corresponding to the third literal. R will create three detours from V into C and back, one for each of those literals. So R will consider each of C's three columns in turn. The literal that corresponds to that column is either some variable v or its negation $\neg v$:

- Suppose R is working on column i and the corresponding literal is v. Then R will go to the gadget for v and choose the first of its columns whose t vertex has not yet been chosen. (Remember that the number of columns in v's gadget is equal to the larger of the number of instances of v or of $\neg v$, so such a column will always be able to be chosen.) Suppose that the vertex labeled $t_{v,j}$ is chosen. R will create a detour from $t_{v,j}$ to C and then back into V to whatever vertex $t_{v,j}$ previously linked to. If we end up choosing the path through v's gadget that corresponds to assigning v the value *True*, then that successor vertex is $f_{v,j}$. So, when working on column i, R will create a detour by adding a vertex from $t_{v,j}$ to $in_{C,i}$ and from $out_{C,i}$ to $f_{v,j}$.
- Suppose, on the other hand, that the corresponding literal is $\neg v$. Then R will go to the gadget for v and choose the first of its columns whose f vertex has not yet been chosen. Suppose that the vertex labeled $f_{v,j}$ is chosen. Just as above, R will create a detour from the chosen vertex into C and then back. But this time it will assume that we will end up choosing the path through v's gadget that corresponds to assigning v the value *False*. In that case, the successor vertex of $f_{v,j}$ is $t_{v,j}$. So, when working on column i, R will create a detour by adding a vertex from $f_{v,j}$ to $in_{C,i}$ and from $out_{C,i}$ vertex to $t_{v,j}$.

To see how these detours work, consider the simple example shown in Figure 28.12. We show the gadget for the variable P (which we've assumed needs just two columns). We also show the gadget for the clause $(P \vee Q \vee S)$. When R considers that gadget's first column, it goes to the gadget for P and finds the first available t vertex. Assume it's the first one. Then it adds to G the two dashed edges.

Notice what effect these two new edges have on our ability to find a Hamiltonian circuit through G. If such a circuit is traversing P's gadget in the *True* direction (i.e., it starts by going from a_P down to $t_{P,1}$), then it can now pass through all the vertices

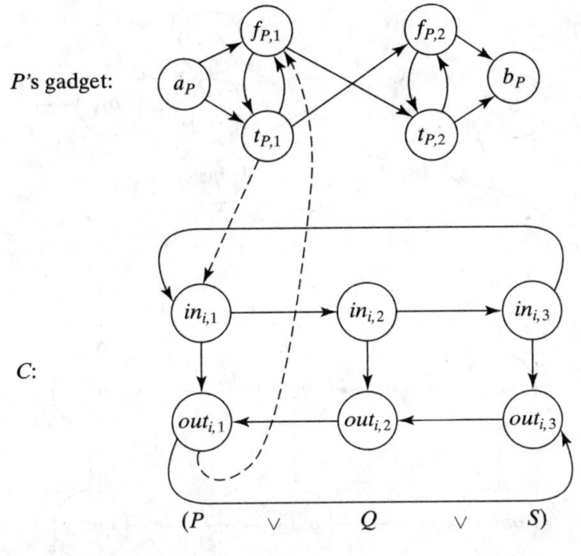

FIGURE 28.12 Combining the variable and the clause gadgets.

of C, leave C, and then continue through the rest of P's gadget. If, on the other hand, such a circuit is traversing P's gadget in the *False* direction, it cannot. It can enter C, but when it leaves it would have to return to a vertex ($f_{P,1}$) that it has already visited.

Let Bf be a Boolean formula. We can define a reduction R from 3-SAT to DIRECTED-HAMILTONIAN-CIRCUIT as follows:

$R(<Bf>) =$

1. Build the graph G as described above.

2. Return $<G>$.

R runs in polynomial time. To show that it is correct we must show that $<Bf> \in$ 3-SAT iff $R(<Bf>) \in$ DIRECTED-HAMILTONIAN-CIRCUIT.

We first show that $<Bf> \in$ 3-SAT $\rightarrow R(<Bf>) \in$ DIRECTED-HAMILTONIAN-CIRCUIT. If $<Bf> \in$ 3-SAT, then there exists a satisfying assignment A of values to the variables in Bf. We can use that assignment to show that G, the graph that R builds, contains a Hamiltonian circuit. We can construct such a circuit H as follows: Begin by letting H be just a Hamiltonian circuit through V. We have a choice, for each variable gadget, of two paths through it. If A assigns the variable v the value *True*, then choose the path that begins by going to the first t vertex in v's gadget. If, on the other hand, A assigns v the value *False*, then choose the path that begins by going to the first f vertex in v's gadget.

But now we must add to H the vertices in all the clause gadgets. Since A is a satisfying assignment, each clause c must contain at least one literal to which A assigns the value *True*. Pick one. If it is the (unnegated) variable v, look at v's

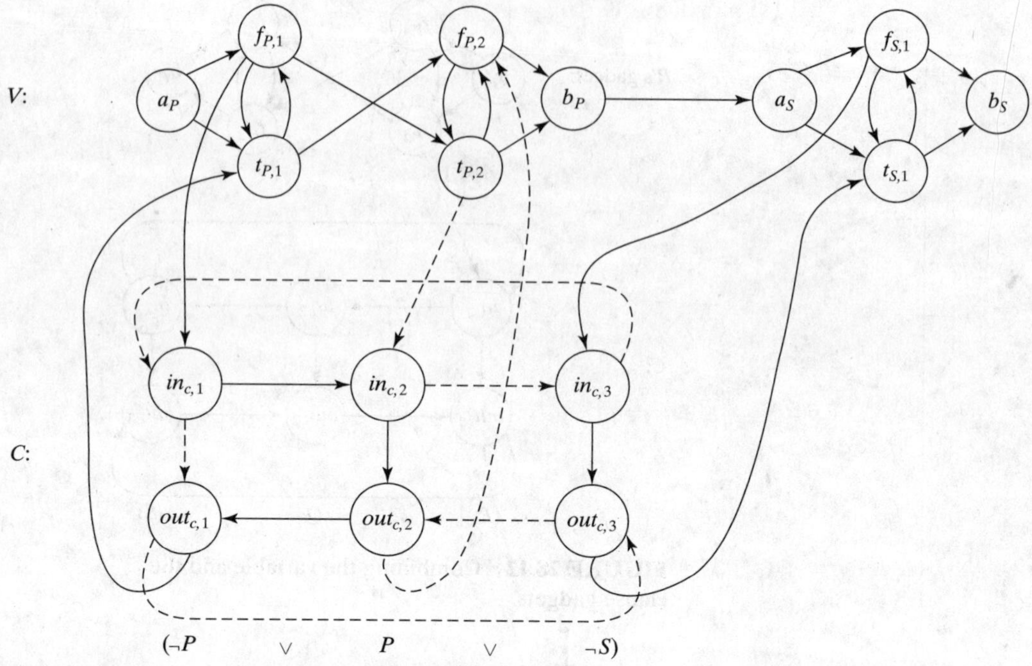

FIGURE 28.13 How the detours work.

gadget. There will be an edge from one of v's t vertices (call it $t_{v,k}$) into c's clause gadget at some *in* vertex $in_{c,i}$, and then back out again (from the same column) to the f vertex ($f_{v,k}$) immediately above $t_{v,k}$. H currently includes an edge from $t_{v,k}$ to $f_{v,k}$. Remove that edge and insert, in its place, the edge from $t_{v,k}$ to $in_{c,i}$. Then add the edges that visit the other two vertices in the top row of c's gadget, followed by the three vertices in its bottom row. Finally add the edge that leaves c's gadget at $out_{c,i}$ and returns to v at $f_{v,k}$.

To see how this works, consider the simple case shown in Figure 28.13. Assume that Bf contains the clause $c = (\neg P \vee P \vee \neg S)$ and that the only variables in Bf are P and S. Then the graph G that R builds will contain the two fragments shown in the figure: V, the variable gadget structure, and C, the gadget for c. Notice that there are three paths into and out of C, one corresponding to $\neg P$, one corresponding to P, and one corresponding to R. (Ignore the distinction between solid and dashed lines for the moment.)

Suppose that P is assigned the value *True* by A and that P is the *True* literal that we pick as we are building H. Because A assigns P the value *True*, H's path through P's gadget will be a_P, then $t_{P,1}$, then $f_{P,1}$, then $t_{P,2}$, and so forth. Initially H contains all the edges in V. But now we remove from it the edge from $t_{P,2}$ to $f_{P,2}$ and replace it by the set of edges shown above as dashed lines. H can still continue its path through V. But now it also detours and visits every vertex in C. And it visits each of them only once because we apply this operation to exactly one of $(\neg P \vee P \vee \neg R)$'s *True* literals.

Now suppose that, for some clause c, the *True* literal that we pick is $\neg v$. Then we do almost the same thing except that now there will be an edge from one of v's f vertices (call it $f_{v,k}$) into c's clause gadget and then back out again to the t vertex (call it $t_{v,k}$) immediately below $f_{v,k}$. H currently includes an edge from $f_{v,k}$ to $t_{v,k}$. Remove that edge and insert, in its place, the edge from $f_{v,k}$ into c's gadget. Then, just as above, add the edges that visit the other two vertices in the top row of c's gadget, followed by the three vertices in its bottom row. Finally add the edge that leaves c's gadget and returns to v at $t_{v,k}$.

H is a Hamiltonian circuit through the graph G that R builds. It includes every vertex in V exactly once. It contains exactly one detour into each clause gadget and that detour visits all six of the vertices in that gadget. So every vertex in G is contained in H exactly once.

It remains to show that $R(<Bf>) \in$ DIRECTED-HAMILTONIAN-CIRCUIT $\rightarrow <Bf> \in$ 3-SAT. If $R(<Bf>) \in$ DIRECTED-HAMILTONIAN-CIRCUIT then the graph G that R builds contains a Hamiltonian circuit we can call H. We use H to construct A, a satisfying assignment of values to the variables of Bf. Building A is simple: Examine each variable gadget in G. If H follows the *True* path through the gadget corresponding to variable v (i.e., it begins by going from a_v to $t_{v,1}$), then assign v the value *True*. If, on the other hand, H follows the *False* path through v's gadget (i.e., it begins by going from a_v to $f_{v,1}$), then assign v the value *False*. Since H is Hamiltonian, it goes through each clause gadget exactly once. And, since it is Hamiltonian, one of the following two things must be true, for each clause gadget, given the way G was constructed:

- H connects to the clause gadget in a column that corresponds to a positive literal v and it does so by a detour from a *True* path. In this case, A assigns v the value *True* and so the clause is satisfied.
- H connects to the clause gadget in a column that corresponds to a negated literal $\neg v$ and it does so by a detour from a *False* path. In this case, A assigns v the value *False*. So $\neg v$ is *True* and so the clause is satisfied.

Since each of its clauses is satisfied, Bf is also satisfied.

The reduction R that we just described, from 3-SAT to DIRECTED-HAMILTONIAN-CIRCUIT, only worked because the edges in the graph that R built were directed. But the fundamental question, "Does a Hamiltonian circuit exist?" is just as hard to answer for undirected graphs. We prove that result next, using a very simple reduction from DIRECTED-HAMILTONIAN-CIRCUIT.

THEOREM 28.22 HAMILTONIAN-CIRCUIT is NP-Complete

Theorem: HAMILTONIAN-CIRCUIT = $\{<G> : G$ is an undirected graph and G contains a Hamiltonian circuit$\}$ is NP-complete.

Proof: We must prove that HAMILTONIAN-CIRCUIT is in NP and that it is NP-hard.

HAMILTONIAN-CIRCUIT is in NP: *Ver*, the verifier that we just described in the proof of Theorem 28.21, also works here. It will simply consider undirected edges instead of requiring directed ones.

HAMILTONIAN-CIRCUIT is NP-hard: We prove this by demonstrating a reduction *R* that shows that:

DIRECTED-HAMILTONIAN-CIRCUIT $\leq_P$ HAMILTONIAN-CIRCUIT.

Given a directed graph *G*, *R* will build an undirected graph *G′*. Each of *G*'s vertices will be represented in *G′* by a gadget that contains three vertices connected by two edges. Further, if there is a directed edge in *G* from *v* to *w*, then *G′* will contain an (undirected) edge from the last of the vertices in *v*'s gadget to the first of the vertices in *w*'s gadget. Figure 28.14 shows a simple example.

Let *G* be a directed graph. We can define a reduction *R* from DIRECTED-HAMILTONIAN-CIRCUIT to HAMILTONIAN-CIRCUIT as follows:

R(<*G*>) =

1. Build the graph *G′* as described above.
2. Return <*G′*>.

R runs in polynomial time. To show that it is correct we must show that <*G*> ∈ DIRECTED-HAMILTONIAN-CIRCUIT iff *R*(<*G*>) ∈ HAMILTONIAN-CIRCUIT.

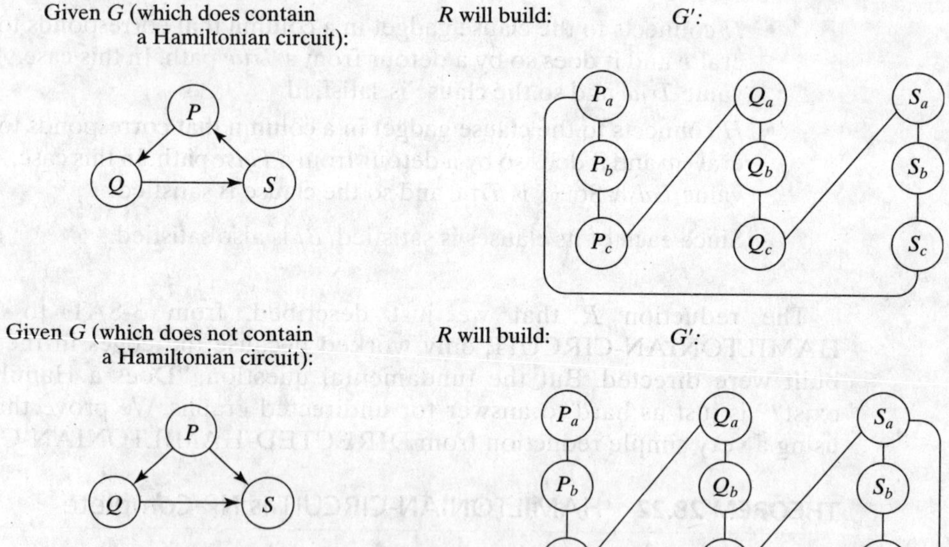

FIGURE 28.14 Reductions from DIRECTED-HAMILTONIAN-CIRCUIT to HAMILTONIAN-CIRCUIT.

We first show that <G> ∈ DIRECTED-HAMILTONIAN-CIRCUIT → R(<G>) ∈ HAMILTONIAN-CIRCUIT. G must contain at least one Hamiltonian circuit, which we will call H. Assume that $H = (v_1, v_2, \ldots, v_k, v_1)$. Then we can describe H', a Hamiltonian circuit through G'. It starts at the top of v_1's gadget, walks down through it, then goes to the top of v_2's gadget, walks down through it, and so forth until it has visited the last vertex of v_k's gadget. It ends by returning to the first vertex of v_1's gadget. In other words,

$$H' = (v_{1a}, v_{1b}, v_{1c}, v_{2a}, v_{2b}, v_{2c}, \ldots, v_{ka}, v_{kb}, v_{kc}, v_{1a}).$$

It remains to show that (R(<G>) ∈ HAMILTONIAN-CIRCUIT) → DIRECTED-HAMILTONIAN-CIRCUIT). Notice that, in any graph that R builds, each b vertex is attached to exactly two edges. So any Hamiltonian circuit through such a vertex comes either down from the top, or up from the bottom, of the corresponding gadget. Pick a gadget. If a Hamiltonian circuit through it goes down from the top, then it must continue to the top of some other gadget. So it must go down through that one as well. And it must continue through all the gadgets, in each case going down from the top. Alternatively, it can move bottom to top through all the gadgets. The key is that it must move in the same direction through all the vertex gadgets. If R(<G>) ∈ HAMILTONIAN-CIRCUIT, then the graph G' that R builds must contain at least one Hamiltonian circuit. Pick one and call it H. Assume that H traverses the G' gadgets top to bottom. (If it goes in the other direction, then, since G' is undirected, there is another Hamiltonian circuit through G' that is identical to H except that it moves in the other direction. Choose it instead.) Note that H can only traverse the gadget for v and then the gadget for w in case there was a directed edge from v to w in the original graph G. So, suppose H visits the gadgets for the vertices $(v_1, v_2, \ldots, v_k, v_1)$, in that order. Then $(v_1, v_2, \ldots, v_k, v_1)$ is a Hamiltonian circuit through G.

We are now in a position to return to the traveling salesman problem, with which we began the previous chapter.

THEOREM 28.23 TSP-DECIDE is NP-complete

Theorem: TSP-DECIDE = {<G, *cost*> : <G> encodes an undirected graph with a positive distance attached to each of its edges and G contains a Hamiltonian circuit whose total cost is less than *cost*} is NP-complete.

Proof: We have already shown (in Theorem 28.10) that TSP-DECIDE is in NP. It remains to prove that it is NP-hard, which we do with a straightforward reduction R that shows that:

$$\text{HAMILTONIAN-CIRCUIT} \leq_P \text{TSP-DECIDE}.$$

Let G be an unweighted, undirected graph with vertices V. R must map G into a weighted, undirected graph plus a cost. We observe that, if there is a Hamiltonian circuit through G, it must contain exactly $|V|$ edges. So suppose that we augment G with edge costs by assigning to every edge a cost of 1. Then, if there is a Hamiltonian circuit in G, its total cost must be equal to $|V|$. Because this is true, we can define R as follows:

$R(<G>) =$

1. From G construct G', a weighted graph. G' will be identical to G except that each edge will be assigned the cost 1.
2. Return $<G', |V|>$.

R runs in polynomial time. And it is correct since G has a Hamiltonian circuit iff G' has one with cost equal to $|V|$.

28.7 The Relationship between P and NP-Complete

So far, every NP language that we have considered has turned out also either to be in P or to be NP-complete. Is it necessarily true that every NP language has that property? The answer is no. In fact, unless P = NP, there must exist languages that don't.

28.7.1 The Gap between P and NP-Complete

Call the class of NP-complete languages NPC. Let NPL = NP − (P ∪ NPC). In other words, NPL is the limbo area between P and NP-complete. Trivially, if P = NP then NPL = ∅. But what if (as seems more likely) P ≠ NP? We can prove the following theorem that tells us that, in that case, NPL is not empty.

THEOREM 28.24 Ladner's Theorem

Theorem: If P ≠ NP, then NPL ≠ ∅.

Proof: The proof relies on the following more general claim that is proved in [Ladner 1975]:

Claim: Let B be any decidable language that is not in P. There exists a language D that is in P and that has the following property: Let $A = D \cap B$. Then $A \notin$ P, $A \leq_P B$, but it is not true that $B \leq_P A$.

Suppose that B is any NP-complete language. Unless P = NP, B is not in P. So there must exist a language D that is in P, and from which we can compute $A = D \cap B$. A must be in NP since membership in D can be decided in polynomial time and membership in B can be verified in polynomial time. So the claim that Ladner proved tells us that:

- $A \notin$ P, but
- it is not true that $B \leq_P A$. Since B is in NP but is not deterministic, polynomial-time reducible to A, A is not NP-complete.

So A is an example of an NP language that is neither in P nor NP-complete. Thus NPL $\neq \varnothing$.

It is possible, using diagonalization techniques, to construct languages that are in NPL. But it remains true that few "natural" languages are in that class. A comprehensive catalogue of NP problems [Garey and Johnson 1979] lists three candidates for membership in NPL:

- COMPOSITES = $\{w : w$ is the binary encoding of a composite number$\}$. Recall that a composite number is a natural number greater than 1 that is not prime.
- LINEAR-PROGRAMMING, which we will describe in Section 28.7.7.
- GRAPH-ISOMORPHISM = $\{<G_1, G_2> : G_1$ is isomorphic to $G_2\}$. Recall that two graphs G and H are isomorphic to each other iff there exists a way to rename the vertices of G so that the result is equal to H.

It is now known that COMPOSITES (see Section 28.1.7) and LINEAR-PROGRAMMING (see Section 28.7.7) are in P.

The jury is still out on GRAPH-ISOMORPHISM. It is easy to show that GRAPH-ISOMORPHISM is in NP. A proposed renaming of the vertices of G_1 so that it matches G_2 is a certificate, which can easily be checked in polynomial time. Recall that the *subgraph* isomorphism language, SUBGRAPH-ISOMORPHISM, which asks whether G_1 is isomorphic to *some subgraph of* G_2 is NP-complete. It appears that the graph isomorphism problem is easier, perhaps because we must compare only G_1 and G_2, not G_1 and all of G_2's subgraphs. But graph isomorphism has not been shown to be in P, nor has it been shown not to be NP-hard (and thus NP-complete).

Problems like GRAPH-ISOMORPHISM are rare, though. So, most of the time, an NP problem will turn out either to be NP-complete or to be in P. The question then is, "Which?" It is interesting to note that sometimes what appears to be a slight change in a problem definition makes the difference between a language that is in P and one that is NP-complete. We'll next consider several examples of this phenomenon.

28.7.2 Two Similar Circuit Problems

Consider the two circuit problems:

- EULERIAN-CIRCUIT, in which we check that there is a circuit that visits every *edge* exactly once.
- HAMILTONIAN-CIRCUIT, in which we check that there is a circuit that visits every *vertex* exactly once.

We have already seen that EULERIAN-CIRCUIT is in P, but HAMILTONIAN-CIRCUIT is NP-complete.

28.7.3 Two Similar SAT Problems

Define 2-conjunctive normal form (2-CNF) analogously to 3-conjunctive normal form (3-CNF) except that each clause must contain exactly two literals. So, for example, $(\neg P \vee R) \wedge (S \vee \neg T)$ is in 2-conjunctive normal form. Now consider:

- 2-SAT = {<*w*> : *w* is a wff in Boolean logic, *w* is in 2-conjunctive normal form and *w* is satisfiable}.
- 3-SAT = {<*w*> : *w* is a wff in Boolean logic, *w* is in 3-conjunctive normal form and *w* is satisfiable}.

2-SAT is in P (which we prove in Exercise 28.5a). But 3-SAT is NP-complete.

28.7.4 Two Similar Path Problems:

Consider the problem of finding the *shortest* path with no repeated edges through an unweighted graph *G*. We can convert this to a decision problem by defining the language:

SHORTEST-PATH = {<*G*, *u*, *v*, *k*>: *G* is an unweighted, undirected graph, *u* and *v* are vertices in *G*, $k \geq 0$, and there exists a path from *u* to *v* whose length is at most *k*}.

SHORTEST-PATH is in P because the following simple marking algorithm decides it in $\mathcal{O}(|<G>|^3)$ time:

shortest-path(*G*: graph with vertices *V* and edges *E*, *u*: vertex, *v*: vertex, *k*: integer) =

1. Mark *u*.
2. For $i = 1$ to $min(k, |E|)$ do:

    For each currently marked vertex *n* do:

        For each edge from *n* to some other vertex *m* do:

            Mark *m*.

3. If *v* is marked then accept; else reject.

We should note here that the simple algorithm *shortest-path* works because we are considering only unweighted graphs. So it suffices simply to count the number of edges that are traversed. If, on the other hand, we want to solve the analogous problem for weighted graphs, the problem is more difficult. But even this problem can also be solved efficiently, for example by using Dijkstra's algorithm 💻.

Finding the shortest path through a weighted graph is important in many applications. The obvious ones include finding routes on a map or routing packets through a network. (I.2) But there are many less obvious ones as well, particularly if we allow weighted edges. For example, consider one problem that an optical character recognition (OCR) system must solve: Find the boundaries between letters. One way to think about doing this is that the goal is to find as straight as possible a path that cuts between the regions occupied by two characters and that touches as few black pixels as possible. To solve this problem, we model the boundaries between pixels as vertices and we add edges that cut through the pixels from one boundary to another. We assign a weight of one to every edge that cuts through a white pixel and we assign a very large weight to every edge that cuts through a black pixel. Then the lowest-cost path between two regions is the most direct path that cuts through the fewest black pixels.

But now consider the problem of finding the *longest* path with no repeated edges through an unweighted graph G. We can convert this to a decision problem by defining the language:

LONGEST-PATH = {<G, u, v, k>: G is an unweighted, undirected graph, u and v are vertices in G, $k \geq 0$, and there exists a path with no repeated edges from u to v whose length is at least k}.

LONGEST-PATH is in NP (since a candidate path can be checked in polynomial time). And it can be shown to be NP-complete.

28.7.5 Two Similar Covering Problems:

Recall that a ***vertex cover*** (also called a ***node cover***) C of a graph G is a subset of the vertices of G with the property that every edge of G touches at least one of the vertices in C. Now define an ***edge cover*** C of a graph G to be a subset of the edges of G with the property that every vertex of G is an endpoint of at least one of the edges in C. Consider the graph G shown in Figure 28.15. The set of heavy edges is an edge cover of G. The set of circled vertices is a vertex cover of it.

Consider the problem of finding the smallest *edge* cover of a graph. We can convert this to a decision problem by defining the following language:

EDGE-COVER = {<G, k>: G is an undirected graph and there exists an edge cover of G that contains at most k edges}.

EDGE-COVER can be shown to be in P. (We leave it as an exercise.) But we have proven that the corresponding vertex-cover language is NP-complete:

- VERTEX-COVER = {<G, k>: G is an undirected graph and there exists a vertex cover of G that contains at most k vertices}.

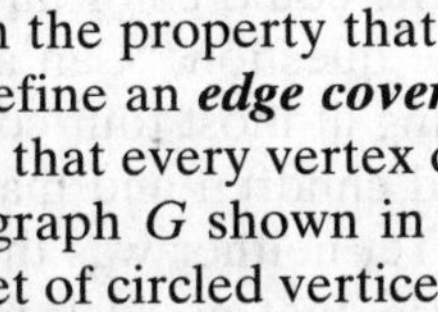

FIGURE 28.15 An edge cover and a vertex cover.

28.7.6 Three Similar Map (Graph) Coloring Problems

Consider the problem of coloring a planar map in such a way that no two adjacent regions (countries, states, or whatever) have the same color. We will allow two regions that share only a single common point to have the same color. So all of the map colorings shown in Figure 28.16 are allowed.

We'll say that a map is ***n-colorable*** or that it can be colored using *n* colors iff it can be colored, according to the rule given above, using no more than *n* distinct colors. Now define the following three languages:

- 2-COLORABLE = {<*m*> : *m* is a 2-colorable map}.
- 3-COLORABLE = {<*m*> : *m* is a 3-colorable map}.
- 4-COLORABLE = {<*m*> : *m* is a 4-colorable map}.

What is the complexity of each of these three languages?

2-COLORABLE is easy. A map is 2-colorable iff it does not contain any point that is the junction of an odd number of regions. We leave the proof of this claim as Exercise 28.21. (The proof of a related claim is given as Exercise A.22.) Map (a) below is 2-colorable. Maps (b) and (c) are not. There is a simple, polynomial-time algorithm to check this requirement. So 2-COLORABLE is in P.

3-COLORABLE 💻 is harder. It can be shown to be NP-complete. We leave the proof of this claim as an exercise.

What about 4-COLORABLE? It turns out that 4-COLORABLE is in P. It can be decided by the trivial algorithm that simply accepts any map that it is given. To see why, we'll sketch the history of the ***4-color problem*** 💻.

In 1852, Francis Guthrie noticed that he could color all the maps he was working with using only four colors. He asked the question, "Can all planar maps be colored (following the rules described above) using at most four colors?" For over a hundred years, the answer to this question eluded children and mathematicians alike. All attempts to find uncolorable maps failed. Yet neither was there a proof of the ***4-color theorem***: the claim, articulated by Guthrie, that no such map exists. A few "proofs" were published, but all were shown to contain flaws.

Then, in 1976, a proof that has stood the test of time was announced by Kenneth Appel and Wolfgang Haken. Interestingly (since we are discussing computation), a computer program played a key role in the development of that proof. Appel and Haken showed that the question of whether all maps are 4-colorable could be reduced to a set of about 1700 special cases. So it remained to check all of them and show that the maps in each case were 4-colorable. Appel and Haken used a computer to do that.

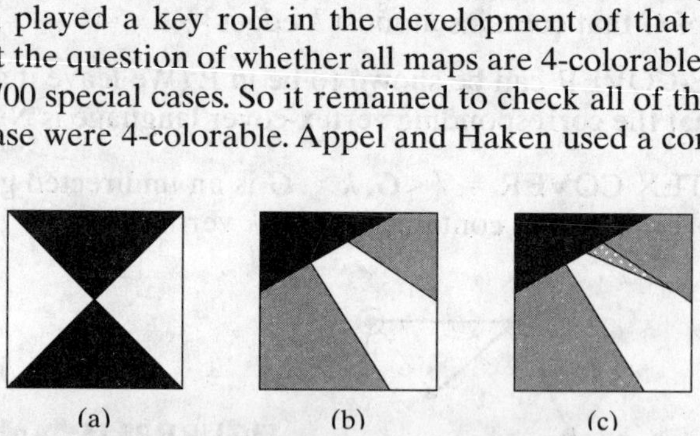

FIGURE 28.16 Legal map colorings.

When their proof was published, there was some concern about the use of a program as part of a proof. What if, for example, the program were incorrect? In the years since the Appel and Haken proof was published, no programming errors have been discovered. Newer, simpler proofs have also been found.

One reason that the 4-color problem is important is that the coloring question applies not just to maps. It applies to a wide range of problems that can be described as graphs. To see why, notice first that a map can be described as an undirected graph in which the vertices correspond to regions and the edges correspond to the adjacency relationships between regions. So there will be an edge between vertices v_1 and v_2 iff the regions that correspond to v_1 and v_2 share a common boundary in the graph. Then the map coloring problem becomes the following graph coloring problem: Given a graph G, assign colors to the vertices of G in such a way that no pair of adjacent vertices are assigned the same color. We can define graph equivalents of the three coloring languages that we defined above.

We will define the ***chromatic number*** of a graph to be the smallest number of colors required to color its vertices, subject to the constraint that no two adjacent vertices may be assigned the same color. In the specific case in which a graph has a chromatic number of two, we'll say that the graph is ***bipartite***.

The 4-color theorem tells us that the chromatic number of any *planar* graph (i.e., one that corresponds to a map on a plane) must be less than five. (More precisely, a graph is ***planar*** iff it can be drawn in such a way that no edges cross.) But, if we do not require planarity, there are graphs of arbitrary chromatic numbers. In particular, any complete graph (i.e., one in which there is an edge between every pair of vertices) with k vertices has the chromatic number k. Define the following language:

CHROMATIC-NUMBER = $\{<G, k> : G$ is an undirected graph whose chromatic number is no more than $k\}$.

CHROMATIC-NUMBER is NP-complete.

> Many optimization problems can be described as graph-coloring problems. We mention two here:
>
> - Consider the problem of scheduling final exams in such a way that no two classes that have any common students share an exam time. We can represent the problem as a graph in which there is a vertex for each class. There is an edge between every pair of classes that share at least one student. Then the number of required exam slots is the chromatic number of that graph.
> - Consider the problem of assigning trains to platforms. Clearly no two trains can be assigned to the same platform at the same time. We can represent the problem as a graph in which there is a vertex for each train. There is an edge between every pair of trains that are scheduled to be in the station at the same time. Then the number of required platforms is the chromatic number of that graph.

Note that CHROMATIC-NUMBER and INDEPENDENT-SET are related. CHROMATIC-NUMBER relates a graph G to the number of distinct colors that are required to color it. INDEPENDENT-SET relates G to the largest number of vertices that can be colored with a single color. So, for example, if the exam scheduling problem were described as an instance of INDEPENDENT-SET, we'd be asking about the maximum number of classes that could share a single exam time.

28.7.7 Two Similar Linear Programming Problems:

Linear programming problems are optimization problems in which both the objective function and the constraints that must be satisfied are linear. We can cast the linear programming problem as a language to be decided by defining:

LINEAR-PROGRAMMING = {<a set of linear inequalities $Ax \leq b$> : there exists a vector X of rational numbers that satisfies all of the inequalities}.

> Linear programming is used routinely to solve industrial resource allocation problems.

The simplex algorithm, invented by George Dantzig in 1947, solves linear programming problems (by finding the vector X if it exists). In the worst case, it may require exponential time. But, in practice, it is highly effective and substantial work over the years since its invention has further improved its performance. For example, we mentioned in the introduction to Chapter 27 that it can be used to solve large instances of the traveling salesman problem. Without a decision procedure that could be guaranteed to halt in polynomial time, however, the question of whether LINEAR-PROGRAMMING was in P remained open. In 1979, Leonid Khachian answered the question by exhibiting a new, polynomial time, linear-programming algorithm. Unfortunately, his algorithm performed worse in practice than did the simplex algorithm, so it remained of only theoretical interest. Then, in 1984, Narendra Karmarkar described a polynomial-time, linear-programming algorithm [Karmarkar 1984] that works well in practice. Both the simplex algorithm and a variety of techniques based on Karmarkar's algorithm are commonly used today.

But now consider a slightly different problem in which we require that a solution be a vector of integers (as opposed to arbitrary rationals). We can describe this problem as the language:

INTEGER-PROGRAMMING = {<a set of linear inequalities $Ax \leq b$> : there exists an integer vector X that satisfies all of the inequalities}.

INTEGER-PROGRAMMING is known to be NP-complete.

28.7.8 A Hierarchy of Diophantine Equation Problems

A Diophantine equation is a polynomial equation in any number of variables, all with integer coefficients. A Diophantine problem then is, "Given a system of Diophantine equations, does it have an integer solution?" Depending on the restrictions that are imposed on the form of a particular problem, it may be undecidable, decidable but intractable, or tractable (i.e., decidable in polynomial time).

- The general Diophantine problem is undecidable, as we saw in Section 22.1.
- If the problem is restricted to equations of the form $ax^2 + by = c$, where a, b, and c are positive integers and we ask whether there exist integer values of x and y that satisfy the equation, then the problem becomes decidable. But it is NP-complete.
- If the problem is restricted to systems in which all the variables are of degree (exponent) 1 or to equations of a single variable of the form $ax^k = c$, and again we ask for integer values of the variable(s), then it is in P.

28.8 The Language Class Co-NP ✸

Given a language L that is in NP, can we say anything about whether $\neg L$ is also in NP? Recall that we are defining the complement of a language to be taken with respect to the universe of strings with the correct syntax whenever it is possible to determine that in polynomial time. So, for example, ¬TSP-DECIDE = {w of the form: <G, *cost*>, where <G> encodes an undirected graph with a positive distance attached to each of its edges and <G> does *not* contain a Hamiltonian circuit whose total cost is less than *cost*}. Is ¬TSP-DECIDE ∈ NP? It is not obviously so. For example, the simple technique we used to prove Theorem 28.1 (that the class P is closed under complement) won't work here. We cannot simply swap accepting and nonaccepting states since, if there were some accepting paths and some rejecting paths, there would then still be some accepting paths and some rejecting ones. So the new machine would accept some strings that are also accepted by the original one. Because the decidable languages are closed under complement, we know that we can build a Turing machine to decide ¬TSP-DECIDE. But the obvious way to do so requires that we explore *all* candidate paths in order to verify that none of them is acceptable. Since the number of candidate paths is $\mathcal{O}(|\text{<}G\text{>}|!)$, we cannot do that in polynomial time. No alternative approach is known to do significantly better. In other words, no nondeterministic polynomial time algorithm to decide ¬TSP-DECIDE is known.

In order to have a place to put ¬TSP-DECIDE, we define the class co-NP (i.e., the complement of some element of NP) as follows:

The Class co-NP: $L \in$ co-NP iff $\neg L \in$ NP.

Another way to think about the relationship between NP and co-NP is the following:

- A language L is in NP iff a qualifying certificate, i.e., one that proves that an input string w is in L, can be checked efficiently.
- A language L is in co-NP iff a disqualifying certificate, i.e., one that proves that an input string w is not in L, can be checked efficiently. For example, a string of the

form <*G*, *cost*> is not in ¬TSP-DECIDE if there exists even one Hamiltonian circuit through *G* whose cost is less than *cost*. Checking such a proposed circuit can easily be done in polynomial time.

EXAMPLE 28.2 Two Co-NP Languages: UNSAT and VALID

Two important languages based on properties of Boolean formulas are in co-NP:

- UNSAT = {<w> : w is a wff in Boolean logic and w is not satisfiable}. UNSAT is the complement of SAT (since we are taking complements with respect to the universe of well-formed expressions).
- VALID = {<w> : w is a wff in Boolean logic and w is valid}. Recall that a wff is valid (equivalently, is a tautology) iff it is true for all assignments of truth values to the variables it contains. So w is valid iff $\neg w$ is not satisfiable. Thus we can determine whether a string w is in VALID by constructing the string $\neg w$ (which can be done in constant time) and then checking whether $\neg w$ is in UNSAT.

No one knows whether NP is closed under complement. In other words, we do not know whether NP = co-NP. For a variety of reasons, it is generally believed that NP ≠ co-NP. We state two such reasons in the next two theorems.

THEOREM 28.25 If NP ≠ Co-NP then P ≠ NP

Theorem: If NP ≠ co-NP then P ≠ NP.

Proof: From Theorem 28.1, we know that the class P is closed under complement. If P = NP, then NP must also be closed under complement. If NP ≠ co-NP then NP is not closed under complement. So it cannot equal P.

We do not know whether NP = co-NP implies that P = NP. It is possible that NP = co-NP but that that class is nevertheless larger than P.

THEOREM 28.26 NP = Co-NP Iff There is Some NP-Complete Language whose Complement is also in NP

Theorem: NP = co-NP iff there exists some language L such that L is NP-complete and $\neg L$ is also in NP.

Proof: We prove the two directions of the claim separately:

If NP = co-NP then there exists some language* L *such that* L *is NP-complete and ¬L is also in NP: There exists at least one language L (for example, SAT) that is NP-complete. By definition, $\neg L$ is in co-NP. If NP $=$ co-NP then $\neg L$ must also be in NP.

If there exists some language* L *such that* L *is NP-complete and* ¬*L is also in NP then NP = co-NP: Suppose that some language L is NP-complete and $\neg L$ is also in NP. Then we can show that NP $\subseteq$ co-NP and co-NP $\subseteq$ NP:

- NP $\subseteq$ co-NP: Let L_1 be any language in NP. Since, by assumption, L is NP-complete, there exists a polynomial-time reduction R from L_1 to L. R is also a polynomial time reduction from $\neg L_1$ to $\neg L$. Since, by assumption, $\neg L$ is in NP, there exists a nondeterministic polynomial-time Turing machine M that decides it. So we can decide $\neg L_1$ in nondeterministic polynomial time by first running R and then running M. So $\neg L_1$ is in NP and its complement, L_1, is in co-NP. Thus every language in NP is also in co-NP.
- co-NP $\subseteq$ NP: Let L_1 be any language in co-NP. Then $\neg L_1$ is in NP. Since, by assumption, L is NP-complete, there exists a polynomial-time reduction R from $\neg L_1$ to L. R is also a reduction from L_1 to $\neg L$. Since, by assumption, $\neg L$ is in NP, there exists a nondeterministic polynomial-time Turing machine M that decides it. So we can decide L_1 in nondeterministic polynomial time by first running R and then M. So L_1 is in NP. Thus every language in co-NP is also in NP.

Despite substantial effort, no one has yet found a single language that can be proven to be NP-complete and whose complement can be proven to be in NP.

28.9 The Time Hierarchy Theorems, EXPTIME, and Beyond

To prove that a language L has an efficient decision procedure, it suffices to exhibit such a procedure, prove its correctness, and analyze its complexity. In general, proving that *no* efficient decision procedure exists is much more difficult. We know however, that there exist some languages that are inherently hard. We know this for two reasons:

- There exists a set of hierarchy theorems that show that adding resources (in terms of either time or space) increases the set of languages that can be decided.
- There exist some specific decidable languages that can be shown to be hard in the sense that no efficient algorithm to decide them exists.

In the next section, we'll describe the hierarchy theorems and their implications. Then we will define one new (and larger) time-complexity class and consider one example of a naturally-occurring language that can be shown to be very hard.

28.9.1 Time Hierarchy Theorems ✸

There exist two time hierarchy theorems. They formalize the intuitive notion that, as we allow a Turing machine to use more and more time, the set of languages that can be decided grows. So, for any fixed time bound, there must be decidable languages that can be decided within the bound but that cannot be decided using "substantially less" time. One of the theorems applies to deterministic Turing machines; the other applies to nondeterministic ones. There is also a corresponding pair of space hierarchy theorems that make the same case for what happens as the amount of space that can be used grows.

The hierarchy theorems are important. In particular, they tell us that, while it is possible that particular pairs of complexity classes may collapse, it is not possible that all of them do. There are time complexity classes that properly contain other ones (and similarly for space complexity classes). Unfortunately, there are two kinds of important questions that the hierarchy theorems cannot answer:

- They do not tell us what languages lie where in the hierarchy. They are proved by diagonalization so they show only that some language must exist. They are not constructive.
- They do not relate deterministic complexity classes to nondeterministic ones. So, for example, they say nothing about whether P = NP. They also do not relate time complexity classes to space complexity classes (such as the ones we will define in the next chapter).

We would like to be able to show that *any* increase in the amount of time that is allowed increases the set of languages that can be decided. Unfortunately, we cannot prove that that is true. The strongest statement that we can prove is that increasing the amount of time by at least a logarithmic factor makes a difference.

We will state and prove the deterministic version of the time hierarchy theorems. The nondeterministic version is similar. The proof that we will do will be by construction of a Turing machine that can do the following two things:

- Compute the value of a *timereq* function, on a given input, and store that value, in binary, on its tape.
- Efficiently simulate another Turing machine for a specified number of steps.

Before we state the theorem and give its complete proof, we'll discuss how to do each of those things.

Time-Constructible Functions

Our goal will be to show that, given a function $t(n)$, there exists some language $L_{t(n)hard}$ that can be decided in $t(n)$ time but not in "substantially less" time. (We'll soon see that "substantially less" will mean by a factor of $1/\log t(n)$.) So we will want to be able to conduct a simulation for at most $t(n)/\log t(n)$ steps. We could do that if we could compute $t(n)$ and write it on the simulator's tape. Then we could divide that number by $\log t(n)$ and use that number as a counter, decrementing it by one for each simulated step and quitting, even if the simulation hasn't yet halted, if the counter ever reaches zero. We will need an efficient representation of $t(n)$'s value. We could choose to use any base other than one. We will choose to represent the value in binary. So what we need is the ability to compute $t(n)$ and store the result in binary. Since n is the length of some Turing machine's input, we can think of that input as though all of its symbols were 1's.

So we can compute $t(n)$ if we can map the string 1^n to the binary representation of $t(n)$. We need this computation not to dominate the simulation itself. So we will require that it be able to be done in $\mathcal{O}(t(n))$ time. So define a function $t(n)$ from the positive integers to the positive integers to be ***time-constructible*** iff:

- $t(n)$ is at least $\mathcal{O}(n \log n)$, and
- the function that maps the unary representation of n (i.e., 1^n) to the binary representation of $t(n)$ can be computed in $\mathcal{O}(t(n))$ time.

Most useful functions, as long as they are at least $\mathcal{O}(n \log n)$, are time-constructible. For example, all polynomial functions that are at least $\mathcal{O}(n \log n)$ are time-constructible. So are $n \log n$, $n\sqrt{n}$, 2^n, and $n!$.

Efficient Bounded Simulation

The proof that we are about to do depends critically on the ability to perform a bounded simulation of one Turing machine by another and to do so efficiently. Any overhead that occurs as part of the simulation will weaken the claim that we are going to be able to make about the impact of additional time on our ability to decide additional languages (because time that gets spent on simulation overhead doesn't get spent doing real work).

The universal Turing machine that we described in Section 17.7 simulates the computation of an arbitrary Turing machine M on an arbitrary input w. But it uses three tapes. If we simply convert that three-tape machine to a one-tape machine as described in Section 17.3.1, then a computation that took $t(n)$ steps on the three-tape machine will take $\mathcal{O}(t(n)^2)$ steps on the corresponding one-tape machine. We can do better. If we look again at the way that the construction of Section 17.3.1 works, we observe that the new, one-tape machine spends most of its time scanning the simulated tapes. First it scans to collect the values under all of the read/write heads. And then it scans again to update each tape in the neighborhood of its read/write head. The fact that the length of any of the tapes may grow as $\mathcal{O}(t(n))$ is what adds the $\mathcal{O}(t(n))$ factor to the time required by the simulation. We can avoid that overhead if we can describe a simulator that uses multiple tapes but that manages them in such a way that it is no longer necessary to scan the length of each tape at each step.

We are about to describe a simulator *BSim* that does that. *BSim* also differs from the universal Turing machine in that it takes a third parameter, a time bound b. It will simulate a machine M on input w for b steps or until M halts, whichever comes first. *BSim* is otherwise like the universal Turing machine that we have already described. In particular, we will assume that the Turing machine that *BSim* simulates is encoded as for the universal Turing machine. This assumption guarantees that *BSim* can simulate any Turing machine, regardless of the size of its tape alphabet.

BSim accepts as input a Turing machine M, an input string w, and a time bound b. It uses a single tape that is divided into three tracks. (As in the construction in Section 17.3.1, multiple tracks can be represented on a single tape by using a tape alphabet that contains one symbol for each possible ordered 3-tuple of track values.) The three tracks will be used as follows:

- Track 1 will hold the current value of M's tape, along with an indication of where its read/write head is.

- Track 2 will hold *M*'s current state followed by *M*'s description (i.e., its transition function).
- Track 3 will hold a counter that is initially set to be the time bound *b*. As each step of *M* is simulated, the counter will be decremented by 1. The simulation will halt if the counter ever reaches 0 (or if *M* naturally halts).

The key to *BSim*'s efficiency is that it will keep the contents of its three tracks lined up so that it can find what it needs by examining only a small slice through the tracks. Suppose that the tracks are as shown in Figure 28.17. The position of *M*'s read/write head is shown as a character in bold.

Each time it needs to make a move, *BSim* needs to check one square on track 1. It also needs to check *M*'s state and it needs to examine *M*'s transition function in order to discover what to do. Because of the way that the tracks are lined up, it can do all of these things by scanning its tape starting in the position shown in bold (i.e., the square that corresponds to the current location of *M*'s read/write head). The number of squares that it must examine on track 2 is a function of the length of *M*'s description, not the length of its input *w* or its working tape. So *BSim* can determine *M*'s next move in $\mathcal{O}(|<M>|)$ steps.

To make *M*'s next move, *BSim* must then:

- Update track 1 as specified by *M*'s transition function. Doing this requires moving at most one square on track 1, so it takes constant time.
- Update *M*'s state on track 2. Doing this requires time that is a function of the length of the state description, which is bounded by $|<M>|$. So it takes $\mathcal{O}(|<M>|)$ time.
- Move the contents of track 2 one square to the right or to the left, depending on which way *M*'s read/write head moved. Doing this takes time that is a function only of *M*. So it also takes $\mathcal{O}(|<M>|)$ time.

All that remains is to describe how *BSim* considers *b*, the bound it has been given. Track 3 contains a counter that has been initialized to a string that corresponds to the binary encoding of *b*. At each of *M*'s steps, *BSim* must:

- Decrement the counter by 1 and check for 0.
- Shift the counter left or right one square so that it remains lined up with *M*'s read/write head. The number of steps required to do this is a function of the length of the counter. The maximum value of the counter is the original bound, *b*. Since the counter is represented in binary, its maximum length is log *b*. So this step takes log *b* time.

BSim runs *M* for no more than *b* steps. Each step takes $\mathcal{O}(|<M>|)$ time to do the computation plus $\mathcal{O}(\log b)$ time to manage the counter. So *BSim* can simulate *b* steps of *M* in $\mathcal{O}(b \cdot (|<M>| + \log b))$ time.

Track 1:	a	b	a	a	b	b	b	**b**	b	a	a	a	a	a	a	b	b	b	a	a	a	a	b	b	b				
Track 2:								*state*, <*M*>																					
Track 3:								*counter*																					

FIGURE 28.17 Lining up the tapes for efficiency.

The Deterministic Time-Hierarchy Theorem

The Deterministic Time-Hierarchy Theorem tells us that changing the amount of available time by a logarithmic factor makes a difference in what can be done. As we'll see, the logarithmic factor comes from the fact that the best technique we have for bounded simulation (as described above) introduces a logarithmic overhead factor. We'll state the theorem precisely using both $\mathcal{O}$ and σ notation. Recall that $f(n) \in \sigma(g(n))$ iff, for every positive c, there exists a positive integer k such that $\forall n \geq k\,(f(n) < c\,g(n))$. In other words, for all but some finite number k of small values, $f(n) < c\,g(n)$.

THEOREM 28.27 Deterministic Time Hierarchy Theorem

Theorem: For any time-constructible function $t(n)$, there exists a language $L_{t(n)hard}$ that is deterministically decidable in $\mathcal{O}(t(n))$ time but that is not deterministically decidable in $\sigma(t(n)/\log t(n))$ time.

Proof: To prove this claim, we will present a technique that, given a function $t(n)$, finds a language $L_{t(n)hard}$ that has the properties that we seek. We'll define $L_{t(n)hard}$ by describing a Turing machine that decides it in $\mathcal{O}(t(n))$ time. So the first requirement will obviously be met. The only thing that remains is to design it so that any other Turing machine that decides it takes at least $t(n)/\log t(n)$ time. We'll use diagonalization to do that. In particular, we'll make sure that the Turing machine that decides $L_{t(n)hard}$ behaves differently, on at least one input, than any Turing machine that runs in $\sigma(t(n)/\log t(n))$ time.

$L_{t(n)hard}$ will be a language of Turing machine descriptions with a simple string consisting of a single 1 and then a string of 0's tacked on to the right. More specifically, every string in $L_{t(n)hard}$ will have the form <*M*>10*. The job of the appendage is to guarantee that L contains some arbitrarily long strings.

The rest of the definition of $L_{t(n)hard}$ is difficult to state in words. Instead, we will define $L_{t(n)hard}$ by describing a Turing machine $M_{t(n)hard}$ that decides it:

$M_{t(n)hard}(w) =$

1. Let n be $|w|$. Compute $t(n)$. Store the result, in binary, on the tape.
2. Divide that number by $\log t(n)$. Store $\lceil t(n)/\log t(n) \rceil$, in binary, on the tape. Call this number b.
3. Check to see that w is of the form <*M*>10*. If it is not, reject.
4. Check that |<*M*>| $< \log b$. If it is not, reject.
5. Reformat the tape into the three tracks required by *BSim*. To do this, leave w on track 1. Copy M's start state and <*M*> to track 2 starting at the left end of w. Copy b to track 3, also starting at the left end of w.
6. Run *BSim*. In other words, simulate M on w (which is of the form <*M*> 10*) for $\lceil t(n)/\log t(n) \rceil$ steps.
7. If M did not halt in that time, reject.
8. If M did halt and it accepted, reject.
9. If M did halt and it rejected, accept.

The key feature of the way that $M_{t(n)hard}$ is defined is the following: Whenever it runs a simulation to completion, it does exactly the opposite of what the machine it just simulated would have done.

We need to show that $L_{t(n)hard}$, the language accepted by $M_{t(n)hard}$, can be decided in $\mathcal{O}(t(n))$ time and that it cannot be decided (by some other Turing machine) in $o(t(n)/\log t(n))$ time.

We'll first show that $M_{t(n)hard}$ runs in $\mathcal{O}(t(n))$ time. In a nutshell, on input $<M, 10^*>$, $M_{t(n)hard}$ uses its time to simulate $t(n)/\log t(n)$ steps of M, using $\mathcal{O}(\log t(n))$ time for each one. We can analyze it in more detail as follows: Step 1 can be done in $\mathcal{O}(t(n))$ time since $t(n)$ is time-constructible. Step 2 can also be done in $\mathcal{O}(t(n))$ time. Step 3 can be done in linear time if we just check the most basic syntax. It isn't necessary, for example, to make sure that all the states in M are numbered sequentially, even though our description of our encoding scheme specifies that. Step 4 can be done in $\mathcal{O}(t(n))$ time. The point of this check is to make sure that the cost of running the simulation in step 6 is dominated by the total length of w, not by the length of $<M>$. Step 5 can be done in linear time.

The core of $M_{t(n)hard}$ is step 6. On input (M, w, b), *BSim* requires $\mathcal{O}(b \cdot (|<M>| + \log b))$ time. But we have guaranteed (in step 4) that $|<M>| < \log b$. So *BSim* requires $\mathcal{O}(b \log b)$ time. We set b, the number of steps to be simulated, to $t(n)/\log t(n)$. Each simulation step will take $\mathcal{O}(\log t(n))$ time. So the total simulation time will be $\mathcal{O}(t(n))$. Giving a bit more detail, notice that, since b is $t(n)/\log t(n)$, we have:

$$timereq(BSim) \in \mathcal{O}\left(\frac{t(n) \cdot \log(t(n)/\log t(n))}{\log t(n)}\right).$$

Since $t(n) > 1$, we have that $timereq(BSim) \in \mathcal{O}(t(n))$. Steps 7, 8, and 9 take constant time. So $M_{t(n)hard}$ runs in $\mathcal{O}(t(n))$ time.

Now we must show that there is no other Turing machine that decides $L_{t(n)hard}$ substantially more efficiently than $M_{t(n)hard}$ does. Specifically, we must show that no such machine does so in time that is $o(t(n)/\log t(n))$. Suppose that there were such a machine. We'll call it $M_{t(n)easy}$. For any constant c, $M_{t(n)easy}$ must, on all inputs of length greater than some constant k, halt in no more than $c \cdot t(n)/\log t(n)$ steps. So, in particular, we can let c be 1. Then, on all inputs of length greater than some constant k, $M_{t(n)easy}$ must halt in fewer than $t(n)/\log t(n)$ steps.

What we are going to do is to show that $M_{t(n)easy}$ is not in fact a decider for $L_{t(n)hard}$ because it is not equivalent to $M_{t(n)hard}$. We can do that if we can show even one string on which the two machines return different results. That string will be $w = <M_{t(n)easy}> 10^p$, for a particular value of p that we will choose so that:

- $|<M_{t(n)easy}>|$ is short relative to the entire length of w. Let n be $|<M_{t(n)easy}> 10^p|$. Then, more specifically, it must be the case that $|<M_{t(n)easy}>| < \log(t(n)/\log t(n))$. We require this so that $M_{t(n)hard}$ will not reject in step 4. Remember that $M_{t(n)hard}$ checks for this condition in order to guarantee that, when *BSim* runs, the overhead, at each step, of managing the counter dominates the overhead of scanning M's description. Let m be $|<M_{t(n)easy}>|$. Then this condition will be satisfied if p is at least 2^{2^m}. (We leave as an exercise the proof that this value works.)

- $|w| > k$. On input $w = <M_{t(n)easy}> 10^p$, $M_{t(n)hard}$ will simulate $M_{t(n)easy}$ on w for $t(|w|)/\log t(|w|)$ steps. For inputs of length at least k, $M_{t(n)easy}$ is guaranteed to halt within that many steps. That means that $M_{t(n)hard}$ will do exactly the opposite of what $M_{t(n)easy}$ does. Thus the two machines are not identical. This condition is satisfied if p is at least k.

So let p be the larger of k and 2^{2^m}. On input $w = <M_{t(n)easy}> 10^p$, the simulation of $M_{t(n)easy}$ on $<M_{t(n)easy}> 10^p$ will run to completion. If $M_{t(n)easy}$ accepts, $M_{t(n)hard}$ rejects. And vice versa. This contradicts the assumption that $M_{t(n)easy}$ decides $L_{t(n)hard}$.

One consequence of the Deterministic Time Hierarchy Theorem is the claim that we made at the beginning of this chapter, namely that the polynomial time complexity classes do not collapse. There are languages that are deterministically decidable in $\mathcal{O}(n^2)$ time but not in linear time. And there are languages that are deterministically decidable in $\mathcal{O}(n^{2000})$ but not in $\mathcal{O}(n^{1999})$ time. So there are languages that are in P but that are not tractable in any useful sense.

Another consequence is that there are languages that are deterministically decidable in exponential time but not in polynomial time.

28.9.2 EXPTIME

In Section 28.5.1, we suggested that there are languages that are NP-hard but that cannot be shown to be NP-complete because they cannot be shown to be in NP. The example that we mentioned was:

- CHESS = {<b>: b is a configuration of an $n \times n$ chess board and there is a guaranteed win for the current player}.

We can describe the complexity of CHESS, other "interesting" games like Go, and many other apparently very difficult languages, by defining the class EXPTIME as follows:

The Class EXPTIME: For any language L, $L \in$ EXPTIME iff there exists some deterministic Turing machine M that decides L and $timereq(M) \in \mathcal{O}(2^{(n^k)})$ for some positive integer k.

We show that a language is in EXPTIME by exhibiting an algorithm that decides it in exponential time. We sketch such an algorithm for chess (and other two person games) in N.2.5. In general, if we can describe an algorithm that decides L by exploring *all* of the paths in a tree whose size grows exponentially with the size of the input, then L is in EXPTIME.

As we did for the class NP, we can define a class of equally hard EXPTIME languages. So we consider two properties that a language L might possess:

1. L is in EXPTIME.
2. Every language in EXPTIME is deterministic, polynomial-time reducible to L.

We'll say that a language is ***EXPTIME-hard*** iff it possesses property 2. If, in addition, it possesses property 1, we'll say that it is ***EXPTIME-complete***. In N.2.3, we'll return to a discussion of the complexity of CHESS. If we make the assumption that, as we add rows and columns to the chess board, we also add pieces, then CHESS can be shown to be EXPTIME-complete.

In Section 29.2, we will define another important complexity class, this time based on space, rather than time, requirements. The class PSPACE contains exactly those languages that can be decided by a deterministic Turing machine whose space requirement grows as some polynomial function of its input. We can summarize what is known about the space complexity classes P, NP, and EXPTIME, as well as the space complexity class PSPACE as follows:

- $\text{P} \subseteq \text{NP} \subseteq \text{PSPACE} \subseteq \text{EXPTIME}$.

It is not known which of these inclusions is proper. However, it follows from the Deterministic Time Hierarchy Theorem that $\text{P} \neq \text{EXPTIME}$. So at least one of them is. It is thought that all of them are.

A consequence of the fact that $\text{P} \neq \text{EXPTIME}$ is that we know that there are decidable problems for which no efficient (i.e., polynomial time) decision procedure exists. In particular, this must be true for every EXPTIME-complete problem. So, for example, CHESS is provably intractable in the sense that no polynomial-time algorithm for it exists. Practical solutions for EXPTIME-complete problems must exploit techniques like the approximation algorithms that we describe in Chapter 30.

28.9.3 Harder Than EXPTIME Problems

Some problems are even harder than the EXPTIME-complete problems, such as CHESS. We will mention one example.

Recall that, in Section 22.4.2, we proved that the language $\text{FOL}_{\text{theorem}} = \{<A, w>: A$ is a decidable set of axioms in first-order logic, w is a sentence in first-order logic, and w is entailed by $A\}$ is not decidable. The proof relied on the fact that there exists at least one specific first-order theory that is not decidable. In particular, it relied on the theory of Peano arithmetic, which describes the natural numbers with the functions *plus* and *times*.

The fact that not all first-order theories are decidable does not mean that none of them is. In particular, we have mentioned the theory of Presburger arithmetic, a theory of the natural numbers with just the function *plus*. Presburger arithmetic is decidable. Unfortunately, it is intractable. [Fischer and Rabin 1974] showed that any algorithm that decides whether a sentence is a theorem of Presburger arithmetic must have time complexity at least $\mathcal{O}(2^{2^{cn}})$.

28.10 The Problem Classes FP and FNP ◆

Recall that:

- A language L that corresponds to a decision problem Q is in P iff there is deterministic polynomial time algorithm that decides, given an arbitrary input x, whether $x \in L$.
- A language L that corresponds to a decision problem Q is in NP iff there is a deterministic polynomial time verifier that decides, given an arbitrary input x and a certificate c, whether c is a certificate for x. Equivalently, L is in NP iff there is a nondeterministic polynomial time algorithm that decides, given an arbitrary input x, whether there exists a certificate for x.

Now suppose that, instead of restricting our attention to decision problems, we wish to be able to characterize the complexity of functions whose result may of any type (for example, the integers). What we'll actually do is to go one step farther, and define the following complexity classes for arbitrary binary relations.

The Class FP: A binary relation Q is in FP iff there is deterministic polynomial time algorithm that, given an arbitrary input x, can find some y such that $(x, y) \in Q$.

The Class FNP: A binary relation Q is in FNP iff there is a deterministic polynomial time verifier that, given an arbitrary input pair (x, y), determines whether $(x, y) \in Q$. Equivalently, Q is in FNP iff there is a nondeterministic polynomial time algorithm that, given an arbitrary input x, can find some y such that $(x, y) \in Q$.

FP is the functional/relational analog of P: If a relation Q is in FP then it is possible, in deterministic polynomial time, given a value x, to find a value y such that (x, y) is in Q. FNP is the functional/relational analog of NP: If a relation Q is in FNP then it is possible, in deterministic polynomial time, to determine whether a particular ordered pair (x, y) is in Q.

As before, checking all values is at least as hard as checking a single value. So we have:

$$\text{FP} \subseteq \text{FNP}.$$

But are they equal? The answer is that FP = FNP iff P = NP.

In Section 28.5, we said that a language is NP-hard iff all other languages in NP are deterministic, polynomial time reducible to it. It is also common to apply the term "NP-hard" to functions. In this case, we'll say that a function is ***NP-hard*** iff its corresponding decision problem is NP-hard. So, for example:

- The language TSP-DECIDE = {<*G*, *cost*> : <*G*> encodes an undirected graph with a positive distance attached to each of its edges and *G* contains a Hamiltonian circuit whose total cost is less than *cost*} is NP-complete (and thus NP-hard). So the function that determines the cost of the lowest cost Hamiltonian circuit in *G* is NP-hard.
- Recall that the chromatic number of a graph is the smallest number of colors required to color its vertices, subject to the constraint that no two adjacent vertices may be assigned the same color. We defined the language CHROMATIC-NUMBER = {<*G*, *k*> : *G* is an undirected graph whose chromatic number is no

more than k}. It is NP-complete. So the function that maps a graph to its chromatic number is NP-hard.

There are, however problems for which the decision version (i.e., a language to be decided) is easy, yet the function version remains hard. Probably the most important of these is the following:

- The language PRIMES = $\{w : w$ is the binary encoding of a prime number$\}$ is in P. But the problem of finding the factors of a composite number has no known polynomial time solution.

Exercises

1. In Section 28.1.5, we described the Seven Bridges of Königsberg problem. Consider the following modification:

The good prince lives in the castle. He wants to be able to return home from the pub (on one of the islands as shown above) and cross every bridge exactly once along the way. But he wants to make sure that his evil twin, who lives on the other river bank, is unable to cross every bridge exactly once on his way home from the pub. The good prince is willing to invest in building one new bridge in order to make his goal achievable. Where should he build his bridge?

2. Consider the language NONEULERIAN = {<G> : G is an undirected graph and G does not contain an Eulerian circuit}.
   a. Show an example of a connected graph with 8 vertices that is in NONEULERIAN.
   b. Prove that NONEULERIAN is in P.

3. Show that each of the following languages is in P.
   a. WWW = $\{www: w \in \{\text{a}, \text{b}\}^*\}$
   b. {<M, w> : Turing machine M halts on w within 3 steps}
   c. EDGE-COVER = {<G, k>: G is an undirected graph and there exists an edge cover of G that contains at most k edges}

4. In the proof of Theorem B.2, we present the algorithm *3-conjunctiveBoolean*, which, given a Boolean wff w, constructs a new wff w', where w' is in 3-CNF.

a. We claimed that w' is satisfiable iff w is. Prove that claim.
b. Prove that *3-conjunctiveBoolean* runs in polynomial time.

5. Consider the language 2-SAT = $\{<w> : w$ is a wff in Boolean logic, w is in 2-conjunctive normal form and w is satisfiable$\}$.
a. Prove that 2-SAT is in P. (*Hint*: Use resolution, as described in B.1.2.).
b. Why cannot your proof from part a be extended to show that 3-SAT is in P?
c. Now consider a modification of 2-SAT that might, at first, seem even easier, since it may not require all of the clauses of w to be simultaneously satisfied. Let 2-SAT-MAX = $\{<w, k> : w$ is a wff in Boolean logic, w is in 2-conjunctive normal form, $1 \leq k \leq |C|$, where $|C|$ is the number of clauses in w, and there exists an assignment of values to the variables of w that simultaneously satisfies at least k of the clauses in $w\}$. Show that 2-SAT-MAX is NP-complete.

6. In Chapter 9, we showed that all of the questions that we posed about regular languages are decidable. We'll see, in Section 29.3.3, that while decidable, some straightforward questions about the regular languages appear to be hard. Some are easy however. Show that each of the following languages is in P.
a. DFSM-ACCEPT = $\{<M, w> : M$ is a DFSM and $w \in L(M)\}$
b. FSM-EMPTY = $\{<M> : M$ is a FSM and $L(M) = \varnothing\}$
c. DFSM-ALL = $\{<M> : M$ is a DFSM and $L(M) = \Sigma^*\}$

7. We proved (in Theorem 28.1) that P is closed under complement. Prove that it is also closed under:
a. union.
b. concatenation.
c. Kleene star.

8. It is not known whether NP is closed under complement. But prove that it is closed under:
a. union.
b. concatenation.
c. Kleene star.

9. If L_1 and L_2 are in P and $L_1 \subseteq L \subseteq L_2$, must L be in P? Prove your answer.

10. Show that each of the following languages is NP-complete by first showing that it is in NP and then showing that it is NP-hard.
a. CLIQUE = $\{<G, k> : G$ is an undirected graph with vertices V and edges E, k is an integer, $1 \leq k \leq |V|$, and G contains a k-clique$\}$.
b. SUBSET-SUM = $\{<S, k> : S$ is a multiset (i.e., duplicates are allowed) of integers, k is an integer, and there exists some subset of S whose elements sum to $k\}$
c. SET-PARTITION = $\{<S> : S$ is a multiset (i.e., duplicates are allowed) of objects, each of which has an associated cost, and there exists a way to divide S into two subsets, A and $S - A$, such that the sum of the costs of the elements in A equals the sum of the costs of the elements in $S - A\}$.
d. KNAPSACK = $\{<S, v, c> : S$ is a set of objects each of which has an associated cost and an associated value, v and c are integers, and there exists some way of choosing elements of S (duplicates allowed) such that the total cost of the chosen objects is at most c and their total value is at least $v\}$

e. LONGEST-PATH = {<G, u, v, k>: G is an unweighted, undirected graph, u, and v are vertices in G, $k \geq 0$, and there exists a path with no repeated edges from u to v whose length is at least k}

f. BOUNDED-PCP = {<P, k> : P is an instance of the Post Correspondence problem that has a solution of length less than or equal to k}

11. Let USAT = {<w> : w is a wff in Boolean logic and w has exactly one satisfying assignment}. Does the following nondeterministic, polynomial-time algorithm decide USAT? Explain your answer.

decideUSAT(<w>) =

1. Nondeterministically select an assignment x of values to the variables in w.
2. If x does not satisfy w, reject.
3. Else nondeterministically select another assignment $y \neq x$.
4. If y satisfies w, reject.
5. Else accept.

12. Ordered binary decision diagrams (OBDDs) are useful in manipulating Boolean formulas such as the ones in the language SAT. They are described in B.1.3. Consider the Boolean function f_1 shown there. Using the variable ordering ($x_3<x_1<x_2$), build a decision tree for f. Show the (reduced) OBDD that *createOBDDfromtree* will create for that tree.

13. Complete the proof of Theorem 28.18 by showing how to modify the proof of Theorem 28.16 so that R constructs a formula in conjunctive normal form.

14. Show that, if P = NP, then there exists a deterministic, polynomial-time algorithm that finds a satisfying assignment for a Boolean formula if one exists.

15. Let R be the reduction from 3-SAT to VERTEX-COVER that we defined in the proof of Theorem 28.20. Show the graph that R builds when given the Boolean formula, $(\neg P \vee Q \vee T) \wedge (\neg P \vee Q \vee S) \wedge (T \vee \neg Q \vee S)$.

16. We'll say that an assignment of truth values to variables ***almost satisfies*** a conjunctive normal form (CNF) Boolean wff with k clauses iff it satisfies at least $k - 1$ clauses. A CNF Boolean wff is ***almost satisfiable*** iff some assignment almost satisfies it. Show that the following language is NP-complete.

- ALMOST-SAT = {<w> : w is an almost satisfiable CNF Boolean formula}

17. Show that VERTEX-COVER is NP-complete by reduction from INDEPENDENT-SET.

18. In Appendix O, we describe the regular expression sublanguage in Perl. Show that regular expression matching in Perl (with variables allowed) is NP-hard.

19. In most route-planning problems, the goal is to find the shortest route that meets some set of conditions. But consider the following problem (aptly named the ***taxicab rip-off problem*** in [Lewis and Papadimitriou 1998]): Given a directed graph G with positive costs attached to each edge, find the longest path from vertex i to vertex j that visits no vertex more than once.

a. Convert this optimization problem to a language recognition problem.

b. Make the strongest statement you can about the complexity of the resulting language.

20. In Section 22.3, we introduced a family of tiling problems and defined the language TILES. In that discussion, we considered the question, "Given a finite set T of tile designs and an infinite number of copies of each such design, is it possible to tile every finite surface in the plane?" As we saw, this unbounded version of the problem is undecidable. Now suppose that we are again given a set T of tile designs. But, this time, we are also given n^2 specific tiles drawn from that set. The question we now wish to answer is, "Given a particular stack of n^2 tiles, is it possible to tile an $n \times n$ surface in the plane?" As before, the rules are that tiles may not be rotated or flipped and the abutting regions of every pair of adjacent tiles must be the same color. So, for example, suppose that the tile set is:

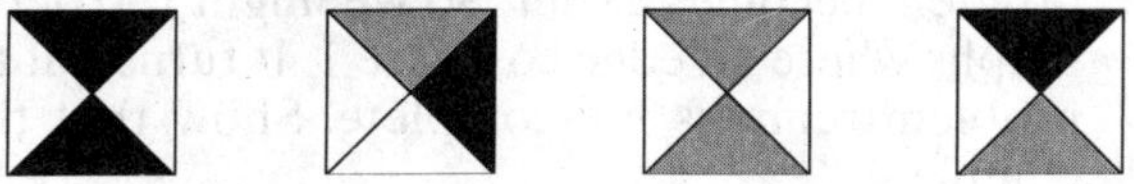

Then a 2×2 grid can be tiled as:

a. Formulate this problem as a language, FINITE-TILES.
b. Show that FINITE-TILES is in NP.
c. Show that FINITE-TILES is NP-complete (by showing that it is NP-hard).

21. In Section 28.7.6, we defined what we mean by a map coloring.

a. Prove the claim, made there, that a map is 2-colorable iff it does not contain any point that is the junction of an odd number of regions. (Hint: Use the pigeonhole principle.)
b. Prove that 3-COLORABLE = {<*m*> : *m* is a 3-colorable map} is in NP.
c. Prove that 3-COLORABLE = {<*m*> : *m* is a 3-colorable map} is NP-complete.

22. Define the following language.

- BIN-OVERSTUFFED = {<*S*, *c*, *k*> : *S* is a set of objects each of which has an associated size and it is *not* possible to divide the objects so that they fit into *k* bins, each of which has size *c*}

Explain why it is generally believed that BIN-OVERSTUFFED is not NP-complete.

23. Let G be an undirected, weighted graph with vertices V, edges E, and a function $cost(e)$ that assigns a positive cost to each edge e in E. A ***cut*** of G is a subset S of the vertices in V. The cut divides the vertices in V into two subsets, S and $V - S$. Define the ***size*** of a cut to be the sum of the costs of all edges (u, v) such that one of u or v is in S and the other is not. We'll say that a cut is ***nontrivial*** iff it is neither $\varnothing$ nor V. Recall that we saw, in Section 28.7.4, that finding shortest paths is easy (i.e., it can be done in polynomial time), but that finding longest paths is not. We'll observe a similar phenomenon with respect to cuts.

a. Sometimes we want to find the smallest cut in a graph. For example, it is possible to prove that the maximum flow between two nodes *s* and *t* is equal to the weight of the smallest cut that includes *s* but not *t*. Show that the following language is in P.

- MIN-CUT = $\{<G, k>$: there exists a nontrivial cut of *G* with size at most $k\}$

b. Sometimes we want to find the largest cut in a graph. Show that the following language is NP-complete.

- MAX-CUT = $\{<G, k>$: there exists a cut of *G* with size at least $k\}$

c. Sometimes, when we restrict the form of a problem we wish to consider, the problem becomes easier. So we might restrict the maximum-cut problem to graphs where all edge costs are 1. It turns out that, in this case, the "simpler" problem remains NP-complete. Show that the following language is NP-complete.

- SIMPLE-MAX-CUT = $\{<G, k>$: all edge costs in *G* are 1 and there exists a cut of *G* with size at least $k\}$

d. Define a ***bisection*** of a graph *G* to be a cut where *S* contains exactly half of the vertices in *V*. Show that the following language is NP-complete. (Hint: The graph *G* does not have to be connected.)

- MAX-BISECTION = $\{<G, k>$: *G* has a bisection of size at least $k\}$

24. Show that each of the following functions is time-constructible.

a. $n \log n$
b. $n\sqrt{n}$
c. n^3
d. 2^n
e. $n!$

25. In the proof of Theorem 28.27 (the Deterministic Time Hierarchy Theorem), we had to construct a string *w* of the form $<M_{t(n)easy}>10^p$. Let *n* be $|<M_{t(n)easy}>10^p|$. One of the constraints on our choice of *p* was that it be long enough that $|<M_{t(n)easy}>| < \log(t(n)/\log t(n))$. Let *m* be $|<M_{t(n)easy}>|$. Then we claimed that the condition would be satisfied if *p* is at least $2^{2^{m}}$. Prove this claim.

26. Prove or disprove each of the following claims.

a. If $A \leq_M B$ and $B \in$ P, then $A \in$ P.
b. If $A \leq_P B$ and *B* and *C* are in NP, then $A \cup C \in$ NP.
c. Let *ndtime*$(f(n))$ be the set of languages that can be decided by some nondeterministic Turing machine in time $\mathcal{O}(f(n))$. Every language in *ndtime*(2^n) is decidable.
d. Define a language to be ***co-finite*** iff its complement is finite. Any co-finite language is in NP.
e. Given an alphabet Σ, let *A* and *B* be nonempty proper subsets of Σ^*. If both *A* and *B* are in NP then $A \leq_M B$.
f. Define the language MANY-CLAUSE-SAT = $\{<w>$: *w* is a Boolean wff in conjunctive normal form, *w* has *m* variables and *k* clauses, and $k \geq 2^m\}$. If P $\neq$ NP, MANY-CLAUSE-SAT $\in$ P.

C H A P T E R 29

Space Complexity Classes

In the last chapter, we analyzed problems with respect to the time required to decide them. In this chapter, we'll focus instead on space requirements.

29.1 Analyzing Space Complexity

Our analysis of space complexity begins with the function *spacereq*(M) as described in Section 27.4.2:

- If M is a deterministic Turing machine that halts on all inputs, then the value of *spacereq*(M) is the function $f(n)$ defined so that, for any natural number n, $f(n)$ is the maximum number of tape squares that M reads on any input of length n.
- If M is a nondeterministic Turing machine all of whose computational paths halt on all inputs, then the value of *spacereq*(M) is the function $f(n)$ defined so that, for any natural number n, $f(n)$ is the maximum number of tape squares that M reads on any path that it executes on any input of length n.

So, just as *timereq*(M) measures the worst-case time requirement of M as a function of the length of its input, *spacereq*(M) measures the worst-case space requirement of M as a function of the length of its input.

29.1.1 Examples

To begin our discussion of space complexity, we'll return to three of the languages that we examined in the last chapter: CONNECTED, SAT, and TSP-DECIDE.

EXAMPLE 29.1 Connected

We begin by showing that CONNECTED = $\{<G> : G$ is an undirected graph and G is connected$\}$ can be decided by a deterministic Turing machine that uses linear space. Recall that a graph is connected iff there exists a path from each vertex to each other vertex.

EXAMPLE 29.1 *(Continued)*

Theorem 28.4 tells us that CONNECTED is in P. The proof exploited an algorithm that we called *connected*. *Connected* works by starting at G's first vertex and following edges, marking vertices as they are visited. If every vertex is eventually marked, then G is connected; otherwise it isn't. In addition to representing G, *connected* uses space for:

- storing the marks on the vertices: This can be done by adding one extra bit to the representation of each vertex.
- maintaining the list L of vertices that have been marked but whose successors have not yet been examined: We didn't describe how L is maintained. One easy way to do it is to add to the representation of each vertex one extra bit, which will be 1 if that vertex is a member of L and 0 otherwise.
- the number *marked-vertices-counter*: Since the value of the counter cannot exceed the number of vertices of G, it can be stored in binary in $\log(|<G>|)$ bits.

So *spacereq*(*connected*) is $\mathcal{O}(|<G>|)$.

CONNECTED is an "easy" language both from the perspective of time and the perspective of space since it can be decided in polynomial time and polynomial (in fact linear) space. Next we consider a language that appears to be harder if we measure time but is still easy if we measure only space.

EXAMPLE 29.2 SAT

Consider SAT $= \{<w> : w$ is a wff in Boolean logic and w is satisfiable$\}$. SAT is in NP, so it can be decided in polynomial time by a nondeterministic Turing machine that, given a wff w, guesses at an assignment of values to its variables. Then it checks whether that assignment makes w *True*. The checking procedure (outlined in the proof of Theorem 28.12), requires no space beyond the space required to encode w. It can overwrite the variables of w with their assigned values. Then it can evaluate subexpressions and replace each one with the value T or F. So SAT can be decided by a nondeterministic Turing machine that uses linear space.

SAT is believed not to be in P. No deterministic, polynomial-*time* algorithm is known for it. But it can be decided by a deterministic, polynomial-*space* algorithm that works as follows:

decideSATdeterministically($<w>$) =

1. Lexicographically enumerate the rows of the truth table for w. For each row do:
   1.1. Evaluate w (by replacing the variables with their values and applying the operators to those values, as described above).
   1.2. If w evaluates to *True*, accept.
2. If no row of the truth table caused w to be *True*, *reject*.

Each step of this procedure requires only linear space. But what about the space that may be required to control the loop? When we analyze algorithms to determine their space requirements, we must be careful to include whatever space is used by a loop index or, more significantly, a stack if one is used. For example, consider a recursive implementation of *decideSATdeterministically* that, at each invocation, evaluates w if all variables have had values assigned. Otherwise, it picks an unassigned variable, assigns it a value, and then recurs. This implementation could require a stack whose depth equals the number of variables in w. Each stack entry would need a copy of w. Since the number of variables can grow linearly with w, we'd have that *spacereq*(*decideSATdeterministically*) is $\mathcal{O}(|w|^2)$. That's polynomial, but not linear.

Fortunately, in the case of *decideSATdeterministically*, it is possible to control the loop using only an amount of space that is linear in the number of variables in w. Let 0 correspond to *False* and 1 correspond to *True*. Assign an order to the n variables in w. Then each row of w's truth table is a binary string of length n. Begin by generating the string 0^n. At each step, use binary addition to increment the string by 1. Halt once the assignment that corresponds to 1^n has been evaluated.

Using this technique, we have that *spacereq*(*decideSATdeterministically*) is $\mathcal{O}(|w|)$. So SAT can also be decided by a deterministic Turing machine that uses linear space.

EXAMPLE 29.3 TSP-DECIDE

Consider TSP-DECIDE = {<*G*, *cost*> : <*G*> encodes an undirected graph with a positive distance attached to each of its edges and *G* contains a Hamiltonian circuit whose total cost is less than *cost*}. We showed, in Theorem 28.10, that TSP-DECIDE is in NP. To prove the theorem, we described a nondeterministic Turing machine, *TSPdecide*, that decides the language TSP-DECIDE by nondeterministically attempting to construct a circuit one step at a time, checking, at each step, to see that the circuit's total cost is less than *cost*. *TSPdecide* uses space to store the partial circuit and its cost. The length of any Hamiltonian circuit can't be longer than the list of edges in *G*, since no edge may appear twice. So the space required to store a partial circuit is a linear function of |<*G*>|. The machine halts if the cost so far exceeds *cost*, so the space required to store the cost so far is bounded by *cost*. Thus we have that *spacereq*(*TSPdecide*) is $\mathcal{O}$(|<*G*>|).

But *TSPdecide* is nondeterministic. How much space would be required by a deterministic machine that decides TSP-DECIDE? We can define such a machine as follows:

decideTSPdeterministically(<*G*, *cost*>) =

1. Set *circuit* to contain just vertex 1.
2. If *explore*(*G*, 0, *circuit*) returns *True* then accept, else reject.

The bulk of the work is then done by the recursive procedure *explore*, which takes a partial circuit as input. It uses depth-first search to see whether it is possible

EXAMPLE 29.3 (*Continued*)

to extend that circuit into one that is complete and whose cost is less than *cost*. Each call to *explore* extends the circuit by one edge. *Explore* is defined as follows:

$explore(\langle G, cost, circuit \rangle) =$

1. If *circuit* is complete and its cost is less than *cost*, return *True*.
2. If *circuit* is complete and its cost is not less than *cost*, return *False*.
3. If *circuit* is not complete then do: /* Try to extend it.
4. For each edge *e* that is incident on the last vertex of *circuit*, or until a return statement is executed, do:
   - **4.1.** If the other vertex of *e* is not already part of *circuit* or if it would complete *circuit* then:

     Call $explore(\langle G, cost + \text{cost of } e, \textit{circuit with e added} \rangle)$.

     If the value returned is *True* then return *True*.
5. No alternative returned *True*. So return *False*.

DecideTSPdeterministically works by recursively invoking *explore*. It needs space to store the stack that holds the individual invocations of *explore*, including their arguments. Some paths may end without considering a complete circuit, but the maximum depth of the stack is $|V| + 1$, since that is the number of vertices in any complete circuit. Each stack record needs space to store a cost and a complete circuit, whose length is $|V| + 1$.

So we have that *spacereq*(*TSPdecidedeterministically*) is $\mathcal{O}(|\langle G \rangle^2|)$. We can actually do better and decide TSP-DECIDE using only linear space by storing, at each invocation of *explore*, just a cost and the one new vertex that is added at that step. Thus, while we know of no deterministic Turing machine that can decide TSP-DECIDE in polynomial time, there does exist one that can decide it in polynomial (in fact, linear) space.

29.1.2 Relating Time and Space Complexity

The examples that we have just considered suggest that there is some relationship between the number of steps a Turing machine executes and the amount of space it uses. The most fundamental relationship between the two numbers arises from the fact that, at each step of its operation, a Turing machine can examine at most one tape square. So we have, for any Turing machine M, that $spacereq(M) \leq timereq(M)$.

But M's time requirement cannot be arbitrarily larger than its space requirement. We are considering only Turing machines that halt on all inputs. If a Turing machine M halts, then it can never re-enter a configuration that it has been in before. (If it did, it would be in an infinite loop.) So the number of steps that M can execute is bounded by the number of distinct configurations that it can enter. We can compute the maximum number of such configurations as follows: Let K be the states of M and let Γ be its tape alphabet. M may be in any one of its $|K|$ states. Define M's active tape to be the smallest tape fragment that contains all the nonblank symbols plus the read/write head. Assuming that $spacereq(M) \geq n$ (i.e., that M actually reads all its input), the number of squares in M's active tape at any point during M's computation is bounded by $spacereq(M)$. Each of those squares may hold any one of the $|\Gamma|$ tape symbols. So the maximum number of distinct tape snapshots is $|\Gamma|^{spacereq(M)}$. And M's read/write head may be on any one of the $spacereq(M)$ tape squares. So the maximum number of distinct configurations that M can enter is:

$$MaxConfigs(M) = |K| \cdot |\Gamma|^{spacereq(M)} \cdot spacereq(M).$$

Let c be a constant such that $c > |\Gamma|$. Then:

$$MaxConfigs(M) \in \mathcal{O}(c^{spacereq(M)}).$$

(We leave the proof of this claim as an exercise.). Using the analysis we have just presented, we can prove the following theorem:

THEOREM 29.1 Relating Time and Space Requirements

Theorem: Given a Turing machine $M = (K, \Sigma, \Gamma, \delta, s, H)$ and assuming that $spacereq(M) \geq n$, the following relationships hold between M's time and space requirements:

$$spacereq(M) \leq timereq(M) \in \mathcal{O}(c^{spacereq(M)}).$$

Proof: *Spacereq*(M) is bounded by *timereq*(M) since M must use at least one time step for every tape square it visits.

The upper bound on *timereq*(M) follows from the fact, since M halts, the number of steps that it can execute is bounded by the number of distinct configurations that it can enter. That number is given by the function *MaxConfigs*(M), as described above. Since $MaxConfigs(M) \in \mathcal{O}(c^{spacereq(M)})$, $timereq(M) \in \mathcal{O}(c^{spacereq(M)})$.

In a nutshell, space can be reused. Time cannot.

29.2 PSPACE, NPSPACE, and Savitch's Theorem

If our measure of complexity is time, it appears that nondeterminism adds power. So, for example, there are languages, such as SAT and TSP-DECIDE, that are in NP but that do not appear to be in P. When we change perspectives and measure complexity in terms of space requirements, the distinction between nondeterministic and deterministic machines turns out almost to disappear.

Recall that we defined the language class P to include exactly those languages that could be decided by a *deterministic* Turing machine in polynomial time. And we defined the class NP to include exactly those languages that could be decided by a *nondeterministic* Turing machine in polynomial time. We'll now define parallel classes based on space requirements.

The Class PSPACE: $L \in$ PSPACE iff there exists some deterministic Turing machine M that decides L and $spacereq(M) \in \mathcal{O}(n^k)$ for some constant k.

The Class NPSPACE: $L \in$ NPSPACE iff there exists some nondeterministic Turing machine M that decides L and $spacereq(M) \in \mathcal{O}(n^k)$ for some constant k.

Savitch's Theorem, which we'll state and prove next, tells us that we needn't have bothered to define the two classes. PSPACE = NPSPACE.

Note that, since every deterministic Turing machine is also a legal nondeterministic one, if a language L can be decided by some deterministic Turing machine that requires $f(n)$ space, then it can also be decided by some nondeterministic Turing machine that requires at most $f(n)$ space. The other direction does not follow. It may be possible to decide L with a nondeterministic Turing machine that uses just $f(n)$ space but there may exist no deterministic machine that can do it without using more than $\mathcal{O}(f(n))$ space. However, it turns out that L's deterministic space complexity cannot be *much* worse than its nondeterministic space complexity. We are about to prove that, assuming one common condition is satisfied, there must exist a deterministic Turing machine that decides it using $\mathcal{O}(f(n)^2)$ space.

The proof that we will do is by construction. We'll show how to transform a nondeterministic Turing machine into an equivalent deterministic one that conducts a systematic search through the set of "guesses" that the nondeterministic machine could have made. That's exactly what we did for TSP-DECIDE above. In that case, we were able to construct a deterministic Turing machine that conducted a straightforward depth-first search and that required only $\mathcal{O}(n^2)$ space to store its stack. But we exploited a specific property of TSP-DECIDE to make that work: We knew that any Hamiltonian circuit through a graph with $|V|$ vertices must have exactly $|V|$ edges. So the depth of the stack was bounded by $|V|$ and thus by $|G|$.

In general, while there is a bound on the depth of the stack, it is much weaker. We can guarantee only that, if a nondeterministic Turing machine M uses $spacereq(M)$ space, then any one branch of a depth-first deterministic Turing machine that simulates M must halt in no more than *MaxConfigs*(M) steps (since otherwise it is in a loop). But $MaxConfigs(M) \in \mathcal{O}(c^{spacereq(M)})$. We can't afford a stack that could grow that deep. There is, however, an alternative to depth-first search that can be guaranteed to require a stack whose depth is $\mathcal{O}(n)$. We'll use it in the proof of Savitch's Theorem, which we state next.

THEOREM 29.2 Savitch's Theorem

Theorem: If L can be decided by some nondeterministic Turing machine M and $spacereq(M) \geq n$, then there exists a deterministic Turing machine M' that also decides L and $spacereq(M') \in \mathcal{O}(spacereq(M)^2)$.

Proof: We require that $spacereq(M) \geq n$, which means just that M must at least be able to read all its input. In Section 29.4, we'll introduce a way to talk about machines that use less than linear *working space*. Once we do that, this constraint can be weakened to $spacereq(M) \geq \log n$.

The proof is by construction. Suppose that L is decided by some nondeterministic Turing machine M. We will show an algorithm that builds a deterministic Turing machine M' that also decides L and that uses space that grows no faster than the square of the space required by M. M' will systematically examine the paths that M could pursue. Since our goal is to put a bound on the amount of space that M' uses, the key to its construction is a technique for guaranteeing that the stack that it uses to manage its search doesn't get "too deep." We'll use a divide-and-conquer technique in which we chop each problem into two halves in such a way that we can solve the first half and then reuse the same space to solve the second half.

To simplify the question that we must answer, we'll begin by changing M so that, whenever it is about to accept, it first blanks out its tape. Then it enters a new, unique, accepting state. Call this new machine M_{blank}. Note that M_{blank} accepts iff it ever reaches the configuration in which its tape is blank and it is in the new accepting state. Call this configuration c_{accept}. M_{blank} uses no additional space, so $spacereq(M_{blank}) = spacereq(M)$.

Now we must describe the construction of M', which, on input w, must accept iff M_{blank}, on input w, can (via at least one of its computational paths) reach c_{accept}. Because we need to bound the depth of the stack that M' uses, we need to bound the number of steps it can execute (since it might have to make a choice at each step). We have already seen that simple approaches, such as depth-first search, cannot do that adequately. So we'll make use of the following function, *canreach*. Its job is to answer the more general question, "Given a Turing machine T running on input w, two configurations, c_1 and c_2, and a number t, could T, if it managed to get to c_1, go on and reach c_2 within t steps?" *Canreach* works by exploiting the following observation: If T can go from c_1 to c_2 within t steps, then one of the following must be true:

1. $t = 0$. In this case, $c_1 = c_2$.
2. $t = 1$. In this case, $c_1 \vdash_T c_2$. (Recall that $\vdash_T$ is the *yields-in-one-step* relation between configurations of machine T.) Whether the single required step exists can be determined just by examining the transitions of T.
3. $t > 1$. In this case, $c_1 \vdash_T \ldots \vdash_T c_k \vdash_T \ldots c_2$. In other words, there is some (at least one) configuration c_k that T goes through on the way from c_1 to c_2. Furthermore, note that, however many configurations there are on the path from c_1 to c_2, there is a "middle" one, i.e., one with the property that half of T's work is done getting from c_1 to it and the other half is done getting from it to c_2. (It won't matter that, if the length of the computation is not an even number, there may be one more configuration on one side of the middle one than there is on the other.)

So *canreach* operates as follows: If $t = 0$, all it needs to do is to check whether $c_1 = c_2$. If $t = 1$, it just checks whether the one required transition exists in T. If $t > 1$, then it considers, as a possible "middle" configuration, all configurations of T that use no more space than $spacereq(T)$ allows for inputs of length $|w|$. It will recursively invoke itself and ask whether T could both go from c_1 to *middle* in $t/2$ steps and from *middle* to c_2 in the remaining $t/2$ steps. (Since $t/2$ may not be an integer, we'll give each invocation $\lceil t/2 \rceil$ steps, where $\lceil t/2 \rceil$ is the ceiling of $t/2$, i.e., the smallest integer that is greater than or equal to $t/2$.) For this approach to work, we must be able to guarantee that there is only a finite number of configurations that T could enter while processing w. We are only going to invoke *canreach* on deciding Turing machines, so we know not only that the number of such configurations is finite but that it is bounded by $MaxConfigs(T)$, which is a function of the number of states in T, the size of its tape alphabet, and $spacereq(T)$, which bounds the number of tape squares that can be nonblank as a function of the length of w.

Canreach will take five arguments: a Turing machine T, an input string w, a pair of configurations, c_1 and c_2, and a nonnegative integer that corresponds to the number of time steps that T may use in attempting to get from c_1 to c_2. Note that T and w won't change as *canreach* recursively invokes itself. Also note that the only role w plays is that its length determines the number of tape squares that can be used. *Canreach* can be defined as follows:

canreach(T: Turing machine, w: string, c_1: configuration, c_2: configuration, t: nonnegative integer) =

1. If $c_1 = c_2$ then return *True*.
2. If $t = 1$ then:
   - **2.1.** If $c_1 \vdash_T c_2$ then return *True*. /* c_1 yields c_2 in one step.
   - **2.2.** Else return *False*. /* In one step, c_1 cannot yield c_2.
3. If $t > 1$, then let *Confs* be the set of all of T's configurations whose tape is no longer than $spacereq(T)$ applied to $|w|$. For each configuration *middle* in *Confs* do:
   - **3.1.** If $canreach(T, w, c_1, middle, \lceil t/2 \rceil)$ and $canreach(T, w, middle, c_2, \lceil t/2 \rceil)$ then return *True*.
4. Return *False*. /* None of the possible *middles* worked.

We can now return to our original problem: Given a nondeterministic Turing machine M, construct a deterministic Turing machine M' such that $L(M') = L(M)$ and $spacereq(M') \in \mathcal{O}(spacereq(M)^2)$. The following algorithm solves the problem:

builddet(M: nondeterministic Turing machine) =

1. From M, build M_{blank} as described above.
2. From M_{blank}, build M'. To make it easy to describe M', define:
   - c_{start} to be the start configuration of M_{blank} on input w.
   - *max-on-w* to be the result of applying the function *maxConfigs* (M_{blank}) to $|w|$. (So *max-on-w* is the maximum number of distinct configurations that M_{blank} might enter when started on w. Thus it is also the maximum number of steps that M_{blank} might execute on input w, given that it eventually halts.)
3. Then $M'(w)$ operates as follows:

   If $canreach(M_{blank}, w, c_{start}, c_{accept}, max\text{-}on\text{-}w)$ then accept, else reject.

Canreach will return *True* iff M_{blank} (and thus M) accepts w. So $L(M') = L(M)$. But it remains to show that $spacereq(M') \in \mathcal{O}(spacereq(M)^2)$.

Each invocation of *canreach* requires storing an activation record. It suffices to store M and w once. But each record must contain a new copy of two configurations and the integer that puts a bound on the number of steps to be executed. Each configuration requires $\mathcal{O}(spacereq(M))$ space, so each invocation record also requires $\mathcal{O}(spacereq(M))$ space. Now all we need to do is to determine the depth of the stack of invocation records. Notice that each invocation of *canreach* cuts the allotted number of steps in half. So the depth of the stack is bounded by $\log_2(max\text{-}on\text{-}w)$. But *max-on-w* is *maxConfigs*(M) applied to $|w|$ and we have that:

$$MaxConfigs(M) \in \mathcal{O}(c^{spacereq(M)}).$$

$$\log_2(MaxConfigs(M)) \in \mathcal{O}(spacereq(M)).$$

So the depth of the stack is $\mathcal{O}(spacereq(M))$ and the total space required is $\mathcal{O}(spacereq(M)^2)$.

Savitch's Theorem has an important corollary, which we state next.

THEOREM 29.3 PSPACE = NPSPACE

Theorem: PSPACE = NPSPACE.

Proof: In one direction, the claim is trivial: If L is in PSPACE, then it must also be in NPSPACE because the deterministic Turing machine that decides it in polynomial time is also a nondeterministic Turing machine that decides it in polynomial time.

To prove the other direction, we note that Savitch's Theorem tells us that the price for going from a nondeterministic machine to a deterministic one is at most a squaring of the amount of space required. More precisely, if L is in NPSPACE then there is some nondeterministic Turing machine M such that M decides L and $spacereq(M) \in \mathcal{O}(n^k)$ for some k. If $k \geq 1$, then, by Savitch's Theorem, there exists a deterministic Turing machine M' such that M' decides L and $spacereq(M') \in \mathcal{O}(n^{2k})$. If, on the other hand, $k < 1$ then, using the same construction that we used in the proof of Savitch's Theorem, we can show that there exists a deterministic M' such that M' decides L and $spacereq(M') \in \mathcal{O}(n^2)$. In either case, $spacereq(M')$ is a polynomial function of n. So L can be decided by a deterministic Turing machine whose space requirement is some polynomial function of the length of its input. Thus L is in PSPACE.

Another corollary of Savitch's Theorem follows.

THEOREM 29.4 P $\subseteq$ NP $\subseteq$ PSPACE

Theorem: P $\subseteq$ NP $\subseteq$ PSPACE.

Proof: Theorem 28.14 tells us that P $\subseteq$ NP. It remains to show that NP $\subseteq$ PSPACE. If a language L is in NP, then it is decided by some nondeterministic Turing machine M in polynomial time. In polynomial time, M cannot use more than polynomial space since it takes a least one time step to visit a tape square.

Since M is a nondeterministic Turing machine that decides L in polynomial space, L is in NPSPACE. But, by Savitch's Theorem, PSPACE = NPSPACE. So L is also in PSPACE.

It is assumed that both subset relationships are proper (i.e., that P $\neq$ NP $\neq$ PSPACE), but no proof of either of those claims exists.

29.3 PSPACE-Completeness

Recall that, in our discussion of time complexity, we introduced two useful language families: We said that a language is NP-hard iff every language in NP is deterministic, polynomial-time reducible to it. And we said that a language is NP-complete iff it is NP-hard and it is also in NP. All NP-complete languages are equivalently hard in the sense that all of them can be decided in nondeterministic, polynomial time and, if any one of them can also be decided in deterministic polynomial time, then all of them can.

In our attempt to understand why some problems appear harder than others, it is useful to define corresponding classes based on space complexity. So we consider the following two properties that a language L might possess.

1. L is in PSPACE.

2. Every language in PSPACE is deterministic, polynomial-time reducible to L.

Using those properties, we will define:

The Class PSPACE-hard: L is PSPACE-hard iff it possesses property 2.

The Class PSPACE-complete: L is PSPACE-complete iff it possesses *both* property 1 and property 2. All PSPACE-complete languages can be viewed as being equivalently hard in the sense that all of them can be decided in polynomial space and:

- If any PSPACE-complete language is also in NP, then all of them are and NP = PSPACE.
- If any PSPACE-complete language is also in P, then all of them are and P = NP =PSPACE.

Note that we have defined PSPACE-hardness, just as we defined NP-hardness, with respect to polynomial-*time* reducibility. We could have defined it in terms of the space complexity of the reductions that we use. But the polynomial-time definition is more useful because it provides a stronger notion of a "computationally feasible" reduction. If all we knew about two languages L_1 and L_2 were that L_1 were polynomial-space reducible to L_2, an efficient (i.e., polynomial-time) solution to L_2 would not guarantee an efficient solution to L_1. The efficiency of the solution for L_2 might be swamped by a very inefficient reduction from L_1 to L_2. By continuing to restrict our attention to deterministic, polynomial-time reductions, we guarantee that if L_1 is reducible to L_2 and an efficient solution to L_2 were to be found, we would also have an efficient solution for L_1.

When we began our discussion of NP-completeness, we faced a serious problem at the outset: How could we find our first NP-complete language? Once we had that one, we could prove that other languages were also NP-complete by reduction from it. We face the same problem now as we begin to explore the class of PSPACE-complete languages. We need a first one.

Recall that, in the case of NP-completeness, the language that got us going and that provided the basis for the proof of the Cook-Levin Theorem, was SAT (the language of satisfiable Boolean formulas). The choice of SAT was not arbitrary. To prove that it was NP-complete, we exploited the expressive power of Boolean logic to describe computational paths. Since every NP language is, by definition, decided by some nondeterministic Turing machine each of whose paths halts in a finite (and polynomially-bounded) number of steps, we were able to define a reduction from an arbitrary NP language L to the specific NP language SAT by showing a way to build, given a deciding machine M for L and a string w, a Boolean formula whose length is bounded by a polynomial function of the length of w and that is satisfiable iff M accepts w.

Perhaps we can, similarly, seed the class of PSPACE-complete languages with a logical language. Because we believe that PSPACE includes languages that are not in NP, we wouldn't expect SAT to work. On the other hand, we can't jump all the way to a first-order logic language like $\text{FOL}_{\text{theorem}} = \{<A, w> : A$ is a decidable set of axioms in first-order logic, w is a sentence in first-order logic, and w is entailed by $A\}$, since it isn't decidable at all, much less is it decidable in polynomial space. In the next section, we will define a new language, QBF, that adds quantifiers to the language of Boolean logic but that stops short of the full power of first-order logic. Then we will show that QBF is PSPACE-complete. We'll do that using a construction that is similar to the one that was used to prove the Cook-Levin Theorem. We'll discover one wrinkle, however: In order to guarantee that, on input w, the length of the formula that we build is bounded by some polynomial function of w, we will need to use the divide-and-conquer technique that we exploited in the proof of Savitch's Theorem.

29.3.1 The Language QBF

Boolean formulas are evaluated with respect to the universe $\{True, False\}$. A particular Boolean well-formed formula (wff), such as $((P \wedge Q) \vee \neg R) \rightarrow S$, is a function, stated in terms of some finite number of Boolean variables. Given a particular set of values as its input, it returns either *True* or *False*. We have defined Boolean-formula languages, like SAT, in terms of properties that the formulas that are in the language must possess. So, for example:

- A wff $w \in$ SAT iff it is satisfiable. In other words, $w \in$ SAT iff *there exists some set of values* for the variables of w such that w evaluates to *True*.
- A wff $w \in$ VALID iff it is a tautology. In other words, $w \in$ VALID iff *for all values* for the variables of w, w evaluates to *True*.

So, while Boolean formulas do not contain quantifiers, we have used quantification in our descriptions of Boolean-formula languages. Now suppose that we add explicit quantifiers to the logical language itself.

Define the language of ***quantified Boolean expressions*** as follows:

- The base case: All wffs are quantified Boolean expressions.

- Adding quantifiers: If w is a quantified Boolean expression that contains the unbound variable A, then the expressions $\exists A\ (w)$ and $\forall A\ (w)$ are quantified Boolean expressions. Exactly as we do in first-order logic, we'll then say that A is bound in w and that the scope of the new quantifier is w.

All of the following are quantified Boolean expressions.

- $(P \wedge \neg R) \rightarrow S$
- $\exists P\ ((P \wedge \neg R) \rightarrow S)$
- $\forall R\ (\exists P\ ((P \wedge \neg R) \rightarrow S))$
- $\forall S\ (\forall R\ (\exists P\ ((P \wedge \neg R) \rightarrow S)))$.

Notice that, because of the way they are constructed, all quantified Boolean expressions are in prenex normal form, as defined in B.2.1. In other words, the expression is composed of a quantifier list followed by a quantifier-free matrix. We'll find this form useful below.

As in first-order logic, we'll say that a quantified Boolean expression is a ***sentence*** iff all of its variables are bound. So, for example $\forall S\ (\forall R\ (\exists P\ ((P \wedge \neg R) \rightarrow S)))$ is a sentence, but none of the other expression listed above is.

A ***quantified Boolean formula*** is a quantified Boolean expression that is also a sentence. Every quantified Boolean formula, just like every sentence in first-order logic, can be evaluated to produce either *True* or *False*. For example:

- $\exists P\ (\exists R\ (P \wedge \neg R))$ evaluates to *True*.
- $\exists P\ (\forall R\ (P \wedge \neg R))$ evaluates to *False*.

We can now define the language that will turn out to be our first PSPACE-complete language:

- QBF = {<w> : w is a true quantified Boolean formula}.

29.3.2 QBF is PSPACE-Complete

QBF, unlike languages like $\text{FOL}_{\text{theorem}}$ that are defined with respect to full first-order logic, is decidable. The reason is that the universe with respect to which existential and universal quantification are defined is finite. In general, we cannot determine the validity of an arbitrary first-order logic formula, such as $\forall x\ (P(x))$, by actually evaluating P for all possible values of x. The domain of x might, for example, be the integers. But it is possible to decide whether an arbitrary quantified Boolean formula is true by exhaustively examining its (finite) truth table.

We'll show next that not only is it possible to decide QBF, it is possible to decide it in polynomial (in fact linear) space.

THEOREM 29.5 QBF is in PSPACE

Theorem: QBF = {<w> : w is a true quantified Boolean formula} is in PSPACE.

Proof: We show that QBF is in PSPACE by exhibiting a deterministic, polynomial-space algorithm that decides it. The algorithm that we present exploits the fact that quantified Boolean formulas are in prenex normal form. So, if w is a quantified Boolean formula, it must have the following form, where each Q is a quantifier (either $\forall$ or $\exists$) and f is a Boolean wff:

$$Qv_1\ (Qv_2\ (Qv_3 \ldots (Qv_n \qquad (f) \ldots).$$

The following procedure, *QBFdecide*, decides whether w is true. It peels off the quantifiers one at a time, left-to-right. Each time it peels off a quantifier that binds some variable v, it substitutes *True* for every instance of v and calls itself recursively. Then it substitutes *False* for every instance of v and calls itself recursively again. At some point, it will be called with a Boolean wff that contains only constants. When that happens, the wff can simply be evaluated.

$QBFdecide(<w>) =$

1. Invoke $QBFcheck(<w>)$.
2. If it returns *True*, accept; else reject.

$QBFcheck(<w>) =$

1. If w contains no quantifiers, evaluate it by applying its Boolean operators to its constant values. The result will be either *True* or *False*. Return it.
2. If w is $\forall v\ (w')$, where w' is some quantified Boolean formula, then:
   - **2.1.** Substitute *True* for every occurrence of v in w' and invoke *QBFcheck* on the result.
   - **2.2.** Substitute *False* for every occurrence of v in w' and invoke *QBFcheck* on the result.
   - **2.3.** If both of these branches accept, then w' is true for all values of v. So accept; else reject.
3. If w is $\exists v\ (w')$, where w' is some quantified Boolean formula, then:
   - **3.1.** Substitute *True* for every occurrence of v in w' and invoke *QBFcheck* on the result.
   - **3.2.** Substitute *False* for every occurrence of v in w' and invoke *QBFcheck* on the result.
   - **3.3.** If at least one of these branches accepts, then w' is true for some value of v. So accept; else reject.

We analyze the space requirement of *QBFdecide* as follows: The depth of *QBFcheck*'s stack is equal to the number of variables in w, which is $\mathcal{O}(|w|)$. At each recursive call, the only new information is the value of one new variable. So the amount of space for each stack entry is constant. The actual evaluation of a variable-free wff w can be done in $\mathcal{O}(|w|)$ space. Thus the total space used by *QBFdecide* is $\mathcal{O}(|w|)$. *QBFdecide* runs in linear (and thus obviously polynomial) space.

We can't prove that a more efficient algorithm for deciding QBF doesn't exist. But the result that we will prove next strongly suggest that none does. In particular, it tells us that a nondeterministic, polynomial-time algorithm exists only if NP = PSPACE and a deterministic, polynomial-time algorithm exists only if P = NP = PSPACE.

THEOREM 29.6 QBF is PSPACE-Complete

Theorem: QBF = {<w> : w is a true quantified Boolean formula} is PSPACE-complete.

Proof: We have already shown that QBF is in PSPACE. So all that remains is to show that it is PSPACE-hard. We'll do that by showing a polynomial-time reduction to it from any language in PSPACE. We'll use approximately the same technique that we used, in the proof of the Cook-Levin Theorem, where we showed that SAT is NP-hard. Let L be any language in PSPACE. L is decided by some deterministic Turing machine M with the property that $spacereq(M)$ is a polynomial. We'll describe a reduction from L to QBF that works by constructing a quantified Boolean formula that describes the computation of M on input w and that is true iff M accepts w.

Just as we did in the proof of the Cook-Levin Theorem, we'll use Boolean variables to describe each of the configurations that M enters while processing w. Our first idea might be simply to construct a Boolean formula exactly as we described in the Cook-Levin Theorem proof. Then we can convert that formula into a quantified Boolean formula by binding each of its variables by an existential quantifier. The resulting quantified Boolean formula will be true iff the original formula is satisfiable.

It remains to analyze the time complexity of the construction. The number of steps required by the construction is a polynomial function of the length of the formula that it constructs. The length of the formula is polynomial in the number of cells in the table that describes the computation of M on w. Each row of the table corresponds to one configuration of M, so the number of cells in a row is $\mathcal{O}(spacereq(M))$, which is polynomial in $|w|$.

But now we have a problem. In the proof of the Cook-Levin Theorem, we knew that the maximum length of any computational path of M was $\mathcal{O}(|w|^k)$. So the maximum number of configurations that would have to be described, and thus the number of rows in the table, was also $\mathcal{O}(|w|^k)$. The problem that we now face is that we no longer have a polynomial bound on the number of configurations that M may enter before it halts. All we have is a polynomial bound on the amount of space M uses. Using that space bound, we can construct a time bound, as we've done before, by taking advantage of the fact that M may not enter a loop. So the maximum number of steps it may execute is bounded by the maximum number of distinct configurations it may enter. That number is

$$MaxConfigs(M) = |K| \cdot |\Gamma|^{spacereq(M)} \cdot spacereq(M) \in \mathcal{O}(c^{spacereq(M)}).$$

So, if we used exactly the same technique we used in the proof of the Cook-Levin Theorem, we'd be forced to describe the computation of M on w with a formula whose length grows exponentially with $|w|$. A polynomial-time reduction cannot build an exponentially long formula.

The solution to this problem is to exploit quantifiers to "cluster" subexpressions so that a whole group of them can be described at once.

To do this, we'll begin by returning to the divide-and-conquer technique that we used in our proof of Savitch's Theorem. As we did there, we will again solve a more general problem. This time, we will describe a technique for constructing a quantified Boolean formula $f(c_1, c_2, t)$ that is true iff M can get from configuration c_1 to configuration c_2 in at most t steps. We again observe that, if M can get from configuration c_1 to configuration c_2 within t steps, then one of the following must be true:

1. $t = 0$. In this case, $c_1 = c_2$. Since each configuration can be described by a formula whose length is polynomial in $|w|$, this condition can also be described by such a formula.
2. $t = 1$. In this case, c_1 yields c_2 in a single step. Using the techniques we used to build $Conjunct_4$ in the proof of the Cook-Levin Theorem, this condition can also be described by a formula whose length is polynomial in $|w|$. Note that, in the proof of the Cook-Levin Theorem, we built a Boolean formula and then asked whether it was satisfiable. Now we build the same Boolean formula and then bind all the variables with existential quantifiers, so we again ask whether any values satisfy the formula.
3. $t > 1$. In this case, c_1 yields c_2 in more than one step. Then there is some configuration we'll call *middle* with the property that M can get from c_1 to *middle* within $\lceil t/2 \rceil$ steps and from *middle* to c_2 within another $\lceil t/2 \rceil$ steps. Of course, as in the proof of Savitch's Theorem, we don't know what *middle* is. But, when we build $f(c_1, c_2, t)$, we can use an existential quantifier to assert that it exists. The resulting formula will only be true if, in fact, *middle* does exist.

Now we just need a space-efficient way to represent $f(c_1, c_2, t)$ in the third case. Suppose that *middle* exists. Then some set of Boolean variables $m_1, m_2, \ldots$ describe it. So we could begin by writing:

$$f(c_1, c_2, t) = \exists m_1\, (\exists m_2 \ldots (f(c_1, middle, \lceil t/2 \rceil) \wedge f(middle, c_2, \lceil t/2 \rceil)) \ldots).$$

We can simplify this by introducing the following shorthand:

- If c is a configuration that is described by the variables $c_1, c_2, \ldots$, let $\exists c\, (p)$ stand for $\exists c_1\, (\exists c_2 \quad (p) \ldots)$ and let $\forall c\, (p)$ stand for $\forall c_1\, (\forall c_2 \quad (p) \ldots)$. Note that since the number of variables required to describe c is polynomial in $|w|$, the length of the expanded formula is a polynomial function of the length of the shorthand one.

This lets us rewrite our definition of f as:

$$f(c_1, c_2, t) = \exists middle\, (f(c_1, middle, \lceil t/2 \rceil) \wedge f(middle, c_2, \lceil t/2 \rceil)).$$

Then we could recursively expand $f(c_1, middle, \lceil t/2 \rceil)$ and $f(middle, c_2, \lceil t/2 \rceil)$, continuing until $\lceil t/2 \rceil$ becomes 0 or 1. We cut the number of computation steps that might have to be described in half each time we do this recursion. But we also replace a single formula by the conjunction of two formulas. So the total length of the formula that we'll build, if we take this approach, is $\mathcal{O}(t)$.

Unfortunately, it becomes obvious that this approach isn't efficient enough as soon as we return to the original, specific problem of describing the computation of M on w. As we did in the proof of Savitch's Theorem, we'll actually work with M_{blank}, a modification of M that accepts by entering a unique accepting configuration that we'll call c_{accept}. Let c_{start} be the starting configuration of M on w. We know that the number of steps that M may execute in getting from c_{start} to c_{accept} is $\mathcal{O}(c^{spacereq(M)})$ and that $spacereq(M)$ is polynomial in $|w|$. The formula that we must build is then:

$$f(c_{start}, c_{accept}, 2^{k \cdot spacereq(M)}).$$

So its length grows exponentially with $|w|$.

To reduce its size, we'll exploit universal quantifiers to enable us to describe the two recursively generated subformulas of $f(c_1, c_2, t)$ as a single formula. To do this, we need to create a new, generic formula that describes the transition, within $\lceil t/2 \rceil$ steps, from an arbitrary configuration we'll call c_3 to another arbitrary configuration we'll call c_4. The names don't matter as long as we describe the two configurations with variables that are distinct from all the variables that we will use to describe actual configurations of M. So the new formula is $f(c_3, c_4, \lceil t/2 \rceil)$. Then we'll want to say that the new formula must be true both when:

- $c_3 = c_1$ and $c_4 = middle$, and
- $c_3 = middle$ and $c_4 = c_2$.

We'll do that by saying that it must be true for all (i.e., both) of those assignments of values to the variables of c_3 and c_4. To do that, we need the following additional shorthands.

- Let $\forall (x, y)(p)$ stand for $\forall x\ (\forall y\ (p))$.
- Let $\forall x \in \{s, t\}(p)$ stand for $\forall x\ ((x = s \vee x = t) \rightarrow p)$.
- Combining these, let $\forall (x, y) \in \{(s_1, s_2), (t_1, t_2)\}(p)$ say that $((x = s_1 \wedge y = s_2) \rightarrow p) \wedge (x = t_1 \wedge y = t_2) \rightarrow p)$.

Note that the length of the expanded versions of one of these shorthands grows at most polynomially in the length of the shortened form. With these conventions in hand, we can now offer a new way to begin to define f:

$$f(c_1, c_2, t) = \exists middle\ (\forall (c_3, c_4) \in \{(c_1, middle), (middle, c_2)\} \\ (f(c_3, c_4, \lceil t/2 \rceil))).$$

We're still using the convention that a configuration name stands for the entire collection of variables that describe it. So this formula asserts that there is some configuration $middle$ such that $f(c_3, c_4, \lceil t/2 \rceil)$ is true both when:

- the variables in c_3 take on the values of the variables in c_1 and the variables in c_4 take on the values of the variables in $middle$, and
- the variables in c_3 take on the values of the variables in $middle$ and the variables in c_4 take on the values of the variables in c_2.

Now we must recursively define $f(c_3, c_4, \lceil t/2 \rceil)$ and we must continue the recursive definition process until $\lceil t/2 \rceil = 0$ or 1.

If we do that, how long is $f(c_{start}, c_{accept}, 2^{k \cdot spacereq(M)})$? The answer is that the number of recursive steps is $\log_2(2^{k \cdot spacereq(M)})$, which is $\mathcal{O}(spacereq(M))$. And now the length of the subformula that is added at each step is also $\mathcal{O}(spacereq(M))$. So the total length of the formula, and thus the amount of time required to construct it, is $\mathcal{O}(spacereq^2(M))$. So we have described a technique that can reduce any language in PSPACE to QBF in polynomial time.

29.3.3 Other PSPACE-Hard and PSPACE-Complete Problems

QBF is not the only PSPACE-complete language. There are others, and many of them exploit the quantifier structure that QBF provides. We mention here some significant problems that are PSPACE-hard, many of which are also PSPACE-complete.

Two-Person Games

A quantified Boolean formula may exploit the quantifiers $\forall$ and $\exists$ in any order. But now consider the specific case in which they alternate. For example, we might write $\exists A\ (\forall B\ (\exists C\ (\forall D\ (P))))$, where P is a Boolean formula over the variables A, B, C, and D. This alternation naturally describes the way a player in a two-player game evaluates moves. So, for example, I could reason that a current game configuration is a guaranteed win for me if there exists *some* move that I can make and then be guaranteed a win. But then, to evaluate what will happen at the next move, I must consider that I don't get to choose the move. My opponent does. So I can only conclude that the next configuration is a win for me if *all* of the possible second moves lead to a win. At the next level, it is again my turn to choose, so I'm interested in the existence of *some* winning move, and so forth.

The theory of asymptotic complexity that we have developed doesn't tell us anything about solving a single problem of fixed size. So it can't be applied directly to games of fixed size. But it can be applied if we generalize the games to configurations of arbitrary size. When we do that, we discover that many popular games are PSPACE-hard. Some of them are also in PSPACE, and so are PSPACE-complete. Some appear to be harder. In particular:

- If the length of a game (i.e., the number of moves that occur before the game is over) is bounded by some polynomial function of the size of the game, then the game is likely to be PSPACE-complete.
- If the length of the game may grow exponentially with the size of the game, then the game is likely not be solvable in polynomial space. But it is likely to be solvable in exponential time and thus to be EXPTIME-complete.

Many real games are interesting precisely because they are too hard to be practically solvable by brute force search. We briefly discuss a few of them, including Sudoku, chess, and Go in N.2.

Questions about Languages and Automata

In Parts II, III, and IV, we described a variety of decision procedures for regular, context-free, and context-sensitive languages. During most of those discussions, we focused simply on decidability and ignored issues of complexity. We can now observe that several quite straightforward questions, while decidable, are hard. These include the following. After each claim, is a source for more information.

Finite state machine inequivalence: We showed, in Chapter 9, that it is decidable whether two FSMs are equivalent. Now define:

- NeqNDFSMs = $\{<M_1, M_2> : M_1$ and M_2 are NDFSMs and $L(M_1) \neq L(M_2)\}$.

NeqNDFSMs is PSPACE-complete [Garey and Johnson 1979].

Finite state machine intersection: We showed, in Chapter 8, that the regular languages are closed under intersection. And we showed, in Chapter 9, that it is decidable whether the language accepted by an FSM is empty. So we know that the following language is decidable:

- 2FSMs-INTERSECT = $\{<M_1, M_2> : M_1$ and M_2 are deterministic FSMs and $L(M_1) \cap L(M_2) \neq \varnothing\}$.

2FSMs-INTERSECT is in P. So it is tractable. But now consider a generalization to an arbitrary number of FSMs:

- FSMs-INTERSECT = $\{<M_1, M_2, \ldots, M_n> : M_1$ through M_n are deterministic FSMs and there exists some string accepted by all of them$\}$.

FSMs-INTERSECT is PSPACE-complete [Garey and Johnson 1979].

Regular expression inequivalence: We showed, in Chapter 6, that there exists an algorithm that can convert any regular expression into an equivalent FSM. So any question that is decidable for FSMs must also be decidable for regular expressions. So we know that the following language is decidable:

- NeqREGEX = $\{<E_1, E_2> : E_1$ and E_2 are regular expressions and $L(M_1) \neq L(M_2)\}$.

NeqREGEX is PSPACE-complete [Garey and Johnson 1979].

Regular expression incompleteness: We showed, in Chapter 9, that it is decidable whether a regular language (described either as an FSM or as a regular expression) is equivalent to Σ^*. So we know that the following language is decidable:

- NOT-SIGMA-STAR = $\{<E> : E$ is a regular expression and $L(E) \neq \Sigma_E^*\}$.

NOT-SIGMA-STAR is PSPACE-complete [Sudkamp 2006].

Regular expression with squaring incompleteness: Define the language of regular expressions with squaring to be exactly the same as the language of regular expressions with the addition of one new operator defined as follows:

- If α is a regular expression with squaring, then so is α^2. $L(\alpha^2) = L(\alpha)L(\alpha)$.

Notice that the squaring operator does not introduce any descriptive power to the language of regular expressions. It does, however, make it possible to write shorter equivalents for some regular expressions. In particular, consider the regular expression that is composed of 2^n copies of α concatenated together (for some value of n). Its length is $\mathcal{O}(2^n)$. Using squaring, we can write an equivalent regular expression, $(\ldots (((\alpha)^2)^2 \ldots)^2$, with the squaring operator applied n times, whose length is $\mathcal{O}(n)$. Since the complexity of any problem that requires reasoning about regular expressions is defined in terms of the length of the expression, this exponential compression of the size of an input string can be expected to make a difference. And it does. Define the language:

- NOT-SIGMA-STAR-SQUARING = {<E> : E is a regular expression with squaring and $L(E) \neq \Sigma_E{}^*$}.

While NOT-SIGMA-STAR (for standard regular expressions) is PSPACE-complete, NOT-SIGMA-STAR-SQUARING is provably not in PSPACE [Sudkamp 2006]. So we know that, since P $\subseteq$ PSPACE, no polynomial-time algorithm can exist for NOT-SIGMA-STAR-SQUARING.

The membership question for context-sensitive languages: In Section 24.1, we described two techniques for answering the question, given a context-sensitive language L and a string w, is $w \in L$? One approach simulated the computation of a linear bounded automaton; the other simulated the generation of strings by a context-sensitive grammar. Unfortunately, neither of those techniques is efficient and it seems unlikely that better ones exist. Define the language:

- CS-MEMBERSHIP = {<G, w> : $w \in L(G)$}.

CS-MEMBERSHIP is PSPACE-complete [Garey and Johnson 1979].

29.4 Sublinear Space Complexity

It doesn't make much sense to talk about algorithms whose time complexity is $\sigma(n)$, i.e., algorithms whose time complexity is less than linear. Such algorithms do not have time to read their entire input. But when we turn our attention to space complexity, it does make sense to consider algorithms that use a sublinear amount of working space (in addition to the space required to hold the original input). For example, consider a program P that is fed a stream of input events, eventually followed by an <*end*> symbol. P's job is to count he number of events that occur before the <*end*>. It doesn't need to remember the input stream. So the only working memory that is required is a single counter, which can be represented in binary. Thus, ignoring the space required by the input stream, $spacereq(P) \in \mathcal{O}(\log n)$.

To make it easy to talk about the space complexity of programs like P and the problems that they solve, we will make the following modification to our computational model. We will consider Turing machines with two tapes:

- a read-only input tape, and
- a read-write working tape.

While the input tape is read-only, it is not identical to the input stream of a finite state machine or of the simple counting example that we just described. The machine may move back and forth on the input tape, thus examining it any number of times.

Now we will define *spacereq*(M) by counting only the number of visited cells of the read-write (working) tape. Notice that, if *spacereq*(M) is at least linear, then this measure is equivalent to our original one since M's input can be copied from the input tape to the read-write tape in $\mathcal{O}(n)$ space.

Using this new notion of space complexity, we can define two new and important space complexity classes: But first we must resolve a naming conflict. We have been using the variable L to refer to an arbitrary language. By convention, one of the complexity classes that we are about to define is named L. To avoid confusion, we'll use the variable $L\#$ for languages when necessary. Now we can state the following definitions:

The Class L: $L\# \in$ L iff there exists some deterministic Turing machine M that decides $L\#$ and $spacereq(M) \in \mathcal{O}(\log n)$.

The Class NL: $L\# \in$ NL iff there exists some nondeterministic Turing machine M that decides $L\#$ and $spacereq(M) \in \mathcal{O}(\log n)$.

We have chosen to focus on $\mathcal{O}(\log n)$ because:

- Many useful problems can be solved in $\mathcal{O}(\log n)$ space. For example:
  - It is enough to remember the length of an input.
  - It is enough to remember a constant number of pointers into the input.
  - It is enough to remember a logarithmic number of Boolean values.
- It is unaffected by some reasonable changes in the way inputs are encoded. For example, it continues not to matter what base, greater than 1, is used for representing numbers.
- Savitch's Theorem can be extended to cases where $spacereq(M) \geq \log n$.

EXAMPLE 29.4 The Balanced Parentheses Language is in L

Recall the balanced parentheses language Bal $= \{w \in \{), (\}^* :$ the parentheses are balanced$\}$. We have seen that Bal is not regular but it is context-free. It is also in L. It can be decided by a deterministic Turing machine M that uses its working tape to store a count, in binary, of the number of left parentheses that have not yet been matched. M will make one pass through its input. Each time it sees a left parenthesis, it will increment the count by one. Each time it sees a right parenthesis, it will decrement the count by one if it was positive. If, on the other hand, the count was zero, M will immediately reject. If, when M reaches the end of the input, the count is zero, it will accept. Otherwise it will reject. The amount of space required to store the counter grows as $\mathcal{O}(\log |w|)$, so $spacereq(M) \in \mathcal{O}(\log n)$.

EXAMPLE 29.5 USTCON: Finding Paths in Undirected Graphs is also in L

Let USTCON $= \{<G, s, t> : G$ is an undirected graph and there exists an undirected path in G from s to $t\}$. In our discussion of finite state machines, we exploited an algorithm to find the states that are reachable from the start state. We used the same idea in analyzing context-free grammars to find nonterminals that are useless (because they aren't reachable from the start symbol). The obvious way to solve USTCON is the same way we solved those earlier problems: We start at s and mark the vertices that are connected to it via a single edge. Then we take each marked vertex and follow edges from it. We halt whenever we have marked the destination vertex t or we have made a complete pass through the vertices and marked no new ones. To decide USTCON then, we accept if t was marked and reject otherwise.

The simple decision procedure that we just described shows that USTCON is in P. But it fails to show that USTCON can be decided in logarithmic space because it requires (to store the marks) one bit of working storage for each vertex in G. An alternative approach shows that USTCON is in NL. Define a nondeterministic Turing machine M that searches for a path from s to t but only remembers the most recent vertex on the path. M begins by counting the vertices in G and recording the count (in binary) on its working tape. Then it starts at s and looks for a path. At each step, it nondeterministically chooses an edge from the most recent vertex it has visited to some new vertex. It stores on its working tape the index (in binary) of the new vertex. And it decrements its count by 1. If it ever selects vertex t, it halts and accepts. If, on the other hand, its count reaches 0, it halts and rejects. If there is a path from s to t, there must be one whose length is no more than the total number of vertices in G. So M will find it. And it uses only logarithmic space since both the step counter and the vertex index can be stored in space that grows logarithmically with the size of G.

It turns out that USTCON is also in L. In other words, there is a deterministic, logarithmic-space algorithm that decides it. That algorithm is described in [Reingold 2005].

What, if anything, can we say about the relationship between L, NL, and the other complexity classes that we have already considered? First, we note that trivially (since every deterministic Turing machine is also a nondeterministic one and since $\log n \in \mathcal{O}(n)$):

$$\mathrm{L} \subseteq \mathrm{NL} \subseteq \mathrm{PSPACE}.$$

But what about the relationship between L and NL in the other direction? We know of no languages that are in NL and that can be proven not to be in L. But neither can we prove that L = NL. The L = NL question exists in an epistemological limbo analogous to the P = NP question. In both cases, it is widely assumed, but unproven, that the answer to the question is no.

As in the case of the P = NP question, one way to increase our understanding of the L = NL question is to define a class of languages that are at least as hard as every language in NL. As before, we will do this by defining a technique for reducing one language to another. In all the cases we have considered so far, we have used polynomial-time reduction. But, as we will see below, NL $\subseteq$ P. So a polynomial-time reduction could dominate a logarithmic space computation. To be informative, we need to define a weaker notion of reduction. The one we will use is called logarithmic-space (or simply log-space) reduction. We will say that a language L_1 is ***log-space reducible*** to L_2 iff there is a deterministic two-tape Turing machine (as described above) that reduces L_1 to L_2 and whose working tape uses no more than $\mathcal{O}(\log n)$ space. Now we can define:

The Class NL-hard: A language $L\#$ is NL-hard iff every language in NL is log-space reducible it.

The Class NL-complete: A language $L\#$ is NL-complete iff it is NL-hard and it is in NL.

Analogously to the case of NP-completeness, if we could find a single NL-complete language that is also in L, we would know that L = NL. So far, none has been found. But there are NL-complete languages. We mention one next.

EXAMPLE 29.6 STCON: Finding Paths in Directed Graphs

Let STCON = $\{<G, s, t> : G$ is a directed graph and there exists a directed path in G from s to $t\}$. Note that STCON is like USTCON except that it asks for a path in a directed (rather than an undirected) graph. STCON is in NL because it can be decided by almost the same nondeterministic, log-space Turing machine that we described as a way to decide USTCON. The only difference is that now we must consider the direction of the edges that we follow.

Unlike in the case of USTCON, we know of no algorithm that shows that STCON is in L. Instead, it is possible to prove that STCON is NL-complete.

So we don't know whether L = NL. We also don't know the exact relationship among L, NL, and P. But it is straightforward to prove the following result about the relationship between L and P.

THEOREM 29.7 L ⊆ P

Theorem: L ⊆ P.

Proof: Any language in L can be decided by a deterministic Turing machine M, where $spacereq(M) \in \mathcal{O}(\log n)$. We can show that M must run in polynomial time by showing a bound on the number of distinct configurations it can enter. Since it halts, it can never enter the same configuration a second time. So we have a bound on the number of steps it can execute. Although M has two tapes, the contents of the first one remain the same in all configurations. So the number of distinct configurations of M on input of length n is the product of:

- the number of possible positions for the read head on the input tape. This is simply n.
- the number of different values for the working tape. Each square of the working tape can take on any element of Γ (M's tape alphabet). So the maximum number of different values of the working tape is $|\Gamma|^{spacereq(M)}$.

- the number of positions of the working tape's read/write head. This is bounded by its length, $spacereq(M)$.
- the number of states of M. Call that number k.

Then, on an input of length n, the maximum number of distinct configurations of M is:

$$n \cdot |\Gamma|^{spacereq(M)} \cdot spacereq(M) \cdot k.$$

Since M is deciding a language in L, $spacereq(M) \in \mathcal{O}(\log n)$. The number k is independent of n. So the maximum number of distinct configurations of M is $\mathcal{O}(n \cdot |\Gamma|^{\log n} \cdot \log n)$ or, simplifying, $\mathcal{O}(n^{1+\log|\Gamma|} \cdot \log n)$. Thus $timereq(M)$ is also $\mathcal{O}(n^{1+\log|\Gamma|} \cdot \log n)$ and thus $\mathcal{O}(n^{2+\log|\Gamma|})$, which is polynomial in n. So the language that M decides is in P.

It is also possible to prove the following theorem, which makes the stronger claim that NL $\subseteq$ P.

THEOREM 29.8 NL $\subseteq$ P

Theorem: NL $\subseteq$ P.

Proof: The proof relies on facts about STCON = $\{<G, s, t> : G$ is a directed graph and there exists a directed path in G from s to $t\}$. STCON is in P because it can be decided by the polynomial-time marking algorithm that we described in our discussion of USTCON in Example 29.5. STCON is also NL-complete, which means that any other language in NL can be reduced to it in deterministic logarithmic space. But any deterministic log-space Turing machine also runs in polynomial time because the number of distinct configurations that it can enter is bounded by a polynomial, as we saw above in the proof that L $\subseteq$ P. So any language in NL can be decided by the composition of two deterministic, polynomial-time Turing machines and thus is in P.

We can summarize what we know as:

$$\text{L} \subseteq \text{NL} \subseteq \text{P} \subseteq \text{PSPACE}.$$

Just as we have done for the other complexity classes that we have considered, we can define classes that contain the complements of languages in L and in NL. So we have:

The Class co-L: $L\# \in$ co-L iff $\neg L\# \in$ L.

The Class co-NL: $L\# \in$ co-NL iff $\neg L\# \in$ NL.

It is easy to show that the class L is closed under complement and thus that L = co-L: If a language $L\#$ is decided by a deterministic Turing machine M, then there exists another deterministic Turing machine M' such that M' decides $\neg L\#$. M' is simply M with the y and n states reversed. $Spacereq(M') = spacereq(M)$. So, if $L\#$ is in the class L, so is its complement.

It is less obvious, but true, that NL = co-NL. The proof follows from the more general claim that we will state as Theorem 29.10 (the Immerman-Szelepcsényi Theorem) in the next section. There we will see that all nondeterministic space complexity classes whose space requirement is at least $\log n$ are closed under complement.

29.5 The Closure of Space Complexity Classes Under Complement

Recall that the class P is closed under complement. On the other hand, it is believed that NP $\neq$ co-NP, although no proof of that exists. When we switch from considering time complexity to considering space complexity, the situation is clearer. Both deterministic and nondeterministic space-complexity classes are closed under complement. The fact that deterministic ones are is obvious (since a deciding machine for $\neg L$ is simply the deciding machine for L with its accepting and rejecting states reversed). The fact that nondeterministic ones are is not obvious.

To make it easy to state the next group of theorems, we will define the following families of languages.

- $dspace(f(n))$ = the set of languages that can be decided by some deterministic Turing machine M, where $spacereq(M) \in \mathcal{O}(f(n))$
- $ndspace(f(n))$ = the set of languages that can be decided by some nondeterministic Turing machine M, where $spacereq(M) \in \mathcal{O}(f(n))$
- $co\text{-}dspace(f(n))$ = the set of languages whose complements can be decided by some deterministic Turing machine M, where $spacereq(M) \in \mathcal{O}(f(n))$
- $co\text{-}ndspace(f(n))$ = the set of languages whose complements can be decided by some nondeterministic Turing machine M, where $spacereq(M) \in \mathcal{O}(f(n))$

THEOREM 29.9 Deterministic Space-Complexity Classes are Closed Under Complement

Theorem: For every function $f(n)$, $dspace(f(n)) = co\text{-}dspace(f(n))$.

Proof: If L is a language that is decided by some deterministic Turing machine M, then the deterministic Turing machine M' that is identical to M except that the halting states y and n are reversed decides $\neg L$. $Spacereq(M') = spacereq(M)$. So, if $L \in dspace(f(n))$, so is $\neg L$.

THEOREM 29.10 The Immerman-Szelepcsényi Theorem and the Closure of Nondeterministic Space-Complexity Classes Under Complement

Theorem: For every function $f(n) \geq \log n$, $ndspace(f(n)) = co\text{-}ndspace(f(n))$.

Proof: The proof of this claim, that the nondeterministic space complexity classes are closed under complement, was given independently in [Immerman 1988] and [Szelepcsényi 1988].

One application of the Immerman-Szelepcsényi Theorem is to a question we asked in Section 24.1, "Are the context-sensitive languages closed under complement?" We are now in a position to sketch a proof of Theorem 24.11, which we restate here as Theorem 29.11.

THEOREM 29.11 Closure of the Context-Sensitive Languages Under Complement

Theorem: The context-sensitive languages are closed under complement.

Proof: Recall that a language is context-sensitive iff it is accepted by some linear bounded automaton (LBA). An LBA is a nondeterministic Turing machine whose space is bounded by the length of its input. So the class of context-sensitive languages is exactly $ndspace(n)$. By the Immerman-Szelepcsényi Theorem, $ndspace(n) = co\text{-}ndspace(n)$. So the complement of every context-sensitive language can also be decided by a nondeterministic Turing machine that uses linear space (i.e., an LBA). Thus it too is context-sensitive.

29.6 Space Hierarchy Theorems

We saw, in Section 28.9.1, that giving a Turing machine more time increases the class of languages that can be decided. The same is true of increases in space. We can prove a pair of space hierarchy theorems that are similar to the time hierarchy theorems that we have already described. The main difference is that the space hierarchy theorems that we can prove are stronger than the corresponding time hierarchy ones because running space-bounded simulations does not require the overhead that appears to be required in the time-bounded case.

Before we can define the theorems, we must define the class of space-requirement functions to which they will apply. So, analogously (but not identically) to the way we defined time constructability, we will define space-constructibility:

A function $s(n)$ from the positive integers to the positive integers is ***space-constructible*** iff:

- $s(n) \geq \log n$, and
- the function that maps the unary representation of n (i.e., 1^n) to the binary representation of $s(n)$ can be computed in $\mathcal{O}(s(n))$ space.

Most useful functions, as long as they are at least $\log n$, are space-constructible.

Whenever we say that, for some Turing machine M, $spacereq(M) \in \sigma(n)$, we are using, as our definition of a Turing machine, the two-tape machine that we described in Section 29.4. In that case, we will take $spacereq(M)$ to be the size of M's working tape.

THEOREM 29.12 Deterministic Space Hierarchy Theorem

Theorem: For any space-constructible function $s(n)$, there exists a language $L_{s(n)hard}$ that is decidable in $\mathcal{O}(s(n))$ space but that is not decidable in $\sigma(s(n))$ space.

Proof: The proof is by diagonalization and is similar to the proof we gave for Theorem 28.27 (the Deterministic Time Hierarchy Theorem). The tighter bound in this theorem comes from the fact that it is possible to describe an efficient space-bounded simulator. The details of the proof, and in particular, the design of the simulator, are left as an exercise.

Exercises

1. In Section 29.1.2, we defined $MaxConfigs(M)$ to be $|K| \cdot |\Gamma|^{spacereq(M)} \cdot spacereq(M)$. We then claimed that, if c is a constant greater than $|\Gamma|$, then $MaxConfigs(M) \in \mathcal{O}(c^{spacereq(M)})$. Prove this claim by proving the following more general claim:

   Given: f is a function from the natural numbers to the positive reals, f is monotonically increasing and unbounded, a and c are positive reals, and $1 < a < c$.

   Then: $f(n) \cdot a^{f(n)} \in \mathcal{O}(c^{f(n)})$.

2. Prove that PSPACE is closed under:
   a. complement.
   b. union.
   c. concatenation.
   d. Kleene star.

3. Define the language:
   - U = {<$M, w, 1^s$> : M is a Turing machine that accepts w within space s}.

   Prove that U is PSPACE-complete.

4. In Section 28.7.3, we defined the language 2-SAT = {<w> : w is a wff in Boolean logic, w is in 2-conjunctive normal form and w is satisfiable} and saw that it is in P. Show that 2-SAT is NL-complete.

5. Prove that $A^nB^n = \{a^nb^n : n \geq 0\}$ is in L.

6. In Example 21.5, we described the game of Nim. We also showed an efficient technique for deciding whether or not the current player has a guaranteed win. Define the language:
   - NIM = {<b>: b is a Nim configuration (i.e., a set of piles of sticks) and there is a guaranteed win for the current player}.

   Prove that NIM $\in$ L.

7. Prove Theorem 29.12 (The Deterministic Space Hierarchy Theorem).

CHAPTER 30

Practical Solutions for Hard Problems

It appears unlikely that P = NP. It appears even more unlikely that, even if it does, a proof that it does will lead us to efficient algorithms to solve the hard problems that we have been discussing. (We base this second claim on at least two observations. The first is that people have looked long and hard for such algorithms and have failed to find them. The second is that just being polynomial is not sufficient to assure efficiency in any practical sense.) And things are worse. Some problems, for example those with a structure like generalized chess, are provably outside of P, whatever the verdict on NP is. Yet important applications depend on algorithms to solve these problems. So what can we do?

30.1 Approaches

In our discussion of the traveling salesman problem at the beginning of Chapter 27, we suggested two strategies for developing an efficient algorithm to solve a hard problem:

Compromise on generality: Design an algorithm that finds an optimal solution and that runs efficiently on most (although not necessarily all) problem instances. This approach is particularly useful if the problems that we actually care about solving possess particular kinds of structures and we can find an algorithm that is tuned to work well on those structures. We have already considered some examples of this approach:

- Very large real instances of the traveling salesman problem can be solved efficiently by iteratively solving a linear programming problem that is a relaxed instance of the exact problem. Although, in principle, it could happen that each such iteration removes only a single tour from consideration, when the graph corresponds to a real problem, large numbers of tours can almost always be eliminated at each step.
- Some very large Boolean formulas can be represented efficiently using ordered binary decision diagrams (OBDDs), as described in B.1.3. That efficient representation makes it possible to solve the satisfiability (SAT) problem efficiently. The OBDD representation of a randomly constructed Boolean formula may not be

compact. But OBDDs exploit exactly the kinds of structures that typically appear in formulas that have been derived from natural problems, such as digital circuits.

Compromise on optimality: Design an approximation algorithm that is guaranteed to find a good (although not necessarily optimal) solution and to do so efficiently. This approach is particularly attractive if the error that may be introduced in finding the solution is relatively small in comparison with errors that may have been introduced in the process of defining the problem itself. For example, in any real instance of the traveling salesman problem, we must start by measuring the physical world and no such measurement can be exact. Or consider the large class of problems in which we seek to maximize (or minimize) the value of some objective function that combines, into a single number, multiple numbers that measure the utility of a proposed solution along two or more dimensions. For example, we might define a cost function for a proposed stretch of new divided highway to be something like:

$$\begin{aligned} cost(s) = {} & 4 \cdot dollar\text{-}cost(s) - 2 \cdot number\text{-}of\text{-}lives\text{-}saved\text{-}by(s) \\ & - 1.5 \cdot commuting\text{-}hours\text{-}saved\text{-}per\text{-}week(s). \end{aligned}$$

Since the objective function is only an approximate measure of the utility of a new road, an approximately optimal solution to a highway system design problem may be perfectly acceptable.

Compromise on both: For some problems, it turns out that if we make some assumptions about problem structure then we can find very good, but not necessarily optimum solutions very quickly. For example, suppose that we limit the traveling salesman problem to graphs that satisfy the triangle inequality (as described in Section 27.1). Real world maps meet that constraint. Then there exist algorithms for finding very good solutions very quickly.

A fourth approach, useful in some kinds of problems is:

Compromise on total automation: Design an algorithm that works interactively with a human user who guides it into the most promising regions of its search space.

> When applied to many practical problems, including verifying the correctness of both hardware and software systems, automatic theorem provers face exponential growth in the number of paths that must be considered. One way to focus such systems on paths that are likely to lead to the desired proofs is to let a human user guide the system. (H.1.1)

In most of these approaches, we are admitting that we have no efficient and "direct" algorithm for finding the answer that we seek. Instead, we conduct a search through a space that is defined by the structure of the problem we are trying to solve. In the next two sections we will sketch two quite different approaches to conducting that search. In particular, we'll consider:

- ***Approach 1:*** The space is structured randomly. Exploit that randomness.
- ***Approach 2:*** The space isn't structured randomly and we have some knowledge about the structure that exists. Exploit that knowledge.

30.2 Randomized Algorithms and the Language Classes BPP, RP, Co-RP and ZPP

For some kinds of problems, it is possible to avoid the expensive behavior of an exhaustive search algorithm by making a sequence of random guesses that, almost all of the time, converge efficiently to an answer that is correct.

EXAMPLE 30.1 Quicksort

We'll illustrate the idea of random guessing with a common algorithm that reduces the expected time required to sort a list from $\mathcal{O}(n^2)$ to $\mathcal{O}(n \log n)$. Given a list of n elements, define *quicksort* as follows:

quicksort(*list*: a list of n elements) =

1. If n is 0 or 1, return *list*. Otherwise:
2. Choose an element from *list*. Call it the *pivot*.
3. Reorder the elements in *list* so that every element that is less than *pivot* occurs ahead of it and every element that is greater than *pivot* occurs after it. If there are equal elements, they may be left in any order.
4. Recursively call *quicksort* with the fragment of *list* that includes the elements up to, but not including *pivot*.
5. Recursively call *quicksort* with the fragment of *list* that includes all the elements after *pivot*.

Quicksort always halts with its input list correctly sorted. At issue is the time required to do so. Step 3 can be done in $\mathcal{O}(n)$ steps. In fact, it can usually be implemented very efficiently. When step 3 is complete, *pivot* is in the correct place in *list*.

In the worst case, *quicksort* runs in $\mathcal{O}(n^2)$ time. This happens if, at each step, the reordering places all the elements on the same side of *pivot*. Then the length of *list* is reduced by only 1 each time *quicksort* is called. In the best case, however, the length of *list* is cut in half each time. When this happens, *quicksort* runs in $\mathcal{O}(n \log n)$ time.

The key to *quicksort*'s performance is a judicious choice of *pivot*. One particularly bad strategy is to choose the first element of *list*. In the not uncommon case in which *list* is already sorted, or nearly sorted, this choice will force worst-case performance. Any other systematic choice may also be bad if *list* is constructed by a malicious attacker with the goal of forcing worst-case behavior. The solution to this problem is to choose *pivot* randomly. When that is done, *quicksort*'s expected running time, like its best case running time, is $\mathcal{O}(n \log n)$.

In the next section, we'll take the idea of random guessing and use it to build Turing machines that decide languages.

30.2.1 Randomized Algorithms

A ***randomized algorithm*** (sometimes called a ***probabilistic algorithm***) is one that exploits the random guessing strategy that we have just described. Randomized algorithms are used when:

- The problem at hand can usually be solved without exhaustively considering all paths to a solution.
- A systematic way of choosing paths would be vulnerable to common kinds of bad luck (for example, being asked to sort a list that was already sorted) or to a malicious attacker that would explicitly construct worst-case instances if it knew how to do so.

> Randomized algorithms are routinely exploited in cryptographic applications. (J.3)

We can describe randomized algorithms as Turing machines. Call every step at which a nondeterministic Turing machine must choose from among competing moves a ***choice point***. Define a ***randomized Turing machine*** to be a nondeterministic Turing machine M with the following properties.

- At every choice point, there are exactly two moves from which to choose.
- At every choice point, M (figuratively) flips a fair coin and uses the result of the coin toss to decide which of its two branches to pursue.

Note that the constraint of exactly two moves at each choice point is only significant in the sense that it will simplify our analysis of the behavior of these machines. Any nondeterministic Turing machine can be converted into one with a branching factor of two by replacing an n-way branch with several two-way ones.

Since the coin flips are independent of each other, we have that, if b is a single path in a randomized Turing machine M and the number of choice points along b is k, then the probability that M will take b is:

$$\Pr(b) = 2^{-k}.$$

Note that every deterministic Turing machine is a randomized Turing machine that happens, on every input, to have zero choice points and thus a single branch whose probability is 1.

Now consider the specific case in which the job of M is to decide a language. A standard (nonrandomized) nondeterministic Turing machine accepts its input w iff there is at least one path that accepts. A randomized Turing machine only follows one path. It accepts iff that path accepts. It rejects iff that path rejects. So the probability that M accepts w is the sum of the probabilities of all of M's accepting paths. The probability that M rejects w is the sum of the probabilities of all of M's rejecting paths. Alternatively, it is $1 - \Pr(M \text{ accepts})$.

If the job of a randomized Turing machine M is to accept the language L, then there are two kinds of mistakes it could make: It could erroneously accept a string that is not in L, or it could erroneously reject one that is. We would like to be able to place a bound on the likelihood of both kinds of errors. So:

- We'll say that M accepts L with a ***false positive*** probability, ε_P, iff $(w \notin L) \rightarrow (\Pr(M \text{ accepts } w) \leq \varepsilon_P)$.
- We'll say that M accepts L with a ***false negative*** probability, ε_N, iff $(w \in L) \rightarrow (\Pr(M \text{ rejects } w) \leq \varepsilon_N)$.

If M is a randomized Turing machine, we define *timereq*(M) and *spacereq*(M) as for standard Turing machines. In both cases, we measure the complexity of the worst case of M's performance on an input of size n.

We're now in a position to define a set of complexity classes based on acceptance by randomized Turing machines. In the next section, we'll define four such classes, all of them focused on accepting in polynomial time. It is possible to define other classes as well. For example, we could talk about languages that can be accepted by randomized Turing machines that use logarithmic space.

30.2.2 The Language Classes BPP, RP, Co-RP, and ZPP

Our goal is to recognize a language with reasonable accuracy in a reasonable amount of time. When we use randomization to do that, there are two kinds of failure modes that we must consider:

- The algorithm always runs efficiently but it may (with small probability) deliver an incorrect answer. Algorithms with this property are called ***Monte Carlo algorithms***.
- The algorithm never returns an incorrect answer but it may (with small probability) be very expensive to run. Algorithms with this property are called ***Las Vegas algorithms***.

We can define complexity classes based on imposing constraints on both kinds of failures. We begin with the first. Define:

The Class BPP: $L \in$ BPP iff there exists some probabilistic Turing machine M that runs in polynomial time and that decides L with a false positive probability, ε_P, and a false negative probability, ε_N, both less than $1/2$. The name BPP stands for **B**ounded-error, **P**robabilistic, **P**olynomial time.

A randomized Turing machine that decides a language in BPP implements a Monte Carlo algorithm. It is allowed to make both kinds of errors (i.e., false positives and false negatives) as long as the probability of making either of them is less than $1/2$. We can characterize such a machine in terms of a single error rate $\varepsilon = max(\varepsilon_P, \varepsilon_N)$. The requirement that ε be less than or equal to $1/2$ may seem too weak. It's hard to imagine saying that M decides L if it only gets it right about half the time. But it is possible to prove the following theorem.

THEOREM 30.1 Reducing the Error Rate

Theorem: Let M be a randomized, polynomial-time Turing machine with error rate ε that is a constant equal to $max(\varepsilon_P, \varepsilon_N)$. If $0 < \varepsilon < 1/2$ and $f(n)$ is any polynomial function, then there exists an equivalent randomized, polynomial-time Turing machine M' with error rate $2^{-f(n)}$.

Proof: The idea is that M' will run M some polynomial number of times and return the answer that appeared more often. If the runs are independent, then the probability of error decreases exponentially as the number of runs of M increases. For a detailed analysis that shows that the desired error bound can be achieved with a polynomial number of runs of M, see [Sipser 2006].

So, for example, the definition of the class BPP wouldn't change if we required ε to be less than 1/10 or 1/3000 or $\frac{1}{2^{3000}}$. Note that the latter is substantially less than the probability that any computer on which M runs will experience a hardware failure that would cause it to return an erroneous result.

The class BPP is closed under complement. In other words, BPP = co-BPP since false positives and false negatives are treated identically.

Sometimes it is possible to build a machine to accept a language L and to guarantee that only one kind of error will occur. It may be possible to examine a string w and to detect efficiently some property that proves that w is in L. Or it may be possible to detect efficiently some way in which w violates the membership requirement for L. So define:

The Class RP: $L \in$ RP iff there exists some randomized Turing machine M that runs in polynomial time and that decides L and where:

- if $w \in L$ then M accepts w with probability 1-ε_N, where $\varepsilon_N < \frac{1}{2}$, and
- if $w \notin L$ then M rejects w with probability 1 (i.e., with false positive probability $\varepsilon_P = 0$).

The name RP stands for **R**andomized, **P**olynomial time.

If L is in RP, then it can be decided by a randomized Turing machine that may reject when it shouldn't. But it will never accept when it shouldn't. Of course, it may also be possible to build a machine that does the opposite. So define the complement of RP:

The Class co-RP: $L \in$ co-RP iff there exists some randomized Turing machine M that runs in polynomial time and that decides L and where:

- if $w \in L$ then M accepts w with probability 1 (i.e., with false negative probability $\varepsilon_N = 0$), and
- if $w \notin L$ then M rejects w with probability 1-ε_P, where $\varepsilon_P < \frac{1}{2}$.

Note that, as in the definition of BPP, the error probabilities required for either RP or co-RP can be anything strictly between 0 and $\frac{1}{2}$ without changing the set of languages that can be accepted.

In the next section, we will present a randomized algorithm for primality testing. An obvious way to decide whether a number is prime would be to look for the existence of a factor that proves that the number isn't prime. The algorithm we will present doesn't do that, but it does look for the existence of a certificate that proves that its input isn't prime. If it finds such a certificate, it can report, with probability 1, that the input is composite. If it fails to find such a certificate, then it reports that the input is prime. That report has high probability of being the correct answer. We will use our algorithm to show that the language PRIMES = $\{w : w$ is the binary encoding of a prime number$\}$ is in co-RP and the language COMPOSITES = $\{w : w$ is the binary encoding of a composite number$\}$ is in RP.

But first let's consider what appears to be a different approach to the use of randomness. Suppose that we want to require an error rate of 0 and, in exchange, we are willing to accept a nonzero probability of a long run time. We call algorithms that satisfy this requirement Las Vegas algorithms. To describe the languages that can be accepted by machines that implement algorithms with this property, define:

The Class ZPP: $L \in$ ZPP iff there exists some randomized Turing machine M such that:

- if $w \in L$ then M accepts w with probability 1,
- if $w \notin L$ then M rejects w with probability 1, and
- there exists a polynomial function $f(n)$ such that, for all inputs w of length n, the expected running time of M on w is less than $f(n)$. It is nevertheless possible that M may run longer than $f(n)$ for some sequences of random events.

The name ZPP stands for **Z**ero-error, **P**robabilistic, **P**olynomial time.

There are two other, but equivalent ways to define ZPP:

- ZPP is the class of languages that can be recognized by some randomized Turing machine M that runs in polynomial time and that outputs one of three possible values: *Accept*, *Reject*, and *Don't Know*. M must never accept when it should reject nor reject when it should accept. Its probability of saying *Don't Know* must be less than $^1/_2$. This definition is equivalent to our original one because it says that, if M runs out of time before determining an answer, it can quit and say *Don't Know*.
- ZPP = RP $\cap$ co-RP. To prove that this definition is equivalent to our original one, we show that each implies the other:
  - $(L \in \text{ZPP}) \rightarrow (L \in \text{RP} \cap \text{co-RP})$: If L is in ZPP, then there is a Las Vegas-style Turing machine M that accepts it. We can construct Monte Carlo-style Turing machines M_1 and M_2 that show that L is also in RP and in co-RP, respectively. On any input w, M_1 will run M on w for its expected running time or until it halts. If M halts naturally in that time, then M_1 will accept or reject as M would have done. Otherwise, it will reject. The probability that M will have halted is at least $^1/_2$, so the probability that M_1 will falsely reject a string that is in L is less than $^1/_2$. Since M_1 runs in polynomial time, it shows that L is in RP. Similarly, construct M_2 that shows that L is in co-RP except that, if the simulation of M does not halt, M_2 will accept.
  - $(L \in \text{RP} \cap \text{co-RP}) \rightarrow (L \in \text{ZPP})$: If L is in RP, then there is a Monte Carlo-style Turing machine M_1 that decides it and that never accepts when it shouldn't. If L is in co-RP, then there is another Monte Carlo-style Turing machine M_2 that decides it and that never rejects when it shouldn't. From these two, we can construct a Las Vegas-style Turing machine M that shows that L is in ZPP. On any input w, M will first run M_1 on w. If it accepts, M will halt and accept. Otherwise M will run M_2 on w. If it rejects, M will halt and reject. If neither of these things happens, it will try again.

Randomization appears to be a useful tool for solving some kinds of problems. But what can we say about the relationships among BPP, RP, co-RP, ZPP and the other complexity classes that we have considered? The class P must be a subset of all four of the randomized classes since a standard, deterministic, polynomial-time Turing machine that doesn't happen to have any choice points satisfies the requirements for a machine that accepts languages in all of those classes. Further, we have already shown that ZPP is a subset of both RP and co-RP. So all of the following relationships are known.

- $\text{P} \subseteq \text{BPP}$
- $\text{P} \subseteq \text{ZPP} \subseteq \text{RP} \subseteq \text{NP}$
- $\text{P} \subseteq \text{ZPP} \subseteq \text{co-RP} \subseteq \text{co-NP}$
- $\text{RP} \cup \text{co-RP} \subseteq \text{BPP}$

There are two big unknowns. One is the relationship between BPP and NP. Neither is known to be a subset of the other. The other is whether P is a proper subset of BPP. It is widely conjectured, but unproven, that BPP = P. If this is true, then randomization is a useful tool for constructing practical algorithms for some problems but it is not a technique that will make it possible to construct polynomial-time solutions for NP-complete problems unless P = NP.

30.2.3 Primality Testing

One of the most important applications of randomized algorithms is the problem of primality checking. We mentioned above that PRIMES = $\{w : w$ is the binary encoding of a prime number$\}$ is in co-RP and COMPOSITES = $\{w : w$ is the binary encoding of a composite number$\}$ is in RP. In this section, we will see why.

Recall that the obvious way to decide whether an integer p is prime is to consider all of the integers between 2 and $\sqrt{p}$, checking each to see whether it divides evenly into p. If any of them does, then p isn't prime. If none does, then p is prime. The time required to implement this approach is $\mathcal{O}(\sqrt{p})$. But n, the length of the string that encodes p, is $\log p$. So this simple algorithm is $\mathcal{O}(2^{n/2})$. It has recently been shown that PRIMES is in P, so there exists a polynomial-time algorithm that solves this problem exactly.

But, well before that result was announced, randomized algorithms were being used successfully in applications, such as cryptography, that require the ability to perform primality checking quickly. One idea for a randomized algorithm that would check the primality of p is to pick randomly some proposed factors of p and check them. If any of them is a factor, then p is composite. Otherwise, claim that p is prime. The problem with this idea is that, if p is large, most numbers may fail to be factors, even if p is composite. So it would be necessary to try a very large number of possible factors in order to be able to assert with high probability that p is prime. There is a better way.

The randomized algorithm that we are about to present is similar in its overall structure to the factor-testing method that we just rejected. It will randomly choose some numbers and check each to see whether it proves that p is not prime. If none of them does, it will report that p is (highly likely to be) prime. Its effectiveness relies on a few fundamental facts about modular arithmetic. To simplify the rest of this discussion, let $x \equiv_p y$, read "x is equivalent to y mod p" mean that x and y have the same remainder when divided by p.

The first result that we will use is known as ***Fermat's Little Theorem*** 🖳. It tells us the following:

- If p is prime, then, for any positive integer a, if $gcd(a, p) = 1$, $a^{p-1} \equiv_p 1$.

Recall that the greatest common divisor (gcd) of two integers is the largest integer that is a factor of both of them. We'll say that p passes the Fermat test at a iff $a^{p-1} \equiv_p 1$. For example, let $p = 5$ and $a = 3$. Then $3^{(5-1)} = 81 \equiv_5 1$. So 5 passes the fermat test at 3, which it must do since 5 is prime and 3 and 5 are relatively prime. But now let $p = 8$ and $a = 3$. Then $3^{(8-1)} = 2187 \equiv_8 3$. So 8 fails the Fermat test at 3, which is consistent with the theorem, since 8 is not prime. Whenever p fails the Fermat test at a, we'll say that a is a ***Fermat witness*** that p is composite.

Fermat's Little Theorem tells us that if p is prime, then it must pass the Fermat test at every appropriately chosen value of a. Can we turn this around? If p passes the Fermat test at some value a, do we know that p is prime? The answer to this question is no. If p is composite and yet it passes the Fermat test at a, we will say that a is a ***Fermat liar*** that p is prime.

Fermat's Little Theorem is the basis for a simple randomized algorithm for deciding the primality of p. We'll randomly choose values for a, looking for a witness that p is composite. We'll only consider values that are less than p. So, if p is prime, $gcd(a, p)$ will always be 1. Thus our algorithm will not have to evaluate gcd. If we fail to find a witness that shows that p is composite, we'll report that p is probably prime. Because liars exist, we can increase the likelihood of finding such a witness, if one exists, by increasing the number of candidate witnesses that we test. So we'll present an algorithm that takes two inputs, a value to be tested and the number of possible witnesses that should be checked. The output will be one of two values: *composite* and *probably prime*.

simpleFermat(p: integer, k: integer) =

1. Do k times:

  1.1. Randomly select a value a in the range $[2: p-1]$.

  1.2. If it is not true that $a^{p-1} \equiv_p 1$, then return *composite*.

2. All tests have passed. Return *probably prime*.

Modular exponentiation can be implemented efficiently using the technique of successive squaring that we describe in Example J.1. So *simpleFermat* runs in polynomial time. All that remains is to determine its error rate as a function of k. With the exception of a small class of special composite numbers that we will describe below, if p is composite, then the chance that any a is a Fermat liar for it is less than $^1/_2$. So, again with the exception we are about to describe, the error rate of *simpleFermat* is less than $1/2^k$.

But now we must consider the existence of composite numbers that pass the Fermat test at all values. Call such numbers ***Carmichael numbers*** 🖳. Every value of a is a Fermat liar for every Carmichael number, so no value of k will enable *simpleFermat* to realize that a Carmichael number isn't prime.

However, there is a separate randomized test that we can use to detect Carmichael numbers. It is based on the following fact: If p is prime, then 1 has exactly two square roots (mod p): 1 and -1. If, on the other hand, p is composite, it is possible that 1 has three or more square roots (mod p). For example, let $p = 8$. Then we have:

- $1^2 = 1$.
- $3^2 = 9 \equiv_8 1$.
- $5^2 = 25 \equiv_8 1$. Note that $5 \equiv_8 -3$.
- $7^2 = 49 \equiv_8 1$. Note that $7 \equiv_8 -1$.

So we can write the four square roots of 1 (mod 8) as $1, -1, 3, -3$. For every Carmichael number n, 1 has more than two square roots (mod n). For example, the smallest Carmichael number is 561. The square roots of 1 (mod 561) are $1, -1(560)$, $67, -67(494), 188(-373), 254$, and $-254(-307)$.

While *simpleFermat* cannot distinguish between primes and Carmichael numbers, a randomized test based on finding square roots can. We could design such a test that just chooses random values and checks to see whether they are square roots of 1 (mod p). If any is, then p isn't prime. And, unlike with *simpleFermat*, there exist witnesses even for Carmichael composite numbers. But there's a more efficient way to find additional square roots if they exist. Suppose that we have done the *simpleFermat* test at a and a has passed. Then we know that $a^{p-1} \equiv_p 1$. Taking the square root of both sides, we get that $a^{(p-1)/2}$ is a square root of 1 (mod p). If $a^{(p-1)/2} \equiv_p 1$, we haven't learned anything. But then we can again take the square root of both sides and continue until one of the following things happens.

1. We get a root that is -1. We're not interested in finding square roots of -1. So we give up, having failed to show that any additional roots exist. It is possible that p is prime or that it is composite.
2. We get a noninteger. Again, we simply stop as in case 1.
3. We get a root that is neither 1 nor -1. We have shown that p is composite.

So (taking all results (mod p)) we check:

- a^{p-1} (and, as in *simpleFermat*, assert composite if we get any value other than 1), then
- $a^{(p-1)/2}$ (and assert composite if we get any value other than 1 or -1), then
- $a^{(p-1)/4}$ (and assert composite if we get any value other than 1 or -1), and so forth, quitting as described above.

The most efficient way to generate this set of tests is in the opposite order. But, to do that, we need to know where to start. In particular, we need to know when the result (if we were going in the order we described above) would no longer be an integer. Suppose that $p - 1$ is represented in binary. Then it it can be rewritten as $d \cdot 2^s$, where d is odd. (The number s is the number of trailing 0's and the number d is what is left after the trailing 0's are removed.) The number of times that we would be able to take the square root of a^{p-1} and still get an integer is s. So we compute (mod p) the reverse of the sequence we described above:

$$a^{d \cdot 2^0}, a^{d \cdot 2^1}, \ldots, a^{d \cdot 2^s}.$$

Then we check the sequence right to left. If the last element is not 1, then a fails the simple Fermat test and we can report that p is composite. Otherwise, as long as the values are 1, we continue. If we encounter -1, we must quit and report that we found no evidence that p is composite. If, on the other hand, we find some value other than 1 or -1, we can report that p is composite.

Using this idea, we can state the following algorithm, which is generally known as the Miller-Rabin test :

Miller-Rabin(p: integer, k: integer) =

1. If $p = 2$, return *prime*. Else, if p is even, return *composite*.

2. Rewrite $p - 1$ as $d \cdot 2^s$, where d is odd.

3. Do k times:

3.1. Randomly select a value a in the range $[2: p - 1]$.

3.2. Compute the following sequence (mod p):

$$a^{d \cdot 2^0}, a^{d \cdot 2^1}, \ldots, a^{d \cdot 2^s}.$$

3.3. If the last element of the sequence is not 1, then a fails the simple Fermat test. Return *composite*.

3.4. For $i = s - 1$ down to 0 do:

If $a^{d \cdot 2^i} = -1$, then exit this loop. Otherwise, if it is not 1, then return *composite*.

4. All tests have passed. Return *probably prime*.

Miller-Rabin runs in polynomial time and can be shown 💻 to have an error rate that is less than $1/4^k$. So it proves the claim, made above, that the language COMPOSITES is in RP. The efficiency of the algorithm can be improved in various ways. One is to check the elements of the sequence as they are generated. It's harder to see how to do that correctly, but it can cut out some tests. In fact, the algorithm is generally stated in that form.

> While randomized algorithms provide a practical way to check for primality and thus to find large prime numbers, they do not tell us how to factor a large number this is known not to be prime. Modern cryptographic techniques, such as the RSA algorithm, rely on two important facts: Generating primes can be done efficiently, but no efficient technique for factoring composites is known. (J.3)

30.3 Heuristic Search

For some problems, randomized search works well. But suppose that we have some useful information about the shape of the space that we are attempting to search. Then it may make sense not to behave randomly but instead to exploit our knowledge each time a choice needs to be made.

30.3.1 An Introduction to Heuristic Search

A large class of important problems can be described generically as:

- a space of states that correspond to configurations of the problem situation.
- a start state.
- one or more goal states. If there are multiple goal states, then the set of them must be efficiently decidable.
- a set of operators (with associated costs) that describe how it is possible to move from one state to another.

Many puzzles are easy to state in this way. For example:

- In the 15-puzzle, which we described in Example 4.8, the states correspond to arrangements of tiles on the board. An instance of the puzzle specifies a particular arrangement of tiles as the start state. There is a single goal state in which the tiles are arranged in numeric order. And there is a set of legal moves. Specifically, it is possible to move from one state to another by sliding any tile that is adjacent to the empty square into the empty square.
- In the game Instant Insanity®, which we describe in N.2.2, the states correspond to the arrangement of blocks to form a stack. The start state describes a set of blocks, none of which is in the stack. There is a set of goal states (since a goal state is any state in which there is a stack that contains all the blocks and the colors are lined up as required). And there is a set of operators that correspond to adding and removing blocks from the stack.

More significantly, many real problems can also be described as state space search. For example, an airline scheduling problem can be described as a search through a space in which the states correspond to partial assignments of planes and crews to routes. The start state contains no assignments. Any state that assigns a plane and a crew to every flight and that meets some prescribed set of constraints is a goal state. The operators move from one state to the next by making (or unmaking) plane and crew assignments.

Now suppose that we are given a state space search problem and asked to find the shortest (cheapest) path from the start state to a goal. One approach is to conduct a systematic search through the state space by applying operators, starting from the start state. The problem with this technique is that, for many problems, the number of possible states and thus the number of paths that might have to be examined grows exponentially with the size of the problem being considered. For example, if we generalize the 15-puzzle to the n-puzzle (where $n = k^2 - 1$ for some positive integer k), then the number of distinct puzzle states is $(n + 1)!$ It can be shown that the problem of finding the shortest sequence of moves that transforms a given start state into the goal state is NP-hard.

In Section 28.7.4, we showed, by exhibiting a $\mathcal{O}(n^3)$ algorithm to decide it, that the language SHORTEST-PATH = $\{<G, u, v, k>: G$ is an unweighted, undirected graph, u, and v are vertices in G, $k \geq 0$, and there exists a path from u to v whose length is at most $k\}$ is in P. And we pointed out that the extension of SHORTEST-PATH to the case of weighted graphs is also in P. So why can't an instance of the n-puzzle (and other problems like it) be solved in polynomial time? The problem is to find the shortest path from the start state to a goal state and we appear to know how to do that efficiently.

The answer is simple. An instance of SHORTEST-PATH must contain an *explicit* description of the entire space that is to be searched. The vertices of G correspond to the states and the edges of G correspond to the operators that describe the legal moves from one state to the next. When we say that SHORTEST-PATH is in P, we mean that the amount of time that is required to search the space and find the shortest path is a polynomial function of the length of that *complete* state description.

But now consider an instance of the n-puzzle. It can be described much more succinctly. Instead of explicitly enumerating all the board configurations and the moves between them, we can describe just the start and goal configurations, along with a function that defines the operators. This function, when given a state, returns a set of successor states and associated costs. What we do not have to do is to list explicitly the $(n + 1)!$ states that describe configurations of the puzzle. An exhaustive search that requires considering that list would require time that is exponential in the length of the succinct description that we want to use, even though it would have been polynomial in the length of the explicit description that is required for an instance of SHORTEST-PATH.

Simple problems like the n-puzzle and Instant Insanity, as well as real problems, like airline scheduling, are only solvable in practice when:

- there exists a succinct problem description, and
- there exists a search technique that can find acceptable solutions without expanding the entire implicitly defined space.

We've already described a way to construct succinct problem descriptions as state space search. It remains to find efficient algorithms that can search the spaces that are defined in that way. For many problems, if we want an optimal solution and we have no additional information about how to find one, we are stuck. But for many problems, additional information is available. All we have to do is to find a way to exploit it.

A ***heuristic*** is a rule of thumb. It is a technique that, while not necessarily guaranteed to work exactly all of the time, is useful as a problem-solving tool. The word "heuristic" comes from the Greek word εὑρίσκ-ειν (*heuriskein*), meaning to "to find" or "to discover," which is also the root of the word "eureka," derived from Archimedes' reputed exclamation, *heurika* (meaning "I have found"), spoken when he had just discovered a method for determining the purity of gold. Heuristics typically work because they exploit relevant knowledge about the problem that they are being used to solve.

A ***heuristic search algorithm*** is a search algorithm that exploits knowledge of its problem space to help it find an acceptable solution efficiently. One way to encode that knowledge is in the operators that are supplied to the program. For example, instead of defining operators that correspond to all the legal moves in a problem space, we might define only operators that correspond to generally "sensible" moves. Another very useful way is to define a ***heuristic function*** whose job is to examine a state and return a measure of how "desirable" it is. That score can then be used by the search algorithm as it chooses which states to explore next. It is sometimes useful to define heuristic functions that assign high scores to states that merit further exploration. In other cases, it is useful to define heuristic functions that measure cost. For example, we might assign to a state a score that estimates the cost of getting from that state to a goal. When we do this, we assign low scores to the states that most merit further consideration.

30.3.2 The $A*$ Algorithm

In this section, we will describe one very general and effective heuristic search algorithm. The **A* *algorithm*** finds the cheapest path from a start state to a goal state in a succinctly described state space. It exploits a version of ***best-first search*** in which a heuristic function that evaluates states as they are generated guides the algorithm so that it looks first in the part of the space that is most likely to contain the desired solution.

> The $A*$ algorithm is widely used to plan routes for the agents in video games. (N.3.2)

Because what we are trying to do is to find a cheapest path, the score we would like to be able to compute, for any state n is:

$f^*(n)$ = cost of getting from the start state to a goal state via a path that goes through n.

We can break $f^*(n)$ into two components,

$$f^*(n) = g^*(n) + h^*(n), \text{ where:}$$

- $g^*(n)$ is the cost of getting from the start state to n, and
- $h^*(n)$ is the cost of getting the rest of way, i.e., the cost of getting from n to a goal.

If we have generated the state n, then we know the cost of at least one way of getting to it. So we have an estimate of $g^*(n)$. But we don't know $h^*(n)$. If, however, we have information about the problem that allows us to estimate $h^*(n)$, we can use it. We'll denote an estimate of a function by omitting the * symbol. So we have:

$$f(n) = g(n) + h(n).$$

The function $f(n)$ will be used to guide the search process. The function $h(n)$ will evaluate a state and return an estimate of the cost of getting from it to a goal.

In the rest of this discussion, we will assume two things:

- There is some positive number c such that all operator costs are at least c. We make this assumption because, if negative costs are allowed, there may be no cheapest path from the start state to a goal. It is possible, in that case, that any path could be made cheaper by repeating some negative cost operator one more time. And if costs can keep getting smaller and smaller, then the cheapest path to a goal might be one with an infinite number of steps. No procedure that halts will ever be able to output such a path.
- Every state has a finite number of successor states.

The most straightforward version of the A^* algorithm conducts a search through a tree of possible paths. In this version, we ignore the possibility that the same state might be generated along several paths. If it is, it will be explored several times. We'll present this version first. Then we'll consider a graph-based version of the technique. In this second algorithm, we will check, when a state is generated, to see if it has been generated before. If it has, we will collapse the paths. The second version is more complex to state, but it may be substantially more efficient at solving problems in which it is likely that the same state could be reached in many different ways.

To see the difference, consider the partial search shown in Figure 30.1. Suppose that, given the search as shown in (a), the next thing that happens is that state C is considered, its successors are generated, and one of its successors is the state labeled E. The tree-search version of A^* won't notice that E has already been generated another way. It will simply build a new search tree node, as shown in (b), that happens to correspond to the same state as E. If it decides that E is a good state to continue working from, it may explore the entire subtree under E twice, once for E and once for E'. On the other hand, the graph-search version of A^* will notice that it has generated E before. It will build the search graph shown as (c).

A^* is a best-first search algorithm. So it proceeds, at each step, by generating the successors of the state that looks most promising as a way to get cheaply to a goal. To see how it works, consider the search shown in Figure 30.2. State A is the start state. It is expanded (i.e., its successors are generated) first. In this example, shown in (a), it has two successors: B, which costs 1 to generate, and C, which costs 3 to generate. Let's say that the value of $h(B)$ is 3, so $f(B) = g(B) + h(B) = 1 + 3 = 4$. Similarly, if $h(C)$ is 2, then $f(C) = 3 + 2 = 5$. The expression $(g + h)$ for each state is shown directly under it.

A^* maintains a set, called OPEN, of the nodes (corresponding to states) that have been generated but not yet expanded. So OPEN is now $\{B, C\}$. A^* chooses to expand next the element of OPEN that has the lowest f value. That element is B. So B's successors are generated, producing the search tree shown in (b). Notice that the cost of getting to D is $1 + 2$; the cost of getting to E is $1 + 3$. OPEN is now $\{C, D, E\}$. The state with the lowest f value is C, so it is expanded next. Suppose it has one successor, F. Then the search tree is as shown in (c). F will be expanded next, and so forth, until a goal (a state with an h value of 0) is expanded.

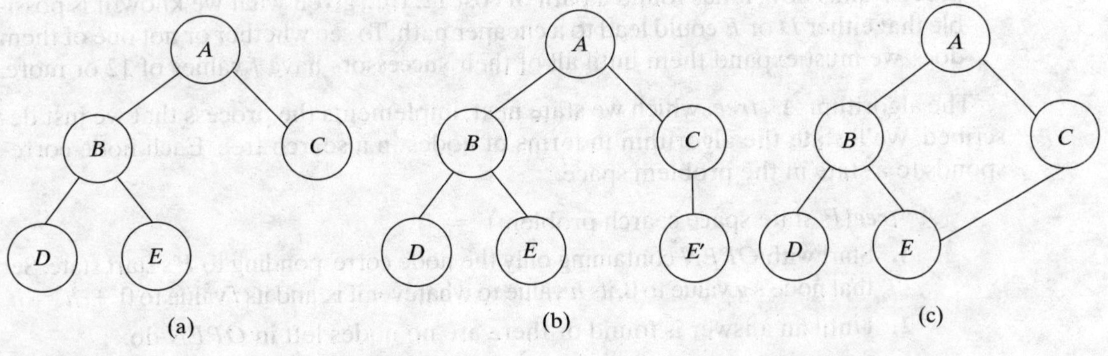

FIGURE 30.1 Tree search versus graph search.

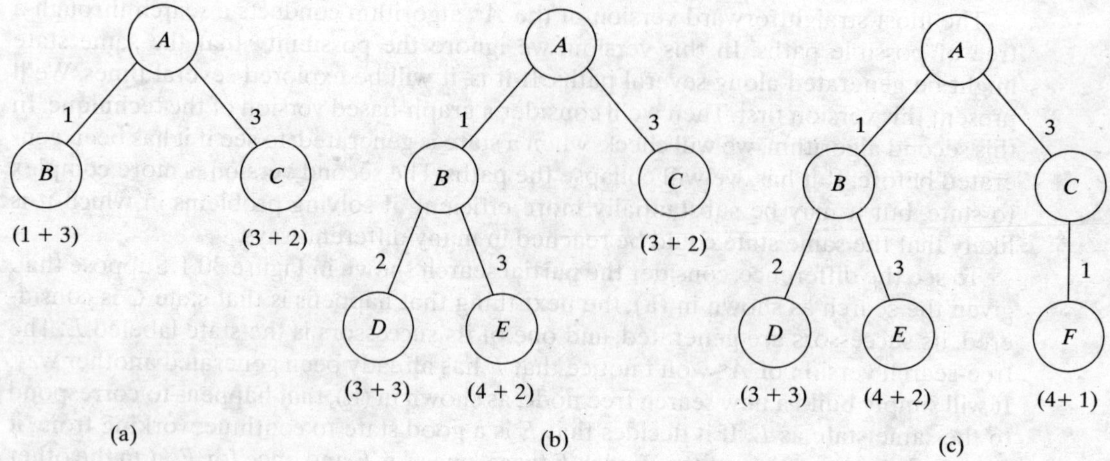

FIGURE 30.2 Best-first search.

Note two things about the process that we have just described:

- If the subtree under *B* had remained promising, none of the subtree under *C* would have been generated. If the subtree under *C* remains promising, no more of the subtree under *B* will be generated. If *C* does turn out to be on the shortest path to a goal, we wasted some time exploring the subtree under *B* because $h(B)$ underestimated the cost of getting to a goal from *B*. In so doing, it made *B* look more promising than it was. The better *h* is at estimating the true cost of getting to a goal, the more efficient *A** will be.
- The search process cannot stop as soon as a goal state is generated. Goal states have *h* values of 0. But a goal state may have a high value of $f = g + h$ if the path to it was expensive. If we want to guarantee to find the shortest path to a goal, the search process must continue until a goal state is chosen for expansion (on the basis of having the lowest total *f* value). To see why this is so, return to the situation shown above as (c). Suppose that *F* has a single successor *G*, it costs 8 to go from *F* to *G*, and *G* is a goal state. Then we have $f(G) = g(G) + h(G) = 12 + 0 = 12$. If the search process quits now, it has found a path of cost 12. But, given what we know, it is possible that either *D* or *E* could lead to a cheaper path. To see whether or not one of them does, we must expand them until all of their successors have *f* values of 12 or more.

The algorithm *A*-tree*, which we state next, implements the process that we just described. We'll state the algorithm in terms of nodes in a search tree. Each node corresponds to a state in the problem space.

A-tree*(*P*: state space search problem) =

1. Start with *OPEN* containing only the node corresponding to *P*'s start state. Set that node's *g* value to 0, its *h* value to whatever it is, and its *f* value to $0 + h = h$.

2. Until an answer is found or there are no nodes left in *OPEN* do:

2.1. If there are no nodes left in *OPEN*, return *Failure*. There is no path from the start state to a goal state.

2.2. Choose from *OPEN* a node such that no other node has a lower *f* value. Call the chosen node *BESTNODE*. Remove it from OPEN.
2.3. If BESTNODE is a goal node, halt and return the path from the initial node to *BESTNODE*.
2.4. Generate the successors of *BESTNODE*. For each of them do:
Compute *f*, *g*, and *h*, and add the node to *OPEN*.

If there exist any paths from the start state to a goal state, *A*-tree* will find one of them. So we'll say that *A*-tree* is ***complete***.

But we can make an even stronger claim: We'll say that $h(n)$ is ***admissible*** iff it never overestimates the true cost $h^*(n)$ of getting to a goal from n. If h is admissible, then *A*-tree* finds an optimal (i.e., cheapest path). To see why this is so, consider the role of h:

- If h always returns 0, it offers no information. *A*-tree* will choose *BESTNODE* based only on the computed cost of reaching it. So it is guaranteed to find a path with a lowest cost. If, in addition to h being 0, all operator costs are the same, then *A*-tree* becomes breadth-first search.
- If $h(n)$ always returns $h^*(n)$, i.e., the exactly correct cost of getting to a goal from n, then *A*-tree* will walk directly down an optimal path and return it.
- If $h(n)$ overestimates $h^*(n)$, then it effectively "hides" a path that might turn out to be the cheapest. To see how this could happen, consider the search trees shown in Figure 30.3. After reaching the situation shown in (b), *A*-tree* will halt and return the path (with cost 5) from A to B to D. But suppose that there is an operator with a cost of 1 that can be applied to C to produce a goal. That would produce a path of cost 4. *A*-tree* will never find that path because the h estimate of 12 blocked it from being considered.
- But if $h(n)$ errs in the other direction and underestimates the true cost of getting to a goal from n, its error will be discovered when the observed cost of the path exceeds the estimated cost without a goal being found. When that happens, *A*-tree* will switch to a cheaper path if there is one.

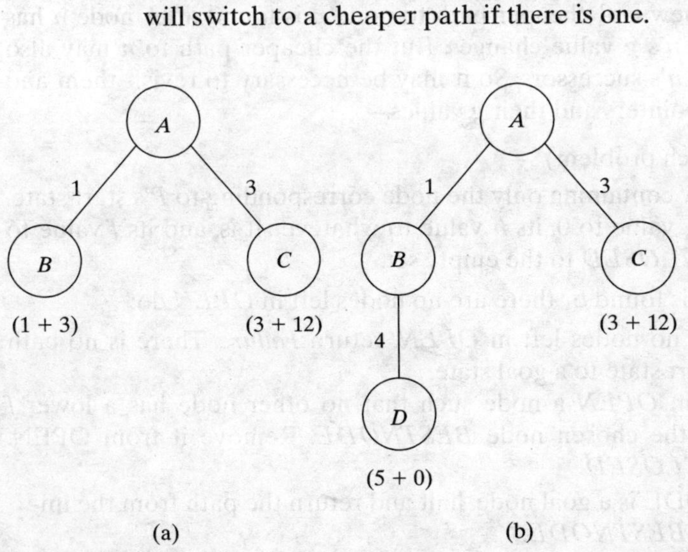

FIGURE 30.3 What happens if h overestimates h^*.

So the only way that *A*-tree* can find and return a path that is more expensive than some other path it could have found is the case in which h overestimates the true cost h^*.

Some simple heuristic functions are always admissible. For example, if the true cost of getting between points A and B is the distance between them along roads in a plane, then Euclidean distance (the length of a straight line between two points) is admissible. And, of course, the heuristic function that simply returns 0 is always admissible. But, for some problems, it may be hard to find a heuristic function that is informative but never runs the risk of overestimating true costs. In those cases, the following further observation is important. We'll call it the ***graceful decay of admissibility***: If h rarely overestimates h^* by more than δ, then *A*-tree* will rarely find a solution whose cost is more than δ greater than the cost of the optimal solution. So, as a practical matter, *A*-tree* will find very good paths unless h makes large errors of overestimation.

So we have that *A*-tree* is optimal in one sense: It finds the best solutions. Search algorithms that are optimal in this sense are called ***admissible***. So *A*-tree* is admissible. But is its own performance optimal or might it be possible to find cheapest paths by exploring a smaller number of nodes? The answer is that *A*-tree* is not optimal in this sense. The reason is that it may explore identical subtrees more than once. As we suggested above, the way to fix this problem is to let it search a state graph rather than a state tree.

We'll give the name *A** to the version of *A*-tree* that searches a graph. We present it next. *A** differs from *A*-tree* in the following ways.

- *A** exploits two sets of nodes: *OPEN*, which functions as in *A*-tree* and contains those nodes that have been generated but not expanded, and *CLOSED*, which contains those nodes that have already been expanded.
- Both *A*-tree* and *A** must be able to trace backward from a goal so that they can return the path that they find. *A*-tree* can do that trivially by simply storing bi-directional pointers as it builds its search tree. But *A** searches a graph. So it must explicitly record, at each node, the best way of getting to that node from the start node. Whenever a new path to node n is found, its backward pointer may change.
- Suppose that, in *A**, a new and cheaper path to node n is found after node n has been expanded. Clearly n's g value changes. But the cheaper path to n may also mean a cheaper path to n's successors. So it may be necessary to revisit them and update their backward pointers and their g values.

*A**(*P*: state space search problem) =

1. Start with *OPEN* containing only the node corresponding to *P*'s start state. Set that node's g value to 0, its h value to whatever it is, and its f value to $0 + h = h$. Set *CLOSED* to the empty set.

2. Until an answer is found or there are no nodes left in *OPEN* do:

2.1. If there are no nodes left in *OPEN*, return *Failure*. There is no path from the start state to a goal state.

2.2. Choose from *OPEN* a node such that no other node has a lower f value. Call the chosen node *BESTNODE*. Remove it from OPEN. Place it in *CLOSED*.

2.3. If BESTNODE is a goal node, halt and return the path from the initial node to *BESTNODE*.

2.4. Generate the successors of *BESTNODE*. But do not add them to the search graph until we have checked to see if any of them correspond to states that have already been generated. For each *SUCCESSOR* do:

2.4.1. Set *SUCCESSOR* to point back to *BESTNODE*.

2.4.2. Compute $g(SUCCESSOR) = g(BESTNODE) +$ the cost of getting from *BESTNODE* to *SUCCESSOR*.

2.4.3. See if *SUCCESSOR* corresponds to the same state as any node in *OPEN*. If so, call that node *OLD*. Since this node already exists in the graph, we can throw *SUCCESSOR* away and add *OLD* to the list of *BESTNODE*'s successors. But first we must decide whether *OLD*'s backward pointer should be reset to point to *BESTNODE*. It should be if the path we have just found to *SUCCESSOR* is cheaper than the current best path to *OLD* (since *SUCCESSOR* and *OLD* are really the same node). So compare the *g* values of *OLD* and *SUCCESSOR*. If *OLD* is cheaper (or just as cheap), then we need do nothing. If *SUCCESSOR* is cheaper, then reset *OLD*'s backward point to *BESTNODE*, record the new cheaper path in *g(OLD)*, and update *f(OLD)*.

2.4.4. If *SUCCESSOR* was not in *OPEN*, see if it is in *CLOSED*. If so, call the node in *CLOSED OLD* and add *OLD* to the list of *BESTNODE*'s successors. Check to see if the new path or the old path is better just as in step 2.4.3, and set the backward pointer and *g* and *f* values appropriately. If we have just found a better path to *OLD*, we must propagate the improvement to *OLD*'s successors. This is a bit tricky. *OLD* points to its successors. Each successor in turn points to its successors, and so forth, until each branch terminates with a node that either is still in *OPEN* or has no successors. So, to propagate the new cost downward, do a depth-first traversal of the search graph, starting at *OLD*, and changing each node's *g* value (and thus also its *f* value), terminating each branch when it reaches either a node with no successors or a node to which an equivalent or better path had already been found. Note that this condition doesn't just allow the propagation to stop as soon as the new path ceases to make a difference to any further node's cost. It also guarantees that the algorithm will terminate even if there are cycles in the graph. If there is a cycle, then the second time that a given node is visited, the path will be no better than the first time and so propagation will stop.

2.4.5. If *SUCCESSOR* was not already in either *OPEN* or *CLOSED*, then compute its *h* and *f* values, put it in *OPEN*, and add it to the list of *BESTNODE*'s successors.

*A**, like *A*-tree*, is complete; it will find a path if one exists. If *h* is admissible, then *A** will find a shortest path. And the graceful decay of admissibility principle applies to *A** just as it does to *A*-tree*.

In addition, we can now say something about the efficiency with which A^* finds a shortest path. Let $c(n_1, n_2)$ be the cost of getting from n_1 to n_2. We'll say that $h(n)$ is ***monotonic*** iff, whenever n_2 is a successor of n_1 (meaning that it can be derived from n_1 in exactly one move), $h(n_1) \leq c(n_1, n_2) + h(n_2)$. If f is monotonic, then A^* is optimal in the sense that no other search algorithm that uses the same heuristic function and that is guaranteed to find a cheapest path will do so by examining fewer nodes than A^* does. In particular, in this case it can be shown that A^* will never need to reexamine a node once it goes on CLOSED. So it is possible to skip step 2.4.4.

Unfortunately, even with these claims, A^* may not be good enough. Depending on the shape of the state space and the accuracy of h, it may still be necessary to examine a number of nodes that grows exponentially in the length of the cheapest path. However, if the maximum error that h may make is small, the number of nodes that must be examined grows only polynomially in the length of the cheapest path. More specifically, polynomial growth is assured if:

$$|h^*(n) - h(n)| \in \mathcal{O}(\log h(n)).$$

A^* is just one member of a large family of heuristic search algorithms. See [Pearl 1984] or [Russell and Norvig 2002] for a discussion of others. For example, A^*, like its cousin, breadth-first search, uses a lot of space. There exist other algorithms use less.

> Generalized chess is provably intractable (since it is EXPTIME-complete). Even the standard chess board is large enough that it isn't possible to search a complete game tree to find a winning move. Yet champion chess programs exist. They, along with programs that play other classic games like checkers and Go, exploit a heuristic search algorithm called *minimax*, which we describe in N.2.5.

Exercises

1. In Exercise 28.23, we defined a cut in a graph, the size of a cut and a bisection. Let G be a graph with $2v$ vertices and m edges. Describe a randomized, polynomial-time algorithm that, on input G, outputs a cut of G with expected size at least $mv/(2v-1)$. (*Hint:* Analyze the algorithm that takes a random bisection as its cut.)

2. Suppose that the A^* algorithm has generated the following tree so far:

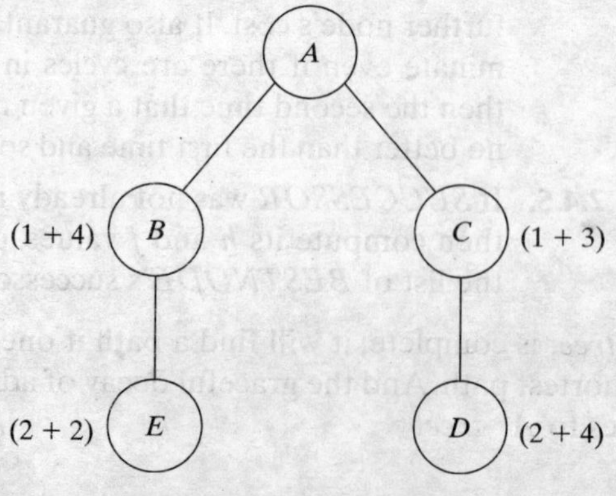

Assume that the nodes were generated in the order, A, B, C, D, E. The expression (g, h) associated with each node gives the values of the functions g and h at that node.

a. What node will be expanded at the next step?

b. Can it be guaranteed that A^*, using the heuristic function h that it is using, will find an optimal solution? Why or why not?

3. Simple puzzles offer a way to explore the behavior of search algorithms such as A^*, as well as to experiment with a variety of heuristic functions. Pick one (for example the 15-puzzle of Example 4.8 or see) and use A^* to solve it. Can you find an admissible heuristic function that is effective at pruning the search space?

CHAPTER 31

Summary and References

In Part IV, we saw that some problems are uncomputable in principle: For example, no effort on the part of the engineers of the world can make the halting problem solvable. In Part V, we've considered only problems that *are* computable in principle. But we've seen that while some are computable in practice, others aren't, at least with the techniques available to us today. In the years since the theory of NP-completeness was first described, a substantial body of work has increased our understanding of the ways in which some problems appear to require more computational resources than others. But that work has left many questions unanswered. While it is known that not all of the complexity classes that we have considered can collapse, it is unknown whether some of the most important of them can. In particular, we are left with the Millennium Problem 💻, "Does P = NP?"

References

The traveling salesman problem, along with other related combinatorial problems, has been studied by mathematicians since the nineteenth century. The problem has been given a variety of names. For example, Karl Menger [Menger 1932] called it "Das Botenproblem" or the Messenger Problem, so named, he said "since this problem is encountered by every postal messenger, as well as by many travelers". The application to a survey of Bengal farmers was described in [Mahalanobis 1940]. Julia Robinson appears to have been the first to publish a discussion of the problem with the name traveling salesman problem [Robinson 1949]. The use of linear programming to solve the TSP was introduced in [Dantzig, Fulkerson, and Johnson 1954]. See [Corman, Leiserson, Rivest, and Stein 2001] for a description of a straightforward minimum spanning tree-based algorithm that, when the triangle inequality holds, finds a solution to the TSP whose distance is no more than twice the distance of an optimal solution. The existence of an algorithm that tightens that bound to 1.5 was proved in [Christofides 1976]. For a comprehensive discussion of the TSP, see [Lawler, Lenstra, Rinnooy Kan, and Shmoys 1985].

The Complexity Zoo 💻 was created and is maintained by Scott Aaronson.

Strassen's algorithm for matrix multiplication was presented in [Strassen 1969]. The Coppersmith-Winograd algorithm was presented in [Coppersmith and Winograd 1990].

The Knuth-Morris-Pratt string search algorithm was discovered by Don Knuth and Vaughan Pratt and, independently, by Jim Morris. They published it jointly as [Knuth, Morris, and Pratt 1977].

Kruskal's algorithm was originally described in [Kruskal 1956]. For a good discussion of it, along with Prim's algorithm, an alternative for finding minimum spanning trees, see [Corman, Leiserson, Rivest, and Stein 2001].

Shor's algorithm for factoring using quantum computing was described in [Shor 1994].

[Hartmanis and Stearns 1965] introduced the idea of defining language complexity classes based on the running time, stated in terms of the length of the input, of deciding Turing machines. In 1993, Hartmanis and Stearns won the Turing Award for this work. The citation read, "In recognition of their seminal paper which established the foundations for the field of computational complexity theory."

The notion of NP-completeness and the proof of Theorem 28.16 (now commonly called the Cook-Levin Theorem) were introduced in [Cook 1971] and [Levin 1973]. In 1982, Cook won the Turing Award for this work. The citation read, "For his advancement of our understanding of the complexity of computation in a significant and profound way. His seminal paper, "The Complexity of Theorem Proving Procedures," presented at the 1971 ACM SIGACT Symposium on the Theory of Computing, laid the foundations for the theory of NP-Completeness. The ensuing exploration of the boundaries and nature of NP-complete class of problems has been one of the most active and important research activities in computer science for the last decade."

[Karp 1972] showed that SAT was not the only NP-complete language. That paper presents a landmark list 💻 of 21 other NP-complete problems. Karp won the 1985 Turing Award, "For his continuing contributions to the theory of algorithms including the development of efficient algorithms for network flow and other combinatorial optimization problems, the identification of polynomial-time computability with the intuitive notion of algorithmic efficiency, and, most notably, contributions to the theory of NP-completeness. Karp introduced the now standard methodology for proving problems to be NP-complete which has led to the identification of many theoretical and practical problems as being computationally difficult."

For a comprehensive discussion of NP-completeness, see [Garey and Johnson 1979]. Also there you will find a well-organized list of NP-hard problems, along with what is known of their complexity class and the references to the appropriate results. The list includes many problems that are known to be PSPACE-complete or EXPTIME-complete. The proof we present of Theorem 28.24 (Ladner's Theorem) is based on the one presented in [Garey and Johnson 1979]. Any NP-completeness claims that are made in this book and for which other references are not provided are discussed in [Garey and Johnson 1979]; further references are given there.

The literature on individual NP-complete languages includes:

- HAMILTONIAN-CIRCUIT: The proof we gave of Theorem 28.22 is patterned after the one given in [Hopcroft, Motwani and Ullman 2001].
- SUDOKU: A proof that SUDOKU is NP-complete was given in [Yato and Seta 2002].

For a description of the first proof of the four-color theorem, see [Appel and Haken 1977].

The proof we present for Theorem 28.26 (NP = co-NP iff there exists some language L such that L is NP-complete and $\neg L$ is also in NP) was taken from [Hopcroft, Motwani and Ullman 2001].

The proof we present of Theorem 28.27 (the Deterministic Time Hierarchy Theorem) was modeled closely after the one in [Sipser 2006].

The statement of the Linear Speedup Theorem that we give as Theorem F.3, as well as its proof, are taken from [Sudkamp 1998].

Savitch's Theorem (Theorem 29.2) was stated and proved in [Savitch 1970]. The proof that we present of Theorem 29.6 is modeled on the one presented in [Sipser 2006].

Quicksort was first described in [Hoare 1961]. An early version of the Miller-Rabin primality test was described in [Miller 1976] and later modified in [Rabin 1980].

For a more comprehensive discussion of heuristic search, including the A^* algorithm and its cousins, see [Russell and Norvig 2002]. The A^* algorithm was introduced in [Hart, Nilsson and Raphael 1968]. Its description was amended slightly in [Hart, Nilsson and Raphael 1972].

APPENDIX A

Review of Mathematical Background: Logic, Sets, Relations, Functions, and Proof Techniques

Throughout this book, we rely on a collection of important mathematical concepts and notations. We summarize them here. For a deeper introduction to these ideas, see any good discrete mathematics text, for example [Epp 2003] or [Rosen 2003].

A.1 Logic

We assume familiarity with the standard systems of both Boolean and quantified logic, so this section is just a review of the definitions and notations that we will use, along with some of the most useful inference rules.

A.1.1 Boolean (Propositional) Logic

A ***proposition*** is a statement that has a truth value. The language of ***well-formed formulas*** (***wffs***) allows us to define propositions whose truth can be determined from the truth of other propositions. A wff is any string that is formed according to the following rules.

- A propositional symbol (e.g., P) is a wff. (Propositional symbols are also called ***variables***, primarily because the term is shorter. We will generally find it convenient to do that, but this use of the term should not be confused with its use in the definition of first-order logic.)
- If P is a wff, then $\neg P$ is a wff.
- If P and Q are wffs, then so are $P \vee Q$, $P \wedge Q$, $P \rightarrow Q$, and $P \leftrightarrow Q$.
- If P is a wff, then (P) is a wff.

Table A.1 A truth table for the common Boolean operators.

P	Q	$\neg P$	$P \wedge Q$	$P \wedge Q$	$P \rightarrow Q$	$P \leftrightarrow Q$
True	*True*	*False*	*True*	*True*	*True*	*True*
True	*False*	*False*	*True*	*False*	*False*	*False*
False	*True*	*True*	*True*	*False*	*True*	*False*
False	*False*	*True*	*False*	*False*	*True*	*True*

Other binary operators, such as XOR (exclusive or) and NAND (not and), can also be defined, but we will not need them.

The definitions of the operators are given by the truth table shown in Table A.1. It shows how the truth value of a proposition can be computed from the truth values of its components. (Note that the symbol $\vee$ means inclusive or.)

We can divide the set of all Boolean wffs into three useful categories, as a function of when they are true:

- A Boolean wff is ***valid*** if and only if it is true for all assignments of truth values to the variables it contains. A valid wff is also called a ***tautology***.
- A Boolean wff is ***satisfiable*** if and only if it is true for at least one assignment of truth values to the variables it contains.
- A Boolean wff is ***unsatisfiable*** if and only if it is false for all assignments of truth values to the variables it contains.

EXAMPLE A.1 Using a Truth Table

The wff $P \vee \neg P$ is a tautology (i.e., it is valid). We can easily prove this by extending the truth table shown above and considering the only two possible cases (P is *True* or P is *False*):

P	$\neg P$	$P \vee \neg P$
True	*False*	*True*
False	*True*	*True*

The wff $P \vee \neg Q$ is satisfiable. It is *True* if either P is *True* or Q is *False*. It is not a tautology, however. The wff $P \wedge \neg P$ is unsatisfiable. It is *False* both in case P is *True* and in case P is *False*.

We'll say that two wffs P and Q are ***equivalent***, which we will write as $P \equiv Q$, iff they have the same truth values regardless of the truth values of the variables they contain. So, for example, $(P \rightarrow Q) \equiv (\neg P \vee Q)$.

In interpreting wffs, we assume that $\neg$ has the highest precedence, followed by $\wedge$, then $\vee$, then $\rightarrow$, then $\leftrightarrow$. So:

$$(P \vee Q \wedge R) \equiv (P \vee (Q \wedge R)).$$

Parentheses can be used to force different interpretations.

The following properties (defined in Section A.4.3) of the Boolean operators follow from their definitions in the truth table given above.

- The operators $\vee$, $\wedge$, and $\leftrightarrow$ are commutative and associative.
- The operators $\vee$ and $\wedge$ are idempotent (e.g., $(P \vee P) \equiv P$).
- The operators $\vee$ and $\wedge$ distribute over each other:
  - $P \wedge (Q \vee R) \equiv (P \wedge Q) \vee (P \wedge R)$.
  - $P \vee (Q \wedge R) \equiv (P \vee Q) \wedge (P \vee R)$.
- ***Absorption laws***:
  - $P \wedge (P \vee Q) \equiv P$.
  - $P \vee (P \wedge Q) \equiv P$.
- ***Double negation***: $\neg\neg P \equiv P$.
- ***de Morgan's Laws***:
  - $\neg(P \wedge Q) \equiv (\neg P \vee \neg Q)$.
  - $\neg(P \vee Q) \equiv (\neg P \wedge \neg Q)$.

We'll say that a set A of wffs ***logically implies*** or ***entails*** a conclusion Q iff, whenever all of the wffs in A are true, Q is also true.

An ***axiom*** is a wff that is asserted *a priori* to be true. Given a set of axioms, rules of inference can be applied to create new wffs, to which the inference rules can then be applied, and so forth. Any statement so derived is called a ***theorem***. Let A be a set of axioms plus zero or more theorems that have already been derived from those axioms. Then a ***proof*** is a finite sequence of applications of inference rules, starting from A.

A proof is a syntactic object. It is just a sequence of applications of rules. We would like, however, for proofs to tell us something about truth. They can do that if we design our inference rules appropriately. We'll say that an inference rule is ***sound*** iff, whenever it is applied to a set A of axioms, any conclusion that it produces is entailed by A (i.e., it must be true whenever A is). An entire proof is sound iff it consists of a sequence of inference steps each of which was constructed using a sound inference rule. A set of inference rules R is ***complete*** iff, given any set A of axioms, all statements that are entailed by A can be proved by applying the rules in R. If we can define a set of inference rules that is both sound and complete then the set of theorems that can be proved from A will exactly correspond to the set of statements that must be true whenever A is.

The truth table we presented above is the basis for the construction of sound and complete inference rules in Boolean logic. Some useful rules are:

- ***Modus ponens***: From the premises $(P \rightarrow Q)$ and P, conclude Q.
- ***Modus tollens***: From the premises $(P \rightarrow Q)$ and $\neg Q$, conclude $\neg P$.

- ***Or introduction***: From the premise P, conclude $(P \vee Q)$.
- ***And introduction***: From the premises P and Q, conclude $(P \wedge Q)$.
- ***And elimination***: From the premise $(P \wedge Q)$, conclude P or conclude Q.

Any two statements of the form P and $\neg P$ form a ***contradiction***.

A.1.2 First-Order Logic

The primitives in Boolean logic are predicates of no arguments (i.e., Boolean constants). It is useful to extend our logical system to allow predicates of one or more arguments and to allow the use of variables. So, for example, we might like to write $P(China)$ or $Q(x, y)$. ***First-order logic***, often called simply ***FOL*** (or sometimes first-order predicate logic, first-order predicate calculus, or FOPC), allows us to do that.

We will use symbols that start with lowercase letters as variables and symbols that start with uppercase letters as constants, predicates, and functions.

An expression that describes an object is a ***term***. So a variable is a term and an n-ary function whose arguments are terms is also a term. Note that if n is 0, we have a constant.

We define the language of ***well-formed formulas (wffs)*** in first-order logic to be the set of expressions that can be formed according to the following rules.

- If P is an n-ary predicate and each of the expressions $x_1, x_2, \ldots, x_n$ is a term, then an expression of the form $P(x_1, x_2, \ldots, x_n)$ is a wff. If any variable occurs in such a wff, then that variable is ***free*** (alternatively, it is not bound).
- If P is a wff, then $\neg P$ is a wff.
- If P and Q are wffs, then so are $P \vee Q$, $P \wedge Q$, $P \rightarrow Q$, and $P \leftrightarrow Q$.
- If P is a wff, then (P) is a wff.
- If P is a wff, then $\forall x\ (P)$ and $\exists x\ (P)$ are wffs. Any free instance of x in P is ***bound*** by the quantifier and is then no longer free. $\forall$ is called the universal quantifier and $\exists$ is called the existential quantifier. In the wff $\forall x\ (P)$ or $\exists x\ (P)$, we'll call P the ***scope*** of the quantifier. It is important to note that when an existentially quantified variable y occurs inside the scope of a universally quantified variable x (as, for example, in statement 4 below), the meaning of the wff is that for every value of x there exists some value of y but it need not be the same value of y for every value of x. So, for example, the following wffs are not equivalent:
  - $\forall x\ (\exists y\ (Father\text{-}of(y, x)))$, and
  - $\exists y\ (\forall x\ (Father\text{-}of(y, x)))$.

For convenience, we will extend this syntax slightly. When no confusion will result, we will allow the following additional forms for wffs:

- $\forall x < c\ (P(x))$ is equivalent to $\forall x\ (x < c \rightarrow P(x))$
- $\forall x \in S\ (P(x))$ is equivalent to $\forall x\ (x \in S \rightarrow P(x))$
- $\forall x, y, z\ (P(x, y, z))$ is equivalent to $\forall x\ (\forall y\ (\forall z\ (P(x, y, z))))$
- $\forall x, y, z \in S\ (P(x, y, z))$ is equivalent to $\forall x \in S\ (\forall y \in S\ (\forall z \in S\ (P(x, y, z))))$

The logical framework that we have just defined is called ***first-order*** because it allows quantification over variables but not over predicates or functions. It is possible to define higher-order logics that do permit such quantification. For example, in a higher-order logic we might be able to say something like $\forall P\ (P(John) \rightarrow P(Carey))$. In other words, anything that is true of *John* is also true of *Carey*. While it is sometimes useful to be able to make statements such as this, the computational and logical properties of higher-order systems make them very hard to use except in some restricted cases.

A wff with no free variables is called a ***sentence*** or a ***statement***. All of the following are sentences.

1. $Bear(Smoky)$
2. $\forall x\ (Bear(x) \rightarrow Animal(x))$
3. $\forall x\ (Animal(x) \rightarrow Bear(x))$
4. $\forall x\ (Animal(x) \rightarrow \exists y\ (Mother\text{-}of(y, x)))$
5. $\forall x\ ((Animal(x) \wedge \neg Dead(x)) \rightarrow Alive(x))$

A ***ground instance*** is a sentence that contains no variables. All of the following are ground instances: *Bear*(*Smoky*), *Animal*(*Smoky*), and *Mother-of*(*BigEyes*, *Smoky*). In computational logic systems, it is common to store the ground instances in a different form than the one that is used for other sentences. They may be contained in a table or a database, for example.

Returning to sentences 1–5 above, 1, 2, and 4, and 5 are true in our everyday world (assuming the obvious referent for the constant *Smoky* and the obvious meanings of the predicates *Bear*, *Animal*, and *Mother-of*). On the other hand, 3 is not true.

As these examples show, determining whether or not a sentence is true requires appeal to the meanings of the constants, functions, and predicates that it contains. An ***interpretation*** for a sentence w is a pair (D, I). D is a universe of objects. I assigns meaning to the symbols of w: It assigns values, drawn from D, to the constants in w and it assigns functions and predicates (whose domains and ranges are subsets of D) to the function and predicate symbols of w. A ***model*** of a sentence w is an interpretation that makes w true. For example, let w be the sentence, $\forall x\ (\exists y\ (y < x))$. The integers (along with the usual meaning of $<$) are a model of w since, for any integer, there exists some smaller integer. The positive integers, on the other hand, are an interpretation for w but not a model of it. The sentence w is false for the positive integers since there is no positive integer that is smaller than 1.

A sentence w is ***valid*** iff it is true in all interpretations. In other words, w is valid iff it is true regardless of what the constant, function, and predicate symbols "mean". A sentence w is ***satisfiable*** iff there exists *some* interpretation in which w is true. A sentence w is ***unsatisfiable*** iff it is not satisfiable (in other words, there exists no interpretation in which it is true). Any sentence w is valid iff $\neg w$ is unsatisfiable.

EXAMPLE A.2 Valid, Satisfiable, and Unsatisfiable wffs

Let w_1 be the wff:

$$\forall x\ ((P(x) \wedge Q(Smoky)) \rightarrow P(x)).$$

The wff w_1 is valid because it is true regardless of what the predicates P and Q are or what object *Smoky* refers to. It is also satisfiable since it is true in at least one interpretation.

Let w_2 be the wff:

$$\neg(\forall x\ (P(x) \lor \neg(P(x)))).$$

The wff w_2 is not valid. It is also unsatisfiable since it is false in all interpretations, which follows from the fact that $\neg w_2$ is valid.

Finally, let w_3 be the wff:

$$\forall x\ (P(x, x)).$$

The wff w_3 is not valid but it is satisfiable. Suppose that the universe is the integers and P is the predicate *LessThanOrEqualTo*. Then P is true for all values of x. But, again with the integers as the universe, suppose that P is the predicate *LessThan*. Now P is false for all values of x. Finally, let the universe be the set of all people and let P be the predicate *HasConfidenceInTheAbilityOf*. Now P is true of some values of x (i.e., of those people who have self confidence) and false of others.

A set A of axioms ***logically implies*** or ***entails*** a conclusion c iff, in every interpretation in which A is true (i.e., in every model of A), and for all assignments of values to the free variables of c, c must be true.

As in Boolean logic, a proof in first-order logic starts with a set A of axioms and theorems that have already been proved from those axioms. Rules of inference are then applied, creating new statements. Any statement derived in this way is called a ***theorem***. A ***proof*** is a finite sequence of applications of inference rules, starting from the axioms and given theorems.

As in Boolean logic, we will say that an inference rule is ***sound*** iff, whenever it is applied to a set A of statements (axioms and given theorems), any conclusion that it produces is entailed by A (i.e., it must be true whenever A is). A set of inference rules R is ***complete*** iff, given any set A of statements, all statements that are entailed by A can be proved by applying the rules in R. As in Boolean logic, we seek a set of inference rules that is both sound and complete.

> Resolution is a single inference rule that is used as the basis for many automatic theorem proving and reasoning programs. It is sound and refutation-complete. By the latter, we mean that if $\neg ST$ is inconsistent with the axioms and if both the axioms and $\neg ST$ have been converted to a restricted syntax called clause form, resolution will find the inconsistency and thus prove ST. (B.2.2)

For Boolean logic, truth tables provide a basis for defining a set of sound and complete inference rules. It is less obvious that such a set exists for first-order logic. But it does, as was first shown by Kurt Gödel in his Completeness Theorem [Gödel 1929]. More specifically, Gödel showed that there exists some set of inference rules R such that, given any set of axioms A and a sentence c, there is a proof of c, starting with A and applying the rules in R, iff c is entailed by A. Note that all that we are claiming here is that, if there is a proof, there is a procedure for finding it. We are not claiming that there exists a procedure that decides whether or not a proof exists. In fact, as we show in Section 22.4.2, for first-order logic no such decision procedure can exist.

All of the inference rules that we have and will present are sound. The individual inference rules that we have so far considered are not, however, complete. For example, modus ponens is incomplete. But a complete procedure can be constructed by including all of the rules we listed above for Boolean logic, plus new ones, including, among others:

- ***Quantifier exchange***:
  - From $\neg\exists x\ (P)$, conclude $\forall x\ (\neg P)$.
  - From $\forall x\ (\neg P)$, conclude $\neg\exists x\ (P)$.
  - From $\neg\forall x\ (P)$, conclude $\exists x\ (\neg P)$.
  - From $\exists x\ (\neg P)$, conclude $\neg\forall x\ (P)$.
- ***Universal instantiation***: For any constant C, from $\forall x\ (P(x))$, conclude $P(C)$.
- ***Existential generalization***: For any constant C, from $P(C)$, conclude $\exists x\ (P(x))$.

EXAMPLE A.3 A Simple Proof

Assume the following three axioms:

[1] $\forall x\ (P(x) \wedge Q(x) \rightarrow R(x))$.

[2] $P(X_1)$.

[3] $Q(X_1)$.

We prove $R(X_1)$ as follows:

[4]	$P(X_1) \wedge Q(X_1) \rightarrow R(X_1)$.	(Universal instantiation, [1].)
[5]	$P(X_1) \wedge Q(X_1)$.	(And introduction, [2], [3].)
[6]	$R(X_1)$.	(Modus ponens, [5], [4].)

A first-order ***theory*** is a set of axioms and the set of all theorems that can be proved, using a set of sound and complete inference rules, from those axioms. A theory is ***logically complete*** iff, for every sentence P in the language of the theory, either P or $\neg P$ is a theorem. A theory is ***consistent*** iff there is no sentence P such that both P and $\neg P$ are theorems. If, on the other hand, there is such a sentence, then the theory contains a ***contradiction*** and is ***inconsistent***.

We are often interested in the relationship between a theory and some set of facts that are true in some view we may have of the world (for example the facts of arithmetic or the facts a robot needs in order to move around). Let w be a world plus an interpretation (that maps logical objects to objects in the world). Now we can say that a theory is ***sound*** with respect to w iff every theorem (in the theory) corresponds to a fact that is true (in w). We say that a theory is ***complete*** with respect to w iff every fact that is true (in w) corresponds to a theorem (in the theory). We will assume that any first-order logic statement in the language of w is either true or false in the world that w describes. So, if a theory is complete with respect to w it must be the case that, for any sentence P, either P corresponds to a sentence that is true in w, in which case it is a theorem, or P corresponds to a sentence that is false in w, in which case $\neg P$ is a theorem. So any theory that is complete with respect to an interpretation and a set of facts is also logically complete.

By the way, while the language of first-order logic has the property that every statement is either true or false in any world, not all languages share that property. For example, English doesn't. Consider the English sentence, "The king of France has red hair." Is it true or false (in the world as we know it, given the standard meanings of the words)? The answer is neither. It carries the (false) presupposition that there is a king of France and then makes a claim about that individual. This problem disappears, however, when we convert the English sentence into a related sentence in first order logic. We might try:

- $\exists x\,(King\text{-}of(x, France) \wedge Haircolor\text{-}of(x, Red))$: This sentence is false in the world.
- $\forall x\,(King\text{-}of(x, France) \rightarrow Haircolor\text{-}of(x, Red))$: This sentence is true in the world (trivially, since there are no values of x for which $King\text{-}of(x, France)$ is true).

There are interesting first-order theories that are both consistent and complete with respect to particular interpretations of interest. One example is Presburger arithmetic, in which the universe is the natural numbers and there is a single function, *plus*, whose properties are axiomatized. There are other theories that are incomplete because we have not yet added enough axioms. But it might be possible, eventually, to find a set of axioms that does the job.

However, many interesting and powerful theories are not both consistent and complete and they will never become so. For example, Gödel's Incompleteness Theorem [Gödel 1931], one of the most important results in modern mathematics, shows that *any* theory that is derived from a decidable (a notion that we explain in Chapter 17) set of axioms and that characterizes the standard behavior of the constants 0 and 1, plus the functions *plus* and *times* on the natural numbers, cannot be both consistent and complete. In other words, if any such theory is consistent (and it is generally assumed that the standard theory of arithmetic is), then there must be some statements that are true (in arithmetic) but not provable (in the theory). While it is of course possible to add new axioms and thus make more statements provable, there will always remain some true but unprovable statements unless either the set of axioms becomes inconsistent or it becomes infinite and undecidable. In the latter case, the fact that a proof exists is not very useful since it has become impossible to tell whether or not a statement is an axiom and thus can be used in a proof.

Do not be confused by the fact that there exists both a Completeness Theorem and an Incompleteness Theorem. The terminology is unfortunate since it is based on two different notions of completeness. The Completeness Theorem states a fact about the framework of first-order logic itself. It says that there exists a set of inference rules (and, in fact, more than one such set happens to exist) such that, given any set A of axioms, the theorems that are provable from A are exactly the set of sentences that are entailed by A. The Incompleteness Theorem states a fact about theories that can be built within any logical framework. It says that there exist theories (the standard one about arithmetic with *plus* and *times* being one example) that, assuming consistency, are incomplete in the sense that there are sentences that are true in the world but that are not theorems. Such theories are also logically incomplete: There exist sentences P such that neither P nor $\neg P$ is a theorem.

A.2 Sets

Most of the structures that we will consider are based on the fundamental notion of a set.

A.2.1 What is a Set?

A ***set*** is simply a collection of objects. The objects (which we call the ***elements*** or ***members*** of the set) can be anything: numbers, people, strings, fruits, etc. For example, all of the following are sets.

- $S_1 = \{13, 11, 8, 23\}$
- $S_2 = \{8, 23, 11, 13\}$
- $S_3 = \{8, 8, 23, 23, 11, 11, 13, 13\}$
- $S_4 = \{\text{apple, pear, banana, grape}\}$
- $S_5 = \{$January, February, March, April, May, June, July, August, September, October, November, December$\}$
- $S_6 = \{x : x \in S_5 \text{ and } x \text{ has 31 days}\}$
- $S_7 = \{$January, March, May, July, August, October, December$\}$
- $\mathbb{N}$ = the nonnegative integers (also called ***the natural numbers***)
- $S_8 = \{i : \exists x \in \mathbb{N}\ (i = 2x)\}$
- $S_9 = \{0, 2, 4, 6, 8, \ldots\}$
- S_{10} = the even natural numbers
- S_{11} = the syntactically valid C programs
- $S_{12} = \{x : x \in S_{11} \text{ and } x \text{ never gets into an infinite loop}\}$
- $S_{13} = \{$finite length strings of a's and b's$\}$
- Z = the integers $(\ldots -3, -2, -1, 0, 1, 2, 3, \ldots)$

In the definitions of S_6, S_8, and S_{12}, we have used the colon notation. Read it as "such that." So, for example, read the definition of S_6 as, "the set of all values x such that x is an element of S_5 and x has 31 days." We have used the standard symbol $\in$ for "element of." We will also use $\notin$ for "not an element of." So, for example, $17 \notin S_1$ is true.

Remember that a set is simply a collection of elements. So if two sets contain precisely the same elements (regardless of the way we actually defined the sets), then they are identical. Thus S_6 and S_7 are the same set, as are S_8, S_9, and S_{10}.

Since a set is defined only by what elements it contains, the order in which we list its elements does not matter. Thus S_1 and S_2 are the same set. Also note that a given element is either in a set or it isn't. Duplicates do not matter. So sets S_1, S_2, and S_3 are equal.

One useful technique for describing a set S that is a subset of an existing set D is to define a function (we'll define formally what we mean by a function in Section A.4) that can be used to determine whether or not a given element is in S. Such a function is called a ***characteristic function***. Formally, a function f with domain D is a characteristic function for a set S iff $f(x) = True$ if x is an element of S and *False* otherwise. For example, we used this technique to define set S_6.

We can use programs to define sets. There are two ways to use a program to define a set S:

- Write a program that generates the elements of S. We call the output of such a program an ***enumeration*** of S.
- Write a program that ***decides*** S by implementing the characteristic function of S. Such a program returns *True* if run on some element that is in S and *False* if run on an element that is not in S.

It seems natural to ask, given some set S, "What is the size of S?" or "How many elements does S contain?" We will use the term ***cardinality*** to describe the way we answer such questions. So we'll reply that the cardinality of S, written $|S|$, is n, for some appropriate value of n. For example, $|\{2, 7, 11\}| = 3$. In simple cases, determining the cardinality of a set is straightforward. In other cases, it is more complicated. For our purposes, however, we can get by with three different kinds of answers:

- a natural number (if S is finite),
- "countably infinite" (if S has the same number of elements as there are integers), or
- "uncountably infinite" (if S has more elements than there are integers).

We will formalize these ideas in Section A.6.8.

The smallest set is the unique set that contains no elements. It is called the ***empty set***, and is written $\varnothing$ or $\{\ \}$. The cardinality of the empty set, written $|\varnothing|$, is 0.

When we are working with sets, it is very important to keep in mind the difference between a set and the elements of a set. Given a set that contains more than one element, this distinction is usually obvious. It is clear that $\{1, 2\}$ is distinct from either the number 1 or the number 2. It sometimes becomes a bit less obvious, though, with ***singleton sets*** (sets that contain only a single element). But it is equally true for them. So, for example, $\{1\}$ is distinct from the number 1. As another example, consider $\{\varnothing\}$. This is a set that contains one element. That element is in turn a set that contains no elements (i.e., the empty set). $\{\{1, 2, 3\}\}$ is also a set that contains one element.

A.2.2 Relating Sets to Each Other

We say that A is a ***subset*** of B (which we write as $A \subseteq B$) iff every element of A is also an element of B. Formally, $A \subseteq B$ iff $\forall x \in A\ (x \in B)$.

The symbol we use for subset ($\subseteq$) looks somewhat like $\leq$. This is no accident. If $A \subseteq B$, then there is a sense in which the set A is "less than or equal to" the set B, since all the elements of A must be in B, but there may be elements of B that are not in A.

Given this definition, notice that every set is a subset of itself. This fact turns out to offer a useful way to prove that two sets A and B are equal: First prove that A is a subset of B. Then prove that B is a subset of A. We will have more to say about this later in Section A.6.7.

We say that A is ***proper subset*** of B (written $A \subset B$) iff $A \subseteq B$ and $A \neq B$. The ***Venn diagram*** shown in Figure A.2(a) illustrates the proper subset relationship between A and B. Notice that the empty set is a subset of every set (since, trivially, every element of $\varnothing$, all none of them, is also an element of every other set). And the empty set is a *proper* subset of every set other than itself.

It is useful to define some basic operations that can be performed on sets.

- The ***union*** of two sets A and B (written $A \cup B$) contains all elements that are contained in A or B (or both). Formally, $A \cup B = \{x: (x \in A) \vee (x \in B)\}$. We can easily visualize union using a Venn diagram, as shown in Figure A.1(b). The union of sets A and B is the entire hatched area in the diagram.
- The ***intersection*** of two sets A and B (written $A \cap B$) contains all elements that are contained in both A and B. Formally, $A \cap B = \{x: (x \in A) \wedge (x \in B)\}$. In the Venn diagram shown in Figure A.1(b), the intersection of A and B is the double hatched area in the middle.
- The ***difference*** of two sets A and B (written $A - B$ or A/B) contains all elements that are contained in A but not in B. Formally, $A/B = \{x: (x \in A) \wedge (x \notin B)\}$. In the Venn diagrams shown in Figure A.1(c) and (d), the hatched region represents A/B.

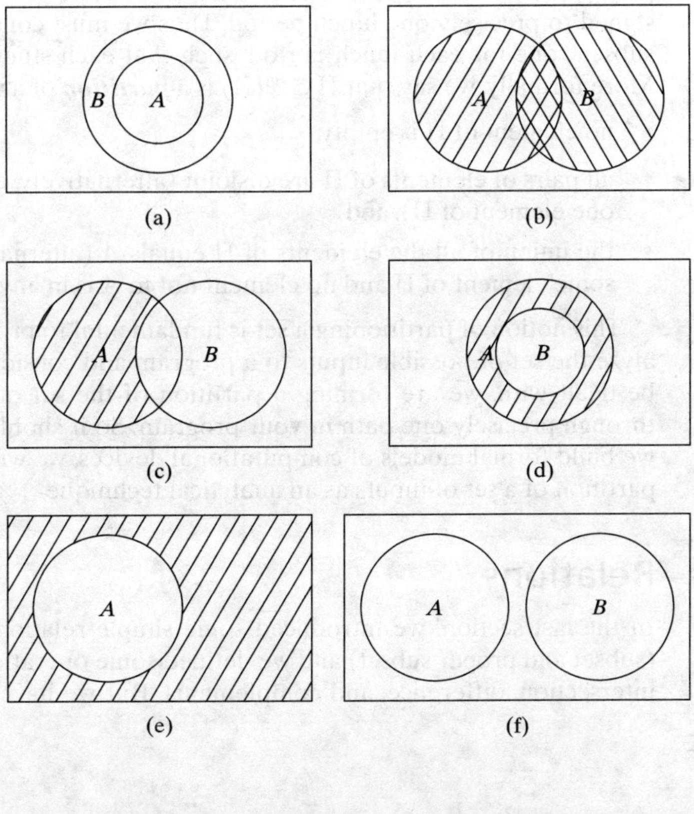

FIGURE A.1 Venn diagrams that illustrate relations and functions on sets.

- The ***complement*** of a set A with respect to a specific universe U (written as $\neg A$) contains exactly those elements of U that are not contained in A (i.e., $\neg A = U - A$). Formally, $\neg A = \{x: (x \in U) \wedge (x \notin A)\}$. For example, if U is the set of residents of Austin and A is the set of Austin residents who like barbeque, then $\neg A$ is the set of Austin residents who don't like barbeque. The complement of A is shown as the hatched region of the Venn diagram shown in Figure A.1(e).
- Two sets are ***disjoint*** iff they have no elements in common (i.e., their intersection is empty). Formally, A and B are disjoint iff $A \cap B = \varnothing$. In the Venn diagram shown in Figure A.1(f), A and B are disjoint.

Given a set A, we can consider the set of all subsets of A. We call this set the ***power set*** of A, and we write it $\mathcal{P}(A)$. For example, let $A = \{1, 2, 3\}$. Then:

$$\mathcal{P}(A) = \{\varnothing, \{1\}, \{2\}, \{3\}, \{1, 2\}, \{1, 3\}, \{2, 3\}, \{1, 2, 3\}\}.$$

The power set of A is interesting because, if we're working with the elements of A, we may well care about all the ways in which we can combine those elements.

Now for one final property of sets. Again consider the set A above. But this time, rather than looking for all possible subsets, let's just look for a single way to carve A up into subsets such that each element of A is in precisely one subset. For example, we might choose any of the following sets of subsets:

$$\{\{1\}, \{2, 3\}\} \quad \text{or} \quad \{\{1, 3\}, \{2\}\} \quad \text{or} \quad \{\{1, 2, 3\}\}.$$

We call any such set of subsets a partition of A. Partitions are very useful. For example, suppose we have a set S of students in a school. We need for every student to be assigned to precisely one lunch period. Thus we must construct a partition of S: a set of subsets, one for each lunch period, such that each student is in precisely one subset. More formally, we say that $\Pi \subseteq \mathcal{P}(A)$ is a ***partition*** of a set A iff:

- no element of Π is empty,
- all pairs of elements of Π are disjoint (alternatively, each element of A is in at most one element of Π), and
- the union of all the elements of Π equals A (alternatively, each element of A is in some element of Π and no element not in A is in any element of Π).

This notion of partitioning a set is fundamental to programming. Every time we analyze the set of possible inputs to a program and consider the various cases that must be dealt with, we are forming a partition of the set of inputs: Each input must fall through precisely one path in your program. So it should come as no surprise that, as we build formal models of computational devices, we will rely heavily on the idea of a partition of a set of inputs as an analytical technique.

A.3 Relations

In the last section, we introduced some simple relations that can hold between sets (subset and proper subset) and we defined some operations (functions) on sets (union, intersection, difference, and complement). But we haven't yet defined formally what we mean by a relation or a function. We will do that now. (By the way, the reason we introduced relations and functions on sets in the last section is that we are going to use sets as the basis for our formal definitions of relations and functions and we will need the simple operations we just described as part of our definitions.)

A.3.1 What is a Relation?

An ***ordered pair*** is a sequence of two objects. Given any two objects, x and y, there are two ordered pairs that can be formed. We write them as (x, y) and (y, x). As the name implies, in an ordered pair (as opposed to in a set), order matters (unless x and y happen to be equal).

The ***Cartesian product*** of two sets A and B (written $A \times B$) is the set of all ordered pairs (a, b) such that $a \in A$ and $b \in B$. For example, let A be a set of people: {Dave, Sara, Billy}, and let B be a set of desserts: {cake, pie, ice cream}. Then:

$$\begin{aligned} A \times B = \{ & \text{(Dave, cake), (Dave, pie), (Dave, ice cream),} \\ & \text{(Sara, cake), (Sara, pie), (Sara, ice cream),} \\ & \text{(Billy, cake), (Billy, pie), (Billy, ice cream)}\}. \end{aligned}$$

As you can see from this example, the Cartesian product of two sets contains elements that represent all the ways of pairing some element from the first set with some element from the second. Note that $A \times B$ is not the same as $B \times A$. In our example:

$$\begin{aligned} B \times A = \{ & \text{(cake, Dave), (pie, Dave), (ice cream, Dave),} \\ & \text{(cake, Sara), (pie, Sara), (ice cream, Sara),} \\ & \text{(cake, Billy), (pie, Billy), (ice cream, Billy)}\}. \end{aligned}$$

If A and B are finite, then the cardinality of their Cartesian product is given by:

$$|A \times B| = |A| \cdot |B|.$$

A ***binary relation*** over two sets A and B is a subset of $A \times B$. For example, let's consider the problem of choosing dessert. We could define a relation that tells us, for each person, what desserts he or she likes. We might write the *Dessert* relation, for example as:

$$\textit{Dessert} = \{\text{(Dave, cake), (Dave, ice cream), (Sara, pie), (Sara, ice cream)}\}.$$

In other words, Dave likes cake and ice cream, Sara likes pie and ice cream, and Billy seems not to like sinful treats.

Not all relations are binary. We define an ***n-ary relation*** over sets $A_1, A_2, \ldots A_n$ to be a subset of $A_1 \times A_2 \times \ldots \times A_n$. The n sets may be different, or they may be the same. For example, let A be a set of people:

$$A = \{\text{Dave, Sara, Billy, Beth, Mark, Cathy, Pete}\}.$$

Now suppose that Sara and Dave are the parents of Billy, Beth and Mark are the parents of Cathy, and Billy and Cathy are the parents of Pete. Then we could define a 3-ary (or *ternary*) relation *Child-of*, where the first element of each 3-tuple is the mother, the second is the father, and the third is the child. So we would have the following subset of $A \times A \times A$:

$$\{(\text{Sara, Dave, Billy}), (\text{Beth, Mark, Cathy}), (\text{Cathy, Billy, Pete})\}.$$

Notice a couple of important properties of relations as we have defined them. First, a relation may be equal to the empty set. For example, if Dave, Sue, and Billy all hate dessert, then the *Dessert* relation would be { } or $\varnothing$.

Second, there are no constraints on how many times a particular element may occur in a relation. In the *Dessert* example, Dave occurs twice, Sue occurs twice, Billy doesn't occur at all, cake occurs once, pie occurs once, and ice cream occurs twice. Given an n-ary relation R, we'll use the notation $R(x_1, \ldots, x_{n-1})$ for the set that contains those elements with the property that $(x_1, \ldots, x_{n-1}, x_n) \in R$. So, for example $Dessert(\text{Dave}) = \{\text{cake, ice cream}\}$.

An n-ary relation R is a subset of the cross product of n sets. The sets may all be different, or some of them may be the same. In the specific case in which all the sets are the same, we will say that R is a relation on the set A.

Binary relations are particularly useful and are often written in the form $x_1\ R\ x_2$. Common binary relations include $=$ (equality, defined on many domains), $<$ (defined on numbers and some other domains), and $\leq$ (also defined on numbers and some other domains). For example, the relation $<$ on the integers contains an infinite number of elements drawn from the Cartesian product of the set of integers with itself. For instance, $2 < 7$.

The ***inverse*** of a binary relation R, written R^{-1}, is simply the set of ordered pairs in R with the elements of each pair reversed. Formally, if $R \subseteq A \times B$, then $R^{-1} \subseteq B \times A = \{(b, a): (a, b) \in R\}$. If a relation is a way of associating with each element of A with a corresponding element of B, then think of its inverse as a way of associating with elements of B their corresponding elements in A. Every relation has an inverse. For example, the inverse of $<$ (in the usual sense, defined on numbers) is $>$.

If we have two or more binary relations, we may be able combine them via an operation we'll call composition. For example, if we knew the number of fat grams in a serving of each kind of dessert, we could ask for the number of fat grams in a particular person's dessert choices. To compute this, we first use the *Dessert* relation to find all the desserts each person likes. Next we get the bad news from the *Fatgrams* relation, which probably looks something like this:

$$\{(\text{cake}, 30), (\text{pie}, 25), (\text{ice cream}, 15)\}.$$

Finally, we see that the composed relation that relates people to fat grams is $\{(\text{Dave}, 30), (\text{Dave}, 15), (\text{Sara}, 25), (\text{Sara}, 15)\}$. Of course, this only worked because, when we applied the first relation, we got back desserts. Then our second relation has desserts as its first component. We couldn't have composed *Dessert* with *Less than*, for example.

Formally, we say that the ***composition*** of two relations $R_1 \subseteq A \times B$ and $R_2 \subseteq B \times C$, written $R_2 \circ R_1$, is:

$$R_2 \circ R_1 = \{(a, c) : \exists b\ ((a, b) \in R_1 \wedge ((b, c) \in R_2)\}.$$

Note that this definition tells us that, to compute $R_2 \circ R_1$, we first apply R_1, then R_2. In other words we go right to left. Some definitions go the other way. Obviously we can define it either way, but it is important to be consistent. Using the notation we have just defined, we can represent the people to fat grams composition described above as *Fatgrams* ∘ *Dessert*.

A.3.2 Representing Binary Relations

Binary relations are particularly important. If we're going to work with them, and, in particular, if we are going to compute with them, we need some way to represent them. We have several choices. To represent some binary relation R, we could:

1. List the elements of R. For example, consider the *Mother-of* relation in a family in which Doreen is the mother of Ann, Ann is the mother of Catherine, and Catherine is the mother of Allison. Then we can write:

   $$\textit{Mother-of} = \{(\text{Doreen, Ann}), (\text{Ann, Catherine}), (\text{Catherine, Allison})\}.$$

   Clearly, this approach only works for finite relations.
2. Encode R as a computational procedure. As with any set, there are at least two ways in which a computational procedure can define R. It may:
   - enumerate the elements of R, or
   - implement the characteristic function for R by returning *True* when given a pair that is in R and *False* when given anything else.
3. Encode R as an adjacency matrix. Assuming a finite relation $R \subseteq A \times B$, we can build an adjacency matrix to represent R as follows:
   - Construct a Boolean matrix M (i.e., a matrix all of whose values are *True* or *False*) with $|A|$ rows and $|B|$ columns.
   - Label each row for one element of A and each column for one element of B.
   - For each element (p, q) of R, set $M[p, q]$ to *True*. Set all other elements of M to *False*.

   If we let 1 represent *True* and blank represent *False*, the adjacency matrix shown in Table A.2 represents the relation *Mother-of* defined above.

Table A.2 Representing a relation as an adjacency matrix.

	Doreen	***Ann***	***Catherine***	***Allison***
Doreen		1		
Ann			1	
Catherine				1
Allison				

4. Encode R as a directed graph. If R is a relation on the set A, we can build a directed graph to represent R as follows:
   - Construct a set of vertices (often called nodes), one for each element of A that appears in any element of R.
   - For each ordered pair in R, draw an edge from the first element of the pair to the second.

The directed graph shown in Figure A.2(a) represents our example relation *Mother-of* defined above. If there are two elements x and y, and both (x, y) and (y, x) are in R, we will usually draw the graph as shown in Figure A.2(b). The directed graph technique can also be used if R is a relation over two different sets A and B. But in this case, we must construct vertices for elements of A and for elements of B. So, for example, we could represent a *Fatgrams* relation as shown in Figure A.2(c).

A.3.3 Properties of Binary Relations on Sets

Many useful binary relations have some kind of structure. For example, it might be the case that every element of the underlying set is related to itself. Or it might happen that if x is related to y, then y must necessarily be related to x. There is one special kind of relation, called an equivalence relation that is particularly useful. But before we can define it, we need first to define each of the individual properties that equivalence relations possess.

A relation $R \subseteq A \times A$ is ***reflexive*** iff, $\forall x \in A\ ((x, x) \in R)$. For example, consider the relation *Address* defined as "lives at same address as". We will make the simplifying assumption that everyone has only one address. *Address* is a relation over a set of people. Clearly every person lives at the same address as him or herself, so *Address* is reflexive.

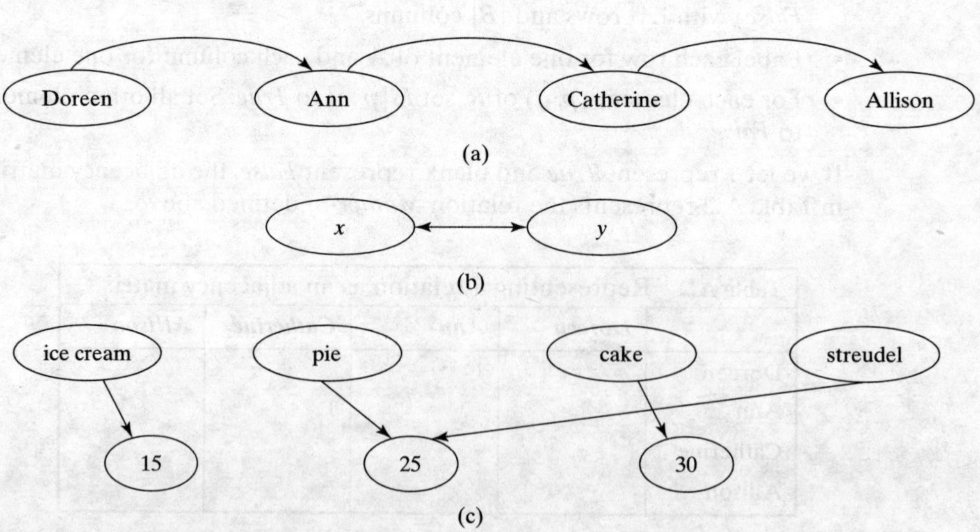

FIGURE A.2 Representing relations as graphs.

1		
	1	
		1

FIGURE A.3 Representing a reflexive relation.

So is the $\leq$ relation on the integers. For every integer x, $x \leq x$. But the $<$ relation is not reflexive: In fact, for no integer x, is $x < x$. Both the directed graph and the matrix representations make it easy to tell if a relation is reflexive. In the graph representation, every vertex will have, at a minimum, an edge looping back to itself. In the adjacency matrix representation, there will be ones all along the major diagonal, and possibly elsewhere as well. Figure A.3 illustrates both cases.

A relation $R \subseteq A \times A$ is ***symmetric*** iff $\forall x, y\ ((x, y) \in R \rightarrow (y, x) \in R)$. The *Address* relation we described above is symmetric. If Joanna lives with Ann, then Ann lives with Joanna. The $\leq$ relation is not symmetric (since, for example, $2 \leq 3$, but it is not true that $3 \leq 2$). The graph representation of a symmetric relation has the property that, between any two vertices, either there is an arrow going in both directions or there is no arrow going in either direction. So we get graphs with components that look like the one shown in Figure A.4(a). If we choose the matrix representation, we will end up with a ***symmetric matrix*** (i.e., if you flip it on its major diagonal, you'll get the same matrix back again). In other words, if we have a matrix with 1's as shown in the matrix of Figure A.4(b), then there must also be 1's in all the squares marked with an * in that matrix.

A relation $R \subseteq A \times A$ is ***antisymmetric*** iff $\forall x, y\ (((x, y) \in R \wedge x \neq y) \rightarrow (y, x) \notin R)$. The *Mother-of* relation we described above is antisymmetric: If Ann is the mother of Catherine, then one thing we know for sure is that Catherine is not also the mother of Ann. Our *Address* relation is clearly not antisymmetric. There are, however, relations that are neither symmetric nor antisymmetric. One example is the *Likes* relation on the set of people: If Joe likes Bob, then it is possible that Bob likes Joe; it is also possible that he doesn't. Note that antisymmetric is not the same as not symmetric. The relation $\varnothing$ is both symmetric and antisymmetric.

A relation $R \subseteq A \times A$ is ***transitive*** iff $\forall x, y, z\ (((x, y) \in R \wedge (y, z) \in R) \rightarrow (x, z) \in R)$. A simple example of a transitive relation is $<$. *Address* is another one: If Bill lives with

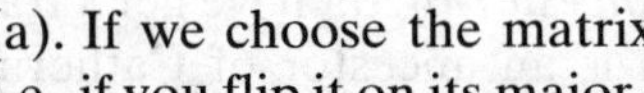

(a)

	*	*		
1				1
1				
	*			

(b)

FIGURE A.4 Representing a symmetric relation.

Table A.3 Important properties of relations.

Properties	***Domain***	***Example***
None	People	*Mother-of*
Just reflexive	People who can see	*Would-recognize-picture-of*
Just symmetric	People	*Has-ever-been-married-to*
Just transitive	People	*Ancestor-of*
Just reflexive and symmetric	People	*Hangs-out-with* (assuming we can say one hangs out with oneself)
Just reflexive and transitive	Numbers	$\leq$
Just symmetric and transitive	Anything	$\varnothing$
All three	Numbers	$=$
"	People	*Address*

Stacy and Stacy lives with Lee, then Bill lives with Lee. *Mother-of* is not transitive. But if we change it slightly to *Ancestor-of*, then we get a transitive relation. If Doreen is an ancestor of Ann and Ann is an ancestor of Catherine, then Doreen is an ancestor of Catherine.

The three properties of reflexivity, symmetry, and transitivity are almost logically independent of each other. We can find simple, potentially useful relations that possess seven of the eight possible combinations of these properties. We show them in Table A.3 (which we'll extend to include antisymmetry in Exercise A.10).

To see why we can't find a nontrivial (i.e., different from $\varnothing$) example of a relation that is symmetric and transitive but not reflexive, consider a simple relation R on $\{1, 2, 3, 4\}$. As soon as R contains a single element that relates two unequal objects (e.g., $(1,2)$), it must, for symmetry, contain the matching element $(2, 1)$. So now we have $R' = \{(1, 2), (2, 1)\}$. To make R' transitive, we must add $(1, 1)$ and $(2, 2)$. Call the resulting relation R''. Then R'' would be reflexive, except that neither 3 nor 4 is related to itself. In fact, they are related to nothing. We cannot find an example of a relation R that is symmetric and transitive but not reflexive if we insist that all elements of the domain be related under R to something.

A.3.4 Equivalence Relations

Although all but one of the combinations we just described are reasonable, one combination is of such great importance that we give it a special name. Given a domain A, a relation $R \subseteq A \times A$ is an ***equivalence relation*** iff it is reflexive, symmetric and transitive. *Equality* (for numbers, strings, or whatever) is an equivalence relation (no coincidence, given the name). So is our *Address* (lives at same address) relation.

Equality is a very special sort of equivalence relation because it relates an object only to itself. It doesn't help us much to carve up a large set into useful subsets. But other equivalence relations may serve as very useful ways to carve up a set. To see why, consider a set A, with five elements, which we can draw as a set of vertices as shown in

Figure A.5(a). Having done that, we can build an equivalence relation R on A. First, we'll relate each vertex to itself. That will make the relation reflexive. Once that is done, we'll have the relation shown in Figure A.5(b).

Now let's add one additional element, $(1, 2)$, to R. As soon as we do that, we must also add $(2, 1)$, since R must be symmetric. At this point, we have the relation shown in Figure A.5(c). Suppose we now add $(2, 3)$. We must also add $(3, 2)$ to maintain symmetry. In addition, because we have $(1, 2)$ and $(2, 3)$, we must add $(1, 3)$ for transitivity. And then we need $(3, 1)$ to restore symmetry. That gives us the relation shown in Figure A.5(d).

Notice what happened here. As soon as we related 3 to 2, we were also forced to relate 3 to 1. If we hadn't, we would no longer have had an equivalence relation. See what happens now if you add $(3, 4)$ to R.

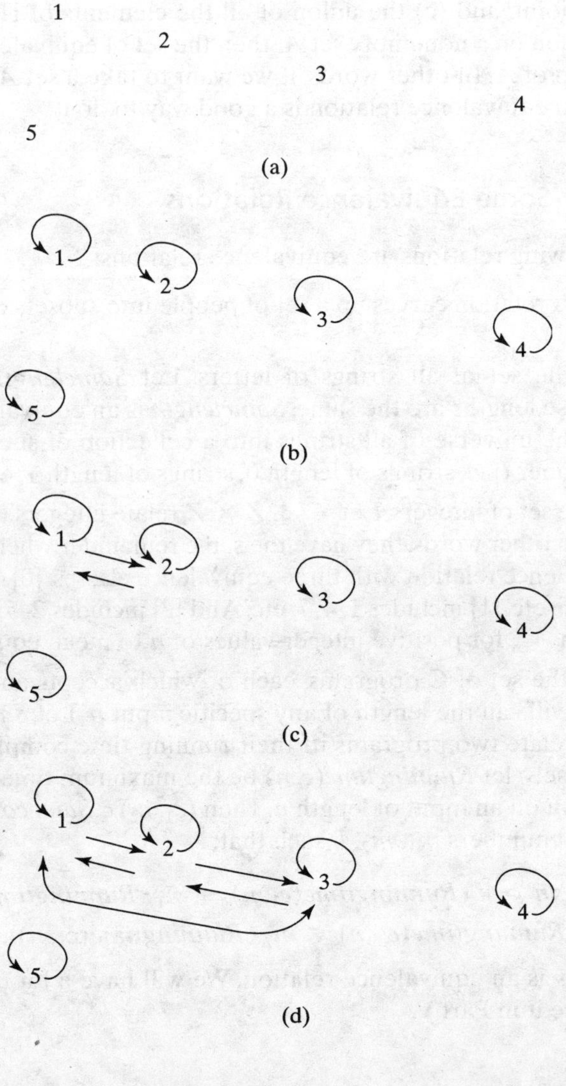

FIGURE A.5 Building an equivalence relation.

What we've seen in this example is that an equivalence relation R on a set S carves S up into a set of clusters or islands, which we'll call ***equivalence classes***. This set of equivalence classes has the following key property:

$$\forall s, t \in S\ ((s \in class_i \wedge (s, t) \in R) \rightarrow t \in class_i).$$

In other words, all elements of S that are related under R are in the same equivalence class. To describe equivalence classes, we'll use the notation $[x]$ to mean the equivalence class to which x belongs. Or we may just write [description], where description is some clear property shared by all the members of the class. Notice that, in general, there may be lots of different ways to describe the same equivalence class. In our example, for instance, [1], [2], and [3] are different names for the same equivalence class, which includes the elements 1, 2, and 3. In this example, there are two other equivalence classes as well: [4] and [5].

Recall that Π is a partition of a set A iff (a) no element of Π is empty; (b) all members of Π are disjoint; and (c) the union of all the elements of Π equals A. If R is an equivalence relation on a nonempty set A, then the set of equivalence classes of R constitutes a partition of A. In other words, if we want to take a set A and carve it up into a set of subsets, an equivalence relation is a good way to do it.

EXAMPLE A.4 Some Equivalence Relations

All of the following relations are equivalence relations:

- The *Address* relation carves up a set of people into subsets of people who live together.
- Let A be the set of all strings of letters. Let $Samelength \subseteq A \times A$ relate strings whose lengths are the same. *Samelength* is an equivalence relation that carves up the universe of all strings into a collection of subsets, one for each natural number (i.e., strings of length 0, strings of length 1, etc.).
- Let Z be the set of integers. Let $\equiv_3 \subseteq Z \times Z$ relate integers that are equivalent modulo 3. In other words, they have the same remainder when divided by 3. $\equiv_3$ is an equivalence relation with three equivalence classes, [0], [1], and [2]. [0] includes 0, 3, 6, etc. [1] includes 1, 4, 7, etc. And [2] includes 2, 5, 8, etc. We will use the notation $\equiv_n$ for positive integer values of n to mean equivalent modulo n.
- Let CP be the set of C programs, each of which accepts an input of variable length. We will call the length of any specific input n. Let $Samecomplexity \supset CP \times CP$ relate two programs iff their running-time complexity is the same. More, precisely, let $Runningtime(c, n)$ be the maximum time required for program c to run on an input of length n. Then $(c_1, c_2) \in Samecomplexity$ iff there exist natural numbers m_1, m_2, k such that:

$$\forall n > k\ (Runningtime(c_1, n) \leq m_1 \cdot Runningtime(c_2, n) \wedge$$
$$Runningtime(c_2, n) \leq m_2 \cdot Runningtime(c_1, n)).$$

Samecomplexity is an equivalence relation. We will have a lot more to say about relations like it in Part V.

Not every relation that connects "similar" things is an equivalence relation. For example, define *Similarcost*(x, y) to hold if the price of x is within \$1 of the price of y. Suppose X_1 costs \$10, X_2 costs \$10.50, and X_3 costs \$11.25. Then $Similarcost(X_1, X_2)$ and $Similarcost(X_2, X_3)$, but not $Similarcost(X_1, X_3)$. *Similarcost* is not transitive, although it is reflexive and symmetric. So *Similarcost* is not an equivalence relation.

A.3.5 Orderings

Important as equivalence relations are, they are not the only special kind of relation worth mentioning. Let's consider two more.

A ***partial order*** is a relation that is reflexive, antisymmetric, and transitive. Let R be a partial order defined on a set A. Then the pair (A, R) is a ***partially ordered set***. If we write out any partial order as a graph, we'll see a structure like the ones in the following examples. Notice that, to make the graph relatively easy to read, we'll adopt the convention that we don't write in the links that are required by reflexivity and transitivity. But, of course, they are there in the relations themselves.

EXAMPLE A.5 *Subset-of* is a Partial Order

Consider the relation *Subset-of*, defined on the set of all sets. *Subset-of* is a partial order, since it is reflexive (every set is a subset of itself), transitive (if $A \subseteq B$ and $B \subseteq C$, then $A \subseteq C$) and antisymmetric (if $A \subseteq B$ and $A \neq B$, then it must not be true that $B \subseteq A$). A small piece of *Subset-of* can be drawn as:

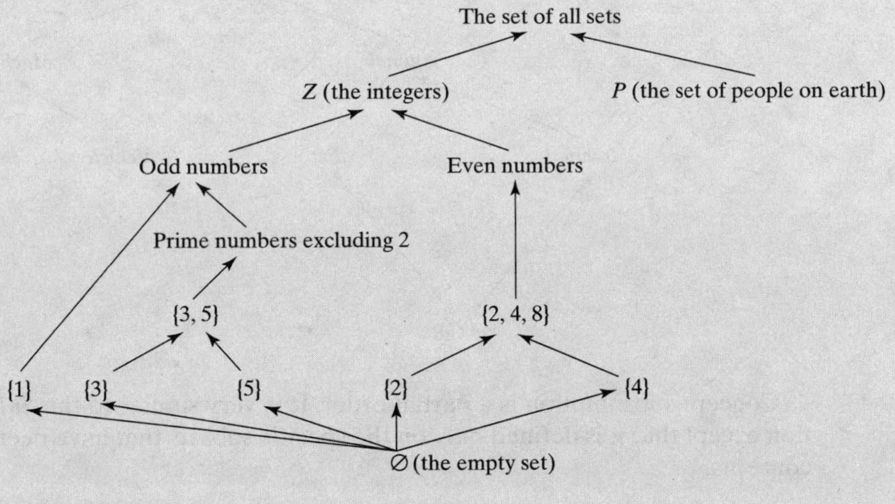

Read an arrow from x to y as meaning that (x, y) is an element of *Subset-of*. So, in this example, $\{3\}$ is a subset of $\{3, 5\}$. Note that in a partial order, it is often the case that there are some elements (such as $\{3, 5\}$ and $\{2\}$) that are not related to each other at all (since neither is a subset of the other). Remember in reading this picture that we have omitted the reflexive and symmetric arrows.

EXAMPLE A.6 *Proper-Subset-of* is Not a Partial Order

Now consider the relation *Proper-subset-of*. It is not a partial order because it is not reflexive. For example $\{1\} \not\subset \{1\}$.

In many kinds of applications, it is useful to organize the objects we are dealing with by defining a partial order that corresponds to the notion of one object being more or less general than another. Such a relation may be called a ***subsumption relation***.

EXAMPLE A.7 Concepts Form a Subsumption Relation

Consider a set of concepts, each of which corresponds to some significant set of entities in the world. Some concepts are more general than others. We'll say that a concept x is ***subsumed*** by a concept y (written $x \leq y$) iff every instance of x is also an instance of y. Alternatively, y is at least as general as x. A small piece of this subsumption relation for some concepts that might be used to model the meanings of common English words is:

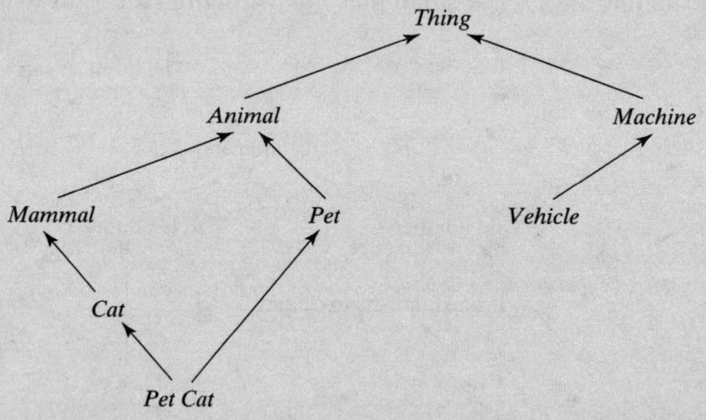

Concept subsumption is a partial order. It is very similar to the *Subset-of* relation except that it is defined only on the specific subsets that have been defined as concepts.

Subsumption relations are useful because they tell us when we have new information. If we already know that some object X_1 is a cat, we learn nothing new when told that it is an animal.

EXAMPLE A.8 Logical Statements Form a Subsumption Lattice

A first-order logic sentence P is subsumed by another sentence Q (written $P \le Q$) iff, whenever Q is true P must be true, regardless of the values assigned to the variables, functions, and predicates of P and Q. For example: $\forall x\,(P(x))$ subsumes $P(X_1)$, since, regardless of what the predicate P is and what axioms we have about it, and regardless of what object X_1 represents, if $\forall x\,(P(x))$ is true, then $P(X_1)$ must be true. Why is this a useful notion? Suppose that we are building a theorem-proving or reasoning program. If we already know $\forall x\,P(x)$, and we are then told $P(X_1)$, we can throw away this new fact. It doesn't add to our knowledge (except perhaps to focus our attention on the object X_1), since it is subsumed by something we already knew. A small piece of the subsumption relation on sentences is shown in the following graph:

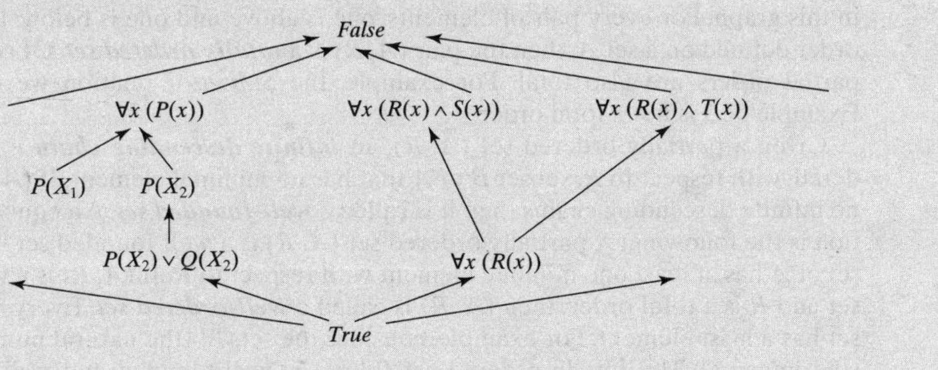

The subsumption relation on sentences is a partial order.

The symbol $\le$ is often used to denote a partial order. Let $\le$ be an arbitrary partial order defined on some domain A. Any element x of A such that $\forall y \in A\,((y \le x) \rightarrow (y = x))$ is a ***minimal element*** of A with respect to $\le$. In other words, x is a minimal element if there are no other elements less than or equal to it. Similarly, any element x of A such that $\forall y \in A\,(x \le y \rightarrow y = x)$ is a ***maximal element*** of A with respect to $\le$. There may be more than one minimal (or maximal) element in a partially ordered set. For example, the partially ordered set of concepts in Example A.7 has two minimal elements, *Pet Cat* and *Vehicle*. If there is a unique minimal element it is called the ***least element***. If there is a unique maximal element it is called the ***greatest element***. The set of logical sentences ordered by subsumption has a greatest element, *False*, which subsumes everything. It makes the strongest, and in fact, unsatisfiable claim. There is also a least element, *True*, which makes the weakest possible claim, and is subsumed by all other sentences.

A ***total order*** $R \subseteq A \times A$ is a partial order that has the additional property that $\forall x, y \in A\,((x, y) \in R \vee (y, x) \in R)$. In other words, every pair of elements must be related to each other one way or the other. The classic example of a total order is $\le$ (or $\ge$, if you prefer) on the integers. The $\le$ relation is a partial order and, given any two

FIGURE A.6
Drawing a total order as a graph.

integers x and y, either $x \leq y$ or $y \leq x$. If we draw any total order as a graph, we'll get something that looks like the graph in Figure A.6 (again without the reflexive and transitive links shown).

This is only a tiny piece of the graph, of course. It continues infinitely in both directions. But notice that, unlike our earlier examples of partial orders, there is no splitting in this graph. For every pair of elements, one is above and one is below. If R is a total order defined on a set A, then the pair (A, R) is a ***totally ordered set***. Of course, not all partial orders are also total. For example, the *Subset-of* relation we described in Example 32.5 is not a total order.

Given a partially ordered set (A, R), an ***infinite descending chain*** is a totally ordered, with respect to R, subset B of A that has no minimal element. If (A, R) contains no infinite descending chains then it is called a ***well-founded set***. An equivalent definition is the following: A partially ordered set (A, R) is a well-founded set iff every subset of A has at least one minimal element with respect to R. If (A, R) is a well-founded set and R is a total order, then (A, R) is called a ***well-ordered set***. Every well-ordered set has a least element. For example, consider the sets $\mathbb{N}$ (the natural numbers) and Z (the integers). The totally ordered set $(\mathbb{N}, \leq)$ is well-founded and well-ordered. Its least element is 0. The totally ordered set $(Z, \leq)$ is neither well-founded nor well-ordered, since it contains an infinite number of infinite descending chains, such as $3, 2, 1, 0, -1, -2, \ldots$.

Table A.4 reviews some of our examples.

Well-founded and well-ordered sets are important. Well-ordered sets provide the basis for proofs by induction (as we'll see in Section A.6.5). Well-founded sets (that are often also well-ordered) provide the basis for proofs that loops and recursively defined functions halt (as we'll see in Section A.7.1).

Table A.4 Checking for well-foundedness and well-orderedness.

(A, R)	***Well-founded?***	***Well-ordered?***
The set of sets with respect to the *subset-of* relation	Yes	No
The set of concepts with respect to *subsumption*	Yes	No
The set of first-order sentences with respect to *subsumption*	Yes	No
The set of natural numbers under $\leq$	Yes	Yes
The set of integers under $\leq$	No	No

A.4 Functions

Relations are very general. They allow an object to be related to any number of other objects at the same time (as they are, for example, in our *Dessert* relation). Sometimes we want a more restricted notion, in which each object is related to a unique other object. For example, (at least in an ideal world without criminals or incompetent bureaucrats) each United States resident is related to a unique social security number. To capture this idea we need functions.

A.4.1 What is a Function?

We begin with the common definition of a function: A ***function*** f from a set A to a set B is a binary relation that is a subset of $A \times B$, with the additional property that:

$$\forall x \in A\ ((((x, y) \in f \land (x, z) \in f) \rightarrow y = z) \land \exists y \in B\ ((x, y) \in f)).$$

In other words, each element of A is related to exactly one element of B.

The *Dessert* relation we defined earlier is not a function since Dave and Sara each occur twice. We haven't restricted each person to precisely one dessert. A simple relation that *is* a function is the successor function *succ* defined on the integers:

$$succ(n) = n + 1.$$

Of course, we cannot write out all the elements of *succ* (since there are an infinite number of them), but *succ* includes:

$$\{\ldots, (-3, -2), (-2, -1), (-1, 0), (0, 1), (1, 2), (2, 3) \cdots\}.$$

It is useful to define some additional terms to make it easy to talk about functions. We start by writing:

$$f: A \rightarrow B,$$

which means that f is a function from the set A to the set B. We call A the ***domain*** of f and B the ***codomain*** or ***range*** of f. We may also say that f is a function from A to B. Using this notation, we can write function definitions that have two parts, the first of which specifies the domain and range and the second of which defines the way in which the elements of the range are related to the elements of the domain. So, for example, we define the successor function on the integers (denoted as Z) by writing:

$$succ: Z \rightarrow Z,$$
$$succ(n) = n + 1.$$

If $x \in A$, then we write:

$$f(x),$$

which we read as, "f of x", to indicate the element of B to which x is related. We call this element the ***image*** of x under f or the ***value*** of f for x. Note that, given the definition of a function, there must be exactly one such element. We will also call x the ***argument*** of f. For example we have that:

$$succ(1) = 2,\ succ(2) = 3, \ldots$$

Thus 2 is the image (or the value) of the argument 1 under *succ*.

We will also use the notation $f(x)$ to refer to the function f (as opposed to f's value at a specific point x) whenever we need a way to refer to f's argument. So, for example, we'll write, as we did above, $succ(n) = n + 1$.

The function *succ* is a ***unary function***. It maps from a single element (a number) to another element. We are also interested in functions that map from ordered pairs of elements to a value. We call such functions ***binary functions***. For example, integer addition is a binary function:

$$+: (Z \times Z) \rightarrow Z.$$

Thus + includes elements such as ((2, 3), 5), since 2 + 3 is 5. We could also write:

$$+((2, 3)) = 5.$$

We have used double parentheses here because we are using the outer set to indicate function application (as we did above without confusion for *succ*) and the inner set to define the ordered pair to which the function is being applied. But this is confusing. So, generally, when the domain of a function is the Cartesian product of two or more sets, as it is here, we drop the inner set of parentheses and simply write:

$$+(2, 3) = 5.$$

The ***prefix notation*** that we have used so far, in which we write the name of the function first, followed by its arguments, can be used for functions of any number of arguments. For the specific, common case of binary functions, it is often convenient to use an alternative: ***infix notation***, in which the function name (often called the operator) is written, between its two arguments:

$$2 + 3 = 5.$$

So far, we have considered unary functions and binary functions. But just as we could define n-ary relations for arbitrary values of n, we can define n-ary functions. For any positive integer n, an ***n*-ary function** f is a function that is defined as:

$$f: (S_1 \times S_2 \ldots \times S_n) \rightarrow R.$$

For example, let Z be the set of integers. Then,

$$quadraticequation: (Z \times Z \times Z) \rightarrow F$$

is a function whose domain is an ordered triple of integers and whose range is a set of functions. The definition of *quadraticequation* is:

$$quadraticequation(a, b, c) = ax^2 + bx + c.$$

What we did here is typical of function definition. First we specify the domain and the range of the function. Then we define how the function is to compute its value (an element of the range) given its arguments (an element of the domain).

Whenever the domain of a function f is an ordered n-tuple of elements drawn from a single set S, we may (loosely) say that the domain of f is S. In this case, we may also say that f is a function of n arguments. So, for example, we may talk about the binary function + on the domain $\mathbb{N}$ (when, properly, its domain is $\mathbb{N} \times \mathbb{N}$).

Recall that, in the last section, we said that we could compose binary relations to derive new relations. Clearly, since functions are just special kinds of binary relations, if we can compose binary relations we can certainly compose binary functions. Because a function returns a unique value for each argument, it generally makes a lot more sense to compose functions than it does relations, and you'll see that although we rarely compose relations that aren't functions, we compose functions all the time. So, following our definition above for relations, we define the ***composition*** of two functions $f \subseteq A \times B$ and $g \subseteq B \times C$, written $g \circ f$, as:

$$g \circ f = \{(a, c) : \exists b\, ((a, b) \in f \text{ and } (b, c) \in g)\}.$$

Notice that the composition of two functions must necessarily also be a function. We mentioned above that there is sometimes confusion about the order in which relations (and now functions) should be applied when they are composed. To avoid this problem, we will introduce a new notation $g(f(x))$. We use the parentheses here to indicate function application, just as we did above. So $g \circ f(x) = g(f(x))$. This notation is clear. Apply g to the result of first applying f to x. This notation reads right to left as does our definition of the $\circ$ notation.

A.4.2 Properties of Functions

Some functions possess properties that may make them particularly useful for certain tasks. The definition that we gave for a function at the beginning of this section required that, for $f : A \rightarrow B$ to be a function, it must be defined for every element of A (i.e., every element of A must be related to some element of B). This is the standard mathematical definition of a function. But, as we pursue the idea of "computable functions" (i.e., functions that can be implemented on some reasonable computing platform), we'll see that there are functions whose domains cannot be effectively defined.

For example, consider a function *steps* whose input is a Java program and whose result is the number of steps that are executed by the program on the input 0. This function is undefined for programs that do not halt on the input 0. As we'll see in Chapter 19, there can exist no program that can check a Java program and determine whether or not it will halt on the input 0. So there is no program that can look at a possible input to *steps* and determine whether that input is in *steps*'s domain. In Chapter 25, we will consider two approaches to fixing this problem. One is to extend the range of *steps*, for example by adding a special value, *Error*, that can be the result of applying *steps* to a program that doesn't halt on input 0. The difficulty with this approach is that *steps* becomes uncomputable since there exists no algorithm that can know when to return *Error*. Our alternative is to expand the domain of *steps*, for example to the set of all Java programs. Then we must acknowledge that if *steps* is applied to certain elements of its domain (i.e., programs that don't halt), its value will be undefined.

In order to be able to talk about functions like *steps*, we'll introduce two new terms. We'll say that $f: A \rightarrow B$ is a ***total function*** on A iff it is a function that is defined on all elements of A (i.e., it is a function in the standard mathematical sense). We'll say that $f: A \rightarrow B$ is a ***partial function*** on A iff f is a subset of $A \times B$ and every element of A is related to no more than one element of B. In Chapter 25 we will return to a discussion of partial functions. Until then, when we say that f is a function, we will mean that it is a total function.

A function $f: A \rightarrow B$ is ***one-to-one*** iff no two elements of A map to the same element of B. *Succ* is one-to-one. For example, the only number to which we can apply *succ* and derive 2 is 1. *Quadraticequation* is also one-to-one. But + isn't. For example, both +(2, 3) and +(4, 1) equal 5.

A function $f: A \rightarrow B$ is ***onto*** iff every element of B is the value of some element of A. Another way to think of this is that a function is onto iff all of the elements of B are "covered" by the function. As we defined it above, *succ* is onto. But let's define a different function *succ'* on $\mathbb{N}$ (the natural numbers), rather than the integers. So we define:

$$succ' : \mathbb{N} \rightarrow \mathbb{N}.$$
$$succ'(n) = n + 1.$$

succ' is not onto because there is no natural number i such that $succ'(i) = 0$.

The easiest way to envision the differences between an arbitrary relation, a function, a one-to-one function, and an onto function is to make two columns (the first for the domain and the second for the range) and think about the kind of matching problems you probably had on tests in elementary school.

Consider the six matching problems shown in Figure A.7. In each, we'll consider ways of relating the elements of the first column (the domain) to the elements of the second column (the range). Example 1 describes a relation that is not a (total) function because C is an element of its domain that is not related to any element of its range. Example 2 describes a relation that is not a function because there are three values associated with A. The third example is a function since, for each object in the first column, there is a single value in the second column. But this function is neither one-to-one (because X is derived from both A and B) nor onto (because Z is not the image of anything). The fourth example is a function that is one-to-one (because no element of the second column is related to more than one element of the first column). But it still isn't onto because Z has been skipped: Nothing in the first column derives it. The fifth example is a function that is onto (since every element of column two has an arrow coming into it), but it isn't one-to-one, since Z is derived from both C and D. The sixth and final example is a function that is both one-to-one and onto. By the way, see if you can modify either example 4 or example 5 to make it both one-to-one and onto. You're not allowed to change the number of elements in either column, just the arrows. You'll notice that you can't do it. In order for a function to be both one-to-one and onto, there must be equal numbers of elements in the domain and the range.

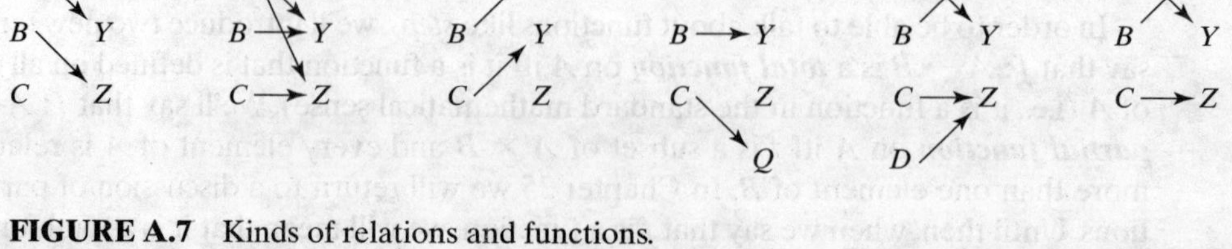

FIGURE A.7 Kinds of relations and functions.

The *inverse* of a binary function f is the relation that contains exactly the ordered pairs in f with the elements of each pair reversed. We'll write the inverse of f as f^{-1}. Formally, if $f \subseteq A \times B$, then $f^{-1} \subseteq B \times A = \{(b, a): (a, b) \in f\}$. Since every function is a relation, every function has a relational inverse, but that relational inverse may or may not also be a function. For example, look again at example 3 of the matching problem above. Although it is a function, its inverse is not. Given the argument X, should we return the value A or B? Now consider example 4. Its inverse is also not a function, since there is no value to be returned for the argument Z. Example 5 has the same problem example 3 does. Now look at example 6. Its inverse is a function. Whenever a function is both one-to-one and onto, its inverse will also be a function and that function will be both one-to-one and onto. Such functions are called ***bijections***. Bijections are useful because they enable us to move back and forth between two sets without loss of information. Look again at example 6. We can think of ourselves as operating in the $\{A, B, C\}$ universe or in the $\{X, Y, Z\}$ universe interchangeably since we have a well defined way to move from one to the other. And if we move from column one to column two and then back, we'll be exactly where we started.

It is sometimes useful to talk about functions that map one object to another but, in so doing, do not fundamentally change the way that the objects behave with respect to some structure (i.e., some set of functions that we care about). A ***homomorphism*** is a function that maps the elements of its domain to the elements of its range in such a way that some structure of the original set is preserved. So, considering just binary functions, if f is a homomorphism and # is a binary function in the structure that we are considering, then it must be case that $\forall x, y\, (f(x) \# f(y) = f(x \# y))$. The structure of unary and higher order functions must also be preserved in a similar way.

Given a particular function f, whether or not it is a homomorphism depends on the structure that we are considering. So, for example, consider the integers, along with one function, addition. Then the function $f(x) = 2x$ is a homomorphism because $2x + 2y = 2(x + y)$. But, if the structure we are working with also contains a second function, multiplication, then f is no longer a homomorphism because, unless x or y is $0, 2x \cdot 2y \neq 2(x \cdot y)$.

If a homomorphism f is also a bijection, then it is called an ***isomorphism***. If two objects are isomorphic to each other, then they are indistinguishable with respect to the defining structure. For example, consider the set of undirected graphs, along with all of the standard graph operations that determine size and paths. If G is an arbitrary graph, let $f(G)$ be exactly G except that the symbol # is appended to the name of every vertex. This function f is an isomorphism. The two graphs shown in Figure A.8 are isomorphic.

When the intersection of the domain and the range of a function f is not empty, it is sometimes useful to find elements of the domain that are unchanged by the application

FIGURE A.8 Two isomorphic graphs.

of f. A ***fixed point*** of a function f is an element x of f's domain with the property that $f(x) = x$. For example, 1 and 2 are fixed points of the factorial function since $1! = 1$ and $2! = 2$. The factorial function has no other fixed points.

A.4.3 Properties of Binary Functions

Any relation that uniquely maps from each element of its domain to some element of its range is a function. The two sets involved can be anything and the mapping can be arbitrary. However, most of the functions we actually care about behave in some sort of regular fashion. It is useful to articulate a set of properties that many of the functions that we'll study have. When these properties are true of a function, or a set of functions, they give us techniques for proving additional properties of the objects involved. In the following definitions, we will consider an arbitrary binary function # defined over a set A. As examples, we'll consider functions whose actual domains are ordered pairs of sets, integers, strings, and Boolean expressions.

- A binary function # is ***commutative*** iff $\forall x, y \in A\ (x \# y = y \# x)$. Examples:

  $i + j = j + i.$ (integer addition)

  $A \cap B = B \cap A.$ (set intersection)

  $P \wedge Q \equiv Q \wedge P.$ (Boolean *and*)

- A binary function # is ***associative*** iff $\forall x, y, z \in A\ ((x \# y) \# z = x \# (y \# z))$. Examples:

  $(i + j) + k = i + (j + k).$ (integer addition)

  $(A \cap B) \cap C = A \cap (B \cap C).$ (set intersection)

  $(P \wedge Q) \wedge R \equiv P \wedge (Q \wedge R).$ (Boolean *and*)

  $(s \| t) \| w = s \| (t \| w).$ (string concatenation)

- A binary function # is ***idempotent*** iff $\forall x \in A\ (x \# x = x)$. Examples:

  $min(i, i) = i.$ (integer minimum)

  $A \cap A = A.$ (set intersection)

  $P \wedge P \equiv P.$ (Boolean *and*)

- The ***distributivity*** property relates two binary functions: A function # distributes over another function % iff $\forall x, y, z \in A\ (x \# (y \% z) = (x \# y) \% (x \# z))$. Examples:

  $i \cdot (j + k) = (i \cdot j) + (i \cdot k).$ (integer multiplication over addition)

  $A \cup (B \cap C) = (A \cup B) \cap (A \cup C).$ (set union over intersection)

  $P \wedge (Q \vee R) \equiv (P \wedge Q) \vee (P \wedge Q).$ (Boolean *and* over *or*)

- ***Absorption laws*** also relate two binary functions to each other: A function # absorbs another function % iff $\forall x, y \in A\ (x \# (x \% y) = x))$. Examples:

  $A \cap (A \cup B) = A.$ (Set intersection absorbs union.)

  $P \vee (P \wedge Q) \equiv P.$ (Boolean *or* absorbs *and*.)

  $P \wedge (P \vee Q) \equiv P.$ (Boolean *and* absorbs *or*.)

It is often the case that when a function is defined over some set A, there are special elements of A that have particular properties with respect to that function. In particular, it is worth defining what it means to be an identity and to be a zero:

- An element a is an ***identity*** for the function # iff $\forall x \in A\ ((x \# a = x) \wedge (a \# x = x))$. Examples:

$i \cdot 1 = i.$	(1 is an identity for integer multiplication.)
$i + 0 = i.$	(0 is an identity for integer addition.)
$A \cup \varnothing = A.$	($\varnothing$ is an identity for set union.)
$P \vee False \equiv P.$	(*False* is an identity for Boolean *or*.)
$s \parallel "" = s.$	("" is an identity for string concatenation)

Sometimes it is useful to differentiate between a ***right identity*** (one that satisfies the first requirement above) and a ***left identity*** (one that satisfies the second requirement above). But for all the functions we'll be concerned with, if there is a left identity, it is also a right identity and vice versa, so we will talk simply about an identity.

- An element a is a ***zero*** for the function # iff $\forall x \in A\ ((x \# a = a) \wedge (a \# x = a))$. Examples:

$i \cdot 0 = 0.$	(0 is a zero for integer multiplication.)
$A \cap \varnothing = \varnothing.$	($\varnothing$ is a zero for set intersection.)
$P \wedge False \equiv False.$	(*False* is a zero for Boolean *and*.)

Just as with identities, it is sometimes useful to distinguish between left and right zeros, but we won't need to.

Although we're focusing here on binary functions, there's one important property that unary functions may have that is worth mentioning here:

- A unary function \$ is a ***self inverse*** iff $\forall x\ (\$(\$(x)) = x)$. In other words, if we compose the function with itself (apply it twice), we get back the original argument. Examples:

$-(-(i)) = i.$	(Multiplying by $-$ is a self inverse for integers.)
$1/(1/i) = i$ if $i \neq 0.$	(Dividing into 1 is a self inverse for integers.)
$\neg\neg A = A.$	(Complement is a self inverse for sets.)
$\neg(\neg p) = p.$	(Negation is a self inverse for Booleans.)
$(S^R)^R = s.$	(Reversal is a self inverse for strings.)

A.4.4 Properties of Functions on Sets

The functions that we have defined on sets satisfy most of the properties that we have just considered. Further, as we saw above, some set functions have a zero or an identity. We'll summarize here (without proof) the most useful properties that hold for the functions we have defined on sets:

- Commutativity: $A \cup B = B \cup A.$
  $A \cap B = B \cap A.$

- Associativity: $(A \cup B) \cup C = A \cup (B \cup C)$.
  $(A \cap B) \cap C = A \cap (B \cap C)$.
- Idempotency: $A \cup A = A$.
  $A \cap A = A$.
- Distributivity: $A \cup (B \cap C) = (A \cup B) \cap (A \cup C)$.
  $A \cap (B \cup C) = (A \cap B) \cup (A \cap C)$.
- Absorption: $(A \cup B) \cap A = A$.
  $(A \cap B) \cup A = A$.
- Identity: $A \cup \varnothing = A$.
- Zero: $A \cap \varnothing = \varnothing$.
- Self Inverse: $\neg\neg A = A$.

In addition, we will want to make use of the following theorems that can be proven to apply specifically to sets and their operations (as well as to Boolean expressions, with $\vee$ substituted for $\cup$ and $\wedge$ substituted $\cap$):

- De Morgan's Laws: $\neg(A \cup B) = \neg A \cap \neg B$.
  $\neg(A \cap B) = \neg A \cup \neg B$.

A.5 Closures

We say that a binary relation R on a set A is ***closed under*** property P iff R possesses P. For example, the relation $\leq$ as generally defined on the integers is closed under *transitivity*.

Sometimes, if a relation R is not closed under P we may want to ask what elements would have to be added to R so that it would possess P. So, let R be a binary relation on a set A. A relation R' is a ***closure*** of R with respect to some property P iff:

- $R \subseteq R'$,
- R' is closed under P, and
- there is no smaller relation R'' that contains R and is closed under P. (One relation R_1 is smaller than another relation R_2 iff $|R_1| < |R_2|$.

In other words, to form the closure of R with respect to P we add to R the minimum number of elements required to establish P. So, for example, the ***transitive closure*** of a binary relation R is the smallest relation R' that contains R but is transitive. Thus, if R contains the elements (x, y) and (y, z), the transitive closure of R must also contain the element (x, z).

EXAMPLE A.9 Forming Transitive and Reflexive Closures

Let $R = \{(1, 2), (2, 3), (3, 4)\}$.

- The transitive closure of R is $\{(1,2), (2,3), (3,4), (1,3), (1,4), (2,4)\}$.
- The reflexive closure of R is $\{(1,2), (2,3), (3,4), (1,1), (2,2), (3,3), (4,4)\}$.

EXAMPLE A.10 The Transitive Closure of *Parent-of*

The transitive closure of *Parent-of* is *Ancestor-of*.

Under some conditions (which will hold in all the cases we consider), it is possible to prove that a relation R has a unique closure under the property P. (See Section A.8 for a discussion of this issue.)

We can define the closure of a set with respect to a function in a similar manner. Let f be a function of n arguments. We say that a set A is ***closed under*** f iff, whenever all n of f's arguments are elements of A, the value of f is also in A. For example, the positive integers are closed under addition. The positive integers are not closed under subtraction since, for example $7 - 10 = -3$.

As we did for relations, we may again want to consider, whenever a set A is not closed under some function $f: X \rightarrow Y$, how A could be augmented (with additional elements drawn from X) so that it would be closed. Let f be function of n arguments drawn from a set A. A set A' is a ***closure*** of A under f iff:

- $A \subseteq A'$,
- A' is closed under f, and
- there is no smaller set A'' that contains A and is closed under f.

EXAMPLE A.11 Closures under Functions

- $\{0\}$ is not closed under the successor function *succ*, since $succ(0) = 1$. The closure of $\{0\}$ under *succ* is $\mathbb{N}$ (the natural numbers).
- $\mathbb{N}$ is closed under addition (since the sum of any two natural numbers is a natural number). So the closure of $\mathbb{N}$ under addition is simply $\mathbb{N}$.
- $\mathbb{N}$ is not closed under subtraction. For example, $5 - 7$ is not a natural number. The closure of $\mathbb{N}$ under subtraction is Z (the integers).
- Z is not closed under division. Its closure under division is Q (the rational numbers) plus a special element that is the result of dividing by 0.
- Q is not closed under limits. Its closure under limits is R (the real numbers).
- R is not closed under square root. Its closure under square root is C (the complex numbers).
- The set of even length strings of a's and b's is closed under concatenation.
- The set of odd length strings of a's and b's is not closed under concatenation. For example the string aaa concatenated with the string aaa is aaaaaa, whose length is not odd. The closure of the odd length strings of a's and b's under concatenation is the set of all strings of a's and b's.

EXAMPLE A.11 (*Continued*)

- Let A be the set of all strings of a's. So $A = \{a, aa, aaa, aaaa, aaaaa, \ldots\}$. Let S be the set that contains all subsets SS of A where SS contains an odd number of elements. So $S = \{\{a\}, \{aa\}, \{aaa\}, \ldots, \{a, aa, aaa\}, \ldots\}$. S is not closed under union, since, for example $\{a\} \cup \{aa\} = \{a, aa\}$, which is not in S, since it contains an even number of elements. The closure of S under union is the set of all nonempty finite sets in $\mathcal{P}(A)$.

Given a set S and a property P, we may want to compute the closure of S with respect to P. For example, we will often want to compute the transitive closure of a binary relation R on a set A. This is harder than it seems. We can't just add a fixed number of elements to R and then quit. Every time we add a new element, such as (x, y), we have to look to see whether there is some element (y, z). If so, we also have to add (x, z). And, similarly, we must check for any element (w, x) that would force us to add (w, y). If R is infinite, there is no guarantee that this process will ever terminate. Theorem A.5 (presented in Section A.8) guarantees that a unique closure exists but it does not guarantee that the closure will contain a finite number of elements and thus be computable in a finite amount of time.

We can, however, guarantee that the transitive closure of any *finite* binary relation is computable. How? A very simple approach is the following algorithm for computing the transitive closure of a binary relation R with n elements on a set A. If t is an ordered pair, then *t.first* will refer to the first element of the pair and *t.second* will refer to the second element.

computetransitiveclosure(R: relation) =

1. *trans* = *R*. /* Initially *trans* is just the original relation.

/* We need to find all cases where (x, y) and (y, z) are in *trans*. Then we must
/* insert (x, z) into *trans* if it isn't already there.

2. *addedSomething* = *True*. /* Keep going until we make one whole pass. without adding any new elements to *trans*.

3. While *addedSomething* = *True* do:

3.1. *addedSomething* = *False*.

3.2. For each element *t1* of *trans* do:

For each element *t2* of *trans* do: /* Compare *t1* to every other element of *trans*.

If *t1.second* = *t2.first* then do: /* We have(x, y) and (y, z).

If(*t1.first*, *t2.second*) $\notin$ *trans* then do: /* We have to add (x, z).

Insert(*trans*, (*t1.first*, *t2.second*)).

addedSomething = *True*.

This algorithm is straightforward and correct, but it may be inefficient. There are more efficient algorithms. In particular, if we represent a relation as an adjacency matrix, we can do better using Warshall's algorithm 🖫, which finds the transitive closure of a relation over a set of n elements using approximately $2n^3$ bit operations.

In Section A.8, we present a more general definition of closure that includes, as special cases, the two specific definitions presented here. We also elaborate on some of the claims that we have just made.

A.6 Proof Techniques

In this section we summarize the most important proof techniques that we will use in the rest of this book.

A.6.1 Proof by Construction

Suppose that we want to prove an assertion of the form $\exists x\ (Q(x))$ or $\forall x (\exists y\ (P(x, y)))$. One way to prove such a claim is to show a (provably correct) algorithm that finds the value that we claim must exist. We call that technique ***proof by construction***.

For example, we might wish to prove that every pair of integers has a greatest common divisor. We could prove that claim by exhibiting (as we do in Example 27.6) a correct greatest common divisor algorithm. In exhibiting such an algorithm, we show not only that the greatest common divisor exists (since the algorithm provably finds one for every input pair), we show something more—a method to determine the greatest common divisor for any pair of integers. While this is a stronger claim than the one we started with, it is often the case that such stronger claims are easier to prove.

A.6.2 Proof by Contradiction

Suppose that we want to prove some assertion P. One approach is to assume, to the contrary, that $\neg P$ were true. We then show, with that assumption, that we can derive a contradiction. The law of the excluded middle says that $(P \vee \neg P)$. If we accept it, and we shall, then, since $\neg P$ cannot be true, P must be.

EXAMPLE A.12 There is an Infinite Number of Primes

Consider the claim that there is an infinite number of prime numbers. Following Euclid, we prove this claim by assuming, to the contrary, that the set P of prime numbers is finite. So there exists some value of n such that $P = \{p_1, p_2, p_3, \ldots p_n\}$. Let:

$$q = (p_1 p_2 p_3 \ldots p_n) + 1.$$

Since q is greater than each p_i, it is not on the list of primes. So it must be composite. In that case, it must have at least one prime factor, which must then be an

EXAMPLE A.12 (*Continued*)

element of P. Suppose that factor is p_k, for some $k \leq n$. Then q must have at least one other factor, some integer i such that:

$$\begin{aligned} q &= ip_k. \\ (p_1p_2p_3\ldots p_n) + 1 &= ip_k. \\ (p_1p_2p_3\ldots p_n) - ip_k &= -1. \end{aligned}$$

Now observe that p_k divides both terms on the left since it is prime and so must be in the set $\{p_1, p_2, p_3, \ldots p_n\}$. Factoring it out, we get:

$$\begin{aligned} p_k(p_1p_2p_{k-1}p_{k+1}\ldots p_n - i) &= -1. \\ p_k &= -1/(p_1p_2p_{k-1}p_{k+1}\ldots p_n - i). \end{aligned}$$

But, since $(p_1p_2p_{k-1}p_{k+1}\ldots p_n - i)$ is an integer, this means that $|p_k| < 1$. But that cannot be true since p_k is prime and thus greater than 1. So q is not composite. Since q is greater than 1 and not composite, it must be prime, contradicting the assumption that all primes are in the set $\{p_1, p_2, p_3, \ldots p_n\}$.

Notice that this proof, in addition to being a proof by contradiction, is constructive. It exhibits a specific example that contradicts the initial assumption.

EXAMPLE A.13 $\sqrt{2}$ is Irrational

Consider the claim that $\sqrt{2}$ is irrational. We prove this claim by assuming, to the contrary, that $\sqrt{2}$ is rational. In that case, it is the quotient of two integers, i and j. So we have:

$$\sqrt{2} = i/j.$$

If i and j have any common factors, then reduce them by those factors. Now we have:

$$\begin{aligned} \sqrt{2} &= k/n, \text{ where } k \text{ and } n \text{ have no common factors.} \\ 2 &= k^2/n^2. \\ 2n^2 &= k^2. \end{aligned}$$

Since 2 is a factor of k^2, k^2 must be even and so k is even. Since k is even, we can rewrite it as $2m$ for some integer m. Substituting $2m$ for k, we get:

$$\begin{aligned} 2n^2 &= (2m)^2. \\ 2n^2 &= 4m^2. \\ n^2 &= 2m^2. \end{aligned}$$

So n^2 is even and thus n is even. But now both k and n are even and so have 2 as a common factor. But we had reduced them until they had no common factors. The assumption that $\sqrt{2}$ is rational has led to a contradiction. So $\sqrt{2}$ cannot be rational.

A.6.3 Proof by Counterexample

Consider any claim of the form $\forall x\ (P(x))$. Such a claim is false iff $\exists x\ (\neg P(x))$. We can prove that it is false by finding such an x.

EXAMPLE A.14 Mersenne Primes

Let M be the set of numbers of the form $2^n - 1$ for some positive integer n. M is also called the set of ***Mersenne numbers***. Now consider only those cases in which n is prime. (In fact, some authors restrict the term Mersenne number only to those cases.) Consider two statements:

1. If n is prime, then $2^n - 1$ is prime.
2. If $2^n - 1$ is prime, then n is prime.

Statement 2 is true. But what about statement 1? Hundreds of years ago, some mathematicians believed that it was true, although they had no proof of it. Then, in 1536, Hudalricus Regius refuted the claim by showing a counterexample: $2^{11} - 1 = 2047$ is not prime. But that was not the end of false conjectures about these numbers. The elements of M that are also prime are called ***Mersenne primes***, after the monk Marin Mersenne, who, in 1644, made the claim that numbers of the form $2^n - 1$ are prime if $n = 2, 3, 5, 7, 13, 17, 19, 31, 67, 127$, and 257, but are composite for all other positive integers $n \leq 257$. Mersenne's claim was shown to be false by counterexample, over two hundred years later, when it was discovered that $2^{61} - 1$ is also prime. Later discoveries showed other ways in which Mersenne was wrong. The correct list of values of $n \leq 257$ such that $2^n - 1$ is prime is 2, 3, 5, 7, 13, 17, 19, 31, 61, 89, 107, and 127.

EXAMPLE A.15 All it Takes is One Counterexample

Consider the following claim:

Let A, B, and C be any sets. If $A - C = A - B$ then $B = C$.

We show that this claim is false with a counterexample: Let $A = \varnothing$, $B = \{1\}$, and $C = \{2\}$. $A - C = A - B = \varnothing$. But $B \neq C$.

A.6.4 Proof by Case Enumeration

Consider a claim of the form $\forall x \in A\ (P(x))$. Sometimes the most straightforward way to prove that P holds for all elements of A is to divide A into two or more subsets and then to prove P separately for each subset.

EXAMPLE A.16 The Postage Stamp Problem

Suppose that the postage required to mail a letter is always at least 6¢. Prove that it is possible to apply any required postage to a letter given only 2¢ and 7¢ stamps.

We prove this general claim by dividing it into two cases, based on the value of n, the required postage:

1. If n is even (and 6¢ or more), apply $n/2$ 2¢ stamps.
2. If n is odd (and 6¢ or more), then $n \geq 7$ and $n - 7 \geq 0$ and is even. 7¢ can be applied with one 7¢ stamp. Apply one 7¢ stamp and $(n - 7)/2$ 2¢ stamps.

A.6.5 Mathematical Induction

The ***principle of mathematical induction*** states:

If:	$P(b)$ is true for some integer base case b, and
	for all integers $n \geq b$, $P(n) \rightarrow P(n+1)$
Then	for all integers $n \geq b$, $P(n)$

A proof, using mathematical induction, of an assertion P about some set of positive integers greater than or equal to some specific value b, has three parts.

1. A clear statement of the assertion P.
2. A proof that that P holds for some base case b, the smallest value with which we are concerned. Often, $b = 0$ or 1, but sometimes P may hold only once we get past some initial unusual cases.
3. A proof that, for all integers $n \geq b$, if $P(n)$ then it is also true that $P(n + 1)$. We'll call the claim $P(n)$ the ***induction hypothesis***.

EXAMPLE A.17 The Sum of the First n Odd Positive Integers is n^2

Consider the claim that that the sum of the first n odd positive integers is n^2. We first check for plausibility:

$$\begin{aligned}
(n = 1)\ 1 &= 1 = 1^2. \\
(n = 2)\ 1 + 3 &= 4 = 2^2. \\
(n = 3)\ 1 + 3 + 5 &= 9 = 3^2. \\
(n = 4)\ 1 + 3 + 5 + 7 &= 16 = 4^2, \text{ and so forth.}
\end{aligned}$$

The claim appears to be true, so we should prove it. Let $Odd_i = 2(i - 1) + 1$ denote the ith odd positive integer. Then we can rewrite the claim as:

$$\forall n \geq 1 \left(\sum_{i=1}^{n} Odd_i = n^2 \right).$$

The proof of the claim is by induction on n:

- Base case: Take 1 as the base case. $1 = 1^2$.
- Prove: $\forall n \geq 1 \left(\left(\sum_{i=1}^{n} Odd_i = n^2 \right) \rightarrow \left(\sum_{i=1}^{n+1} Odd_i = (n+1)^2 \right) \right)$.

Observe that the sum of the first $n + 1$ odd integers is the sum of the first n of them plus the $n + 1^{st}$, so:

$$\sum_{i=1}^{n+1} Odd_i = \sum_{i=1}^{n} Odd_i + Odd_{n+1}$$

$$= n^2 + Odd_{n+1}. \quad \text{(Using the induction hypothesis.)}$$

$$= n^2 + 2n + 1. \quad \text{(Since } Odd_{n+1} \text{ is } 2(n + 1 - 1) + 1 = 2n + 1.)$$

$$= (n + 1)^2.$$

Mathematical induction lets us prove properties of positive integers. But it also lets us prove properties of other things if the properties can be described in terms of integers. For example, we could talk about the cardinality of a finite set, or the length of a finite string.

EXAMPLE A.18 The Cardinality of the Power Set of a Finite Set

Let A be any finite set. We prove the following claim about the cardinality of the power set of A:

$$|\mathcal{P}(A)| = 2^{|A|}.$$

The proof is by induction on $|A|$, the cardinality of A.

- Base case: Take 0 as the base case. $|A| = 0$, $A = \varnothing$, and $\mathcal{P}(A) = \{\varnothing\}$, whose cardinality is $1 = 2^0 = 2^{|A|}$.
- Prove: $\forall n \geq 0$ (($|\mathcal{P}(A)| = 2^{|A|}$ for all sets A of cardinality n) $\rightarrow$ ($|\mathcal{P}(A)| = 2^{|A|}$ for all sets A of cardinality $n + 1$)).

We do this as follows. Consider any value of $n \geq 0$ and any set A with $n + 1$ elements. Since $n \geq 0$, A must have at least one element. Pick one and call it a. Now consider the set B that we get by removing a from A. $|B|$ must be n. So, by the induction hypothesis, $|\mathcal{P}(B)| = 2^{|B|}$. Now return to $\mathcal{P}(A)$.
It has two parts: those subsets of A that include a and those that don't. The second part is exactly $\mathcal{P}(B)$, so we know that it has $2^{|B|} = 2^n$ elements. The first part (all the subsets that include a) is exactly all the subsets that don't include a with a

EXAMPLE A.18 *(Continued)*

added in). Since there are 2^n subsets that don't include a and there are the same number of them once we add a to each, we have that the total number of subsets of our original set A is 2^n (for the ones that don't include a) plus another 2^n (for the ones that do include a), for a total of $2(2^n) = 2^{n+1}$, which is exactly $2^{|A|}$.

Mathematical induction can be used to prove properties of a linear sequence of objects by assigning to each object its index in the sequence.

EXAMPLE A.19 Generalized Modus Tolens

Recall the inference rule we call modus tollens: From $(P \rightarrow Q)$ and $\neg Q$, conclude $\neg P$. We can use mathematical induction to prove a generalization of modus tollens to an arbitrary chain of implications. Suppose that we know, for any value of $n \geq 2$, two things:

$\forall i$, where $1 \leq i < n - 1$, $(P_i \rightarrow P_{i+1})$ /* In a chain of n propositions,
/* each implies the next.

$\neg P_n$ /* The last proposition is known
/* to be false.

Then generalized modus tollens will let us conclude that all the preceding propositions are also false, and so, in particular, it must be the case that:

$$\neg P_1.$$

We can use induction to prove this rule. To make it easy to describe the rule as we work, we'll introduce the notation $P \vdash Q$ to mean that, from P, we can derive Q. Using this notation, we can state concisely the rule we are trying to prove.

$$\forall n \geq 2 \; (((\forall i < n \; (P_i \rightarrow P_{i+1})) \land \neg P_n) \vdash \neg P_1)$$

The proof is by induction on n, the number of propositions.

- Base case: Take 2 as the base case. We have $P_1 \rightarrow P_2$ and $\neg P_2$. So, using modus tolens, we conclude $\neg P_1$.
- Prove that if the claim is true for n propositions it must be true for $n + 1$ of them:

$$(((\forall i < n \; (P_i \rightarrow P_{i+1})) \land \neg P_n) \vdash \neg P_1) \rightarrow (((\forall i < n + 1 \; (P_i \rightarrow P_{i+1})) \land \neg P_{n+1}) \vdash \neg P_1)$$

$((P_n \rightarrow P_{n+1}) \wedge \neg P_{n+1}) \vdash \neg P_n$	(Modus tollens)
$((\forall_i < n\, (P_i \rightarrow P_{i+1})) \wedge \neg P_n) \vdash \neg P_1$	(Induction hypothesis)
$((\forall i < n\, (P_i \rightarrow P_{i+1})) \wedge (P_n \rightarrow P_{n+1}) \wedge \neg P_{n+1}) \vdash \neg P_1$	(Chaining)
$((\forall i < n + 1\, (P_i \rightarrow P_{i+1})) \wedge \neg P_{n+1}) \vdash \neg P_1$	(Simplification)

Mathematical induction relies on the fact that any subset of the nonnegative integers forms a well-ordered set (as defined in Section A.3.5) under the relation $\leq$. Once we have done an induction proof, we know that $A(b)$ (where b is typically 0 or 1, but it could be some other starting value) is true and we know that $\forall n \geq b\, (A(n) \rightarrow (A(n+1))$. Then we claim that $\forall n \geq b\, (A(n))$. Suppose that the principle of mathematical induction were not sound and there existed some set S of nonnegative integers $\geq b$ for which $A(n)$ is false. Then, since S is well-ordered, it has a least element, which we can call x. By definition of S, x must be equal to or greater than b. But it cannot actually be b because we proved $A(b)$. So it must be greater than b. Now consider $x - 1$. Since $x - 1$ is less than x, it cannot be in S (since we chose x to be the smallest value in S). If $x - 1$ is not in S, then we know $A(x - 1)$. But we proved that $\forall n \geq 0\, (A(n) \rightarrow A(n + 1))$, so $A(x - 1) \rightarrow A(x)$. But we assumed $\neg A(x)$. So that assumption led us to a contradiction and thus must be false.

Sometimes the principle of mathematical induction is stated in a slightly different but formally equivalent way:

If: $A(b)$ is true for some integer value b, and
for all integers $n \geq b$ (($A(k)$ is true for all integers k where $b \leq k \leq n) \rightarrow A(n + 1)$),

Then: for all integers $n \geq b\, (A(x))$.

This form of mathematical induction is sometimes called ***strong induction***. To use it, we prove that whenever A holds for all nonnegative integers starting with b, up to and including n, it must also hold for $n + 1$. We can use whichever form of the technique is easiest for a particular problem.

A.6.6 The Pigeonhole Principle

Suppose that we have n pigeons and k holes. Each pigeon must fly into a hole. If $n > k$, then there must be at least one hole that contains more than one pigeon. We call this obvious observation the ***pigeonhole principle***. More formally, consider any function $f: A \rightarrow B$. The pigeonhole principle says:

If $|A| > |B|$ then f is not one-to-one.

The pigeonhole principle is a useful technique for proving relationships between sets. For example, suppose that set A is the set of all students who live in the dorm. Set

B is the set of rooms in the dorm. The function f maps each student to a dorm room. So, if $|A| > |B|$, we can use the pigeonhole principle to show that some students have roommates. As another everyday use of the principle, consider: If there are more than 366 people in a class, then at least two of them must share a birthday. The pigeonhole principle is also useful in proving less obvious claims.

EXAMPLE A.20 The Coins and Balance Problem

Consider the following problem: You have three coins. You know that two are of equal weight; the third is different. You do not know which coin is different and you do not know whether it is heavier or lighter than the other two. Your task is to identify the different coin and to say whether it is heavier or lighter than the others. The only tool you have is a balance, with two pans, onto which you may place one or more objects. The balance has three possible outputs: left pan heavier than right pan, right pan heavier than left pan, both pans the same weight. Show that you cannot solve this problem in a single weighing.

There are six possible situations: There are three coins, any one of which could be different, and the different coin can be either heavier or lighter. But a single weighing (no matter how you choose to place coins on pans) has only three possible outcomes. So there is at least one outcome that corresponds to at least two situations. Thus one weighing cannot be guaranteed to determine the situation uniquely.

A.6.7 Showing That Two Sets Are Equal

A great deal of what we do when we build a theory about some domain is to prove that various sets of objects in that domain are equal. For example, in our study of automata theory, we are going to want to prove assertions such as the following.

- The set of strings defined by some regular expression α is identical to the set of strings defined by some second regular expression β.
- The set of strings that will be accepted by some given finite state machine M is the same as the set of strings that will be accepted by some new finite state machine M' that has fewer states than M has.
- The set of languages that can be defined using regular expressions is the same as the set of languages that can be accepted by a finite state machine.
- The set of problems that can be solved by a Turing Machine with a single tape is the same as the set of problems that can be solved by a Turing Machine with any finite number of tapes.

So we become very interested in the question, "How does one prove that two sets are identical?" There are lots of ways and many of them require special techniques that apply in specific domains. But it is worth mentioning two very general approaches here.

Sometimes we want to compare apples to apples. We may, for example, want to prove that two sets of strings are identical, even though they may have been derived differently. In this case, one approach is to use the set identity theorems that we have already described. Suppose, for example, that we want to prove that:

$$A \cup (B \cap (A \cap C)) = A.$$

We can prove this as follows:

$$\begin{aligned} A \cup (B \cap (A \cap C)) &= (A \cup B) \cap (A \cup (A \cap C)). && \text{(Distributivity)} \\ &= (A \cup B) \cap ((A \cap C) \cup A). && \text{(Commutativity)} \\ &= (A \cup B) \cap A. && \text{(Absorption)} \\ &= A. && \text{(Absorption)} \end{aligned}$$

Sometimes, even when we're comparing apples to apples, the theorems we have listed are not enough. In these cases, we need to use the definitions of the operators. Suppose, for example, that we want to prove that:

$$A - B = A \cap \neg B.$$

We can prove this as follows (where U stands for the universe with respect to which we take complement):

$$\begin{aligned} A - B &= \{x : x \in A \text{ and } x \notin B\}. \\ &= \{x : x \in A \text{ and } (x \in U \text{ and } x \notin B)\}. \\ &= \{x : x \in A \text{ and } x \in U - B\}. \\ &= \{x : x \in A \text{ and } x \in \neg B\}. \\ &= A \cap \neg B. \end{aligned}$$

Sometimes, though, our problem is more complex. We may need to compare apples to oranges. In other words, we may need to compare sets that aren't even defined in the same terms. For example, we will want to be able to prove that A: {the set of languages that can be defined using regular expressions} is the same as B: {the set of languages that can be accepted by a finite state machine}. This seems very hard: Regular expressions, which we describe in Chapter 6, are strings that look like:

a*(b ∪ ba)*

Finite state machines, which we describe in Chapter 5, are collections of states and rules for moving from one state to another. How can we possibly prove that A (defined in terms of regular expressions) and B (defined in terms of finite state machines) are the same set? The answer is that we can show that any two sets are equal by showing that each is a subset of the other. So, to prove that $A = B$, we will show first that, given a regular expression, we can construct a finite state machine that accepts exactly the strings that the regular expression describes. That gives us $A \subseteq B$. But there might still be some finite state machines that don't correspond to any regular expressions. So we then show that, given a finite state machine, we can construct a regular expression that defines exactly the same strings that the machine accepts. That gives us $B \subseteq A$. In Section 6.2, we describe both of these proofs and use them to prove the claim, called Kleene's Theorem, that $A = B$. We will use the same technique several more times throughout the book.

A.6.8 Showing That a Set is Finite or Countably Infinite

Next, let's return briefly to the question, "What is the cardinality of a set?" In this book, we will be concerned with three cases:

- finite sets,
- countably infinite sets, and
- uncountably infinite sets.

We will use the following definitions for the terms "finite" and "infinite":[14]

A set A is ***finite*** and has cardinality $n \in \mathbb{N}$ (the natural numbers) iff either $A = \varnothing$ or there is a bijection from $\{1, 2, \ldots n\}$ to A, for some value of n. Alternatively, a set is finite if we can count its elements and finish. The cardinality of a finite set is simply a natural number whose value is the number of elements in the set.

A set is ***infinite*** iff it is not finite. The first infinite set we'll consider is $\mathbb{N}$, the natural numbers. Following Cantor, we'll call the cardinality of $\mathbb{N}$ $\aleph_0$. (Read this as "aleph null". Aleph is the first symbol of the Hebrew alphabet.)

Now consider an arbitrary set A. We'll say that A is ***countably infinite*** and also has cardinality $\aleph_0$ iff there exists some bijection $f: \mathbb{N} \rightarrow A$. And we need one more definition: A set is ***countable*** iff it is either finite or countably infinite. We use the term "countable" because the elements of a countable set can be counted with the integers.

To prove that a set A is countably infinite, it suffices to find a bijection from $\mathbb{N}$ to it.

EXAMPLE A.21 There is a Countably Infinite Number of Even Numbers

The set E of even natural numbers is countably infinite. To prove this, we offer the bijection:

$$Even: \mathbb{N} \rightarrow E,$$
$$Even(x) = 2x.$$

So we have the following mapping from $\mathbb{N}$ to E:

$\mathbb{N}$	E
0	0
1	2
2	4
3	6
…	…

[14] An alternative is to begin by saying that a set A is infinite iff there exists a one-to-one mapping from A into a proper subset of itself. Then a set is finite iff it is not infinite. With the axiom of choice, these two defintions are equivalent.

The last example was easy. The bijection was obvious. Sometimes it is less so. In harder cases, a good way to think about the problem of finding a bijection from ℕ to some set A, is to turn it into the problem of finding an enumeration of A.

An ***enumeration*** of a set A is simply a list of the elements of A in some order. Each element of A must occur in the enumeration exactly once. Of course, if A is infinite, the enumeration will be infinite. But as long as we can guarantee that every element of A will show up eventually, we have an enumeration.

THEOREM A.1 Infinite Enumeration and Countable Infinity

Theorem: A set A is countably infinite iff there exists an infinite enumeration of it.

Proof: We prove the if and only-if parts separately.

If A is countably infinite, then there exists an infinite enumeration of it: Since A is countably infinite, there exists a bijection f from ℕ to it. We construct an infinite enumeration of A as follows (where the only slight issue is that we number the elements of an enumeration starting with 1 and the natural numbers start with 0): For all $i \geq 1$, the ith element of the enumeration of A will be $f(i - 1)$. So the first element of the enumeration will be the element that 0 maps to, the second element of the enumeration will be the element that 1 maps to, and so forth.

***If there exists an infinite enumeration* E *of* A *, then* A *is countably infinite*:** Define $f: \mathbb{N} \rightarrow A$, where $f(i)$ is the $(i + 1)^{\text{st}}$ element of the list E. The function f is a bijection from ℕ to A, so A is countably infinite.

We can use Theorem A.1 both to show that a set is countably infinite (by exhibiting an infinite enumeration of it) and to show that a set is not countably infinite (by showing that no infinite enumeration of it exists).

THEOREM A.2 Finite Union

Theorem: The union U of a finite number of countably infinite sets is countably infinite.

Proof: The proof is by enumeration of the elements of U. We need a technique for producing that enumeration. The simplest thing to do would be to start by enumerating all the elements of the first set, then all the elements of the second, etc. But, since the first set is infinite, we will never get around to considering any of the elements of the other sets. We need another technique. We take the first element from each of the sets, then the second element from each, and so forth, checking before inserting each element to make sure that it is not already there.

Using a technique similar to the one we just used to prove Theorem A.2, it is easy to show that, for any fixed n, the set of ordered n-tuples of elements drawn from a countably infinite set must also be countably infinite. So, for example, the rational numbers are countably infinite.

	Set 1	Set 2	Set 3	Set 4	...
Element 1	1	2	4	7	
Element 2	3	5	8		
Element 3	6	9			
...	10				

FIGURE A.9 Systematically enumerating the elements of an infinite number of infinite sets.

THEOREM A.3 Countably Infinite Union

Theorem: The union U of a countably infinite number of countably infinite sets is countably infinite.

Proof: The proof is by enumeration of the elements of U. Now we cannot use the simple enumeration technique that we used in the proof of Theorem A.2. Since we are now considering an infinite number of sets, if we tried that technique we'd never get to the second element of any of the sets. So we follow the arrows as shown in Figure A.9. The numbers in the squares indicate the order in which we select elements for the enumeration. This process goes on forever, but it is systematic and it guarantees that, if we wait long enough, any element of any of the sets will eventually be enumerated. Note that, before we actually enter any element into the enumeration, we must check to make sure that it has not already been generated.

It turns out that there are a lot of countably infinite sets. Some of them, like the even natural numbers, appear at first to contain fewer elements than $\mathbb{N}$ does. Some of them, like the union of a countable number of countable sets, appear at first to be bigger. But in both cases there is a bijection from $\mathbb{N}$ to the elements of the set, so the cardinality of the set is $\aleph_0$.

A.6.9 Showing That a Set is Uncountably Infinite: Diagonalization

But not all infinite sets are countably infinite. There are sets with more than $\aleph_0$ elements. There are more than $\aleph_0$ real numbers, for example. As another case, consider an arbitrary set S with cardinality $\aleph_0$. Now consider $\mathcal{P}(S)$ (the power set of S). $\mathcal{P}(S)$ has cardinality greater than $\aleph_0$. To prove this, we need to show that, although $\mathcal{P}(S)$ is infinite, there exists no bijection from $\mathbb{N}$ to it. To do this, we will use a technique called ***diagonalization***.

Diagonalization is a kind of proof by contradiction. To show that a set A is not countably infinite, we assume that it is, in which case there would be some enumeration of it. Every element of A would have to be on that list somewhere. But we show how to construct an element of A that cannot be on the list, no matter how the list was constructed. Thus there exists no enumeration of A. So A is not countably infinite.

THEOREM A.4 The Cardinality of the Power Set

Theorem: If S is a countably infinite set, $\mathcal{P}(S)$ (the power set of S) is infinite but not countably infinite.

Proof: $\mathcal{P}(S)$ must be infinite because, for each of the infinitely many elements s of S, the set $\{s\}$ is an element of $\mathcal{P}(S)$.

Elem 1 of S	Elem 2 of S	Elem 3 of S	Elem 4 of S	Elem 5 of S	Elem 6 of S	......
1			1	1		......

(a)

	Elem 1 of S	Elem 2 of S	Elem 3 of S	Elem 4 of S	Elem 5 of S	Elem 6 of S	....
Elem 1 of $\mathcal{P}(S)$	1 (1)						.....
Elem 2 of $\mathcal{P}(S)$		1 (2)					.....
Elem 3 of $\mathcal{P}(S)$	1	1	(3)				.....
Elem 4 of $\mathcal{P}(S)$			1	(4)			.....
Elem 5 of $\mathcal{P}(S)$	1		1		(5)		.....
Elem 6 of $\mathcal{P}(S)$		1	1			(6)	.....
....							.....

(b)

¬(1)	¬(2)	¬(3)	¬(4)	¬(5)	¬(6)	......

(c)

FIGURE A.10 Using diagonalization to show the uncountability of a power set.

But now we must prove that $\mathcal{P}(S)$ is not countably infinite. The proof is by diagonalization. Since S is countably infinite, by Theorem A.1, there exists an infinite enumeration of it. We can use that enumeration to construct a representation of each subset SS of S as an infinite binary vector that contains one element for each element of the original set S. If SS contains element 1 of S, then the first element of its vector will be 1, otherwise 0 (which we'll show as blank to make our tables easy to read). Similarly for all the other elements of S. Of course, since S is countably infinite, the length of each vector will also be countably infinite. Thus we might represent a particular subset SS of S as the infinite vector shown in Figure A.10(a).

Now, assume that $\mathcal{P}(S)$ is countably infinite. Then there is some enumeration of it. Pick any such enumeration, and write it as shown in Figure A.10(b) (where each row represents one element of $\mathcal{P}(S)$ as described above. Ignore for the moment the numbers enclosed in parentheses.) This table is infinite in both directions. Since it is an enumeration of $\mathcal{P}(S)$, it must contain one row for each element of $\mathcal{P}(S)$. But it doesn't. To prove that it doesn't, we will construct L, an element of $\mathcal{P}(S)$ that is not on the list. To do this, consider the numbers in parentheses along the diagonal of the matrix of Figure A.10(b). Using them, we can construct L so that it corresponds to the vector shown in Figure A.10(c). What we mean by ¬(1) is that if the square labeled (1) is a 1 then 0; if the square labeled (1) is a 0, then 1.

So we've constructed the representation for an element of $\mathcal{P}(S)$. It must be an element of $\mathcal{P}(S)$ since it describes a possible subset of S. But we've built it so that it differs from the first element in the list of Figure A.10(b) by whether or not it includes element 1 of S. It differs from the second element in the list by whether or not it includes element 2 of S. And so forth. In the end, it must differ from every element in the list in at least one place. Yet it represents an element of $\mathcal{P}(S)$. Thus we have a contradiction. The list was not an enumeration of $\mathcal{P}(S)$. But since we made no assumptions about it except that it was an enumeration of $\mathcal{P}(S)$, no such enumeration can exist. In particular, if we try to fix the problem by simply adding our new element L to the list, we can just turn around and do the same thing again and create yet another element that is not on the list. Thus there are more than $\aleph_0$ elements in $\mathcal{P}(S)$.

If a set S is infinite but not countably infinite then we will say that it is ***uncountably infinite***. So, for example, $\mathcal{P}(\mathbb{N})$ is uncountably infinite, since, by Theorem A.4, the power set of any countably infinite set is infinite but not countably infinite. The real numbers are uncountably infinite, which can be shown with a proof that is very similar to the one we just did for the power set except that it is a bit tricky because, when we write out each number as an infinite sequence of digits (just as we wrote out each set above as an infinite sequence of 0's and 1's), we have to consider the fact that several distinct sequences may represent the same number.

Not all uncountably infinite sets have the same cardinality. There are more elements in the power set of the real numbers than there are real numbers, for example.

A.7 Reasoning about Programs

An ***algorithm*** is a detailed procedure that accomplishes some clearly specified task. A ***program*** is an executable encoding of an algorithm. Not all algorithms halt. For example, a monitoring system might be designed never to halt but to run constantly, looking for some pattern of events to which some sort of response is required. So not all programs are designed to halt. However, we will focus on the class of programs whose job is to accept input, compute, and halt, having produced appropriate output. Useful programs of this sort possess two kinds of properties:

1. Correctness properties, including:
   - the program eventually halts, and
   - when it halts, it has produced the desired output.
2. Performance properties, including:
   - time requirements, and
   - space requirements.

Entire books have been written on techniques for proving these properties. We summarize here just the few techniques that we will find the most useful in the rest of this book.

A.7.1 Proving Correctness Properties

We will first consider the problem of proving that a program halts. Then we'll look at techniques that can be used to show that a program's result satisfies its specification.

Proving that a Program Halts

When we describe a program to solve a problem, we would like to be able to prove that the program always halts. One of the main results of the theory that we will develop in this book is that there can exist no algorithm to solve the halting problem, which we can state as, "Answer the following question: Given the text of some program M and some input w, does M halt on input w?" So there can exist no general purpose algorithm that considers an arbitrary program and determines whether or not it halts on even one input, much less on all inputs. However, that does not mean that there are not particular programs that can be shown to halt on all inputs.

Any program that has no loops and no recursive function calls halts when it reaches the end of its code. So we focus our attention on proving that loops and recursive functions halt. In a nutshell, any such proof must show that the loop or the recursion executes some finite number of steps. Sometimes, particularly in the case of for loops, we can simply state the maximum number of steps.

EXAMPLE A.22 Termination of a For Loop

Consider the following very simple program P:

P(some arguments) =
    For $i = 1$ to 10 do:
        Compute something.

As long as the compute step of P does not modify i, we can safely claim that this loop executes at most 10 times. (It could possibly execute fewer if it exits prematurely.)

When dealing with while and until loops and with recursive functions, it may not be possible to make such a straightforward statement. In proving that any such program P halts, we will generally rely on the existence of some well-founded set (S, R) such that:

- There exists some bijection between each step of P and some element of the set S,
- The first step of P corresponds to a maximal (with respect to R) element of S,
- Each successive step of P corresponds to a smaller (with respect to R) element of S, and
- P halts on or before it executes a step that corresponds to a minimal (with respect to R) element of S.

EXAMPLE A.23 Choosing a Well-Founded Set

Consider the following simple program P that acts on a finite-length string:

P(s: string) =
    While $length(s) > 0$ do:
        Remove the first character from s and call it c.

EXAMPLE A.23 (*Continued*)

if $c =$ a return *True*.
Return *False*.

Let $S = \{0, 1, 2, \ldots, |s|\}$. $(S, \leq)$ is a well-founded set whose least element is 0. Associate each step of the loop with $|s|$ as the step is about to be executed. The first pass through the loop is associated the initial length of s, which is the maximum value of $|s|$ throughout the computation. $|s|$ is decremented by one each time through the loop. P halts when $|s|$ is 0 or before (if it finds the character a). So the maximum number of times the loop can be executed is the initial value of $|s|$.

If we cannot find a well-founded set that corresponds to the steps of a loop or a recursively defined function, then it is likely that that program fails to halt on at least some inputs.

EXAMPLE A.24 When We Can't Find a Well-Founded Set

Consider the following program P, along with the claim that, given some positive integer n, P always halts and finds and prints the square root of n:

```
P(n: positive integer) =
    r = 0.
    Until r*r = n do:
        r = r + 1.
    Print(r).
```

We could try to prove that P always halts by using the well-founded set $(\mathbb{N}, \leq)$. Associate each step of the loop with $n - r^2$. On entrance to the loop, this difference must be in $\mathbb{N}$ since n is in $\mathbb{N}$ and $r = 0$. The difference decreases at each step through the loop, as r increases. If r ever equals the square root of n, the difference will be 0 and the loop will terminate. But, if n is not a perfect square, there is no guarantee that the difference will not simply become more and more negative. So there is no bijection between $n - r^2$ and $\mathbb{N}$. There is one between $n - r^2$ and Z (the integers), but Z has no minimal element and so is not well-founded. As it turns out, there is no well-founded set that can be put in one-to-one correspondence with the steps of this loop, which cannot be guaranteed to halt.

Proving that a Program Computes the Correct Result

Given that a program halts, does it halt with the correct result? We will find two techniques particularly useful for proving that it does.

1. Loop invariants, which we will introduce briefly here.
2. Induction, which we reviewed in Section A.6.5.

Often the most straightforward way to analyze any sort of iterated process is to focus not on what the process does but rather on what it doesn't do. So we'll describe some key property that does not change at any step of the process's execution.

EXAMPLE A.25 The Coffee Can Problem

Consider the following problem, which we'll call the ***coffee can problem*** [Gries 1989]: We have a coffee can that contains some white beans and some black beans. We perform the following operation on the beans:

Until no further beans can be removed do:
  Randomly choose two beans.
  If the two beans are the same color, then throw both of them away and add a new black bean.
  If the two beans are different colors, then throw away the black one and return the white one to the can.

It is easy to show that this process must halt. After each step, the number of beans in the can decreases by one. When only one bean remains, no further beans can be removed.

But what can we say about the one remaining bean? Is it white or black? The answer is that if the original number of white beans is odd, the remaining bean is white. Otherwise the remaining bean is black. To see why this is true, we note that our bean culling process preserves white bean parity. In other words, if the number of white beans starts out even, it stays even. If the number of white beans starts out odd, it stays odd. To prove that this is so, we consider each action that the culling process can perform. There are three:

- Two white beans are removed and one black bean is added.
- Two black beans are removed and one black bean is added.
- One black bean is removed.

In each of these, an even number of white beans is removed and white bean parity is preserved. So, if the number of white beans is initially odd, the number of white beans can never become zero and a white bean must be the sole survivor. If, on the other hand, the number of white beans is initially even, it can never become one. Thus any sole survivor must be black.

The white bean parity property that we just described is an example of a ***loop invariant***: a predicate I that describes a property that doesn't change during the execution of an iterative process. To use a loop invariant I to prove the correctness of a program, we must prove each of the following.

- I is true on entry to the loop.
- The truth of I is maintained at each pass through the loop. By this we mean that, if I is true at the beginning of a particular pass through the loop, then it must also be

true at the end of that pass. Note, however, that I may fail to hold at some point partway through the loop.

- I, together with the loop termination condition, imply whatever property we wish to prove is true on exit from the loop.

EXAMPLE A.26 Finding a Loop Invariant

Consider the following program P:

P(s: string) =
  count = 0.
  For i = 1 to length(s) do:
    If the ith character of s is a then:
      count = *count* + 1.
  Print (*count*).

Prove that the value of *count*, on exit from the loop, is the number of a's in s. Call this claim C. We will use a loop invariant to prove C.

We'll use the notation $\#_{\text{a}}(s)$ to mean the number of a's in the string s. Let:

$$I = [\#_{\text{a}}(s) = count + \#_{\text{a}}(\text{the last } (length(s) + 1 - i) \text{ characters of } s)].$$

In other words, the total number of a's in s is equal to the current value of *count* plus the number of a's in that part of s that has not so far been examined by the loop. We show:

- I is true on entry to the loop: $i = 1$ and $count = 0$. So we have:

  $\#_{\text{a}}(s) = 0 + \#_{\text{a}}$ (the last ($length(s)$) characters of s), which is true.

- I is maintained at each step through the loop: If the ith character of s is an a, then *count* is incremented by 1. But i is also incremented, so the number of a's in the last $(length(s) + 1 - i)$ characters of s is decremented by 1, leaving $count + \#_{\text{a}}(\text{the last } (length(s) + 1 - i) \text{ characters of } s)$ unchanged. If the ith character of s is not an a, then the value of both *count* and the number of a's in the last $(length(s) + 1 - i)$ remains unchanged.

- I, together with the loop termination condition, imply C: On exit from the loop, $i = length(s) + 1$. So we have:

$$\begin{aligned} I \wedge [i = length(s) + 1] &\equiv [\#_{\text{a}}(s) = count + \#_{a}(\text{the last } (length(s) + 1 - i) \\ &\qquad \text{characters of } s)] \wedge [i = length(s) + 1]. \\ &\equiv [\#_{\text{a}}(s) = count + \#_{a}(\text{the last } (length(s) + 1 - \\ &\qquad (length(s) + 1)) \text{ characters of } s)]. \\ &\equiv [\#_{\text{a}}(s) = count + \#_{a} (\text{the last 0 characters of } s)]. \\ &\equiv \#_{\text{a}}(s) = count. \end{aligned}$$

So, on exit from the loop, *count* is equal to the number of a's in s. Thus C is true. Note that a separate proof is required to show that the loop does in fact terminate.

EXAMPLE A.27 Finding a Loop Invariant for a Program that Doesn't Halt

Consider the following program P, which differs from our other examples since it is not designed to halt:

```
P() =
    s = "".
    Loop:
        Print(s).
        s = s || a.
```

Prove that P will print all and only the finite length strings composed of 0 or more a's (and no other characters). We will use a loop invariant to prove that P prints only strings composed exclusively of a's. We will use induction to prove that P will eventually print every string composed only of a's. The loop invariant we need is I = [s contains no characters other than a].

We show:

- I is true on entry to the loop the first time: s is the empty string and so contains no characters that are not a.
- I is maintained at each step through the loop: s is unchanged through the loop except to have a single a added to the end of it. So if it contained only a's at the top of the loop, it will contain only a's at the bottom.
- We are not concerned with what happens when the loop in P terminates, since it doesn't. So we can skip the step in which we show that some statement is true on exit from the loop.

Since I must be true at the top of the loop, it is true when the print statement executes, so only strings composed exclusively of a's will be printed.

Now we need to show that P will eventually print any string s that is composed of no characters other than a. We do this by induction on $|s|$:

- Base step: Let $|s| = 0$. P prints s the first time through the loop.
- Induction hypothesis: P prints all strings of a's of length n. Note that, for any value of n, there is only one such string. Call it a^n.
- Prove that P prints all strings of a's of length $n + 1$. There is only one such string, namely $a^n a$. By the induction hypothesis, P generates a^n. When it does that, the variable s is equal to a^n. The next thing P does is to concatenate one more a onto s, which then equals $a^n a$, and print it.

So, for all $n \geq 0$, P prints the string composed exactly of n a's.

A.7.2 Analyzing Complexity

Whenever we present a program P, we may want to ask the question, "How long will it take P to run?" or, "How much memory will P use?" Generally the answer depends on the size of the input. So our answer will usually be stated as a function of some number that corresponds to a reasonable measure of the size of the input. If the input is a string, we can use the length of the string. If the input is a structure like a list or an array, we can use the number of elements in the structure. If the input is a number, we will typically use the length of the binary or decimal encoding of the number.

In Part V of this book we present a formal theory of both time and space complexity. Here we present an informal treatment of the approach to time complexity that we will describe there.

We will describe the time complexity of a program P as a function of the size of its input, which we'll call n. We are typically not interested in how long it takes P to run on small inputs. Rather we are concerned with how quickly execution time grows as n grows. While in some cases we are concerned with an exact count of the number of steps that P must execute, we are often willing to ignore constant factors and instead to concentrate on whether P's execution time

- is constant (i.e., it is independent of n),
- grows linearly with n,
- grows faster than n but at a rate that can be described by some polynomial function of n (for example, n^2), or
- grows at a rate that is faster than any polynomial function of n (for example 2^n).

Suppose that we have a program that, on input of length n, executes $n^3 + 2n + 3$ steps. As n increases, the n^3 term dominates the other two. So we would like to ignore the slower growing terms of the function $n^3 + 2n + 3$ and characterize the time required to execute this program as the simpler function n^3. To do that, we introduce the notion of asymptotic dominance of one function by another.

Let $f(n)$ and $g(n)$ be functions from the natural numbers to the positive reals. Then we'll say that the function $g(n)$ ***asymptotically dominates*** the function $f(n)$ iff there exists a positive integer k and a positive constant c such that:

$$\forall n \geq k\ (f(n) \leq c\, g(n)).$$

In other words, ignoring some number of small cases (all those of size less than k), and ignoring some constant factor c, $f(n)$ is bounded from above by $g(n)$.

We will use the symbol $\mathcal{O}$ to denote the asymptotic dominance relation, so $\mathcal{O}(g(n))$ is the set of all functions that are asymptotically dominated by $g(n)$. Thus, if $g(n)$ asymptotically dominates $f(n)$, we will write:

$$f(n) \in \mathcal{O}(g(n)).$$

This claim is read, "f is big-O of g". It is also often written $f(n) = \mathcal{O}(g(n))$, although that statement is not literally correct since $\mathcal{O}(g(n))$ is a set of functions, not a function.

EXAMPLE A.28 $\mathcal{O}$

$n^3 + 2n + 3 \in \mathcal{O}(n^3)$, since we can let $k = 2$ and $c = 2$ and observe that for all $n \geq 2$, $n^3 + 2n + 3 \leq 2n^3$.

Now we can return to the problem of characterizing the execution time of a program P. Let $f(n)$ be a function that describes the time required to execute P as a function of n, where n is some reasonable measure of the size of P's input. We'll say that P runs in time $\mathcal{O}(g(n))$ iff $f(n) \in \mathcal{O}(g(n))$.

EXAMPLE A.29 Using $\mathcal{O}$ to Measure Time Complexity: A Linear Example

Consider again the program P from Example A.26:

```
P(s: string) =
        count = 0.
        For i = 1 to length(s) do:
            If the ith character of s is a then:
                count = count + 1.
        Print (count).
```

Let n = length(s). The number of program steps that P executes is at most $2 + 2n \in \mathcal{O}(n)$. So the execution time of P grows linearly in the length of its input.

EXAMPLE A.30 Using $\mathcal{O}$ to Measure Time Complexity: A Quadratic Example

Consider the following program P, which returns *True* if any two elements of its input vector are the same and *False* otherwise:

```
P(v: vector of integers) =
    For i = 1 to length(v) do:
        For j = i + 1 to length(v) do:
            If v[i] = v[j] then return True.
    Return False.
```

Let n = length(v). In the worst case, P goes through the outer loop n times. At each pass, unless it finds a match, it goes through the inner loop on average $n/2$ times. So the number of program steps that P executes is at most $1 + n(1 + 2n/2) = 1 + n + n^2 \in \mathcal{O}(n^2)$. So the execution time of P grows as the square of the length of its input.

Suppose that a program P, on input of size n, runs in time $f(n) = 2 + 4n$. Then $f(n) \in \mathcal{O}(n)$. But notice that it is also true that $f(n) \in \mathcal{O}(n^2)$ and $f(n) \in \mathcal{O}(2^n)$, since both n^2 and 2^n also asymptotically dominate $2 + 4n$. In Chapter 27 we will define Θ, a relation that is similar to $\mathcal{O}$ except that it is stricter. Specifically,

$$f(n) \in \Theta(g(n)) \text{ iff } f(n) \in \mathcal{O}(g(n)) \text{ and } g(n) \in \mathcal{O}(f(n)).$$

So $2 + 4n \in \Theta(n)$, but $2 + 4n \notin \Theta(n^2)$ because $n^2 \notin \mathcal{O}(n)$.

Discussions of the complexity of algorithms should use Θ, whenever possible, since we want the tightest bound we can find. But that is not the convention. As we did in both Example A.29 and Example A.30, we will use the standard convention of writing $f(n) \in \mathcal{O}(g(n))$ instead of $f(n) \in \Theta(g(n))$, but, whenever we can, we will choose values for $g(n)$ such that the claim that $f(n) \in \Theta(g(n))$ would also be true.

In analyzing the algorithms that we will consider in Parts II through IV of this book, we will use the $\mathcal{O}$ relation as we have just defined it. In Chapter 27, we will have more to say about $\mathcal{O}$ and similar relations such as Θ.

A.8 A General Definition of Closure ✹

In Section A.5 we introduced closures. We elaborate on that discussion here. We begin by reviewing what we said there. Imagine some set S and some property P. If we care about making sure that S has property P, we could do the following.

1. Examine S for P. If it has property P, we quit.
2. If it doesn't, then add to S the smallest number of additional elements required to satisfy P.

We will say that S is closed with respect to P iff it possesses P. And, if we have to add elements to S in order to satisfy P, we'll call a smallest such expanded S that does satisfy P a closure of S with respect to P.

EXAMPLE A.31 Some Relations and Their Closures

1. Let S be a set of friends we are planning to invite to a party. Let P be, "S should include everyone who is likely to find out about the party" (since we don't want to offend anyone). Let's assume that if you invite Bill and Bill has a friend Bob, then Bill may tell Bob about the party. This means that if you want S to satisfy P, then you have to invite not only your friends, but your friends' friends, and their friends, and so forth. If you move in a fairly closed circle, you may be able to satisfy P by adding a few people to the guest list. On the other hand, it's possible that you'd have to invite the whole city before P would be satisfied. It depends on the connectivity of the *Friendof* relation in your social setting. The problem is that whenever you add a new person to S, you have to

turn around and look at that person's friends and consider whether there are any of them who are not already in *S*. If there are, they must be added, and so forth. There is one positive feature of this problem, however. Notice that there is a unique set that does satisfy *P*, given the initial set *S*. There aren't any choices to be made.

2. Let *S* be a set of six people. Let *P* be, "*S* can enter a baseball tournament." This problem is different from the previous one in two important ways. First, there is a clear limit on how many elements we have to add to *S* in order to satisfy *P*. We need nine people and when we've got them we can stop. But notice that there is not a unique way to satisfy *P* (assuming that we know more than nine people). Any way of adding three people to *S* will work.
3. Let *S* be the *Address* relation (which we defined earlier as "lives at same address as"). Since relations are sets, we should be able to treat *Address* just as we've treated the sets of people in our last two examples. We know that *Address* is an equivalence relation. So we'll let *P* be the property of being an equivalence relation (i.e., reflexive, symmetric, and transitive). But suppose we are only able to collect facts about living arrangements in a piecemeal fashion. For example, we may learn that *Address* contains (Dave, Stacy), (Jen, Pete), (John, Bill). Immediately we know, because *Address* must be reflexive, that it must also contain (Dave, Dave), (Stacy, Stacy), (Jen, Jen), (Pete, Pete), (John, John), (Bill, Bill). And, since *Address* must also be symmetric, it must contain (Stacy, Dave), (Pete, Jen), (Bill, John). Now suppose that we discover that Stacy lives with Jen. We add (Stacy, Jen). To make *Address* symmetric again, we must add (Jen, Stacy). But now we also have to make it transitive by adding (Dave, Jen), (Jen, Dave).
4. Let *S* be the set of positive integers. Let *P* be, "The sum of any two elements of *S* is also in *S*." Now we've got a property that is already satisfied. The sum of any two positive integers is a positive integer. This time, we don't have to add anything to *S* to establish *P*.
5. Let *S* again be the set of positive integers. Let *P* be, "The quotient of any two elements of *S* is also in *S*." This time we have a problem. 3/5 is not a positive integer. We can add elements to *S* to satisfy *P*. If we do, we end up with exactly the positive rational numbers.

To use closures effectively, we need to define precisely what we mean when we say that a set *S* is closed under *P* or that the closure of *S* under *P* is *T*. We present here a set of definitions that include all but one of the specific cases that we just described. The definitions of closure that we presented in Section A.5 are special cases of the ones presented here. The one requirement that must be met in order to apply these definitions to a closure problem is that we must be able to describe the property *P* that is to be maintained as a relation.

Let n be an integer greater than or equal to 1. Let R be an n-ary relation on a set A. Thus elements of R are of the form $(d_1, d_2, \ldots, d_n)$. We say that a subset S of A is ***closed under*** R iff, whenever:

- $d_1, d_2, \ldots d_{n-1} \in S$ (all of the first $n - 1$ elements are already in the set S), and
- $(d_1, d_2, \ldots d_{n-1}, d_n) \in R$ (the last element is related to the $n - 1$ other elements via R).

it is also true that $d_n \in S$.

A set S' is a ***closure*** of S with respect to R (defined on A) iff:

- $S \subseteq S'$,
- S' is closed under R, and
- $\forall T\ ((S \subseteq T$ and T is closed under $R) \rightarrow |S'| \leq |T|)$.

In other words, S' is a closure of S with respect to R if it is an extension (i.e., a superset) of S that is closed under R and if there is no smaller set that also meets both of those requirements. Note that we cannot say that S' must be the smallest set that will do the job, since we do not yet have any guarantee that there is a unique such smallest set (recall the softball example above).

These definitions of closure are a very natural way to describe our first example above. Drawing from a set A of people, you start with S equal to your friends. Then, to compute your invitee list S', you simply take the closure of S with respect to the relation *Friendof*, which will force you to add to S' your friends' friends, their friends, and so forth.

These definitions also apply naturally to our fifth example, the positive integers under division. The smallest set that contains the positive integers and that is closed under division is the positive rationals. So the closure under division of the positive integers is the positive rationals.

Now consider our second example, the case of the baseball team. Here there is no relation R that specifies, if one or more people are already on the team, that some specific other person must also be on. The property we care about is a property of the team (set) as a whole and not a property of patterns of individuals (elements). Thus this example, although similar, is not formally an instance of closure as we have just defined it. This turns out to be significant and leads us to the following definition:

Any property that asserts that a set S is closed under some relation R is called a ***closure property*** of S.

THEOREM A.5 Closures Exist and are Unique

Theorem: If R is a closure property, as just defined, on a set A and S is a subset of A, then the closure of S with respect to R exists and is unique.

Proof: Omitted.

Stating the theorem another way, if its conditions are met then there exists a unique minimal set S' that contains S and is closed under R. Of all of our examples above, the baseball example is the only one that cannot be described in the terms of this definition of a closure property. The theorem that we have just stated (without proof) guarantees, therefore, that it will be the only one that does not have a unique minimal solution.

The definitions that we have just provided also work to describe our third example, in which we want to compute the closure of a relation (since, after all, a relation is a set). All we have to do is to come up with relations that describe the properties of being reflexive, symmetric, and transitive. To help us see what those relations need to be, let's recall our definitions of symmetry, reflexivity, and transitivity:

- A binary relation $R \subseteq A \times A$ is ***reflexive*** iff, for each $a \in A$, $(a, a) \in R$.
- A binary relation $R \subseteq A \times A$ is ***symmetric*** iff, whenever $(a, b) \in R$, so is (b, a).
- A binary relation $R \subseteq A \times A$ is ***transitive*** iff, whenever $(a, b) \in R$ and $(b, c) \in R$, $(a, c) \in R$.

Looking at these definitions, we can come up with three relations, *Reflexivity*, *Symmetry*, and *Transitivity*. All three are relations on relations, and they will enable us to define these three properties using the closure definitions we've given so far. All three definitions assume a base set A on which the relation that we are interested in is defined:

- For any a in A, $((a, a)) \in$ *Reflexivity* and no other elements are. Notice the double parentheses here. *Reflexivity* is a unary relation, where each element is itself an ordered pair. It doesn't really "relate" two elements. It is simply a list of ordered pairs. To see how it works to define reflexive closure, imagine a set $A = \{x, y\}$. Now suppose we start with a relation R on $A = \{(x, y)\}$. Clearly R isn't reflexive: The *Reflexivity* relation on A is $\{((x, x)), ((y, y))\}$. *Reflexivity* is a unary relation. So n, in the definition of closure, is 1. Consider the first element $((x, x))$. We consider all the components before the nth (i.e., first) and see if they are in A. This means we consider the first zero components. Trivially, all zero of them are in A. So the nth (the first) must also be. This means that (x, x) must be in R. But it isn't. So to compute the closure of R under *Reflexivity*, we add it. Similarly for (y, y).
- For any a and b in A, $a \neq b \rightarrow [((a, b), (b, a)) \in Symmetry]$ and no other elements are. This one is a lot easier. Again, suppose we start with a set $A = \{x, y\}$ and a relation R on $A = \{(x, y)\}$. Clearly R isn't symmetric: *Symmetry* on $A = \{((x, y), (y, x)), ((y, x), (x, y))\}$. But look at the first element of *Symmetry*. It tells us that for R to be closed under *Symmetry*, whenever (x, y) is in R, (y, x) must also be. But it isn't. To compute the closure of R under *Symmetry*, we must add it.
- For any a, b and c and in A, $[a \neq b \wedge b \neq c] \rightarrow [((a, b), (b, c), (a, c)) \in Transitivity]$ and no other elements are. Now we will exploit a ternary relation. Whenever the first two elements of it are present in some relation R, then the third must also be if R is transitive. This time, let's start with a set $A = \{x, y, z\}$ and a relation R on $A = \{(x, y), (y, z)\}$. Clearly R is not transitive: The *Transitivity* relation on A is $\{((x, y), (y, z), (x, z)), ((x, z), (z, y), (x, y)), ((y, x), (x, z), (y, z)), ((y, z), (z, x), (y, x)), ((z, x), (x, y), (z, y)), ((z, y), (y, x), (z, x))\}$. Look at the first element of it. Both of the first two components of it are in R. But the third isn't. To make R transitive, we must add it.

We can also describe the closure of the positive integers under division with a closure property: Let A be the positive rationals, let S be the positive integers and let R be *Quotientclosure*, defined as:

- For any a, b and c and in A, $[a/b = c] \rightarrow [(a, b, c) \in Quotientclosure]$.

So there exists a unique closure of S with respect to *Quotientclosure*. In this case, that closure is A.

We now have a general definition of closure that makes it possible to prove the existence of a unique closure for any set and any relation R. The only constraint is that this definition works only if we can define the property we care about as an n-ary relation for some finite n. There are cases of closure where this is not possible, as we saw above in the baseball team example, but we will not consider them further.

Exercises

1. Prove each of the following:

a. $((A \wedge B) \rightarrow C) \leftrightarrow (\neg A \vee \neg B \vee C)$.

b. $(A \wedge \neg B \wedge \neg C) \rightarrow (A \vee \neg(B \wedge C))$.

2. List the elements of each of the following sets:

a. $\mathcal{P}(\{\text{apple, pear, banana}\})$.

b. $\mathcal{P}(\{\text{a}, \text{b}\}) - \mathcal{P}(\{\text{a}, \text{c}\})$.

c. $\mathcal{P}(\varnothing)$.

d. $\{\text{a}, \text{b}\} \times \{1, 2, 3\} \times \varnothing$.

e. $\{x \in \mathbb{N}: (x \leq 7 \wedge x \geq 7)\}$.

f. $\{x \in \mathbb{N}: \exists y \in \mathbb{N}\ (y < 10 \wedge (y + 2 = x))\}$ (where $\mathbb{N}$ is the set of nonnegative integers).

g. $\{x \in \mathbb{N}: \exists y \in \mathbb{N}\ (\exists z \in \mathbb{N}\ ((x = y + z) \wedge (y < 5) \wedge (z < 4)))\}$.

3. Prove each of the following:

a. $A \cup (B \cap C \cap D) = (A \cup B) \cap (A \cup D) \cap (A \cup C)$.

b. $A \cup (B \cap C \cap A) = A$.

c. $(B \cap C) - A \subseteq C$.

4. Consider the English sentence, "If some bakery sells stale bread and some hotel sells flat soda, then the only thing everyone likes is tea." This sentence has at least two meanings. Write two (logically different) first-order logic sentences that correspond to meanings that could be assigned to this sentence. Use the following predicates: $P(x)$ is *True* iff x is a person; $B(x)$ is *True* iff x is a bakery; $S_B(x)$ is *True* iff x sells stale bread; $H(x)$ is *True* iff x is a hotel; $S_S(x)$ is *True* iff x sells flat soda; $L(x, y)$ is *True* iff x likes y; and $T(x)$ is *True* iff x is tea.

5. Let P be the set of positive integers. Let $L = \{\text{A, B}, \ldots, \text{Z}\}$ (i.e., the set of upper case characters in the English alphabet). Let T be the set of strings of one or more upper case English characters. Define the following predicates over those sets.

- For $x \in L$, $V(x)$ is *True* iff x is a vowel. (The vowels are A, E, I, O, and U.)
- For $x \in L$ and $n \in P$, $S(x, n)$ is *True* iff x can be written in n strokes.

- For $x \in L$ and $s \in T$, $O(x, s)$ is *True* iff x occurs in the string s.
- For $x, y \in L$, $B(x, y)$ is *True* iff x occurs before y in the English alphabet.
- For $x, y \in L$, $E(x, y)$ is *True* iff $x = y$.

Using these predicates, write each of the following statements as a sentence in first-order logic:

a. A is the only upper case English character that is a vowel and that can be written in three strokes but does not occur in the string STUPID.

b. There is an upper case English character strictly between K and R that can be written in one stroke.

6. Choose a set A and predicate P and then express the set $\{1, 4, 9, 16, 25, 36, \ldots\}$ in the form:

$$\{x \in A : P(x)\}.$$

7. Find a set that has a subset but no proper subset.

8. Give an example, other than one of the ones in the book, of a reflexive, symmetric, intransitive relation on the set of people.

9. Not equal (defined on the integers) is (circle all that apply): reflexive, symmetric, transitive.

10. In Section A.3.3, we showed a table that listed the eight possible combinations of the three properties: reflexive, symmetric and transitive. Add antisymmetry to the table. There are now 16 possible combinations. Which combinations could some nontrivial binary relation possess? Justify your answer with examples to show the combinations that are possible and proofs of the impossibility of the others.

11. Using the definition of $\equiv_p$ (equivalence modulo p) that is given in Example A.4, let R_p be a binary relation on $\mathbb{N}$, defined as follows, for any $p \geq 1$:

$$R_p = \{(\mathtt{a}, \mathtt{b}) : \mathtt{a} \equiv_p \mathtt{b}\}.$$

So, for example R_3 contains (0, 0), (6, 9), (1, 4), etc., but does not contain (0, 1), (3, 4), etc.

a. Is R_p an equivalence relation for every $p \geq 1$? Prove your answer.

b. If R_p is an equivalence relation, how many equivalence classes does it induce for a given value of p? What are they? (Any concise description is fine.)

c. Is R_p a partial order? A total order? Prove your answer.

12. Let $S = \{w \in \{\mathtt{a}, \mathtt{b}\}^*\}$. Define the relation *Substr* on the set S to be $\{(s, t) : s$ is a substring of $t\}$.

a. Choose a small subset of *Substr* and draw it as a graph (in the same way that we drew the graph of Example A.5).

b. Is *Substr* a partial order?

13. Let P be the set of people. Define the function:

$$father\text{-}of : P \rightarrow P.$$

$$father\text{-}of(x) = \text{the person who is } x\text{'s father}$$

a. Is *father-of* one-to-one?

b. Is it onto?

14. Are the following sets closed under the following operations? If not, give an example that proves that they are not and then specify what the closure is.

a. The negative integers under subtraction.

b. The negative integers under division.

c. The positive integers under exponentiation.

d. The finite sets under Cartesian product.

e. The odd integers under remainder, mod 3.

f. The rational numbers under addition.

15. Give examples to show that:

a. The intersection of two countably infinite sets can be finite.

b. The intersection of two countably infinite sets can be countably infinite.

c. The intersection of two uncountable sets can be finite.

d. The intersection of two uncountable sets can be countably infinite.

e. The intersection of two uncountable sets can be uncountable.

16. Let $R = \{(1,2), (2,3), (3,5), (5,7), (7,11), (11,13), (4,6), (6,8), (8,9), (9,10), (10,12)\}$. Draw a directed graph representing R^*, the reflexive, transitive closure of R.

17. Let $\mathbb{N}$ be the set of nonnegative integers. For each of the following sentences in first-order logic, state whether the sentence is valid, is not valid but is satisfiable, or is unsatisfiable. Assume the standard interpretation for $<$ and $>$. Assume that f could be any function on the integers. Prove your answer.

a. $\forall x \in \mathbb{N}\ (\exists y \in \mathbb{N}\ (y < x))$

b. $\forall x \in \mathbb{N}\ (\exists y \in \mathbb{N}\ (y > x))$

c. $\forall x \in \mathbb{N}\ (\exists y \in \mathbb{N}\ f(x) = y)$

18. Let $\mathbb{N}$ be the set of nonnegative integers. Let A be the set of nonnegative integers x such that $x \equiv_3 0$. Show that $|\mathbb{N}| = |A|$.

19. What is the cardinality of each of the following sets? Prove your answer.

a. $\{n \in \mathbb{N} : n \equiv_3 0\}$

b. $\{n \in \mathbb{N} : n \equiv_3 0\} \cap \{n \in \mathbb{N} : n \text{ is prime}\}$.

c. $\{n \in \mathbb{N} : n \equiv_3 0\} \cup \{n \in \mathbb{N} : n \text{ is prime}\}$

20. Prove that the set of rational numbers is countably infinite.

21. Use induction to prove each of the following claims:

a. $\forall n > 0 \left(\sum_{i=1}^{n} i^2 = \frac{n(n+1)(2n+1)}{6} \right)$.

b. $\forall n > 0\ (n! \geq 2^{n-1})$. Recall that $0! = 1$ and $\forall n > 0 (n! = n(n-1)(n-2)\cdots 1)$.

c. $\forall n > 0 \left(\sum_{k=0}^{n} 2^k = 2^{n+1} - 1 \right)$.

d. $\forall n \geq 0 \left(\sum_{k=0}^{n} r^k = \frac{r^{n+1} - 1}{r - 1} \right)$, given $r \neq 0, 1$.

e. $\forall n \geq 0 \left(\sum_{k=0}^{n} f_k^2 = f_n \cdot f_{n+1} \right)$, where f_n is the nth element of the Fibonacci sequence, as defined in Example 24.4.

22. Consider a finite rectangle in the plane. We will draw some number of (infinite) lines that cut through the rectangle. So, for example, we might have:

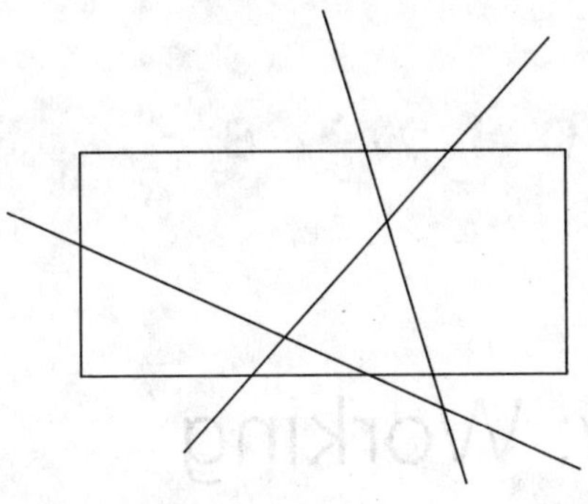

In Section 28.7.6, we define what we mean when we say that a map can be colored using two colors. Treat the rectangle that we just drew as a map, with regions defined by the lines that cut through it. Use induction to prove that, no matter how many lines we draw, the rectangle can be colored using two colors.

23. Let $div_2(n) = \lfloor n/2 \rfloor$ (i.e., the largest integer that is less than or equal to $n/2$). Alternatively, think of it as the function that performs division by 2 on a binary number by shifting right one digit. Prove that the following program correctly multiplies two natural numbers. Clearly state the loop invariant that you are using.

```
mult(n, m: natural numbers) =
    result = 0.
    While m ≠ 0 do
        If odd(m) then result = result + n.
        n = 2n.
        m = div2(m).
```

24. Prove that the following program computes the function *double*(s) where, for any string s, *double*(s) = *True* if s contains at least one pair of adjacent characters that are identical and *False* otherwise. Clearly state the loop invariant that you are using.

```
double(s: string) =
    found = False.
    for i = 1 to length(s) - 1 do
        if s[i] = s[i + 1] then found = True.
    return(found).
```

APPENDIX B

The Theory: Working with Logical Formulas

Boolean formulas describe circuits. First-order logic formulas encode software specifications and robot plans. We need efficient and correct techniques for manipulating them. In this appendix, we present some fundamental theoretical results that serve as the basis for such techniques. We'll begin with Boolean formulas. Then we'll consider the extension of some of the Boolean ideas to first-order logic.

B.1 Working with Boolean Formulas: Normal Forms, Resolution and OBDDs

In this section we discuss three issues that may arise when working with Boolean (propositional) formulas:

- conversion of an arbitrary Boolean formula into a more restricted form (a normal form),
- boolean resolution, a proof by refutation technique, and
- efficient manipulation of Boolean formulas.

B.1.1 Normal Forms for Boolean Logic

Recall that a normal form for a set of data objects is a restricted syntactic form that simplifies one or more operations on the objects. When we use the term "normal form," we generally require that every object in the original set have some equivalent (with respect to the operations for which the normal form will be used) representation in the restricted form.

In this section we define three important normal forms for Boolean formulas and we prove that any Boolean formula has a corresponding formula in each of those normal forms. We begin with some definitions:

A ***literal*** in a Boolean formula is either an atomic proposition (a simple Boolean variable), or an atomic proposition preceded by a single negation symbol. So P, Q, and $\neg P$ are all literals. A ***positive literal*** is a literal that is not preceded by a negation symbol. A ***negative literal*** is a literal that is preceded by a negation symbol.

A ***clause*** is either a single literal or the disjunction of two or more literals. So P, $P \vee \neg P$, and $P \vee \neg Q \vee R \vee S$ are all clauses.

Conjunctive Normal Form

A well-formed formula (wff) of Boolean logic is in ***conjunctive normal form*** iff it is either a single clause or the conjunction of two or more clauses. The following formulas are in conjunctive normal form.

- P
- $P \vee \neg Q \vee R \vee S$
- $(P \vee \neg Q \vee R \vee S) \wedge (\neg P \vee \neg R)$

The following formulas are not in conjunctive normal form.

- $P \rightarrow Q$
- $\neg(P \vee \neg Q)$
- $(P \wedge \neg Q \wedge R \wedge S) \vee (\neg P \wedge \neg R)$

THEOREM B.1 Conjunctive Normal Form Theorem

Theorem: Given w, an arbitrary wff of Boolean logic, there exists a wff w' that is in conjunctive normal form and that is equivalent to w.

Proof: The proof is by construction. The following algorithm *conjunctiveBoolean* computes w' given w:

conjunctiveBoolean(w: wff of Boolean logic) =

1. Eliminate $\rightarrow$ and $\leftrightarrow$ from w, using the fact that $P \rightarrow Q$ is equivalent to $\neg P \vee Q$.
2. Reduce the scope of each $\neg$ to a single term, using the facts:
   - Double negation: $\neg(\neg P) = P$.
   - deMorgan's laws:
     - $\neg(P \wedge Q) \equiv (\neg P \vee \neg Q)$.
     - $\neg(P \vee Q) \equiv (\neg P \wedge \neg Q)$.
3. Convert w to a conjunction of clauses using the fact that both $\vee$ and $\wedge$ are associative and the fact that $\vee$ and $\wedge$ distribute over each other.

EXAMPLE B.1 Boolean Conjunctive Normal Form

Let w be the wff $P \rightarrow \neg(R \vee \neg Q)$. Then w can be converted to conjunctive normal form as follows.

- Step 1 produces $\neg P \vee \neg(R \vee \neg Q)$.
- Step 2 produces $\neg P \vee (\neg R \wedge Q)$.
- Step 3 produces $(\neg P \vee \neg R) \wedge (\neg P \vee Q)$.

Conjunctive normal form is useful as a basis for describing 3-conjunctive normal form, as we are about to do. It is also important because its extension to first-order logic formulas is useful, as we'll see below, in a variety of applications that require automatic theorem proving.

3-Conjunctive Normal Form

A well-formed formula (wff) of Boolean logic is in ***3-conjunctive normal form*** (***3-CNF***) iff it is in conjunctive normal form and each clause contains exactly three literals. So the following formulas are in 3-conjunctive normal form:

- $(\neg Q \vee R \vee S)$.
- $(\neg Q \vee R \vee S) \wedge (\neg P \vee \neg R \vee \neg Q)$.

3-conjunctive normal form is important because it allows us to define 3-SAT $= \{w : w$ is a wff in Boolean logic, w is in 3-conjunctive normal form and w is satisfiable$\}$. 3-SAT is important because it is NP-complete and reduction from it can often be used to show that a new language is also NP-complete.

THEOREM B.2 3-Conjunctive Normal Form Theorem

Theorem: Given a Boolean wff w in conjunctive normal form, there exists an algorithm that constructs a new wff w' that is in 3-conjunctive normal form and that is satisfiable iff w is.

Proof: The following algorithm *3-conjunctiveBoolean* computes w' given w:

3-conjunctiveBoolean(w: wff in conjunctive normal form) =

1. If, in w, there are any clauses with more than three literals, split them apart, add additional variables as necessary, and form a conjunction of the resulting clauses. Specifically, if $n > 3$ and there is a clause of the following form:

$$(l_1 \vee l_2 \vee l_3 \vee \ldots \vee l_n),$$

then it will be replaced by the following conjunction of $n - 2$ clauses that can be constructed by introducing a set of literals $Z_1 - Z_{n-3}$ that do not otherwise occur in the formula:

$$(l_1 \vee l_2 \vee Z_1) \wedge (\neg Z_1 \vee l_3 \vee Z_2) \wedge \ldots \wedge (Z_{n-3} \vee l_{n-1} \vee l_n)$$

2. If there is any clause with only one or two literals, replicate one of those literals once or twice so that there is a total of three literals in the clause.

In Exercise 28.4, we prove that w' is satisfiable iff w is. We also prove that *3-conjunctiveBoolean* runs in polynomial time.

EXAMPLE B.2 Boolean 3-Conjunctive Normal Form

Let w be the wff $(\neg P \vee \neg R) \wedge (\neg P \vee Q \vee R \vee S)$. We build the 3-conjunctive normal form wff w' as follows:

- The first clause can be rewritten as $(\neg P \vee \neg R \vee \neg R)$.
- The second clause can be rewritten as $(\neg P \vee Q \vee Z_1) \wedge (\neg Z_1 \vee R \vee S)$.

So the following formula w' is satisfiable iff w' is:

$$(\neg P \vee \neg R \vee \neg R) \wedge (\neg P \vee Q \vee Z_1) \wedge (\neg Z_1 \vee R \vee S).$$

Disjunctive Normal Form

We now consider an alternative normal form in which conjunctions of literals are connected by disjunction (rather than the other way around). A well-formed formula (wff) of Boolean logic is in ***disjunctive normal form*** iff it is the disjunction of one or more disjuncts, each of which is either a single literal or the conjunction of two or more literals. All of P, $\neg P \wedge \neg R$, and $P \wedge \neg Q \wedge R \wedge S$ are disjuncts, and all of the following formulas are in disjunctive normal form.

- P
- $P \vee \neg Q \vee R \vee S$
- $(P \wedge \neg Q \wedge R \wedge S) \vee (\neg P \wedge \neg R)$

Disjunctive normal form is the basis for a convenient notation for writing queries against relational databases. (H.5)

THEOREM B.3 Disjunctive Normal Form Theorem

Theorem: Given w, an arbitrary wff of Boolean logic, there exists a wff w' that is in disjunctive normal form and that is equivalent to w.

Proof: The proof is by a construction similar to the one used to prove Theorem B.1. The following algorithm *disjunctiveBoolean* computes w' given w:

disjunctiveBoolean(w: wff of Boolean logic) =

1. Eliminate $\rightarrow$ and $\leftrightarrow$ from w, using the fact that $P \rightarrow Q$ is equivalent to $\neg P \vee Q$.

2. Reduce the scope of each $\neg$ in w to a single atomic proposition using the facts:
   - Double negation: $\neg(\neg P) = P$.
   - deMorgan's laws:
     - $\neg(P \wedge Q) \equiv (\neg P \vee \neg Q)$.
     - $\neg(P \vee Q) \equiv (\neg P \wedge \neg Q)$.
3. Convert w to a disjunction of disjuncts using the fact that both $\vee$ and $\wedge$ are associative and the fact that $\vee$ and $\wedge$ distribute over each other.

EXAMPLE B.3 Boolean Disjunctive Normal Form

Let w be the wff $P \wedge (Q \rightarrow \neg(R \wedge T))$. Then w can be converted to disjunctive normal form as follows.

- Step 1 produces: $P \wedge (\neg Q \vee \neg(R \wedge T))$.
- Step 2 produces: $P \wedge (\neg Q \vee \neg R \vee \neg T)$.
- Step 3 produces: $(P \wedge \neg Q) \vee (P \wedge \neg R) \vee (P \wedge \neg T)$.

B.1.2 Boolean Resolution

Two of the most important operations on Boolean formulas are:

1. ***Satisfiability checking***: Given a wff ST, is it satisfiable or not? Recall that a wff is satisfiable iff it is true for at least one assignment of truth values to the variables it contains.
2. ***Theorem proving***: Given a set of axioms A and a wff ST, does A entail ST? Recall that A entails ST iff, whenever all of the wffs in A are true, ST is also true.

But note that A entails ST iff $A \wedge \neg ST$ is unsatisfiable. So an algorithm for determining unsatisfiability can also be exploited as a theorem prover. The technique that we present next is significant not just because it can be used to reason about Boolean logic formulas. More importantly, its extension to first-order logic launched the field of automatic theorem proving.

Resolution: The Inference Rule

The name "resolution" is used both for an inference rule and a theorem-proving technique that is based on that rule. We first describe the inference rule. Let Q, $\neg Q$, P and R be wffs. Then define:

Resolution: From the premises: $(P \vee Q)$ and $(R \vee \neg Q)$,

Conclude: $(P \vee R)$.

The soundness of the resolution rule is based on the following observation: Assume that both $(P \vee Q)$ and $(R \vee \neg Q)$ are *True*. Then:

- if Q is *True*, R must be *True*.
- if $\neg Q$ *True*, P must be *True*.

Since either Q or $\neg Q$ must be *True*, $P \vee R$ must be *True*. To prove resolution's soundness, it suffices to write out its truth table. We leave that as an exercise.

Resolution: The Algorithm

We next present a theorem-proving technique called resolution. It relies on the inference rule called resolution that we just defined. The core of the prover is an algorithm that detects unsatisfiability. So a resolution proof is a proof by contradiction (often called refutation). A resolution proof of a statement ST, given a set of axioms A, is a demonstration that $A \wedge \neg ST$ is unsatisfiable. If $\neg ST$ cannot be true given A, ST must be.

The resolution procedure takes as its input a list of clauses. So, before it can be used, we must convert the axioms in A to such a list, as follows.

1. Convert each formula in A to conjunctive normal form.

2. Build L, a list of the clauses that are constructed in step 1.

EXAMPLE B.4 Making a List of Clauses

Suppose that we are given the set A of axioms as shown in column 1. We convert each axiom to conjunctive normal form, as shown in the second column.

Given Axioms	Converted to Conjunctive Normal Form
P	P
$(P \wedge Q) \rightarrow R$	$\neg P \vee \neg Q \vee R$
$(S \vee T) \rightarrow Q$	$(\neg S \vee Q) \wedge (\neg T \vee Q)$
T	T

Then the list L of clauses constructed in this process is: $P, \neg P \vee \neg Q \vee R, \neg S \vee Q, \neg T \vee Q$, and T.

To prove that a formula ST is entailed by A, we construct the formula $\neg ST$, convert it to conjunctive normal form, and add all of the resulting clauses to the list of clauses produced from A. Then resolution, which we describe next, can begin.

A pair of ***complementary literals*** is a pair of literals that are not mutually satisfiable. So two literals are complementary iff one is positive, one is negative, and they contain the same propositional symbol. For example, Q and $\neg Q$ are complementary literals. We'll say that two clauses C_1 and C_2 contain a pair of complementary literals iff C_1 contains one element of the pair and C_2 contains the other. For example, the clauses $(P \vee Q \vee \neg R)$ and $(T \vee \neg Q)$ contain the complementary literals Q and $\neg Q$.

Consider a pair of clauses that contain a pair of complementary literals, which, without loss of generality, we'll call Q and $\neg Q$. So we might have $C_1 = R_1 \vee R_2 \vee \ldots \vee R_j \vee Q$ and $C_2 = S_1 \vee S_2 \vee \ldots \vee S_k \vee \neg Q$. Given C_1 and C_2, resolution (the inference rule) allows us to conclude $R_1 \vee R_2 \vee \ldots \vee R_j \vee S_1 \vee S_2 \vee \ldots \vee S_k$. When we apply the resolution rule in this way, we'll say that we have ***resolved*** the ***parents***, C_1 and C_2, to generate a new clause, which we'll call the ***resolvent***.

The resolution algorithm proceeds in a sequence of steps. At each step it chooses from L two clauses that contain complementary literals. It resolves those two clauses together to create a new clause, the resolvent, which it adds to L. If any step generates an unsatisfiable clause, then a contradiction has been found. For historical reasons, the ***empty clause*** is commonly called *nil*, the name given to an empty list in ***Lisp***, the language in which many resolution provers have been built. The empty clause is unsatisfiable since it contains no literals that can be made *True*. So if it is ever generated, the resolution procedure halts and reports that, since adding $\neg ST$ to A has led to a contradiction, ST is a theorem given A.

> We'll describe Lisp and illustrate its use for symbolic reasoning, including theorem proving, in G.5.

We can state the algorithm as follows:

resolve-Boolean(A: set of axioms in conjunctive normal form, ST: a wff to be proven) =

1. Construct L, the list of clauses from A.
2. Negate ST, convert the result to conjunctive normal form, and add the resulting clauses to L.
3. Until either the empty clause (*nil*) is generated or no progress is being made do:
   - **3.1.** Choose from L two clauses that contain a pair of complementary literals. Call them the parent clauses.
   - **3.2.** Resolve the parent clauses together. The resulting clause, called the resolvent, will be the disjunction of all the literals in both parent clauses except for one pair of complementary literals.
   - **3.3.** If the resolvent is not *nil* and is not already in L, add it to L.
4. If *nil* was generated, a contradiction has been found. Return success. ST must be true.
5. If *nil* was not generated and there was nothing left to do, return failure.

EXAMPLE B.5 Boolean Resolution

Given the axioms that we presented in Example B.4, prove R. The axioms, and the clauses they generate are shown in the following table.

Given Axioms	**Generate the Clauses**
P	P
$(P \wedge Q) \rightarrow R$	$\neg P \vee \neg Q \vee R$
$(S \vee T) \rightarrow Q$	$\neg S \vee Q$
	$\neg T \vee Q$
T	T

We negate R. The result is already in conjunctive normal form, so we simply add it to the list of clauses:

$$\neg R.$$

We illustrate the resolution process by connecting each pair of parent clauses to the resolvent that they produce.

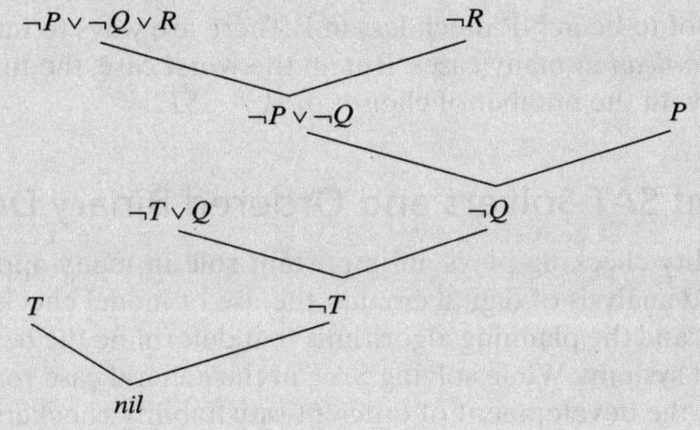

In the simple example that we just did, *Resolve-Boolean* found a proof without trying any unnecessary steps. In general, though, it conducts a search through a space of possible resolvents. Its efficiency can be affected by the choice of parents in step 3.1. In particular, the following strategies may be useful.

- ***Unit preference***: All other things being equal, choose one parent that consists of just a single clause. Then the resolvent will be one clause shorter than the other parent and thus one clause closer to being the empty clause.
- ***Set-of-support***: Begin by identifying some subset S of L with the property that we can prove that any contradiction must rely on at least one clause from S. For example, if we assume that the set of axioms is consistent, then every contradiction must rely on at least one clause from $\neg ST$. So we could choose S to be just the clauses in $\neg ST$. Then, in every resolution step, choose at least one parent from S and then add the resolvent to S.

Resolve-Boolean's efficiency can also be affected by optimizing step 3.3. One way to do that is based on the observation that, if the resolvent is subsumed by some clause already in L, adding it to L puts the process no closer to finding a contradiction. It should simply be discarded. For example, if P is already in L, it makes no sense to add $P \vee P$

or $P \vee Q$. At the extreme, if the resolvent is a tautology, it is subsumed by everything. So adding it to L puts the process no closer to finding a contradiction. It should simply be discarded. For example, it never makes sense to add a clause such as $P \vee \neg P$.

It is possible to prove that the procedure *resolve-Boolean* is sound. It is also possible to prove that, as long as *resolve-Boolean* systematically explores the entire space of possible resolutions, it is ***refutation-complete***. By that we mean that if $A \wedge \neg ST$ is unsatisfiable, *resolve-Boolean* will generate *nil* and thus discover the contradiction.

But it is important to keep in mind the complexity results that we present in Chapter 28. We prove, as Theorem 28.16, that the language SAT = {<w> : w is a wff in Boolean logic and w is satisfiable} is NP-complete. No polynomial-time algorithm for deciding it is known and it is unlikely that one exists. Unsatisfiability checking appears to be even harder since unsatisfiability, unlike satisfiability, cannot be verified just by checking one set of assignments of values to the propositional symbols. As we see in Section 28.7, the language UNSAT = {<w> : w is a wff in Boolean logic and w is not satisfiable} is in co-NP (i.e., it is the complement of a language in NP). But it is thought not to be in NP, much less in P. There are ways to improve the performance of *resolve-Boolean* in many cases. But, in the worst case, the time it requires grows exponentially with the number of clauses in $A \wedge \neg ST$.

B.1.3 Efficient SAT Solvers and Ordered Binary Decision Diagrams

Satisfiability checking plays an important role in many applications 💻, including the design and analysis of digital circuits, the use of model checking to verify properties of programs, and the planning algorithms that determine the behavior of robots and other intelligent systems. While solving SAT in the general case remains hard, substantial research on the development of efficient satisfiability checkers (or SAT solvers) has led to the development of practical systems that work very well. In this section, we'll describe one technique that plays an important role in many efficient SAT solvers. What we'll do is to describe a new normal form for Boolean formulas. Its advantage is that it often produces a compact representation that can be exploited efficiently.

For many applications, we will find it useful to think of a Boolean formula P as a Boolean function of its inputs, so we'll use that notation in the rest of this example, rather than the wff notation that we introduced in A.1.1. So let f be a Boolean function of any number of variables. We'll encode *True* as 1 and *False* as 0.

One straightforward way to represent f is as a truth table, as we did in A.1.1. An alternative is as an ***ordered binary decision tree***. In any such tree, each non-terminal node corresponds to a variable and each terminal node corresponds to the output of the function along the path that reached that node. From each nonterminal node there are two edges, one (which we'll draw to the left, with a dashed line) corresponds to the case where the value of the variable at the parent node is 0. The other (which we'll draw to the right, with a solid line) corresponds to the case where the value of the variable at the parent node is 1. To define such a tree for a binary function f, we begin by defining a total ordering $(v_1 < v_2 < \cdots < v_n)$ on the n variables that represent the inputs to f. Any ordering will work, but the efficiency of the modified structure that we will present below may depend on the ordering that has been chosen. Given an ordering, we can draw the tree with v_1 at the root, v_2 at the next level, and so forth.

As an example, consider the function $f_1(x_1, x_2, x_3) = (x_1 \vee x_2) \wedge x_3$. We can represent f_1, as shown in Figure B.1, as either a truth table or as a binary decision tree (where the tree is built using the variable ordering $(x_1 < x_2 < x_3)$.

The size of both the truth table representation and the binary decision tree for a function f of n variables is $\mathcal{O}(2^n)$. Any program M that reasons about f by manipulating either of those representations (assuming it must consider all of f) will consume at least $\mathcal{O}(2^n)$ space and $\mathcal{O}(2^n)$ time. So $timereq(M) \in \Omega(2^n)$ and $spacereq(M) \in \Omega(2^n)$. If we could reduce the size of the representation, it might be possible to reduce both the time and space requirements of any program that uses it.

If we choose the decision tree representation, it is often possible to perform such a reduction. We can convert the tree into a directed acyclic graph, called an ***ordered binary decision diagram*** or ***OBDD***. OBDDs, along with algorithms for manipulating them, were introduced in [Bryant 1986]. Our discussion of them is modeled after [Bryant 1992] and the examples we show here were taken from that paper.

We can optimize an OBDD by guaranteeing that none of its subtrees occurs more than once. Starting from the bottom, we will collapse all instances of a duplicate subtree into a single one. We'll then adjust the links into that unique tree appropriately. So we begin by creating only two terminal nodes, one labeled 0 and the other labeled 1. Then we'll move upward collapsing subtrees whenever possible. In the tree we just drew for f_1, for example, observe that the subtree whose root is x_3, whose left branch is the terminal 0 and whose right branch is the terminal 1 occurs three times. So the three can be collapsed into one. After collapsing them, we get the diagram shown in Figure B.2(a). At this point, notice the two nodes shown with double circles. Each of them has the property that its two outgoing edges both go to the same place. In essence, the value of the variable at that node has no effect on the value that f_1 returns. So the node itself can be eliminated. Doing that, we get the diagram shown in Figure B.2(b).

The process we just described can be executed by the following function *createOBDD*:

createOBDDfromtree(*d*: ordered binary decision tree) =

1. Eliminate redundant terminal nodes by creating a single node for each label and redirecting edges as necessary.
2. Until one pass is made during which no reductions occurred do:

x_1	x_2	x_3	f_1
0	0	0	0
0	0	1	0
0	1	0	0
0	1	1	1
1	0	0	0
1	0	1	1
1	1	0	0
1	1	1	1

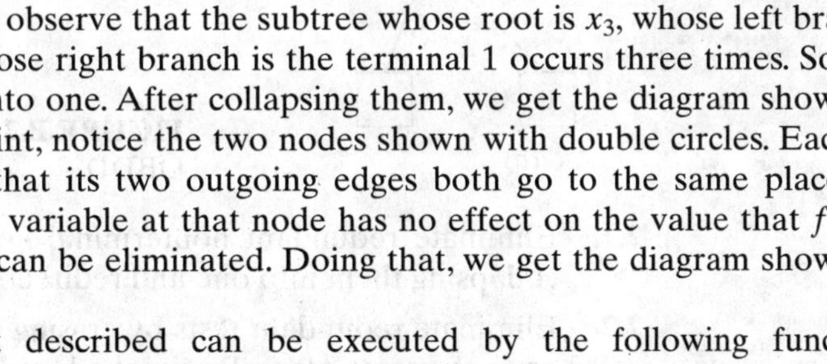

FIGURE B.1 Representing a function as a truth table or a binary decision tree.

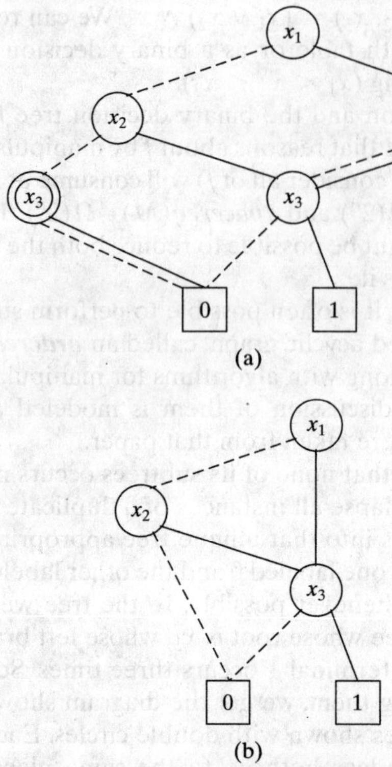

FIGURE B.2 Collapsing nodes to get an efficient OBDD.

2.1. Eliminate redundant nonterminal nodes (i.e., duplicated subtrees) by collapsing them into one and redirecting edges as necessary.

2.2. Eliminate redundant tests by erasing any node whose two output edges go to the same place. Redirect edges as necessary.

This process will create a maximally reduced OBDD, by which we mean that there is no smaller one that describes the same function and that considers the variables in the same order. It is common to reserve the term OBDD for such maximally reduced structures. Given a particular ordering $(v_1 < v_2 < \cdots < v_n)$ on the n variables that represent the inputs to some function f, any two OBDDs for f will be isomorphic to each other (i.e., the OBDD for f is unique up to the order in which the edges are drawn). Thus the OBDD structure is a canonical form for the representation of Boolean functions, given a particular variable ordering.

Since the OBDD for a function is unique up to isomorphism, some operations on it can be performed in constant time. For example, a function f corresponds to a valid wff (i.e., one that is a tautology) iff its OBDD is identical to the one shown in Figure B.3(a). A function f corresponds to a satisfiable wff iff its OBDD is not identical to the one shown in Figure B.3(b).

If the only way to build a reduced OBDD were to start with a decision tree and reduce it by applying *createOBDDfromtree*, it would not be practical to work with functions of a large number of variables, even if the reduced OBDD were of manageable size. Fortunately, it is possible 💻 to build a reduced OBDD directly, without starting with a complete decision tree.

FIGURE B.3 Exploiting canonical forms.

The size of the OBDD that can be built for a function f may depend critically on the order that we impose on f's inputs. For example, in the original decision tree that we built for f_1 above, we considered the inputs in the order x_1, x_2, x_3. We could have produced a slightly smaller OBDD (one with one fewer edge) if we had instead used the order x_3, x_1, x_2. We leave doing that as an exercise.

In some cases though, the effect of variable ordering is much more significant. Particularly in many cases of practical interest, in which there are systematic relationships within clusters of variables, it is possible to build a maximally reduced OBDD that is substantially smaller than the original decision tree. Consider the Boolean function:

$$f_2(a_1, b_1, a_2, b_2, a_3, b_3) = (a_1 \wedge b_1) \vee (a_2 \wedge b_2) \vee (a_3 \wedge b_3).$$

We'll consider two different variable orderings and the OBDDs that can be created for them. The first ordering, shown in Figure B.4(a), respects the relationship between the a, b pairs. The second, shown in Figure B.4(b), does not and pays a price.

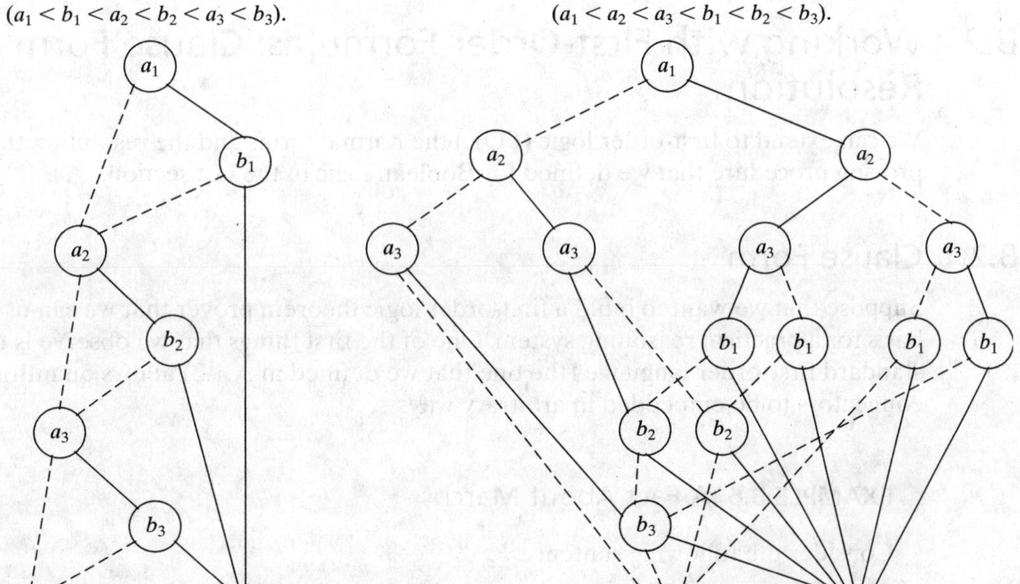

FIGURE B.4 The order of the variables matters.

Fortunately, for many classes of important problems there exist heuristics 💻 that find the variable orderings that make small structures possible. Unfortunately, however, there are problems for which no small OBDD exists. For example, consider a circuit that implements binary multiplication. Let f be the Boolean function corresponding to either of the two middle digits of the result of an n-bit multiplication. The size of any OBDD for f grows exponentially with n.

Programs that solve problems for which small OBDDs exist may have manageable requirements for both time and space. In particular, it is known that most common operations on OBDDs can be done in time that is $\mathcal{O}(nm)$, where n and m are sizes of the input OBDDs. So the OBDD structure improves the expected performance (with respect to both time and space) of many algorithms on many practical problems.

> Model checkers based on OBDDs are routinely used to prove properties of systems whose state description contains 10^{20} states. (H.1.2)

However, because small OBDDs do not exist for all problems, the structure does not change the worst-case complexity of those problems. Theorem 28.5.2 (the Cook-Levin theorem) tells us that Boolean satisfiability is NP-complete. No polynomial algorithm for solving it for all cases is known. So, if we can impose no constraints on the form of the input, the worst-case time complexity of any algorithm is likely to be $\mathcal{O}(2^n)$. While there is no proof that it is not possible to do better than that, it appears unlikely that we can.

B.2 Working with First-Order Formulas: Clause Form and Resolution

We can extend to first-order logic (FOL) the normal forms and the resolution theorem-proving procedure that we defined for Boolean logic in the last section.

B.2.1 Clause Form

Suppose that we want to build a first-order logic theorem prover that we can use as the basis for a practical reasoning system. One of the first things that we observe is that the standard first-order language (the one that we defined in A.1.2) allows quantifiers and connectors to be embedded in arbitrary ways.

EXAMPLE B.6 A Fact About Marcus

Consider the following sentence F:

$$\forall x\ ((Roman(x) \wedge Know(x, Marcus)) \rightarrow$$
$$(Hate(x, Caesar) \vee \forall y\ (\exists z\ (Hate(y, z)) \rightarrow Thinkcrazy(x, y)))).$$

F says that any Roman who knows Marcus either hates Caesar or thinks that anyone who hates anyone is crazy. So if we knew that Paulus was a Roman who knew Marcus and who didn't hate Caesar, we could use *F* to conclude that Paulus thinks that anyone who hates anyone is crazy. Or, if we knew that Paulus was a Roman who knew Marcus, and that Augustus hates Flavius but Paulus doesn't think Augustus is crazy, then we could use *F* to conclude that Paulus hates Caesar. Or, if we knew that Paulus knows Marcus, doesn't hate Caesar, and doesn't think that Augustus, who hates Flavius is crazy, then we could use *F* to conclude that Paulus is not a Roman.

Each of the arguments that we have just described requires a different way of matching the other facts we already know against the fact about Marcus's friends. We'd like one technique that works for all of them.

One approach to solving this problem is to exploit the idea of a normal form, just as we did in dealing with Boolean logic formulas. In particular, we can extend the notions of conjunctive and disjunctive normal forms, to first-order logic. Now we must be concerned both with the structure of the logical connectors (just as we were for Boolean logic) as well as the structure of the quantifiers and variables. The motivation for the definition of the normal forms we are about to describe is the need to build theorem-proving programs. The syntax for an arbitrary sentence in first-order logic allows a great deal of flexibility, making it hard to write programs that can reason with all the facts that they may be given.

A sentence in first-order logic is in ***prenex normal form*** iff it is of the form:

$$<quantifier\ list><matrix>,$$

where $<quantifier\ list>$ is a list of quantified variables and $<matrix>$ is quantifier-free.

EXAMPLE B.7 Prenex Normal Form

$\forall x\ (\exists y\ ((P(x) \land Q(y)) \rightarrow \forall z\ (R(x, y, z)))$ is not in prenex normal form.

$\forall x \exists y \forall z\ (P(x) \land Q(y) \rightarrow R\ (x, y, z))$ is in prenex normal form. Its matrix is $(P(x) \land Q(y) \rightarrow R\ (x, y, z))$.

Any sentence can be converted to an equivalent sentence in prenex normal form by the following procedure.

1. If necessary, rename the variables so that each quantifier binds a lexically distinct variable.
2. Move all the quantifiers to the left, without changing their relative order.

We define the terms literal, clause, and conjunctive normal form for sentences in first-order logic analogously to the way they were defined for Boolean logic:

- A ***literal*** is either a single predicate symbol, along with its argument list, or it is such a predicate preceded by a single negation symbol. So $P(x, f(y))$ and $\neg Q(x, f(y), 2)$ are literals. A ***positive literal*** is a literal that is not preceded by a negation symbol. A ***negative literal*** is a literal that is preceded by a negation symbol.
- A ***clause*** is either a single literal or the disjunction of two or more literals.
- A sentence in first-order logic is in ***conjunctive normal form*** iff its matrix is either a single clause or the conjunction of two or more clauses.

A ***ground instance*** is a first-order logic expression that contains no variables. So, for example, *Major-of*(*Sandy*, *Math*) is a ground instance, but $\forall x\ (\exists y\ ((Major\text{-}of(x, y)))$ is not.

A sentence in first-order logic is in ***clause form*** iff:

- it has been converted to prenex normal form,
- its quantifier list contains only universal quantifiers,
- its quantifier list is no longer explicitly represented,
- it is in conjunctive normal form, and
- there are no variable names that appear in more than one clause. This last condition is important because there will no longer be explicit quantifiers to delimit the scope of the variables. The only way to tell one variable from another will be by their names.

EXAMPLE B.8 Clause Form

The following sentence is not in clause form:

$$\forall x\ (P(x) \rightarrow Q(x)) \wedge \forall y\ (S(y)).$$

When it is converted to prenex normal form, we get:

$$\forall x\ \forall y\ (P(x) \rightarrow Q(x)) \wedge S(y).$$

Then, when it is converted to clause form, we get the conjunction of two clauses:

$$(\neg P(x) \vee Q(x)) \wedge S(y).$$

We are going to use clause form as the basis for a first-order, resolution-based proof procedure analogous to the Boolean procedure that we defined in the last section. To do that, we need to be able to convert an arbitrary first-order sentence w into a new sentence w' such that w' is in clause form and w' is unsatisfiable iff w is. In the proof of the next theorem, we provide an algorithm that does this conversion. All of the steps are straightforward except the one that eliminates existential quantifiers, so we'll discuss it briefly before we present the algorithm.

Let *Mother-of*(y, x) be true whenever y is the mother of x. Consider the sentence $\forall x\ (\exists y\ ((Mother\text{-}of(y, x)))$. Everyone has a mother. There is not a single individual who is the mother of everyone. But, given a value for x, some mother exists. We can eliminate the existentially quantified variable y using a technique called ***Skolemization***, based on an idea due to Thoralf Skolem [Skolem 1928]. We replace y by a function of x.

We know nothing about that function. (We don't know, for example, that it is computable.) We know only that it exists. So we assign the function a name that is not already being used, say f_1. Then:

$$\forall x\ (\exists y\ ((Mother\text{-}of(y, x))) \text{ becomes } \forall x\ ((Mother\text{-}of(f_1(x), x)).$$

Multiple existential quantifiers in the same sentence can be handled similarly, but it is important that a new function be created for each existential quantifier. For example, consider the predicate *Student-data*(x, y, z) that is true iff student x enrolled at date y and has major z. Then:

$$\forall x\ (\exists y\ (\exists z\ (Student\text{-}data(x, y, z)))) \text{ becomes } \forall x\ (Student\text{-}data(x, f_2(x), f_3(x))).$$

The function $f_2(x)$ produces a date and the function $f_3(x)$ produces a major. Now consider the predicate *Sum*(x, y, z), that is true iff the sum of x and y is z. Then:

$$\forall x\ (\forall y\ (\exists z\ (Sum(x, y, z)))) \text{ becomes } \forall x\ (\forall y\ (Sum(x, y, f_4(x, y)))).$$

In this case, the value of z that must exist (and be produced by f_4) is a function of both x and y. More generally, if an existentially quantified variable occurs inside the scope of n universally quantified variables, it can be replaced by a function of n arguments corresponding to those n variables. In the simple case in which an existentially quantified variable occurs inside the scope of no universally quantified variables, it can be replaced by a constant (i.e., a function of no arguments). So:

$$\exists x\ (Student(x)) \text{ becomes } Student(f_5).$$

The functions that are introduced in this way are called ***Skolem functions*** and ***Skolem constants***.

Skolemization plays a key role in theorem-proving systems (particularly resolution-based ones) because the Skolemization of a sentence w is unsatisfiable iff w is. But note that we have not said that a Skolemization is necessarily equivalent to the original sentence from which it was derived. Consider the simple sentence, $\exists x\ (P(x))$. It can be Skolemized as $P(f_1)$. But now observe that:

- $\exists x\ (P(x)) \rightarrow \exists x\ (P(x))$ is valid (i.e., it is a tautology). It is true in all interpretations.
- $\exists x\ (P(x)) \rightarrow P(f_1)$ is satisfiable since it is *True* if $P(f_1)$ is *True*. But it is not valid, since it is *False* if P is true for some value of x that is different from f_1 but *False* for f_1.

So $\exists x\ (P(x))$ and $P(f_1)$ are not logically equivalent.

The proof of the Clause Form Theorem, which we state next, exploits Skolemization, in combination with standard logical identities, as the basis of an algorithm that converts any first-order sentence w into another sentence w' that is in clause form and that is unsatisfiable iff w is.

THEOREM B.4 Clause Form Theorem

Theorem: Given w, a sentence in first-order logic, there exists a clause form representation w' such that w' is unsatisfiable iff w is.

Proof: The proof is by construction. The following algorithm *converttoclauseform* computes a clause form representation of w:

converttoclauseform(w: first-order sentence) =

1. Eliminate $\rightarrow$ and $\leftrightarrow$, using the fact that $P \rightarrow Q$ is equivalent to $\neg P \vee Q$.
2. Reduce the scope of each $\neg$ to a single term, using the facts:
   - Double negation: $\neg(\neg P) = P$.
   - deMorgan's laws:
     - $\neg(P \wedge Q) \equiv (\neg P \vee \neg Q)$.
     - $\neg(P \vee Q) \equiv (\neg P \wedge \neg Q)$.
   - Quantifier exchange:
     - $\neg\forall x\,(P(x)) \equiv \exists x\,(\neg P(x))$.
     - $\neg\exists x\,(P(x)) \equiv \forall x\,(\neg P(x))$.
3. Standardize apart the variables so that each quantifier binds a unique variable. For example, given the sentence:

   $$\forall x\,(P(x)) \vee \forall x\,(Q(x)),$$

   the variables can be standardized apart to produce:

   $$\forall x\,(P(x)) \vee \forall y\,(Q(y)).$$

4. Move all quantifiers to the left without changing their relative order. At this point, the sentence is in prenex normal form.
5. Eliminate existential quantifiers via Skolemization, as described above.
6. Drop the prefix since all remaining quantifiers are universal.
7. Convert the matrix to a conjunction of clauses by using the fact that both $\vee$ and $\wedge$ are associative and the fact that $\vee$ and $\wedge$ distribute over each other.
8. Standardize apart the variables so that no variable occurs in more than one clause.

EXAMPLE B.9 Converting the Marcus Fact to Clause Form

We now return to F, the statement about Marcus's friends that we introduced in Example B.6:

$$\forall x\,((Roman(x) \wedge Know(x, Marcus)) \rightarrow$$
$$(Hate(x, Caesar) \vee \forall y\,(\exists z\,(Hate(y, z)) \rightarrow Thinkcrazy(x, y)))).$$

We convert F to clause form as follows:

- Step 1: Eliminate $\rightarrow$. This step produces:

$$\forall x\,(\neg(Roman(x) \wedge Know(x, Marcus)) \vee (Hate(x, Caesar) \vee \forall y\,(\neg\exists z\,(Hate(y, z)) \vee Thinkcrazy(x, y)))).$$

- Step 2: Reduce the scope of $\neg$. This step produces:

$$\forall x\,(\neg Roman(x) \vee \neg Know(x, Marcus) \vee (Hate(x, Caesar) \vee \forall y\,(\forall z\,(\neg Hate(y, z)) \vee Thinkcrazy(x, y)))).$$

(Notice that the existential quantifier disappeared)

- Steps 3 and 4: Standardize apart and shift the quantifiers to the left. These steps produce:

$$\forall x\,\forall y\,\forall z\,(\neg Roman(x) \vee \neg Know(x, Marcus) \vee (Hate(x, Caesar) \vee \neg Hate(y, z) \vee Thinkcrazy(x, y))).$$

- Steps 5–8: These last steps produce:

$$\neg Roman(x) \vee \neg Know(x, Marcus) \vee Hate(x, Caesar) \vee \neg Hate(y, z) \vee Thinkcrazy(x, y).$$

EXAMPLE B.10 Handling Existential Quantifiers and Standardizing Apart

We convert the following sentence to clause form:

$$\forall x\,(Person(x) \rightarrow (\exists y\,(Mother\text{-}of(y, x)) \wedge \exists y\,(Father\text{-}of(y, x)))).$$

- Step 1: Eliminate $\rightarrow$. This step produces:

$$\forall x\,(\neg Person(x) \vee (\exists y\,(Mother\text{-}of(y, x)) \wedge \exists y\,(Father\text{-}of(y, x)))).$$

- Step 2: Reduce the scope of $\neg$. This step is not necessary.
- Step 3: Standardize apart the variables so that each quantifier binds a unique variable.

$$\forall x\,(\neg Person(x) \vee (\exists y_1\,(Mother\text{-}of(y_1, x)) \wedge \exists y_2\,(Father\text{-}of(y_2, x))))$$

- Step 4: Move all quantifiers to the left without changing their relative order.

$$\forall x\,\exists y_1\,\exists y_2\,(\neg Person(x) \vee (Mother\text{-}of(y_1, x) \wedge Father\text{-}of(y_2, x)))$$

- Step 5: Eliminate existential quantifiers via Skolemization.

$$\forall x\,(\neg Person(x) \vee (Mother\text{-}of(f_1(x), x) \wedge Father\text{-}of(f_2(x), x)))$$

- Step 6: Drop the prefix since all remaining quantifiers are universal.

$$\neg Person(x) \vee (Mother\text{-}of(f_1(x), x) \wedge Father\text{-}of(f_2(x), x))$$

- Step 7: Convert the matrix to a conjunction of clauses.

$$(\neg Person(x) \vee Mother\text{-}of(f_1(x), x)) \wedge (\neg Person(x) \vee Father\text{-}of(f_2(x), x))$$

EXAMPLE B.10 *(Continued)*

- Step 8: Standardize apart the variables so that no variable occurs in more than one clause.

$$(\neg Person(x_1) \vee Mother\text{-}of(f_1(x_1), x_1)) \wedge$$
$$(\neg Person(x_2) \vee Father\text{-}of(f_2(x_2), x_2))$$

Now the two clauses can be treated as independent clauses, regardless of the fact that they were derived from the same original sentence.

The design of a theorem prover can be simplified if all of the inputs to the theorem prover have been converted to clause form.

EXAMPLE B.11 Using the Marcus Fact in a Proof

We now return again to *F*, the statement about Marcus's friends that we introduced in Example B.6:

$$\forall x\ ((Roman(x) \wedge Know(x, Marcus)) \rightarrow$$
$$(Hate(x, Caesar) \vee \forall y\ (\exists z\ (Hate(y, z)) \rightarrow Thinkcrazy(x, y)))).$$

When we convert this statement to clause form, we get, as we showed in the last example, the formula that we will call F_C:

$$(F_C) \qquad \neg Roman(x) \vee \neg Know(x, Marcus) \vee Hate(x, Caesar)$$
$$\vee \neg Hate(y, z) \vee Thinkcrazy(x, y).$$

In its original form, *F* is not obviously a way to prove that someone isn't a Roman. But, in clause form it is easy to use for that purpose. Suppose we add the following facts.

- *Know*(*Paulus*, *Marcus*)
- ¬*Hate*(*Paulus*, *Caesar*)
- *Hate*(*Augustus*, *Flavius*)
- ¬*Thinkcrazy*(*Paulus*, *Augustus*)

We can now prove that Paulus is not a Roman. Paulus knows Marcus, doesn't hate Caesar, and doesn't think that Augustus, who hates Flavius is crazy. The general statement about Marcus's friends must hold for all values of *x*. In the case of Paulus, we've ruled out four of the five literals that could make it true. The one that remains is ¬*Roman*(*Paulus*). Note that to implement the reasoning that we just did, we need a way to match literals like *Know*(*Paulus*, *Marcus*) and ¬*Know*(*x*, *Marcus*). We'll present unification, a technique for doing that, in the next section.

B.2.2 First-Order Logic Resolution

First-order logic is undecidable. We stated that result as Theorem 22.4: The language $\text{FOL}_{\text{theorem}} = \{<A, w> : A$ is a decidable set of axioms in first-order logic, w is a sentence in first-order logic, and w is entailed by $A\}$ is not in D. As a proof, we sketched Turing's proof. So there is no algorithm to *decide* whether or not a statement is a theorem. But, as we showed in Theorem 22.3, the language $\text{FOL}_{\text{theorem}}$ is semidecidable by an algorithm that constructs a lexicographic enumeration of the valid proofs given A. Given a statement w, that algorithm will *discover* a proof if one exists. To make theorem-proving useful in practical problem domains, however, we need techniques that are substantially more efficient at, least in many cases, than the exhaustive enumeration method. Fortunately, such techniques exist. And finding even better ones remains an active area of research. Keep in mind, however, that every first-order logic theorem prover has the limitation that, if asked to prove a nontheorem, it may not be able to tell that no proof exists.

In this section we describe one important proof technique—the extension to first-order logic of the resolution algorithm that we presented for Boolean logic in B.1.2. First-order resolution was introduced in [Robinson 1965] and has served, since then, as the basis for several generations of automatic theorem-proving programs. It is sound (i.e., it can prove only theorems that are entailed by the axioms it is given). And it is refutation-complete, by which we mean the following: Given a set of axioms A and a sentence ST, if ST is a theorem then $A \wedge \neg ST$ will derive a contradiction and the resolution algorithm, assuming it uses a systematic strategy for exploring the space of possible resolution steps, will (eventually) find it. We note, however, that first-order resolution is not complete in the sense that there may be theorems that will not be generated by any resolution step.

> First-order logic resolution is the basis for logic programming languages such as Prolog. (M.2.3) It has played a key role in the evolution of the field of artificial intelligence. (M.2) It has been used to solve problems in domains ranging from program verification. (H.1.1) to medical reasoning. One noteworthy application in mathematics was the proof of the Robbins Algebra Conjecture, which had outwitted mathematicians for 60 years.

A first-order logic resolution theorem prover works in essentially the same way a Boolean one does. It begins with A, a set of axioms that have been converted to clause form. To prove a statement ST, it negates ST, converts the result to clause form, and adds it to A. Then, at each resolution step, it chooses two parent clauses that contain complementary literals, resolves the two clauses together, creates a resolvent, and adds it to A. If the unsatisfiable clause *nil* is ever generated, a contradiction has been found.

Unification

The only new issue that we must face is how to handle variables and functions. In particular, what does it now mean to say that two literals are complementary? As before, two literals are complementary iff they are inconsistent. Two literals are inconsistent iff one of them is positive, one of them is negative (i.e., begins with ¬), they both contain the same predicate, and they are about intersecting sets of individuals. In other words, two literals are inconsistent, and thus complementary, iff they make conflicting claims about at least one individual. To check for this, resolution exploits a matching process called ***unification***. Unification takes as its arguments two literals, each with any leading ¬ removed. It will return *Fail* if the two literals do not match, either because their predicates are different or because it is not certain that the intersection of the sets of individuals that they are about is not empty. It will succeed if they do match. And, in that case, it will return a list of substitutions that describes how one literal was transformed into the other so that they match and the nonempty intersection was found.

When are two literals about intersecting sets of individuals? Recall that all clause variables are universally quantified. So the domains of any two variables overlap. For example, $P(x)$ and $\neg P(y)$ are complementary literals. One says P is true of everyone; the other says that P is false of everyone. The domain of any one variable necessarily includes all specific values. So $P(x)$ and $\neg P(Marcus)$ are complementary since P cannot be true of everyone but not true of *Marcus*. $P(Caesar)$ and $\neg P(Marcus)$ are not complementary since P can be true of *Caesar* but not of *Marcus*. $P(f(Marcus))$ and $\neg P(f(Marcus))$ are complementary, but $P(f(Marcus))$ and $\neg P(f(Caesar))$ are not. While it is possible that $f(Marcus)$ and $f(Caesar)$ refer to the same individual, it is not certain that they do. Unification will handle functions by recursively invoking itself. It will check that function symbols match in the same way that it checks that predicate symbols match.

If the same variable occurs more than once in a literal, any substitutions that are made to it must be made consistently to all of its occurrences. So the unification algorithm must, each time it makes a substitution, apply it to the remainder of both literals before it can continue. For example, consider unifying $Know(x, x)$ (everyone knows him/her/itself) and $Know(Marcus, Marcus)$. Unification will match the first x with the first *Marcus*, substituting *Marcus* for x. It will then substitute *Marcus* for the second occurrence of x before it continues. It will succeed when it next matches *Marcus* with *Marcus*. But now consider unifying $Know(x, x)$ and $Know(Marcus, Caesar)$. The second literal, $Know(Marcus, Caesar)$, is not about knowing oneself. Unification will fail in this case because it will substitute *Marcus* for x, apply that substitution to the second x, and then fail to match *Marcus* and *Caesar*.

Each invocation of the unification procedure will return either the special value *Fail* or a list of substitutions. We will write each list as $(subst_1, subst_2, \ldots)$. We will write each substitution as sub_1/sub_2, meaning that sub_1 is to be written in place of sub_2. If unification succeeds without performing any substitutions, the substitution list will be *nil* (the empty list). We are now ready to state the unification procedure:

unify-for-resolution(lit_1, lit_2: variables, constants, function expressions or positive literals) =

1. If either lit_1 or lit_2 is a variable or a constant then:

1.1. Case (checking the conditions in order and executing only the first one that matches):

lit_1 and lit_2 are identical: Return *nil*. /* Succeed with no substitution required.

lit_1 is a variable that occurs in lit_2: Return *Fail*. /* These two cases implement the occur check. See note below.

lit_2 is a variable that occurs in lit_1: Return *Fail*. "

lit_1 is a variable: Return (lit_2/lit_1).

lit_2 is a variable: Return (lit_1/lit_2).

otherwise: Return *Fail*. /*Two different constants do not match.

2. If the initial predicate or function symbols of lit_1 and lit_2 are not the same, return *Fail*.

3. If lit_1 and lit_2 do not have the same number of arguments, return *Fail*.

4. *substitution-list* = *nil*.

5. For $i = 1$ to the number of arguments of lit_1 do:

5.1. Let *S* be the result of invoking *unify-for-resolution* on the ith argument of lit_1 and of lit_2.

5.2. If *S* contains *Fail*, return *Fail*.

5.3. If *S* is not equal to *nil* then:

5.3.1. Apply *S* to the remainder of both lit_1 and lit_2.

5.3.2. Append *S* to *substitution-list*.

6. Return *substitution-list*.

In step 1.1, *unify-for resolution* performs a check called the ***occur check***. Consider attempting to unify $f(x)$ with $f(g(x))$. Without the occur check, the function expression $g(x)$ could be unified with x, producing the substitution $g(x)/x$. But now there is no way to apply that substitution consistently to the new occurrence of x. In this case, the problem might simply not be noticed, with the consequence that any theorem prover that uses the result of the unification may produce an unsound inference. The problem is even clearer in the following case: Consider attempting to unify $f(x, x)$ with $f(g(x), g(x))$. Without the occur check, $g(x)$ could be unified with x, again producing the substitution $g(x)/x$. But now, the unification algorithm must apply that substitution to the remainder of the two clauses before it can continue. So $(, x)$ and $(, g(x))$ become $(, g(x))$ and $(, g(g(x)))$. But now it has to substitute again, and so forth. Unfortunately, the occur check is expensive. So some theorem-proving programs omit it and take a chance.

EXAMPLE B.12 Unification Examples

We show the result of *unify-for-resolution* in each of the following cases:

	Inputs	Result	Substitution
[1]	*Roman*(x), *Roman*(*Paulus*).	Succeed	*Paulus*/x.
[2]	*Roman*(x), *Ancient*(*Paulus*).	Fail	
[3]	*Roman*(*father-of*(*Marcus*)), *Roman*(x).	Succeed	*father-of*(*Marcus*)/x.
[4]	*Roman*(*father-of*(*Marcus*)), *Roman*(*Flavius*).	Fail	
[5]	*Roman*(x), *Roman*(y).	Succeed	x/y.
[6]	*Roman*(*father-of*(x)), *Roman*(x).	Fail (fails occur check)	
[7]	*Likes*(x, y), *Likes*(*Flavius*, *Marcus*).	Succeed	*Flavius*/x, *Marcus*/y.

Notice that *unify-for-resolution* is conservative. It returns a match only if it is certain that its two arguments describe intersecting sets of individuals. For example, *father-of*(*Marcus*) and *Flavius* may (but do not necessarily) refer to the same individual. Without additional information, we do not want resolution to assert a contradiction between *Roman*(*father-of*(*Marcus*)) and ¬*Roman*(*Flavius*).

One other property of *unify-for-resolution* is worth noting: Consider unifying *Roman*(x) with *Roman*(y). The algorithm as given here returns the substitution x/y. We could, equivalently, have defined it so that it would return y/x. That choice was arbitrary. But we could also have defined it so that it returned the substitution *Marcus*/x, *Marcus*/y. That substitution effectively converts a statement that had applied to all individuals into one that applies only to *Marcus*. This restricted statement is entailed by the more general one, so a theorem prover that exploited such a match would still be sound. But proving statements would become more difficult because resolution is going to look for contradictions. General statements lead to more contradictions than specific ones do. So we can maximize the performance of a resolution theorem prover if we exploit a unification algorithm that returns what we will call a ***most general unifier***, namely a substitution with the property that no other substitution that preserves soundness imposes fewer restrictions on the values of the variables. The algorithm that we have presented always returns a most general unifier.

We can now define complementary literals analogously to the way they were defined for Boolean logic. Two literals are ***complementary literals*** iff they unify and one of them is the negation of the other. So, for example ¬*Roman*(x) and *Roman*(*Paulus*) are complementary literals. Just as in the case of Boolean logic, the conjunction of a pair of complementary literals is unsatisfiable.

Resolution: The Algorithm

Now that we have a way to identify complementary literals, we can define the resolution algorithm for first-order logic. It works the same way that resolution works in Boolean logic except that two new things need to happen after each resolution step:

- The substitution that was produced when the two complementary literals were unified must be applied to the resolvent clause. To see why this is important, consider resolving $P(x) \vee Q(x)$ with $\neg Q(Marcus)$. The first clause says that, for all values of x, at least one of P or Q must be true. The second one says that, in the specific case of *Marcus*, Q is not true. From those two clauses, it follows that, in the specific case of *Marcus*, P must be true. It does not follow that P must be true of all values of x. The result of unifying $Q(x)$ with $\neg Q(Marcus)$ is the substitution *Marcus/x*. So we can construct the result of resolving these two clauses by first building the clause that is the disjunction of all literals except the two complementary ones. That gives us $P(x)$. We then apply the substitution *Marcus/x* to that, which produces $P(Marcus)$.
- We must guarantee that the variable names in the resolvent are distinct from all the variable names that already occur in any of the clauses in L. If this is not done, it is possible that later resolution steps will treat two different variables that just happen to have the same name as though they were a single variable to which consistent substitutions must be applied. For a concrete example of the problem that this can cause, see Exercise B.8.

resolve-FOL(*A*: set of axioms in clause form, *ST*: a statement to be proven) =

1. Construct L, the list of clauses from A.
2. Rename all variables in ST so that they do not conflict with any variables in L.
3. Negate ST, convert the result to clause form, and add the resulting clauses to L.
4. Until either the empty clause (called *nil*) is generated or no progress is being made do:
   4.1. Choose from L two clauses that contain a pair CL of complementary literals. Call them the parent clauses.
   4.2. Resolve the parent clauses together to produce a new clause called the resolvent:
      4.2.1. Initially, let the resolvent be the disjunction of all of the literals in both parent clauses except for the two literals in CL.
      4.2.2. Apply to all of the literals in the resolvent the substitution that was constructed when the literals in CL were unified.
      4.2.3. Rename all of the variables in the resolvent so that they do not conflict with any of the variables in L.
   4.3. If the resolvent is not *nil* and is not already in L, add it to L.
5. If *nil* was generated, a contradiction has been found. Return success. ST must be true.
6. If *nil* was not generated and there was nothing left to do, return failure. ST may or may not be true. But no proof of ST has been found.

EXAMPLE B.13 FOL Resolution

Assume that we are given the following axioms (in clause form):

(F_C) $\neg Roman(x) \vee \neg Know(x, Marcus) \vee Hate(x, Caesar) \vee \neg Hate(y, z) \vee Thinkcrazy(x, y)$.
$\neg Hate(Cornelius, Caesar)$.
$Hate(Augustus, Flavius)$.
$\neg Thinkcrazy(Cornelius, Augustus)$.
$Roman(Cornelius)$.

We will use resolution to prove $\exists x\ (\neg Know(x, Marcus))$.

We negate $\exists x\ (\neg Know(x, Marcus))$, producing $\neg(\exists x\ (\neg Know(x, Marcus)))$ or $\forall x\ (Know(x, Marcus))$. Converting this to clause form (and standardizing apart the variables), we get:

$$Know(x_1, Marcus).$$

Resolution can now proceed as follows. (But note that this is just one path it could pursue. It could choose parent clauses in a different order.) We show, at each resolution step, the substitution that the unification process produced. Note also that the variable names have been standardized apart at each step.

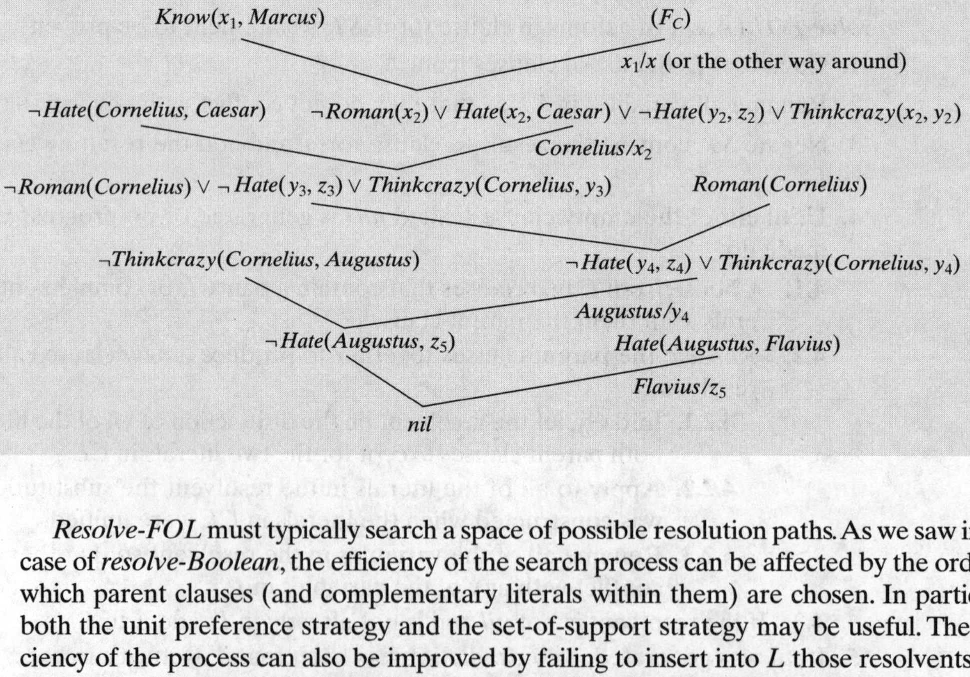

Resolve-FOL must typically search a space of possible resolution paths. As we saw in the case of *resolve-Boolean*, the efficiency of the search process can be affected by the order in which parent clauses (and complementary literals within them) are chosen. In particular both the unit preference strategy and the set-of-support strategy may be useful. The efficiency of the process can also be improved by failing to insert into L those resolvents that put the process no closer to finding a contradiction (for example because they are subsumed by clauses that are already present). Other optimizations are also possible. Even with them, however, the size of the search space that must be explored may grow too fast to make resolution a practical solution for many kinds of problems. One way to cut down the space is to limit the form of the clauses that are allowed. For example, logic programming languages, such as Prolog, work only with Horn clauses, which may have at most one positive literal. See M.2.3 for a brief introduction to Prolog and some of its applications.

Resolution: The Inference Rule

Recall that, in our discussion of resolution in Boolean logic, we pointed out that resolution is both an inference rule and an algorithm for checking unsatisfiability. The same is true for resolution in first-order logic. Using the definitions of unification and substitution that we have just provided, we can state resolution as an inference rule. Let $Q, \neg Q, P_1, P_2, \ldots, P_n$ and $R_1, R_2, \ldots, R_n$ be literals, let *substitution-list* be the substitution that is returned by *unify-for-resolution* when it unifies Q and $\neg Q$, and let *substitute*(*clause*, *substitution-list*) be the result of applying *substitution-list* to *clause*. Then define:

- ***Resolution***: From the premises: $(P_1 \vee P_2 \vee \ldots \vee P_n \vee Q)$ and $(R_1 \vee R_2 \vee \ldots \vee R_m \vee \neg Q)$,
  Conclude: *substitute*($(P_1 \vee P_2 \vee \ldots \vee P_n \vee R_1 \vee R_2 \vee \ldots \vee R_m)$, *substitution-list*).

Exercises

1. Convert each of the following Boolean formulas to conjunctive normal form.
   a. $(a \wedge b) \rightarrow c$
   b. $\neg(a \rightarrow (b \wedge c))$
   c. $(a \vee b) \rightarrow (c \wedge d)$
   d. $\neg(p \rightarrow \neg(q \vee (\neg r \wedge s)))$

2. For each of the following Boolean formulas w, use *3-conjunctive Boolean* to construct a formula w' that is satisfiable iff w is.
   a. $(a \vee b) \wedge (a \wedge \neg b \wedge \neg c \wedge d \wedge e)$
   b. $\neg(a \rightarrow (b \wedge c))$

3. Convert each of the following Boolean formulas to disjunctive normal form.
   a. $(a \vee b) \wedge (c \vee d)$
   b. $(a \vee b) \rightarrow (c \wedge d)$

4. Use a truth table to show that Boolean resolution is sound.
5. Use resolution to show that the following premises are inconsistent:

   $a \vee \neg b \vee c$, $b \vee \neg d$, $\neg c \vee d$, $b \vee c \vee d$, $\neg a \vee \neg b$, and $\neg d \vee \neg b$.

6. Prove that the conclusion $b \wedge c$ follows from the premises: $a \rightarrow (c \vee d)$, $b \rightarrow a$, $d \rightarrow c$, and b.
   a. Convert the premises and the negation of the conclusion to conjunctive normal form.
   b. Use resolution to prove the conclusion.

7. Consider the Boolean function $f_1(x_1, x_2, x_3) = (x_1 \vee x_2) \wedge x_3$ that we used as an example in B.1.3. Show how f_1 can be converted to an OBDD using the variable ordering $(x_3 < x_1 < x_2)$.

8. In this problem, we consider the importance of standardizing apart the variables that occur in a first-order sentence in clause form. Assume that we are given a single axiom, $\forall x\ (Likes(x, Ice\ cream))$. And we want to prove $\exists x\ (Likes(Mikey, x))$. Use resolution to do this but do not standardize apart the two occurrences of x. What happens?

9. Begin with the following fact from Example B.6.

[1] $\forall x\ ((Roman(x) \wedge Know(x, Marcus)) \rightarrow$
$(Hate(x, Caesar) \vee \forall y\ (\exists z\ (Hate(y, z)) \rightarrow Thinkcrazy(x, y))))$.

Add the following facts.

[2] $\forall x\ ((Roman(x) \wedge Gladiator(x)) \rightarrow Know(x, Marcus))$
[3] $Roman(Claudius)$
[4] $\neg\exists x\ (Thinkcrazy(Claudius, x))$
[5] $\neg\exists x\ (Hate(Claudius, x))$
[6] $Hate(Isaac, Caesar)$
[7] $\forall x\ ((Roman(x) \wedge Famous(x)) \rightarrow (Politician(x) \vee Gladiator(x)))$
[8] $Famous(Isaac)$
[9] $Roman(Isaac)$
[10] $\neg Know(Isaac, Marcus)$

a. Convert each of these facts to clause form.
b. Use resolution and this knowledge base to prove $\neg Gladiator\ (Claudius)$.
c. Use resolution and this knowledge base to prove $Politician(Isaac)$.

10. In M.2.3, we describe a restricted form of first-order resolution called SLD resolution. This problem explores an issue that arises in that discussion. In particular, we wish to show that SLD resolution is not refutation-complete for knowledge bases that are not in Horn clause form. Consider the following knowledge base B (that is not in Horn clause form).

[1] $P(x_1) \vee Q(x_1)$
[2] $\neg P(x_2) \vee Q(x_2)$
[3] $P(x_3) \vee \neg Q(x_3)$
[4] $\neg P(x_4) \vee \neg Q(x_4)$

a. Use resolution to show that B is inconsistent (i.e., show that the empty clause *nil* can be derived).
b. Show that SLD resolution cannot derive *nil* from B.

A P P E N D I X   C

The Theory: Finite State Machines and Regular Languages

In this appendix, we will do, in gory detail, one proof of the correctness of a construction algorithm.

Theorem 5.3 asserts that, given a nondeterministic FSM M that accepts some language L, there exists an equivalent deterministic FSM that accepts L. We proved this theorem by construction. We described the following algorithm:

ndfsmtodfsm(M: NDFSM) =

1. For each state q in K do:

    Compute *eps*(q). /* These values will be used below.

2. $s' = eps(s)$

3. Compute δ':

  3.1. *active-states* $= \{s'\}$. /* We will build a list of all states that are reachable from the start state. Each element of *active-states* is a set of states drawn from K.

  3.2. $\delta' = \varnothing$.

  3.3. While there exists some element Q of *active-states* for which δ' has not yet been computed do:

    For each character c in Σ do:

      new-state $= \varnothing$.

      For each state q in Q do:

        For each state p such that $(q, c, p) \in \Delta$ do:

          new-state = *new-state* $\cup$ *eps*(p).

    Add the transition (Q, c, *new-state*) to δ'.

    If *new-state* $\notin$ *active-states* then insert it into *active-states*.

4. K' = *active-states*.

5. $A' = \{Q \in K' : Q \cap A \neq \varnothing\}$.

From any NDFSM M, *ndfsmtodfsm* constructs a DFSM M', which we claimed is both (1) deterministic and (2) equivalent to M. We prove those claims here.

Proving 1 is trivial. By the definition in step 3 of δ', we are guaranteed that δ' is defined for all reachable elements of K' and all possible input characters. Further, step 3 inserts a single value into δ' for each state, input pair, so M' is deterministic.

Next we must prove 2. In other words, we must prove that M' accepts a string w iff M accepts w. We constructed the transition function δ' of M' so that M' mimics an "all paths" simulation of M. We must now prove that that simulation returns the same result that M would. In particular, δ' defines each individual step of the behavior of M'. We must show that a sequence of steps of M' mimics the corresponding sequence of steps of M and then that the results of the two sequences are identical.

So we begin by proving the following lemma, which asserts that entire sequences of moves of M' behave as they should:

- ***Lemma***: Let w be any string in Σ^*, let p and q be any states in K, and let P be any state in K'. Then:

$$(q, w)|\text{-}_M{}^* (p, \varepsilon) \text{ iff } (eps(q), w)|\text{-}_{M'}{}^* (P, \varepsilon) \text{ and } p \in P.$$

In other words, if the original NDFSM M starts in state q and, after reading the string w, can land in state p (along at least one of its paths), then the new machine M' must behave as follows: When started in the state that corresponds to the set of states the original machine M could get to from q without consuming any input, M' reads the string w and lands in one of its new "set" states that contains p. Furthermore, because of the only-if part of the lemma, M' must end up in a "set" state that contains only states that M could get to from q after reading w and following any available ε-transitions.

To prove the lemma we must show that δ' has been defined so that the individual steps of M', when taken together, do the right thing for an input string w of any length. Since we know what happens one step at a time, we will prove the lemma by induction on $|w|$.

We must first prove that the lemma is true for the base case, where $|w| = 0$ (i.e., $w = \varepsilon$). To do this, we actually have to do two proofs, one to establish it for the *if* part of the lemma, and the other to establish it for the *only if* part:

Base step, if part: Prove that $(q, w)|\text{-}_M{}^* (p, \varepsilon)$ if $(eps(q), w)|\text{-}_{M'}{}^* (P, \varepsilon)$ and $p \in P$. Or, turning it around to make it a little clearer:

$$[(eps(q), w)|\text{-}_{M'}{}^* (P, \varepsilon) \text{ and } p \in P] \rightarrow [(q, w)|\text{-}_M{}^*(p, \varepsilon)].$$

If $|w| = 0$, then, since M' contains no ε-transitions, M' makes no moves. So it must end in the same state it started in, namely $eps(q)$. So $P = eps(q)$. If P contains p, then $p \in eps(q)$. But, given our definition of the function *eps*, that means exactly that, in the original machine M, p is reachable from q just by following ε-transitions, which is exactly what we need to show.

Base step, only if part: We need to show:

$$[(q, w)|\text{-}_M{}^* (p, \varepsilon)] \rightarrow [(eps(q), w)|\text{-}_{M'}{}^* (P, \varepsilon) \text{ and } p \in P].$$

If $|w| = 0$ and the original machine M goes from q to p with only w as input, it must go from q to p following just ε-transitions. In other words $p \in eps(q)$. Now consider the new machine M'. It starts in $eps(q)$, the set state that includes all the states that are reachable from q via ε transitions. Since M' contains no ε-transitions, it will make no moves at all if its input is ε. So it will halt in exactly the same state it started in, namely $eps(q)$. So $P = eps(q)$ and thus contains p. So M' has halted in a set state that includes p, which is exactly what we needed to show.

Next we'll prove that, if the lemma is true for all strings w of length k, where $k \geq 0$, then it is true for all strings of length $k + 1$. Any string of length $k + 1$ must contain at least one character. So we can rewrite any such string as zx, where x is a single character and z is a string of length k. The way that M and M' process z will thus be covered by the induction hypothesis. We use the definition of δ', which specifies how each individual step of M' operates, to show that, assuming that the machines behave identically for the first k characters, they behave identically for the last character also and thus for the entire string of length $k + 1$. Recall the definition of δ':

$$\delta'(Q, c) = \bigcup\{eps(p) : \exists q \in Q\ ((q, c, p) \in \Delta)\}.$$

To prove the lemma, we must show a relationship between the behavior of:

- the computation of the NDFSM M: $(q, w)|\text{-}_M{}^* (p, \varepsilon)$, and
- the computation of the DFSM M': $(eps(q), w)|\text{-}_{M'}{}^* (P, \varepsilon)$ and $p \in P$.

Rewriting w as zx, we have:

- the computation of the NDFSM M: $(q, zx)|\text{-}_M{}^* (p, \varepsilon)$, and
- the computation of the DFSM M': $(eps(q), zx)|\text{-}_{M'}{}^* (P, \varepsilon)$ and $p \in P$.

Breaking each of these computations into two pieces, the processing of z followed by the processing of the single remaining character x, we have:

- the computation of the NDFSM M: $(q, zx)|\text{-}_M{}^* (s_i, x)|\text{-}_M (p, \varepsilon)$, and
- the computation of the DFSM M': $(eps(q), zx)|\text{-}_{M'}{}^* (Q, x)|\text{-}_{M'} (P, \varepsilon)$ and $p \in P$.

In other words, after processing z, M will be in some set of states S, whose elements we'll write as s_i. M' will be in some "set" state that we will call Q. Again, we'll split the proof into two parts:

Induction step, if part: We must prove:

$$[(eps(q), zx)|\text{-}_{M'}{}^* (Q, x)|\text{-}_{M'} (P, \varepsilon) \text{ and } p \in P] \rightarrow [(q, zx)|\text{-}_M{}^* (s_i, x)|\text{-}_M (p, \varepsilon)].$$

If, after reading z, M' is in state Q, we know, from the induction hypothesis, that the original machine M, after reading z, must be in some set of states S and that Q is precisely that set. Now we just have to describe what happens at the last step when the two machines read x. If we have that M', starting in Q and reading x lands in P, then we know, from the definition of δ' above, that P contains precisely the states that M could land in after starting in any state in S and reading x. Thus if $p \in P$, p must be a state that M could land in if started in s_i on reading x.

Induction step, only if part: We must prove:

$$[(q, zx)|\text{-}_M{}^* (s_i, x)|\text{-}_M(p, \varepsilon)] \rightarrow [(eps(q), zx)|\text{-}_{M'}{}^* (Q, x)|\text{-}_{M'} (P, \varepsilon) \text{ and } p \in P].$$

By the induction hypothesis, we know that if M, after processing z, can reach some set of states S, then Q (the state M' is in after processing z) must contain precisely all the states in S. Knowing that, and our definition of δ', we know that from Q, reading x, M' must be in some set state P that contains precisely the states that M can reach starting in any of the states in S, reading x, and then following all ε transitions. So, after consuming w (i.e., zx), M', when started in $eps(q)$, must end up in a state P that contains all and only the states p that M, when started in q, could end up in.

Now that we have proved the lemma, we can complete the proof that M' is equivalent to M. Consider any string $w \in \Sigma^*$.

If $w \in L(M)$ (i.e., the original machine M accepts w) then the following two statements must be true.

1. The original machine M, when started in its start state, can consume w and end up in an accepting state. This must be true given the definition of what it means for a machine to accept a string.
2. $(eps(s), w)|\text{-}_{M'}{}^* (Q, \varepsilon)$ for some Q containing some $a \in A$. In other words, the new machine, when started in its start state, can consume w and end up in one of its accepting states. This follows from the lemma, which is more general and describes a computation from any state to any other. But if we use the lemma and let q equal s (i.e., M begins in its start state) and $p = a$ for some $a \in A$ (i.e., M ends in an accepting state), then we have that the new machine M', when started in its start state, $eps(s)$, will consume w and end in a state that contains a. But if M' does that, then it has ended up in one of its accepting states (by the definition of A' in step 5 of the algorithm). So M' accepts w (by the definition of what it means for a machine to accept a string).

If $w \notin L(M)$ (i.e., the original machine M does not accept w) then the following two statements must be true:

1. The original machine M, when started in its start state, will not be able to end up in an accepting state after reading w. This must be true given the definition of what it means for a machine to accept a string.
2. If $(eps(s), w)|\text{-}_{M'}{}^* (Q, \varepsilon)$, then Q contains no state $a \in A$. In other words, the new machine, when started in its start state, cannot consume w and end up in one of its accepting states. This follows directly from the lemma.

Thus M' accepts precisely the same set of strings that M does.

APPENDIX D

The Theory: Context-Free Languages and PDAs

In this appendix, we will provide the proofs of three claims that we made introduced in Part III, during our discussion of the context-free languages.

D.1 Proof of the Greibach Normal Form Theorem

In this section, we prove the result that we stated as Theorem 11.2, namely that, given a context-free grammar G, there exists a Greibach normal form grammar G' such that $L(G') = L(G) - \{\varepsilon\}$.

Recall that a grammar $G = (V, \Sigma, R, S)$ is in Greibach normal form iff every rule in R has the form:

$$X \rightarrow a\beta, \text{ where } a \in \Sigma \text{ and } \beta \in (V - \Sigma)^*.$$

So the following kinds of rules violate the Greibach normal form constraints:

- Epsilon productions, i.e., productions of the form $A \rightarrow \varepsilon$: Given a grammar G, ε-rules can be removed by the procedure *removeEps* that we defined in Section 11.7.4. The resulting grammar G' will have the property that $L(G') = L(G) - \{\varepsilon\}$.
- Unit productions, i.e., productions of the form $A \rightarrow B$, where B is a single element of $V - \Sigma$: Given a grammar G, unit productions can be removed by the procedure *removeUnits* that we defined in Section 11.8.3. The resulting grammar G' will have the property that $L(G') = L(G)$.
- Productions, such as $X \rightarrow AaB$, whose right-hand sides have terminal symbols in positions other than the left-most: Given a grammar G, these productions can be

removed by the procedure *removeMixed* that we defined in Section 11.8.3. The resulting grammar G' will have the property that $L(G') = L(G)$. Note that *removeMixed* actually goes farther than we need to, since it removes all terminals except those that stand alone on a right-hand side. So it will rewrite the rule $X \rightarrow \text{a}AB$, even though it is in Greibach normal form.

- Productions, such as $X \rightarrow AB$, whose right hand side begins with a nonterminal symbol: We must define a new procedure to handle these productions.

The process of converting a grammar to Chomsky normal form removes all rules in the first three of these classes. So the algorithm that we are about to present for converting a grammar G to Greibach normal form will begin by converting G to Chomsky normal form, using the algorithm that we presented in Section 11.8.3. Note, however, that Greibach normal form allows rules, such as $X \rightarrow \text{a}A$ and $X \rightarrow \text{a}ABCD$, that are not allowed in Chomsky normal form. So there exist more efficient Greibach normal form conversion algorithms than the one we are about to describe.

Our algorithm will also exploit the following operations that we have described elsewhere:

- Rule substitution allows nonterminals to be replaced, in right-hand sides, by the strings that they can derive. Suppose that $G = (V, \Sigma, R, S)$ contains a rule r of the form $X \rightarrow \alpha Y \beta$, where α and β are elements of V^* and $Y \in (V - \Sigma)$. Let $Y \rightarrow \gamma_1 | \gamma_2 | \ldots | \gamma_n$ be all of G's Y rules. And let G' be the result of removing from R the rule r and replacing it by the rules $X \rightarrow \alpha\gamma_1\beta, X \rightarrow \alpha\gamma_2\beta, \ldots, X \rightarrow \alpha\gamma_n\beta$. Then Theorem 11.3 tells us that $L(G') = L(G)$.

- The procedure *removeleftrecursion*, which we defined in Section 15.2.2 as part of our discussion of top-down parsing, removes direct left-recursion and replaces it by right-recursion. So, for example, if the A rules of G are $\{A \rightarrow A\text{b}, A \rightarrow \text{c}\}$, *removeleftrecursion* will replace those rules with the rules $\{A \rightarrow \text{c}A', A \rightarrow \text{c}, A' \rightarrow \text{b}A', A' \rightarrow \text{b}\}$. Note that the right-hand side of every rule that is introduced by *removeleftrecursion* begins with either a terminal symbol or an element of $(V - \Sigma)$. None of these right-hand sides begins with an introduced nonterminal (such as A').

EXAMPLE D.1 Using Substitution to Convert a Very Simple Grammar

To see how these procedures are used, consider the following grammar, which is in Chomsky normal form but not in Greibach normal form.

$$S \rightarrow AB$$
$$A \rightarrow XY \mid \text{c}$$
$$X \rightarrow \text{a}$$
$$Y \rightarrow \text{b}$$
$$B \rightarrow \text{c}$$

To convert this grammar to Greibach normal form, we:

- use rule substitution to replace the rule $S \rightarrow AB$ with the rules $S \rightarrow XYB$ and $S \rightarrow \mathtt{c}B$ (since A can derive XY and c). The second of these new rules is in Greibach normal form.
- use rule substitution on the first of the new rules and replace it with the rule $S \rightarrow \mathtt{a}YB$ (since X can derive a). This new rule is in Greibach normal form.
- use rule substitution to replace the rule $A \rightarrow XY$ with the rule $A \rightarrow \mathtt{a}Y$ (since X can derive a). This new rule is in Greibach normal form.

Since the remaining three rules are already in Greibach normal form, the process ends with the grammar containing the rules $\{S \rightarrow \mathtt{a}YB, S \rightarrow \mathtt{c}B, A \rightarrow \mathtt{a}Y, X \rightarrow \mathtt{a}, Y \rightarrow \mathtt{b}, B \rightarrow \mathtt{c}\}$.

EXAMPLE D.2 Dealing with Left Recursion

But now consider the following grammar.

$$S \rightarrow SA \mid BA$$
$$A \rightarrow \mathtt{a}$$
$$B \rightarrow \mathtt{b}$$

The first rule is left-recursive. If we apply rule substitution to it, we get two new rules, $S \rightarrow SSA$ and $S \rightarrow BAA$. But now we still have a rule whose left-hand side begins with S. We can apply rule substitution again, but no matter how many times we apply it, we will get a new rule whose left-hand side begins with S. To solve this problem, we must exploit *removeleftrecursion* to eliminate direct left-recursion before we apply rule substitution. Doing that, we get the following.

$$S \rightarrow BAS' \mid BA$$
$$A \rightarrow \mathtt{a}$$
$$B \rightarrow \mathtt{b}$$
$$S' \rightarrow AS' \mid A$$

Now, to convert this grammar to Greibach normal form, we:

- use rule substitution to replace the rule $S \rightarrow BAS'$ with the rule $S \rightarrow \mathtt{b}AS'$. This new rule is in Greibach normal form.
- use rule substitution to replace the rule $S \rightarrow BA$ with the rule $S \rightarrow \mathtt{b}A$. This new rule is in Greibach normal form.

EXAMPLE D.2 *(Continued)*

- use rule substitution to replace the rule $S' \rightarrow AS'$ with the rule $S' \rightarrow \mathrm{a}S'$. This new rule is in Greibach normal form.
- use rule substitution to replace the rule $S' \rightarrow A$ with the rule $S' \rightarrow \mathrm{a}$. This new rule is in Greibach normal form.

The remaining two rules are already in Greibach normal form, so the process terminates.

More realistic grammars typically contain more than a few nonterminals and those nonterminals may derive each other in arbitrary ways. To handle such grammars, we need a systematic way to organize the substitutions that will be performed.

So the conversion algorithm we will exploit is the following. It will return a new grammar it calls G_G.

converttoGreibach(G: CFG in Chomsky normal form) =

1. Choose an ordering of the nonterminals in G. Any ordering will work as long as the start symbol comes first. Let G_G initially be G.
2. Rewrite the rules of G_G so that each rule whose left-hand sides is one of G's original nonterminals is in one of the following two forms:
   - $X \rightarrow a\beta$, where $a \in \Sigma$ and $\beta \in (V - \Sigma)^*$ (in other words, the rule is in Greibach normal form), or
   - $X \rightarrow Y\beta$, where $Y \in V - \Sigma$ and Y occurs after X in the ordering defined in step 1.

   Call the constraint we have just described the ***rule-order constraint***. Note that, if any of G's rules are directly left-recursive, this step will add some new rules whose left-hand sides are new nonterminals. We will not require that these new rules satisfy the rule-order constraint, since the new nonterminals are unnumbered. But note that no newly introduced nonterminal will occur as the first symbol in any rule's right-hand side.
3. Consider each of G's original nonterminals, starting with the highest numbered one, and working backwards. For each such nonterminal N, perform substitutions on the rules in G_G so that the right-hand sides of all N rules begin with a terminal symbol.
4. Consider each nonterminal N that was introduced by *removeleftrecursion*. Perform substitutions on the rules of G_G so that the right hand sides of all N rules start with a terminal symbol.
5. Return G_G.

The grammar G_G that *converttoGreibach* returns will be in Greibach normal form. And $L(G_G) = L(G)$. We'll now describe how to perform steps 2, 3, and 4. Define A_k to be the kth nonterminal, as defined in step 1.

Step 2: We will first rewrite all the A_1 rules so that they meet the rule-order constraint. Then we'll do the same for the A_2 rules, and so forth. For each k, as we begin to transform the rules for A_k, we assume that all rules for nonterminals numbered from 1 to $k - 1$ already satisfy the rule-order constraint.

Any A_k rule whose right-hand side starts with a terminal symbol already satisfies the constraint and can be ignored. But we must consider all A_k rules of the form:

$$A_k \rightarrow A_j\beta.$$

Group those rules into the following three cases and consider them in this order:

i. $j > k$: No action is required.

ii. $j < k$: Replace the rule $A_k \rightarrow A_j\beta$ by the set of rules that results from substituting, for A_j, the right-hand sides of all the A_j rules. Since all A_j rules have already been transformed so that they satisfy the rule-order constraint, the right-hand sides of all A_j rules start with either terminal symbols or nonterminals numbered greater than j. They may still be numbered less than k, however. If any of them are, repeat the substitution process. Since the indices must increase by at least 1 each time, it will be necessary to do this no more than $k - 1$ times.

iii. $j = k$: All such rules are of the form: $A_k \rightarrow A_k\beta$. They are directly left-recursive. Use *removeleftrecursion* to remove the left-recursion from all A_k rules. Recall that *removeleftrecursion* will create a new set of A_k rules. The right-hand side of each such rule will begin with a string that corresponds to the right-hand side of some nonrecursive A_k rule. But, as a result of handling all the rules in case ii, above, all of those right-hand sides must start with either a terminal symbol or a non-terminal symbol numbered above k. So all A_k rules now satisfy the rule-order constraint.

EXAMPLE D.3 Performing Step 2 of the Conversion Algorithm

We'll begin with the following grammar in Chomsky normal form.

$$S \rightarrow SB \mid AB \mid \mathsf{d}$$
$$A \rightarrow SA \mid \mathsf{a}$$
$$B \rightarrow SA$$

We'll order the three nonterminals S, A, B. So first we must rewrite the three S rules so that they satisfy the rule-order constraint. The second and third of them already do. But we must rewrite the first one, which is left-recursive. Using *removeleftrecursion*, we get the new grammar.

$$S \rightarrow AB \mid ABS' \mid \mathsf{d} \mid \mathsf{d}S'$$
$$A \rightarrow SA \mid \mathsf{a}$$
$$B \rightarrow SA$$
$$S' \rightarrow B \mid BS'$$

EXAMPLE D.3 *(Continued)*

Now we consider the A rules. The second one starts with a terminal symbol, but the first one violates the rule-order constraint since A is numbered 2 and S is numbered 1. We use rule substitution and replace it with four new rules, one for each S rule. That produces the following set of A rules.

$$A \rightarrow ABA \mid ABS'A \mid \mathrm{d}A \mid \mathrm{d}S'A \mid \mathrm{a}$$

But now the first two of these are left-recursive. So we use *removeleftrecursion* and get the following set of A and A' rules. The A rules now satisfy the rule-order constraint.

$$A \rightarrow \mathrm{d}A \mid \mathrm{d}AA' \mid \mathrm{d}S'A \mid \mathrm{d}S'AA' \mid \mathrm{a} \mid \mathrm{a}A'$$

$$A' \rightarrow BA \mid BAA' \mid BS'A \mid BS'AA'$$

Finally, we consider the single B rule, $B \rightarrow SA$. It fails to satisfy the rule-order constraint since B is numbered 3 and S is numbered 1. We use rule substitution and replace it with four new rules, one for each S rule. That produces the following set of B rules.

$$B \rightarrow ABA \mid ABS'A \mid \mathrm{d}A \mid \mathrm{d}S'A$$

The first two of these fail to satisfy the rule-order constraint since B is numbered 3 and A is numbered 2. So we use rule substitution again. The first B rule is replaced by the rules:

$$B \rightarrow \mathrm{d}ABA \mid \mathrm{d}AA'BA \mid \mathrm{d}S'ABA \mid \mathrm{d}S'AA'BA \mid \mathrm{a}BA \mid \mathrm{a}A'BA.$$

And the second B rule is replaced by the rules:

$$B \rightarrow \mathrm{d}ABS'A \mid \mathrm{d}AA'BS'A \mid \mathrm{d}S'ABS'A \mid \mathrm{d}S'AA'BS'A \mid \mathrm{a}BS'A \mid \mathrm{a}A'BS'A.$$

At this point, the complete grammar is the following (where the B rules are broken up just for clarity).

$$S \rightarrow AB \mid ABS' \mid \mathrm{d} \mid \mathrm{d}S'$$

$$A \rightarrow \mathrm{d}A \mid \mathrm{d}AA' \mid \mathrm{d}S'A \mid \mathrm{d}S'AA' \mid \mathrm{a} \mid \mathrm{a}A'$$

$$B \rightarrow \mathrm{d}A \mid \mathrm{d}S'A$$

$$B \rightarrow \mathrm{d}ABA \mid \mathrm{d}AA'BA \mid \mathrm{d}S'ABA \mid \mathrm{d}S'AA'BA \mid \mathrm{a}BA \mid \mathrm{a}A'BA$$

$$B \rightarrow \mathrm{d}ABS'A \mid \mathrm{d}AA'BS'A \mid \mathrm{d}S'ABS'A \mid \mathrm{d}\,S'AA'BS'A \mid \mathrm{a}BS'A \mid \mathrm{a}A'BS'A$$

$$S' \rightarrow B \mid BS'$$

$$A' \rightarrow BA \mid BAA' \mid BS'A \mid BS'AA'$$

This grammar satisfies the rule-order constraint. But it is substantially larger and messier than the original grammar was. This is typical of what happens when a grammar is converted to Greibach normal form.

At the end of step 2, all rules whose left-hand sides contain any of G's original nonterminals satisfy the rule-order constraint. Note also that step 2 preserves the three properties initially established by conversion to Chomsky normal form: There are no ε-rules, there are no unit productions, and, in every right-hand side, all symbols after the first must be nonterminals.

Step 3: Let n be the number of original nonterminals in G. Then A_n is the last of them (given the order from step 1). The right-hand sides of all A_n rules must begin with a terminal symbol. This must be true since there are no original nonterminals numbered higher than n. Now consider the A_{n-1} rules. Their right-hand sides must begin with a terminal symbol or A_n. Use substitution to replace all the rules whose right-hand sides start with A_n. After doing that, the right hand sides of all the A_{n-1} will all start with terminal symbols. Continue working backwards until the A_1 rules have been processed in this way. This step also preserves the three properties initially established by conversion to Chomsky normal form. So, at the end of this step, all rules whose left-hand sides contain any of G's original nonterminals are in Greibach normal form.

Step 4: The *removeleftrecursion* procedure introduces new nonterminal symbols and new rules with those symbols as their left-hand sides. So there will be new rules like $S' \rightarrow AS' | A$. The new nonterminals are independent of each other, so the right-hand sides of all of their rules consist only of terminals and original nonterminals. If r is one of those rules and r is not already in Greibach normal form then it is $N \rightarrow A_j\beta$ for some original nonterminal A_j. As a result of step 3, all A_j rules are already in Greibach normal form. So a single substitution for A_j will replace r by a set of N rules in Greibach normal form. This step preserves all of the properties that were true at the end of step 3. So, at the end of this step, G_G is in Greibach normal form.

EXAMPLE D.4 Performing Steps 3 and 4 of the Conversion

We'll continue with the grammar from Example D.3. After step 2, it was as follows.

$S \rightarrow AB \mid ABS' \mid \mathrm{d} \mid \mathrm{d}S'$

$A \rightarrow \mathrm{d}A \mid \mathrm{d}AA' \mid \mathrm{d}S'A \mid \mathrm{d}S'AA' \mid \mathrm{a} \mid \mathrm{a}A'$

$B \rightarrow \mathrm{d}A \mid \mathrm{d}S'A$

$B \rightarrow \mathrm{d}ABA \mid \mathrm{d}AA'BA \mid \mathrm{d}S'ABA \mid \mathrm{d}S'AA'BA \mid \mathrm{a}BA \mid \mathrm{a}A'BA$

$B \rightarrow \mathrm{d}ABS'A \mid \mathrm{d}AA'BS'A \mid \mathrm{d}S'ABS'A \mid \mathrm{d}S'AA'BS'A \mid \mathrm{a}BS'A \mid \mathrm{a}A'BS'A$

$S' \rightarrow B \mid BS'$

$A' \rightarrow BA \mid BAA' \mid BS'A \mid BS'AA'$

EXAMPLE D.4 *(Continued)*

Step 3: All the B rules must be in Greibach normal form. It turns out that, in this example, the A rules are also. But then we must consider the S rules. The first two of them have right-hand sides that do not begin with terminal symbols. So they must be rewritten using substitution. After doing that, the complete set of S rules is as follows.

$$S \rightarrow \text{d}AB \mid \text{d}AA'B \mid \text{d}S'AB \mid \text{d}S'AA'B \mid \text{a}B \mid \text{a}A'B$$

$$S \rightarrow \text{d}ABS' \mid \text{d}AA'BS' \mid \text{d}S'ABS' \mid \text{d}S'AA'BS' \mid \text{a}BS' \mid \text{a}A'BS'$$

$$S \rightarrow \text{d} \mid \text{d}S'$$

Step 4: We must use substitution on both of the S' rules. The two of them will be replaced by the following set of S' rules.

$$S' \rightarrow \text{d}A \mid \text{d}S'A$$

$$S' \rightarrow \text{d}ABA \mid \text{d}AA'BA \mid \text{d}S'ABA \mid \text{d}S'AA'BA \mid \text{a}BA \mid \text{a}A'BA$$

$$S' \rightarrow \text{d}ABS'A \mid \text{d}AA'BS'A \mid \text{d}S'ABS'A \mid \text{d}S'AA'BS'A \mid \text{a}BS'A \mid \text{a}A'BS'A$$

$$S' \rightarrow \text{d}AS' \mid \text{d}S'AS'$$

$$S' \rightarrow \text{d}ABAS' \mid \text{d}AA'BAS' \mid \text{d}S'ABAS' \mid \text{d}S'AA'BAS' \mid \text{a}BAS' \mid \text{a}A'BAS'$$

$$S' \rightarrow \text{d}ABS'AS' \mid \text{d}AA'BS'AS' \mid \text{d}S'ABS'AS' \mid \text{d}S'AA'BS'AS' \mid \text{a}BS'AS' \mid \text{a}A'BS'AS'$$

And similarly for the A' rules. We'll skip writing them all out. There are 14 (the number of B rules) $\cdot$ 4 (the number of A' rules) = 56 of them.

So the original, 6-rule grammar in Chomsky normal form becomes a 118-rule grammar in Greibach normal form.

THEOREM D.1 Greibach Normal Form Grammar

Theorem: Given a context-free grammar G, there exists a Greibach normal form grammar G_G such that $L(G_G) = L(G) - \{\varepsilon\}$.

Proof: The proof is by construction, using the algorithm *converttoGreibach* described above.

D.2 Proof that the Deterministic Context-Free Languages are Closed Under Complement

In this section, we prove the result that we stated as Theorem 13.10.

THEOREM D.2 Closure Under Complement

Theorem: The deterministic context-free languages are closed under complement.

Proof: The proof is by construction. The construction exploits techniques that we used to prove several other properties of the context-free languages, but now we must be careful to preserve the property that the PDA we are working with is deterministic.

If L is a deterministic context-free language over the alphabet Σ, then $L\$$ is accepted by some deterministic PDA $M = (K, \Sigma \cup \{\$\}, \Gamma, \Delta, s, A)$. We need to describe an algorithm that constructs a new deterministic PDA that accepts $(\neg L)\$$. The algorithm will proceed in two main steps:

1. Convert M to an equivalent PDA M'''' that is in a constrained form that we will call ***deterministic normal form***.
2. From M'''', build $M\#$ to accept $(\neg L)\$$.

The design of deterministic normal form is motivated by the observation that a deterministic PDA may fail to accept an input string w for any one of several reasons.

1. Its computation ends before it finishes reading w.
2. Its computation ends in an accepting state but the stack is not empty.
3. Its computation loops forever, following ε-transitions, without ever halting in either an accepting or a nonaccepting state.
4. Its computation ends in a nonaccepting state.

If we attempt to build $M\#$ by simply swapping the accepting and nonaccepting states of M, we will build a machine that correctly fails to accept every string that M would have accepted (i.e., every string in $L\$$). But it cannot be guaranteed to accept every string in $(\neg L)\$$. To do that, we must also address issues 1 – 3 above. Converting M to deterministic normal form will solve those problems since any deterministic PDA in restricted normal form will, on any input $w\$$:

- read all of w,
- empty its stack, and
- halt.

One additional problem is that we don't want to accept $\neg L(M)$. That includes strings that do not end in \$. We must accept only strings that do end in \$ and that are in $(\neg L)\$$.

Given a deterministic PDA M, we convert it into deterministic normal form in a sequence of steps, being careful, at each step, not to introduce nondeterminism.

In the first step, we will create M', which will contain two complete copies of M's states and transitions. M' will operate in the first copy until it reads the end-of-input symbol \$. After that, it will operate in the second copy. Call the states in the first copy the pre\$ states. Call the states in the second copy the post\$ states. If q is a pre\$ state, call the corresponding post\$ state q'. If q is an accepting state, then add q' to the set of accepting states and remove q from the set. If M contains the transition $((q, \$, \alpha), (p, \beta))$ and q is a pre\$ state, remove that transition and replace it with the transition $((q, \$, \alpha), (p', \beta))$. Now view M' as a directed graph but ignore the actual labels on the transitions. If there are states that are unreachable from the start state, delete them. If M was deterministic, then M' also is and $L(M') = L(M)$.

If M' ever follows a transition from a post\$ state that reads any input then it must not accept. So we can remove all such transitions without changing the language that is accepted. Remove them. Now all transitions out of post\$ states read no input. So they are one of the following:

- stack-ε-transitions: $((p, \varepsilon, \varepsilon), (q, \gamma))$ (nothing is popped), or
- stack-productive transitions: $((p, \varepsilon, \alpha), (q, \gamma))$, where $\alpha \in \Gamma^+$ (something is popped).

Next we remove all stack-ε-transitions from post\$ states. To construct an algorithm to do this, observe:

- since M' is deterministic, if it contains the stack-ε-transition $((p, \varepsilon, \varepsilon), (q, \gamma))$ then it contains no other transitions from p.
- if $((p, \varepsilon, \varepsilon), (q, \gamma))$ ever plays a role in causing M' to accept a string then there must be a path from q that eventually reaches an accepting state and clears the stack.

So we can eliminate the stack-ε-transition $((p, \varepsilon, \varepsilon), (q, \gamma))$ as follows: First, if q is accepting, make p accepting. Next, delete $((p, \varepsilon, \varepsilon), (q, \gamma))$ and replace it by transitions that go directly from p to wherever q could go, skipping the move to q. So consider every transition $((q, \varepsilon, \alpha), (r, \beta))$. If $\alpha = \varepsilon$, then add the transition $((p, \varepsilon, \varepsilon), (r, \beta\gamma))$. Otherwise, if $\gamma = \varepsilon$ then add the transition $((p, \varepsilon, \alpha), (r, \beta))$. Otherwise, suppose that γ is $\gamma_1\gamma_2 \ldots \gamma_n$. If $\alpha = \gamma_1\gamma_2 \ldots \gamma_k$ for some $k \leq n$, then add the transition $((p, \varepsilon, \varepsilon), (r, \beta\gamma_{k+1} \ldots \gamma_n))$. In other words, don't bother to push the part that the second transition would have popped off. If $\alpha = \gamma\eta$ for some $\eta \neq \varepsilon$, then add the transition $((p, \varepsilon, \eta), (r, \beta))$. In other words, skip pushing γ and then popping it. Just pop the rest of what the second transition would pop. If any new stack-ε-transitions from p have been created, then replace them as just described except that, if the process creates a transition of the form $((p, \varepsilon, \varepsilon), (p, \gamma'))$, where γ' is not shorter than γ from the first transition that was removed, then the new transition is not describing a path that can ever lead to M' clearing its stack and accepting. So simply delete it. Continue until all stack-ε-transitions have been removed. With a bound on the length of the string that gets pushed when a new transition is created, this process must eventually halt. Since there was no nondeterminism out of q, there won't be nondeterminism out of p when p simply copies the transitions from q.

At this point, M' has the following properties.

- Every transition out of a post\$ state pops at least once character off the stack.
- No transition out of a post\$ state reads any input.
- All accepting states are post\$ states.

Next, we consider problem 2 as described above (M doesn't accept because its stack isn't empty). That problem would go away if our definition of acceptance were by accepting state alone, rather than by accepting state and empty stack.

Recall that, in Example 12.14, we presented an algorithm that constructs, from any PDA that accepts by accepting state and empty stack, an equivalent one that accepts by accepting state alone. The resulting PDA has a new start state s' that pushes a new symbol # onto the stack. It also has a single accepting state, a new state q_a, which is reachable only when the original machine would have reached an accepting state and had an empty stack. Our next step will be to apply that algorithm to M' to produce M''. Once we've done that, we can later make q_a nonaccepting and thus reject every string in $L\$$. At the same time, we are assured that doing so will not cause M'' to reject any string that was not in $L\$$, since no such string can drive M'' to q_a. The only issue we must confront is that the algorithm of Example 12.14 may convert a deterministic PDA into a nondeterministic one because transitions into q_a may compete with other transitions that were already present (as one does in the example we considered when we presented the algorithm). But that cannot happen in the machine M'' that results when the algorithm is applied to M'. Each new transition into the new state q_a has the form $((a, \varepsilon, \#), (q_a, \varepsilon))$, where a is a post\$ state. No transition in M' pops # since # is not in its stack alphabet. And there are no stack-ε-transitions from a post\$ state in M' (because all such transitions have already been eliminated). So we can guarantee that M'' is equivalent to M' and is still deterministic. We also know that, whenever M'' is in any state except the new start state s' and the new accepting state q_a, there is exactly one # on the stack and it is on the bottom.

Note that we have not switched PDA definitions. We will still accept by accepting state and empty stack. So it will be necessary later to make sure that the final machine that we build can empty its stack on any input it needs to accept.

Next we consider problem 1 (M halts without reading all its input). We must complete M'', by adding a dead state, in order to guarantee that, from any configuration in which there may be unread input characters (i.e., any configuration with a pre\$ state), M'' has a move that it can make. The problem is that it is not sufficient simply to assure that there is a move for every input character. Consider for example a PDA $M\#$, where $\Sigma = \{\mathtt{a}, \mathtt{b}\}$, $\Gamma = \{\#, 1, 2\}$, and the transitions from state q are $((q, \mathtt{a}, 1), (p, 2))$ and $((q, \mathtt{b}, 1), (r, 2))$. If $M\#$ is in state q and the character on the top of the stack is 2, $M\#$ cannot move.

We can't solve this problem just by requiring that there be some element of Δ for each (input character, stack character) pair because we allow arbitrarily long strings to be popped from the stack on a single move. For example, again let $\Sigma = \{\mathtt{a}, \mathtt{b}\}$ and $\Gamma = \{\#, 1, 2\}$. Suppose that the transitions from state q are:

$$((q, \mathtt{a}, 12), (p, 2)),$$

$$((q, \mathtt{a}, 21), (p, 2)),$$

$$((q, \mathtt{b}, 122), (r, 2)), \text{and}$$

$$((q, \mathtt{b}, 211), (r, 2)).$$

If the top of the stack is 22 and the next input character is a or b, $M\#$ cannot move.

So our next step is to convert M'' into a new machine M''' with the following property: Every transition, except the one from the start state s', pops exactly one symbol. Note that this is possible because, in every state except s' and the one accepting state q_a, # is on the bottom of the stack. And there are no transitions out of q_a. So there always exists at least one symbol that can be popped. To build M''' we use a slight variant of the technique we used in the algorithm *convertPDAtorestriced* that we described in Section 12.3. We replace any transition that popped nothing with a set of transitions, one for each element of Γ''. These transitions pop a symbol and then push it back on. And we replace any transition that popped more than one symbol with a sequence of transitions that pops them one at a time. To guarantee that no nondeterminism is introduced when we do this, it is necessary to be careful when creating new states as described in step 6. If, from some state q, there is more than one transition that pops the same initial sequence of characters, all of them must stay on the same path until they actually pop something different or read a different input character.

Next we add two new dead states, d and d'. The new dead state d will contain strings that do not end in \$. The new dead state d' will contain strings that do end in \$. For every character $c \in \Sigma$, add the transition $((d, c, \varepsilon), (d, \varepsilon))$. So, if M''' ever goes to d, it can loop in d and finish reading its input up until it hits \$. Then add the transition $((d, \$, \varepsilon), (d', \varepsilon))$. So M''' moves from d to d' when it encounters \$. Finally, we must make sure that, from d', M''' can clear its stack. So, for every symbol γ in Γ, add the transition $((d', \varepsilon, \gamma), (d', \varepsilon))$. After adding those transitions, every symbol except # can be removed. Note that none of these new transitions compete with each other, so M''' is still deterministic.

Now we can modify M''' so that it always has a move to make from any pre\$ state. To do this, we add transitions into the new dead states. M''' always has a move from s', so we don't have to consider it further. In order to guarantee that M''' will always be able to make a move from any other pre\$ state q, it must be the case that, for every (q, c, γ), where q is a pre\$ state, $c \in \Sigma \cup \{\$\}$, and $\gamma \in \Gamma'''$, there exists some (p, α) such that either:

- $\Delta_{M'''}$ contains the ε-transition $((q, \varepsilon, \gamma), (p, \alpha))$, or
- $\Delta_{M'''}$ contains the transition $((q, c, \gamma), (p, \alpha))$.

Since M''' is deterministic, it is not possible for $\Delta_{M'''}$ to contain both those transitions. Now consider any stack symbol γ and state q. If M''' contains an ε-transition $((q, \varepsilon, \gamma), (p, \alpha))$, no others from q that pop γ are required. If it does not, then there must be one for each character c in $\Sigma \cup \{\$\}$. If there is no transition $((q, \$, \gamma), (p, \alpha))$, then we add to M''' the transition $((q, \$, \gamma), (d', \varepsilon))$. If, for any other character c, there is no transition $((q, c, \gamma), (p, \alpha))$, then we add to M''' the transition $((q, c, \gamma), (d, \varepsilon))$.

At this point, we know that, until it has read all its input, M''' will always have a move to make. And we know that any string that drives it to d' is in $(\neg L)\$$. So, in the complement machine we are eventually trying to build, d' should accept any strings it sees. To do that, it must first clear the stack.

Next we make sure that, from every post\$ state except q_a, M''' always has a move it can make. There is no input to be read, so we must assure that, for every post\$ state q (except q_a) and every stack symbol $\gamma \in \Gamma$, there is a move. When M would have died, M''' needs to move to a state that knows that \$ has been read and that can clear the stack (so that its complement will eventually be able to accept). That state is d'. So, if (q, ε, γ) is a triple for which no move is defined, add the transition $((q, \varepsilon, \gamma), (d', \varepsilon))$.

Next, we must make sure that M''' never gets into a loop that is not making progress toward at least one of the two things that must occur before it can accept: emptying the stack and consuming the input. M''' determines its next move by considering only its current state, the top stack symbol and the current input character. Any transition that reads an input character makes progress, so we need only worry about those that do not. Suppose that some triple (q, ε, γ) matches against M''''s current configuration. If that triple ever matches again and no progress has been made, then none will ever be made because M''', since it is deterministic, will simply do the same thing the second time. So we must find all the triples with the property that, when they match M''''s configuration, no progress occurs. Call these triples ***dead triples***. We now build a new machine M'''' which is identical to M''' except that all dead triples that originate in a pre\$ state will drive M'''' to d and all dead triples that originate in a post\$ state will drive M'''' to d'. So $M'''' = M'''$, except:

- if (q, ε, γ) is a dead triple and q is a pre\$ state then delete any transition $((q, \varepsilon, \gamma), (p, \beta))$ and replace it by $((q, \varepsilon, \gamma), (d, \varepsilon))$.
- if (q, ε, γ) is a dead triple and q is a post\$ state then delete any transition $((q, \varepsilon, \gamma), (p, \beta))$ and replace it by $((q, \varepsilon, \gamma), (d', \varepsilon))$.

Now M'''' has the following properties.

1. On input w\$, if M's computation would have ended before all of w\$ were read, M'''' will be able to reach state d' and have the stack empty except for #.
2. On input w\$, if M's computation would have looped forever, following ε-transitions, without ever halting in either an accepting or a nonaccepting state, M'''' will be able to reach state d' and have the stack empty except for #.
3. On input w\$, iff M's computation would have accepted, M'''' will be in state q_a and its stack will be empty.
4. On any input that does not end in \$, M'''' will be in some pre\$ state.

Our final step will be to construct M# that accepts $(\neg L)$\$. We'll do that by starting with M'''', making q_a nonaccepting, and creating a path by which d' can pop the remaining # and go to an accepting state. But, before we can do that, we must consider two remaining cases.

- On input w\$, M would have finished reading w\$ but not emptied its stack.
- On input w\$, M would have finished reading w\$ and landed in a nonaccepting state.

We need to make sure that, in both of those cases, our final machine will be able to accept. Note that we only want to accept after reading \$, so we need only worry about what M'''' should do once it has reached some post\$ state. We first guarantee that M'''' can clear its stack except for #. We do that as follows: For every post\$ state q in M'''' (except q_a) and every symbol c in Γ, if M'''' does not contain a transition for the triple (q, ε, c), add the transition $((q, \varepsilon, c), (d', \varepsilon))$. (If M'''' already contains a transition for the triple (q, ε, c) then that transition must be on a path to clearing the stack or it would already have been eliminated.)

It's now the case that every string of the form w\$, where $w \in \Sigma^*$, will drive M'''' to some post\$ state and either the state is q_a, in which case the stack will be empty, or the state is something else, in which case the stack contains exactly #. So our next step is to add a new state d''. From every post\$ state q except q_a and any states from which there is a transition into q_a, add the transition $((q, \varepsilon, \#), (d'', \varepsilon))$. Since there were no transitions on # from any of those states, the resulting machine is still deterministic.

At this point, M'''' is in deterministic normal form. We can now define:

convertPDAtodetnormalform(M: deterministic PDA) =

1. Return M'''', constructed as described previously.

Note that M'''' still accepts L\$ and it is deterministic. It is also in restricted normal form (as defined in Section 12.3.2).

All that remains is to build $M\#$ to accept $(\neg L)$\$. Let $M\# = M''''$ except that d'' will be the only accepting state. There are no transitions out of d'', so there is never competition between accepting and taking some transition. All and only strings of the form w\$, where $w \in \Sigma^*$ and w\$ was not accepted by M will drive $M\#$ to d'' with an empty stack. So $M\#$ accepts $(\neg L)$\$ and it is deterministic.

D.3 Proof of Parikh's Theorem

The background for Parikh's Theorem and the definitions of ψ and Ψ are given in Section 13.7.

THEOREM D.3 Parikh's Theorem

Theorem: Every context-free language is letter-equivalent to some regular language.

Proof: We will break the proof into two parts. We will first show that, for every context-free language L, $\Psi(L)$ is semilinear. Then we will show that if $\Psi(L)$ is semilinear then L is letter-equivalent to some regular language.

For purposes of the following discussion, define:

- The sum of two vectors v_1 and v_2, written $v_1 + v_2$, to be the pairwise sum of their elements. So $(1, 2) + (5, 7) = (6, 9)$.
- The product of an integer n and a vector $v = (i_1, i_2, \ldots i_k)$, written nv, to be $(ni_1, ni_2, \ldots ni_k)$. So $4(1, 2) = (4, 8)$.

A set V of integer vectors of the form $(i_1, i_2, \ldots i_k)$ is ***linear*** iff there exists a finite basis set B and a second finite set C of vectors $c_1, c_2, \ldots$, such that:

$V = \{v: (v = b + n_1c_1 + n_2c_2 + \ \ldots \ + n_{|C|}c_{|C|}),$ where $n_1, n_2, \ldots, n_{|C|}$ are integers, $b \in B$, and $c_1, c_2, \ldots, c_{|C|} \in C$.

For example:

- $\{(2i, i) : 0 \leq i\} = \{(0, 0), (2, 1), (4, 2), (6, 3), \ldots\}$ is linear: $B = \{(0, 0)\}$ and $C = \{(2, 1)\}$.
- $\{(i, j) : 0 \leq i \leq j\} = \{(0, 0), (0, 1), (0, 2), (1, 3), \ldots, (3, 8), \ldots\}$ is linear: $B = \{(0, 0)\}$ and $C = \{(0, 1), (1, 1)\}$.

A set V of integer vectors of the form $(i_1, i_2, \ldots i_k)$ is ***semilinear*** iff it is the finite union of linear sets. For example, $V = \{(i, j) : i < j \text{ or } j < i\}$ is semilinear because $V = V_1 \cup V_2$, where:

- $V_1 = \{(0, 1), (0, 2), \ldots, (1, 2), (1, 3), \ldots, (3, 8), \ldots\}$ is linear: $B = \{(0, 1)\}$ and $C = \{(0, 1), (1, 1)\}$, and
- $V_2 = \{(1, 0), (2, 0), \ldots, (2, 1), (3, 1), \ldots, (8, 3), \ldots\}$ is linear: $B = \{(1, 0)\}$ and $C = \{(1, 0), (1, 1)\}$.

The core of the proof of Parikh's Theorem is a proof of the claim that if a language L is context-free, then $\Psi(L)$ is semilinear. In fact, sometimes that claim, which we prove next, is called Parikh's Theorem.

Let L be an arbitrary context-free language. Then L is defined by some context-free grammar $G = (V, \Sigma, R, S)$. Let $n = |V - \Sigma|$ (i.e., the number of nonterminals in G) and let b be the branching factor of G (i.e., the length of the longest right hand side of any rule in R). Every string in L has at least one parse tree that can be generated by G. For each such string, choose one of its "smallest" parse trees. In other words, choose one such that there is no other one with fewer nodes. Let T be the set of all such chosen trees. So T contains one smallest tree for each element of L. For any parse tree t, let *yield*(t) be the string that is yield of t.

Let t be an arbitrary element of T. Then either:

- The tree t contains no paths that contain repeated nonterminals. By the same argument we used in the proof of the Pumping Theorem, the maximum length of the yield of t is b^n. Call the subset of T that contains all such trees *Short*. *Short* contains a finite number of elements (because there is a bound on the length of the yields and each yield may correspond to only one tree).
- The tree t contains at least one path that contains at least one repeated nonterminal, as shown in Figure D.1. As we did in the proof of the Pumping Theorem, we can choose one such path and find the first repeated nonterminal, coming up from the bottom, along that path. Call the subtree rooted at the upper instance [1] and the subtree rooted at the lower instance [2]. We can excise the subtree rooted at [1] and replace it by the subtree rooted at [2]. Call the resulting

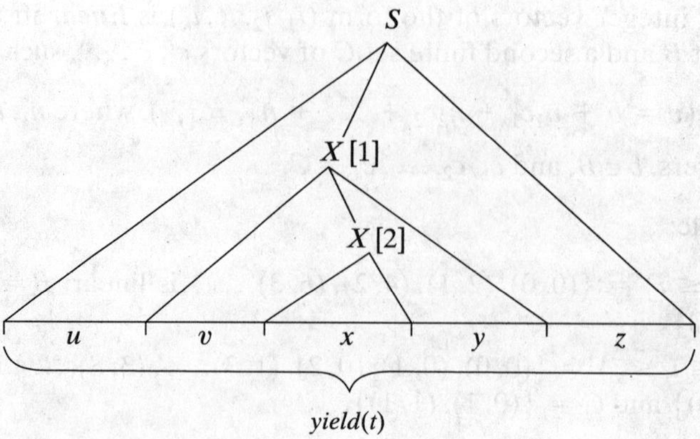

FIGURE D.1 A parse tree whose height is greater than n.

tree t'. There exist values for u, v, x, y, and z such that $yield(t) = uvxyz$, $yield(t') = uxz$, $vy \neq \varepsilon$, $|vxy| \leq b^{n+1}$, $|uxz| < |uvxyz|$, and uxz is also in L. If t' still contains any paths that contain any repeated nonterminals, then another vy can be pumped out to yield yet another shorter string in L, and so forth until a string whose parse tree is in *Short* is produced.

Let t be an arbitrary element of *Short*. We will define $produce(t)$ to be the smallest set of strings that includes $yield(t)$ plus all the longer strings in L that pump down to $yield(t)$. Or think of it as the smallest set that includes $yield(t)$ and all the longer strings that can be generated by pumping into t.

Since there is a bound on $|vy|$, the number of distinct values for vy is finite. For any tree t in *Short*, define $pumps(t)$ to be the set of vy strings that can be pumped out of any element of $produce(t)$ by a single pumping operation. The value of $pumps(t)$ depends only on t and the rules of G.

We now return to describing strings just by the number of each character that they contain. Let w be an element of $produce(t)$. Then w contains all the characters in $yield(t)$. It also contains all the characters in each vy pair that was pumped out of w in the process of shrinking w down to $yield(t)$. Let VY be a list of all those vy pairs (so repeats are included) and let q be the length of VY (i.e., the number of times some string vy was pumped out of w to produce $yield(t)$). Note that each element of VY must be an element of $pumps(t)$. Then:

$$\psi(w) = \psi(yield(t)) + \sum_{i=1}^{q} \psi(VY_i).$$

We can now prove that $\Psi(produce(t))$ is linear, with:

$$B = \{\psi(yield(t))\} \text{ and } C = \left\{c: \exists w \in pumps\ (t) \left(c = \psi\ (w)\right)\right\}.$$

For this to be true, it must be the case that:

- Let w be an arbitrary element of *produce*(t). Then $\psi(w)$ is a linear combination of $\psi(yield(t))$, the single vector in B, and some finite number of vectors $c_1, c_2, \ldots$, all of which are drawn from C. We just saw that that is true.
- Let v be an arbitrary vector that is a linear combination of $\psi(yield(t))$ and some finite number of vectors $c_1, c_2, \ldots$, all of which are drawn from C. Then there must exist some string w in *produce*(t) such that $\psi(w) = v$. This follows from the fact that the Pumping Theorem tells us that any vy string that can be pumped out can also be pumped in any number of times.

Now we can prove that $\Psi(L)$ is semilinear. There are a finite number of elements in *Short*. Every string in L is an element of *produce*(t) for some t in *Short*. So $\Psi(L)$ is the finite union of linear sets:

$$\Psi(L) = \bigcup_{t \in Short} \Psi(produce(t)).$$

The last step in the proof of Parikh's theorem is to show that, given any semilinear set v, there exists a regular language L such that $\Psi(L) = V$. Let ψ^{-1} be a function that maps from an integer vector v to the lexicographically first string w such that $\psi(w) = v$. For example, if $\Sigma = \{\mathtt{a}, \mathtt{b}, \mathtt{c}\}$, then $\psi^{-1}((2, 1, 3)) = \mathtt{aabccc}$.

We begin by showing that, given any *linear* set V_1, there exists a regular language L_1 such that $\Psi(L_1) = V_1$. Since V_1 is linear, it can be described by the sets B and C. From them we can produce a regular expression that describes L_1. Let $B = \{b_1, b_2, \ldots\}$ and let $C = \{c_1, c_2, \ldots\}$. Then define $R(V_1)$ to be the regular expression:

$$(\psi^{-1}(b_1) \cup \psi^{-1}(b_2) \cup \cdots)(\psi^{-1}(c_1) \cup \psi^{-1}(c_2) \cup \cdots)^*.$$

If L is the language defined by $R(V_1)$, then $\Psi(L) = V_1$.

For example, if $\Sigma = \{\mathtt{a}, \mathtt{b}, \mathtt{c}\}$, and V is defined by $B = \{(1, 2, 3)\}$ and $C = \{(1, 0, 0), (0, 0, 1)\}$, then $R(V) = (\mathtt{abbccc})(\mathtt{a} \cup \mathtt{c})^*$.

Now we return to the problem of showing that, given any *semilinear* set V, there exists a regular language L such that $\Psi(L) = V$. If V is semilinear then it is the finite union of linear sets $V_1, V_2, \ldots$. Then L is the language described by the regular expression:

$$R(V_1) \cup R(V_2) \ldots$$

So we have:

- If L is context-free then $\Psi(L)$ is semilinear.
- If $\Psi(L)$ is semilinear then there is some regular language L' such that $\Psi(L') = \Psi(L)$.

Thus, if L is context-free, L is letter-equivalent to some regular language.

APPENDIX E

The Theory: Turing Machines and Undecidability

In this appendix, we will prove some of the claims that were made but not proved in Part IV.

E.1 Proof that Nondeterminism Does Not Add Power to Turing Machines

In this section we complete the proof of Theorem 17.2.

THEOREM 17.2 Nondeterminism in Deciding and Semideciding Turing Machines

Theorem: If a nondeterministic Turing machine $M = (K, \Sigma, \Gamma, \Delta, s, H)$ decides a language L, then there exists a deterministic Turing machine M' that decides L. If a nondeterministic Turing machine M semidecides a language L, then there exists a deterministic Turing machine M' that semidecides L.

Discussion: The proof is by construction of M'. When we sketched this proof in Section 17.3.2, we suggested using breadth-first search as the basis for the construction. The main obstacle that we face in doing that is bookkeeping. If we use breadth-first search, then M' will need to keep track of the partial paths that it is exploring. One approach would be for it to start down path 1, stop after 1 move, remember the path, go one move down path 2, remember it, and so forth, until all paths have been explored for one step. It could then return to path 1 (which has been stored somewhere on the tape), explore each of its branches for one more move, store them somewhere, find path 2 on the tape, continue it for one more move, and so forth. But this approach has two drawbacks:

- the amount of memory (tape space) required to keep track of all the partial paths grows exponentially with the depth of the search, and
- unlike conventional computers with random access memory, the work required for a Turing machine to scan the tape to find each path in turn and then shift everything to allow for insertion of new nodes into a path could dominate all the work that it would do in actually exploring paths.

Iterative deepening, a hybrid between depth-first search and breadth-first search, avoids both the infinite path pitfall of depth-first search and the exponentially growing memory requirement of breadth-first search. The idea of iterative deepening is simple. We can state the algorithm as follows:

$ID(T$: search tree$)$ =

1. $d = 1$. /* set the initial depth limit to 1.

2. Loop until a solution is found:

2.1. Starting at the root node of T, use depth-first to explore all paths in T of depth d.

2.2. If a solution is found, exit and return it.

2.3. Otherwise, $d = d + 1$.

Iterative deepening avoids the infinite path pitfall of depth-first search by exploring each path to depth d before trying any path to depth $d + 1$. So, if there is a finite-length path to a solution, it will be found. And iterative deepening avoids the memory pitfall of breadth-first search by throwing away each partial path when it backs up. Of course, we do pay a price for that: Each time we start down a path of length $d + 1$ we recreate that path up to length d. That seems like a heavy price, but let's look at it more closely.

Consider a tree such as the one shown in Figure E.1. Each node in the tree represents a configuration of M and each edge represents a step in a computational path that M might follow. Observe first that, in iterative deepening, the nodes at the top of the tree get generated a lot of times. The nodes at the very bottom get generated only once, the ones at the level above that only twice, and so forth. Fortunately, there aren't very many nodes at the top of tree. In fact, the number of nodes at any level d is larger than the *total* number of nodes at all previous levels by approximately a factor of $(b - 1)$, where b is the branching factor of the tree.

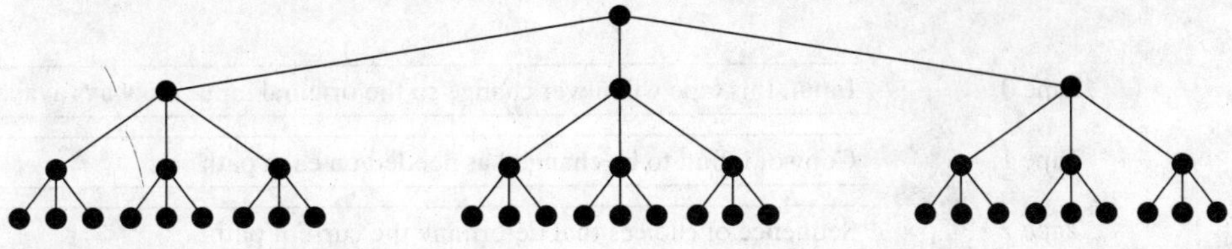

FIGURE E.1 A simple search tree.

So starting over every time is not as bad as it at first seems. In fact, the relatively inefficient implementation of iterative deepening that we will use examines only a factor of approximately h (the height of the tree that is eventually explored) more nodes than does a simple breadth-first search to the correct depth. See E.2 for a proof of this claim.

Proof: We can now return to the task of proving that, for any nondeterministic Turing machine $M = (K, \Sigma, \Gamma, \Delta, s, H)$, there exists an equivalent deterministic Turing machine M'. The proof is by construction of a deterministic M' that simulates the execution of M. M' will operate as follows: Start with the initial configuration of M. Use iterative deepening to try longer and longer computational paths. If any path eventually accepts, M' will discover that and accept. If all paths reject, M' will discover that and reject. So, if M is a deciding Turing machine, M' will always halt. If M is only a semidecider, however, then M' may loop forever.

All that remains is to describe how to perform iterative deepening on a Turing machine. Iterative deepening is usually implemented as a form of bounded depth-first search. For each depth-limited search, a stack is used to keep track of the path so far and the search process backs up whenever it reaches its depth limit. To simplify our implementation, we will choose an approach that does not require a stack. Instead we will create each path, starting from the root, each time.

M' will use three tapes, as shown in Figure E.2. Tapes 1 and 2 correspond to the current path. To see how M' works, we will first define a subroutine P that uses tapes 1 and 2 and follows one specific path for some specified number of steps. Then we will see how M' can invoke P on a sequence of longer and longer paths.

Suppose we want to specify some one specific path through the search tree that M explores. To do this, we first need to be able to write down the set of alternatives for each move in some order so that it makes sense to say, "Choose option 1 this time. Choose option 2 the second time, and so forth." Imagine that we have that. (We will describe such a method shortly.) Then we could specify any finite path as a ***move vector***: a finite sequence of integers such as "2, 5, 1, 3", which we will interpret to mean: "Follow a path of length 4. For the first move, choose option 2. For the next, choose option 5. For the third, choose option 1. For the fourth, choose option 3. Halt." The Turing machine P that we mentioned above, the one that follows one particular finite path and reports its answer, is then a machine that follows a move vector such as "2, 5, 1, 3."

So now we need a way for P to interpret a move vector. To solve this problem we first observe that there is a maximum number B of branches at any point in M's

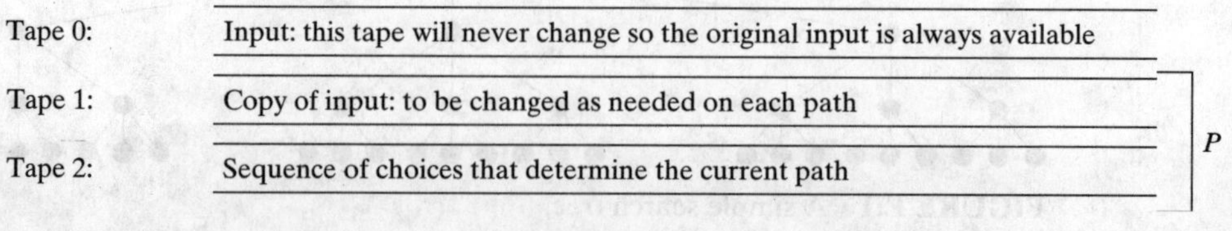

FIGURE E.2 Iterative deepening on a three-tape Turing machine.

Table E.1(a) A table that lists all of M's move choices.

	1	*2*	*3*	...	*B*
(state 1, char 1)	move choice 1	move choice 2			
(state 1, char 2)	move choice 1	move choice 2	move choice 3	move choice 4	
...	move choice 1				
(state 2, char 1)	move choice 1	move choice 2	move choice 3		
...	move choice 1	move choice 2			
(state $\|K\|$, char $\|\Gamma\|$)	move choice 1				

(a)

	1	*2*	*3*	...	*B*
(state 1, char 1)	move choice 1	move choice 2	move choice 1	move choice 2	move choice 1
(state 1, char 2)	move choice 1	move choice 2	move choice 3	move choice 4	move choice 1
...	move choice 1	move choice 1	move choice 1	move choice 1	move choice 1
(state 2, char 1)	move choice 1	move choice 2	move choice 3	move choice 1	move choice 2
...	move choice 1	move choice 2	move choice 1	move choice 2	move choice 1
(state $\|K\|$, char $\|\Gamma\|$)	move choice 1	move choice 1	move choice 1	move choice 1	move choice 1

(b)

execution. For its next move, M chooses from among $|K|$ states to go to, from among $|\Gamma|$ characters to write on the tape, and between moving left and moving right. Thus

$$B = 2 \cdot |K| \cdot |\Gamma|.$$

Since there are only at most B choices at each point, the largest number that can occur in any move vector for M is B. Of course, it will often happen that Δ offers M many fewer choices given its current state and the character under its read/write head. Suppose that we imagine organizing Δ so that, for each (q, c) pair, we get a list (in some arbitrary order) of the moves that M may make if it is in state q and c is under the read/write head. We can enter that information into an indexable table T as shown in Table E.1(a). We assume that we can sequentially number both the states and the elements of Γ. Each move choice is an element of $(K \times \Gamma \times \{\rightarrow, \leftarrow\})$. But what happens if P is told to choose move j and fewer than j choices are available? To solve this problem, we will fill out T by repeating the sequence of allowable moves as many times across each row as necessary to fill up the row. So T will actually be as shown in Table E.1(b).

There are two important things about each row in this table:

- Every entry is a move that is allowed by Δ, and
- every move that is allowed by Δ appears at least once.

Also notice that, given a particular nondeterministic Turing machine M, we can build this table and it will contain a finite number of cells. In addition, there is a finite number $|K|$ of different states that M can be in at any point in following some path. So, given M, we can build a new Turing machine P to follow one of M's paths and we can encode all of the move table, as well as the current simulated state of M, in P's finite state controller.

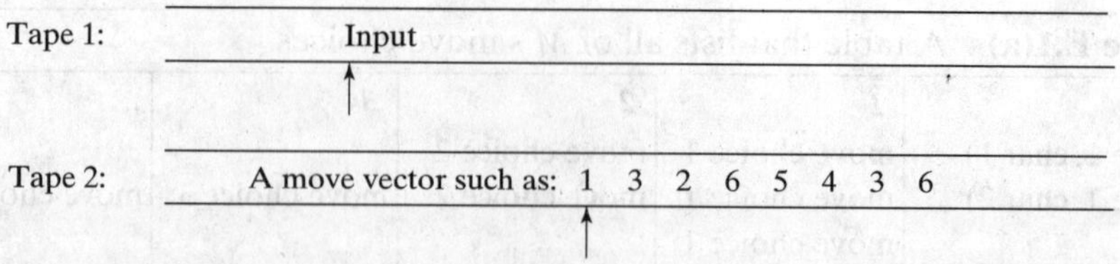

FIGURE E.3 Using two tapes to simulate one path of fixed length.

We are now ready to define P (the Turing machine that follows one finite path that M could take). P uses two tapes, as shown in Figure E.3. The table T and the current (simulated) state of M are encoded in the state of P, which operates as follows.

1. For $i = 1$ to length of the move vector on Tape 2 do:

1.1. Determine c, the character under the read/write head of Tape 1.

1.2. Consider q, the current simulated state of M. If q is a halting state, halt. Otherwise:

1.3. Determine v, the value of square i of the move vector.

1.4. Look in T to determine the value in the row labeled (q, c) and the column labeled v. Call it m.

1.5. Make move m (by writing on tape 1, moving tape 1's read/write head, and changing the simulated state as specified by m).

Whatever happens, P halts after at most n steps, where $n = |\text{Tape } 2|$.

Now that we have specified P, we are ready to specify M', the deterministic Turing machine that is equivalent to M. M' uses three tapes: Tape 0 holds the original input to M. It will not change throughout the computation. Tapes 1 and 2 will be used by instantiations of P. M''s job is to invoke P with all paths of length 0, then all paths of length 1, all paths of length 2, and so forth. For example, suppose that $B = 4$. Then the value on Tape 2 at the first several calls by M' to P will be: ε; 1; 2; 3; 4; 1,1; 1,2; 1,3; 1,4; 2,1; . . .; 2,4; 3,1; . . .; 3,4; 4,1; . . .; 4,4; 1,1,1; 1,1,2; . . .

To see how M' can use P, let's first consider the simplest case, namely the one in which M' is a semideciding machine that will accept if any path of M accepts; otherwise it will simply loop looking for some accepting path. In this case, M' operates as follows on input w.

1. Write ε (corresponding to a path of length 0) on Tape 2.

2. Until P accepts do:

2.1. Copy w from Tape 0 to Tape 1.

2.2. Invoke P (i.e., simulate M for $|\text{Tape } 2|$ steps following the path specified on Tape 2).

2.3. If P discovers that M would have accepted then halt and accept.

2.4. Otherwise, generate the lexicographically next string on Tape 2.

Next we consider what must happen if M is to be able to reject as well as to accept. It can only reject if every path eventually halts and rejects. So now we need to design M' so that it will halt as soon as one of the following things happens:

- It discovers a path along which M halts and accepts. In this case, M' accepts.
- It has tried all paths until they halt, but all have rejected. In this case, M' rejects.

The first of these conditions can be checked as described above. The second is a bit more difficult. Suppose that M' discovers that M would halt and reject on the path 2, 1, 4. M must continue to try to find some accepting path. But it restarts every path at the beginning. How is it to know not to try 2, 1, 4, 1, or any other path starting with 2, 1, 4? It's hard to make it do that, but we can make it notice if it tries every path of length n, for some n, and all of them have halted.

If every path of M halts, then there is some number n that is the maximum number of moves made by any path before it halts. M' should be able to notice that every path of length n halts. At that point, it need not consider any longer paths. So we'll modify M' so that, in its finite state controller, it remembers the value of a Boolean variable we can call *nothalted*, which we'll initialize to *False*. Whenever M' tries a path that hasn't yet halted, it will set *nothalted* to *True*. Now consider the procedure that generates the lexicographically next string on tape 2. Whenever it is about to generate a string that is one symbol longer than its predecessor (i.e., it is about to start looking at longer paths), it will check the value of *nothalted*. If it is *False*, then all paths of the length it was just considering halted. M' can quit. If, on the other hand, *nothalted* is *True*, then there was at least one path that hasn't yet halted. M' needs to try longer paths. The variable *nothalted* must be reset to *False*, and the next longer set of paths considered. So M' operates as follows on input w:

1. Write ε (corresponding to a path of length 0) on Tape 2.
2. Set *nothalted* to *False*.
3. Until P accepts or rejects do:
  3.1. Copy w from Tape 0 to Tape 1.
  3.2. Invoke P (i.e., simulate M for |Tape 2| steps following the path specified on Tape 2).
  3.3. If P discovers that M would have accepted then accept.
  3.4. If P discovers that M would not have halted, then set *nothalted* to *True*.
  3.5. If the lexicographically next string on Tape 2 would be longer than the current one then:
    Check the value of *nothalted*. If it is *False*, then reject. All paths of the current length halted but none of them accepted.
    Otherwise, set *nothalted* to *False*. We'll try again with paths of the next longer length and see if all of them halt.
  3.6. Generate the lexicographically next string on Tape 2.

If M is a semideciding Turing machine, then M' will accept iff M would. If M is a deciding Turing machine, all of its paths must eventually halt. If one of them accepts, M' will find it and accept. If all of them reject, M' will notice when all paths of a given length have halted without accepting. At that point, it will reject. So M' is a deciding machine for $L(M)$.

E.2 An Analysis of Iterative Deepening

Consider a complete tree T with branching factor b and height h. Assume that each node of T, including the root, corresponds to a state and each edge corresponds to a move from one state to another. We want to compare the number of moves that will be considered for each of three search strategies.

We first consider a straightforward ***breadth-first search***. There are b^d edges between nodes at level $d - 1$ and nodes at level d. So the number of moves that will be considered by breadth-first search, to depth h, will be:

$$\sum_{d=1}^{h} b^d = \frac{b(b^h - 1)}{b - 1} = \mathcal{O}(b^h).$$

Now suppose that we use standard ***iterative deepening***, defined as follows:

$ID(T$: search tree$)$ =

1. $d = 1$. /* Set the initial depth limit to 1.

2. Loop until a solution is found:

2.1. Starting at the root node of T, use depth-first to explore all paths in T of depth d.

2.2. If a solution is found, exit and return it.

2.3. Otherwise, $d = d + 1$.

Assume that ID halts with a solution at depth h. Then the number of moves that it considered is,

$$\text{at least: } \sum_{d=1}^{h-1}\left(\sum_{k=1}^{d} b^k\right) + h, \text{and at most: } \sum_{d=1}^{h}\left(\sum_{k=1}^{d} b^k\right) = \frac{b^{h+2} - (h + 1)b^2 + hb}{(b - 1)^2} = \mathcal{O}(b^h).$$

The lower bound comes from the fact that ID must have explored at least one path at depth h or it would have halted at depth h–1. The upper bound corresponds to it finding a solution on the very last path in the tree. To see where that upper bound formula comes from, notice that ID makes one pass through its loop for each value of d, so we must sum over all of them. On the dth pass, it does a simple depth-first search of a tree of depth d and branching factor b.

Now consider a variant of iterative deepening in which, instead of doing a backtracking search at each depth limit d, we start each path over again at the root. So each path of length 1 is considered. Then each path of length 2 is considered, starting each from the root. Then each path of length 3 is considered, starting from the root, and so forth. This is the technique we used in Section 36.1 to prove Theorem 17.2. Because reaching each of the b^d nodes at level d requires d moves, the number of moves that this algorithm considers is,

$$\text{at least: } \sum_{d=1}^{h-1} d\, b^d + h, \text{ and at most: } \sum_{d=1}^{h} d\, b^d = \frac{hb^{h+2} - (h + 1)b^{h+1} + b}{(b - 1)^2} = \mathcal{O}(hb^h).$$

E.3 The Power of Reduction

Define a ***planar grid*** to be a set of lines with two properties:

- No two lines are co-linear, and
- each line is either parallel or perpendicular to every other one.

We'll call each position at which two lines intersect a ***grid point*** or just a ***point***. Now consider the following problem from [Dijkstra EWD-1248]:

> Show that, for any finite set of grid points in the plane, we can colour each of the points either red or blue such that on each grid line the number of red points differs by at most 1 from the number of blue points.

An instance of this problem could be the grid shown in Figure E.4(a). The selected grid points are shown as circles. One way to attack the problem is directly: We could prove the claim using operations on the grid. An alternative is to reduce the problem to one that is stated in some other terms that give us useful tools for finding a solution.

[Misra 1996] suggests reducing this grid problem to a graph problem. The reduction described there works as follows: Given a grid and a finite set of points on the grid, construct a graph in which each grid line becomes a vertex and there is an edge between two vertices iff the corresponding grid lines share one of the given points. The graph that is produced from our example grid is shown in Figure E.4(b).

Notice that the number of edges in the constructed graph is finite (since the number of points in the grid problem is finite). The problem to be solved is now to show that there exists a way to color the *edges* of the graph in such a way that the polarity of each vertex is at most one. Define the ***polarity*** of a vertex to be the absolute value of the difference between the number of red and blue edges incident on it. We'll show that the required coloring exists by describing an algorithm to construct it.

Observe that, in any graph that this reduction builds, each vertex corresponds either to a vertical or to a horizontal grid line. Since each edge connects a "vertical" vertex to a "horizontal" vertex, the graph must be bipartite. (In other words, it is possible to divide the vertices into two sets, in this case the "horizontal" ones and the "vertical" ones, in such a way that no edge is incident on two vertices in the same set.)

Now we can exploit anything we know about bipartite graphs. In particular, we'll use the fact that, in a bipartite graph, every cycle has an even number of edges. So, in any cycle, we can color the edges alternately, red and blue, without affecting the polarity of any vertex. Hence, we may remove all cycles from the graph (in arbitrary order) and solve the coloring problem over the remaining edges. After removing the cycles, we are left with an acyclic undirected graph (i.e., a tree or a forest of trees).

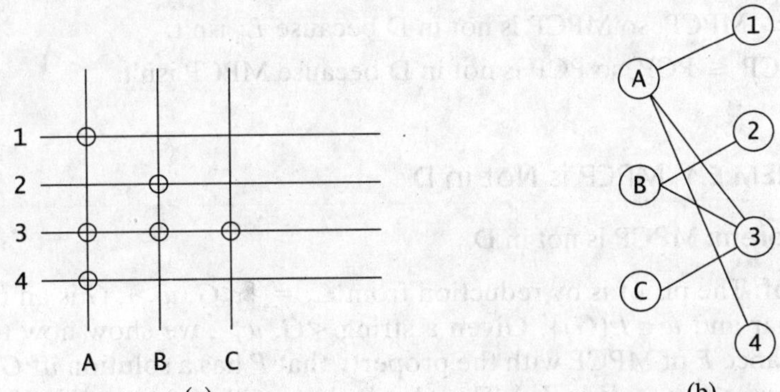

FIGURE E.4 A grid problem and its corresponding graph version.

If the forest is not connected, then each maximal connected tree within it can be colored independently of the others since no pair of such trees shares any vertices. To color each tree, begin by designating some vertex to be the root. Color the edges incident on the root alternately. Then pick any vertex that has both colored and uncolored incident edges. If there is no such vertex then all edges have been colored. Otherwise, the vertex has exactly one colored edge, say red, incident on it; color the incident uncolored edges alternately starting with blue, so as to meet the polarity constraint.

E.4 The Undecidability of the Post Correspondence Problem

In Section 22.2, we defined the language:

- PCP = {<*P*> : *P* is an instance of the Post Correspondence problem and *P* has a solution}.

Theorem 22.1 asserts that PCP is in SD/D. We proved that it is in SD by presenting the algorithm, M_{PCP}, that semidecides it. We will now present the proof that it is not in D.

We begin by defining a related language MPCP (modified PCP). An instance of MPCP looks exactly like an instance of PCP. So it is a string <*P*> of the form:

$$<P> = (x_1, x_2, x_3, \ldots, x_n)(y_1, y_2, y_3, \ldots, y_n), \text{ where } \forall j \ (x_j \in \Sigma^+ \text{ and } y_j \in \Sigma^+).$$

The difference between PCP and MPCP is in the definition of a solution. A solution to an MPCP instance is a finite sequence $1, i_2, \ldots i_k$ of integers such that:

$$\forall j \ (1 \leq i_j \leq n \text{ and } x_1 x_{i_2} \ldots x_{i_k} = y_1 y_{i_2} \ldots y_{i_k}).$$

In other words, the first index in any solution must be 1.

Recall that Theorem 23.3 tells us that the language L_a = {<*G*, *w*> : *G* is an unrestricted grammar and $w \in L(G)$} is not in D. We will show that PCP is not in D in two steps. We will prove that:

- $L_a \leq$ MPCP, so MPCP is not in D because L_a isn't.
- MPCP $\leq$ PCP, so PCP is not in D because MPCP isn't.

THEOREM E.1 MPCP is Not in D

Theorem: MPCP is not in D.

Proof: The proof is by reduction from L_a = {<*G*, *w*> : *G* is an unrestricted grammar and $w \in L(G)$}. Given a string <*G*, *w*>, we show how to construct an instance *P* of MPCP with the property that *P* has a solution iff *G* generates *w* (and thus <*G*, *w*> is in L_a). The idea is that we'll construct the *X* and *Y* lists of *P* so that they can be used to build up strings that describe derivations that *G* can produce. We'll make sure that it is possible to build the same string from the two lists exactly in case G can generate w.

Let $G = (V, \Sigma, R, S)$ be an unrestricted grammar. Suppose that G can derive w. Then there is a string of the following form that describes the derivation:

$$S \Rightarrow x_1 \Rightarrow x_2 \Rightarrow \ldots \Rightarrow w$$

Let % and & be two symbols that are not in V. We'll use % to mark the beginning of a derivation and & to mark the end. Using this convention, a derivation will look like:

$$\%S \Rightarrow x_1 \Rightarrow x_2 \Rightarrow \ldots \Rightarrow w\&$$

From G and w, the reduction that we are about to define will construct an MPCP instance with the property that both the X list and the Y list can be used to generate such derivation strings. We'll design the two lists so that when we use the X list we are one derivation step ahead of where we are when we use the Y list. So the only way for the two lists to end up generating the same derivation string will be to choose a final index that lets Y catch up. We'll make sure that that can happen only when the final generated string is w.

Specifically given $G = (V, \Sigma, R, S)$ and w, we will build the X and Y lists as shown in Table E.2. The entry that is listed on line one must be on line one. Since any solution to an MPCP problem must be a sequence that starts with 1, we thus guarantee that any solution must generate a string that begins with $\%S \Rightarrow$. The other entries may occur in any order. Notice that the entries that correspond to the rules of G are "backwards." This happens because the X-generated string is one derivation ahead of the Y-generated one.

To see how this construction works, we'll consider a simple example. Let $G = (\{S, A, B, \mathsf{a}, \mathsf{b}, \mathsf{c}\}, \{\mathsf{a}, \mathsf{b}, \mathsf{c}\}, R, S)$, where $R =$

$$S \rightarrow AB\mathsf{c}$$
$$S \rightarrow ABS\mathsf{c}$$
$$AB \rightarrow BA$$
$$B\mathsf{c} \rightarrow \mathsf{bc}$$
$$BA \rightarrow \mathsf{a}$$
$$A \rightarrow \mathsf{a}$$

Given G and the string $w = \mathsf{ac}$, the reduction will build the MPCP instance shown in Table E.3. G can derive ac. So this MPCP instance has a solution, (1, 9, 15, 11, 6, 15, 13, 6, 2), shown in Figure E.5.

To complete the proof, we must show that the MPCP instance, P, that is built from the input, <G, w>, has a solution iff G can derive w. The formal argument can be made by induction on the length of a derivation. We omit it. The general idea is as we suggested above. Any MPCP solution starts with the index 1. Given the lists as we have described them, this means that the X-generated string starts out with one more derivation step than does the Y-generated string. The only way for the Y-generated string to "catch up" is to use the second entry in the table. If that is done, then the final generated string can only be w. In between the first index and the last one, all the table entries have been constructed so that all and

Table E.2 Building an MPCP instance from a grammar and a string.

	X	Y		*Comment*
1	$\%S \Rightarrow$	$\%$		Get started, with X one step ahead.
	&	$\Rightarrow w$ &		End, with Y doing its last step and catching up.
	c	c	For every symbol c in V	Copy characters that don't change.
	β	α	For every rule $\alpha \rightarrow \beta$ in R	Apply each rule. X will generate β when Y is one step behind and so is generating α.
	$\Rightarrow$	$\Rightarrow$		

Table E.3 An example of building an MPCP instance from a grammar and a string.

	X	Y		X	Y
1	$\%S \Rightarrow$	%	9	ABc	S
2	&	$\Rightarrow$ ac&	10	ABSc	S
3	S	S	11	BA	AB
4	A	A	12	bc	Bc
5	B	B	13	a	BA
6	c	c	14	a	A
7	b	b	15	$\Rightarrow$	$\Rightarrow$
8	a	a			

only derivations that match the rules in G can be generated. So the two lists will correspond iff G can generate w.

So we have that $L_a \leq$ MPCP. Let $R(<G, w>)$ be the reduction that we have just described. If there existed a Turing machine M that decided MPCP, then $M(R(<G, w>))$ would decide L_a. But L_a is not in D, so no decider for it exists. So M does not exist either and MPCP is not in D.

	1	9	15	11	6	15	13	6	2
X	$\% S \Rightarrow$	ABc	$\Rightarrow$	BA	c	$\Rightarrow$	a	c	&
Y	%	S	$\Rightarrow$	AB	c	$\Rightarrow$	BA	c	$\Rightarrow$ ac&

FIGURE E.5 This MPCP instance has (1, 9, 15, 11, 6, 15, 13, 6, 2) as a solution.

THEOREM E.2 PCP is Not in D

Theorem: PCP is not in D.

Proof: The proof is by reduction from MPCP. In moving from MPCP to PCP, we lose the constraint that a solution necessarily starts with 1. But we can effectively retain that constraint by modifying the X and Y lists so that the only sequences that will cause the two lists to generate the same string must start with 1. Given an MPCP instance $<X, Y>$, we will create a PCP instance $<A, B>$ with the property that $<X, Y>$ has a solution iff $<A, B>$ does. The new lists $<A, B>$ will differ from the original ones in two ways: Each list will contain two new strings and each string will be made twice as long by inserting a special symbol after each original symbol (in the case of the X list) or before each original symbol (in the case of the Y list).

Let $MP = <X, Y>$ be an instance of MPCP with alphabet Σ and size n. Let ¢ and \$ be two characters that are not in Σ. We will build $P = <A, B>$, an instance of PCP with alphabet $\Sigma \cup \{¢, \$\}$ and size $n + 2$ as follows.

- Assume that: $X = x_1, x_2, \ldots x_n$ and $Y = y_1, y_2, \ldots y_n$.
- We construct: $A = a_0, a_1, a_2, \ldots a_n, a_{n+1}$ and $B = b_0, b_1, b_2, \ldots b_n, b_{n+1}$.

For values of i between 1 and n, construct the elements of the A and B lists as follows.

- Let a_i be x_i except that the symbol ¢ will be inserted *after* each symbol of x_i. For example, if x_i is aab then a_i will be a¢a¢b¢.
- Let b_i be y_i except that the symbol ¢ will be inserted *before* each symbol of y_i. For example, if y_i is aab then b_i will be ¢a¢a¢b.

Then let: $a_0 = ¢a_1$,
$a_{n+1} = \$$,
$b_0 = b_1$, and
$b_{n+1} = ¢\$$.

For example:

- If: $X =$ a, baa and $Y =$ ab, aa
- Then: $A =$ ¢a¢, a¢, b¢ a¢ a¢, \$ and $B =$ ¢a¢ b, ¢ a¢ b, ¢ a¢ a, ¢ \$

Now we must show that $MP = <X, Y>$ has an MPCP solution iff $P = <A, B>$ has a PCP solution:

- If $MP = <X, Y>$ has an MPCP solution, then it is of the form $(1, j_2, j_3, \ldots j_k)$, for some k. In that case, the sequence $(0, j_2, j_3, \ldots j_k, n + 1)$ is a solution to $P = <A, B>$. The string that this new sequence produces will be identical to the string that the original sequence produced except that there will be the symbol ¢ between each pair of other symbols and the string will start with ¢ and end with ¢\$. We choose the first element of the sequence to be 0 rather than 1 to create the initial ¢ in the A-generated list, and we add the final element, $n + 1$, so that the B-generated sequence can catch up and contain the final ¢.

- If $P = \langle A, B\rangle$ has a PCP solution S, then it must be of the form $(0, \langle main\ part\rangle, n + 1)$, where $\langle main\ part\rangle$ is all of S minus its first and last elements. We know that S has to start with 0 because every string in the B list starts with the symbol ¢. The only string in the A list that starts with the symbol ¢ is the first one (which we've numbered 0). So the only way that the strings that are generated from the two lists can match is for the first index to be 0. We know that S must end with $n + 1$ because every string in the A list except the last ends with ¢. But no string in the B list does. But B's $n + 1^{st}$ element provides that final ¢ and it provides nothing else except the final \$. The string that S produces is identical, if we remove all instances of ¢ and \$, to the string that the sequence $(1, \langle main\ part\rangle)$ would produce given $\langle X, Y\rangle$. This is true because we constructed elements 1 through n of $\langle A, B\rangle$ to be identical to the corresponding elements of $\langle X, Y\rangle$ except for the insertion of ¢ and \$. And we guaranteed, again ignoring ¢ and \$, that $a_0 = a_1 = x_1$. So the sequence $(1, \langle main\ part\rangle)$ generates the same string from both the X and Y lists and its first element is 1. So it is an MPCP solution for $MP = \langle X, Y\rangle$.

So we have that MPCP $\leq$ PCP. Let $R(\langle X, Y\rangle)$ be the reduction that we have just described. If there existed a Turing machine M that decided PCP, then $M(R(\langle X, Y\rangle))$ would decide MPCP. But MPCP is not in D, so no decider for it exists. So M does not exist either and PCP is not in D.

A P P E N D I X F

The Theory: Complexity

In this appendix, we will prove some of the claims that were made but not proved in Part V.

F.1 Asymptotic Dominance

In this section we prove the claims made in Section 27.5.

F.1.1 Facts about $\mathcal{O}$

We will prove separately each of the claims made in the theorem. The basis for these proofs is the definition of the relation $\mathcal{O}$: $f(n) \in \mathcal{O}(g(n))$ iff there exists a positive integer k and a positive constant c such that:

$$\forall n \geq k\ (f(n) \leq cg(n)).$$

Let f, f_1, f_2, g, g_1, and g_2 be functions from the natural numbers to the positive reals, let a and b be arbitrary real constants, and let $c, c_0, c_1, \ldots c_k$ be any positive real constants.

Fact 1: *f(n)* ∈ *𝒪(f(n))*

Let $k = 0$ and $c = 1$. Then $\forall n \geq k\ (f(n) \leq cf(n))$.

Fact 2: Addition

1. $\mathcal{O}(f(n)) = \mathcal{O}(f(n) + c_0)$ (if we make the assumption, which will always be true for the functions we will be considering, that $1 \in \mathcal{O}(f(n))$).

   We first note that, for any function $g(n)$, if $g(n) \in \mathcal{O}(f(n))$ then it must also be true that $g(n) \in \mathcal{O}(f(n) + c_0)$ since $f(n) \leq f(n) + c_0$. Now we show the other direction. Since $1 \in \mathcal{O}(f(n))$, there must exist k_1 and c_1 such that:

$$\forall n \geq k_1 \, (1 \leq c_1 f(n))$$
$$(c_0 \leq c_0 c_1 f(n)). \quad (1)$$

If $g(n) \in \mathcal{O}(f(n) + c_0)$ then there must exist k_2 and c_2 such that:

$$\forall n \geq k_2 \, (g(n) \leq c_2(f(n) + c_0)).$$

Combining that with (1), we get:

$$\forall n \geq max(k_1, k_2) \, (g(n) \leq c_2(f(n) + c_0 c_1 f(n))$$
$$\leq (c_2 + c_0 c_1)(f(n))).$$

So let $k = max(k_1, k_2)$ and $c = c_2 + c_0 c_1$. Then,

$$\forall n \geq k \, (g(n) \leq cf(n)).$$

2. If $f_1(n) \in \mathcal{O}(g_1(n))$ and $f_2(n) \in \mathcal{O}(g_2(n))$ then $f_1(n) + f_2(n) \in \mathcal{O}(g_1(n) + g_2(n))$.

If $f_1(n) \in \mathcal{O}(g_1(n))$ and $f_2(n) \in \mathcal{O}(g_2(n))$, then there must exist k_1, c_1, k_2 and c_2 such that:

$$\forall n \geq k_1 \, (f_1(n) \leq c_1 g_1(n)).$$
$$\forall n \geq k_2 \, (f_2(n) \leq c_2 g_2(n)).$$

So: $$\forall n \geq max(k_1, k_2) \, (f_1(n) + f_2(n) \leq c_1 g_1(n) + c_2 g_2(n)$$
$$\leq max(c_1, c_2)(g_1(n) + g_2(n))).$$

So let $k = max(k_1, k_2)$ and $c = max(c_1, c_2)$. Then,

$$\forall n \geq k \, (f_1(n) + f_2(n) \leq c(g_1(n) + g_2(n))).$$

3. $\mathcal{O}(f_1(n) + f_2(n)) = \mathcal{O}(max(f_1(n), f_2(n)))$.

We first show that if $g(n) \in \mathcal{O}(f_1(n) + f_2(n))$ then $g(n) \in \mathcal{O}(max(f_1(n), f_2(n)))$. If $g(n) \in \mathcal{O}(f_1(n) + f_2(n))$, then there must exist k_1 and c_1 such that:

$$\forall n \geq k_1 \, (g(n) \leq c_1(f_1(n) + f_2(n))$$
$$\leq 2c_1 \cdot max(f_1(n), f_2(n))).$$

So let $k = k_1$ and $c = 2c_1$. Then,

$$\forall n \geq k \, (g(n) \leq c \, max(f_1(n), f_2(n))).$$

Next we show that if $g(n) \in \mathcal{O}(max(f_1(n), f_2(n)))$ then $g(n) \in \mathcal{O}(f_1(n) + f_2(n))$. If $g(n) \in \mathcal{O}(max(f_1(n), f_2(n)))$, then there must exist k_1 and c_1 such that:

$$\forall n \geq k_1 \, (g(n) \leq c_1 \, max(f_1(n), f_2(n))$$
$$\leq c_1 \, (f_1(n) + f_2(n))).$$

So let $k = k_1$ and $c = c_1$. Then,

$$\forall n \geq k \, (g(n) \leq c(f_1(n) + f_2(n))).$$

Fact 3: Multiplication

1. $\mathcal{O}(f(n)) = \mathcal{O}(c_0 f(n))$.

We first show that, if $g(n) \in \mathcal{O}(f(n))$, then $g(n) \in \mathcal{O}(c_0 f(n))$. If $g(n) \in \mathcal{O}(f(n))$, then there must exist k_1 and c_1 such that:

$$\forall n \geq k_1 \, (g(n) \leq c_1 f(n)).$$

So let $k = k_1$ and $c = c_1/c_0$. (Thus $c_1 = c\, c_0$.) Then,

$$\forall n \geq k \, (g(n) \leq c\, c_0 f(n)).$$

Next we show that, if $g(n) \in \mathcal{O}(c_0 f(n))$, then $g(n) \in \mathcal{O}(f(n))$. If $g(n) \in \mathcal{O}(c_0 f(n))$, then there must exist k_1 and c_1 such that:

$$\forall n \geq k_1 \, (g(n) \leq c_1 c_0 f(n)).$$

So let $k = k_1$ and $c = c_1 c_0$. Then,

$$\forall n \geq k \, (g(n) \leq c f(n)).$$

2. If $f_1(n) \in \mathcal{O}(g_1(n))$ and $f_2(n) \in \mathcal{O}(g_2(n))$ then $f_1(n) f_2(n) \in \mathcal{O}(g_1(n) g_2(n))$.

If $f_1(n) \in \mathcal{O}(g_1(n))$ and $f_2(n) \in \mathcal{O}(g_2(n))$, then there must exist k_1, c_1, k_2 and c_2 such that:

$$\forall n \geq k_1 \, (f_1(n) \leq c_1 \, g_1(n)), \text{ and}$$
$$\forall n \geq k_2 \, (f_2(n) \leq c_2 \, g_2(n)).$$

Thus: $\quad \forall n \geq max(k_1, k_2) \, (f_1(n) f_2(n) \leq c_1 c_2 \, g_1(n) \, g_2(n)).$

So let $k = max(k_1, k_2)$ and $c = c_1 c_2$. Then,

$$\forall n \geq k \, (f_1(n) f_2(n) \leq c \, g_1(n) g_2(n)).$$

Fact 4: Polynomials

1. If $a \leq b$ then $\mathcal{O}(n^a) \subseteq \mathcal{O}(n^b)$.

If $g(n) \in \mathcal{O}(n^a)$, then there must exist k_1 and c_1 such that:

$$\forall n \geq k_1 \, (g(n) \leq c_1 n^a \leq c_1 n^b) \qquad (\text{since } (a \leq b) \rightarrow (n^a \leq n^b)).$$

So let $k = k_1$ and $c = c_1$. Then:

$$\forall n \geq k \, (g(n) \leq c n^b).$$

2. If $f(n) = c_j n^j + c_{j-1} n^{j-1} + \ldots c_1 n + c_0$, then $f(n) \in \mathcal{O}(n^j)$.

$$\forall n \geq 1 \, (c_j n^j + c_{j-1} n^{j-1} + \ldots c_1 n + c_0 \leq c_j n^j + c_{j-1} n^j + \ldots c_1 n^j + c_0 \, n^j$$
$$\leq (c_j + c_{j-1} + \ldots c_1 + c_0) \, n^j).$$

So let $k = 1$ and $c = (c_j + c_{j-1} + \ldots c_1 + c_0)$. Then:

$$\forall n \geq k\ (f(n) \leq cn^j).$$

Fact 5: Logarithms

1. For a and $b > 1$, $\mathcal{O}(\log_a n) = \mathcal{O}(\log_b n)$.

Without loss of generality, it suffices to show that $\mathcal{O}(\log_a n) \subseteq \mathcal{O}(\log_b n)$. If $g(n) \in \mathcal{O}(\log_a n)$, then there must exist k_1 and c_1 such that:

$$\forall n \geq k_1\ (g(n) \leq c_1 \log_a n).$$

Note that $\log_a n = \log_a b \log_b n$. So let $k = k_1$ and $c = c_1 \log_a b$. Then,

$$\forall n \geq k\ (g(n) \leq c \log_b n).$$

2. If $0 < a < b$ and $c > 1$ then $\mathcal{O}(n^a) \subseteq \mathcal{O}(n^a \log_c n) \subseteq \mathcal{O}(n^b)$.

First we show that $\mathcal{O}(n^a) \subseteq \mathcal{O}(n^a \log_c n)$. For any $n \geq c$, $\log_c n \geq 1$, so $n^a \leq n^a \log_c n$. If $g(n) \in \mathcal{O}(n^a)$, then there must exist k_1 and c_1 such that:

$$\forall n \geq k_1\ (g(n) \leq c_1 n^a).$$

So let $k = max(k_1, c)$ and $c_0 = c_1$. Then,

$$\forall n \geq k\ (g(n) \leq c_0 n^a \log_c n).$$

Next we show that $\mathcal{O}(n^a \log_c n) \subseteq \mathcal{O}(n^b)$. First, notice that, for $p > 0$ and $n \geq 1$, we have,

$$\log_e n = \int_1^n x^{-1}\, dx \leq \int_1^n x^{-1+p}\, dx = \frac{1}{p}(n^p - 1) < \frac{1}{p} n^p.$$

In particular, for $p = b - a$, we have:

$$\log_e n < \frac{1}{b-a} n^{b-a}.$$

If $g(n) \in \mathcal{O}(n^a \log_c n)$, then there must exist k_1 and c_1 such that:

$$\forall n \geq k_1\ (g(n) \leq c_1 n^a \log_c n).$$

So, for all $n \geq max(1, k_1)$, we have that:

$$g(n) \leq cn^a \log_c n = cn^a \log_c e \log_e n < \frac{c \log_c e}{b-a} n^a n^{b-a} \leq \frac{c \log_c e}{b-a} n^b.$$

So let $k = max(1, k_1)$ and $c_0 = \dfrac{c \log_c e}{b-a}$. Then,

$$\forall n \geq k\ (g(n) \leq c_0 n^b).$$

Fact 6: Exponentials (including the fact that exponentials dominate polynomials)

1. If $1 < a \le b$ then $\mathcal{O}(a^n) \subseteq \mathcal{O}(b^n)$.

If $g(n) \in \mathcal{O}(a^n)$, then there must exist k_1 and c_1 such that:

$$\begin{aligned}\forall n \ge k_1\, (g(n) &\le c_1 a^n \\ &\le c_1 b^n) \qquad \text{(since } (a \le b) \rightarrow (a^n \le b^n)\text{)}.\end{aligned}$$

So let $k = k_1$ and $c = c_1$. Then,

$$\forall n \ge k\, (g(n) \le cb^n).$$

2. If $a \ge 0$ and $b > 1$ then $\mathcal{O}(n^a) \subseteq \mathcal{O}(b^n)$.

If $a = 0$, then we have that $\mathcal{O}(1) \subseteq \mathcal{O}(b^n)$, which is trivially true. We now consider the case in which $a > 0$. First notice that, if $p \ge 1$ and $n \ge p$, then,

$$\begin{aligned}\log_e n = \int_1^n \frac{1}{x}dx &= \int_1^p \frac{1}{x}dx + \int_p^n \frac{1}{x}dx \\ &\le \log_e p + \int_p^n \frac{1}{p}dx \\ &\le \log_e p + \frac{n-p}{p} \\ &\le \log_e p + \frac{n}{p}.\end{aligned}$$

If, in particular, $p = max\left(\frac{a}{\log_e b}, 1\right)$, then $\frac{1}{p} \le \frac{\log_e b}{a}$, $p \ge 1$ and:

$$\begin{aligned}\log_e n &\le \log_e p + \frac{\log_e b}{a} n \\ a \log_e n &\le a \log_e p + \log_e b \cdot n.\end{aligned}$$

And:

$$\begin{aligned}n^a = e^{a \cdot \log_e n} &\le e^{a \cdot \log_e p + \log_e b \cdot n} \\ &\le p^a \cdot b^n.\end{aligned}$$

If $g(n) \in \mathcal{O}(n^a)$, then there must exist k_1 and c_1 such that:

$$\forall n \ge k_1\, (g(n) \le c_1 n^a).$$

So, again letting $p = max\left(\frac{a}{\log_e b}, 1\right)$, let $k = max(k_1, p)$ and $c = c_1 p^a$. Then,

$$\forall n \ge k\, (g(n) \le cb^n).$$

3. If $f(n) = c_{j+1}2^n + c_jn^j + c_{j-1}n^{j-1} + \dots c_1n + c_0$, then $f(n) \in \mathcal{O}(2^n)$.

From Fact 4.2, we have that $c_jn^j + c_{j-1}n^{j-1} + \dots c_1n + c_0 \in \mathcal{O}(n^j)$. From Fact 6.2, we have that $n^j \in \mathcal{O}(2^n)$. So, using the transitivity property that we prove in 8, we have that $c_jn^j + c_{j-1}n^{j-1} + \dots c_1n + c_0 \in \mathcal{O}(2^n)$. So there must exist k_1 and k_2 such that:

$$\begin{aligned} \forall n \geq k_1 \,(c_jn^j + c_{j-1}n^{j-1} + \dots c_1n + c_0 &\leq k_2 2^n \\ c_{j+1}2^n + c_jn^j + c_{j-1}n^{j-1} + \dots c_1n + c_0 &\leq c_{j+1}2^n + k_2 2^n \\ &\leq (c_{j+1} + k_2)2^n). \end{aligned}$$

So let $k = k_1$ and $c = c_{j+1} + k_2$. Then,

$$\forall n \geq k\,(f_1(n) \leq c2^n).$$

Fact 7: Factorial dominates exponentials: If $a \geq 1$ then $\mathcal{O}(a^n) \subseteq \mathcal{O}(n!)$

First notice that, if $a \geq 1$, then:

$$\begin{aligned} a^n = \prod_{k=1}^{n} a &= \prod_{k=1}^{\lceil a\rceil-1} a \cdot \prod_{k=\lceil a\rceil}^{n} a \leq \prod_{k=1}^{\lceil a\rceil-1} a \cdot \prod_{k=\lceil a\rceil}^{n} k \\ &\leq \prod_{k=1}^{\lceil a\rceil-1} a \cdot \frac{\prod_{k=1}^{\lceil a\rceil-1} k}{\prod_{k=1}^{\lceil a\rceil-1} k} \cdot \prod_{k=\lceil a\rceil}^{n} k \\ &\leq \prod_{k=1}^{\lceil a\rceil-1} \frac{a}{k} \cdot \prod_{k=1}^{n} k \\ &\leq \prod_{k=1}^{\lceil a\rceil-1} \frac{a}{k} \cdot n!. \end{aligned}$$

If $g(n) \in \mathcal{O}(a^n)$, then there must exist k_1 and c_1 such that:

$$\forall n \geq k_1\,(g(n) \leq c_1a^n).$$

So let $k = k_1$ and $c = c_1 \prod_{k=1}^{\lceil a\rceil-1} \frac{a}{k}$. Then,

$$\forall n \geq k\,(g(n) \leq cn!).$$

Fact 8: Transitivity: If $f(n) \in \mathcal{O}(f_1(n))$ and $f_1(n) \in \mathcal{O}(f_2(n))$ then $f(n) \in \mathcal{O}(f_2(n))$

If $f(n) \in \mathcal{O}(f_1(n))$ and $f_1(n) \in \mathcal{O}(f_2(n))$, then there must exist k_1, c_1, k_2 and c_2 such that:

$$\forall n \geq k_1\,(f(n) \leq c_1f_1(n)).$$
$$\forall n \geq k_2\,(f_1(n) \leq c_2f_2(n)).$$

So let $k = max(k_1, k_2)$ and $c = c_1c_2$. Then,

$$\forall n \geq k\ (f(n) \leq cf_2(n)).$$

F.1.2 Facts about σ

We will prove separately the two claims made in the theorem. The basis for these proofs is the definition of the relation σ: $f(n) \in \sigma(g(n))$ iff, for every positive c, there exists a positive integer k such that:

$$\forall n \geq k\ (f(n) < cg(n)).$$

Let f and g be functions from the natural numbers to the positive reals. Then,

1. $f(n) \notin \sigma(f(n))$:

Let $c = 1$. Then there exists no k such that $\forall n \geq k\ (f(n) < cf(n))$.

2. $\sigma(f(n)) \subset \mathcal{O}(f(n))$:

If $g(n) \in \sigma(f(n))$ then, for every positive c_1, there exists a k_1 such that: $\forall n \geq k\ (g(n) < cf(n))$. To show that $g(n) \in \mathcal{O}(f(n))$, it suffices to find a single c and k that satisfy the definition of $\mathcal{O}$. Let $c = 1$ and let k be the k_1 that must exist if $c_1 = 1$.

F.2 The Linear Speedup Theorem

In Section 27.5 we introduced the theory of asymptotic dominance so that we could describe the time and space requirements of Turing machines by the rate at which those requirements grow, rather than by some more exact measure of them. One consequence of this approach is that constant factors get ignored. This makes sense for two reasons. The first is that, in most of the problems we want to consider, such factors are dominated by much faster growing ones, so they have little impact on the size of the problems that we can reasonably solve.

But a second reason is the one that we will focus on here: All but the most efficient Turing machines can be sped up by any constant factor. The idea behind this claim is simple. At each step of its operation, a Turing machine visits one tape square. If we can compress the contents of the tape so that they fit on fewer squares, we can reduce the number of steps that a Turing machine must execute to process the tape. Compressing a tape is easy. We simply increase the size of the tape alphabet. That enables us to encode a chunk of squares from the original tape into a single square of the new one.

EXAMPLE F.1 Encoding Multiple Tape Squares as a Single Square

Let M be a Turing machine whose tape alphabet is $\{0, 1, \square\}$. We can build a new Turing machine M' that uses the tape alphabet $\{$A-Z, a-z, 0-9, α-$\omega\}$. Using the new alphabet, we can encode four squares of M's tape as a single square on the tape

M' will use. Initially, we'll include in the encoding at least one blank on either side of the input (plus more on the right for padding if necessary). If M ever moves off its input, new squares can be encoded as necessary. So, for example:

If the tape of M is: ... ❑❑❑000000000001000010❑❑ ...

Then the tape of M' might be: C 8 8 f π

If we design the transitions of M' appropriately, it will be able to do in one step what it takes M four steps to do.

The compression idea that we have just described is the basis of the Linear Speedup Theorem that we are about to present. Before we go into the details of the theorem and its proof, one caveat is in order. While this theorem is of some theoretical interest, its application to real computers is limited. Real computers have a fixed size alphabet (generally consisting of two binary symbols). So the sort of compression that we are using here cannot be applied. However, it is worth noting that other compression algorithms (that exploit patterns in particular kinds of input strings and are thus able to reduce the number of bits required) are routinely used in many kinds of real applications.

THEOREM F.1 The Linear Speedup Theorem

Theorem: Let M be a k-tape Turing machine where $k > 1$ and $timereq(M) = f(n)$. Given any constant $c > 0$, there exists another k-tape Turing machine M' such that $L(M) = L(M')$ and

$$timereq(M') \leq \left\lceil \frac{f(n)}{c} \right\rceil + 2n + 2 \cdot \lceil 6c \rceil.$$

Notice that c is a factor by which we reduce the time a computation requires. So, if we want to say that the new program takes half as long, we set c to 2. In some statements of the theorem, c is a multiplicative factor. Using those versions, we'd set c to $\frac{1}{2}$ in that case. The two formulations are equivalent.

Proof: We prove the claim by describing the operation of M'. M' will begin by making one pass across its input tape to encode it as described in Example F.1. It will store the encoded string on tape 2 and blank out tape 1. During the rest of its operation, it will use tape 1 as M would have used tape 2 and vice versa. The number of symbols to be collapsed into one at this step is determined by c, the speedup that is desired. We'll call this collapsing factor m and set it to $\lceil 6c \rceil$.

Next M' simulates the execution of M. The idea here is that, since M' encodes m symbols as one, it can process m symbols as one. Unfortunately, on any one tape, the m symbols that M' needs may be spread across two of the new encoded tape squares: They may fall on the current square plus the one to its right or they may fall on the current square plus the one to its left. So M' must make one move to the left, then one back, and then one more to the right and then back before it can be sure that it has all the information it needs to make the move that simulates m moves of M. We illustrate this with the following example. Let $k = 2$ and $m = 5$. Each tape square actually contains a single symbol that encodes five original symbols, but we've shown them here with the original sequences so that it is possible to see how the simulation works. Suppose that, at some point in its computation, M has entered some state q and its tapes contain the following fragments:

Tape 1:	...	0 0 1 0 0	0 1 1 0 0	1 1 1 0 1	1 0 0 0 0	0 0 0 1 0	...
					↑		
Tape 2:	...	0 0 1 1 1	1 1 0 0 0	0 0 1 1 1	1 1 1 0 1	1 1 0 1 1	...
			↑				

If the next five moves of M move the read/write head on tape 1 to the right five times and they move the read/write head on tape 2 to the left five times, M' will need to examine both one encoded square to the left and one encoded square to the right before it will have enough information to simulate all five of those moves.

So M' simulates M by doing the following:

1. Move one square to the left on each of the tapes and record in the state the encoded symbol it finds on each of the k tapes.
2. Move one square back to the right on each tape and record in the state the encoded symbol it finds on each of the k tapes.
3. Move one more square to the right on each tape and record in the state the encoded symbol it finds on each of the k tapes.
4. Move one square back to the left on each tape.

At this point, the read/write heads of M' are back where they started and the state of M' includes the following vector of information that captures the current state of M:

$(q,$	M's state.
$L_1, C_1, R_1, t_1,$	The relevant contents of tape 1: L_1 is the encoded square to the left of the one that contains M's simulated read/write head. C_1 is the encoded square that contains M's simulated read/write head. R_1 is the encoded square to the right of the one that contains M's simulated read/write head. t_1 (an integer between 1 and m) is the position within C_1 of M's simulated read/write head.

$L_2, C_2, R_2, t_2,$ Tape 2: similarly

…

$L_k, C_k, R_k, t_k)$ Tape k: similarly

5. Using this information, make one move that alters the C squares as necessary and moves each read/write head as required to simulate M. Also update M's state.
6. Make one more move if necessary. If, on some tape, M's simulated read/write head moved off the C square, it will be necessary to make this second move in order to alter the contents of either the L or R square to match what M would have done. But note that, on any given tape, it will only be necessary to work with the current square plus one to the left *or* the current square plus one to the right. So two moves suffice to make all necessary changes to the tapes.

The first phase, encoding the input tape, requires that M make one complete pass through the input and then move back to the left. It may have to use up to m padding blanks. So, in the worst case, on an input of length n this phase requires $2(n + m)$ steps. The second phase, simulating M, requires at most six steps for every m steps that M would have executed. So, if $timereq(M) = f(n)$, then,

$$timereq(M') \leq \left\lceil \frac{6f(n)}{m} \right\rceil + 2(n + m).$$

Since $m = \lceil 6c \rceil$, we then have,

$$timereq(M') \leq \left\lceil \frac{f(n)}{c} \right\rceil + 2n + 2 \cdot \lceil 6c \rceil.$$

APPENDICES G – Q:

Applications

In appendices G through Q, we describe applications of the techniques that have been covered throughout the book. Most of the discussion is organized around a collection of key application areas that make use of more than one of the ideas that we have discussed. We will consider all in the following list, although we will barely scratch the surface of each.

- Programming languages: syntax and compilers
- Functional programming
- Tools for programming and software engineering, including techniques for verifying the correctness of programs and of hardware designs
- Network protocols, network modeling, and the Semantic Web
- Computer system security, cryptography, hackers and viruses
- Computational biology
- Natural language processing
- Artificial intelligence and computational reasoning
- Music
- Classic games and puzzles
- Interactive video games

Then we will look at three of the specific tools that we have introduced. We will briefly survey some of their applications that lie outside the particular application areas that we will already have covered. The three tools are

- regular expressions,
- finite state machines and transducers, and
- grammars.

APPENDIX G

APPLICATIONS: PROGRAMMING LANGUAGES AND COMPILERS

The ideas that we have discussed throughout this book form the foundation of modern programming. Programming languages are typically described with context-free grammars. Regular expression matchers are built into many modern programming environments. Finite state transition diagrams enable visual programming.

G.1 Defining the Syntax of Programming Languages

Most programming languages are mostly context-free. There are some properties, such as type constraints, that cannot usually be described within the context-free framework. We will consider those briefly in Section G.2. But context-free grammars provide the basis for defining most of the syntax of most programming languages.

G.1.1 BNF

It became clear early on in the history of programming language development that designing a language was not enough. It was also necessary to produce an unambiguous language specification. Without such a specification, compiler writers were unsure what to write and users didn't know what code would compile. The inspiration for a solution to this problem came from the idea of a rewrite or production system as described years earlier by Emil Post. (See Section 18.2.4.) In 1959, John Backus confronted the specification problem as he tried to write a description of the new language ALGOL 58. Backus later wrote [Backus 1980], "As soon as the need for precise description was noted, it became obvious that Post's productions were well-suited for that purpose. I hastily adapted them for use in describing the syntax of IAL [Algol 58]." The notation that he designed was modified slightly in collaboration with Peter Naur and used in the definition, two years later, of ALGOL 60. The ALGOL 60 notation became known as BNF, for Backus Naur form or Backus Normal form. For the definitive specification of ALGOL 60, using BNF, see [Naur 1963]. Just as the ALGOL 60 language influenced the design of generations of procedural programming languages, BNF has served as the basis for the description of those new languages, as well as others.

The BNF language that Backus and Naur used exploited these special symbols:

- ::= corresponds to $\rightarrow$,
- | means or, and
- < > surround the names of the nonterminal symbols.

EXAMPLE G.1 Standard BNF

Our term/factor grammar for arithmetic expressions would be written as follows in the original BNF language:

```
<E> ::= <E> + <T> | <T>
<T> ::= <T> * <F> | <F>
<F> ::= id | (<E>)
```

While it seems obvious to us now that formal specifications of syntax are important and BNF seems a natural way to provide such specifications, the invention of BNF was an important milestone in the development of computing. John Backus received the 1977 Turing Award for "profound, influential, and lasting contributions to the design of practical high-level programming systems, notably through his work on FORTRAN, and for seminal publication of formal procedures for the specification of programming languages." Peter Naur received the 2005 Turing Award "For fundamental contributions to programming language design and the definition of Algol 60, to compiler design, and to the art and practice of computer programming."

Since its introduction in 1960, BNF has become the standard tool for describing the context-free part of the syntax of programming languages, as well as a variety of other formal languages: query languages, markup languages, and so forth. In later years, it has been extended both to make better use of the larger character codes that are now in widespread use and to make specifications more concise and easier to read. For example, modern versions of BNF

- often use $\rightarrow$ instead of ::=.
- provide a convenient notation for indicating optional constituents. One approach is to use the subscript $_{\text{opt}}$. Another is to declare square brackets to be metacharacters that surround optional constituents. The following rules illustrate three ways to say the same thing:

$$S \rightarrow T \mid \varepsilon$$
$$S \rightarrow T_{\text{opt}}$$
$$S \rightarrow [T]$$

- may include many of the features of regular expressions, which are convenient for specifying those parts of a language's syntax that do not require the full power of the context-free formalism.

These various dialects are called Extended BNF or EBNF.

EXAMPLE G.2 EBNF

In standard BNF, we could write the following rule that describes the syntax of an identifier that must be composed of an initial letter, followed by zero or more alphanumeric characters:

```
<identifier> ::= <letter> | <letter> <alphanumseq>
<alphanumseq> ::= <alphanum> | <alphanum> <alphanumseq>
<alphanum> ::= <letter> | <digit>
```

In EBNF, it can be written as:

```
identifier = letter (letter | digit)*
```

But note, this is a simple example that illustrates the point. In any practical system, the parsing of tokens, such as identifiers, is generally handled by a lexical analyzer and not by the context-free parser.

G.1.2 Railroad Diagrams

Context-free grammars fill reference books on every programming language that has been created since BNF was used to define ALGOL 60. Sometimes more modern definitions look superficially different from BNF, since other notations have been developed over the years. For example, ***railroad diagrams*** (also called syntax diagrams or railway tracks) are graphical renditions of the rules of a context-free grammar. Railroad diagrams have the same expressive power as does BNF, but they are sometimes easier to read.

EXAMPLE G.3 A Railroad Diagram for a Switch Statement

Consider the following BNF specification for a switch statement like the one in Java (where the subscript$_{\text{OPT}}$ indicates an optional constituent):

```
<switch-statement> ::= SWITCH (<int-expression> |
                                <enum-type>} ) {<case-list>}
<case-list> ::= <case-body> <default-clause>OPT
<case-body> ::= <case-item> |<case-item> <case-body>
<case-item> ::= CASE <value> : <stmt-list> BREAKOPT
<default-clause> ::= DEFAULT : <stmt-list>
```

We assume that <`stmt-list`>, which is used in other places in the grammar, is defined elsewhere.

Here's the corresponding railroad diagram (again assuming that `<stmt-list>` is defined elsewhere):

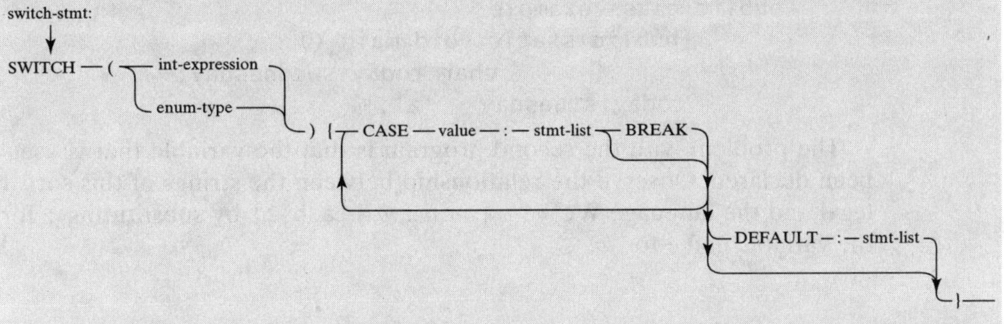

Terminal strings are shown in upper case. Nonterminals are shown in lower case. To generate a switch statement, we follow the lines and arrows, starting from switch-stmt. The word SWITCH appears first, followed by (. Then one of the two alternative paths is chosen. They converge and then the symbols) and { appear. There must be at least one case alternative, but, when it is complete, the path may return for more. The BREAK command is optional. So is the DEFAULT clause, in both cases because there are detours around them.

G.2 Are Programming Languages Context-Free?

So far, we have considered the use of context-free grammars to specify the syntax of individual statements. They are also used to specify the structure of entire programs. However, there are global properties of programs that cannot be described within the context-free framework. Recall that, in Section 13.3, we showed that WcW $= \{wcw : w \in \{\mathtt{a},\mathtt{b}\}^*\}$ is not context-free. The structure of the strings in WcW is very similar to the declaration-use pattern that is common in typed programming languages.

EXAMPLE G.4 Why Java Isn't Context Free

Here's a syntactically legal Java program:

```
public class example
        {public static void main ()
                {    char todayistuesday;
        todayistuesday = 'a';}}
```

EXAMPLE G.4 (*Continued*)

Here's a string that is not a syntactically legal Java program:

```
public class example
      {public static void main ()
            {       char todayiswednesday;
      todayistuesday = 'a';}}
```

The problem with the second program is that the variable that is used hasn't been declared. Observe the relationship between the strings of this sort that are legal and the language WcW = $\{wcw : w \in \{a, b\}^*\}$ by substituting ; for c and the variable name for w.

To prove that Java is not context-free, let:

J = {syntactically legal Java programs} ∩ <prelude> `string` a*b*; a*b* = 'a';}}.

We've used the shorthand <prelude> for some particular opening string that will transform the remaining fragment into a legal Java program. So J includes a set of Java programs that declare a single variable whose name is in a*b* and then do a single operation, namely assigning to that variable the value 'a'.

By Theorem 13.7, if Java were context free then J would also be context-free since it would be the intersection of a context-free language with a regular language. But we can show that J is not context-free using the Pumping Theorem. Let:

w = <prelude> `string` $a^k b^k$; $a^k b^k$ = 'a';}}
| 1 |2|3|4|5|6| 7 |

If either v or y contains any portions of regions 1, 4, or 7, then set q to 2. The resulting string violates the form constraint of J. If either v or y overlaps the boundary between regions 2 and 3 or regions 5 and 6, then set q to 2. The resulting string violates the form constraint of J. It remains to consider the following cases:

- (2, 2), (2, 3), (3, 3), (5, 5), (5, 6), (6, 6), (3, 5): Set q to 2. The resulting string s will have a declaration for one variable and a use of another, thus violating the type constraints of Java. So $s \notin$ {syntactically legal Java programs}.
- (2, 5), (2, 6), (3, 6): Violate the requirement that $|vxy| \leq k$.

There is no way to carve w into $uvxyz$ such that all the conditions of the Pumping Theorem are met. So J is not context-free. So Java is not context-free.

Recall that, in Exercise 13.3, we considered another aspect of type checking: guaranteeing that each invocation of a declared procedure contains the same number of parameters as the declaration. We saw that a simple language that exhibits a similar property is not context free. Because of these issues, type checking typically cannot be done with a context-free parser.

G.3 Designing Programming Languages and Their Grammars

So far, we have discussed the syntax of programming languages as though it were a natural phenomenon over which we have no control. In Appendix L, we'll consider English; it is such a phenomenon and we have no control. But programming languages are artificial things, designed by people to serve a particular purpose. It makes sense to design them so that they have the properties we want. Clearly we want them to be expressive, easy to use, and hard to make mistakes in (alternatively, easy to check for mistakes). We also want to design the syntax so that:

- The language is not inherently ambiguous. If this is true, then we will be able to design an unambiguous grammar that will generate exactly one parse tree (and thus one interpretation) for each string in the language.
- The language can be parsed efficiently (i.e., deterministically). This requirement imposes a stronger constraint than does the need to avoid ambiguity.
- The syntax is straightforward. We want to be able to write a grammar that serves to document the syntax in a way that is readable by programmers.

The issue of ambiguity is particularly important and it is enlightening to contrast English with useful artificial languages in this regard. For example, while English does not allow the use of parentheses to force a particular parse structure, most programming languages do. While English does not exploit rules like operator precedence, and instead allows great flexibility in organizing sentences, most programming languages do exploit such rules and are defined by grammars that force a single interpretation in all cases. So, while many English sentences are highly ambiguous, most programming language statements are not. Contrast:

> The boy and the girl with the red wagon bought a pencil and a book with a floppy cover,

with

$$17 + 12*(4*8)*4 + 7.$$

The English sentence is ambiguous given any reasonable grammar of English. The arithmetic expression is ambiguous given some arithmetic expression grammars. But, as we saw in Example 11.19, it is straightforward to design an unambiguous grammar for arithmetic expressions.

Unfortunately, some convenient programming language constructs present challenges to the design of unambiguous grammars. The most common is the `if` statement that allows an optional `else` clause. We discussed this problem, generally known as the dangling `else` problem, in Example 11.20. Recall the following statement that we presented there:

`if` cond$_1$ `then` `if` cond$_2$ `then` st$_1$ `else` st$_2$

The problem is that, if we use a straightforward grammar that makes `else` clauses optional, then this statement has two parses (and thus two meanings):

`if` cond$_1$ `then` [`if` cond$_2$ `then` st$_1$ `else` st$_2$]

`if` cond$_1$ `then` [`if` cond$_2$ `then` st$_1$] `else` st$_2$

The designers of any programming language that has this construct must solve the problem in one of two ways:

- Rely on delimiters to disambiguate nested `if` statements. Languages such as Algol 68, Modula-2, Ada, Lisp, and Scheme take this approach. For example, in Algol 68, one would write:

```
if i = 0 then
   if j = 0 then
      x := 0
      fi          /* In Algol 68, each delimiter x had a matching close
                  /* delimiter xR. So if/fi.
   else x := 1
   fi
```

  Or, in Scheme, one would write:

```
(if (= i 0) (if (= j 0) (set! x 0)) (set! x 1))
```

  It is clear, in both these cases, that the single `else` clause (which sets x to 1) goes with the first `if`.

- Dispense with delimiters and substitute an arbitrary decision that can be encoded in the grammar. Languages such as C and Java take this approach, which we illustrated with a fragment of a Java grammar in Example 11.20. Of course, the main drawback to this approach is that programmers may not always be aware which arbitrary decision will be made; they may write their code assuming that something different will happen. So this approach can lead to programmer errors, which can sometimes be caught by audit rule checkers.

So there are cases like the dangling `else` problem that are known to create ambiguity. And there are examples of grammars that can be shown (as we did in Example 11.18) to be unambiguous. Unfortunately, the undecidability results of Section 22.5 make it clear that there can exist no general tools that can tell the difference. So, in particular, there exist no general tools that can:

- decide whether a proposed language is inherently ambiguous, or
- decide whether a proposed grammar is ambiguous.

G.4 Compilers for Programming Languages

The job of a compiler can be broken down into the following pieces:

- lexical analysis,
- syntactic analysis,
- code generation and optimization, and
- error checking, which must be done at each step of the process.

Both lexical analysis and syntactic analysis are driven primarily by the theory that has been presented in this book, which also tells us something about what kinds of error checking are possible. In addition, the computability results we have presented have implications for our ability to design effective optimizers.

G.4.1 Lexical Analysis

The job of a lexical analyzer is to transform a string of input characters into a string of tokens (typically corresponding to the smallest meaningful units in the language). The character patterns that correspond to the allowable tokens are generally described with regular expressions. See Section 15.1 for a discussion of how lexical analysis is done and the tools that are available for building lexical analyzers.

G.4.2 Syntactic Analysis

The job of a syntactic analyzer is twofold:

- to transform a sequence of tokens into a parse tree that represents the structure of the input and that can be used as the basis for generating code, and
- to check for errors.

We've seen that most of the syntactic structure of most programming languages can be described with a context-free grammar. But there are features, for example type constraints, that cannot. So one approach might be to move outward in the language hierarchy. For example, we might use a context-sensitive grammar instead of a context-free one. That would solve many of the problems, but it would introduce a new one. Recall, from Chapters 24 and 29, that the best known algorithm for examining a string and deciding whether or not it could be generated by an arbitrary context-sensitive grammar takes time that is exponential in the length of the input string. Some programs are very long and compilers need to be fast, so that is not an acceptable solution. As a result, the way practical syntactic analyzers work is to:

- exploit a context-free grammar that describes those features that it can.
- use a deterministic parser such as one of the ones described in Sections 15.2.3 and 15.3.3.
- augment the parser with specific code, for example a symbol table, to handle the noncontext-free features of the language.

G.4.3 Optimization

Optimizing compilers play an important role in the development of modern software. But, unfortunately, the undecidability results that we have discussed, particularly the ones we summarized in Section 21.5, describe some clear limits on what these compilers can do.

For example, consider the problem of dead code elimination. Programmers do not intentionally write code that can never be reached at run time. But programs that have been around for a while tend to accrete such dead code as a result of changes that affect overall control flow. Is it possible to build a compiler that checks for dead code and simply eliminates it? The answer is no, and it follows directly from Theorem 21.13, which tells us that the language $\{<M, q>$: Turing machine M reaches q on some input$\}$ is not in D.

G.4.4 Compile-Time Error Checking

It is safer and substantially more efficient to detect errors at compile time, rather than waiting until run time to do so. The theory that has been presented in this book provides substantial insight into ways of doing this. It also defines limits on what any sort of compile-time error-checking process can do.

Errors that Can be Caught by a Context-Free Parser

Some errors are easy to detect. They can be caught by a context-free parser because they result in strings that are outside the language that is generated by the grammar on which the parser operates. For example, given the expression grammar that we have used throughout this book, the expressions `id id` and `id ++` are syntactically ill-formed.

Ill-formed strings present a challenge to parser designers, however. It is generally unsatisfactory to find the first error in a program, stop, and report that the parser failed. Instead the parser should try to find a point (perhaps a statement boundary), from which it can partially start over. Then it can continue reading the rest of the program and checking for additional errors. To start over, the parser needs to figure out how much input to skip and how much of what is on its stack should be popped and discarded. See [Aho, Sethi, and Ullman 1988] for a discussion of various ways of doing this.

Error Questions that are Decidable but not by a Context-Free Parser

As we have already discussed, context-free grammars are unable to capture the type constraints imposed by most programming languages. However, all of the following questions are decidable.

- Given a program P, are all the variables in P declared?
- Given a program P, are all the variables in P used only in operations that are defined for their type?
- Given a program P, do all the function calls in P have the correct number of arguments?

Undecidable Error Questions

Unfortunately, as we saw in Chapter 21 and, in particular in Section 21.5, there are other questions about the correctness of programs that are not decidable. The most basic is:

1. Given a program *P*, does *P* halt on all inputs? So no compiler can offer to find all infinite loops in programs.

But there are others. For example, we showed, in Theorem 21.13, that it is undecidable whether a program reaches some particular state (place in the code) on any input. The question is also undecidable if we ask about a particular input or about all inputs. So all of the following questions are undecidable.

2. Given a program *P* and a variable *x*, is *x* always initialized before it is used?
3. Given a program *P* and a file *f*, does *P* always close *f* before it exits?
4. Given a program *P* and a section of code *s* within *P*, is *s* dead code (i.e., code that can never be reached)?

Some other undecidable questions include:

5. Given a program *P* and a division statement with denominator *x*, is *x* always nonzero when the statement is executed?
6. Given a program *P* with an array reference of the form *a*[*i*], will *i*, at the time of the reference, always be within the bounds declared for the array?
7. Given a program *P* and a database of objects *d*, does *P* perform the function *f* on all elements of *d*?

We will show that question 5 is undecidable. The proofs of questions 2, 3, 6, and 7 are left as exercises in Chapter 21.

THEOREM G.1 "Does a Program Divide by Zero?" is Undecidable

Theorem: The language L_2 = {<*M*, *s*> : *s* is the statement number of a division statement to be executed by Turing machine *M* and, whenever *M* executes statement *s*, the denominator is nonzero} is not in D.

Proof: We show $H \leq L_2$ and so L_2 is not in D. Define:

R(<*M*, *w*>) =

1. Construct the description <*M#*> of a new Turing machine *M#*(*x*) that, on input *x*, operates as follows:
   - **1.1.** Erase the tape.
   - **1.2.** Write *w* on the tape.
   - **1.3.** Run *M* on *w*.
   - **1.4.** $x = 1/0$.
2. Return <*M#*, 1.4>).

$\{R, \neg\}$ is a reduction from H to L_2. If *Oracle* exists and decides L_2, then $C = \neg Oracle(R(<M, w>))$ decides H. R and $\neg$ can be implemented as Turing machines. And C is correct. Note that there are no explicit division statements in M (since division is not a primitive Turing machine operation). So the only division statement in $M\#$ is in step 1.4. Thus:

- If $<M, w> \in$ H: M halts on w, so $M\#$ makes it to step 1.4, where it attempts to divide by 0. *Oracle* rejects, so C accepts.
- If $<M, w> \notin$ H: M does not halt on w, so $M\#$ gets stuck in step 1.3. It never executes step 1.4, so, trivially, it is true that on all attempts the denominator is nonzero. So *Oracle* accepts and C rejects.

But no machine to decide H can exist, so neither does *Oracle*.

While, as we have just seen, there are program errors that cannot be guaranteed to be caught and there are program properties that cannot be proven to hold, there are many useful situations in which it is possible to prove that a program meets some or all of its specifications. We return to this topic in the next chapter, where we will discuss a variety of tools that support both programming and software engineering.

G.5 Functional Programming and the Lambda Calculus

In the 1930's, Alonzo Church, Alan Turing, and others were working on the problem that had come to be known as the Entscheidungsproblem. They sought an answer to the question, "Does there exist an algorithm to decide whether a sentence in first-order logic is valid?" They all realized that to answer the question, particularly in the negative, they needed a formal definition of what an algorithm was. Turing's proposal most closely matched the procedural approach to computing that seemed natural to most early programmers. Thus the theory that we have been discussing is based primarily on Turing machines.

But Church's proposal, the lambda calculus, laid the groundwork for an alternative approach to programming that has had an important influence on the modern programming language landscape. In this approach, called ***functional programming***, one defines a program as a function to be computed, rather than as a sequence of specific operations (possibly with side effects) to be performed.

In 1960, John McCarthy published a paper [McCarthy 1960] in which he described ***Lisp***, a language that was directly inspired by the lambda calculus. Today Lisp is the second oldest surviving programming language. (The oldest is Fortran.) Lisp remains the programming language of choice for many kinds of symbolic computing applications. It is the platform that supports a variety of production tools, including Emacs, a flexible and extensible text editor, knowledge-based systems like Scone and KM, the music composition tool Common Music, and a user extension language for the popular computer-aided design tool AutoCAD®, just to name a few. It also inspired the design of an entire family of functional programming languages, including modern languages like ML and Haskell.

The easiest way to begin to understand Lisp is to consider some examples, but one caveat is required. Lisp is no longer a single language. It is a whole language family, each member of which has a different syntax. For illustrative purposes, we will use an easy-to-read syntax close to that of early Lisp systems; the various modern Lisp dialects will differ in some details.

We begin with a simple expression.

```
(LAMBDA (X) (TIMES X X))
```

This expression defines a function of one argument that returns the square of its argument. We often want not just to define functions but to give them names by which they can be referred. We can assign our function the name SQUARE by writing the following.

```
(DEFINE (SQUARE (LAMBDA (X) (TIMES X X))))
```

Since that syntax is clunky, there is an easier one.

```
(DEFUN SQUARE (X) (TIMES X X))
```

In this alternative syntax, it is no longer necessary to write LAMBDA explicitly. DEFUN takes three arguments: the name of the function, a list of the names of the function's arguments, and the body of the function. Named functions can call themselves recursively. So we can write the following.

```
(DEFUN FACTORIAL (X)
      (COND ((EQUAL X 1) 1)
            (T (TIMES X (FACTORIAL (SUB1 X))))))
```

Read this definition as follows: Define the function FACTORIAL of one argument X. To compute it, evaluate a CONDitional expression with two branches. If X equals 1, then return 1. Otherwise (written as T, standing for *True*), return the result of multiplying X times (X−1)! The FACTORIAL function is in many ways a toy; it could easily be implemented with a loop in most programming languages, including modern dialects of Lisp. But it illustrates, for a simple case, the power of recursion. We'll mention less trivial applications shortly.

In the early dialects of Lisp, there were only two kinds of objects: primitive objects, called atoms, and lists. Numbers, strings, and Booleans were all atoms. In this view, anything with an internal structure is a list. A list is written as a sequence of objects enclosed in parentheses. So, for example, (A B C) is a list that contains three atoms. A list may contain another list as one of its elements. So, for example, we could have (A B (C D)), which is a list of three elements, the last of which is a list of two elements. The following list corresponds to a complete binary tree with a root node labeled A and a height of 3. The first element of each list is the label of the root node to which the list corresponds. The next two elements describe the node's two subtrees.

```
(A (B (D E))(C (F G)))
```

Notice now that the definition we wrote for the FACTORIAL function is a list (with sublists). In Lisp, programs are represented as lists, the data type that Lisp is best at manipulating, as we'll see below. To parse a program is easy: The tree structure of a program is exactly its structure as a set of nested lists. So it is straightforward in Lisp for programs to manipulate and modify other programs. Early Lisp programmers took advantage of this and wrote functions that explicitly manipulated the code of other functions. We'll see one example of this below, although it is now generally regarded as bad software practice. But the fact that Lisp allowed programs to access other programs and the environments in which they were executed led to the development, within Lisp, of arguably the most powerful macro facility in any modern programming language.

Modern dialects of Lisp have evolved substantially more sophisticated data typing systems than the simple, atoms and lists model that McCarthy introduced. But the notion that programs (functions) are data objects remains a key feature of the language and a major source of the flexibility that gives Lisp its power.

In the Lisp programming environment, computation occurs when an expression (an atom or a list) is evaluated. Constants (including numbers, as well as the Boolean constants T and F) evaluate to themselves. Variables evaluate to their values. Lists are evaluated by treating the first element as a function and the remaining elements as the arguments to which the function should be applied. So, for example, we might write:

```
(FACTORIAL 5)
```

This expression, when evaluated, will apply the FACTORIAL function to the value 5 and return 120. Before a function can be applied to its arguments, each of them must be evaluated. This wasn't obvious in the (FACTORIAL 5) case because the atom 5 evaluates to 5. But if the variable X has the value 3, then (FACTORIAL X) will return 6.

Lists can be written, as we have been doing, as constants that are specified by the programmer and they can be read as input. Or they can be constructed within a program. Lisp provides a set of primitives for constructing lists and for taking them apart. The function LIST takes any number of arguments and puts them together to make a list. So we could write the following.

```
(LIST 'A (FACTORIAL 5))
```

When evaluated, that expression will build a list with two elements. The first will be the symbol A. (Remember that arguments are evaluated before functions are applied to them. The quote mark suppresses that evaluation. If we had omitted the quote mark in front of A, A would have been treated as a variable and evaluated. Then its value, whatever it is, would have become the first element of the new list.) The second element of the list will be the result of evaluating (FACTORIAL 5). So the new list will be (A 120).

The function CONS (for constructor) adds an element to the front of an existing list. So we could write the following expression, which will return the list (B A 120).

```
(CONS 'B '(A 120))
```

Lists can be broken apart into their pieces using two primitive functions whose names are historical accidents: CAR returns the first element of the list it is given. CDR returns its input list with the first element removed. So:

```
(CAR '(B A 120)) evaluates to B.
(CDR '(B A 120)) evaluates to (A 120).
```

In most programming environments, the semantics of the language are implemented in a black box runtime environment that cannot be accessed at the program level. This isn't true in Lisp. Functions don't just look like lists. They *are* lists and operations can be performed on them. The most important operation that can be performed on functions is evaluation. Lisp provides functions, including EVAL, APPLY, and FUNCALL, that can be invoked from within any Lisp program. These functions explicitly evaluate expressions. For example, EVAL takes a single argument and evaluates it. To see how it works, suppose that we want to read in P, a polynomial function of one variable, and then apply it to several values. Then we might input the following list, corresponding to the polynomial $7x^2 - 2x + 3$.

```
(PLUS (DIFFERENCE (TIMES 7 (SQUARE X)) (TIMES 2 X)) 3)
```

Note that functions in Lisp are written in prefix notation. (Modern Lisps use the more compact symbols +, *, and − though.) Suppose that the variable P now has that list as its value and the variable X has the value 4. Then the following expression will return the value 107.

```
(EVAL P)
```

Functions can also be passed as parameters to other functions. Suppose, for example, that we want to write a program that takes two inputs, a function and a list. We want our program to apply the function to each element of the list and return a new list with the resulting values. For example, if given SQUARE and the list (4 3 7), it should return (16 9 49). The Lisp function MAPCAR does exactly this. Given a function F and a list L, it first applies F to the first element of L, namely (CAR L). Then it applies it to the second element of L, namely (CAR (CDR L)). And so forth. It returns a new list that contains the values that it produced. So we can write the following expression.

```
(MAPCAR F L)
```

If F has the value (LAMBDA (X) (* X X)) and L has the value (4, 3, 7), the result of EVALing our expression will be (16, 9, 49). Suppose, on the other hand, that F has as its value a function that returns, for any letter in the Roman alphabet, its successor (letting the successor of Z be A). And suppose that L has the value (C A T). Then EVALing (MAPCAR F L) will produce (D B U).

Modern dialects of Lisp provide an even more powerful mechanism for treating functions as first-class objects. They enable programs to construct and exploit ***closures***, i.e., function definitions coupled with evaluation environments that bind values to variables. To see how closures can be used, consider the following example. BOSS wants a list of candidates whose score on some dimension called KEY is at least THRESHOLD. To get the list, BOSS executes (GETSOME THRESHOLD). GETSOME considers many criteria and has access to various sources of candidates. Each such source maintains its own list of possible candidates and it accepts two inputs, the number of candidates desired and a function (of a single argument) that describes a test to be performed on candidates; only those that pass the test will be suggested. Let's call one of the sources WELL. GETSOME can be defined as follows.

```
(DEFUN GETSOME (THRESHOLD)
   ...                                          /* Consider other things.
   (WELL  K #'(LAMBDA (X)  (AND (TEST1)
                                (TEST2)
                                (> (KEY X) THRESHOLD))))
   ...                                          /* Consider other things.
                  )
```

When the expression (WELL ...) is evaluated, the first thing that happens is that its arguments are evaluated. Its first argument evaluates to the value of the variable K. It is assumed to be a number. Its second argument begins with the symbol #', which is shorthand for a function (called FUNCTION) that forms a closure by capturing the current values of all of the free variables in the enclosed expression. In this case, there is a single such variable, THRESHOLD. So the closure that is formed contains the function described by the LAMBDA expression plus the current value of THRESHOLD. Without closures, one could imagine simply passing THRESHOLD as another argument to WELL. But WELL may be called by many different kinds of customers. It doesn't know what THRESHOLD is. All it knows how to do is to select candidates it wants to recommend and then apply a single test to see which ones will be acceptable to its customer. Its customer (in this case GETSOME) must therefore describe all of the tests it cares about as a single function that can be applied to a candidate.

We've now seen enough to be able to comment on some of the key ideas that underlie Lisp and that play a key role in modern high-level programming languages:

- In Lisp, the most important data structure is the list. Lists can be constructed by programs at run time. Their sizes and structures need not be declared in advance. It is very easy to write programs that manipulate dynamic lists and trees. So, for example, we were able above to read in a polynomial function of arbitrary length and then EVAL it. There is no need to declare in advance what the size of any structure is. Thus Lisp had to provide run-time storage allocation and garbage collection. (We should point out here, though, that Lisp was not the first list processing language. That title belongs to the IPL family of languages 💻.)
- In Lisp, one describes a computation as a function to be evaluated. While Lisp was not the first list-processing language, it was the first functional one. Lisp provided a few primitive functions and it allowed programmers to define new ones. To make this possible, Lisp introduced:
  - ***conditional expressions:*** The Lisp COND function, which can have any number of branches, is the precursor of the modern if-then-else or case statement. We take such control statements for granted, but at the time that Lisp was first described, Fortran, for example, only had a conditional go to statement.
  - ***recursion:*** Another reason that Lisp introduced run-time storage allocation and garbage collection was to make recursion possible.

- ***functions as first-class objects:*** Functions can be manipulated by other functions and passed to other functions as arguments. In early implementations of Lisp, the runtime manipulation of functions was possible because the language was interpreted, rather than compiled. The job of the interpreter was to transform a list into something executable and then run it. While this execution model was flexible, it was also slow. Modern implementations of Lisp also provide compilers, with the consequence that, while Lisp maintains its flexibility, it no longer necessarily incurs a runtime performance penalty.

- Lisp functions are lists, a data type that Lisp programs can manipulate. Because they are lists, they can be stored within other data structures and they can be parsed easily at either compile time or run time.

In defining Lisp, McCarthy did more than just create a new and arguably convenient way to program. He also made clear the connection between the power of the new language and the fundamental notions of computability as investigated by Turing and Church. In particular, McCarthy showed that the class of functions that can be computed in Lisp is exactly the computable functions (i.e., exactly the set that can be computed by some Turing machine).

The Lisp language, as originally described by McCarthy, evolved into a family of dialects that became the programming languages of choice for the development of many kinds of artificial intelligence (AI) systems. The next few examples illustrate some of the reasons that Lisp was, and is, so well suited to the needs of AI programmers.

EXAMPLE G.5 Search: Exploiting Recursion and Function Objects

Lisp's natural control structure is recursion. This contrasts with the iterative control structures that were the mainstay of other early programming languages. What many AI programs do is search and search can easily be described recursively. To evaluate a situation to see whether it can lead to a solution to a problem, we generate all of the situations that can be reached via a single action from the current one. If any of them is a goal, we have found our answer. Otherwise, we call the evaluation procedure recursively on each of the successor states. In Section 30.3.2, we describe A^*, a general-purpose, best-first search algorithm that does this, and in N.2.5, we describe *minimax*, an alternative that is tailored specifically to searching two-person game trees.

While recursion is key in implementing almost any search algorithm, another feature of Lisp is also important in implementing best-first search algorithms like A^* and *minimax*: The input to all such programs is a problem definition, which must contain two functions: *successors*, which computes a node's successors and assigns costs to individual moves, and h, a heuristic evaluation function. In Lisp, it is easy to write A^* or *minimax* once and then to pass it, as parameters, the functions that it needs.

EXAMPLE G.6 Representing Parse Trees as Lists

To see why list-like structures that need not be declared in advance are useful in AI, consider the natural language (NL) understanding problem. An NL understanding program must accept as input one or more sentences. In Lisp, this is easy. The input text can be represented as a list of words. So assuming that we have defined symbols that correspond to the words in our dictionary, we might, for example, have:

```
(the smart cat smells chocolate)
```

An early step in understanding sentences is usually to parse them. Recall that, in Example 11.11, we showed the following parse tree:

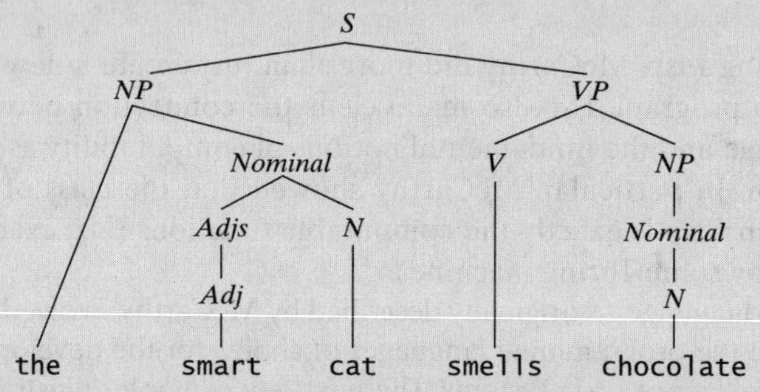

This tree can easily be represented as a Lisp list, in which each node is a list. The first element of the list is the label attached to the node. The remaining elements are node's subtrees. So we have:

```
(S   (NP (the) (Nominal (Adjs (Adj (smart)))(N(cat))))
     (VP (V (smells))(NP(Nominal (N (chocolate)))))   )
```

EXAMPLE G.7 Representing Logical Formulas as Lists

In many task domains, knowledge can be represented as sentences in first-order logic. These sentences, in turn, can easily be represented as Lisp lists. For example, the sentence:

$$\forall x\, (\exists y\, (P(x) \wedge R(x) \rightarrow Q(y)))$$

can be represented as the list:

```
(FORALL X
    (EXISTS Y
        (IMPLIES (AND (P X)
                      (R X))
            (Q Y))))
```

The sentence can then be evaluated by recursively evaluating its subexpressions.

EXAMPLE G.8 Automatic Programming

In Lisp, there is no distinction between programs and data. Lisp programs, like everything else, are lists. This turns out to be particularly useful if one wants to build programs that can write or modify other programs. So, for example, one subfield of AI is called ***automatic programming*** or ***program synthesis*** 💻. Its goal is to automate the task of writing code to solve a problem whose specifications have been provided. Of course, the problem of deciding what code to write remains hard, but in Lisp it is straightforward to build up a program by composing lists. And the code that is built in that way can be run, as part of the coding and debugging process, in exactly the same way that any Lisp expression is evaluated.

EXAMPLE G.9 Learning to Improve Performance

An important characteristic of an intelligent system is its ability to learn and to improve its performance on the basis of experience. If a performance program is written in Lisp, then a learning program, also written in Lisp, can modify the performance program using Lisp's basic list operations. For example, suppose that we want to build a program that evaluates its environment and, on the basis of what it sees, decides how to perform a task. We might write such a program in Lisp using the following structure:

```
(COND ( (AND (condition1)
             (condition2)
             (condition3))      (action A))
      ( (OR  (condition4)
             (condition5))      (action B))  )
```

Now suppose that we want to learn to perform the task better. There are several things that we might want to be able to do. We might discover a new special case that requires a new action. The alternatives that are listed in a Lisp COND statement are evaluated in the order in which they are written. So we could describe the special case by adding a new branch at the beginning of the COND expression, producing:

```
(COND ( (condition6)            (action C))
      ( (AND (condition1)
             (condition2)
             (condition3))      (action A))
      ( (OR  (condition4)
             (condition5))      (action B))  )
```

EXAMPLE G.9 (*Continued*)

Note that we're not simply claiming that a programmer can make this change. A Lisp program that notices that the change is necessary can use CONS to add the new condition to the front of the list of branches. Or we might want to generalize the behavior of our program so that it works in some additional environments. One way to do that would be to change the AND on line 2 to an OR. Another way would be to remove one or more of conditions 1, 2, and 3. These changes can easily be made by the learning program to the list representation of the performance program. Then the new program can be run and evaluated to see whether the change improved its performance.

EXAMPLE G.10 Procedural Knowledge

The core of any AI program is its knowledge base. Some knowledge can naturally be thought of as declarative. For example, John's phone number is a string of digits, his age is a number, his mother's name is a string, and his birthday wish list is a list of objects. But in real applications, the values for even these simple attributes, much less more complex ones, may not always be known. Instead, what may be available are procedures for computing values as they are needed. Thus it may make sense to store, as the value of John's phone number, a function closure that was created in a context in which it was known what city he lives in. The function searches that city's phone book to find John's number. Similarly, the value for John's birthday wish list might be a procedure that executes in an environment that knows his hobbies and his favorite foods.

As originally defined, Lisp was a purely functional language. All computation occurred by evaluating functions. There existed no operations that caused side effects. Most modern dialects have been extended to allow side effects in various ways. In addition to input and output functions, there are typically functions that assign values to variables and functions that destructively modify lists (as opposed simply to creating new ones). There may also be a way to describe a sequence of actions that should be performed. So most modern Lisps are not purely functional.

But there are arguments for purely functional programming. In particular, when side effects are allowed, constructing correctness proofs may be hard. In the years since McCarthy's original description of Lisp, a variety of other purely functional languages have been defined. These languages, of which ***Haskell*** is probably the most widely used, owe an intellectual debt to Lisp, as well as to other developments in the area of high-level programming language design.

APPENDIX H

Applications: Tools for Programming, Databases and Software Engineering

The formal structures that we have been discussing have inspired the design of many different kinds of tools that programmers use every day. We have already discussed the design of high-level programming languages and the construction of compilers for them. In Appendix O, we'll discuss the use of regular expressions in modern programming environments. In this appendix, we'll briefly describe some other kinds of useful tools whose design is rooted in the theory that we have described.

H.1 Proving Correctness Properties of Programs and Hardware

Consider the problem of proving that a particular software program or hardware device correctly implements its specification. In the rest of this discussion, we will use the term "system" to describe both software and hardware systems.

If the answer to the Entscheidungsproblem that we introduced in Chapter 18 had been yes (in other words, if there did exist a procedure to determine whether an arbitrary sentence in first-order logic is valid), then it might be possible to:

1. Write a first-order logic sentence that corresponds to the specifications for a system.
2. Write another first-order logic sentence that describes what the system actually does. An effective way to do this is in two steps:
   - **2.1.** Define a set of first-order logic axioms that describe the primitive operations that a system can perform. For example, we could describe the behavior of an individual gate in a hardware circuit or an individual statement in some particular programming language.

2.2. Derive from those axioms and the definition of a particular system (its logic design or its code) the required sentence that describes the system's behavior

3. Build a theorem proving program that could determine whether the sentence from step 2 entails the sentence from step 1. (In other words: Given a system that behaves as described in the sentence from step 2, must the sentence from step 1 be true? Put another way: Does the system satisfy the specification?)

But, as we saw in Chapter 19, the answer to the Entscheidungsproblem is no. That result, proved independently by Turing and by Church in the mid 1930s, coupled with the Incompleteness Theorem published by Kurt Gödel at about the same time, dashed the hopes of mathematicians that they might find a completely syntactic basis for mathematics. It also means that it won't be possible to build a completely automatic, general-purpose, first-order logic-based verification system that can be guaranteed to halt and return *True* precisely in case the target system satisfies its specification and *False* otherwise.

Early interest in the Entscheidungsproblem was motivated by a concern with issues in mathematics and philosophy. Now, with the advent of modern computers, we have a new and more practical need for a syntactically-based theorem-proving method: We build huge and complex pieces of hardware and software and we trust them to perform critical functions. If we could build programs that could produce formal proofs of the correctness of those critical systems, we would have an increased basis for the trust we place in them. (We say an increased basis for the trust, rather than total trust, because there would still be issues like the extent to which the formal specification corresponds to our goal for our systems, the correctness of the proof-generator itself, and limits to our ability to describe, all the way down to the electrons, the behavior of the hardware on which our systems run). Fortunately, the negative results of Church and Turing do not doom all efforts to build mechanical verification systems. It is true that we showed, in Chapter 21, that there are some program properties, including some that could be part of many reasonable specifications, that are undecidable. These properties include:

- Given a program P, does P halt on all inputs? Does P halt on some particular input w? Does P halt on any inputs?
- Given a program P, does P ever output anything?
- Given two programs P_1 and P_2, are they equivalent?

Nevertheless, there are useful correctness properties that can be proved, at least of some programs and devices. For example, while it is not possible to decide whether an arbitrary program always halts, it may be possible to prove that a particular one does. To construct such targeted proofs, we require a logical language that can be used to represent specifications and to describe the behavior of systems. In particular, we must find a logical language that meets all of the following requirements.

- It is expressive enough to make it possible to encode both specifications and descriptions of system behavior.

- Its decidability properties are strong enough to make it useful.
- The complexity of its decision procedures is acceptable for the size problems we wish to solve.

These issues trade off and there does not appear to be a single approach that worst best for all kinds of problems. But there are two general approaches, each of which has proven to be effective for some classes of important problems:

- deductive verification systems, in which steps 1 through 3 are done but step 3 is typically only semiautomatic—a human user must guide the theorem prover; and
- model checking systems, which are usually fully automatic but are limited to reasoning about systems that can be described with finite (and thus decidable) models.

H.1.1 Deductive Verification

Deductive verification systems find proofs in much the same way mathematicians do. The core of all such systems is a theorem prover that begins with a set of axioms and then applies rules of inference to derive conclusions. The theorem prover may also be augmented with a set of conventional programs that perform tasks such as the computation of standard arithmetic operations. Effective verification systems must cope with two realities of the task:

- expressively powerful logical systems (including standard first-order logic) are undecidable, and
- the number of legal proofs grows exponentially with the length of the proof so, even when a proof exists, a brute force approach to finding it will take too long.

Modern deductive verification systems solve those problems by choosing a carefully designed logical language and then exploiting an interactive theorem prover. A human user guides the theorem prover in one or more of the following ways.

- The user describes the steps (lemmas) that should be solved on the way to a complete proof. If the theorem prover is unable to complete a step, the user can provide additional information.
- The user tells the theorem prover what substitutions to perform as the variables and constants of one expression are matched against those of another.

Interactive verification systems of this sort have been used both to find faults and to prove correctness in a wide variety of critical applications. Some examples include:

- The discovery of flaws in the design of control software for an observatory.
- The analysis of cryptographic protocols (e.g., Bluetooth) for security properties.

But the fact that people must be part of the verification process has meant that the spread of this approach into practical system construction has been limited by the scarcity of people who understand the required logical language and who are skilled at providing the assistance that the theorem prover needs.

H.1.2 Model Checking

Suppose that the system (software or hardware) whose correctness we would like to prove can be modeled with a finite number of states. Perhaps (as is often the case with hardware) it was originally designed as a finite state machine. Or perhaps it was designed some other way but its state can be described by a finite number of variables and each of those variables can take on a finite number of values. In the latter case, it is straightforward. to build a finite state machine that describes the operation of the system. Many concurrent systems, for example, can be modeled in this way since there are typically only a finite number of shared variables, each of which can be described as taking on values from only a finite set. Further, it is sometimes the case that, although in principle a variable may take on some unbounded set of values, any logical errors in the design of the system in which the variable occurs can be detected by considering only some well-crafted subset of those values.

When it is possible to create such finite system descriptions, a powerful class of programs called model checkers ([Clarke and Emerson 1981], [Quielle and Sifakis 1982], [Clarke, Grumberg and Peled 1999]) can be used to check for system correctness. The basic idea is that we compare a finite description of our system to an appropriately crafted logical statement that describes the system's specification. The system is correct iff it satisfies (i.e., is a model of) the specification. Thus the name model checking. Undecidability is not a problem for model checkers (since finite descriptions can be described in Boolean logic, which is decidable). But combinatorial explosion is a problem and current research in model checking is focused on ways of reducing that explosion in practice.

The primary use of model checkers has been to prove the correctness of digital circuits and concurrent programs. Since those systems are not intended to halt, the examples we will present in this section all describe infinite computations.

The first step in using a model checker is to construct a finite state model of the system whose correctness we wish to prove. Suppose that v is the set of variables in the system. Then we create, in our model, one state for each possible assignment of values to the variables in v. For example, suppose that v contains the variables x, y, and z and each of them can take on the values 0 and 1. Then the model we build will have eight states corresponding to the eight ways of assigning values to those variables. So, for example, one such state would correspond to the valuation $(x = 0; y = 0; z = 0)$. More generally, we can describe each state by a set of atomic propositions that are true in it. So, for example, we could use propositions such as $(x = 0)$. In the examples that follow, we will assume that all system variables are binary and we will use propositions with names corresponding to the variables. The proposition a will be true iff the variable a has the value *True* (or 1). This technique can easily be extended to handle any variable that ranges over a finite number of values by encoding those values in binary. When modeling real systems, it will often happen that some states correspond to valuations that cannot occur. Since those states will not be reachable from any start state, it is not necessary to represent them in the model.

The two other important things we need to do are to specify the system's start state(s) and to specify how it moves from one state to the next. So a complete model of a system Y can be given as a five-tuple (called a ***Kripke structure***) $M = (S, S_0, P, R, L)$, where:

- S is a finite set of states designed, as described above, to correspond to the possible assignments of values to the variables of Y.
- S_0, a subset of S, is the set of start states of Y.
- P is a non-empty set of atomic propositions that describe properties (such as the fact that the variable $x = 0$) that may hold in the various states of S.
- R is a transition relation. It is a subset of $S \times S$. The pair $(q_1, q_2) \in R$ iff Y can go directly from q_1 to q_2. Since Y does not halt, it must be the case that, for every state q_1 in S, there exists at least one state q_2 such that $(q_1, q_2) \in R$. Note that we do not require that R be a function. So it is possible to model systems whose behavior is nondeterministic.
- L is a function that labels each state in S with the set of propositions that are true in it. So L maps from S to $\mathcal{P}(P)$.

EXAMPLE H.1 Modeling a Simple, Two-Switch System

Consider a very simple system with two switches. One is the *a* switch and it can be on or off. The other is the *b/c* switch. It can be off or it can be thrown to *b* or *c*, but that can happen only if it's currently off. Once it's ever thrown to *c*, it can't be changed. The *a* switch can only go off if *c* is on. The system starts out with the *a* switch on and the *b/c* switch off. We can model this system with the Kripke structure $M = (\{\{a\}, \{a, b\}, \{a, c\}, \{c\}\}, \{\{a\}\}, \{a, b, c\}, R, L)$, where L assigns to each state the labels we're using as the state's name and R is given by:

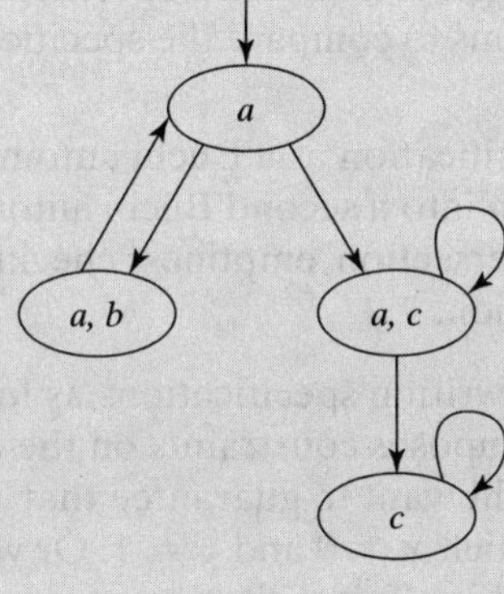

A computation of a system Y, described by a Kripke structure M, is a path through the states of M. Since computations don't end, any such path will be infinite. Since a state may have more than one successor, we can describe all paths that Y could follow, from some start state q, as a computation tree rooted at q.

EXAMPLE H.2 The Two-Switch System's Computation Tree

Consider again the system we described in Example H.1. Its computation tree, starting from state $\{a\}$ contains:

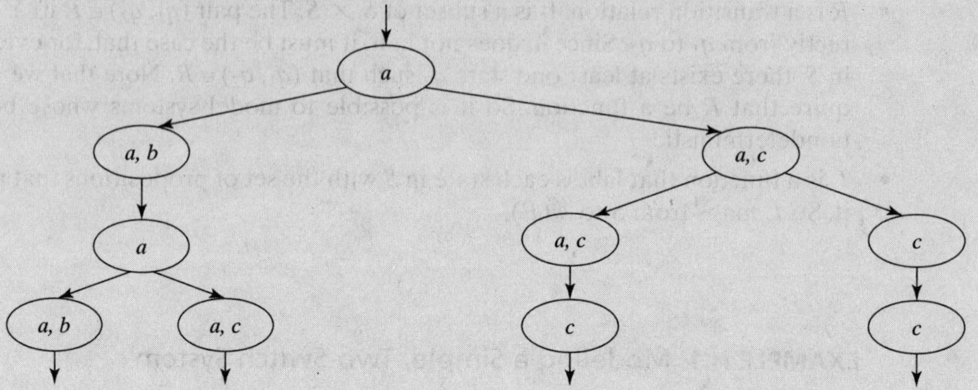

Steps two and three in using a model checker are to state the specification and then to show that, on every computation path, the system model satisfies the specification. The technique that is used to perform step three depends on the language that is used to define the specification in step two. We'll consider two approaches:

- Use a temporal logic to define the specification and apply one of a family of model checking algorithms to compare the specification to the Kripke structure that models the system.
- Describe the specification as a Büchi automaton, convert the Kripke structure that models the system into a second Büchi automaton, and use operations on automata (complement, intersection, emptiness checking) to decide whether the system satisfies the specification.

We first consider writing specifications as logical formulas. Typically, the specification for a system Y imposes constraints on the computational paths that Y can follow. For example, we might want to guarantee that Y never enters a state that corresponds to the situation in which $x = 0$ and $y = 1$. Or we might want to guarantee that, once x becomes 0, y never does. To facilitate stating such requirements, the logical language that is used in model checking systems is typically some form of temporal logic, in which it is possible to describe constraints on the future states of the system given its current state. Formulas in temporal logic may describe properties that must be true of states, including properties that must be true along paths that can emerge from those states.

There are two main kinds of temporal logics that are used in model checkers:

- Linear time logics, in which there is always a unique future, and

- Branching time logics, in which, given a particular moment in time, multiple futures are possible. Branching time logics typically provide quantifiers that can range over paths. Common quantifiers are:
  - **A** (for all computation paths), and
  - **E** (for some computation path, i.e., there exists some computation path).

Temporal logics provide operators that can be applied to propositions. The following operators are present in the branching time logical language CTL* 💻, and are typical:

- **G** *P*, which holds iff *P* is always true (is true **g**lobally),
- **F** *P*, which holds iff *P* will eventually (at some time in the **f**uture) become true,
- **X** *P*, which holds iff *P* holds in the ne**x**t state,
- P_1 **U** P_2, which holds iff P_2 eventually becomes true and, at every state until then, P_1 is true (P_1 **u**ntil P_2), and
- P_1 **R** P_2, which holds iff P_2 holds in every state up to and including the first state in which P_1 is true (P_1 **r**eleases P_2). It is possible that P_1 may never become true, however.

EXAMPLE H.3 Some Simple Specifications of the Two-Switch System

We return again to the system we described in Example H.1. This time we'll consider some possible specifications and see whether the system satisfies them:

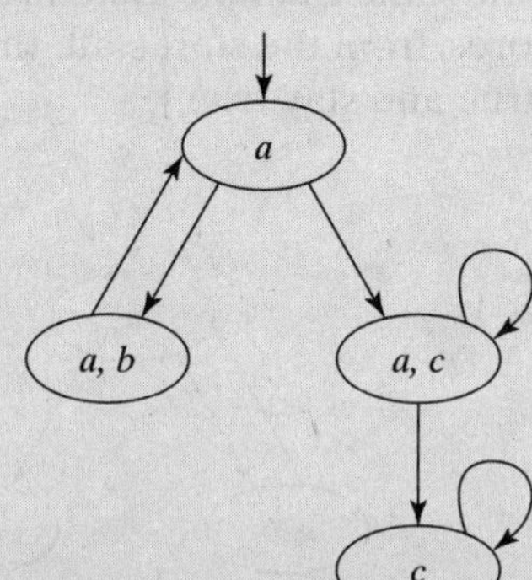

$a \vee c$	This holds in all states.
EG $(a \vee c)$	(There exists a path such that $a \vee c$ always.) This holds in all states.
EF c	(There exists a path such that eventually c.) This holds in all states.
EG c	(There exists a path such that c always.) This holds only in $\{a, c\}$ and $\{c\}$.
Ec**R**a	(There exists a path where a until released by c.) This holds in all states except $\{c\}$.

Now we have, for a system Y, a Kripke structure M that describes Y's implementation and a temporal logic formula f that describes the requirements (specifications) for Y. The final step in determining the correctness of Y is to decide whether the implementation conforms to the specification. We would like to prove that there is no path through M that fails to satisfy f. If, on the other hand, there is such a path, we would like to report it. The fact that model checkers can do more than "just say no" is one reason that they are particularly useful in practice: A counterexample tells the system's developers exactly where the system can fail and thus points the way to solution to the problem. Further, if a specification requires that there exist a path with some desirable property, the model checking process will find and report such a "witness."

The most straightforward algorithms for model checking work with an explicit representation of the Kripke structure $M = (S, S_0, R, P, L)$ that describes the implementation. The idea is that we will consider the states in S and we will annotate each of them with those subformulas from the specification f that can be shown to hold in it. The annotation process begins with the labels that are already attached to the states by the labeling function L. Then it considers the subformulas in f, starting with the most primitive, builds up longer and longer annotations, and propagates them through M. If all subformulas hold in all start states, then all computation paths satisfy f.

EXAMPLE H.4 Evaluating a Specification of the Two-Switch System

We'll continue with the same example system. Suppose that the specification for it is **EG** c. (In other words, from the start state there exists a path along which c will eventually become true and stay true.)

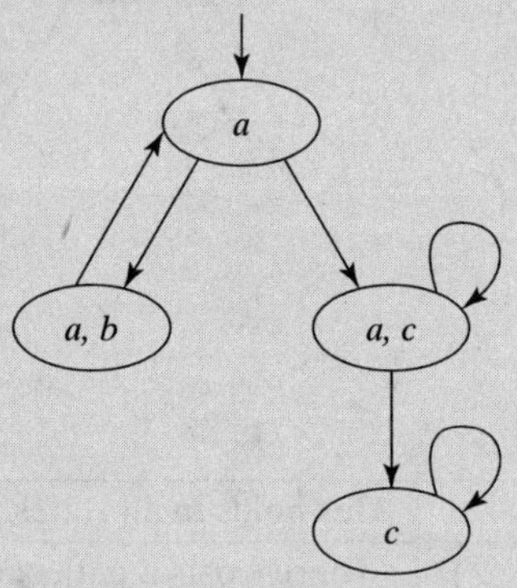

- c holds in state $\{c\}$.
- **EG** c also holds in $\{c\}$.
- Thus **EG** c also holds in $\{a, c\}$.
- Thus **EG** c also holds in $\{a\}$, which is the only start state, so this implementation satisfies **EG** c.

The details of any model checking algorithm depend on the temporal logic language that is used for the specification. But, for example, for CTL*, the language we discussed above, there exists a model checking algorithm and its complexity is $\mathcal{O}(|f| \cdot (|S| + |R|))$, where f is the formula that describes the specification. So it is linear in both the size of the formula f and the size of the Kripke structure M. For large systems, though, this isn't good enough because the number of states in M may be $\mathcal{O}(2^{|v|})$, where v is the number of variables in the system that M is modeling.

To solve this problem we need a technique that does not require the explicit construction of M before we can start. Suppose that instead of describing a system Y as a set of states and transitions between them, we could describe Y as a Boolean function. Then we could use an ordered binary decision diagram (OBDD), as described in B.1.3, as an efficient way to represent Y.

To start, we'll describe each state as the Boolean function that describes the condition under which Y is in that state. So, for example, suppose that there are three atomic propositions (v_1, v_2, v_3) in our model. Then we'll represent the state shown in Figure H.1(a) as $v_1 \wedge \neg v_2 \wedge v_3$. Now consider any transition in a Kripke structure, as for example the transition from state (1) to state (2) shown in Figure H.1(b). We can think of this transition as a relation between the sets of propositions that are true in state (1) and those that are true in state (2).

To describe it that way, we need a second set of proposition names. We'll use the original set A to describe the propositions that hold in state (1) and a new set A' to describe those that hold in state (2). Then we can describe the transition relation using its characteristic function (i.e., a Boolean function whose value is *True* for each element of the relation and *False* otherwise). Using this idea, we construct, for the single transition shown above, the Boolean function:

$$v_1 \wedge \neg v_2 \wedge v_3 \wedge v_1' \wedge v_2' \wedge \neg v_3'.$$

From the functions that describe individual transitions, we can construct a single function that is true for an entire transition relation. It is true whenever any of the transition relations is true. So, for the simple two-state, two-transition structure of Figure H.1(c), we can construct the Boolean function:

$$(v_1 \wedge \neg v_2 \wedge v_3 \wedge v_1' \wedge v_2' \wedge \neg v_3') \vee (v_1 \wedge v_2 \wedge \neg v_3 \wedge v_1' \wedge v_2' \wedge \neg v_3').$$

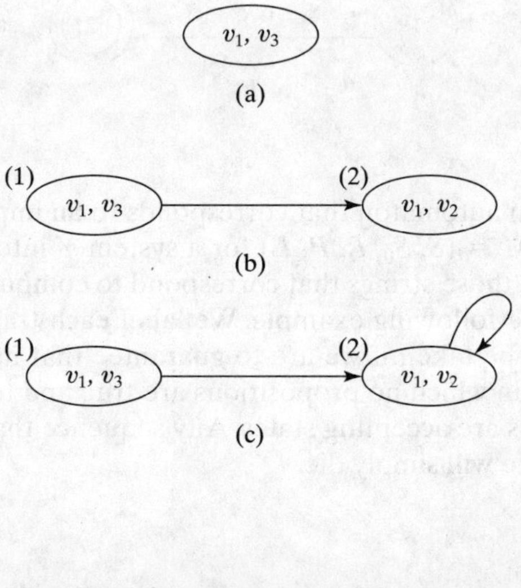

FIGURE H.1 States can be described as Boolean expressions.

This representation doesn't look smaller than the original state model, but that's primarily because the original state model was already small. In cases where the state model is enormous, the OBDD representation of the corresponding Boolean function is often small and it is possible to construct that representation directly from Y's description (as a logic circuit or as a program), without first creating the Kripke structure (and thus representing all possible combinations of variable values explicitly). This insight has led to the development of a more powerful class of verification programs called ***symbolic model checkers***, which exploit system models described as Boolean functions, which in turn are represented as OBDDs.

As we pointed out in B.1.3, there are some systems (e.g., an n-bit multiplier) whose OBDD representation grows as $\mathcal{O}(2^{|n|})$. But most useful systems don't have that property and symbolic model checkers are now routinely used to prove the correctness of systems whose Kripke structure contains 10^{20} or more states.

An alternative approach to model checking is automata-based. In this approach, both the specification and the Kripke structure that describes the implementation are described as Büchi automata (automata that accept infinite strings, as described in Section 5.12). We use Büchi automata here because strings that correspond to computations will be infinite.

Representing many kinds of specifications as Büchi automata is straightforward. Recall that, in Example 5.39, we showed the Büchi automaton for a single simple requirement, mutual exclusion. We can do the same thing for many other important properties.

EXAMPLE H.5 A Büchi Automaton for a Simple Liveness Property

The following Büchi automaton corresponds to a simple liveness property. As in Example 5.39, we use the atomic propositions: CR_0 ($process_0$ is in its critical region) and CR_1 ($process_1$ is in its critical region). This time, we require that $process_0$ eventually enter its critical region:

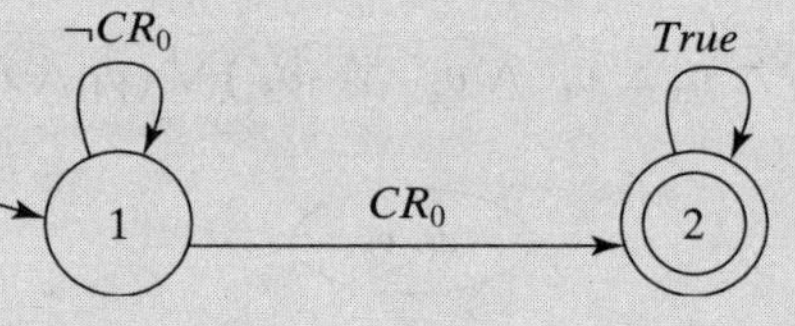

Next we need a Büchi automaton that corresponds to an implementation. Converting a Kripke structure $M = (S, S_0, R, P, L)$ for a system Y into a Büchi automaton B that accepts all and only those strings that correspond to computations of Y is straightforward, as shown in the following example. We label each transition with the condition under which it can be taken if we are to guarantee that its annotation holds. We create a new start state in which no propositions are true and transitions from it to all elements of S_0. All states are accepting states. Any sequence that would correspond to a path that Y cannot take will simply die.

EXAMPLE H.6 Converting a Kripke Structure to a Büchi Automaton

Returning again to our two-switch example, we can convert the Kripke structure to a Büchi automaton as shown here. As we did in labeling the states, we will label the transitions with the propositions that must be true. All others must be false. So, for example, $a \wedge b$ should be read as equivalent to $a \wedge b \wedge \neg c$.

Kripke structure:

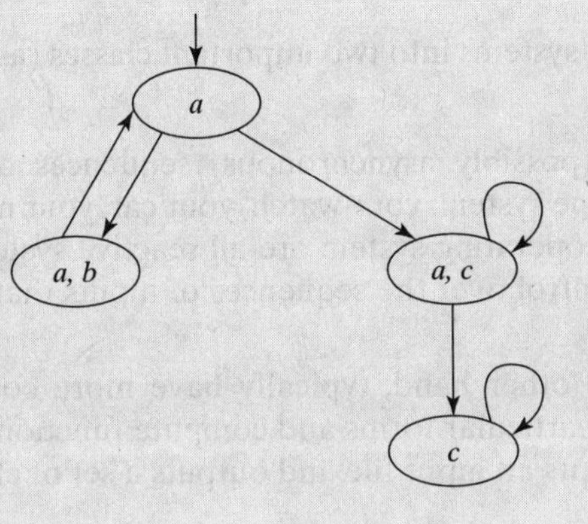

Büchi automaton:

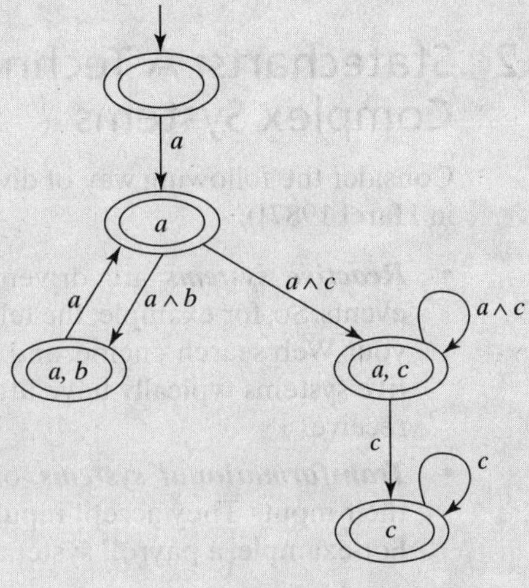

Given two Büchi automata, B_{SPEC}, which corresponds to Y's specification, and B_{IMP}, which corresponds to the Kripke structure that describes an implementation, we're ready to decide whether B_{IMP} satisfies B_{SPEC}. We proceed as follows: Construct B_{BAD}, a Büchi automaton that accepts the complement of $L(B_{SPEC})$. So B_{BAD} accepts exactly the strings that violate the specification Next, construct B_{BOTH}, a Büchi automaton that accepts the intersection of $L(B_{BAD})$ and $L(B_{IMP})$. Finally, test whether $L(B_{BOTH})$ is empty. If it is not, then there are computation sequences that are possible in the implementation but that are not allowed by the specification. If it is empty, then there are no such computations and we have proved that the system satisfies its specification. Note that this procedure works because the class of languages accepted by Büchi automata is closed under both complement and intersection and there exists a decision procedure for the emptiness question. It is also possible to skip the complement step if the user enters the negative specification directly.

Using these techniques, model checkers have been used to:

- Prove the correctness of general-purpose processor chips.
- Prove the correctness of special-purpose processors such as for video game consoles.

- Prove that a logic optimizer has not altered the functionality of a circuit. This is done by showing that the functions for the two circuits (the original one and the optimized one) are identical.
- Prove the correctness of network protocols, including, for example, the alternating bit protocol described in I.1.2.
- Prove the correctness of critical real time systems such as the controllers for aircraft and space exploration vehicles. For example, the SPIN 💻 model checking system found five previously undetected concurrency errors in the plan execution module of the controller for a space-craft that NASA launched in 1998.

H.2 Statecharts: A Technique for Specifying Complex Systems

Consider the following way of dividing systems into two important classes (as described in Harel 1987]):

- ***Reactive systems*** are driven by (possibly asynchronous) sequences of external events. So, for example, the telephone system, your watch, your car, your microwave, your Web search engine, and your operating system are all reactive systems. Reactive systems typically have little control over the sequences of inputs that they may receive.
- ***Transformational systems***, on the other hand, typically have more control over their inputs. They accept inputs in particular forms and compute functions of them. For example, a payroll system accepts an input file and outputs a set of checks.

While the distinction between these two kinds of systems is not hard and fast, it is useful. In particular, it highlights one reason that designing reactive systems is hard (the fact that arbitrary sequences of inputs must be handled properly). And it suggests a way to build tools that are particularly well-suited for the design of those systems: Let the tool provide explicit support for describing the way that the system's state changes as inputs are received.

In Chapter 5 we used this approach to system design when we built finite state machines. But what about real systems with real complexity? Can they too be modeled with a finite number of states? It turns out that often they can. And, in other cases, they can be modeled with a finite number of states plus a set of variables that can take on arbitrary values.

A family of design tools based on statecharts 💻, as described in [Harel 1987] and [Harel and Politi 1998], exploits this observation. A ***statechart*** is a hierarchically structured finite state machine. The hierarchical structure makes it possible to:

- view a system design at whatever level of detail is necessary.
- describe a system design using fewer transitions than would be required in a flat structure. This happens because a single transition from a parent state implicitly describes a whole family of transitions from its child states.

Statecharts differ from finite state machines, as we've been using them, in one additional important way: Suppose that a complex reactive system is made up of a set of components that act independently (or mostly independently) of each other as they respond to different kinds of input signals. For example, imagine a cell phone that must simultaneously listen for incoming calls while allowing its user to manage the local phonebook. The "state" of such a system must reflect the states of all of its components. Rather than forcing an explicit enumeration of all such state combinations as a way to describe the overall system's state, statecharts allow the specification of parallel state sets. A complex system can then be described as being in multiple states at once and the total number of states that are required in the description becomes the sum of the numbers of the separate states, rather than their product.

Statecharts have been widely used in a variety of software design contexts, including real-time systems, simulations, and user interfaces. Statechart capabilities are now part of many software design and implementation systems, including general-purpose tools such as the Unified Modeling Language (UML) 💻, as well as specialized languages that have been crafted to support the design of particular kinds of reactive systems. For example, SCXML 💻 is a statechart-based tool that supports the design of voice and multimodal interfaces. The details of how one specifies a set of states vary from one system to the next. Typically there exists both a graphical language and a text-based one (generally based on some form of XML). In the example that we are about to present, we use a representative kind of graphical language.

To see how statecharts work, consider the problem of designing a digital watch. We'll substantially simplify the problem, which is described in much more realistic detail in [Harel 1987]. Statecharts can be used to construct designs either top-down or bottom-up. We'll sketch a top-down approach. At the top level, our watch has three states, shown in Figure H.2.

When the watch is turned on, it enters the displaying state, in which it displays the date and time. If an alarm is triggered, it will enter the alarm-beeping state, where it will stay until some button (any button) is pushed. When that happens, it will return to the displaying state. If the set button is pushed from the displaying state, the watch enters the setting state, in which the date, time, and alarms can be set. When the done button is pushed, it returns to the displaying state. If an alarm is triggered while the watch is in the setting state, it will immediately enter the alarm-beeping state. The only way to return to the setting state is to enter it in the usual way. So the watch will forget any settings that have not yet been saved. If the set button is pushed while an alarm is beeping, it will be ignored (since there is no transition labeled set button pushed from the alarm-beeping state).

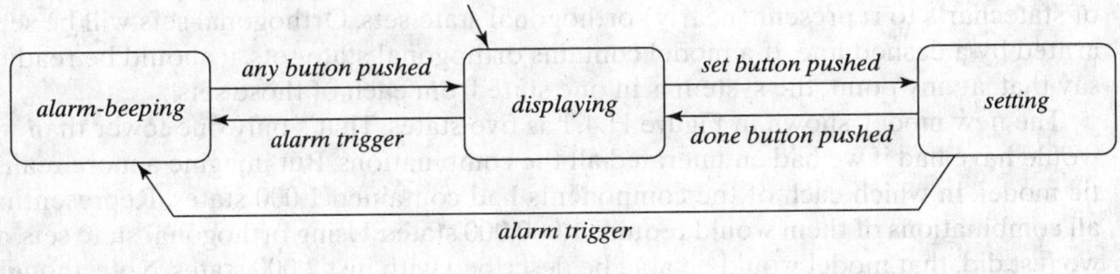

FIGURE H.2 A simple, top-level model of a watch.

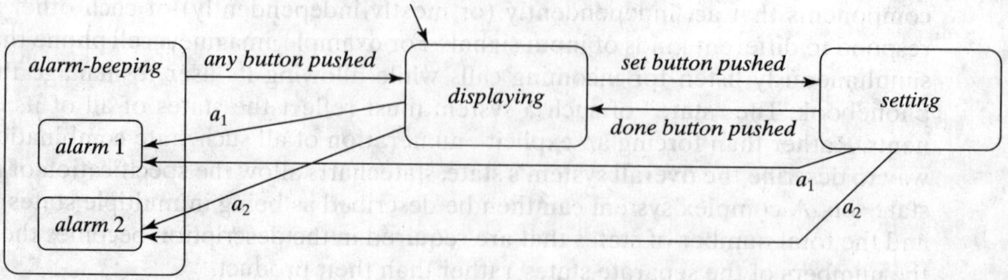

FIGURE H.3 Zooming in to the alarm-beeping state.

One might easily take issue with several things about the design that we have just described. For example, perhaps, if the set button is pushed from the alarm-beeping state, the watch should go directly to the setting state. The point of this example is not to argue for this particular design. It is to show the way that a statechart makes clear what a particular design is and what decisions were made in constructing it.

Of course, to build a watch, we need a more detailed design than the one we have just presented. To provide it, we must zoom in to each of the top-level states. Zooming into the alarm-beeping state, we might see the statechart shown in Figure H.3.

Now we see that this watch has two separate alarms, either of which may be set. We've used the symbol a_1 to mean that the first alarm has been triggered and a_2 to mean that the second one has. Notice the way in which we used the statechart's hierarchical structure mechanism to reduce the number of transitions, compared to the number that would be required in a flat machine: The transition from the alarm-beeping state back to the displaying state does not need to be duplicated for both of the alarm substates. Instead it is attached once to the parent state. Transitions are assumed to be inherited, unless overwritten, from parent state to child states.

Now suppose that the watch has a background light, which can be in one of two states, on or off. By default, it will be off, but it will go on if either the light button or the set button is pressed (the latter on the assumption that the user may need the light in order to see well enough to perform any settings). So now, at any point, the watch is in some state within its main controller, as sketched in Figure H.2, and it is in one of the light states. We could model that by creating a second copy of the main control box, with one copy corresponding to the light being on and the other corresponding to it being off. But that doubles the number of states. Instead, we can exploit the ability of statecharts to represent (nearly) orthogonal state sets. Orthogonal sets will be separated by a dashed line. If a model contains orthogonal state sets, it should be read to say that, at any point, the system is in one state from each of those sets.

The new model, shown in Figure H.4, has five states. That's only one fewer than we would have had if we had enumerated all the combinations. But imagine a more realistic model, in which each of the components had contained 1,000 states. Representing all combinations of them would require 1,000,000 states. Using orthogonal state sets, as we just did, that model would be able be described with just 2,000 states. Note, though, that we have not thrown away the ability to describe interactions between/among

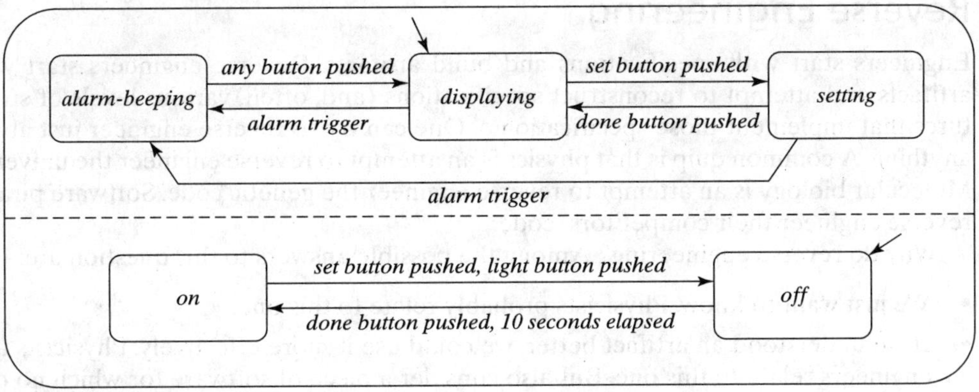

FIGURE H.4 Describing the watch as two orthogonal state sets.

orthogonal states when they occur. So, in our simple example, a single event, *set button pushed*, can cause a state change in both components of the model.

H.3 Model-Based Test Case Generation

We've now seen two uses for models that describe the desired behavior of systems that we wish to build:

- Models can be used to verify the correctness of an implementation.
- Models can be exploited as design tools.

We'll now briefly mention a third:

- Models can be used to generate test suites.

The goal of test case generation is to construct a set of tests that, collectively, increase our confidence that the behavior of a system under test conforms to some set of desired properties. Suppose that we have a model that describes those properties. Then it is possible to exploit that model in an automated tool for generating test cases. A variety of techniques can be used to do this 💻; the details depend, among other things, on the formalism in which the model is written. We'll mention just one idea here.

Suppose that we have a finite model of the sort that can be used as input to a model checker. If the model checker discovers a counterexample (i.e., an execution path that does not satisfy the specification), we know that there is a bug and can go about fixing it. But the model checker will typically find many paths, called witnesses, that do satisfy the specification. Unfortunately, we are still not certain that no bugs occur along those paths since the system model is almost always an abstract description that ignores details of the system's implementation. It is those details that need to be checked by testing. So one way to generate test cases is to choose inputs that force the system under test down the witness paths.

H.4 Reverse Engineering

Engineers start with specifications and build artifacts. Reverse engineers start with artifacts and attempt to reconstruct specifications (and, often, various levels of structures that implement those specifications). One can try to reverse engineer just about anything. A common quip is that physics is an attempt to reverse engineer the universe. Molecular biology is an attempt to reverse engineer the genetic code. Software pirates reverse engineer their competitors' code.

Why do reverse engineering? Among the possible answers to this question are:

- We just want to know. Physicists probably relate to this one.
- If we understood an artifact better, we could use it more effectively. Physicists and engineers relate to this one. But also consider a piece of software for which no one has yet bothered to write a manual or a piece of software with undocumented features. Suppose, for example, that we want a system we are building to share files with another system but the group that built the other system never described the internals of their file structure. If we could reverse engineer that other system, we could discover how its file structure works.
- We've got an artifact that's broken and we want to understand its structure so we can fix it. This one drives research in molecular biology. It also comes up a lot with legacy software, which can easily become obsolete even if it doesn't directly "break". For example, the number of bits allocated to some field may no longer be enough. But we don't know what the consequences would be if we changed it.
- We've got an artifact that is old and clunky. We want to replace it with a newer, sleeker version but first we have to figure out exactly what it does. This one comes up all the time with legacy software.
- We want to steal our competitors' ideas. This is why we have patent law.

We'll focus here on the specific problem of reverse engineering of software. The problem is one of analysis and the artifacts we need to analyze are strings. So this seems like a natural application for many of the ideas that we have been discussing. We'll briefly mention two techniques, one based on extending our notion of regular expressions, the other on the use of island grammars.

H.4.1 Hierarchical Regular Expressions

In Section 11.9, in our introduction to island grammars, we sketched some of the problems that arise when we try to analyze legacy software. In a nutshell, any approach that requires exact matching will probably fail because of errors, the interleaving of different languages, dialect differences, and irrelevant code, among other things. Further, there are applications that, by their nature, need to be fast and cheap. For example, suppose that we are trying to analyze code in order to figure out how expensive it would be to make some proposed change. We require that this feasibility analysis be cheaper and faster than the more complete analysis that will probably be required if we decide to go ahead with the update. What we need is a good technique for what is often called ***lightweight analysis***.

A robust lightweight analysis tool needs to be flexible. It needs to be able to find instances of patterns that describe the parts of the code that matter. And it needs to be able to ignore the rest. Regular expressions are very good at this. For example, we could write the regular expression:

(a ∪ b)* aaabba (a ∪ b)*,

which will match any occurrence of aaabba, while skipping over everything else.

But, in a realistic software engineering environment, the regular expressions that we would have to write to get the job done become too complex to work with. One approach to solving this problem [Murphy and Notkin 1996] is to organize the regular expressions hierarchically. In this approach, we still allow only regular expressions that can be compiled into finite state machines that can, in turn, be used to implement the actual search process. This means that the search process can be fast. So the use of regular expressions that we are suggesting here contrasts with the use of extended regular expression notations, for example in Perl and in much of the Unix world.

To see what hierarchical regular expressions can do, consider the following example (from [Murphy and Notkin 1996]):

```
[ <type> ] <functionName> \( [ {<formalArg> }1 ] \) [ { <type>
    <argDecl> ; }1 ] \{
<calledFunctionName> \( [ { <parm> }1 ] \)
```

To read these patterns, note two conventions: Expressions enclosed in square brackets are optional. Reserved tokens, like brackets and parentheses, can be quoted using \.

The job of these two regular expressions is to extract static call relationships among functions. The first pattern looks for function definitions. It will match an optional type statement, followed by a function name, an open parenthesis, an optional list of formal parameters, a close parenthesis, an optional list of type declarations for the formal parameters (each terminated by a semicolon), and an opening curly brace, which marks the beginning of the function body. The names in angle brackets just give names to the tokens that they match. Once these pieces have been matched, we assume that a function body comes next, followed by a closing curly brace. We want to find, within that function body, instances of calls to other functions. We don't care about any other code. So we use the second pattern, which is a daughter of the first. Once the first pattern matches, the second one may also match. But, at the same time, additional instances of the first pattern will also be sought. It isn't necessary, for example, to find the matching right curly brace first. So the pattern matching is robust, even in the face of mismatched delimiters in the code.

H.4.2 Island Grammars

While regular expressions are useful, they lack, for example, the ability to match properly nested delimiters. And they don't describe a way to build anything like a parse tree of the code fragments that do match. Context-free grammars do both of those things. But parsing with context-free grammars, as generally described (for example in Chapter 15), is not robust. Parsers must find exact matches between input strings and grammars. To solve the various problems that are generally faced in reverse engineering, on the other hand, we require parsers that are robust in the face of all of the issues that we mentioned above.

So one idea is to use island grammars, of the sort that we described in Section 11.9. As part of that discussion, we sketched a simple island grammar modeled after one in [Moonen 2001]. Its purpose, just like that of the regular expressions we presented above, is to find function invocations. But because island grammars are variants of context-free grammars, it can find expressions with balanced delimiters and it can build parse trees of those expressions.

Island grammars have proved useful in analyzing both old code (legacy software that may be written in obsolete languages and that has mutated, over the years, beyond recognition by its original writers) and much newer material, in particular World Wide Web pages, where straight text is typically interleaved with code in one or several programming and markup languages.

H.5 Normal Forms for Data and for Querying Relational Databases

In Section 11.8, we introduced the idea of a normal form and we mentioned two useful normal forms for context-free grammars: Chomsky normal form and Greibach normal form. Throughout the rest of Part III we used those forms on several occasions to make it easy to define algorithms that operate on grammars. We also introduced restricted normal form for PDAs and used it to simplify the design of algorithms that operate on PDAs. Later, in Section 28.4, we introduced two normal forms for Boolean formulas and we exploited them in our proof that SAT (the language of satisfiable Boolean formulas) is NP-complete.

But the idea of a normal form as a way to simplify the design and implementation of an algorithm is useful in a much wider variety of contexts than those. For example, normal forms are widely used in the design both of databases and their interfaces. In this section, we sketch one way in which a normal form can be used in the design of a graphical user interface for relational databases.

Programmers can write database queries in programming languages such as SQL (which we discuss briefly in Q.1.1). But nonprogrammers also use databases. They need an interface tool that is easy to use and they are typically able to get by with substantially less expressive power than languages like SQL offer.

The Query by Example (or QBE) grid was proposed, in [Zloof 1975], as a tool for such users; it has since been implemented in commercial relational database systems. The QBE idea is simple. Imagine a grid such as the one shown in Figure H.5(a). The column headings correspond to fields in database tables or in other queries. A user creates a grid by dragging field names into the grid; each name creates a new column. So the grid we just considered could have been built by a user of a database that records a company's suppliers, along with each supplier's products and their prices.

Once a grid with all the required fields has been created, the user can write a particular query by inserting values into the cells of the grid. So, for example, one could write the simple query shown in Figure H.5(b). The constraints in the nonblank cells in a row of the grid are ANDed together to form a query. So this grid corresponds to the query, "Find all records where Category is fruit and Supplier is Aabco."

Disjunctive queries can be constructed by using more than one row. The constraints from multiple rows are ORed together to form a complete query. So the grid shown in Figure H.5(c) corresponds to the query, "Find all records where Category is fruit or Category is vegetable."

ANDs and ORs can be combined. The constraints from each row are first ANDed together. Then the rows are ORed together. So, for example, consider the query:

```
(Category=fruit AND Supplier=Aabco) OR (Category=vegetable AND
Supplier=Bortrexco).
```

It can be written as the QBE grid shown in Figure H.5(d). But now consider the query:

```
(Category=fruit OR Category=vegetable) AND (Supplier=Aabco OR
  Supplier=Bortrexco).
```

If we try to write this query directly in a QBE grid, we realize that, because the QBE interpreter first ANDs all constraints within a row and then ORs together all the rows, every QBE query is effectively in disjunctive normal form. In other words, each query is a disjunction of subexpressions each of which is a conjunction of primitive constraints. But, to every logical expression, there corresponds an equivalent expression in disjunctive normal form. (We proved this claim for Boolean logic as Theorem B.3. The corresponding claim for first-order logic can be proved similarly.) So we can rewrite our query as:

```
(Category=fruit AND Supplier=Aabco) OR
(Category=fruit AND Supplier=Bortrexco) OR
(Category=vegetable AND Supplier=Aabco) OR
(Category=vegetable AND Supplier=Bortrexco).
```

From this form, it can easily be written as the QBE grid shown in Figure H.5(e).

The QBE grid is a simple structure and it is easy for people to learn to use. It is more expressively powerful than its obvious structure predicts because disjunctive normal form is, just as its name suggests, a *normal form*. In other words, while not all logical expressions are in that form, all of them can be converted into an equivalent expression that is.

Category	Supplier	Price

(a)

Category	Supplier	Price
fruit	Aabco	

(b)

Category	Supplier	Price
fruit		
vegetable		

(c)

Category	Supplier	Price
fruit	Aabco	
vegetable	Bortrexco	

(d)

Category	Supplier	Price
fruit	Aabco	
fruit	Bortrexco	
vegetable	Aabco	
vegetable	Bortrexco	

(e)

FIGURE H.5 Representing queries in QBE grids.

APPENDIX I

Applications: Networks

The theory that we have described in this book is useful in describing, at many levels, the structure of networks and the way they can be used. We'll introduce a few of them:

- the definition of network communication protocols,
- monitoring and maintaining networks,
- exploiting network resources for problem solving—the Semantic Web, and
- network security (or the lack of it)—hackers and viruses.

We'll discuss the first three of these issues in this chapter. We'll talk about the remaining one in the next chapter, in the larger context of computer security.

I.1 Network Protocols

The job of a network is to enable efficient and reliable communication between hosts. To make any kind of physical network suitable for practical use requires solving all of the following problems:

- error control: Messages may be corrupted or lost or reordered as they are being sent.
- flow control: The receiving host may not be able to process messages as fast as the sending host can send them.
- bandwidth limitation: The network itself has a limit on how fast data can be transmitted. If data are sent faster than they can be transmitted, they will be lost. So it is particularly important that the network never be forced to sit idle since idle time throws away capacity.

To solve these problems requires the definition of one or more communication ***protocols***, i.e., shared conventions for the transmission of data in one direction and acknowledgements (that the data have been received) in the other direction. Rather than attempting to describe all of the required functionality as a single protocol, it is now common practice to provide a protocol stack. Protocols at layer *n* of the stack make

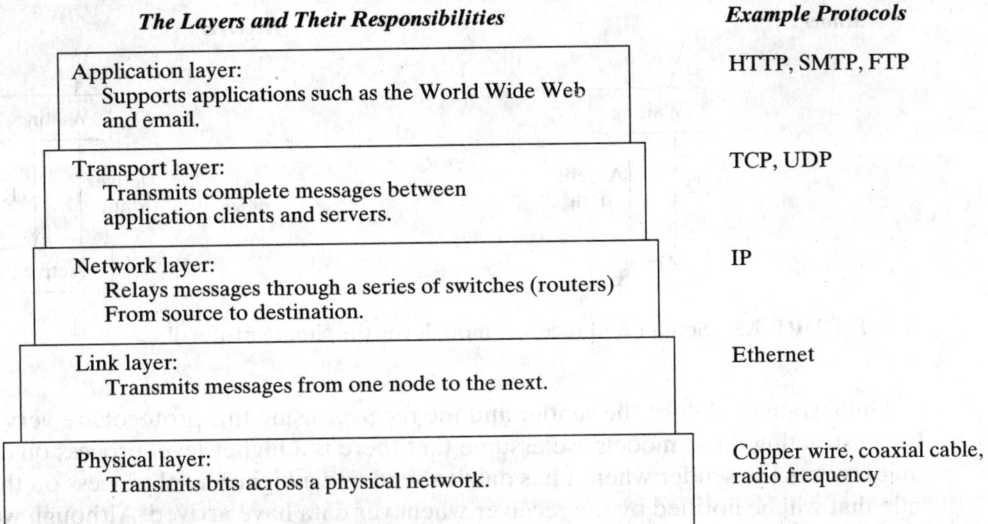

FIGURE I.1 The Internet protocol stack.

use of the functionality provided at layers n-1 and below. For example, the Internet protocol stack has five layers, as shown in Figure I.1.

Many kinds of communication protocols can usefully be modeled as communicating finite state machines that never halt. Each process (machine) simply loops forever, sending and receiving messages. So, more precisely, the models that we are about to build are Büchi automata, as described in Section 5.12, but without the distinction between accepting and nonaccepting states. In the rest of this section, we will show automata that correspond to the explicit communication actions that are required by a few important network communication protocols. Note that, in all of these models, the finite state automata will capture just the communication state of the corresponding processes. Additional state is required to encode the data that are being transmitted.

The most basic protocol we can imagine is illustrated in Figure I.2. The horizontal axis corresponds to time. The sender simply sends data messages (indicated by the boxes labeled D) whenever it is ready to do so. The hope is that the receiver receives them (at some time after they are sent).

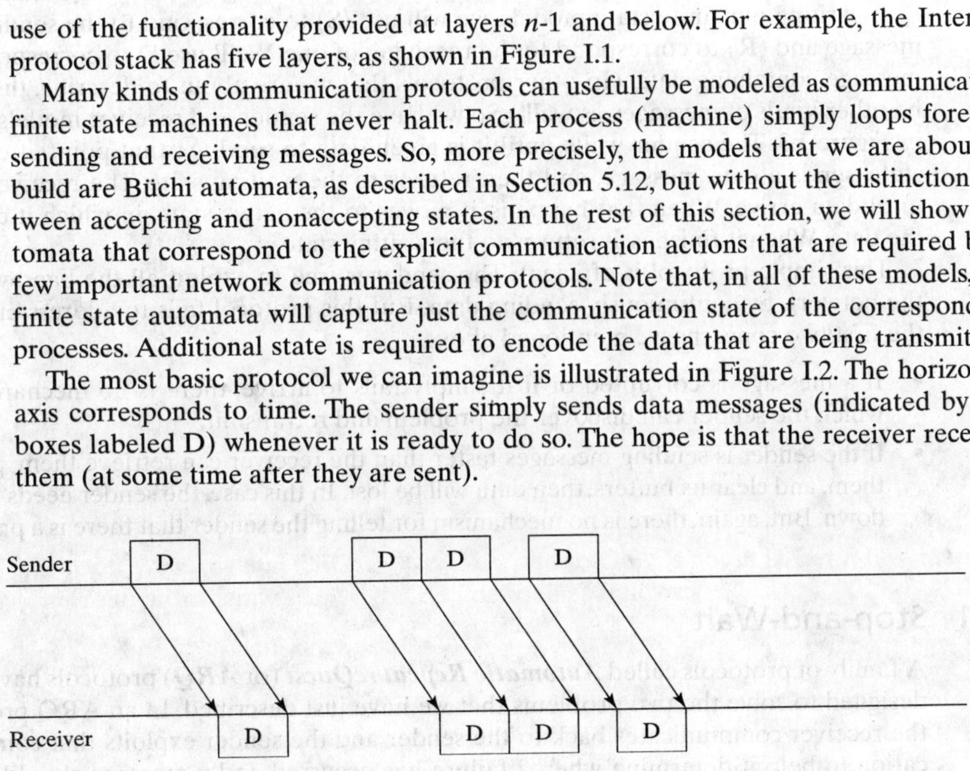

FIGURE I.2 A very simple protocol.

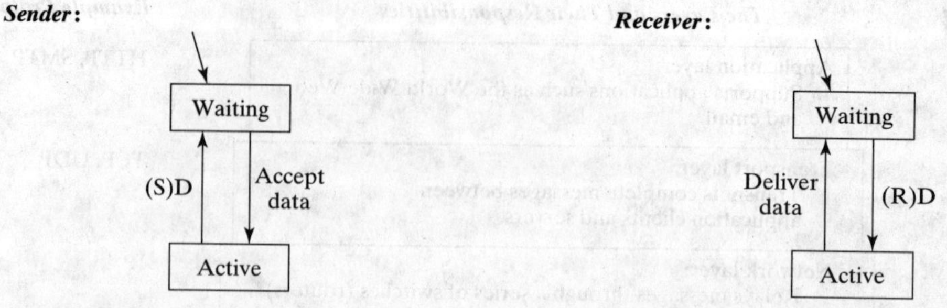

FIGURE I.3 Sender and receiver models for the simple protocol.

Finite state models of the sender and the receiver using this protocol are very simple. In constructing these models, we assume that there is a higher level process on one side that invokes the sender when it has data to send and a higher level process on the other side that will be notified by the receiver whenever data have arrived. Although we won't handle this part of the process in the models we are about to build, we can note that the sender will maintain a FIFO (first-in, first-out) queue of messages that it has been told to send. Each time it is ready, it will remove and send the message at the head of that queue.

In writing our finite state models, we will use (S) to correspond to the sending of a message and (R) to correspond to the receiving of one. We'll use D to correspond to a message containing data. (In other protocols that we are about to describe, there will be other kinds of messages as well.) So we have the sender and receiver models shown in Figure I.3. The sender waits until it is given data to send. At that point, it changes state, sends a data message, and then returns to the waiting state. The receiver waits until data arrive. When that happens, it moves to the active state, in which it delivers the data. When it finishes, it returns to the waiting state.

This simple protocol is efficient. The sender is free to exploit all the bandwidth of the network by continuously sending data. But this protocol fails to address either of the first two concerns we mentioned above.

- If a message is corrupted or if it simply fails to arrive, there is no mechanism by which the sender can discover the problem and retransmit.
- If the sender is sending messages faster than the receiver can retrieve them, process them, and clear its buffers, then data will be lost. In this case, the sender needs to slow down. But, again, there is no mechanism for telling the sender that there is a problem.

I.1.1 Stop-and-Wait

A family of protocols called ***Automatic Repeat reQuest*** (or ***ARQ***) protocols have been designed to solve the two problems that we have just described. In an ARQ protocol, the receiver communicates back to the sender and the sender exploits that communication to help it determine when a failure has occurred and a message should be retransmitted. A simple subfamily of ARQ protocols is called ***Stop-and-Wait***.

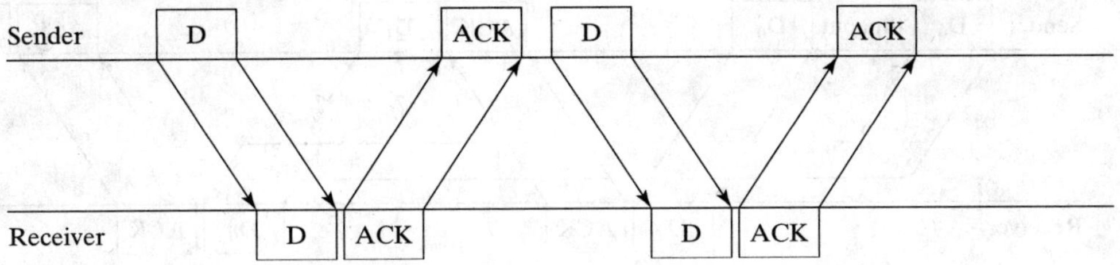

FIGURE I.4 The ARQ protocol.

A very basic Stop-and-Wait protocol is illustrated in Figure I.4. Now there are two kinds of messages—data messages (labeled D) and acknowledgement messages (labeled ACK). The sender waits for an acknowledgement that one message has been received before sending the next one.

With just one additional state in each model, we can describe the behavior of senders and receivers using this new protocol, as shown in Figure I.5.

The Stop-and-Wait protocol that we have just described solves the flow control problem that existed for the simpler case. The sender will never send a second message until it knows that the receiver has successfully delivered the data from the first one. And it solves one error control problem: If a data message is lost, the sender will retransmit it after it times out waiting for an ACK. If a data message is corrupted and the receiver can tell that (for example by using checksum bits), the receiver can simply fail to send an ACK, the sender will time out, and the message will be resent. There are also variants of the Stop-and-Wait protocol in which explicit negative ACK messages (NACKs) are sent when a message arrives corrupted.

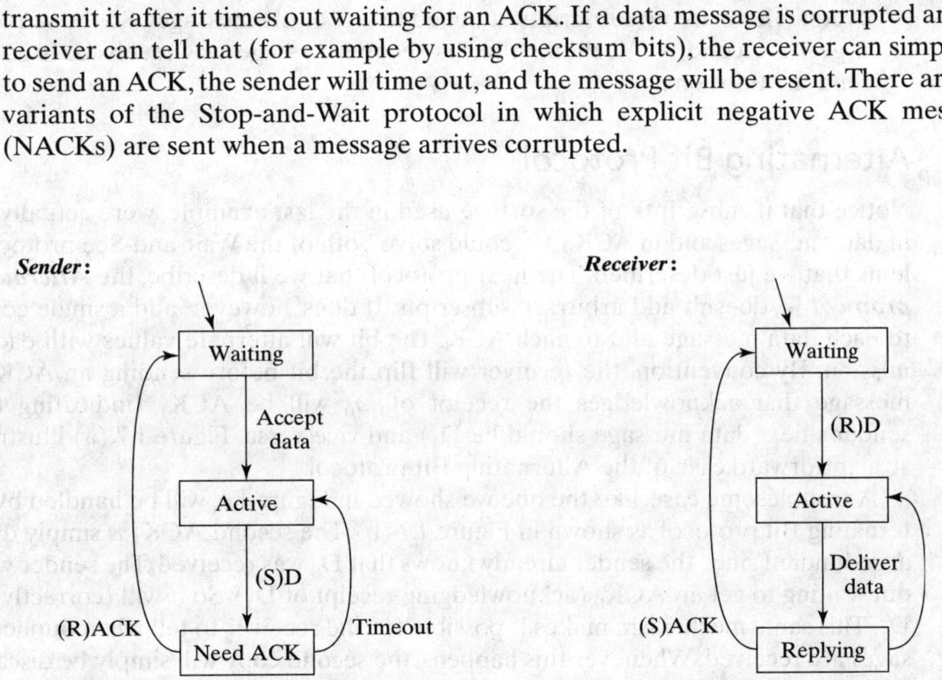

FIGURE I.5 Sender and receiver models for the Stop-and-Wait protocol.

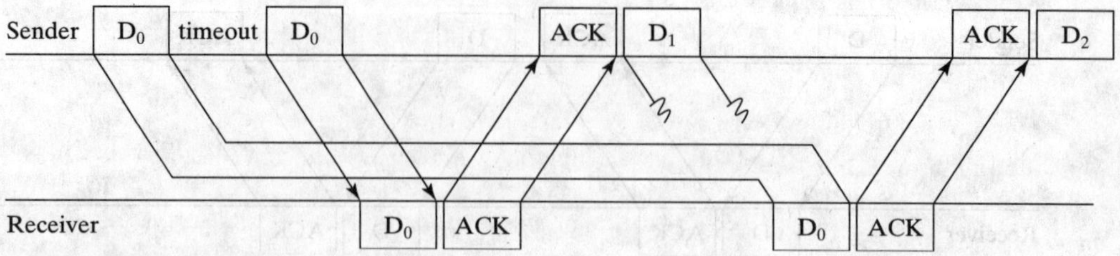

FIGURE I.6 What happens when a delayed message eventually shows up and its ACK is confused with another.

But other error control problems remain:

- If a data message arrives successfully but its corresponding ACK message gets lost, the sender will time out and then resend the data message. But then the receiver will receive two copies of the same message. It has no way to know that it has just gotten a second copy of the first message rather than a first copy of a next message.
- Suppose that the sequence of events shown in Figure I.6 occurs. The first data message (labeled D_0) is delayed until after the sender times out waiting for it to be acknowledged. So that first message will be resent. It arrives and an acknowledgement is sent and received. So the sender sends a second data message (labeled D_1). It gets lost. But, meanwhile, the original copy of the first message arrives and is acknowledged. The subscripts in the figure are just to enable us to envision the events. There are no subscripts attached to any of the messages. So the sender, when it gets a second ACK, thinks that its second message was received. It goes on to send the third one.

I.1.2 Alternating Bit Protocol

Notice that if subscripts, of the sort we used in the last example, were actually present in data messages and in ACKs, we could solve both of the Wait-and-See protocol problems that we just described. The next protocol that we'll describe, the ***Alternating Bit protocol*** 💻, doesn't add arbitrary subscripts. It does, however, add a single control bit to each data message and to each ACK. The bit will alternate values with each transmission. By convention, the receiver will flip the bit before sending an ACK, so the message that acknowledges the receipt of D_0 will be ACK_1 (indicating that the sender's next data message should be D_1) and vice versa. Figure I.7 (a) illustrates the straightforward case of the Alternating Bit protocol.

A troublesome case, like the one we showed in Figure I.6, will be handled by the Alternating Bit protocol as shown in Figure I.7 (b). The second ACK_1 is simply discarded as redundant since the sender already knows that D_0 was received. The sender will timeout waiting to get an ACK_0 (acknowledging receipt of D_1). So it will (correctly) resend D_1. This same mechanism makes it possible for the receiver to tell when duplicate messages are received. Whenever this happens, the second copy will simply be discarded.

To describe the behavior of senders and receivers that exploit this new protocol requires two copies of each of the states that were needed for the Stop-and-Wait protocol. One copy corresponds to handling data whose control bit is 0; the other to handling

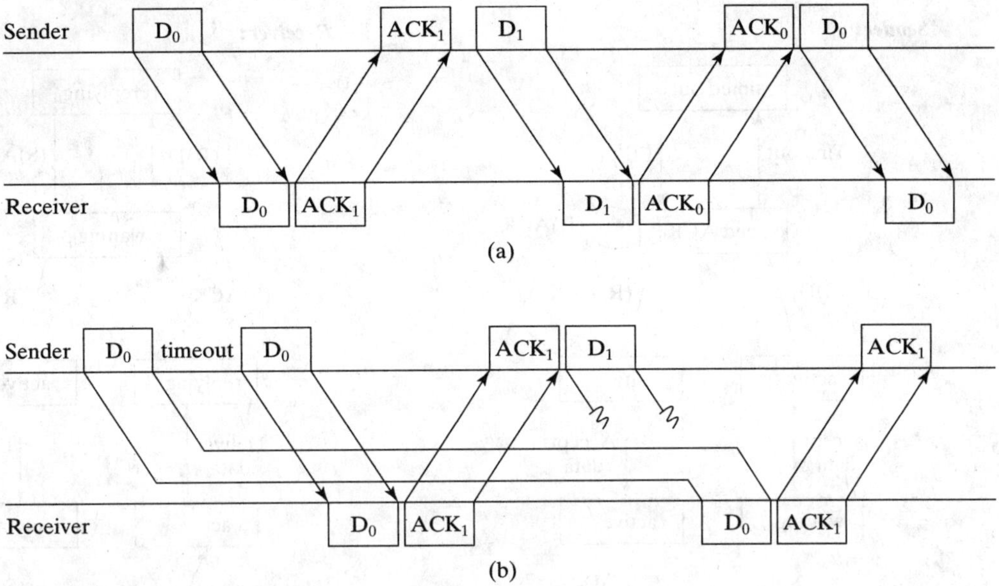

FIGURE I.7 The Alternating Bit protocol.

data whose control bit is 1. The new models are shown in Figure I.8. Both the sender's and receiver's start state is waiting$_0$.

The Alternating Bit protocol does not solve all error control problems. For example it does not address the problem of messages that are received but corrupted. It also won't work if a message is delayed long enough that its parity matches that of a more recently transmitted message. But its most serious problem, as a practical protocol, is throughput. As with any Wait-and-See protocol, the network must sit idle while the sender waits for the receiver to process a message and for an ACK to be sent and received.

I.1.3 Sliding Window Protocol

The wasted bandwidth problem can be solved by a more sophisticated ARQ technique, the ***Sliding Window protocol***, that assigns sequence numbers (rather than alternating bits) to the messages that a sender sends to a receiver. As before, data messages are initially entered into a FIFO queue that is maintained by the sender. They are assigned sequence numbers as they enter the queue and they will be transmitted in the order in which they enter the queue.

Any specific use of the Sliding Window protocol begins by choosing a window size w. The window is then placed over the first w messages. We'll say that those messages are in the ***send window***. The sender may send (without waiting for acknowledgements) any message that is in the send window. The send window can, in turn, be shifted to the right as ACK messages are received.

The Sliding Window protocol is used for sending messages on the Internet. It is illustrated in Figure I.9. Each box corresponds to a data message to be sent from the sender to the receiver. Messages that have been sent are shown in the sender's queue with diagonal hatch lines. Messages that have been received are shown with hatched

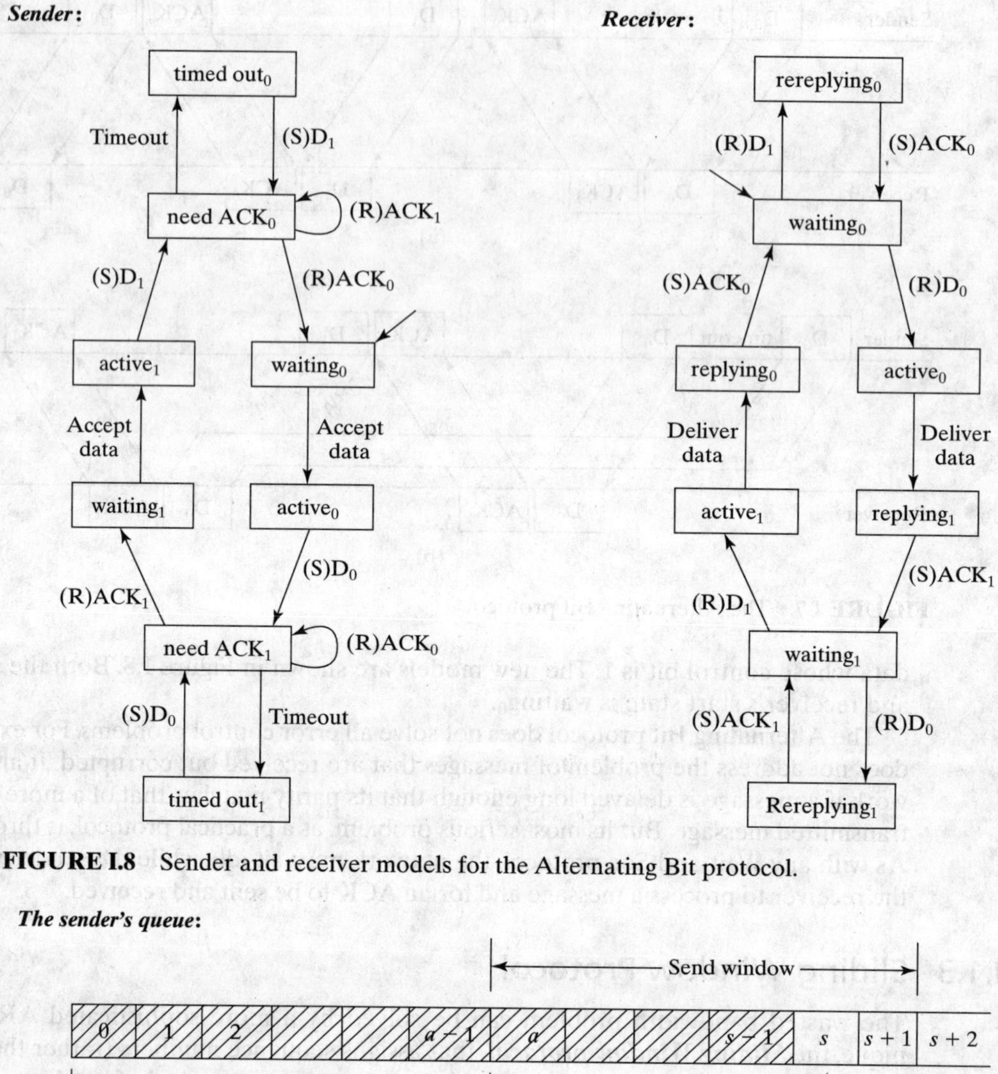

FIGURE I.8 Sender and receiver models for the Alternating Bit protocol.

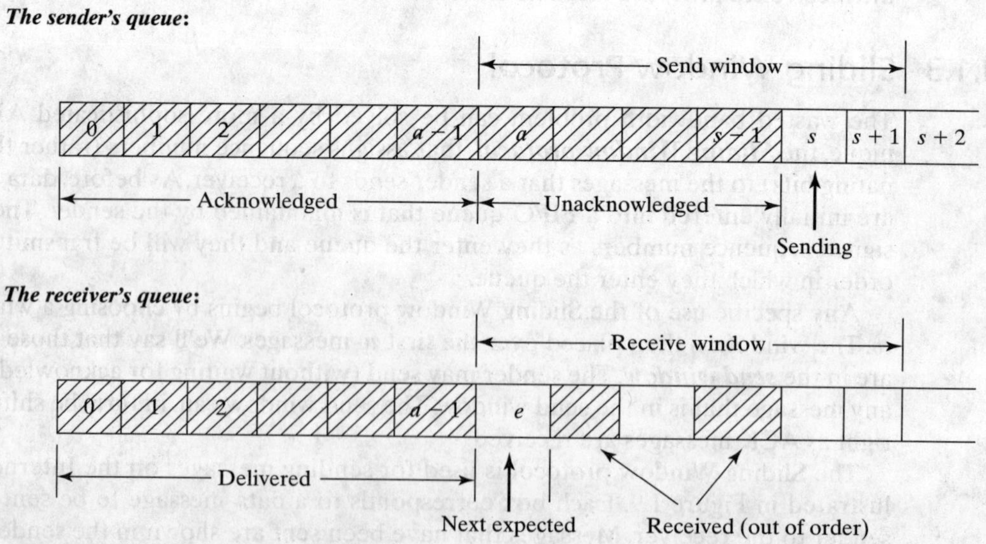

FIGURE I.9 The Sliding Window protocol.

lines in the receiver's queue. The sender begins transmitting by sending, in order, the messages in the send window (i.e., the first w messages). It will not wait for an acknowledgement of message n before sending message $n + 1$. It will, however, expect to be told of the arrival of all data messages it sends and it will resend any message on which it times out before it receives an ACK that acknowledges that message.

In any ***cumulative acknowledgement protocol***, of which the Sliding Window protocol is one example, an ACK_n message acknowledges receipt of all data messages numbered up to $n - 1$. So, as shown in the diagram, the receiver may have received some messages that have not been acknowledged; they won't be until all the messages before them in the sequence have been successfully received. This means that, if the sender receives an ACK_n message, then it knows that all messages numbered up to $n - 1$ have been received. At that point, the send window can be slid to the right so that the lowest numbered message it contains is n. Each time the window slides, the sender may resume sending messages. It need only stop and wait when it has sent all messages in the current send window. For a more formal treatment of cumulative acknowledgement protocols, including Sliding Window, see [Gouda 1998].

The Sliding Window protocol cannot usefully be modeled as a finite state machine because of the need to store the message sequence numbers. (Of course, if we assume a maximum word size for storing those numbers, we *could* build a corresponding FSM, but it would be too complex to be useful as an analysis tool.) As we'll see in the next section though, we can continue to use finite state machines as tools for describing higher-level protocols, including ones that are used on the Internet and that exploit the Sliding Window protocol. We'll simply take advantage of the fundamental structure of a protocol stack and treat the action of correctly sending a message as an atomic event without worrying about how it happens.

I.1.4 TCP

In the Internet protocol stack, the transport layer sits immediately below the application layer. So the transport layer protocol is invoked by application protocols such as HTTP, SMTP, and FTP. A practical transport layer protocol must be efficient and it must address some issues that we have not considered up until this point. For example, it must enable data messages to be sent in both directions between two hosts.

The transport layer protocol used by the Internet is the ***Transmission Control Protocol*** (or ***TCP***). A TCP connection is established by a three-step handshake procedure: One host initiates the connection, the other acknowledges it, and the originator then confirms the acknowledgement. Once a connection is open, data can be transmitted between the two hosts until it is closed.

Internet standards are defined by a set of documents called RFCs. The functional specification of TCP can be described as a simple finite state transducer, shown in Figure I.10, exactly as it appears in [RFC 793] 💻 as Figure 6.

The model is described, again in [RFC 793], as follows:

> A connection progresses through a series of states during its lifetime. The states are: LISTEN, SYN-SENT, SYN-RECEIVED, ESTABLISHED, FIN-WAIT-1, FIN-WAIT-2, CLOSE-WAIT, CLOSING, LAST-ACK, TIME-WAIT, and the

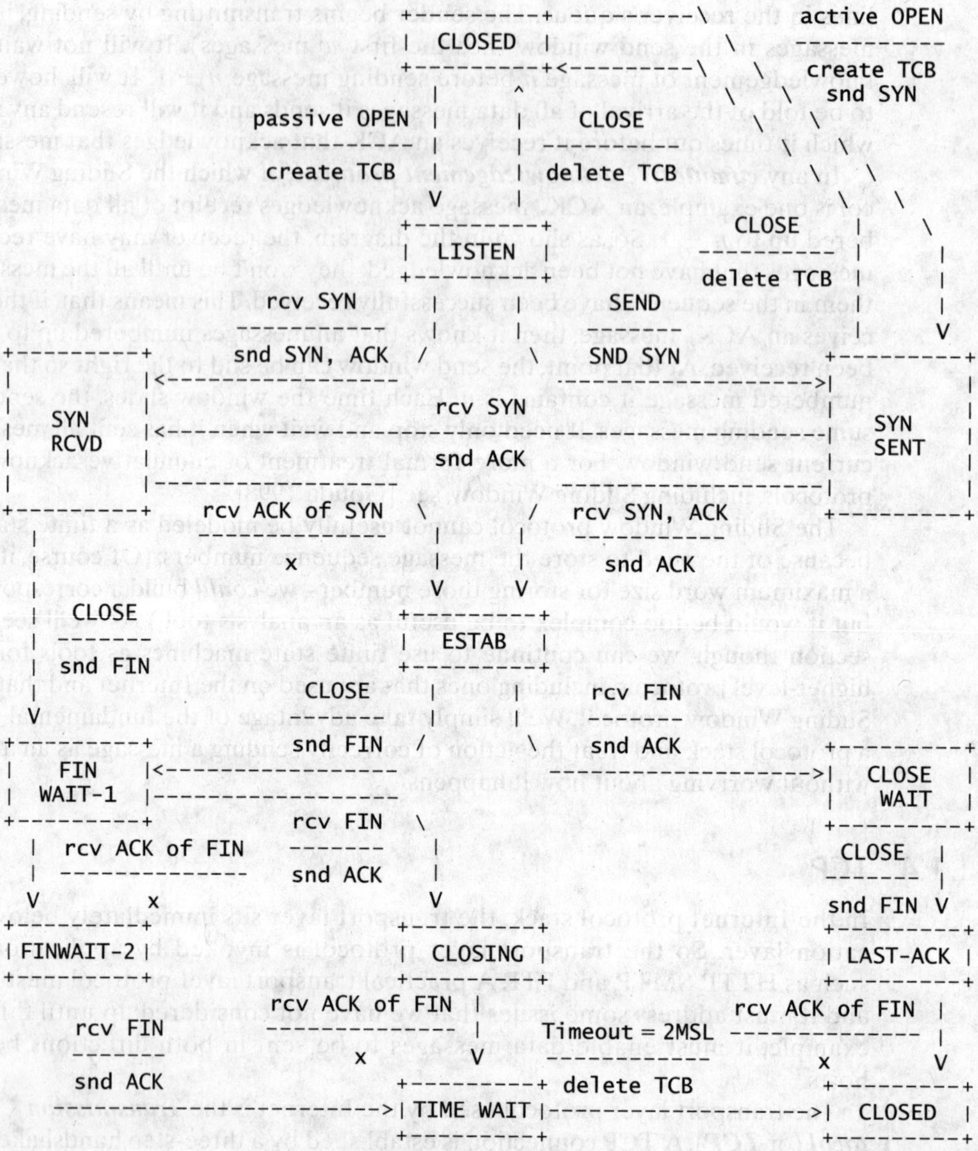

FIGURE I.10 A finite state transducer model of TCP.

fictional state CLOSED. CLOSED is fictional because it represents the state when there is no TCB [Transmision Control Block], and therefore, no connection. Briefly the meanings of the states are:

- LISTEN — represents waiting for a connection request from any remote TCP and port.
- SYN-SENT — represents waiting for a matching connection request after having sent a connection request.

- SYN-RECEIVED — represents waiting for a confirming connection request acknowledgment after having both received and sent a connection request.
- ESTABLISHED — represents an open connection, data received can be delivered to the user. The normal state for the data transfer phase of the connection.
- FIN-WAIT-1 — represents waiting for a connection termination request from the remote TCP, or an acknowledgment of the connection termination request previously sent.
- FIN-WAIT-2 — represents waiting for a connection termination request from the remote TCP.
- CLOSE-WAIT — represents waiting for a connection termination request from the local user.
- CLOSING — represents waiting for a connection termination request acknowledgment from the remote TCP.
- LAST-ACK — represents waiting for an acknowledgment of the connection termination request previously sent to the remote TCP (which includes an acknowledgment of its connection termination request).
- TIME-WAIT — represents waiting for enough time to pass to be sure the remote TCP received the acknowledgment of its connection termination request.
- CLOSED — represents no connection state at all.

A TCP connection progresses from one state to another in response to events. The events are the user calls, OPEN, SEND, RECEIVE, CLOSE, ABORT, and STATUS; the incoming segments, particularly those containing the SYN, ACK, RST and FIN flags; and timeouts.

Each transition in this diagram has a label of the form $\frac{<event>}{<action>}$, where $<event>$ is the event that causes the transition to occur and $<action>$ is the action that is executed when the transition is taken. The diagram ignores error conditions and other actions that are not directly connected to the state changes.

I.2 Modeling Networks as Graphs

It is natural to model a network as a graph in which the processors correspond to vertices and the links correspond to edges. As soon as we do that, it becomes clear that many of the problems that we need to solve when we build and analyze networks correspond to the graph problems that we discussed in Part V. We'll mention a few examples here.

Consider the problem of designing a physical network that connects a set of points. We want to find the cheapest way to build the network. We can show that there is an efficient algorithm for solving this problem. Let G be a graph whose vertices correspond to the points and whose edges correspond to the costs of laying cable (or wires, or whatever) between pairs of points. Recall that a spanning tree T of G is a subset of the edges of G such that:

- T contains no cycles, and
- every vertex in G is connected to every other vertex using just the edges in T.

If G is a weighted graph, then the cost of a spanning tree is the sum of the costs (weights) of its edges. Define a tree T to be a minimum spanning tree of G iff it is a spanning tree and there is no other spanning tree whose cost is lower than that of T. In Section 28.1.6, we described the minimum spanning tree problem as the language MST = {<G, *cost*> : G is an undirected graph with a positive cost attached to each of its edges and there exists a minimum spanning tree of G with total cost less than *cost*}. We showed that MST is in P. We described one efficient technique, Kruskal's algorithm, for finding minimum spanning trees.

The cheapest way to build a network that connects the points in G is to lay cable along a minimum spanning tree of G. So the network design problem can be reduced to the minimum spanning tree problem. Since we have an efficient way to solve MST, we have an efficient way to design our network.

Next we consider the problem of finding the optimal route for a message through a network. Again we'll describe the network as a graph G. Let the vertices of G correspond to network nodes and let the edges correspond to network links. We can reduce the message routing problem to the problem of finding the shortest path, from source to destination, through G. In Section 28.7.4, we described the language:

- SHORTEST-PATH = {<G, u, v, k>: G is an unweighted, undirected graph, u, and v are vertices in G, $k \geq 0$, and there exists a path from u to v whose length is at most k}.

We showed that SHORTEST-PATH is in P. Unfortunately, SHORTEST-PATH is not exactly what we need to solve the message routing problem because it is stated in terms of unweighted, rather than weighted, graphs. We need to use weights to describe the costs of the individual network links. But, as we mentioned in Section 28.7.4, there also exist efficient algorithms for finding paths through weighted graphs.

Next we consider the problem of checking a network to verify that all links are working properly. The shortest way to traverse all the links in a network is via an Eulerian circuit. Recall that an Eulerian circuit through a graph G is a path that starts at some vertex s, ends back in s, and traverses each edge in G exactly once. In Section 28.1.5 we described the problem of finding an Eulerian circuit as the language:

- EULERIAN-CIRCUIT = {<G> : G is an undirected graph and G contains an Eulerian circuit}.

We showed that EULERIAN-CIRCUIT is in P. So there exists an efficient algorithm for solving the link checking problem.

So far, our theory has yielded positive results for the network problems we have wished to solve. Unfortunately, that is not always so, as we'll see in our final example.

Consider the problem of finding a minimal set of network nodes at which we can place monitors so that we can observe the status of every network link. Again, we'll describe the network as a graph G, whose vertices correspond to network nodes and whose edges correspond to network links. Recall that a vertex cover C of a graph G with vertices v and edges E is a subset of v with the property that every edge in E touches at least one of the vertices in C. We can reduce the problem of finding a minimal set of monitor sites to the problem of finding a smallest vertex cover of G. In Section 28.6.5, we described the vertex cover problem as the language:

- VERTEX-COVER = $\{<G, k> : G$ is an undirected graph and there exists a vertex cover of G that contains at most k vertices$\}$.

Unfortunately, we showed that VERTEX-COVER is NP-complete. So it is unlikely that there exists an efficient algorithm for solving it.

I.3 Exploiting Knowledge: The Semantic Web

Networks enable two or more computers, and their users, to communicate. The World Wide Web enables millions (possibly billions) of computers, and their users, to communicate. Hard problems get solved by building software layers on top of the fundamental communication protocols that we have already described.

Hypertext structure turns a *set* of documents into a *web* of documents that people can explore. HTML, which we describe in Q.1.2, is a standard hypertext markup language that makes the documents of the world accessible to the *people* of the world. But what about making information available to the *programs* of the world? It is no longer possible for people to manage the amount of information that is available on the World Wide Web. We need programs to help. It is common to describe such programs as ***intelligent agents***.

We (people) can exploit the contents of the Web because we can read text, interpret tables, recognize images, and watch videos. In other words, we assign meaning to Web objects. At some point, it may be possible to build automated agents that can read the current contents of the Web in much the same way people do. In Appendices L and M we describe just a few of the research questions that must be solved to make that happen. In the meantime, if we want automated agents to work for us on the Web, we must annotate the Web with meanings that are stated in machine-usable forms. And then we must provide a set of inference rules and procedure(s) for exploiting those meanings to solve problems.

As an example of what we might like an agent to be able to do, consider the Web pages for two local quilt guilds, shown in Figure I.11. By reading these pages, people would be able to answer questions such as:

- Find quilt guilds in Texas. The fact that Hometown is in Texas can be gleaned from the map and, since Texas is the Lone Star State, Nimble Fingers is in Texas.
- Find quilt guilds that meet during the day.
- Find a list of email addresses for presidents of quilt guilds in the American southwest.
- Find quilt shows this fall in Texas.

Keyword-based search engines aren't able to discriminate the correct answers to these questions from many other pages that happen to contain words and phrases like

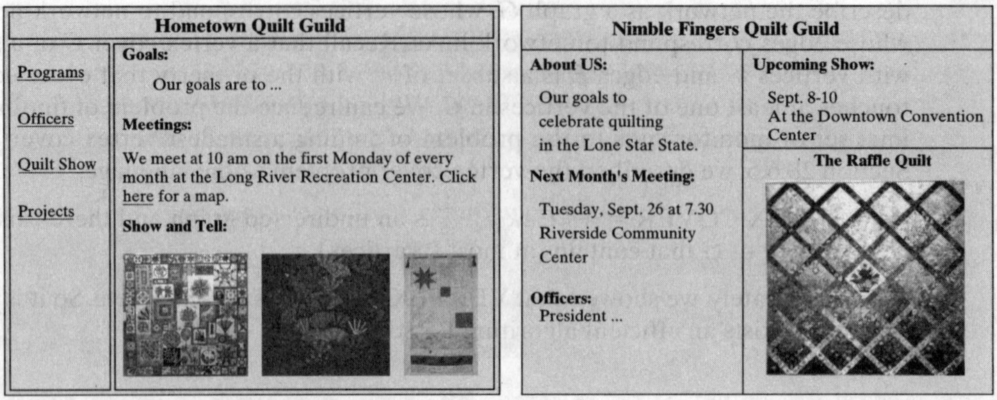

FIGURE I.11 Two quilt guild Web pages.

"quilt guild," "quilt show," and "Texas." To reason correctly about these questions requires having effective access to the contents of the relevant Web pages. It also requires having background knowledge about what the terms on the pages "mean." For example, it's necessary to know that 10 a.m. is "during the day" but 7:30 p.m. is not, that Texas is in the American Southwest, and that September is a fall month.

The ***Semantic Web*** [Berners-Lee, Hendler and Lassila 2001] is a vision for the transformation of the World Wide Web into a knowledge store (or knowledge base) that supports the construction of agents that can answer questions like the ones we just considered. To make the Semantic Web a reality requires the solution of a host of technical problems. We focus here on two:

- common description (markup) languages. If knowledge is to be used, its structure and its meaning must be described. If knowledge is to be shared, one or more *standard* description languages need to be defined.
- an inference engine. If knowledge is to be used, there must exist some technique(s) for reasoning with it so that facts can be combined to solve a user's problem.

Issues that we have discussed in this book play important roles in the design of solutions to both of these problems. In particular:

- to solve the common description languages problem requires that we:
  - design one or more languages that are expressively adequate for the job yet retain the decidability and tractability properties that we need.
  - exploit formal techniques for describing the languages so that users around the world can share them.
- to solve the inference engine problem requires that we design one or more knowledge representation frameworks that are expressively adequate but that do not crumble in the face of the undecidability and intractability results that characterize full first-order logic.

In the rest of this section we'll sketch the definition of a layered set of languages that can be used to define Web objects and assign meaning to them. Each layer will be able to exploit the capabilities of the layers beneath it. One way to think of the languages that we are about to describe is that, while most current Web languages (such as HTML) are designed to support a common way of *displaying* content on the Web, the new languages must be designed to support a common way of *automated reasoning* with that content.

I.3.1 The Language of Universal Resource Identifiers (URIs)

Any language for describing the Web must start with a sublanguage for describing the Web's fundamental units, as well as other, non-Web objects that relate to Web objects in useful ways. Call these resources. A Web page can be uniquely identified by its Web address, stated as a URL (universal resource locator). A URL contains an access method and an actual path that will find an object on the Web. But what about things that aren't Web pages? For example, we might want to be able to say that the creator of a particular Web page is a person (not a web location) whose name is Chris, who lives in New York, and who works for Jingle Co. To do this, we need a way to refer to Chris, New York, and the Jingle Co.

To make that possible, we'll define a new language, the language of universal resource identifiers. A ***universal resource identifier*** (or ***URI***) specifies a resource. Some URIs actually describe how to find their associated resource on the Web. For example, every URL is also a URI. Other kinds of URIs simply provide a "hook" that enables statements to be made about the resource, whether we know how to find it or not.

A URI (as its name suggests), identifies an object. That object may be a file or some other structure that contains smaller units. In that case, we may want to be able to refer to those smaller units individually. We use the fragment notation to do that. A fragment is the symbol #, followed by a fragment name. So, for example, if `http://www.mystuff.wow/products.html` contains descriptions of all my products, then `http://www.mystuff.wow/products.html#widget` might point directly to the description of my widgets.

The syntax for the language of URIs can be described with a BNF-style, context-free grammar. (In fact, this language is also regular and so it could be defined with a regular grammar or a regular expression.) We'll use here the convention that all special characters are metacharacters rather than terminal symbols. So, to use one as a terminal symbol, it will be quoted. We'll also use the common convention that any sequence that is enclosed by a [ ] pair is optional. Recall that | separates alternatives, and Kleene star means zero or more occurrences are allowed. A complete grammar for URIs on the Web is too long to present, but a simplified excerpt is shown as follows:

<URI> → *<URIbody>* ["#"*<Fragment>*]
<URIbody> → *<Scheme>* ":" *<Hier-part>* ["?"*<Query>*]
<Scheme> → `ftp` | `http` | `https` | `mailto` | `news` | ...
<Hier-part> → "//" *<Authority><Path-Absolute>* |
"//"*<Authority><Path-Empty>* |
<Path-Absolute> |

<*Path-Empty*>|
<*Path-Rootless*>
<*Authority*> → [<*User-info*>"@"]<*Host*>[":"<*Port*>]
<*Path-Absolute*> → "/" [<*Segment-1*>("/" <*Segment*>)*>]
<*Segment-1*> → <*a segment with at least one character*>

EXAMPLE I.1 Parsing URIs

Using the grammar excerpt that we just presented, we can produce the following parse tree:

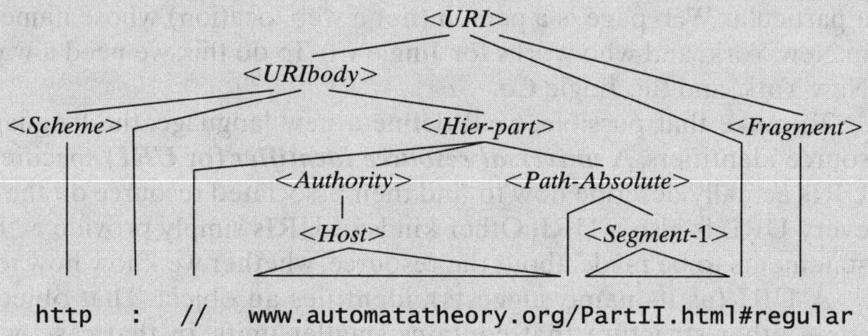

I.3.2 RDF

Now that we have a way to name Web objects, we need a markup language that can be used to describe their properties so that they can be exploited. We'll call such descriptions ***metadata***, i.e., information about other data sources (e.g., Web pages).

There is today no single standard metadata language for the Web. What we'll do here is to describe one interconnected family of such languages. All of them are evolving standards maintained by the World Wide Web Consortium (W3C). The bottom layer of this language family is RDF (Resource Description Framework).

Each RDF statement is a triple that asserts a value for some property of some Web resource. Remember that a Web resource is anything that can be named with a URI, so it could be a Web page or something (like a person, a city, a business or a product) that is external to the Web but to which we can give a name. Taken together, a set of RDF statements can be used to describe a set of relevant properties of some useful collection of Web resources. Typically such an RDF description will describe how some collection of Web pages relate to each other and how they relate to some collection of external objects.

Like any language, RDF has a syntax and a vocabulary. Both are substantially more flexible than in any of the languages that we've considered so far.

- The syntax: We'll begin by describing RDF syntax abstractly in terms of triples. The meaning of an RDF expression is defined by a semantic interpretation function that applies to triples. But we also need a "concrete" syntax, i.e., a form for writing strings that describe those triples. At least two such forms are in common use. Each of them comes with a compiler that maps strings to triples. The Web community doesn't have to agree on a concrete syntax, as long as it agrees on the abstract one.
- The vocabulary: It is completely unrealistic to assume that all users of the Web will want to agree on a single vocabulary to be used in describing Web resources and their properties. Anyone who wants to do so can define an RDF vocabulary and place it in a resource somewhere. Then anyone who has access to that resource can use one of its terms by referring to the resource and then to some specific term.

Every RDF statement is a triple. So it has three parts:

- a *subject* (the thing about which a statement is being made),
- a *predicate* (a property or attribute that the subject possesses), and
- an *object* (the value of the predicate for the subject).

The meaning of each triple is that *subject* has a property named *predicate* and the value of that property is *object*. The meaning of an RDF expression is the assertion of the conjunction of all of the triples that it describes. So RDF is a logical language with limited expressive power. In particular,

- all predicates are binary. (In other words, each predicate relates exactly two things: its subject and its object). This is not a real limitation, though, since other predicates can be converted into sets of binary ones.
- the only logical connective is AND (since an RDF expression is just a list of triples, all of which are asserted to be true). Neither disjunction nor negation is allowed.

So, ignoring all issues of syntax, and even of how entities get named, we might use RDF to specify triples like:

- (*mywebpage*, *created-by*, *me*).
- (*me*, *lives-in*, *cityofAustin*).
- (*Hometown Quilt Guild*, *organization-focus*, *quilting*).

At its core, RDF is thus a very simple language. One uses it to write triples. There is, however, one way in which its definition is more complex than is the definition of many other kinds of formal languages. RDF is a language for describing properties of objects on the Web. So there is no central control of what objects exist or what they are called. RDF must provide a naming convention that handles the distributed and dynamic nature of things on the Web. Its solution to this problem is to use URIs as names. Specifically, subjects, predicates, and objects are described as follows.

- Subjects: RDF statements are "about" resources. So the subject of every triple must be a URI, with one exception: There may be "blank" nodes that exist only as placeholders within RDF expressions. These nodes are "blank" in the sense that they have no name outside the immediate expression in which they occur. Blank nodes may be the subject of an RDF statement. So, for example, we may want to say that the Web page *w* was created by someone who lives in Maine but we don't know who that person is. We can create a blank node `_:1` and then say:

$$(w, created\text{-}by, \_:1)$$

$$(\_:1, lives\text{-}in, stateofMaine)$$

- Predicates: It is tempting to allow (as suggested by the examples that we have presented so far) simple predicate names like *lives-in*, *created-by*, *works-for*, etc. But doing so would pose two problems:
  - Where would we define the meanings of those strings?
  - The (world-wide) community of World Wide Web users will never be able to agree on a set of predicate names. It must be possible for smaller communities of users (including communities of one) to define the predicates they need without having to worry about what everyone else has done.

RDF solves both of these problems by requiring that every predicate be a URI. Anyone who can define a URI can define an RDF predicate. We'll say more shortly about how this system works.

- Objects: An object may be a named resource (specified by a URI), a blank node, or an element of a primitive data type such as string or integer. We'll notice, by the way, that strings get used as objects much less frequently than one might think. For example, we won't want to say that Chris lives in "Maine." Chris clearly doesn't live in a string. We'll want to say that Chris lives in a state whose name is "Maine."

Since URIs play such an important role in RDF, let's say a bit more about them before we show a few concrete RDF examples.

Entities and predicates in RDF are named by URIs. So they can be defined (using the RDF Schema language that we'll describe later) by anyone who can create a Web resource. Then they can be used by anyone who has access to that resource. A single Web file typically contains the definitions of a collection of related things, each of which can be uniquely identified within that file by a fragment name. So, suppose that we have defined a set of terms to be used in describing craft organizations. Then individual predicates might have names like:

```
http://www.myisp.net/regusers/mytown/me/
    craft-stuff#organization-focus
http://www.myisp.net/regusers/mytown/me/
    craft-stuff#meeting-place
```

Next, we observe that URIs (like the ones we just wrote) tend to be long. But many of the ones a particular RDF expression uses may share a common prefix like:

```
http://www.myisp.net/regusers/mytown/me/craft-stuff#
```

Users don't want to have to write that whole string every time they write a subject, predicate, or object in an RDF expression. The solution to this problem is the use of namespaces (as they are defined in the markup language XML). To define a namespace, we simply associate some (generally short, mnemonic) name with a string that is a prefix of some set of URIs that we want to use. Using XML syntax (which is one common way in which RDF is written), we can define a namespace by writing, for example:

```
xmlns:crafts="http://www.myisp.net/regusers/mytown/me/
    craft-stuff#"
```

This XML namespace (ns) definition maps the string `crafts` to the long URI shown to the right of the equal sign. RDF then allows the use of what it calls qualified names or QNAMES whenever a URI is required. A QNAME has the form:

<name space>":"*<local name>*

RDF will form a full URI from a QNAME by appending *<local name>* to the string to which *<name space>* maps. So, having defined the namespace `crafts` as we just did, the QNAME `crafts:meeting-place` is equivalent to:

```
http://www.myisp.net/regusers/mytown/me/
    craft-stuff#meeting-place
```

The definition of the RDF language says nothing about what vocabularies can be used in RDF expressions. Whenever a URI is required, any syntactically valid URI is acceptable. We'll have more to say later about how RDF vocabularies (of predicates and things to which predicates apply) can be defined (for example, how we could have defined the craft organization vocabulary). For now, though, we'll just mention that there are some public vocabulary definitions that are commonly used in writing RDF expressions. Each of them has a URI and each of those has a standard namespace definition. As a shorthand, we'll use those definitions, but remember that in real RDF code you must explicitly define each namespace first. The namespaces we'll use are:

- `rdf` – contains terms that have special meaning in RDF.
- `rdfs` – contains terms that have special meaning in RDFS (RDF Schema), a language that we'll describe below. RDFS is a language for describing RDF vocabularies.
- `owl` – contains terms that have special meaning in the inference language OWL that we'll describe below.
- `dc` – contains a vocabulary called the Dublin Core. The Dublin Core vocabulary has been designed for attaching common kinds of metadata to document-like network objects. So it contains, for example, the predicates `Title`, `Creator`, `Subject`, `Publisher`, `Language`, and so forth.
- `foaf` – contains a vocabulary called Friend of a Friend (thus foaf). The foaf vocabulary contains terms that are useful for describing people. So it contains, for example, the predicates `name`, `title`, `homepage`, `interest`, `weblog`, and `schoolHomepage`.

So, for example, if we write `dc:Publisher` as a predicate, it is simply a shorthand for a URI that happens to point to a place on a Web page defined by the Dublin Core Initiative. As it turns out, on that Web page is some machine-readable information (written in the language RDF Schema, to be described below) that can help an agent actually interpret, in a useful way, a triple that uses this predicate.

We've said that we can think of the abstract syntax of RDF as a set of triples. But what about its "concrete syntax"? In other words, what sequence of symbols must users write if they want to define an RDF expression? The answer is that users can exploit any concrete syntax for which a translator into abstract syntax exists. One approach is to use the simple triple language Notation3 (also called N3). We illustrate that next.

EXAMPLE I.2 Writing RDF in N3

A very natural way to write RDF is to use the triple language N3. In this example, we will use seven namespaces. In N3, namespaces are defined with the `@prefix` command. So we'll write those first, then we'll list triples.

```
@prefix rdf:      <the location of the rdf definitions>.
@prefix dc:       <the location of the Dublin Core definitions>.
@prefix foaf:     <the location of the Friend of a Friend definitions>.
@prefix fooddb:   <the location of a fictional food description resource>.
@prefix mystuff:  <the location of a fictional resource I've created. It defines things
                   I care about.>.
@prefix myco:     <the location of a fictional resource that defines significant things in
                   my company>.
@prefix places:   <the location of a fictional resource that defines places like cities
                   and states>.
myco:bigreport     dc:Creator                   myco:person521.
myco:person521     rdf:type                     foaf:Person.
myco:person521     foaf:firstName               "Chris".
myco:person521     mystuff:favoritefood         fooddb:chocolate.
fooddb:chocolate   rdf:type                     fooddb:food
fooddb:chocolate   fooddb:caloriesperounce      150.
myco:person521     places:birthplace            [places:cityplaces:
                                                 Boston;
                                                 places:stateplaces:
                                                 MA].
```

What we've said here is that a particular report called `bigreport` in `myco` was created by someone whose identifier in `myco` is `person521`. That someone is a person in the sense defined in `foaf`. (To say this, we used the RDF-defined predicate `type`, which relates a thing to a class of which it is a member.) `Person521`'s first name is the string "Chris". Chris's favorite food (in the sense in which I defined it in `mystuff`) is something that is defined in `fooddb` and called `chocolate` there. Chocolate's calories per ounce (in the sense defined in `fooddb`) is the number 150. Finally, `person521` was born in an unnamed place, indicated by an unnamed structure in brackets, whose city is Boston and whose state is MA (both as defined in `places`).

A common alternative to N3 is RDF/XML, which exploits the markup language XML that we describe in Q.1.2. This form is attractive to many users because they are already familiar with XML and XML parsers are readily available.

Whatever concrete syntax is used to describe it, an RDF expression corresponds to a list of triples. So another natural way to think of it is as a labeled, directed graph. The vertices of the graph correspond to entities (on the Web or in the world). The edges name properties that those entities can possess.

EXAMPLE I.3 Representing RDF Triples as a Graph

Here's the graph that corresponds to the triples that were defined in Example I.2:

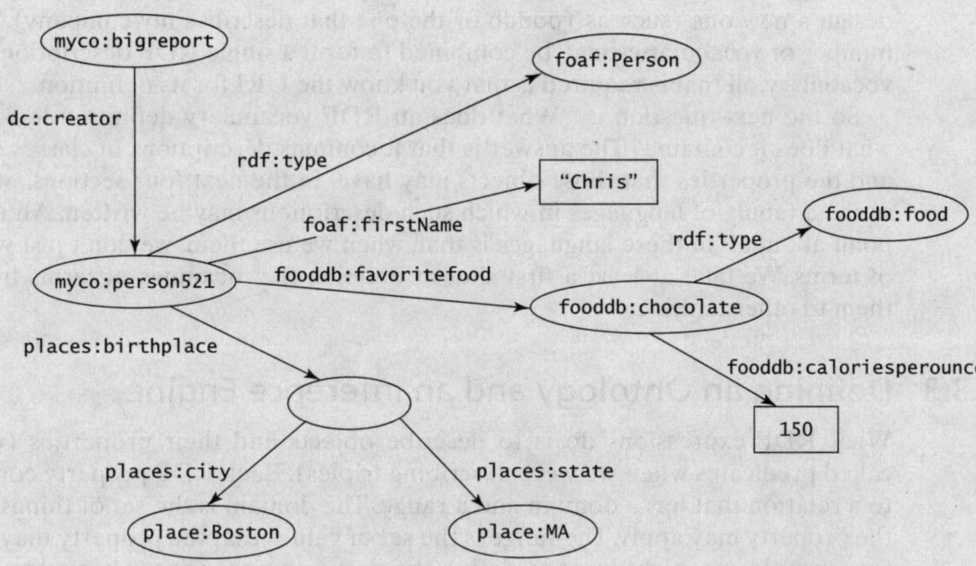

It is perhaps more obvious in the graph representation than it was in the triples form that whenever an RDF expression exploits a term that has been defined in some other namespace, it connects with what is already known in that other namespace. So, for instance, we wrote the triple that asserted that chocolate has 150 calories per ounce. If that fact were already asserted in `fooddb`, we could have used it without explicitly mentioning it.

Application programs can query RDF descriptions by writing their own code or by using any of a number of query languages, many of which are very similar to the ones that are used to query relational databases. The results that are returned in response to such queries will be a set of Web resources that match the query. So, for example, we'd like "Chris" to be returned in response to a query that asked the first name of the creator of `bigreport`. We'd also like to be able to reason in less trivial ways with the facts that have been provided. For example, I might want to find other people who live near me and who like high-calorie food. In the next section we'll talk about the issues that arise when we attempt to define reasoning engines that work with RDF.

RDF expressions describe properties of various kinds of resources. But where do those RDF expressions reside on the Web? There are at least two possible answers. They may sit in separate files with distinct URIs that name them. Those files may be private or they may be publicly available and searchable. Another possibility, though, is that they may be embedded inside the objects that they describe. It is becoming increasingly common for Web languages to provide a way to incorporate metadata, such as RDF descriptions, inside objects that are written in those languages.

Let's now return to the question of RDF's vocabulary. As we said in the introduction to our discussion of RDF, a key feature of the language is that there is not one universal, fixed vocabulary. There are some standard vocabularies but anyone is free to design a new one (such as `fooddb` or the one that describes my company). Then any number of vocabularies may be combined to form a single RDF description. To use a vocabulary, all that is required is that you know the URI for its definition.

So the next question is, "What does an RDF vocabulary definition look like and what does it contain?" The answer is that it contains descriptions of classes of objects and the properties that those objects may have. In the next four sections, we will describe a family of languages in which such descriptions may be written. An important point about all of these languages is that, when we use them, we don't just write a list of terms. We take at least a first shot at defining the meanings of terms by relating them to other terms.

I.3.3 Defining an Ontology and an Inference Engine

What RDF expressions do is to describe objects and their properties (which we called predicates when we were describing triples). Each RDF property corresponds to a relation that has a domain and a range. The domain is the set of things to which the property may apply. The range is the set of values that the property may have. So, for example, we might want to define the property `org-name`, whose domain is the set of organizations and whose range is the set of strings. To define a property, we need to define its domain and its range. In order to be able to do that, we must also be able to define classes, such as organizations. And we need to make sure that these definitions are constructed in a way that makes it possible to reason with them. For example, we must be able to answer the question, "Does object A, with properties P_1 and P_2 satisfy the description provided by query Q, which specifies properties P_3 and P_4?" Note that it's not sufficient to do the trivial check of determining whether P_1 is identical to P_3 and P_2 is identical to P_4. For example, P_1 might be the property of being a golden retriever and P_3 might be the property of being a dog. Clearly P_1 satisfies P_3, even though they are not the same. So we must construct definitions that support the kinds of inference that we want to be able to do.

At this point, anyone who is familiar with object-oriented programming, databases or artificial intelligence (AI) observes, "This is familiar territory." Object-oriented programming languages, database schema languages and AI knowledge representation languages are all designed to allow the definition of classes and their properties.

In object-oriented programming, the most important properties are methods, i.e., procedures that can be applied to members of a class. In the case of database schema languages and AI knowledge representation languages, declarative properties play a more important role. The job of these properties is to permit inference about both classes and their elements. The design of a family of representation languages that can be used to define the meaning of RDF expressions is based on a long tradition of work in the tradition of declarative representation languages.

But the World Wide Web environment creates some new challenges. For example, inference engines in many database environments can reasonably make what is called the ***closed world assumption***. They assume that all the relevant objects and their properties are present in the database. If an object or a property is missing from the database, it is presumed not to exist in the world. For example, a program that is querying an airline database can assume that, if a flight is not listed, it doesn't exist. In the distributed knowledge environment of the World Wide Web, however, the closed world assumption is rarely justified. For example, if I query the Web with my uncle's name but fail to find him mentioned, it doesn't mean that he doesn't exist. We'll say that, in the Web environment, we must often make the ***open world assumption***.

Another important difference between most database and artificial intelligence systems on the one hand, and the World Wide Web environment on the other, is that no one individual or organization has sole responsibility for defining the system. We will consider some of the important implications of this difference below.

An ***ontology***, as used in the context of an automated reasoning system, is a formal specification of the objects in a domain and their relationships to each other. An ontology consists of a set of classes, typically arranged in a subclass/superclass hierarchy. It may describe specific individuals that are members of those classes. It typically describes properties, both of classes and of individuals. Those properties may include quite general ones, like `part-of`, as well as more specific ones like `caloriesperounce`. The properties themselves typically have properties, including, at a minimum, their domain and range. So an RDF vocabulary is an ontology.

Despite the rich corpus of work that has been done in the broad area of knowledge-based systems, the architects of the Semantic Web faced some hard choices as they set about the task of building an ontology language that could support both defining the Web's objects and reasoning with them. The perfect language would be expressively powerful, defined by a clear formal semantics, decidable, computationally tractable, and easy for people to use. Unfortunately, the key results that we presented in Theorem 22.4 and Theorem 28.16 again rear their ugly heads:

- First-order logic is attractive because it has a clear, formal semantics. It is expressively powerful enough for many tasks. While it isn't expressively perfect, other, more powerful logics are even less computationally tractable than first-order logic is.
- But first-order logic is not, in general, decidable (Theorem 22.4) and it is possible to define theories that are incomplete (as shown by Gödel).
- And even Boolean logic appears, in general, to be intractable (Theorem 28.16).

So compromises are required. There isn't one set of compromises that is perfect for all tasks. Yet standards are crucial if the potential of the Web as a shared resource is going to be exploited. Three decisions have made it possible for the task of defining a set of representation standards for the Semantic Web to proceed:

- There won't be a single ontology. For all the reasons that we have already mentioned, individual users and user communities will be free to define ontologies that suit their needs. To make this possible, though, there must be a standard ontology-definition language(s) that those users can exploit.
- Languages will be defined in layers. Rather than waiting until all of the issues and tradeoffs can be resolved, standards for parts of the problem will be released as they are agreed upon. We've already described the lowest level, the URI language, and the second level, RDF. After a brief introduction to description logics, we will sketch the next two layers, RDFS and OWL.
- At the highest level(s), there is simply no one right answer for all problems. So alternative, but upward compatible languages will be provided. Users who stick to the less expressive subsets can be assured decidability and, in some cases, tractability. Users who choose to use the more expressive languages will be responsible for finding domain-appropriate compromises that deal with the decidability and tractability issues that those languages present.

I.3.4 Description Logics

The development path that we are about to describe, from RDFS to OWL, is based on a knowledge representation framework called ***description logic*** (or DL)[15]. Most DL languages are sublanguages of first-order logic, tailored to the task of defining and reasoning with classes, instances, and their properties. The most important reasoning operations are typically:

- subsumption checking: Given the definitions of two classes, does one subsume the other? (Class A subsumes class B iff every element of B is an element of A. Stated another way, A subsumes B iff A is at least as general as B.)
- classification: Given a set of classes, arrange them, based on their descriptions, into a subsumption graph. Think of a subsumption graph as a subclass/superclass hierarchy. We showed one instance of such a graph in Example A.7.
- realization: Given an ontology and a description of some particular entity in terms of a set of properties, find the classes to which the entity belongs. In other words, find the classes whose definitions are consistent with the definition of the entity.
- consistency/satisfiability checking: Given a set of two or more descriptions, are they consistent? Alternatively, could there exist a nonempty set of objects that satisfies all of those descriptions? Note that inconsistency checking is a special case of subsumption checking in which the proposed subsumer is the empty set. Any set that is subsumed by the empty set is also necessarily empty.

[15] For a comprehensive treatment of description logics, see [Baader, et al. 2003], particularly the first chapter: [Nardi and Brachman 2003].

The details of the definition of a DL language matter. Depending on how classes, properties, and instances are allowed to be described, a DL logic may:

- share the problems of full first-order logic. In other words, it may be undecidable and it may allow the definition of theories that are incomplete.
- be decidable but apparently intractable.
- be decidable in polynomial time.

So what is the right DL language for the Semantic Web? There is no one right answer. The tradeoff is between expressive power and the desirable computational properties of decidability and tractability. Then what should a standards committee do? We won't attempt to answer that question. But we will describe what the Semantic Web committees did do:

- They worked for several years without agreeing on a single common language. But they needed to release a standard in order to allow work on defining useful ontologies to proceed.
- So they released the definition of RDFS (a Resource Description Framework Schema language). Oversimplifying a complex issue, RDFS is merely a subset of the language that everyone knew would eventually be required. But it is a subset that people could agree on after only a few years of discussion.
- Meanwhile, work continued and a sequence of other languages were defined and standards for them were released. The ideas from some of the earlier such languages evolved into the OWL family of languages. OWL has three dialects that range from expressively weak and computationally easy to expressively powerful and computationally undecidable. Users are free to choose to use exactly the language features that they need and no more.

In the next two sections, we'll sketch the definitions of RDFS and the three OWL dialects, showing how the issues of computability and tractability influenced those definitions.

I.3.5 RDFS: A Resource Description Framework Schema Language

The Resource Description Framework Schema language, RDF Schema, or simply RDFS, permits the definition of RDF vocabularies, i.e., classes, instances, and properties that correspond to relations among them. RDFS programs are written in RDF syntax. (In other words, they consist of sets of triples.) They may exploit the constructs that are defined in the RDF namespace (`rdf`), as well as the concepts that are defined in the RDFS namespace (`rdfs`). They may also, of course, exploit constructs that are defined in any other namespace for which a URI is known.

The mechanism by which classes and properties are defined in RDFS differs in one important way from the mechanism by which they are defined in most object-oriented systems, including most database schema languages. In those systems, the focus is on classes. Someone defines a class by listing its properties. In RDFS, on the other hand, the focus is on properties. A user defines a property by specifying (using the domain and range properties defined below) the classes to which it applies. The advantage of this property-oriented approach in the distributed environment of the World Wide Web is that classes are not "owned" by particular users. One user may declare a class and then define some properties whose domain and/or range is equal to that class. Another user, working on a different problem, may define new properties that apply to that same class. So, for example, one user might define the property `caloriesperounce` with domain `fooddb:food` and range `number`. Someone else, taking a completely different point of view, might define the property `wheninseason`, also with the domain `fooddb:food` but this time with range `timeofyear`. While one user owns the URI for `fooddb:food`, neither user "owns" the definition of the class food. Both of them may use each other's properties if they want to and if they know the URIs of the resources in which the properties are defined.

RDF and RDFS, between them, define some fundamental classes:

- `rdfs:class`: The class of all classes. The members of a class are called its instances. Every class is an instance of `rdfs:class`. (So, in particular, `rdfs:class` is an instance of itself.)
- `rdfs:resource`: The class that contains everything that an RDF program can talk about. Every other class is both an instance and a subclass of `rdfs:resource`, which, in turn, is an instance of `rdfs:class`. In other ontologies, this most general class is typically called something like "thing".
- `rdf:property`: The class of properties that can be used to define classes, instances, and other properties.
- `rdfs:literal`: The class of literal values such as strings and numbers.

RDFS distinguishes between a class and the set of its instances. So, for example, the class that contains all cats that reside at the White House may be different from the class that contains all cats owned by the President, even if those two classes happen to contain the same instances.

RDF and RDFS provide some built-in properties (i.e., instances of the class `rdf:property`) that can be used in class and instance definitions. These include:

- `rdfs:subClassOf`: Relates two classes. If A is a subclass of B, then every instance of A is also an instance of B. The `subClassOf` property (relation) is transitive, so if A is a subclass of B, and B is a subclass of C, then every instance of A is also and instance of C.
- `rdf:type`: Relates an instance and a class. If A `rdf:type` B, then A is an instance of B. In other ontologies, this property is often called `instance-of`.

RDFS (unlike RDF) allows users to define new properties by, in turn, defining their properties. Built-in properties that can be used to define other properties include:

- `rdfs:subPropertyOf`. So, for example, `color` might be declared to be a subproperty of `physicalcharacteristic`. The `subPropertyOf` property (relation) is transitive.

- `rdfs:domain`: If *P* `rdfs:domain` *C*, then the domain of the relation (property) *P* is the class *C*. So the only resources that can possess property *P* are instances of the class *C*. In terms of triples, this means that the subject of any triple whose predicate is *P* must be an instance of *C*.
- `rdfs:range`: If *P* `rdfs:range` *C*, then the range of the relation (property) *P* is the class *C*. So all values of the property *P* are instances of the class *C*. Again, in terms of triples, this means that the object of any triple whose predicate is *P* must be an instance of *C*.

RDFS also provides mechanisms for defining:

- Containers: open ended structures that contain other resources. Containers may be viewed as (unordered) bags (i.e., sets with duplicates allowed), as sequences (where order matters), or in some other way.
- Collections: closed structures that contain other resources. A collection is described as a list of its members.

An RDFS program, just like an RDF program, is a list of triples. The meaning of such a program is to assert the conjunction of the assertions made by each of the individual triples. So, viewed as a logical language, RDFS is first-order logic with some very important restrictions, including:

- Only binary predicates can be represented as triples. Properties that might naturally be stated in first-order logic using unary predicates are typically described in RDFS using the `rdf:type` property. So, for example, instead of saying *food (chocolate)*, in RDFS we say `chocolate rdf:type food`.
- The only logical connector that is allowed is conjunction. (And it is not written explicitly. Rather all the triples are interpreted to be conjoined.) In particular, negation, disjunction, and implication cannot be represented.
- There are no explicitly quantified variables.

So RDFS, while useful, is inadequate for many practical representation and reasoning tasks. To support those tasks, additional mechanisms must be provided. The OWL family of languages, to be described next, provides some of those mechanisms.

On the other hand, RDFS, as a logical language, allows the specification of theories that are incomplete and undecidable. One culprit is the fact that a class may also be treated as an individual. So a set (a class) may be both a subset of and an element of another set. Without a distinction between sets and elements, definitions, such as this one, known as Russell's paradox, are possible:

> Let *S* be the set of all sets that are not members of themselves. Is *S* an element of *S*? The answer to this question cannot be yes, since if *S* is an element of *S*, it fails to meet the requirement for membership in *S*. But the answer also cannot be no, since if *S* is not an element of *S* then it does meet *S*'s requirement for membership and it must therefore be in *S*.

The design of the OWL family of languages also addressed the desire to eliminate this problem.

I.3.6 OWL

OWL, like RDFS, is a language for publishing and sharing ontologies on the World Wide Web. OWL is designed to support both the construction of ontologies and the implementation of reasoning engines (theorem provers) that can reason with the knowledge that its ontologies contain.

Building an OWL ontology for a particular task may be substantially easier than building that ontology in a more traditional environment because it is rarely necessary to start from scratch. Many OWL ontologies 🖳 already exist on the Web and new ontologies can be built simply by adding to the existing ones.

An OWL ontology, just like an RDFS one, is simply a set of RDF triples. What OWL offers, that RDFS doesn't, is primarily:

- the ability to express more complex relationships among classes, and
- the ability to specify more precise constraints on classes and their properties.

So, for example, in OWL, one can:

- describe constraints on the number of values that a property may possess for objects of a particular class. For example, a person can have only one mother but any number of children. In OWL, a property is "functional" iff each subject (i.e., an element of the property's domain) has at most one value for the property. A property is "inverse-functional" iff each object (i.e., an element of the property's range) may be the value of the property for no more than one subject. So, for example, `USsocialsecuritynumber` is a functional property of people (since each person has only one). It is also inverse-functional since each number is the social security number of at most one person.
- describe constraints on the values that a property may possess for objects of a particular class. (Note that this is different from specifying the range of the property since the range applies to the property regardless of the class of the individual to whom the property applies. So, for example, the value of the mother property for a person must be a person, while the value of the mother property of a cat must be a cat, and so forth.)
- write statements that enable the system to infer that any object that possesses a given set of property values is necessarily a member of some class.
- define new classes in terms of existing classes by using the operations union, intersection, and complement.
- assert that two classes are necessarily disjoint.
- define a class by enumerating its elements.
- declare that a property is transitive, symmetric, one-to-one, one-to-many, or many-to-one.
- assert equality and inequality.

In providing these abilities, OWL must give all its users the power they need for the applications they are building while making, as strongly as possible, guarantees of completeness, decidability and tractability.

Since expressive power trades off against completeness, decidability and tractability, there is no single language that can meet all of these goals for all users (and their applications). So OWL is not a single language but a family of upward compatible languages:

- OWL Full is the most expressively powerful of the OWL dialects. But the expressiveness comes at a price. A particular theory that is expressed in OWL Full may be consistent, complete and decidable, but there is no guarantee that it is. In this sense, OWL Full is analogous to first-order logic: There are first-order logic theories, such as Presburger arithmetic, a theory of the natural numbers with *plus* as the only operator, that are complete and decidable. But not every first-order logic theory is. It is known that no decision procedure for OWL Full can exist.
- OWL DL (where the DL stands for Description Logic) is a compromise between expressiveness and desirable computational properties. More specifically, OWL DL is intended to be a maximal subset of OWL Full for which not only a complete inference procedure but also a decision procedure is known to exist. OWL DL supports all of the language constructs of OWL Full, but it imposes some constraints on how they are used.
- OWL Lite is expressively the weakest dialect of OWL. As a result, its inference procedure guarantees better worst-case performance than do the corresponding procedures of its more expressive cousins. It is designed to support the definition of a straightforward ontology based on a hierarchy of classes and subclasses.

OWL Full is a superset of RDFS. OWL Lite and OWL DL are both supersets of a subset of RDFS. In particular, while RDFS allows an object to be both a class and an instance, neither OWL Lite nor OWL DL does (and so the Russell paradox would not be expressible in them).

OWL DL achieves its completeness and decidability properties by imposing constraints, including the following, on the way that the OWL vocabulary may be used.

- Type separation is enforced (as mentioned above). A class cannot also be an instance or a property. A property cannot also be an instance or a class.
- A property must either be an objectProperty (i.e., a relation between instances of two classes) or a data type property (i.e., a relation between an instance of a class and an RDF literal or a built-in XML Schema data type). It may not be both.
- No cardinality constraints can be placed on transitive properties or their inverses or any of their superproperties.
- Statements about equality and inequality can only be made about named individuals.

The fact that OWL DL is decidable (and thus consistency checking is possible) makes it a useful tool in domains where consistency is critical. In the next section we'll mention one system, Galen, that takes advantage of this ability.

OWL Lite uses a subset of the OWL vocabulary. It imposes all the same constraints on vocabulary use that OWL DL does. And it imposes additional constraints, including:

- The only values that are allowed as cardinality constraints on properties are 0 and 1. So, for example, it is not possible to say that the number of members of a soccer team must be at least 11.

- Classes cannot be defined using the union or complement operator (applied to other classes). So, for example, it is not possible to define a class `commonpet` as the union of the `dog` and `cat` classes.
- Only explicitly named classes and properties may be used with the intersection operator to form new classes or properties.
- Classes cannot be defined by enumerating their elements. So, for example, it is not possible to define the class `dayofweek` by listing the seven days of the week.
- Classes cannot be asserted to be the same or to be disjoint.
- It is not possible to assert that any instance of a given class must have some particular value for a given property. So, for example, it is not possible to require that every element of the class `UScitizen` must have the value `United States` for the `citizenof` property.

I.3.7 Exploiting The Semantic Web

Metadata resources on the Web are growing daily 💻. Many are based on RDF, RDF Schema, and OWL, as we have described them here. Many are based on other representational systems. Some use other languages derived from description logic; others use languages that are more similar to relational databases. At the core of many of these efforts is the development of common ontologies that enable entire communities of users to share Web resources. We've already mentioned a few of these ontologies, for example the Friend of a Friend (foaf) and Dublin Core vocabularies. We'll mention a few more here.

The need to share data is acute and well-understood within the biomedical research community. Several ontology-construction projects have been driven by the need to make this possible. For example:

- The objective of the Gene Ontology (GO) Consortium 💻 is to address the need for consistent descriptions, in a species-independent way, of gene products in different databases. To meet this need, the GO project has developed three ontologies, each of which enables the description of gene products from one important perspective: associated biological processes, cellular components, and molecular functions. GO exploits both XML and RDF/XML.
- The objective of the GALEN 💻 project is make it easier to build useful clinical (medical) applications by providing a common knowledge base of clinical terminology. The core of this knowledge base is an ontology that is intended to contain all and only the sensible medical concepts. Dictionaries (in many languages) can then connect words to concepts. The first implementation of GALEN was built using a representation language that was designed explicitly to support the GALEN project. The GALEN ontology has since been translated into OWL. More specifically, it exploits OWL DL. Because OWL DL is decidable, it is possible (although it may require running overnight) to answer the question, "Is this version of the GALEN ontology consistent?"

Consider the problem of adding location information to various kinds of Web resources. For example, a user might like to find only those blogs that originate in some particular location. There exists an RDF vocabulary for describing basic geographical information in a way that would make that possible.

Consider the wide range of physical devices that are used to access the World Wide Web. They range from computers with large display screens and full sound capability to handheld devices that are used in settings where sound is not appropriate and bandwidth may be limited. Further, the users of those devices have their own preferences for things ranging from language to font size. One way to make it possible to customize information delivery for all of those situations is for clients to describe, for example in RDF, their characteristics and preferences.

Thesauri categorize words using relationships similar to the ones used in many useful kinds of ontologies. So it may be natural to represent thesaurus information in an ontology language such as RDF or OWL. Wordnet is a large, online lexical reference system that organizes English nouns, verbs, adjectives and adverbs into synonym sets that correspond to underlying lexical concepts. Those lexical concepts are, in turn, organized by relations such as *hypernym* (more general concept), *hyponym* (more specific concept), and *hasinstance*. The Wordnet lexicon has been encoded in RDF/OWL to make it accessible to a wide assortment of other metadata projects.

A P P E N D I X J

Applications: Security

In the modern world, security is an important feature of almost every system we use. We protect physical locations with locks and burglar alarms. We protect computers with safe operating systems and sophisticated virus checkers. We protect sensitive communications by encrypting them. The theory described in this book has something to say about all of those techniques.

J.1 Physical Security Systems as FSMs

Imagine a conventional intrusion-detection security system of the sort that is found in all kinds of buildings, including houses, offices, and banks. Such systems can naturally be modeled as finite-state machines.

Some intrusion-detection systems are complex: They may, for example, divide the region that is being protected into multiple zones. Then the state of each zone may be partially or completely independent of the states of the other zones. But we can easily see the essential structure of such systems by considering the simple DFSM shown in Figure J.1. The inputs to this FSM are user commands and timing events: arm (turn on

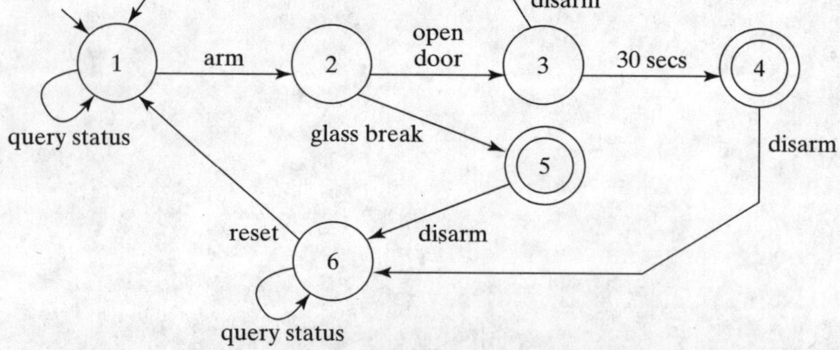

FIGURE J.1 A simple physical security system.

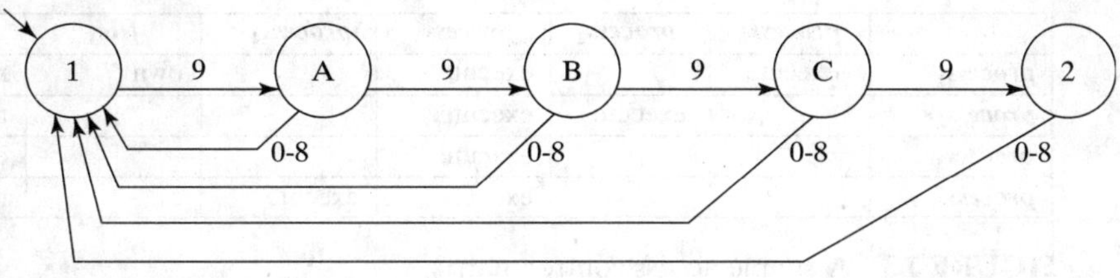

FIGURE J.2 The code-entering fragment of a security system.

the system), disarm (turn off the system), query the status of the system, reset the system, open a door, activate the glass-break detector, and 30 seconds elapse. The job of this machine is to detect an intrusion. So we have labeled the states that require an alarm as accepting states. State 6 differs from state 1 since it displays that an alarm has occurred since the last time the system was reset and it will not allow the system to be armed until a reset occurs.

A realistic system has many more states. For example, suppose that alarm codes consist of four digits. Then the single transition from state 1 to state 2 is actually a sequence of four transitions, one for each digit that must be typed in order to arm the system. Suppose, for example, that the alarm code is 9999. Then we can describe the code-entering fragment of the system as the DFSM shown in Figure J.2.

Note that we have not specified what happens if the query button is pushed in states A-C. One of the questions that that system designer must answer is whether the query function is allowed in the middle of an arming sequence.

J.2 Computer System Safety

Consider a complex computer system. It includes files that some users, but not others, have access to. It includes processes (like print pay checks) that some users are allowed to run but most are not. Is it decidable whether such a system is safe? For example is it decidable, given the operations that are possible in the system, whether an unauthorized user could acquire access to the paycheck printing system? The answer to this question depends, of course, on the operations that are allowed.

To build a model of the protection status of a system, we'll use three kinds of entities:

- Subjects: Active agents, generally processes or users.
- Objects: Resources that the agents need to exploit. These could include files, processes, devices, etc. Notice that processes can be viewed both as subjects (entities capable of doing things) and as objects (entities that other entities may want to invoke).
- Rights: Capabilities that agents may have with respect to the objects. Rights could include read access, write access, delete access or execute access for files, execute access for processes, edit, compile, or execute access for source code, check or change access for a password file, and so forth.

	$process_1$	*$process_2$*	*$process_3$*	*$process_4$*	*$file_1$*	*$file_2$*
$process_1$	execute		execute		own	read
$process_2$		execute	execute			read
$process_3$			execute			own
$process_4$			execute	execute		read

FIGURE J.3 A simple access control matrix.

We can describe the current protection status of a system with an ***access control matrix***, A, that contains one row for each agent and one column for each protected object. Each cell of this matrix contains the set of rights that the agent possesses with respect to the object. Figure J.3 shows a simple example of such a matrix.

The protection status of a system must be able to evolve along with the system. We'll assume the existence of the following primitive operations for changing the access matrix:

- Create subject (x) records the existence of a new subject x, such as a new user or process.
- Create object (x) records the existence of a new object x, such as a process or a file.
- Destroy subject (x).
- Destroy object (x).
- Enter r into $A[s, o]$ gives subject s the right r with respect to object o.
- Delete r from $A[s, o]$ removes subject s's right r with respect to object o.

We will allow commands to be constructed from these primitives, but all such commands must be of the following restricted form:

command-name($x_1, x_2, \ldots, x_n$) =
  if r_1 in $A[\ldots, \ldots]$ and
    r_2 in $A[\ldots, \ldots]$ and
    …
    r_j in $A[\ldots, \ldots]$
  then
    operation$_1$
    operation$_2$
    …
    operation$_m$

In other words, the command may check that particular rights are present in selected cells of the access matrix. If all conditions are met, then the operation sequence is executed. All the operations must be primitive operations as defined above. So no additional tests, loops, or branches are allowed. The parameters $x_1, x_2, \ldots, x_n$ must each be bound to some subject or some object. The rights $r_1, r_2, \ldots r_j$ are hard-coded into the definition of a particular command.

Define a ***protection framework*** to be a set of commands that have been defined as described above and that are available for modifying an access control matrix. Define a ***protection system*** to be a pair (*init*, *framework*). *Init* is an initial configuration that is described by an access control matrix that contains various rights in its cells. *Framework* is a protection framework that describes the way in which the rights contained in the matrix can evolve as a result of system events.

In designing a protection framework, our goal is typically to guarantee that certain subjects maintain control over certain rights to certain objects. We will say that a right has ***leaked*** iff it is added to some access control matrix cell that did not already contain it. We will say that a protection system is ***safe*** with respect to some right *r* iff there is no sequence of commands that could, if executed from the system's initial configuration, cause *r* to be leaked. We'll say that a system is ***unsafe*** iff it is not safe. Note that this definition of safety is probably too strong for most real applications. For example, if a process creates a file it will generally want to assign itself various rights to that file. That assignment of rights should not constitute leakage. It may also choose to allocate some rights to other processes. What it wants to be able to guarantee is that no further transfer of unauthorized rights will occur. That more narrow definition of leakage can be described in our framework in a couple of ways, including the ability to ask about leakage from an arbitrary point in the computation (e.g., after the file has been created and assigned initial rights) and the ability to exclude some subjects (i.e., those who are "trusted") from the matrix when leakage is evaluated. For simplicity, we will consider just the basic model here.

- Given a protection system S = (*init*, *framework*) and a right *r*, is it decidable whether S is safe with respect to *r*?

It turns out that if we impose an additional constraint on the form of the commands in the system then the answer is yes. Define a protection framework to be ***mono-operational*** iff the body of each command contains a single primitive operation. The safety question for mono-operational protection systems is decidable. But such systems are very limited. For example, they do not allow the definition of a command by which a subject creates a file and then gives itself some set of rights to that file.

So we must consider the question of decidability of the more general safety question. Given an arbitrary protection system S = (*init*, *framework*) and a right *r*, is it decidable whether S is safe with respect to *r*? Now the answer is no, which we can prove by reduction from $H_\varepsilon = \{<M> : \text{Turing machine } M \text{ halts on } \varepsilon\}$. The proof that we are about to present was originally given in [Harrison, Ruzzo, and Ullman 1976], which was concerned with protection and security in the specific context of operating systems. It is also presented, in the larger context of overall system security, in [Bishop 2003].

The key ideas in the proof are the following:

- It is possible to encode the configuration of an arbitrary Turing machine M as an access control matrix we'll call A. To do this will require a set of "rights" as follows:
  - One for each element of M's tape alphabet.
  - One for each state of M. These must be chosen so that there is no overlap in names with the ones that correspond to tape alphabet symbols. Let q_f be the "right" that corresponds to any of M's halting states.

We call these objects "rights" (in quotes) because, although we will treat them like rights in a protection system, they are not rights in the standard sense. They do not represent actions that an agent can take. They are simply symbols that will be manipulated by the reduction.

Each square of *M*'s tape that is either nonblank or has been visited by *M* will correspond to one cell in the matrix *A*. The cell that corresponds to $square_i$ of *M*'s tape will contain the "right" that corresponds to the current symbol on $square_i$ of the tape. In addition, the matrix will encode the position of *M*'s read/write head and its state. It will do that by containing, in the cell that is currently under the read/write head, the "right" that corresponds to *M*'s current state.

- It is possible to describe the transition function of a Turing machine as a protection framework (a set of commands, as described above, for manipulating the access control matrix).
- So the question, "Does *M* ever enter one of its halting states when started with an empty tape?" can be reduced to the question, "If *A* starts out representing *M*'s initial configuration, does a symbol corresponding to any halting state ever get inserted into any cell of *A*?" In other words, "Has any halting state symbol leaked?"

So, if we could decide whether an arbitrary protection system is safe with respect to an arbitrary right *r*, we could decide H_ε. But we know, from Theorem 21.1, that H_ε is not in D.

The only question we are asking about *M* is whether or not it halts. If it halts, we don't care which of its halting states it lands in. So we will begin by modifying *M* so that it has a single halting state q_f. The modified *M* will enter q_f iff the original *M* would enter any of its halting states. Now we can ask the specific question, "Does q_f leak?"

To make it easier to represent *M*'s configuration as an access control matrix, we will assume that *M* has a one-way (to the right) infinite tape, rather than our standard, two-way infinite tape. By Theorem 17.5, any computation by a Turing machine with a two-way infinite tape can be simulated by a Turing machine with a one-way infinite tape, so this assumption does not limit the generality of the result that we are about to present.

To see how a configuration of *M* is encoded as an access control matrix, consider the simple example shown in Figure J.4 (a). *M* is in state q_5 and we assume that it started on the blank just to the left of the beginning of the input, so there are four nonblank or examined squares on *M*'s tape. This configuration will be represented as the square access control matrix *A*, shown in Figure J.4 (b). *A* contains one row and one column for each tape square *s* that is nonblank or has been visited:

Notice that, primarily, only cells along *A*'s major diagonal contain any rights. The cell $A[i, i]$ contains the "right" that corresponds to the contents of tape square *i*. Since the read/write head is on square 3, $A[3, 3]$ also contains the "right" corresponding to the current state, q_5. The only other "rights" encode the sequential relationship among the squares on the tape. If s_i immediately precedes s_j, then s_i "owns" s_j. Finally, the cell that corresponds to the right-most nonblank or visited tape square contains the "right" *end*.

It remains to show how the operation of *M* can be simulated by commands that modify *A*. Given a particular *M*, we can construct a set of such commands that exactly

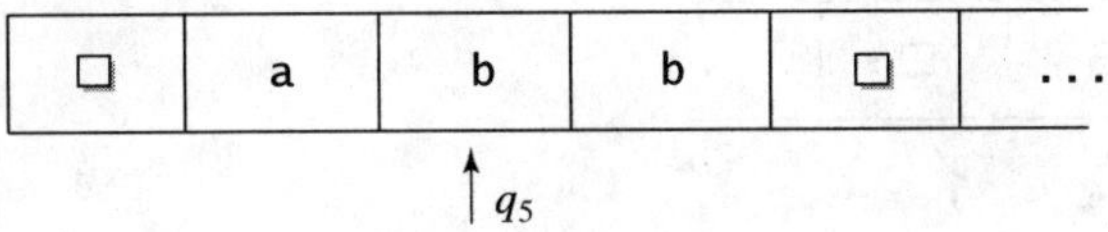

(a)

	s_1	s_2	s_3	s_4
s_1	□	*own*		
s_2		a	*own*	
s_3			b, q_5	*own*
s_4				b, *end*

(b)

FIGURE J.4 Representing a Turing machine configuration as an access control matrix.

mimic the moves that M can make. For example, suppose that, in state q_5 reading b, M writes an a, moves left, and goes to state q_6. We construct the following command:

```
stateq5readingb(x1, x2) =
    if own in A[x1, x2] and        /* This command can only apply to
                                      two adjacent tape squares,
                                      where
       q5 in A[x2, x2] and         /* the one to the right is
                                      currently under the read/write
                                      head and M is in q5, and
       b in A[x2, x2]              /* there is a b under the
                                      read/write head
    then
       delete q5 from A[x2, x2]    /* Remove the old state info
       delete b from A[x2, x2]     /* and the current symbol under
                                      the read/write head.
       enter a into A[x2, x2]      /* Write the new symbol under the
                                      read/write head.
       enter q6 into A[x1, x1]     /* Move the read/write head one
                                      square to the left and go to
                                      state q6.
```

We must construct one such command for every transition of M. We must also construct commands that correspond to the special cases in which M tries to move off the tape to the left and in which it moves to the right to a previously unvisited blank tape square. The latter condition occurs whenever M tries to move right and the current tape square has the "right" *end*. In that case, the appropriate command must first create a new object and a new subject corresponding to the next tape square.

The simulation of a Turing machine M begins by encoding M's initial configuration as an access control matrix. For example, suppose that M's initial configuration is as shown in Figure J.5(a). Then we let A be the access control matrix shown in Figure J.5(b).

There are a few other details that we must consider. For example, since we are going to test whether q_f ever gets inserted into A during a computation, we must be sure that

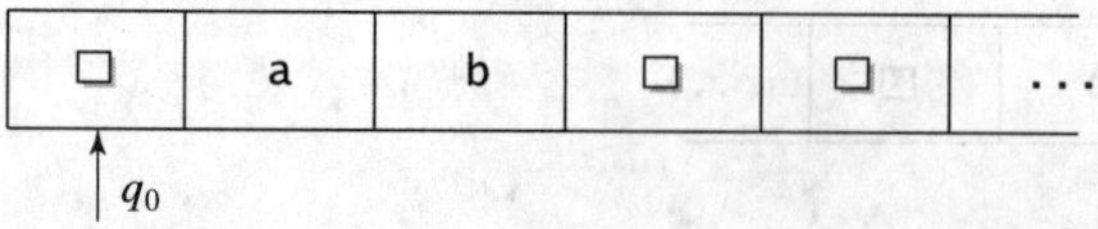

(a)

	s_1	s_2	s_3
s_1	□, q_0	*own*	
s_2		a	*own*
s_3			b, *end*

(b)

FIGURE J.5 Encoding an initial configuration as an access control matrix.

q_f is not in A in the initial configuration. So if M starts in q_f, we will first modify it so that it starts in some new state and then makes one transition to q_f.

Notice that we have constructed the commands in such a fashion that, if M is deterministic, exactly one command will have its conditions satisfied at any point. If M is nondeterministic then more than one command may match against some configurations.

We can now show that it is undecidable whether, given an arbitrary protection system S = (*init*, *framework*) and right r, S is safe with respect to r. To do so, we define the following language and show that it is not in D:

- Safety = $\{<S, r> : S \text{ is safe with respect to } r\}$.

THEOREM J.1 "Is S is Safe with Respect to r?" is Undecidable

Theorem: The language Safety = $\{<S, r> : S \text{ is safe with respect to } r\}$ is not in D.

Proof: We show that $H_\varepsilon = \{<M> : \text{Turing machine } M \text{ halts on } \varepsilon\} \leq$ Safety and so Safety is not in D because H_ε isn't. Define:

$R(<M>) =$

1. Make any necessary changes to M:

1.1. If M has more than one halting state, then add a new unique halting state q_f and add transitions that take it from each of its original halting states to q_f.

1.2. If M starts in its halting state q_f, then create a new start state that simply reads whatever symbol is under the read/write head and then goes to q_f.

2. Build S:

2.1. Construct an initial access control matrix A that corresponds to M's initial configuration on input ε.

2.2. Construct a set of commands, as described above, that correspond to the transitions of M.

3. Return $<S, q_f>$.

$\{R, \neg\}$ is a reduction from H_ε to Safety. If *Oracle* exists and decides Safety, then $C = \neg Oracle(R(<M>))$ decides H_ε. R and $\neg$ can be implemented as a Turing machines. And C is correct. By definition, S is unsafe with respect to q_f iff q_f is not present in the initial configuration of A and there exists some sequence of commands in S that could result in the initial configuration of S being transformed into a new configuration in which q_f has leaked, i.e., it appears in some cell of A. Since the initial configuration of S corresponds to M being in its initial configuration on a blank tape, M does not start in q_f, and the commands of S simulate the moves of M, this will happen iff M reaches state q_f and so halts. Thus:

- If $<M> \in H_\varepsilon$: M halts on ε, so q_f eventually appears in some cell of A. S is unsafe with respect to q_f, so *Oracle* rejects. C accepts.
- If $<M, w> \notin H_\varepsilon$: M does not halt on w, so q_f never appears in some cell of A. S is safe with respect to q_f, so *Oracle* accepts. C rejects.

But no machine to decide H_ε can exist, so neither does *Oracle*.

Does the undecidability of Safety mean that we should give up on proving that systems are safe? No. There are restricted models that are decidable. And there are specific instances of even the more general model that can be shown to have specific properties. This result just means that there is no general solution to the problem.

J.3 Cryptography

Effective encryption systems, or the lack of them, have changed the course of history. Modern techniques for encoding sensitive financial information have enabled the explosion of electronic commerce. Throughout history, the evolution of cryptographic systems has been a game of cat and mouse; as code breaking techniques were developed, new encoding methods had to be developed.

Before computers, any useful cryptographic scheme was necessarily computationally trivial. It had to be because both senders and receivers implemented their algorithms by hand. With the advent of computers, things changed. Senders and receivers, as well as enemies and eavesdroppers, all have access to substantial and equivalent computational resources. But computational complexity is still important. What is now required is a scheme with two properties: There must exist efficient algorithms for encoding a message and for decoding it by the intended recipient. And there must not exist an efficient algorithm for decoding the message by anyone else. The facts about computing with prime numbers, as we describe them in Part V, provide the basis for a system that possesses both of these properties.

In all but the simplest cryptographic systems, the algorithms that will be used, both for encryption and decryption, are fixed and known to everyone. But those algorithms take two inputs, the text to be encoded or decoded and a key. In a ***symmetric key system***, sender and receiver use the same key. Symmetric key systems suffer from the following pitfalls: No message can be sent unless there has been some prior agreement on a key. Even if there has been such an agreement, if the same key is used over an extended period of time, an eavesdropper may be able to infer the key and break the code. For example, the eavesdropper might be able to collect statistics on the frequency of letter combinations in the encoded text and compare them to frequencies in typical unencoded texts in order to infer relationships between the two. But in order to change keys, there must be some way to transmit new keys (securely) between senders and receivers.

Public key systems, first introduced in the 1970s, get around all of those problems. The most widely used public key system is the ***RSA algorithm*** [Rivest, Shamir and Adleman 1978]. Following convention, we'll assume that Bob and Alice wish to exchange secure messages and that Eve is attempting to eavesdrop. We'll call the original (unencrypted text) the ***plaintext*** and the encrypted text the ***ciphertext***. The most general way to describe RSA, and related algorithms, is as follows:

Assume that Alice wants to send a message to Bob. Then:

1.1. Bob chooses a key, *private*, known only to him. This key may need to possess some specific mathematical properties in order to be effective, so Bob may need to exploit a function *choose* that guarantees to return an appropriate private key. Bob exploits a function *f* to compute his public key, *public* = *f*(*private*).

1.2. Bob publishes *public* (either completely publicly or by sending it, unencrypted, to Alice).

1.3. Alice exploits Bob's public key to compute *ciphertext* = *encrypt*(*plaintext*, *public*) and she sends *ciphertext* to Bob.

1.4. Bob exploits his private key to compute *plaintext* = *decrypt*(*ciphtertext*, *private*). In order for this last step to work, *encrypt* and *decrypt* must be designed so that one is the inverse of the other.

If there exist efficient algorithms for performing all four of these steps, then Bob and Alice will be able to exchange messages. But what about Eve? Might she also be able to decrypt Alice's message? We assume that Eve knows the algorithms *encrypt* and *decrypt*. So she could easily eavesdrop if she could infer Bob's private key from his public one or if she could compute *decrypt* without knowing Bob's private key. The RSA algorithm exploits the mathematical properties of modular arithmetic and the computational properties of prime numbers to guarantee that Bob and Alice can perform their tasks efficiently but Eve cannot.

Alice uses the RSA algorithm to send a message to Bob as follows. Assume that all messages are represented as binary strings. Let $j \pmod{k}$, read "j modulo k," mean the remainder when j is divided by k. The greatest common divisor of two numbers i and j, written $gcd(i, j)$ is the largest number that evenly divides both i and j. Then we have:

1. Bob constructs his public and private keys:

1.1. Bob chooses two large prime numbers p and q. From them, he computes $n = p \cdot q$.

1.2. Bob finds a value e such that $1 < e < p \cdot q$ and $gcd(e, (p-1) \cdot (q-1)) = 1$. (In other words, he finds an e such that e and $(p-1) \cdot (q-1)$ are relatively prime.)

1.3. Bob computes a value d such that $d \cdot e \pmod{(p-1)\cdot(q-1)} = 1$. In RSA terminology, this value d, rather than the original numbers p and q, is referred to as Bob's private key.

2. Bob publishes (n, e) as his public key.

3. Alice breaks her message *plaintext* into segments such that no segment corresponds to a binary number that is larger than n. Then, for each *plaintext* segment, Alice computes *ciphertext* = *plaintext*^{e} (mod n). Then she send *ciphertext* to Bob.

4. Bob recreates Alice's original message by computing *plaintext* = *ciphertext*^{d} (mod n).

The RSA algorithm is effective because:

- The functions *encrypt* and *decrypt* are inverses of each other. The proof follows from Euler's generalization of Fermat's Little Theorem (as described in Section 30.2.4). The generalization is called Euler's Totient Theorem or sometimes just Euler's Theorem.
- Bob can choose primes efficiently using the following algorithm:

  1.1. Randomly choose two large numbers as candidates.

  1.2. Check the candidates to see if they are prime. This can be done efficiently using a randomized algorithm, as described in Section 30.2.4. There is a tiny chance that a nonprime could be thought to be prime, but the probability of this happening can be reduced so that it is substantially lower than the probability of a transient hardware failure causing an error in the transmission process.

  1.3. Repeat steps 1 and 2 until two primes have been chosen. By the Prime Number Theorem, the probability of a number near x being prime is about $1/\ln x$ (where ln is the natural logarithm, i.e., the log base 2.71828..., of x). So, for example, suppose Bob wants to choose a 1000 bit number. The probability of a randomly chosen number near 2^{1000} being prime is about 1/693. So he may have to try 1000 or so times for each of the two numbers that he needs.

- Bob can check *gcd* efficiently (using Euclid's algorithm, as described in Example 27.6), so he can compute e.
- Bob can compute d efficiently, using an extension of Euclid's algorithm that exploits the quotients that it produces at each step.
- Alice can implement *encrypt* efficiently. It is not necessary to compute *plaintext*^{e} and then take its remainder mod n. Modular exponentiation can be done directly by successive squaring, as shown in the example below.
- Similarly, Bob can implement *decrypt* efficiently.
- Eve can't recreate *plaintext* because:
  - she can't simply invert *encrypt* because modular exponentiation isn't invertible. She could try every candidate *plaintext* and see if she gets one that produces *ciphertext*, but there are too many of them for this to be feasible.

- she can't compute d from n and e. No efficient algorithm for factoring n into p and q is known, so she can't solve the problem that way. And if there were some other way for her to compute d efficiently, that algorithm could be used as an efficient algorithm for computing p and q. And again, no such efficient algorithm is known.

EXAMPLE J.1 The RSA Algorithm

We can illustrate the RSA algorithm with a simple message from Alice to Bob. In practice, messages will be longer and keys should be large numbers. We'll use short ones here so that it is easier to see what is going on.

1. Bob is expecting to receive messages. So he constructs his keys as follows:

1.1. He chooses two prime numbers, $p = 19$ and $q = 31$. He computes $n = p \cdot q = 589$.

1.2. He finds an e that has no common divisors with $18 \cdot 30 = 540$. The e he selects is 49.

1.3. He finds a value $d = 1069$. Notice that $1069 \cdot 49 = 52{,}381$. Bob needs to assure that the remainder, when 52,381 is divided by 540, is 1. And it is: $52{,}381 = 540 \cdot 97 + 1$. Bob's private key is now 1069.

2. Bob publishes (589, 49) as his public key.

3. Alice wishes to send the simple message "A." The ASCII code for A is 65. So Alice computes 65^{49} (mod 589). She does this without actually computing 65^{49}. Instead, she exploits the following two facts:

$$n^{i+j} = n^i \cdot n^j.$$
$$(n \cdot m)(\text{mod } k) = (n\ (\text{mod } k) \cdot m\ (\text{mod } k))(\text{mod } k).$$

Combining these, we have:

$$n^{i+j}\ (\text{mod } k) = (n^i(\text{mod } k) \cdot n^j(\text{mod } k))(\text{mod } k).$$

So, to compute 65^{49}, first observe that 49 can be expressed in binary as 110001. So $49 = 1 + 16 + 32$. Thus $65^{49} = 65^{1+16+32}$. The following table lists the required powers of 65:

$$65^1\ (\text{mod } 589) = 65.$$
$$65^2\ (\text{mod } 589) = 4225\ (\text{mod } 589) = 102.$$
$$65^4\ (\text{mod } 589) = 102^2\ (\text{mod } 589) = 10404\ (\text{mod } 589) = 391.$$
$$65^8\ (\text{mod } 589) = 391^2\ (\text{mod } 589) = 152881\ (\text{mod } 589) = 330.$$
$$65^{16}\ (\text{mod } 589) = 330^2\ (\text{mod } 589) = 108900\ (\text{mod } 589) = 524.$$
$$65^{32}\ (\text{mod } 589) = 524^2\ (\text{mod } 589) = 274576\ (\text{mod } 589) = 102.$$

$$\begin{aligned}
\text{So we have that: } 65^{49} \pmod{589} &= 65^{(1+16+32)} \pmod{589}.\\
&= (65^1 \cdot 65^{16} \cdot 65^{32})(\text{mod } 589).\\
&= ((65^1 \pmod{589}) \cdot (65^{16} \pmod{589}) \cdot\\
&\quad (65^{32} \pmod{589}))(\text{mod } 589).\\
&= (65 \cdot 524 \cdot 102)(\text{mod } 589).\\
&= ((34060 \pmod{589}) \cdot 102)(\text{mod } 589).\\
&= (487 \cdot 102)(\text{mod } 589).\\
&= 49674 \pmod{589}.\\
&= 198.
\end{aligned}$$

Alice sends Bob the message 198.

4. Bob uses his private key (1069) to recreate Alice's message by computing $198^{1069} \pmod{589}$. Using the same process Alice used, he does this efficiently and retrieves the message 65.

For the details of the mathematical claims that have just been made, as well as some additional points that should be considered in choosing good keys, see any good cryptography book, for example [Trappe and Washington 2006].

J.4 Hackers and Viruses

In this section, we'll briefly touch on two other network security issues: The first is virus detection. We'll see that the undecidability results that we proved in Chapter 21 tell us that the definitive virus detector cannot exist. The second involves the difference between the average-case and worst-case time complexity of some important algorithms. This difference may allow hackers to launch denial of service attacks and to observe "secret" behavior of remote hosts.

J.4.1 Virus Detection

Given a known computer virus V, consider the problem of detecting an infection by V. The most straightforward approach to solving this problem is just to scan incoming messages for the text $<V>$. But viruses can easily evade this technique by altering their text in ways that have no effect on the computation that V performs. So, for example, source code could be modified to add blanks in meaningless places or to add leading 0s to numbers. Executable code could be modified by adding jump instructions that just jump to the next instruction.

So the practical virus detection problem must be stated as, "Given a known virus V and an input message M, does M contain the text of a program that computes the same thing V computes?" By Theorem 21.8, we know that the equivalence question is undecidable for Turing machines. Using that result, we showed, in Theorem 21.12, that the equivalence question for arbitrary programs is also undecidable. So there exists no algorithm that can, in the general case, decide whether a program P, contained in some message M, is equivalent to a given virus V.

So we can't solve the virus problem by making a list of the known viruses and comparing new code to them. What about going the other way? Suppose that, instead of making a list of forbidden operations, we allowed users to define a "white list" of the operations that are to be allowed to run on their machines. Then the job of a virus filter is to compare incoming code to the operations on the white list. Any code that is equivalent to some allowed operation can be declared safe. But now we have exactly the same problem. No test for equivalence exists.

J.4.2 Exploiting the Difference Between the Worst Case and the Average Case

Some widely used algorithms have the property that their worst-case time complexity is significantly different than their average-case time complexity. For example:

- Looking up an entry in a hash table may take, on average, constant time. But if all the entries collide and hash to the same table location, the time required becomes $\mathcal{O}(n)$ where n is the number of entries in the table.
- Looking up an entry in a binary search tree may take, on average $\mathcal{O}(\log n)$ time. But the tree may become unbalanced. In the worst case, it becomes a list and lookup time again becomes $\mathcal{O}(n)$
- Matching regular expressions (often called regexes) of the sort that are supported by Unix utilities and programming languages like Perl may take close to constant time on average. But these regex languages allow expressions that are not regular expressions in the sense in which we defined them in Chapter 6. Any of the regular expressions that we considered there can be converted to a finite state machine that can be guaranteed to perform a match in linear time. But the added flexibility that is provided in the practical tools (see Appendix O for a description of one of them) means that languages that are not regular can be defined. So no finite state machine can be built to accept them. In the worst case, matching some of these patterns may require a backtracking search and so the time required may be exponential in the length of the input string.

Hackers can exploit these facts. For example:

- One way to launch a denial of service attack against a target site S is to send to S a series of messages/requests that has been crafted so that S will exhibit its worst-case performance. If S was designed so that it could adequately respond to its traffic in the average case, it will no longer be able to do so.

- One way to get a peek inside a site S and observe properties that were not intended to be observable is to time it. For example, it is sometimes possible to observe the time required by S to perform decryption or password checking and so to infer its private key or a stored password.

APPENDIX K

Applications: Computational Biology

Proteins and DNA, the building blocks of every living organism, can naturally be described as strings. In Section 18.2.9, we described an experiment in DNA computing. In it, synthesized DNA molecules are treated as strings and operations on them are used to solve a simple graph search problem. Of more practical interest, at least so far, is the fact that significant sets of real DNA and protein molecules can be modeled as languages. So, not surprisingly, several of the techniques (including FSMs, regular expressions, HMMs, and context-free grammars) that have been described in this book play an important role in modern computational biology. In Section 5.12.1, we described the use of an HMM to model a problem in population genetics. In this chapter, we will discuss several other application areas.

K.1 A (Very) Short Introduction to Molecular Biology and Genetics

We begin this chapter with a very short introduction to the biological concepts that are required for an understanding of the way that the computational models we have discussed are being used by biologists. We skip many important details. For more information, follow the Web links suggested here, or consult [Alberts et al 2002] or any good modern text on molecular biology.

K.1.1 Proteins

Proteins are the building blocks of living organisms. A protein is a large molecule that is composed of a sequence of amino acids. There are 20 amino acids that occur in proteins. They are shown in Table K.1, along with their standard, one-letter symbols.

Amino acids are typically divided into classes: hydrophobic (h-phob), hydrophilic (h-phil), and polar, with the polar molecules further divided into positively (pos) and negatively (neg) charged. The class to which an amino acid belongs can have an effect on its function in a protein. Table K.1 shows the class to which each amino acid belongs.

Table K.1 Amino acids.

Amino acid	*Sym*	*Class*	*Amino Acid*	*Sym*	*Class*	*Pattern Symbols*	*Symbol*
Alanine	A	h-phob	Leucine	L	h-phob	Aspartic acid or	B
Arginine	R	pos	Lysine	K	pos	Asparagine	
Asparagine	N	h-phil	Methionine	M	h-phob	Glutamine or	Z
Aspartic acid	D	neg	Phenylalanine	F	h-phob	Glutamic acid	
Cysteine	C	h-phil	Proline	P	h-phob	any amino acid	X
Glutamine	Q	h-phil	Serine	S	h-phil		
Glutamic acid	E	neg	Threonine	T	h-phil		
Glycine	G	h-phob	Tryptophan	W	h-phob		
Histidine	H	pos	Tyrosine	Y	h-phil		
Isoleucine	I	h-phob	Valine	V	h-phob		

It also shows a set of symbols that are sometimes used in specifying patterns of amino acid sequences.

Amino acids share a common chemical structure. Each contains a carbon atom, to which is attached an amino group (NH_2), a carboxyl group (COOH), and a side chain, also called the functional group. Amino acids contain different functional groups, and it is that part of the molecule that causes them to behave differently. Amino acids combine to form proteins when the amino group of one amino acid molecule bonds with the carboxyl group of another, releasing one molecule of water (H_2O) and forming a bond called a peptide linkage. For example, three amino acid molecules, joined by two peptide linkages would look roughly as shown in Figure K.1 (ignoring the details of what the peptide linkages, shown as ovals, actually look like, and letting the ?'s represent the functional groups of each of the amino acids).

The part of each amino acid that remains after peptide bonds have been formed is called an amino acid residue. So, to be exact, a protein is a sequence of amino acid residues. For simplicity, however, proteins are often described simply as sequences of amino acids and we will follow that convention.

The sequence of amino acids that makes up a protein is called the protein's ***primary structure***. If each amino acid is assigned a distinct symbol, as shown in the table above, then the primary structure of a protein can be described as a string. So, for example, the string QTS corresponds to the sequence Glutamine, Threonine, Serine. Notice that the two ends of the sequence illustrated below are different. There is an amino (NH_2) group on one end and a carboxyl (COOH) group on the other. If we adopt the convention that a protein molecule will be described with its amino group on the left, then there is a unique string that corresponds to each protein.

Proteins vary in size. The smallest ones may contain fewer than a hundred amino acids. The largest may contain thousands. A typical protein may contain between 300 and 500 of them.

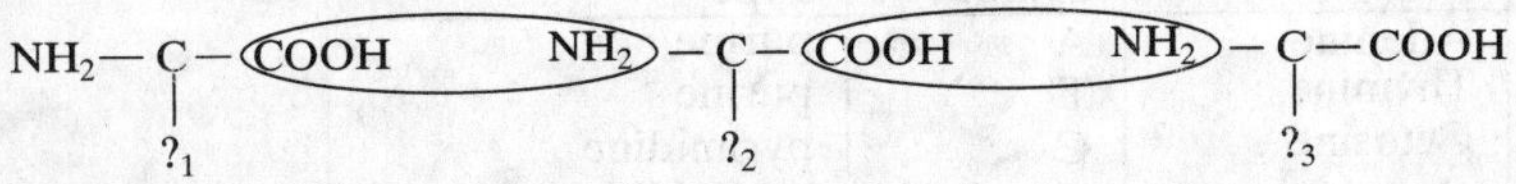

FIGURE K.1 Putting amino acids together to form proteins.

While a protein can be described as a two-dimensional (primary) structure that is simply a chain of amino acids, every physical protein also has a three-dimensional structure that is formed as the amino acid chain folds and wraps around itself. This three-dimensional shape is called the protein's ***secondary structure*** 💻. The secondary structure of a protein is determined by its primary structure, as well as by environmental factors, such as temperature. Each protein has a natural secondary structure, and it must exhibit that structure in order to perform its function within a living organism. Sometimes, when the structure is broken, as for example, by changing the temperature, it can be rebuilt if the natural environment is restored. Sometimes, however, it cannot. For example, the proteins in a cooked egg cannot be "uncooked" and returned to their natural structure. Proteins that have formed abnormal secondary structures will typically behave abnormally. For example, it is believed that an accumulation of abnormally shaped proteins called prions is responsible for causing mad cow disease.

The work of a protein is done at some number of specific locations called ***functional sites***. It is there that other molecules can attach to the protein. In order for a protein to do its job, it must be folded so that its functional sites are exposed and the sites themselves must exist (i.e., contain a sequence of amino acids with the chemical properties that are necessary for whatever job the site is required to perform). But it turns out that some variations in the exact amino acid sequence that makes up a protein molecule can be tolerated without affecting the ability of the protein to function correctly. Such variation can be introduced by mutations. So if we examine a particular protein, for example the blood protein hemoglobin, in multiple organisms, we will find similar but not identical molecules.

The similarity among related molecules may be able to be described as a set of motifs, where a ***motif*** is a relatively short region that has been conserved (left unchanged) by the evolutionary process. If the same motif occurs in very different organisms, then it is likely that it is significant, in the sense that it corresponds to a sequence whose structure is necessary in order for the protein to function properly.

K.1.2 DNA

DNA is the blueprint for living organisms. Each molecule of DNA is composed of two strands, held together by weak hydrogen bonds and arranged as a helix. Each of the strands is made up of a sequence of nucleotides, each of which in turn is composed of three parts: deoxyribose (a sugar), a phosphate group, and one of four bases, shown in Table K.2, along with the symbols that are used to represent them.

The four bases are divided into two chemical classes, also shown in the table below. Each base has a complement, which is the other base in the same class. So A and T are complements, as are C and G. When a double strand of DNA is examined as a sequence of base pairs (one nucleotide from each strand), each base is paired with its complement. Figure K.2 shows a fragment of a DNA molecule.

Table K.2 The nucleotides that make up DNA.

Base	*Symbol*	*Type*
Adenine	A	purine
Thymine	T	purine
Cytosine	C	pyrimidine
Guanine	G	pyrimidine

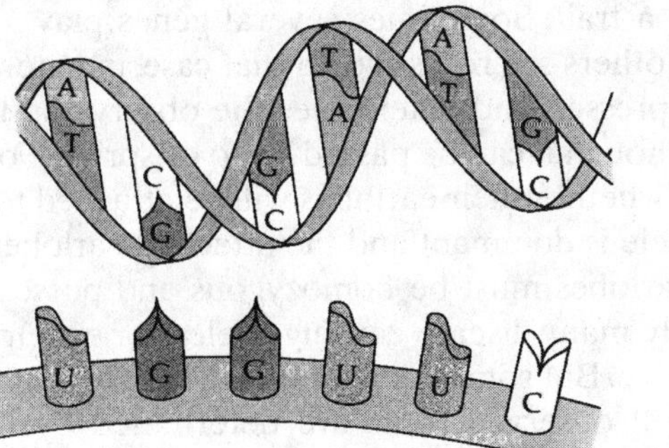

FIGURE K.2 A DNA double helix.

The sequence of base pairs in the DNA of an individual is called the individual's ***genome***. Since the DNA of individuals from the same species is almost identical, the genome of an individual can be considered to be representative of the species, so we can also talk about the genome of a species.

DNA molecules encode the program (set of instructions) that an organism uses to manufacture the proteins that it needs. Since a protein is a sequence of amino acids, the program that builds it can be encoded as a sequence of subprograms, one for each amino acid in the sequence. There are 20 amino acids and only four different nucleotides, so it takes a sequence of three nucleotides to specify a single amino acid. Such a sequence of three nucleotides is called a ***codon***. There are $4^3 = 64$ different codons and only 20 amino acids, so there is redundancy in the way that amino acids are specified. Some amino acids are described by more than one codon. So, in particular, note that some changes to a codon will have no effect on the protein that the codon defines.

A sequence of codons that contains the blueprint for a protein or some other important molecule (such as RNA) is called a ***gene*** and is said to ***code for*** that protein or molecule.

The DNA of an individual is organized as a set of double-helix strands called ***chromosomes***. The human genome, for example, is arranged into 46 chromosomes. Sexually reproducing organisms are ***diploid***, meaning that the chromosomes in all but the egg and sperm cells occur in pairs. Each organism inherits one member of each pair from each parent. Generally both members of the pair contain the same sequence of genes, although there may be exceptions. For example, humans have 23 chromosome pairs, of which 22 are matching. In addition, females have a pair of X chromosomes, while males have one X and one Y.

Differences between individuals within a species are the result of differences in their genes (as well as differences in environmental factors). When a gene occurs in more than one form, those forms are called ***alleles***. So, for example in humans, there are three alleles (called A, B, and O) of a gene that codes for an important blood protein. Each person possesses two genes for this blood protein (one from each parent). Those two genes may be the same or they may be different. So each person's ***genotype*** (the actual genes they possess) for this trait must be one of the six values: AA, AB, AO, BB, BO, and OO. (Order doesn't matter.) Individuals with two identical genes, (i.e., two genes that correspond to the same allele) are called ***homozygous*** with respect to that gene. Individuals with two different genes are called ***heterozygous*** with respect to that gene.

The observable traits of an individual represent its ***phenotype***. The phenotype is determined by the genotype in a variety of ways. Sometimes a single gene is responsible for determining a trait. Sometimes several genes play a role. Sometimes one allele is dominant while others are recessive. In that case, in heterozygous individuals, the dominant allele is expressed and determines the observable trait, while the recessive allele has no affect, although it can be passed on to offspring. For example, people have a gene that determines whether their earlobes will be attached to their skull or hang freely. The free earlobes allele is dominant and the attached earlobes allele is recessive. So anyone with attached earlobes must be homozygous and possess two genes for attached earlobes. Fortunately, many disease-causing alleles, for example the one that causes cystic fibrosis, are recessive. But some, for example the allele that causes Huntington's disease, is dominant. Not all observed traits are determined by the simple dominant/recessive model. For example, in the case of the ABO blood protein, none of the alleles is dominant. Any individual who possesses an A gene will have red blood cells with antigen A on the surface. An individual with a B gene will have red blood cells with antigen B on the surface. A person with one of each will produce both antigen A and antigen B. A person with neither the A nor the B gene (i.e., someone who is homozygous with two O genes) will produce neither antigen. So there are four phenotypes: A (corresponding to the genotypes AA and AO), B (corresponding to the genotypes BB and BO), AB (corresponding to the genotype AB), and O (corresponding to the genotype OO).

While genes are the key to the function of DNA, most of the DNA that is present in the chromosomes of living creatures codes for nothing. For example, about 97% of the human genome is noncoding. A small amount of that noncoding DNA appears to serve some function, for example in regulating the activity of the coding regions. But we do not know what, if any, function is served by most noncoding DNA. Noncoding DNA is important when we compare DNA sequences across related organisms since mutations in nonessential DNA can occur without affecting the fitness of the organism. So, while functional DNA sequences are more likely to be conserved across individuals within a species and across related species, other segments may vary, sometimes substantially. These variations make it possible to do DNA testing to identify individuals. They can also be used to infer genetic closeness of species: The more changes there are in the DNA sequences, the longer ago the species shared a common ancestor.

K.1.3 RNA

RNA is chemically very similar to a single strand of DNA. There are two important differences:

- The four bases that are present in RNA nucleotides are adenine (A), guanine (G), cytosine (C) and uracil (U). The first three are also present in DNA. The last, uracil, occurs in place of thymine. C and G are complementary (just as they are in DNA). A and U are also complementary.
- RNA nucleotides contain a different sugar molecule (ribose) than do those in DNA.

In a living cell, RNA plays several important roles, including:

- Messenger RNA transports the encoding of a protein from the cell's nucleus (where the DNA is) to the site of protein synthesis.
- Transfer RNA transports individual amino acid molecules to the building site during protein synthesis.

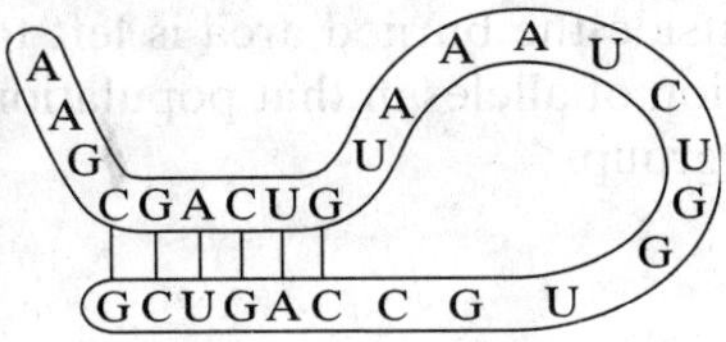

FIGURE K.3 An RNA molecule folding.

- Ribosomal RNA makes up a substantial part of the ribosomes, the cell's protein factories.
- Catalytic RNA functions like an enzyme and is involved in a variety of cell functions.

RNA molecules, unlike DNA ones, do not form double strands. But a single RNA strand does fold around itself, creating a secondary structure that is important to the function of the molecule. In particular, if two subsequences that contain complementary bases fold so that they align next to each other, they form hydrogen-bonded base pairs in much the same way that two DNA strands do. We call these bonded subsequences ***stems***. The unaligned subsequences between the stems will then form loops, and unaligned subsequences at the end will simply hang out as tails.

Consider, for example, the RNA sequence AAGCGACUGUAAAUCUGGUGCCAGUCG. It is likely to fold to form the structure shown in Figure K.3. The lines indicate hydrogen bonds between complementary bases in a stem. In this example, a stem containing six base pairs has formed. Stems generally arrange themselves in a helix, in much the same way that the paired strands in a DNA molecule do.

K.1.4 Genetics and Evolution

The genomes of living creatures are under constant evolutionary pressure from three natural stochastic processes:

- mutation, which occurs when DNA is imperfectly copied during reproduction,
- natural selection, which occurs when fitter (i.e., better-adapted) individuals have higher survival and reproduction rates than their less well-adapted cousins, and
- genetic drift 💻, which occurs when the relative frequencies of competing alleles changes, either as a result of sampling bias or as the result of random (i.e., not based on fitness) events. Sampling bias is particularly likely to occur in small populations (and many species exist in relatively small, isolated populations). Suppose that there exists a gene with two alleles, a and A, that occur with frequency .5 each. Assuming sexual reproduction, one gene from each parent is passed on to the next generation. That gene is chosen at random from the two that the parent possesses. It is likely that in the next generation, the relative frequencies of the two alleles will not be exactly .5, but will instead be something like .4955 or .5045. At the next generation, it could become slightly more weighted. And so forth. If it ever reaches 0/1, there is no going back. Genetic drift also occurs when some individuals are selected more because they are lucky than because they are fit. Suppose, for example, that there is a fire that rages through a large portion of the natural habitat of a population and all the individuals in the fire-ravaged area are destroyed. A small group that

happened to be lucky enough to be outside the burned area is left to reproduce. There is no guarantee that the distribution of alleles in that population is identical to the distribution in the original larger group.

K.1.5 Summary

The computational theory that we have described in this book is well-suited to biological applications for two important reasons:

- proteins, DNA, and RNA can straightforwardly be represented as strings.
- naturally occurring stochastic processes apply to them.

K.2 The Sequence Matching Problem

There now exist sophisticated techniques for analyzing DNA and protein molecules and for determining the sequence of amino acids or nucleotides that they contain. This process is called mapping or sequencing. In 2003, the human genome project 💻 completed its goals of describing the approximately 3 billion base pairs and identifying the approximately 30,000 genes that make up human DNA. The genomes of other organisms, ranging from the bacterium *E. coli* to chimpanzees, have also been mapped, as have many of the proteins that are found throughout nature.

Consider a set of related organisms. They will share many of their proteins, as well as much of their DNA and RNA. But, when molecules are looked at as sequences of amino acids or nucleotides, they will be similar but not identical for two reasons:

- Mutations can occur during reproduction. Those changes will, in turn, cause changes to the proteins that make up the organism, resulting in individual differences within a species, as well as the more significant differences that can be observed across species.
- Many mutations have no effect on the function of the protein, DNA, or RNA molecules that they modify. So they may be passed on, without effect, to the descendants of the original organism in which they occurred. Thus even very similar organisms may possess different DNA and different proteins.

Proteins are very long molecules and DNA strands are even longer. So, to analyze them, it makes sense to break them apart into shorter (hopefully significant) subsequences. There are a variety of techniques available for doing this. The important thing about these techniques is that they cut up long sequences in predictable ways. For example, there is a family of enzymes called restriction enzymes, each of which cuts double-stranded DNA only in places that contain a particular nucleotide sequence. So if similar DNA molecules are subjected to the same processes, they will produce similar sequences.

Comparing DNA, RNA, or protein sequences can help to answer the following kinds of questions:

- Given an organism (from which we have a DNA, RNA, or protein sequence), how is it related to other organisms? The closer the match between the sequences, the more closely related the organisms are likely to be.

- Given a DNA, RNA, or protein sequence, what function does it perform? What parts of the sequence are important in the performance of the function? If the sequence is very similar to sequences in other organisms, or even other molecules in the same organism, and we already know what those molecules do, we may have an answer. Or, if we find similar sequences in other molecules, perhaps it is possible to figure out what all of them do by looking for similarities in what we know about all of them.
- Given a DNA, RNA, or protein sequence from a diseased organism and one from a healthy organism, what is the difference? This may help us understand the cause or a potential treatment for the disease.

There now exist large databases 💻 of known protein, DNA, and RNA sequences from known organisms. But a substantial computational problem remains: comparing sequences to each other. Generally the goal of such comparisons is to find related sequences that are evolutionarily as close as possible to each other. In other words, we want to find sequences from which the current sequence could have evolved with the smallest number of mutations. Because the sequences can be described as strings, another way to describe the problem is as string matching. Because related sequences are not necessarily identical, the problem is one of approximate string matching. For a good introduction to the variety of computational techniques that have been developed to solve this problem, see [Durbin et al. 1998].

All of these techniques rely on the notion of ***alignment***: Two or more sequences are aligned if they are arranged in a way that minimizes some notion of evolutionary distance. One strategy, for example, is to maximize the number of positions that contain the same amino acid or nucleotide. But each alignment algorithm exploits its own specific measure of closeness. For example, some rate pairs of amino acids as either identical or different, while others consider amino acids in the same class (as shown in the amino acid table we presented above) to be more similar than ones in different classes. Some alignment algorithms are global: They try to align entire sequences so that as many symbols as possible match. Other algorithms are local: They try to find smaller subsequences that match exactly or almost exactly, even if the rest of the alignment produced by that match isn't very good.

EXAMPLE K.1 Aligning Amino Acid Sequences

Consider the four amino acid sequences:

AGHTYWDNR, AGHDTYENNRY, YPAGQDTYWNN, AGHDTTYWNN

In this simple case, a straightforward alignment is:

```
    A G H   T   Y W D N R
    A G H D T   Y E N N R Y
Y P A G Q D T   Y W N N
    A G H D T T Y W N N
```

Similar (but not necessarily identical) sequences can be aligned as shown above. Such sequences are probably related (both genetically and functionally). But they may differ as a result of three kinds of mutations:

- substitution: For example, in the third sequence above, Q has been substituted for H. In evaluating the closeness of an alignment, some substitutions are typically assigned higher distances (and so alignments that include them are ranked as less close) than others. Sometimes the distance is based on chemical and structural properties of the corresponding amino acids or nucleotides. But in one common scheme, the PAM family of distance matrices for amino acids, the distances are based on the probability that one amino will replace another during evolution. The Q/H substitution in the third sequence has very low evolutionary distance (i.e., it is very likely to occur), while the E/W substitution in the second sequence has a high one.
- deletion: For example, the D is missing from the first sequence above.
- insertion: For example, an extra T has been inserted in the fourth sequence above.

In the rest of this section, we consider a collection of techniques for solving the following problems:

1. Given two sequences, find the best alignment between them.
2. Given one new sequence and a database of known sequences, find the known ones that are most likely to be related to the new one.
3. Given one or more patterns that describe related families of sequences, compare the pattern to an individual sequence or to a database of sequences and find close matches.

K.3 DNA and Protein Sequence Matching Using the Tools of Regular Languages

We begin by describing three techniques that can be used to solve alignment problems involving proteins and DNA.

- Deterministic FSMs are used in BLAST, a very fast query engine that operates on huge databases and solves problem 2 above.
- Regular expressions can be used to specify motifs, or patterns that describe a related set of sequences. These patterns are used to solve problem 3 above.
- Hidden Markov models can be used both for pairwise matching (problem 1 above), as well as to model known families of sequences and to compute the probability that other sequences are related to that family (problem 3 above).

All of these techniques make the assumption that the mutations that caused the variation among related sequences occurred, for the most part, independently of each other. This independence assumption makes it possible to rely on techniques that are based on models of regular languages. In Section K.4, we will consider phenomena, such as sequence evolution and secondary structure prediction of RNA, in which distant parts of a sequence interact with each other. To solve such problems it will be necessary to use more powerful formal structures, such as stochastic context-free grammars.

K.3.1 Finite State Machines in BLAST

The first problem we will consider is the following: Given a protein or DNA sequence, find other sequences that have high-scoring local matches with it. The BLAST [Altschul, Gish, Miller, Myers, and Lipman 1990] search engine is widely used to solve this problem. There are several versions of BLAST. Some of them now do global as well as local matches. The BLAST family of search engines uses a variety of heuristic techniques to search huge databases and find the sequences that are most likely to be biologically significant matches for the query string.

The core of the original BLAST system is a three step process:

1. Select a reasonably small number w (usually between 4 and 20). Examine the query string and select the substrings of length w that are good candidates for producing local matches with it.
2. Using the set of substrings found in step 1 (called words), build a DFSM that can be used to scan a database of known sequences and identify those sequences that have high-scoring local matches with one of the words. Run the resulting DFSM against the database and find the sequences that match.
3. Examine the matches found in step 2 and see if it is possible to extend any of them to build longer matching sequences. Assign scores to all of those extended matches and return those sequences with a local match score above some predetermined cutoff.

The implementation of step 2 can take advantage of the observation that we made at the end of Section 6.2.4: Given a finite set of keywords K, it is straightforward to build a DFSM that matches all instances of elements of K. If we had to view the set K as an arbitrary regular expression, build an NDFSM, and then convert it to a deterministic one, the construction step could take time that grows exponentially in the size of K. But a variant of the algorithm *buildkeywordFSM*, which we described in Section 6.2.4, builds the required deterministic FSM in time that is proportional to the sum of the lengths of the words in K. We need a variant of *buildkeywordFSM* because we actually need a finite state transducer, not simply a recognizer. The job of the transducer is to output *each instance* of a match when it finds it. In experiments that were done in the early stages of the implementation of BLAST, other techniques for implementing step 2 were tried, but the FSM approach yielded the highest performance in searching large databases. Some later versions of BLAST now use other techniques, but some retain the original FSM approach.

K.3.2 Regular Expressions Specify Protein Motifs

Given a collection of proteins that are already known to be related, and a sequence alignment of them, we can define a ***motif***, a conserved sequence of amino acids, that we may know or hypothesize corresponds to some function of the proteins in which these sequences occur.

EXAMPLE K.2 Detecting Motifs

Suppose that we have the following fragments (which are smaller than the ones that are generally considered, but they illustrate the idea):

E	S	**G**	H	**D**	**T**					Y	Y	**N**	**K**	N	R
		M		**D**	**T**	T	T	T	T	S	W	**Q**	**S**		
	R	**G**	S	**D**	**T**	T	T			P	D	**M**	**T**		
	A	**G**	P		**T**	T				W	R	**N**	**T**		
K	Q	**G**	E	**D**	**T**	T				D	G	**M**	**T**		
	A	**G**	M	**D**	**T**	T				K	P	**Q**	**T**		
		M		**D**	**T**					R	W	**N**	**S**		
		1	2	3	4					5	6	7	8	9	

This example appears to contain a short motif, shown in bold. Notice that small variations (in particular, things that we believe do not affect function) may be allowed.

Once we have defined a motif, we would like to search to find occurrences of it in other protein sequences. So we need a notation in which to describe the motif. Regular expressions are often used to do this. Not all systems use exactly the same regular expression syntax, but most use something similar to the syntax of Perl (Appendix O) or Python.

EXAMPLE K.3 Describing Motifs with Regular Expressions

Continuing with the example we started above, we see that:

- The motif begins with G or with M, but if it starts with M then the M is the first element of the sequence.
- Position 3 is D, but it is optional.
- Position 4 is T, which may be replicated some number of times.
- Position 7 can be anything except P (purine). It would be hard to hypothesize this from this small a sample, but such an observation could be part of a motif that was derived from a larger sample, so we include it here to illustrate the idea.
- Position 8 must be K, S or T.

EXAMPLE K.3 (*Continued*)

To describe this motif with a Perl/Python-style regular expression, we would write:

```
(G|(^M)) X D? T T* X X [^P] [KST]
```

X is a shorthand for [ARND...], so it matches any amino acid. The character ^ means the left end of the sequence if it occurs outside []. Inside [], it means not one of the characters listed.

The exact syntax that is used to specify these patterns varies across systems. For example, Prosite 💻, a database of motifs, uses a different format, but the structure of the pattern expressions is the same.

K.3.3 HMMs for Sequence Matching

While regular expressions are a good way to define motifs that are derived from a set of very similar sequences, the technique degrades when the set of sequences becomes fairly diverse. As new sequences are added to the set, more and more special cases must be included in the regular expression, and there is no way to indicate that some of them are rare, truly special cases, while other variants are found in almost all sequences in the family. If this process continues long enough, the motif will become so general that it will match many unrelated sequences. And there is no notion of, "close match," as opposed to, "This one is a stretch."

To solve this problem, we need a new technique for describing related families of sequences. In particular, we need a technique that can capture the variations among the members of the family and that records the probabilities associated with those variations. We'll call such a representation a ***profile***. Given a set of profiles describing a set of sequence families, we would like to be able to consider a new sequence and compute the probability that it could have been derived from each of the known families. We'll then hypothesize that it belongs to the family with the highest probability of generating it.

To build a profile for a family, we'll assume an initial ancestral sequence and then describe the mutations that produced the other members of the family. We'll associate a probability with each such mutation. Then, given a new sequence s and a profile p, we can compute the probability that s evolved from the ancestral sequence of p and thus belongs to the family that is descended from that sequence. So, while the attempt to match a regular expression against a sequence produces one of only two results, match or fail, matching a sequence against a probabilistic profile produces some value in the range 0 to 1.

We begin by considering just the case in which all members of a family are identical except for substitutions of one amino acid for another. Then we can build a simple hidden Markov model (or HMM, as described in Section 5.11.2) that corresponds to the profile of a family. Such a hidden Markov model is called a ***profile HMM***. To describe a family of sequences of length n, we will build a profile HMM $M = (K, O, \pi, A, B)$, where:

- K is a set of n states, one for each position in the sequence.
- O is the output alphabet, namely the set of amino acid or nucleotide symbols.
- π contains the initial state probabilities. $\pi[1] = 1$ and all other values of π are 0.
- A contains the transition probabilities. $\forall i < n\ (A[i, i+1] = 1)$ and all other values of A are 0.
- B contains the output probabilities. So, for any symbol a, if the probability that the ith symbol is an a is p, then $B[i, a] = p$.

So the state structure of M for a four-element sequence family would be as shown in Figure K.4(a). M will start in state 1 and then move to 2, then 3, then 4. Associated with each state is a vector that lists, for each output symbol, the probability that M will generate it when it is in that state. Suppose, for example, that almost always the first element of a sequence in this family is a `W` but rarely it may be a `K` instead. Then, $B[1, \texttt{W}]$ might be .95, $B[1, \texttt{K}]$ might be .05, and, for all other values v, $B[1, v]$ would be 0.

Given a new sequence, the probability that it was generated by M (and so is related to the sequences that were used to define M) can be computed using the ***forward algorithm***, described in Section 5.11.2.

But substitutions are not the only mutations that can occur. Elements can be deleted from a sequence and new ones can be added. So we need to expand the HMM to include states that correspond to deletions and insertions. We can do that by building a profile HMM with the structure shown in Figure K.4(b). The match states at the bottom, represented as squares, correspond to an original ancestral sequence. The fact that new elements could have been added to that sequence is encoded in a set of insertion states, shown as diamonds. Each time the machine enters an insertion state, it outputs one symbol according to the output probabilities associated with that state. Notice that there is a transition from each insertion state back to itself since more than one element may be inserted at any point. The fact that elements may have been deleted from the original sequence is encoded in a set of deletion states, shown as circles. All the output probabilities associated with deletion states are 0. So if the machine enters a deletion state instead of the corresponding match state, one symbol from the original sequence will fail

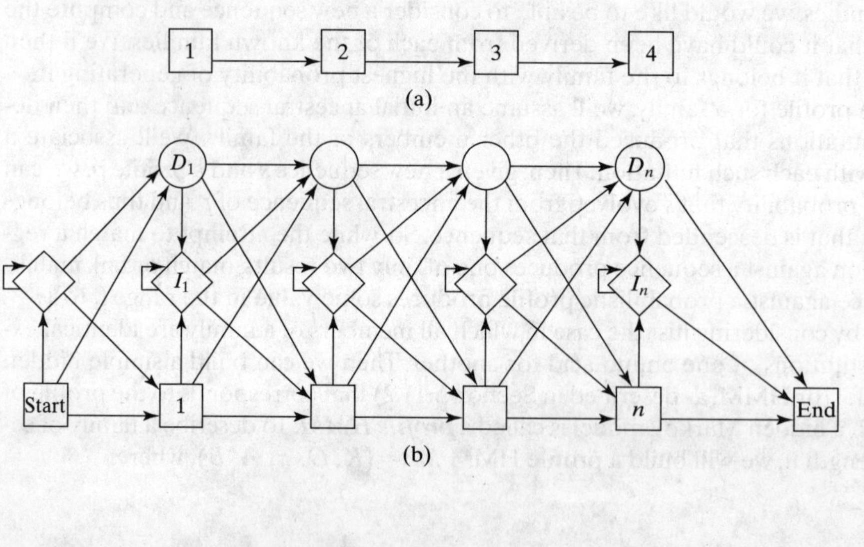

FIGURE K.4 An HMM that describes a protein sequence family.

to appear in the output sequence. We've shown all possible transitions among the three kinds of states. The probabilities associated with those transitions (as well as the output probabilities associated with the match and insertion states) must be acquired from a training set of sequences that the model is designed to describe.

Given a collection of profile HMMs of this sort and a new sequence s, we can use the forward algorithm to find the HMM with the highest likelihood of outputting s.

We can also use profile HMMs to find an optimal alignment of a new sequence with a known family. We can recast this problem as follows: Given a profile HMM M and a sequence s, what path through M has the highest probability of outputting s? This problem can be solved with the ***Viterbi algorithm***, as described in Section 5.12.2.

K.4 RNA Sequence Matching and Secondary Structure Prediction Using the Tools of Context-Free Languages

So far, we have considered the problem of aligning and matching DNA and protein sequences. We have been able to define useful techniques for solving those problems using the tools of regular languages. The reason this was possible is that we were able to make the assumption that whatever mutations occurred and caused the variations among the sequences in a family occurred independently of each other. The facts of primary structure (sequence) evolution of DNA and proteins by and large support that assumption.

But now let's consider RNA. The secondary (three-dimensional) structure of an RNA molecule is usually critical to its function. Because of the way that RNA molecules fold, a change to a single nucleotide in a stem (paired) region could completely alter the molecule's shape and thus its function. So it turns out that, for many RNA molecules, secondary structure is more likely to be conserved than primary (sequence) structure is. If secondary structure is to be conserved, then any change to one nucleotide in a stem must be matched by a corresponding change to the paired nucleotide.

Let's return to the example RNA fragment that we considered in Section K.1.3:

AAGCGACUGUAAAUCUGGUGCCAGUCG

We saw that this fragment is likely to fold to form the structure shown in Figure K.5(a), which contains one stem that is six base pairs long (shown with the lines between the paired bases). We can also represent the paired bases in the stem as shown in Figure K.5(b).

Suppose that there were a mutation and the U in position (counting from the left) 8 were replaced by C. Then, in order to preserve the folding structure, the A in position 23 would also have to change (to G). On the other hand, any number of substitutions could occur in the loop region without changing the secondary structure of the molecule. It is quite common to find related RNA molecules whose sequences are very different but whose secondary structure (and thus function) have been conserved.

The nested dependencies that determine secondary structure cannot be described by a regular expression or recognized by a finite state machine. But they can be described by a context-free grammar. Notice that the structure is very similar to other nested structures (for example matched parentheses and palindromes) that we have already described with CFGs.

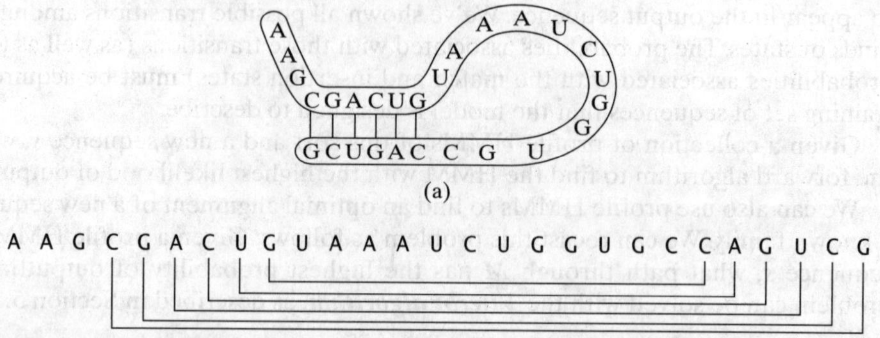

(b)

FIGURE K.5 An RNA molecule folding.

The real story on RNA folding is more complicated than what we have just described. So, before we attempt to write a grammar that describes a family of strings with the same secondary structure, we will add one more twist: Complementary pairs (C - G and A - U) are the most likely to form base pairs that build stems. But other pairs can also be joined to form base pairs. In particular, G - U, although less likely than the complementary pairs to bond, can do so not infrequently. So what we need, to model this phenomenon, is a stochastic context-free grammar of the sort we described in Section 11.10, coupled with an appropriate stochastic parser.

The rules for a fragment of a stochastic CFG that describes RNA sequences with a three nucleotide tail, a six base pair stem, and a seven nucleotide loop would then be something like the following (with the probabilities shown in brackets):

<family> → *<tail><stemloop>* [1] /* *<stemloop>* builds a six base pair stem plus a loop.

<tail> → *<base><base><base>* [1]

<stemloop> → C *<stemloop-5>* G [.23] /* *<stemloop5>* builds a five base pair stem plus a loop.

<stemloop> → G *<stemloop-5>* C [.23]

<stemloop> → A *<stemloop-5>* U [.23]

<stemloop> → U *<stemloop-5>* A [.23]

<stemloop> → G *<stemloop-5>* U [.03]

<stemloop> → U *<stemloop-5>* G [.03]

<stemloop-5> → ...

There are two kinds of questions we would like to be able to answer with a grammar such as this:

- Given a new sequence *s* and a grammar *G* that describes a family of known sequences, what parse tree describes the most likely way in which *G* could have generated *s*? That parse predicts s's secondary structure. To answer this question requires a stochastic parser that is the context-free equivalent of the Viterbi algorithm.

- Given a new sequence s and a grammar G that describes a family of known sequences, what is the probability that G generated s via some path? The answer to this question allows us to compare families and find the one to which s is most likely to belong? To answer this question requires the context-free equivalent of the forward algorithm for HMMs.

As with all probabilistic models, to be able to answer any of these questions requires that we obtain, typically from a set of training instances, the probabilities associated with the rules of the grammar.

The discussion presented here has barely scratched the surface of this problem. For substantial additional detail, see [Durbin et al. 1998] and .

K.5 Complexity of the Algorithms Used in Computational Biology

Obvious approaches to many of the problems we have sketched here are computationally intractable. For example, consider the problem of sequencing a large DNA or protein molecule. Since it is difficult to do that directly, the standard procedure is to clone the molecule and then break the copies randomly into smaller molecules that can be sequenced individually. Then it remains to figure out how the smaller molecules were connected in the original one. Thinking of the molecules as strings, our goal is to find a single string that contains each of the shorter strings as a substring. Clearly we can find one such string simply by concatenating together all of the shorter strings. But we assume that that is not the original string. Instead we assume that the most likely original string is the shortest string that contains each of the observed substrings. Finding the shortest common superstring of a set of strings is NP-hard. When we convert that problem to a decision problem we get the language:

- SHORTEST-SUPERSTRING(<S, k> : S is a set of strings and there exists some superstring T such that every element of S is a substring of T and T has length less than or equal to k}.

SHORTEST-SUPERSTRING is NP-complete.

As another example, consider the problem of predicting how proteins will fold. Obvious approaches require search. In some cases, it is possible to prove that no more efficient algorithm exists. For example [Berger and Leighton 1998] shows that the protein-folding problem, given the hydrophobic-hydrophilic model of protein structure, is NP-complete.

APPENDIX L

Applications: Natural Language Processing

Why should we care about the formal properties of a language like English? More than 375 million people speak English as their first language. The number would be even larger if we had picked Chinese instead. Why do computers need to be involved?

Millions of words of text are posted on the Internet every day. People can read any one page of that easily, but none of us can sort through that mountain of words to find the one page we're interested in. Computers are good at that. If programs could read English and Spanish and Chinese, real automated query agents could exist. To build such programs, we need an understanding of the phenomenon: What are the sentences of English (or Spanish or Chinese) and how are they structured? The formal theory we have presented is just a small beginning of that analysis, but it is a beginning. In this section, we summarize a few of the ways in which our theory can be applied in natural language processing (NLP) systems. For a comprehensive treatment of modern NLP techniques, see [Jurafsky and Martin 2000]. For more on statistical techniques in particular, see [Manning and Schütze 1999].

L.1 Morphological Analysis

The first step in almost any approach to processing natural language sentences is to find the words and look them up in a dictionary. For English, this is only slightly more difficult than it sounds. For some other languages, it is substantially more so. Although we will limit this discussion to English, we'll still be able to see most of the major issues.

A ***morpheme*** is the smallest linguistic unit to which meaning can be assigned. Consider words like `animal`, `destroy`, and `cacophony`. Each of these words is composed of a single morpheme and exists in any reasonable dictionary of English. But now consider:

- `loudly`: the simple word `loudly` is composed of two morphemes:
  - loudly + ly (adverb).
- `likes`: unfortunately, there are two ways to analyze the simple word `likes`:
  - like (noun) + s (plural).
  - like (verb) + s (third person singular).

- leaves: there may be three or more different morphological analyses:
  - leaf (noun) + s (plural).
  - leave (noun, as in military leave) + s (plural).
  - leave (verb) + s (third person singular).
- disparagingly: this single word can be decomposed into three (and sometimes even more) morphemes:
  - disparag- (verb) + ing (progressive) + ly (adverb).
- skies: sometimes the stem is changed when it combines with an affix. Here the final y of sky is rewritten as ie before an s is added:
  - sky (noun) + e + s (plural).
- toys: but whether the y changes depends on the preceding letter:
  - toy (noun) + s (plural).
- went: sometimes neither the root nor the standard form of the affix is anywhere to be found:
  - go (verb) + ed (past).
- fish: there are two noun analyses (plus a verb one) because the plural affix is rendered as the empty string:
  - fish (noun), with no affixes, so the default "unmarked" form, singular, is meant.
  - fish (noun) + (plural).
  - fish (verb).
- women: sometimes (although rarely in English) the root word changes internally instead of simply adding an affix before or after it:
  - woman (noun) + (plural).
- unfriendly: affixes can be added to both the front and the end of a root.
  - un (negative) + friend + ly (adverb).

Depending on the dictionary, some or all of these words may be found. But new words come into the language on a regular basis and the process by which new words are formed by adding affixes is productive, meaning that the instant the word blog appears, so do the words blogger, blogging, blogged, unblog and so forth. (Just as an aside, as this paragraph was written, none of those words were in the dictionary that the spell checker was using.) So it makes sense to encode the regular rules for adding affixes, rather than to require that all inflected forms be entered explicitly in the dictionary. Further, there are languages, for example Finnish and Turkish, in which there may be hundreds or thousands of forms of a single verb. It would be completely impractical to list them all.

If our task is to read and interpret English text, then we need a technique for analyzing words in their surface form (the form, such as leaves in which they appear in text) and translating them into the form we'll call lexical (in which a word is represented as a root form, the main meaning unit listed in the dictionary, plus one or more affixes that modify the main meaning). If, on the other hand, we are building an application that must generate English sentences or text (for example in a conversational system, or a text summary system, or the output side of a machine translation system), then we need a way to map from lexical (meaning) form to surface form. It makes sense, from a software engineering perspective, as well as from a linguistic one, to attempt to capture the facts about those mappings in a single representation that can be used in either direction.

We can do this with a bidirectional finite state transducer of the sort that we described in Section 5.10. Such a system is called a two-level morphological analyzer 🖳. For a good description of the evolution of this idea in linguistics, see [Karttunen and Beesley 2001]. We show here a very tiny fragment of a morphological transducer for English. While a practical one might have 100,000 or more transitions, it does not need to be built by hand. It can be compiled from a dictionary and a set of rules that describe the order in which affixes can be applied, as well as the spelling alternations (like converting `y` to `i`) that English requires. For more detail on how to make this work in practice, see [Jurafsky and Martin 2000]. In our example, we use the notation *a*/*b*, just as we did in Section 5.10. In this case, *a*/*b* means that the symbol *a* occurs in the surface form and the symbol *b* occurs in the lexical form. When the symbol is the same on both levels, we will write it simply as *a*. We use # in surface forms to indicate a word boundary. We use the following symbols in lexical forms: +N (noun), +V (verb), +ADJ (adjective), +SG (singular), +PL (plural), and +3SG (3rd person singular, for verbs).

EXAMPLE L.1 A Tiny Morphological Transducer

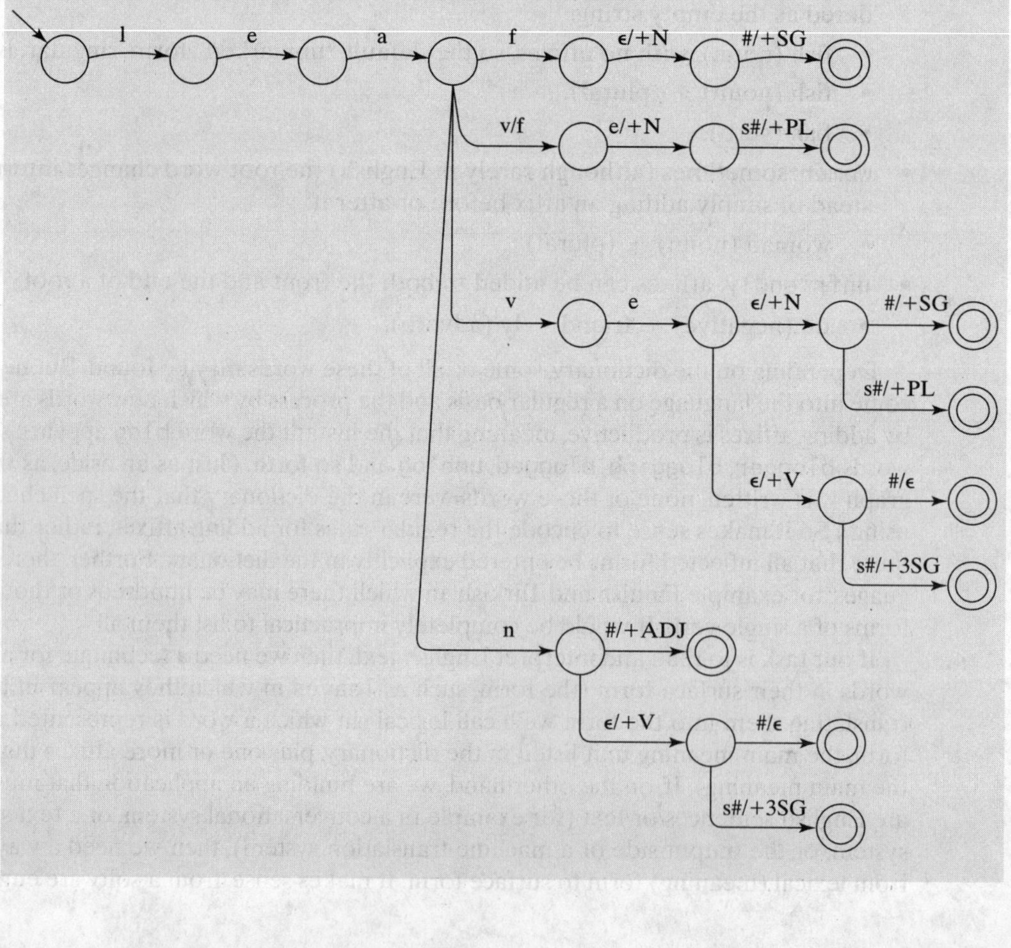

This simple transducer can, for example, perform the following mappings in either direction:

- `leaf#` ⇔ leaf + N + SG
- `leave#` ⇔ leave + N + SG
- `leave#` ⇔ leave + V
- `leaves#` ⇔ leaf + N + PL
- `leaves#` ⇔ leave + N + PL
- `leaves#` ⇔ leave + V + 3SG
- `lean#` ⇔ lean + ADJ
- `lean#` ⇔ lean + V

Note that when the transducer that we just built is run in the surface form to lexical form direction it is nondeterministic. It may output more than one lexical form and those forms may have different part of speech tags (e.g., N or V). But, of course, a straightforward dictionary lookup can also report more than one possible part of speech for a single word. In the next section, we consider a technique for resolving that ambiguity.

L.2 Part of Speech Tagging

Consider the problem of parsing an English sentence such as `Store ice in the cooler.` We'd like to do that using a grammar of the sort we presented in Example 11.6. The rules of that grammar are written using part of speech (POS) tags, such as N(oun), V(erb), and Adj(ective). So, before those rules can be applied to a sentence, it is necessary to tag each word with the part of speech that corresponds to the way the word is functioning in that sentence. We can begin by looking the words up in a dictionary or by using a morphological analyzer of the sort we just described. If we do that for the words in `Store ice in the cooler`, we'll get the values shown in Table L.1.

We've simplified a bit here. Practical NLP systems use tag sets with somewhere between 45 and 200 tags, so the classes that we have labeled N, V, and Adj would be further subdivided, thus making the disambiguation problem even more difficult.

Table L.1 Words and their part of speech tags.

`store`	N, V
`ice`	N, V
`cooler`	N, Adj

To build a part of speech (POS) tagger, we need to make use of two kinds of information:

- Given a word, what tags can be applied and how likely is each of them? For example, while the word `store` can be either a noun or a verb, it is more likely to be a noun than it is to be a verb.
- Given a particular sentential context, what tag is most likely to come next? For example, a verb rarely comes after the word `the`.

There are two approaches one can take to capturing that information and encoding it in an effective POS tagging system.

- Create a set of rules that describe the facts. Match the rules against input sentences to build a tag sequence.
- Build a hidden Markov model (HMM). Use the Viterbi algorithm that we discussed in Section 5.11.2 to find the path that is most likely to have produced the observed sequence of words. We'll briefly sketch that approach here.

Consider the sentence we are analyzing. Imagine that whatever process generated it actually generated a sequence of parts of speech. We want to know what that sequence is but we cannot observe it directly. All we can observe is the sequence of words that were generated from those parts of speech. So we can build an HMM in which the (hidden) states correspond to parts of speech, the outputs correspond to the words, and the probabilities describe the likelihood of one part of speech following another and the likelihood that a particular part of speech will be realized as a particular word.

So we can build a straightforward HMM for POS tagging as follows:

- Let K contain one state for each part of speech tag.
- Let O be the set of possible words.
- Let π describe the probabilities, for each tag, of a sentence starting with that tag.
- Let A describe the transition probabilities, i.e., the probability, given some tag t_1, that the next tag will be t_2.
- Let B describe the output probabilities, i.e., the probability, given some tag t, that the word that corresponds to that tag is word w.

The probabilities in π, A, and B have to come from somewhere. Fortunately, there are large datasets (generally called ***corpora***) of sentences that have already been tagged, so they can be used to train the HMM.

The model that we have just described is called a ***bigram tagger***. It decides on the tag for the current word by considering just a single preceding word. We could extend the idea and create states that correspond to a sequence of two tags. Then, in A, we'd capture the probability that tag t_2 follows a particular sequence of two prior tags. We'll call such a model a ***trigram tagger***.

While the overall problem of NLP is far from solved, the POS tagging piece of the problem is very nearly so. Current POS taggers report accuracies in the range of 97% (i.e., 97% of the words are tagged correctly). Some taggers can be set to return not just the single POS sequence (i.e., path through the HMM) with the highest score, but some specified number of highest scoring sequences. Those paths can be presented to a parser, which can then be asked to select the one that is consistent with the rules of the grammar.

L.3 The Grammar of English

In this section, we consider the problem of building a formal model for the syntax (grammar) of English. We will attempt to answer the question, "How powerful does such a model have to be in order to describe the facts about grammatically correct English sentences?"

L.3.1 Is English Regular?

If the set of grammatical English sentences is finite, then it is regular. It is finite if there is a finite number of words and a longest grammatical sentence. At any particular point in time and for any specific dialect of English, there exists the longest word ever used and the longest sentence ever spoken or written. But, in principle, the next day someone could add a bit to that longest sentence to make a yet longer one. Just as an example that shows that there are sentences that are much longer than whatever upper limit you probably have in mind, consider the 630 word sentence shown in Figure L.1. It announces a local government's intention to move a path.

In Example 8.19, we assumed that there was no bound on the length of English sentences and we gave one proof that English is not regular. That proof was based on the structure of sentences such as `The rat that the cat saw ran`. It is possible to do different but similar proofs based on other naturally recursive structures in English.

For example, consider the following argument from [Chomsky 1957], based on a fragment of a grammar for English sentences:

$S \rightarrow$ `if` S `then` S

$S \rightarrow$ `either` S `or` S

$S \rightarrow$ `the man who said` S `is arriving today`

Any grammatical sentence that combines the constructs defined by those three rules must properly nest all if/then and either/or pairs. For example, the following string is grammatical:

```
If either the man who said if it rains then we can't go is
arriving today or the man who said if it's sunny then we must
go is arriving today then we must go.
```

By the way, while it is very unlikely that anyone would ever write such a sentence, and if they did, they would almost certainly use commas, keep in mind that English was first a spoken language, in which pauses and inflection make it possible to utter sentences like this one and have them be understandable.

A path from a point approximately 330 metres east of the most south westerly corner of 17 Batherton Close, Widnes and approximately 208 metres east-south-east of the most southerly corner of Unit 3 Foundry Industrial Estate, Victoria Street, Widnes, proceeding in a generally east-north-easterly direction for approximately 28 metres to a point approximately 202 metres east-south-east of the most south-easterly corner of Unit 4 Foundry Industrial Estate, Victoria Street, and approximately 347 metres east of the most south-easterly corner of 17 Batherton Close, then proceeding in a generally northerly direction for approximately 21 metres to a point approximately 210 metres east of the most south-easterly corner of Unit 5 Foundry Industrial Estate, Victoria Street, and approximately 202 metres east-south-east of the most north-easterly corner of Unit 4 Foundry Industrial Estate, Victoria Street, then proceeding in a generally east-north-east direction for approximately 64 metres to a point approximately 282 metres east-south-east of the most easterly corner of Unit 2 Foundry Industrial Estate, Victoria Street, Widnes and approximately 259 metres east of the most southerly corner of Unit 4 Foundry Industrial Estate, Victoria Street, then proceeding in a generally east-north-east direction for approximately 350 metres to a point approximately 3 metres west-north-west of the most north westerly corner of the boundary fence of the scrap metal yard on the south side of Cornubia Road, Widnes, and approximately 47 metres west-south-west of the stub end of Cornubia Road be diverted to a 3 metre wide path from a point approximately 183 metres east-south-east of the most easterly corner of Unit 5 Foundry Industrial Estate, Victoria Street and approximately 272 metres east of the most north-easterly corner of 26 Ann Street West, Widnes, then proceeding in a generally north easterly direction for approximately 58 metres to a point approximately 216 metres east-south-east of the most easterly corner of Unit 4 Foundry Industrial Estate, Victoria Street and approximately 221 metres east of the most southerly corner of Unit 5 Foundry Industrial Estate, Victoria Street, then proceeding in a generally easterly direction for approximately 45 metres to a point approximately 265 metres east-south-east of the most north-easterly corner of Unit 3 Foundry Industrial Estate, Victoria Street and approximately 265 metres east of the most southerly corner of Unit 5 Foundry Industrial Estate, Victoria Street, then proceeding in a generally east-south-east direction for approximately 102 metres to a point approximately 366 metres east-south-east of the most easterly corner of Unit 3 Foundry Industrial Estate, Victoria Street and approximately 463 metres east of the most north easterly corner of 22 Ann Street West, Widnes, then proceeding in a generally north-north-easterly direction for approximately 19 metres to a point approximately 368 metres east-south-east of the most easterly corner of Unit 3 Foundry Industrial Estate, Victoria Street and approximately 512 metres east of the most south easterly corner of 17 Batherton Close, Widnes then proceeding in a generally east-south, easterly direction for approximately 16 metres to a point approximately 420 metres east-south-east of the most southerly corner of Unit 2 Foundry Industrial Estate, Victoria Street and approximately 533 metres east of the most south-easterly corner of 17 Batherton Close, then proceeding in a generally east-north-easterly direction for approximately 240 metres to a point approximately 606 metres east of the most northerly corner of Unit 4 Foundry Industrial Estate, Victoria Street and approximately 23 metres south of the most south westerly corner of the boundary fencing of the scrap metal yard on the south side of Cornubia Road, Widnes, then proceeding in a generally northern direction for approximately 44 metres to a point approximately 3 metres west-north-west of the most north westerly corner of the boundary fence of the scrap metal yard on the south side of Cornubia Road and approximately 47 metres west-south-west of the stub end of Cornubia Road.

FIGURE L.1 A very long English sentence.

So, continuing with the example: If English were regular, then we could apply the following substitution to English sentences and the resulting language would also be regular:

- Replace every instance of `if`, `either` and `the man who said` by (.
- Replace every instance of `then`, `or` and `is arriving today` by).

To help make this example clearer, let's also substitute `c` for each instance of a sentence that contains no embedded sentences. With these substitutions, the sentence we just wrote would be rewritten as:

$$((((c)\ c\ ))((c)\ c\ ))\ c.$$

If English were regular, the substituted language that we just defined would also be regular since the regular languages are closed under letter substitution. But we can show that the substituted language is not regular by a Pumping Theorem proof that is almost identical to the one we used in Example 8.10 to show that the language of balanced parentheses is not regular. So English is not regular either.

Even if we could impose some upper limit on the length of English words and sentences, and thus be able to argue that English is regular because it is finite, describing English as a regular language isn't very useful. For many applications, we would like to be able to parse English sentences into syntactic structures that correspond to the sentences' meanings. For example, consider the small fragment of an English grammar that we gave in Example 11.6:

$S \rightarrow NP\ VP$

$NP \rightarrow \texttt{the}\ Nominal \mid \texttt{a}\ Nominal \mid Nominal \mid ProperNoun \mid NP\ PP$

$Nominal \rightarrow N \mid Adjs\ N$

$N \rightarrow \texttt{cat} \mid \texttt{dogs} \mid \texttt{bear} \mid \texttt{girl} \mid \texttt{chocolate} \mid \texttt{rifle}$

$ProperNoun \rightarrow \texttt{Chris} \mid \texttt{Fluffy}$

$Adjs \rightarrow Adj\ Adjs \mid Adj$

$Adj \rightarrow \texttt{young} \mid \texttt{older} \mid \texttt{smart}$

$VP \rightarrow V \mid V\ NP \mid VP\ PP$

$V \rightarrow \texttt{like} \mid \texttt{likes} \mid \texttt{thinks} \mid \texttt{shot} \mid \texttt{smells}$

$PP \rightarrow Prep\ NP$

$Prep \rightarrow \texttt{with}$

Given the sentence, "`The smart older cat smells chocolate`", this grammar could be used by a parser to produce the parse tree shown in Figure L.2. That tree corresponds to a natural way of assigning meaning to the sentence. There is one object, the cat, about whom we know something, namely that she smells chocolate.

It is possible to build a regular grammar to describe this tiny subset of English. But every rule in that grammar must be of one of the following forms: $A \rightarrow \mathrm{a}B$, $A \rightarrow \mathrm{a}$, or $A \rightarrow \varepsilon$. So any parse tree generated by such a grammar must be shaped like the one shown in Figure L.3. The structures that correspond to semantically meaningful units, like the smart older cat, have disappeared.

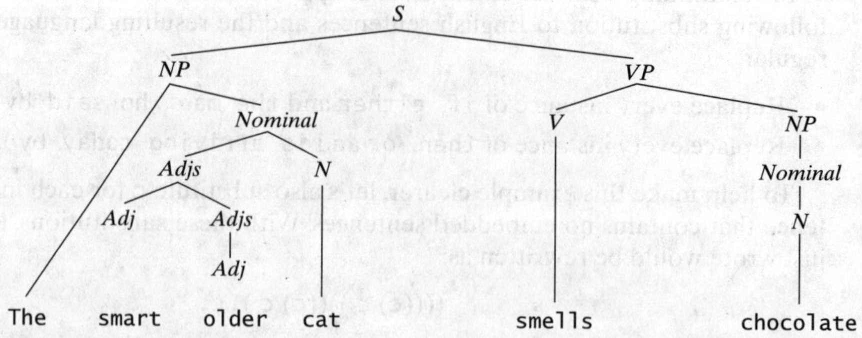

FIGURE L.2 The structure of a parse tree corresponds to the meaning of a sentence.

Because, as in the example that we just considered, there may be a difference between being able to construct a grammar that generates the strings in a language and being able to construct a grammar that creates useful parse trees for its strings, we will divide the question, "Does there exist a grammar for language L?" into two parts. Does there exist a grammar with:

- the necessary ***weak generative capacity***, which we define to be the ability to generate all and only the strings in L, and
- the necessary ***strong generative capacity***, which we define to be the ability not only to generate all and only the strings in L but also to generate, for each of them, at least one meaningful parse tree.

Summarizing our discussion so far:

- If English is finite, then:
  - Regular grammars have the weak generative capacity to describe it.
  - Regular grammars to not have the strong generative capacity to describe it.

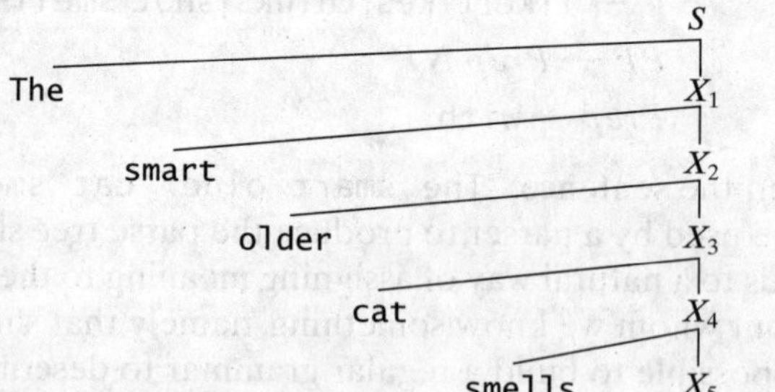

FIGURE L.3 A parse tree that loses semantically meaningful structure.

- If English is not finite, then:
  - Regular grammars have neither the weak nor the strong generative capacity to describe it.

While regular grammars do not do a good job of capturing the complete structure of English sentences, it turns out that finite state machines (FSMs) can be used effectively in applications where a complete analysis of each sentence is not required. Suppose, for example, that we want to scan large text databases and look for sentences that contain patterns that involve objects (as described by noun phrases) that are related by particular verbs of interest. We might, for example, be looking for articles that talk about corporate takeovers or articles that talk about elections in South America. In these kinds of problem domains, systems based on the idea of cascaded FSMs 💻, in which one FSM runs, creates output, and then passes that output onto the next FSM, have been shown to be useful.

At this point, we can summarize the bottom line: While finite state machines are useful for some aspects of English processing, for example morphological analyzers such as the ones we described in section L.1, as well as applications where an incomplete analysis is adequate for the task, they are not enough to solve the entire problem.

L.3.2 Can English Be Described with a Markov Model?

Although finite state machines are not powerful enough to describe all of the rules that distinguish grammatical English sentences from ungrammatical ones, Markov models (FSMs augmented with probabilistic information) can do a very good job of generating English text that appears almost natural 💻. This idea was suggested in [Shannon 1948]. We can build letter-level models, which consider the previous k letters as a basis for generating the next one. Or we can build word-level models, which predict each word based on the previous k words. A model that uses k prior outputs (letters or words) is called a kth order model. A first-order model is sometimes called a ***bigram*** model (since it is based on the probabilities associated with pairs of outputs). A second-order model is ***trigram*** model, and so forth.

In one of his *Programming Pearls* columns [Bentley 2000], Jon Bentley describes his experiment (down to the level of providing code) in building Markov models of English 💻. Let's first consider predicting letters. Using probabilities acquired from 990 Kb of the text of this book, Bentley's Markov model produced the following example strings:

- (k = 1): a a idjume Thicha lanbede f nghecom isonys rar t r ores aty Ela ancuny, ithi, witheis weche
- (k = 2): Ther to for an th she con simach a so a impty dough par we forate for len postrit cal nowillopecide allexis inteme numbectionsityFSM Cons onste on codere elexpre ther
- (k = 3): Ouput that the collowing with to that we'll in which of that is returesult is alway ther is id, the cal on the Prove be and N.

- (k = 4): Notice out at least to steps if new Turing derived for explored. What this to check solved each equal string it matrix (i, k, y must be put part can may generated grammar in D.
- (k = 5): So states, and Marting rules of strings. We may have been regions to see, a list. If ? ? unrestricted grammars exist a devices are constructive-state i back to computation
- (k = 6): We'll have letter substituted languages that L(G) since we drop the address to the rule1 were counterexample, that is that we are true when we switched in how we
- (k = 7): If it does a context-free language 3. If the model of which corresponding b's. M must have chosen strings as a tree such characters of some p.

While this may seem like a silly exercise, note that, by $k = 3$, very word-like strings appear. This observation served as the basis for Typo [Morris and Cherry 1975], an effective early spell checking system. Typo had to fit into a very small amount of memory, so it was impossible to store a dictionary. Instead, it computed trigram frequencies and used them to find letter sequences that were very unlikely to occur in correctly spelled English words.

Now let's consider building word-level Markov models. Again using probabilities acquired from 990 Kb of the text of this book, Bentley's Markov model produced the following example strings:

- (k = 1): there exists at the idea was presented for some finite state 3 together. So U begins in this approach, it is labeled with wj as some model to position-list, solve-15 can reduce every derivation becomes M1 and the number of A building efficient algorithms.
- (k = 2): The language to be if the various grammar formalisms in which they were deposited make no moves are possible. The competition can come from somewhere. Fortunately, there are edges from level nodes to level nodes. Now suppose that we do with a successful value.
- (k = 3): Compare A and w. If equal, accept (i.e., go to n). Nondeterministic Semi-deciding Next we must decide what it means for a nondeterministic Turing machine M that decides it. From M, we can build a Turing machine because, with grammars, we do not have to worry about a dead state.
- (k = 4): Again, let st be the working string at any point in its computation it will have executed only a finite number of squares can be nonblank. And, even if M never halts, at any point in its computation it will have executed only a finite number of choices at each derivation step and since each path that is generated must eventually end, the Turing machine M that computes it.
- (k = 5): Is there any computational solution to the problem? • If there is, can it be implemented using some fixed amount of memory? • If there is no such element, then choose will: • Halt and return False if all the actions halt and return False. • Fail to halt if there is no mechanism for determining that no elements of S

that satisfy P exist. This may happen either because v and y are both nonempty and they both occur in region n.

- ($k = 6$): Consider a programming language that requires that variables be declared before they are used. If we consider just a single variable w, then a program that declares w and then uses it has a structure very similar to the strings in the language L are formed. The set of all possible strings over an alphabet Σ is written Σ^*. This notation exploits the Kleene star operator, which we will define more generally below.

Notice that, by $k = 4$, most of what is generated is literal text from the training corpus. At this point most of the *n*-gram probabilities are 0. With a larger, more heterogeneous training corpus, this phenomenon would be less marked.

[Copeland and Haemer 2001] describes one concrete use for randomly generated text: testing text-processing software. Random text will push the software into obscure corners that the designers may not have considered but that may show up eventually in real text.

Another clever use of randomly generated text exploits the fact that Markov models can generate text that seems "natural" except to people. Consider the problem of generating spam that will make it through a spam filter. We'll call the spam message that we want to send *S*. We can't simply send *S* as text. If we do that, filters can be trained to recognize and filter it. But, at least with current technology, spam filters can't read images. So we can hide *S* in an image. But spam filters can be tuned to reject messages that contain nothing but images. They can also be tuned to recognize and reject text that is completely random. But, using a Markov model of English, it is possible to produce, for each copy of *S* that we want to send, a new paragraph of text that can pass any statistical test of Englishness. This technique can produce a message like, "There was something gipsy-like and agreeable in the dinner, after confident in the character and behaviour of the girl who never was then, of not having been to sleep at all, and by the uncommon Well, I dont know, replied Steerforth, coolly. You may as well This was formerly the castle of the redoubted giant Despair, That affair of the first bond for four thousand five hundred grammar; so that, for a brother and sister, we made a most uneven pair."

L.3.3 Is English Context-Free?

If regular grammars are not powerful enough for English and probabilistic FSMs only approximate English, what about context-free grammars? Suppose that we want to build a computational grammar of English that could be used as part of any of a wide class of applications including spoken English interfaces, machine translation systems, and text-based information retrieval engines. Is it possible to build a context-free grammar for English that possesses the following three properties:

1. weak generative capacity: In other words, is English formally context-free?
2. strong generative capacity: In other words, does there exist a context-free grammar that generates parse trees that can reasonably be used to derive meanings from English sentences?

3. good engineering: In other words, is the grammar modular? Does it capture appropriate generalizations so that important structural concepts, such as Noun Phrase, can be described only once? Is it easy to build and maintain?

We'd like the answers to these questions to be yes. As we've seen, there exist straightforward and relatively efficient parsers for context-free grammars. Since such parsers do not exist for unrestricted grammars, the question of whether English is effectively context-free is important.

In a nutshell, the answers to questions 1 through 3 above appear to be yes, mostly, and no, respectively. As a result, most computational grammars of English start with a context-free core and then add exactly enough additional mechanism to handle the phenomena that cannot easily be captured in a pure context-free system.

Is English Formally Context-Free?

We begin by attempting to answer the first question, "Is English formally context-free?" Much of English clearly can be described by a (very greatly enhanced) version of the simple context-free grammar that we gave in Example 11.6. We require enhancements to deal with a variety of constructs that are missing from our simple grammar. For example, English allows several kinds of embedded structures, including the ones (if/then, either/or, and the man who said *S*) that we used in our argument that English wasn't regular. Those structures are easily described by a context-free grammar. The three rules we gave for those structures when we introduced them are context-free. Although the last of them is clearly a special case rule that we wouldn't want in a real grammar, we'll keep it here for convenience. So we could generate, for our sentence about the man and the rain, the parse tree shown in Figure L.4. In drawing it, we use the convention that a triangle describes a subtree with whose internal structure we are not currently concerned.

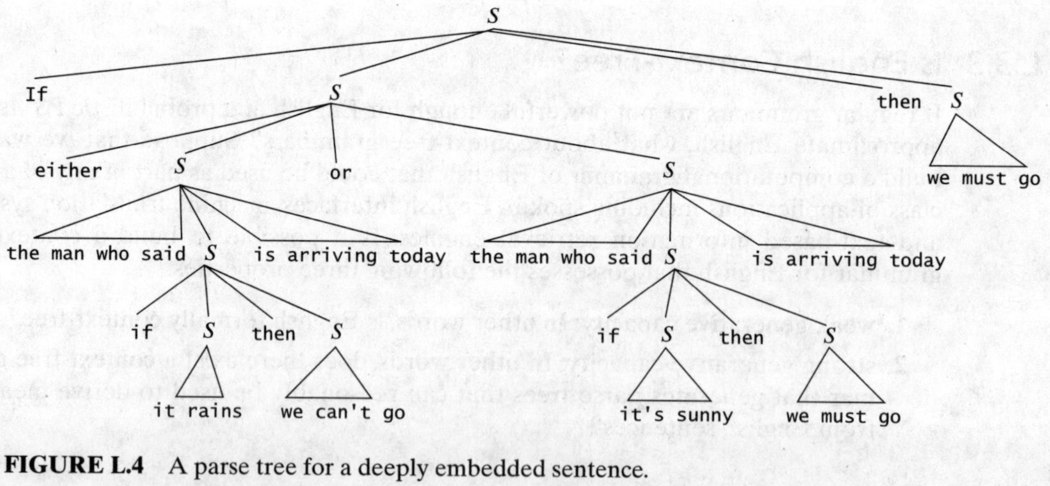

FIGURE L.4 A parse tree for a deeply embedded sentence.

But English also appears to allow structures that are not properly nested. It is those structures that have formed the basis for some arguments that English is not formally context-free. For example, consider the `respectively` construct:

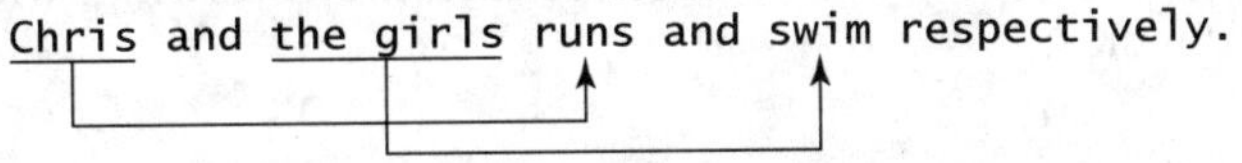

The relationships between the nouns and the verbs in this sentence are shown with arrows. Instead of being nested, the lines cross. Patterns such as this are called ***cross-serial dependencies***, and they cannot naturally be described with context-free rules. Recall that we observed cross serial dependencies in two noncontext-free languages that we considered in Chapter 13: WcW and WW.

Suppose that there is no bound on the number of nouns and verbs that can occur in a `respectively` construction in English, and further suppose that there is some relationship that must hold between each noun and its corresponding verb. In particular, in English, present tense verbs must agree with their subjects in number. So the first of the following sentences would be grammatical. The second wouldn't (which we indicate by preceding it with *):

```
Chris and the girls runs and swim respectively.
* Chris and the girls runs and swims respectively.
```

With these assumptions, it appears that English is not context-free. We can prove that claim as follows: If English is context-free, then any subset that is formed by intersecting English with a regular language must also be context free (by Theorem 13.7). Let:

L = {English sentences} ∩

{`Chris` (`and` (`Chris` ∪ `the girls`))* `runs` (`and` (`run` ∪ `runs`))* `respectively`}.

For any sentence w in L, let s be the string of noun phrases and conjunctions at the beginning of w and let s_{verb} be s with each noun phrase replaced by its matching verb. Then the entire sentence is of the form:

ss_{verb} `respectively.`

L is the set of all strings of that form. We can show that L is not context-free by using the context-free Pumping Theorem in a proof analogous to the one we used in Example 13.6 to show that WW = $\{ww : w \in \{\mathtt{a}, \mathtt{b}\}^*\}$ is not context-free.

The problem with this argument, and many like it, has been pointed out in [Pullam and Gazdar 1982] and [Pullum 1984]. Although the mathematics are correct, the empirical observations about English are not. In principle, each noun in one of our `respectively` sentences should agree with its corresponding verb. But, when native speakers are asked which of the following sentences is more grammatical, they choose the second rather than the first:

```
Jan and Pat runs and swims, respectively.
Jan and Pat run and swim, respectively.
```

So far, no convincing arguments that English is not context-free have been discovered. However, there are arguments that some other languages are not. One of those arguments was presented in [Shieber 1985] and in [Huybregts 1984]. It concerns Swiss German, which includes sentences like the following, which do contain cross serial dependencies:

```
Jan   säit   das  mer   em Hans    es huus       hälfed aastriiche.
```

Jan says that we Hans/DAT the house/ACC helped paint.

In English, we'd indicate the direct and indirect objects with word order. So, in this case, we'd say, "Jan says that we helped Hans paint the house." In Swiss German, on the other hand, word order is more flexible; instead the nouns themselves are marked for their syntactic function in the sentence. The subject of a sentence will end with a nominative marker; the direct object will end with an accusative (ACC) marker; and an indirect object will end with a dative (DAT) marker. The verb "help" requires a dative object and the verb "paint" requires an accusative one. So there is only one interpretation of this sentence, the one shown with the arrows, in which Hans got helped and the house got painted.

Of the three questions that we asked a couple of pages ago, we have now answered the first: Context-free grammars appear to have the weak generative capacity to describe English but not all other languages.

Can Context-Free Grammars Generate Good Parse Trees for English?

We now move on to the second question: Do context-free grammars have the strong generative capacity to describe English? As we said above, the answer to this question is, "mostly". We've already seen a few examples of reasonable trees that can be built by the simple context-free rules that we've so far considered.

But there are structures that are hard to capture with context-free rules. Consider the following sentence:

```
What did Will say he ate for lunch?
```

The problem in building a parse tree for this sentence is that it contains a gap. The object of the verb `ate` is the word `what`, which comes all the way at the other end of the sentence. So the structure that we would like to build corresponds to:

```
What did Will say he ate ______ for lunch?
```

Describing structures such as this with a natural context-free grammar is difficult.

A second issue, which we considered briefly in Example 11.22, is that many English sentences are syntactically ambiguous. So any reasonable context-free grammar of English may be able to generate not just the correct parse tree (i.e., the one that corresponds to the intended meaning of the sentence) but also one or more additional parse trees, each of which corresponds to some other, unintended meaning. We'll return to this issue in the next section.

Is Using A Pure Context-Free Grammar Good Engineering?

Let's now consider our third question: Can we build a context-free grammar for English that is also a sound engineering artifact? For example, how good is the small grammar that we have been considering? We begin by observing that our grammar generates, among other things, the following sentences:

```
Chris likes the cat.
* The dogs likes the cat.
```

The first of these is English. The second is not because its subject fails to agree with its verb in number. So we have found an error in our grammar: It overgenerates because it fails to account for the constraint that, in English present tense sentences, the subject and the verb must agree. The problem arises from the first rule in the grammar:

$S \rightarrow NP\ VP$

Once an *S* has been divided into the two constituents *NP* and *VP*, the subsequent derivations of the two subtrees proceed independently.

We could fix this problem by replacing our single *S* rule by a pair of rules:

$S \rightarrow SNP\ SVP$ /* *S* is a single *NP* followed by a single *VP*.

$S \rightarrow PNP\ PVP$ /* *S* is a plural *NP* followed by a plural *VP*.

But then we'd also have to create two copies of the rules for forming *NP*s and two copies of the rules for forming *VP*s, one for singular phrases and one for plural phrases. This is theoretically possible, of course, but it is very bad engineering.

The problem is made worse by the fact that there are other similar phenomena. Consider the following sentences:

```
The girl likes herself.
* The girl likes himself.
```

We could solve this problem by again splitting the grammar so that we have the top-level rules:

$S \rightarrow MNP\ MVP$ /* *S* is a masculine *NP* followed by a *VP* whose object, if reflexive, is masculine.

$S \rightarrow FNP\ FVP$ /* *S* is a feminine *NP* followed by a *VP* whose object, if reflexive, is feminine.

But now we have four kinds of *NP*s and four kinds of *VP*s. This is even worse engineering.

Unfortunately, these aren't the only phenomena of this sort. Consider the following pairs of sentences:

```
This cat likes chocolate.
* These cat likes chocolate.
```

`The cat likes chocolate.`
`* The cat sleeps chocolate.`

The problem in the first pair of sentences is that, while most English modifiers are not marked for number, a few, including the demonstratives `this` and `these` are. We can solve this problem similarly to the way we solved the problem of subject/verb agreement. The problem in the second pair of sentences is that verbs have properties that determine the arguments that can be provided to them. Transitive verbs, including `likes`, may take a direct object (such as `chocolate`). But intransitive verbs, including `sleeps`, may not have a direct object. Again, we can solve this problem by creating new classes of verbs and replicating all the parts of the grammar that describe what verbs can do. But the size of the grammar that we'll build, if we take this approach, grows exponentially in the number of distinctions that we make as we try to solve these problems.

What Parsing Techniques Work?

So what should we try next? One idea is to move outward in the language hierarchy. Suppose that, instead of trying to describe English with a context-free grammar, we used a context-sensitive one. All of the problems that we just examined could be solved in a reasonable way if we did that. But then we'd have a new problem. Recall from Chapters 24 and 29 that the best known algorithm for examining a string and deciding whether or not it could be generated by an arbitrary context-sensitive grammar takes time that is exponential in the length of the input string. That's a heavy price to pay to be able to handle the relatively small number of features that cannot easily be described with a context-free grammar. As a result, the way practical English parsers work is to:

- Give up trying to handle constraints like agreement within the set of context-free rules.
- But don't jump all the way to context-sensitive ones. Instead, start with a set of context-free rules and augment them with features that must match in order for constituents to be combined.

In particular, a common approach is to exploit a feature grammar (often called a unification grammar) of the sort described in Section 24.3. So, for example, we might handle the subject/verb agreement problem by rewriting our first grammar rule as shown in Example 24.3:

[CATEGORY S] →	[CATEGORY NP	[CATEGORY VP
	NUMBER x_1	NUMBER x_1
	PERSON x_2]	PERSON x_2]

Now each constituent (a complete sentence, a noun phrase, or a verb phrase) is augmented with two features, `person` and `number`. The values for the `person` and `number` features of the NP and the VP must match since they are specified with the same variable. They are then shared with the S.

If the number of feature/value pairs is finite, then it is possible to compile a grammar, written in this way, into a standard context-free grammar that uses a distinct nonterminal or terminal symbol for each feature collection. But, in the case of a realistic English grammar, the compiled grammar would be very large. In Chapter 15, we saw that there exist algorithms (for example *CKY* and *Earleyparse*) that can parse a string of length n, given an arbitrary context-free grammar G, in time that is $\mathcal{O}(n^3)$ if we take the size of G to be a constant. If, on the other hand, we consider the size of G, then the time required to run either algorithm grows as $\mathcal{O}(n^3 \cdot |G|^2)$. It has generally been found to be substantially more efficient to use a feature-based grammar directly, rather than to attempt to compile it into a context-free (and very much larger) one.

L.3.4 Ambiguity

If we want to build programs that can analyze English sentences, it is not sufficient to construct grammars with the weak generative capacity to generate all and only the syntactically legal English sentences. Any useful grammar must also assign, to each sentence, a parse tree whose structure corresponds to the semantically significant constituents of the sentence.

The fragment of an English grammar that we have been using allows prepositional phrases to be attached both to noun phrases and to verb phrases. Because a prepositional phrase can be attached to a noun phrase, it is possible to produce a semantically meaningful parse tree for the sentence, `Chris likes the girl with the cat`. The tree shown in Figure L.5 makes it clear that there is a girl with a cat and Chris likes her.

Unfortunately, because a prepositional phrase can be attached to a verb phrase, it is also possible to produce the parse tree shown in Figure L.6. It corresponds to a nonsensical interpretation in which Chris uses a cat to like the girl.

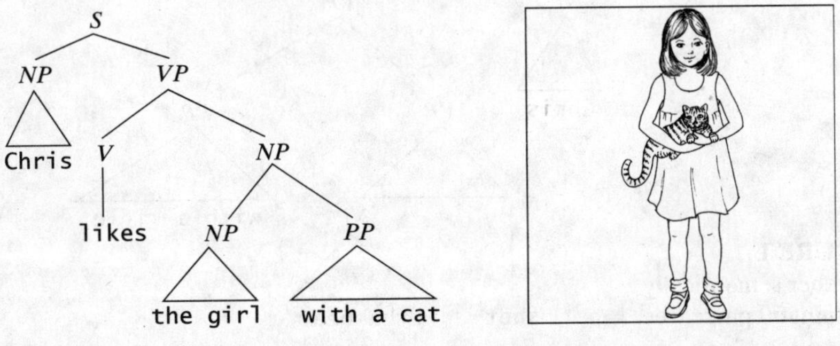

FIGURE L.5 A semantically meaningful parse tree.

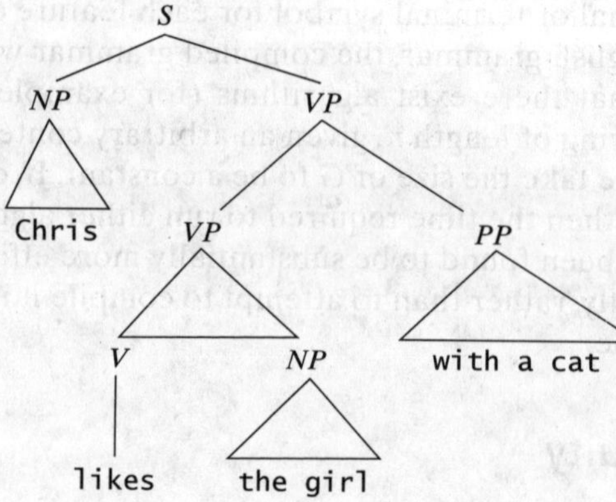

FIGURE L.6 A nonsensical parse tree.

But the ability to attach prepositional phrases to verb phrases is what makes it possible to construct a semantically coherent parse tree for the sentence, `Chris shot the bear with a rifle`. That tree, shown in Figure L.7, makes clear that the rifle is the instrument that was used in the shooting. Again though, it is also possible to attach the prepositional phrase to the nearest noun phrase. So our grammar can produce the (in most contexts) nonsensical parse tree shown in Figure L.8.

The problem we must face is that any English grammar that is powerful enough to produce the parse trees that we want is likely to contain attachment ambiguities similar to the dangling else problem that occurs in many programming languages. Because of those ambiguities, it is typically possible to produce parse trees that do not correspond to the intended meaning of some sentences. For programming languages, the solution to ambiguity problems is to design them away. So, for example, in Section G.3, we discussed two techniques for designing away the dangling else problem.

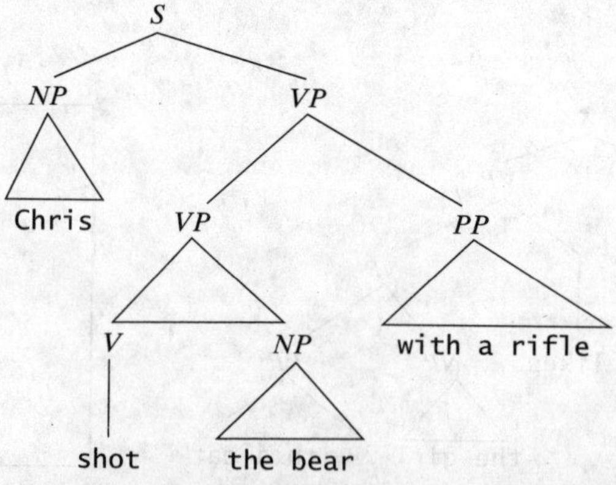

FIGURE L.7 Another semantically meaningful parse tree.

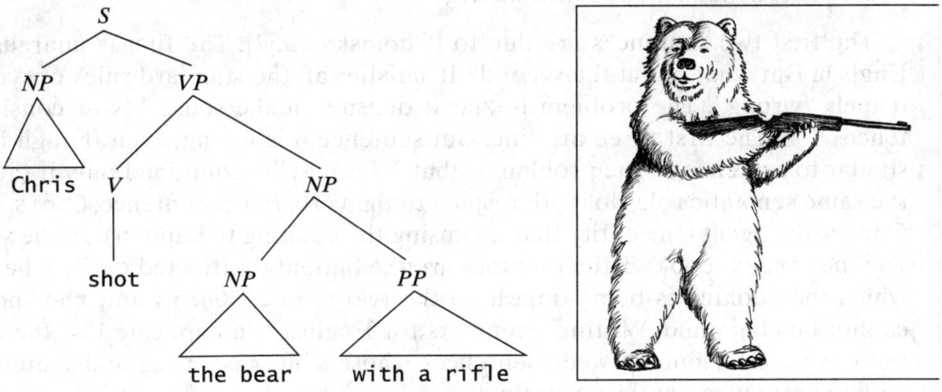

FIGURE L.8 Another nonsensical parse tree.

For English, however, we don't get to make the rules. The language is a naturally occurring phenomenon and all we can do is describe it. This means that we must generally accept a grammar that can generate multiple parse trees for many sentences. Then we require some additional mechanism for choosing the correct one. This almost always requires appeal to some model of the domain of discourse. The model may be a statistical one that has been built by examining a large corpus of English sentences (possibly accompanied by hand-built parse trees). In Section 11.10, we introduced stochastic context-free grammars, which are one way in which such probabilistic information can be encoded and exploited during parsing. An alternative is to exploit an explicit model of facts about the world. So, for example, we could encode the fact that rifles are used for shooting. In I.3.3, we discussed one way to do this: Build an ontology that describes objects and their properties. An alternative is to build a rule-based system of the sort we describe in M.3.

L.3.5 Other Reasons English Syntax is Hard

We conclude this brief discussion of English grammar with three final issues, which are illustrated by the following sentences:

1. * `Furiously sleep ideas green colorless.`
2. `Colorless green ideas sleep furiously.`
3. `Chris cooked.`
4. `The potatoes cooked.`
5. `Chris and the girls cooked.`

6. * `Chris and the potatoes cooked.`
7. ? `The window needs cleaned.`

The first two sentences are due to [Chomsky 1957]. The first is unarguably not English. But what about the second? It satisfies all the standard rules of syntax. Yet it feels "wrong". The problem is that it doesn't "make sense." Now consider sentences 3–6. The first three are fine. But sentence 6 is wrong, even though it is very similar to sentence 5. The problem is that *NP*'s may be conjoined only if they all fill the same semantic role slot with respect to the verb. In the sentence, `Chris cooked`, Chris is the agent (the entity that is causing the cooking to happen). In the sentence, `The potatoes cooked`, the potatoes are the patient or affected entity (the thing to which the cooking is being done). So the two phrases, `Chris` and `the potatoes` cannot be conjoined. Writing grammars for English is complicated by the fact that there is no clear line between sentences whose syntax is wrong and sentences that violate various semantic constraints.

Last, consider sentence 7. In western Pennsylvania, this sentence is regarded as perfectly fine English. In most of the rest of the world, it isn't. All natural languages that have more than a few speakers have more than one dialect. It is hard to write a formal grammar for a language whose elements we cannot agree on.

L.3.6 Stochastic Grammars

Stochastic context-free grammars play an important role in computational linguistics because it is not possible to build practical, unambiguous grammars for natural languages such as English. Lacking the ability to find a single parse, the next best thing is to find the most likely one 💻.

L.4 Building a Complete NL System

A complete system that analyzes natural language text typically performs all of the following tasks:

- morphological analysis and part of speech tagging,
- syntactic parsing of each sentence,
- semantic interpretation of individual sentences, and
- interpretation of sentences in the larger context of the rest of the text.

These processes may be done in stages, or they may be integrated in a variety of ways. We discussed the first step, morphological analysis and part of speech tagging earlier in this chapter. We summarized some of the issues involved in natural language parsing in Section 15.4. In particular, we introduced the notion of bottom-up chart parsing, which forms the basis for many NL parsers. The last two tasks are beyond the scope of the techniques that we have described in this book. In particular, semantic interpretation must be done in a way that supports the particular application of which the NL system is part. Generally it must rely on some model of the task domain and it may require the ability to reason about objects in that model. In I.3.3 and M.2, we comment briefly on the implications of our undecidability results for our ability to build arbitrary reasoning engines.

L.5 Speech Understanding Systems

So far, we have discussed natural language processing as though language were exclusively a written phenomenon. But now imagine talking to your computer rather than typing. Consider the levels of analysis required to make that idea a reality. A speech understanding program must solve all of the problems that we have already mentioned:

- morphological analysis and part of speech tagging,
- syntactic parsing of each sentence,
- semantic interpretation of individual sentences, and
- interpretation of sentences in the larger context of the rest of the text.

And it must solve new ones, including:

- word recognition from a sound wave, and
- recovery from the kinds of errors that people often make when they talk. For example, consider the following utterance, which might not be unusual in an airline reservation system:

```
I need to get there by uh noon no er make that eleven.
```

Hidden Markov models (HMMs) are widely used to build practical speech understanding systems 🖳. For a good introduction, see [Rabiner 1989] or [Jurafsky and Martin 2000]. Two approaches are common:

- Use HMMs for word recognition from sound waves. Then use other techniques as appropriate to build the larger system. In this approach, we train a collection of HMMs, one for each word (or possibly phrase) in the active lexicon. Then, given an observed sound sequence, we use the forward algorithm to solve the evaluation problem. In other words, we find the HMM that has the highest probability of having emitted that sound sequence. We assert that the word or phrase that we heard is the word that corresponds to that highest-scoring HMM. This approach is useful for isolated word recognition.
- Use an integrated HMM model of the entire process by which a concept to be communicated is mapped to a sentence and then a string of sounds. Now, to understand an utterance, we use the Viterbi algorithm to solve the decoding problem, i.e., we find the maximum likelihood path through the network. This approach is useful for

continuous speech processing, where there are no pauses (and thus no clear boundaries) between words.

We'll sketch here the use of HMMs for isolated word recognition, which is an instance of the evaluation problem that we outlined in Section 5.11.2: Given an observation sequence O and a set of HMMs that describe a collection of possible underlying models, choose the HMM that is most likely to have generated O. To solve this problem, we need:

- a set of HMMs, one for each word (or possibly common phrase) that may have been said, and
- an observed sequence of sounds.

When we hear a word, we generally hear a continuous sound wave, such as the one shown in Figure L.9. It was generated when the word cacophony was uttered. The x-axis in the figure represents time (in milliseconds). The y-axis represents the amplitude of the sound wave. A sound wave can be analyzed at several levels:

- The sound wave is digitized by sampling at some rate. The signal corresponding to cacophony was sampled at 22,050 Hz.
- The samples are combined into slightly larger chunks, called frames. A frame may correspond to, say, 10 milliseconds of the signal. Each frame is then described by a set of feature/value pairs. The features capture the properties of the signal that are important for interpreting it. For example, they may describe how much of the energy in the signal occurs in each of several frequency bands.
- A sequence of frames will correspond to a phone. A ***phone*** is an abstraction of a sound. So some of the physical variation that will not affect interpretation is thrown

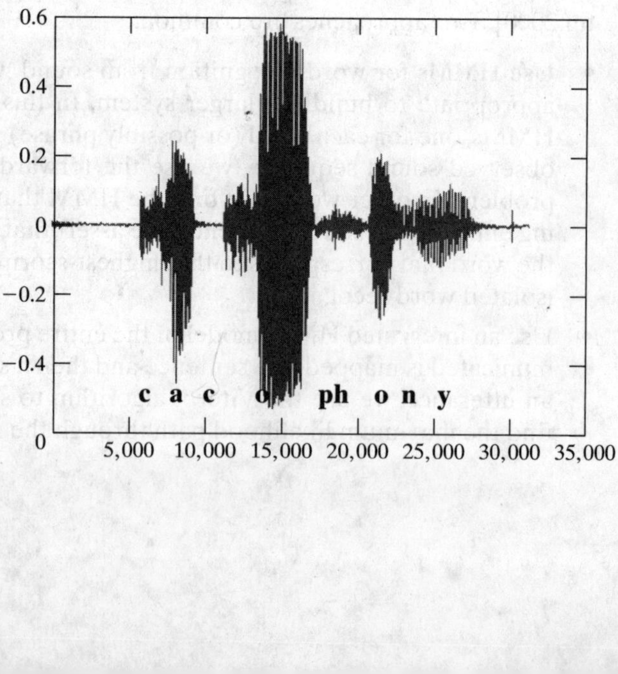

FIGURE L.9 A sound wave corresponding to the word cacophony.

away. Phones can be represented using one of a small number of standard phonetic alphabets. One such alphabet, the IPA alphabet, contains over 100 symbols plus over 50 marks that can be added to those symbols. For example, it includes the symbols [p] as in penguin, as in weather, [θ], as in thin, [i] as in lily, and [I] as in lily, and [$\wedge$], as in cup. An alternative alphabet, the ARPAbet, is widely used in speech processing systems. It has about 50 phones.

- The phones can be mapped to phonemes in a particular language such as English. A ***phoneme*** corresponds to a set of phones that function identically with respect to a particular language. For example, in English, there is no functional difference between an aspirated `p` and an unaspirated `p` (with or without a puff of air at the end). In other words, there are no two words that differ only in one having an aspirated `p` and the other having an unaspirated one. In Thai, on the other hand, that difference is as important as the difference between `b` and `p` in English. So aspirated and unaspirated `p` correspond to the same phoneme in English but not in Thai.
- A sequence of phonemes forms a word.

One reasonable way to build an HMM for the word recognition task is to let the states correspond to phones. Then each word model describes the various phone sequences that could correspond to that word. Associated with each state (phone) is a list of frames that could describe the sound that would be generated by a speaker when uttering that phone. Since there is variability across speakers, there may be more than one such frame. The confusion matrix, B, will contain the probability, for each frame, that it is the one that is uttered.

To get better accuracy, it may be useful to create three states for each phone: beginning, middle, and end. That lets us describe a phone, say [t], as a silence followed by a burst of air. For an even more accurate model, we may want to write out the basic phone sequence for a word and then apply a model that describes coarticulation effects. These affects occur because we can't pronounce one phone and then another without letting our mouth and tongue move continuously from their first position to their second. While they're moving, other sounds may be produced, or the desired sound may be altered, effectively due to laziness. (Say the words `mitt` and `mitten` to yourself, with you hand in front of your mouth. Can you hear that the `t` in `mitt` is aspirated but the `t` in `mitten` is not?) These effects are independent of the particular word that is being spoken, however. So we can build individual word models at the phone level, then apply a richer model of what goes on when each individual phone is spoken, and then apply a coarticulation model to describe how phones are combined into a single speech signal. The end result is an HMM whose states correspond to phones and whose observable outputs correspond to frames that describe physical sounds. The state structures of these HMMs are typically built by hand, but the probabilities of the state transitions, as well as the output probabilities, can be extracted from labeled training data. The initial probabilities for each of the word models can also be extracted from training data so that the final decision about which word was spoken is conditioned on the prior probability that anyone would speak that word. In more sophisticated models, those probabilities can depend on some number of prior words of context.

So, greatly oversimplifying the picture, an HMM for the two words, `hit` and `hot` is shown in Figure L.10. The nodes labeled `Start` and `End` are the same for both words, so they haven't been expanded. The difference between the two words is the vowel in the middle, so we show beginning, middle, and end states for them. The rectangular boxes connected to those states correspond to what is observed when the words are spoken. In a real system, those observations will be described as sets of physical parameters. We've just written numbers that are suggestive of those real values. For example, we see that the middle states of the two vowels are different, as

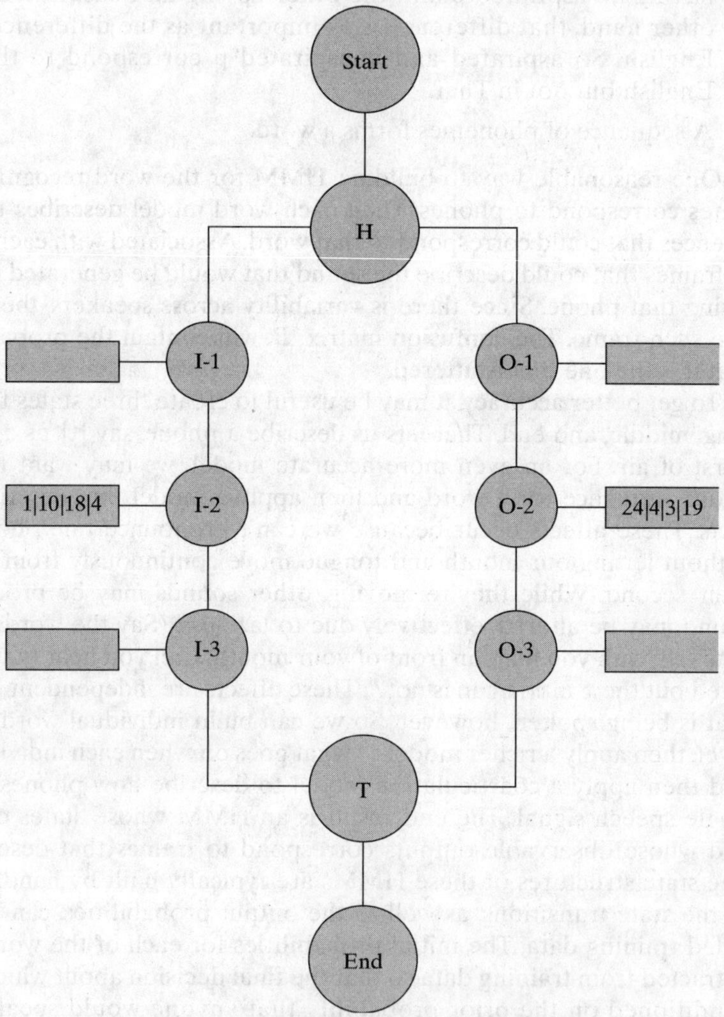

FIGURE L.10 A simplified HMM for two words, `hit` and `hot`.

indicated by the fact that `I-2` has small values for the first and fourth parameters, and large values for the first and second, while `O-2` has the situation reversed. At recognition time, most of the acoustics for the two words will be the same, but when the system reaches `I-2/O-2`, it will be able make a decision based on whether large parameter values occur in the middle of the sound or at the edges. Note that, if similar values for all four parameters are observed, it is likely that the word that was spoken is neither `hit` nor `hot`.

APPENDIX M

Applications: Artificial Intelligence and Computational Reasoning

In 1936, before there were computers, Alan Turing described the formal model of computation that we now call a Turing machine. In 1950, when there were only handfuls of computers on the planet (and the computer at Manchester, the one with which Turing was most familiar, had about 20k of memory), Turing again wrote a visionary paper [Turing 1950], in which he suggested that, within about fifty years, there would exist a computer that could pass what has come to be called the ***Turing test*** 💻. Although Turing's version of the test (which he called the Imitation Game) was a bit different, in its modern form it can be stated as follows: Imagine an interrogator who can type English questions to two agents, A and B, who are in another room. A and B in turn type responses to the interrogator's questions. The interrogator knows that one of the two agents is a person and the other is a computer. His job is to figure out which is which. The job of both A and B is to try to convince the interrogator that they are human. The computer passes the test if it wins and fools the interrogator into thinking it is the person. The specific prediction that Turing made was, "I believe that in about fifty years time it will be possible to programme computers with a storage capacity of about 10^9 to make them play the imitation game so well that an average interrogator will not have more than 70 per cent chance of making the right identification after five minutes of questioning." This time, Turing has turned out not to be quite right. There exist a lot of interactive chatbots 💻 that are capable of playing the game according to Turing's rules. None of them has yet "won" the game. Try conversing with a couple of them and see if they could fool you.

Turing introduced his game as a way of making the question, "Can a machine think?" concrete enough that it could be answered. The game is flawed in many ways as a test of cognition. In his paper, Turing raised several objections and replied to them. Additional objections have been put forward over the years. Some of the most serious objections include:

- A key aspect of human intelligence is our ability to perceive the world. The test doesn't measure sensory perception. So, for example, there is no way for the interrogator to hand one of the agents a picture and ask what it's a picture of.

- A program with a huge store of canned questions and answers might be able to fool the interrogator, but surely it doesn't think. This argument is often called the Chinese room argument [Searle 1980]. Imagine a person who speaks no Chinese but who is locked in a room with filing cabinets full of slips of paper. On each slip of paper is written, in Chinese, a question and an answer. Now suppose that an interrogator slides questions, also written in Chinese, under the door. The job of the person inside the room is to find the slip that matches the question, copy down the answer, as given on the slip, and slide it back out the door. To an outside observer it may appear that the person in the room knows Chinese and can think about answers to questions. But, since we know that (s)he doesn't know any Chinese, we know that all that is happening is symbol lookup, not thinking. Might it be that, even if a program could pass the Turing test, it isn't thinking anymore than the person in the room was?

While these arguments have merit and human intelligence is complex, they don't obscure the fact that Turing's fundamental claim was that computers are sufficiently powerful, in principle, to be able to act "intelligently". And while Turing was overly optimistic in how long it would take before computers rivaled humans in the sort of everyday intelligence that his imitation game measures, he was right that computers can be programmed to perform many of the kinds of tasks that we think of as requiring intelligence when people do them. In fact, almost as soon as there were computers, there were programs that proved simple theorems, played games (such as checkers and chess), and attempted to recognize patterns in faces, symbols, and drawings.

Did those programs exhibit "artificial intelligence"? What counts as "artificial intelligence"? It's impossible to provide a rigorous definition of either "artificial" or "intelligence", much less both of them. We'll begin instead with a more than 20 year old, pragmatic definition from [Rich and Knight 1991]: ***Artificial intelligence*** (AI) is the study of how to make computers do things that, at the moment, people do better. Using that definition, yes, those early programs exhibited AI. To do justice, though, to much of the modern work that is being done on the boundary between AI, databases, and the World Wide Web, it will be useful to expand our definition as follows: Artificial intelligence (AI) is the study of how to make computers do things that people are better at or would be better at if they could extend what they do to a World Wide Web-sized amount of data and not make mistakes.

Over half a century has elapsed since Turing's paper on intelligent machines. Over those years, it has become clear that one reason that people can do so much is that they know a lot. Work on the early problems, as well as new ones, has led to the development of a variety of techniques for acquiring and representing knowledge and for reasoning with it. These techniques have been applied to the creation of programs that read English, navigate highways, examine pictures, play games, and diagnose diseases (to name just a few of the hundreds of problem domains that have been considered). Substantial research is now devoted to the construction of intelligent agents: systems that exploit large knowledge sources and act for their users to solve problems in one or more domains. We discussed, for example, one branch of this work in I.3, where we described the design of the Semantic Web.

Large books, for example [Russell and Norvig 2002], can barely scratch the surface of this area and we can do only a small fraction of that in a few pages here. But the theory that we have developed in this book has a lot to say about how we might go about building an intelligent system. One of the most important aspects of human intelligence is our ability to exploit language. In Appendix L, we considered ways in which the theory of formal languages, as we have developed it here, informs the study of natural language. But, in that discussion, we largely ignored the fact that linguistic utterances are, by and large, about something. In this chapter we will survey a few of the ways that the theory that we have built informs our attempt to build programs that know something and that can use what they know to solve problems. For more examples, see:

- A discussion of the programming language Lisp, whose design was inspired by Church's work on the lambda calculus and whose structure is particularly well-suited to expressing many kinds of AI programs. (G.5)
- A discussion of the use of finite state machines in the design of a controller for an intelligent, soccer-playing robot. (P.4)
- A discussion of the impact of complexity on the design of programs that play games like chess and Go. (N.2.5)
- A discussion of various techniques that are used in the design of intelligently acting agents in computer games. (N.3)
- A discussion of the impact of the undecidability of first-order logic and the intractability of Boolean logic on the design of the Semantic Web. (I.3)

M.1 The Role of Search

Search appears to play a significant role in the design of intelligent programs. For example, theorem-proving programs search a space of possible proofs. Game-playing programs search a space of possible moves. Natural language understanding programs search a space of possible sentence parses and then possible meanings that can be assigned to those parses. Medical diagnosis programs search a space of possible interpretations of the observed symptoms. Alternatively, we can view intelligent behavior as pattern matching in which a large set of patterns have been compiled into a structure that is able to yield answers without obvious search. Much of what goes on in human cognition may be able to be described in this way. But, in this view, we have simply traded search in one space for search in another. Instead of searching in a space of problem solutions, it becomes necessary to train the pattern matchers. And that process requires search in a space of pattern arrangements. For example, neural net-based systems search a space of weights that are attached to the connections between nodes.

While some of the search problems that we would like to solve in AI are undecidable (theorem-proving in first-order logic, for example), the main way in which the theory that is presented in this book impacts AI is the complexity of search algorithms. In Section 30.3, we considered the problem of searching a space that is too large to enumerate explicitly. That discussion applies widely in AI. For example, the ***A**** search algorithm, which we presented there, has been used extensively in AI applications, as have been a variety of extensions and modifications of it. Specialized search algorithms have also been developed to solve particular kinds of problems. For example, ***resolution*** (as described in B.2.2) is important as a way to limit search in theorem-proving programs. Another example is the ***minimax*** algorithm, described in N.2.5, which manages search in game trees.

In the rest of this chapter, we will consider the two main problems that must be solved if we are to build intelligent systems. We must find a way to encode, acquire, and evolve the huge amount of knowledge that appears to be required for all but the most trivial tasks, and we must find a way to manage search in one or more spaces that are defined by that knowledge. Over the years, several approaches to the knowledge representation problem have been developed. We'll focus our discussion on two of them—logical systems and rule-based systems. We've chosen those two because they represent important applications of the theory that we have been discussing. But we should point out that other promising approaches exist. In particular, statistical approaches, including both high-level, symbolic techniques as well as neural net models, are widely used in many applications.

M.2 A Logical Foundation for Artificial Intelligence

One approach to building artificial reasoning systems is to encode the relevant knowledge in a logical language and to use the rules of logical inference to solve problems. In other words, we solve problems by proving theorems. One appeal of this approach, as opposed, say, to encoding knowledge procedurally in the code that uses it, is that knowledge can be stated independently of how it is to be used. That means that the same knowledge base may be able to be used for multiple applications. For an excellent introduction to the logical approach to knowledge representation, see [Brachman and Levesque 2004].

M.2.1 The Fundamental Issues

To use a logical representation as the basis for building an intelligent software solution to a problem, we must satisfy the same requirements that we considered in the design of automatic program verification systems. So we need a logical system that meets all of the following requirements:

1. It is expressive enough to make it possible to encode the knowledge required to solve the problem.
2. Its decidability properties are strong enough to make it useful.
3. Its complexity is acceptable for the size problems we wish to solve.

Practical reasoning programs generally choose a system that starts with first-order logic (FOL), which may then be extended, to add expressive power, or restricted, to add tractability and perhaps decidability.

Extensions to FOL may include one or more higher-order techniques, appropriately chosen to support the task at hand. For example, many general purpose systems support first-order logic plus equality. Other systems are enhanced to support reasoning about time and belief.

Another important extension to FOL allows ***nonmonotonic reasoning***. To define what we mean by that, note first that reasoning in standard first-order logic is monotonic, in the sense that adding an axiom may make some additional statements provable. But no statements that were provable without the new axiom cease to be provable with it. Suppose, though, that our logic allows statements such as, "If x is a bird, assume it can fly unless you know that it is a penguin or that it is a baby or that it has a broken wing or that it fell into an oil slick". Now, with just the fact that Tweety is a bird, we will be able to conclude that Tweety can fly. But if the fact that Tweety is a penguin is added later, that conclusion will no longer be justified. We'll say that a logical system is nonmonotonic iff the addition of one or more axioms may remove some sentence from the set of theorems. Default reasoning of the sort we just saw in the Tweety example is one of the most common uses for nonmonotonic reasoning. It plays an important role in applications that must reason with incomplete information.

Going the other direction, it often makes sense to exploit a logical language that is weaker than FOL. Weaker languages may possess decidability and tractability problems that FOL lacks. In M.2.3, we'll mention one such language, the language of Horn clauses. In Section I.3.4, we mentioned another, description logics.

M.2.2 A Brief History of Theorem-Proving Systems and Their Applications

The title "first artificial intelligence program" probably belongs to a theorem prover. The Logic Theorist (or just LT) [Newell, Shaw and Simon 1957] debuted at the 1956 summer Dartmouth conference that is generally regarded as the birthday of the field called AI 💻. LT did what mathematicians do: It proved theorems. It proved, for example, most of the theorems in Chapter 2 of *Principia Mathematica* [Whitehead and Russell 1910, 1912, 1913]. LT used three rules of inference: substitution (which allows any expression to be substituted, consistently, for any variable), replacement (which allows any logical connective to be replaced by its definition, and vice versa), and detachment (which allows, if A and $A \rightarrow B$ are theorems, to assert the new theorem B). LT began with the five axioms given in *Principia Mathematica*. From there, it began to prove *Principia*'s theorems. For example, in about 12 minutes it produced the following proof, for Theorem 2.45:

$\neg(p \vee q) \rightarrow \neg p$	(Theorem 2.45, to be proved.)
1. $A \rightarrow (A \vee B)$	(Theorem 2.2.)
2. $p \rightarrow (p \vee q)$	(Subst. p for A, q for B in 1.)
3. $(A \rightarrow B) \rightarrow (\neg B \rightarrow \neg A)$	(Theorem 2.16.)
4. $(p \rightarrow (p \vee q)) \rightarrow (\neg(p \vee q) \rightarrow \neg p)$	(Subst. p for A, $(p \vee q)$ for B in 3.)
5. $\neg(p \vee q) \rightarrow \neg p$	(Detach right side of 4, using 2.)
Q. E. D.	

(Note that both upper and lower case symbols correspond to variables.) The inference rules that LT used are not complete and the proofs it produced are trivial by modern standards. For example, given the axioms and the theorems prior to it, LT tried for 23 minutes but failed to prove theorem 2.31:

$$[p \vee (q \vee r)]) \rightarrow [(p \vee q) \vee r].$$

LT's significance lies in the fact that it opened the door to the development of more powerful systems.

The designers of LT did not face difficult representational issues. LT's job was to prove theorems that had already been stated in the language of first-order logic. But the use of theorem provers is not limited to domains that start out looking like mathematics. For example, theorem provers have been used to reason about the semantics of natural language sentences. So attempts have been made to find logical representations of almost everything that we can talk about.

Practically useful theorem provers must work with large sets of facts (axioms) and with a stronger set of inference rules than LT used. So, even if the representation question can be answered and first-order logic can be shown to be expressively powerful enough, two important issues remain:

Undecidability: First-order logic, given a complete inference procedure, and with no restrictions on the axioms that may be presented, is undecidable, as we showed in Theorem 22.4. So, while there are algorithms that find proofs when they exist, any such algorithm cannot be guaranteed to halt and fail when asked to prove a nontheorem.

Intractability: First-order logic is typically computationally intractable. It is at least as hard as Boolean logic and we showed, in Theorem 28.16 (the Cook-Levin Theorem), that Boolean satisfiability is NP-complete. The language of quantified Boolean formulas (QBF) that we defined in Section 29.3.1 also involves a representational system that is weaker than first-order logic. While it allows quantifiers, it does not allow functions, so it can describe only finite domains. Yet we showed that QBF appears not even to be in NP; it is PSPACE-complete. And decidable theories in full first-order logic can be even harder. For example, we pointed out, in Section 28.9.3, that any algorithm that decides Presburger arithmetic has time complexity at least $\mathcal{O}(2^{2^{cn}})$.

The problem is that finding a proof requires searching a space of possible proofs and, in real problem contexts, with realistic axiom sets, that space is huge. Substantial research over the half century since LT appeared has been devoted to techniques for pruning the space of proofs that must be examined. [Davis and Putnam 1960] defined conjunctive normal form (B.2) for first-order logic and showed that it could be used as the basis for a theorem-prover that was substantially more efficient than the others that were available at the time. But the most significant breakthrough occurred with the development of the resolution technique that we described in B.2.2. Resolution-based theorem provers have been used to prove mathematical theorems, to verify the correctness of programs and to reason in domains such as engineering design and medicine. In many important domains, however, resolution, as we have described it, is still not efficient enough because the space of possible proofs is too large.

To deal with these issues, practical, logic-based systems make compromises. In the next section, we describe one approach to making such compromises.

M.2.3 Horn Clauses, Logic Programming and Prolog

Suppose that we are willing to consider only axioms with one of the following two forms:

- Implication rules: Each such rule contains no existentially quantified variables. It contains one instance of the logical connector $\rightarrow$. It also contains zero or more positive literals anded together on its left-hand side and precisely one positive literal on its right hand side. So $\forall x\ ((P(x))$ is an implication rule with a trivial (empty) left-hand side. $\forall x\ ((P_1(x) \wedge P_2(x) \wedge \ldots \wedge P_n(x)) \rightarrow R(x))$ is an implication rule with a nonempty left-hand side.
- Basic facts: $R(A)$, for some specific individual A.

Further suppose that we are willing to limit the form of the statements that we will attempt to prove. All variables must be existentially quantified, all literals must be positive, and the only logical connector that is allowed is $\wedge$. So the following could be a goal to be proved:

- $\exists x, y\ (P_1(x, y) \wedge P_2(x) \wedge \ldots \wedge P_n(y))$.

Given these constraints, it is possible to build a theorem prover that exploits a single reasoning process, ***backward chaining***. Backward chaining works by starting with a goal (a statement to be proved). Note that the goal may be a conjunction of subgoals. The backward chainer chooses one subgoal and looks to see if it matches a basic fact. If it does, that subgoal is proved; it requires no further action and the prover can move on to the next subgoal. Otherwise, the backward chainer looks to see if the subgoal matches the right-hand side of some implication rule. If it does, the matched subgoal will be replaced by the set of literals that make up the left-hand side of that rule. That establishes each of those literals as a new subgoal. This process continues until all subgoals have been proved.

A significant property of the backward chaining process that we will describe is that the proofs that it finds are constructive in the following sense: The proof that some value of x exists will include an explicit statement of such a value.

EXAMPLE M.1 Backward Chaining

Suppose that we are given the following knowledge base, which is composed of some implication rules that describe our company's hiring policy (statements [1]–[5]) and some basic facts of the sort that would be encoded in a recruiter's database (statements [6]–[10]).

[1] $\forall x\ (Famous(x) \rightarrow Great\text{-}hire(x))$

[2] $\forall x\ (Good\text{-}major(x) \wedge Great\text{-}grades(x) \wedge Did\text{-}internship(x) \rightarrow Great\text{-}hire(x))$

[3] $\forall x\ (Major(x, ComputerScience) \rightarrow Good\text{-}major(x))$

[4] $\forall x\,(Major(x, Engineering) \rightarrow Good\text{-}major(x))$

[5] $\forall x\,(\forall y\,(GPA(x, y) \wedge Greater\text{-}than(y, 3.5) \rightarrow Great\text{-}grades(x))$

[6] $Major(John, English)$

[7] $Major(Ellen, ComputerScience)$

[8] $GPA(Ellen, 3.9)$

[9] $Did\text{-}internship(John)$

[10] $Did\text{-}internship(Ellen)$

We want to find someone great to hire. We will attempt to do that by proving $\exists x\,(Great\text{-}hire(x))$ and, in the process, finding such an x. So we set it as a goal. No facts match the goal. So we look for an implication rule whose right-hand side matches it. There are two, so we must pick one. We'll use a simple strategy: Try the rules in the order in which they occur in the knowledge base. So we choose statement [1]. Using it, we rewrite the original goal as a new one. The easiest way to envision this process is as a goal tree (not a very bushy one just yet):

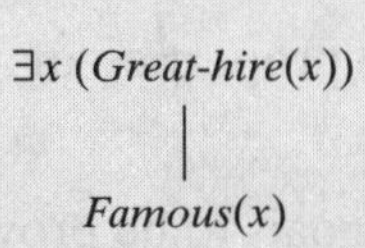

The new goal cannot be satisfied with the knowledge that we have. So we must back up. This time, we apply statement [2] to the original goal, producing:

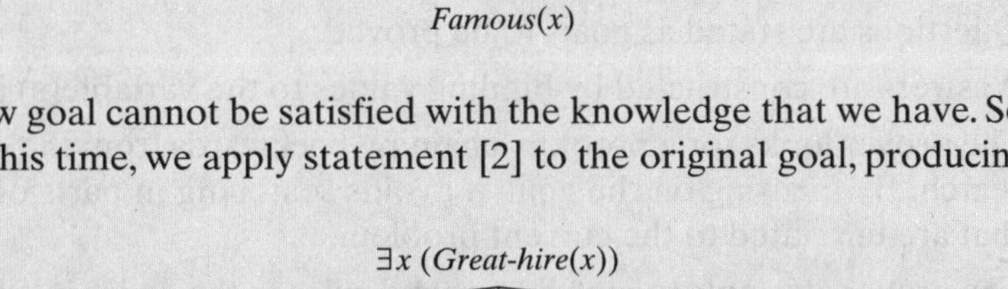

We next tackle the first new subgoal. We choose the first rule ([3]) whose right-hand side matches it, and we get:

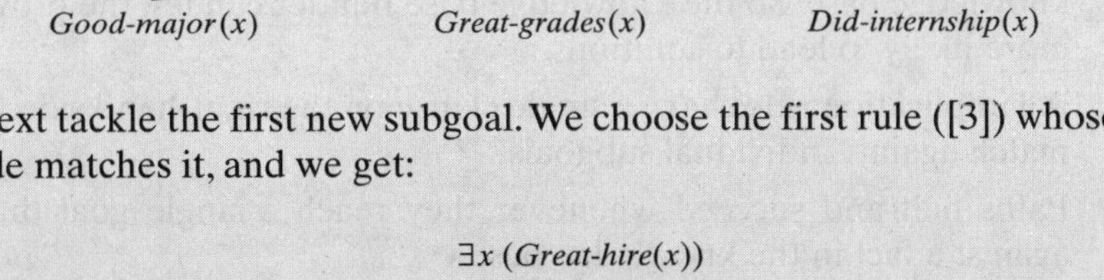

Continuing to explore the current path, we exploit fact [7]. This time we must unify (match) the variable x with the constant *Ellen*. When we do that, we will have to apply the resulting substitution to the rest of the goal tree since we must find a single value

EXAMPLE M.1 (*Continued*)

of x that satisfies all three subgoals. Also, we'll remember this substitution because it will be used to construct the answer to the original question. Doing this, we get:

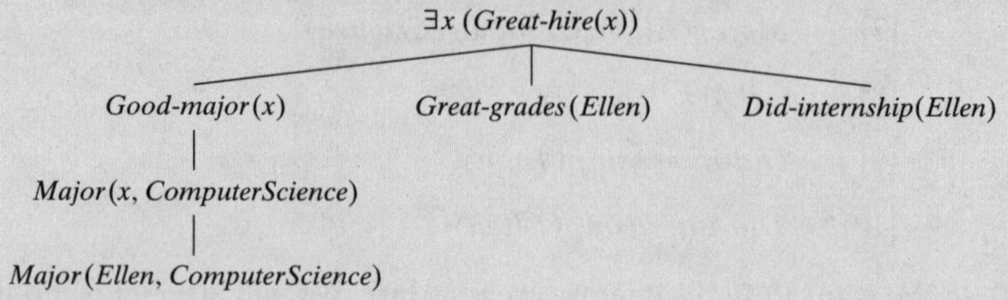

The left-most branch reports that it has succeeded since it matched against a fact in the knowledge base. So we now back up and begin working on the second subgoal. The rest of the process proceeds in a similar way (by immediately matching facts). So all three branches will succeed with the substitution of *Ellen* for x. The answer *Ellen* can be reported.

Note the following key properties of the theorem-proving process that we just sketched:

- Questions are stated as goals to be proved.
- Answers are constructed by binding values to the variable(s) in the question.
- The prover looks for a proof by chaining backwards from the goal, using depth-first search. By focusing on the goal, it avoids searching in parts of the knowledge base that are unrelated to the current problem.
- The prover attempts to match facts and rules in the order in which they occur in the knowledge base. So the knowledge base builder can tell the prover which paths are more likely to lead to solutions.
- All implication rules have a single clause on the right-hand side. So right-hand sides match against individual subgoals.
- Paths halt and succeed whenever they reach a single goal that can be matched against a fact in the knowledge base.
- Paths halt and fail whenever it can be determined that there is no sentence in the knowledge base that can match the current goal.

Horn Clauses and SLD Resolution

Recall, from B.2.1, that a ***clause*** is either a single literal or a disjunction of literals. Now define the following kinds of clauses.

- A ***Horn clause*** is a clause with at most one positive literal.
- A ***positive Horn clause*** is a Horn clause with exactly one positive literal. A positive Horn clause is also called a ***definite clause***.

- A ***negative Horn clause*** is a Horn clause with no positive literals.
- The ***empty clause*** (which we call *nil*) is a Horn clause with no literals.

The efficiency of resolution can be improved when it is restricted to Horn clauses. If we observe the restrictions that we stated at the beginning of this section, then, when our knowledge base and goal are converted to clause form, all of the clauses that will be produced will be Horn clauses. This must be so since:

- An implication rule must be of the form $\forall x, y, \ldots ((P_1(\ldots) \wedge P_2(\ldots) \wedge \ldots \wedge P_n(\ldots)) \rightarrow R(\ldots))$. Such a rule, when converted to clause form, will be a positive Horn clause. It will contain zero or more negative literals (corresponding to the literals on the left-hand side of the original rule) and exactly one positive literal (corresponding to the single literal on the right-hand side of the original rule). So it will look like:

$$\neg P_1(\ldots) \vee \neg P_2(\ldots) \vee \ldots \vee \neg P_n(\ldots) \vee R(\ldots).$$

- A basic fact is a ground instance of the form $R(A)$, for some specific individual A. Such facts are already in clause form and they are positive Horn clauses since they contain no negative literals and exactly one positive one.
- A goal must be of the form $\exists x, y, \ldots (P_1(\ldots) \wedge P_2(\ldots) \wedge \ldots \wedge P_n(\ldots))$. To use resolution to prove a goal, we begin by negating it, producing $\forall x, y, \ldots (\neg(P_1(\ldots) \wedge P_2(\ldots) \wedge \ldots \wedge P_n(\ldots)))$. Converting that to clause form, we get a negative Horn clause (i.e., one with no positive literals):

$$\neg P_1(\ldots) \vee \neg P_2(\ldots) \vee \ldots \vee \neg P_n(\ldots)).$$

We'll say that a set of clauses is in ***Horn clause form***, or that it is a ***Horn clause knowledge base*** iff it is a set of clauses all of which are Horn clauses. Given a Horn clause knowledge base, a resolution theorem prover can start with a negative clause (corresponding to a negated goal) and use backward chaining in exactly the way that we used it in Example M.1. In particular, such a theorem prover can avoid considering those parts of its knowledge base that cannot be relevant to its current goal. To see why this works, observe the following facts about resolution with Horn clauses:

- At each resolution step, at least one parent clause must be positive (so that there exists a pair of complementary literals).
- Resolution of a negative clause with a fact will create a resolvent that is also a negative clause. Further, the number of literals in the new negative clause will be one less than the number in the parent negative clause.
- Resolution of a negative clause with a rule will create a resolvent that is also a negative clause. The one positive literal in the rule will form a complementary pair with one negative literal in the negative clause. So the number of literals in the new negative clause will be the sum of the number of literals in the two parents minus two.
- Resolution of a rule with either another rule or a fact will create a resolvent that is also a rule (which will be represented as a positive clause). The positive literal from

one of the parents must be complementary to a negative literal in the other parent. That leaves the positive literal from the other parent as the only positive literal in the resolvent.

So the property of being a Horn clause knowledge base is preserved by resolution.

It is important to point out that Horn clause form differs from clause form (as defined in B.2.1) in a very important way. Given an arbitrary sentence s in first-order logic, there exists a clause form representation s' of s with the property that s' is unsatisfiable iff s is. In other words, clause form is a normal form, in our usual sense. Every logical sentence has an equivalent (with respect to unsatisfiability) representation in clause form. But that is not so for Horn clause form. There are first-order sentences that cannot be expressed as Horn clauses. A simple such example is $\neg P(A) \rightarrow R(A)$. Converting this sentence to clause form, we get $P(A) \vee R(A)$, which is not a Horn clause because it contains two positive literals.

So Horn clause form is not as expressive as full first-order logic. But it is important because it is possible to prove the following additional fact about Horn clause resolution:

- If c is any negative Horn clause (including *nil*) and c is entailed by some set S of Horn clauses, then there is a resolution proof of c with the property that every resolvent that is created by the proof has, as its two parents, one positive clause in S and one negative clause. At the first resolution step, this negative clause must, of course, be one of the clauses in S. At each step after that, the negative clause must have been the one that was produced at the previous resolution step.

This fact is the basis for an efficient, restricted form of resolution called ***SLD resolution***. At the first step of an SLD resolution proof, one parent clause must be a positive clause and one must be a negative clause. At each step after the first, one parent clause must be a previously generated negative clause (i.e., one that was not in the original knowledge base) and one must be some positive clause from the original knowledge base. So for example, using SLD resolution, we will never resolve two positive clauses (i.e., rules or facts) together. Nor will we resolve two clauses neither of which was in the original knowledge base (i.e., two clauses derived by prior resolution steps).

SLD resolution is refutation complete for Horn clauses. (It is not, however, refutation complete for arbitrary sets of clauses. See Exercise B.9.) So, if there exists a way to derive *nil* from a Horn clause knowledge base S, then there exists a way to derive it from S using the SLD strategy. No other ways of choosing parent clauses need to be considered. Notice that SLD resolution implements the set-of-support strategy that we described in B.1.2. Notice also that SLD resolution can be thought of as backward chaining from one initial goal, just as we described in Example M.1. Some search and backtracking may still be required since there may be more than one way to resolve the most recent negative clause against the rest of the knowledge base and it may not be immediately obvious which one (if any) will succeed in producing a contradiction. But the search is focused only on possible parent clause pairs that include one positive clause that existed in the original knowledge base and one negative clause that is directly descended from a single initial negative clause.

Logic Programming and Prolog

Now consider an idea: *A* set of logical statements can be thought of as a program that solves problems by proving theorems about potential solutions. ***Logic programming*** is an approach to programming that takes this view. Clearly logic programming only makes sense as a way to solve real problems if it can exploit an efficient theorem-proving engine.

The most widely used logic programming language is Prolog. Modern Prolog systems contain a wide assortment of tools. For example, they may support object-oriented programming, graphical interfaces, and Web-based application development. But the core of every Prolog system is a Horn clause-based, resolution theorem prover that exploits SLD resolution. Despite the expressive limits of Horn clauses, Prolog has proven to be a useful, relatively high-level language for expressing rules in many different kinds of domains, ranging from circuit design, to help desks to Web brokers. We'll mention an application to music in N.1.2.

Prolog programs may be interpreted or compiled. In either case, we need to be able to talk about how a program will be executed. We'll use the term Prolog virtual machine to describe the mechanism by which a Prolog program is run. A Prolog program consists of a knowledge base (of implication rules and basic facts, all of which can be written as positive Horn clauses) and a goal (with the restricted form described above). Since reasoning is done using resolution, the Prolog virtual machine, given a goal G, begins by negating G to produce the only negative clause in its knowledge base. Then the Prolog virtual machine uses depth-first search and SLD resolution to reason backwards from $\neg G$. So, at each resolution step, the negative clause that was created at the previous step will be one of the parent clauses unless all ways of resolving with it have already been tried. In that case, the prover will back up to the next most recently generated negative clause and look for an alternative way to use it as a parent clause. This process continues until either the empty clause, *nil*, is generated or there is nothing left to do. If *nil* is generated, (i.e., a contradiction and thus a proof has been found), then the variable bindings that led to the contradiction of the knowledge base with $\neg G$ can be returned. So, when the Prolog virtual machine proves a goal of the form $\exists x, y, \ldots (P_1(\ldots) \wedge P_2(\ldots) \wedge \ldots \wedge P_n(\ldots))$, it also returns values for the variables $x, y, \ldots$ that make $(P_1(\ldots) \wedge P_2(\ldots) \wedge \ldots \wedge P_n(\ldots)$ true.

When resolving with a negative clause G, the Prolog virtual machine will consider the literals in G one at a time, left to right. To work on each of those literals, it will consider the knowledge base clauses in the order in which they were written.

EXAMPLE M.2 The Order in Which a Prolog Program Considers Resolvents

Suppose that the most recently generated negative clause is $\neg R(x) \vee \neg P(x) \vee \neg S(x)$, and suppose that the knowledge base contains the following clauses:

[1] $\neg T(x) \vee P(x)$.

[2] $\neg G(x) \vee P(x)$.

EXAMPLE M.2 *(Continued)*

[3] $\neg H(x) \vee R(x)$.
[4] $\neg B(x) \vee S(x)$.
[5] $H(x)$.

The Prolog virtual machine will first look for a way to use $\neg R(x)$ as a complementary literal. So it will resolve $\neg R(x) \vee \neg P(x) \vee \neg S(x)$ with [3], producing the new negative clause $\neg H(x) \vee \neg P(x) \vee \neg S(x)$. It will next try to use $\neg H(x)$ as a complementary literal, so it will resolve with [5], producing $\neg P(x) \vee \neg S(x)$. Next it will try to use $\neg P(x)$. There are two rules that contain the literal $P(x)$. It will try [1] first, producing $\neg T(x) \vee \neg S(x)$. It will continue from here until it either proves *nil* or hits a dead end. In the latter case, it will back up the first negative clause for which some alternative resolution step exists.

Notice that the control strategy that the Prolog virtual machine uses enables knowledge base builders to encode, in their knowledge bases, information about which facts and rules are more likely to be useful. The more useful clauses get written ahead of the less useful ones. So, on average, we can expect that the Prolog virtual machine finds proofs faster than would a prover that was working without any such "hints".

Different dialects of Prolog differ in their syntax. In the examples that we are about to present, we will use the syntax as defined in [Clocksin and Mellish 1981]. Variables are written in upper case and constants in lower case. A Prolog program consists of a goal, plus a knowledge base of implication rules and basic facts. The syntax of each of these pieces is shown next. Variables in rules and facts are universally quantified. Variables in goals (also called queries) are existentially quantified. The logical connective AND is written as a comma.

- A goal, such as, $\exists x\, (P(x) \wedge Q(x) \wedge T(x))$, is written in Prolog as:

  ```
  ?- p(X), q(X), t(X).
  ```

  So, for example, the following are legal Prolog goals:

  ```
  ?- know(marcus, caesar).              /* Does Marcus know Caesar?
  ?- know(marcus, X)                    /* Does Marcus know anyone
                                           (and, if so, whom)?
  ?- know(X, Y), know(Y, marcus)        /* Does anyone know someone
                                           who knows Marcus?
  ```

- Implication rules can all be written as positive Horn clauses. But, in a Prolog program, they are written in their more natural form, except that the right hand side and left-hand side are reversed (suggesting the way that the rules are used in backward chaining). So the mapping between implication rules, Horn clause form, and Prolog syntax is:

  - Implication rule: $\forall x\, ((P(x) \wedge Q(x) \wedge \ldots \wedge T(x)) \rightarrow R(x))$.
  - Horn clause form: $\neg P(x) \vee \neg Q(x) \vee \ldots \vee \neg T(x) \vee R(x)$.
  - Prolog rule syntax: `r(X) :- p(X), q(X), ..., t(X).`

Read the symbol `:-` as "if". Read a comma as "and". So the Prolog rule we just showed can naturally be read as, "R must be true if $P, Q, \ldots,$ and T are." Alternatively, it can be thought of as saying, "Rewrite the goal R as the set of subgoals $P, Q, \ldots, T$ and then attempt to prove them." An example of an implication rule written in Prolog syntax is:

```
living-ancestor-of(X, Y) := mother-of(X, Y), alive(X).
```

This rule corresponds to the implication rule, $\forall x\, ((Mother\text{-}of(x, y) \wedge Alive(x)) \rightarrow Living\text{-}ancestor\text{-}of(x, y))$.

- A fact, such as $GPA(Ellen, 3.9)$ is written in Prolog as `gpa(ellen, 3.9)`. The facts that a Prolog program uses may be listed explicitly in the program itself or they may be contained in one or more databases to which the program refers.

EXAMPLE M.3 Prolog Implements Backward Chaining Using Resolution

To see how the Prolog virtual machine conducts a depth-first search using resolution, we'll return to our hiring example. The implication rules and the facts of Example M.1 can be written as a Prolog program as follows:

```
great-hire(X) :- famous(X).
great-hire(X) :- good-major(X), great-grades(X),
                 did-intern(X).
good-major(X) :- major(X, computer-science).
good-major(X) :- major(X, engineering).
great-grades(X) :- gpa(X, Y), greater-than(Y, 3.5).
major(john, english).
major(ellen, computer-science).
gpa(ellen, 3.9).
did-intern(john).
did-intern(ellen).
```

This program creates the following list of Horn clauses:

$\neg Famous(x) \vee Great\text{-}hire(x))$.

$\neg Good\text{-}major(x) \vee \neg Great\text{-}grades(x) \vee \neg Did\text{-}intern(x) \vee Great\text{-}hire(x)$.

$\neg Major(x, ComputerScience) \vee Good\text{-}major(x)$.

$\neg Major(x, Engineering) \vee Good\text{-}major(x)$.

$\neg GPA(x, y) \wedge \neg Greater\text{-}than(y, 3.5) \vee Great\text{-}grades(x)$.

$Major(John, English)$.

$Major(Ellen, ComputerScience)$.

EXAMPLE M.3 ***(Continued)***

GPA(*Ellen*, 3.9).
Did-intern(*John*).
Did-intern(*Ellen*).

We again want to prove, $\exists x\ (Great\text{-}hire(x))$. We state that goal in Prolog as:

```
?- great-hire(X).
```

The Prolog virtual machine negates the goal and creates the negative Horn clause, $\neg Great\text{-}hire(x)$. Resolution then answers the question by producing the following proof:

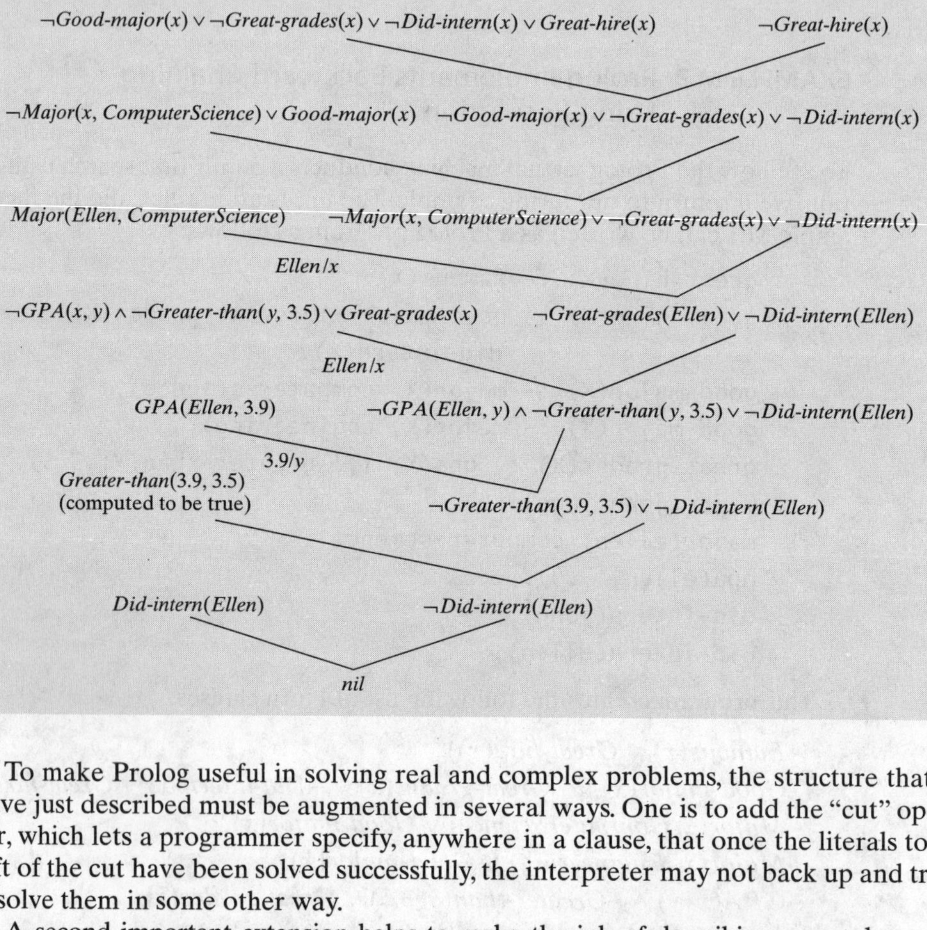

To make Prolog useful in solving real and complex problems, the structure that we have just described must be augmented in several ways. One is to add the "cut" operator, which lets a programmer specify, anywhere in a clause, that once the literals to the left of the cut have been solved successfully, the interpreter may not back up and try to resolve them in some other way.

A second important extension helps to make the job of describing a complex world tractable. To see how it works, we'll first describe an assumption that is reasonable in many domains: The ***closed world assumption*** says that the only facts that are true are those that have been explicitly declared. If a database (or knowledge base) satisfies the closed world assumption, then if we want to prove $\neg P$, it suffices to look for P and fail to find it. In many domains, it may not be reasonable to make the closed world assumption for all predicates, but there may be some (even many) predicates for which it does make sense.

For example, we can assume that a travel database contains all scheduled airline flights. We can assume that a university registrar's database contains all scheduled classes. We can assume that a company's personnel database contains all of the company's employees. Finally, suppose that we want to build a planning agent that must limit its actions to things that are legal. In most systems of law, we don't list legal things. What we do is to write laws that define illegal activities. Then anything that is not explicitly illegal is legal (until someone figures out how to ban it). So suppose that we have the following Prolog rule:

```
choose-action(X) :- reasonable-cost(X), legal(X).
```

Assuming also a list only of illegal actions, how can the Prolog interpreter, given a proposed action X, show that X is legal? The answer is that the Prolog interpreter provides an operator (generally \+) that implements a form of reasoning called ***negation as failure***. The negation as failure inference rule says that P may be concluded if it is not possible to prove $\neg P$. So, we could write:

```
legal(X):- \+ illegal(X).
```

Note that the negation as failure rule is a form of ***nonmonotonic reasoning***. The addition of a fact (for example the assertion that some new activity is illegal) could make it no longer possible to prove a claim that could, before the addition of the new fact, have been proved. Thus Prolog programs can implement reasoning that cannot be described in standard first-order logic.

M.2.4 Do Undecidability and Intractability Doom a Logical Approach to Artificial Intelligence?

The techniques that we have just described, plus others, make it possible to build logic-based reasoning systems that can solve a wide variety of problems. But we know that first-order logic is not powerful enough to describe all the things that we might want to say to a general-purpose reasoning system. For example, since it is monotonic, it doesn't let us describe and exploit the fact that birds fly *unless* there is something special about them. To use this fact, we'd want to be able to conclude that Tweety flies if all we know about him is that he is a bird. We'd also want to be able to undo that conclusion if we later find out that Tweety has had his wings clipped. As another example of the limits of first-order logic, consider reasoning about belief. Suppose that $P(Felix)$ is a predicate and we want to assert that Linus believes it to be true. Then we might like to be able to write, $believes(Linus, P(Felix))$. But in first-order logic, predicates cannot be arguments to other predicates. To solve these and other problems, a variety of more expressively powerful logical systems have been developed.

Suppose that we want to build an artificial agent with human-like capabilities and that we have succeeded in building a logical theory that captures enough relevant knowledge about the world (a wild stretch from the current state of the art). If for no other reason than that the world is changing, the theory that we will build will necessarily be incomplete (in the sense that there are statements that are true in the world but unprovable in the theory). So suppose further that we have also developed techniques for acquiring (learning) new information as it is required.

Are we, nevertheless, doomed? In particular, we know that first-order logic (even without the enhancements mentioned above) is undecidable and intractable. Does this mean that any attempt to build a powerful logical reasoning agent must necessarily fail? We might guess that the answer to this question is no. After all, despite his proof fifteen years earlier of the undecidability of the Entscheidungsproblem, Alan Turing forecast in the middle of the last century that, by the turn of the century, intelligent programs would exist.

Although we have not yet succeeded in building an artificial system that rivals the intelligent behavior of people, the negative results that we have presented throughout this book do not necessarily doom our attempt to do so. To see why they don't, consider:

The undecidability issue: Theorem 22.4 tells us that no algorithm exists that *always* halts and decides whether a statement *s* is a theorem in some particular logical theory. So, given any theorem-deciding algorithm that we might attempt to write, there will be some statements on which the algorithm will fail to halt. But Theorem 22.4 does not say that we can't build an algorithm that halts with the correct result much (or even most) of the time we actually call it. In particular, theoremhood in first order logic is semidecidable. So, if our program attempts to prove statements that are theorems, it will always succeed (assuming we wrote it correctly). We can imagine building a program that, with enough knowledge, rarely tries to prove something that turns out to be false. More generally, we can build theorem provers with the property that, if we consider only statements that have been constructed because they say something relevant to the task at hand, it is overwhelmingly likely that they will be either provable or disprovable. Further, we can prevent our agent from getting hopelessly stuck by imposing an effort limit on each proof attempt. If a proof cannot be found within the assigned amount of time, the agent can give up and try something else.

We started with the goal of building an intelligent agent, perhaps one that could rival people in performing some or all of the things we do. It is hard to compare people to Turing machines, primarily because people have sophisticated perceptual systems and Turing machines don't. We are only beginning to understand how to construct realistic computational models of those human systems. But there is no reason to believe that people have any special oracle-like capability that would enable us to compute a logical function that a Turing machine could not compute. The fact is that the undecidability of first-order logic limits the way people use logic just as it limits what programs can do. Yet we solve hard problems all the time. Appropriately designed programs, once we understand how to build them, will be able to do the same thing.

The intractability issue: The intractability claims that we have made about logical systems are claims about worst-case performance. There exist techniques, such as the ones we've described, that succeed much of the time, particularly when there is structure to the space that needs to be searched. So there may be relevant conclusions that will not be found soon enough to be useful. But that happens to people too.

The bottom line: There are reasons, beyond the undecidability and intractability of FOL, that artificial intelligence remains difficult and appears to require techniques beyond the logical ones that we have been discussing. We suggested in Section M.1, for example, that statistical techniques can be useful, both for representing knowledge and for acquiring it. Even with those techniques, though, no program has yet passed the Turing test or equaled the ability of people to analyze photographs.

But the reason that no AI program has done these things is not that FOL is undecidable and even simpler logics are intractable. The proofs we have presented for our undecidability and intractability results do not depend on the physical mechanism by which computation is performed. So they apply to people, as well as to machines. And people remain the existence proof that intelligence is possible.

M.2.5 A Complete and Decidable Legal System?

Going the other way, the negative results that we have presented do tell us that we cannot expect a mechanized logical system to solve all the problems inherent in the less formal systems that people have built up over the centuries. We consider here one example.[16]

When we say that our society is based on the rule of law, we assume that we can write a set of specific laws with four important properties:

- The laws capture the rules by which we want to live. So it must be the case that all allowable actions are legal and all unallowable actions are not legal. (This requirement assumes that we can all agree on how we want to live. We'll ignore that issue here.)
- The set of laws is consistent. In other words, we must guarantee that there is no action A that can be shown to be both legal and illegal.
- The set of laws is finite and reasonably maintainable. So, for example, we must reject any system that requires a separate law, for each specific citizen, mandating that that citizen pay taxes.
- It is possible to answer the question, "Given an action A, is A legal?"

Will we ever be able to write a single set of laws that satisfies all of those goals?

To do so requires that there be some deductive system in which we can:

- Describe each individual law.
- Derive conclusions about the legality of specific actions using some collection of rules of inference applied to the set of laws.

If we could be content with, say, the following set of laws, then we could create a decidable system:

- Mr. Smith must pay his taxes this year.
- Either Ms. Jones or Ms. Garcia must fix the potholes this year.

We can represent these laws in Boolean logic (for example, with the two axioms: SPT and $JFP \vee GFP$. Since Boolean logic is decidable, we can prove, for example that $SPT \wedge JFP$ is legal, while $(\neg JFP \wedge \neg GFP)$ is not legal.

---

[16] The question we describe here was suggested by Ben Kuipers.

But clearly this won't do. We require a first-order logical system so that we can write laws such as:

- $\forall x\ (\forall y\ (citizen(x) \wedge year(y) \wedge alive(x, y) \rightarrow paytaxesforyear(x, y)))$.
- $\forall y\ (\exists x\ (year(y) \rightarrow fixespotholes\ (x, y)))$.

There are, of course, first-order theories that are complete and thus decidable. But we know, from Section 22.4.2, that any consistent first-order theory that is powerful enough to describe the integers, along with addition and multiplication, cannot be either complete or decidable. We cannot describe our modern legal and business system without those capabilities, plus a myriad of others. (If you doubt this, take a look at last year's income tax forms.) Thus we cannot construct a decidable system of laws.

M.3 A Rule-Based Foundation for Artificial Intelligence and Cognition

In the early days of the development of formal models of computation, Emil Post proposed [Post 1943] a family of computational models based on the idea of rewrite systems (alternatively called production systems or rule-based systems). We mentioned one of them, Post production systems in Chapter 18. While it has turned out that Turing's model has proved more useful than Post's as a basis for analyzing computability, Post's ideas have served as the inspiration for at least five families of important computational systems: We have already described the use of grammars to define languages. In particular, Post's ideas inspired the design of BNF as a tool for defining context-free languages.

The other four families of ***rule-based systems*** that we will mention have arisen from the fact that it is natural to model many kinds of human cognitive processes as rewrite (or production rule) systems. So we will consider:

- The use of production-rule architectures as models not just of what people can do but of how they do it. Rules of this sort are thus used to define ***cognitive models*** of people.
- The use of production rules to encode the knowledge that people use when they solve many kinds of problems that require specific expertise. Rules of this sort are used by programs that have come to be called ***expert systems***.
- The use of production rules to encode the ***business practice rules*** by which organizations function.
- The use of production rules to describe the behavior of ***nonplayer characters*** (NPCs) in interactive games. We'll discuss this application in N.3.3, where we'll see rules being used in much the same way in which they are used to encode human knowledge in expert systems.

But rule-based systems are not limited to these problem areas. For example, there is a rule-based system that enhances voice signals over noise in hearing aids.

M.3.1 The Architecture of a Rule-Based System

A rule-based system has three main components:

- a knowledge base, which typically contains a collection of rules and a collection of basic facts,
- working memory, and
- an interpreter, often called an inference engine, that controls the way in which rules and facts are applied to solve a problem.

The Knowledge Base

In a rule-based system, problem-solving knowledge is encoded primarily as a set of rules that can be thought of as condition/action pairs. Whenever a rule's left-hand side matches the current problem situation, its right-hand side can be used to make progress toward finding a solution. The rules typically appeal to facts about the problem domain and the entities in it. So the rule base is generally augmented with a declarative knowledge base that can be represented in a standard database format, in a logical description language, or in some other knowledge-representation formalism.

The way in which rules are written varies across rule-based systems, primarily as a function of the knowledge the rules encode and how they are going to be used to solve problems. We've already seen one way to represent rules: as Prolog programs. The Prolog approach may be appropriate when the facts can be stated in Prolog's logical language and when problem-solving is to be done by backward chaining. We'll briefly mention a few other examples that illustrate the kinds of knowledge and reasoning that rule-based systems can encode. In all of them, we'll describe rules in English so that they make sense to us. The internal representation will depend on the tools that are used to build the system.

EXAMPLE M.4 Financial Planning

Rule-based systems have been used in a variety of financial applications. Consider the following two simplified rules from a financial planning system:

If: age >50, and
time-to-retirement <10 years, and
children to support,
Then: personal-state is conservative.

If: personal-state is conservative, and
financial state is aggressive, and
risk-tolerance is high.
Then: buy x% bonds, y% stocks, and z% cash.

Notice that these rules can be chained together to enable the system to reason from basic facts, provided by the user, to a conclusion that describes an appropriate action.

EXAMPLE M.5 Computing Damage Claims in a Civil Suit

Sometimes, although we require a single answer, many factors may affect how that answer should be computed. Then we can write a collection of rules, each of which modifies the answer in some appropriate way. For example, a rule-based system that provides advice on the size of a damage claim that it would make sense to seek in a civil suit might have rules like:

If: disfiguring injury,
Then: add $100,000 to damages.

If: work-time-lost >3 weeks,
Then: add $75,000 to damages.

EXAMPLE M.6 Medical Diagnosis

Rule-based systems have been widely used in expert systems that perform diagnosis tasks, ranging from medicine to computer system repair. In these systems, there is often some degree of uncertainty that should be attached to the conclusion of each rule. In this simple example rule, read (.8) to mean that on some scale (sometimes 0 to 1, sometimes −1 to 1, depending on the system), the certainty that should be attached to the conclusion of this rule is .8.

If: spots, and
fever, and
aches,
Then: chicken pox (.8).

Working Memory

In order for a rule to be applied, its left-hand side must match against something and its right-hand side must act on something. Those somethings are called ***working memory***. When we use a grammar to derive a string, working memory is simply a single string, which we have been calling the working string. In other kinds of rule-based systems, working memory may have a more complex structure. It may start out empty. Assertions may be added to it as data are provided, either by a user or by some other input mechanism. As rules fire, the contents of the working memory will change.

The Inference Engine

Rules are applied to the contents of working memory and results are computed by the action of a rule interpreter that is usually called an ***inference engine***. Recall that, in Section 11.1, we presented a very general definition of a rule-based system. We pointed out there that, to build a particular rule-based system, it is necessary to define a rule interpreter that specifies how and when rules will be applied. The design of such an interpreter requires an answer to each of the following questions.

- ***Efficient matching***: How can the left-hand sides of a large rule base be compared efficiently against the contents of working memory? Many inference engines solve this problem be exploiting the RETE algorithm, which we will describe briefly below.
- ***Conflict resolution***: A conflict occurs whenever there is more than one way to match the rules against working memory. How will such conflicts be resolved so that a single rule can be chosen to be applied next?
- ***Direction of reasoning***: In what direction will reasoning proceed? One simple answer is to use forward chaining and to reason from observables to conclusions. An alternative is to use backward chaining (as in Prolog) and to reason from goals back to observables. Various hybrid approaches may also make sense.

Strategies for conflict resolution and reasoning direction vary as a function of the problem that is being solved. For example, in some task domains, it makes sense to resolve conflicts using a recency heuristic in which rules that match against facts that have recently been added to working memory will be given priority over rules that match against older information. But that heuristic isn't appropriate in some other domains.

Efficient matching is, however, an issue that is important in any rule-based system that exploits a nontrivial-sized rule base or working memory. Many widely used inference engines solve the matching problem by exploiting some version of the RETE algorithm 💻 [Forgy 1982]. The name RETE comes from the Latin word *rete*, which means net or network. Two key ideas underlie the design of RETE:

- Instead of simply placing rules in a flat list and treating all of the left-hand sides as independent patterns to be matched, it makes sense to build a tree. The nodes of the tree correspond to patterns that occur in left-hand sides of rules. The leaf nodes correspond to complete left-hand sides, so they point to the associated right-hand sides.
- Working memory doesn't change very often. Thus, by and large, the rules that matched the last time we checked will still match. So, instead of starting from scratch and comparing each left-hand side against working memory each time a rule must be selected, let each node in the pattern tree keep track of the working memory elements that match it. Whenever working memory changes, update the appropriate values at the tree nodes.

Inference engines can be implemented independently of the specific rule sets that will run on them. There exist a variety of commercial tools 💻 that include inference engines and that can be tailored for use in rule-based systems that solve particular tasks.

M.3.2 Cognitive Modeling

One of the earliest uses of rule-based systems was to the design of programs that were intended to model various aspects of human cognitive performance. Such models have turned out to be important, both in the study of cognitive psychology and in the design of programs that require sophisticated interfaces with people. For example, rule-based cognitive models have been used as the basis for the design of tutoring systems 💻 that can form guesses about the misconceptions of students. Then they tailor their instruction to the specific goal of repairing those misconceptions. Another important application has been to the design of agents in interactive video games 💻. Here the goal is to construct agents whose behavior seems human to the game's human players.

Research on general cognitive architectures has led to the development of several software platforms that are used to create systems that model human intelligent behavior. Two of the most comprehensive and influential such architectures are SOAR 💻 (described in [Newell 1990] and [Laird, Newell and Rosenbloom 1987]) and ACT-V 💻 (described in [Anderson and Lebiere1998] and [Anderson et al. 2004]). At the heart of these systems is the principle that intelligent action arises from perceiving the environment and then responding to what has been observed. So these architectures exploit a production-rule system to model the way in which such responses are constructed. When left-hand sides of rules match against working memory (which may organized into submemories, such as a long and a short-term memory), right-hand sides describe appropriate conclusions and actions.

M.3.3 Expert Systems

The term "expert system" is generally used to describe a program that performs a task that is more traditionally performed by a human expert. This contrasts with other kinds of AI programs, for example image understanders and common sense reasoners, that do things that even children can do well. Expert systems exploit many techniques for representing task domain knowledge and for reasoning with it. But one of the most important techniques is rule-based systems. It turns out that, for many kinds of problems, the wisdom that experts have accumulated can be captured in a set of pattern/action rules of the sort we showed in Examples M.4, M.5 and M.6.

Rule-based expert systems have been used to solve real problems in domains 💻 as varied as:

- airplane maintenance,
- quality control in manufacturing,
- insurance underwriting,
- clinical decision support,
- identifying archeological artifacts,
- pest control in agriculture, and
- education.

Commercial tools 💻 support the construction of such systems by providing a domain-independent inference engine, as well as support for eliciting rules from human experts and for building interfaces between the rule base and other data sources.

M.3.4 Rule-Based Systems for Modeling Business Practices

Every successful, complex organization operates (most of the time) systematically. So there exists a set of rules, whether they are written down or not, that describe what the organization does and how it does it.

EXAMPLE M.7 Some Simple Business Rules

A human resources rule set might include the following:

If: an employee has been employed fewer than two years,
Then: vacation time per year is two weeks.

If: an employee has been employed two or more years,
Then: vacation time per year is three weeks.

If: an employee fails to show up for work for three consecutive days without calling in,
Then: (s)he can be fired.

A sales rule set might include the following:

If: a customer is a repeat customer,
Then: do not do a credit check.

If: a customer orders more than $1000 worth of merchandise in a single order,
Then: give a 10% discount.

An inventory-management rule set might include the following:

If: the inventory of widgets has been below 100 for more than two days,
Then: notify the inventory manager.

If: the inventory of fradgets goes below 1000,
Then: notify the inventory manager immediately.

Getting employees to articulate these rules, particularly in any sort of formal way, can be hard. But, for a variety of reasons, including regulatory ones, businesses are increasingly attempting to do just that. There exists a growing family of commercial tools to help them. As with expert system tools, these business practice rules engines assist with extracting rules from employees, checking rule sets for consistency, and applying rules to help solve problems.

APPENDIX N

Applications: Art and Entertainment: Music and Games

In 1968, the album *Switched on Bach* 💻 hit the pop charts and almost overnight, at least in the United States, just about everyone had heard of electronic music. But the use of machines as entertainers substantially precedes the modern digital computer. Some may have occurred as early as the second century B.C. We know that Leonardo da Vinci built mechanical musical instruments in the 16th century. By the end of the 20th century, it was no longer possible to imagine the worlds of entertainment and the arts as distinct from the worlds of digital media and computation. In this section, we'll briefly sketch some of the ways in which the techniques that have been presented in this book are used in music and in games. In Q.2.1, we'll mention one other entertainment application: the use of context-free grammars to model ballroom dances.

N.1 Music

It is natural to think of music as a language. So it should not be surprising that many of the tools that we have described can be used to model various styles of music and to help create them. We mention a few of them here. For a comprehensive survey, see [Roads 1996]. But first we'll consider a short digression to answer the question, "Why?" What good does it do to make a formal model of a style of music? Roughly the answer has three parts (suggested by [Roads 1985]):

- Musicologists strive to understand the nature of particular musical forms and styles. If they can build formal models of their analyses, they can test them. And, once tested, the model(s) can be used to help determine, for example, the origins of works whose composer and/or date is not clear from the historical record.
- Composers want new ways to create new music.
- Some people think it is fun.

N.1.1 Using Markov and Hidden Markov Models

Composers have been using Markov models since well before the advent of the computer; in fact, they've been using them since before Markov described them. Perhaps the most famous early example is the *Musikalisches Würfelspiel* (or *Musical Dice Game*) 🖳, published in 1792 and (almost certainly erroneously) attributed to Mozart. While the origin of this particular game is unclear, it is known that games of this sort were widely popular in 18th century Europe. The definition of a dice-game composition consists of:

- a numbered set of short musical phrases, and
- a table with 11 rows and some number (8 in the case of the *Musikalisches Würfelspiel*) of columns. Each entry in the table contains the number of one of the musical phrases.

To "compose" a piece that consists of k phrases, a player rolls a pair of dice k times. Each roll produces a number between 2 and 12. The player uses the first roll to choose a row in the table and then selects the phrase whose number appears in column 1. The second roll is used to select a second phrase from column two, and so forth. You can try it yourself 🖳.

The *Musikalisches Würfelspiel* is a 0th order Markov model (since it uses no history in deciding what to do next). The probabilities associated with each choice are simply the probabilities of rolling each of the numbers between 2 and 12. Thus the computational requirements of the game make it easy to play by hand (although it was also implemented by Lejaren Hiller and John Cage in the program HPSCHD 🖳 [Hiller 1972].)

Since the mid 1950's, with the advent of digital computers, more sophisticated Markov models, typically of higher order, have been possible. Such models have been used to create music in a wide variety of genres 🖳. Models have been trained on nursery tunes, the songs of Stephen Foster, hymn tunes, and the works of Mozart and Hayden, to name a few.

To build a Markov model of a particular musical style, it is necessary to do the following:

1. Collect a corpus of example pieces from the chosen style.
2. Select one or more important features (such as pitch or note duration) and encode each piece as a sequence of features.
3. Build the model by defining a state set (corresponding to the features that were selected in step 2) and training it using the technique described in Section 5.11.1.

Once one or more models have been constructed, it/they can be used for either or both of the following tasks:

- Composing of new pieces in a selected style: To do this, simply run the model that corresponds to the desired style, allowing it to generate notes according to the probabilities that it acquired during the training process.

- Composer or style identification: Given two or more models, each corresponding to a composer or style, a piece whose origin is uncertain can be analyzed to see which model is most likely to have generated it.

The first piece of music composed by a digital computer is the *Illiac Suite for String Quartet* 🖳, written in 1956 by a program created by Lejaren Hiller and Leonard Isaacson. The four movements of the Suite correspond to four composition experiments conducted by Hiller and Isaacson. The first three movements are based on traditional compositional techniques, implemented on a machine. But the fourth movement is completely different. It was created by a succession of more and more powerful Markov models, the last of which was 4th order. Once the piece was written, it was transcribed and played by musicians on conventional instruments. The *Illiac Suite* had a huge impact on computer music, not just for what it was but also because its creators chose to document the techniques they used in substantial detail [Hiller and Isaacson 1959].

In creating the *Illiac Suite*, Hiller and Isaacson used Markov models to generate notes but not to generate sounds. It was soon obvious that that could be done too. So in 1963, Hiller, along with Robert Baker, used a computer to write *Computer Cantata* [Hiller and Baker 1964]. Again Markov models of up to 4th order were used. The models that generated the musical elements were trained on Charles Ives's *Three Places in New England*. But the *Cantata* also exploited a sequence of Markov models that had been trained on English sentences. They were used to generate "singing." The 4th order model was able to create some sounds that seemed English-like.

Hiller and Baker used the creation of *Computer Cantata* as a tested for a more general, computer-composition tool that they were building. That tool, MUSICOMP, became the first in a long string of tools that enable composers to create electronic music.

The stochastic techniques that Hiller pioneered have been used, particularly for electronic sound generation, by many composers in the years since the first appearance of the *Illiac Suite* and the *Computer Cantata*. Good introductions to them appear in computer music textbooks, for example [Moore 1990]. These techniques are appealing to some composers because they "may also produce unanticipated possibilities, where the bonds of a restrictive and inaccurate acoustic theory and of a limited aural imagination may be broken," [Jones 1981].

As with any computational problem, a key issue in using Markov models to describe music is representation. A piece of music can naturally be described as a sequence of events. So one way to represent it as a Markov model is to build a single model whose states correspond to atomic events (at some level of granularity). But musical events are complex. For example, a single note has pitch (which may be described, for example, as a range and an average), length, intensity, a concluding period of silence, and a harmonic envelope. So another idea is to describe each musical event as a vector of parameters, each of which describes some aspect of the note. Then a set of Markov models can be used to control, separately, the vector elements. An example of the use of this technique the piece *Macricisum*, by Kevin Jones [Jones 1981]. It was created using a set of nine Markov models.

But now suppose that we wish to train our models on music that is a noisy rendition of the music that was composed. For example, suppose that, instead of reading a score, we are listening to a singer sing. Now the probability that we will hear a particular note is a function of both the probability that that note was intended by the composer and the probability that the singer rendered the written note in a particular way. In this case, we can use a hidden Markov model (HMM). The states, and the transitions between them, will describe the music as it is written. The output probabilities will describe the likelihood of each written note being performed in a particular way. HMMs of this sort can be used in a variety of applications. For example, suppose that we have a database of compositions/songs, each represented as an HMM. Then we can build a retrieval system that allows a user to hum a song. The system can then identify and retrieve the song by using the forward algorithm (as described in Section 5.11.2) to choose the HMM that is most likely to correspond to the hummed tune.

HMMs can also be used in composition. Suppose that we are given one musical line (say a melody or a base line) and the task is to generate other lines in either harmony or counterpoint with it. We build an HMM whose states correspond to relationships between a given note and the one that we propose to generate to coincide with it. The probabilities associated with the transitions correspond to the likelihood of one such relationship following another. We train the network on a corpus of harmonized works drawn from the style we want to emulate. We then use the Viterbi algorithm to find the most likely path through the network given a particular input line. That path will define an output line that can be played along with the original one.

N.1.2 Using Grammars and Rule-Based Systems

While purely stochastic systems have proven to be interesting, they fail to capture everything about the organization of interesting music:

> It is mostly agreed that musical structures are hierarchical. This hierarchical organization implies that the various parts of a piece of music belong together so that small parts are joined, such that they form greater parts, which are joined such that they form greater parts, which are joined such that they form greater parts, and so on. These structural units are called *constituents*. With respect to the hierarchical constituent structure, there is a clear similarity between music and language. What kind of descriptions are appropriate for such structures? [Sundberg and Lindblom 1991, pp. 245–246].

Grammars and, more generally, rule-based systems, can be effective tools for associating structures with strings. Soon after the development of formal linguistic grammars in the 1950s, musicians and musicologists began exploiting grammatical formalisms, both to analyze existing music and to compose new pieces. The question then arose, "What kind of grammar best suits the task?" Following the Rule of Least Power (see Section 3.3.4), it makes sense to choose the weakest adequate formalism. Regular grammars can assign only simple structures in which one terminal symbol is generated at each branch of a parse tree. So they were never seriously considered for this task.

Context-free grammars have been considered. But it turns out that they cannot describe even very straightforward musical structures. We'll present one simple example, taken from [West, Howell and Cross 1991]. Sonata (or, sometimes, sonata allegro) form was commonly used, starting in the late 18th century, to define the structure of the first and sometimes also the last movement of a symphony, a sonata, or a concerto. A simple attempt to describe sonata form with a context-free grammar might begin like this:

$$<movement> \rightarrow <part_1><part_2>$$
$$<part_1> \rightarrow <section_1><section_2><section_3><section>^*$$
$$<part_2> \rightarrow <section_1><section>^*<section_1><section_2><section_3><section>^*$$

But we immediately have two problems, both of which are fundamental to the use of context-free grammars:

- Both occurrences of $section_1$ in $part_2$ must be based on the same theme as $section_1$ in $part_1$. Similarly for the two fragments labeled $section_2$. So, ignoring the musical variations that are allowed, we have the same problem that we had in trying to write a context-free grammar for WW $= \{ww : w \in \{\mathtt{a}, \mathtt{b}\}^*\}$ and for describing the type checking constraints imposed by programming languages like Java.
- There are what linguists call suprasegmental properties (like intonation) that are not captured by the breakdown of the piece into sections. $Part_1$ starts in a home key. There is then movement away from the home key through $section_2$ and $section_3$. In $part_2$, the motion is in the other direction, back to the home key by the end of the second occurrence of $section_1$. These larger properties cannot be described by a context-free grammar that must generate each subconstituent independently of all the others.

As a result, most grammars of music exploit more powerful formalisms, primarily ones that are equivalent in power to unrestricted grammars and to Turing machines.

When rules can contain multiple symbols in their left-hand sides, contextual constraints can be described. We'll mention one example, taken from a much larger body of work whose goal is to describe, for Western musicians, nonwestern musical traditions. Formal systems have been appealing in this arena since people are working in traditions with which they are not familiar. It thus becomes important to construct theories that can be validated without appeal to intuitions that are probably not well formed. [Kippen and Bel 1992] presents a grammar that describes the rules by which improvisation is done in North Indian tabla drumming. One of the constituents in the grammar is named V_1. It can be realized in one of three ways, named *dha*, *ti*, and -. It turns out that the way it is realized is dependent on its context. So the grammar contains rules such as the ones shown in Figure N.1.

Kippen and Bel call these rules "context-sensitive," as indeed they are. But the overall grammar that they describe is an unrestricted grammar in our sense, not a context-sensitive one, since length-reducing rules are employed.

contexts that generate *ti*:	contexts that generate *dha*:	contexts that generate -:
$dha\ V_1\ dha \rightarrow dha\ ti\ dha$	$kt\ V_1\ tr \rightarrow kt\ dha\ tr$	$dha\ V_1\ tr \rightarrow dha$ - tr
$dha\ V_1\ V_1 \rightarrow dha\ ti\ V_1$	$kt\ V_1\ V_1 \rightarrow kt\ dha\ V_1$	$dha\ V_1\ dha \rightarrow dha$ - dha
etc.	etc.	etc.

FIGURE N.1 Context-dependent tabla rules.

The language of music appears to share many structural features with natural languages and many of those features are hard to describe without substantial formal power. Linguists have, over the years, defined grammatical frameworks that have the formal expressive power of unrestricted grammars but that offer particular kinds of representational advantages for describing linguistic data. Musicologists have adopted many of those formalisms and put them to their own use.

Starting in the mid 1960s, the transformational grammar formalism described in [Chomsky 1965] became popular. The key idea in transformational grammar is that a sentence has a deep structure that corresponds naturally to its meaning. It also has a surface structure (namely what we hear or read). While these two are not the same, there is a systematic relationship between them. A transformational grammar, then, has two parts: a set of context-free rules that define the deep structure of a sentence and another set of transformational rules that describe how the deep structure is to be realized as a linguistic form. It is the existence of the transformational component that gives these grammars the expressive power of an unrestricted grammar. Transformational rules can be used to do many kinds of things. For instance, they can move constituents around. A simple example from English illustrates this idea. Consider the sentence, "What did Mary see in the park?" The object of the verb "see" is the interrogative pronoun "what." It got moved from its natural place after "see" to the sentence-initial position in which interrogative pronouns occur in English.

Transformations that describe the relationship between an underlying structure and a surface form appear to be a natural way to describe many aspects of the structure of many kinds of music. This notion was articulated by Heinrich Schenker 💻 (see, for example, [Schenker 1935]) well before it became possible to write formal grammars that could be run on computers. So the transformational model has been used to describe many genres of music. For example, [Baroni et al 1984] describes work on grammars for the melodies of Lutheran hymn tunes, the melodies of French chansons, and Bach's chorale harmonies. [Camilleri 1984] describes a similar effort to construct a grammar for the initial phrases of Schubert's Lieder. Other work has modeled folks tunes and jazz.

Early efforts at defining grammars of music were conducted by hand. People examined music, attempted to extract recurrent patterns, and then wrote grammars that described those patterns. But if the goal is to construct a grammar that accurately describes the patterns that characterize an existing corpus of work, then it makes sense to use as large a corpus as possible and to extract the grammar rules automatically. Once the grammar has been written, it can be used as the basis for an analysis of the existing corpus or as a way to generate new works. Many genres of classical Western tonal music have been analyzed in this way. Twentieth century jazz has been extensively studied in order to extract rules that describe successful improvisation strategies. One of the most widely used musical pattern extractors and composers is David Cope's EMI system [Cope 1996]. It has been used to write music in the styles of Bach, Beethoven, Mozart, Stravinsky, Gershwin, Joplin, and Cope himself. EMI represents its grammars in a formalism called an augmented transition network (or ATN). An ATN is essentially a finite state machine except that arbitrary computational actions, including recursive calls to the state machine itself, may be performed as tests on any of the arcs that connect one state to another. ATNs have the same computational power as do Turing machines.

Rule-based systems that do not behave exactly as grammars do have also been used both to analyze and to generate music. This approach is appealing when dealing with musical genres that appear to be describable by some fixed set of rules. Some kinds of early Western music, for example, have that property. Sixteenth century counterpoint is a good case study. Fux's *Gradus ad Parnassum*, published in 1725, offered a set of rules and guidelines that characterize species counterpoint [Fux 1725]. [Schottstaedt 1989] describes a program for generating counterpoint according to the rules that Fux laid out. Associated with each rule is a penalty that should attach to any composition each time it breaks the rule. So, for example, Schottstaedt lists the following rules and their penalties:

Parallel fifths are not allowed. (Infinite penalty.)
Avoid direct motion to a perfect fifth. (Penalty is 200.)
Avoid unisons in two-part counterpoint. (Penalty is 100.)
Avoid tritones near the cadence in Lydian mode. (Penalty is 13.)

Schottstaedt's program composes counterpoint by running a best-first search process through a space of possible compositions. It uses the penalties as its heuristic function for evaluating competing notes. Another example of a rule-based system that composes in a well-understood style is CHORAL [Ebcioglu 1992], which creates harmonies to accompany the melodies of Bach chorales.

One way to represent production rules is as a Prolog program (as described in M.2.3). For a description of this approach to describing music, see [Schaffer and McGee 1997]. A simple example shown there is the following rule, which encodes the definition of a passing tone:

```
nonharmonic_tone(passing_tone)  :-
    approached(step),
    resolved(step),
    registral_direction(same).
```

Other approaches to writing musical grammars have also been exploited. For example, L-systems 🖳 can be used to model a process in which basic musical characteristics, like pitch and duration, are encoded as symbols and then transformed into music.

N.2 Classic Games and Puzzles

By the late 1940s, the idea of a stored-program, electronic computer had been born and development efforts were well underway. By then, also, Alan Turing and others had begun talking about computer chess. At the start of the 1950's, Claude Shannon, sometimes called the father of information theory, published the first paper [Shannon 1950] on computer chess. By the mid 1950s, there were several programs that played at least partial games of chess. A few years later, Allen Newell and Herbert Simon, pioneers in the then-new field of artificial intelligence, wrote, "Within ten years a computer will be the world's chess champion, unless the rules bar it from competition," [Simon and Newell 1958]. The rules imposed no such bar. But a computer did not beat the human world chess champion until 1997, when Deep Blue beat Garry Kasparov. Why did it take so long?

The theory of complexity that we describe in Part V does not apply directly to chess. Nor does it apply to Go, Sudoku, or most of the other classic games and puzzles with which we are familiar. It doesn't apply because most of those games have fixed-size boards and the theory we have built describes complexity as a function of increasing problem size. But chess and its cousins are hard for the same reason that the sort of combinatorial problems to which our theory does apply are hard: There does not appear to exist an algorithm for solving the problem without searching a large space of individual moves. For example, in the middle of a chess game, the branching factor (the number of alternative moves) is about 35. It is typically estimated that playing master-level chess requires looking ahead about eight moves. So choosing a move using lookahead requires examining about $35^8 \approx 2 \cdot 10^{12}$ moves. For the game of Go, the situation is even worse. The branching factor is greater (over 300 at some points in the game) and it is substantially harder to write an evaluation function that can examine an intermediate board position and determine how good it is. While tables of opening and closing moves can help reduce search (at least in the case of chess), no one has yet found a way to avoid search in the general case of these classic games.

Complexity theory can help to explain the observed difficulty of writing programs to play these games if we generalize the games to boards of arbitrary size. This isn't a totally off-the-wall idea. For example, one early (1956) "chess"-playing program used just a 6×6 board in order to make the problem tractable. Using this idea, we have defined, for example, the language that contains descriptions of generalized chess configurations from which the current player has a guaranteed win.

- CHESS = {<*b*>: *b* is a configuration of an $n \times n$ chess board and there is a guaranteed win for the current player}

N.2.1 Nim

In Example 21.5, we considered the game of Nim. We can describe Nim as a language as follows.

- NIM = {<*b*>: *b* is a Nim configuration (i.e., a set of piles of sticks) and there is a guaranteed win for the current player}

Recall that, in Example 21.5, we described a straightforward algorithm for deciding, in any game of Nim, whether the current player has a move that leads to a guaranteed win. Our algorithm doesn't require actually searching the space of possible move sequences. It proves that NIM is in P (and, in fact, in L).

People get bored pretty quickly with Nim (particularly once they know the trick). It appears that, for games and puzzles, greater complexity is a desirable feature.

N.2.2 NP-Complete Puzzles

The generalizations of many popular puzzles have been shown to be NP-complete. We'll mention a few of them here.

Sudoku

Sudoku ▭ is typically played on a 9×9 grid. The goal is to complete a partially filled-in grid, such as the one shown in Figure N.2. The rules of the game require that, in any solution, each of the digits 1 through 9 must occur exactly once in each row, in each column, and in each marked 3×3 subgrid.

In order to be able to talk about the complexity of a Sudoku problem as a function of the size of its input, we generalize the standard Sudoku game to an $n \times n$ grid, where n is a perfect square. We then require that each of the numbers from 1 to n occur in each row, in each column, and in each of the n subgrids divided as above. Then, to turn the problem into a decision problem, we restate it as follows.

- SUDOKU = {<b>: b is a configuration of an $n \times n$ grid and b has a solution under the rules of Sudoku}

The problem becomes one of deciding whether a solution exists. Clearly completing the grid can be no easier than deciding whether such a completion is possible.

Sudoku is typical of a large class of one-person games or puzzles. It can be solved by a straightforward search process in which it suffices to find a single solution. In the case of Sudoku, we need to find a single way of filling in the grid that meets the requirements of the game. Of course, experts tend to do very little actual search as they exploit a variety of heuristics that prune the space of alternatives, often to the point that no search is required. Those heuristics break down, however, for larger versions of the puzzle. Whether or not heuristics work to simplify the problem some of the time, the search approach suggests a straightforward way to show that SUDOKU is in NP: It can be verified in polynomial time by a deterministic Turing machine that considers a proposed solution and simply checks that all the constraints are satisfied.

Sudoku is a variant of an older puzzle called Latin squares ▭, which considers only the row and column (but not the subgrid) constraints. The problem of deciding whether

	5			9	4	2	1	
4							8	
	3		7					
				2				4
2			4		6			8
6				3				
					8		6	
	7							3
	6	8	9	5			4	

FIGURE N.2 A game of Sudoku.

c	a	b
a	g	e
d	o	g

FIGURE N.3 A crossword grid.

an instance of an $n \times n$ Latin squares puzzle has a solution is NP-complete [Colbourn 1984]. SUDOKU has been shown [Yato 2002] to be NP-complete by reduction from the Latin squares problem.

Crossword Puzzles

Next we consider the problem of constructing a crossword puzzle. More specifically, define:

- CROSSWORD-PUZZLE-CONSTRUCTION = {<a finite set $W \subseteq \Sigma^+$ of words, an $n \times n$ matrix B, each square of which is blank or black>: it is possible to form a valid crossword puzzle by filling every blank square of B with a symbol in Σ in such a way that every contiguous string of letters, running both horizontally and vertically, is a word in W}.

For example, if n is 3, all squares of B are blank, and the list of words is age, ago, beg, cab, cad, dog, then it is possible to construct the grid shown in Figure N.3. CROSSWORD-PUZZLE-CONSTRUCTION is NP-complete. (See [Garey and Johnson 1979].)

Instant Insanity

The last example that we'll consider is the Parker Brothers® puzzle known as Instant Insanity®. The puzzle consists of a set of four plastic cubes. There is a set of four colors C, and each of the six sides of each of the cubes is painted one of the colors in C. A solution to the puzzle is an arrangement of the cubes into a single column in such a way that, on each of the four sides of the column, each color in C appears exactly once. We can describe the generalized puzzle as the language:

- INSTANT-INSANITY = {<a set B of n blocks and a set C of n colors> : the blocks in B can be stacked in a single vertical column and, on each of the four sides of the column, each color in C appears exactly once}.

INSTANT-INSANITY is NP-complete [Garey and Johnson 1979].

N.2.3 Two-Person Games

But now consider two-person games, like chess and Go (and checkers and backgammon and so forth). Suppose that we have the fragment of a game tree shown in Figure N.4. To make it easy to follow the discussion that we are about to present, we'll assume that we always evaluate moves from a single perspective. We'll pick the perspective of the first player, whom we'll call $player_1$. Let's say that, at A, it is $player_1$'s turn. $Player_1$ will consider its alternatives and attempt to find the best one. We'll call this a maximizing step. But then something different happens at the next step. $Player_2$ gets to choose a move. So suppose that $player_1$ chooses to move to C. Then $player_2$ will choose move D or E or

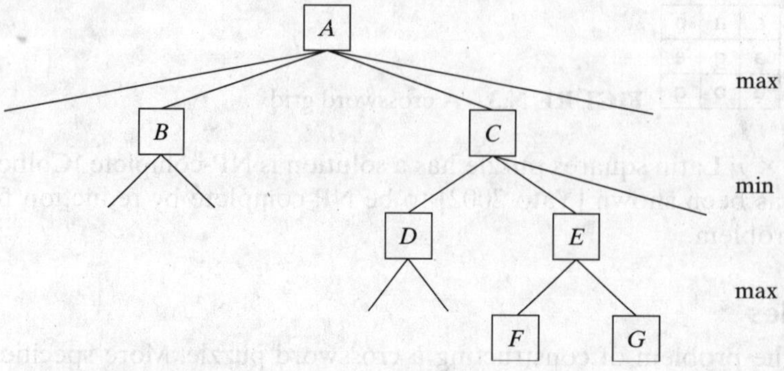

FIGURE N.4 A game tree when there are two players, a maximizer and a minimizer.

one of their alternatives. When it does so, it will choose the worst move (from $player_1$'s perspective). So we'll call this a minimizing level. Then it's $player_1$'s turn again and it will again attempt to maximize, and so forth.

Now suppose that $player_1$ is considering a proposed move sequence, say A, C, E, G. $Player_1$ can't verify that it can win by choosing to go from A to C just by examining that sequence. Maybe A, C, E, G does lead to a win. But if A, C, D leads to a loss, then $player_1$ cannot be guaranteed a win just by choosing to move to C. The problem is that the second move isn't under its control.

So CHESS is not obviously in NP since we no longer have a simple verifier for it (of the sort that we have for SUDOKU).

Another way to think about the reason that we have failed to show CHESS to be in NP is to think about a nondeterministic decider (as opposed to a deterministic verifier). Recall how a nondeterministic Turing machine works. It accepts a string iff there is *any* path that accepts. But now consider the problem of deciding whether there is a guaranteed win for $player_1$. When it is $player_1$'s turn, it suffices to find any move that is guaranteed to be a win for it. But, when it is $player_2$'s turn, it is necessary to show that *every* move that $player_2$ might choose guarantees the win we seek for $player_1$. So we can't solve the CHESS problem by (nondeterministically) finding a single path that leads to a win.

There are, however, two ways we can solve it. The first is to conduct, deterministically, a depth-first search of the tree of possible moves. Each branch ends whenever one side wins or a draw is declared. As the search backs up, it can compute win/lose/draw values for each intermediate node once the values for all of its daughter nodes are known. At each maximizing step, the win/lose/draw value is the maximum of the values of the daughter nodes. At each minimizing step, it is the minimum of those values. If the starting node gets assigned the win value, then it corresponds to a guaranteed win for $player_1$ and the algorithm will accept. Otherwise, it will reject.

Let's analyze the space complexity of this approach. The search requires $\mathcal{O}(n^2)$ space to store one board configuration. The total amount of space required to conduct the search depends on the number of moves that must be considered (and thus the depth of the search stack). Let the maximum number of moves be given by some function $f(n)$. Then conducting the depth-first search can be done in $\mathcal{O}(f(n) \cdot n^2)$ space. So what is $f(n)$? If the search process ever generates a board configuration that duplicates one that appeared earlier in the same path, the path can quit. Its options are the same the second time as they were the first time. So the length of any search path is bounded by the number of board configurations it may encounter. How many such configurations are there? That depends on exactly what we mean when we say that we generalize the game to an $n \times n$ board. If we just add board squares but do not add any pieces, then $f(n)$ is a polynomial. If we take that definition for CHESS, then it is in PSPACE. And, in that case, it can be shown to be PSPACE-complete. If, on the other hand, we make the perhaps more reasonable assumption that the number of pieces grows with n, then $f(n)$ grows exponentially with n and CHESS appears not to be in PSPACE. It is, in that case, EXPTIME-complete [Fraenkel and Lichtenstein 1981].

An analysis similar to the one that we just did for CHESS can also be applied to the game of Go. First we must generalize the standard game to a board of arbitrary size. Doing that, we can define the language:

- GO = {<b>: *b* is a configuration of an $n \times n$ Go board and there is a guaranteed win for the current player}.

GO is PSPACE-hard [Lichtenstein and Sipser 1980], so no efficient algorithm for it is likely to exist. Saying anything more precise about the computational complexity of GO is complicated by the fact that the rules of the game vary and the details of the rules appear to affect GO's complexity class. For example, using Japanese rules and the simple "ko" rule (which makes it illegal to make a move that causes the board configuration to return to its immediately preceding configuration), GO is EXPTIME-complete [Robson 1983]. Using some other rule sets, the complexity class of GO remains an open question.

It is worth noting, however, that while CHESS and GO do not appear to be in PSPACE, there are two-person games that are. They are games for which it is possible to place a polynomial bound on the number of moves that can occur in one game. So, for example, Amazons, Hex, and Othello are all PSPACE-complete.

N.2.4 Alternating Turing Machines

An alternative approach to analyzing languages like CHESS is suggested by the observation that, at alternating levels of a game search tree, we need to ask, "Is there at least one winning path from here?" and then, "Are all paths from here winning?" Define an ***alternating Turing machine*** to be a nondeterministic Turing machine with one difference: Whenever a nondeterministic choice is made, the machine specifies the condition under which it will accept. It may choose to:

- accept whenever at least one daughter path accepts, or
- accept only if all daughter paths accept.

Note that it can make different choices at different branch points. We can easily build an alternating Turing machine to decide CHESS. At maximizing levels, it suffices to find one accepting path. At minimizing levels, all paths must win.

What is the complexity of the alternating Turing machine that decides CHESS? To answer that question, we begin by defining a set of complexity classes for alternating Turing machines:

- AP (alternating polynomial time): For any language L, $L \in$ AP iff there exists some alternating Turing machine M that decides L in polynomial time.
- APSPACE (alternating polynomial space): For any language L, $L \in$ APSPACE iff there exists some alternating Turing machine M that decides L in polynomial space.
- AL (alternating logarithmic space): For any language L, $L \in$ AL iff there exists some alternating Turing machine M that decides L in logarithmic space.

A significant result is that alternation buys one complexity class [Chandra, Kozen and Stockmeyer 1981]. More specifically:

- AL = P: Alternating logarithmic space is exactly as powerful as deterministic polynomial time.
- AP = PSPACE: Alternating polynomial time is exactly as powerful as polynomial space.
- APSPACE = EXPTIME: Alternating polynomial space is exactly as powerful as exponential time.

Without assuming a polynomial bound on the number of moves that may have to be considered, we know that CHESS is EXPTIME-complete. So, given the result we just described, we can conclude that it is also APSPACE-complete. Similarly, since, using Japanese rules and the simple ko rule, GO is EXPTIME-complete, it is also APSPACE-complete.

Alternating Turing machines are more useful, however, in cases where the complexity of a problem is not already known. When the alternating Turing machine model naturally matches the structure of a problem (as it does in chess, for example), it may be easier to determine the problem's alternating Turing machine complexity than it would be to determine its complexity with respect to the standard model. But then, using the result we just described, its standard complexity class can be inferred.

N.2.5 Game Programs that Win: The Minimax Search Algorithm

So far, we have been considering ways of constructing an exact answer to the question, "Can $player_1$ win?" and we've seen that it is hard. But the analysis that we have done suggests that there may be a way to get an approximate answer and, at the same time, play a very good game of chess or checkers.

The backbone of most programs that play two-person games is the ***minimax*** algorithm (so named because it alternately minimizes and maximizes the values of the moves that are considered). In principle, *minimax* could be used to search a complete game tree, following each move sequence until it ends in a win, a loss, or a draw. In practice, however, complete trees are too large for that to be feasible. For example, Claude Shannon (mentioned above as the author of the first paper on computer chess in 1950), estimated that a typical chess game takes 40 moves (for each player) and that there is an average of about 30 choices at each point. So the total number of moves that would be examined in a complete game tree would be about $(30 \cdot 30)^{40} \approx 10^{118}$. Modern estimates put the size of a chess game tree at about 10^{123}. For comparison, the number of atoms in the observable universe is estimated to be about 10^{79}.

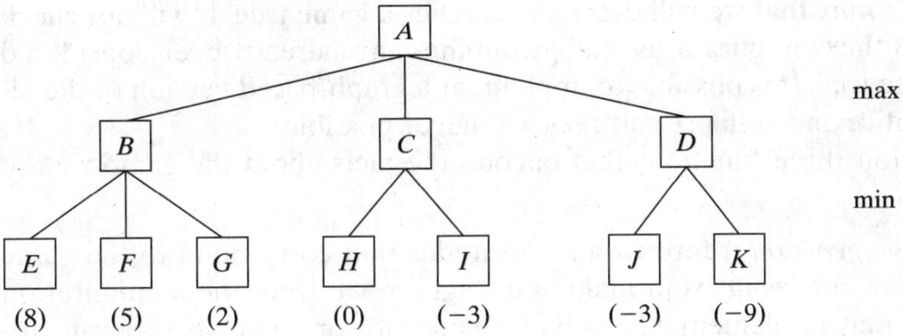

FIGURE N.5 A game tree in which a static evaluation function has been applied to each leaf node.

So practical programs look ahead as many moves (typically called ***ply***) as they can, given the time they are allotted. They examine the game configurations that result, applying to each a heuristic function, generally called a ***static evaluation function***, that measures how promising the configuration is. Then they choose a move based on those scores. When *minimax* is used in that way, it becomes a ***heuristic search*** technique of the sort described in Section 30.3. Like other heuristic search algorithms, it is an approximation technique. It isn't guaranteed to return an optimal result. But optimality isn't generally required in games. It suffices to find a move that is *good enough to win*.

To see how *minimax* works, consider the two-ply search tree shown in Figure N.5. Below each leaf node is shown the value of the static evaluation function applied to that node. We will assume that all evaluations are done from the perspective of $player_1$, whose turn it is to move from position *A*. High scores are good for $player_1$.

The job of *minimax* is to generate this tree and to apply the static evaluation function to each leaf node. Then it must propagate scores upward so that it can make the optimal choice from position *A*. Positions *E*, *F*, and *G* send their scores up to *B*. Since the player who chooses from position *A* is a maximizing player, the player who chooses from *B* is a minimizer, who will choose to go to *G*, which makes *B*'s score 2. Positions *H* and *I* send their scores up to *C*. Again, this is a minimizing level, so the choice from *C* is *I* and *C*'s score becomes −3. Positions *J* and *K* send their scores up to *D*, whose score becomes −9. From *A*, then, there is a choice of three moves: *B* (with a score of 2), *C* (with a score of −3), and *D* (with a score of −9). From *A*, the maximizing player will choose *B*, which sets *A*'s score to 2. Figure N.6 shows the tree after all scores have been propagated.

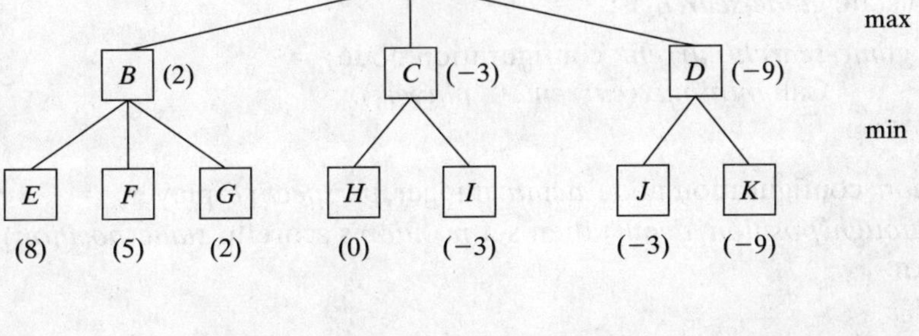

FIGURE N.6 A game tree in which values have been propagated up the tree.

The version of *minimax* that we will describe searches a game tree. It will not check to see whether any of the configurations that it examines have already been considered somewhere else in the tree. It is possible to implement a graph-based version of the algorithm that does notice and collapse subtrees whenever possible.

Minimax will exploit three functions that encode the facts about the game we are playing:

- The function *move-gen*(*node*) returns a set of nodes that correspond to the game configurations that can result from making a single move from the configuration stored at *node*. It may implement a legal move generator or it may incorporate additional heuristic information and generate only moves that appear plausible from the current position.
- The function *static*(*node*) returns the result of applying a static evaluation function to the configuration contained in *node*. For chess, for example, *static* might be a measure of piece advantage, mobility, and control of the center. We will define *static* so that it always evaluates from the perspective of $player_1$.
- The function *deep-enough*(*node*, *depth-so-far*) returns *True* if the path that currently ends at *node* is as deep as we want to go in the search and *False* otherwise. In its simplest form, *deep-enough* just counts to some fixed depth limit and then returns *True*. In more sophisticated implementations, it considers additional factors. For example, it's not a good idea to stop searching at a point that is likely to be half-way through a piece exchange.

Each node of the tree that *minimax* explores will have three fields: *position* (a description of a game configuration), *score* (if it is known), and *best-successor* (if one is known).

A straightforward way to describe *minimax* is as a recursive procedure. To choose a move from position *A*, *minimax* will invoke *move-gen*(*A*). Then it will call itself on each of the resulting nodes. Whenever a branch gets deep enough, *static* will evaluate its final node and the resulting value will be passed back up to the parent node. If *minimax* is called from the perspective of a maximizing player, then each call it makes on successor nodes will bc from the perspective of a minimizing player, and vice versa. *Minimax* will not return a value. Its job, given *A*, is to fill in *A*'s *score*. And, unless *A* is at the last ply of the search tree, it must also fill in *A*'s *best-successor*.

To implement these ideas, we'll define a procedure, *game-search*, whose job is to create the first invocation of *minimax*. *Game-search* can be called with a starting game configuration, or it can be called at any point during a game, in which case it is given the current configuration as input. It calls *minimax* with its input configuration, a *depth* (so far) count of 0, and a *perspective*, that of $player_1$. When *game-search* ends, *best-successor* of the starting node will be filled in with the move that should be chosen (if there is one). We can state *game-search* as:

game-search(*current*: configuration node) =
Call *minimax*(*current*, 0, $player_1$).

Then *minimax* is:

minimax(*position*: configuration node, *depth*: integer, *perspective*: player) =

1. If *deep-enough*(*position*, *depth*) then set *position*'s score to *static*(*position*) and return.

2. Set *successors* to the set returned by *move-gen(position)*.
3. If *successors* is empty then there aren't any moves to make so set *position*'s score to *static(position)* and return.
4. If *successors* is not empty then examine them and choose the best. To do this, do:

    4.1. For each element *move* of *successors* do: /* Fill in a *score* for *move*.

    Call *minimax*(*move*, $depth + 1$, *opposite*(*perspective*)).

    4.2. Considering the scores of all the moves in *successors*:

    If $perspective = player_1$, set *chosen* to an element of *successors* with the highest *score*.

    If $perspective = player_2$, set *chosen* to an element of *successors* with the lowest *score*.

5. Set *position*'s *score* to the *score* of *chosen*.
6. Set *position*'s *best-successor* to *chosen*.

Heuristic information plays an important role in *minimax* since it enables the algorithm to choose a move without having to search all the way to the end of the game. And it's possible also that heuristics are embedded in *move-gen*. But *minimax* is still required to search all the subtrees that *move-gen* creates.

Now recall *A**, the heuristic search algorithm that we introduced in Section 30.3.2. It exploits heuristic information that enables it to ignore large parts of its search space. We'd like a way for *minimax* to do the same thing. For example, look again at the game tree of Figure N.6. Once the subtree rooted at *B* has been examined, *minimax* knows that $player_1$, a maximizer, is guaranteed a move, *B*, with a score of 2. But it continues and looks at the alternatives in hopes of doing better. It considers *C* next, and first notices that *C* has the successor *H*, whose score is 0. At this point, without looking at any of *H*'s alternatives, $player_2$, a minimizer, knows that it is guaranteed that *C*'s score can be made no higher than 0. $Player_1$ already knows it can get a 2 from *B*. So it can decide immediately that it won't go to *C*. It doesn't have to examine *I* or any other successors that *C* might have. We'll call 2 an ***alpha cutoff***. It corresponds to the lower bound that a maximizing player can count on. Of course, in our simple example, using an alpha cutoff lets us skip expanding just a single node. But suppose that the search were going to eight ply. Then using the cutoff would save expanding a possibly large subtree under *I*. Next, notice that, if we extend the tree another ply, we can see that it is possible to exploit a second threshold, which we'll call a ***beta cutoff***. It corresponds to the upper bound that a minimizing player can count on.

The ***minimax-with-α-β-pruning*** algorithm takes advantage of the *alpha* and *beta* cutoffs that we have just described. To see how it works, consider the game tree shown in Figure N.7. The choice of a move from *D* is made by a maximizing player, so *D* gets a score of 5, which is passed back to *B*. The minimizing player who chooses from *B* is thus guaranteed a score of ≤5. So *beta* is set to 5 and passed down to *E*. The choice from *E* is made by a maximizing player. *J* gets a score of 7, which is passed back to *E*. *E* is thus guaranteed a score of ≥7. But the *beta* value at *E* is 5, corresponding to the fact

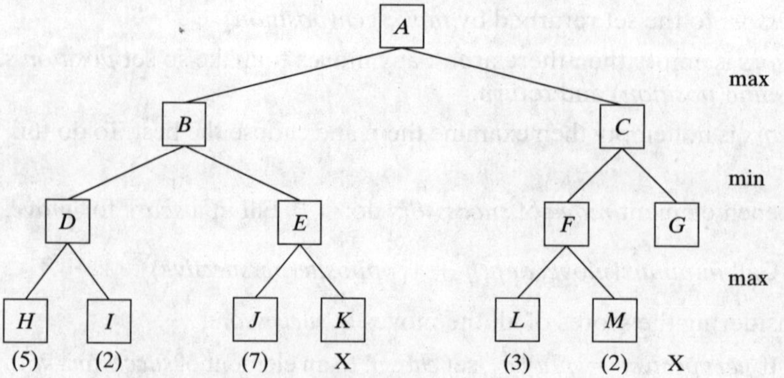

FIGURE N.7 A deeper game tree, in which *alpha* and *beta* cutoffs can be used.

that the minimizing player above *E* is guaranteed a score of no more than 5 by going to *D*. Because $7 > 5$, a *beta* cutoff occurs and the rest of the successors of *E* need not be considered because the move from *B* to *E* will never be chosen.

At this point, we know that *B*'s score is 5 and it is passed back up to *A*. So we know that *A* is guaranteed a score of ≥ 5. That becomes the value of *alpha*. It is passed down to *C*. The choice at *F* is made by a maximizing player, so *F*'s score becomes 3. It is passed up to *C*. So *C* is now guaranteed a score of ≤ 3. But *A* is guaranteed a score (as reflected in *alpha*) of at least 5 by going to *B*. Because $3 < 5$, an *alpha* cutoff occurs and the rest of the successors of *C* can be ignored because the move from *A* to *C* will never be chosen.

Summarizing, we see that *alpha* cutoffs correspond to guarantees for maximizing players. They get set (to reflect the best option so far) at maximizing levels and they get used to cut off search at minimizing levels. Similarly, *beta* cutoffs correspond to guarantees for minimizing players. They get set at minimizing levels and they get used to cut off search at maximizing levels. Both cutoffs must be provided at both levels.

The order in which moves are examined now matters. So we will let *move-gen* return an ordered list, rather than a set, of moves.

As before, we'll assume that the player to movc first is a maximizing player. Since no information is available yet, *alpha* at the top node starts out as the minimum value that *static* can compute. Similarly, *beta* at the top node starts out as the maximum value that static can compute. We can describe *game-search-α-β* and *minimax-with-α-β* as follows:

game-search-α-β(current: configuration node) =

1. Return *minimax-with-α-β(current*,
   0,
   $player_1$,
   minimum value *static* can compute,
   maximum value *static* can compute).

minimax-with-α-β(position: configuration node, *depth*: integer, *perspective*: player, *alpha*, *beta*: integers) =

1. If *deep-enough*(*position*, *depth*) then set *position*'s score to *static*(*position*) and return.

2. Set *successors* to the list returned by *move-gen(position)*.
3. If *successors* is empty then (there aren't any moves to make so) set *position*'s *score* to *static(position)* and return.
4. If *successors* is not empty and perspective $=$ $player_1$ (maximizing) then do:
   - **4.1.** Set *chosen* to the first element of *successors*.
   - **4.2.** Do the following for each element *move* of *successors*, stopping if a cutoff occurs:

     Call *minimax(move, depth* + 1, *opposite(perspective), alpha, beta)*.

     If *move*'s *score* > *chosen*'s *score* then set *chosen* to *move*.

     If *move's score* ≥ *beta* then all other elements of *successors* can be skipped. Cut off and exit the loop.

     If *move*'s *score* > *alpha* then set *alpha* to *move*'s *score*.
5. If *successors* is not empty and *perspective* $=$ $player_2$ (minimizing) then do:
   - **5.1.** Set *chosen* to the first element of *successors*.
   - **5.2.** Do the following for each element *move* of *successors*, stopping if a cutoff occurs:

     Call *minimax(move, depth* + 1, *opposite(perspective), alpha, beta)*.

     If *move*'s *score* < *chosen*'s *score* then set *chosen* to *move*.

     If *move's score* ≤ *alpha* then all other elements of *successors* can be skipped. Cut off and exit the loop.

     If *move*'s *score* < *beta* then set *beta* to *move*'s *score*.
6. Set *position*'s *score* to the *score* of *chosen*.
7. Set *position*'s *best-successor* to *chosen*.

The difference in performance between *minimax* and *minimax-with-*α-β depends on the order in which moves are considered. If the best moves are considered last, *minimax-with-*α-β cannot prune any subtrees. It gets its best performance when the best moves are always considered first. Of course, if we always knew the best move before we searched the tree, we wouldn't need to search at all. But it is possible to use heuristics, such as the function *static*, to make informed guesses about the order in which to consider moves. Without using *alpha-beta* cutoffs, *minimax* must search $\mathcal{O}(b^n)$, nodes, where b is the average branching factor of the tree and n is the depth of the search. If the best move is always considered first, then *minimax-with-*α-β searches $\mathcal{O}(b^{n/2})$ nodes [Knuth and Moore 1975]. So, in a fixed amount of time, it can search to twice the depth that *minimax* can.

Neither heuristic search nor the use of cutoffs alters the fact that games like chess and go are hard, as suggested by the fact that their generalizations are EXPTIME-complete. But a chess-playing program has beaten a reigning world champion. No Go-playing program has yet come close to doing that. Why does Go appear harder than chess? The answer is that constants do sometimes matter. There came a time when there existed exactly enough computing power to search a chess game tree fast enough to win some games against a champion. The game trees for Go (which is typically played on a 19 by 19 board) are bushier and deeper than those in chess. And it is much harder to evaluate a Go position that isn't yet a win or a loss and determine how likely it is to turn into one. So there is not yet enough computing power to enable a program to win a championship match. Of course, people can't search any faster than a computer can. In fact, they search a lot slower. This suggests that the way to build a winning Go program is to look for approaches that rely less on search and more on particular patterns and heuristics that are crafted especially to the game. Research on Go is focused on doing exactly that.

N.3 Interactive Video Games

Three of the techniques that we have discussed in this book are widely used in the construction of interactive computer games. We'll mention each of them briefly, but there is much more that could be said 💻. For a more comprehensive discussion of these and other techniques, see any good book, such as [Champandard 2004], on the role of artificial intelligence in game development.

N.3.1 Finite State Machines

Finite state machines are used in a variety of ways to define the behavior of interactive games. In P.4, we mention one example, the use of an FSM to describe the behavior of a soccer-playing robot. In this section, we'll mention another.

Many interactive games are structured as finite state machines. Often they are deterministic machines. The advantage of DFSMs is that they are predictable. This means that human players can learn how the games work and so can improve their performance relative to the machines. Other games use nondeterministic FSMs. Their advantage is that they are unpredictable. So they create more plausible opponents and are thus more appealing to play.

In either case, the states of the machine correspond to situations, typically ones in which an agent is doing (or not doing) something. The inputs to the machine correspond to events. But, just like the single characters that are the inputs to the simple language-recognizing machines we have been building, the inputs that correspond to game events can be represented by a finite set of symbols. The job of FSMs, when used in this context, is not to decide a language but rather to describe the behavior of the game. So, properly, we should say that we are using finite state transducers rather than machines. That terminology is, however, rarely used in this context.

In Figure N.8, we show a toy example. In most real games, the nonplayer characters (NPCs) are controlled by a set of FSMs, each of which describes one aspect of behavior. For example, one might be responsible for weapon selection, one might choose a target, and a third might control movement. In addition, realistic applications often exploit probabilities associated with the transitions. In such machines, each of a set of competing transitions is chosen with the probability that is attached to it.

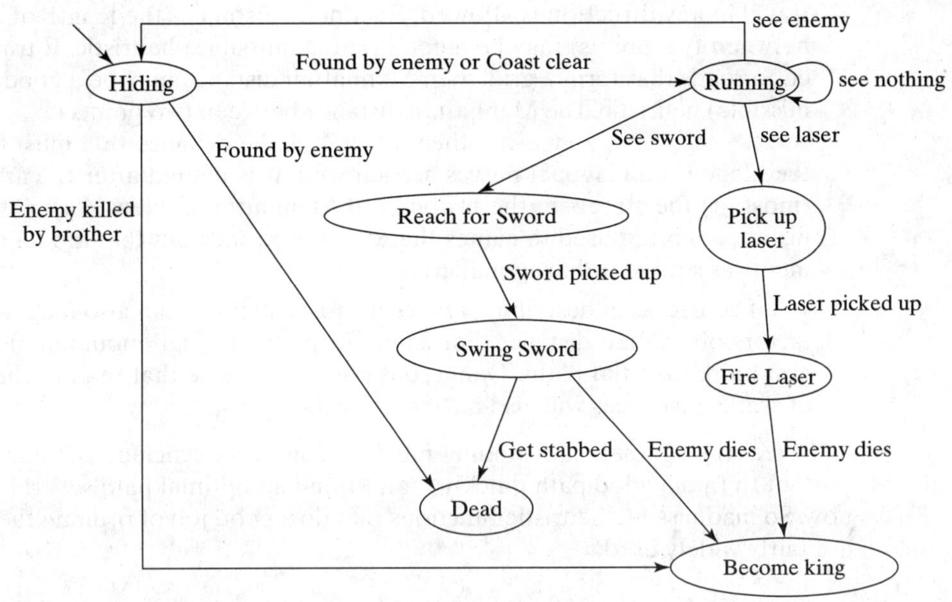

FIGURE N.8 A finite state model of a game character.

N.3.2 Heuristic Search and the *A** Algorithm

Consider the problem of computing the movements of the nonplayer characters (NPCs) in an interactive game. One very simple approach to solving this problem is just to let the characters move in what appears to be the correct direction and hope that they don't run into obstacles. Generally a better approach is to plan a route in advance, taking advantage of maps and other terrain information.

Because paths are being computed in real time, as a game is being played, we want an efficient algorithm for computing the best path to be followed for each player. The A^* algorithm, as described in Section 30.3.2, is widely used to do this 💻.

Recall that the A^* algorithm implements a kind of heuristic search. It makes use of two sorts of cost information:

- The costs that are associated with each of the operators that generate new states: In the game environment, the simplest way to define these costs is the actual distance traveled. If we do that, we'll find the shortest path from the current state to a goal. But other factors besides distance can be added. For example, moves that go through dangerous territory can be assigned higher cost than moves that go through areas that are known to be safe. Moves that reveal to the enemy our knowledge of the terrain can be assigned higher costs than moves that give nothing away, and so forth.
- Estimates of future costs, as provided by the heuristic function: These are guesses about how much it will cost to move from the current state to a goal. The simplest way to make such estimates is to use some kind of geometric distance. If

travel in any direction is allowed, Euclidean distance (the length of a straight line between two points) may be a good (and admissible) heuristic. If travel is restricted to roads that form a grid, then Manhattan distance may be a good (and also admissible) heuristic. The Manhattan distance between two points (x_1, y_1) and (x_2, y_2) is $|x_1 - x_2| + |y_1 - y_2|$. In other words, it is the distance that must be traveled in the plane if no diagonal moves are allowed. It is named after the arrangement of (most of) the streets in the borough of Manhattan in New York City. Manhattan distance is often used in games that don't use roads but that model their environments as square or hexagonal grids.

Of course, as in describing real costs, cost estimates can also include estimates of factors other than distance. For example, paths through mountainous terrain may cost more than flat paths. Dangerous paths and those that require the expenditure of scarce resources will also have high cost.

In real-time games, path-finding must be done very efficiently. It may be more important to find a good path quickly than to find an optimal path several minutes from now. So inadmissible heuristic functions that do a good job of pruning the search space are fairly widely used.

N.3.3 Rule-Based Systems that Control NPCs in Interactive Games

In M.3, we sketched the origin of rule-based systems as descendants of one of the earliest formal models of computation. We also described their basic architecture. Rule-based systems (or RBSs) deserve mention in the context of game development because they have proved to be useful for describing the behavior of non-player characters (NPCs) in interactive games. Rules can be used to define a variety of kinds of behaviors. For example, they can be used for problem solving, in much the same way they are used by expert systems. There might, for instance, be rules such as:

If: The laser is gone,
Then: Someone else has it.

If: It is night and the power is out,
Then: The enemy cannot see me.

Rules can also be used to define behaviors, again in much the same way in which they are used in expert systems. There might, for instance, be rules such as:

If: I have just hit a wall,
Then: Turn to the right and keep walking.

If: A grenade has just been thrown,
Then: Duck.

If: I have a shotgun and I do not have ammunition for a shotgun,
Then: Find ammunition.

Rule-based systems of varying degrees of sophistication are being used to build NPCs. Simple systems consist of sets of rules such as the ones we just described. Another approach is to start with SOAR (described in M.3.2), a comprehensive, rule-based cognitive architecture whose goal is to model human behavior. The idea is that agents based on SOAR will exhibit convincingly human-level behavior.

APPENDIX O

Applications: Using Regular Expressions

Patterns are everywhere. Regular expressions describe patterns. So it's easy to see that regular expressions could be useful in a wide variety of applications. We have already discussed some important uses of regular expressions, including the description of lexical analyzers that are used by context-free parsers and the description of protein motifs that are to be matched against protein sequence databases. In Q.1.2, we'll describe their use in defining XML document types. In this appendix, we briefly highlight the use of regular expressions in programming environments and, more broadly, in computer system tools.

A quick look through the manuals for many programming languages (such as Perl, Python, and Java), as well as systems utilities (such as the Unix file searching program grep or the mailing list management system Majordomo), will turn up a chapter on regular expressions (or "regexes"). But we must be careful. While these systems share a name and some syntax with the pattern language that we described in Chapter 6 and they were certainly inspired by that language, they are, both formally and practically, quite different. In these systems, it is possible, as we'll see below, to write regular expressions that describe languages that are not regular. The added power comes from the presence of variables, whose values may be strings of arbitrary length.

For example, consider the regular expression language that is supported in Perl. Table O.1 shows some of the most important constants and operators in that language. Notice that all of the operators that exist in the regular expression language of Chapter 6 are present here, although union is represented differently. Some new operators, such as replication, word boundary, and nonword boundary, are simply convenient shorthands for patterns that can easily be written in our original language. Much of the rest of the syntax is necessary because of the large character set, including nonprinting characters, that may occur in real texts. But the most important difference between the two languages is the ability to assign a value to a variable. Then the variable can be used in a pattern and we can require that it match the same substring each time it occurs.

Table O.1 Regular expressions in Perl.

Syntax	Name	Description
abc	Concatenation	Matches a, then b, then c, where a, b, and c are any regexs
a|b|c	Union (Or)	Matches a or b or c, where a, b, and c are any regexs
a*	Kleene star	Matches 0 or more a's, where a is any regex
a+	At least one	Matches 1 or more a's, where a is any regex
a?		Matches 0 or 1 a's, where a is any regex
a{n, m}	Replication	Matches at least n but no more than m a's, where a is any regex
a*?	Parsimonious	Turns off greedy matching so the shortest match is selected
a+?	"	"
.	Wild card	Matches any character except newline
^	Left anchor	Anchors the match to the beginning of a line or string
$	Right anchor	Anchors the match to the end of a line or string
[a-z]		Assuming a collating sequence, matches any single character in range
[^a-z]		Assuming a collating sequence, matches any single character not in range
\d	Digit	Matches any single digit, i.e., string in [0-9]
\D	Nondigit	Matches any single nondigit character, i.e., [^ 0-9]
\w	Alphanumeric	Matches any single "word" character, i.e., [a-zA-Z0-9]
\W	Nonalphanumeric	Matches any character in [^a-zA-Z0-9]
\s	White space	Matches any character in [space, tab, newline, etc.]
\S	Nonwhite space	Matches any character not matched by \s
\n	Newline	Matches newline
\r	Return	Matches return
\t	Tab	Matches tab
\f	Formfeed	Matches formfeed
\b	Backspace	Matches backspace inside []
\b	Word boundary	Matches a word boundary outside []
\B	Nonword boundary	Matches a non-word boundary
\0	Null	Matches a null character
\nnn	Octal	Matches an ASCII character with octal value nnn
\xnn	Hexadecimal	Matches an ASCII character with hexadecimal value nn
\cX	Control	Matches an ASCII control character
\char	Quote	Matches char; used to quote symbols such as . and \
(a)	Store	Matches a, where a is any regex, and stores the matched string in the next variable
\1	Variable	Matches whatever the first parenthesized expression matched
\2		Matches whatever the second parenthesized expression matched
...		For all remaining variables

It is possible to write many useful regular expressions without exploiting variables, as we can see in the next two examples:

EXAMPLE O.1 Spam Detection

The following regular expression matches the subject field of at least some email messages that are likely to be spam:

```
\badv\ (?ert\) ?\b
```

EXAMPLE O.2 Email Addresses

The following regular expression scans text looking for valid email addresses:

```
\b[A-Za-z0-9_%-]+@[A-Za-z0-9_%-]+(\.[A-Za-z]+){1,4}\b
```

But, using variables, it is possible to do things that would not be possible without them, as we can see in the next two examples.

EXAMPLE O.3 WW

Recall the language WW = $\{ww : w \in \{\texttt{a}, \texttt{b}\}^*\}$. The following regular expression matches all and only strings in WW:

```
^([ab]*)\1$
```

The pattern `[ab]*` can match any string of a's and b's. Whatever it matches is stored in the variable `1` (because `[ab]*` is the first pattern in parentheses in the expression). Then `\1` will match a second occurrence of the same string of a's and b's. The anchors `^` and `$` force the pattern to start at the beginning of the target string and end at the end of it. So this pattern matches all and only strings in WW.

EXAMPLE O.4 Finding Duplicated Words

Suppose that we want to proof read some text that we are writing. One common error is to duplicate a simple word like `the`. The following regular expression matches duplicated words:

```
\b([A-Za-z]+)\s+\1\b
```

By using variables, it is possible to define languages that are not regular. This means that it is no longer possible to compile an arbitrary regular expression into a deterministic finite state machine that can decide whether the expression matches against an input string. While every deterministic finite state machine runs in time that is linear in the length of its input, we cannot make this claim for a regex matcher when variables are allowed. In fact, it can be shown that regular expression matching in Perl (where variables are allowed) is NP-hard. To see why search may be required, consider again the regex of Example 46.3. When it is attempting to match against a string w, it may have to try each position in w as it searches for a place to stop matching `[ab]*` and start matching `\1`.

Most regular expression languages, including the one we just described in Perl, support not just string matching but also string manipulation. For example, it is easy to write a Perl expression that works like a production in a Post system (see Section 18.2.4). The first part of the expression defines a pattern to be matched and the second part describes a string that should be substituted for the matched substring. The Perl syntax for string substitution is:

$$\$variable = \sim \textsf{s}/\textit{regex}/\textit{result}/;$$

When such a command is executed, the first substring in *\$variable* that matches *regex* will be replaced by *result*. If the symbol `g` (for global) is inserted after the last /, all instances of *regex* will be replaced by *result*.

EXAMPLE O.5 Deleting Duplicated Words

Continuing with the duplicated word example, we might want to write a substitution command that deletes the second occurrence of any duplicated word (plus the white space in between the words). We could do that, assuming a text string in `$text`, as follows:

```
$text =~ s/\b([A-Za-z]+)\s+\1\b/\1/g;
```

EXAMPLE O.6 A Simple Chatbot

Regular expression substitution can be used to build a simple chatbot. For example, suppose that whenever the user types an expression of the form *<phrase1>* `is` *<phrase2>*, we want our chatbot to reply with the expression `Why is` *<phrase1><phrase2>*? So, on input, "The food there is awful," our chatbot would reply, "Why is the food there awful?" We could do this, again assuming that the input text is stored in the variable `$text`, as follows:

```
$text =~ s/^ ([A-Za-z]+)\sis\s([A-Za-z]+)\.?$/Why is \1 \2?/;
```

APPENDIX P

Applications: Using Finite State Machines and Transducers

In this appendix, we illustrate some examples of early (i.e., before the advent of modern computers in the middle of the 20th century) finite state machines. Then we consider some current applications of FSMs.

P.1 Finite State Machines Predate Computers

The history of finite state machines (also called finite state automata) substantially predates the history of anything we would now call a "computer". The Oxford English Dictionary [OED 1989] lists the following among its definitions of the word, "automaton":

> 3. A piece of mechanism having its motive power so concealed that it appears to move spontaneously; 'a machine that has within itself the power of motion under conditions fixed for it, but not by it' (W. B. Carpenter). In 17–18th c. applied to clocks, watches, etc., and transf. to the Universe and World; now usually to figures which simulate the action of living beings, as clock-work mice, images which strike the hours on a clock, etc.

Automata, in this sense, have fascinated people for millennia.

P.1.1 The Antikythera Mechanism

The Antikythera Mechanism, built in Greece around 80 BC, is perhaps the earliest known example of a sophisticated mechanical automaton. Crafted in bronze, it contained at least 30 precision gears inside a wooden case that was covered with writing. It was discovered in 1901, as part of a shipwreck off the Greek island of Antikythera.

FIGURE P.1 A fragment of the Antikythera Mechanism.

After about 2,000 years under water, the device is fragmented and corroded, as can be seen from the photograph in Figure P.1. Thus its exact function is unclear.

It appears, however, to have been an astronomical calculator that was substantially more sophisticated than any others that are known to have been built for at least another 1,000 years. Using modern techniques, researchers have been able to analyze the mechanism and to build a model that describes a likely hypothesis for how the mechanism worked. Figure P.2 (a) shows a front view of that model; Figure P.2 (b) shows a rear view.

P.1.2 The Prague Orloj

Another spectacular example of an early automaton is the Prague orloj, shown in Figure P.3(a). The orloj is an astronomical clock mounted on a wall of the old town city hall. The original clock was built in 1410. At that point, it consisted of just an astronomical

(a) (b)

FIGURE P.2 Two views of a modern reconstruction of the Antikythera Mechanism.

(a) (b)

FIGURE P.3 The Prague orloj.

dial, whose state was controlled by three gears (with 365, 366 and 379 cogs) on the same axle. The state of the dial represented the positions of the sun, the moon, and the stars. Later, a calendar dial was added beneath the original one. Later still, three sets of figures were added:

- A set of four figures that represent threats to the city: a skeleton representing death, a Turk, a miser, and vanity. While these figures do not move, they do have moving parts. They are shown, next to the original astronomical dial, in Figure P.3(b).
- A set of four figures that represent virtues: an angel, a chronicler, a philosopher, and an astronomer. These figures do not move at all.
- The twelve Apostles.

As the hour is about to chime, the skeleton tolls the bell. Then the Apostles parade through two small doors above the original dial. Then, as the clock chimes, the Turk shakes his head, the miser watches his bag of money, and vanity admires itself in the mirror.

The Prague orlog, as well as other early mechanical clocks, is typical of a simple class of finite automata that accept no input except the passage of time.

FIGURE P.4 An abacus.

P.1.3 The Abacus

The abacus, shown in Figure P.4, on the other hand, does accept input. In one form or another, the abacus has been in use for over 2,000 years. It is a computer whose inputs (bead movements) correspond to the steps required to perform a calculation and whose state corresponds to the result of performing the calculation.

Modern computers are, in some sense, finite state devices, since the actual universe (or at least the part of it that we can observe) does not contain an infinite number of molecules that could be used to encode memory. But we model them as Turing machines because there is no *a priori* upper bound on the amount of memory. New tapes or disks can always be provided. But the abacus is different. When an abacus is built, the largest number it can record is fixed. So it truly is a finite state computer.

P.1.4 Programmable Automata and the Jacquard Loom

A loom is a finite state machine whose states correspond to configurations of the warp threads. A weaver works a loom by throwing a shuttle, wound with the weft threads, back and forth through the warp. By raising and lowering the warp threads, the weaver can create a pattern. The shuttle will fly below all raised warp threads and above all lowered ones. A simple pattern can be created from a two state machine: In the first state, all the even numbered threads are raised. The shuttle is thrown, and then the machine enters the second state, in which only the odd numbered threads are raised. The shuttle is thrown and the machine returns to state one.

But more intricate patterns require long sequences of states, in each of which a carefully selected set of warp threads has been raised. Since a loom may be required to weave one pattern one week and a different pattern another week, the patterns cannot be built into the loom itself. It must be programmable.

During the 18th century, weavers tried various techniques, other than by hand, for raising and lowering the warp threads. In 1801, Joseph Marie Jacquard created the loom that bears his name. An example of a Jacquard loom is shown in Figure P.5. Jacquard's idea was to encode each pattern as a loop of punched cards. Each card encoded one row of the pattern. The cards passed by a set of pins, which could go through the card in the positions of the holes. Each hole controlled a hook, which was attached to one or more warp threads. If the hook was raised, it pulled up the warp threads to which it was attached.

FIGURE P.5 A Jacquard loom.

Each loop of cards defines a specific finite state machine with *n* states, where *n* is the number of cards in the loop. Every such machine has an input alphabet that consists of the single symbol `next`, which is executed by the weaver after each time the shuttle is thrown. Each time it gets the `next` signal, the loom moves from one state (warp configuration) to the next.

P.2 The Towers of Hanoi: Regular Doesn't Always Mean Tractable

The Towers of Hanoi problem 💻 was invented by François Édouard Anatole Lucas, who published it in 1883 under the name of M. Claus. To solve the problem, it is required to move a stack of disks from one pole to another while obeying a couple of simple rules. An example of a starting configuration is shown in Figure P.6.

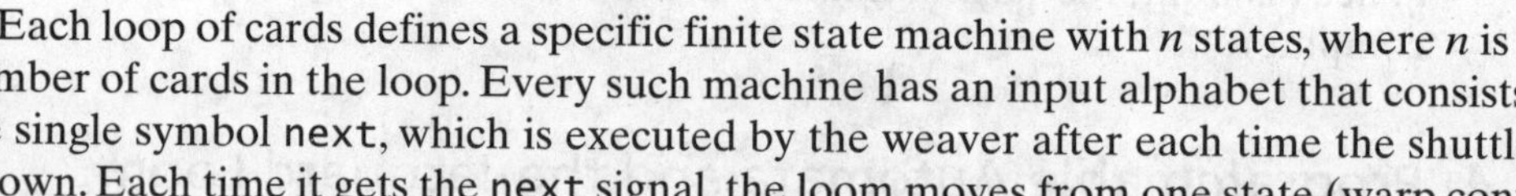

FIGURE P.6 The Towers of Hanoi.

Various stories have been created to go along with the problem. One version is the following:

> In a monastery in India there are three poles and 64 golden disks, each of a different diameter. When God created the universe, he stacked the disks on the first of the poles, with the largest on the bottom. The remaining disks were stacked in order of size, with the smallest on the top. The monks were given the task of moving all 64 disks to the last pole. But the disks are sacred, so there are important rules that must be followed. Whenever a disk is removed from a pole, it must immediately be placed on some other pole. No disks may be placed on the ground or held. Further, a disk may never be placed on top of a smaller disk. The monks were told that they must begin working immediately, taking turns around the clock. When they finish, the world will end.

It is, in principle, possible for the monks to accomplish this task. The following simple procedure solves an arbitrary Towers of Hanoi problem with n disks:

towersofHanoi(n: positive integer) =

1. If $n = 1$ then move the disk to the goal pole.
2. Else:

   2.1. Move the top $n - 1$ disks to the pole that is neither the current one nor the goal.

   2.2. Move the bottom disk to the goal pole.

   2.3. Move the $n - 1$ disks that were just set aside to the goal pole.

Fortunately, even if the story of the monks and the end of the world is true, no one need worry. Using the procedure that we just described, it will take the monks $2^{64} - 1$ moves to accomplish the task. So, at one move per second, it would take 584,542,046,090 years, 228 days, 15 hours, 14 minutes, 45 seconds. That's approximately $6 \cdot 10^{11}$ years. The universe, on the other hand, has existed for probably about $12 \cdot 10^9$ years (since the Big Bang).

Of course, this analysis assumes that the monks cannot find a more efficient strategy. They might, quite reasonably, look for a nonrecursive solution. People are quite bad at maintaining recursion stacks in their heads. So imagine the three poles arranged in a circle (whether they actually are or not). Then let's say that the "next" pole is the next one in clockwise order and the "previous" pole is the previous one, again in clockwise order. A clever monk might come up with the following solution:

towersofHanoicircle(n: positive integer) =

1. Move the smallest disk to the next pole.
2. Until all disks form a single stack on some pole other than the starting one do:

   2.1. Make the only legal move that does not involve the smallest disk.

   2.2. Move the smallest disk to the next pole.

If the number of disks is odd, this technique will move all of the disks from the starting pole to the next one. If the number of disks is even, it will move all of the disks from the starting pole to the previous one.

This technique seems quite different from the first. It can easily be implemented, even by a child, for small values of n. But it actually requires exactly the same number of moves as does the recursive technique. And no better technique exists.

So the shortest solution to the 64-disk problem is very long. Nevertheless, the system of poles and disks can easily be modeled as a nondeterministic finite state machine. The start state is the one in which all 64 disks are stacked on the first pole. The accepting state is the one in which all 64 disks are stacked properly on the goal pole. Because there is a finite number of disks and the position of each disk can be uniquely described by naming one of the three poles, the number of distinct states of the system, and thus of the machine we'll build to model it, is finite. Finite but not tractable: This system has 3^{64} states (because each of the 64 disks can be on any one of the three poles). The transitions of the machine correspond to the legal moves (i.e., those that satisfy the rule that all disks must be on a pole and that no disk may be on top of a smaller one). Each transition can be labeled with one of six symbols: 12 (meaning that the top disk from pole 1 is removed and placed on pole 2), 13, 21, 23, 31, and 32. To make the machine as simple as possible, we have left out transitions that pick up a disk and put it right back in the same place.

We can define the Towers of Hanoi language to be the set of strings that correspond to move sequences that take the system from its start state to its accepting state. The Towers of Hanoi language is regular because it is accepted by the Towers of Hanoi FSM as we just described it. And it is infinite, since there is no limit to the number of times a disk can be moved between poles. But the shortest string in the language has length $2^{64} - 1$ (namely the length of the optimal sequence of moves that solves the problem).

P.3 The Arithmetic Logic Unit (ALU)

In most computer chip designs, the ALU performs the fundamental operations of integer arithmetic, Boolean logic, and shifting. The ALU's operation can be modeled as a finite state transducer, using either a Moore machine (in which outputs are associated with states) or a Mealy machine (in which outputs are associated with transitions).

P.3.1 An Adder

As an example, consider a simple binary adder, shown in Figure P.7. Two numbers can be added by adding their digits right to left. So we can describe an adder as a Mealy machine whose input is a stream of pairs of binary digits (one digit from each of the two numbers to be added). The machine has two states, one of which corresponds to a carry-in bit of 0 and the other of which corresponds to a carry-in bit of 1. When the machine is reset, it enters the state corresponding to no carry (i.e., a carry-in bit of 0). This simple one-bit adder can be embedded into a larger system that adds numbers of any fixed number of bits.

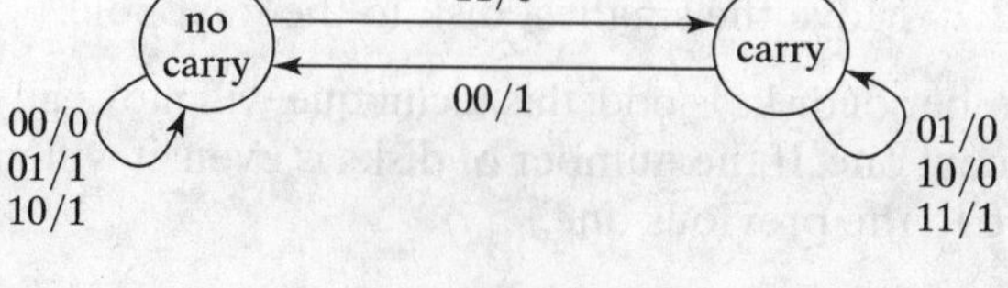

FIGURE P.7
A binary adder.

P.3.2 A Multiplier

Binary adders can also be used as building blocks for binary multipliers. Figure P.8 shows a schematic diagram that describes the behavior of an 8-bit multiplier. The multiplier can be implemented as the finite state transducer shown in Figure P.9.

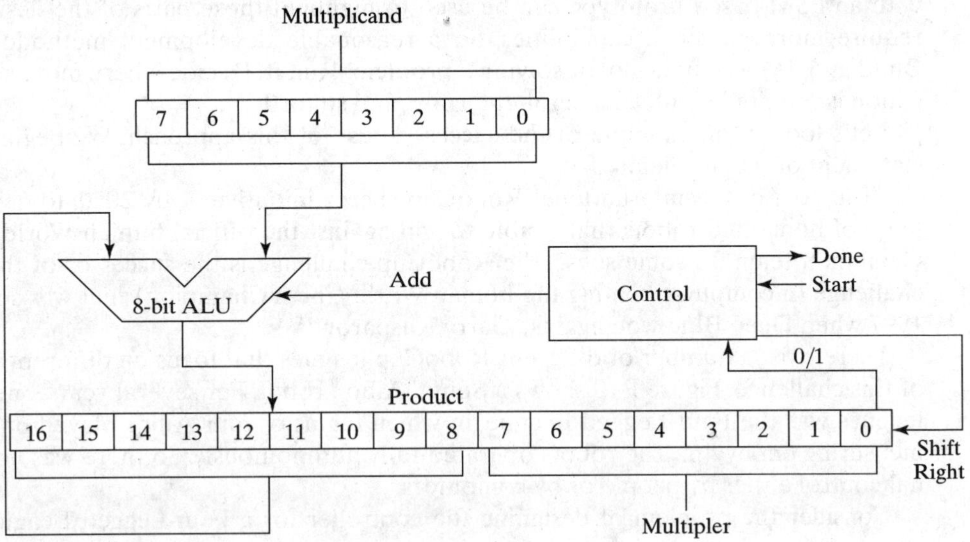

FIGURE P.8 A schematic diagram for an 8-bit multiplier.

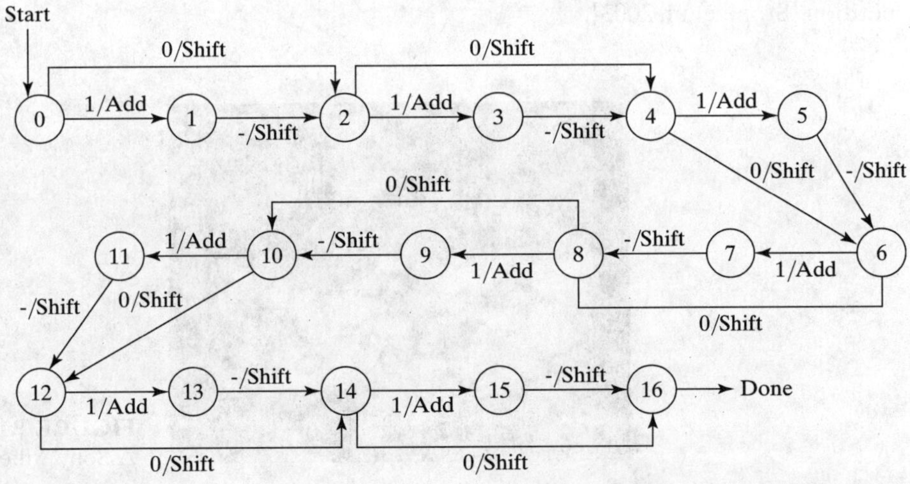

FIGURE P.9 The finite state transducer that implements the multiplier.

P.4 Controlling a Soccer-Playing Robot

A finite state machine may not be the best way to model all of the complexity that is required to solve many kinds of hard problems. But an FSM may be a good way to start. There exist good tools for building FSMs and for displaying them graphically so that their structure is obvious to their designers. The process of articulating the states helps designers understand the large-scale structure of their problem. Experiments with an FSM-based prototype can be used to highlight those parts of the design that require more powerful capabilities. So a reasonable development methodology is: Build an FSM as a first shot at solving a problem. Run it. Decide where more sophistication is required. Add it. Experiment again, and so forth.

Let's look at an example of the successful use of this approach. We begin with a statement of the problem:

"The goal of the international RoboCup soccer initiative is, by 2050, to develop a team of humanoid robots that is able to win against the official human World Soccer Champion team. In some sense, the RoboCup challenge is the successor of the chess challenge (a computer beating the human World Chess Champion) that was solved in 1997 when Deep Blue won against Garry Kasparov."[17]

There exist a number of different RoboCup leagues that focus on different aspects of this challenge. Figure P.10 shows a Sony® Aibo® robot. For several years, one of the leagues was the Four-Legged League, in which teams of four Aibos played on a field measuring 6m by 4m. The robots operated fully autonomously. So there was no external control either by people or by computers.

Consider the problem of designing the controller for a Four-Legged League team member. Clearly each robot must perceive its environment and then decide how to act. No simple controller will make a robot competitive with a human player at either task. But a simple controller may provide the basis for a first-generation prototype. Figure P.11 shows a finite state machine that was used to define the behavior of an attacking player for the Austin Villa team 💻 in 2003, the first year that it entered the Four-Legged competition [Stone et al. 2003].

FIGURE P.10
A Sony Aibo robot.

[17]This description is a very slightly edited version of the description on the RoboCup 2006 website 💻.

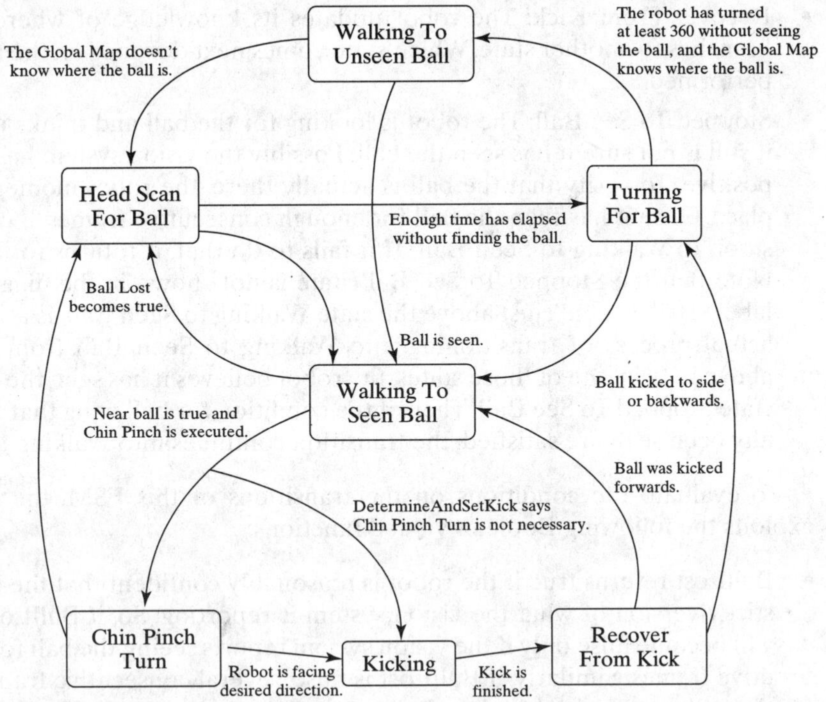

FIGURE P.11 A finite state controller for an Aibo soccer player.

The states of this machine correspond to simple behaviors. The transitions between the states depend on input from the robot's perceptual systems: vision and localization, as well as its global map and its joint angles. The states can be described as follows:[18]

- Head Scan for Ball: This is the first of a few states designed to find the ball. While in this state, the robot stands in place, scanning the field with its head.
- Turning For Ball: The robot is turning in place with the head in a fixed position (pointing ahead but tilted down slightly).
- Walking To Unseen Ball: The robot cannot see the ball itself but one of its teammates communicates to it the ball's location. Then the robot tries to walk toward the ball. At the same time, it scans with its head to try to find the ball.
- Walking to Seen Ball: The robot can see the ball and is walking toward it. The robot keeps its head pointed toward the ball and walks in the direction in which its head is pointing. As the robot approaches the ball, it captures the ball by lowering its head right before making the transition to the Chin Pinch Turn state.
- Chin Pinch Turn: The robot pinches the ball between its chin and the ground. It then turns with the ball to face in the direction in which it is trying to kick.
- Kicking: The robot is kicking the ball.

[18]These descriptions are slightly edited versions of the ones that appeared in [Stone et al. 2003].

- Recover From Kick: The robot updates its knowledge of where the ball is and branches to another state. Which state comes next depends on the kick that was just performed.
- Stopped To See Ball: The robot is looking for the ball and thinks it has seen it. But it still is not sure it has seen the ball. Possibly the vision system has returned a false positive. To verify that the ball is actually there, the robot momentarily freezes in place. Once it has seen the ball for enough consecutive frames, it can take the transition to Walking to Seen Ball. If it fails to do that, it returns to its previous state. Note that the Stopped To See Ball state is not shown in the diagram. Instead the label "Ball is seen", just above the state Walking to Seen Ball, is a shorthand for the actual process of transitioning into Walking to Seen Ball from the three states above it. If, in one of those states, the robot believes it has seen the ball, it enters the state Stopped To See Ball. Then, if the condition for believing that the ball has actually been seen are satisfied, the transition continues into Walking to Seen Ball.

To evaluate the conditions on the transitions of this FSM, the robot controller exploits the following Boolean-valued functions:

- BallLost returns true if the robot is reasonably confident that the ball is lost. It is a sticky version of what the vision system is reporting. So, if BallLost is true, then it will become false only if the vision system reports seeing the ball for several consecutive frames. Similarly, if BallLost is false, several consecutive frames of not seeing the ball are required for it to become true.
- NearBall is used when the robot is walking toward the ball. It returns true when the robot is close enough to the ball to be able to begin capturing the ball with a chin pinch motion.
- DetermineAndSetKick is used when making a transition out of WalkingToSeenBall. It determines whether or not a chin pinch turn is necessary. It also computes the angle through which the robot should turn before it kicks, as well as which kick should be executed.

APPENDIX Q

Applications: Using Grammars

The *Oxford English Dictionary* (2nd Edition, 1989) gives, as its fifth definition of the word "grammar", the following:

a. The fundamental principles or rules of an art or science. *b.* A book presenting these in methodical form. (Now rare; formerly common in the titles of books.)

It goes on to mention the following examples:

- E. Newman's book, *The Grammar of Entomology*, 1856.
- Owen Jones's book, *Grammar of Ornament*, 1870.
- W. Sharp, in Rosetti, 1882, said, "The young poet may be said to have reached the platform of literary maturity while he was yet learning the grammar of painting."
- An article in *The Listener*, 18 September, 1958, said, "Reizenstein's dissonances do not make one 'sit up' in the way Haydn's do if we attend to his musical grammar."
- An article in *The Times*, 5 March, 1963, said, "The grammar of the film was established."

We have been using a more restricted, technical definition of the term. But its wider use is not disconnected from our narrower one. Grammars, as we have defined them, can be used to describe a wide variety of phenomena. We have already seen that context-free grammars can be used to describe some or all of the structure of:

- Artificial languages that have been designed to facilitate people's interaction with computers. For example, we've mentioned the programming languages Algol, Lisp, and Java.
- Naturally occurring phenomena. For example, we have considered written/spoken languages such as English and Chinese, as well as other natural symbol systems such as DNA and protein sequences.

In this appendix, we will consider other uses for context-free grammars. We will also mention the use of one other formalism, the Lindenmayer (or simply L) system.

Q.1 Describing Artificial Languages Designed for Person/Machine Interaction

Imagine that you need a language that can support person/machine communication or machine/machine communication. Consider the language classes that we have discussed. We can rate them on a star system, as shown in Figure Q.1. Regular languages do not have enough expressive power for many applications. For example, in the regular framework it is not possible to require that delimiters be matched. The decidable languages, on the other hand, have all the power it is possible to get. But there are few decision procedures and the ones that do exist are, quite often, unacceptably slow. The context-free framework is a reasonable compromise in many cases.

Most programming languages are mostly (except for type-checking) context-free. We discussed them in appendix G. In this section we consider other common kinds of context-free languages.

Q.1.1 Query Languages

Query languages allow users to write logical expressions that describe objects that are to be retrieved. For example, SQL is a widely used query language for relational database systems. A simple SQL query is the following:

```
SELECT DISTINCTROW A.x, A.y, A.z
    FROM A INNER JOIN B ON A.x = B.x
    WHERE (((A.z) = "m") AND ((B.w) ="c"))
              OR
          (((A.z) = "n"))
```

There exist context-free grammars that describe the syntax of the various dialects of SQL 💻. Regular expressions (or regular grammars) are not powerful enough because, among other things, they cannot describe the language of Boolean expressions. For example notice the use of balanced parentheses in the Boolean expression that occurs in the WHERE clause of the query that we just wrote. It is, on the other hand, straightforward to write a context-free grammar for such expressions. Using the same techniques that we used in Example 11.19 to define a grammar of arithmetic expressions, we saw, in Exercise 11.10, that we can write an unambiguous Boolean expression grammar that forces left associativity and that implements conventional precedence rules.

	Expressive power	Decision procedures: existence	Decision procedures: efficiency
Regular languages	*	* * * * *	* * * * *
Context-free languages	* * *	* * *	* * *
Decidable languages	* * * * *	*	

FIGURE Q.1 Comparing three classes of languages.

Q.1.2 Markup Languages: HTML and XML

Markup languages allow users to annotate documents with tags that identify functional components within a document. By defining standard, agreed-upon tags, markup languages allow multiple users and application programs to perform operations on the same document. For example, a menu document might contain units that are marked with a price tag. Then a menu formatting and printing program could right justify each price on its line. And a restaurant-cataloguing program could extract the prices from the restaurant's menu and use them to assign a price category to the restaurant.

The Hypertext Markup Language (HTML) powers the World Wide Web by providing a standard language in which hypertext documents on the Web can be described. An HTML document is simply a text string, but that text string describes a set of structural elements, each of which is delimited by a starting tag and its matching closing tag. The text between the starting and closing tags will be displayed according to the definition of the element class that is delimited by those tags. Since elements may be nested within other elements, HTML is not regular (for the same reason that the language of balanced parentheses isn't). It is context-free and can be described with a context free grammar. Each element definition defines a new kind of delimiter (a matched pair of tags). A syntactically valid HTML text must nest the delimiters correctly.

EXAMPLE Q.1 A Grammar for a Fragment of HTML

Consider the following syntactically legal fragment of HTML. This fragment contains a `ul` or unordered list (generally displayed with bullets before each item). The list contains two items (each marked as an `li`, for list item), the first of which contains a nested unordered list:

```
<ul>
      <li>Item 1, which will include a sublist</li>
            <ul>
                    <li>First item in sublist</li>
                    <li>Second item in sublist</li>
            </ul>
      <li>Item 2</li>
</ul>
```

This fragment could have been generated by the following context-free grammar (which ignores many details, including the fact that an `li` can occur only inside a list):

```
HTMLtext → Element HTMLtext | ε     /* Text is a sequence
                                       of elements.
Element → UL | LI | ... (and other kinds of elements that
                         are allowed in the body of an
                         HTML document)
```

EXAMPLE M.1 *(Continued)*

```
UL → <ul> HTMLtext </ul>          /* The <ul> and </ul>
                                     tags must match.

LI → <li> HTMLtext </li>          /* The <li> and </li>
                                     tags must match.
```

In HTML, the set of legal tags (e. g., `ul`, `/ul`, `li`, and `/li`) is fixed and determined by the language designers. So it can be built into a grammar such as the one we just described. But the idea of annotating text with structural tags is useful in all kinds of contexts, not just the display of text on the Web. To exploit this idea, it's necessary to allow users to define new tags to suit their needs.

The Extensible Markup Language (XML) does exactly that. Users write definitions of new document types by specifying the set of legal elements and the tags that delimit them. Those elements can then be processed by application programs. So some tags may be used to indicate how an element should be displayed (as in HTML). But others could be used to define fields in a database, to provide a basis for sorting the elements, and so on. In I.3.2, we mention RDF, a language for annotating Web resources so that they can function as part of the Semantic Web. One way to write RDF expressions is in XML.

There are a couple of formalisms that can be used to define new kinds of XML documents. We'll briefly consider document type definitions (DTDs). Each DTD effectively extends the grammar of the base system to include problem-specific elements and tags.

EXAMPLE Q.2 Writing a Document Type Definition

Suppose that we want to define a document type that will be used for homework assignments handed out to a class. Each such document may contain some or all of the following fields: sequence number, title, due date, body. We can describe this class of documents with the following DTD:

```
<!DOCTYPE homework [
  <!ELEMENT seq   (#PCDATA)>      /* #PCDATA (parsed character
  <!ELEMENT title (#PCDATA)>         data) is a built-in type.
  <!ELEMENT due   (#PCDATA)>
  <!ELEMENT body  (#PCDATA)>  ]>
```

So a homework document may be composed of four kinds of elements. Each element will be delimited with one of the four tags, `seq`, `title`, `due`, and `body`, that we just defined. An example of a homework document that is consistent with this definition is:

```
<homework>
  <seq>2</seq>
```

```
    <title>Regular Expressions</title>
    <due>Friday</due>
    <body>1. Write a regular expression for the language of
      strings of a's and b's that start with a.
      2. Write a regular expression for the language of
      strings of a's, b's, and c's with at most one a.</body>
  </homework>
```

The advantage of a structured document such as this, over a more standard, straight text document, is that someone else who also has access to the DTD can easily skim piles of documents and extract specific pieces of information, say, for example, the titles.

Of course, real documents are more complicated. There are typically elements that occur inside other elements, elements that must occur at least once, elements that may occur only once, optional elements, elements that may occur only if some other element also occurs, and so forth. So the language in which DTDs are written functions very much like Extended BNF (EBNF), described in G.1.1. The DTD specification language, like EBNF, augments the standard context-free grammar formalism with regular expressions for describing regular fragments of the target language.

The next example extends the homework document type and illustrates the use of the regular expression operators concatenation (represented by a comma), union (represented as |), Kleene star, and at-least-one (represented as +).

EXAMPLE Q.3 A More Flexible Document Type Definition

In this version, we describe the structure of the body of a homework assignment. It is made up of zero or more problems. Each problem specifies the number of points and then a description (the comma indicates concatenation). The description may either be an arbitrary string (in the case of a single-part problem), or a list of one or more parts.

```
<!DOCTYPE homework [
  <!ELEMENT seq         (#PCDATA)>
  <!ELEMENT title       (#PCDATA)>
  <!ELEMENT due         (#PCDATA)>
  <!ELEMENT body        (problem*)>      /* zero or more problems.
    <!ELEMENT problem   (points,
                         description)>  /* a points element
                                           followed by a
                                           description.
```

EXAMPLE M.1 *(Continued)*

```
      <!ELEMENT points      (#PCDATA)>
      <!ELEMENT description (#PCDATA |
                             multipart)> /* a single-part ques-
                                            tion can be any sort
                                            of text.  Or the
                                            question may be mul-
                                            tipart.
          <!ELEMENT multipart  (part+)> /* At least one part.
               <!ELEMENT part  (#PCDATA)>   ]>
```

Although the DTD syntax is different from the one we have been using for grammar rules, it provides the same information that grammar rules do. Each element declaration in a DTD effectively augments the grammar that defines the strings that are legal in an XML document that has been written to conform to that DTD.

EXAMPLE Q.4 Viewing a DTD as a Grammar

Consider again the simple DTD of Example Q.2:

```
<!DOCTYPE homework [
  <!ELEMENT seq       (#PCDATA)>
  <!ELEMENT title     (#PCDATA)>
  <!ELEMENT due       (#PCDATA)>
  <!ELEMENT body      (#PCDATA)>  ]>
```

That DTD defines four new kinds of elements by effectively adding the rules:

$$Element \rightarrow seq \mid title \mid due \mid body$$

Each element must be delimited by the appropriate tags, so the DTD also adds the following rules:

seq → <seq>\#*PCDATA*</seq>
title → <title>\#*PCDATA*</title>
due → <due>\#*PCDATA*</due>
body → <body>\#*PCDATA*</body>

Some XML parsers, called validating parsers, check documents to make sure that they contain only the elements that are defined in the current DTD. But, for efficiency, there are also nonvalidating parsers, which check only that the core syntax has been followed and that tags are properly nested.

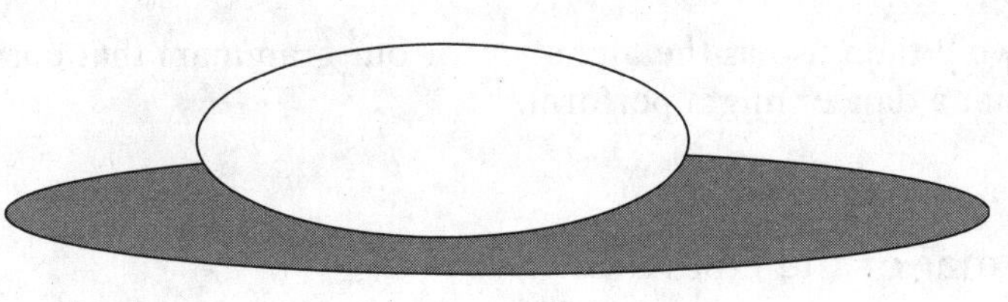

FIGURE Q.2 A picture drawn with a graphics metalanguage.

XML has been used to define specialized markup languages for hundreds, and probably even thousands, of specialized application environments 🖳.

Q.1.3 Graphics Metalanguages: SVG

Pictures, like the one shown in Figure Q.2, do not look like strings. So sets of pictures do not appear to be languages. But programs that draw such pictures must be told what to do. Strings in graphics metalanguages provide such instructions. So while the pictures aren't strings, their descriptions are.

Many graphics languages exist 🖳, some as stand-alone languages and others as extensions of more general programming languages and environments. With the advent of the World Wide Web, came the need for standards in this arena, as in many others.

The Scalable Vector Graphics (or SVG) language is one proposed standard. SVG 🖳 is a language for describing two-dimensional graphics (including interactive and animated graphics) in XML. The following SVG program drew the figure shown above:

```
<svg width="100%" height="100%" version="1.1"
   xmlns="http://www.w3.org/2000/svg">
  <ellipse cx="240" cy="100" rx="200" ry="25"
    style="fill:grey;stroke:black"/>
  <ellipse cx="220" cy="70" rx="100" ry="40"
    style="fill:white;stroke:black"/>
</svg>
```

SVG can be described with a context-free grammar.

Q.2 Describing Naturally Occurring Phenomena

Many kinds of naturally occurring phenomena can usefully be described using grammars of various sorts. We sketch two of them here. We should point out before we start, though, that there many kinds of naturally occurring phenomena that cannot easily be described within the context-free framework. In N.1.2 we briefly mention some of the reasons that they are rarely used in music, for example.

Q.2.1 Dance

Dancers move in three dimensional space and in time. Context-free grammars define languages that are composed of one-dimensional strings. But such strings can be used to describe the essential characteristics of many kinds of dances if we start by defining a set of primitives (which we'll then use as the alphabet for our grammar) that correspond to the basic moves that a dancer might perform.

EXAMPLE Q.5 A Grammar of the Foxtrot

When dancing a foxtrot, one can take either slow (S) steps (that take two beats) or quick (Q) steps (that take a single beat). Each step may start with either the left (L) or the right (R) foot. And each step may move forward (F), sideways (W), or backwards (B), or it may close (C), i.e., bring the feet together. These basic symbols can be combined to form an alphabet that corresponds to the individual steps that can make up a dance.

One popular foxtrot form is called the box rhythm. The following grammar rule (slightly adapted from the larger grammar described in [Herbison-Evans 2006] 💻) describes it (for the man):

$$B \rightarrow LS\ RQW\ LQC\ RS\ LQW\ RQC$$

The dancer takes six steps: slow, quick, quick, slow, quick quick. The man always starts with his left foot, then alternates feet.

Q.2.2 The Development of Plants

In Section 24.4, when we introduced Lindenmayer systems (typically called just L-systems), we pointed out that they were created by the biologist Aristid Lindenmayer as part of his work on plant development and growth. There we showed a simple L-system that described highly stylized tree structures. But much more realistic structures can also be produced 💻.

References

Other textbooks on automata theory, language theory, and the theory of computation also cover the material described in this book. See [Sipser 2006], [Hopcroft, Motwani and Ullman 2001], [Lewis and Papadimitriou 1998], and [Martin 2003]. Many of the examples and proofs in this book are modeled after those presented in these earlier texts.

References that exist on the Web are indicated with the symbol 🖳. Current links to them can be found on the Web site for this book, in the final section entitled Bibliography.

Ackermann, Wilhelm, 1928. "Zum Hilbertschen Aufbau der Reellen Zahlen," *Mathematical Annals*, 99, pp. 118–133. Translated as "On Hilbert's construction of the real numbers," in *From Frege to Gödel: A Source Book in Mathematical Logic 1879–1931*, Jean van Heijenoort (ed), Harvard University Press, 1967.

Adleman, Leonard M., 1994. "Molecular Computation of Solutions to Combinatorial Problems" 🖳, *Science*, 266, pp. 1021–1024.

Adleman, Leonard M., 1998. "Computing with DNA" 🖳, *Scientific American*, August, pp. 34–41.

Agrawal, Manindra, Neeraj Kayal, and Nitin Saxena, 2004. "PRIMES is in P" 🖳, *Annals of Mathematics*, 160(2), pp. 781–793.

Aho, Alfred V. and Margaret J. Corasick, 1975. "Efficient String Matching: An Aid to Bibliographic Search," *Comm. ACM*, 18(6), pp. 333–340.

Aho, Alfred V., Ravi Sethi, and Jeffrey D. Ullman, 1988. *Compilers: Principles, Techniques, and Tools*, Addison-Wesley.

Alberts, Bruce, Alexander Johnson, Julian Lewis, Martin Raff, Keith Roberts, and Peter Walter, 2002. *Molecular Biology of the Cell, Fourth Edition*, Garland Publishing.

Altschul S. F., W. Gish, W. Miller, E. W. Myers, and D. J. Lipman, 1990. "Basic Local Alignment Search Tool" 🖳, *Journal of Molecular Biology*, Oct 5, 215(3), pp. 403–410.

Anderson, John R. and Christian Lebiere, 1998. *The Atomic Components of Thought,* Erlbaum.

Anderson, John R., Daniel Bothell, Michael D. Byrne, Scott Douglass, Christian Lebiere, and Yulin Qin, 2004. "An Integrated Theory of the Mind" 🖳, *Psychological Review*, 111(4), pp. 1036–1060.

Appel, Kenneth and Wolfgang Haken, 1977. "The Solution of the Four-Color Map Problem," *Scientific American,* 237, pp. 108–121.

Baader, Franz, Diego Calvanese, Deborah McGuinness, Daniele Nardi, and Peter Patel-Schneider, 2003. *The Description Logic Handbook*, Cambridge University Press.

Backus, John, 1980. "Programming in America in the 1950s—Some Personal Impressions", in *A History of Computing in the Twentieth Century*, Nicholas Metropolis and J. Howlett (eds), Academic Press, pp. 125–135.

Bar-Hillel, Yehoshua, M. Perles, and Eliahu Shamir, 1961. "On Formal Properties of Simple Phrase-structure Grammars," *Zeitschrift für Phonetik, Sprachwissenschaft und Kommunikationsforschung*, 14, pp. 143–172.

Baroni, Mario and Laura Callegari, 1984. *Musical Grammars and Computer Analysis*. Florence: Leo S. Olschki.

Baroni, Mario, Rosella Brunetti, Laura Callegari, and Carlo Jacoboni, 1984. "A Grammar for Melody. Relationships between Melody and Harmony," in [Baroni and Callegari 1984], pp. 201–218.

Baum, Leonard E., Ted Petrie, George Soules and Norman Weiss, 1970. "A Maximization Technique Occurring in the Statistical Analysis of Probabilistic Functions of Markov Chains," *Annals of Mathematical Statistics,* 41, pp. 164–171.

Bentley, Jon, 2000. *Programming Pearls,* Second Edition, Addison-Wesley.

Berger, Bonnie and Tom Leighton, 1998. "Protein Folding in the Hydrophobic-Hydrophilic (HP) Model is NP-complete," *J. Computational Biology*, 5(1), Spring, pp. 27–40.

Berger, Robert, 1966. "The Undecidability of the Domino Problem," *Mem. Amer. Math. Soc.* 66, 1–72.

Berners-Lee, Tim, James Hendler, and Ora Lassila, 2001. "The Semantic Web," *Scientific American*, May, pp. 34–43.

Berners-Lee, Tim and Noah Mendelsohn, 2006. *The Rule of Least Power*.

Berlekamp, Elwyn R, John H. Conway, and Richard K. Guy, 1982. *Winning Ways for your Mathematical Plays*, volume 2, Chapter 25, Academic Press.

Bishop, Matt, 2003. *Computer Security*, Addison-Wesley.

Brachman, Ronald J. and Hector J. Levesque, 2004, *Knowledge Representation and Reasoning*, Morgan Kaufmann.

Bryant, Randal E., 1986. "Graph-based Algorithms for Boolean Function Manipulation", *IEEE Transactions on Computers*, C-35-8, pp. 677–691.

Bryant, Randal E., 1992. "Symbolic Boolean Manipulation with Ordered Binary Decision Diagrams", *ACM Computing Surveys*, 24(3), September, pp. 293–318.

Büchi, J. Richard, 1960a. "On a Decision Method in Restricted Second Order Arithmetic," *Proc. of the International Congress on Logic, Methodology and Philosophy of Science*, Stanford University Press, pp. 1–11.

Büchi, J. Richard, 1960b. "Weak Second-order Arithmetic and Finite Automata," *Z. Math Logik Grundlag. Math.* 6, pp. 66–92.

Camilleri, Lelio, 1984. "A Grammar of the Melodies of Schubert's Lieder," in [Baroni and Callegari 1984], pp. 229–236.

Cantor, David G., 1962. "On the Ambiguity Problem in Backus Systems," *J. ACM*, 9(4), pp. 477–479.

Carroll, John A., 1983. "An Island Parsing Interpreter for the Full Augmented Transition Network Formalism," *Proceedings of the First Conference of the European Chapter of the Association for Computational Linguistics*, Pisa, Italy, pp. 101–105.

Champandard, Alex J., 2004. *AI Game Development: Synthetic Creatures with Learning and Reactive Behaviors*, New Riders.

Chandra, Ashok K., Dexter C. Kozen, and Larry J. Stockmeyer, 1981. "Alternation," *Journal of the ACM*, 28(1), pp. 114–133.

Chomsky, Noam, 1956. "Three Models for the Description of Language," *I.R.E. Transactions on Information Theory*, vol. IT-2, September, pp. 113–124.

Chomsky, Noam, 1957. *Syntactic Structures*. Mouton.

Chomsky, Noam and George A. Miller, 1958. "Finite-state Languages," *Information and Control*, 1, pp. 91–112.

Chomsky, Noam, 1959. "On Certain Formal Properties of Grammars", *Information and Control*, 2(2), pp. 137–167.

Chomsky, Noam, 1962. "Context-free Grammar and Pushdown Storage," *Quarterly Progress Report*, 65, pp. 187–194, M.I.T. Research Laboratory in Electronics, Cambridge, Mass.

Chomsky, Noam and M. P. Schutzenberger, 1963. "The Algebraic Theory of Context-free Languages," *Computer Programming and Formal Systems*, North Holland, pp. 118–161.

Chomsky, Noam, 1965. *Aspects of the Theory of Syntax*, MIT Press.

Christofides, Nicos, 1976. "Worst-case Analysis of a New Heuristic for the Traveling Salesman Problem." Technical report, Graduate School of Industrial Administration, Carnegie-Mellon University, Pittsburgh PA.

Church, Alonzo, 1936. "An Unsolvable Problem of Elementary Number Theory," *American Journal of Mathematics*, 58, pp. 345–363. Reprinted in [Davis 1965].

Clarke, Edmund M. and E. Allen Emerson, 1981. "Design and Synthesis of Synchronization Skeletons Using Branching Time Temporal Logic," *Logic of Programs: Workshop, Yorktown Heights, NY*. *Lecture Notes in Computer Science* 131, Springer, pp. 52–71.

Clarke, Edmund M., E. Allen Emerson, and A. P. Sistla, 1983. "Automatic Verification of Finite-state Concurrent Systems Using Temporal Logic Specifications," *Proc. of the 10th Annual ACM Symposium on Principles of Programming Languages*, January, pp. 117–126.

Clarke, Edmund M., Orna Grumberg, and Doron Peled, 1999. *Model Checking*, MIT Press.

Clocksin, William F. and Christopher S. Mellish, 1981. *Programming in Prolog*, Springer Verlag.

Colbourn, Charles J., 1984. "The Complexity of Completing Partial Latin Squares," *Discrete Applied Mathematics*, 8, pp. 25–30.

Cook, Stephen C., 1971. "The Complexity of Theorem-proving Procedures," *Third ACM Symposium on Theory of Computing*, ACM, pp. 151–158.

Coppersmith, Don and Shmuel Winograd, 1990. "Matrix Multiplication via Arithmetic Progression," *Journal of Symbolic Computation*, 9(3), pp. 251–280.

Cope, David, 1996. *Experiments in Musical Intelligence*, A-R Editions, Inc., Computer Music and Digital Audio Series, Vol. 12.

Copeland, Jeffrey and Jeffrey Haemer, 2001. "Nonsense", *SW Expert*, October, pp. 32–35.

Corman, Thomas H., Charles E. Leiserson, Ronald L. Rivest, and Clifford Stein, 2001. *Introduction to Algorithms*, Second Edition, MIT Press.

Culik, Karel II, 1996. "An Aperiodic Set of 13 Wang Tiles." *Disc. Math.* 160, 245–251.

Dantzig, George B., Ray Fulkerson, and Selmer M. Johnson, 1954. "Solution of a Large-scale Traveling Salesman Problem," *Operations Research*, 2, pp. 393–410.

Davis, Martin D. and Hilary Putnam, 1960. "A Computing Procedure for Quantification Theory," *Journal of the ACM*, 7(3), pp. 201–215.

Davis, Martin D., 1965. *The Undecidable*, Raven Press.

Dedekind, Richard, 1888. *Was sind und was sollen die Zahlen?* F. Vieweg, Braunschweig. Translated by W. W. Beman and W. Ewald, in Ewald, William Bragg (ed.), *From Kant to Hilbert. A Source Book in the Foundations of Mathematics*, vol. 2, Oxford University Press, pp. 787–832, 1996.

Dijkstra, Edsger, EWD-1248 🖳.

Durbin, Richard, Sean Eddy, Anders Krogh, and Graeme Mitchison, 1998. *Biological Sequence Analysis: Probabilistic Models of Proteins and Nucleic Acids: A tutorial introduction to hidden Markov models and other probabilistic modelling approaches in computational sequence analysis,* Cambridge University Press.

Du, Ding-Zhu and Ker-I Ko, 2001. *Problem Solving in Automata, Languages, and Complexity*, John Wiley and Sons.

Earley, Jay, 1970. "An Efficient Context-free Parsing Algorithm" 🖳, *Comm. of the ACM*, 13(2), February, pp. 94–102.

Ebcioğlu, Kemal, 1992. "An Expert System for Harmonizing Chorales in the Style of J. S. Bach," in Mira Balaban, Kemal Ebcioğlu and Otto Laske (eds.), *Understanding Music with AI: Perspectives on Music Cognition*, AAAI Press/MIT Press, pp. 294–334.

Ehrenfeucht, Andrzej, Juhani Karhumaki, and Grzegorz Rozenberg, 1982. "The (Generalized) Post Correspondence Problem with Lists Consisting of Two Words is Decidable," *Theoret. Comput. Sci.*, 21(2), pp. 119–144.

Epp, Susanna, 2003. *Discrete Mathematics with Applications*, Brooks Cole.

Evey, R.J., 1963. "Application of Pushdown Store Machines," *Proceedings of the 1963 Fall Joint Computer Conference*, pp. 215–217, AFIPS Press.

Fischer, Michael J. and Rabin, Michael O., 1974. "Super-Exponential Complexity of Presburger Arithmetic." *Complexity of Computation. Proceedings of a Symposium in Applied Mathematics of the American Mathematical Society and the Society for Industrial and Applied Mathematics. Held in New York, April 18–19, 1973* (Ed. R. M. Karp). Providence, RI: Amer. Math. Soc., pp. 27–41.

Floyd, Robert W., 1962. "On Ambiguity in Phrase Structure Languages," *Comm. ACM*, 5(10), pp. 526–534.

Forgy, Charles L., 1982. "Rete: A Fast Algorithm for the Many Pattern/Many Object Pattern Match Problem," *Artificial Intelligence,* 19, pp. 17–37.

Fux, Johann Joseph, 1725. *The Study of Counterpoint from Johann Joseph Fux's Gradus ad Parnassum*, translated and edited by Alfred Mann. W. W. Norton and Company. 1971.

Fraenkel, Aviezri S. and David Lichtenstein, 1981. "Computing a Perfect Strategy for $n \times n$ Chess Requires Time Exponential in n," *J. Combinatorial Theory Series A*, 31, pp. 199–214.

Gardner, Martin, 1970. "Mathematical Games" 🖳, *Scientific American*, 223, pp. 120–123, October.

Garey, Michael and David Johnson, 1979. *Computers and Intractability—A Guide to the Theory of NP-completeness*, Freeman.

Gillman, Leonard and Allen J. Rose, 1984. *APL: An Interactive Approach*, John Wiley & Sons.

Ginsburg, Seymour and H. Gordon Rice, 1962. "Two Families of Languages Related to ALGOL," *J. ACM*, 9(3), pp. 350–371.

Ginsburg, Seymour and Gene F. Rose, 1963. "Some Recursively Unsolvable Problems in ALGOL-like Languages," *J. ACM*, 10(1), pp. 29–47.

Ginsburg, Seymour, 1966. *The Mathematical Theory of Context-Free Languages*, McGraw-Hill.

Gödel, Kurt, 1929. "Über die Vollständigkeit des Logikkalküls," doctoral dissertation, University of Vienna.

Gödel, Kurt, 1931. "Über formal unentscheidbare Sätze der Principia Mathematica und verwandter Systeme, I," *Monatshefte für Mathematik und Physik*, 38, pp. 173–198. Translated as "On formally undecidable propositions in *Principia Mathematica* and related systems, I," in *From Frege to Gödel: A Source Book in Mathematical Logic 1879–1931*, Jean van Heijenoort (ed), Harvard University Press, 1967. There is also a translation into English and modern notation by Martin Hirzel 💻.

Gouda, Mohamed, 1998. *Elements of Network Protocol Design*, Wiley Interscience.

Greibach, Sheila A., 1965. "A New Normal Form Theorem for Context-free Phrase Structure Grammars," *J. ACM,* 10(2), pp. 175–195.

Greibach, Sheila A., 1981. "Formal Languages: Origins and Directions," *Annals of the History of Computing*, 3(1), January, 1981.

Gries, David, 1989. *The Science of Programming*, Springer.

Harel, David, 1987. "Statecharts: A Visual Formulation for Complex Systems," *Science of Computer Programming*, 8(3), pp. 231–274 💻.

Harel, David and Michal Politi, 1998. *Modeling Reactive Systems with Statecharts: The Statemate Approach*, McGraw-Hill.

Harrison, Michael, Walter L. Ruzzo, and Jeffrey D. Ullman, 1976. "Protection in Operating Systems," *Comm. of the ACM*, 19(8), August, pp. 461–471.

Harrison, Michael. A., 1978. *Introduction to Formal Language Theory*, Addison-Wesley.

Hart, Peter E., Nils J. Nilsson, and Bertram B. Raphael, 1968. "A Formal Basis for the Heuristic Determination of Minimum Cost Paths." *IEEE Transactions on Systems Science and Cybernetics SSC4*, (2), pp. 100–107.

Hart, Peter E., Nils J. Nilsson, and Bertram B. Raphael, 1972. "Correction to 'A Formal Basis for the Heuristic Determination of Minimum Cost Paths.'" *SIGART Newsletter*, 37, pp. 28–29.

Hartmanis, Juris and John E. Hopcroft, 1968. "Structure of Undecidable Problems in Automata Theory," in *Proc. Ninth Symposium Switching and Automata Theory*, IEEE, pp. 327–333.

Hartmanis, Juris and Richard E. Stearns, 1965. "On the Computational Complexity of Algorithms," *Transactions of the American Mathematical Society*, 117, pp. 285–306.

Herbison-Evans, Don, 2006. "A Revised Grammar for the Foxtrot" 💻.

Hilbert, David and Wilhelm Ackermann, 1928. *Grundzüge der theoretischen Logik*, Springer-Verlag.

Hiller, Lejaren and Leonard Isaacson 1959. *Experimental Music*, McGraw-Hill.

Hiller, Lejaren and Robert Baker, 1964. "Computer Cantata: A Study in Compositional Method," *Perspectives of New Music*, 3(1), pp. 62–90.

Hiller, Lejaren, 1972. *Computer Programs Used to Produce the Composition HPSCHD*. Technical Report No. 4, National Science Foundation Project No. GK-14191, State University of New York, Buffalo.

Hoare, C. A. R., 1961. "Partition: Algorithm 63", "Quicksort: Algorithm 64," and "Find: Algorithm 65." *Comm. ACM*, 4(7), pp. 321–322.

Hopcroft, John E. and Jeffrey D. Ullman, 1969. *Formal Languages and their Relation to Automata Theory*, Addison-Wesley.

Hopcroft, John E., Rajeev Motwani, and Jeffrey D. Ullman, 2001. *Introduction to Automata Theory, Languages, and Computation*, Addison Wesley.

Howell, Peter, Robert West, and Ian Cross, 1991. *Representing Musical Structure*, Academic Press.

Immerman, Neil, 1988. "Nondeterministic Space is Closed Under Complementation", *SIAM Journal on Computing* 17, pp. 935–938.

Johnson, C. Douglas, 1972. *Formal Aspects of Phonological Description*, Mouton.

Johnson, Stephen C., 1979. "Yacc: Yet Another Compiler-Compiler", In *UNIX Programmer's Manual*. Holt, Rinehart, and Winston.

Jones, Kevin, 1981. "Compositional Applications of Stochastic Processes," *Computer Music Journal*, 5(2). Reprinted in Curtis Roads (ed.), *The Music Machine*, MIT Press, 1989.

Jurafsky, Daniel and James H. Martin, 2000. *Speech and Language Processing: An Introduction to Natural Language Processing, Computational Linguistics, and Speech Recognition*, Prentice-Hall.

Kaplan, Ronald M., and Martin Kay, 1994. "Regular Models of Phonological Rule Systems," *Computational Linguistics*, 20(3), pp. 331–378, written in 1980.

Karmarker, Narendra, 1984. "A New Polynomial-time Algorithm for Linear Programming," *Combinatorica*, 4(4), pp. 373–395.

Karp, Richard M., 1972. "Reducibility Among Combinatorial Problems," In *Complexity of Computer Computations*, Proc. Sympos. IBM Thomas J. Watson Res. Center, Yorktown Heights, N.Y., Plenum, pp. 85–103.

Karttunen, Laurie and Kenneth Beesley, 2001. "A Short History of Two-level Morphology".

Kasami, Tadao, 1965. "An Efficient Recognition and Syntax Algorithm for Context-free Languages," Scientific Report AFCRL-65-758, Air Force Cambridge Research Lab, Bedford, MA.

Khoussainov, Bakhadyr and Anil Nerode, 2001. *Automata Theory and its Applications*, Birkhäuser.

Kippen, Jim and Bernard Bel, 1992. "Modelling Music with Grammars," in *Computer Representations and Models in Music*, Academic Press, pp. 207–238.

Kleene, Stephen C., 1936a. "General Recursive Functions of Natural Numbers," *Math. Annals*, 112, pp. 727–742. Reprinted in [Davis 1965].

Kleene, Stephen C., 1936b. "λ-definability and Recursiveness," *Duke Math. Journal*, 2, pp. 340–353.

Kleene, Stephen C., 1956. "Representation of Events in Nerve Nets and Finite Automata," in C. E. Shannon and J. McCarthy, *Automata Studies*, Princeton University Press, pp. 3–42.

Kleene, Stephen C., 1964. *Introduction to Metamathematics*, Van Nostrand.

Knuth, Donald E., 1968. "Semantics of Context-free Grammars," *Theory of Computing Systems*, 2(2), pp. 127–145.

Knuth, Donald E. and Ronald W. Moore, 1975. "An Analysis of Alpha-beta Pruning," *Artificial Intelligence*, 6(4), pp. 293–326.

Knuth, Donald E., James H. Morris, Vaughn R. Pratt, 1977. "Fast Pattern Matching in Strings," *SIAM Journal of Computing,* 6(2), pp. 323–350.

Koskenniemi, Kimmo, 1983. *Two-Level Morphology: A General Computational Model for Word-Form Recognition and Production*. PhD thesis, University of Helsinki. Publications of the Department of General Linguistics, University of Helsinki, No. 11. Helsinki.

Kruskal, Joseph Bernard, 1956. "On the Shortest Spanning Subtree and the Traveling Salesman Problem," in *Proceedings of the American Mathematical Society*, 7, pp. 48–50.

Kuroda, S. Y., 1964. "Classes of Languages and Linear-bounded Automata," *Information and Control*, 7, pp. 207–223.

Ladner, Richard E., 1975. "On the Structure of Polynomial-time Reducibility," *JACM*, 22(1), pp. 155–171.

Lagarias, Jeff, 1985. "The 3x + 1 Problem and Its Generalizations", *American Mathematical Monthly*, 92, pp. 3–23.

Laird, John, Allen Newell, and Paul Rosenbloom, 1987. "Soar: An Architecture for General Intelligence," *Artificial Intelligence*, 33, pp. 1–64.

Landweber, Peter S., 1963. "Three Theorems on Phrase Structure Grammars of Type 1," *Information and Control,* 6, pp. 131–136.

Lawler, Eugene L., Jan Karel Lenstra, A. H. G. Rinnooy Kan, and D. B. Shmoys, 1985. *The Traveling Salesman Problem: A Guided Tour of Combinatorial Optimization.* John Wiley & Sons.

Lee, Lillian, 2002. "Fast Context-free Parsing Requires Fast Boolean Matrix Multiplication", *J. ACM*, 49(1), pp. 1–15.

Lesk, Michael and E. Schmidt, 1979. *Lex–A Lexical Analyzer Generator*, In *UNIX Programmer's Manual.* Holt, Rinehart, and Winston.

Levin, Leonid A., 1973. "Universal Sorting Problems," *Problemi Peredachi Informatsii*, 9(3), pp. 265–266.

Lewis, Harry R. and Christos H. Papadimitriou, 1998. *Elements of the Theory of Computation*, Prentice-Hall.

Lichtenstein, David and Michael Sipser, 1980. "GO is Polynomial-space Hard," *JACM*, 27(2), April, pp. 393–401.

Lindenmayer, Aristid, 1968. "Mathematical Models for Cellular Interactions in Development," *Journal of Theoretical Biology* 18, pp. 280–315.

Linz, Peter, 2001. *An Introduction to Formal Languages and Automata*, Jones and Bartlett.

Mahalanobis, P. C., 1940. "A Sample Survey of the Acreage Under Jute in Bengal," *Sankhyu* 4, pp. 511–530.

Manning, Christopher and Hinrich Schütze, 1999. *Foundations of Statistical Natural Language Processing*, The MIT Press.

Markov, Andrei, 1951. "Theory of Algorithms," *Trudy Mat. Inst. Steklov.*, 38 , pp. 176–189.

Markov, Andrei A. and N.M. Nagorny, 1988. *The Theory of Algorithms* (English translation), Kluwer Academic Publishers.

Martin, John C., 2003. *Introduction to Languages and the Theory of Computation*, McGraw-Hill.

Matiyasevich, Yuri, 1970. "Enumerable Sets are Diophantine," *Doklady Akademii Nauk SSSR*, 191, pp. 279–282, 1970. English translation in *Soviet Mathematics. Doklady,* vol. 11, no. 2.

McCarthy, John, 1960. "Recursive Functions of Symbolic Expressions", *Comm. A.C.M.*, 3(4), pp. 184–195.

McCulloch, Warren S. and Walter Pitts, 1943. "A Logical Calculus of the Ideas Immanent in Nervous Activity," *Bull. Math. Biophysics*, 5, pp. 115–133.

Mealy, George H., 1955. "A Method for Synthesizing Sequential Circuits," *Bell System Technical Journal*, 34(5), pp. 1045–1079.

Menger, Karl, 1932. "Das botenproblem," in K. Menger (ed), *Ergebnisse eines Mathematischen Kolloquiums* 2, Teubner, Leipzig, pp. 11–12.

Miller, Gary L., 1976. "Riemann's Hypothesis and Tests for Primality," *J. Comp. Syst. Sci.* 13(3), pp. 300–317.

Minsky, Marvin L., 1961. "Recursive Unsolvability of Post's Problem of 'tag' and Other Topics in Theory of Turing Machines," *Ann. of Math.* 74, pp. 437–455.

Misra, Jay, 1996. "Coloring Grid Points, Without Rabbits or Snakes".

Misra, Jay, 2004. *Theory in Programming Practice*.

Moonen, Leon, 2001. "Generating Robust Parsers Using Island Grammars," *Proceedings of the 8th Working Conference on Reverse Engineering*. IEEE Computer Society Press, pp. 13–22.

Moore, Edward F., 1956. "Gedanken Experiments on Sequential Machines," in C. E. Shannon and J. McCarthy, *Automata Studies*, Princeton University Press, pp. 129–153.

Moore, F. Richard, *Elements of Computer Music*, Prentice-Hall, 1990.

Morris, Robert, and Cherry, Lorinda L., 1975. "Computer Detection of Typograhical Errors," *IEEE Trans. On Professional Communication*, PC-18, 1, March, pp. 54–64.

Murphy, Gail C. and David Notkin, 1996. "Lightweight Lexical Source Model Extraction," *ACM Transactions on Software Engineering and Methodology*, 5(3), July, pp. 262–292.

Myhill, John, 1957. "Finite Automata and the Representation of Events," *WADC Technical Report* 57-624, Wright Patterson Air Force Base, Ohio, pp. 112–137.

Nardi, Daniele and Ronald J. Brachman, 2003. "An Introduction to Description Logics", in Franz Baader et al (eds.), *The Description Logic Handbook*, Cambridge University Press.

Naur, Peter (ed), 1963. "Revised Report on the Algorithmic Language ALGOL 60," *CACM*, 6, p. 1; *The Computer Journal*, 9, p. 349; *Num. Math.*, 4, p. 420.

Nerode, Anil, 1958. "Linear Automaton Transformations," *Proc. Amer. Math. Soc.*, 9, pp. 541–544.

Newell, Allen, J.C. Shaw, and Herbert Simon, 1957. "Empirical Explorations with the Logic Theory Machine," *Proceedings of the Western Joint Computer Conference*, 15, pp. 218–239. Reprinted in Edward A. Feigenbaum and Julian Feldman (eds.), *Computers and Thought*, McGraw-Hill, 1963.

Newell, Allen, [1990]. *Unified Theories of Cognition*, Harvard University Press.

Ochoa, Gabriella, 1998. "On Genetic Algorithms and Lindenmayer Systems," in *Parallel Problem Solving From Nature (PPSN V), Lecture Notes in Computer Science 1498*, Springer-Verlag, pp 335–344.

Oettinger, Anthony G., 1961. "Automatic Syntactic Analysis and the Pushdown Store," *Struc. Lang. Math. Aspects; Proc. Symp. Appl. Math*, 12, pp. 104–129.

Ogden, William F., 1968. "A Helpful Result for Proving Inherent Ambiguity," *Mathematical Systems Theory,* 2(3), pp. 31–42.

Parikh, Rohit J., 1966. "On Context-free Languages," *J. ACM*, 13(4), pp. 570–581.

Päun, Gheorghe, Grzegor Rozenberg, and Arto Salomaa, 1998. *DNA Computing: New Computing Paradigms*, Springer.

Pearl, Judea, 1984. *Heuristics: Intelligent Search Strategies for Computer Problem Solving*, Addison-Wesley.

Péter, Rózsa, 1967. *Recursive Functions*, translated by István Földes, Academic Press.

Post, Emil, 1943. "Formal Reductions of the General Combinatorial Decision Problem," *American Journal of Mathematics,* 65, 197–215.

Post, Emil L., 1946. "A Variant of a Recursively Unsolvable Problem," *Bulletin of the American Mathematical Society*, 52, pp. 264–268.

Post, Emil L., 1947. "Recursive Unsolvability of a Problem of Thue," *J. Symbolic Logic*, 12, pp. 1–11. Reprinted in [Davis 1965].

Pullam, Geoffrey K. and Gerald Gazdar, 1982. "Natural Languages and Context-free Languages," *Linguistics and Philosophy*, 4, pp. 471–504.

Pullam, Geoffrey K., 1984. "On Two Recent Attempts to Show that English is Not a CFL," *Computational Linguistics*, 10:3–4, July-December.

Prusinkiewicz, Przemyslaw and Aristid Lindenmayer 1990. *The Algorithmic Beauty of Plants*, Springer-Verlag 🖳.

Presburger, Mojzesz, 1929. "Uber die Vollstaendigkeit eines gewissen Systems der Arithmetik ganzer Zahlen, in welchem die Addition als einzige Operation hervortritt," *Comptes Rendus du I Congrés de Mathématiciens des Pays Slaves.* Warsaw, Poland, pp. 92–101.

Queille, Jean-Pierre. and Joseph Sifakis, 1982. "Specification and Verification of Concurrent Systems in CESAR," *Proceedings of the Fifth International Symposium in Programming. Lecture Notes in Computer Science* 137, Springer, pp. 337–351.

Rabin, Michael O. and Dana Scott, 1959. "Finite Automata and Their Decision Problems," *IBM Journal of Research and Development*, 3, pp. 114–125.

Rabin, Michael O., 1980. "Probabilistic Algorithm for Testing Primality," *Journal of Number Theory*, 12(1), pp. 128–138.

Rabiner, Lawrence R., 1989. "A Tutorial on Hidden Markov Models and Selected Applications in Speech Recognition" 🖳, *Proc. IEEE*, 77(2), pp. 257–286.

Rado, Tibor, 1962. "On Non-Computable Functions," *The Bell System Technical Journal*, 41(3), pp. 877–884.

Ratner, Daniel and Manfred K. Warmuth, 1986. "Finding a Shortest Solution for the N × N Extension of the 15-Puzzle is Intractable," *AAAI-86*, pp. 168–172.

Reingold, Omer, 2005. "Undirected ST-connectivity in Log-space," *Proceedings of the* 37th *Annual ACM Symposium on the Theory of Computing*, Baltimore, Md., pp. 376–385.

Rendell, Paul, 2000. *This is a Turing Machine Implemented in Conway's Game of Life*.

RFC 793, Postel, J., "Transmission Control Protocol," RFC 793, Sept. 1981.

Rice, H. Gordon, 1953. "Classes of Recursively Enumerable Sets and Their Decision Problems," *Transactions of the American Mathematical Society*, 74, pp. 358–366.

Rich, Elaine and Kevin Knight, 1991. *Artificial Intelligence*, McGraw-Hill.

Rivest, Ron, Adi Shamir and Leonard Adleman, 1978. "A Method for Obtaining Digital Signatures and Public Key Cryptosystems," *Comm. ACM*, 21, pp. 120–126.

Roads, Curtis, 1985. "Research in Music and Artificial Intelligence," *ACM Computing Surveys*, 17(2), pp. 163–190.

Roads, Curtis, 1996. *The Computer Music Tutorial*, MIT Press.

Robinson, Julia B., 1949. "On the Hamiltonian Game (A Traveling-salesman Problem)," *RAND Research Memorandum* RM-303.

Robinson, J. Alan, 1965. "A Machine-oriented Logic Based on the Resolution Principle," *J. ACM*, 12, pp. 23–41.

Robson, J. M., 1983. "The Complexity of Go," *Proc. IFIP*, pp. 413–417.

Roggenbach, Markus, [2002]. "Determinization of Büchi Automata", in E. Grädel et al. (eds), *Automata, Logics, and Infinite Games*, LNCS 2500, Springer-Verlag, pp. 43–60.

Rosen, Kenneth H., 2003. *Discrete Mathematics and Its Applications*, McGraw-Hill.

Russell, Stuart and Peter Norvig, 2002. *Artificial Intelligence: A Modern Approach*, Prentice-Hall.

Savitch, Walter J., 1970. "Relationships Between Nondeterministic and Deterministic Tape Complexities," *J. Computer and Systems Sciences*, 4(2), pp. 177–192.

Schaffer, John and Deron McGee, 1997. *Knowledge-Based Programming for Music Research*, A-R Editions, Inc.

Scheinberg, Stephen, 1960. "Note on the Boolean Properties of Context-free Languages," Information and Control, 3(4), pp. 372–375.

Schenker, Heinrich, 1935. *Der freie Satz* (*Free Composition*). Originally published in Vienna: Universal Edition, 1935. English edition, E. Oster (ed. and trans), Longman, Inc. 1979.

Schottstaedt, William, 1989. "Automatic Counterpoint," in Max V. Matthews and John R. Pierce (eds), *Current Directions in Computer Music Research*, MIT Press.

Schutzenberger, Marcel-Paul, 1963. "On Context-free Languages and Pushdown Automata," Information and Control, 6(3), pp. 246–264.

Searle, John, 1980. "Minds, Brains, and Programs," *Behavioral and Brain Sciences*, 3, pp. 417–424.

Senizergues, Geraud, 2001. "L(A) = L(B)? Decidability Results from Complete Formal Systems," *Theoretical Computer Science,* 251, pp. 1–166.

Shannon, Claude E., 1948. "A Mathematical Theory of Communication", *Bell System Technical Journal*, 27, pp. 379–423 and 623–656, July and October.

Shor, Peter, 1994. "Polynomial-Time Algorithms for Prime Factorization and Discrete Logarithms on a Quantum Computer", *Proceedings of the 35th Annual Symposium on Foundations of Computer Science*, pp. 124–134.

Simon, Herbert A and Allen Newell, 1958. "Heuristic Problem Solving: The Next Advance in Operations Research," *Operations Research*, January-February, pp. 1–10.

Sipser, Michael, 2006. *Introduction to the Theory of Computation*, Second Edition, PWS Publishing Company.

Skolem, Thoralf, 1928. "Über die mathematische Logik," *Norsk Matematisk Tidsskrift*, 10, pp. 125–142. Translated as "On Mathematical Logic," in *From Frege to Gödel: A Source Book in Mathematical Logic 1879–1931*, Jean van Heijenoort (ed), Harvard University Press, 1967.

Sokol, Joel, 2004. "An Intuitive Markov Chain Lesson from Baseball".

Stock, Oliviero, Rino Falcone, and Patrizia Insinnamo, 1988. "Island Parsing and Bidirectional Charts," *Proceedings 12th Conference on Computational Linguistics*, (ACL), pp. 636–641.

Stone, Peter, Kurt Dresner, Selim Erdoğan, Peggy Fidelman, Nicholas Jong, Nate Kohl, Gregory Kuhlmann, Ellie Lin, Mohan Sridharan, Daniel Stronger, and Gurushyam Hariharan, 2003. "UT Austin Villa 2003: A New RoboCup Four-Legged Team." Technical Report, The University of Texas at Austin, Artificial Intelligence Lab, UT-AI-TR-03-304, October, 2003.

Strassen, Volker, 1969. "Gaussian Elimination is Not Optimal," *Numerische Mathematik*, 14(3), pp. 354–356.

Sudkamp, Thomas A., 1998. *Languages and Machines*, Addison-Wesley.

Sundberg, Johan and Björn Lindblom, 1991. "Generative Theories for Describing Musical Structure," in [Howell, West and Cross 1991], pp. 245–272.

Szelepcsényi, Róbert, 1988. "The Method of Forced Enumeration for Nondeterministic Automata," *Acta Informatica* 26, pp. 279–284.

Taylor, R. Gregory, 1988. *Models of Computation and Formal Languages*, Oxford University Press.

Thomas, Wolfgang, 1990. "Automata on Infinite Objects," in *Handbook of Theoretical Computer Science*, Jan Van Leeuwen(ed), MIT Press, pp. 135–191.

Trappe, Wade and Lawrence C. Washington, 2006. *Introduction to Cryptography with Coding Theory*, Prentice-Hall.

Turing, Alan, 1936. "On Computable Numbers, With an Application to the Entscheidungsproblem", *Proceedings of the London Mathematical Society*, Series 2, 42, pp 230–265. Errata appeared in Series 2, 43 (1937), pp 544–546. Reprinted in [Davis 1965].

Turing, Alan, 1950. "Computing Machinery and Intelligence", *Mind*, 59, pp. 433–460.

Valiant, Leslie G., 1975. "General Context-free Recognition in Less Than Cubic Time," *J. of Computer and System Sciences*, 10, pp. 308–315.

Viterbi, Andrew J., 1967. "Error Bounds for Convolutional Codes and an Asymptotically Optimum Decoding Algorithm," *IEEE Transactions on Information Theory* IT-13, pp, 1260–1269.

Wang, Hao, 1961. "Proving Theorems by Pattern Recognition II," *Bell System Tech. Journal*, 40, pp. 1–42.

West, Robert, Peter Howell, and Ian Cross, 1991. "Musical Structure and Knowledge Representation," in [Howell, West, and Cross 1991].

Whitehead, Alfred North, and Bertrand Russell, 1910, 1912, 1913. *Principia Mathematica*, 3 vols. Cambridge University Press.

Wolfram, Stephen, 2002. *A New Kind of Science*, Wolfram Media, Inc.

Yato, Takayuki and Takahiro Seta, 2002. "Complexity and Completeness of Finding Another Solution and Its Application to Puzzles", *IPSJ SIG Notes,* 2002-AL-87-2.

Younger, Daniel H., 1967. "Recognition and Parsing of Context-free Languages in Time n^3," *Information and Control*, 10(2), pp. 189–208.

Zloof, Moshé M., 1975. "Query by Example," *Proc. National Computer Conference* (NCC), AFIPS, 44, pp. 431–438.

INDEX